Published by
Argus Specialist Publications
Argus Books Ltd.,
Wolsey House, Wolsey Road,
Hemel Hempstead, Herts.

On the cover: Woodworker ran a "squares and rounds" Competition in conjunction with the 1986 Bristol Woodworker Show. This chess table by Aubrey Gill was one of a healthy entry and was described in the August 1986 issue.

WOODWORKER VOLUME 90 INDEX

12 monthly copies January 1986 – December 1986

January pp 1-88
A striking example of marquetry work by *Masquerade* author Kit Williams graces the cover, supported by an article on the unusual approach he adopts to this and other subjects.

February pp 89-176
This cover features a burr jarrah bowl by Richard Raffan (p.149), an elegant sycamore desk by Robin Williams (p.108) and a charming bird and blossom carving by Andrew Armitage (p.117)

March pp 177-264
Exceptional for *Woodworker* is a cover devoted to part of a painted wood table, but the painting demonstrates broken colour techniques, explained in this and the following issues.

April pp 265-352
If you've ever wanted to build an open canoe, this is the issue. Plans etc. are included and the complete Ojibwa craft is shown on the cover, with Japanese plane-making and old and new tools.

May pp 353-440
A desk by Nick Allen in bird's eye maple and stained veneers, photographed from an unusual angle, and the book jacket of 'World Woods in Colour' make this an unusual cover.

June pp 441-528
Giant turning – pieces up to 40 in. diameter and 48 in. high – are illustrated by a sample bowl some 3ft high. There is also an interesting boss from the rebuilding of York Minster and a sample sachet of BRIWAX!

July pp 529-616
The larch-tiled roof of a small Transylvanian church links with a glimpse of Rumanian timber buildings on pages 548 and 549. There is also an inset picture of a Sjöberg workbench offered at a special reader price.

August pp 617-704
Four chess-boards, one with chessmen in place, surround an oval table, all of outstanding workmanship and all exhibits from the Bristol Woodworker Show, which is reported on the inside pages.

September pp 705-800
A single-subject cover showing a French cooper tapering barrel staves relates to an article on page 772 on modern makers of traditional clogs and barrels and another on French-based Paul Davis' work on page 780.

October pp 801-896
Examples of parquetry work and a free sample pack of nine veneer panels are backed by introductory articles and designs for parquetry and marquetry on pages 820, 838 and 870 to tempt readers to try their hand.

November pp 897-992
An unusual steam-bent country style stacking chair under construction by David Colwell forms an interesting cover, attached to which was a sample pack of fluted beech dowels.

December pp 993-1088
A shaker design for a table swift, photographed by Paul Rocheleau, features on this cover. A table swift is a device for winding a skein of wool or other yarn into a ball.

AUTHOR INDEX

Anderson, Paul 1039
Anstey, Peter 20, 831
Applegate, David 504
Armitage, Andrew 117
Ashby, Tim 460, 503, 962
Austin, Paul 1058
Barker, Judith 34, 124, 208, 340, 386, 480
Beckett, Herbert 581
Benfield, Roy 347
Bernascone, T.F. 71
Binnington, Peter & Francis 721
Blizzard, Richard 690
Booth, Adrian 284, 632
Bridgewater, Alan & Gill 240, 418, 685, 838
Brown, Bill 155
Bulger, Martin 1009
Burrough, Max 54
Buse, Roger 334
Cain, Tubal 494
Cleaver, Idris 56
Clewlaw, Dr. Bob 120
Cliffe, Charles 352
Coldwell, Eric 926
Condick, Glyn 674, 777, 861
Coolen, Rene 714
Corcoran, Jim 153
Darlow, Mike 61
Davis, Dennis 296
Davis, Paul 780, 870
Deane, Tony 548
Dines, Peter 1062
Edwards, Michael 682
Entwistle, Richard 556

Fell, Alan 908
Foden, Michael 601
Folb, Stanley 201, 546
Fossel, Theo 841
Fowler, Kerry 649, 833
Gliddon, David 235
Grant, Bob 113, 171
Greenhalgh, Graham 131
Greer, Paul 833
Grierson, Martin 1012
Harcourt, Geoffrey 836
Hemsley, John 876, 916, 1053
Hewitt, Graham 393, 474
Hicks, Ron 626
Hill, Jack 737
Horsefield, Charles 667
Hosker, Ian 196, 292, 832
Howe, Stuart 374
Howlett, Peter 736, 740
Hughes, Luke 735
Hurrell, Steven 583
Iles, Ashley 45, 115, 257, 345, 381, 485, 600, 665, 757, 881
Ingham, Eric 427
Jaffa, George 509
Jones, Arthur 7, 95, 183, 271, 359, 447, 535, 623, 709, 805, 901, 997
Kell, Richard 382
Key, Ray 512
Kingshott, Jim 942
Kitto, John 672
Lapworth, Frank 587
Leach, Noel 165, 207

Mallinson, Peter 596
Markham, Leonard 414, 456
Mathews, Simon 550
McAllister, Neil 596
Meinert, Friedbert 730
Middleton, Rik 808, 972, 1000
Montesquieu, Marie-Laure de 772
Moorwood, William 331
Moss, Terry 629
Murdoch, Colin 49
O'Donnell, Michael 1070
O'Neill, Hugh 64, 363, 743, 802
Paffett, James 133
Pearce, Grant 953
Peters, Alan 464
Raffan, Richard 912
Reed, Les 820
Reffell, Ted 856
Rendell, Guy 966
Ripley, Mark 110
Roberts, Trevor 546
Robinson, Waring 244
Rowlinson, Dennis 1031
Sattin, Tony 26
Saunders, David 1066
Savage, David 103, 190, 236, 287, 432, 467, 565, 656, 717
Sear, Roger 590
Sprigg, June 1019
Stevenson, Marc & Tony 412
Stokes, Gordon 193, 711
Stuttle, Leslie 750, 813
Syson, Leslie 598

Taylor, Vic 150, 216, 306, 396, 453, 553, 644, 759, 852, 956, 1036
Thomas, Alan 30, 288, 355, 491, 493
Thom, Edward 542
Thornton, Emma 831
Townsend, Phil 653
Trussell, John 303

Turner, John 1043
Unwin, Harry 431
Walker, Bill 129
Watts, William 72
Wearing, Bob 33, 161, 233, 281, 430, 511, 575, 674, 755, 825, 945, 1005, 1045
Webb, Alex 202, 325

White, John 39
White, Mary 904
Wintle, Malcolm 949
Wood, Arthur 761
Wood, Tony 338, 422, 604, 650, 726, 846
Zielinski, Lech 680

SUBJECT INDEX

A

Advent Calendar 1009
American's furniture 24
Arley Hall workshop 146
Art Ducko 682
Atkins, Mick, woodcarver 201
Audio cabinet 20

B

Balkan timber buildings 548
Bandsaw to build 39, 355
Bar, oak 153
Barrels, French 773
Biscuit jointing 926
Blanks for bowls 1070
Books 68, 172, 259, 309, 369, 573, 648, 855, 921, 1055
   Beginner's Guide to Woodworking 68
   Book of Toymaking 855
   Collins Complete Do It Yourself Manual 573
   Complete Guide to Decorative Wood-working, The 1055
   Complete Home Improvement Manual 855
   Contemporary American Woodworkers 1055
   Craftman's Guide to Wood Polishing & Finishing Techniques 259
   Design Courses in Britain 1986 309, 573
   D.I.Y. Designer Furniture 556
   Federal Furniture 921
   Fine Woodworking on . . . series 573
   Guide to Making Wooden Toys that move 573
   Gluing & Cramping 921
   Handbook of Hardwoods, The 172
   High Relief Wood Carving 173
   Illustrated Handbook of Furniture Restoration, The 259
   Japanese Woodworking Tools – Selection, Care & Use 260
   Jobs in Carpentry & Joinery 573
   Korean Furniture 68
   Making Authentic Craftsman Furniture 855
   Making Country – Rustic Furniture 173
   Making Small Wooden Boxes 1055
   Making Whirligigs & Other Wind Toys 260
   Making Wooden Boxes with a Bandsaw 172
   Mauchline Ware 68
   Measured Shop Drawings for American Furniture 369
   Performing Wooden Toys 648
   Picture-framing Made Easy 855
   Practical Carpentry 573
   Practical Woodwork Book, The 309, 573
   Practice of Woodworking, The 648
   Projects in Wood 369
   Radial Arm Saw Technique 1055
   Shaker Design 921
   Timber in Construction 172
   Tool Grinding & Sharpening Handbook 68
   Turning Wood with Richard Raffan 309, 855
   Two Hundred Years of History & Evolution of Woodworking Machines 259
   Vaughans, East End Furniture Makers, The 68
   Walking & Working Sticks 855
   Woodcarvers' Pattern & Design Book 921
   Woodcarving – An Introduction 855
   Woodframe Furniture Restoration 369

Woodwork Skills 309, 573
   Working in Wood – Making Boxes & Small Chests 172
   World Woods in Colour 855
Boulle marquetry 838
Bowls 148
Bowls, giant size 512
Bowl turning 1070
Bristol tools 284
Bristol Woodworker Show report 632
British Craft Centre, turned bowls 148
Buckinghamshire College Show 831
Bust stand 113
Buying timber wisely 30, 491

C

Cabinet, small tall 110
Calendar, advent 1009
Candlestick, giant 856
Canoe 296
Carved figures 503
Carved netsuke mouse 240
Carving, a career 201
Carving flowers 117
Chair design 962
Chair, spinning 761
Chairs, steam-bent 916
Cheese smoker 1043
Chiffonier table 870
Child's back-stool 761
Child's chair 1031
Chimney chest 393
Chinese-style occasional table 244
Chippendale 598
Chisels 656
Chisels, Japanese 338, 422
Chucks, multi-jaw 61
Chunky chair 1031
Classical modern furniture 1012
Clock, novel 1039
Clocks 72
Clogs, French 772
Coats of many colours 196, 292
Collecting 287
College work 730, 735, 828
College work & the High Street 740
Combination hand vice 171
Convertible desk/dressing table 750
Coopering 347
Corner cabinet 926
Courses, turning 362
Cramps 281
Cricket bats 509
Cricket table 202
Cribbage board 303
Cupboard, country style 325

D

Decoy ducks 596, 683
Designs for DIY 556
Designs on the market 372
Desk/dressing table, convertible 750
Desk, oak 49
Diary 179, 266, 354
Disabled children's woodwork 427
Disc-sanding table 347
Display cabinet, upright 1062
Doctor in woodwork 546
Dolphins, carved 629

Doors, ledge & brace 288
Dowel box 352
Dowelling jig 581
Dresser 966
Ducks, sitting 596
Dust – Health & Safety 120, 583
Dutch chest 714

E

Easel & Donkey 131
Easel & paintbox 129
Ellipses, jig for 431
Extending table 504

F

Faceplate, intermediate 825
Fireplace chest 393
Folding screen 1058
Folding wardrobe 813
French woodwork 772, 780

G

Garden work centre 690
Gilding 721
Grand furniture saga 150, 306, 396, 453, 556, 644, 759, 852, 956, 1036
Green wood turning 680
Grinling Gibbons flowers 242
Guard for sawbench 71
Guild Notes 52, 96, 184, 273, 360, 479, 563, 655, 747, 867, 976
   Associate/Amateur/Professional membership 273
   Australian turner's contact 1051
   Back issues offered 655
   Bowl auction 52
   Bristol meeting 273
   British Woodturners' Guild? 184
   Carvers sought 52
   Christmas get-together? 976
   Courses 52, 53, 97, 185, 272, 360, 479, 563, 655, 747, 867, 976, 1051
   Crafts Council map 563
   Crafts Council register 685
   Duty free 273
   Experience sought 976
   Guild publicity 184
   Guild wooden badges? 184
   Herefordshire group 1051
   House name-boards 976
   Indian experience 976
   Jewel box 867
   Local representative volunteers 1051
   London Gallery at WW Show 1051
   Lovespoons 52
   Membership categories 273
   Miniature furniture 52
   Mosquito Aircraft Museum 360, 479
   New Guild administrator 655
   New Guild secretary 96
   Newquay invitation 747
   Old unusual tools 273
   Photographic hints 747
   Railway coach restoration 867
   Sales outlets 360, 747, 976
   School for Woodland Industry 184, 273, 867
   South London Kity K5 user 747
   South Wirral group 655

"Things To Do", Brixham 563
Turning demonstration 184
West London/South Bucks turners 1051
West Midlands branch 563
Woodland Trust 96
Woodworker Show 52, 563
Work experience requested 360
1930s books sought 52

H

Hand veneering 103, 190
Hatton, Sid, woodcarver 1066
Health & Safety – dust 120
Hi-fi/bookshelf/display cabinet 20
Hi-fi cabinet, traditional 626
Hinged table 504
History of furniture 150, 306, 396, 453, 553,
    644, 759, 852, 956, 1036
Holes in corners 493
Hooke Park Forestry school 236
House Models 26

I

Independent Designers' Federation 106
Indian boxes 418
Inventive designs 372
Irish-based furniture maker 653
Ivory box 497

J

Jacobean hi-fi cabinet 626
Japan 334
Japanese chisels 338, 422
Japanese saws 604, 650
Japanese twisted dovetail 464
Japanese wooden planes 726, 846
Jewel cabinet 714
Jig sander 861
Jigsaw sander 777
Jointing thin boards 233
Juror furore 835

K

King's makers 598
Knobs, making professional 161
Kuh, Peter, furniture 24

L

Lamination former 430
Lathe choice 743
Leeds Polytechnic show 833
Letters 13, 174, 261, 349, 515, 569, 661, 799,
    895, 991
    Anti-dust moustache 13
    Antique fittings sought 515
    Bandsaw accident 516
    Bandsaw motor 662, 991
    'Beginners Guide to Woodturning' 261
    Belts for inshave & gouge sharpening 14
    Bleaching oak 895
    Bows 515
    Carpet tape to hold wood 261
    Carving career 515
    Chisel-mortise machine 13
    Chisels & steels 895
    Chisels from files 991
    Comfort in chairs 1088
    Cost of tools 352
    'Craft of Woodturning' review 13
    De-clogging abrasives 799
    Decoration in furniture 14
    Designs & dust 1088
    Disston spirit-level saw 263
    Drawknife 800, 992
    Drilling with a mortiser 895
    Duck carving 991
    Edison router address sought 569
    External staircases 175
    Ferropine address wanted 1088
    Folk toys, moving 515
    French lathe description 14
    Gas engines 661
    Golden mean comment 351
    Hand veneering 569, 799, 895
    Induction motor hazard 992
    Japanese tools 661
    Light press from drill stand 261
    L.M. Saws of Derby 351
    Locked faceplate prevention 13
    Long-hole augers 174
    'Machine Guide' comment 174
    Magnetic secret drawers 261
    MDF availability 261
    MDF edge sealing 349
    Metal criticisms 175
    Miniature furniture information 174
    Moisture meters 800
    Morris men, The 261
    Mortise miller bit 569
    Mosquito aircraft 570, 799
    Multi-plane spare parts 662
    Mystery bedheads 516
    Noise, workshop 570, 799
    Outdoor workshop 13
    Planes & planing 351
    Polish lathes 13
    'Practice of Woodturning' review 896
    Radial-arm saw safety tip 263
    Radial-arm wide cuts 1088
    Removing hard putty 13
    Router cutter tip 261
    Safety at the WW Show 175
    Safety spectacles 895
    Saw filing 14
    Saw sharpening 351, 516
    Sharing workshop offer 895
    Simple workbenches 992
    Smokers' bow chair query 261
    Spring guard query 349
    Steels, modern 991
    Stobart books 569
    Stripping 991
    Successful farthingale chairs 175
    Sycamore finishing 263
    Tales out of steel 799, 1088
    'The Vaughans' author comment 349, 515
    Three-legged chair 349
    Thumb-hole in saw 992
    Tools of the trade 991
    Too many lathes 1088
    Turning course criticised 351, 515
    Turning course praised 515
    Unusable iroko 349, 569
    Winding doors 662
    Window weather strip 895
    Women in woodworking 349
    Woodturning improvisation 661
    Wrong clock photo 263
    Wuidart sharpening tool 13
    WW readers survey 263
    Yew 515
Livery cupboard 325
London College of Furniture show 831

M

Machining Wood 34, 124, 208, 340, 386, 480,
    667
Making a wooden plane 1000, 1005
Making time (clocks) 72
Manchester Central College show 737
Marks, shipping 155
Marquetry by Kit Williams 16
MDF turned bust stand 113
Middlesex Polytechnic show 730
Model houses 26
Morris & Co. furniture 54
Mosquito aircraft 374
Mouse, netsuke 240
Multi-jaw chucks 61
Munrow Collection exhibition 354

N

Netsuke mouse 240

O

Oak bar 153
Oak desk 49
Occasional table 244
Ojibwa canoe 296
Old tools 284, 287
Ornamental turning 494, 601

P

Painted finishes 196, 292
Painter's donkey 131
Parnham show 738
Parquetry 820
Planes, wooden 808, 1000, 1005
Planing stops 1045
Planing thin strips 1065
Playing card box 303
Pressure guard 71
Propeller making 942
Pulleys 674

Q

Question Box 9, 98, 187, 275, 436, 449, 537,
    676, 767, 863, 935, 1073
    Alder turning 674
    Ash & beech seasoning 768
    Arch-top door & window 189
    Bagpipe drones 537
    Ball-jointed vice 439
    Bandsaw blade guides 439
    Bandsaw blade sharpening 439
    Bandsaw motors 437
    Bandsaw or circular saw? 277
    Bandsaw tensioning 437
    Bench, unusual 767
    Bending timber 864
    Bird carving identification 439
    Blue streaks in pine 279
    Bowling woods finish 767
    Bow window, double-glazed 537
    Cabinet files 539
    Cabinet glazing bars 11
    Cabriole legs 450
    Card table framing 437
    Cat plate-warmer 10
    Cedar & yew drying
    Cellulose finishing 863
    Cellulose lacquer spraying 275
    Charles II chair joints 187
    Chuck plates 439
    Colouring mahogany 863
    Colouring MDF 863
    Colour-matching timbers 936
    Conversion in a small workshop 936
    Curved alcove 99
    Cutting new saw teeth 675
    Danish oil 451
    Dowel staining 279
    Drying for carving 538
    Ebonising problems 440
    Electric motors 98
    Ellipse turning 277
    Exterior plywood treatment 9
    Face masks 189
    Finishing oak notice-boards 768
    Flutes on taper legs 275
    Fruit stains in ash 537
    Garden seat 438
    Golden oak stain 279
    Grey colouring 537
    Guitar fingerboard 864
    Hardwood window frames 99
    Hinge-back saw 676
    Holm oak 935
    Horse-chestnut burrs 768
    Japan lacquer 935
    Keruing preservative 936
    Kitchen furniture finish 9
    Laburnum veneer 449
    Laminated irons 440
    Lathework flexing 101, 439
    Mahogany drying 450

Mahogany period finishes 677
Microwave seasoning 539
Millers Falls plane iron 676
Moisture meters 450
Myrtlewood 277
Noise from workshop 437
Oak bleaching 677
Oak exterior finish 768, 1073
Oak panel renovation 537, 1073
Oak, staining 279
Oak, yellow stains 451
Oxford picture-frames 675
Painted wooden toys 100
Parabola plotting 1074
Pergola, arched 449
Pine stains 279
Pipe stems 9
Plane identification 451
Polish on polyurethane 935
Rabbet/rebate planes 935
Radial-arm saw use 10
Refinishing car dash 538
Removing stains from oak 768
Reusing weathered oak 863
Rhododendron wood 539
Rip-fence alignment 277
Rosewood 436, 936
Rotted oak 279
Rust 865
Sandstone grinding wheel 187
Scraper sharpening 539, 676
Scratch-stock blades 864
Screwdriver blades 440
Screw thread for spinning wheel 11
Silicone v. wax polish 98
Snooker cue 100
Sound insulation 437
Spiers plane 98
Spindle-moulder safety 439
Spraying lacquer (courses) 101
Stail engine 864
Stain matching 538
Steadies, lathe 101, 439
Stripping acrylic finish 768
Swivels for bookcases 767
Sycamore/beech bed finish 9
Sycamore drying 1074
Teak colour restoration 438
Teak finishing 1073
Threads in wood 11, 865, 1073
Three-phase electricity 98
Timber marks 436
Turning books 436
Turning chipboard 677
TV snack tables 538
Veneer crazing 1073
Violin chinrests 189
Warped cupboard door 437
Wetting wood 676
Wooden toys 100
Weathered oak finish 101
Windows 99
Window weatherproofing 450
Yew & cedar drying 279
Yew seasoning 767, 1074
18th Century gilded mirror frame 10

R

Radial-arm saw 34
Reforestation 354
Router slide 953
Routing for tambours 33
Routing gauges 945
Rocking horses 412
Royal College of Art show 735
Rycotewood show 833

S

Sash window, double-hung 474
Sawbench pressure guard 71
Saw table 672

Scarf joints 949
School for Woodland Industry 236, 331
School for Woodcarving 1878–1937 1053
Scraper holder 674
Scratch tool, metal 575
Screen, folding 1058
Screwing the unscrewable 133
Secretaire in apple 542
Settle 216
Shaker design 1019
Shipping marks 155
Shop talk 5, 92, 181, 193, 268, 355, 445, 531,
    550, 620, 707, 803, 899, 995
    AEG battery screwdriver 621, 707
    AEG Maxi-26 Universal 711
    Al-Ko Multiworker 5
    Al-Ko planer/thicknesser 445
    Ashby Design Planscope 181
    Black & Decker cordless tools 620
    Black & Decker hammer drill 533
    Bondseal drill sharpener 707
    Bosch battery circular saw 181
    Bosch belt-sander 899
    Bosch plunging router 445
    Bosch reciprocating power saw 268
    Bosch router bits 803
    Branding irons 268
    Brimarc Sjöberg offer 620
    Burgess workshop range 445
    Carrymate for doors, sheets 620
    Carving machine 621
    Clock movements 531
    Combination augers 533
    Copying lathes, Symtec 269
    Coronet now Record Ridgway 445
    Courses 803
    Craft Supplies catalogue 995
    Cuprinol colour restoration 445
    Deca Dynamic scroll saw 899
    Diamond slurry sharpener 803
    Dominion planer/thicknesser 621
    Don White courses 445
    Dust extractor, P & J. 899
    Ebac wood dryer 531
    Elu crosscut/mitre saw 92
    Elu heavy duty drills 803
    Elu power saws 193
    Evo-stik Impact 2 268
    Exacta expanding rule 355
    Fercell mobile dust extractor 620
    Fercell woodwaste refiner 803
    Fercell woodwaste space heater 899
    Fimagen board 92, 181
    Fine Woodworking on . . . series 445, 803
    Fire & Timonox paints 355
    Fluid Wood (Apr.1) 269
    Forestar portable bandsaw 93
    Frame clamp 92, 445
    French polishing 92
    French polish price cut 268
    Glasurit Beck door finish 181
    Gluepot 803
    Gordon Stokes smoothing tool 355
    Holmes bench sander 92
    Homemaster table-top universal 5
    Irwin power bits 620
    James Inns Sherwood lathe 5
    Japanese plane 93
    Jaydee edgebander 899
    Kity Combi-star 899
    Langlow strippers 93
    Leather tool pouch 445
    London College of Furniture 355
    Luna C-frame sander 93
    Magomagh cupboard workshop 995
    Makita power tools offer 531
    Martek drill sharpener 93
    Merton College courses, 268
    Metal bender, Tubemate 268
    Microporous stains 803
    Miniature furniture kits 803
    Multico mortiser 803

    Multico planer/thicknesser 269
    Musical instrument courses 268
    Nitromors strippers 93
    Nobex mitre saw 899
    Oval art mat cutter 268
    Peerless plane 899
    Poster, woods in colour 355
    Powermate workstation 620
    Power table for Workmate 707
    'Quick Reference Guide' to hardboards
        etc.355
    ResiWood gap filler 531
    Rocking horse maker 531
    Ronseal spraycans 620
    Rotary planes availablity 995
    Ryobi thicknesser 899
    Samco mini-router 92
    Sandvik saw competition 707, 803, 899
    Sandvik tool box saw & squares 619
    Sanko saw bench 445
    'Saws & Sawing' 707
    Scantool grinder 533
    Sears radial-arm saw 455
    Shopsmith universal 707
    Siaco abrasives 269
    Siaco hand-sanding tool 531
    Siaco sanding disc free gift 445
    Skil rechargeable screwdriver 533
    Slot 'n' dot sanding disc 445
    Spindle moulder cutter block 707
    Spinet plans 995
    Spiral self-tapping inserts 181
    Startrite bandsaw 533
    Startrite planer/thicknesser 803
    Startrite tooling set offer 899
    Tool Book, The 5
    TRADA free pest leaflet 899
    Triton power-saw converter 445
    Triton power-tool table 803
    Universal woodworking stand 551
    Valspar paints 355
    Veneering manual & catalogue 531
    Vitrex ratchet screwdriver 533
    Wadkins planer/sizer 533
    West Dean College courses 268
    Wolfcraft machining table 531
    Wooden toymaking symposium 533
    Woodturning courses 181
    'Woodworker Manual of Finishing &
        Polishing' 620
    Woodworker Planbook 181
    Woodworker Plans Service 533
    3M respirator 92
Shrewsbury College show 832
Side-table/settle 216
Smoker for cheese 1043
Spinning chair 761
Spinning wheels 587, 590
Squares & Rounds results 639
Steam bending 916
Steam bent chest 418
Stripping finishes 165
Student work 730, 735, 828
Suffolk College Show 736

T

Table, chiffonier 870
Table for portable saw 672
Table, occasional 244
Table-top seat 216
Tales out of steel 41, 115, 257, 345, 381,
    485, 600, 665, 757, 881
Tambours, routing for 33
TAPA plan packs 962
Tapering jigs 755
Television/video cabinet 908
Thin board jointing 233
Third World tools 876
This month 2, 90, 179, 266, 354, 443, 530,
    618, 706, 802, 898, 994

Accident statistics 994
Alan Peters furniture 266
American jobs caution 706
Basketmaking 91
BBC ideas programme 618
Bristol WW Show prize draw 619
Bristol Woodworker Show 179
British Toy Fair 3
British Woodworking Federation Training 994
Briwax, sample 443
Caribbean Art Now Show 802
Carved chair 91
Change of Editor 2
Chaos, London showroom 898
Chess exhibition at V & A 267
Chinese ball 2
Computer kitchens 91
Course comments sought 530
CPVE 618
Crafts Council grants 898
Crafts Council Munrow exhibition 354
Design conference 443
Design & Industries Association prizes 994
Designer salesperson 618
Design for Profit conference 802
Desk, American cherry 2
Diary 179, 266, 354, 443, 530, 619, 706, 802, 898, 994
Dowel pack 898
Earthlife exhibition 619, 898
Erddig furniture 530
Expobois '86 91
Fieldhazel Ltd. 90
Friends of the Earth 3, 179, 266, 443, 531
Herring fishing carving 179
Hire tools 91
'Images of lust' photo 179
International Tropical Timber Organisation 898
Irradiation of Timber 706

Jumping Jack 443
Mitred clamp (1946) 179
National Marquetry Exhibition 443
National Miniature Fair 443
Norwegian design seminar 898
Obituaries – Bill Brown 266
                    Max Burrough 443
                    Peter Child 266
Portable power tool safety 898
Railway sleeper sculptures 898
Reader survey 91
Reforestation 354, 443
Selling furniture 618
Show news 267, 531, 618, 706
Skill-build joinery award 531
Sjöberg workbench winner 898
Small piece prize winner 898
Stag design winners 2
Style '86 2
Timber Trades Federation 3, 179, 266
Tools for self-reliance 706
Tropical timber products 3
Turning green 706
Two-handed screwdrivers 706
V & A Eye for Industry exhibition 994
Veneer pack 802
VSO woodworkers wanted 443
Walking stick competition 706
Whittle-in-the-woods event 802
Wooden school in U.S.A. 530
Wood sculpture symposium 706
Woodworker chair award 994
Woodworker circulation 354, 443
Woodworker Show, Bristol 354
Woodworker Show, draw winners 2, 90
York Minster oak 898
Timberline 7, 95, 183, 271, 359, 447, 535, 623, 709, 805, 901, 997
Tools for self-reliance 876
Tools of the trade 432, 467, 565, 656, 717
Transylvanian timber buildings 548

Turning containers 382
Turning courses 363
Turning, giant candlestick 856
Turning, lathe choice 743
'Turning Wood' 912
Twisted dovetail 464

V
Veneering, hand 103, 190

W
Walking stick growing 841
Wardrobe, folding 813
Waste, avoiding in finishes 207
Waste removal 583
Waterstones 1045
Watertight boxes 418
West Dean College 649
Williams, Kit, marquetry 16
Winding strips 511
Workbench of the future 1026
Workshop, Arley Hall 146
Workshop, Bob Wearing's 33, 161, 233, 281, 430, 511, 575, 674, 755, 825, 945, 1045
Woodcarver Sid Hatton 1066
Woodcuts 460
Wooden planes 808, 972, 1000, 1005
Wooden Wonder (Mosquito) 374
Wood skill centre 147
Woodwaste 583
Woodworking Wheeze 71, 133, 207, 352, 431, 493, 581, 674, 777, 861, 953, 1065
Woodworker circulation 354
Woodworker Show, Bristol 354, 632
Woodworker Show, comment 64
Woodworker Show preview 904

Y
Yew, turned 235
York Minster restoration 456

ADVERTISERS' INDEX

A
Abrams & Mundy Ltd. 80, 138, 224, 314, 521
Adcock, Harry 80, 138, 224, 315, 401, 519, 695, 885
Advertising Standards Authority 954
AEG (UK) Ltd. 425, 490, 582, 816, 922, 1042
Air Plants Ltd. 586
Apollo Products 46, 104, 220, 273, 410, 487, 579, 666, 764, 874, 961, 996
Argus Books Ltd. 658, 765, 1024
Argus Specialist Exhibitions 178, 270, 282, 357, 390, 442, 625, 729, 770, 817, 970
Arrowsmith, John 79, 137, 225, 315, 402, 521, 609, 696, 789, 885, 981
Art Veneers Co., Ltd. 84, 142, 229, 319, 793, 824, 891, 986
Ashby Design Workshop 87, 144, 231, 322, 408, 527
Ashford Tool Centre 665, 742, 859, 955, 1046
Asles 58, 159, 258, 924, 998
ASP Ltd. 162, 454, 488, 540, 631, 725, 866, 923
AVFS 425
Axminster Power Tool Centre, 8, 166, 188, 330, 356, 472, 540, 638, 844, 845, 910, 911, 1056, 1057
A–Z Tool Sales Ltd. IBC July, IBC Aug, 739, 843, 934, IBC Dec

B
BDM 1030
Bedford Saw & Tool Co., Ltd. 881, 1030
Benmail 212, 301, 385, 444, 572, 670, 778, 880, 933, 1024

Boddy's, John, Fine Wood & Tool Store Ltd. 12, 79, 106, 137, 180, 225, 276, 314, 358, 401, 446, 521, 535, 609, 664, 697, 748, 790, 818, 907, 1061
Breanainn Enterprises 701
Buck & Ryan 819, 868, 925
Buckinghamshire College 615, 702, 794
Builders' Direct Mail 94, 348, 552, 753, 818
Burch & Hills 1060
Burgess Power Tools Ltd. 508

C
Canaan Carbides Ltd. 720, 865, 954, 1029
Case, H. (Hardware) Ltd. 42, 156, 204, 323, 380, 506, 555, 688, 771, 804, 805, 806, 807, 862, 900, 901, 902, 903, 955, 996, 997, 998, 999
CCB (Woodworking Machinery) Co., Ltd. 69, 174, 179, 303, 431.
Charltons Timber Centre 28, 94, 204, 291, 380, 493, 586, 689, 710, 879, 903, 1047
Charnwood 397, 452, 628, 806, 827, 954
Child, Peter 59, 119, 258, 350, 417, 490, 581, 648, 765, 796, 807, 892, 937, 985, 1060
Christchurch Power Tools 689, 779, 878, 965, 1019
Chronos Ltd. 594, 948
Clam-Brummer Ltd. 907, 1061
Cleveland Woodcraft 82, 140, 666, 778, 806, 907, 1014
Corbett Tools 50, 159, 248
Coronet Lathe & Tool Co., Ltd. 733
Craft Materials Ltd. 58, 159, 258, 302, 416, 486, 580, 654, 764, 862, 925, 1048

Craft Supplies 48, 158, 210, 323, 367, 471, 532, 678, 716, 810, 937, 1018
Craft Tools & Tackle Ltd. 44, 168, 192, 337, 1038
Creative Woodcraft 948
Cutwell Tools Ltd. 555, 647, 763, 782, 859
Cutwell Woodworking 679, 939, 1046

D
Data Powertools Ltd. 280, 440, 482, 574, 671, 742, 859, 955, 1038
Decoy Art Studios 701, 795, 889, 988
DeWalt 29, 42, 160, 176, IFC Apr, 959, 961, 1025, 1029
Dew, Anthony 580, 663, 782
D.I.Y. Supply 490, 594, 1054
Dodd Machine Tools Ltd. 666, 778, 850
Dunlop Powerbase IFC Nov, IFC Dec

E
Early Music Shop 570
Ebac Ltd. 199, 776
Edgemaster Drills 933
Elektra Beckum (UK) Ltd. 67, 132, 262, OBC Apr, 367, OBC June, 568, IFC Sept, IBC Oct, OBC Dec
Elu Power Tools IFC Jan, 19, IBC Jan, IBC Feb, 264, IFC May, 379, 444, 570, 758, IFC Oct, 933, 937, 939, 1017, 1019, 1025
Euromodels 23
Excell Machine Tools 70, 154, 210, 348, 429, 473, 544, 663, 728, 818, 901, 998

F

Flack, Henry (1860) Ltd. OBC Feb, 204, 324, 458, 634, OBC Aug, OBC Oct, 924
Fox 1061

G

Garndyrrys Woodworking Supplies 489
Geinine Brown Styled Garments 989
General Woodwork Supplies 79, 137, 225, 314, 401, 519, 608, 695, 886, 980
Gilks, Nigel, Cabinetmakers 796
Gill & Hoxby Ltd. 878, 974, 1068
Graham Engineering 59, 132, 310, 486, 635
Guild of Woodworkers 119, 168

H

Hallam Tools Ltd. 612
Hall J. & Son 695
Heath Saws 63, 156, 206, 291, 379, 458, 589, 634, 779, 869, 971, 1046
Hegner (UK) Ltd. 83, 141, 228, 318, 405, 526, 615, 700, 792, 891, 985
Howard & Dean Ltd. 301, 416, 486, 893, 989
Hobbies (Dereham) Ltd. 88
Holtham, Alan 7, 95, 183, 271, 359, 473, 532, 623, 709, 861, 900, 1004
Home Workshop, The, Ltd. 807, 874, 938, 961 1030, 1042
Horological Solvents 881
Hosking, W. 429, 959
Hoyle, J.W. Ltd. 578, 646, 762, 906, 1017
Hunt, David, Tools, Ltd. 50, 159, 258, 302, 417, 463, 589, 679, 774, 875, 964, 1060

I

Iles, Ashley, (Edge Tools) Ltd. 47, 114, 214, 336, 380, 508, 536, 621, 710, 848, 925, 1048
Infonet Ltd. 69, 160, 350, 426, 480, 594, 692, 763, 992
Islington Health Authority 527

J

Janik Enterprises 796, 892, 985
Jarrett & Son 665, 939
Jaydee (Machine Sales) Ltd. 664
JCN Ltd. 70

K

Kent Power Tools Ltd. 679, 774, 875, 974, 1019
Kity U.K. 12, 59, 70, 106, 114, 156, 180, 200, 218, 276, 344, 350, 362, 379, 417, 447, 452, 489, 534, 562, 689, 741, 848, 1004
Kraftkabin Ltd. 487, 574, 663

L

Ledbury Craft Accessories 532, 621, 765, 805
Lervad (UK) Ltd. 47, 94, 206, 902, 1087
Limehouse Timber 116, 301, 315, 402 452, 520, 610, 696, 790, 869, 885, 979
Lord, Isaac, Ltd. 678, 769, 810, 964, 1014
Lucas, E.W. & Co., Ltd. 48, 128, 218, 346, 410, 502, 564, 635, 848, 959, 999
Luckhurst, Bruce 230, 321, 407, 525
Luna Tools & Machinery Ltd. 44, OBC Jan, 116, 159, 192, OBC Mar, 324, 337, 417, OBC May, 442, 486, 580, OBC July, 624, 654, 707, 764, OBC Sept, 824, 879, 964, OBC Nov, 1008, 1054

M

Machine Sales (Southampton) Ltd. 888, 983, 1082
Magomagh IBC Mar, IBC May, IBC Sept
Marquetry Society 392
Martek Ltd. 544, 1017
Mathews Brothers (Woodworkers) Ltd. 152, 256, 346, 516, 595, 688, 782, 878, 965, 1068
Merlin 23, 159, 248, 302

Mills, A. (Acton) Ltd. 15, 158, 246, 308, 395, 478, 489, 536, 625, 748, 826, 940 1069
Milestone Company, The 58, 159, 258
Minirad 324
M.J. Woodworking 506
M & M Distributors Ltd. (Triton) IFC June, 874, 902, 998
Model Wheel 1049
Moordown Power Tools Ltd. 46, 152, 220
Multistar Machine & Tool Ltd. 36, 262, 506, 580, 741, 881, 907, 1030
Myford Ltd. 122, 156, 753, 860
Myland, John, Ltd. 69, 102, 182, 278, 366, 451, 552, 628, 728, 894, 938, 1008

N

Naerok Ltd. 48, 128, 214, 346, 392
Nolanward Ltd. 15, 164, 260, 344
Nortec 1038

O

Ocean West 1034

P

P. & J. Dust Extraction Ltd. 582, 666, 765, 804, 939, 1054
Phoenix Antique Furniture Restoration Ltd. 796
Plant, W.M. 59, 555, 688, 782, 869, 875, 964, 1019
Pollard, A. & Son 23, 154, 348, 578, 764, 989, 1050

R

Rawdon Machine Sales Ltd. 86, 143, 230, 321, 407, 525, 614, 702, 794, 890, 946, 987
Record Marples Ltd. IFC Aug
Redbridge, London Borough of 85
Ridgway, Wm., & Sons Ltd. IFC May, IBC Apr, IFC July, 716
Robbins Ltd. 88, 145, 232, 320, 409, 528, 608, 697, 790, 884, 981
Roberts & Lee 720, 932
Roberts, Tyrone R. 232
Roger's 36, 168, 192, 336, 361, 482, 571, 647, 862, 947, 1035

S

Sanlin Leisure Marketing 58, 152, 220, 308, 424, 493, 532, 692, 742, 826, 932, 1087
Sarjents Tools 60, IBC Feb, 352, 368, 444, 514, 574, 658, 769, 851, 958, 960, 1054
Saw Centre, The 82, 140, 227, 317, 404, 522, 611, 887, 982
Scientific Instruments Ltd. (Hobbymat) 163, 207
Scott & Sargeant 28, 122, 200, 336, 358, 448, 562, 646, 746, 837, 920, 1052
Skycrafts 990
Smith, J.J. (Woodworking Machinery) Ltd. 273, 426, 514, 544, 628, 1018
Smiths Woodworkers Ltd. 44, 104, 186
Solent Tools Ltd. 4, 218, 274, 425, 471, 579, 662, 708, 858, 974
South West Power Tools 294, 411, 506, 589, 634, 771, 878, 924, 1061
Spencer, Margaret, & Co. 892, 986
Stanley, David, Auctions 88, 526
Startrite Machine Tool Co., Ltd. 38, 74, IBC June, 766, 854, IBC Nov
Steerdown Ltd. 647, 764, 850, 965, 999
Stobart & Son Ltd. 70, 158, 258, 346, 417, 446, 572, 648, 764, 807, 932
Suffolk College of Further Education 614
Sumaco 6, 154, 162, 212 , 234, 310, 385, 502, 578, 713, 756, 850, 873, 906, 1034, 1039
Swann-Morton 154, 337, 506, 564, 748, 971

T

Tabwell Tools 246, 294, 421, 463, 555, 689, 774, 875, 924, 1044

Taylor Bros. (Liverpool) Ltd. 36, 104, 291, 411, 458, 595, 679, 774, 868, 925, 1014
Taylor, Henry (Tools) Ltd. 280, 440, 482, 574, 671, 763, 859, 939, 1038
Tedbar Tinker Ltd. 319, 405, 523, 612, 699, 792, 888, 983
Thatcher, W., & Son Ltd. 50, 173, 248, 416, 594, 707, 964
Thomas & Willis Ltd. 350, 417, 488, 581, 666, 765, 804, 925, 1060
Tilgear 44, 58, 158, 220, 248, 258, 302, 310, 323, 348, 410, 416, 426, 429, 463, 486, 489, 516, 536, 562, 572, 580, 594, 625, 654, 663, 671, 692, 710, 742, 762, 778, 782, 807, 824, 865, 879, 907, 937, 955, 971, 990, 999 1018, 1038, 1050, 1068
Timber Purchasing 1050
Tomkinson, Eric 260, 302, 417
Tool Centre 156, 206, 291, 421, 463, 589, 688, 771, 819
Toolmail (GMC) Ltd. 286, 380, 458, 595, 634, 771, 869, 965, 1014, 1029
Treebridge Ltd. 50, 132, 258, 348, 417, 516, 580, 850, 959, 1025
Trend Cutting Tools 28, 94, 246, 302, 411, 516, 552, 654, 710, 903, 1050
Truebridge 1034
Turtle, L.H. 1047
Tyme Machines 362, 906
Tyzack, Cecil W. Ltd. 50, 164, 248, 260, 280, 410, 446, 571, 624, 728, 769, 804, 902, 996

V

Vamac 128, 214
Voluntary Service Overseas 988

W

Wadkin plc 348
Walker & Anderson 798, 892, 990
Warner Auctions 320, 526, 701, 796
Warren Machine Tools (Warco) 38, 112, 182, 278, 366, 514, 564, 779, 819, 971, 1060
Waymek 1025
Wessex Timber 665, 778, 806, 932, 1068
West Bromwich College of Commerce & Technology 595
Wheelers Ltd. 80
Whitehill Spindle Tools 46, 114, 210, 336, 411, 502, 582, 624, 716, 868, 900, 996
Williams Distributors (Tools) Ltd. 83, 141, 228, 318
Willis 58, 116, 204, 579
Winstick 84, 142, 229
Woodcraft Supply of Lewes 508
Woodcraft Supply (UK) Ltd. 63, 206
Woodfit Ltd. 46, 102, 186, 294, 397, 473, 571, 666, 804, 948, 997
Woodplan 50, 173, 248, 302, 416, 698
Woodward, J.D. 983
Woodworker Plans Service 304, 370, 487, 577, 670, 749, 880, 941, 1048
Woodworker Squares & Rounds Competition 107, 195, 283, 371
Woodworking Machines of Switzerland 58, 173, 192, 302, 426, 489, 572, 671, 754, 862, 955

X

X.R. Machines Ltd. 580, 646, 753, 806, 1042

The magazine for the craftsman
~ and the aspiring craftsman!

January 1986
Vol. 90
No. 1106

16 **Thoroughly modern magic**
Kit Williams — artist and wizard in paint and wood. We talk to the *Masquerade* man. *Aidan Walker*

24 **The quiet American**
A craftsman from Kansas in a Devon workshop owes much to the Cotswold tradition. *Aidan Walker*

26 **The building contractor**
Miniature architecture: Bruce Coombes models famous buildings to order — and for his own pleasure. *Tony Sattin*

30 **Buying timber wisely: 4**
Our roving investigator continues his assessment of big suppliers for smaller buyers. *Alan Thomas*

34 **MACHINING WOOD Your expert guide: 3**
The radial-arm saw: what to expect from it, and how to maximise its versatility. Our authoritative series continues

45 **Tales out of steel**
Get to know the buffing lasses, and follow a master-toolmaker and storyteller into Sheffield's colourful past. *Ashley Iles*

Editor Peter Collenette
Deputy editor Aidan Walker
Editorial assistant Kerry Fowler
Advertisement Manager Paul Holmes
Graphics Jeff Hamblin
Guild of Woodworkers Aidan Walker, Kerry Fowler
Editorial, advertisements and Guild of Woodworkers
1 Golden Square, London W1R 3AB, telephone 01-437 0626

Subscriptions and back issues Infonet Ltd, 10-13 Times House, 179 Marlowes, Hemel Hempstead, Herts HP1 1BB; telephone Hemel Hempstead (0442) 48434
Subscriptions per year UK £16.90; overseas outside USA (accelerated surface post) £21.00, USA (accelerated surface post) $28, airmail £48
UK trade SM Distribution Ltd, 16-18 Trinity Gardens, London SW9 8DX; telephone 01-274 8611
North American trade Bill Dean Books Ltd, 151-49 7th Avenue, PO Box 69, Whitestone, New York 11357; telephone 1-718-767-6632
Printed in Great Britain by Ambassador Press Ltd, St Albans, Herts
Mono origination Multiform Photosetting Ltd, Cardiff
Colour origination Derek Croxson Ltd, Chesham, Bucks
© Argus Specialist Publications Ltd 1985
ISSN 0043 776X

Argus Specialist Publications Ltd
1 Golden Square, London W1R 3AB; 01-437 0626

● *This extraordinary fretworked clock was only one of the wonders at the 1985 Woodworker Show, Alexandra Pavilion – p64*

54 **The Morris men**
A tribute to a giant in design history, and an appraisal of the craftsmen he inspired. *Max Burrough, Idris Cleaver*

61 **The gripping story**
A professional turner evaluates engineer's chucks and explains an important invention. *Mike Darlow*

64 **Show business**
Woodworker Show 1985 report: personal views of the best exhibits and the best buys in the showcase of the year. *Hugh O'Neill, Martin Bulger*

72 **Making time**
Award-winning clocks, the business of making them, and the business of business. *William Watts*

● *On the point of turning the page to see more of Gordon Brown's ballet carvings . . .*

PROJECTS
All with fully detailed working drawings

20 **Audio artifice**
The hi-fi bookcase is a stately and up-to-date solution to many a living-room's problems. *Peter Anstey*

39 **A bandsaw you can build**
Everything you need to know to make the workshop machine you really need. *John White*

49 **Solid value**
Try your frame-and-panelling skills on a sturdy oak desk in traditional style. *Colin Murdoch*

On the cover: The feet of Spring twinkle beneath her bejewelled frock (pp16-18)

REGULARS

2 **This month** looks at the woodworking world

5 **Shoptalk** reviews products and services

7 **Timberline**
The woods to buy and the woods to try. Our inside view of the market. *Arthur Jones*

9 **Question box**
Our experts answer a selection of the craft's countless queries

13 **Letters — now up front**
Readers' views aired and (sometimes!) voices raised

33 **Bob Wearing's Workshop**
A tambour-routing jig

52 **Guild notes**
News, ideas and courses for craftspeople at all levels

68 **Books**

Woodworker
This month

PETER COLLENETTE writes: By the time you read this, Aidan Walker will be *Woodworker's* editor and I shall be at it no longer. My career would disgrace a frenzied grasshopper, and I'm leaving to seek fresh challenges. But I'll be well content if they're even half as enjoyable or rewarding as the 23 months I've spent with our community of readers, contributors, advertisers, contacts, and just plain friends — together and as individuals.

I know Aidan will give it all he's got (which is plenty). *Woodworker* is a unique magazine, and editing it has been a unique privilege. I hope and believe that it'll just get better still; and I wish it, and you, the very best. Thank you all.

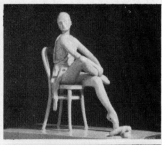

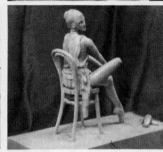

Dance on The four ballet sculptures **left** are part of *Sur Les Pointes*, an exhibition of Gordon Brown's work at the Lyre Room, Royal Festival Hall, London, 28 December-15 January. It coincides with the London Festival Ballet's production of 'The Nutcracker'.

Winners!

FEW VISITORS to the Woodworker Show will have missed our sales stand (there was even a handy computer terminal so you could see your new subscription go straight into its electronic maw).

And, if you saw the stand, you saw the tempting prizes that adorned it — even if you didn't fill out an entry of your own.

The draw was free to all who bought anything, and it took place at the end of the Show. As a result . . .

● Mr Eagle, a civil engineer from Wallers Ash near High Wycombe, won the unique **radial-arm saw** made by **Warren Machine Tools**;

● An **AEG bandsaw** went to Vicky Coghill, a joiner from London's Holloway;

● Mr J. Corrigan of Co. Tipperary gets an **AEG cordless drill/screwdriver**; P. L. Steares of Wadhurst, Sussex, gets an **AEG jigsaw**; and Mr R. Horrex, retired in Eastbourne, finds himself wielding an **AEG electronic reversible drill.**

Many congratulations to all, and we hope they get excellent use from such excellent products.

Something fishy? From the *Horsham Guardian*, 17 Oct 1985

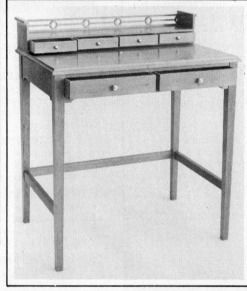

Making good Sara Wilkinson and Chris Vickers of the London College of Furniture sent us their photos in quick response to our moan in October's *Woodworker* — not enough LCF pix. Sarah's superb desk (**left**) is in American cherry with sterling silver handles.

Stag right 23-year old Clair Hunter won the Stag Furniture Group's Design Award for her bookshelf unit (**left**); Bucks College student Robert Rowlands' glazed display cabinet (**far left**) was highly commended. The pieces were displayed at Style 86, London's autumn furniture show.

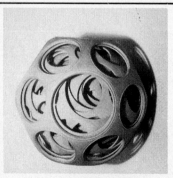

Tweddle medal The Society of Ornamental Turners' highest award for 1985 was won by Mr F. Kottek of Vienna for this extraordinary 27-section, 6¼ diameter Chinese ball that needed 26 different tools to make! The word is he's planning something bigger . . .

Fair do The British Toymakers Guild's Annual Toy Fair runs from 26-28 January at Kensington New Town Hall, Hornton St, London W8. From internationally acclaimed dolls to skittles via Noah's Arks: more information on 01-761 2957

Annual manual
The 1985 *Woodworker Annual* is to be read with relish; it boasts a record 976 pages of woodworking wisdom. £18.50+ £1.85 p&p from Argus Books, Wolsey House, Wolsey Rd, Hemel Hempstead, Herts HP2 4SS, or bookshops

Trade off?

'A million spiders died for this door', says one of the stickers that **Friends of the Earth** are aiming to plant on tropical timber products in the high street.

'There's no way,' says Allan Robinson of the **Timber Trades Federation,** 'that stopping someone buying a desk in Wigan will save a rain forest in Brazil. Not a million desks.'

FoE and the TTF were doing well, negotiating an agreement on FoE's suggested code of conduct for timber importers and users; the TTF claims it is fairly and squarely behind a sensible and responsible use of tropical hardwoods — whose accelerating despoliation ultimately affects the survival of us all.

The stickers put the cat among the pigeons.

'They didn't tell us' says the TTF. 'We did,' say the FoE; 'we'd been planning the campaign for some time. We don't feel that this campaign is incompatible with the theme of accord with the TTF — we're aiming it at retailers, who by and large have been unsympathetic to our 'seal of approval' stickers for products made from the right timbers correctly forested. We are two organisations that work in different ways. FoE feel that the public must be woken up to the urgency of the issue; if logging goes on in the way it is, there won't *be* a timber trade in 10 years' time.

'The FoE are going for the drama, the emotive element,' says Robinson. 'If you wanted to preserve rain forests in the way they do, you'd have to move 270 million people out tomorrow.'

Arthur Jones' *Timberline* column (WW/Sep 85) mentions just some of the research into the confused and complex issues. Population explosion, food, water and fuel; local logging practices, governmental policies; all are ingredients of a potentially explosive recipe.

FoE and the TTF both know this. TTF believe they have a better line on the ear of the money-men, the policy-makers, than a 'radical' campaign group like the FoE; FoE believe things only change when public pressure works upwards — from retailers, to importers, to exporters who find they can't sell their products, to governments.

Clearly, there's room — and need — for them both; clearly there's been a lack of communication. Clearly, constructive cooperation is what's needed, and clearly both sides in what we hope is a temporary tiff are committed to it. There are some good ideas floating about; no one would object, surely, to a £1 levy for each tropical-hardwood product sold. That £1 would come from the importer, the manufacturer, the retailer and even the customer; it would go into a fund for research and development of solutions to the enormous problems. Everyone, too, would surely like to see a wider range of less well-known hardwoods available to furniture makers and buyers, beautiful and useable hardwoods that are often burnt in a single-minded search for mahogany.

The point is not that there are two sides to the argument, but merely two ways of trying to get something done. The TTF's way may be slow, the FoE's way may annoy the wrong people. But we're convinced they do want the same thing — as does everyone who loves wood, trees, and when it comes down to it, air, water and life itself.

We're behind anything that gets these two uneasy bedfellows back together, and wholeheartedly support a responsible use of what none of us could do without — wood.

If we're blind to the trees, in our own lifetime there won't be a wood (or in this case, a tropical forest) to be seen. ■

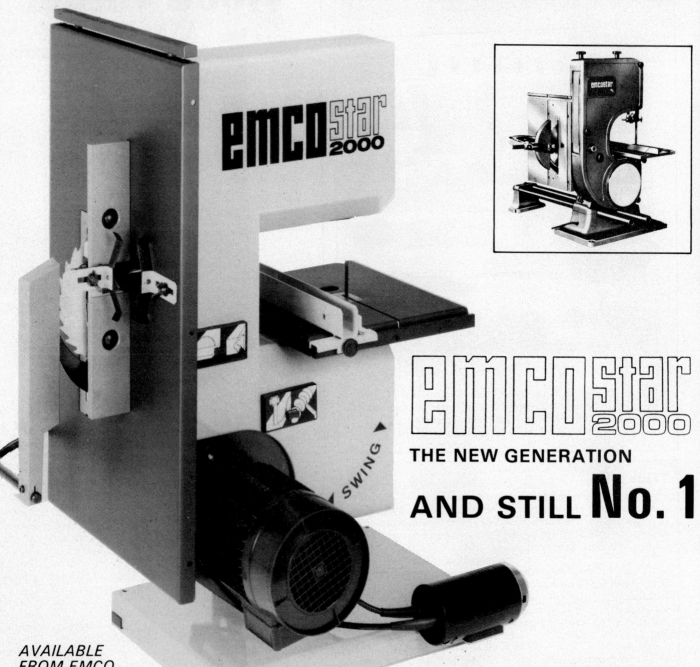

Shoptalk

If you keep your *Woodworkers* (and most people do), you ought to be looking at buying a **binder.** It comes with the title on the spine, it holds a year's issues, and it costs £5.20 all-inclusive from ASP Reader Services, PO Box 35, Wolsey House, Wolsey Rd, Hemel Hemel Hempstead, Herts HP2 4SS. Please make cheques and POs out to ASP Ltd, and allow 21 days for delivery.

You know what a partwork is. It's like a magazine except for the fact that one day it deliberately stops. You're supposed to get hooked on issue 1 and collect the lot. The pile of print that results by the end contains a great deal of miscellaneous information on the chosen subject — which is usually, for some reason, cookery, gardening, war, cars, sex, sewing or DIY. At least you've bought it even if you never read it.

That's not all. The canny publishers make sure they milk the same cow at least twice if not three or four times. So, if you bought a partwork called *Jobmate*, don't buy **The Tool Book** which has just been published by Orbis at £8. Everything in it has appeared in print before.

Nonetheless, it contains a lot of perfectly good information about woodworking, including detailed accounts of how to get the most from all the main hand and power tools — plus information about cutting joints (from butt to dovetail), gluing up, routing, sharpening and even turning. The format includes acres of nice clear colour pictures in step-by-step sequences. Builders' tools and simple metalworking are covered as well.

It's good value.

A TABLE-TOP UNIVERSAL: the Homemaster costs £430+VAT.
● CZ Scientific Instruments Ltd, 2 Elstree Way, Borehamwood, Herts WD6 1NH, tel. 01-953 1688

MORE CHOICE; Al-Ko's 5005 Multiworker is a saw, planer or spindle moulder; it uses a flexible accessory shaft. £450+VAT.
● Al-Ko Britain Ltd, 1 Industrial Estate, Medomsley Rd, Consett, Co. Durham DH8 6SZ, tel. (0207) 590295

AEG WOODWORKING are cutting their prices by 8-12%.
● AEG *Telefunken*, 217 Bath Rd, Slough, Berks SL1 4AW, tel. Slough 872101.

As a hobbyist woodworker, **writes Charles Hammond,** my interest in woodturning was originally at a craft fair: I was immediately attracted to the prospect of completing a job within an evening!

The first challenge, as ever, was how much I should spend, and what I could get for the outlay. I was looking for satisfactory quality and suitability in what would be my first machine. Brochures and leaflets became my main reading, followed by more and more informed discussions with all and sundry. In the end I decided to get a four-speed Sherwood lathe, 36in between centres (see also W. T. Odd's recommendation in the September issue). A very pleasant and informative visit to the maker, James Inns of Nottingham, confirmed my choice. I selected a ½hp motor.

The Sherwood has been effectively developed since I bought mine some six years ago, and the specification now includes a ¾in spindle with sealed bearings, a choice of morse taper or UNF centre, 7½in swing over the bed and an interesting range of sturdy and practical accessories. Headstock steady-stays are available for turning over 15in diameter, and the weight of the lathe is impressive at nearly ½ cwt.

A stout bench was called for, and I made one from excellent reclaimed timber. To ensure complete rigidity I bolted it to the floor and the wall. The headstock was bolted to the bench with an additional 1in block underneath, and the motor mounted on a 2in block of pine in line with the lathe pulleys. I mounted an 80-grit 6x1in grinding-wheel on the outward

end, and an extra tool-rest holder with short tool-rest completed the facility. I was ready to start turning.

In use, the lathe has consistently proved a strong, reliable, true and versatile machine with a total lack of vibration at all speeds. Work has ranged from thimbles and lace-bobbins to 5x5x27in between centres, and even a 12x4in bowl disc! All adjustments to the tool-rest holder, cross-slide, tool-rest and tailstock are made with a double-ended spanner, but since I'm not doing production runs I don't consider this a real drawback. In fact, with the bed being a round steel bar (1¼in in diameter), the flexibility in positioning the tool-rest is a positive advantage for between-centres turning. With reasonable care, I have not found the open belt drive a

hazard, but a top pulley guard is now available and I intend to fit one: after all, a moment's inattention — or an interruption — can cause a wholly avoidable accident.

Two refinements I have added are a reversing switch and a ¼in keyway cut into the bed bar with a complementary locating pin threaded through the rear side of the tailstock to facilitate instant centring. I am presently discussing with the makers the provision of a dividing head and a sanding table, which should altogether make a most comprehensive prospect for the wide-ranging amateur — even for small lathe capacity in a trade workshop.

● James Inns, Unit 3 Welbeck Workshops, Alfred Close, Nottingham NG3 1AD, tel. (0602) 585643.

Timberline

Arthur Jones presents the month's inside news of supplies

For many readers, prices quoted in this column have an unrealistic air. Sometimes we hear grumbles after a price for a particular timber has been published: 'Tell me where I can buy the timber for that price! My dealer is asking at least three times as much for exactly the same spec as you have quoted.'

We are both right. I almost always give the overseas price quoted to the UK importer, though on the CIF basis which includes insurance and freight charges. The aim is to give you an idea of how the international market is moving (comparison is always to corresponding CIF overseas prices) so a trend can be identified and you will know whether future prices are going to be moving up or down.

In the same way information on logging and sawmilling conditions abroad is always given simply to provide a warning of possible imminent shortages. If you favour samba and want to use only that species, it's important to know if supplies will be interrupted.

But back to the prices quoted for the UK importer. There are immediate additions to his costs as he moves the wood from the port to his yard, with charges for sorting, storage and financing. The woodworker is most unlikely to be buying from the importer, though these days you might be buying from a firm owned by one of them; the big groups in timber are moving into the lower regions of selling to get closer to the customer.

The woodworker is more likely to be buying from the timber or builder's merchant, rather than the importer. Already costs will have been added — both for transport and storage in the merchant's yard, and also for the conversion work on the larger sizes.

Here is the main difference between the merchant and the superstore or DIY branch outlet. Find the right merchant and he will meet your needs for size, species and finish precisely (though it has to be admitted there are a lot of merchants who still don't want to bother with an average woodworker's order).

Another big advantage of using a friendly timber merchant is that there is usually a wide knowledge of timbers to draw from, whereas most superlengths and thicknesses (often in shrink-wrapping so you can't inspect each piece closely). The assistant (if one can be found) is also unlikely to know wood, and certainly there is no question of any advisory or cutting service. Things may be a little better in the true DIY shop, though, where the assistant may have some knowledge.

All these extra services cost money, so often the superstore can actually quote you a cheaper rate than the merchant. By this stage, however, we're already talking of a final selling price which can easily be three times the rate quoted in this column!

Those who like to use native timbers will be interested in the rapid increases in the production of softwoods from our own woodlands. The area of productive woodlands continues to increase (up by 19,000 hectares in the last forest year), and it's now around the 2m hectare mark. Sawmill production is forecast to reach 2.8cu. m. by the end of this decade and a staggering 7m cu. m. by 2025, so there will soon be far more native softwood on offer compared with imported.

In the current softwood market woodworkers continue to reap the benefit of the lowest possible prices being quoted by overseas shippers — most of them aren't making any money on their sawn softwood. Coupled with this feature of the international market is the still high level of softwood stocks in the country, so it's worth shopping around among the suppliers for softwood.

It is interesting to note a continued rise in particle-board consumption, which stands in contrast to other sectors of the timber market. A lot of the extra business has been in chipboard made in the UK, largely because of the favourable sterling rate, but some of the chipboard from Communist countries is now being quoted at highly competitive rates, and reports suggest the quality is good. So look out for Czech chipboard! ∎

Question box

Our panel of experts solve your woodworking problems

Q *Some of my pupils made a set of letters for the school name out of old desk-tops -five-ply birch plywood. Although they were primed, undercoated and painted, the ply was obviously not exterior-grade because the laminations have separated after only a year.*

I have been given some exterior plywood to make a new sign which I intend to varnish either with Ronseal or yacht varnish. Will this treatment prevent splitting of the laminations, or will I have to treat the cut edges of the plywood with additional protection?

Leslie Ross, Evesham

A I'm surprised that the original 5-ply birch letters deteriorated so quickly. Coating exterior wood with primer, undercoat and gloss paint normally gives greater durability than a clear varnish. The laminations of the plywood would only split if the wood was absorbing moisture; it could be that when the letters were painted, you didn't paint the back of them, nor paint over the screws that were used to fix them.

If you want to varnish the new letters, it's important that you apply at least one coat to their backs and a minimum of three coats to the front and the edges, even though the new letters will be made from exterior plywood. You should also apply varnish over the screws to make sure that the moisture doesn't get in there.

I'd recommend a yacht varnish, preferably one based on tung oil (china wood oil) as polyurethanes tend to break down and peel from the surface after about 18 months. Tung oil varnishes have very good exterior durability. I would also suggest that you re-coat the letters at regular intervals before the bare wood becomes exposed.

Ronald E. Rustin

Q *I am coming to the end of a four-year project – the construction of a double bed from some large pieces of sycamore and beech. My problem concerns a finish that would do this piece of furniture justice. I don't just want to coat the wood with varnish, but would like to produce a finish that will protect the wood yet still retain its natural feel.*

What are the relative merits and disadvantages of finishing systems such as sealers, waxes, oils and so on? How does one go about surface preparation for such finishes?

Peter W. H. Olden, Glasgow

A I assume you want to finish your bed in its natural colour. A factory-made bed would be given a spray finish which would give good protection but not the desired feel. Varnish gives a thicker layer on the surface and would also be unsuitable. Oil polishing gives a durable finish, but as each application has a darkening effect, you may find the bed becoming darker than you wanted. A sealer will seal the pores of the wood and thereby prevent dirt from soiling its surface.

Whatever finish is used, it's essential to prepare the surface of the wood thoroughly because any small defects or blemishes will be highlighted by the finish. Use a steel cabinet scraper to remove all plane-marks and rough areas of wild grain, and then rub down with progressively finer grades of abrasive paper until the wood is as smooth as silk. On the assumption that you don't stain, you should now brush on two coats of white french polish all over the areas to be polished. This will seal the surface against dirt and also help to achieve a more rapid build-up of wax.

When the white polish is completely hard after a few hours, lightly smooth away any little specks or 'nibs' with 7/0 garnet paper. Wipe away all the dust and then rub on an even coat of a light-coloured wax polish with a clean rag. Allow the polish to stand for about 15 minutes and then polish briskly in the direction of the grain with a clean soft duster. Four or five such waxings will give you a deep mellow shine through which you will still be able to feel the wood's texture. Wax and white french polish are available from finish suppliers, whose names you can get from the Yellow Pages or the advertisements in *Woodworker*.

Charles Cliffe

Q *I take commissions for kitchens, and would appreciate your advice on the following points.*

● *Could you recommend a cellulose semi-matt finish that can be sprayed?*

● *Are there any special preparations before spraying? What method would be advisable?*

● *What type of equipment do you recommend before spraying? What method would be advisable?*

● *What type of equipment do you recommend for this type of work? I have no airline, and only a moderate budget for the necessary sprayer.*

I would be most appreciative of your advice.

John Deacon, Winchester

A You will find my two articles — 'Spray finishing — the basics' (WW/April and May 84), helpful.

In answer to your first question, I would suggest a pre-catalysed lacquer, available in either satin or semi-gloss finish, will give you the finish you require. The lacquer must be sprayed on a clean non-greasy surface and is ready to use from the tin; add a little pre-catalysed thinner to obtain the correct viscosity for your spray-gun. This finish will dry off in 15 minutes and be 'stack-hard' within the hour. It takes a few more days for the lacquer to cure fully. This is classified as a non-reversible finish, that is, it won't dissolve in its own solvent. Pre-cat lacquer, as it's known, is available from all trade suppliers.

In answer to your second question, there are a number of basic points to remember when using any modern finishing materials;

● Take special care in the preparation of the surface;

● Use only cellulose stoppers and sealers — no beeswax;

● Use no oil or spirit stains or shellac-based products under these lacquers;

● Use water stains only;

● Have plenty of ventilation, and take great care of fire. Most cellulose lacquers and thinners have a low flashpoint;

● Use a face-mask while you are spraying.

The simplest solution to your last query would be a small portable spray unit with a compressor which can be used for workshop or site work. They can be obtained for about £150 from various suppliers who advertise in trade magazines; one such is J. W. Bollom & Co. Ltd, tel: 01-658 2299. They are easy to operate and require only a 13 amp outlet. Happy spraying!

Noel Leach

Q *Thank you for the informative article a few months ago (WW/June 85), on the manufacture of smoking pipes. The replacement of broken and chewed pipe stems is becoming an expensive business in this country; where does one purchase basic stem pieces and what type of machine or lathe is required to prepare and fit the stems?*

Martin Wright, Pretoria, South Africa

A As far as South Africa is concerned, I have no record of supplies of mouth-pieces being available locally, and suggest that is something that can only be discovered locally.

Otherwise, I suggest you get in touch with Messrs John Redman Ltd., 123/5/7 Whitecross St, London EC1Y 8JJ.

As far as a lathe is concerned, you would need a good stock which includes a 'dead' pulley, driven by an electric motor, probably around 1½hp. The dead pulley is so you don't have to stop the motor all the time. A fitted leather belt driving the lathe should be able to slide from the dead to the live spindle.

The type of chuck used is generally only found in the pipe trade; however, there are some woodworking chucks that can be adapted. It should be a screw chuck that can open up to, say, 20-25mm, with three or four jaws to keep the stem steady. It would be ideal to have a back stopper as well, which would steady the stem but also help to ensure that the centre is constant. You would, of course, need some good chisels and a T-stand to cut the pegs. This is done by shaving away layers of vulcanite until the required diameter is reached, which is why you would have to stop the spindle so often.

Alternatively, and provided that the chuck is correct, a turret lathe can be altered, but this would mean that you would have to check the position of your cutters every time. This is all right for quantity production but repairers in the UK still hand-turn the push; they find that each pipe to be repaired needs a different diameter push.

I hope this will help you to start with; you would do well to subscribe to the pipe enthusiasts' journal, *Pipeline*, 18 Kay Ave, Meadowlands Park, Weybridge Rd, Addlestone, Surrey KT15 2PE, UK.

Jacques Cole

Question box

Q *The photo shows a mirror frame which was resilvered in 1921. I've been told it dates from 1720, and the gilding on plaster is of French origin; I can't trace a mention of it in any book, although I have seen one book of mirrors which showed a similar piece, made by Mallett of London in 1750.*

I have cleaned the veneer with fine steel wool and wax. I was advised to rub the gold with a match very gently, but it's too stubborn – it appears to be gold paint. I have one or two broken pieces; at one time the bottom was sawn across, possibly to fit on to a bureau. I'd like to put it into original condition – could you tell me of a book which would show the original? What was the plaster used for the mouldings? Are they gold leaf?

W. E. A. Booth, Sandy, Beds

A The nearest design I have seen to your looking-glass is for a Chippendale fretwork mirror frame in *Reproducing Antique Furniture*, by Franklin H. Gottshall, obtainable from Stobart & Son Ltd, 65-73 Worship St, London EC2A 2EL.

The maker's name you mention I have assumed to be William Hallett (1707-81) who was a fashionable cabinetmaker around the middle of the 18th century, but I cannot find that he published any books of designs. If you are in London I suggest you visit the Victoria & Albert Museum library, as they have practically every book ever published on furniture.

No doubt the base to the gilding is gesso, but it sounds to me as if it has been touched up with one or other of the gold paints, which are not to be recommended as they all eventually tarnish. I must dissuade you most strongly against attempting to re-gild it yourself as it is a highly skilled job requiring special equipment and immense expertise, so if you think the job warrants it, have it done professionally.

Vic Taylor

Q *I need guidance on the correct and safe way to use a small radial-arm saw. The instructions with my Minirad say the saw should be pulled across the work, and most books on woodworking machines say this too. I note that with the Eumenia it is recommended to push the saw and I have seen it done.*

I have tried pushing on my own saw and find it easier to use, although the cut is not as clean. A pushing cut, theoretically, should have a tendency to lift the wood but I haven't found this difficulty. With a pulling cut there is an uncomfortable tendency for the saw to run across the wood and stall the motor unless it is held back.

Could you comment on the techniques for using a radial-arm for cross cutting?

D. G. Catt, Haverfordwest

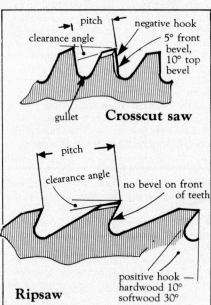

A Pulling the saw across the work is the usual method with a radial-arm, and it's also the safest, because the material is pushed down on the table and back against the fence while the blade cuts.

The problem of the saw's tendency to run across the wood and jam in the cut is caused by teeth of the wrong shape. For cross-cutting, particularly on a radial-arm saw, a saw with negative hook on the teeth is needed — the front of the teeth slope back in relation to a radial line drawn from the centre of the blade. The fronts of the teeth also need to be sharpened with a bevel, and a large clearance angle filed on top of the teeth. This combination will give a sharp point to sever the fibres of the wood and minimise break-out.

But don't use this type of blade for cutting along the grain. You need a saw with positive hook and a straight front to the teeth.

It's also important when crosscutting bowed or warped timber to put the convex side down on the table. If the edge is also curved, then the convex side must be put against the fence. Otherwise the cut will collapse on to the blade as it cuts, and it will jam.

Ken Taylor

● **See our 'Machining Wood' series in this issue.**

Q *During a visit to Crathie's Castle in Scotland last summer, I noticed this strange timber object on the nursery hearth. A guide told me it was a Victorian plate-warmer, but I find that hard to accept. It is possible to stack plates horizontally or vertically – it may have been used as a plate-rack, with the plates facing inwards. The photo shows as close a copy as I was able to make from memory; the size of the sphere is about 60mm, and the length of the arms about 190mm. Can you tell me anything about it?*

Peter Madge, Croydon, Australia

● **Top:** Mr Madge's 'cat': **Above:** T. Rowlandson, The Catastrophe, *from* The Fashionable Fireplace *published by Leeds City Art Galleries, 1985*

A The object is in fact a 'cat', a piece of domestic furniture which was used in the 18th and 19th centuries as a stand on which plates were balanced at the side of a hob grate to keep warm. 'Cats' were made from both metal and easily-turned wood; I suspect that at some stage an enterprising woodcarver found the shape of a metal example intriguing and reproduced it in wood, just as you have done. Wood was probably not such a practical material for the purpose. We have a number of wooden examples in our collections.

The name probably comes from the fact that whichever way you throw the object, it always lands on its feet, like its namesake.

John Batty, National Trust for Scotland

Question box

Q I'm in the process of making a spinning wheel and one of the components involves the production of a ½in. wooden thread (internal and external).

As this will probably be a one-off job the thought of parting with £30-£40 for a wood screwcutter and tap gives me the horrors.

I've thought of making a set from a ½in Whitworth nut and bolt, but even at 12 tpi I think it's too fine for a wood screw. Can you help?

J. Broome, Solihull

A Your problem is common to most amateurs making a spinning wheel. You are quite right, it is not practicable to cut your wood thread using a Whitworth tap and die, and making the tap is a formidable engineering project.

My recommendation is that you turn a nice hardwood handle, fitted with a brass ferrule. Drill and tap this ½in BSW, using the taper tap only. Screw in tightly a piece of threaded brass rod, which can be further secured either by filing two large flats and using an epoxy resin glue, or by drilling through and fitting a metal pin.

The corresponding nut can be let into the bed of the spinning wheel — better still, let in a large handmade brass square nut. This arrangement will both work well and look well.

Screwed rod and brass can always be obtained by post from K. R. Whiston Ltd., New Mills, Stockport, SK12 4PT.

Bob Wearing

Q Could you please give me some information about making glazing bars? I want to put them in the doors at the top of a bureau bookcase I have made.

I have a number of old Victorian planes, some of which were used for this purpose; I do have most up-to-date woodworking machines but not a spindle moulder. I want to make bars out of mahogany, and use the traditional 13-panes-of-glass configuration.

I have recently found a small block of beech among my collection of Victorian tools, which I think is a jig for cutting the angles for glazing bars, but I'm not certain about this. I would be grateful for any help; I have been a subscriber to Woodworker since 1964.

Terry Stokes, Wellington

A There is no book that I know of that deals with making cabinet glazing-bars. You don't give the sectional size of your bars; let's assume they are ¾x⅜in.

It is unlikely that a suitable moulding plane would be found for small mouldings such as this. A router could be inverted (cut a hole through a table-top) and used as a miniature spindle, but with such small sections — and mahogany at that — there would be a risk of breakage. You would then have to resort to the scratch stock. Figs. 1, 2 and 3 show the stages of working using a 'sticking rod'. The rebate is easily worked, but for the moulding, note that most of the waste is removed by a plane and/or chisel, and the stock is used just to complete the profile. The bars should be cut just a little longer than the minimum lengths required, so you can pin them if necessary, to prevent movement while working. Also of course, a suitable stop is necessary on the sticking rod.

Do you have any curved bars to make? A good method is this; first, cut out the required curved piece of material in the square. Now glue this to paper and glue the paper onto a flat surface, and, using the stock on a swivel, take out the groove (fig. 5). Now part-off and re-glue with groove down (fig. 6); then, having removed the bulk of material with a chisel, swivel-stock to profile (fig. 7). Finally, bend a strip of thin ply into the groove (fig. 8).

Sometime about the mid 70s, I had a Workshop Miscellany feature in *Woodworker* in which I dealt with the crossing-over and jointing of glazing bars. You should have this among your back numbers. Three-way jointing of glass bars appeared in 'Question Box', WW/September 1983.

The block of beech you mention is indeed a mitre-cutting template; depending on the size of your bars, you might be able to use this.

Stan Thomas

Fig.4 Block the bar up to work the same profile on the reverse

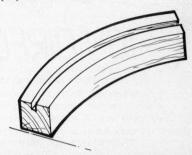

Fig.5 Work a groove in a curved piece, paper-glued

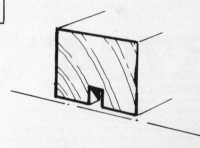

Fig.6 Turn over, re-glue and chisel the bulk of the waste

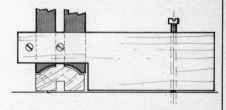

Fig.7 Work the curved profile with a fixed-pivot swivel stock

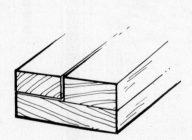

Fig.1 Set the blank on the 'sticking rod'

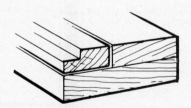

Fig.2 Work the rebate

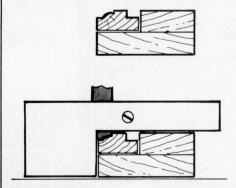

Fig.3 Turn and work the mould with plane, chisel and scratch stock

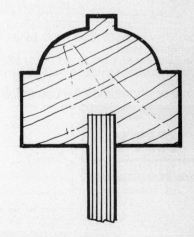

Fig.8 Bend a strip of thin ply into the groove

Letters

CONGRATULATIONS! A publishing breakthrough in the woodworking field. For supercilious mealy-mouthedness, Tobias Kaye's review of John Sainsbury's *The Craft of Woodturning* (WW/Nov 85) takes the cake.

What a miserable, unwarranted put-down. John's 'fluence' has touched many a woodturner, his writing has brought a host of new converts into the fold and helped sustain old hands, and he doesn't deserve this sort of treatment. Whatever happened to the notion of constructive criticism?

Whether this review was an attempt at self-aggrandisement or merely the expression of a joyless soul I don't know, but I feel that if Tobias can't do better he should put his pen on 'hold'.

Phil Reardon, Boroughbridge

WHILE IT IS POSSIBLE to remove old hard putty with a chisel (WW/Oct), it is extremely hard work and the chances of damaging the frame are very great if one is working with very fragile glazing-bars on old cabinets. A much more satisfactory method is to use a hot soldering iron to gently soften and push out the putty.

When working with a cracked pane there is no problem about breaking the glass by touching it, but some old glass is very fragile and great care should be taken to keep the iron from touching the glass on any pane which you intend to keep for re-use. The best iron to use is a high-wattage type with about a 7mm tip filed to a chisel. Keep it blunt and do not use a lot of pressure; the heat does the work for you.

The job is still demanding, but with a little care the clean result is well worthwhile. If you wish to experiment, Nitromors will remove old hard putty, but the effect on any finish around the frame does not bear thinking about.

David H Walton, Crowland, Lincs.

IN REPLY to the letter from Jack Barratt in your November issue, I write to say to him 'Welcome to the club', and is the following any help?

In preparation for my own retirement I recently built what my wife now calls 'the cabin' but what is really a small machine-shop housing a Robland 210 combination, a radial-arm saw and a bandsaw. I wanted somewhere I could vacate after creating the dust which machining makes, moving to an unpolluted workshop with the prepared materials. As this building would be seen from the sitting-room, my wife stipulated that it should not look like a garden shed.

Construction was as follows:
● A 6in-thick reinforced-concrete raft 15x10 was poured on to a bed of hardcore covered with a waterproof membrane.
● I made the front and back in sections which were coach-bolted together and subsequently bolted to two end-frames made from 2x2in studding and clad with ¾in shiplap. The two doors were bought at auction at a very reasonable price.

● Three 4x2in roof beams were laid front to back and three 2x2in purlins along the length, covered in heavy-duty mineral felt on 20mm chip-board.
● Power was supplied from a switched fuse-box in the house to another in the 'cabin', from which I ran three twin-socket outlets and three 4ft fluorescent light-fittings.
● Walls and roof were insulated and lined with 'paper ply' (the stuff with which caravans are lined) in simulated ash planking, giving a nice light appearance. The floor was sealed with red 'tennis court' paint to eliminate surface erosion when sweeping up.
● For £5 I acquired a 9ft 'black heat' tubular heater and thermostat which effectively keep the place from freezing up in winter — thanks to the insulation.

Admittedly I used a lot of reclaimed timber, and had a few items in stock such as bolts, door furniture, window stays and some glass, but the total cost was approximately £550 and included everything from the hire of the concrete-mixer to three coats of Sadolin for protection. I look forward to many happy hours in my 'playroom' in future.

Patrick Neill, Newmarket

I'M A RETIRED FOREMAN JOINER; I started life as a cabinetmaker and have worked with wood for some 52 years, as I still do. Some years ago the dust affected my nose in various ways, and my late uncle asked me, 'Why don't you grow a moustache, Harry?'

I did so, and from that day to this I've never had any more sores in my nose. Nature's remedy may be a tip worth passing on to other craftsmen.

Harry Parsons, Heathfield

Peter Collenette writes: As a whiskery yet wheezy woodworker I've sadly never found that my moustache improves matters. Maybe I'm unlucky — or merely a freak. But the makers of masks do say that a beard will always prevent their equipment from working properly.

IN THE OCTOBER ISSUE Peter Boddy was enquiring about a Wuidart sharpening tool. I suggest he contacts Wuidart Engineering Ltd, Clifton Rd, Shefford, Beds.

With regard to the locked aluminium face-plate of Roy Benfield, I overcame the same problem by taking the advice of Gordon Stokes, who recommended the use of a flexible washer behind the face-plate. I keep three nylon washers about 1mm thick: one to fall on the floor and be lost in the shavings and sawdust, one hanging on a hook as a replacement, and one actually in place on the machine but waiting for a chance to fall on the floor and be lost.

D. J. Kirby, Cheltenham

IN TWO RECENT ISSUES you have shown Charles Cliffe demonstrating the art of french polishing with his various mixtures decanted into soft-drink bottles. This is a most unwise practice, especially when he is instructing amateurs. They may well have children or grandchildren around who could easily find the 'pop' bottles and drink the contents, with most unfortunate results. It might be as well if you reminded your readers of the dangers.

Jennifer M. Langley, Wrexham

Charles Cliffe replies: All my bottles are clearly labelled, and in my workshop are well out of the reach of small children. Moreover, the workshop is always kept locked in my absence. I cannot see that there is any danger in using soft-drink bottles, particularly when they are so plainly labelled as those on p659 of the September issue.

I WAS VERY INTERESTED in your October 'Question Box' item about mortising machines.

Herewith a photograph of our pride and joy at Grange special school, Kempston, Bedfordshire: a chisel-mortise machine made by F. W. Reynolds & Co., Southwark Street, London, named 'The Monarch' — Serial no. 928.

We bought it for £10, 15 years ago, from a local antique dealer as a rusty heap of heavy metal. Our boys cleaned, painted and restored it to its original glory. To say we would not be without it in our craft room is an understatement. It is a vital piece of equipment, very safe, and even boys and girls of small stature use it with ease.

We would recommend it to any craft teacher, especially for children with learning difficulties, because it opens up great possibilities in that we are able to mortice without failure.

Jack Holt, Grange School, Kempston

Letters

IN HIS ARTICLE on design in October's *Woodworker*, David Field makes some astonishing remarks.

His own furniture is undecorated. Decoration in former days, he considers, was a means of concealing inaccuracies when craftsmen lacked machines and abrasive papers, and found true surfaces and accurate joints too difficult to achieve. He says the cabriole leg of a Chippendale chair was shaped because the inaccuracies in straight legs would be too easily seen, so he is including the 18th century in his survey. Has he ever looked closely at good 18th century furniture? If so, he will have seen perfectly fair surfaces combined with perfectly controlled decoration.

The fact is that, in spite of (or was it because of?) their lack of machines, the better furniture-makers of that period achieved a mastery of materials based on a commitment to making which is very seldom equalled today — though perhaps one sees it in the work of Mr. Field's mentor David Pye. It was this mastery, or the overflowing of it, which culminated in the ribband-back of a Chippendale chair and such marvels of decoration.

Mr. Field also overlooks the fact that the designers of these masterpieces were not the workmen who made them, and so the designers had no interest in concealing faults.

No one wants modern designers to copy the work of a former age. One longs to see work which is fresh but as elegant as that of the 18th century. What would the furniture-makers of that age have made of David Field's folding table featured in *Woodworker*? 'Easy to make', as your commentary says — yes; but 'elegant'? Hardly!

J.M.G. Crossley, Oakham

David Field replies: Mr Crossley's letter obviously highlights the problems associated with taking a project and part of a chapter from a book as a taster — they can be read out of context. However, it would be helpful to the debate if Mr Crossley had read the article carefully before reaching in rage for his pen. I am glad that he finds my remarks 'astonishing', for a great deal of care went into the preparation of the book. I have studied and looked at furniture very carefully. I will answer his comments point by point.

Firstly, most of my furniture *is* decorated. The table on the cover uses diamond matching, crossbanding, inlays and stringing (an extension of Sheraton, perhaps?). The boxwood stringing protects vulnerable veneered edges. The inlay on the surface allows cross-grain shrinkage of very wide veneers, with resultant gaps, to be concealed. It is not a sell-out but a deliberate design detail to cope with the inevitable results of working in this manner. The decoration therefore allows perfect joints to be achieved (no glue-lines) and endorses the geometry of the piece without destroying the effect of the diamond matching. Furthermore, it allows a workshop to pro-

duce an article of very high quality at realistic price.

This is not something new and was as much a reality in the 18th century as it is now. It is, first, a contemporary example of a practice which is centuries old and one of the hallmarks of good design thinking — precisely understood by the designers of the 'classical masterpieces' mentioned: i.e., decoration resulting from the need for a tolerance in manufacture (for whatever reason, be it the nature of the material or limited technique).

With this in mind, I challenge Mr Crossley to take a rule (not a vernier caliper) to some of his revered 'classical' pieces. He will find my points well-founded. There are, of course, some very well-made pieces, but these are by no means the norm. I offer a further challenge also, and suggest that the workmanship practised by some makers from small workshops today is of a higher calibre than at any time in history — there being currently a preoccupation with perfection rarely seen in the past.

One of the reasons for the book is to encourage makers beginning to reach a mature knowledge of technique to embark upon the activity of *designing* for themselves. But this is a slow process, and the projects in the book vary from the simple (e.g. the folding table) to those that will challenge the very best makers. It is my experience that a simple object executed well will encourage more ambitious attempts later on. The folding table, whilst not 'elegant' in 18th-century terms, has its own direct simplicity determined from a structural need for stability and rigidity. The maker is encouraged, in the book, to adapt and adjust this formula to achieve his/her own results — perhaps even elegance!

I hope Mr Crossley will buy the book, especially if he is a maker himself. It must be remembered that Chippendale and Sheraton were the foremost furniture designers of their day, their work reflecting and influencing the cultural attitudes and aspirations of that period. There are designers and makers featured in the book who are attempting with integrity and sensitivity to do the same for our culture, and it is insulting to them to have their work derided by a blinkered view which dismisses anything new, reveres everything old and fails totally to see the complacency in the work or attitudes which result from such a standpoint.

David Field

MAY I PLEASE COMMENT on Mr Whitrick's second letter on saw filing (WW/Aug 85)?

I feel he is being a little too dogmatic on the subject of the 90° angle to the depth. A famous writer around the turn of the century, Paul Hasluck, quite distinctly shows in his *Handyman's Book* the saw-file being held upward at an angle of about 80°, end view. Often in the mechanical trades a slight bias in one direction can be a good thing:

butt joints shot hollow rather than rounded, lathe face-plates flat to concave, etc.

Likewise, Bernard E. Jones of *Practical Woodworking* fame suggests that rip-saws be filed a little out of square, say 5° or 10° in plan, on the (to me) realistic grounds that the grain of timber is always more or less curved; thus the rip-saw must act as a pseudo-crosscut some of the time.

F. Seward, London

I WAS AMUSED at Roger Buse's letter regarding 'pockwood'. A leaflet describes a lathe of French manufacture:

'The model T115 only little wood lathe which can copy on model wood piece or carved model, with a steady a regulated at different rungs. Ideal machine for the artisan and for the exactins amateur. This wood lathe is simple and strong. It has mecanic copier which allow the reproduction of the all forms, with an advance of manuel wagon. Which is soft grace at the guidage by billard rollings of precision. The tightly of the wagon is do by two soroped joints in melting.'

(In all fairness, I don't think I would do any better translating from English to French!)

John Greenwell, Leighton Buzzard

● No printing errors, we promise!

BEING A SLIGHT SPASTIC down the left side of my body I have no sense of touch in my left hand, or individual use of the fingers. I bought myself an inshave, but was having great difficulty in honing it to a sharp edge. On two occasions I slipped when trying and needed hospital attention.

Considering how the convex bevel could be sharpened, I thought of a modified belt-sander, with the belt loose so that it would mould to the shape of the bevel.

When I contacted English Abrasives asking about the availability of belts for the purpose, to my surprise they replied enclosing one of their Super Sander foam drum sanders and several belts, and asking me to evaluate this for the job. The fine belt (150 grit) ground the bevel to the perfect shape, and after I had deliberately blunted it I obtained a reasonable edge — but not, however, as good as I had hoped.

I contacting English Abrasives again, and they suggested that they make up some special belts for it. These were 400 grit, and polished the bevel to an almost mirror finish with a very sharp edge. If the drum is stiffened by inserting by inserting a strip of flexible plastic, the same width, between the drum and the belt, it also sharpens turning gouges in seconds, leaving the bevel concave.

When a large company gives service like this to an individual, they deserve praise.

Michael Perryman, Redhill

15

Thoroughly modern magic

Myth and marquetry, realism and romance mingle in Kit Williams' work. Aidan Walker talked to him

Kit Williams' book *Masquerade*, the riddle-me-ree recipe (with fine-art instructions) for a wild-bejewelled-hare-chase, has sold 2 million copies. This man has, by choice or chance, successfully managed to dip into a well of mass imagination — all sorts of psychic depths have been stirred by the book and the search. What sort of mystical character was this? And on top of that, what has he got to do with *Woodworker*?

The second question is easier to answer. Kit is a woodworker, as well as a painter, a jeweller, a writer, a metalworker, and an inventor. He is also hospitable and modest — showing neither the false self-deprecation nor the overweening self-elevation that would be understandable, if not excusable, in someone of his achievement.

I was to talk to him about the techniques with wood — specifically marquetry — that he used to give depth and focus to the range of paintings in his latest 'bee book'; of which, until May this year, only one titled copy existed, in a sealed and highly decorated wooden box. Under a small marquetry panel, guarded by a gold queen bee, the title remained a secret for a year and a day after publication; Kit's challenge to his readers' creativity was to work out the title and then express it in any medium other than words — bake it, crochet it, do it in stained glass, stainless steel, whatever — and the winner of the box and the only titled book would be the one that delighted him most.

Kit is entirely self-educated ('self-impressed', he calls it) and all his skills are self-taught. The same topic recurs in discussion of writing, painting, rectangles, working drawings and even workshop machinery; the victory over limitations and restrictions. *Masquerade* uses riddles and measured prose to illustrate the paintings, to get people to look at art more closely and to direct emphasis away from concrete, static definitions. Technical training, he maintains, by its very nature teaches as much about what you can't do as what or how you can; measured drawings for the workshop require you to work out every detail accurately in the first instance, allowing little room for development, refinement, addition or subtraction. Machinery, in its own way, beguiles the designer into conceiving and executing something that suits the machine, not the idea.

Excellent marquetarian and jeweller though he is, Kit is primarily a painter. I didn't ask whether he saw himself as an artist or a craftsman — there's no doubt he's both, and just as little uncertainty about the precision and imagination he

brings to anything he does. He disclaims excellence, preferring to claim only an unusual facility for teaching hand and eye to co-ordinate. For the crafts that he calls 'other people's' — by which I assumed he meant anything to which he turns his hand other than painting — he just says, 'Perhaps I use them more creatively than they do.' Not perhaps as modest as might be in this respect, although objectively it's fair comment. He would suggest that his highly individual use of these crafts owes a great deal to not having a formal training; I would suggest it's down to the intense power of his imagination.

● *The 'ancient tree, naked and hunched,'* (**far left**) *is surrounded with a veneer concoction including bird's-eye maple and burr walnut; the bees* **below** *are sand-shaded.* **Above,** *the prize book-box*

Thoroughly modern magic

Although he consciously fits himself into the craft tradition of 'minimum resources, maximum resourcefulness', his marquetry technique, for instance, owes nothing to tradition. It's more like inlay than marquetry; rather than cut out shapes, tape them together and stick them down, he lays the background veneer complete and then cuts bits out of it. A bee, for example, would be examined to see which part of the body was most overlapped, and that part would go in first. He cuts out the shape, cuts round it on the background, cuts the background out and glues the piece in with acetone glue. The next segment is then cut, and overlap-fitted over both the background and the first piece, and so on. He described how he worked and explained his learning-and-doing method, gleaned from the father of a boyhood friend; do a little drawing, enough to work out the bit you start with, and go on from there, fitting everything to the first piece. Kit himself lays conscious emphasis on the 'find the key piece' approach; look, learn, and there's nothing you can't do — as long as it's one-off. For production, of course, you need to think every angle out on paper before you start.

Sitting in the round-roofed summer-house, built using massive oak beams salvaged from the demolition of a local manor house, he becomes animated on the topic. 'If something has been done under conditions that you can re-create or better, you should be able to do it. There are people sitting in gutters in India casting bronze; what about tool steel? That's a comparatively recent invention, you know; the Vikings didn't have it. How do you build a longship without tool steel? People are so dependent on technology, they'll find every excuse for not doing something — haven't got the equipment, haven't got the time. They didn't even have developed ideas of perspective when they built cathedrals, but they built them.'

The summerhouse's radial rafters are lined with thick hazel twigs, bent green, and the stone tiles are laid on them and fixed with green oak pegs. 'Green oak — look — hard as nails. Ancient buildings have been taken down with oak pegs still in first-class condition. Good as galvanised nails any day.' Did he prefer to use oak pegs merely for the sake of doing it the old way? 'No, not at all.' He pointed across the garden to the roof of his new studio, built in old stone and tile to match his house. 'They're using nails, but they're cladding the inside with plasterboard. I don't want to sit here and look up at a load of nails lining the roof. Besides, it's pleasurable to feel yourself part of a tradition.'

The oak pegs lead to the subject of the right wood for the right use. 'There are many different kinds of wood, all suited ideally to one particular purpose. Look at a cartwheel or a windsor chair — they use a variety of types, all with their own properties just right for the part they play in the construction. There's even a self-lubricating timber — did you know that ships used to be built with lignum vitae bearings for their iron prop-shafts?'

He loves wood, and finds the exertion that woodwork requires a refreshing change from the mental intensity and physical tension of his demanding, super-realistic painting. Materials like timber, gold and paint seem more human to him ('Gold talks back at you like wood'), and have more warmth than baser metals, ceramics or textiles; the processes that the first three require also leave less to chance. He prefers to be in complete control of a constructive/creative project, and finds no attraction in the 'offer your work to God' gamble of the kiln or the printing screen. The marquetry frames sprang from 'a desire to encapsulate, envelop, put arms round a piece of work' and wood offers a harmonious compliment to the myriad colours of paint. The frames themselves include and expand the idea of the painting; a village cricket team's deep square leg is watching intently from the marquetry boundary. In

his painting Kit is trying to get the actual quality of 'real sky, real flesh, real grass'. You can get any colour you want by mixing paints, a fact that gives almost unlimited scope for getting it wrong, and for inadvertently drawing attention to the fact. Out of all the nuances, only one is the right one; but marquetry isn't attempting that illusion. It asks you to look at and appreciate the wood, how burr walnut makes a good lion's mane or an obscure Brazilian mahogany re-creates the fur. All the colours, says Kit, 'are harmonious, like autumn'.

He uses a Startrite 352 bandsaw and a little Elu router, permanently held in an open frame that serves as a small table for mini-spindle moulding. Just about the only other machine in the workshop is a hefty bench-grinder, used more often as a sander, a buffer and a lathe. A lathe? 'Yes — this is the headstock, I fit it into this drill-chuck.' A heavy-duty Jacobs chuck mounts on the grinder, and a beautiful precision-made centre-point headstock fits into that. The tailstock? Kit waves his hand round the workshop. The practical philosophy of the

self-educated and highly artful bodger would raise many a turner's eyebrow. 'Oh — anything that comes to hand: you can turn things as long as the space is wide, if you get it lined up right.'

Pre-*Masquerade* (it was published in 1979) was a period in which Kit was comparatively highly productive in woodwork. He is particularly interested in concealed springs: a two-lid, two-drawer box containing objects and pictures of 'a highly erotic nature' was designed so it couldn't just be picked up and opened by anyone round the house. Once you finally got inside, it was as if you deserved its feast of desire.

'The way I work', Kit seems to want you to believe, owes a lot to the Iron Age. 'I love the Iron Age, they were such good craftsmen.' The independently inventive, enquiring individual is Kit's model, but his only formal training is as a computer engineer, taken in the 60s when science was the romance of the age — but you can't do science on your own, and it changes too fast: there's no humanity in it.

There is a box puzzle which he designed to fend off boredom on a long plane journey to Japan. He wanted to develop a machine-made mass-marketable puzzle, and came up with a maze; a box with a secret drawer, which opens to reveal a gold artefact ('About three quid's worth'), but only when the lead ball inside has been positioned correctly. (Lead to gold — alchemy, 1980's-style.) Each of the four sides are engraved on the outside with the Japanese characters for earth, air, water and fire, whose slashes and strokes are reproduced as routed grooves on the core-cube inside. You have to get the lead ball from one end to the other of each character — it's inside the box, you can only do it by sound and feel — when it drops over on to the next face, and finally through a hole in the centre where it must be positioned to jam closed a pair of locking cams. If the ball doesn't sit right, you press on a spring-loaded panel in one end of the cube to no avail; if you get it in place, the cams stay closed and allow the secret drawer to be pushed out. Yes, instructions do come with it. He was to mass-produce it in association with a Japanese consortium, who wanted it made in plastic: no chance, said Kit, wood or not at all. It was to be not at all.

His riddles have entwined, entrapped and obsessed two million buyers and easily twice that many readers; I asked him to do the box puzzle to show me how it works. 'There are two kinds of puzzle people,' he said, applying the screwdriver, 'the inventors and the doers (or undoers); the explorers and the followers. I sat down and designed something that was difficult to do — I'm buggered if I'm going to spend my time actually solving it.' ∎

● Thanks to Eric Lister and Jessica, of the Portal Gallery, 16a Grafton St, London W1, for their help in preparing this feature, and also to Jonathan Cape, 30 Bedford Sq, London WC1, for the colour transparencies.

Precision sawing's a push-over with our new pull-over

The **Elu** PS174 Crosscut/Mitre Saw introduces an entirely new and unique approach to precision sawing. It is designed for bench or floor-level operation and will appeal to a wide spectrum of professional users — builders, shopfitters, flooring contractors, signmakers etc., in fact any operation where timber or plastics need to be cut with accuracy using an easily transportable machine.

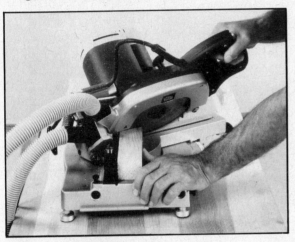

Down

The **Elu** PS174 will crosscut, mitre, bevel and cut combination mitres. On narrow workpieces, the machine is operated like a conventional mitre saw with the sawhead lowered straight down into the work and then allowed to spring-return to its upright position. The safety guard retracts only as far as is necessary to cut the material.

Across

Where the PS174 really comes into its own is on wider material, the telescoping arm giving the machine much wider cutting capacity than an ordinary mitre saw even having a much larger blade.

The whole design of the PS174 exudes quality. The extreme rigidity of its die-cast aluminium construction ensures accurate cutting of widths up to 250mm (174mm in 45° mitre setting) to a depth of 52mm (40mm in 45° bevel setting), which is ample capacity for most applications. Bevel and mitre angle adjustment is simple and quick with clear scales and the most common mitre angles have machined locations for convenience.

Up and away

Once the job is done, the PS174 weighs only 12.5kg and is therefore easily carried to the next job, even if it's up a ladder.

The **Elu** PS174 is available in both 115V and 220V AC, featuring a powerful 1200 watt low-noise universal motor. Dust extraction tubes are available as optional accessories, as are side support extensions to facilitate cutting of longer material.

The **Elu** PS174 is not like any other mitre saw you have ever seen. Check it out at your **Elu** dealer and see how it can make your cutting a real push-over.

Audio artifice

Peter Anstey's hi-fi, bookshelf and display unit is an accomplished amateur answer to a tough domestic brief

After many years' hard wear, our sitting-room furniture was beginning to look its age. So my wife challenged me to design and make a new combination piece which would fulfil several functions at once.

We are music lovers, and our first requirement was for a good hi-fi unit which would also provide plenty of space for records, tapes and equipment. We also had a whole lot of treasured books for which shelf space was now inadequate. Our third requirement was for some kind of showcase in which my wife, who is a potter, could display her pieces. Whatever the design solution, it had to be reasonably compact, since at 12x16ft our sitting-room is by no means large.

A good deal of thought and measurement led finally to a variation on the traditional dresser. The piece was made in two halves. The lower comprised a three-section cupboard to house standard-width audio units and record-storage facilities behind vertical space-saving tambour doors, with ample drawer space beneath for tapes and other equipment. The upper consisted of a matching three-section bookcase and display cabinet with glass-fronted doors; the two outer sections have fixed shelving for books, and the central section has adjustable shelves for general display purposes. I used recessed bookcase strip. Rigid assembly of the upper and lower halves was achieved by knock-down fittings — four brass countersunk machine-screws passed through holes at each end of the base of the cabinet and screwed into threaded collars let into the surface of the cupboard.

I make no special claim for the design except that it is simple and functional, with few gimmicks. But it may hold an interest for other woodworkers in its fairly extensive challenge to basic woodworking skills. In my case (apart from occasional access to equipment at Bucks College, High Wycombe, to whose wood-machining instructors my absorbing interest in woodworking owes a great deal), machinery was limited to a circular saw and table, a hand planer, a home-built router table with heavy-duty router (see *Woodworker* July 1984, p422, for a portable design), and a belt sander.

In my description I've taken basic cabinetmaking skills and techniques for granted. I've concentrated instead on those elements of the project which proved most taxing as well as calling for improvisation.

Building the carcase

My own cabinetmaking interests tend towards solid-wood construction. Since I'm fortunate in having access to quality

● *'Amateur', in this case, means first-class!*

supplies of ash and seasoning facilities for a combined cost of under £5 per cubic foot, I chose ash as the basic material throughout. material throughout.

Preparing the carcase members was the most time-consuming part of the project, since it involved choosing matching strips planed to a standard 20mm thickness (the finished size after sanding was 18mm), edge-planing them accurately, and then jointing them. I have found the simplest method of satisfactory jointing to be that of grooving both edges on the router with a ¼in straight cutter and then gluing them with a ¼in plywood fillet inserted along the full length of the grooves. This gives great strength and at the same time minimises the danger of damaging the prepared edges. It is, of course, important to join adjacent strips so that any residual tendency to bow or twist is cancelled out.

Every woodworker has his or her own preference for carcase joints. Mine is for lapped dovetails, which were used in this case. Dovetails finished to a good professional standard are never easy for the ama-

teur — never mind what the manufacturers of various so-called foolproof devices tell you. My own solution involves using a router with a dovetail bit mounted upside-down on my home-built router table, which also incorporates and adjustable fence with millimetre scale and a second smaller fence clamped to it at right-angles. This allows the workpiece to be held rigidly and fed into the dovetail cut at precise intervals.

I have also found dovetail dado joints to be particularly valuable in a solid-wood carcase of this type, since their interlocking strength and total rigidity check the slightest tendency of the carcase members to move. Shelf dados must of course be stopped half an inch or so before one end of the cut, so that the joint will not be visible at the front of the shelf.

A few notes on the central record-storage section of the audio unit. Solid wood and dovetail joints are not practicable for the ⅜in dividers here; they are best made of ply or chipboard, edged with ash lippings, with ⅛in tenons and grooves for the joints. Also, since the appropriate design height and depth for vertical record racks are no more then 14-15in, some compromise is needed within a unit where the basic module to accommodate a wide range of audio equipment is some 2-3in higher and deeper. This is achieved by setting back the racks 1½-2in from the front of the unit — a requirement, in any case, for the tambour doors — and by gluing a 2½in facing strip at right-angles to the upper horizontal cross-member of the racks; this projects above and behind the tambour when fully raised, and neatly conceals the unused space.

Tambour details

The apparent complexity of tambour door construction may deter many people from attempting it, but I have not found it as difficult as the textbooks imply. The most important thing is to make all the tambour slats (over 100 are needed) exactly the same size — 16¾x½inx6mm being the design measurements; in addition the distance between each pair of guide channels must, as nearly as possible, be constant throughout.

A good way of making the slats accurately is to prepare a number of pieces of selected timber, straight-grained and without any tendency to bow, to the correct length and thickness and at least, say, 6in wide. Then set the longitudinal fence on the circular-saw table to ½in width of cut, and feed each piece through with consecutive passes against the fence until the required number of slats (102 for the three doors) have been cut. All that's needed for finishing is to round off the front edges of each slat and smooth with fine sandpaper. Rounding off is best done on a spindle-moulder, but if you don't have one the router table and fence can easily be adapted to give satisfactory results, using a small quarter-round concave cutter.

Once the slats have been accurately finished, assembling the tambours is straightforward. First, carry out any varnishing or finishing treatment on the faces of the slats before gluing them to a backing sheet of good-quality plastic leathercloth; this helps to keep them clean and vertically flexible. Second, prepare the leathercloth to the exact size of the finished tambour (16¾in square) with a small overlap all round, marking out the position of each slat with parallel pencilled lines measured accurately against verticals left and right. This is an essential precaution when gluing, since the smooth running of the tambour depends on its being perfectly rectangular. Third, use PVA glue to fix the slats to the backing, making sure of a good butt-joint between the base of each slat and its neighbour. Finally, clamp the result firmly between two solid blockboards or equivalent pieces cut to the same size as the tambour, trimming off the leathercloth at the edges once the glue is dry.

The tambour guide channels, illustrated here, proved the most challenging element of the project. Each of the six channels, made of beech for toughness and smooth-

● The curved section of the tambour guide channel is shown with the fascia strip removed. The gap in the channel accommodates the fascia and allows the tambour to slide in

● Cutting the circular groove in the beech roundel which is then cut into quadrants for the guide-channel corners. The roundel, carried on dowel, is lowered over the router cutter in the ply slot

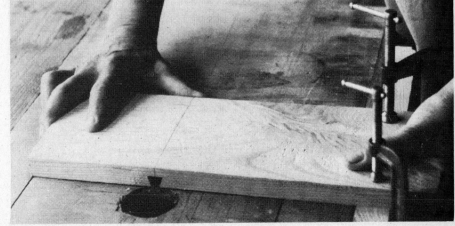
● Dovetail dadoes are cut on the router table; the straight piece clamped to the end runs against the table as a guide fence

21

Audio artifice

ness, was constructed in three sections — vertical and horizontal, with a linking curved central section. The basic profile of the channel is a rectangle 27mm wide and 9mm deep, with a central groove 7mm square. The channels are planed off diagonally on both sides between their bottom edges and the top edges of the grooves, which gives a triangular appearance, At the front of the carcase, this enables them to provide neat and unobtrusive receding extensions of the vertical dividers to which they are attached. The channel grooves are drilled and countersunk at their bases to accept small screws which reinforce the channels when glued to the carcase. The problem of constructing an accurate curved groove for the central section of each channel is solved as shown in the drawing. A spokeshave, fretsaw and sandpaper will be found useful for finishing the curved slope on each side of the groove.

A further important tambour design detail should also be mentioned. This comprises three flush-fitting ash fascia strips at the top of each door-frame, which are invisibly secured to the carcase by means of ⅝in square supporting strips screwed from behind and below. These fascias serve to conceal the tambour mechanism while providing stops for the bottom tambour slat in each case. The bottom slat (cross-section ⅞in high by ½in deep) projects approximately 10mm in front of the rest of the tambour and provides a solid base for the door-handle. Its side edge profile follows the outer slope of the guide channel, thus anchoring the slat firmly in the channel and neatly finishing off the front appearance of the unit.

Drawer construction

Many woodworkers will have ruefully experienced, as I have, the problems of getting drawers to fit accurately and run smoothly. With a piece such as this, where the drawers support a good deal of weight and are a key element in the design, metal side runners were an obvious choice. Construction, in softwood, followed the standard method involving lapped dovetails at each corner, with a plywood base in routed grooves. I added an oversize facing piece in solid ash, which could be exactly finished to the size of its drawer-hole and then fitted once the drawers themselves were mounted and running smoothly. The technique here is to pre-drill and countersink each drawer-front from behind with suitably spaced holes, from behind with suitably spaced holes, then mount each fascia in its drawer hole, hold it firmly against the drawer from the rear, and clamp the two tightly together. The alignment of each facing piece should now be exact, so that it can be screwed to the drawer from the inside via the pre-drilled holes.

Glass-fronted doors

A final word on the glass-fronted doors of the display cabinet, for which 4mm glass must be used and on which, for aesthetic reasons, the same handles were used as on the drawers — in this case mounted vertically instead of horizontally. Standard mortise-and-tenon joints were used for the door-frames (profile 1½inx16mm), with an internal rebate of 10x10mm and mitred fillets 6x10mm to fix the glass in position. Nailing panel pins into the hardwood fillets with the glass *in situ* proved difficult, the solution being to pre-drill the fillets with a slightly oversize drill before gluing and then tapping in ¾in panel pins.

The measure of success for any piece of craftsmanship is how well it looks in its surroundings and how well it does its intended job. For us, the piece wins on both counts, and its clear polyurethane semi-matt finish, with white adhesive plastic sheet for the internal face of the plywood backing, provides an excellent foil for our decor and furnishings. ■

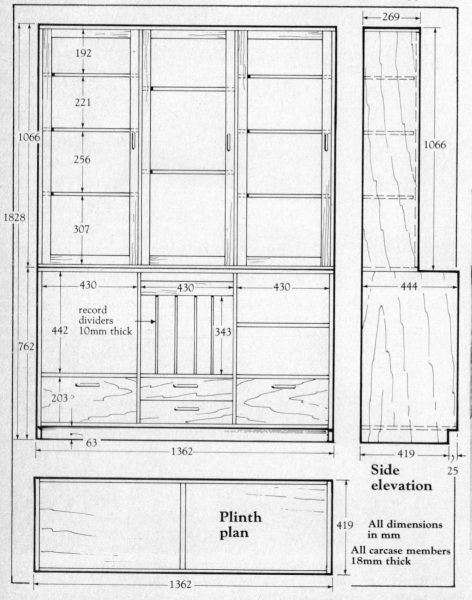

● *Shelf-ends are dovetail-tenoned to fit the dovetail housings; the side fence is adjusted to give a glue fit*

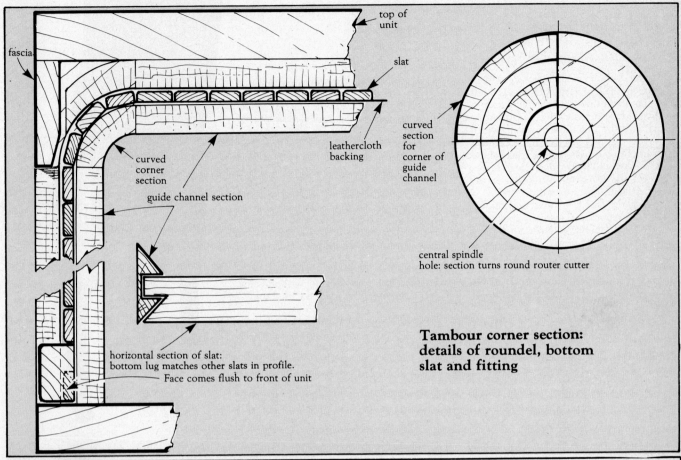

top of unit

fascia

slat

leathercloth backing

curved corner section

guide channel section

curved section for corner of guide channel

horizontal section of slat:
bottom lug matches other slats in profile.
Face comes flush to front of unit

central spindle hole: section turns round router cutter

Tambour corner section: details of roundel, bottom slat and fitting

The quiet American

A transatlantic transplant is making his name in fine English furniture. Aidan Walker went to see him

Peter Kuh, an ex-architecture student from the University of Kansas, stands fair in the middle of a strong tradition of English furniture-making. An afternoon in his workshop at Otterton Mill, which houses several practising craftspeople near the south Devon coast, revealed that behind his shy, slow-talking manner there lurk a sharp wit and some very firm ideas on the one-man furniture business.

He didn't finish his architecture training. Unhappy about the evident communication problem between the originator of a design and its builder, and impatient with the latest in a long line of silly projects (an elephant house), he decided to quit. Since he was leaving anyway, he reasoned with his mentors, could he build a chair instead of design an elephant house?

'It was a total write-off,' recalls Peter, 'a totally academic chair.' He had no machines, almost no hand-tools, and even less woodworking knowledge; he bought a waney-edge lump of oak and set to with a will. No great exponent of machine woodworking, he claims this experience taught him a lesson on what machines can do. 'Everyone should make at least one piece of furniture totally by hand.'

Peter worked for a builder in 1971-2, and later in a Boston furniture factory doing mainly unskilled work. He used a timely inheritance to pay for a year's training with Simon Watts, a cabinetmaker in Vermont. The year was particularly useful in providing time for him to develop hand skills and to get acquainted with the running of a small workshop. Having had some difficulties with his own apprentices, he sees both sides of the argument over paying for a 'practising' training. Why pay someone for the privilege of producing for them? 'I think workshop training is the best possible situation to learn the trade in,' he says. 'Unfortunately, there are far too few places for apprentices. If you're paying the boss, he can't put pressure on you to produce — and he can't fire you. I don't really want to take pupils, because I want to give the orders. I *want* to pay anyone that works here.'

Peter moved to England in 1975 to work with Alan Peters ('The hardest-working human being I think I've ever met'), initially on a provisional offer of six weeks' training. He stayed for two years.

'You must have impressed him.'

'I think I depressed him. When I arrived I thought I knew what I was doing. I feel dwarfed by Alan's commitment to his work.' He started his own business in 1977, well-positioned for the designer-craftsman network that seems strongest in that part of the country. He's been at Otterton Mill ever since.

His workshop is public, by an unwritten agreement with the Mill that in return for very favourable rent he will leave his doors open for visitors to walk round. It's 'not altogether an easy trade-off'; he reckons he gets about 10% of his orders from people who just walk in, but he has also given up counting the number of people 'whose only reaction is that my work is very expensive — compared to G-plan or MFI. Occasionally I find people are actually helping me with designs.' He was working on the height-adjusting mechanism for his music-stand, possibly his most publicised piece, and pays tribute to an engineer who walked in, got talking and ended up sending him a long letter and a detailed drawing. 'The ones I don't enjoy are the ones who come in, hold up a hand with missing fingers, and say: "I'm a woodworker too!"'

Apart from Peters, whose insistence on quality of workmanship and honesty of design he holds in extremely high regard, Peter also cites Edward Barnsley's work as an influence. 'I like curves much better than straight lines. Here we are trying to make something as beautiful as the tree which the wood originally came from; I like the elegance afforded by small-section components, I like inlay. People consider my work strongly traditional, but I'm not interested in fashion. I tend to ignore it, I don't look at exhibitions that much. I tend to work in a vacuum, which has its good and bad points.' He does, however, have a taste for the extreme — 'the over-the-top quality' which some regard as typically American.

The fact that his work undoubtedly stands in a high English tradition is a problem when it comes to acceptance in exhibitions. 'Modern galleries refuse to acknowledge the usefulness or worth of traditionally based work. Some won't even have it if it looks traditional.' As any craft

● *Peter's chair designs blend ergonomics and style*

worker should be, he is aware of the assistance available through local and national grants, and has made several unsuccessful applications. 'The Crafts Council and the regional arms of the Arts Council can really influence the way things go; it'd be a shame if they put all their money behind space-age stuff.' His latest application for a grant is currently under assessment.

Peter is excited, on the other hand, about 'my own contribution to space-age furniture', a bathroom chair in ash whose laminated components curve in three dimensions. Other chairs, the music-stand — indeed much of his work — curves in two, but this is a first attempt at compound shapes. The back-rest comes round to form the front legs. It is experimental, and Peter is highly appreciative of the client's willingness to pay the design development costs. With any batch work (he does sets of dining-chairs and machines 10 music-stands at a time), he will produce one piece to finished standard so the clients can see what they're getting before he makes the whole lot; he uses mock-ups and prototypes, but still sees the design side as 'the intimidating side. I might do two weeks' work and end up with nothing'. It's obviously a great advantage — almost a luxury — to have a client who is prepared to subsidise something like the bathroom chair; it eventually took 160 hours to produce.

Comfort and ergonomics, thankfully, are strict parameters for Peter's chair designs. For this one, he started with templates of an average human back-shape, made up from

● *Meticulous stringing and elegant shaping of the drop-leaf table-legs confer quiet distinction*

standardised data, and worked out dimensions accordingly; then he had to devise a jigging system to hold springy laminates in place in their compound curves. ('Alan Peters calls it "torturing wood"!') Try-outs at laminating the main, single back/legs member exposed gluing problems. The solution uses a three-dimensional jig on a gridded piece of blockboard, which consists of triangulated former-posts standing out to the precise positions where most clamping stress is taken. Peter had to measure out into the air to the positions where aesthetic and practical factors determined the key points of the structure, the grid ensuring symmetry. $\frac{1}{8}$in ash laminates were glued and bound together with bicycle inner tubes, a cramping system that evolved to eliminate separation at the twistiest bits. The single piece was held in the middle and bent either way to clamp to the former-posts; the seat and vertical lumbar support 'stile' were comparatively simple laminating jobs. For 160 hours' work, £600 doesn't seem so expensive.

Which brings us to the old chestnut of sales and marketing. How does a one-man business make money? Committed as he is to impeccable craftsmanship and finish, Peter has found selling bulk orders to shops difficult because he can't make it pay if he works on it himself, and can't in all conscience pass the work that apprentices turn out. A bread-board deal has faded away because the profit margins were too low,

● No fewer than 10 jigs are used in batch-producing the adjustable-height music-stand

although he had a CoSIRA trainee with him long enough to produce 300 in a year. 'I don't think I made a penny on them, apart from the few I sold through the workshop.' Similarly, a batch-production scheme for stools has died the death because 'young people come unstuck with my fussy insistence on precision.'

I suspect that Peter would rather not bother with selling as such at all. 'I was never brought up as a businessman. I'm basically anti-capitalist, but here I am running a business. When I set up in 1977 I didn't have a clue about how to sell a piece of furniture, and I had absolutely no business training. My approach was basically to copy Alan Peters' most visible selling method. I got into as many exhibitions as I could with various galleries and the Devon Guild of Craftsmen. On average I showed work in four or five exhibitions a year with usually one in a prestigious place like the Crafts Council gallery or the Prescote Gallery; in retrospect this is a wise marketing method since these exhibitions tend to attract people who are seriously interested in the work shown and who can often afford it. Another advantage of exhibitions is that the mark-up is usually low compared to that in exotic shops. I've always preferred to sell where the mark-up is low for the simple reason that if I discount my prices too much I end up losing money on the things I've made . . . I've done enough of that to know how soul-destroying it is.

'Once I had a foot-hold after a few years of exhibiting as extensively as possible, I had accumulated a small clientele; four to six customers who liked my work, trusted me not to overcharge and came back almost every year for something else.

'Aside from putting work in front of people either in my workshop or at exhibitions, the way that I market is really to discuss the qualities of design and construction which I put into the piece in which they are interested . . . in other words, I try to convince them I have a considerable amount of expertise and that they can trust me with their commission. For those who are only partially converted, this sometimes sways them my way. I am uncertain that I lose some customers by not having a line of chat to bring them on to my side; my social skills fail me here.

'Marketing, I believe, also includes selling work at the right price. Estimating is tricky and it can only be done reliably after some experience. I always keep time-sheets, and refer to them for estimates. If you don't price work correctly you end up working long hours just to keep your bank balance up to zero. You must be brave enough to quote prices which seem absurdly high at times, but of course you mustn't price yourself out of work. You have to apply intuition here as well — you can't simply apply a hard-and-fast rule of, say, £10 an hour or nothing. You might lose an important job that way that will pay off in other areas — good photos, publicity,

● 'The bathroom chair represents what I love and hate most about this crazy job.' Peter's contribution to 'space-age furniture'

opportunities to do experimental work.

He is adamant that 'the best part and also the worst' of the one-man set-up is that you're totally in command of the entire process. 'This is what attracted me to design/making — you constantly hear architects complain that the builder has screwed up their design. I do think co-operatives are a good idea — a proper co-op — because all the overheads are shared. Being on your own all the time can also drive you crazy, which is another good reason for a good co-op.' But then, setting up and keeping a co-op running demands commitment to the idea, and time that a solitary furniture-maker will never have. Just a few orders, and Peter will be working flat-out for months to fill them.

He makes no bones of the fact that the last two years have been hard. 'I sat down and evaluated the whole thing last winter,' he says: 'and decided that, despite the financial difficulties, the rewards were sufficient. All I want to do in my life is make half a dozen pieces with a timeless quality — I'd feel I was a lucky human being if I achieved that.'

'What struck me about Peter,' says Alan Peters, 'was that he has a great, dogged perseverance. I've seen many people with a great desire to be designer-craftsmen, but so few survive. Peter persists. He's still there, and there are lots of high-flyers who've fallen by the wayside.

'If there's one word to describe what I aim to achieve in design, workmanship and my dealings with customers,' says Peter, 'it's integrity.' If compliments were paid in cash, and a craftsman's honesty were bankable, Peter Kuh would be a very rich man. ■

● Peter Kuh, Endgrain, Otterton Mill, Otterton, Budleigh Salterton, Devon, (0395) 68031. The Mill is a working museum, open from 10.30 to 5.30 daily, and shorter hours in the winter.

The building contractor

Tony Sattin went to see a man who shrinks the best of British architecture to tabletop size

The first and most striking thing about Bruce Coombes is his passion for his work. Whether pointing out the model buildings ranged around his showroom-workshop in Frome, Somerset, or flicking through his albums of past commissions, he is animated. He loves talking about his models and the history that surrounds them.

This is not an idle observation, because one of the essential qualities for a modelmaker — Bruce Coombes specialises in building model period houses and architectural structures to scale — is enthusiasm: enough enthusiasm to survive the hours of painstaking research and weeks of delicate construction. Most of his stock models have taken between six and eight weeks to complete.

Born in London in 1917, he completed a tool-and-die apprenticeship and gained experience in several different fields before he started teaching technical studies and crafts at Bloomfield School, Woolwich, in the late sixties. It was there that he began making models — as teaching aids, to help bring history alive and to demonstrate construction techniques through the centuries. He has now made a series of models of Tudor, Georgian and Victorian houses, which have been bought by the Schools Loan Service. They are made from a variety of woods, including oak and mahogany; the windows are glazed either with glass or, if the models are to be used by children, with Perspex. His unusual scale is $5/16$ or $3/8$ in to the foot.

Another educational series he has developed demonstrates road communications with fine scale models of a coaching inn, toll-house, blacksmith's forge, wheelwright's shop and village store. And, to give movement to the series, there's a working $1/12$-scale model of a Royal Mail coach, its wooden structure mounted with iron shackles on to timber axle-cases. The wheelwright's shop is an excellent example of the lengths to which Bruce Coombes will go to recreate a building and its contents. Open the doors to the workshop, and inside are the workbenches and tools of the trade — all fixed to the surfaces and racks in case they get lost or broken.

By the early 1970s Bruce had moved to a school in Bath, and it was then that the *Sunday Times* carried a feature on his models. The subsequent attention and flood of commissions allowed him to retire from teaching and devote all his time to developing his talent for modelmaking. But

● *Bruce Coombes has a particular passion for miniature inns because of the social history which fills every corner.* **Below** *is the Spaniards, a well-known north-London landmark*

the commercial demand for his work didn't make him change his techniques. Although his workshop now houses an engineer's lathe, a woodworker's lathe, a bandsaw and a small drilling machine, he doesn't do anything with them that he wasn't already doing with hand tools. 'All the machines do', he points out, 'is make things quicker.' Unlike many other areas of woodworking, modelmaking doesn't have to involve any great expense, and it can be done on the smallest of worktops.

His new market allowed him to expand his range, and he was commissioned to produce scale models of a number of private houses for their owners. Of one of them — Duart Castle, in Mull, Scotland, made on a scale of $3/16$in for its owner Lord Charles Maclean — he is especially proud. For such a commission Bruce, usually assisted by his wife, likes to spend some time at the house, not only to measure (they take the dimensions and descriptions of every room and passage) but also to get a feel for the place. 'You have to use a certain amount of discretion when reconstructing,' he insists; but you also have to know the building you are intending to model.'

Models of houses and public buildings are usually intended as presents. One proud father commissioned a model of Burbage's Globe theatre (1599) to commemorate his son's appearance in one of Shakespeare's plays.

Commercial organisations also showed an interest, and a number of companies (both in England and abroad) have commissioned models. Some form part of a promotion — the Japanese purchased models of a Cotswold stone house, a Tudor half-timbered house, a Victorian artisan's house and a Georgian shop, to display at British Week in Tokyo in 1975, and a department store in New York commissioned a stunning Tudor house as a central display piece. Some are emblems for products — the Black & White whisky company ordered a working model of a horse-drawn whisky dray.

Bruce Coombes has also executed a number of models of inns and taverns, usually for the licensee or landlord. This area of his work obviously excites him, and he does a great deal of research for it. 'I like to know the stories that come with the inns.' His models are exact and carry some of the history of the real buildings with them. His enthusiasm for the inns reflects his deep interest in social history; and, as he says, 'Every inn has got some history attached to it.' Along the shelves of his showroom are models of the Spaniards Inn, the much sung-about Bull and Bush in north London, and the King's Head in Aylesbury. Some are intended as educational pieces, and so a section of the roofing can be detached to reveal the structure — built, as in the original, of oak (although he uses pine if it's not going to be seen).

His sense of history pervades his work altogether. Both his Nuremberg kitchen and his grocery shop are meticulously accurate in their furnishings and details; pans and kettles are made from copper or brass, and each packet is properly labelled. It is through these pieces that the modelling tradition can be traced: like the other models in the range — an English butcher's shop, a Victorian bathroom, a milliner's shop and a pleasure-garden kiosk — the grocer's shop was first made as a training aid for young ladies before marriage; it was to give them an idea of how a household was run and provided for, and to show them things they might never have seen otherwise.

By the end of the 19th century, toymakers in Nuremberg were reproducing the buildings as toys for children. The doll's- or baby-houses, as they were called, were originally designed for boys to play with, although they have a more general appeal now. The people who commission the models in this range do so for their value and appeal as collectors' items, and

● *A Coombes interior is carefully detailed down to counters, labels, pots and pans*

only occasionally for use as toys. (Bruce also provides miniatures, mostly furniture and brass- and copper-ware, for members of the International Doll's-House Club.)

The ability of Bruce Coombes' models to record social and industrial history is clearly shown in his scale reconstruction of Bridgewater Docks as they were in 1900, showing the warehouses, railway lines and roads, which is now exhibited at Bridgewater's Admiral Blake Museum. The list of his other commissions includes models of Newcomen's steam-engine, canal scenes (complete with lock-keeper's house, lock gates and barge or narrowboat), a complete medieval village for the Loch Lomond Bear Park, and a number of buildings for the army's officer training colleges. There seems no end to the different ways his models are used. This was obviously one of the things that first attracted Bruce Coombes to modelmaking, and it has continued to fascinate him.

At one time he called himself an artist-craftsman because, he argued, he was a craftsman in skill and an artist by inheritance (from his father and grandfather) and by training (at the Harrow and Lime Grove schools of art). But he seems to have little time for or interest in that kind of debate now.

He calls himself a historical modelmaker and a specialist — less provocative, perhaps, but just as apt.

In keeping with a noticeable trend among independent specialists in a whole variety of occupations, Bruce has recently opened a shop (he works behind it) at 17 Paul Street, Frome, Somerset. It is strange but pleasing to see a window filled with models in a row of shops selling more mundane products such as clothes and food. Inside he is busy at work on his latest commission, for the Castle Cary Museum: a Roman temple, based on the one uncovered at the Creech Hill site, which is typical of rural Roman temples found all over the country. Piled on his worktop are books on Roman architecture and guides to Roman sites and archeological digs. If you go in you might find him researching a design for the mosaic on the floor, or wondering whether there should be a frieze beside the architrave, or just gazing at his already completed models — reminders not only of ages gone by, but of life-styles that went with them. ∎

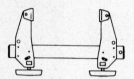
28

You never saw better!

The DeWalt Powershop will transform your woodworking capability. Its unique combination of precision, versatility and ease of use, long appreciated by professionals, is increasingly convincing the home woodworker and tradesman to make the DeWalt Powershop the centre-piece in his workshop.

The quiet, maintenance-free induction motor has a full 1½hp output to cope effortlessly with even the toughest hardwood.

In its standard form, the DeWalt Powershop will perform all the basic sawcuts, with the two models offering a choice of 380mm or 465mm crosscut capacity (640/730mm max. ripping width). Combined with the range of optional attachments, it becomes a complete workshop.

The DeWalt Powershop makes even the most demanding woodworking project easier, quicker and more accurate.

How much longer can you get by without one?

Price guide for DW1251 Powershop around £395.00 inc. VAT. (DW1501=£459.00 inc. VAT).

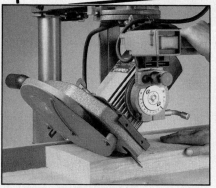

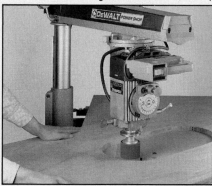

PRECISION

The cast iron arm and substantial steel support column complement the clamping levers and machined locations for the most common cutting angles to ensure superb rigidity.

Calibrated scales are provided for setting accurately the cutting angle required. Once set, the robust Powershop will hold in that position for repeated cuts to produce identical workpieces.

Consistent accuracy is the hallmark of DeWalt, and the Powershop is fully adjustable to maintain accuracy throughout its long life.

VERSATILITY

The Powershop's standard equipment provides for crosscutting, bevels, mitres and ripcuts, as well as dishing, hollowing and circle-cutting, while the optional attachments enable grooving, tenoning, rebating, edge-moulding, curved and straight sanding and even drilling.

With the special mounting bracket, most Elu plunging routers can also be secured to the Powershop, giving enormous scope for accurate decorative work. With all this versatility you can tackle even the most ambitious woodworking projects with confidence.

EASE OF USE

Despite its versatility, the Powershop needs access only on three sides (unlike a traditional sawbench) so it can be positioned conveniently on an existing bench or on its optional legstand against the wall of your workshop, leaving more space free for other activity.

All operations with the Powershop are conducted with ease, accuracy and safety. Simple, yet positive controls enable quick adjustment of the depth and angle of cut.

Even the most complicated woodworking joints can be easily mastered with the DeWalt Powershop.

For a free copy of the Powershop Colour Wallchart and the name of your nearest participating dealer, write to:-

 **DeWALT ® POWERSHOP**
THERE'S NO BETTER WAY TO WORK WITH WOOD

DeWalt Powershop Offer, Dept. ', Black & Decker Professional Products Division, Westpoint, The Grove, Slough, Berkshire SL1 1QQ. or Telephone (0753) 74277 and ask for "Service & Information Centre".

Buying timber wisely :4

Alan Thomas continues his nationwide tour of the timber merchants who care

Wheelers appears just the sort of timber yard that small-time buyers would do well to avoid. It is huge — £4.4m turnover, and 15 acres of yards and sheds buried in an enormous industrial estate. It has one of those forbidding entrance barriers operated by a security man.

But anyone who quails at this exterior would be entirely wrong. The chap wanting a fiver's worth of wood really is as welcome as a builder about to order hundreds of roof trusses.

Wheelers has been established in the area of Sudbury, Suffolk since 1860, when it began to supply building materials including home-made bricks. Since then the company has infiltrated every corner of the building trade — and also gone wholeheartedly into the DIY market, with a very large showroom devoted to the faced chipboards, fitted furniture, kitchens and bathrooms which form the backbone of the trade. And there is an equally sizeable tool shop which holds the better class of hand and power equipment.

But to many potential customers, turning up in their family saloons for that notional fiver's worth and getting a courteous nod from the gateman as he raises his barrier, Wheelers means oak. Lots and lots of oak. Logs of it, planks of it, drying sheds and kilns full of it — all scenting the air with that unmistakable vinegary smell. Wheelers stock other species, but it is the oak which impresses visitors.

Much of the present Wheeler enthusiasm for native-grown hardwoods stems from current managing director Stephen Goody, and he was quick to recognise that present-day Britain offers considerable business potential for suppliers who are willing not to place a lower limit on the value of individual orders. The slump has left many craftsmen and would-be craftsmen with time on their hands, and a lot of them have turned to woodworking. Some are now established small businesses; others are in a no-man's-land where their home workshop keeps them occupied and produces the occasional saleable piece. 'I know', says Stephen Goody, of a joinery business not far from here which employed maybe 120 people. It closed down almost overnight, but over a period several of their tradesmen have become regular customers here.

'Of course, you don't get much oak for a fiver these days! On the other hand, our prices are lower than many retailers' because we supply them. As a broad indication, I'd say our price for selected sawn oak is currently around £30 to £33 a cubic foot. If you want it put through our mill and finish-planed that adds £7.'

Why is oak so expensive?

'Is it expensive? The landowner who grew it wants a return, or there's no incentive to re-plant. Then we take a gamble on the inside of a tree: there can be a lot of wastage — wood that's just not usable; the net yield from oak is about 70%. Elm and ash are much better, at about 90%, because oak sapwood is no use.

'You see, there's no comparison at all with softwoods, which are what most people think of as wood. They're close-grown on otherwise useless land and can be cut in 40 years. For oak it's nearer 120 years. Then there's the drying. Oak is more difficult, takes more time, and is vastly more labour-intensive. Identifying prime-quality planks takes a tremendous amount of inspection time.'

Once Wheelers went all over the country to collect suitable trees, but now East Anglia and Sussex are the main sources for oak, sweet chestnut, ash, and even elm still. Some beech is bought in, too. Many users will be surprised to learn that Britain has more oak maturing than it actually uses, and — so far as anyone can tell — there is more than enough to last into the next century. But, if this happy state is to continue, felling and re-planting must become continuous: there's no point in leaving a tree standing so long that it goes past its prime.

Perhaps the most spectacular use for Wheeler oak is in renovating, renewing and matching tudor-style timber-framed buildings. 'In this area builders use a fair amount of fresh-sawn oak for that kind of work,' says Stephen Goody, ' and we can supply up to 18in square by 20ft long. Prices are much lower for heavy structural material, of course; probably less than half what they are for the joinery and cabinet grades.

'Joinery takes an increasing amount, and I think that within five years hardwoods will be in quite common use for secondary fixings. Reproduction furniture-making is amazingly buoyant, too. A lot of low-grade

beech, ash, and to some extent sycamore, goes to firms making upholstered furniture. And fencing is very significant: oak is durable in that application.'

Since Wheelers converts it own butts, there are many lying in the yard, although numbers fall as winter recedes ('You don't cut oak in the summer'). And there is plenty of sawn wood slowly air-drying. 'It is of absolutely paramount importance to dry it in stick before kilning if you're going to maintain quality,' insists Stephen Goody. 'We use new sticks every time to prevent staining.' After air-drying down to, say, 17 or 18% moisture content, the vacuum kiln takes 24 hours to the inch to reduce content down to 12%. Heated platens control any tendency to twist in the kiln.

● Acres of oak and English hardwoods at Wheelers. Native timbers come mainly from East Anglia and Sussex

Apart from the larger square sections, much of the timber is sawn through-and-through into 2in planks, and it can be bought in that form. When it is, any defects are measured out and the remainder charged accordingly. This is why square-edged appears to be more expensive than waney-edged, and Stephen Goody points out that, while defects — notably sapwood and the almost inevitable splits down the middle — are still present in the planks, they are also costing rent in the drying sheds: it all adds to the final cost. On the plus side, he also remarks that, when buyers order sizes to be finished at the mill, the machinists naturally do more selecting as they work: if a concealed defect comes to light, a substitute piece will be found.

Wheelers, like most other sellers, prefer buyers to go along and choose for themselves. Finished, racked timber is stored in drive-in warehouses, so that customer selection and loading are independent of the weather. Anyone used to racks of planed-all-round softwoods, 2x1in, 3x¾in and so on, will find it odd to come face-to-face with a similar choice of dimensions and quantity in oak, ash and chestnut. In addition to this regular stock there is a sizeable and often changing selection of boards, run-ons, and ends surplus to special orders.

Rough-sawn planks and planks in stick are less conveniently, if still temptingly, housed in a collection of sheds, and so huge is the choice that customers are quite likely to be told to browse and come out when they've found what they want.

Unlike many merchants, Stephen Goody is keen to have even small buyers call during the week. If they know what they want, there will be enough labour to help them find it. On Saturday mornings, though, the main pressure is off, and staff are able to spend more time solving the problems of the chap who just wants a bit of wood.

A recurring difficulty, says Stephen, is that of getting a finish. 'Are amateurs aware of the snags there can be in working and finishing some woods?' he asks. 'They look at furniture made with plenty of machining facilities, and think they can get the same results with hand tools. This is one of the reasons why we like to talk to customers about their projects, and often we steer them away from something that they originally wanted to something else that will be much the same for a lot less work.'

And he repeats the standard advice: 'Please don't try to "help" us by lumping all the dimensions together in the hope of saving us time and you money. It is always better to give us a proper cutting list. Then we can both save.'

Apart from the native hardwoods, Wheelers also hold iroko and Brazilian mahogany, and builder's sections in both. Then there is the softwood stock: as importers the company can pick and choose, and they hold all grades from carcassing upwards. 'Pine sawn for finishing at home can be supplied from clear to very knotty.'

Where possible, it's obviously a good idea to collect personally, but the firm's already intensive delivery service to builders and factories can be harnessed for more modest consumers.

As part of his crusade for native hardwoods Stephen Goody is willing to organise evening tours of Wheelers. Provided they give some notice, small parties are welcome to see for themselves how logs are cut, kilned, and machined.
Wheelers Ltd, Chilton, Sudbury, Suffolk CO10 6XH, tel. (0787) 73391. Mon-Fri 8-5, Sat 8.30-12.30.

Your average timber merchant was set up to sell timber: Treework Services began at the other end, cutting down trees and having to dispose of them.

Operating from a positively concealed series of sheds in a worked-out quarry at Backwell, near Bristol, Treework has been a single entity for less than two years; but its several partners have been in the business and collaborating with each other for more than a decade. While most people in timber reckon to have a feeling for the stuff, and the trees from which it comes, the Treework team have an almost passionate concern for the environment generally and woodlands in particular. This regard colours their conversation and appears to have a marked effect on their business.

According to John Emery and Neville Fry, two of the partners, tree-felling is often considered to be vandalism. But, says Neville, 'You could equally put it the other way round, for timber users contribute to the regeneration of a natural resource. Felling is an essential element in the process. Without human intervention, woodland rapidly degenerates into scrub. By taking out the right trees at the right time it is possible to use the money they produce to keep woodland in good condition.'

Broadly the business divides into three areas: tree surgery, woodland renovation, and the supply of kiln-dried native hardwoods ('Consultancy, too,' adds Neville). John Emery reckons that about half of the quality wood they sell comes from their own felling. Each scheme is worked out to suit individual sites and owners. 'Usually', says John, 'a woodland has been managed at some time but allowed to fall into neglect. So the trees will tend to mature at the same time: they're overcrowded, with a lot of undergrowth, and poorly formed. Judicious thinning improves the aesthetic appeal and renovation ensures the survival of the woodland. And the timber extracted helps to finance the work.'

Having got trees lying on the ground, Treework has to find a use for them. 'We find markets, from firewood up,' says Neville Fry. 'Did you realise that about a third of the hardwoods grown in this country go to the coalmines? Timber for fencing we pass on to specialist contractors — fencing is a very competitive business with tight margins, and we couldn't compete. But probably some of the wood will be of use to Treework. Even so, we can't hog all the best, because we have to preserve our reputation as honest brokers when other merchants are interested in buying parcels of timber.'

What the partners are looking for in the supply end of their business, says John Emery, is good quality planking-grade timber. 'Veneer is the very topmost grade, but usually only one log will be as good as

● *Loading a kiln at Treework Services – these English hardwoods have already been in stick for some time*

that. The veneer-makers want to buy by the lorry load, though, so often we plank the log.'

Where it is simply too awkward to get a butt back to the works, portable chainsaw-milling equipment is taken to the tree, but there is wastage and thick planks result. Whenever possible, logs are cut up by a specialist milling company, which at least makes it easier to get stock to the quarry by way of an unavoidable network of one-vehicle-wide lanes.

● *Treework will also machine your timber to size*

Treework seems even to have found its own sorts of customers. 'Some don't care about where the wood comes from,' says John. 'But, at the other extreme, two of our buyers want a promise from us that they are buying native hardwoods, and that the timber was cut as part of a scheme of re-planting. One user won't touch imported hardwood because of the environmental implications, and explains to his clients why he won't use anything but native species. He says they usually agree, and he hasn't lost any work as a result. There is unease among woodworkers about what is happening to the world's forests, and it makes customers feel great that by using material from our sources they are actually doing something to help.'

If all this sounds a bit far-fetched, not to say high-flown, Neville Fry could also produce a customer who made prestige furniture for British use in Japan, and who had to guarantee the wood was British also.

The partners estimate that about half their customers earn a living at woodwork, and that they are mostly concerns employing one to five people — probably making furniture and fitted kitchens. An interesting demand comes from DIYers who are looking for single pieces of 'feature' timber — for a mantelpiece, for example, or a fancy window-sill. Giving these one-off buyers exactly what they want and being helpful about it will, John and Neville like to think, help spread the good word generally, and may even coax people back to buy wood for more adventurous projects.

John Emery thinks Treework have about a couple of thousand cubic feet of timber currently air-drying; Neville Fry reckons it's more like 3000. They both agree it's time for a stocktaking, but that about one-third of the stock and turnover is in oak and ash. The rest mainly consists of elm, sweet chestnut, yew and sycamore. However, their forays into small plantations and large gardens often produce rarer timbers; ask, and it may well be that enough acacia, or apple, or box, or lime, or plane, or tulipwood, or any of a dozen other home-grown exotica, will be available. Stock prices are based on thickness — for instance, waney-edged oak 1½in thick would be £18.50 per cubic foot, with increasing discounts as quantities rise. On the same basis ash comes out at £13, and sycamore is £12.50.

Finding that waney-edged planks work out cheaper, Treework's customers not surprisingly tend to buy in that form. But such material can present a daunting sight to the possessor of average home-workshop facilities. However, the yard is perfectly willing to saw wood to required dimensions for an extra charge, and it is sometimes possible to cut chosen planks to size while a customer waits. Even more attractive to some potential buyers is the firm's willingness to plane material to a cutting list.

Going further still, John Emery outlines their workshop time-hire scheme: for £6 and hour, users can have the run of a big bandsaw, crosscut and circular saws, a 24in over-and-under planer, and a mortiser. Obviously prior arrangements are essential, and normally working hours Monday to Friday, plus Saturday morning, are the available time.

An ingenious scheme now making gradual but satisfactory progress is the woodworkers' agency. On the premise that many craftsmen are too busy making to go out and sell, while many potential clients don't know how to contact suitable makers, the partners have begun a self-defined task: raising public awareness of work being done in native hardwoods, and of the people who do it.

Each member on the agency list pays only £50 a year, so the budget is not large, but it does go some way to providing the sort of public-relations activities which busy craftsmen tend to neglect: maintaining a presence at county and similar shows, preparing presentation folders of work, and the like. In addition, a room at the Treework headquarters is given over to photographic displays of work by members — and, of course, samples of the woods available. The agency idea is frankly experimental. So long as it is self-financing, say the partners, that will be good enough.

Treework Services have undertaken their low-cost woodland renovation schemes in Sussex, Surrey, Wales and of course the southwest generally. Customers for the end product are also widely spread, but probably 80% are within 30 miles of Backwell. There are no regular delivery services for small customers, but good use is made of transport hired to take large consignments. Part-loads are almost invariably delivered within 10 days of ordering.

● Wheelers keep large stocks of planed-all-round material; here is an assortment of oak lengths and sections, left over from larger orders

● Buyers can rent workshop time at Treework, where there is a full range of massive machinery for you to use

Native hardwoods, feel John and Neville, will be scarce around the first quarter of the next century, in reflection of the woodland neglect during and immediately after the Great War. It is not right, they claim, to compare prices of home-grown against those for imported: in too many exporting countries there is no requirement to re-plant, and labour is very cheap. Neville, however, foresees the price gap narrowing as such nations realise what they are doing to a valuable resource, and come into line with more enlightened thinking. ■

Treework Services Ltd, Cheston Combe, Church Town, Backwell, Avon, tel. (0275) 833917. Intending visitors really would be well advised to telephone first for a copy of the firm's price-list-cum-maps. Six full days' opening each week, 9-5.30, with lunch 1-2.

Routing for tambours

Bob Wearing's Workshop

Bob suggests a simple template for a tricky routing task

Few of us nowadays want to plough or scratch out the grooves for tambours. The power router is so quick, neat and accurate that it's obviously the tool to use when it's available. And many workers will use it — but not to the full.

Most will be happy to work the straight grooves with the router, but lack the confidence to work the corner quarter-circles. Working these freehand is somewhat risky, particularly on expensive material or when much work has already been done, so generally these curves are chiselled out, a time-consuming though thoroughly safe method. Some routers are provided with a pivot-pin for circular work, but the radius required for a tambour is usually too small to be arranged.

Help is however at hand in the form of this simple jig or template. To make it, first collect the data from the working drawing (fig. 1): width of groove, depth of groove (not required immediately), distance in from the edge, proposed radius, and diameter of the router's guide-bush.

Make the template from an accurately squared piece of plywood very slightly thicker than the height of the guide-bush; the size will vary to suit the particular router. It must be big enough to permit the router movement required and also give room for two cramps to hold it in place.

Fig. 2 shows the construction. I mark out with a fine ballpoint pen because it gives a consistent thin line. Mark out the two centre-lines to give point C. Draw a circle centred on C which is the centre-line of the groove. Stab in two centres, P1 and P2. Choose a convenient radius and strike two arcs B from P1 and P2; bisect the right-angle at the centre, extending beyond C. Stab another centre D on this 45° line about ¼in (6mm) from C. This distance is related to the width of the tambour slats, and a test groove on some scrap material will confirm it. Now drill two holes of the diameter of the guide-bush, centred on P1 and P2. From the centres C and D draw arcs connecting the outside and inside edges of the two holes. Shade in the waste and then saw out carefully with a coping-saw and file accurately to the lines. Drill C to take a panel pin.

Set a gauge to the distance between C and the edge of the template, gauge two lines from the two edges of the actual job (fig. 1), and lightly stab their intersection. Locate the template on this point by a pin through C. Do not hammer the pin in. Square up the template with one edge of the job and secure it there with two cramps or hand-screws, which must be positioned clear of the router's path.

Now simply fit the required cutter, generally ¼in or 6mm, adjust the depth and proceed to cut the groove — two cuts are better than one heavy one.

The extra removed from the inside of the curve makes it easier for the slats to nego-tiate the corners. Test out the groove; if the fit is not an easy one, move D back slightly and re-draw the inside curve with an increased (flatter) radius. Having confidence in the template, I prefer to cut the curves first and then join up with the straight grooves.

Finish by drilling a hanging hole, as the template may well be useful again. Write on it the width of slat used. ∎

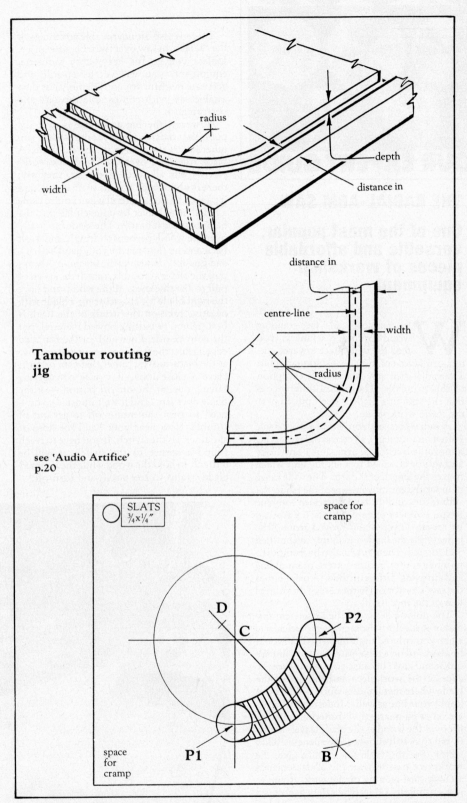

Tambour routing jig

see 'Audio Artifice' p.20

MACHINING WOOD

YOUR EXPERT GUIDE

THE RADIAL-ARM SAW

One of the most popular, versatile and affordable pieces of workshop equipment

With almost all free-standing woodworking machinery, you feed the workpiece towards cutters or blades spinning in a stationary unit. The radial-arm saw is a notable exception to this principle. The radical difference is that the spinning blade is itself pulled over the static workpiece.

A radial-arm saw consists of a work-table (often on four legs), a vertical pillar carrying a movable horizontal arm, and a saw-blade and motor attached to a sliding unit which moves the length of the arm. The wide range of independent movements of the blade, the sliding unit and the horizontal arm combine to suit a variety of applications; the arm can be raised, lowered and moved around the pillar while the blade and motor can be tilted and rotated. There might also be facilities to mount a router, router cutters, or moulding and grooving cutters on the arm, using either the saw's motor or (in the case of the router) that of the tool itself.

The unique design of the radial-arm saw makes it ideal for crosscutting, particularly when you're handling long pieces that would be awkward on a table-saw. Cuts to a line are quick and easy, because you can just see the edge of the workpiece and the tips of the blade where metal meets wood — and (you hope) your line as well. Modern radial-arms are very well-guarded, with mechanisms that lift over the wood as the blade travels across it, but they still allow a convenient visibility factor that the table-saw cannot give; the workpiece passing over the blade demands an awkward craning of the neck, if you're just cutting to a line. The safety aspect is a subject of much controversy, of course, but there remains no doubt that the radial-arm is good news for quick 'one-off' cuts in a busy workshop. It's also efficient for repeat-cutting, where a stop-block is clamped to the fence to give an accurate length; again blade-and-line visibility is an advantage. If you're doing a lot of this work, chamfer the bottom edge of your stop-block because dust can collect against it and reduce the length of your supposedly uniform pieces!

There is also an unarguable advantage of the radial-arm saw over the table-saw: price. Unless you go for heavy-duty industrial equipment, you will get a versatile and accurate machine for considerably less than a table-saw with comparable capacity and performance.

However, the big argument is over the potential hazards that, some claim, are inherent in the design of the machine. A blade travelling over the top of the workpiece spells all sorts of danger, they say; there is undoubtedly some truth in this, and it pays to be extra-careful when you're using a radial-arm. Never let yourself fall into the habit of using it hastily. The blade can 'walk' over the wood, perhaps shifting it, pulling it back and up (and maybe your hand with it), and possibly damaging the machine. Always pull the slider smoothly, match the speed of pull to the thickness of the wood, and have the right blade for crosscutting; a blade with negative rake on the fronts of the teeth is best. If you're cutting bowed material, put the convex side down and/or the rounded edge against the fence so the cut will open up as the blade moves, rather than jam on to it. Have a close look, if you're considering buying one, at the on/off button — if the blade does jam (and it isn't unusual), you'll need to turn the motor off to get out of trouble. How near your hand (or nose or shoulder!) is the switch? If you have to reach round a corner to the switch, it will be difficult to hold the wood while the jammed blade strains to free itself, and turn off.

● **Above:** *A radial-arm saw with all guards removed. The blade/motor unit rises and falls, slides on the arm and tilts; it's important to get the table set up accurately.* **Below:** *a straight mitre cut with the arm swung at 45°. Note the hefty back-fence*

The riskiest part of the radial-arm saw, in a sense, is its very convenience. It's just too tempting to slap a piece of wood down and be pulling the blade over it almost before you've shifted your hand . . . no woodworking machine should ever be used carelessly, but safety margins are greater with some than others.

Careful setting-up of a radial-arm saw is vital to its efficient and accurate performance. This involves sensitive and painstaking installation, to get all the calibrations spot on; almost everything is adjustable, so if a dial says 90° and you're getting an 88° cut, you can sort it out. Start by levelling the table, and then line it with hardboard or a piece of thin ply, making sure no panel pins go in where the blade might travel. Unless you're doing dado or grooving cuts (where the height adjustment is useful), the blade needs to project through the bottom of the wood, and there's no point in replacing the thick ply or chipboard table regularly! The bottom surface of the workpiece must be hard against the table to prevent spelching, so when the hardboard or ply is badly scored, moved it around or replace it. The wooden fence at the back of the table is the same; the blade goes behind it, so blade-width kerfs are cut out of it whenever and wherever you re-position the blade. The notches can be quite useful for positioning pieces to be cut at first, but the inevitable vibration of the blade soon widens them, and you can't rely on this as a system of measurement for long. It's also important to realise that the different angles at which the blade can be set will eventually combine to create a selection of wedges in the fence, ready to be cut loose, jam between the blade and work or fence, bounce off and fly past your head — if you're lucky. Wear safety glasses and change the fence when it needs it.

When setting the machine up for use, *read the manufacturer's instructions thoroughly.* Make sure you know exactly how to adjust the machine and its guards, and are familiar with the locking devices and the panic button. Note the direction of rotation of the saw, and make sure it's mounted the right way round. Don't use extra-heavy blades, as they can put a strain on the motor bearings. Do trial runs with the moving parts, getting the feel of how it all works; level up the table, square up the arm to the fence, and check the various cuts for accuracy. The best way of doing this is to cut one piece in two, turn one half over, and see if the two pieces placed end-to-end still make a dead straight line. For mitre cuts, check that the two halves of one piece cut at 45° go together to make a perfect right-angle. Compound mitres, too, are easily done but tricky to set up; the blade itself is working on two angles, given by the arm's rotation and the tilt of the blade/motor unit. Get one dead right and then go on to the other.

In design terms, it looks as if there are more sources of inaccuracy in these machines, because it would be natural for the arm to drop slightly at its extremity, and accuracy be lost at the outer end. While hairline adjustments are more difficult at the saw's limits of extension, the better machines are remarkably dependable, and there is always some adjustment you can make. There are machines on the market with support for the arm at both ends, but current models are on the small side.

Ripping — cutting along the grain — is a great deal less pleasant on radial-arm saws than crosscutting, and in truth it is a function to which the design does not lend itself. If you can only afford one saw, however, you can still get reasonably effective ripping; just remember to wear

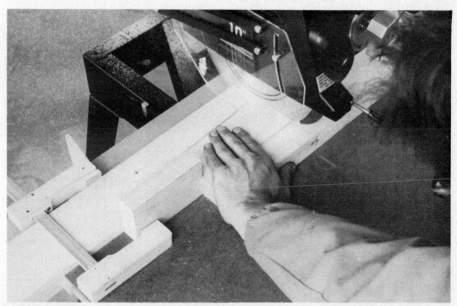

● **Above:** *Repeat crosscutting to a pre-set length with a clamped block.* **Below:** *A compound mitre cut*

● **Below:** *Handles and catches vary from machine to machine. Here, the release catch is held while the arm is swung round*

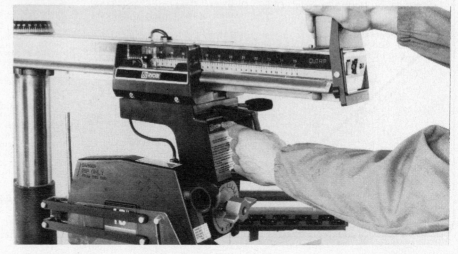

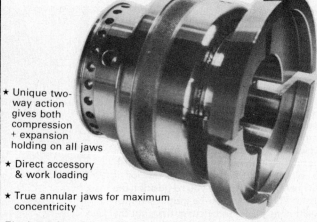

your eye-protectors, because the blade's direction of rotation means the dust and chips fly straight back at you. Attempts to extract or deflect airborne waste are only partly successful, because it's difficult to enclose and guard a sliding blade efficiently. Most saws have 'in-rip' and 'out-rip' positions, which basically mean that the motor is either toward the fence for the wider cuts or further away from it for the narrower ones. The blade/motor unit locks anywhere on the arm, and even with the smaller machines you can rip widths up to 24in. Again, be especially safety-conscious; there are grip-teeth devices (varying from machine to machine) which prevent kickback of the workpiece, and a safety hold-down should also be incorporated; the natural tendency is for the blade to lift

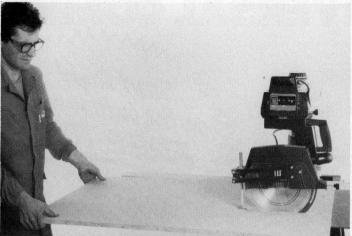

● *Left:* Panel cutting or ripsawing can be uncomfortable to eyes and face! Blade-guarding and enclosing systems vary in effectiveness

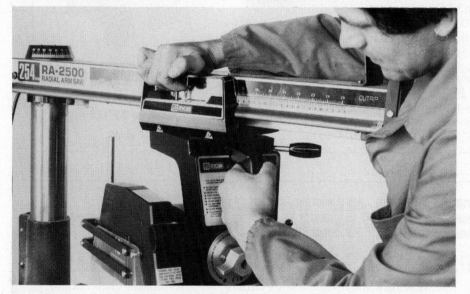

● **Above:** Another release mechanism swings the blade/motor unit on its own axis.

This series was written by Judith Barker. Ken Taylor of the London College of Furniture checked it for completeness and accuracy. Aidan Walker planned it and demonstrated the techniques. Derek Wales took the pictures. But Luna Tools and Machinery made it possible. They provided vital financial support – and for photography and demonstration they lent their machines, their space, and the help and advice of staff member Joe Wickens. So we give our warmest thanks to Luna's MD Gerry Baker for his unhesitating and generous co-operation. Luna are at 20 Denbigh Hall, Bletchley, Milton Keynes, Bucks MK3 7QT, tel. Milton Keynes (0908) 70771.

the wood off the table. The height of both these mechanisms (sometimes they are one and the same) is critical for their proper function, which in turn means that the thickness of the wood must be constant. If it varies in thickness, the grip-teeth/hold-down will chatter when it goes loose and jam when it gets too tight. Don't be tempted to save a walk round the table to collect cut pieces by ripping half a length, pulling it back and cutting to make the line meet halfway; to do this you'll need to have the safety teeth too loose to do their job properly, and you're asking for your bit of wood to savage you mercilessly. Use two push-sticks; remember also that the blade is turning in different directions on 'in-rip' and 'out-rip', and feed the work from the right side of the table.

Manufacturers claim that the radial-arm saw's undoubted versatility is further enhanced by the capability of carrying grooving and moulding devices, either cutters in blocks or a separately-powered electric router. It's quite a good idea to turn your hand-held router into an overhead machine on the arm of the saw, but cutter-blocks are generally too small for optimum

moulding and the motor-speeds too low for the best result. Better than nothing of course, but if you do use these facilities, make a number of small cuts rather than one big one, feed the work quite slowly, and make sure your cutters are in tip-top condition. In ordinary cutting terms alone, thousands of satisfied radial-arm saw users find they get excellent value from the machine's compactness, convenience, adaptability, and, above all, price. ■

● Use two push-sticks if you can!

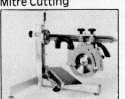

A bandsaw you can build

Follow John White's immaculate drawings and you'll end up with a machine you know inside-out

These plans are (or should be) self-explanatory.

No doubt readers can improve on the design in some respects — indeed, I did so myself when I made both the top and rear wheels adjustable to allow for possible reductions in blade length caused by breakage and re-welding. This feature does not appear on the drawings: but I've found that the top wheel allows enough adjustment in any case.

Other requirements not shown in the plans are the motor guard, and the case fittings for securing the main guard. The design of the motor guard depends on the motor. I mounted the electrics on the motor guard via a plug-and-socket arrangement, so that both guard and electrics can be removed at once.

The main frame and base are made from

● *Handsome and strong – and all John paid for was the ply and the pulley!*

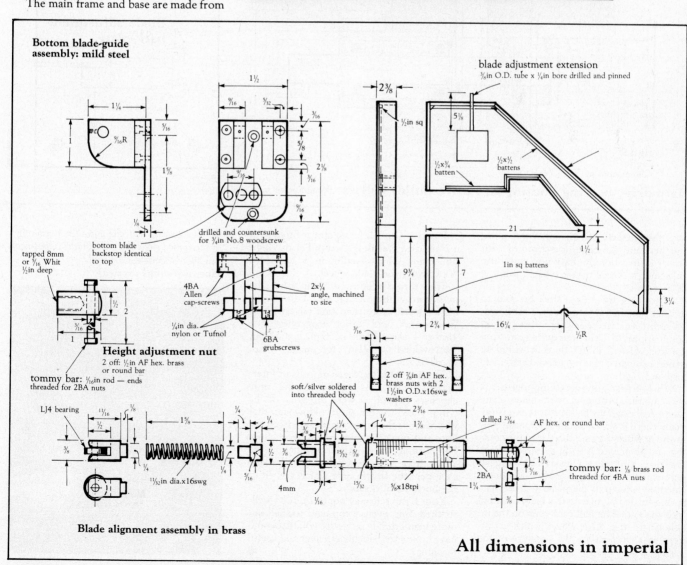

Bottom blade-guide assembly: mild steel

drilled and countersunk for ¾in No.8 woodscrew

bottom blade backstop identical to top

tapped 8mm or ⁵⁄₁₆ Whit ½in deep

4BA Allen cap-screws

¼in dia. nylon or Tufnol

6BA grubscrews

2x¼ angle, machined to size

Height adjustment nut
2 off: ½in AF hex. brass or round bar

tommy bar: ⁵⁄₁₆in rod — ends threaded for 2BA nuts

blade adjustment extension
⅜in O.D. tube x ¼in bore drilled and pinned

½in sq

½x¾ batten

½x½ battens

1in sq battens

½R

LJ4 bearing

¹¹⁄₃₂in dia.x16swg

4mm

soft/silver soldered into threaded body

2 off ⅞in AF hex. brass nuts with 2 1½in O.D.x16swg washers

drilled ²³⁄₆₄

AF hex. or round bar

⅝x18tpi

2BA

tommy bar: ⅛ brass rod threaded for 4BA nuts

Blade alignment assembly in brass

All dimensions in imperial

39

A bandsaw you can build

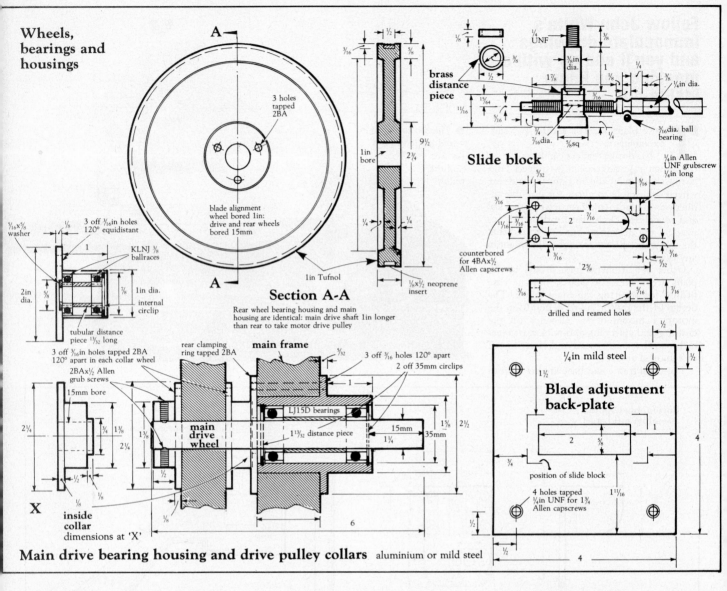

Wheels, bearings and housings

A

3 holes tapped 2BA

1in bore

blade alignment wheel bored 1in: drive and rear wheels bored 15mm

9½

2¾

1in Tufnol

Section A-A

1in

A

Rear wheel bearing housing and main housing are identical: main drive shaft 1in longer than rear to take motor drive pulley

⅛x½ neoprene insert

brass distance piece

UNF

⅜in dia.

¹⁵⁄₆₄

₃⁄₁₆dia. ball bearing

¼in dia.

Slide block

¼in Allen UNF grubscrew ¼in long

2

counterbored for 4BAx½ Allen capscrews

2⅝

drilled and reamed holes

¼in mild steel

Blade adjustment back-plate

2

position of slide block

4 holes tapped ¼in UNF for 1¼ Allen capscrews

4

⁵⁄₁₆x⅝ washer

3 off ³⁄₁₆in holes 120° equidistant

KLNJ ⅜ ballraces

2in dia.

1in dia.

internal circlip

tubular distance piece 1¹³⁄₃₂ long

3 off ³⁄₁₆in holes tapped 2BA 120° apart in each collar wheel

rear clamping ring tapped 2BA

main frame

2BAx½ Allen grub screws

15mm bore

main drive wheel

LJ15D bearings

1¹³⁄₃₂ distance piece

3 off ³⁄₁₆ holes 120° apart

2 off 35mm circlips

15mm

35mm

2½

2¼

X

inside collar dimensions at 'X'

6

Main drive bearing housing and drive pulley collars aluminium or mild steel

---

two thicknesses of ¾in plywood glued together, and the edges are trimmed with veneer strips. For the base you could use only one thickness if you rebated it into a 2x1in frame.

As you can see, I used shelf brackets to secure the main frame to the base. Although I'd seen them used elsewhere, this method didn't appeal to me at first: quite apart from the look of it, I didn't think it would be strong enough. Yet it has proved extremely firm and rigid.

When I first put everything together, I encountered problems with blade alignment. Although the ball-races are precision-made there is still a certain amount of play in them; when they are fitted into the housing and then into a 9½in-diameter wheel, the play multiplies considerably. I dealt with this by designing the blade-alignment assembly shown in the plans — basically a spring-loaded plunger with a ball-race fitted into the end. The ball-race runs on the inside of the top blade wheel, which is thus kept in alignment by the pressure of the spring. Simple, as they say, but effective.

I used a ⅓hp 1425rpm motor fitted with a 2¾in-diameter A-section pulley driving a 5in pulley. This results in a speed of 800rpm on the blade wheel.

The throat depth is 19in and the maximum cutting height 4in. You can get blades from more than one advertiser in *Woodworker* and other magazines. For timber I use a blade of 6tpi, ¼x0.025in, butt-welded at 91in; for metal, 14tpi, ³⁄₁₆x0.025in.

The job took me three months of inter-mittent work. As for cost, the only expenses I incurred were the price of the ¾in ply and the 5in pulley. However, that was because the other parts came from the 'bits and pieces' corner of my workshop. For example, the cleaning brush behind the main drive wheel was part of a draught-excluder (the bristle type which you fit to the bottoms of doors).

Your scrap pile may not be quite so well-stocked. But, even if you have to shell out more than I did, I can assure you that you'll have built a thoroughly efficient and useful machine. ■

● *Crosscutting with the mitre fence running in the routed slot. The turned brass adjustment nuts show themselves off well.*
More drawings overleaf

A bandsaw you can build

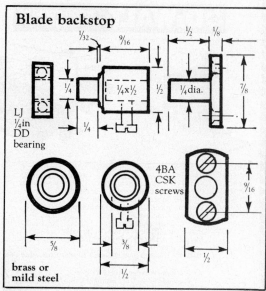

Blade backstop

LJ ¼in DD bearing

¼ dia.

4BA CSK screws

brass or mild steel

● **Left:** *Design of the motor guard would vary according to the motor used. John mounted the electrics on the guard so that both switch and guard come off in one*

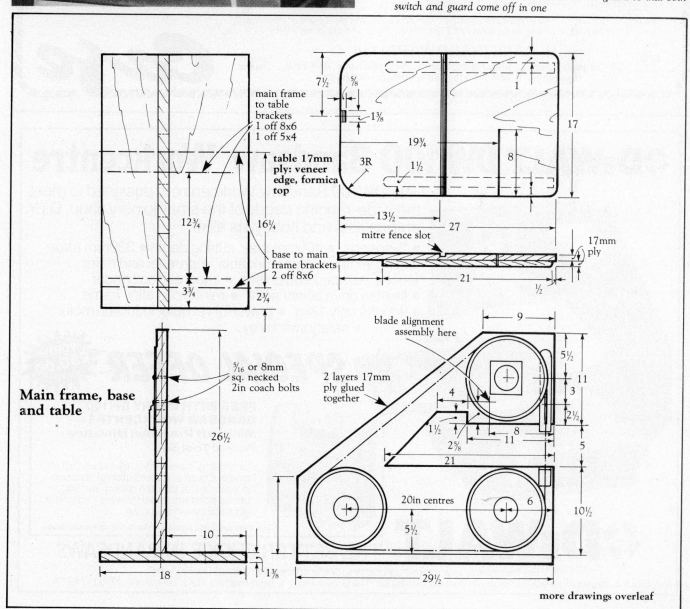

main frame to table brackets
1 off 8x6
1 off 5x4

table 17mm ply: veneer edge, formica top

base to main frame brackets
2 off 8x6

mitre fence slot

17mm ply

blade alignment assembly here

2 layers 17mm ply glued together

20in centres

Main frame, base and table

⁵⁄₁₆ or 8mm sq. necked 2in coach bolts

more drawings overleaf

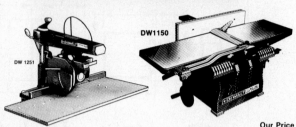

42

A bandsaw you can build

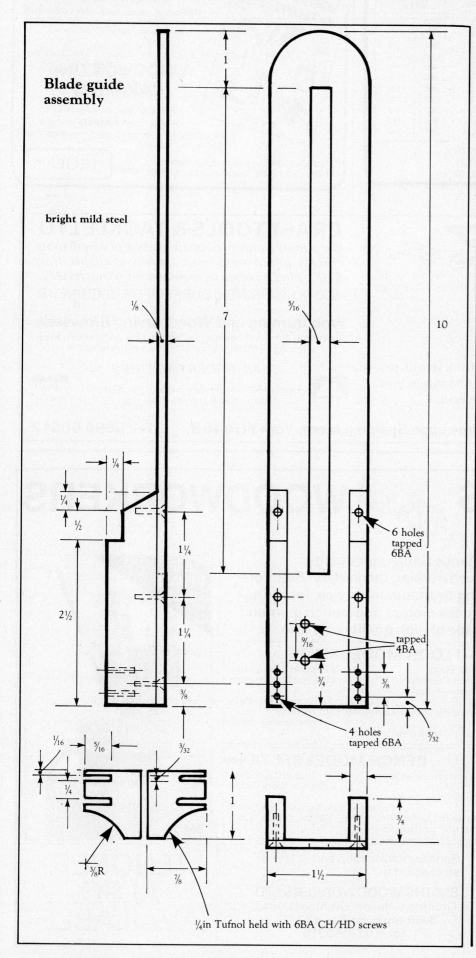

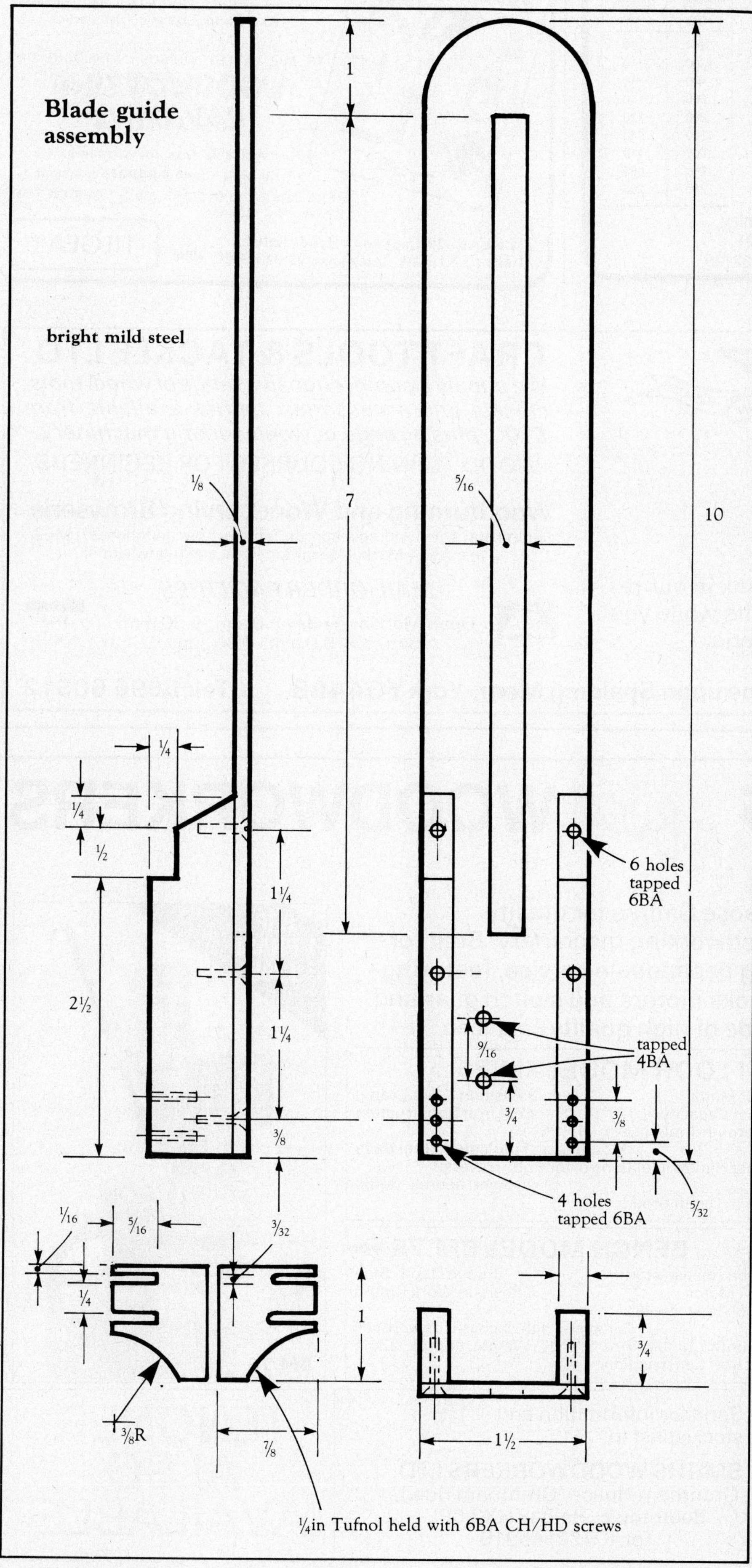
Blade guide assembly
bright mild steel
1
7
10
1/8
5/16
1/4
1/4
1/2
1 1/4
1 1/4
2 1/2
6 holes tapped 6BA
9/16
tapped 4BA
3/4
3/8
3/8
5/32
4 holes tapped 6BA
1/16
5/16
3/32
1/4
1
3/4
3/8R
7/8
1 1/2
1/4in Tufnol held with 6BA CH/HD screws

REMEMBER... *Woodworker* depends on woodworkers. We're willing and eager to tell the world what you're making, doing, exhibiting — even thinking. Our only aim is to produce the magazine you want to read. We're looking for photos, drawings (rough sketches will do) and words on any woodworking subject from ovolo mouldings to overhead routers. And we're on the end of the phone. We're waiting to hear from you!

Peter Collenette
Aidan Walker

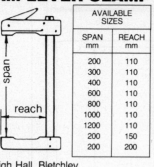

 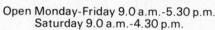
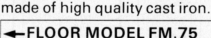

Tales out of steel

Ashley Iles unfolds his story of Sheffield's vanished prime

At the bottom of St Phillips Road, Sheffield, stands an 18-storey block of flats inhabited by people living in desperate isolation with fond memories of the days when they were a community in their neat little Coronation-Street-style houses. The previous occupants of the site were Brooks & Crooks, cutlery manufacturers, and long may they be remembered for cutlery now sold at fancy prices in antique shops.

The factory was a rectangular five-storey building where work started on the ground floor and went up, floor by floor, through all the trades I mentioned last month, plus buffing. One enormous electric motor was the sole source of power for all the machines in the works. Each floor had a full-length line-shaft with a pulley to each machine. At the end of each line-shaft was another pulley, and through a system of belts all the line-shafts were connected to the electric motor. The belts started at 2ft wide, ending on the top floor at about 3in wide. Steel went in on the ground floor and finished goods went out of the top-floor warehouse.

I knew a couple of grinders at Brooks & Crooks, and often took the opportunity to look round. On one visit I learned that the factory inspector had called and made them put an emergency switch on each machine to stop the main motor in case of an accident. This was particularly stupid because everything went on for five minutes after the button was pushed. A bit of stick to knock the belt off would have been far more sensible.

If an accident did occur, the grinding shop of the 50s was not exactly the place for heart transplants. But when you got something in your eye you didn't go to the eye department of the Royal Hospital (possibly the best in the country). You went to the nearest grinder. A grinder, of course, would go to another grinder, who would leave the wheel and fumble in his waistcoat pocket for a box of matches. Striking one, he would let it burn for an exact length of time and then pull it through his unwashed finger and thumb — making a sort of black artist's paintbrush. With this instrument in his hand he would look into your eye and say something like 'I can see the little bleeder, it's at quarter past nine'; then, with one quick flick, it was out. I

often had this treatment, though no way would I do it for anyone else. The golden rule is to get it out the day you get it in. I have seen some horrible sights the day after.

On the third floor were the buffing lasses, a race apart, in full regalia. Their shins were covered in a full newspaper held top and bottom with string. A sort of back-to-front lambing gown extended down below the newspaper; the hair, almost certain to be in large curlers, was covered by a scarf and tied under the chin. A thick bandage round the first finger of each hand was preferred to gloves. Imagine a woman dressed by a committee; that would be a buffing lass.

Their proper title was 'mirror-polishers'; the 'mirror' was the surface of the steel when they had buffed it to reflect your face. The black sheen on a knife is known as 'colour', and getting this colour is the art of the mirror-polisher. Only when you try it yourself do you realise how skilled the job is. I've never been able to do it (except on brass, which is easy); but from 16 onwards those girls could mirror-polish table-knives at around 6s a gross and talk to the girl on the next machine at the same time. Despite their appearance at work, in the evening they were bobby-dazzlers — hence the curlers all day.

There was very little familiarity between these girls and the men. Whereas under normal circumstances there is the risk of a slap in the face, with a buffing lass there was the danger of going through a window (third-floor) unconscious. When they set up on their own account as outworkers they were as formidable as MT at Question Time. Each knew exactly how long it took to do a gross and, if the money didn't match, the firm she was working for had big trouble.

In fact women played an equal role in the trades to men. When I made my own handles I had a widow working for me part-time. She was a well-bred, genteel type, a Penelope Keith character, and certainly not to be pushed around. She knew the handle trade inside out and could do anything. On a semi-automatic turning machine, where the work is fed into a revolving cutterhead, she could do three gross of carver-pattern handles an hour and then french-polish a gross in the afternoon. The secret was spit. For the final rub with a cloth while the polishing lathe was running, she would spit on the rag; one sweep across the handle and it came up like glass. She taught my wife how to do it, and also how to get paid in cash.

Back to Brooks & Crooks. At that time firms were going bust all over the place. (I went to an auction where one tool company

bought a name, trade-mark and goodwill for £115. They thought they'd also got the names and addresses of all the customers, but I'd bought them for 5s in a filing cabinet 10 lots before. Any business consultant will tell you that you're in business to find a customer, and charge you £200 for the advice.) When Brooks & Crooks packed up in 1957, the last item in the catalogue read 'Steam engine in cellar'. I went down to the cellar and saw a 300hp twin-cylinder double-action masterpiece of north-Yorkshire engineering, the type which preceded the main-drive electric motor. The auctioneer couldn't get a bid; I could have had it for a quid, but there was no way of getting it out. They'd installed the engine and then built the factory round it, and as far as I know it's still there in the foundations of the flats.

'Please don't think you're a craftsman the day you master the skew-chisel'

Last month I told you something of the hand forgers, and I am now going to let you in on a closely guarded trade secret. Although Longfellow's 'Village Blacksmith' was a man of immense stature and physique who performed Herculean tasks from dawn to sunset, actually it isn't like that at all. When you know how, it's easy.

Smithing is based on the scientific law that for every force there is an equal and opposite force. Pick up a hammer and strike a blow. Note the difference between up and down; up is where the hard work is — so you only go up once per heat. There's a recoil after the blow, and the rest of the time you keep the hammer bouncing. Get the idea? If you have to turn the steel on edge or alter the position, you still keep the hammer bouncing on the right-hand side of the anvil. Only one hard blow is struck per heat; not many people know that.

Everyone, on the other hand, knows you should strike while the iron is hot — but the problem is keeping it hot. The steel should only be in contact with the anvil when the hammer hits it. While the hammer is going up and down, you lift the steel $\frac{1}{2}$in clear of the anvil so that the heat is not dissipated.

Thirdly, it's the shoulder that keeps the hammer bouncing; the arm just keeps it the right distance away from you. From shoulder to hammer-head, the arm and hammer are one. The inward slope of the hammer face throws the weight to the shoulder. It takes a bit of practice — and there's no harm in making it look like hard work, especially if you have an audience or your customer is watching. But, while my brother — a joiner — would arrive home from a day's 'floor-bumping' absolutely shattered, I would be out dancing till midnight.

Finally, the anvil itself is worth a mention.

46

Tales out of steel

It doesn't matter what is used for a base — stone, concrete, wood: but it must be set in horse manure. Anything but horse manure will set solid, and the percussion (unable to dissipate through the anvil) will return up the hammer-shaft, in time causing paralysis.

The story of the Sheffield tool trade is not only that of the men who made the tools; it leads on to the craftsmen who used them. Among these were numbered my own forebears.

My grandfather Joseph Iles was a carpenter of vast experience. After rearing eight children he settled down at the Bristol Waggon Works, making wheelbarrows at 1s 6d a time piecework. He had all the angles for wheelbarrows set out with blocks of wood on the inside of the drawer-front on his bench. He would rest the stock of his bevel on the top of the drawer and pick up each angle from the blocks.

They sacked him at 62 for smoking in the yard. Without more ado he went to his bench, unscrewed all the blocks and threw them on the fire. He spent the rest of his life in penury sharpening saws at 6d a time, but to his dying day had the satisfaction of knowing that the Bristol Waggon Works never made another wheelbarrow. No wonder my father became a trades-union leader.

My father was the first craftsman I knew. He was a patternmaker and a very good one. He started at the Bristol Waggon Works as an apprentice before moving to Stothert & Pitts of Bath, then to several motor-car works (including Wolseley), and to Hadfields of Sheffield in 1912. He got full money at 19 by lying about his age (full money was supposed to be at 23). Just one more move, to a larger steelworks, and he married and settled down for life.

All is well in a steelworks until a mill breaks down. Then bedlam reigns in the maintenance shops until it's working again. As my father had a turn of speed on the bench he was usually chosen for the break-downs, and often worked all night and weekends. It frequently fell to me, as a small boy, to take his Sunday lunch in a basket. I shall never forget one Sunday when he had in the lathe a lagged-up barrel — 6ft long, 4ft in diameter — and was skimming it up with his trying-plane. Please don't think you're a craftsman the day you master the skew-chisel.

In the pattern-shop I got personal tuition from my father on what can only be described as one each from the Wadkin catalogue, including the big miller with 500 cutters, and the reason why I still have 10 fingers is that I was shown the correct use of woodworking machinery.

All the patternmakers worked to a strict code. When saws or planer blades were changed, the isolator was knocked off and a danger sign hung on the rheostat. There was hell to pay, too, if you were caught using a circular saw without a push-stick. I shall never forget my father jabbing a push-stick into a running saw and then holding it under my nose, saying, 'Look, son, no blood.' Amateurs buying saws and planers should get advice from an experienced machinist.

Spindle-moulders were the worst. My father was secretary of the Allied Trades Council; once, when addressing a mass meeting of machinists, he asked them to signify if they had had an accident on a spindle-moulder. The show of hands was 50%; and they were pros. Bandsaws and lathes are comparatively safe — though the lathe arouses fear in many people. Last year, demonstrating woodturning in the USA, I approached a man who was showing a lot of interest and asked him if he'd like to have a go. He recoiled in horror. I tried to soften him up by asking what his job was, and the answer came: 'A test pilot.' ∎

47

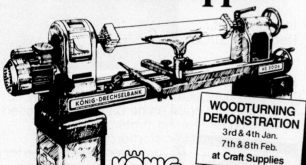

48

Solid value

Colin Murdoch's design for an oak desk is both sensible and distinguished

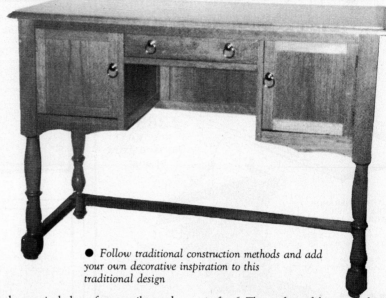

● *Follow traditional construction methods and add your own decorative inspiration to this traditional design*

Oak has always been my favourite wood because it seems to gleam and radiate warmth, and this oak writing-desk will be a lasting and valued piece.

It's practical and attractive, a pleasing addition to any living-room or study, and its sturdiness means it can be well-used by all members of the household. The brass fixtures blend in nicely with the satin finish of the oak.

The construction of the desk is straightforward, but accurate measuring is essential when you are making the door-frames and drawer.

The first step was to make the two end sections. Cutting the material for the legs (720x50x50mm) and turning them to shape was the first job, then the mortices were cut. There are eight on the front and seven on the rear legs, including a groove as shown in fig. 1. The three rails are made from material measuring 510x30x20mm, and the grooves which accept the oak ply are done with a plough plane. The small middle rail (510x20x8mm) supports the shelf and also strengthens the oak ply panel. Both sections are clamped up dry first, to ensure a tight fit and to check for square. After this both the end sections can be glued.

The back section should now be made, the whole thing using material measuring 30x20mm. The frame is made as shown in fig. 2. The frame is clamped up dry with the middle panel in place — leave the two end panels out at this stage. Glue can now be applied and the frame set aside.

The next stage is to make the top front rail and the back foot-rail. The small bare-faced dovetail joints were cut in the front

rail for the vertical door-frame stiles and front-to-back frame members, as shown in the three-dimensional drawing; then the whole carcase was clamped and later glued together, including the back panels set aside earlier.

The rest of the frames were made from material 20x20mm in section, except for the shelf support which is 20x8. Further construction details are shown on the three-dimensional drawing. Great accuracy is needed in making this part of the desk. Again the frames and panels are dry-assembled before gluing; this was a two-man job and quite a number of sash-cramps were needed.

The drawer and door-frames can now be made and fitted, both of traditional construction. You can also fit the oak ply shelves in the cupboards. The top can be made from solid oak, or oak-veneered blockboard with solid edging as this one was. Details are given

in fig. 6. The surface of the top is taken down with a scraper, after which a decorative edge is routed round.

Great care should be taken in finishing the desk. The carcase was given four coats of polyurethane varnish, and the top six coats. After each coat, the surface should be cut back using wet-and-dry paper, and the final coat toned down with steel wool and wax. This takes away the gloss and leaves a smooth satin finish.

I hope you'll find this desk as satisfying to make as to own! ■

more drawings overleaf

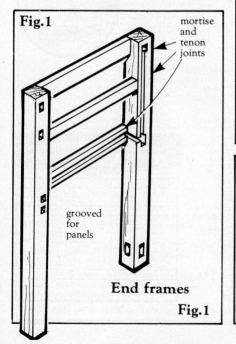

End frames
Fig.1

mortise and tenon joints

grooved for panels

Fig. 1

Fig.2
Back frame

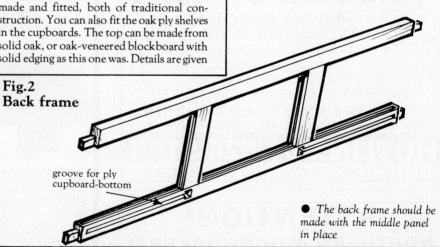

groove for ply cupboard-bottom

● *The back frame should be made with the middle panel in place*

Cutting list
Finished sizes in mm

4 legs	720	x	50	x	50
3 rails: 1 front, 2 back	1040		30		20
1 bottom foot-rail	1040		40		25
2 bottom cupboard rails	430		40		25
2 top cupboard rails	430		30		20

The door- and side-frames and drawer-front are made from timber 20mm thick; the shelves inside the cupboards from oak-veneered plywood; and the top from 24mm solid oak or oak-veneered 24mm blockboard, edged with solid oak lipping wide enough to take a routed decorative detail.

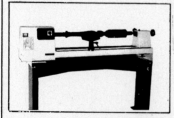
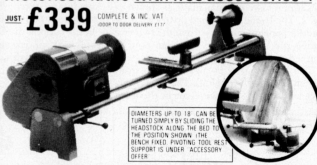

Solid value

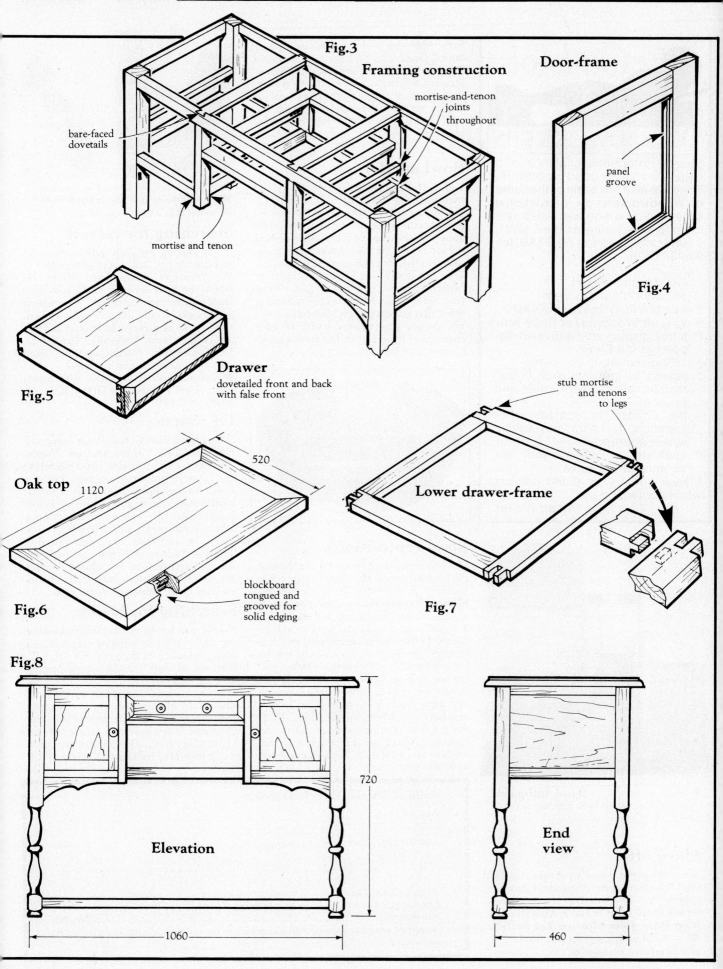

Fig.3

Framing construction

mortise-and-tenon joints throughout

Door-frame

bare-faced dovetails

panel groove

mortise and tenon

Fig.4

Drawer
dovetailed front and back with false front

Fig.5

stub mortise and tenons to legs

Oak top 1120

520

Lower drawer-frame

blockboard tongued and grooved for solid edging

Fig.6

Fig.7

Fig.8

720

Elevation

End view

1060

460

Guild notes

Guild of WOODWORKERS

Shared information, advice and help are vital to good woodwork. They are also the basis of the **Guild of Woodworkers**: an international organisation which welcomes new members — whatever their skills. 1 Golden Sq, London W1R 3AB, tel. 01-437 0626.

Guild members get
- priority on our courses
- free publicity in *Woodworker*
- 15% off Woodworker Show entry
- a free display area and meeting-point at the Show
- 15% discount on our plans
- access to and inclusion in our register of members' skills and services
- the chance to contact other members for help and advice where appropriate
- specially arranged tool insurance at low rates

Please quote your Guild number when contacting us.

Aidan Walker

● *Small is beautiful . . . **David Applegate's** charming pieces drew Show compliments galore*

Show off

Many delightful pieces were exhibited by Guild members at the Alexandra Palace — very fine too. Thanks to **David Applegate, Stan Kimm, John Walker, Alan Dixon, John Price, John Ellis** and **Ted Reffell** for providing such an excellent display — and benefiting themselves too, of course.

Remember that this is a regular opportunity! Guild members get the chance to show their work on our stand at the Show. Mention will be made of it early next year, so if you want to put your prize pieces on display, get in touch around next April. We need photos to be able to judge quality — and size!

Bowl auction

Ted Reffell, whose three bowls graced the stand, started woodturning last January. The quality of his work was for all to see; he had a charming idea about what should be done after the show with his highly-figured walnut bowls. He would like them to be sold and the proceeds donated to charity. Ted's bowls will be sold by postal auction; reserve price for each one is £15. Write your bid and your idea for a charity to me at this office, and the highest offer gets a bowl. The money goes to the charity of your choice, and thanks go to Ted for his good-hearted impulse.

Local rep(osition)

Much interest was expressed at the Show in the form for people who want to meet other members in their area. It was devised by **Michael Perryman**, to whom our thanks are due for his imagination and energy; fill it in and send it back, and we'll be able to collate the response geographically and thus identify the areas where meetings can be held. We had over 150 of these forms, and ran out of them before the end of the last day — just goes to show there are people out there wanting to meet their fellow-members and fellow-woodworkers. Keep those forms pouring in — or fill in the coupon on this page and return it to this office — and we'll soon have a map covered with blue pins!

● *New member **Sid Lye** carves traditional Welsh lovespoons and also happens to be Woodworker's trusted typesetter!*

Searching for carvers

'I am looking for high quality pieces of woodcarving to sell in my new gallery in East Yorkshire,' writes **Colin Saxton**. He would be interested to hear from professional, semi-professional and amateur carvers who would like to display and sell their work; he is prepared to meet and talk to people from Yorkshire, Lancashire, Derbyshire and Nottinghamshire. Send him a photo in the first instance.
● Colin Saxton, 16 Crowther Way, Swanland, North Humberside HU14 3QD, tel. (0482) 631179.

Of course

'May I thank **Bob Grant, Peter Sarac** and **Charles Cliffe**,' writes **Andrew Nicols**, 'for their very enjoyable hand veneering and french polishing courses. Being a complete beginner to these areas of woodwork I wondered what I'd let myself in for, but I needn't have worried. For anyone in a similar position, my advice is: have a go — you'll be surprised what you can do!' Thanks Andrew for that entirely unsolicited testimonial. See **Guild courses** for new dates to work with Bob, Charles and our other illustrious instructors.

Searching for books

Cardiff member **E. M. Phadraig** is looking for copies of some indispensable standard texts, published in the early 30s by B. T. Batsford: *Modern Practical Joinery, Modern Pracical Carpentry, Modern Practical Masonry, Modern Practical Stair-building and handrailing, Modern Cabinetwork, Furniture and Fitments,* and *Plastering: Plain and Decorative.* If you have any of these titles, or know where they can be found, please get in touch with Mr Phadraig at 20 Penarth Rd, Cardiff.

Guild of Woodworkers local groups

Name ....

Address ....

....

....

Are you prepared to have the first meeting at your home, if you are at the centre of a group? .... Yes/No

Details of your local group will be sent when the information has been collected and sorted

Guild courses

Furniture restoration — Eric Burger

17-19 January, 9.30-5, Bournemouth, £70+ VAT.
Still a few places left on this comprehensive course. Note it's for three days, which allows you to take a piece of your own, strip it, repair joints and veneers, cut in patches or do any other necessary work; then fill, re-stain, touch in, and refinish. Don't worry if you have no particular task to perform on a piece of your own; Eric will see you through these and other techniques in his professional workshop.

Power routing — Roy Sutton

8 February, 10-5 Herne Bay, £25+VAT. Like all our courses, a day chock-full of experience under the guidance of an expert. Roy's reputation for teaching every routing trick in the book is a national one, so we're proud and pleased to add him to our list of Guild instructors. Housing, grooving, rebating, straight and circular moulding, tenoning, mortising, rule-joints and templates: plus devising and using jigs. Buffet lunch, refreshments and materials are all included in the price.

Design and workshop drawing — Bob Grant

22 February, 9.30-5, Oxford, £25+VAT. Yet another excellent idea from Bob, whose expertise in this area is illustrated by the fact that he is head of Craft, Design and Technology at a comprehensive school. All facilities are there for you to practise free-hand sketching, use grid paper and drawing boards, learn workshop geometry (such as setting out ellipses), make and use rods and templates, and conquer the complexities of this essential adjunct to your craft.

Survival metalwork — Bob Grant

15 March, 9.30-5, Oxford, £25+VAT. Here is your chance to learn the details of a subject which many woodworkers consider obscure — to their cost. Grind your own cutters and tools, get the sharpest of sharp edges, learn hardening, tempering and silver soldering (for broken bandsaw blades); repair tool bodies, drill and tap holes, turn brass and aluminium. Once you've spent this day with Bob, you'll wonder how you ever got on without your new-found skills!

French polishing — Charles Cliffe

3-4 April, 9.30-5, £35+VAT, Bexleyheath. Two full days on one of our most popular subjects; Charles (who you may have seen demonstrating his prowess at the Show) deals with all aspects of preparation, staining, and application of this much-prized finish. Get to grips with the cabinet-scraper too; bring your own if you have one, and a piece of furniture to ask advice about if you want to.

Hand veneering — Bob Grant

12 April, 9.30-5, Oxford, £35+VAT. Cabinetwork, clockmaking, restoration; these and many other fine woodwork skills need veneers and veneering. Bob's one-day symposium is just the thing to set you up. You lay a panel with veneer, mitre a cross-banding, and inlay lines round it; then apply the balancer veneer to the back. Bob shows examples of cartouches, and demonstrates the scratch-stock; **Peter Sarac,** local harpsichord maker and cabinetmaker, will also be there to advise. Bring a veneer hammer if you have one; cost of materials is included in the price.

French polishing — Ian Hosker

19-20 April, 10-5, Chester, £40+VAT. For those in the north who want to know the craft. Teacher and practising professional Ian will take you through surface preparation (for new and old pieces), the variety of stains and colouring techniques, grainfilling, shellac finishes, fadding, bodying in, spiriting off, and reviving polished surfaces. The price includes materials you will use, but if you want Ian to make you up a **polishing kit** to take away, **add another £8 when you book.**

● Whittling by **Trevor Dixon.** He is anxious to get a group together; contact him at 6 Field Close, Melton Mowbray, Leics

Easter School — Manchester!

The Guild of Woodworkers proudly presents, in association with the School of Furniture, **Manchester Central College,** a selection of three courses over the Easter holiday. All three are for five days, 23-27 March, 9.30-5, £125+VAT.

Country chairmaking — Jack Hill

Jack is no stranger to anyone interested in country furniture, or anyone, for that matter, who enjoys his individual blend of wit and wisdom at the Woodworker Show. Now an established lecturer at the College, Jack will be teaching traditional country chairmaking techniques using cleft and sawn wood. He will be demonstrating steam-bending and explaining the use of the various jigs; you'll be doing lathe turning or using the **Fred Lambert** rounders and machines, and everyone will complete at least one piece of furniture.

Introduction to cabinetmaking — Robert Cooksey and Keith Parry

Robert (BA Des, LCG) and Keith (AIWSc) are an experienced furniture maker and a wood-machinist respectively. Robert has exhibited his work widely; Keith's speciality is prototype and development work. They'll be giving an introduction to basic machine preparation and hand-making techniques in fine furniture; the course is for the enthusiastic beginner and people with some experience who are anxious to improve. You'll be making a small piece which you should finish by the end of the week.

Traditional upholstery — Ken Jones and John Shepherd

Ken (LCG) and John have a combined 42 years' experience in upholstery. They will be leading an introduction to use of the traditional methods and materials (tacks and webbing, not foam and staples!), and teaching you to develop your hand-skills; a basic frame will be available for individual practice, or bring a piece of your own, stripped, repaired, and ready for work.
● **Richard Hill,** senior lecturer at the College, will be administrating the courses, but **all enquiries to this office** for the above three courses. The College is also running a five-day course in finishing during the same week, which will include two days' demonstrations of spray techniques. **Get in touch with them direct.** Manchester Central College School of Furniture, Lower Hardman St, Manchester M3 3ER, tel. (061) 831 7791.

The Morris men

Towards the end of last century, something happened in English furniture – something whose effects continue today. This is the tale of a man, his ideas, his work, and some of his successors

Max Burrough offers an appreciation of the most famous Arts and Crafts genius of them all

William Morris was gifted in many ways apart from the practical. By the time he was seven, in 1841, he had read all Scott's novels, and wrote both poetry and prose with apparent ease. Despite his academic leanings, though, his school-companions noted his restless fingers, and that he got relief by making nets for hours on end! He originally intended to take holy orders when he left school, but abandoned the idea and signed articles with the well-known Oxford architect G. E. Street.

During this time he practised many crafts — wood-engraving, clay-moulding, carving in wood and stone, and illuminating, among others. He always considered what he later called 'the noble craft of house-building' to be man's finest employment but he found working at a drawing-board tedious in the extreme, and left the office to pursue an art career in London. While living with his friend Burne-Jones in Red Lion Square, Morris sketched, and had a local firm make, some furniture described as 'intensely mediaeval'. According to the diary of the man now believed to have been responsible for the actual making, oak, walnut, pitch pine, lime and mahogany were all to be used. Besides at least one large cabinet, the pieces included high-backed chairs and a round table.

In 1857 Morris and a few friends returned to Oxford to paint the upper walls and roof of the new debating hall of the Union Society. Morris stayed on in Oxford with the ailing Burne-Jones, and during this time experimented with various handicrafts; he carved a block of freestone, drew and coloured designs for stained-glass windows, modelled from life in clay and began his first experiments in embroidery.

He married in 1859 and had his friend Philip Webb draw up plans for a house to be built in an apple orchard in Kent; in 1860 the young couple moved into Red House — determined, as one friend said, 'to make it the most beautiful place on earth'. This task gave Morris the opportunity to discard any thought of current Victorian furnishing, and he and his friends set to designing and making everything for the house. Here, apparently, Morris practised what he subsequently preached in his lecture 'The Lesser Arts of Life'.

A great settle from Red Lion Square was taken and set up in the drawing-room, and Webb and others designed plainer pieces, including an oak dining-table and other tables and chairs, so that from the beginning the furniture was of two distinct kinds. Here is an extract from that famous lecture:

'So I say that our furniture should be good citizen's furniture, solid and well made in workmanship, and in design should have nothing about it that is not easily defensible, no monstrosities or extravagances, not even of beauty, lest we weary of it. As to matters of construction, it should not depend on the special skill of a picked workman, or the super-excellence of his glue, but be made on the proper principles of the art of joinery. Also I think that except for very removable things like chairs, it should not be so very light as to be nearly imponderable, it should be made of timber rather than walking sticks. Moreover, I must need think of furniture as of two kinds: one part of it being chairs, dining and working tables and the like, the necessary workaday furniture in short, which should be, of course, both well-made and well-proportioned, but simple to the last degree . . .

'But besides this kind of furniture, there is the other kind, of what I should call state-

furniture, which I think is proper even for a citizen; I mean sideboards, cabinets, and the like, which we have quite as much for beauty's sake as for use. We need not spare ornament on these, but may make them as elegant and elaborate as we can with carving, inlaying or painting . . . **,**

It was during busy weekends, when the house was full of friends, happy and working, that the idea of the firm Morris and Company surfaced. It was possibly inspired by the Great Exhibitions, planned for 1862. Soon a dozen men and boys (who came from a London boys' home) were employed. Webb designed most of the important furniture, and large schemes of decoration were carried out for rich clients. But at the same time the Sussex chairs (5/- each) and cheaper furniture and wallpapers were produced, so the artist Walter Crane could well write: 'The great advantage and charm of the Morrisian method is that it lends itself to either simplicity or splendour. You might be almost as plain as Thoreau, with a rush-bottomed chair, a piece of matting, or an oaken trestle table; or you might have gold and lustre gleaming from the sideboard, jewelled light in the windows, and the walls hung with arras tapestry.' The expensive pieces designed by Webb (later by George Jack) display the

● One movement – many faces. The mahogany cabinet (**left**), designed by C.R. Ashbee and made by the Guild of Handicraft in 1898-9, has a holly interior. The mahogany secretaire (**above**) and escritoire (**right**) were designed by George Jack (photos Sotheby's, Cheltenham Art Gallery, The National Trust)

best of Victorian cabinet-making; the firm also made and sold furniture 'of the best forms of the Chippendale and Queen Anne period, especially in regard to carved drawing-room and dining-room chairs'.

In 1875 the original parners disbanded and Morris became sole owner of the firm. In 1877 a showroom was opened in Oxford Street, and many records survive of Morris's autocratic attitude to customers. William Rosetti wrote: 'Mr Morris laid down the law and all his clients had to

comply willy-nilly with his dictates. The products were first class, the artistic quality of the handicraft excellent, and the prices high. There were no concessions to other types of taste, and of course, none at all to bad taste. Reduction in prices was out of the question.' Well might Morris, in a lecture delivered in 1880, say: 'Have nothing in your house that you do not know to be useful or believe to be beautiful'.

William Morris died in 1890, when W. A. S. Benson took over the dictatorship of the firm, which closed in 1939/40. Unfortunately it was not until 1890 that the firm's furniture was stamped with the name and number. Undoubtedly, Morris's furniture, and his philosophy of life influenced many people, notable C. R. Ashbee, Ernest Gimson and the Barnsleys and Ambrose Heal, all of whose work and influence can

be traced to the present day.

A little-known impression of Morris was given by a woman who worked for him as a carpet weaver. He was a short man with a big red and brown beard; he always had a walking stick — you could hear him coming! He was a peculiar man but I think he was good at heart. He jumped about — it was very irritating for the man who had to follow him. Dealing with a rug or a piece of glass he used to dance around like a cat on hot bricks. When I used to see them going down to Merton Abbey station — (Morris, Burne-Jones and William de Morgan) they were always screaming with laughter. They were all talked about quite a bit, but I don't think Morris was really liked by the upper ten, because he was a Socialist.'

For all his dream of Utopia, his prose, poetry and romances, Morris was essentially a practical person who never lost touch with humanity. 'He was not ashamed of being a tradesman; he gloried in it. That was a new thing in his day.' As W. R. Lethaby, the first Principal of the Central School of Arts and Crafts said, 'he was a workmaster — Morris the maker'.

● The William Morris Gallery is at the Water House, Lloyd Park, Forest Rd, London E17.

Books

J. W. Mackall, *The Life of William Morris*, Longmans, Green & Co, London 1899
P. Henderson, *William Morris, His Life, Work and Friends* Thames and Hudson, London 1967
R. Watkinson, *William Morris as Designer* Studio Vista, London 1967
T. Bradley, *William Morris and His World* Thames and Hudson 1978

The Morris men

Idris Cleaver introduces some lesser-known Arts-and-Craftsmen who are only now getting the recognition they deserve

During the past 20 years or so, we have been seeing and hearing a great deal of the work of the Cotswold school of designer-craftsmen led by Ernest Gimson and the Barnsleys, but little is mentioned about some of the lesser-known craftspeople originally inspired by William Morris and the Arts and Crafts movement. They worked quietly and unobtrusively to produce handmade furniture of the highest quality in various parts of the country, in single-person workshops or with the help of a few apprentices and assistants.

Three such men were originally A. Romney Green's assistants (WW/June 83). They all left to set up their own workshops and produce furniture which is only now beginning to be fully recognised as a contribution to the Arts and Crafts movement. **W. Stanley Davies** moved into a purpose-built workshop in Windermere; **Eric Sharpe** set up on his own in Martyr Worthy, Winchester, and **Robin Nance** moved to St Ives, Cornwall.

Stanley W. Davies

Stanley Davies was an Oxford history graduate until he came under the influence of A. Romney Green. During the first world war he served with the Friends' War Victims' Relief Unit in France, an experience which fundamentally affected his whole attitude to life. He decided to move away from the academic career which his parents had persuaded him to follow, and devote himself to making beautiful things that would bring joy and happiness to maker and owner. In order to do this he entered Romney Green's workshops in Hampshire.

He soon revealed his gift. One example of his craftsmanship is a parabolic wheatsheaf-back chair which he made and Green designed, on permanent display at the Cheltenham Art Gallery and Museum.

His early designs were naturally influenced to some extent by Romney Green, but he soon developed his own personal and distinctive style. There is little doubt that his small walnut cabinet, with its specially selected matching panels and exposed joints at the corners of the carcase, showed Davies' familiarity with the work of the Gimson/Barnsley Cotswold school, although it is doubtful whether Davies ever met either Gimson or Barnsley.

After two years with Green he left in 1922 to start his own workshop, which he had specially built in Windermere in the Lake District. It took Davies some time to develop his own design style, and it was not until after the second world war that his work was in greatest demand. The total

● *This 'swan' chair was made by Eric Sharpe in 1943*

output from his workshop exceeded 2000 pieces; each with a distinctive style that came from keeping close to the basic principles of woodwork and developing from sound tradition.

The desire was to import a timeless value to the work rather than follow fashion. The lightness and apparent simplicity of his pieces reveal the beauty of the wood, the skill of the workmanship, and the structural emphasis of the design. The woods he used were mainly English oak, chestnut, cherry and cedar, with some imported timbers such as mahogany. Unless the customer specifically requested it he always gave a natural finish to the wood; he considered this to be the only 'true' finish for his English oak and chestnut cabinets. It did indeed allow him to express his genius through original and ingenious chamfering. He put chamfers on existing chamfers and worked twisted chamfers on the octagonal feet of some of his sideboards and desks. He did not altogether approve of pieces of wood (such as inlay) used solely for decoration, considering that the decorative effect should only be achieved by what he called 'structural design'. The character of the design should be governed by the construction and not by structurally unnecessary applied decoration.

He enunciated his whole philosophy of craftwork in a series of radio talks and articles. In a radio talk in 1933 he spoke of 'the truth in construction and finish which is true to the nature of wood; careful joints which can hold together without glue; careful selection of timber because of its natural strengths and weaknesses; a careful finish which does not alter the natural colour of the wood, and sensible simple design. Good art is not laboured in appearance; rather it should give a feeling of ease and simplicity. Sparing use of thoughtful

and sensitive decoration can be very effective, specially when the craftsman has put into it something of himself.'

He thought it was sensible to use machines for first sawing logs into boards, but he saw 'no sense in getting machines to do work which men enjoy doing by hand, and not only enjoy, but find great opportunity for their skill, inventiveness and artistic ability in the doing of it'. He was always fearful that the machine might influence the design and reduce the individual responsibility of the craftsman. Towards the end of his life, though, he was forced to introduce a few small machines in an attempt to reduce costs. He felt strongly that furniture should not be called 'handmade' if machines were used for anything other than sawing or planing; also that the craftsman should see his work through from start to finish, true to the Arts and Crafts principles. Despite the increased demand for his work in the post-war years, Davies would never employ more than seven assistants as he felt that was the maximum number he could control.

Eric Sharpe

From 1921 to 1929 Eric Sharpe was a pupil of and assistant to A. Romney Green, first in London and later when he moved to Christchurch, Hampshire. At the end of this period he set up his own workshops in Martyr Worthy, Winchester, where I first met him, when I visited his workshop with Edward Barnsley. Sharpe and Barnsley were close friends, and both had been pupils at Bedales School.

Sharpe, also greatly influenced by Romney Green, first became acquainted with the work of the Cotswold school after he had set up on his own. It was through the now almost forgotten designer-craftsman Malcolm Powell that he first came across the work of Gimson and the Barnsleys, and there is little doubt that they had a profound influence on him thereafter.

His work soon attracted the attention of architects who commissioned him to make domestic furniture, a number of church works, and special ceremonial and memorial pieces. These included the cabinet to

● *A stationery cabinet designed by Stanley Davis*

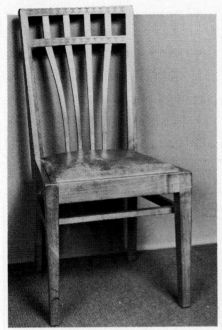

● *This chair is probably by Romney Green (photos Cheltenham Art Gallery)*

house Winchester Cathedral's book of names of the fallen in the second world war; the Bidder Memorial chair (the Mistress' Chair for Girton College, Cambridge); the high table of Newnham College, Cambridge, in 1940; and the casket for the freedom of the City of London presented to Winston Churchill in 1943.

Perhaps the most prestigious of his pieces was the presidential chair presented to the Pharmaceutical Society of Great Britain by the Australian Societies in 1933. At the presentation meeting Sharpe gave a description of the chair, explaining its design and the woods of which it was made; he used a sample species from every one of the colonies in Australia and New Zealand, the top rail carrying a map in which each colony was represented by a piece of its own native wood.

Unlike Davies, he was very fond of incised lettering in wood, and used a great deal of carving in his work for churches. His essay on 'Woodwork' in *Fifteen Craftsmen on their Crafts*, edited by Jon Farleigh, gives an appraisal of Gimson's work which shows his obvious admiration for it.

Robin Nance

Nance was also trained by Romney Green until he started his own workshop in 1933 in St Ives, Cornwall. Most of his work is handmade, well designed, of good material and of sound workmanship, as is to be expected after such training. He uses machines only in the early stages of his work, which is aimed at producing furniture mainly for customers of limited means; his pieces are much sought after by tourists in the area. Although he rarely employs more than four craftsmen, he does not limit himself to furniture, and whenever required he undertakes work commissioned and designed by architects.

THE CONTINUING STORY

The work of the Barnsleys and Gimson changed the course of modern furniture not only in Britain but also in Europe and America, **writes Idris Cleaver** — and Edward Barnsley (now 85) has been continuing and refining that tradition since 1923, when he set up his own workshops in Froxfield, Hampshire.

For some of those 62 years I had the privilege of working there. So I was especially pleased and excited to be able to attend the workshops' recent open day.

It was because the financing of five-year apprenticeships proved too much, even for Barnsley, that the Edward Barnsley Educational Trust was set up five years ago, so that apprentices could continue to train at Froxfield. During the visit we saw them at work, together with the older craftsmen, and is was good to see them continuing the workshop's superlative standards.

Overall administration continues to be the responsibility of Edward Barnsley; his architect son Jon Barnsley supervises the work, and has adapted many of his father's drawings without in any way departing from their personal and distinctive style. The high standard of work produced, and still expected of the apprentices, is assured by the presence and guidance of George Taylor, a master-craftsman by any standard. Still actively making the magnificent pieces which one has come to expect from him, he is the last remaining man originally apprenticed to Barnsley over 50 years ago — and soon to retire. Oscar Dawson, the other remaining craftsman, died sadly and unexpectedly some months ago.

The first three apprentices were taken on in 1981, and new ones will be appointed each year from now on. Applications are, as expected, heavily over-subscribed. This year the trustees decided that the next apprentice should be chosen from local candidates, if a promising one were available — and last year Darren Harvey, a 16-year-old from Cowplain who was

● *Edward Barnsley and two apprentices watch George Taylor at work*

● *A writing-table by apprentice Colin Eden-Eadon*

● *More apprentice work – a box for timber specimens*

working for the Youth Opportunities Scheme, was selected by interview after a two-week trial period in the workshop. His apprenticeship was confirmed subject to a satisfactory six-month probationary period, and he has proved a very promising craftsman. New applications are currently being considered; four candidates have been selected for interview, and are to be given a week's trial in the workshop before the final choices are made. Richard Elderton remains in charge of the apprentices' training, in collaboration with George Taylor and Jon Barnsley.

In spite of the progress already made, the trustees have plans for very necessary extensions, and are appealing for funds. The first priority is a display and archive room with a dry timber store beneath it. Thanks to a grant and gifts of books a fairly good reference library has been started, but many more books are needed (and would be greatly appreciated).

The trust has obviously learnt from past experience with Gimson's workshop drawings, which have only now (about 65 years after his death) been filed and catalogued for Cheltenham Museum and Art Gallery. A research assistant has been busy at Froxfield, evolving a definitive system of classifying and cataloguing Barnsley's drawings, numbering them, and filing them in order. The trust hopes they will be available for inspection by scholars, students, historians and craftsmen some time in 1986. ∎

● Readers of *Woodworker* may like to know that they will be welcome to visit the workshop at any time, provided they ring up in advance to make an appointment.

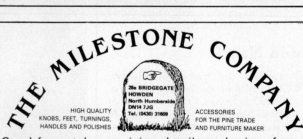
58

British Code of Advertising Practice

Advertisements in this production are required to conform to the British Code of Advertising Practice. In respect of mail order advertisements where money is paid in advance, the code requires advertisers to fulfil orders within 28 days, unless a longer delivery period is stated. Where goods are returned undamaged within seven days, the purchaser's money must be refunded. Please retain proof of postage/despatch, as this may be needed.

Mail Order Protection Scheme

If you order goods from Mail Order advertisements in this magazine and pay by post in advance of delivery WOODWORKER will consider you for compensation if the Advertiser should become insolvent or bankrupt, provided:

(1) You have not received the goods or had your money returned; and

(2) You write to the Publisher of this publication, summarising the situation not earlier than 28 days from the day you sent your order and not later than two months from that day.

Please do not wait until the last moment to inform us. When you write, we will tell you how to make your claim and what evidence of payment is required.

We guarantee to meet claims from readers made in accordance with the above procedure as soon as possible after the Advertiser has been declared bankrupt or insolvent (up to a limit of £2,000 per annum for any one Advertiser so affected and up to £6,000 per annum in respect of all insolvent Advertisers. Claims may be paid for higher amounts or when the above procedure has not been complied with, at the discretion of this publication, but we do not guarantee to do so in view of the need to set some limit to this commitment and to learn quickly of readers' difficulties).

This guarantee covers only advance payment sent in direct response to an advertisement in this magazine (not, for example, payment made in response to catalogues etc., received as a result of answering such advertisements). Classification advertisements are excluded.

MAIL ORDER ADVERTISING

The gripping story

Mike Darlow shares his experience of multi-jaw chucks for woodturning and explains an important idea

● **Fig.1:** *Mike's chuck-plates allow unusual freedom in designing bowl-bases. The three bowls on the left all have walls whose thickness is constant to within* $\frac{1}{16}$*in*

E ngineer's chucks are used extensively in metal turning, but rarely in woodturning. The role for these chucks in woodturning needs some clarification; there has also been a major advance in equipment that turners should know about.

Two sorts of engineer's chucks are in common use: independent, in which there are usually four jaws, each independently radially adjustable; and self-centring, or scroll, in which the jaws move radially in unison. Scroll chucks are available with two, three, four, or six jaws, three being the most common and cheapest for a given size of chuck. Four-jaw scroll chucks have some advantages over three-jaw, but they are considerably more expensive; with the better brands of chuck various interchangeable jaw-types are available — inside-gripping, outside-gripping, bar, two-piece hard, and blank.

Although I strongly advocate a larger role for engineer's chucks, their relative neglect is not without foundation. They have both advantages and disadvantages;
● They are heavy, and so hobby lathes will not cope with the really useful 6 and 8in sizes;
● They are expensive. Also, if they aren't available as a standard extra for your lathe they will need to be machined to suit, or a backing plate will need to be made so they can be mounted on your particular headstock spindle;
● There are potentially dangerous projections from the front, and often from the perimeter, of the chuck. They should be used with a guard wherever possible;
● Their jaws grip on only a small area of the workpiece which is therefore liable to be crushed, and thus might loosen or even fly out;
● Occasionally the scroll mechanism will choke up with wood dust, and the chuck will then have to be disassembled and cleaned;
● **But** they are precise, very quick to adjust, and have a large range of adjustment.

Engineer's chucks — weight and sizes

Body diameter	Centre-hole diameter	Weight
4in	1.00in	6.6lbs
5	1.38	10.3
6	1.81	17.8
7.87	2.16	31.3

Independent chucks

Four-jaw independent chucks can be used for gripping irregularly-shaped workpieces or for holding workpieces non-concentric-ally with the lathe axis. However, the short projection of the jaws from the face of the chuck may reduce the possible use of even these minor roles.

Scroll chucks with inside-gripping jaws

Inside-gripping jaws may be used to grip the perimeter walls of an axial hole or recess in a workpiece. However the most frequently used surfaces of inside-gripping jaws are the outside-gripping ones. These are unfortunately usually narrowed (fig. 2), resulting in an even smaller gripping area. This can however be increased in several ways;
● Use a chuck with more jaws — one reason for preferring four- to three-jaw chucks;
● Grip the workpiece with the full axial length of the jaws. Therefore in a highly stressed situation such as cup-chucking, the diameter of the workpiece where it is being held shouldn't be greater than the chuck's centre hole;
● Increase the width of the outside-gripping surfaces. Bar-jaws (fig. 2) may be available, or soft blank jaws can be machined and hardened; there are four main ways in which bar-jaws are used for gripping.
1 To hold work for cup-chucking. This is quicker than any other method but the large diameter of the chuck compared with the workpiece impedes access to the work's left-hand end.
2 To hold work for drilling with the bit held in a Jacob's chuck mounted in the tailstock.
3 To give a solid hold at the end when turning slender items. As the chuck gives excellent axial alignment, holding the left-hand end of a slender workpiece in the jaws reduces the tendency for it to deflect under the tool. This may eliminate the need for a steady. Four-jaw chucks are especially useful here, as square-

● **Fig.2:** *Engineer's scroll chucks, with inside- and outside-gripping jaws. The bar jaws on the right give greater grip*

section wood can be held without the need for preliminary turning.
4 For holding other chucks and faceplates by their bosses. This can be very time-saving and allows the use of equipment which is not compatible with your lathe.

Scroll chucks with outside-gripping jaws

The potential uses of outside-gripping jaws are many, but their gripping area is small. Several methods can be used to overcome this;
● An annular spring-steel ring is placed around the workpiece or projecting spigot. As the ring has a small length cut out, the ring diameter will decrease and grip the workpiece as the jaws are tightened. This principle can obviously be used in reverse

The gripping story

with inside-gripping jaws. As the possible adjustment is small and the workpiece shape is restricted, the ring idea is not used very much.

● The workpiece may be screwed or glued on to a disc or faceplate which is then held in the chuck. For example, when roughing bowls we often screw a machined thick steel disc onto the top face of the wooden blank and hold the disc in the outside-gripping jaws for turning the outside of the bowl. If a short parallel-sided spigot is turned on the base of the bowl, this can then be gripped directly by the chuck jaws, and the inside of the bowl then turned. Alternatively, or where the bowl is large and would tend to pull out of the jaws, the bowl base can be screwed onto the steel disc and the disc then held by the scroll chuck so the inside of the bowl can be hollowed out. Using this chuck-and-disc system is considerably faster than conventional methods, since you aren't continually screwing faceplates on and off the lathe spindle.

● Chuck-plates can be used.

● **Fig.3:** The parts of a chuck-plate, showing both sides. You can see the bottom part of a two-piece jaw screwed on to the segment **top left**; segments of a supplementary jaw and plate on the **right**

● **Fig.4:** Use a chuck-guard with engineer's chucks whenever you can

● **Fig.5:** Chuck-plates and supplementaries for 6¼in and 12in chucks. The big one will hold workpieces of up to 36in diameter!

Chuck-plates

When scroll-chuck jaws are gripping waste wood, any local crushing will not matter. However, in some applications the workpiece will need to be gripped on a finished surface, and the chuck-plates described below (for which a patent is pending) overcome this serious shortcoming.

The plates are made of a rigid material such as steel and are sectors of a circle in plan. They fix on to suitably machined and tapped chuck-jaws (the bottom halves of two-piece jaws are already suitable). Plates of an easily turnable material such as wood or fibreboard are then screwed onto the chuck-plates. These supplementary plates,

made up by the turner, may be of several thicknesses glued together and can have an outside diameter considerably greater than the chuck (fig. 6). Obviously the mass of these supplementary plates needs to be kept compatible with the chuck size and lathe speed. An annular rib is provided on the chuck-plates to retain the supplementary plates in position under varying radial stresses.

The chuck-plate apparatus can be used for either outside- or inside-gripping. For outside-gripping, (figs. 6 and 7) a recess is turned in the supplementary plates to the correct diameter, the chuck opened slightly, the workpiece inserted, and the jaws tightened. This is particularly useful in bowl-turning for holding the rim while the base

is turned and sanded and allows great freedom in base design (fig. 1).

Inside gripping is worked out in much the same way except that a spigot is turned on, or fixed to, the supplementary plates which can then be used to grip the perimeters of holes or recesses in the workpieces.

Using engineer's chucks as much as we do, we have found the chuck-plates give great versatility to our work, and allow us to specialise in large and unusually-shaped bowls. Don't despair if you don't have an enormous lathe — the chuck-plate system is quite compatible with the better hobby lathes, which will accept 4 and 5in engineer's chucks. ■

● Mike Darlow is a professional wood-turner in Sydney, Australia.

● **Fig.7 below:** *The same chuck-plate and supplementary plate as* **left** *seen from behind. No hobby lathe this!*

● **Fig.6:** *A recess equal to the bowl-rim's maximum diameter is turned in the supplementary plates; the jaws must close tight and the speeds must be below 500rpm*

Show business

Hugh O'Neill gives a very personal view of the woodworking event of the year

We are moving into an age of excellence! The recent words of Bob Tyrell, director of the Social Futures Group of the Henley Centre for Forecasting, were ringing in my ears as I gathered my first impressions of the 1985 Woodworker Show at Alexandra Pavilion.

There were two types of buyer at the Show, although there should really have been three. Busiest of all the stands were those where gadgets were being demonstrated by professional barkers. Drills that 'would put a hole through anything'; dovetail routers and guides for use with electric drills; a flexible sanding-disc that will grind away tool steel without marking; even a video demonstration of a device for cutting tomatoes (I suppose some woodworkers do eat!).

There will always be 'bodgers' — individuals who will use any means available to achieve a quick, passable result. There will also be those craftsmen in one area of woodworking who use gadgets and 'bodge' when working in another. The demonstrations were not all show; at least, I hope so for the sake of those members of the 'audience' who ended up walking off with coloured boxes under their arms.

We probably all came away with one gadget or another. I fell for the offset dovetail saw from **Craftbray**. This natty little device with a swing-round handle enables you to make inboard or outboard flush cuts, for taking off extra length on dowels and so on. I have a couple of chests-of-drawers to restore and this little gem will greatly simplify the task of cutting away the worn channels in the drawer-rails. It would cost me more than the £5 (a special Show price) I spent to cut up an old saw-blade and make myself a runner block.

There weren't quite the same crowds round the stands where you could buy the tools of excellence, but there were enough and they were mainly serious buyers. I asked **Craft Supplies** what was generating the most interest on their stand, and the answer was: 'Everything! We're selling everything we brought with us!' Their half-dozen sales assistants certainly worked flat out all day.

Roger's must have confounded many sceptics. 'We've already sold one, and have interest in another,' they said, pointing to a £250 boxed set of 10 Japanese carving tools. 'And we might have sold that £995 plane. We've sold a large number of the individual chisels at about £40 each.'

All the tool stands were busy. There were the browsers looking for 'anything useful' among the plastic-packaged, moderately priced, adequate-quality CK range tools on the **Darlac Products** stand; there were the

● *This Gimson-style silver-medal winning cabinet by Wing Commander Landells boasts walnut, cherry, kingwood and ebony*

delvers into the Aladdin's cave of **Simble's** of Watford; there were the many dedicated users buying chisels and gouges from **Ashley Iles.** Interestingly, although Ashley Iles were doing extremely good business, their generous 'Show offers' on boxed sets of tools were being ignored. Customers were largely making their own selections from individual items, often from the trays of unhandled blades. I talked to some of the buyers, and it emerged that they weren't trying to save a few coppers by buying blades without handles; this was their means of ensuring they got the size, shape and quality of handle that they wanted and that the fine blades demanded.

So, quality was being sought, and was being bought.

The volume sales were of tools and timber. There was much less interest in fittings — clock movements, tile inserts, pepper-mill mechanisms and the like. 'Those are usually bought mail-order,' one of **John Boddy's** assistants explained.

The third type of buyer wasn't there — at least not on the day I went, or not in any noticeable numbers. Where were the professionals who might be interested in the larger machines? On the day I was there, customers on the stands of two manufacturers selling big combination units were few.

Of the larger pieces of equipment that were being bought, bandsaws of medium capacity and upwards stood out. Perhaps this isn't surprising — I wish I hadn't bought a DIY-size machine when I made my purchase two years ago. Going round the timber suppliers at the Show emphasised this regret; bowl-turning blanks abounded and the prices were well-nigh unbounded! For some of the pre-cut circular blanks of exotics, they were exorbitant. I bought a plank of wenge from **Limehouse Timber** — it wasn't cheap, but it will give me eight

turning blanks. The same money wouldn't quite have bought three discs on another stand. It wouldn't take long to pay off the £200-300 for a large-capacity bandsaw compared with £100 for something that just doesn't have the required depth of cut. But then, I would have had difficulty doing some of the fine furniture-making that has been possible with my Burgess. Decisions, decisions!

For me the star item of the show was a reflection of the same problem. The lathe I use is typical 'hobbyist' equipment, only just capable of turning out a good job(!). Looking at it, and at several others at the Show, I became disenchanted with the general flimsiness and concern for sleek appearance at the cost of practicality, exhibited by more than half the lathes on offer. The light-gauge tubular-steel bed-rails of some were just adequate, but I cringed at aluminium. Fittings are often the most inadequate castings, many in brittle zinc alloy. The component range for many is limited and vastly over-priced; for the price of a simple screw and a cup-chuck for one you can buy a complete Duplex chuck

● *Richard Willis' writing desk, in delicately inlaid Brazilian mahogany, drew admiration*

set. Should you be unfortunate enough to break anything, you probably won't be able to obtain spares. Elu can't supply a replacement screw for their screw-chuck — I had to buy the whole damn thing! So when I came across the prototype Maxima lathe on the **Multistar** stand, I just stood and drooled.

OK, it's in a different price-bracket, and it may not be everybody's ideal. It has an angular, functional appearance and is fabricated from thick steel plate, just the sort of thing to appeal to the engineer in me. As I looked, the man next to me said: 'Why didn't they round it off there and make that smoother? They could have done a lot to improve the aesthetics.'

Aesthetics is all very well, but I want something that works, takes punishment, and produces results uncomplainingly. The Maxima has a five-speed drive, a 360° swing-head, a bed-length of 'what you want' and a side-turning capacity of about 4ft. Allan Batty, leading woodturning tutor at John Boddy's, has contributed some ideas to the design; it is obviously produced by people who understand woodturning.

From talking to a number of lathe suppliers, it emerged that it was the stronger, better-quality machines from specialist manufacturers that were selling. Without doubt there is enormous interest in turning, and woodturning courses across the country are reporting good business. All of which made me feel disappointed with the amount of turned work on sale or exhibition. There were a few nice pieces but little spectacular.

Allan Batty believes that (woodworking) amateurs — those not making a full-time living from a craft — are achieving a higher standard of workmanship than the professionals. Amateurs can afford to invest time in a piece; but, however much time you spend, it cannot overcome a basic deficiency in skills. They *must* have the skills!

The exhibition did display enormous skills. I felt that the 12-string guitar by **Phil Chambers** of Sutton was the absolute epitome of excellence. It won the Woodworker Challenge Cup for Musical Instru-

● *J. Gray's turntable fire engine won the gold medal in the toys section. The hosereel turns, the ladder extends, the steering steers . . .*

ments, a Gold Medal, and a Very Highly Commended in the English Abrasives Award for Finishing. 'Follow that!', as they say.

The instrument cried out to be played. The purfling looked as though it had grown as part of the wood of the soundboard. The inside of the rosewood back had been fine-finished almost to a polish; and the cross-struts and joint-bandings were so smooth that there was not a whisker to interrupt the sound-flow.

I stood and absorbed the two spinning-wheels for some time; the gold-medal winner was again perfection, but somehow I preferred the other, slightly more chunky one. Possibly it was the contrast of the ivory fittings.

Where do you start in trying to comment upon the many superb carvings? For me, the

● *Editor Peter Collenette (right) searches for a hand to shake – Mr F. Taylor took a gold medal for his barometer, and took care of Alan Townsend's marquetry cup for him*

The exhibits in the clocks section of the Show were interesting and varied, **writes Martin Bulger.** The long-case clock by **William Watts** was a worthy winner, not least because of his masterly use of the untraditional bubinga. **G. Chappell's** walnut long-case clock also displayed superb craftsmanship — the subtly designed veneered front was particularly pleasing to the eye.

N. Miller deserves the highest praise for his truly incredible fretworked clock (**right**); nor was **Gordon Foote** to be outdone, showing some ingenious fretwork in (of all things) thin stout-heart plywood. Personally, I thought it deserved a better base. William Watts' second clock, smooth and well-produced in iroko, completed an attractive trio in the mantel bracket-clock section.

The two clocks in the 'others' section were **R. Miller's** pleasant wall clock in oak and **S. Jackson's** 'Inspiration' clock, which, although lacking quality in the finish, must be applauded for its adventurousness and defiance of tradition. Definitely a conversation piece — for instance, should it stand on the floor, a large shelf, or a low table? Guaranteed to keep the household interior design team busy . . .

real display of excellence was the marquetry, whose standard must rival anything that there is or ever has been in this field. Despite the quality of the reproductions of paintings from the Louvre, I had to agree with the judges who gave first place to a picture of five sparrows on a window-sill. The choice of woods gave this piece a remarkable clarity and depth of perspective.

Some of the work, I felt, was ordinary — nothing took my fancy amongst the clocks. One piece of furniture that required a second look, though, was the silver-medal winner — a wall-mounted Gimson-style cabinet by **Wing Cmdr Landells.** This is an interesting piece, just the sort of item you might expect to find in a stately home in another 200 years. However, for today I'm not so sure. Mainly in walnut with a cherry lining, but also featuring kingwood and ebony, it had just too much variety of material and colour, which could be distracting.

In view of the all-too-frequently totally impractical, 'art-for-art's-sake' pieces we see from the students of some colleges of furniture and design, it was very pleasing to see the **college stands** at the show. Craftsmanship, interesting design and functionality were all well-represented. I could have lived with any of the work, particularly the spalted-beech chest from **Shrewsbury's Will Price.** I would also be happy to put any piece of restoration into the hands of

Show business

the students from **Manchester College!**

The demonstrating craftsmen give enormous pleasure. **Stuart King** held my attention as he fashioned a shovel with an antique swan-neck hand-adze. His stand, laid out with old tools and bits and pieces, had an evocative atmosphere which put me immediately in mind of a Chilterns bodger at work somewhere above High Wycombe.

The notice on **Theo Fossel's** stand advertises evening classes in stickmaking (beer supplied!). Theo, tall and thin, with his pointed face and country clothes, looks for all the world like a caricature of one of his own decorated sticks! I didn't realise how popular stickmaking and dressing had become. Theo will train over 70 people this year, his catalogue of fittings is into reprint, and the Stickmakers Guild he founded already has 550 members.

Visit the stand of the **Tool and Trades History Society,** with tools going back 300 and more years, and you come away asking yourself 'What's changed?' Then you look at the design and quality of work and you know the answer. Each year there are newly discovered timbers, improvements in tools, new gadgets. But it isn't the changes we go for. It is to see and handle the items we only see in catalogues; it is to make comparisons between manufacturers; it is to buy or order the odd thing or two (big and small) that we've been thinking about for some time, and indulge in a few extravagances. It is to be tempted by and succumb to the special 'Show offers', some of which represent extraordinarily good value. We get design ideas from the work of others. We go to talk to suppliers, who — busy as they are — still have time to share a few thoughts with us, and help us solve the odd problem. We find a few things we didn't know about — a particular finish, perhaps. And we meet a few friends who show up year after year. See you next time? ∎

● **Above:** 'Kneecaps', a marquetry tour-de-force by Alan Townsend, deservedly won the gold medal and the 'World of Wood' Cup; Anton Mikuz' relief carving 'Springtime' (**left**) pulses with raw strength. Waring Robinson's occasional table (**below**), subtly shaped and finished, won the cabinetmaking gold medal and the Robbins Rose Bowl

● AEG/Warren Machine Tools prize draw: how many hands fill an ancient bushel? Jim Murray (**left**) and Roger Warren share the lucky dip. See 'This Month' for the winners

● *The magnificent sofa table* **below** *was made by Guild of Woodworkers member John Walker, and displayed on the Guild stand.* **Right:** *Stuart King puts in some hard work in his replica woodware workshop (WW/Oct 85); and (*****below right*****) Maurice Lund's carving kept a constant stream of onlookers fascinated*

Books

Edward Reynolds Wright and Man Sill Pai
Korean Furniture
Kodansha/Harper & Row, £60 hardback
Reviewed by Peter Collenette

For most readers, Korea is a very long way away — and £60 is more than you'd ever spend on a book, no matter how close to home the subject. Still, this is a beautiful and absorbing volume.

Western woodworkers have borrowed from China, and to a lesser extent Japan, for at least 250 years. Only rarely has much of the original style survived the journey west, but that borrowing (like the growing buzz over Japanese tools) testifies to the repeated discovery of a woodworking tradition as strong and sophisticated as our own. And, while Eastern approaches are different enough to intrigue and excite, they are not so different as to alienate and baffle.

Korean traditional furniture greatly resembles that of Japan and China but has, likewise, its own character. This book, whose production is first-class and which appears an almost ideal introduction, depicts nothing to rival China's famous chairs, but is crammed with fascinating cabinet work ranging from small boxes to chests-of-drawers and tables.

The basic technique is framing and panelling. There's hardly any veneer work or moulding, and squares and rectangles predominate. Yet this directness is not crudity, and a luscious display of grain and colour in local timbers, such as zelkowa (very like elm) and persimmon, ensures that it's not dull. Many modern designer-craftspeople will find it powerfully inspiring.

If (my only quibble) the book had been written by a woodworker instead of two very conscientious scholars, I'd almost say it were worth the price.

John Baker
Mauchline Ware
Shire Publications, £1.25 paperback
Reviewed by Stuart King

Collecting is a funny thing. It can give enormous pleasure not only to the collector but to others who are allowed access to the private hoard.

John Baker is a collector who obviously likes to share his enthusiasm and knowledge. The history of Mauchline (pronounced 'Mochlin') ware, sometimes known simply as Scottish woodware, to some extent parallels that of its English cousin from Tunbridge Wells. It appears that snuff-talking was behind it all. A man called John Sandys invented a wooden snuffbox with an ingenious secret hinge. It proved very popular, but his secret was not to last and soon he had many imitators. Some of the best boxes were beautifully painted by local artists.

With the decline of snuff-taking, other avenues were explored — and what a lot there were. The most instantly recognisable Mauchline ware is perhaps the highly polished sycamore souvenirs, usually dec-orated with transfers and later with photo-graphs. Pictures of famous buildings, sea-side views and street scenes adorned small boxes, darning mushrooms, eggcups, needle-cases and more. These pieces found their way into almost every tourist spot there was — not only in Great Britain but in Canada, Australia, South Africa and the United States.

Apart from the naturally finished items there was also 'fern ware' and tartan ware. If they intrigue you, it's all in this nicely illustrated 32-page book.

Gordon Stokes
Beginner's Guide to Woodworking
(revised edition)
Pelham, £8.95 hardback
Reviewed by Tobias Kaye

Very practical, instructive and well-thought-out, Gordon Stokes' book is permeated with the delightful perspective of many years' experience in turning and teaching the craft.

The enjoyment of reading it is enhanced by dry remarks such as this: 'There is so far as I know no market for long shavings . . . but those who really want some need only turn wet wood'.

His remarks on safety are also realistic. I sometimes wonder if I shall be able to claim, as he can, an unblemished 40-year record — especially as I use the engineer's chuck he warns against. Such chucks are not exorbitantly expensive compared with complete universal chucks, and they are both versatile and wonderfully accurate. But they are dangerous. Stick to woodturner's chucks and you won't need a regular finger-count.

Gordon Stokes states that grinding is a controversial issue, and his methods certainly differ from mine. While I respect them and am sure that he gets excellent results, I wonder if the easiest way to avoid burning a tool is to learn how to balance it on your finger while grinding. I would rather use the adjustable rest seen in the photos, and learn not to push too hard.

I also question his rejection of high-speed-steel tools. True, they are more expensive, but as they need less grinding they last that much longer. If his arguments were taken to their logical conclusion one would have to say 'The softer the steel, the better the tool'. Though a marginally better edge is obtained on a softer steel, it's lost so quickly that I can't see the advantage.

My main criticism will be very important to some and not at all to others.

To me, turning is a continuous pursuit of aesthetic excellence, in which one makes the very finest distinctions between 'good' and 'not good enough'. Gordon Stokes, however, is not an exponent of High Design; his shapes are somewhat mundane. I do not like turning that merely serves as support for glossy mass-produced goodies — a category into which a few of his products fall.

That said, this book deals very thoroughly with all the necessary tech-niques. So I recommend it to those who do not aspire to the more 'artistic' types of woodturning. I shall lend it to many of the enquirers who come to me for help in starting or in improving technique.

Anthony Vaughan
The Vaughans: East End Furniture Makers
ILEA, County Hall, London SE1 7PB
Reviewed by David Savage

This is one of those books that now flourish under the title of local history. The Geffrye Museum, in what was the heart of the London furniture trade, has generously and rightly encouraged the publication of little books recounting a past era.

This one concentrates on a single family which made its living from furniture. Sadly, however, in comprehending the East End trade — with its multiplicity of tiny shops, day-workers, pieceworkers, piece-masters, milling shops, upholsterers and polishers — a book such as this is little help.

Mr Vaughan does fill it with reference material of all sorts, some indeed informative about the time and place: vivid personal recollections with descriptions of workshops and processes now long gone, and some stories (secondhand) which are wonderfully evocative of the sweatshop system — also gone, and un-lamented. The Vaughans themselves, however, do not make such informative or interesting read-ing. As piece-masters and gaffers of some-times large concerns, they were seldom en-gaged at the point of production.

An amateur historian has here tried to write the history of his own family, and it lacks clarity, objectivity and style. For those really interested in the history of the trade, it contains many jewels. Unfortunately, Mr Vaughan does not present them for our emjoyment; we must dig to find them.

Glenn Davidson
Tool Grinding and Sharpening Handbook
Blandford Press, £5.95
Reviewed by David Savage

Without really sharp tools it's impossible for the craftsman to produce work of any quality. Dull tools are slow to use, inac-curate and dangerous, while a keen edge will give the effortless ease associated with skilled craftsmanship.

This is one of those valuable and rare textbooks that is seldom read, but always kept for reference, because it contains com-plete information within its own narrow area — namely, electric grinders. So long as sharpening is effected by the use of a grinding wheel, this book covers it. Honing is rather sketchily touched upon; but, if you want to know how to use your grinder with-out blue-ing your precious tools, Mr David-son will tell you how. Personal safety and the sharpening of drill bits, lathe toolbits, circular saws, router bits and hand-held cutting tools each have a separate chapter.

69

70

I thought it would be worth making a pressure guard to fit my saw-bench, **writes T. F. Bernascone.** It is of beech, with a sliding stock of teak, and the sliding rod that retains the guard is of brass, threaded OBA at each end. No particular reason for the beech, teak or OBA — they just happened to be available. Similarly, dimensions would vary to suit the saw-bench and workpiece, so I have given no figures.

A captive OBA nut is fixed to the guard, and the same fixtures are in the saw-table to enable the guard-slide to be positioned. The spring applying pressure to the guard is a large terry-clip, bent so the ends slide in a groove in the guard's back. I enlarged the hole in the base of the clip so the brass rod can pass through, and the base of the clamped spring is held by a brass plate. It works very well, holds timber nicely against the fence, and keeps fingers out of the way without having to resort constantly to the awkward two-push-stick trick. ∎

● *Easily home-made, this pressure guard will prove a big help for accuracy and safety*

A PRESSURE GUARD FOR A SAW-BENCH

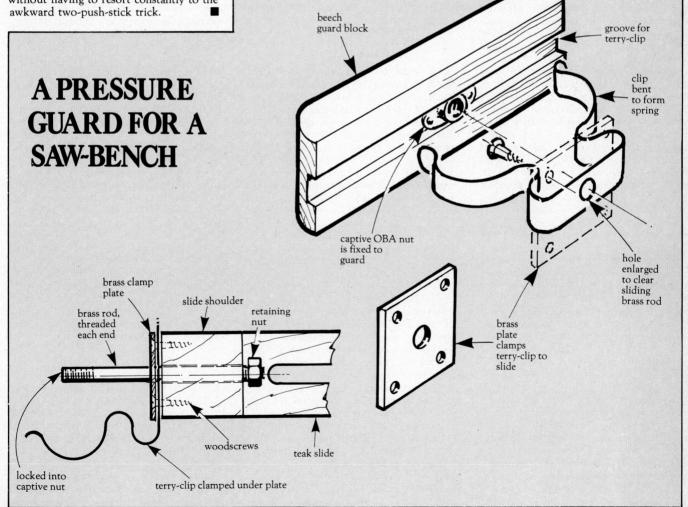

beech guard block

groove for terry-clip

clip bent to form spring

captive OBA nut is fixed to guard

hole enlarged to clear sliding brass rod

brass clamp plate

slide shoulder

retaining nut

brass rod, threaded each end

brass plate clamps terry-clip to slide

woodscrews

teak slide

locked into captive nut

terry-clip clamped under plate

Making time

Celebrated clockmaker
William Watts comments
on the craft, the business,
the past and the future

Craftspeople are remarkable survivors. In what is arguably an age of mediocrity, craftwork from all disciplines is alive and well, as the success of exhibitions like the Woodworker Show indicates. Work is being done today which undoubtedly equals the very best of former ages.

It's inconceivable that the patron exists who would willingly pay the astronomical prices that endless hours of true craftsmanship demand, but there are other means of survival. *Woodworker's* classified columns give a clue, where woodturners, french-polishers, instrument-makers and others are offering short courses, and sometimes accommodation as well. Perhaps the craft worker survives because he or she sees the money that people are ready to spend on what they use as leisure activities?

It was via this route I first entered the craft world, enrolling on one of Juliet Barker and Roland Gentle's violin-making courses in Cambridge. It wasn't long before I realised that I wasn't going to be able to make instruments as well as I wanted by just going to a one-week course every year; so I looked for full-time courses.

The local choice was limited, but armed with splendid testimonial support from Cambridge I duly presented myself for interview at one establishment. It was a strange experience, conducted by a young woman in an elderly and very shabby continental car, and I wasn't really surprised not to be given a place. The following year I tried once again, armed as before with the most impeccable references, but this time offering to pay my own fees (more than £3000 p.a.) since I thought that Government cutbacks in education might be a reason for my lack of success. How I envy Edward Park's happy experience (WW/June 85) at Merton College! My own, at the hands of no less than four unfriendly and unhelpful interlocutors who were all tutors at this particular college, was gruesome in the extreme. All appeared dedicated to the idea that I ought not to have been there in the first place. The interview was characterised by gritty and abrasive comments from my interviewers, which I now interpret as the result of nervousness and inexperience. I wasn't at all surprised not to receive even the courtesy of a letter saying my application had failed.

Time is a great healer and a little bit of ego-puncturing is good for us all at times. After a short period of self-indulgent anger I gradually came to the conclusion that I hadn't thought the matter through properly. To be able to earn a living at making and repairing instruments might require an application of time, effort and money that in truth I really did not have.

I've had a lifelong interest in clocks so it was natural to explore the possibilities of craftwork in this direction. One of the benefits of exposure to violin-making techniques was the awareness that the millimetre is in fact a noble dimension. How often Juliet or Roland would say: 'It's greatly oversize, you need to take off at least half a millimetre', and I would smile inwardly; but no more. With a hardwood such as maple or bubinga, that ½mm will represent an age of scraping to size!

My first clock was entered in the 1984 Woodworker Show at Alexandra Pavilion, and (with beginner's luck) was awarded the Silver Challenge Trophy. The intangible rewards were the most pleasurable; I came into contact with a great number of enthusiasts who took the trouble to find me and discuss techniques of design and application, giving their time and expertise without stint. A natural progression was to wonder whether there might be commercial outlets for my clocks — several people having enquired what the prices were; so I began to examine the marketplace.

The close parallel between clocks and violins is that the market for modern examples of both is narrow. Given a choice, most musicians would prefer an instrument several hundred years old and most clock buyers would consider the investment value of an old timepiece an over-riding consideration. Genuine antiques in either field are becoming more and more difficult to find and costly to buy; I reasoned that there must be people of taste with enough cash to buy a clock for 10% of the cost of a genuine Tompion or Fromanteel, which is still entirely hand-crafted like the original.

There wasn't much point in offering mass-produced movements from the Black Forest, or quartz types from Japan, since this would negate the whole idea of something unique and individual that justified the necessarily high price. Surprisingly, there are still highly skilled clockmakers who will hand-craft movements and dials to special order, and I have been fortunate enough to meet Stephen Kelly of Exeter, who has been a clockmaker for over 60 years. With infinite skill and patience, Mr Kelly has translated my ideas into practical form, and I like to think that a similar happy working relationship must have existed between the clockmakers of old and their casemakers.

I always enjoy reading articles about craftspeople's business, and am especially interested in how they market their work. There is something quite indefinable about the mechanics of acquiring a fine piece. Firstly it must have a perceived value; if this appears more than the asking price, then the auguries for the sale are good. Design, detail workmanship and finish are also crucial, and perhaps (least likely of all) a genuine need for the buyer to have the piece in question. If all this adds up to a powerful urge to buy, the craftsman's situation is indeed a happy one and you only have to handle your necessarily high asking price with a certain diffidence and reluctance not to oversell too heavily. However, where pricing is the dominant factor, the craftsman is in a very vulnerable position since you know you simply can't compete on level terms, and the buyer is probably not in a position to pay what's being asked. Perhaps this is why I've consciously sought out the commercial buyer for my work — pricing is usually of secondary importance to these people. They are busy, they know what they want and they are usually prepared to pay when they find what they are looking for.

I believe it's only a fringe benefit to have had a commercial background before taking up craftwork. Basically business is very simple and straightforward; the issues are clear-cut and can be resolved in a clear-cut manner, yes or no. I've often thought a housewife running a home and raising a family has far and away a more difficult task than a businessman; she's making a variety of snap decisions every moment of her day, some of which are matters of life and death — although she probably doesn't see it that way. I would say, delegate as much as possible on to the broad shoulders of your accountant or other advisor, leaving as much of your time as possible for creativity. It's a trial and a disappointment for your letters to be unanswered, but it happens all the time. In such cases I try to take the view that perhaps my letter wasn't written as well as it might have been, so I might try again. Letters and phone calls are costly and I try to keep both to a minimum.

It's really strange how the mind can leap from deciding to enter the world of crafts to discussing the marketing of the finished product. There is a whole world in between of discovery and the acquisition of know-how (usually by painful trial and error!); so here are a few of my own experiences.

My first sizeable project was a fitted kitchen in pine. There was a great deal of repetition work with doors and drawers, and the tool I used most of all was a Black & Decker ½in drill mounted on a stand. I used a wheel-cutter for my tenons and rebates, and dug the mortises out with a mallet and chisel. On and off, the work took about six months, and my wife was very patient and long-suffering. It's one thing to learn how to use tools from books, but some things have to be experienced at first hand for the message to sink in, and the behaviour of wet wood is one. I wasn't at all prepared for the movement which occurred because of shrinkage, and I've had to learn the hard way that, no matter how old a prize piece of wood might be, it's rarely stable. A tip from James Krenov's *A Cabinetmaker's Notebook* was literally worth its weight in gold — he says that wood needs a minimum of two or three weeks in the workshop environment to settle down after re-sawing.

My first sizeable tool was a Sears radial-arm saw. In theory, this was the ultimate in universals and I bought many attachments to give a wide range of options — routing, sanding, moulding, shaping, and so on. But I soon found the only function it performed really well was crosscutting. It proved impossible for the locks in the carriage, yoke and arm to set really tightly and so I couldn't perform any truly accurate work. The retailers (Hawards of Tunbridge Wells) tried hard to correct this situation, but without success. A well-learned lesson was that all universals are a compromise, and ever since I have purchased a single tool for a specific purpose.

Most beginners find hand-sawing and planing really hard work, especially with hardwood, and the two most useful of my power tools are an Arco saw-bench with a 12in TCT rip-blade and a Scheppach Solo thicknesser and planer. These tools reduce preparation time to a fraction of that needed for hand labour, and yet they leave a perfect finish. Quoting Krenov again, there should be no unease about using power tools for hand-crafted work since this gives you more time for design, cutting joints, accurate gluing and so on.

A really useful tool has been the Lion mitre-trimmer, without which much of my work on clocks would be difficult or indeed impossible. I read somewhere that mitres are always a disappointment and my initial experience confirmed this. No matter how beautifully the mitres matched when dry, they always seemed to slip when glued ... My (almost!) infallible method now is to glue 'dog-ears' on each pair of mitres, which have previously been cut across with a ¼in router bit to take a key. When the glue has set I use Crab cramps across the 'dog-ears', and the specially designed shoes on the cramps ensure an absolutely true and tight bond which is of course strengthened by the ½x¼in key. My bracket clock in the 1985 Woodworker Show has no less than 28 such joints and the only problem really is the time required for the glue to dry; perhaps it isn't commercial, but it works.

The router has proved a wonderful tool. My Bosch POF 50 on a Type S7 table has been the workhorse for all my mouldings,

● *Bill Watts' lovely bracket clock in iroko won a silver medal at the 1985 Woodworker Show*

grooves and rebates. I discovered early on that for very accurate work one has to ensure that the table is really flat; mine had bowed slightly and the 1-2mm of play across the length always resulted in a poor cut. Not wishing to replace the table-top (it is drilled and calibrated for the movable fence), I cramp a trued-up straight-edge on to it, which gives me a good flat surface.

My experience with cutters is that those made by Stanley from the USA are far and away the best. All the one I have bought that are made in England have suffered from vibration, which I believe is due to the wings' being out of balance. Cutters from Israel were well balanced but not as sharp as the American ones. Another problem is sharpening TCT bits. Even when serviced by

How to finish...

first... ..with a planer that's prized for its surfacing performance and tough durability. The Startrite PT260 has a lever action infeed table for rapid adjustments against scale and an easily adjusted safety cutterblock.

second... ..a thicknesser with real power and precision. A lockable handwheel raises and lowers the robust table against an easily read scale calibrated in Imperial and Metric units. Thicknessing guard and chip deflector are standard.

third... ..and for no extra charge, a quality rebater with 15mm capacity. Lever action on infeed table allows instant depth change. Safety holding device is standard Startrite equipment.

and fourth. ..bevels and chamfers make it a clean sweep for Startrite. The large rigid and easily adjusted fence allows angles up to 45° to be cut with sure precise control along the metre long table.

STARTRITE

The Startrite PT260 sweeps the board! Surfacing, thicknessing, rebating and bevelling — the famous four-way finish is yours if you Startrite! This quality machine is solidly built, attractively finished and ready for action with sealed for life bearings on the two knife steel planer block. With all the internal wiring ready connected, just plug in for PT260 productivity. **INTERBUILD EXHIBITION STAND 7242**

To: **STARTRITE MACHINE TOOL CO. LTD.**

Waterside Works, Gads Hill, Gillingham, Kent ME7 2SF.

600 ®
THE 600 GROUP

Please send me colour brochure and price details.

Name_____

Address_____

Making time

the makers, they never seem to be as good as new. I spoke to Jim Phillips, the MD of Trend Cutting Tools, about this, and he was very helpful, suggesting that my POF 50 was much too small for my work and perhaps a larger router would iron out the vibration. I take his point but wonder why the Stanley cutters seem to work so well with my existing kit?

I use a Japanese water-stone grinder for sharpening my chisels and plane-irons, which is very functional. However, I fully agree with the review (WW/Feb 85) which concluded that this particular model was crudely made and very much overpriced, and it ought not to be necessary to make major adjustments for the machine to operate correctly. I also have to say that my chisels are razor-sharp after a session with the grinder, and are a joy to use subsequently.

Volumes might be written about the pitfalls of buying — wood, tools, whatever. I tend to buy more than I need of practically everything. Sometimes this is good, since well-stored wood is as good as money in the bank earning interest. Other items, however, don't store well, and I dread to think of the french polish I have bought which deteriorated before it was all used up. There are of course great savings to be made when buying in bulk, but you have to take all the contributing factors into the equation — cashflow, storeability, saleability and so on.

Buying wood is a minefield for the unwary. Retail prices are horrendous, but I sometimes buy this way if I see a unique example of figuring which I need and must have. I have bought whole logs which I have had quartered and sawn; the initial prices were very low (or appeared so), but if you take cost like transport and cutting into account the waste is considerable. The prices charged by reputable dealers for straight-edged boards no longer appear excessive!

An experience with cutting a piece of bubinga is perhaps worth relating. An 8x3in baulk had been set up on a German-built bandsaw with the intention of cutting ⅝in finished boards. The saw had a 50hp motor and a 4in blade with 2in TCT teeth, yet it suddenly stalled; four teeth were sheared off, two of which penetrated the baulk to a depth of 1½in. The operator (one of the tutors at a leading technical college) examined the surfaces for a foreign object like a nail or bullet, but could find nothing. He concluded that the wood was simply too dense for the saw on auto-feed and I still have the piece of wood where the teeth entered as a souvenir of an uncomfortable moment! I have since become very fond of bubinga; it looks good, takes a marvellous polish and is stable. Its density is an asset, since anything made with it will always sit firmly on the ground. It follows of course that hand-tools require frequent sharpening when you use them on such timber.

Surface finishing is a subject all on its own. I think I spend more time polishing my clocks than making them, and I sometimes

wonder whether this is true of other makers. Initially I spent about four days on a polishing course in Paignton; it is really quite surprising how much can be covered in so short a time. We covered staining, matching and restoration and learned enough to realise the enormous amount of work to be done to obtain even an average finish. My favourite standard finish is to french-polish up to a medium gloss, flat down with grade 0000 wire wool, polish with Fiddes' burnishing cream, and finally coat with carnauba wax, polishing with a soft rag. The result is a lovely soft, glossy finish which is extremely durable and requires only a bare minimum of maintenance. I make my own french polishes and waxes with materials from Fiddes of Cardiff.

A pet hate of mine is to pay for a trade catalogue. I don't charge for mine, and it seems preposterous to make such a charge even if it's offset against a subsequent purchase. It's interesting to observe that the level of pricing, whoever the supplier, is very much the same even allowing for the special offers. The wary buyer shops around and gets the best deal coupled with good service. There are many bargains to be had at the Woodworker Shows in London and Bristol. I've purchased router cutters, Crab clamps, timber, veneers, power tools and so on at a fraction of the regular prices at these shows, and it's well worth taking your credit card just in case.

I read a lot, buying the books if my cashflow allows, or borrowing from the library if not. I also visit museums and country houses to sketch and examine interesting clocks at close quarters. It's strange how often the same examples of masterworks are featured in so many different books, perhaps because the supply is finite and the numbers limited. The net result is that one soon becomes adept at recognising features of a particular maker's work — all part of the 'learning curve'. My first clock took over a year to construct, but the latest was completed in a little over five weeks.

I believe that the craftsmen of olden times were often badly let down by their glue, and we're fortunate to have today's powerful adhesives. Also a craftsman rarely seemed to bother about cleaning up out-of-sight surfaces, even in the best work. These are about the only criticisms I would dare to make of these wonderful old timers(!). One needs to have only a poor perception of excellence to realise the abundant skills they applied in all areas; design, construction, finish, everything. Perhaps too few were good business-people, so they mostly worked for a pittance and lived in poverty. The one commodity they had in abundance was time, and though the hours were long they made good use of them. Then as now the best would achieve recognition and they set standards which guide and inspire us to this day. I like to dream that my clocks too might be treasured 300 years from now — it is a form of immortality, after all! ∎

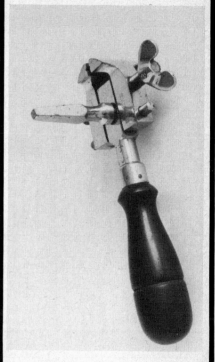

shop guide

AVON

BATH   Tel. Bath 64513
JOHN HALL TOOLS   ★
RAILWAY STREET

Open: Monday-Saturday
9.00 a.m.-5.30 p.m.
H.P.W.WM.D.A.BC.

BRISTOL   Tel. (0272) 741510
JOHN HALL TOOLS LIMITED   ★
CLIFTON DOWN SHOPPING CENTRE
WHITELADIES ROAD
Open: Monday-Saturday
9.00 a.m.-5.30 p.m.
H.P.W.WM.D.A.BC.

BRISTOL   Tel. (0272) 629092
TRYMWOOD SERVICES
2a DOWNS PARK EAST, (off North View)
WESTBURY PARK
Open: 8.30 a.m.-5.30 p.m. Mon. to Fri.
Closed for lunch 1.00-2.00 p.m.
P.W.WM.D.T.A.BC.

BRISTOL   Tel. (0272) 667013
WILLIS
157 WEST STREET
BEDMINSTER
Open Mon.-Fri. 8.30 a.m.-5.00 p.m.
Sat. 9 a.m.-4 p.m.
P.W.WM.D.CS.A.BC.

BEDFORDSHIRE

BEDFORD   Tel. (0234) 59808
BEDFORD SAW SERVICE   K
39 AMPTHILL ROAD

Open: Mon.-Fri. 8.30-5.30
Sat. 9.00-4.00
H.P.A.BC.W.CS.WM.D.

BERKSHIRE

COOKHAM   Tel. (06285) 20350
CHURCH'S TIMBER
STATION HILL

Open: Mon-Sat 8.30 a.m.-5.30 p.m.
Wed 8.30 a.m.-1.00 p.m.
H.P.W.T.CS.MF.A.

READING   Tel. (0734) 591361
HOME CARE CENTRE
26/30 KING'S ROAD

Open: Monday-Saturday
9.00 a.m.-5.30 p.m.
H.P.W.D.A.WM.BC.

READING   Tel. Littlewick Green
DAVID HUNT (TOOL   2743
MERCHANTS) LTD
KNOWL HILL, NR. READING   ★
Open: Monday-Saturday
9.00 a.m.-5.30 p.m.
H.P.W.D.A.BC.

BERKSHIRE

READING   Tel. Reading 661511
WOKINGHAM TOOL CO. LTD.
99 WOKINGHAM ROAD

Open: Mon-Sat 9.00 a.m.-5.30 p.m.
Closed 1.00-2.00 p.m. for lunch
H.P.W.WM.D.CS.A.BC.

BUCKINGHAMSHIRE

SLOUGH   Tel. (06286).5125
BRAYWOOD ESTATES LTD   ★
158 BURNHAM LANE

Open: 9.00 a.m.-5.30 p.m.
Monday-Saturday
H.P.W.WM.CS.A.

MILTON KEYNES   Tel. (0908)
POLLARD WOODWORKING   641366
CENTRE   ★
51 AYLESBURY ST., BLETCHLEY
Open: Mon-Fri 8.30-5.30
Saturday 9.00-5.00
H.P.W.WM.D.CS.A.BC.

HIGH WYCOMBE   Tel. (0494)
SCOTT SAWS LTD.   24201/33788
14 BRIDGE STREET   ★

Mon.-Sat. 8.30 a.m.-6.00 p.m.

H.P.W.WM.D.T.CS.MF.A.BC.

HIGH WYCOMBE   Tel. (0494)
ISAAC LORD LTD   22221
185 DESBOROUGH ROAD   KE

Open: Mon-Fri 8.00 a.m.-5.00 p.m.
Saturday 9.00 a.m.-5.00 p.m.
H.P.W.D.A.

CAMBRIDGESHIRE

CAMBRIDGE   Tel. (0223) 63132
D. MACKAY LTD.   E★
BRITANNIA WORKS, EAST ROAD

Open: Mon.-Fri. 8.30 a.m.-1 p.m./2.00-
5.00 p.m. Sat. 8.30 a.m.-1.00 p.m.
H.P.W.D.T.CS.MF.A.BC.

CAMBRIDGE   Tel. (0223) 247386
H. B. WOODWORKING   K
105 CHERRY HINTON ROAD
Open: 8.30 a.m.-5.30 p.m.
Monday-Friday
8.30 a.m.-1.00 p.m. Sat.
H.P.W.WM.D.CS.A.

PETERBOROUGH   Tel. (0733)
WILLIAMS DISTRIBUTORS   64252
(TOOLS) LIMITED   K
108-110 BURGHLEY ROAD
Open: Monday to Friday
8.30 a.m.-5.30 p.m.
H.P.A.W.D.WH.BC.

CHESHIRE

NANTWICH   Tel. Crewe 67010
ALAN HOLTHAM   K★
THE OLD STORES TURNERY
WISTASON ROAD, WILLASTON
Open: Tues.-Sat. 9.00 a.m.-5.30 p.m.
Closed Monday
P.W.WM.D.T.C.CS.A.BC.

CHEADLE   Tel. 061491 1726
ERIC TOMKINSON   ★
86 STOCKPORT ROAD
Open: Mon.-Fri. 9.00 a.m.-4.00 p.m.
Saturday 9.00 a.m.-1.00 p.m.
H.P.W.D.MF.A.BC.

CLEVELAND

MIDDLESBROUGH   Tel. (0642)
CLEVELAND WOODCRAFT   813103
(M'BRO), 38-42 CRESCENT ROAD   K

Open: Mon-Sat 9.15 a.m.-5.30 p.m.

H.P.T.A.BC.W.WM.CS.D.

CORNWALL

HELSTON   Tel. Helston (03265) 4961
SOUTH WEST   Truro (0872) 71671
POWER TOOLS   Launceston
MONUMENT ROAD   (0566) 3555
   K
H.P.W.WM.D.CS.A.

TRURO   Tel. (0872) 71671
TRURO POWER TOOLS   E★
30 FERRIS TOWN

Open Mon.-Sat. 8.00 a.m.-12.30 p.m./
1.30 p.m.-5.00 p.m.
H.P.W.WM.D.CS.MF.A.BC.

CUMBRIA

CARLISLE   Tel. (0228) 36391
W. M. PLANT
ALLENBROOK ROAD
ROSEHILL, CA1 2UT
Open: Mon.-Fri. 8.00 a.m.-5.15 p.m.
Sat. 8.00 a.m.-12.30 noon
P.W.WM.D.CS.A.

DERBYSHIRE

DERBY   Tel. (0332) 41862
HAZLEHURSTS LTD.   E★
LONDON ROAD AND CANAL STREET

Open: Mon.-Sat. 8.30 a.m.-5.30 p.m. (retail)
Mon.-Fri. 8.00 a.m.-5.00 p.m. (trade)
H.P.W.MF.A.BC.

BUXTON   Tel. (0298) 871636
CRAFT SUPPLIES   K★
THE MILL, MILLERSDALE

Open: Mon-Sat 9.00 a.m.-5.00 p.m.

H.P.W.D.T.CS.A.BC.

DEVON

BRIXHAM   Tel. (08045) 4900
WOODCRAFT SUPPLIES   E★
4 HORSE POOL STREET

Open: Mon.-Sat. 9.00 a.m.-6.00 p.m.

H.P.W.A.D.MF.CS.BC.

PLYMOUTH   Tel. (0752) 330303
WESTWARD BUILDING SERVICES   ★
LTD., LISTER CLOSE, NEWNHAM
INDUSTRIAL ESTATE, PLYMPTON
Open: Mon-Fri 8.00 a.m.-5.30 p.m.
Sat. 8.30 a.m.-12.30 p.m.
H.P.W.WM.D.A.BC.

DORSET

BOURNEMOUTH   Tel: (0202) 420583
POWER TOOL SERVICES
(Sales, spares, repairs)
849-851 CHRISTCHURCH ROAD
BOSCOMBE
Open: Mon.-Fri. 9.00 a.m.-5.30 p.m.
Sat. 9.00 a.m.-5.00 p.m.
H.P.W.CS.K.A.

ESSEX

LEIGH ON SEA   Tel. (0702)
MARSHAL & PARSONS LTD.   710404
1111 LONDON ROAD   EK

Open: 8.30 a.m.-5.30 p.m. Mon-Fri
9.00 a.m.-5.00 p.m. Sat.
H.P.W.WM.D.CS.A.

ILFORD
CUTWELL TOOLS LTD.   ★
774-776 HIGH ROAD

Mon.-Fri. 9.00 a.m.-5.00 p.m.
and also by appointment.
P.W.WM.A.D.CS.

GLOUCESTER

TEWKESBURY   Tel. (0684)
TEWKESBURY SAW CO. LTD.   293092
TRADING ESTATE, NEWTOWN   K

Open: Mon-Fri 8.00 a.m.-5.00 p.m.
Saturday 9.30 a.m.-12.00 p.m.
P.W.WM.D.CS.

HAMPSHIRE

SOUTHAMPTON   Tel. (0703)
H.W.M.   776222
THE WOODWORKERS
303 SHIRLEY ROAD, SHIRLEY
Open: Tues-Fri 9.30 a.m.-6.00 p.m.
Sat 9.30 a.m.-4.00 p.m.
H.P.W.WM.D.CS.A.BC.T.

★Shops offering a mail order service are denoted in this Guide by an asterisk.

shopguide

HAMPSHIRE

ALDERSHOT   Tel. (0252) 334422
POWER TOOL CENTRE   **K**
374 HIGH STREET
Open Mon.-Fri. 8.30 a.m.-5.30 p.m.
Sat. 8.30 a.m.-12.30 p.m.

H.P.W.WM.D.A.BC.

PORTSMOUTH   Tel. (0705)
EURO PRECISION TOOLS LTD   667332
259/263 LONDON ROAD, NORTH END   ★
   E
Open: Mon-Fri 9.00 a.m.-5.30 p.m.
Sat. 9.00 a.m.-1.00 p.m.
H.P.W.WM.D.A.BC.

SOUTHAMPTON   Tel: (0703)
POWER TOOL CENTRE   332288
7 BELVIDERE ROAD   **K★**
Open Mon.-Fri. 8.30-5.30

H.P.W.WM.D.A.BC.CS.MF.

HUMBERSIDE

GRIMSBY   Tel. Grimsby (0472)
   58741 Hull (0482) 26999
J. E. SIDDLE LTD. (Tool Specialists)   ★
83 VICTORIA STREET
Open: Mon-Fri 8.30 a.m.-5.30 p.m.
Sat. 8.30 a.m.-12.45 p.m. & 2 p.m.-5 p.m.
H.P.A.BC.W.WMD.

KENT

WYE   Tel. (0233) 813144
KENT POWER TOOLS LTD.
UNIT 1, BRIAR CLOSE
WYE, Nr. ASFORD

H.P.W.WM.D.A.CS.

**If you wish to be
in the shop guide,
'phone 01-437 0699**

LANCASHIRE

PRESTON   Tel. (0772) 52951
SPEEDWELL TOOL COMPANY   **E★**
62-68 MEADOW STREET PR1 1SU
Open: Mon.-Fri. 8.30 a.m.-5.30 p.m.
Sat. 8.30 a.m.-12.30 p.m.

H.P.W.WM.CS.A.MF.BC.

ROCHDALE   Tel. (0706) 342123/
C.S.M. TOOLS   342322
4-6 HEYWOOD ROAD   **E★**
CASTLETON
Open: Mon-Sat 9.00 a.m.-6.00 p.m.
Sundays by appointment
W.D.CS.A.BC.

LANCASTER   Tel. (0524) 32886
LILE TOOL SHOP   **K**
43/45 NORTH ROAD
Open: Monday to Saturday
9.00 a.m.-5.30 p.m.
Wed 9.00 a.m.-12.30 p.m.
H.P.W.D.A.

LANCASHIRE

BURY   Tel. (061 764 6769
HOUSE OF HARBRU   ★
101 CROSTONS ROAD
ELTON
Open: Mon.-Fri. 9.00 a.m.-5.00 p.m.
Send 2 × 1st class stamps for catalogue
MF.

MANCHESTER   Tel. (061 789)
TIMMS TOOLS   0909
102-104 LIVERPOOL ROAD
PATRICROFT M30 0WZ
Weekdays 9.00 a.m.-5.30 p.m.
Sat. 9.00 a.m.-1.00 p.m.
H.P.A.W.

LINCOLNSHIRE

LINCOLN   Tel. (0522) 689369
SKELLINGTHORPE SAW SERVICES LTD.
OLD WOOD, SKELLINGTHORPE
Open: Mon to Fri 8 a.m.-5 p.m.
Sat 8 a.m.-12 p.m.
H.P.W.WM.D.CS.A.*.BC.
Access/Barclaycard

LONDON

ACTON   Tel. (01-992) 4835
A. MILLS (ACTON) LTD   ★
32/36 CHURCHFIELD ROAD W3 6ED
Open: Mon-Fri 9.00 a.m.-5.00 p.m.
Saturdays 9.00 am.-1.00 p.m.
H.P.W.WM.

LONDON   Tel. 01-723 2295-6-7
LANGHAM TOOLS LIMITED
13 NORFOLK PLACE   LT
LONDON W2 1QJ

LONDON   Tel. (01-567) 2922
G. D. CLEGG & SONS   ★
83 UXBRIDGE ROAD, HANWELL W7 3ST
Mon-Sat 9.15 a.m.-5.30 p.m.
Closed for lunch 1.00-2.00p.m.
Early Closing 1.00 p.m. Wed.
H.P.A.W.WM.D.CS.

NORBURY   Tel. (01-679) 6193
HERON TOOLS & HARDWARE LTD.
437 STREATHAM HIGH ROAD SW16
Open Mon-Fri 8.30 a.m.-5.00 p.m.
Wednesday 8.30 a.m.-1.00 p.m.
Sat. 9.00 a.m.-1.00 p.m.
H.P.W.A.

LONDON   Tel. (01-636) 7475
BUCK & RYAN LTD   ★
101 TOTTENHAM COURT ROAD W1P ODY

Open: Mon.-Fri. 8.30 a.m.-5.30 p.m.
Saturday 8.30 a.m.-4.00 p.m.

H.P.W.WM.D.A..

WEMBLEY   Tel. 904-1144
ROBERT SAMUEL LTD.   (904-1147
7, 15 & 16 COURT PARADE   after 4.00)
EAST LANE, N. WEMBLEY   ★
Open Mon.-Fri. 8.45-5.15; Sat. 9-1.00
Access, Barclaycard, AM Express, & Diners
H.P.W.CS.E.A.D.

LONDON

WOOLWICH   Tel. (01-854) 7767/8
A. D. SHILLMAN & SONS LTD
108-109 WOOLWICH HIGH STREET
SE18
Open: Mon-Sat
8.30 p.m.-5.30p.m.
H.P.W.CS.A.

HOUNSLOW   Tel. (01-570)
Q.R. TOOLS LTD   2103/5135
251-253 HANWORTH ROAD

Open: Mon-Fri 8.30 a.m.-5.30 p.m.
Sat. 9.00 a.m.-1.00 p.m.
P.W.WM.D.CS.A.

FULHAM   Tel. (01-385) 5109
I. GRIZZARD LTD.   **E**
84a-b LILLIE ROAD, SW6 1TL
Open: Mon-Sat 9.00-5.30 p.m.
Half day Thursday

H.P.A.BC.W.CS.WM.D.

MERSEYSIDE

LIVERPOOL   Tel. (051-207) 2967
TAYLOR BROS (LIVERPOOL) LTD   **K**
195-199 LONDON ROAD
LIVERPOOL L3 8JG
Open: Monday to Friday
8.30 a.m.-5.30 p.m.
H.P.W.WM.D.A.BC.

MIDDLESEX

ENFIELD   Tel. (01-363) 2935
GILL & HOXBY LTD.   **K**
133-137 ST. MARKS ROAD EN1 1BB

Mon.-Sat. 8.30 a.m.-6.00 p.m.
Early closing Wednesday 1.00 p.m.
H.P.W.WM.T.CS.A

RUISLIP   Tel. (08956) 74126
ALLMODELS ENGINEERING LTD.   **E★**
91 MANOR WAY

Open: Mon-Sat 9.00 a.m.-5.30 p.m.

H.P.W.A.D.CS.MF.BC.

CROWMARSH   Tel. (0491) 38653
MILL HILL SUPPLIES   **E★**
66 THE STREET
Open: Mon.-Fri. 9.30 a.m.-5.00 p.m.
Thurs. 9.30 a.m.-7.00 p.m.
Sat. 9.30 a.m.-1.00 p.m.
P.W.D.CS.MF.A.BC.

FARNHAM   Tel. (0252) 725427
A.B.E. CO. LTD. (Quick Hire)   ★
GOODS SHED
STATION APPROACH, FARNHAM
Open Mon.-Fri. 8.00 a.m.-5.30 p.m.
Sat. 8.00 a.m.-5.30 p.m.
H.P.W.D.CS.A.BC.

---

*An Asterisk ★
denotes a Mail
Order Service.*

NORFOLK

NORWICH   Tel. (0603) 898695
NORFOLK SAW SERVICES
DOG LANE, HORSFORD
Open: Monday to Friday
8.00 a.m.-5.00 p.m.
Saturday 8.00 a.m.-12.00 p.m.
H.P.W.WM.D.CS.A.

KINGS LYNN   Tel. (0553) 2443
WALKER & ANDERSON (Kings Lynn) LTD.
WINDSOR ROAD, KINGS LYNN   **K**
Open: Monday to Saturday
7.45 a.m.-5.30 p.m.
Wednesday 1.00 p.m. Saturday 5.00 p.m.
H.P.W.WM.D.CS.A.

NORWICH   Tel. (0603) 400933
WESTGATES WOODWORKING   **Tx**
61 HURRICANE WAY,   975412
NORWICH AIRPORT INDUSTRIAL ESTATE
Open: 9.00 a.m.-5.00 p.m. weekdays
9.00 a.m.-12.30 Sat.
P.W.WM.D.BC.   **K**

KING'S LYNN   Tel: 07605 674
TONY WADDILOVE, UNIT A   ★
HILL FARM WORKSHOPS
GREAT DUNHAM, (Nr. Swaffham)
Open: Tues. — Fri. 10.00 a.m. to 5.30 p.m.
Sat. 9.00 a.m. to 5.00 p.m.
H.P.W.D.T.MF.A.BC.*

GT. YARMOUTH   Tel. (0493)
ANGLIA POWER TOOLS   850388
3 DENESIDE, NR30 2HL

Open: Monday to Saturday
8.30 a.m. 5.30 p.m.
H.P.W.D.CS.A.

NOTTINGHAMSHIRE

NOTTINGHAM   Tel. (0602) 225979
POOLEWOOD   and 227064/5
EQUIPMENT LTD.   (06077) 2421 after hrs
5a HOLLY LANE, CHILLWELL
Open: Mon-Fri 9.00 a.m.-5.30 p.m.
Sat. 9.00 a.m. to 12.30 p.m.
P.W.WM.D.CS.A.BC.

OXON

WITNEY   Tel. (0993) 3885,
TARGET TOOLS (SALES,   & 72095 OXON
TARGET   HIRE & REPAIRS)   ★
TOOLS   SWAIN COURT
   STATION INDUSTRIAL ESTATE
Open: Mon.-Sat. 8.00 a.m.-5.00 p.m.
24 hour Answerphone
BC.W.M.A.

SHROPSHIRE

TELFORD   Tel. Telford (0952)
ASLES LTD   48054
VINEYARD ROAD, WELLINGTON   **EK★**

Open: Mon. Fri. 8.30 a.m.-5.30 p.m.
Saturday 8.30 a.m.-4.00 p.m.
H.P.W.WM.D.CS.BC.A.

SOMERSET

TAUNTON   Tel. (0823) 85431
JOHN HALL TOOLS   ★
6 HIGH STREET

Open Monday-Saturday
9.00 a.m.-5.30 p.m.
H.P.W.WM.D.CS.A.

77

shopguide

SOMERSET

TAUNTON   Tel: Taunton 79078
KEITH MITCHELL ★
TOOLS AND EQUIPMENT
66 PRIORY BRIDGE ROAD
    Open: Mon-Fri 8.30 a.m.-5.30 p.m.
Saturday 9.00 a.m.-4.00 p.m.
H.P.W.WM.D.CS.A.BC.

STAFFORDSHIRE

TAMWORTH   Tel. (0827) 56188
MATTHEWS BROTHERS LTD. K
KETTLEBROOK ROAD
    Open: Mon-Sat 8.30 a.m.-6.00 p.m.
Demonstrations Sunday mornings by
appointment only
H.P.WM.D.T.CS.A.BC.

SUFFOLK

IPSWICH   Tel. (0473) 40456
FOX WOODWORKING KE★
142-144 BRAMFORD LANE
    Open: Tues., Fri., 9.00 a.m.-5.30 p.m.
Sat. 9.00 a.m.-5.00 p.m.

H.P.W.WM.D.A.BC.

SUSSEX

ST. LEONARD'S-ON-SEA   Tel.
DOUST & MONK (MONOSAW)-(0424)
25 CASTLEHAM ROAD 52577

Open: Mon.-Fri. 8.00 a.m.-5.30 p.m.
Most Saturdays 9.00 a.m.-1.00 p.m.
H.P.W.WM.D.CS.A.

BOGNOR REGIS Tel. (0243) 863100
A. OLBY & SON (BOGNOR REGIS) LTD.
"TOOLSHOP," BUILDERS MERCHANT
HAWTHORN ROAD K
    Open: Mon-Thurs 8 a.m.-5.15 p.m. Fri.
8 a.m.-8 p.m. Sat 8 a.m.-12.45 p.m.
H.P.W.WM.D.T.C.A.BC.

WORTHING   Tel. (0903) 38739
W. HOSKING LTD (TOOLS & KE★
MACHINERY)
28 PORTLAND RD, BN11 1QN
    Open: Mon.-Sat. 8.30 a.m.-5.30 p.m.
Closed Wednesday
H.P.W.WM.D.CS.A.BC.

TYNE & WEAR

NEWCASTLE UPON TYNE   Tel.
J. W. HOYLE LTD. (0632) 617474
CLARENCE STREET NE2 1YJ K★
    Open: Mon 8.00 a.m.-5.00 p.m.
Saturday 9.00 a.m.-4.30 p.m.

H.P.A.BC.W.CS.WM.D.

TYNE & WEAR

NEWCASTLE   Tel. (0632) 320311
HENRY OSBOURNE LTD. E★
50-54 UNION STREET

    Open: Mon-Fri 8.30 a.m.-5.00 p.m.

H.P.W.D.CS.MF.A.BC.

WEST MIDLANDS

BIRMINGHAM   Tel. (021-554) 5177
ROTAGRIP E★
16 LODGE ROAD, HOCKLEY
    Open: Mon.-Fri. 9.00 a.m.-5.00 p.m.
Sat. 9.00 a.m.-12.00 p.m.

H.P.W.CS.A.BC.T.MF.

WOLVERHAMPTON   Tel. (0902)
MANSAW SERVICES 58759
SEDGLEY STREET K★
    Open: Mon.-Fri. 9.00 a.m.-5.00 p.m.

H.P.W.WM.A.D.CS.

YORKSHIRE

BOROUGHBRIDGE   Tel. (09012)
JOHN BODDY TIMBER LTD 2370
FINE WOOD & TOOL STORE ★
RIVERSIDE SAWMILLS
    Open: Mon.-Thurs. 8.00 a.m.-6.00 p.m.
Fri. 8.00am-5.00pm Sat. 8.00am-4.00pm
H.P.W.WM.D.T.CS.MF.A.BC.

SHEFFIELD   Tel. (0742) 441012
GREGORY & TAYLOR LTD KE
WORKSOP ROAD
    Open: 8.30 a.m.-5.30 p.m.
Monday-Friday
8.30 a.m.-12.30 p.m. Sat.
H.P.W.WM.D.

HARROGATE   Tel. (0423) 66245/
MULTI-TOOLS 55328
158 KINGS ROAD K★

    Open: Monday to Saturday
8.30 a.m.-6.00 p.m.

H.P.W.WM.D.A.BC.

LEEDS   Tel. (0532) 574736
D. B. KEIGHLEY MACHINERY LTD. ★
VICKERS PLACE, STANNINGLEY
PUDSEY LS2 86LZ
    Mon. 9.00 a.m.-5.00 p.m.
Sat. 9.00 a.m.-1.00 p.m.

P.A.W.WM.CS.BC.

YORKSHIRE

HUDDERSFIELD   Tel. (0484)
NEVILLE M. OLDHAM 641219/(0484)
UNIT 1 DALE ST. MILLS 42777
DALE STREET, LONGWOOD ★
    Open: Mon-Fri 8.00 a.m.-5.30 p.m.
Saturday 9.30 a.m.-12.00 p.m.
P.W.WM.D.A.BC.

YORKSHIRE

THIRSK   Tel. (0845) 22770
THE WOOD SHOP ★
TRESKE SAWMILLS LTD.
STATION WORKS
    Open: Seven days a week 9.00-5.00

T.H.MF.BC.

KEIGHLEY   Tel. (0535) 663325
EUROMAIL (TOOLS) ★
PO BOX 13
108 EAST PARADE
    Open 9.15 a.m.-5.00 p.m.
Not Tuesday but inc. Saturday
H.P.W.A.BC.

CLECKHEATON   Tel. (0274)
SKILLED CRAFTS LTD. 872861
34 BRADFORD ROAD ★

    Open: 9.00 a.m.-5.00 p.m. Monday
Saturday Lunch 12.00 a.m.-1.00 p.m.
H.P.A.W.CS.WM.D.

LEEDS   Tel. (0532) 790507
GEORGE SPENCE & SONS LTD.
WELLINGTON ROAD
    Open: Monday to Friday
8.30 a.m.-5.30 p.m.
Saturday 9.00 a.m.-5.00 p.m.
H.P.W.WM.D.T.A.

SCOTLAND

EDINBURGH   Tel. 031-337-5555
THE SAW CENTRE ★
38 HAYMARKET EH12 5JZ
    Mon.-Fri. 8.30 a.m.-5.30 p.m.
Sat. 9.00 a.m.-1.00 p.m.
H.P.W.WM.D.CS.A.

PERTH   Tel. (0738) 26173
WILLIAM HUME & CO K
ST. JOHN'S PLACE
    Open: Monday to Saturday
8.00 a.m.-5.30 p.m.
8.00 a.m.-1.00 p.m. Wednesday
H.P.A.BC.W.CS.WM.D.

SCOTLAND

CULLEN   Tel: (0542) 40563
GRAMPIAN WOODTURNING SUPPLIES AT
BAYVIEW CRAFTS
Open Mon.-Sat. 9.00 a.m.-5.30 p.m. Sunday
10.00 a.m.-5.30 p.m. Open later July/Aug.
Sept. Demonstrations SAT/SUN or by
H.W.D.MF.BC. appointment

TAYSIDE   Tel: (05774) 293
WORKMASTER POWER TOOLS LTD. ★
DRUM, KINROSS
    Open Mon.-Sat. 8.00 a.m.-8.00 p.m.
Demonstrations throughout Scotland by
appointment
P.W.WM.D.A.BC.

GLASGOW   Tel. 041-429-4444/
THE SAW CENTRE 4374 Telex: 777886
650 EGLINTON STREET E★
GLASGOW G5 9RP
    Mon.-Fri. 8.00 a.m.-5.00 p.m.
Sat. 9.00 a.m.-1.00 p.m.
H.P.W.WM.D.CS.A.

WALES

CARDIFF   Tel. (0222) 595710
DATAPOWER TOOLS LTD,
MICHAELSTON ROAD,
CULVERHOUSE CROSS
    Open: Mon.-Fri. 8.00 a.m.-5.00 p.m.
Sat. 9.00 a.m.-1.00 p.m.
H.P.W.WM.D.A.

CARMARTHEN   Tel. (0267) 237219
DO-IT-YOURSELF SUPPLY K
BLUE STREET, DYFED
    Open: Monday to Saturday
9.00 a.m.-5.30 p.m.
Thursday 9.00 a.m.-5.30 p.m.
H.P.W.WM.D.T.CS.A.BC.

CARDIFF   Tel. (0222) 396039
JOHN HALL TOOLS LIMITED ★
CENTRAL SQUARE

    Open: Monday to Saturday
9.00 a.m.-5.30 p.m.

H.P.W.WM.D.A.BC.

SWANSEA   Tel. (0792) 55680
SWANSEA TIMBER & PLYWOOD CO. LTD.
57-59 OXFORD STREET ★

    Open: Mon to Fri 9.00 a.m.-5.30 p.m.
Sat. 9.00 a.m.-1.00 p.m.
H.P.W.D.T.CS.A.BC.

KEY: CS CUTTING OR SHARPENING SERVICES

KEY: MF MATERIAL FINISHES

KEY: BC BOOKS/CATALOGUES

79

WOOD SUPPLIERS

THE WOODSTORE
Suppliers of Native Hardwoods
MOST HOMEGROWN SPECIES IN STOCK
LARGE AND SMALL QUANTITIES
SUPPLIED FRESH SAWN, AIR DRIED
AND KILN DRIED
MACHINING FACILITIES AVAILABLE
Send sae for Price List to

TREEWORK SERVICES LTD
CHESTON COOMBE, CHURCH TOWN,
BACKWELL, Nr. BRISTOL
OR PHONE FLAX BOURTON
(027583) 3917 OR 3078
We also offer a tree milling service

SEASONED NORTH
AMERICAN LONG LEAF
PITCH PINE AVAILABLE

Converted from timber beams to
your specification or in our standard
sizes. From timber originally imported circa 1880.

Traditional and modern mouldings
available.

Largest sixes section 14" × 12".

Architraving and Skirting all in stock
*FOR A LIMITED PERIOD SPECIAL
SUPPLY WITCH ELM.*

J. R. NELSON & CO

"The Saw Mill,"
Wills Farm,
Newchurch, Kent.

Tel: Hamstreet (023373) 3361

NORTH HEIGHAM
SAWMILLS

**Good, Kiln-Dried stocks of most
Home-Grown timbers, and exotic,
Imported Hardwoods.**
Stocks include: Apple, ash, beech,
blackwood, box, cedar, cherry,
cocobolo, ebony, elm, holly,
lemonwood, lignum, lime, mahogany, maple, oak, padauk, pear,
plane, rosewood, satinwood, sycamore, walnut, yew, zelkova.
*Please send S.A.E. for priced stock
list to:*
**North Heigham Sawmills, Paddock
St. (off Barker St.), NORWICH NR2
4TW. Tel: Norwich 622978.**

DESIGNS IN WOOD
by Phil Osborne
**THE ULTIMATE WOOD SERVICE
IN SOUTH WALES**

Oak, Ash, Beech and Mahogany a Speciality
at realistic prices. Also wood cut to one's
own cutting list, fully finished.
For details and quotations apply to:
**Designs in Wood, Unit L2, Hirwaun
Industrial Estate, Hirwaun, Mid-Glam.
Tel: 0685 814111**

OAK AND ELM
Prime oak and elm kiln dried, also
other British hardwoods. Cutting
and Planing Service. Large or small
quantities. Table tops and work tops
made to measure.
**NEW HALL TIMBER, Duddleston,
Ellesmere, Shropshire.
Tel: (0691) 75244**

LIMEHOUSE TIMBER

*See the wood
from the trees!*
Select from our stock of
English and imported
hardwoods, Russian
redwoods, veneers and
exotics. Send 17p
stamp for stock list.
*A unique source in London
for all wood users.
Cutting lists prepared.*
Open 9-5, Mon.-Fri. 9-3 Sat.
**5 Grenade Street,
London E14 8HL. 01-987 6289**

ELM BURR BLANKS
12" × 12" × 4"; 12" × 12" × 3"
Small Quantity of Yew and
Cherry. Offers!
BEARD BROS.
Tel: Hoar Cross 292, Staffs.

ENGLISH HARDWOODS
IN DEVON
All species. Trade prices, Woodturners,
carvers blocks from £1 quality oak
Specialist 1" to 4"
*(This months special offer
monkeypuzzle, clean £5 cu.ft.)*
Mr. Baker, Pethers, Crown Hill,
Halberton, Tiverton. Tel: 0884 820152.

VENEERS, all types. SAE list. S. Gould
(Veneers), 22 Spencer Road, N. Wembley,
Middx. HA0 3SF. 01-904-7954.   T/C

Homegrown Hardwoods
in London
15 species — kiln dried
**1-5 Chance Street,
London E1 6JT.
Tel: 729 5736**

OPEPE — LIMITED QUANTITY 44" x 1½"
square sawn. Pack of 15 pcs. — £10.30 D/d
C.W.O. or £5.50 collected. American Red Oak
10 fts. x 3" x 1" kiln dried £3.75 each, collected
ex-works: T. T. Smith Ltd., Portersfield Road,
Cradley Heath, West Midlands. 0384-69581.

18TH CENTURY pitch pine, superb quality.
Bandmilled to your requirements. Most
English hardwoods stocked, air and kiln dry.
Tel. Will Tyers, cabinet maker for price list —
(0468) 21292 (Nr. Lancaster).

HARDWOOD blanks for turning. SAE for lists.
G. W. Monk Pantllidiart W, Brynafnan,
Llanafan, Aberystwyth, Dyfed, Wales.

HARD & SPECIALIST WOODS, air and kiln
dried. Priced stock list. Items prepared to
your cutting list. Minns, Unit 5, West Way,
Oxford (0865) 247840.

HAMPSHIRE HARDWOODS, wide range of
English and exotic timber in many shapes and
sizes for turning, carving, etc. Most air-dried.
Ring: Liss 892750 evenings/weekends.

YEW, CHERRY, walnut, cedar, quarter-sawn
oak, lime, elm, ash. Air-dried 1"-4". Flint, The
Needles, Hirdon. Telephone (074789) 237.

ENGLISH HARDWOODS. Oak specialists,
also Ash, Beech, Cherry, Yew. Over 3000
cu.ft. Send for stock list to W. H. Mason & Son
Ltd., The Sawmills, Wetmore Road, Burton-
on-Trent, Staffs. Telephone 64651.

EXOTIC WOODS African blackwood, Ebony
Padauk, Paurosa, Rosewood, Burrelm Satinwood, Wenge, Yew, Zebrano. Many others:
Chart evenings/Saturdays. Reading (0734)
695336.

BERKSHIRE HARDWOODS. Kiln dried
English hardwoods. Ash, beech, cherry,
chestnut, oak, yew. Small quantities a
speciality. Some machining available. Bowl
blanks. Crowthorne 772157/773586
(evenings).

MICK JONES TIMBER has available 250ft°
prime square edged oak, kiln dried to 12½%. 1"
and ¾" thick. Only £15.50 to clear in large or
small quantities. Welshpool, Powys. ME1 FOD
(093884) 253.

AIR DRIED English Hardwoods: Chestnut £22
per cubic ft. Walnut £30 per cubic ft. Oak £22
per cubic ft. Elm £18 per cubic ft. Cherry £22
per cubic ft. Ash £20 per cubic ft. Yew £22 per
cubic ft. All prices ex stock and include VAT.
Tel: Bath 315504 anytime.

Wood Supplies Advertisement Coupon
Send to: Classified Ad Dept. A.S.P. Ltd., 1 Golden Square, London, W.1.

FROM _____

_____

_____

I enclose remittance to the value of _____ to cover _____ inset or retain.

Private & Trade Rate, 46p per word.
(VAT inclusive) minimum £6.90.
Display Box rates s.c.c. £8,
(minimum 2.5cm (+ VAT)

Classified Advertisements

FOR SALE

87

WOODWORKER
Style . . . tradition . . . and the love of wood

February 1986   Vol. 90   No. 1107

103 The craft of cabinetmaking
Hand veneering — how and where to start. *David Savage*

107 Squares and Rounds
Win a £500 table-saw or a fine lathe in our craft competition!

108 Industrious Design Force
A number of sparkling British designers are banding together to get extra business strength and show the world what they can do

113 MDF turns noble
An 18th-century bust needed a lift, and got what it needed from a favourite fibreboard. *Bob Grant*

115 Tales out of steel
Quirky reminiscences from a toolmaker's Sheffield past. *Ashley Iles*

120 Not so dusty?
Amid disturbing Health & Safety reports, we get a doctor's view of dusty damage. *Bob Clewlow*

124 MACHINING WOOD Your expert guide: 4
The bandsaw; a versatile machine which cuts hundreds of ways. We explain as many of them as we can fit in.

● *Birds and flowers from Andrew Armitage's superb carved garden on p117*

146 A tale of two workshops
Two approaches to serious business in different parts of the country. *Debra Chalmers-Brown, Norma Johnston*

148 Round, rough and smooth
Three innovative woodturners with styles as different as they are challenging. It may be wood, but is it art?

150 The grand furniture saga: 2
From the fall of the Roman Empire to mediaeval beds. *Vic Taylor*

153 Crossing the bar
One man, one machine and a site-job in solid oak do not an easy living make. *Jim Corcoran*

155 Up to the mark
A guide to timber-shippers and countries of origin for the knowledge seekers. *Bill Brown*

166 Many a strip
How to know what you're up against when you put new life into a tired surface. *Noel Leach*

169 Plane speaking
The art and science of the smoothing-plane, plus a test of a top-quality tool. *Fraser Budd*

171 Combination curio
A quaint device which has all sorts of solutions in the handle — or does it? *Bob Grant*

PROJECTS
A selection of things to make — all with detailed plans

110 Hand-made and handsome
This small tall cabinet needs a feel for the rustic and a sense of texture. *Mark Ripley*

117 The carver's garden
How to carve and colour flowers with very particular delicacy. *Andrew Armitage*

129 Three legs and a paintbox
First of two for outdoor artists — a clever pack-up-and-carry box easel with adjustable legs. *Bill Walker*

131 Four legs and an easel
The artist's donkey — a docile animal to stretch your skills in the workshop. *Graham Greenhalgh*

On the cover: Richard Raffan's burr jarrah bowl (p149) above Robin Williams' sculpted sycamore desk (p108) and Andrew Armitage's stunning carving (p117)

REGULARS
90 This Month takes a view on the world of woodwork

92 Shoptalk takes a line on buying

96 Guild Notes
Courses and opinions for people at all levels of the craft

98 Question Box
Ask, and your woodworking question will be answered

133 Woodworking wheeze of the month
Screw-fixing things that never seemed possible. *James Paffett*

161 Bob Wearing's Workshop
Making professional knobs

172 Books

174 Letters
Readers and writers in a full and frank exchange of views!

Editor Aidan Walker
Deputy editor Owen Watson
Editorial assistant Kerry Fowler
Advertisement manager Paul Holmes
Graphics Jeff Hamblin
Technical illustrator Peter Holland
Guild of Woodworkers Owen Watson, Kerry Fowler

Editorial, advertisements and Guild of Woodworkers
1 Golden Square, London W1R 3AB, telephone 01-437 0626

Unfortunately we cannot accept responsibility for loss of or damage to unsolicited material. We reserve the right to refuse or suspend advertisements, and regret we cannot guarantee the bone fides of advertisers.

Subscriptions and back issues Infonet Ltd, 10-13 Times House, 179 Marlowes, Hemel Hempstead, Herts HP1 1BB; telephone Hemel Hempstead (0442) 48434

Subscriptions per year UK £16.90; overseas outside USA (accelerated surface post) £21.00, USA (accelerated surface post) $28, airmail £48

UK trade SM Distribution Ltd, 16-18 Trinity Gardens, London SW9 8DX; telephone 01-274 8611

North American trade Bill Dean Books Ltd, 151-49 7th Avenue, PO Box 69, Whitestone, New York 11357; telephone 1-718-767-6632

Printed in Great Britain by Ambassador Press Ltd, St. Albans, Herts.
Mono origination Multiform Photosetting Ltd, Cardiff
Colour origination Derek Croxson Ltd, Chesham, Bucks

© Argus Specialist Publications Ltd 1986
ISSN 0043 776X

Argus Specialist Publications Ltd
1 Golden Square, London W1R 3AB; 01-437 0626

Quick on the draw Furniture testing at a recent BSI press day at the Furniture Industry Research Association

Index finder

Our 1985 index is now ready. Subscribers will find theirs with this issue; otherwise, send £1.25 to Argus Specialist Publications, Reader Services, Wolsey House, Wolsey Rd, Hemel Hempstead, Herts HP2 4SS.

Propping up the pits

If you thought that wood in collieries went out with pit ponies, **writes Paul Greer,** you'd be put right by a company that has just set up near Barnsley. Fieldhazel Ltd is near Cortonwood, where the recent pit strike began. The company, whose opening was attended by the Prince of Wales and TV news, was set up by redundant workers from the National Coal Board's central workshops, and makes ventilation doors and the collapsible stone-dust barriers which isolate underground areas in case of fire. The main advantages of wood for these purposes are price and portability.

Both products, which are bought by the National Coal Board, represent fairly rudimentary carpentry, as the aim is utility rather than beauty. The men's knowledge of mining, and the fact that they did the same jobs when employed by the NCB, has meant that they haven't had to be retrained.

More refined products are a possibility; Fieldhazel has been able to produce medical stretchers better than those currently used by the NCB — so much so that even a fairly substantial price hike has been no deterrent to sales.

Arthur Shaw, who is due to become involved with the company when he is made redundant from the NCB, is hopeful about these developments. 'I anticipate that we shall expand enough to need more staff in 1986. Everyone has put in extra hours during the evenings and weekends; we were all familiar with running a large concern — so running a small venture has proved relatively easy. I only wish it had happened ten years ago.'

When the NCB's central workshops were closed, the men were offered the option of jobs at other workshops with the NCB, or redundancy payments. As the jobs they were offered were in a trade different from their own, they took the money.

They were assisted by the NCB's Enterprise Scheme, the premises are rate-free, and the NCB have loaned pieces of specialised equipment. All this has reduced the amount of cash they had to take out of their redundancy payments.

The seven workers' ages range from 23 to 52 — the youngest is chairman! Two or three of the workers concentrate on sales and accounts, but there is no hierarchy. Everybody lends a hand on the shop floor when things get busy.

● Fieldhazel Ltd, Bolton Rd, Wath-upon-Dearne, Rotherham, South Yorkshire, tel. (0709) 879063.

Old and yew

What of the bow?
The bow was made in England
Of true wood, of yew wood,
The wood of English bows;
For men who are free
Love the old yew-tree
And the land where the yew-tree grows.

> Marching song of the
> White Company,
> Conan Doyle

For most of us, **writes Anne McBride,** the yew tree's sombre foliage and dramatic outline are associated with churchyards and cemeteries. In the hands of skilled workers, however, this slow-growing and incredibly hard wood can achieve a handsomely marbled effect and a rich golden sheen. It is a favourite for the cabinetmaker.

There is, however, a practical reason why ancient yew trees stand near ancient churches. In medieval times, when the defence of the realm depended mainly upon the skill of yeoman archers, a royal decree made it compulsory to practise at the butt on Sundays and holy days. There are still in existence sandstone churches with grooves in the porchway, caused by archers sharpening their arrows as they prepared to take their turn at practice after mass.

Yew was the most favoured wood for the 6ft English longbow, and as the leaves are poisonous to livestock, the trees were only allowed to grow in enclosed places well away from pastureland. It is also likely that the only area big enough and well-enough placed for the compulsory practice sessions would be next to the village church. Most highly prized was the slow-growing mountain yew, which produced the finest traditional English longbow. If the staves are cleft, and not sawn, the entire butt of a good tree may be used.

Ancient accounts maintain that the best part of the tree is that pale sapwood just under the bark, with a little of the darker heartwood as well. The qualities of both are indispensable; the sapwood is resistant to stretch, and so suitable for the back of the bow (the convex side when it is bent); the heartwood, which resists compression, is right for the inside of the bow.

The feats of the bowmen of England bear testimony not only to skill and courage, but also to that unique combination of qualities found in the English yew.

Happy as Larry The winners of our Show prizes get their just deserts. **Top,** Craig Warren (left) of **Warren Machine Tools** bestows a Eumenia radial-arm on a gleeful Roger Eagle; **bottom,** Jim Murray of **AEG Telefunken** offers a piece of hilarious blockboard to joiner Vicky Coghill, along with her handsome AEG bandsaw. Many thanks to AEG and Warren for their generosity, and also to David Hoxby of Gill and Hoxby, 135-137 St Marks Rd, Enfield, for his hospitality

Carved choir Let the mahogany sing . . . Huw Roberts' *Côr Meibion Bro Mahogany* is all set to make a big impression. The wooden choir, complete with stage, curtains, lighting and piano took him 15 months and an estimated 600 hours to carve

Showing baskets David Drew, basketmaker, at work. The home-grown willow rods that he uses 'white' or stripped are left to root in water, after which they are stripped by pulling through a cleft stick. See his work at the Crafts Council Gallery, 12 Waterloo Place, London SW1 until 30 March

Peters in Cheltenham

An exhibition of master furniture-maker Alan Peters' work runs until 8 February at the Cheltenham Art Gallery, Clarence St, Cheltenham, Glos GL50 3NX, tel. (0242) 37431.

Rent-a-wound?

Cleveland County Council have been checking maintenance standards of DIY tools for hire, and have found it severely lacking. Following complaints from hirers who had been involved in 'unnecessary accidents' (when would an accident be necessary, one wonders), the Trading Standards Department hired 15 tools from 12 firms — chainsaws, circular saws, hedge trimmers and so on — and got 10 without the legally-required safety instructions, and eight inadequately maintained tools reckoned to be potentially dangerous. Faults included badly-wired and/or damaged plugs, broken and missing cord-restraints, and corrosion.

The DIY boom has encouraged a lot of comparatively inexperienced people to go out and hire tools that need a wary user; be warned!

Readers researched

To all those who took the time and trouble to fill in our readership survey in October's *Woodworker*, many thanks. The collated results make fascinating reading, and have caused a few brains to overheat with some startling mental arithmetic. 87% of you read nearly all of the magazine; is it a surprise to learn that 0% of you read none of it?

Those of you that want more specific articles, be assured that you will get them. 90% of *Woodworker* readers keep their copies for more than a year, and nearly two-thirds of you look at them at least once every three months.

What about the money you spend? Hold your breath. We took minimum figures all down the line — if you put that you spent £500 plus, we counted it as £500. Personal expenditure of *Woodworker* buyers — readers are more, remember — adds up to a minimum of £5¼ *million*, with your businesses spending over £10¼ million! The actual amounts are probably twice these figures . . .

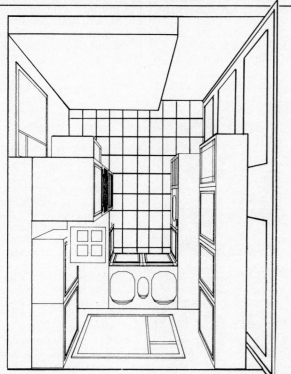

A byte in the kitchen

Magnet and Southerns are now using computers to plan their kitchens, print a breakdown costing, and give views from different angles. It's a customer service; they reckon a kitchen plan can be done in 20 minutes. Easy enough with a systematic range of sizes and units, of course — anyone out there use computers yet to do complex drawings?

● Magnet & Southerns, Royd Ings Ave, Keighley, West Yorkshire BD21 4BY, tel. (0535) 661133.

. . . and in France

Expobois 86 is an enormous woodworking exhibition in Paris Le Bourget, 20-25 March. The organisers claim it'll be providing high-tech answers to the problems facing furniture makers who use solid woods — problems likely to become more acute in the future.

● More information from Genevieve Brulet, Chambre de Commerce de Française de Grande-Bretagne, 54 Conduit St, London W1, tel. 01-439 1735.

Shoptalk

French polishing, **writes Charles Cliffe,** is one of the most difficult tasks. Many woodworkers find their finish does not match their cabinet-making skills.

To help non-polishers in their search for a quality finish requiring the minimum of skill, John Myland Ltd are now selling a special french polish under the name of Gedge's Brushing French Polish.

It is light in colour, and its darkening effect is slight, so it can be safely used on marquetry work without fear of changing the colour significantly. It brushes easily, although care is needed to apply an even coat without 'runs'.

New work is glasspapered smooth and stained in the usual way. The polish tin is well shaken and a small quantity is poured into a shallow glass jar or similar container. A polisher's mop is used to brush on a coat, which will be quite dry in half an hour. Then the surface is lightly sanded smooth with fine garnet or OOO wire wool, dusted off and given a second coat of polish. This in turn is papered smooth when hard and followed by a third coat. It is usually possible to apply all three coats within one hour.

The work is ready for waxing after the final coat has hardened and been lightly sanded. Mylands have produced their 'Centenary' brand of wax polish to mark their 100 years as polish manufacturers; it is a light-coloured high-grade wax polish,

which can safely be used on valuable antiques and high quality furniture. Using a clean piece of rag, the wax is applied evenly and thinly over the french-polished surface and allowed to stand for five minutes or more. It is then buffed with a soft duster. After three or four such waxings a most attractive deep shine is produced. The finish also resists alcohol- and ring-marks from hot dishes. However, if such marks do appear, they can easily be remedied by further waxing.

Work that needs re-polishing should have the old finish removed, and be glasspapered thoroughly before being polished in the same way as new work. I stripped some walnut-veneered drawer-fronts completely of the original crazed finish, and then glasspapered them smooth. The first coat restored much of the walnut's colour and life. The subsequent two coats slightly deepened the colour, as well as improving the shine. The waxings gave a mellowness to the finish which was not only attractive but most appropriate to an older piece of furniture enjoying a facelift.

In all, the combination of Brushing Polish and Centenary wax will do much to raise your finish from the 'amateur' class to the 'professional'.

● John Myland Ltd, 80 Norwood High St, London SE27 9NW, tel. 01-670 9161. Brushing Polish: 1 lt £6.32, 5lt £31.62; Centenary wax: 13oz £2.59, 7lb £12.65, all inc VAT.

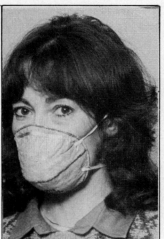

MODELLED HERE from 3M's spring collection is the 9915 disposable respirator. A free sample is available through Martyn Billing at 3M.

● 3M UK Ltd, 3M House, P.O. Box 1, Bracknell, Berks RG12 1JU, tel. (0344) 426726

SAMCO'S MINI-ROUTER was the only overhead machine at the '85 Woodworker Show; a measly £1297+VAT.
● ccb, 31-39 Napier Court, Wardpark North, Cumbernauld G68 0LE, tel. Cumbernauld 38222

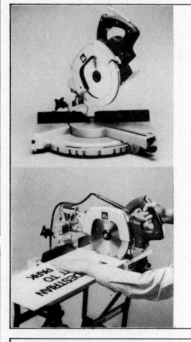

A PULL-OVER SAW? That's what Elu have christened their new PS 174 Crosscut/Mitre saw, which can cut 45° mitres in material up to 174mm wide. Narrow material is cut with the normal snip-off action; with wider pieces the blade is plunged in and then pulled towards you. Maximum depth of cut is 52mm. Watch out for a Woodworker test.
● Black & Decker Professional, Westpoint, The Grove, Slough, Berks SL1 1QQ, tel. (9753) 74277

Clamping up frames and furniture can be a tricky operation, so a new **frame clamp** from Vitrex should be of interest. It differs from the Stanley product in that here is both coarse and fine tightening adjustment, and corner jaws are supplied that will both keep the strap away from the wood, and set the angles on the piece to be glued. The jaws are set for either rec-

tangles, hexagons, or octagons, but for the latter two you will need to buy extra jaws. It handles work from 100-900mm square, and also round, oval, or even irregular objects.

● JEM Marketing, 180 Princes Avenue, Palmers Green, London N13 6HL, tel. 01-889 1415. £14.95 inc VAT, p&p, and three corner jaws.

Into the gap between chipboard and MDF comes Fimagen, a new product that claims to have almost the machinability of MDF at a lower price. Our

research teams will be reporting on it in March's *Woodworker*.
● Tafinsa Ltd, 76 Great Portland St, London W1N 5AL, tel. 01-637 5701.

A NEW BENCH SANDER from Holmes Machinery to complement their heavyweight pedestal model. The 'Star' comes in two sizes, each with two speeds.
● Holmes Machinery, 15 Geralds Rd, Terriers, High Wycombe, Bucks HP13 6BN, tel. (0494) 33118

A PLANE with an unplain price: £995 to be exact. From Chiyozuru Sadahide, a Japanese master of plane blades, and sold through Rogers Tools. Before you gasp, remember that pre-war Norris planes used to cost two week's wages...
● Roger's Tools, 47 Walsworth Rd, Hitchin, Herts, tel. (0461) 34177

A PORTABLE BANDSAW: the Forestor 900 with the optional bolt-on rolling table in action. Forestor claim it is the only true wide bandsaw in the world that can be hauled to the site, and powered by, a tractor. Other attractions include one-person operation and no need for foundations to house the bottom bandreel; prices start at £2847+VAT.
● Forestor Ltd, 35 West Hill, London SW18 1RB, tel. 01-874 0044

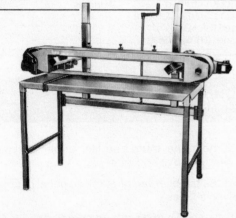

THIS C-FRAME SANDER from Luna doesn't restrict the length of workpieces for face-and-edge sanding – the belt moves up and down, not the table. It's available table- or wall-mounted, with a single-phase 1.1kw motor.
● Luna Tools, 20 Denbigh Hall, Bletchley, Milton Keynes MK3 7QT, tel. (0908) 70771

EASY AS SHARPENING a pencil is the claim for this drill-sharpener. It takes steel and masonry bits (a green silicon-carbide wheel is supplied) up to 12.5mm, with a variety of possible grinding angles and a depth setter to prevent over-grinding. £29.90 inc. p&p, drill not supplied.
● Martek Ltd, PO Box 20, Redruth, Cornwall TR15 2UF

● Langlow, PO Box 32, Asheridge Rd, Chesham, Bucks HP5 2QF, tel. (0494) 784866

WOMEN IN WOODWORK have finally caught the eye of Langlow and Nitromors – simultaneously, **writes Kerry Fowler.** Both are promoting a range of strippers and cleaners aimed specifically at women. Woodworker doesn't usually print can-and-bottle pix; but we think it's interesting that their 'aesthetic' packaging aims to catch the feminine eye, and real woman-appeal is judged to be in child-proof caps and 'simple instructions'.

● Nitromors Ltd, Alexandra Park, Bristol BS16 2BQ, Tel. (0272) 656271

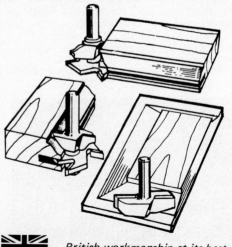

Timberline

Arthur Jones presents the month's buzz from the timber trade

Every year the European softwood importers and exporters gather to compare notes and make trading forecasts. Usually the aim is to pinpoint any potential shortages so that producers can step up production to meet increased demand, but in the past couple of years the idea has been rather to show that demand is reduced and less output is needed for the market.

The attempts to achieve balance have not been too successful; competition has been intense and prices low. No doubt you will all protest that timber prices are high, but the fact is that there have been few increases over the past couple of years, and it's doubtful that any other raw material can match this record.

Most mill outputs are now under control, and the slump in the whitewood market brought dramatic reductions, so stocks in both Sweden and Finland are on the low side this winter. We can expect to see some more increases in whitewood prices. Altogether the main European softwood countries expect their sales to rise by about 2% in 1986, but there is no question of any shortage. There will be plenty of softwood around, but expect some price rises as the producers get into a better position to sell outputs which match demand, rather than have huge stocks on their hands and be forced into price-cutting.

The UK report to the conference admitted that the forecasts for 1985 had been too optimistic, with stocks higher and sales down. There were all sorts of reasons for the errors in the estimates, ranging from severe winter conditions in Europe to high interest and mortgage rates, not to mention weak sterling. The truth remains that the guesstimates were wrong.

Importers cut back their buying to match the changed market (they saw consumption drop by 10% in the first half of the year), and the revised sales for 1985 have been put at 6,150,000cu. m., more than 6% down on the estimate and over 7% down on sales in 1984. Finding bargains in softwood is going to be hard in 1986.

The problem of acid rain was discussed at the conference and it was reported that sanitation fellings are already taking place.

On the subject of conservation, the UK Timber Trade Federation has established guidelines and policies to be advanced in government circles. One of the measures will be the encouragement of tropical-hardwood countries to promote newer commercial species to make better use of forest potential, and to use non-commercial species for their own development. The point is that the international hardwood trade uses only a minimal quantity of the timber felled in developing countries.

Support will be given for an international code of conduct based on sound sustainable forest yields and ecological forest management. A Regional Development Fund will be established to strengthen the forestry services in developing countries, and this money will be raised by what will be, in effect, a tax. So woodworkers will be helping; you will have no choice!

A labelling scheme to identify the origin of tropical hardwoods in finished products will be devised, with manufactured items also showing where they were made. This could obviously affect woodworkers who market their goods, though it will be a long time before any of these ideas become reality — assuming international agreement can be reached.

Now a look at the hardwood market, where Brazilian mahogany and lauan continue to attract most interest. Mahogany prices have risen and will continue to rise over the next few months; stockists have put up their prices in advance of increases paid by importers in the latest contracts, though the mahogany bought in these deals will not be in the yards for many months. There is no abundance of lauan in prospect and prices are rising. West African mahogany is dearer and not freely available in the UK, but supplies are coming from West Africa far more freely now. Utile has become more popular as an alternative, and both samba and sipo have been bought in larger quantities. ∎

Guild notes

● *Guild member Peter Hurst made this unusual writing-table for an American serviceman from an old photo. Peter has no formal training!*

Backlog

Normal service should have been resumed by now, but our apologies to those of you who found us a little tardy late last year with memberships and letters. As you may have read elsewhere in *Woodworker*, Peter Collenette departed from the editor's chair, and Aidan Walker stepped into his still-warm clogs. There was a gap in appointing someone to take over his role, hence the delay. Anyway, enough of the excuses! **Owen Watson** is your new secretary, assisted by **Kerry Fowler**. Aidan will still be around, of course, to help field the technical wobblies you lob at us.

No trees, no wood

A world without trees is hard to imagine, writes **Steven Hurrell**. This may not be too far away; the rate at which some of the world's forests are being chewed away is a frightening reality. The decline of trees in our countryside starts a chain reaction that effects wildlife, plants, human recreation, woodworkers, and life itself. Although we cannot stop the present level of timber consumption (for which we are partly responsible), we can have an influence on the replenishment and care of our woodlands.

In the last 30 years, almost half of Britain's ancient woods have disappeared. More than 140,000 miles of hedgerows have been destroyed to make way for farmland!

● *Peter Scott's drawing courtesy of Woodland Trust*

When you consider an average oak wood can support over 4000 different species of birds, animals, insects and plants, you soon realise we have a duty to secure wood for the future — not just for our own benefit, but for that of the world and its occupants.

The Woodland Trust's prime objectives are the conservation, restoration and re-establishment of broad-leaved woodlands for the benefit of wildlife, plants and the enjoyment of the public. Its membership currently stands at 50,000, and it spent £462,000 on the acquisition of new woodland in 1984. The Woodland Trust is firmly established, so much so that they claim to acquire, on average, a wood every two weeks, 'from a few hilltop trees to hundreds of acres in national parks'. Trust forests are usually open to the public.

Now Harpic (they make the stuff that sends you clean round the bend), in co-operation with the Woodland Trust, are sponsoring an appeal to plant and care for up to 20,000 new trees. By collecting and returning four tokens from the special packs, Harpic will donate £1 to the Woodland Trust to fund the planting and care of a 3ft sapling, enter your name in a special Woodland Trust book of commemoration, and send you a certificate of appreciation. The appeal closes on 31 January, 1986; so as you are unlikely to dispose of four packets of Harpic by then, send me what tokens you have (address below). I will have the name of The Guild of Woodworkers inscribed in the book. The planting of new trees by the Woodland Trust does not directly benefit woodworkers as consumers of timber, but it does guarantee that there are trees and wood for tomorrow, for all to enjoy. Joining the Woodland Trust is a step in the right direction for anyone with the remotest connections with wood. An annual subscription of £5 or a lifetime membership of £100 is guaranteed to be used for the purpose for which it's intended.

The practical benefits include information, newsletters, directories of sites and car emblems, but the real advantage is knowledge that you are putting something back.

● **The Woodland Trust,** Autumn Park, Dysart Road, Grantham, Lincolnshire NG31 6LL, tel. (0476) 74297.

● **Steven Hurrell,** 25 Baxter Road, Hingham, Norfolk NR9 4HY.

Guild courses

Manchester Easter School

The Guild, in association with the Manchester Central College School of Furniture, presents three courses over the Easter holiday. All are for 5 days, 23-27 March, 9.30-5, £125+VAT.

Country Chairmaking — Jack Hill

Jack Hill is a well-known name in country furniture, so we are proud to get him to teach traditional country techniques using cleft and sawn wood. You may have seen Jack demonstrating his craft at the Show, and been impressed by his no-nonsense style, coupled with a ready wit. He'll be taking you through steam bending and the various jigs; you'll be using machines of **Fred Lambert's** design, and the aim is that you finish the week with a piece of furniture to take home.

Introduction to cabinetmaking — Robert Cooksey and Keith Parry

Robert (BA Des, LCG) is an experienced furniture maker and has exhibited his work in many places; Keith (AIWSc) is a wood-machinist whose speciality is prototype and development work. They'll be giving an introduction to basic machine preparation, and hand-making techniques in fine furniture. The course is aimed at the enthusiastic beginner, and those who have some experience and want to know more. At the end of the week you should have made a small piece.

Traditional upholstery — Ken Jones and John Shepherd

Can you beat 42 years combined experience in upholstery? Ken (LCG) and John will introduce you to traditional methods and materials (so don't bring your power stapler), and teach you to develop your hand-skills. They will provide a basic frame to practise on, but bring a piece of your own if it is stripped for action.

● Richard Hill, the senior lecturer at the Central College, will be administering the courses. **However, please send all enquiries and bookings to the Guild.** The College is also running a five-day course in finishing in the same week, which will include two days demonstrations of spraying techniques. **For this course, contact them direct** at Manchester Central College School of Furniture, Lower Hardman St, Manchester M3 3ER, tel (061) 831 7791.

GUILD COURSES

● **You must book in advance, and we must have a cheque for the full cost of the course. Make cheques payable to 'Guild of Woodworkers/ASP Ltd'. If you cancel less than two weeks before the advertised date you will forfeit 50% of the cost, unless there are exceptional circumstances.**

Power routing — Roy Sutton

8 February, 10-5, Herne Bay, £25+VAT. Roy has a nationwide reputation for knowing the ins and outs of routing. Housing, grooving, rebating, straight and circular moulding, tenoning, mortising, rule-joints and templates are covered, together with designing and using the jigs which make this tool even more versatile. Buffet lunch, refreshments, and materials are all included in the price.

Design and workshop drawing — Bob Grant

22 February, 9.30-5, Oxford, £25+VAT. Planning your work is very important to avoid waste of wood and effort. Bob, who is head of Craft, Design and Technology at a comprehensive school, will guide you through planning your design on paper. Learn freehand sketching, how to use grid paper and drawing boards, tricks for laying out ellipses and other shapes, and making and using rods and templates.

Survival metalwork — Bob Grant

15 March, 9.30-5, Oxford, £25+VAT. Woodworkers, for better or worse, have to be able to handle steel as well as wood. On this course Bob will show you how to grind your own cutters and tools, get that razor edge, harden steel, and silver solder broken bandsaw blades. He'll be also covering repairing tool bodies, how to drill and tap holes, and turning the softer metals. After this course, you'll have no excuse for not getting the best out of your tools!

French polishing — Charles Cliffe

3-4 April, 9.30-5, Bexleyheath, £35+VAT. A very popular course; Charles Cliffe (who demonstrated his skills at the Show) explains all about preparation, staining, and application of this tricky finish. He'll also be dealing with using a cabinet scraper, so bring your own if you have one. If you have a piece of furniture that you want his advice on, bring it as well.

Hand veneering — Bob Grant

12 April, 9.30-5, Oxford, £35+VAT. Bob and Peter Sarac, a local harpsichord maker and cabinetmaker, will guide you through the difficult art of veneering. He'll show you examples of cartouches, and demonstrate the scratch-stock; you'll be laying a panel with veneer, mitring a cross-banding, inlaying lines round it, and applying a balancer veneer on the back. With the current concern over conserving fine woods, veneering could be considered as ideologically correct as well as producing a beautiful end result! If you have a veneer hammer, bring it; but materials will be provided.

French polishing — Ian Hosker

19-20 April, 10-5, Chester, £40+VAT. Ian is a teacher (and practising professional) who will guide you through preparation of both new and old pieces, staining and colouring techniques, grainfilling, shellac finishes, fadding, bodying in, spiriting off, and giving new life to existing polished surfaces. The fee includes course materials, and Ian will make you up a polishing kit to take away with you **if you include another £8 when you book.** Who said we had a south-east England bias?

BOOKING FORM

I wish to book for the following course(s).
- ☐ **Power routing** 8 February, £25+VAT = £28.75
- ☐ **Design and workshop drawing** 22 February, £25+VAT = £28.75
- ☐ **Survival metalwork** 15 March, £25+VAT = £28.75
- ☐ **Country chairmaking** 23-27 March, £125+VAT = £143.75
- ☐ **Introduction to cabinetmaking** 23-27 March, £125+VAT = £143.75
- ☐ **Traditional upholstery** 23-27 March, £125+VAT = £143.75
- ☐ **French polishing** 3-4 April, £35+VAT = £40.25
- ☐ **Hand veneering** 12 April, £35+VAT = £40.25
- ☐ **French polishing** 19-20 April, £40+VAT = £46

I enclose a cheque/PO for £ ....
made out to 'The Guild of Woodworkers/ASP Ltd'

Name...

Address ....

....

....

Send to The Guild of Woodworkers, 1 Golden Square, London W1R 3AB. The Guild reserves the right to cancel any course.

Question box

Our panel of experts solve your woodworking problems

Q *Why is it wrong to use silicone polish instead of wax polish with wire wool?*
D. J. Kirkby, Cheltenham

A Silicones are produced chemically and are very complex in their production, but when added to furniture polishes they produce an easy, glossy, water-resistant finish. There are a great many on the market, and most of them come in aerosols. A quick spray of the polish onto a substrate followed by a wipe-down with a lint-free cloth produces an easy shine — however, a film is produced and if steel wool is used, it will break into the surface and render it useless.

This doesn't happen when using traditional wax furniture-polish containing beeswax, carnauba wax and turpentine in conjunction with fine steel wool (grade OOO or OOOO). The wax forms a 'slip' with the steel wool which produces a fine semi-matt or satin antique finish on a traditional or cellulose surface.

Two points of interest here. If you value your fingers or eyes, don't use steel wool on turned work in your lathe. Use abrasive papers; they are safer. Also, don't use silicone aerosols if you have cellulose or catalysed lacquers anywhere near, or 'cissing' will result ('Question Box' WW/ July 85).
Noel Leach

Q *I have inherited a plane from my father, which is clearly marked 'Stewart Spiers, Ayr, Scotland'. It's made of steel with rosewood infill and handle – the body is 7¼in long and the handle protrudes a further 1⅝in. The lever-cap and screw appear to be made of brass and the iron is almost 3/16in thick, parallel, made by Hearnshaw Bros, Sheffield.*

My father bought it second-hand in the late thirties. It is a beautiful tool to use and I wondered whether you would consider this as interesting as a Norris. It would seem that the Norris was an improvement on the Spiers – how did this affect the Spiers? Did some craftsmen still prefer to use the old pattern, or did the old Spiers still have some advantages over the Norris?

Peter Tonks, Bromsgrove

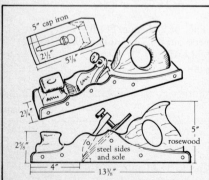

● Not a Norris, but a Spiers; from 'Question Box', WW/July 83

A Spiers (1840-1920) and Norris (1860-1950) are well known for their lead in producing the typical British design of plane which consisted of a metal casing or box filled with wood. The desirability, to woodworkers as well as to collectors, of these planes is so well-established (it is reflected in auction prices running into hundreds for the rarer models in good condition) that nothing I say is going to depress the market! Nevertheless, in the interests of balance, a few things should be pointed out.

It does not seem that Stewart Spiers of Ayr started, or even re-introduced, the manufacture of this type of plane. *Tools & Trades* (the Journal of the Tool And Trades History Society) Vol. 1 illustrates a number of metal, box-construction planes, including one with a very professional-looking decorative stamp around the initials B.H.G. marked 'London 1739'.

Second, they, and other makers such as Holland of Lambeth, Thackeray of Armley, Mathieson of Edinburgh and Glasgow, Slater of Clerkenwell, and Price of Kentish Town produced great quantities, so that these planes are not so rare as they often seem to a new collector coming across his first specimen.

Then there is the question of their technical features which should be looked at objectively in comparison with the much less expensive American Stanley-type plane which has conquered much of the world in the last 120 years. Consider the question of mouth-adjustment: Stanleys can usually be adjusted simply by loosening two screws and moving the iron frog; bits of leather and cardboard found glued to the wooden frogs of many Spiers or Norris planes show that their users have wished that they too were adjustable.

Then there's the adjustment of the cutter itself. As Jerry Glaser pointed out in *Woodworker* June 1983, the normal Norris mechanism employs two concentric screws which produce cumulative, not differential, movement. In other words, the adjustment is 'geared-up' and it moves the cutter too far, too fast. Some Spiers planes did have a screw-cutter adjustment but it was a cheap and flimsy affair.

Finally, consider the British screw-lever-cap in relation to the Stanley cam-lever-cap. Once the Stanley cap has been set, it exerts the same pressure on the cutter every time it is removed and replaced. The pressure exerted by the bronze caps fitted to most Norris and Spiers planes depends entirely on the sensitivity of the user's fingers; too much twist and the cutter adjustment is adversely affected.

However, I admit that most of the British metal planes were made of finer materials, and finished to closer tolerances, than their mass-produced, cast-iron competitors; I love the thick rosewood handles and smoothly-flowing chamfers of my try-plane — a 22in Spiers!
Philip Walker

Q *While I welcome your series on wood-machining, the first article had the characteristic flaw of expert advice, namely a tendency to assume an unreasonable level of knowledge in the reader.*

For example, the article in question states that powerful machines 'on a single-phase supply' should always be wired into a 15amp fused mains outlet. There are surely many other readers who would like to know:
● *What does 'single-phase' mean?*
● *How does one identify it?*
● *Why is it wrong to use a 13amp plug?*
While this is a random example of overestimating the reader's knowledge, the increasing number of electrically-powered machines coming into inexpert hands surely warrants a future Woodworker *article on electrical safety, good practice and DIY hints.*

A. Ely, Loughton

A Your query raises the serious matter of understanding electricity and its associated technology. It's a complex and specialised subject and I consider it wise practice to consult qualified electricians on all electrical matters.

Electrical installations in the UK are thoroughly covered in the Institute of Electrical Engineers' *Regulations for the electrical equipment of buildings*. Further advice may be found in the relevant British Standards, especially BS 5304, *Safeguarding of machinery*. Finally your local electricity board should be able to help you with any queries.

However, in reply to your specific questions:
● Single-phase is a term to explain how electric power is generated, transmitted and distributed. Basically generators at power stations produce a three-phase alternating current at very high voltages (a simple analogy would be water being driven down a pipe). The familiar pylons striding across the country carry this electricity in sets of three cables for the three individual phases (the single cable at the top of the pylon is the neutral wire which serves to complete the circuit back to the generator). Electricity then flows to a series of local switching and transformer stations which step the voltage down for distribution to the consumer.

Industrial users using large amounts of electricity receive a three-phase supply, while domestic users receive a single-phase supply at 240 volts. This load is spread over the three phases by connecting one house in three to each phase. Therefore the manufacturers of light woodworking machines for the amateur home-market use single- and not three-phase motors.
● As the supply to your house is single-phase, there is no need to identify it. In the case of a motor fitted to a woodworking machine, check the manufacturer's plate which should be riveted to the motor casing. This will have the appropriate phase stamped on it and other details such as rpm, horsepower, amps, volts and so on. Single-phase motors, which are normally split-

Question box

phase or capacitor-start types, are fed by two wires, (the live and the neutral) plus an earth wire. The manufacturers supply instructions with new motors which explain how to connect them, but with second-hand motors (possibly with identification plates missing) consult an electrician.

● The advice in the November article about using a 15amp supply is sound. It is really suggesting that you run a separate supply from your house distribution-point (usually located near the meters). It should be independent of your house circuits, running straight to your workshop to avoid putting an overload on your domestic system.

I know that many home woodworkers ignore this advice and have their workshops powered by a lead from the house — but they do run the risk of blowing the main fuse and possibly starting a serious fire. Electric motors take a starting current that is almost twice their rated or running load and this is where the trouble can begin.

It is always wise to check with your local electricity board that the total load you propose can be carried by the incoming main.
Bob Grant

Q *I would welcome some advice on making windows in hardwood. I intend to double-glaze them using units which can be purchased locally, made-to-measure. I assume that the hardwood would be mahogany to simplify annual maintenance.*

I made some windows in softwood some years ago which were very simple in construction, 3x2in all round (no wide cill) with a drip-groove on the bottom. The stop to form a rebate against which the glass was bedded was 1½x⅝in pinned and glued to the frame which was mortised, tenoned and glued. These frames are now rotting and beginning to let the weather in. Should glued joints be used in window construction?

I don't have access to a spindle moulder and want to keep to the lines of modern double-glazed windows; so I think that it would be as well to go for a simple type of frame again. Would you please give me some advice on timber, sizes, weather grooves, the correct strength of opening casements (the extra weight of glass) and how the units should be fixed in the frame? Are there any good books on window construction?

A. Powell, Hornchurch

A Unfortunately you don't mention the size of opening the windows should fit or what the total thickness of the double-glazed units is to be. Both of these factors affect the dimension of the stock to be used so I shall assume that the opening is within the range of normal standard windows and that the sealed glazing units are some ½in thick.

Dealing with your points in turn:
● Timber: oak or teak is preferable, although manufactured hardwood frames are often made from one of the varieties of mahogany.

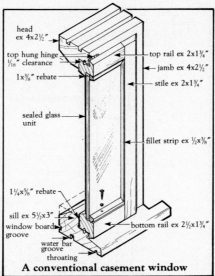

head
ex 4x2½"
top hung hinge
1/16" clearance
1x⅜" rebate
sealed glass unit
1¼x⅝" rebate
sill ex 5½x3"
window board groove
water bar groove
throating
top rail ex 2x1¾"
jamb ex 4x2½"
stile ex 2x1¾"
fillet strip ex ½x⅜"
bottom rail ex 2½x1¼"

A conventional casement window

● The frame: battening pieces of wood to make the rebate isn't a satisfactory way of making up rebated frames. It is sound practice to cut the rebate out of solid stuff (a spindle moulder isn't necessary, they can be stepped out with a circular-saw and cleaned up with a rebate plane). The drawing shows the average sizes. The frame is mortised and tenoned together, then glued, wedged and sometimes pinned. It is important to form a proper sill to the frame 'sunk weathered' to cast off the rainwater and prevent moisture getting under the frame which is particularly vulnerable.

● The weather grooves or capillary grooves are commonly called throats. They serve to arrest water, which would otherwise get in by capillary action, and they also help to reduce draughts. They can be formed with a small round moulding-plane, a plough-plane with a ¼in cutter, a circular saw or a portable router.

● A feature of the sash shown is that it's rebated over the face of the frame to make it weathertight. It can be top- or side-hung to provide the opening. Note that cranked or extension hinges are needed for this type of construction. The sash is mortised and tenoned in the usual manner.

● The double-glazed units are bedded into the sashes with putty and then secured with fillet strips fixed at intervals with countersunk cups and screws — use sherardised steel or brass screws.

● The sketch shows a simplified yet effective modern design but it should be realised that there are many variations on the theme. Many of these are shown in W. B. McKay's *Building Construction* (Metric Series, vol. 1), published by Longmans, which includes full details on the design and construction of windows and is highly recommended.

In general, window design and making is not a simple matter, although it should be well within the scope of the average craftsman. Short-cut expedients in both design and materials always lead to early trouble with weather penetration and rot. The extra time taken to make a 'proper' window is well worth the effort.
Bob Grant

Q *I want to make an alcove or niche (for a large and valuable clock) in a 'plane shell' shape. How do I set about the double curving at the top, and what materials are best?*

H. Reynolds, Amersham

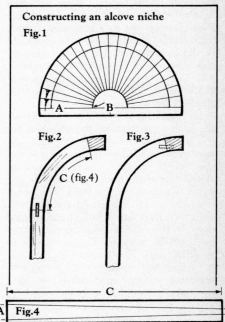

Constructing an alcove niche
Fig.1
Fig.2
Fig.3
C (fig.4)
C
A Fig.4 B

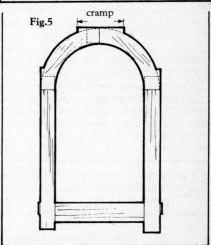

Fig.5
cramp

A Any curved work such as this should be set out full-size in plan and elevation. The plan will give the sections of the segments for the bottom section, which will be cylindrical, and also the taper-thicknesses of the spherical sections (fig. 1). To avoid 'feather edging', the latter should be cut about 3in short, and a semi-circular boss inserted as shown; but note how the two front sections are made parallel, to overlap the boss and join neatly at the crown.

This job can of course be made in two sections, the lower cylindrical, and the upper spherical, and these two then jointed by dowelling (fig. 2). A better job however would be to cut the sections in single continuous lengths (fig. 3). For either method, the taper thicknesses of each sphere segment — from 'springing' (beginning of curve) to head — can be

Question box

marked by sticking a paper pattern on to each segment, and then spokeshaving to this. The paper patterns can easily be found by bending a strip of paper along the curve to find total length, and then marking in top and bottom widths (fig. 4). Having worked the taper, these papered edges will then have to be gouged to radius, and the whole then glasspapered to a nice even surface (semi-dome) after assembly — which should be done on the setting-out rod — and by glue/screwing each segment to its precursor. The base can of course be made of block-board, with a suitable edging strip along its front edge.

Is the niche to be built in to a recess? If so, the outer surface can be left unfinished, but if it is to be free-standing, the segments will have to be rounded — after assembly — and the whole surface coarse-glasspapered across the grain, then finished with fine paper. The inside can be similarly treated; if it is to be painted as opposed to stained, any minor crevices can be filled and painted over. In this case, a softwood such as red deal will be suitable. The lower section could of course be veneered if required, but it would be impossible to veneer the spherical section satisfactorily by hand methods. It would have to be done by a vacuum process.

Fig. 5 shows details of door construction for this job. The classic method of segment-jointing is by hammer-headed key, but for a small job such as this, the open tenons shown would suffice. But note the cramping lugs; these are of course shaped round after the glue has set. To ensure that the door is going to fit the opening, the niche should be placed face-down on a flat surface, a pencil drawn round the inner edge, and the door assembled on this drawn shape.

Stan Thomas

Q *Can you give me any information on making snooker-cues, such as which jigs to use and so on? I would also be grateful if you could tell me of any books on the subject.*

Richard Hearing, Colchester

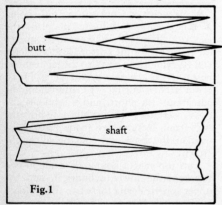

Fig.1

● *The splice between butt and shaft. It might be easier to dispense with the absolute points at the bottom of the splice and use a ⅛in chisel to make the bottom of the butt recess*

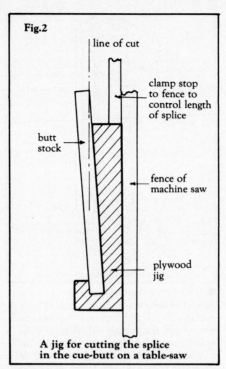

Fig.2

line of cut

clamp stop to fence to control length of splice

butt stock

fence of machine saw

plywood jig

A jig for cutting the splice in the cue-butt on a table-saw

A I can quite understand your fascination with the challenge of making a snooker cue by hand. Most hand-made cues are now made by simply tapering the butt and rebuilding it by gluing on the contrasting layers. However it is the traditional spliced joint which presents the woodworker with a challenge and I'm sure that this is what your question is about.

I'm afraid I can't direct you to any books on the subject but offer the consolation that they would be of little use. However, once you're clear in your mind of the construction involved (fig. 1), the only thing to do is to practise making the joint on short pieces. Few woodworkers would make a satisfactory job at their first attempt.

I can offer you a few hints, the first of which is to warn you of how rapidly the long points of the splice are reduced when you start to round the cue. I would advise you to work with 1¼x1¼in square stock and, assuming the points on the finished cue to be about 6in long, the depth of the splice will need to be about 14in on the original square material.

Both marking out and cutting of this joint needs to be accurate, particularly if the four 'points' are to be the same length — on most commercially-made cues they are not.

The butt is produced by sawing and the shaft by chiselling. There are several methods and it really comes down to individual preference and what tools and equipment you have. The sawing on the butt can be done by hand but a good bandsaw will make the job easier. A circular saw can also be used but it won't get right to the bottom of the splice and will have to be finished off with hand-saw and chisel. If a machine saw is used the simple jig shown in fig. 2 will prove invaluable.

Once you are getting a good fit between the components, clamping isn't a problem.

Once they're driven together, a very tight grip is automatic. However it's advisable to either bind the splice together or make corner-blocks and cramp them diagonally.

The shaping of the cue is done by plane in three stages: a tapering square section; a tapering octagonal section; and a tapering round section. The weight and balance of the cue is finalised by boring a hole into the end of the butt and filling it with lead shot.

John Prince

Q *I want to make some small wooden toys for my grandchildren. What's the best type of wood that won't be dangerous for tiny hands or mouths? Can you recommend any special non-poisonous varnishes or paints?*

W. T. Odd, Wimborne

A You mention grandchildren, tiny hands and mouths, and the need for non-poisonous paints and varnishes, so I'm assuming that the children in question are at the pre-school age of say 1-4 years. Crown Paint Consumer Services assured me that all modern paints, that is those used commercially for painting toys, are required by the Toy Safety Act to meet certain non-toxic, lead-free standards. As I understand it, Crown Plus Gloss comes within these standards. However, if you want a paint product that is completely safe, I recommend Humbrol or Airfix modelmaker's paints. They are fast-drying, finely ground, brilliantly coloured, and most important of all, they are designed with children in mind.

Wood toxicity usually relates to live, 'in the bark' wood, or the dust and juice that is given off by certain woods when they are being converted. I would say that most common woods such as poplar, lime and sycamore could all be chewed, sucked and gnawed by your grandchildren with no ill effect.

As to whether or not they're safe for tiny hands, that is not so straightforward. However with just such problems in mind, when my wife and I started on our book on *Wooden Toys* (currently in preparation) we put a lot of thought into the safety aspects of toy design. We decided to avoid, where possible, all nails, screws, pins and wire, and we also decided to pre-empt all wood-splintering and grain-shattering nasties by making all our toys out of high-quality, fine-grain, multi-layered plywood. I don't mean the horrible ragged, coarse, DIY sheet-wood that's almost unworkable, I mean the traditional ply that has about five layers per ¼in.

Finally, you say you want to make 'small' toys; is this wise bearing in mind that most pre-school children seem to spend their waking hours trying to push bits of toy in their ears and up their noses? Avoid all spiky metal and plastic fixings, and above all, go for designs that are generously rounded.

Alan Bridgewater

Question box

Q *I'm interested in finding a short course that would deal with the principles of spray finishing. There seem to be ample opportunities for french polishing, but no mention of spraying lacquers. I'd be grateful for any advice.*

Tom Poole, Ashburton

A I quite agree. Magazines these days seem to be full of information and courses on french polishing and nothing on modern finishing — baffling when you consider that cellulose finishing has been around since the 1930's. Most manufacturers today use modern finishes because the cellulose finishes will stand up to the rigours of children, heat, steam and stains where french polish will not.

A short course on the subject would not, I'm afraid, be practical because of its complexity. I suggest that you approach a few technical colleges (London College of Furniture or Brunel Technical College, Bristol) to see what courses are available. I can recommend the one-day-a-week City and Guilds Course on modern finishing which lasts for approximately 35 weeks and covers all aspects of modern finishing such as the use of spray-gun, pre-catalysed and acid catalysed lacquers, polyester and polyurethane lacquers, full gloss, semi-gloss and matt finishes, staining, sealing and 'pullovering'. It also deals with Health and Safety regulations.

Noel Leach

Q *I've recently bought a lathe, and am a newcomer to woodturning. After acquainting myself with the basics, I was eager to make something useful, and decided on a dining chair in pine with turned legs. The back rest and legs are made from the same piece.*

Turning the longest pieces (about 3ft) from 2x2in pine, I noticed that the wood seemed to be flexing in the middle, and that the tool was ripping rather than cutting it. I checked that there were no faults in the timber, and that my tools were sharp, and all was as it should have been.

I'm at a loss. Is the wood too wet? Is it too dry? Is it possible to turn such long lengths in softwood? If so how? I'd be grateful for your help, as my family are waiting to see the fruits of my hours in the workshop!

N. A. Howarth, Manchester

A Pine was a somewhat unfortunate choice for your first project, as it is more prone to flex over this length and this diameter. A mild-grained northern temperate hardwood such as beech would probably have given you less trouble.

There is unlikely to be anything wrong with the timber you are using; the flexing you describe is quite normal, so ways of minimising and overcoming the problem have to be found.

Overtightening the tailstock is a common fault when first mounting work between centres, so minimise this. Slot the end for the prong centre, or drive the prong centre into the wood before mounting it in the lathe; this will minimise the need for over-tightening the tailstock. A good-quality revolving cone centre will also help at this end of the lathe. When rounding your square stock, try to take sliding, slicing cuts in the direction of the headstock and tailstock respectively with your gouge and skew chisel. Try to minimise forward-thrusting cuts as these will help to cause flexing, and use only the sharpest tools. All these things help but are unlikely to totally eradicate the problem.

When flexing is minimal, lightly wrap the fingers of the left hand round the work, with only the thumb in contact with the tool. This may be enough to absorb the flexing. If it still isn't steady enough, fixed steadies are the answer.

The one I use is wooden, with a brass-weighted tapered wooden wedge. This pushes forward a pivoting wooden arm with a vee cut at centre-height against the rotating stock/spindle, and prevents flexing. There are several commercially-produced steadies that have ball races, rubber wheels or adjustable metal arms; they all work, but you can make the wooden one yourself; and it is just as efficient and cheaper.

More detail can be found in *The Practical Woodturner* by Fred Pains, *The Craft of Woodturning* by John Sainsbury, *Woodturning* by Geoff Peters, and my own book *Woodturning and Design*, in which there is a section on hand steadying methods.

Ray Key

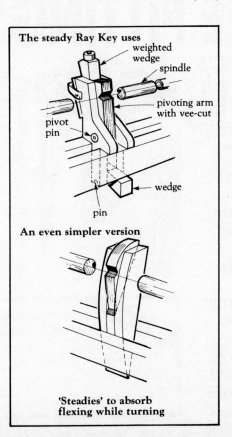

The steady Ray Key uses

weighted wedge

spindle

pivoting arm with vee-cut

pivot pin

wedge

pin

An even simpler version

'Steadies' to absorb flexing while turning

Q *I'm making oak panelling to furbish a small room (12ftx12ft) in traditional style and would like to finish it with a weathered oak effect.*

Charles Hayward's book Staining and Polishing *recommends using American potash and chloride of lime. I would like to know where I can obtain these materials; do they have proper chemical names and are there any other methods to achieve the effect?*

Bryan Knott, Melton Mowbray

A I'd recommend a water stain to obtain the silvery effect of weathered oak that you want.

I've approached a few polish suppliers, but have been unable to locate any stockists of American potash and chloride of lime. I can however give you various methods of producing a weathered oak finish.

One method is to paint the work over with strong lime water. Get some lump-lime and slake it in a tub of water. When the mixture has cooled, take the clear water off the top and using it as a stain, brush it on to the oak. When the panelling is completely dry it can be wax finished.

Another method is to make a solution of caustic soda, about 4oz to a pint of water, and add 2oz of lime. Stir thoroughly and brush on until the medullary rays of the oak turn red. Allow the work to dry and then wash the caustic out of the grain with hot water. When the work is completely dry it is bleached with oxalic acid (2oz to a pint of hot water). Apply the bleach evenly to the oak while it is still hot. Wash down afterwards with clean hot water and you'll have a fine grey colour which will closely resemble old oak.

A less laborious method is to get about ½lb of water-soluble grey powder and stir it into a container of water to produce a weakish stain. Add up to about 10% glue size to act as a 'fix' and brush the mixture evenly over the panelling. When the stain is perfectly dry, seal the open pores of the wood by brushing on two coats of white french polish. When the polish has hardened it is 'de-nibbed' by lightly smoothing with worn, fine abrasive paper. Wipe off all dust and apply wax polish with a clean rag evenly over the panelling. Allow the wax to stand for 15 minutes before polishing briskly with a soft duster. Repeat the process four or five times to obtain a deep mellow shine.

Whatever stain you decide to use, I advise you to experiment on some of the waste wood to make sure you have the colour you want before applying any stain to the panels.

Stains, french polish, and light antique wax polish are obtainable from James Jackson & Co. (London) Ltd, Major Works, 76-89 Alscot Rd, London SE1 5SX, Marrable & Co. Ltd, Delamare Rd, Cheshunt, Herts EN8 9SP, and many others.

Charles Cliffe

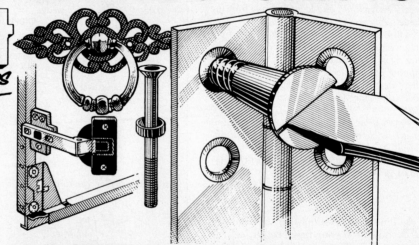
102

The craft of cabinetmaking

Hand veneering: this month and next, David Savage explains how to tackle it and enjoy it. First, the gear you need

Photos John Gollop

Some are born teachers, some aspire to the mantle of guru and some, like myself, have teaching thrust upon them. Jim and Malcolm now share my workshop. They started off on a one-year course in cabinetmaking at another teaching workshop nearby. It closed because of the illness of the principal, and they cast around for a place to spend their remaining six months. Their presence, besides aiding the exchequer, gives me the chance to show off. And veneering is one of the techniques better demonstrated than described.

There is a common misconception, frequently extending even to woodworkers, that veneer is a cheap substitute for solid wood. Dickens named Mr Veneering as a character to represent the superficial, the misleading and deceitful dazzler. However, in the correct place veneering is a wholesome and thoroughly good technique. How else can we economically use rare, exotic and beautiful timbers? There are places, such as the working family dining-table, where veneer might perhaps be a poor choice, but it would be foolish to condemn veneering because it has been, and is being, used commercially to produce only the illusion of quality. Besides, contrary to popular belief, veneered work in a small workshop is usually more time-consuming and almost always more expensive than work in the solid.

Veneering basically takes two forms, distinguished by the equipment used. Caul-veneering requires a press (or, on a small scale, bearers and cramps) to exert pressure on an assembly of groundwork, glue and veneer. One day, one happy day, I shall have a monster veneer-press for everything from storing machined timber to cracking walnuts. Until then I shall lay leaves of veneer by hand using hot glue.

Hand-veneering is ideal for the small workshop, and you can do surprisingly large and complex jobs very quickly once the skill has been acquired. Its limitations really concern the complexity of the design that may be applied. If you have a press, a complex lay-up can be assembled dry, taped together and glued to the ground in one operation. Working by hand, the pieces are laid oversize, each overlapping its neighbour, before being cut and fitted together. This is done with the glue still moist; as it dries there is some danger of shrinkage away from the joints, especially with some species of timber.

First of all the glue — hot glue; nice, old-fashioned, stink-the-place-out, hide or rabbitskin or pearl or call-it-what-you-like

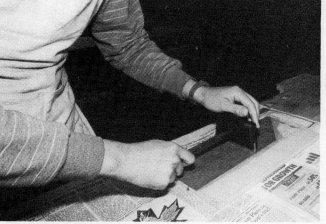

● Animal glue sets as fast as it cools: that's why hand-veneering demands both co-ordination and speed

glue. Wonderful. I don't use hide glue for a lot of jobs, but on occasions there is just nothing to touch it for speed, strength or flexibility. It comes either in a sheet, which you shatter with a mallet inside a plastic bag, or more conveniently in little dark- or light-brown balls or pearls. Now and again you may find hide glue in crystal form in art

shops; it costs about 10 times the usual price.

All these varieties are produced by boiling up animal bits of sundry sorts and species. The lighter-coloured pearls tend to be the most carefully made — House of Harbru are presently selling a well-made glue, the pearls of which are almost amber

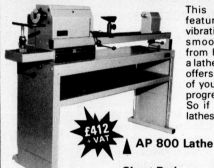
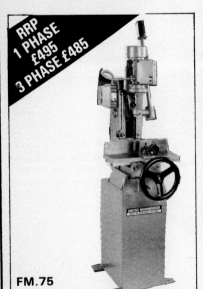
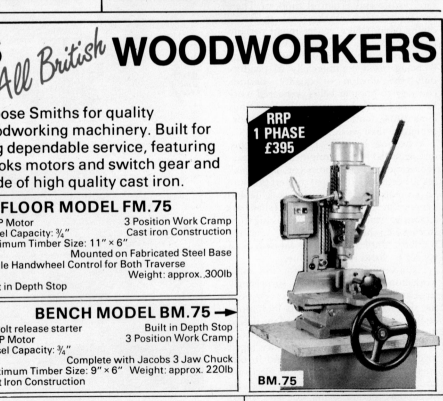

The craft of cabinetmaking

● *Hubble, bubble . . . but don't boil!*

in colour. Do not pay a lot for dark-brown or black pearls: the glue is not so strong. Rabbitskin glue is traditionally the palest, and best reserved for light-coloured veneers. White pigment can also be added, which is handy for camouflaging dark glue-lines.

Soak the glue in cold water for a few hours. Make sure it's covered with water, and stir well and often for the first few minutes, or it will stick together and take too long to soak up the water. Keep it covered with water as it doubles or even trebles in volume. This will take at least two hours (except in the case of finely ground granules), and it is best to allow longer.

Pour off the excess water and use a double-boiler glue-pot. Very good aluminium pots are now made; if your pot is the old cast-iron type, be sure the receptacle is tanned to prevent the glue being discoloured by rust. If you have one of these thermostatically controlled electric glue-pots that heat the water to exactly the right temperature just short of boiling-point, you're quids in and half the fun of glue-making has been stolen from you. We ourselves have various ways of heating the glue-pot — the best, in winter, being the woodburning stove that keeps it bubbling away, gently and at some distance from the bench area. In summer months an ancient Primus stove did duty until very recently, when a Calor-gas ring was drafted in.

The problem with all heat sources is control. Too much heat, and the water in the lower pan boils and froths down the sides of the glue-pot — extinguishing the flame with a loud hiss. The Calor-gas system, which bears great visual similarity to a miniature nuclear reactor, performs this spectacle to a workshop chorus of 'Melt down!'. For strength never, never, never boil the glue. Adjust the consistency by adding water until it flows and brushes out well without being thin and weak. Nobody can explain this precisely, but there is an ideal consistency dependent on temperature and on water content. The expert will adjust it all the time throughout the day as the glue is being used.

This glue is best used so hot that a drop on the back of your hand is painful. Anyone new to it would do well to experience the way the stuff sets. Take hot glue between finger and thumb and rub together. For maybe a minute nothing will happen; maybe this glue is a bad batch? But then, as it chills, quite rapidly the stickiness comes. Continue rubbing and very soon the tack will be complete. At this stage no amount of pressure will get two separate glue surfaces to become one. All your pressure should occur just after the initial no-tack stage but before final chilling.

Once the joint is effected and the glue chilled, the second stage of hardening is by loss of moisture. In a day or two the joint is as hard as it ever will be.

Animal glue, to give it the correct name, is exceptionally strong, with a flexibility that suits timber well. It allows speedy assembly of joints without cramps if the craftsmanship is precise. For hand-veneering it is without equal. However, it has considerable disadvantages — the main one being a vulnerability to dampness and moisture. Your sticky fingers can easily be released by warm water. A hot cup or alcohol spill on a table top has been known to loosen a patch of veneer (though not on my tables, I hasten to add). There again, this capacity to be 'brought back' by heat or moisture can have considerable advantages for the furniture restorer. Indeed, animal glue is the only adhesive that should go anywhere near a prized antique.

Besides the gluing impedimenta, hand-veneering requires several tools that are used for little else. A veneer-hammer, knife and saw, a toothing tool and an electric iron form the basic kit, together with various sponges, cramps, straight-edges, newspapers and buckets of hot water.

The veneer-hammer can be bought — but it's better to make your own, for the tool is a simple one. Its blade is brass, from sheet material $\frac{3}{16}$in thick. Fit it well into the stock as it will have to withstand some pressure. The blade is rounded over and polished smooth. The handle can be made to any convenient length. The word 'hammer' is a slight misnomer, for nothing is struck with the veneer-hammer except perhaps the slumbering student.

The action involves applying pressure to the top of the stock and working the handle to and fro so that the hammer proceeds up the veneer like an indecisive crab. If this is done well, a wave of excess glue is squeezed out ahead of the hammer — leaving a thoroughly attached veneer in its wake.

The veneer-saw, as it comes from the maker, is a totally useless implement — but then, so are most other tools. I very rarely use the side of the saw which has a wide, square kerf. The useful side is the one where the teeth are sharpened by file across the saw in the usual way and then ground to a point down the length of the blade on both sides. This gives them needle-sharp points that will cut veneers easily, with a very narrow kerf. The saw looks an unlikely

weapon for work on delicate veneers, but it does a surprisingly good job if properly sharpened.

The veneer knife is best made from a standard bench or chip-carving knife. Attack the blade with the disc-sander to re-model it. It should be thin, but not so thin that it loses its edge under pressure.

As for the toothing tool . . . In days of yore, there was none of your MDF nonsense. Veneer was laid up on a solid wood ground, usually pine or mahogany, and a toothing-plane both flattened the ground and prepared it for the veneer in one operation. Now we have board material that is dead flat; all that's needed is a tool to scratch the surface. Some I have heard argue that it is unnecessary to deface a perfectly good board, but I still do it. Even more than most man-made boards, MDF has a hard and almost glossy surface; by scratching it in two directions, at right-angles to each other, you form a mechanical key whereby the glue can attach itself more readily. A toothing tool can be made from broken hacksaw blades in a simple wedged handle.

Next month, having assembled the equipment, we might just get down to laying a few leaves of veneer!
● House of Harbru, 101 Crostons Rd, Elton, Bury, Lancs BL8 1AL, tel. 061-764 6769. ■

Peter Collenette writes: Last summer I spent a good and productive weekend in the light, airy fastness of David Savage's workshop in Bideford, Devon. I was learning (though vanity would rather I said 're-learning') how to cut dovetails.

David provides all the materials, some of the tools, the bench, the explanation, the encouragement and the atmosphere needed to make a nice little hardwood box with four dovetailed corners. His instructions are full and authoritative, and leave little to chance or the student's blind guesses. Yet perhaps the main benefit lies in setting aside two days of early starts, free from interruption, for nothing else but concentration and trying to get the job just right.

Even so, you still won't finish it, and a good two months elapsed before I glued up. Gaping mitres told their own sad story; but they didn't reflect on Dave, who is clear about his own methods and imparts them pleasantly yet thoroughly. He does one other weekend course, which deals with making and fitting drawers, and he also takes full-time students. By the time you've got to Bideford (an attractive place), stayed there, and paid Dave for his labours, you'll be lighter in the pocket by about the same amount you'll be heavier in the skills. Details from Dave at 21 Westcombe, Bideford, Devon EX39 3QJ, tel. Bideford (023 72) 79202.

WIN!

● Elektra Beckum's newest precision table-saw

NO PIC YET IT'S TOO NEW!

OR

● The HDM lathe, with a full metre between centres

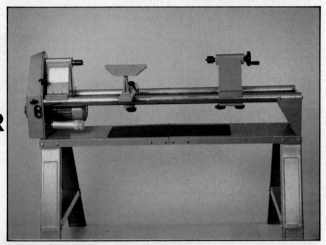

SQUARES AND ROUNDS

There are two types of woodworker — and **Woodworker**, in association with Elektra Beckum, proudly announces a competition for them both. The ones who work in squares — the joiner/cabinetmakers — can win a new table-saw; the ones who work in rounds — the woodturner/carvers — can win over £500 worth of lathe!

THE PRIZES

THE SQUARES

Elektra Beckum's precision table-saw is so new there wasn't even a photo ready by the time we went to press. It has a 700x900mm table, and its motor puts out 3hp at full tilt. The rip-fence is full-length, and it locks front and rear; a crosscut fence is also standard. It comes with a 10in TCT blade, 45° tilt-arbor, and rise-and-fall; it will cost at least £500 retail.

THE ROUNDS

The HDM 1000 lathe's chrome steel bed gives you 1000mm between centres. You can turn bowls up to 15in diameter; it has 4 speeds, and a faceplate and drive dog come as original equipment. The head- and live centre tailstock are both diecast, both with double bearings, and there's a spindle brake. It's worth over £500 with the stand.

THE COMPETITION

What you have to do: make any item (out of wood, of course) that includes a chessboard. It's as simple as that. **But** we'll be judging originality and imagination, as well as craftsmanship; so you can make a chessboard on its own, or you can make something that incorporates one. It can be a chair, a chest, a table or a cabinet — anything as long as it has a built-in chessboard!

What you have to do: the woodturner/carvers are challenged to come up with an ingenious set of chessmen — or draughts, or a set of pieces for any game, ordinary or extraordinary, that can be played on a chessboard. They can be as big as you like and as fantastic as you like; what we're looking for is imagination and craftsmanship.

Final judging of both categories will be at the Bristol Woodworker Show, 16-18 May.

THE RULES

1 Entries must consist of:
● A photograph of your work
● A written description (no more than two A4 sheets) of the idea and the techniques used
● Dimensioned drawings
2 Entries must be sent to **Woodworker Squares and Rounds Competition, 1 Golden Sq, London W1R 3AB** by **Monday 21 April 1986**
3 If you can't finish by 21 April but still want to enter, send a perspective drawing by the closing date instead of the photo,

along with your description and drawings
4 You can't enter both categories
5 Entries selected for final judging will be displayed at the **WOODWORKER SHOW, BRISTOL, 16-18 May, and will be judged there by,** amongst others, master-cabinetmaker **Alan Peters**
6 Decisions of the judges and **Woodworker** magazine are final in all matters concerning the competition

Industrious Design Force

Britain's rich and varied design talent, it's often claimed, is either badly marketed, not marketed at all, or attracted overseas where it's better valued. The Independent Designers' Federation ('This Month' WW/Oct 85) aims to change all that. It is offering business, administration and marketing support for nearly 70 designers (mostly of furniture at present), and the group is growing.

The IDF made its first mark at Style 86, the autumn furniture show at Olympia, London. Their 10,000sq ft corner was full of top-quality craftsmanship. Sure, the work wouldn't be to everyone's taste — but then, how much mass-produced repro can you (or the market) take?

Many of the names in the IDF will already be familiar to dedicated followers of furniture fashion. What's new about it is that they have put themselves under one organisational roof, elected a committee whose executive decisions they trust, and committed themselves to at least some sort of group identity. 'Our very nature as beasts,' says John Coleman, 'is that we are self-employed, and we don't like big groups. Bringing us together is an almost impossible task — but Bill Borland is pulling it off.'

● Not all the IDF's members work is nonsensically trendy (little of it in fact), and all of it is crafted to impeccable standards. **Above** is John Coleman's three-in-one coffee table, commissioned to match an oriental carpet, sycamore-veneered with pear stripes. **Right** is Jakki Dehn's 'music set' – the cabinet was one of a pair commissioned to store sheet music – in black American walnut inlaid with boxwood lines, ivory, mother-of-pearl and holly squares. **Below** is Noel Gaskell's astonishing 'lattice-support' table. **Opposite page: right,** Tom Kealy's traditional Somerset chair uses willow for the seat and back and steam-bent ash for the frame; his writing case **below right** is of paldao with a cherry interior. **Far right,** Noel Gaskell's solution to the lectern problem:

Make no mistake, the IDF is Bill Borland's baby. He wouldn't deny it; as an interior designer, he naturally sees an overall concept and has promoted it with single-minded (and sometimes abrasive) energy. 'I won't be happy until every single member has sold something through my efforts,' he says.

'What about money, Bill? Are you going to be a millionaire through the IDF?'

'Let's just say that if I'm a millionaire, 60-odd others will be too.'

Borland's professed intention is to develop a British design industry as such. The Greater London Enterprise Board and the London Enterprise Agency, among others, have helped it set up (it's a [unique] co-operatively managed limited liability company); and the hope is for mutually beneficial design-and/or-make deals with some of the established manufacturers — the ones who'll listen.

Borland thinks the IDF can take a load off designers' minds, and leave them free to do what they do best while it sells their high-quality work to manufacturers, to the consumer who wants individuality, and to foreign markets. He doesn't believe there's such a thing as a mass market. 'I hate the mass market. I think it's just an idea that's been created.'

As for becoming a member, your work will be judged by one of eight selection panels a year, whose members change each time.

Those with certain tastes choosing their own kind? Perhaps, but the energy behind the idea and its execution is enough to put this modern British design on the world map. It's the IDF's job to choose as representatively and objectively as it can.■

● IDF, Studio A11, The Met, Enfield Rd, London N1 5AZ, tel. 01-241 5104.

Hand-made and handsome

Mark Ripley's small tall
cabinet embodies a
modern approach to
traditional craft. He
shows how it's made

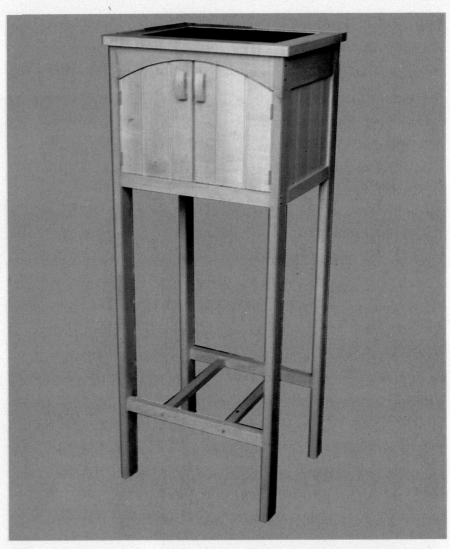

● *Straight from the saw; sycamore au naturel is used in this well-balanced small cabinet*

My training is in contemporary furniture design aimed at mass production, but the bulk of my work
now is in cottage style, with strong
emphasis on traditional forms and techniques. The transition to a traditional
approach occurred when I took several
commissions, all of which had to be made in
my very basic workshop with only a small
bandsaw and hand-tools.

I looked to the time before machines for
my inspiration and methods and found the
results exciting and satisfying. I was also
working (I still am) as a woodwork instructor with handicapped adults and was
thinking in simple terms when designing
projects for them, again to be made with
hand-tools. I do use machines — not to is
inefficient and often boring — but I do so
with care and now that I'm considering full-
time making, I want to maintain a modest
workshop with an emphasis on bench
work.

One reason for this is that high-tech
accuracy is simply inappropriate for this
type of work. Perfection needs to be
measured in human terms, not engineering
ones. I am not advocating rough work,
indeed this piece requires some careful
making just to get it together. It is more a
case of creating something that looks and
feels carefully hand-made, something that
people want to use and will enjoy living
with.

Construction

Sycamore is a sweet-smelling, easily worked
wood which requires some careful selection
because of the grey/blue streaks which you
sometimes find. They aren't easily
detectable in a sawn board, so if possible,
plane the boards first. The overall appearance of a piece will be governed by
timber-selection decisions at this stage; aim
for a balance. The grain is not very pronounced in sycamore, but the colour varies
a lot and I used lighter wood in the panels
and doors than in the framework. The
cutting list should be prepared accurately
with the exception of the side-panels, which
should be left slightly oversize for final
thicknessing and fitting later. The rails that
receive through tenons should be allowed
$\frac{1}{16}$in at each end for finishing after
assembly. All the mortises and tenons
should be marked out; note that the ones in
the sides are $\frac{1}{16}$in wider than those in the
front and back.

However you cut the mortises, it's
advisable to do them before the tenons,

because the slots from a slot-mortiser or
router are sometimes slightly wider than
their cutter. Now is also the time to cut the
stopped grooves in the vertical rails into
which the side-panels fit. I cut the grooves
in the horizontal rails on a small table-saw,
but if you use a router it would be advisable
to cut the grooves before ripping the rails
from the blank board. The bigger workpiece makes it easier because there's better
support for both work and router. When
you are squaring up the through mortises,
cut halfway from each side of the rail to
avoid break-out. These mortises will also
require tapering to take the wedges in the
tenons (fig. 7).

The tenons on this job are small and
sycamore is not very forgiving about gaps so
they do need to be accurate. A well-tuned
bandsaw will cut straight and true and it's
quick and accurate for many jobs in terms
of setting up and machining time. The slots
for the wedges can also be cut with a
bandsaw.

The tenons will ideally fit straight from
the saw with a firm push-fit. This is an ideal

time for trial assembly to check that all
those grooves line up before fitting the
panels.

The side-panels may now be thicknessed
to fit their grooves, I suggest by hand. The
finish straight from a perfectly sharp
smoothing-plane is incomparable and
something that no machine can reproduce.
It will also give a subtle contrast between
the panel and the frame. If you don't have a
table-saw to cut the tongues and grooves
you can use a router, but a circular saw-
blade is the right width and it's probably
easier to work with considering the size of
the pieces.

I like the finish straight from a circular saw
and it's sometimes appropriate to use it,
especially in furniture of this style. It does
need to be used sensitively and whilst the
blade-marks on the frame members inside
the cabinet may be left, those visible from
the outside will need scraping clean with a
sharp chisel. The same effect may be
employed on the fixing-battens for the
doors and the buttons, with the edges
lightly chamfered. The ply panels for top,

bottom and back are veneered in a complementary veneer, or you can use good-quality ply and stain it. All the panels should be fitted dry, but before any gluing, all frame members should be lightly sanded and every edge, including the tenon shoulders, slightly chamfered. All the wedges should be sawn from a slat of mahogany the same thickness as the tenons, after which the stretcher assembly may be glued up. The side-panels and frames can also be assembled, using a light coating of PVA glue. The curve on the top front rail can be drawn by flexing a piece of steel or plastic between three pins tapped into a piece of waste ply or hardwood (fig. 6). Cut this out and use it as a template for the rail itself.

Once this piece is cut and finished, complete the assembly by joining the two side-frames by the front and back rails and stretcher-rails, not forgetting to insert the back and bottom. Allow any excess glue to go off before removing it with a chisel, rather than trying to remove it wet.

The top is a straightforward framework with a ply panel inserted. The doors are constructed in a similar way to the side-panels, but they have staggered tongue-and-groove joints. They are simply assembled with battens. The bottom and sides of the doors should be fitted in the cabinet first, so the precise curve of the top rail can be scribed directly on to the backs to ensure a good fit. The brass hinges are set into the doors; I fit a small magnetic catch to a block behind the top rail.

The buttons to fix the top are best made in a strip to make marking out and drilling easier. Cut the notch out with a bandsaw before removing the button from the strip.

Each handle is bandsawn from a single block (fig. 5), keeping the workpiece as big as possible for as long as possible, and using two specially-designed push-sticks when it gets too small. Use a small fine blade and take great care of your fingers! Each piece should be sanded smooth and reassembled in its former relative position, using contact adhesive for a clean and easy joint. The handles are fixed with screws through the back of the doors.

Fit the dark cork tiles for the top and bottom, ready for gluing with contact adhesive after finishing.

In Denmark some years ago, I was impressed to see furniture totally unfinished, just bare wood, which looked superb. I haven't got that much courage but have left the interior unfinished. The rest is covered with two coats of gloss polyurethane, matt-finished with fine-grade wire wool and dressed with 50/50 boiled linseed oil/white spirit, applied with a cloth and rubbed dry. The cork tiles will also look better with an oil dressing to bring the colour out.

I made this cabinet two years ago on spec as a promotional piece, and after an occasional oiling every few months, it has darkened slightly and is developing a fine silky appearance. ■

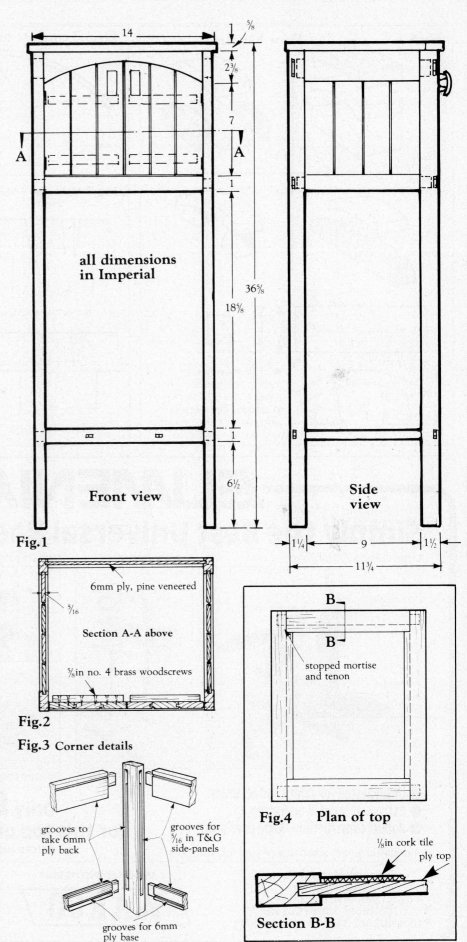

all dimensions in Imperial

Front view

Side view

Fig.1

6mm ply, pine veneered

Section A-A above

⅝in no. 4 brass woodscrews

Fig.2

Fig.3 Corner details

grooves to take 6mm ply back

grooves for ⁵⁄₁₆ in T&G side-panels

grooves for 6mm ply base

B—B

stopped mortise and tenon

Fig.4 Plan of top

⅛in cork tile

ply top

Section B-B

Hand-made and handsome

Fig.5 Door handles

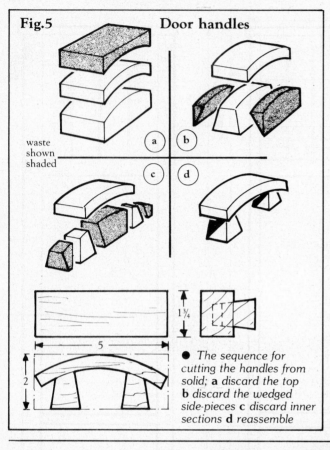

waste shown shaded

1¾

5

2

● The sequence for cutting the handles from solid; **a** discard the top **b** discard the wedged side-pieces **c** discard inner sections **d** reassemble

Fig.6 Template for curved rail

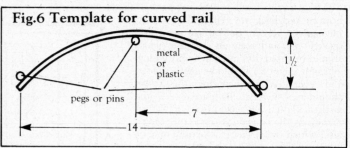

metal or plastic

pegs or pins

1½

7

14

Fig.7 Mahogany wedges in tenons

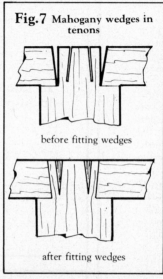

before fitting wedges

after fitting wedges

Fig.8 Buttons

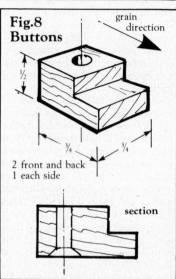

grain direction

½

¾ ¾

2 front and back 1 each side

section

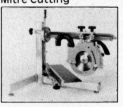
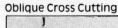

MDF turns noble

An 18th-century bust in an Oxfordshire mansion needed extra height. Bob Grant's solution involved MDF and the lathe

Photos Ray Clayton

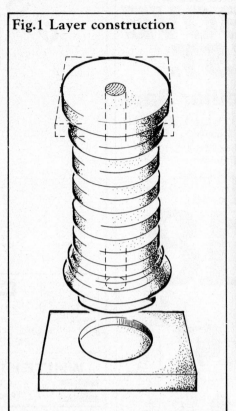

Fig.1 Layer construction

● Why the bust had to be raised – the photo **far left** gives an idea of its ornate surroundings. **Above**, the stand; **fig. 1 (left)** shows its construction

Fig.2

● Enlarging or reducing figures: angle P and distance PC as convenient, ABCD the original figure, A1B1C1D1 the reduced figure

Proportional reduction

If William Kent had been able to get MDF (medium density fibreboard) when he designed the interior of the magnificent hall at Ditchley Park in 1752, he may well have used it for the exquisite panelling and moulding which characterise the place.

The mansion is in rural Oxfordshire, and although it is overshadowed in fame by its near neighbour, Blenheim Palace, it is nonetheless an important architectural treasure. James Gibbs was the architect and William Kent worked on the interior, whose carvings, painted ceilings and gold leaf create an effect of breathtaking grandeur.

One of the hall's treasures, a marble bust of an unknown lady, resides in a niche opposite the fireplace. She is flanked by Corinthian-style columns and fronted by an ornate marble-topped table. Unsurprisingly the bust has been somewhat lost in the scale of its surroundings.

I was commissioned to make a stand to elevate her and set a better proportion. The bust is about 31in high and needed to be set 14in above the niche base. With aesthetic harmony in mind, I took careful measurements of the flanking columns, and by a process of proportional reduction (fig. 2), I arrived at an exact miniature of the original — albeit minus the flutings.

M'lady weighs in at 112lbs, and while the conventional built-up wood segments for columns would have served, I decided to turn up a pile of 1in MDF discs located on a central ¾in mandrel — all pressed together with an alphabetic resin glue (fig. 1). I decided to trust the MDF to bear the weight and remain stable in service.

The 1in MDF made by Medite (there are other brands) has a stated hardness of 4000N. I arrived therefore, at a block 13x9½x9½in to be turned down to 9in diameter; the square base was added afterwards. I made the sinking for the stub tenon at the bottom of the turned piece by mounting the square base on a faceplate and turning out the centre. MDF turns beautifully, cutting conventionally with gouge and chisel or just scraping. It's a rather dusty operation, but the finish from the tool needs no glasspapering.

Because of its compressed construction, the outer faces of the board are somewhat harder than the core and care has to be taken when turning a stack-laminated block so you don't inadvertently hollow out the softer centre and produce a ribbed effect.

Unlike chipboard or plywood, turning MDF didn't dull the tools' cutting edges; the wear rate is comparable to any medium-working hardwood. Discs of green baize were let into the top and bottom of the column to provide non-slip and scratch surfaces.

The finishing presented no problems. Five light coats of ordinary grey emulsion were sprayed on to get a fine alabaster-type surface. Applying the gold leaf to such a surface was comparatively easy, although as always conditions of temperature and humidity were critical.

M'lady now graces her surroundings from an imperial height. MDF has rapidly found all sorts of uses in the woodworking industry; but how many 18th-century beauties rest on turned columns of this very 20th-century stuff? ■

114

Tales out of steel

Tool-handles, hand-turners as fast as machines, and the dreaded 'rape' — Ashley Iles' Sheffield stories continue

The humble tool-handle could tell a tale or two — and worthy of close scrutiny. With thousands of firms producing tools, the demand for handles can well be imagined. In cutlery the volume was incredible. 'Zylonite' was used for medium-priced handles, which were bored by hand to receive the tang of the blade. The borings gave birth to a little industry on its own. Across the yard from me in Solly St was 'little Harold', whose job was to go round the cutlery firms with a two-wheeled barrow, collecting and bagging the borings. Once a fortnight a 30-ton lorry would appear in the yard. It would be piled high with sacks of borings and set off for Northampton, where the load was used to make soles for shoes. 'There's nowt wasted where they keep em,' as we say in Yorkshire. A lorryload of borings! It gives some indication of the volume of handles.

Handles for tools was just as vast a business but far more romantic and exciting. Here we meet the woodturners producing millions of ash, beech and boxwood handles. Specialist semi-automatic machines had been developed, which had a cutter-block at the back composed of three 'flies', each holding three HSS cutters. The first fly produced the knob for the ferrule. The cutters in the other two flies were ground to the shape of the handle body. The flies had to be perfectly balanced, because the block did 5000rpm. The piece of work to be made into a handle was placed between a fork and centre, like on an ordinary lathe. Then, as it rotated slowly, it was fed into the cutter-block by working a lever. At the actual time of machining a steel guard came down, not, I might add, in case the work came out, but in case a cutter came out. Only one high-tensile set-screw held the cutter. Metal fatigue was the danger.

Once a machine had been set up it could do a leisurely gross an hour. Here I would like to introduce Ernie Pennington — all five foot one of him, complete with a bass voice. At five foot eleven, I felt he was talking into a mike in my navel. The singular thing about Ernie was, he could compete with a machine just turning by hand.

He rented a nice well-lit workshop from Mawhood Bros in Bailey St, making all the handles Mawhoods needed, and for many customers of his own. He employed *four* polishing girls. When I first met him, he boomed out: 'Bloody polio shots, that's my trouble!' All his girls were asking for time off to take their children for polio vaccinations, and he couldn't get the work out. But just imagine a hand-turner keeping four polishing girls going! No overtime, either. Every night he was in the Three Tuns on Leopold Street dressed up to the nines.

'If your finger touched the 'rape' it would cut to the first joint before you even felt anything'

Reg Slack and Gordon Stokes can go a bit in full flood, but watching Ernie turning was like watching a speeded-up movie. The piece of wood was put in while the lathe was running. A few cuts with the gouge and it was shaped. Then a flick over with the hook gate, and a digger finished the ferrule knob. A left-and-right flick with a skew chisel finished the body. Then the end was domed with the skew chisel, parted off, and the handle dropped into his waiting left hand. All the time talking away like mad.

Making boxwood handles was interesting. Boxwood from the trunk of the tree wasn't suitable. Branches and saplings, known as branch boxwood, were used. The sticks were about 6ft long, 2in or so at the thick end down to ¾in at the thin end. English boxwood is brittle and dull in colour — the best came from Salonika in Greece. The turner had to cut to length on a circular saw and grade at the same time. As each length was cut, he had to decide what size handle it would make without waste, and throw it into the right-size box. Much of the thick stuff went for oval screwdriver handles, done on the turning machine with a cam on the drive to produce the oval shape.

So there was a comfortable living in making handles — provided you could hand-turn 5000 a week and keep it up.

From all quarters these days we hear of the need for new small businesses. Our very survival seems to depend on them. I have been fortunate to see many businesses grow from tiny seeds. In Alma Street, Sheffield — a district which by no stretch of the imagination could be termed residential — is the works of Jack Adams Cutlers. The floor area is about the size of a supermarket. Jack is a specialist, a leader in his field of all types of butcher's and kitchen knives, and painter's cutlery. If you want 1000 16in French cook's knives, he's your man. In fact I don't think he would make you less than 1000.

'Just imagine a hand-turner keeping four polishing girls going!'

In 1950 he was a scale tang cutler working alone, outworking for Clark and Wharburton in a rented shop about 30x8ft on the floor above me in Solly St. The scale tang handle is where the tool runs full length and the handle is made by fixing a piece of beech or rosewood (known as a 'scale') on either side, then working it round to a nice polished oval. The tang and scale are bored by hand then riveted together with brass rod. Then the whole thing has to be shaped round as quickly as possible, which entails the use of the 'rape'. Personally I wouldn't be seen dead using one. It is a sort of solid-steel milling cutter, about 14in diameter and 3 or 4in wide. The periphery was ground across the wheel into razor-sharp grooves or teeth, making an instrument like a pile of circular saws. This was fixed on a spindle with a wooden driving-pulley, and it ran in wooden bearings between a pair of puppets. The cutler held the tool to be done on top of the rape and worked freehand with the rape running away from him, working the corners off to a nice even round. It fetched it off beautifully but if your finger touched the rape it would cut to the first joint before you even felt anything.

'Full-backs in the steel warehouse . . .'

Jack had the most foolproof recipe for success ever thought of; sheer unrelenting graft from eight in the morning till nine at night and one o'clock on Saturdays, year after year. I have never in my life seen anyone work like Jack Adams.

I popped into see him a few months ago, and stood in the works looking round. It was just like watching Sheffield Wednesday play. Full-backs in the steel warehouse, centre-forwards on the drop-stamps, half-backs on the blanking presses, wingers grinding and hardening. I could feel it all moving forward to the warehouse goal-mouth. Guess who the captain was? Jack Adams junior (16 the last time I'd seen him), who told me Mr Adams was upstairs in the office. I was shown into a modern executive office and there he was. His trade had given him a slight stoop, his face had a few wrinkles, but everything else was there; intense, unassuming, quick to laugh, but in command at the drop of a hat. As I worked my way back to the M1 it occurred to me that men like him are what Sheffield is all about. ∎

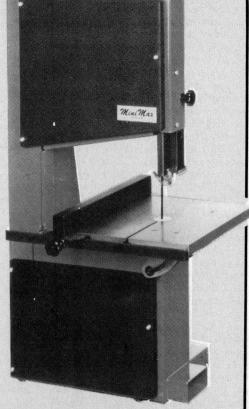

The carver's garden

Andrew Armitage carves and colours all manner of delicate flora and fauna. He explains how

Carving flowers and foliage has one great advantage. There is an almost infinite variety of subjects and, unlike animals and birds, they will sit still long enough for you to copy them in as much detail and accuracy as your skill and patience allow.

Carving free-standing flowers from a solid block can be very difficult and restricted because of the delicacy of the petals and different grain directions in the wood, but if you carve the petals and other parts separately and assemble them with glue, you can produce life-like copies of a wide variety of flora.

Few carvers would have the patience or time to tackle flowers like dahlias or chrysanthemums with hundreds of petals, so choose a subject with something like five to ten petals in a single row for a start. Here are a few good examples:

Wild Flowers buttercup, primrose, dog rose, celandine, marsh marigold, daffodil.
Garden Flowers almond, apple, cherry, clematis, dahlia (coltness type), cistus.
Impatiens begonia (fibrous rooted), viola, narcissus, crocus.

Woods

The colouring process I use is an attempt to reproduce the flowers in their natural shades and, since transparent finishes play a part, the natural colour of the wood is important. For bright shades or pale tints, you need woods nearest to white. They should be free from prominent grain markings, and strong enough to be worked in the thin petal sections. Holly has, so far, proved best for petals although box is even better if its rather strong yellow doesn't restrict the range of colour-shades obtainable.

I use box for the centres of the flowers,

● The living wood: **above left** are long-tailed tits on almond blossom; **above,** 'Flora Allwoodi'; **below,** an almond blossom with vegetable-fibre stamens

for fine stalks and some stamens. Pear is good for leaves and stalks of larger diameter.

CONSTRUCTION
Dahlia (coltness type)

Fig. 1 shows the shape of an 8-petal flower in plan and sections. The outline is transferred with carbon paper on to a piece of holly 1½in thick, including the extra area for holding the piece in the vice (or hand) for carving. I cut the outline out on a band-saw through the thickness of the block, then carve the top surface of the first petal with a gouge to give the cross-sections shown in fig. 1. The block is then turned on its side and a thin slice cut off on the band-saw to give the first petal, carved on the face side only. This is repeated seven times on the same block to get the right number of petals. The back of each petal must now be shaped to give a section about 1mm thick, but tapering at the edges to almost zero thickness. I hold the petal by the extension piece (fig. 1) and shape the back to the correct section with a Dremel moto-tool — the drum sander is the safest attachment to

use. It is shaped with coarse grit and finished with fine. The extension piece is then cut off to give the finished petal. It's important to achieve this very thin cross-section because some petal overlapping occurs with many flowers.

The carver's garden

Flower centre

This is turned in boxwood to the section shown in fig. 1. I cut the slot to take the petals with a 1mm-wide flat chisel, made by grinding the end of an old dental probe. If you want a long stem, the short stem illustrated is cut off and a hole drilled for the new one. The centre of a newly opened flower is a closely-packed mass of stamens which looks from above like a collection of hemispheres about 1.5mm in diameter in close contact. To simulate these, I made a punch from $\frac{1}{8}$in diameter mild-steel rod with a hemispherical depression in the centre of one end, ground in with a dental burr (no.3 round) in the Dremel. Then I ground a taper on the end of the rod to give a sharp edge round the depression (fig. 1). For the stamens round the outer edge, I carve longitudinal grooves with a V-chisel and round off with a riffler or sandpaper. For this type of work, strips of industrial abrasive papers $\frac{1}{8}$-$\frac{1}{2}$in wide and about 4in long glued on to same-size strips of Formica are very good; they have a very long life. If the underside of the flower is visible in the final assembly, bracts should be added. There are five, their shape and position shown in Fig. 1. They are produced in the same way as the petals.

Assembly

The flower centre is held firmly by setting the stalk in a hole of the same diameter drilled in a block of wood, and each petal checked to ensure it fits in the groove. PVA glue is run into the groove from the tip of, for example, a darning needle and the petals inserted. The bracts, if required, are glued in position.

Daffodil

As shown in fig. 2, the principle is the same as for the dahlia. The trumpet is turned in boxwood and finished with chisels or the Dremel tool to give the serrated edge. Enough wood should be left at the base to provide for the bend at the top of the stem, which is worked from pear, and joined to the flower by dowelling and gluing. The spathe is made from boxwood veneer thinned down to almost paper thickness, and I wet it to get the curve to fit round the top of the stem. Then I glue it into position, and hold it to dry by binding it with elastic thread.

Stamens

The daffodil has five stamens almost touching. They are represented by a single piece of boxwood, turned as shown in fig. 2; the top is cut into five segments with the fine saw attachment in the Dremel and finished off with a sanding stick.

Many flowers have large numbers of stamens consisting of fine stalks with a swelling at the tip. These are made from vegetable fibres like the stuff used for brush bristles, and glued in holes drilled in the flower centre with a 0.3mm twist drill in the Dremel. I make the swelling at the tip with a spot of Evostik.

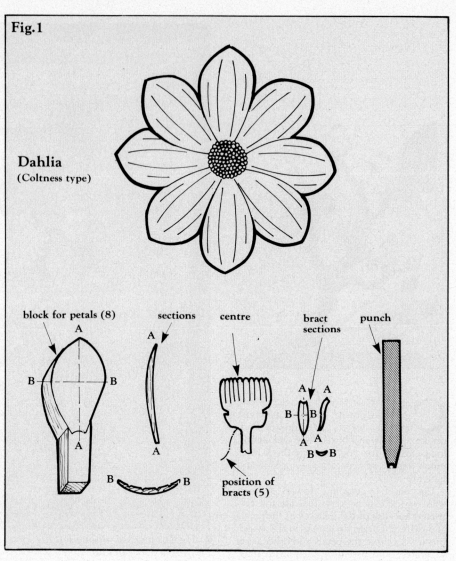

Fig.1

Dahlia
(Coltness type)

block for petals (8)   sections   centre   bract sections   punch

A

B   B

A

position of bracts (5)

Leaves

Holly or pear are fine. I make them the same way as the petals. Variations in size and shape are made to correspond with nature.

Stalks and Twigs

These are usually made from pear, built up from separate pieces cut to outline shape on the bandsaw, and rounded off with the Dremel. The jointing of the sections is shown in fig. 3. Thin stalks, for example ivy leaves, are made from boxwood.

COLOURING

The method I use for colouring my flowers is a compromise between staining and painting. Staining with soluble dyes is not satisfactory because water solutions raise the grain; on the other hand, it's difficult to stop solvent-based stains spreading in small areas, and they don't in general have good light-fastness. Then again the heavy pigmentation of paints entirely obliterates the character of the wood. The compromise uses a polyurethane base (Ronseal clear matt) to which pigments with a degree of transparency are added. Some of these pigments are:

- Monolite yellow G
- Monolite red 2R
- Monolite violet 4R
- Monastral blue B — G
- Monastral green GB.

A wide range of shades can be obtained from mixing these.

To prepare the colours for use, pour about half a teaspoon of Ronseal on to a sheet of plate glass about 12in square, and add very small quantities of pigment according to the depth of shade required. Thoroughly disperse it with a flexible paint scraper, applying pressure in a rotary motion. Sometimes you might need to add a little white spirit to prevent too-rapid drying on the plate or to produce a light wash. Apply a coat of colourless Ronseal to the work first, or variations in absorbency of the wood can produce uneven colouring. Shades can be gradually built up by applying a number of coats, allowing about six hours drying time between each. Very small quantities of pigmented Ronseal can be stored for a few days without drying out by putting them in a small container with a lid in a domestic deep-freeze. Ronseal is liable to dry out and become unusable before the tin is half-empty if it is used frequently in small quantities, and you can also prevent this by storing it immediately after use in the deep freeze. To obtain white or very pale shades, modify the process by adding an opaque white pigment to obscure the natural colour of the wood. Titanium dioxide is best for this, used very sparingly.

Mounting

Blocks of 'Oasis' (a green absorbent material) are often used for mounting flowers, and you can imitate this with a suitably-shaped block of soft wood such as lime, textured over the surface with a glass-engraving bit in a Burgess engraver. Then colour it to match the shade of 'Oasis'.

When the flower arrangement has been decided, holes are drilled to take the stems, and these are glued in position.

Mounting small flowers such as almond blossom on a twig is done by drilling $\frac{1}{16}$in holes in the twig and working the short stems to fit.

And well may your garden grow! ■

● Monolite pigments from I.C.I. Ltd (Organics Division), Sales Division, Smith's Rd, Bolton BL3 2QJ.
● Titanium dioxide from British Titan Products Co. Ltd, 10 Stratton St, London NW1.

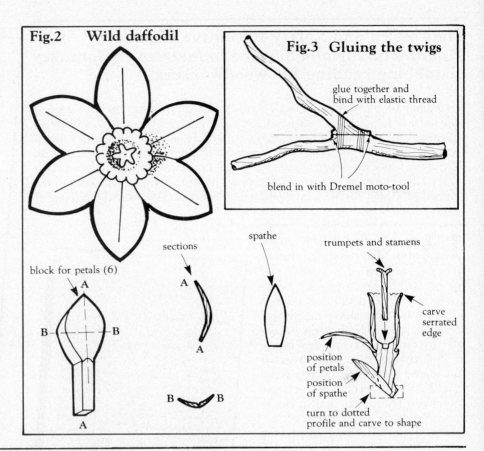

Fig.2 Wild daffodil

Fig.3 Gluing the twigs
glue together and bind with elastic thread
blend in with Dremel moto-tool

block for petals (6)
sections
spathe
trumpets and stamens
carve serrated edge
position of petals
position of spathe
turn to dotted profile and carve to shape

Not so dusty?

The Health and Safety Executive Report
***Manufacturing and Service Industries 1984*, makes
disturbing reading for woodworkers**

*'Two young people were working for a self-employed furniture restorer. He had a
wide range of woodworking machines, some of which were rarely used, with many
unguarded danger points. The major concern was the use of a home-made radiant
heater for flashing off solvents from french-polished furniture. The element of an
electric fire was screwed to a piece of timber approximately the size and shape of a
cricket bat. The element was completely unguarded and was held near to the
polished furniture. An immediate prohibition notice was served and the drying of
french polish is now carried out more safely.'*

13 people died in the timber
and timber-related manu-
facturing industries in 1984, and
six in 1983. The statistics break
down in more detail, of course;
40% of woodworking machinery
accidents in an H&SE study occurred on circular sawing machines;
in 57% of the cases, the inspector
considered the accident was because
guards had been removed or were
defective. There was a dispropor-
tionately high percentage of accidents in small firms employing
up to 25 people.

What about dust?

*'Exposure to wood dust has received
particular attention during the year
because of concern about potential long-
term effects on health,'* says the Report.
*'The problem . . . was most acute in
factories manufacturing reproduction
furniture and generally employing fewer
than 30 people. Inspectors found dust
accumulations on floors three and four
inches deep, piles of shavings several feet
in depth and ledges and fittings covered
with up to seven inches of dust.'* Credit
where it's due — six High Wycombe
factories, inspected in 1977 and 1983,
showed a 'statistically significant decline in
exposure to wood dust'.

The H&SE Woodworking National Industry Group has produced a leaflet on the
subject — a Guide for Employers. The whole
theme of the H&SE's work is that it's up to
the employer to provide safe working conditions. **But:** real detail on the actual hazards
that face the woodworker — self-employed,
small professional, semi-professional and
indeed the enthusiastic amateur — is lacking.
*'Exposure has been associated with the follow-
ing health hazards,'* the leaflet warns; *'● skin
problems ● obstruction of the nose ● asthma
● a rare type of cancer of the nose.'* And, of
course, fire and explosion.

In November's *Woodworker*, we appealed
for a medical angle. Someone out there, we
reasoned, must be a doctor and a reader
who loves wood and woodwork; and **Dr
Bob Clewlow** has replied.

● *The report – does it tell you enough?*

Disc 1 File D
Woodworker January No. 21
Letters
9 on 9½ Goudy to 13½ems

I HAVE BEEN much interested in recent
articles and comments about dust hazards.
I've had to stop working with yew
because the dust always causes me severe
headaches, nausea and chest pains, which
can persist for several weeks. I began to
notice that with each successive exposure
the symptoms became worse, and could
only assume the effect was cumulative. I
concluded that it would be wise to think of
the problem not as an allergy but as
permanent damage.

Although it's always wise to wear a dust-
mask, fine particles remain floating long
after the mask is removed. The main effort
must be to collect the dust effectively at
source. Vacuum-cleaners and dust-
extractors with nozzles close to the source
will remove most of the fine dust which is
the main hazard.

May I recommend some very informative
reading on the subject? 'Toxic Woods' by
Brian Woods and O. P. Galnan,
supplement 13 to the British Journal of
Dermatology, vol. 95, 1976, Blackwell.
Ken Keleher, Whitby

● *Yew dust – readers' letters continue*

WORKING WOOD — AND BREATHING IT

Dr Bob Clewlow deals in depth with the hazard to your health

The traditional image of
woodworking is not usually
associated with industrial disease.
The odd gash or bruise is all the
traditional joiner working with plane,
chisel and mallet expected, but the
introduction of lesser-known timbers,
manufactured boards, and sophisticated
power tools has brought previously

unsuspected dangers to health. Industrial
users are strictly governed by safety
regulations, but the personal
responsibility that these regulations
demand is often neglected — or worse,
ignored — by small businesses and
owners of home workshops.

Any cutting of timber inevitably
produces particles of waste wood. Their
size depends on the nature of the wood
and the operation. In general, the harder
the wood, the finer the dust; routing,
bandsawing, and, obviously, sanding all
produce a very fine waste, which in the
case of sanding is probably mixed with
abrasive powder too. Many power tools
and woodworking machinery generate a
draught which causes the fine dust to be
whipped up into a highly penetrating
aerosol suspension, and it's in this state
that the dust can be damaging. There's
no reason to believe that poisonous fruit
in a timber species leads to a more toxic
dust. Yew and laburnum both produce
toxic berries, but there is no evidence
that their dust is any more toxic than
other timbers. Certain species produce
toxic vapours while they're being
worked; teak can give off an irritating
vapour when friction-heated during
turning, and cocus wood (once used
extensively to make spinning shuttles in
the cotton trade) gives off a volatile
alkaloid when worked, which has an
excessive slowing effect on the heart-rate.

In the early days of mechanisation and
automation in the furniture industry,
workers displayed a very much higher
incidence of nasal cancer, especially
around High Wycombe. The now-
widespread use of efficient dust
extraction plant has minimised this
problem, and I don't think there is a
significant risk to the small workshop user.

The major problems that result from wood dust come generally under two headings: the direct irritating effect, and the effects produced in sensitive subjects. The direct effects are likely to affect anyone coming into contact with dust; the particles enter the nose and pharynx through inhalation, and get in the eyes, when they can cause severe irritation and conjunctival reactions. This can be counteracted by using close-fitting goggles, and a Martindales face mask for particularly dusty operations. Sensitivity to wood dust can produce a severe swelling of the eyelids which may persist for some days and is likely to recur on subsequent exposure.

Skin contact can cause sensitivity problems, and avoidance is difficult. It's hardly practical to carry out the majority of woodworking operations in protective gloves. There are two main types of skin problem associated with handling sensitising substances. The first is an acute sensitivity reaction, when the skin develops a red, raised, itchy blistering rash similar to nettle rash, and is more likely to be due to a direct reaction to oils or resins in the wood than to an allergy. This sort of reaction settles fairly easily with homely remedies. The second type of reaction is more long-standing, and is due to prolonged exposure to one type of dust, to which the worker becomes sensitised. A chronic dry dermatitis then develops, often with cracking and fissures in the skin. This is much more difficult to treat, and requires the attention of a doctor. If it occurs at work, it could be recognised as an industrial dermatitis and thus qualify for industrial compensation. Skin sensitivity problems are not common in wood-handlers, and species likely to cause problems are those producing a very fine dust, for example ebony and rosewood. Interestingly, clarinet players may get reactions in their lips from sensitivity to the grenadilla wood used for reeds. Wood dust and shavings that have been standing for a long period can become damp and form an ideal home for mites. These tiny creatures cause rashes by biting those handling infested material, so this too presents a minor irritation.

Sensitivity to wood dust causes the most serious problems in the respiratory tract, where the damage caused by inhalation of the aerosol-fine dust is worst. The different sections of the lining of the respiratory system, which runs from the nose to the final honeycomb tissues of the lungs themselves, respond differently to toxic substances.

The upper levels are lined with mucous and hair-cells which trap and eliminate foreign particles. The acute feeling of congestion in the head, sneezing and running catarrh that you get when dust enters the nose and throat is because these cells have been temporarily immobilised.

Further down the respiratory tree, in the small air passages, the response is a different one. Here the walls of the small air-tubes are lined with a muscle coat, and the presence of foreign matter, especially organic, causes an allergic constriction of the muscle tubes and a possible attack of bronchial asthma. The sufferer need not necessarily be allergic, though he or she usually would be, and would also need to have been exposed to similar sensitising material in the past. Long-continued exposure to small amounts of organic dust can produce a chronic 'late onset' asthma, which causes persistent shortage of breath, and occurs especially on working days. Asthma due to inhalation of organic dust at work is also now recognised in certain groups of workers as a notifiable industrial disease.

There is a whole group of diseases, known as the **pneumoconioses**, which are a result of dust in the final saccular portions of the lung tissue. Here the response to foreign substances is different again. Cells known as **macrophages** in the tissues absorb the foreign particles, and in doing so generate inflammation, the nature of which depends on the

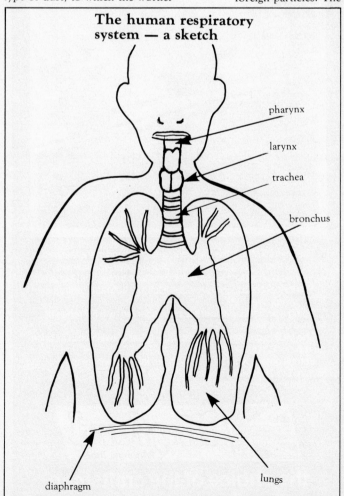

The human respiratory system — a sketch

pharynx

larynx

trachea

bronchus

diaphragm

lungs

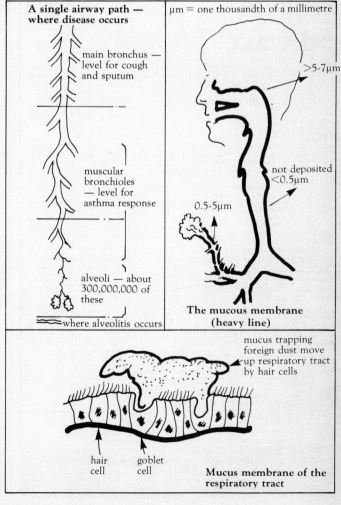

A single airway path — where disease occurs

main bronchus — level for cough and sputum

muscular bronchioles — level for asthma response

alveoli — about 300,000,000 of these

where alveolitis occurs

μm = one thousandth of a millimetre

>5-7μm

not deposited <0.5μm

0.5-5μm

The mucous membrane (heavy line)

mucus trapping foreign dust move up respiratory tract by hair cells

hair cell

goblet cell

Mucus membrane of the respiratory tract

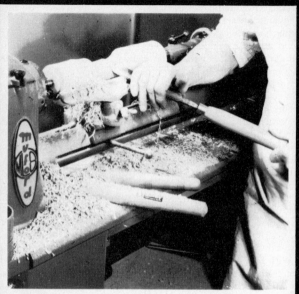
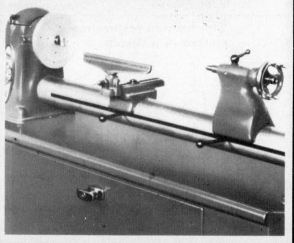

Not so dusty?

inhaled matter. The damage caused by the inhalation of foreign matter depends upon various factors:
- The size of the particle (0.5-5µm)
- The density of the particle in the inhaled air
- The chemical nature of the particle
- Individual tolerance
- Allergic tendency in the person exposed
- Previous exposure to the substance.

Because of the varied chemical structure of wood dusts, there is no constant clinical picture for wood dust pneumoconiosis. There have been reports of dust diseases arising from the inhalation of the dust of mahogany, oak and iroko, but blood tests on the sufferers failed to reveal any allergy to the timber itself. Most allergies to timber or its products are in the group known as **extrinsic allergic alveolitis.** This is a massive inflammatory response in the lung tissues, occurring about eight hours after exposure, and appearing as an acute respiratory difficulty with chest-pains and aching limbs. Although the acute stage may settle quite rapidly, breathlessness and cough may persist for weeks or months, and may progress to permanent lung damage. It's a similar condition to that which occurs in farmer's lung, and results from inhalation of fungus spores in timber. Investigation of the victims very often shows their blood to have antibodies to microscopic fungi in the material they handle. The description given by the correspondent mentioned in 'This Month', *Woodworker* Nov. 85, of his troubles turning an old piece of yew sounds very much like this condition, and could well be explained by his old and dusty timber. Because of the potential in these sorts of disorders for permanent and serious chest disease, it's

important for anyone with respiratory problems who is exposed to wood dust to seek medical advice quickly and to tell the doctor that dust inhalation might be a cause of the symptoms.

Many workshop hazards are self-evident, and with reasonable methods can be avoided or eliminated. It seems that medical authorities in the past have failed to recognise the possible hazards of wood dust, or they have been overlooked on the shop floor (except by industrial timber users). It's more than possible that wood dust can prove a health risk not only for those with allergic tendencies or chest disease, but for healthy people too.

Some protection can be given by commercial face-masks, but many of the smaller particles can pass through their pores. Dust extraction machinery is hardly practicable for the home user, though it may suit the small commercial workshop. If you experience serious chest problems on exposure to wood dust, you should seek medical advice and be sure to point out the nature of the exposure. If you do have serious chest disease, you'll have to avoid that particular timber; you might even have to avoid wood dust altogether, which means — god forbid — you might have to give up woodwork; unless, of course, you can come up with strictly dust-free techniques! ∎

References
Franklin, *Medicine* Oct 82
Hutchinson, *Health in Industry* (Penguin)
Oxford Textbook of Medicine
Schleuter, Fink et al, *Annals Int. Medicine*, 77, p.907
J. Slavin, *Allergy & Clinical Immunology*, 1978
Turner Warwick, *Thoracic Medicine*.

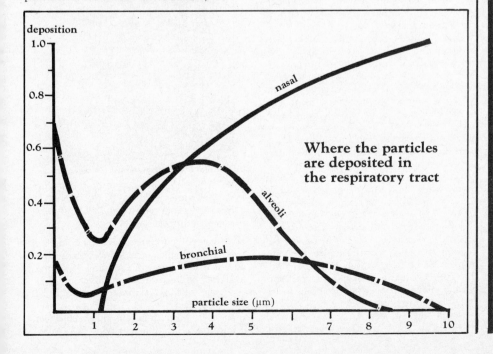

deposition

Where the particles are deposited in the respiratory tract

nasal

alveoli

bronchial

particle size (µm)

MACHINING
WOOD

PART 4

YOUR EXPERT GUIDE

THE BANDSAW
Economical, versatile, and (comparatively!) safe — the bandsaw is many a woodworker's first and only piece of workshop machinery. Here are some of the many ways it can be used

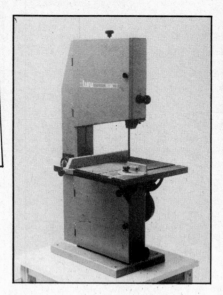

● A two-wheel machine offers you greater capacity and easier blade adjustment, at the expense of price and space. **Right:** doors open to reveal the works

While sawing in a straight line is basic to all wood-machining, there comes a point when the woodworker wants a free hand. The bandsaw is the machine that allows you to wander from the straight and narrow in order to cut curves, circles and odd-shaped patterns, as well as the familiar straight line.

Bandsaws come in all sizes. Larger models are floor-standing, smaller ones can be bench-mounted, and a 'small' two-wheeled type like the one in the photographs is best mounted on a low table. Whatever the size, they all operate on the same principle: a narrow steel band with one cutting edge runs continuously around two (or three) large rubber-lined wheels; the saw, held under tension, cuts as the lower, driving wheel (usually mounted directly on the motor) pulls it down through the workpiece.

The top wheel is adjustable, and getting its position right is essential. Before you start work, read the manufacturer's instructions carefully and make sure you know how to make all the adjustments.

Setting up

The tension of the blade is dependent on the position of the top wheel, usually adjusted by a knob on top of the machine. The tension should allow about 6mm (¼in) sideways movement of the blade (either side of the centre) when you hold it on the upward (outside) run and move it from side to side. This is so for all-size blades, apart from the massive industrial ones which need 9mm movement. Have the upper guard raised to maximum height to check the tension. Correct blade tension is very important: if it's too loose, the blade will wander, or worse, come off the wheels; if it's too tight,

it will snap, usually at the point where the two ends of the band are welded together. Raise or lower the top wheel to achieve the right tension, and remember that saws that have been broken and repaired will be shorter, so the top wheel will need to come down a bit.

The tracking of the blade needs a careful eye to check that the blade always runs over the central part of the wheel, known as the crown. Turn the wheel by hand to ensure that the tracking is consistently central throughout the wheel movement; don't adjust it with the machine running under power. A knob in the back of the top-wheel housing tips the wheel back or forth. Also be sure that the thrust-wheels and blade-guides aren't bearing on the blade when you check the tracking.

Once blade tension and tracking are checked and adjusted, you must set the blade-guides and thrust-wheels, or bearings, above and below the table. This setting should be checked each time you use the bandsaw and whenever you make any other changes or adjustments to the wheels and blades; there are various designs of guide and bearings, which usually need an Allen key or a spanner to set them. Remove the guards, and set the thrust-bearings 1mm behind the blade. The blade should touch them when it's cutting, with enough pressure to make them turn: if the blade is set too tight against them, they will score, and the blade will overheat; if it doesn't touch the thrust-wheels, the blade will be bending too much. Set the guides fractionally off the body of the blade, just behind the gullets of the teeth. They prevent wander; make sure there's no rubbing from one side or the other.

Keep the upper thrust-and-guide assembly as close to the workpiece as you

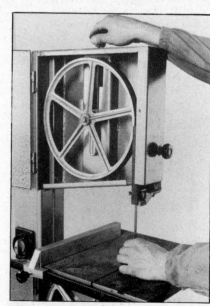

● Adjusting the blade tension with the knob on top. Hold the blade mid-way between table and top-guard; it should move about ¼in either way

can when you cut. It helps accuracy, and is a precaution against accidents, because the guards usually move up and down with the assembly to keep the blade covered.

These setting procedures should be followed carefully. Adjusting two-wheel models is easier than it is on three-wheel machines, which can be tricky. Generally,

● *All switches off? Then spin the wheel by hand to see how the blade tracks. A knob at the back adjusts*

three-wheel saws give greater throat-depth for smaller overall size, and they can accommodate wider pieces of wood than a two-wheel type of equal height. They are cheaper and usually less robust; more convenient for finer work, but if you can afford it, two wheels are better.

Blades

Selecting the right saw-blade is also important. In general terms, bigger pieces of wood need wider blades with fewer teeth per inch. The most commonly-used blades are in ¼, ½ and ¾in sizes (often metric), though anything from 3mm to 20mm is available. Narrower blades with more tpi are best for small, thin workpieces and for cutting curves, while the wider blades are better for straight and deep cuts. Blades with hardened teeth are getting quite common now, which last well but can't be sharpened — when they're blunt you bin them. It's a matter of taste which you use, but don't try sharpening and setting bandsaw blades until you're very experienced indeed!

Bandsaw wheels move quite slowly, but the critical factor in cutting speed is the speed of the teeth past a given point — the 'surface speed'. 2000m/min is optimum, but this will vary with motor speed and blade size.

To get the best result, you should have at least three teeth in the workpiece — to cut a ½in board for instance, use a blade with six to eight tpi. In any case, the thickness of the workpiece should always be more than the pitch of (the distance between) the teeth. The main problem with fine blades is that the sawdust doesn't clear and the blade can clog up. Choosing too fine a blade can also cause it to wander, especially ripping along the grain. Other causes of poor cuts from wandering blades are insufficient blade tension, feeding the work too quickly, incorrect setting of blade-guides and badly-set or sharpened teeth.

Cuts, fences and jigs

A major advantage of the bandsaw is that it can make much deeper cuts that a table-saw which with a 12in blade would only

● **Top:** *blade-guides should be fractionally off the blade;* **above and below:** *set the thrust-wheels about 1mm behind the blade*

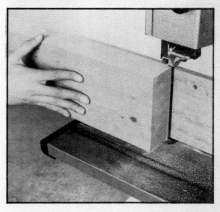

Top: *crosscutting: note the blade-guide assembly close to the wood.* **Above:** *deep cutting with a high auxiliary fence*

have a maximum depth of cut of about 4in (102mm). A medium-size floor-standing two-wheel machine will cut to a depth of 10 or 11in (255-275mm). Bandsaws are good for cutting veneers or slicing pieces where you need to make maximum use of the thickness, since the narrow kerf of the blade allows you to cut very economically.

The bandsaw is popular with carvers and woodturners, who use it for preliminary roughing out, or cutting a blank ready for the lathe. Tilting work-tables also provide a speedy method of making compound mitres, although some loss of accuracy inevitably results from not having such a solid blade.

'Spelch' (breakout) is rarely a problem with the bandsaw since the teeth are comparatively fine and the blades thin. When it does happen, check the wooden insert in the the table. If it's worn, renewing it will help. When you are cutting curves, work out the line carefully in relation to grain direction, because cutting across too much short grain will make a rough finish and possibly a weak component.

The bandsaw can be used for plastics, metal, and other materials with the right blade; it is a comparatively safe machine, but don't be lulled into forming careless habits. Always use pushsticks when practicable, especially during ripping.

For ripping tall pieces or cutting veneers off blocks, a high false fence — accurately squared — should be attached to the rip-fence of the bandsaw table. With deep cuts like these, the wood *must* be fed relatively slowly towards the blade because the large amount of sawdust in the cut needs time to clear. Develop a sense of blade sympathy; if you feed the work too fast, overheating may result.

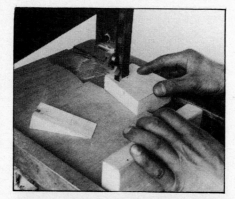

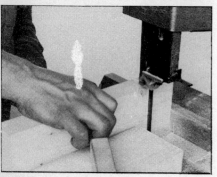

● **Top row, left to right:** *compound mitres are possible, but not so accurate as with a table-saw. Make a jig with two or three steps in it for wedges of different lengths; and use a strong V-jig for cutting your firewood!*

● **Bottom row, left to right:** *cutting tenons needs a wide blade for vertical accuracy. Set a stop and cut the shoulders; reset it, and use an auxiliary fence for the cheeks so the waste won't jam; re-set for the haunches*

When cutting tenons, accuracy is of prime importance. These points will help.
● Use a wide blade for vertical consistency and accuracy.
● Cut the shoulders first, using a block clamped to the table as a length-stop.
● Re-set the saw to cut the cheeks, remembering which side of the blade you are measuring to and which side you are cutting to. Clamp the block on to the table to act as a stop, but not where it will get in the way of the offcuts. Set an auxiliary fence in line with a point just past the back of the blade to ensure that the offcuts from the tenon-cheeks move safely away.

It's a good idea to cut a haunch on the top or bottom of the tenon, again using the auxiliary fence and the clamped block as a length-stop. This gives more strength to joints at the corners of any kind of frame that takes some strain.

The bandsaw's controllability and comparative 'finger-friendliness' makes it a good machine for making cuts at angles to the grain — wedges and tapers, for example. Wedges are easily made using a notched jig and a wide piece of short-grained wood. Place the wood in the notch of the jig and slide the two towards the blade, the jig against the rip-fence. The blade will cut off a small long-grained wedge, the grain running from the narrow to the wide end. Turn the main piece over after each cut to get a series of identical wedges.

Remember — when using jigs near the blade, make sure that nails and screws are well clear of its path.

Curved work

You can make light work of copying curves as well as cutting them. Cut the first curve freehand. If it's relatively shallow, it can be copied very easily by using the auxiliary fence. Set it so it is only a tooth's depth past the front of the blade, leaving a gap of the required width. Feed the curved edge of the workpiece through the gap between the fence and the blade, pressing the curved edge continuously against the fence, which should be the only point of contact.

When you cut irregular stock, there's always a risk that the workpiece will trap in the blade as there is no flat side to press on to the table. For safety's sake as well as for accuracy, it is essential to place the stock in a V-groove jig with wedges to support it. You'll have to go through the front edge of the jig, obviously, so make it strong enough to hold together from the back.

Cutting circles and rings can also be done neatly on the bandsaw, with a little thoughtful preparation. Clamp a baseboard to the work-table; if possible, use an exact square as the workpiece and find its central point by drawing its diagonals. Then pin or secure the central point of the square to the baseboard so that it rotates on top and overhangs slightly on one side. Set the workpiece and baseboard on the table so that the shortest distance from the centre of the workpiece (the middle of a side, not a corner) overhangs the edge of the baseboard and touches the bandsaw blade. Feed the wood carefully towards the blade by

rotating it around the central point. Careful feeding is vital here; if you try to go too fast the blade will twist, and apart from not cutting an accurate circle, it's likely to snap.

If the workpiece is not square, pin through a point as near to the centre as you can get to the baseboard. Then set it on the table so the blade will first cut the side which is the shortest distance from the centre. You must use the side nearest to the centre, or, the blade will fail to cut a perfect circle because the other sides of the workpiece won't reach it.

Wooden rings are cut from circles. Mark an inner circle on a circular blank to give the ring width, then cut through the ring area along the grain, and cut round the inner circle. The central waste area will then drop out. A cut-through point running along the grain will glue back together strongly, but insert a strip of veneer or wood the same width as the kerf in order to keep the ring's shape as accurate as possible.

Tight curves and internal corners can be tackled in several ways on the bandsaw; see the table for the tightest radius a given width of blade will cope with. The most common method of cutting a tight curve is to take little bites back and forth to ensure that the blade has enough room to go round the final tight curve. A warning — don't pull back too far in a cut, or try to pull the blade right out of a cut; you'll pull the blade off the wheels. For perfect internal corners, first cut along the straight lines going into the workpiece. Then make a curve round the first corner (again making several small cuts if necessary) and cut along the back internal line into the second corner. Remove the tiny waste piece left from the curve in the first corner with a final straight cut along the back line to meet the cut already made.

Copying curved shapes where an internal curve comes between two external ones can present problems. The straight fence used in the method of copying simple curves won't allow for internal curvature, so the first step is to cut a curved fence with a tighter radius than the one you are trying to copy. The greater curvature provides space to manoeuvre the workpiece round the fence as you feed it into and away from the blade. Mark an arrow on the jig to show the point nearest to the blade, and set this arrow just 2mm (or the depth of the teeth) from the near edge of the blade. Feed the curved edge of the workpiece towards the blade, pressing continuously against the arrow marked on the jig. This must be the only point of contact throughout the cutting procedure in order to achieve maximum accuracy. Even so, this method is really only good enough for rough copies.

The bandsaw is also useful for cutting curves in two planes, for example, when making cabriole legs or cutting carving blanks. Again careful preparation will make the process simple and safe. The first step is to mark out two profiles of curves or shapes on squared paper. Transfer the curves to two adjoining sides of the workpiece, and cut out the curve on one side; then pin back the waste in its original position, making sure that there are no pins likely to foul the blade on the second cut. Cut the other profile. Pinning back the waste like this makes it easier to get an accurate second cut, as you are still working with a flat-edged workpiece. ∎

Blade width in mm	Minimum cutting radius
6	20
10	45
12.5	55
16	75
20	100
25	180
32	260
40	380

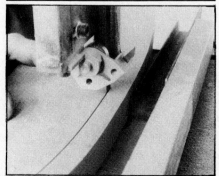
● *Once you have a curve, reproducing it (fairly roughly) is no problem with the auxiliary fence*

● *Cutting curves freehand is best controlled with the workpiece firmly held at both ends*

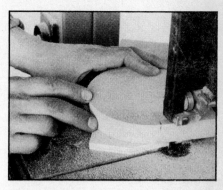
● *Above: a circle-cutting jig. Centre the blank so the blade just cuts the flat sides, and line the centre up with the front of the blade*

*T*his series was written by Judith Barker. Ken Taylor of the London College of Furniture checked it for completeness and accuracy. Aidan Walker planned it and demonstrated the techniques. Derek Wales took the pictures. But Luna Tools and Machinery made it possible. They provided vital financial support – and for photography and demonstration they lent their machines, their space, and the help and advice of staff member Joe Wickens. So we give our warmest thanks to Luna's MD Gerry Baker for his unhesitating and generous co-operation. Luna are at 20 Denbigh Hall, Bletchley, Milton Keynes, Bucks MK3 7QT, tel. Milton Keynes (0908) 70771.

● *Above: for rings, scribe a circle using your marked centre, and cut on to it through long grain. Glue it up with a piece of veneer*

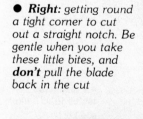
● *Right: getting round a tight corner to cut out a straight notch. Be gentle when you take these little bites, and **don't** pull the blade back in the cut*

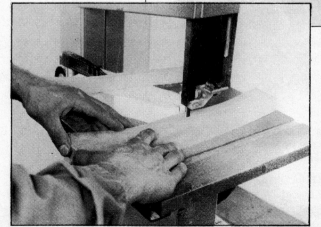

● *Left: reproducing compound curves needs a curved 'fence' of tighter radius than any of the ones on your workpiece*

128

Three legs and a paintbox

Have easel, will travel: two ingenious devices for outdoor arts-and-craftspeople.

Bill Walker's box easel solves a painter's luggage problems

Many people — myself included — paint for a hobby, and attend outdoor summer courses and painting holidays. I've tried to cut down on the amount of gear I lug about on outdoor painting trips by making this combined box and easel. The original has been modified in minor details since it was first made, but this is the basic idea; you will be able to make your own improvements. The commercial type of box easel is quite expensive to buy; I used second-hand wood, some old oak table-legs and a piece of walnut (acquired long ago) for the box. The only things I bought were the coach-bolts and case-clips — even the handle was second-hand.

If you intend to make it well, it's a nice little job for an experienced woodworker, or it would be a good 'design-and-make' test of skill for a beginner.

In this form the easel can take a canvas or board up to 750x600mm (30x24in), and adjust to almost any angle. The legs can be adjusted for standing or sitting. The sizes and design details can be varied to suit individual requirements.

1 Prepare the front, back and the two sides as pairs.
2 Trim the endgrain to exact length on the shooting board.
3 Mark out the dovetail joints, rebates and gauge the cut-off line for the lid (fig. 2).
4 Cut the dovetail joints and the rebates.
5 Assemble the parts dry and test the diagonals for squareness.
6 Clean up the inside surfaces and seal with polyurethane lacquer. When this has dried hard (at least 24 hours),
7 Glue up the carcase with urea formaldehyde resin adhesive.
8 Test for squareness and winding, and leave to set.

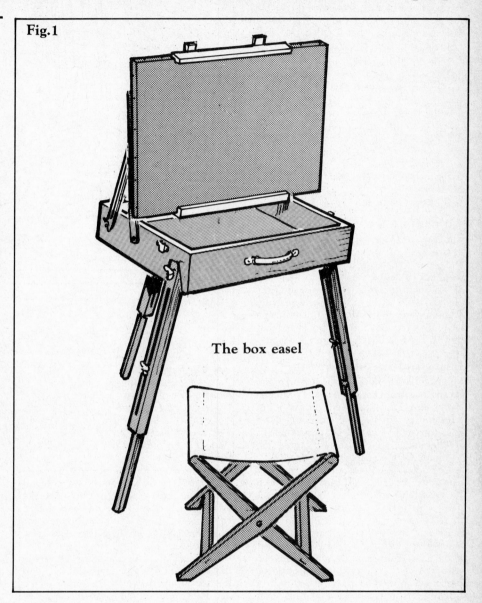

Fig.1

The box easel

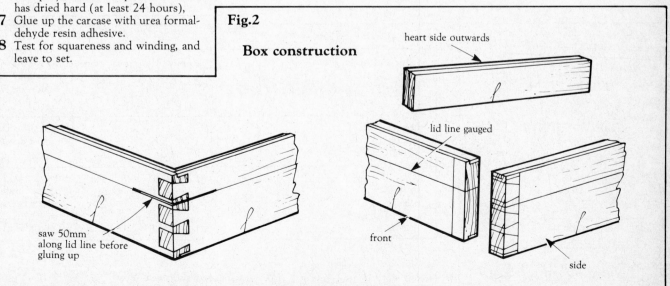

Fig.2

Box construction

heart side outwards

lid line gauged

front

side

saw 50mm along lid line before gluing up

Three legs and a paintbox

● One tip worth remembering — saw about 50mm along the gauged lid-line at each end of all four pieces *before* the box is glued up. This makes cutting off the lid a lot easier later on.

9 After the carcase has set, prepare and fit the plywood top and bottom.

10 Clean up and seal the inside surfaces before fixing with glue, and brass pins punched in.

11 Fill the pin-holes with coloured hard wax stopping.

12 Clean up the outside of the box all round and finish with two or three coats of lacquer.

13 Finally, separate the lid by sawing along the previously gauged line with a fine tenon or dovetail saw.

Adjustable legs

The slots in the top leg sections can be made in two ways.

● Use a portable router to cut grooves from both sides (fig. 4B), or:

● The hand-tool method is to use a fillister plane to build up the section as shown in fig. 4A. Finish all the parts with polyurethane lacquer, wire wool and wax polish, so that they slide smoothly and will not jam in use.

Easel and lid adjustment

Make a full-size mock-up of one end of the box and lid from hardwood or ply offcuts. With thin strips screwed on, you can determine where the hinging- and adjusting-strips should be positioned to give the range of adjustment required (fig. 5). Some experimentation is necessary!

The adjustable holder for the board or canvas can be made to fit in the lid, and it can be left in position when the lid is closed. The constructional details are shown in fig. 3.

As with the legs, all the parts should be smoothly finished, lacquered and wax-polished to ensure smooth adjustments. To minimise wear, it's advisable to bush the bolt-holes in the box with a short piece of brass tubing. It should be a tight fit, but it can be glued in with epoxy resin adhesive.

As the box doesn't have conventional hinges, four case-clips are used to secure the lid when it's closed. The legs and slotted adjusting-strips pack inside the box for transport, along with the palette, paint-box and brushes.

To assemble the easel, sit down with the box on your knees, open the lid and bolt on the legs. When they have been adjusted for height, fit the slotted adjusting-strips to each side and adjust the lid position ■

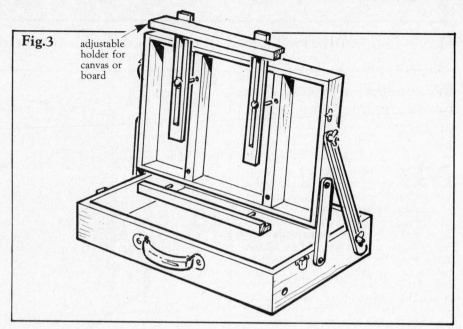

Fig.3 adjustable holder for canvas or board

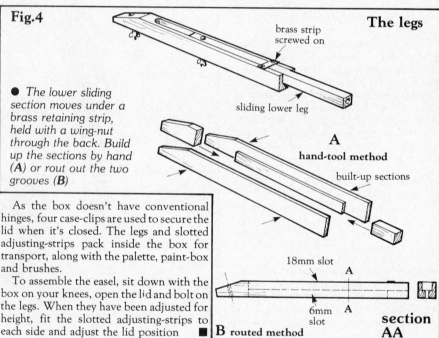

Fig.4

The legs

brass strip screwed on

sliding lower leg

● *The lower sliding section moves under a brass retaining strip, held with a wing-nut through the back. Build up the sections by hand (A) or rout out the two grooves (B)*

A

hand-tool method

built-up sections

18mm slot

6mm slot

B routed method

section AA

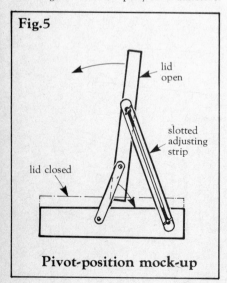

Fig.5

lid open

slotted adjusting strip

lid closed

Pivot-position mock-up

Cutting list — thicknesses net

Box					
front and back	2	450mm x	100mm x	10mm	mahogany
ends	2	400	100	10	mahogany
top and bottom	2	450	400	4	WBP ply
Legs					
upper	3	450	35	35	oak or beech
sliding lower	3	450	20	20	oak or beech
Easel parts					
lid reinforcers	2	400	20	20	oak or beech
slotted	2	350	20	6	oak or beech
rebated	2	350	30	20	oak or beech
Adjusting-strips (slotted)	2	350	20	6	oak or beech
Hinge-strips	2	200	15	6	oak or beech

6 off 50x6mm coach-bolts, washers and wing-nuts
6 off 35x4mm coach-bolts, washers and wing-nuts
4 case-clips, 1 attache-case handle, brass screws and panel pins

Four legs and an easel

And next we have the artist's donkey — a beast of burden with the canvas where the carrot should be. Graham Greenhalgh explains

My father has been a commercial artist for most of his working life, and having retired from illustrating children's books, he decided to 'do some good watercolours'. Having conceived this plan, he asked me to make him an artist's donkey.

You may not have any idea of what such an animal looks like, but I had at least a vague one. I agreed to have a go if he could do me a sketch. He went one better and furnished an artist's catalogue with photos. If anyone reading this thinks materials are expensive in the woodworking game, I suggest they acquire an artist's catalogue. I think donkey prices had something to do with him asking me to make one! To be fair, he did say as I studied photographs and prices, that any old thing would do. I couldn't think of anything that had four legs and an easel except an artist's donkey.

Now came the task of finding some suitable timber. If I could salvage some from an old piece of furniture, it would level the score on the money side; after all, you can't really charge a retired father for something he's always wanted.

I remembered an old wardrobe lying in a friend's workshop, and went to see if it suited the purpose and if I could get it cheap (or free, to be honest). It was solid oak, but at least I didn't have to pay for it. I wouldn't have chosen oak for this particular job, which I think mahogany would do better.

My next task was designing this four-legged oddity. There are two types of donkey, with fixed and folding legs. I decided on the latter. The artist's catalogue provided the overall sizes; length 40in, width 11in, height 17in. The only other thing my father asked for was that the easel could be set vertical almost instantaneously so he could run a wash over the paper. You'll see from the photos and drawing that I decided on a very simple drop-in easel. If it had been for oil painting, I would have had to add a central slat with a top sliding block to grip a canvas. If you want to modify the design, there should be no problem adding the block to the water-colour easel, or even hinging the easel to fold flat on to the top.

The main frame is dovetailed as shown. Square fillets are fixed to the inside, glued and screwed to carry the top. The top was just glued and clamped in and left to dry overnight. The legs are tapered on the inside and were more difficult than I expected to assemble. I found the best way was to clamp the legs to the top flush with the bottom edge, then it was quite easy to screw the stretchers on to the legs, using epoxy glue and screw-cups to avoid the stretcher-ends splitting. For the other parts I used water-

● *Something for the painter who blenches at catalogue prices. The donkey is well-designed and quite simple, but includes the odd tricky detail*

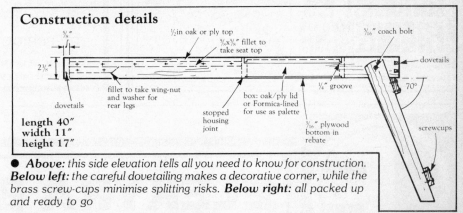

Construction details

⅝"

2⅜"

½in oak or ply top

⅝x⅝" fillet to take seat top

⁵⁄₁₆" coach bolt

dovetails

fillet to take wing-nut and washer for rear legs

dovetails

stopped housing joint

box: oak/ply lid or Formica-lined for use as palette

¼" groove

⁵⁄₁₆" plywood bottom in rebate

70°

screwcups

length 40"
width 11"
height 17"

● *Above: this side elevation tells all you need to know for construction. Below left: the careful dovetailing makes a decorative corner, while the brass screw-cups minimise splitting risks. Below right: all packed up and ready to go*

proof cold-water glue (Cascamite).

As you see from the drawing I incorporated a small box with a sliding top, although this would be a matter of choice. If the donkey is to be used for oil painting, I think I would insert a piece of ¼in plywood into the top with white formica or something similar on both sides. It would act as a loose palette.

When fixing the legs to the top frame, place the legs in the open position and panel-pin them to the top instead of drilling. When you close the legs, you may find they bind on the back of the top stretcher. Adjust the position with a piece

of cardboard and clamp them again in the same way as for assembly. Now drill a ⁵⁄₁₆in hole for the coach-bolts and wing-nut. You will need longer bolts for the back legs to get through the extra fillet that you'll need to give the bolt-and-wing-nut proper strength.

The easel is a simple half-lapped affair with a rebated bottom glued and clamped on. The ⅜x⅜in rebate allows for various thicknesses of ply to be used by the artist.

The whole donkey was given a couple of coats of silk finish polyurethane after I'd taken all the sharp corners from the top with a light to medium garnet paper — it wouldn't do for Dad to get a pain! ■

Photos Alex Allison

132

Screwing the unscrewable ___

WOODWORKING WHEEZE *of the* **month**

S ooner or later, writes **James Paffett**, we are faced with the problem of fastening something to slate, stone or some other intractable material. For example, how can we secure a polished wood plinth to the underside of an alabaster carving? Wouldn't it be nice if only we could form threaded holes in the stuff to take bolts or screws?

In fact, we can do just that quite easily by using polyester resin. We don't even need a tap to cut the thread. The steps are as follows:

1 Drill a clearance hole deep into the stone with a masonry drill, and clean out all the dust.

2 Carefully clean the thread of the screw, and coat it liberally with vaseline. Spread the grease uniformly by running a nut up and down the thread several times.

3 Support the stone, hole uppermost, and fill the hole with liquid polyester resin to which hardener has been added.

4 Drop the screw into the hole and wedge it centrally with pointed matchsticks. Wipe away excess liquid.

5 Allow at least an hour for the resin to set hard.

6 Unscrew the screw. It should come away with very little effort, leaving a perfectly-formed female thread cast in the resin. (Any reluctance to unscrew indicates inadequate greasing beforehand, or a malformed screw).

A screw can be repeatedly screwed and unscrewed from a resin-threaded hole, provided care is taken to avoid damaging the first turn or two of thread on initial entry. The pull-out strength is quite remarkable provided a reasonably coarse thread is used, such as Whitworth, and the hole is reasonably deep, say six screw diameters. For a 1/4in Whitworth screw a hole 1½in deep made with a 5/16in masonry drill is appropriate. Long screws can conveniently be cut from threaded studding, which can be bought by the yard, with a nut brazed on to form the head. Woodscrews are not really satisfactory because of the tapered form and unthreaded shank, but long parallel self-tappers work well enough.

Parallel-sided holes in stone are acceptable, as the shear adhesion between resin and stone seems to be very good. If strength is really critical, it may be reassuring to

● *Make sure it stays in place with a threaded screw – 18th-century sculptors may not have thought of it! (See 'MDF turns noble', p113)*

undercut the hole in the stone a little to stop the resin plug pulling out. This can be done, rather crudely, by rocking the drill about.

I have used this system to hold lumps of stone up to 30lb in weight during sculpturing operations, using a single 3/8in Whitworth bolt and the positioning device described in *Woodworker*, June 1984. Despite a great deal of hammering and rough treatment, I have never had a bolt fail.

The process is not confined to stone; it works well with wood and chipboard. There are times when a woodscrew cannot be made to bite properly — in endgrain, perhaps, or where a knot or splits come in the wrong place, or where a screw has pulled out leaving a ragged crater. In such a case we can drill or carve out an undercut hole, fill it with resin, and form a cast threaded hole in the manner described.

For thread-casting the resin can be used neat, or extended with wood or stone dust. When neat, it forms the threads more precisely, and probably makes for a stronger job; but a powder mix may be preferred if the resin plug is visible and needs to be matched with surrounding material. ■

● A suitable casting material is David's 'Fastglas' resin with 'Fastglas Blue Hardener', available from Halfords.

REMEMBER... *Woodworker* depends on woodworkers. We're willing and eager to tell the world what you're making, doing, exhibiting — even thinking. Our only aim is to produce the magazine you want to read. We're looking for photos, drawings (rough sketches will do) and words on any woodworking subject from ovolo mouldings to overhead routers. And we're on the end of the phone. We're waiting to hear from you!

Aidan Walker
Owen Watson

The quickest and easiest method of reaching all Woodworkers is to advertise in SHOP GUIDE.
Telephone Andrea Smith 01-437 0699 Rate: £12.00 per unit.
Minimum of 6 months

Key: **H** — Hand tools, **P** — Power tools, **W** — Woodworking machinery up to £1,000, **WM** — Woodworking machinery over £1,000,
D — Demonstration available on selected machines, **T** — Timber, **CS** — Cutting or sharpening services, **MF** — Material Finishes, **A** — Attachments
BC — Books/catalogues, ★ — Mail order, **E** — EMCO Leisure Centre. **K** — Kity Woodworking Centre.

AVON

BATH Tel. Bath 64513
JOHN HALL TOOLS
RAILWAY STREET ★

Open: Monday-Saturday
9.00 a.m.-5.30 p.m.
H.P.W.WM.D.A.BC.

BRISTOL Tel. (0272) 741510
JOHN HALL TOOLS LIMITED ★
CLIFTON DOWN SHOPPING CENTRE
WHITELADIES ROAD
Open: Monday-Saturday
9.00 a.m.-5.30 p.m.
H.P.W.WM.D.A.BC.

BRISTOL Tel. (0272) 629092
TRYMWOOD SERVICES
2a DOWNS PARK EAST, (off North View)
WESTBURY PARK
Open: 8.30 a.m.-5.30 p.m. Mon. to Fri.
Closed for lunch 1.00-2.00 p.m.
P.W.WM.D.T.A.BC.

BRISTOL Tel. (0272) 667013
FASTSET LTD
190-192 WEST STREET
BEDMINSTER
Open: Mon.-Fri. 8.30 a.m.-5.00 p.m.
Saturday 9.00 a.m.-1.00 p.m.
H.P.W.WM.D.CS.A.BC.

BRISTOL Tel. (0272) 667013
WILLIS
157 WEST STREET
BEDMINSTER
Open Mon.-Fri. 8.30 a.m.-5.00 p.m.
Sat. 9 a.m.-4 p.m.
P.W.WM.D.CS.A.BC.

BEDFORDSHIRE

BEDFORD Tel. (0234) 59808
BEDFORD SAW SERVICE K
39 AMPTHILL ROAD

Open: Mon.-Fri. 8.30-5.30
Sat. 9.00-4.00
H.P.A.BC.W.CS.WM.D.

BERKSHIRE

COOKHAM Tel. (06285) 20350
CHURCH'S TIMBER
STATION HILL

Open: Mon-Sat 8.30 a.m.-5.30 p.m.
Wed 8.30 a.m.-1.00 p.m.
H.P.W.T.CS.MF.A.

READING Tel. (0734) 591361
HOME CARE CENTRE
26/30 KING'S ROAD

Open: Monday-Saturday
9.00 a.m.-5.30 p.m.
H.P.W.D.A.WM.BC.

BERKSHIRE

READING Tel. Littlewick Green
DAVID HUNT (TOOL 2743
MERCHANTS) LTD ★
KNOWL HILL, NR. READING
Open: Monday-Saturday
9.00 a.m.-5.30 p.m.
H.P.W.D.A.BC.

READING Tel. Reading 661511
WOKINGHAM TOOL CO. LTD.
99 WOKINGHAM ROAD

Open: Mon-Sat 9.00 a.m.-5.30 p.m.
Closed 1.00-2.00 p.m. for lunch
H.P.W.WM.D.CS.A.BC.

BUCKINGHAMSHIRE

SLOUGH Tel. (06286) 5125
BRAYWOOD ESTATES LTD ★
158 BURNHAM LANE

Open: 9.00 a.m.-5.30 p.m.
Monday-Saturday
H.P.W.WM.CS.A.

MILTON KEYNES Tel. (0908)
POLLARD WOODWORKING 641366
CENTRE ★
51 AYLESBURY ST., BLETCHLEY
Open: Mon-Fri 8.30-5.30
Saturday 9.00-5.00
H.P.W.WM.D.CS.A.BC.

HIGH WYCOMBE Tel. (0494)
SCOTT SAWS LTD. 24201/33788
14 BRIDGE STREET ★

Mon.-Sat. 8.30 a.m.-6.00 p.m.

H.P.W.WM.D.T.CS.MF.A.BC.

HIGH WYCOMBE Tel. (0494)
ISAAC LORD LTD 22221
185 DESBOROUGH ROAD KE

Open: Mon-Fri 8.00 a.m.-5.00 p.m.
Saturday 9.00 a.m.-5.00 p.m.

H.P.W.D.A.

CAMBRIDGESHIRE

CAMBRIDGE Tel. (0223) 63132
D. MACKAY LTD. E★
BRITANNIA WORKS, EAST ROAD

Open: Mon.-Fri. 8.30 a.m.-1 p.m./2.00-
5.00 p.m. Sat. 8.30 a.m.-1.00 p.m.
H.P.W.D.T.CS.MF.A.BC.

CAMBRIDGE Tel. (0223) 247386
H. B. WOODWORKING K
105 CHERRY HINTON ROAD
Open: 8.30 a.m.-5.30 p.m.
Monday-Friday
8.30 a.m.-1.00 p.m. Sat.
H.P.W.WM.D.CS.A.

CHESHIRE

NANTWICH Tel. Crewe 67010
ALAN HOLTHAM K★
THE OLD STORES TURNERY
WISTASON ROAD, WILLASTON
Open: Tues.-Sat. 9.00 a.m.-5.30 p.m.
Closed Monday
P.W.WM.D.T.C.CS.A.BC.

CHEADLE Tel: 061491 1726
ERIC TOMKINSON ★
86 STOCKPORT ROAD
Open: Mon.-Fri. 9.00 a.m.-4.00 p.m.
Saturday 9.00 a.m.-1.00 p.m.
H.P.W.D.MF.A.BC.

CLEVELAND

MIDDLESBROUGH Tel. (0642)
CLEVELAND WOODCRAFT 813103
(M'BRO), 38-42 CRESCENT ROAD K

Open: Mon-Sat 9.15 a.m.-5.30 p.m.

H.P.T.A.BC.W.WM.CS.D.

CORNWALL

HELSTON Tel. Helston (03265) 4961
SOUTH WEST Truro (0872) 71671
POWER TOOLS Launceston
MONUMENT ROAD (0566) 3555
K
H.P.W.WM.D.CS.A.

TRURO Tel. (0872) 71671
TRURO POWER TOOLS E★
30 FERRIS TOWN

Open Mon.-Sat. 8.00 a.m.-12.30 p.m./
1.30 p.m.-5.00 p.m.
H.P.W.WM.D.CS.MF.A.BC.

CUMBRIA

CARLISLE Tel. (0228) 36391
W. M. PLANT
ALLENBROOK ROAD
ROSEHILL, CA1 2UT
Open: Mon.-Fri. 8.00 a.m.-5.15 p.m.
Sat. 8.00 a.m.-12.30 noon
P.W.WM.D.CS.A.

DERBYSHIRE

DERBY Tel. (0332) 41862
HAZLEHURSTS LTD. E★
LONDON ROAD AND CANAL STREET

Open: Mon.-Sat. 8.30 a.m.-5.30 p.m. (retail)
Mon.-Fri. 8.00 a.m.-5.00 p.m. (trade)
H.P.W.MF.A.BC.

PETERBOROUGH

PETERBOROUGH Tel. (0733)
WILLIAMS DISTRIBUTORS 64252
(TOOLS) LIMITED K
108-110 BURGHLEY ROAD
Open: Monday to Friday
8.30 a.m.-5.30 p.m.
H.P.A.W.D.WH.BC.

DEVON

BUXTON Tel. (0298) 871636
CRAFT SUPPLIES K★
THE MILL, MILLERSDALE

Open: Mon-Sat 9.00 a.m.-5.00 p.m.

H.P.W.D.T.CS.A.BC.

BRIXHAM Tel. (08045) 4900
WOODCRAFT SUPPLIES E★
4 HORSE POOL STREET

Open: Mon.-Sat. 9.00 a.m.-6.00 p.m.

H.P.W.A.D.MF.CS.BC.

EXETER Tel. (0392) 73936
WRIDES TOOL CENTRE
147 FORE STREET

Open: 9.00 a.m.-5.30 p.m.
Wednesday 9.00 a.m.-1.00 p.m.
H.P.W.WM.A.

PLYMOUTH Tel. (0752) 330303
WESTWARD BUILDING SERVICES ★
LTD., LISTER CLOSE, NEWNHAM
INDUSTRIAL ESTATE, PLYMPTON
Open: Mon-Fri 8.00 a.m.-5.30 p.m.
Sat. 8.30 a.m.-12.30 p.m.
H.P.W.WM.D.A.BC.

DORSET

BOURNEMOUTH Tel: (0202) 420583
POWER TOOL SERVICES
(Sales, spares, repairs)
849-851 CHRISTCHURCH ROAD
BOSCOMBE
Open: Mon.-Fri. 9.00 a.m.-5.30 p.m.
Sat. 9.00 a.m.-5.00 p.m.
H.P.W.CS.K.A.

POOLE Tel: (0202) 686238
MACHINE SALES AND SERVICES ★
(POOLE) LTD.
23 COWLEY ROAD
NUFFIELD INDUSTRIAL ESTATE
Open: Mon.-Fri. 8.30am-5.30pm.
H.P.W.WM.D.CS.A.BC.

ESSEX

LEIGH ON SEA Tel. (0702)
MARSHAL & PARSONS LTD. 710404
1111 LONDON ROAD EK

Open: 8.30 a.m.-5.30 p.m. Mon-Fri
9.00 a.m.-5.00 p.m. Sat.
H.P.W.WM.D.CS.A.

ILFORD
CUTWELL TOOLS LTD. ★
774-776 HIGH ROAD

Mon.-Fri. 9.00 a.m.-5.00 p.m.
and also by appointment.
P.W.WM.A.D.CS.

shopguide

GLOUCESTER

TEWKESBURY Tel. (0684)
TEWKESBURY SAW CO. LTD. 293092
TRADING ESTATE, NEWTOWN **K**

Open: Mon-Fri 8.00 a.m.-5.00 p.m.
Saturday 9.30 a.m.-12.00 p.m.
P.W.WM.D.CS.

HAMPSHIRE

SOUTHAMPTON Tel. (0703)
H.W.M. 776222
THE WOODWORKERS
303 SHIRLEY ROAD, SHIRLEY
Open: Tues-Fri 9.30 a.m.-6.00 p.m.
Sat 9.30 a.m.-4.00 p.m.
H.P.W.WM.D.CS.A.BC.T.

ALDERSHOT Tel. (0252) 334422
POWER TOOL CENTRE **K**
374 HIGH STREET

Open Mon-Fri. 8.30 a.m.-5.30 p.m.
Sat 8.30 a.m.-12.30 p.m.

H.P.W.WM.D.A.BC.

PORTSMOUTH Tel. (0705)
EURO PRECISION TOOLS LTD 667332
259/263 LONDON ROAD, NORTH END ★
  E
Open: Mon-Fri 9.00 a.m.-5.30 p.m.
Sat. 9.00 a.m.-1.00 p.m.
H.P.W.WM.D.A.BC.

SOUTHAMPTON Tel: (0703)
POWER TOOL CENTRE 332288
7 BELVIDERE ROAD **K★**
Open Mon-Fri. 8.30-5.30

H.P.W.WM.D.A.BC.CS.MF.

HUMBERSIDE

GRIMSBY Tel. Grimsby (0472)
  58741 Hull (0482) 26999
J. E. SIDDLE LTD. (Tool Specialists) ★
83 VICTORIA STREET
Open: Mon-Fri 8.30 a.m.-5.30 p.m.
Sat. 8.30 a.m.-12.45 p.m. & 2 p.m.-5 p.m.
H.P.A.BC.W.WMD.

HULL
HUMBERSIDE FACTORING/H.F.C.
SAW SERVICING LTD.
MAIN STREET
Open: Mon-Fri. 8am-5pm.
Saturday 8am-12.00pm.
H.P.W.WM.D.CS.A.BC.K.

KENT

WYE Tel. (0233) 813144
KENT POWER TOOLS LTD.
UNIT 1, BRIAR CLOSE
WYE, Nr. ASFORD

H.P.W.WM.D.A.CS.

LANCASHIRE

PRESTON Tel. (0772) 52951
SPEEDWELL TOOL COMPANY **E★**
62-68 MEADOW STREET PR1 1SU
Open: Mon-Fri. 8.30 a.m.-5.30 p.m.
Sat. 8.30 a.m.-12.30 p.m.

H.P.W.WM.CS.A.MF.BC.

LANCASHIRE

BURY Tel. (061 764 6769
HOUSE OF HARBRU ★
101 CROSTONS ROAD
ELTON
Open: Mon.-Fri. 9.00 a.m.-5.00 p.m.
Send 2 × 1st class stamps for catalogue
MF.

MANCHESTER Tel. (061 789)
TIMMS TOOLS 0909
102-104 LIVERPOOL ROAD ★
PATRICROFT M30 0WZ
Weekdays 9.00 a.m.-5.30 p.m.
Sat. 9.00 a.m.-1.00 p.m.
H.P.A.W.

BLACKPOOL
FLYDE WOODTURNING SUPPLIES
222 HORNBY ROAD (BASEMENT)

H.P.W.WM.A.

ROCHDALE Tel. (0706) 342123/
C.S.M. TOOLS 342322
4-6 HEYWOOD ROAD **E★**
CASTLETON
Open: Mon-Sat 9.00 a.m.-6.00 p.m.
Sundays by appointment
W.D.CS.A.BC.

LANCASTER Tel. (0524) 32886
LILE TOOL SHOP **K**
43/45 NORTH ROAD
Open: Monday to Saturday
9.00 a.m.-5.30 p.m.
Wed 9.00 a.m.-12.30 p.m.
H.P.W.D.A.

LEICESTERSHIRE

HINCKLEY Tel. (0455) 613432
J. D. WOODWARD & CO. (POWER ★
TOOL SPECIALISTS)
THE NARROWS, HINCKLEY
Open: Monday-Saturday
8.00 a.m.-6.00 p.m.
H.P.W.WM.D.CS.A.BC.

LINCOLNSHIRE

LINCOLN Tel: (0522) 689369
SKELLINGTHORPE SAW SERVICES LTD.
OLD WOOD, SKELLINGTHORPE
Open: Mon to Fri 8 a.m.-5 p.m.
Sat 8 a.m.-12 p.m.
H.P.W.WM.D.CS.A.*.BC.
Access/Barclaycard

LONDON

ACTON Tel. (01-992) 4835
A. MILLS (ACTON) LTD ★
32/36 CHURCHFIELD ROAD W3 6ED
Open: Mon-Fri 9.00 a.m.-5.00 p.m.
Saturdays 9.00 a.m.-1.00 p.m.
H.P.W.WM.

LONDON Tel. 01-723 2295-6-7
LANGHAM TOOLS LIMITED
13 NORFOLK PLACE
LONDON W2 1QJ

LONDON

LONDON Tel. (01-567) 2922
G. D. CLEGG & SONS ★
83 UXBRIDGE ROAD, HANWELL W7 3ST
Mon-Sat 9.15 a.m.-5.30 p.m.
Closed for lunch 1.00-2.00p.m.
Early Closing 1.00 p.m. Wed.
H.P.A.W.WM.D.CS.

NORBURY Tel. (01-679) 6193
HERON TOOLS & HARDWARE LTD.
437 STREATHAM HIGH ROAD SW16
Open Mon-Fri 8.30 a.m.-5.00 p.m.
Wednesday 8.30 a.m.-1.00 p.m.
Sat. 9.00 a.m.-1.00 p.m.
H.P.W.A.

LONDON Tel. (01-636) 7475
BUCK & RYAN LTD
101 TOTTENHAM COURT ROAD W1P 0DY

Open: Mon-Fri. 8.30 a.m.-5.30 p.m.
Saturday 8.30 a.m.-4.00 p.m.
H.P.W.WM.D.A..

WEMBLEY Tel. 904-1144
ROBERT SAMUEL LTD. (904-1147)
7, 15 & 16 COURT PARADE after 4.00)
EAST LANE, N. WEMBLEY ★
Open Mon.-Fri. 8.45-5.15; Sat. 9-1.00
Access, Barclaycard, AM Express, & Diners
H.P.W.CS.E.A.D.

WOOLWICH Tel. (01-854) 7767/8
A. D. SHILLMAN & SONS LTD
108-109 WOOLWICH HIGH STREET
SE18
Open: Mon-Sat
8.30 p.m.-5.30p.m.
H.P.W.CS.A.

HOUNSLOW Tel. (01-570)
Q.R. TOOLS LTD 2103/5135
251-253 HANWORTH ROAD

Open: Mon-Fri 8.30 a.m.-5.30 p.m.
Sat. 9.00 a.m.-1.00 p.m.
P.W.WM.D.CS.A.

FULHAM Tel. (01-385) 5109
I. GRIZZARD LTD. **E**
84a-b LILLIE ROAD, SW6 1TL
Open: Mon-Sat 9.00-5.30 p.m.
Half day Thursday

H.P.A.BC.W.CS.WM.D.

LONDON Tel. (01-263) 1536
THOMAS BROTHERS (01-272) 2764
798-804 HOLLOWAY ROAD, N19 **E**
Open: Mon.-Fri. 8.30 a.m.-5.30 p.m. Thurs.
8.30 a.m.-1 p.m. Sat 9 a.m.-5 p.m.
H.P.W.WM.CS.MF.BC.

MERSEYSIDE

LIVERPOOL Tel. (051-207) 2967
TAYLOR BROS (LIVERPOOL) LTD **K**
195-199 LONDON ROAD
LIVERPOOL L3 8JG
Open: Monday to Friday
8.30 a.m.-5.30 p.m.
H.P.W.WM.D.A.BC.

MIDDLESEX

ENFIELD Tel. (01-363) 2935
GILL & HOXBY LTD. **K**
133-137 ST. MARKS ROAD EN1 1BB

Mon.-Sat. 8.30 a.m.-6.00 p.m.
Early closing Wednesday 1.00 p.m.
H.P.W.WM.T.CS.A

RUISLIP Tel. (08956) 74126
ALLMODELS ENGINEERING LTD. **E★**
91 MANOR WAY

Open: Mon-Sat 9.00 a.m.-5.30 p.m.
H.P.W.A.D.CS.MF.BC.

CROWMARSH Tel. (0491) 38653
MILL HILL SUPPLIES **E★**
66 THE STREET
Open: Mon.-Fri. 9.30 a.m.-5.00 p.m.
Thurs. 9.30 a.m.-7.00 p.m.
Sat. 9.30 a.m.-1.00 p.m.
P.W.D.CS.MF.A.BC.

FARNHAM Tel. (0252) 725427
A.B.E. CO. LTD. (Quick Hire) ★
GOODS SHED
STATION APPROACH, FARNHAM
Open Mon.-Fri. 8.00 a.m.-5.30 p.m.
Sat. 8.00 a.m.-5.30 p.m.
H.P.W.D.CS.A.BC.

NORFOLK

NORWICH Tel. (0603) 898695
NORFOLK SAW SERVICES
DOG LANE, HORSFORD
Open: Monday to Friday
8.00 a.m.-5.00 p.m.
Saturday 8.00 a.m.-12.00 p.m.
H.P.W.WM.D.CS.A.

KINGS LYNN Tel. (0553) 2443
WALKER & ANDERSON (Kings Lynn) LTD.
WINDSOR ROAD, KINGS LYNN **K**
Open: Monday to Saturday
7.45 a.m.-5.30 p.m.
Wednesday 1.00 p.m. Saturday 5.00 p.m.
H.P.W.WM.D.CS.A.

NORWICH Tel. (0603) 400933
WESTGATES WOODWORKING Tx
61 HURRICANE WAY, 975412
NORWICH AIRPORT INDUSTRIAL ESTATE
Open: 9.00 a.m.-5.00 p.m. weekdays
9.00 a.m.-12.30 Sat.
P.W.WM.D.BC. **K**

KING'S LYNN Tel: 07605 674
TONY WADDILOVE, UNIT A ★
HILL FARM WORKSHOPS
GREAT DUNHAM (Nr. Swaffham)
Open: Tues. — Fri. 10.00 a.m. to 5.30 p.m.
Sat. 9.00 a.m. to 5.00 p.m.
H.P.W.D.T.MF.A.BC.*

NOTTINGHAMSHIRE

NOTTINGHAM Tel: (0602) 225979
POOLEWOOD and 227064/5
EQUIPMENT LTD. (06077) 2421 after hrs
5a HOLLY LANE, CHILLWELL
Open: Mon-Fri 9.00 a.m.-5.00 p.m.
Sat. 9.00 a.m. to 12.30 p.m.
P.W.WM.D.CS.A.BC.

shopguide

OXON

WITNEY Tel. (0993) 3885,
TARGET TOOLS (SALES, & 72095 OXON
TARGET TOOLS HIRE & REPAIRS) ★
SWAIN COURT
STATION INDUSTRIAL ESTATE
Open: Mon.-Sat. 8.00 a.m.-5.00 p.m.
24 hour Answerphone
B.C.W.M.A.

SHROPSHIRE

TELFORD Tel. Telford (0952)
ASLES LTD 48054
VINEYARD ROAD, WELLINGTON EK★

Open: Mon. Fri. 8.30 a.m.-5.30 p.m.
Saturday 8.30 a.m.-4.00 p.m.
H.P.W.WM.D.CS.BC.A.

SOMERSET

TAUNTON Tel. (0823) 85431
JOHN HALL TOOLS ★
6 HIGH STREET

Open Monday-Saturday
9.00 a.m.-5.30 p.m.
H.P.W.WM.D.CS.A.

STAFFORDSHIRE

TAMWORTH Tel. (0827) 56188
MATTHEWS BROTHERS LTD. K
KETTLEBROOK ROAD
Open: Mon-Sat 8.30 a.m.-6.00 p.m.
Demonstrations Sunday mornings by
appointment only
H.P.WM.D.T.CS.A.BC.

STOKE-ON-TRENT Tel: 0782-48171
F.W.B. (PRODUCTS) LTD.
WHIELDON ROAD, STAFFS.
Open: Mon.-Fri. 8.30am-5.30pm
Saturday 8.30am-12.30pm
H.P.W.WM.A.D

SUFFOLK

IPSWICH Tel. (0473) 40456
FOX WOODWORKING KE★
142-144 BRAMFORD LANE
Open: Tues., Fri., 9.00 a.m.-5.30 p.m.
Sat. 9.00 a.m.-5.00 p.m.

H.P.W.WM.D.A.B.C.

SUSSEX

ST. LEONARD'S-ON-SEA Tel.
DOUST & MONK (MONOSAW)-(0424)
25 CASTLEHAM ROAD 52577

Open: Mon.-Fri. 8.00 a.m.-5.30 p.m.
Most Saturdays 9.00 a.m.-1.00 p.m.
H.P.W.WM.D.CS.A.

BOGNOR REGIS Tel. (0243) 863100
A. OLBY & SON (BOGNOR REGIS) LTD.
"TOOLSHOP," BUILDERS MERCHANT
HAWTHORN ROAD K
Open: Mon-Thurs 8 a.m.-5.15 p.m. Fri.
8 a.m.-8 p.m. Sat 8 a.m.-12.45 p.m.
H.P.W.WM.D.T.C.A.BC.

WORTHING Tel. (0903) 38739
W. HOSKING LTD (TOOLS & KE★
MACHINERY)
28 PORTLAND RD, BN11 1QN
Open: Mon.-Sat. 8.30 a.m.-5.30 p.m.
Closed Wednesday
H.P.W.WM.D.CS.A.BC.

TYNE & WEAR

NEWCASTLE UPON TYNE Tel.
J. W. HOYLE LTD. (0632) 617474
CLARENCE STREET NE2 1YJ K★
Open: Mon-Fri 8.00 a.m.-5.00 p.m.
Saturday 9.00 a.m.-4.30 p.m.

H.P.A.BC.W.CS.WM.D.

NEWCASTLE Tel. (0632) 320311
HENRY OSBOURNE LTD. E
50-54 UNION STREET

Open: Mon-Fri 8.30 a.m.-5.00 p.m.

H.P.W.D.CS.MF.A.BC.

WEST MIDLANDS

BIRMINGHAM Tel. (021-554) 5177
ROTAGRIP E★
16 LODGE ROAD, HOCKLEY
Open: Mon.-Fri. 9.00 a.m.-5.00 p.m.
Sat. 9.00 a.m.-12.00 p.m.

H.P.W.CS.A.BC.T.MF.

WOLVERHAMPTON Tel. (0902)
MANSAW SERVICES 58759
SEDGLEY STREET K★

Open: Mon.-Fri. 9.00 a.m.-5.00 p.m.

H.P.W.WM.A.D.CS.

YORKSHIRE

BOROUGHBRIDGE Tel. (09012)
JOHN BODDY TIMBER LTD 2370
FINE WOOD & TOOL STORE ★
RIVERSIDE SAWMILLS
Open: Mon.-Thurs. 8.00 a.m.-6.00 p.m.
Fri. 8.00am-5.00pm Sat. 8.00am-4.00pm
H.P.W.WM.D.T.CS.MF.A.BC.

SHEFFIELD Tel. (0742) 441012
GREGORY & TAYLOR LTD KE
WORKSOP ROAD
Open: 8.30 a.m.-5.30 p.m.
Monday-Friday
8.30 a.m.-12.30 p.m. Sat.
H.P.W.WM.D.

HARROGATE Tel. (0423) 66245/
MULTI-TOOLS 55328
158 KINGS ROAD K★

Open: Monday to Saturday
8.30 a.m.-6.00 p.m.

H.P.W.WM.D.A.BC.

LEEDS Tel. (0532) 574736
D. B. KEIGHLEY MACHINERY LTD. ★
VICKERS PLACE, STANNINGLEY
PUDSEY LS2 86LZ
Mon.-Fri. 9.00 a.m.-5.00 p.m.
Sat. 9.00 a.m.-1.00 p.m.
P.A.W.WM.CS.BC.

HUDDERSFIELD Tel. (0484)
NEVILLE M. OLDHAM 641219/(0484)
UNIT 1 DALE ST. MILLS 42777
DALE STREET, LONGWOOD ★
Open: Mon-Fri 8.00 a.m.-5.30 p.m.
Saturday 9.30 a.m.-12.00 p.m.
P.W.WM.D.A.BC.

YORKSHIRE

THIRSK Tel. (0845) 22770
THE WOOD SHOP ★
TRESKE SAWMILLS LTD.
STATION WORKS
Open: Seven days a week 9.00-5.00

T.H.MF.BC.

KEIGHLEY Tel. (0535) 663325
EUROMAIL (TOOLS) ★
PO BOX 13
108 EAST PARADE
Open 9.15 a.m.-5.00 p.m.
Not Tuesday but inc. Saturday
H.P.W.A.BC.

CLECKHEATON Tel. (0274)
SKILLED CRAFTS LTD. 872861
34 BRADFORD ROAD ★

Open: 9.00 a.m.-5.00 p.m. Monday
Saturday Lunch 12.00 a.m.-1.00 p.m.
H.P.A.W.CS.WM.D.

LEEDS Tel. (0532) 790507
GEORGE SPENCE & SONS LTD.
WELLINGTON ROAD
Open: Monday to Friday
8.30 a.m.-5.30 p.m.
Saturday 9.00 a.m.-5.00 p.m.
H.P.W.WM.D.T.A.

SCOTLAND

EDINBURGH Tel. 031-337-5555
THE SAW CENTRE ★
38 HAYMARKET EH12 5JZ
Mon.-Fri. 8.30 a.m.-5.30 p.m.
Sat. 9.00 a.m.-1.00 p.m.
H.P.W.WM.D.CS.A.

PERTH Tel. (0738) 26173
WILLIAM HUME & CO K
ST. JOHN'S PLACE
Open: Monday to Saturday
8.00 a.m.-5.30 p.m.
8.00 a.m.-1.00 p.m. Wednesday
H.P.A.BC.W.CS.WM.D.

IRELAND

NEWTOWNARDS Tel: 0247 819800
NORLYN MACHINERY or 812506
UNIT 10, MALCOLMSON IND. EST.
80 BANGOR ROAD, CO. DOWN
Open: Mon-Fri 9.30am-5.30pm
(Closed 1-2pm for lunch)
Any other time by request.
H.W.WM.D.T.MF.A. 24 Hour Service K

SCOTLAND

CULLEN Tel: (0542) 40563
GRAMPIAN WOODTURNING SUPPLIES AT
BAYVIEW CRAFTS
Open Mon.-Sat. 9.00 a.m.-5.30 p.m. Sunday
10.00 a.m.-5.30 p.m. Open later July/Aug.
Sept. Demonstrations SAT/SUN or by
H.W.D.MF.BC. appointment

TAYSIDE Tel: (05774) 293
WORKMASTER POWER TOOLS LTD. ★
DRUM, KINROSS
Open Mon.-Sat. 8.00 a.m.-8.00 p.m.
Demonstrations throughout Scotland by
appointment
P.W.WM.D.A.BC.

GLASGOW Tel. 041-429-4444/
THE SAW CENTRE 4374 Telex: 777886
650 EGLINTON STREET E★
GLASGOW G5 9RP
Mon.-Fri. 8.00 a.m.-5.00 p.m.
Sat. 9.00 a.m.-1.00 p.m.
H.P.W.WM.D.CS.A.

WALES

CARDIFF Tel. (0222) 595710
DATAPOWER TOOLS LTD,
MICHAELSTON ROAD,
CULVERHOUSE CROSS
Open: Mon.-Fri. 8.00 a.m.-5.00 p.m.
Sat. 9.00 a.m.-1.00 p.m.
H.P.W.WM.D.A.

CARMARTHEN Tel. (0267) 237219
DO-IT-YOURSELF SUPPLY K
BLUE STREET, DYFED
Open: Monday to Saturday
9.00 a.m.-5.30 p.m.
Thursday 9.00 a.m.-5.30 p.m.
H.P.W.WM.D.T.CS.A.BC.

CARDIFF Tel. (0222) 396039
JOHN HALL TOOLS LIMITED
CENTRAL SQUARE ★

Open: Monday to Saturday
9.00 a.m.-5.30 p.m.

H.P.W.WM.D.A.BC.

SWANSEA Tel. (0792) 55680
SWANSEA TIMBER & PLYWOOD CO. LTD.
57-59 OXFORD STREET ★

Open: Mon to Fri 9.00 a.m.-5.30 p.m.
Sat. 9.00 a.m.-1.00 p.m.
H.P.W.D.T.CS.A.BC.

WOOD SUPPLIERS

WOOD SUPPLIERS

TIMBERLINE

In addition to our much improved range of over 50 species of fine imported and home grown hardwoods we would like to announce that we now carry comprehensive stocks of the following:

Veneers, decorative lines and bandings, polishes, waxes, stains, adhesives, abrasives and woodwork construction plans. You are always assured of good service and a friendly welcome.

Business hours
Tues.-Sat. 9.30am-5.30pm
Please send large sae for free catalogue quoting ref. WW.
TIMBERLINE,
Unit 7, Munday Works,
58-66 Morley Road,
Tonbridge, Kent TN9 1RP.
Tel: (0732) 355626

THE WOODSTORE

Suppliers of Native Hardwoods
MOST HOMEGROWN SPECIES IN STOCK
LARGE AND SMALL QUANTITIES
SUPPLIED FRESH SAWN, AIR DRIED
AND KILN DRIED
MACHINING FACILITIES AVAILABLE
Send sae for Price List to
TREEWORK SERVICES LTD
CHESTON COOMBE, CHURCH TOWN,
BACKWELL, Nr. BRISTOL
OR PHONE FLAX BOURTON
(027583) 3917 OR 3078
We also offer a tree milling service

SEASONED NORTH AMERICAN LONG LEAF PITCH PINE AVAILABLE

Converted from timber beams to your specification or in our standard sizes. From timber originally imported circa 1880.

Traditional and modern mouldings available.

Largest sizes section 14" × 12".

Architraving and Skirting all in stock
FOR A LIMITED PERIOD SPECIAL SUPPLY WITCH ELM.

"The Saw Mill,"
Wills Farm,
Newchurch, Kent.
Tel: Hamstreet (023373) 3361

NORTH HEIGHAM SAWMILLS

Good, Kiln-Dried stocks of most Home-Grown timbers, and exotic, Imported Hardwoods.
Stocks include: Apple, ash, beech, blackwood, box, cedar, cherry, cocobolo, ebony, elm, holly, lemonwood, lignum, lime, mahogany, maple, oak, padauk, pear, plane, rosewood, satinwood, sycamore, walnut, yew, zelkova.

Please send S.A.E. for priced stock list to:

North Heigham Sawmills, Paddock St. (off Barker St.), NORWICH NR2 4TW. Tel: Norwich 622978.

DESIGNS IN WOOD

by Phil Osborne
THE ULTIMATE WOOD SERVICE IN SOUTH WALES
Oak, Ash, Beech and Mahogany a Speciality at realistic prices. Also wood cut to one's own cutting list, fully finished.
For details and quotations apply to:
**Designs in Wood, Unit L2, Hirwaun Industrial Estate, Hirwaun, Mid-Glam.
Tel: 0685 814111**

selected butts of
British hardwoods, sawn & kilned through & through; veneers and finishes;
quality handtools,
de meester (the master)

54 Chalk Farm Rd London NW1
01-267 0502 (open Sat & Sun)

THE WOOD SHOP

Our Cabinetmaker and Woodturners sawmill specialises in **homegrown,** imported and exotic timbers for the small user.
We can **machine** to your cutting list and **deliver** to your home.
Open 7 days a week, 9 to 5.
Send for new brochure to Treske Sawmills, Station Works
Thirsk YO7 4NY
Tel (0845) 22770
Treske Sawmills

LIMEHOUSE TIMBER

See the wood from the trees!
Select from our stock of English and imported hardwoods, Russian redwoods, veneers and exotics. Send 17p stamp for stock list.
A unique source in London for all wood users.
Cutting lists prepared.
Open 9-5, Mon.-Fri. 9-3 Sat.
**5 Grenade Street,
London E14 8HL. 01-987 6289**

Wood Supplies Advertisement Coupon

***Send to:* Classified Ad Dept. A.S.P. Ltd., 1 Golden Square, London, W.1.**

FROM _____

_____

_____

Private & Trade Rate, 46p per word. (VAT inclusive) minimum £6.90. Display Box rates s.c.c. £8, (minimum 2.5cm (+ VAT)

I enclose remittance to the value of _____ to cover _____ inset or retain.

Classified Advertisements

FOR SALE

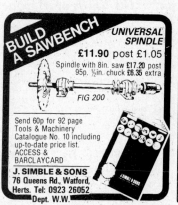

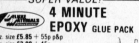

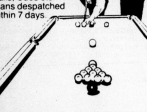
144

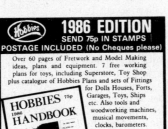

A tale of two workshops

Two stories of two unusual woodwork businesses — both with a healthy sense of public relations

ARLEY HALL WORKSHOP

John Chalmers-Brown produces quality, solid-wood furniture in the old carpenter's workshop at Arley Hall, Cheshire, a Victorian mansion near Great Budworth.

John and his wife Debra, started business in 1981 in a double garage on a housing estate, a far from ideal venue. The neighbours were tolerant, but space was limited, there was nowhere to store wood and hardly enough space to work. The main problem was the lack of contact with members of the public. John and Debra took to hauling furniture and smaller products to local craft fairs and business exhibitions, but after several such ventures decided that the work they sold didn't justify the cost of stands and travelling.

After a great deal of searching, and helped by Bob Adams of CoSIRA they found a building to suit them on the Arley estate. It was rather run down, but the situation was ideal; 700sq ft of space and a captive audience of visitors to the Hall and gardens. They decided to open the workshop for an experimental period during the peak of the tourist season to see if the enterprise was viable; a steady stream of customers buying smaller items would pay overheads, but larger orders were needed if the business was to succeed. They borrowed some trestle tables, covered them in dressmaking material and set up their display stands in June 1984.

The first few months were hard work — long hours for a small return — but gradually orders for larger pieces of furniture began to come in. At the end of the experimental opening period there was no doubt that the workshop would open on a full time basis; the only problem was how to survive the winter months when the Hall and gardens were closed to the public.

That first winter was spent up ladders with paint and brushes. They partitioned off areas of the old carpenter's shop for a showroom, handwork area, machine shop and office; the workshop opened on Good Friday, 1985.

The season was slow to start, but after a few weeks, trade began to pick up and sales of smaller items rose. The next breakthrough came when clients from the previous year began to return and place orders for larger pieces of furniture. John now has a full order book, and more orders come in weekly. He says people don't mind waiting for a piece of furniture that's specially designed to fit a specified space and their own requirements.

In 1981, the only large piece of machinery in the garage was an SCM vertical-spindle moulder. The list now includes a Scheppach HMO-Solo planer/thicknesser, an Elektra Beckum circular saw, a Startrite 352 bandsaw which, after a few teething problems, has proved to be indispensable; and his latest acquisition, a Sumaco mortiser. All are single-phase. These are complemented by a selection of hand power-tools and innumerable handtools. The public's reaction to this equipment is mixed. The realists accept it for what it is — time-saving and therefore cost cutting. The so-called purists mutter to themselves, look round and walk out, but one wonders if they would be prepared to pay today's prices for a piece of furniture made entirely by hand.

Some of John's timber is felled on the Arley estate and air-dried. Most of the wood used for furniture is kiln-dried, bought in from two larger dealers. These are New Hall Timber of Shropshire (found through an advertisement in *Woodworker*) for home-grown hardwoods, and Edward Hughes Ltd of Melling, Liverpool for imported timbers.

John uses a cellulose-based sanding sealer or acid catalyst lacquer and waxes (from Fiddes of Cardiff), both applied by brush. A daunting task, but the standard of finish is high. John uses a full face-mask with a hose drawing air from outside the workshop; it allows him to breathe clear air, and doesn't restrict movement. The unit cost £183, but this set-up may not be any use in a factory; someone would have to guard the air inlet to make sure no-one left their car running next to it! The furniture is polished with one of Fiddes' waxes or beeswax.

It's difficult to make a success of a small business in the present economic climate, but John and Debra are determined to succeed without lowering their standards. One feels that the ghosts of the old Arley carpenters would approve. ∎

Debra Chalmers-Brown
● Arley Hall Workshop, Arley Estate, Northwich, Cheshire.

● A linen chest from the Arley Hall workshop. Note the wooden hinges

146

THE WOOD SKILL CENTRE

Frustration with declining standards of craftsmanship prompted Tim Hocombe, cabinetmaker and wood aficionado, to found the Wood Skill Centre in Plymouth, where craftsmen work together and pass on their skills to apprentices.

Hocombe's opinions of contemporary wood skills and related products are unlikely to endear him to many of his peers. 'Take a look round any woodcraft showroom these days. 50% of the items shouldn't be on display — they don't reach the standards set by generations of woodworkers before us.'

Such sweeping statements are all very well. How can the situation be rectified? His answer is two-fold and entirely practical. Skilled craftsmen at the Centre — woodturners, cabinetmakers and restorers — work to the highest possible standard, and each individual's work is open to constructive criticism from the other members of the group. The Centre is also pursuing an active role in training woodworkers across the range of skills. Apart from having apprentices work in the Centre, Hocombe has initiated a series of lectures introducing the basically competent woodworker to further aspects of wood and its potential. Follow-up evening courses are scheduled for early 1986, where interested people will be able to acquire higher skills working with the Centre's own craftsmen. The curricula will be tailor-made to suit the needs of each individual. Having learnt his craft by 'looking over old men's shoulders' Hocombe appreciates the fundamental necessity of making education interesting, a theme reflected in the format of his teaching courses.

Hocombe, a former social worker, doesn't operate in isolation. Valuable expertise is provided by Richard Crow, who advises on timber. Richard has a huge collection of timber samples from all over the world, and to make best use of his expertise, the Centre offers an appraisal service to help people choose a particular wood for a project, or find out the qualities of a timber they are thinking of using. There are some 30 varieties in stock at the Centre and just about any kind of unusual wood can be found if required.

Pundits may say that in today's highly competitive world the Centre has little hope of commercial success. A look at their order book and the list of recent prestigious clients would soon dispel any doubts about its viability.

The combination of specialists in woodturning, restoring, cabinetmaking and joinery, with design capabilities and unfailing resolve to deliver on time — all under one roof — has made the Centre's working operation an attractive proposal to several clients. Bradbury Wilkinson, for example, an international company which makes engravings for world banks, commissioned

Hocombe and his team to design and make a suite of boardroom furniture for the company's headquarters. The striking results (in olive ash) have enabled the Centre to approach equally prestigious clients for commissions. An international bank is top of the list of forthcoming clients. Other projects have ranged from reproduction Jacobean chests and hi-fi units to a satin-lined padauk box, presented at the inauguration of Plymouth's automatic teller system.

A genuinely unusual idea, brought to life and maintained by the energy of one man. He needs a particular combination of clients and trainees to sustain his vision; and although it's early days yet, it looks like his commitment is attracting them. ∎

Norma Johnston
● Wood Skill Centre, 105 Grenville Rd, St Jude's, Plymouth, tel. (0752) 663363.

● **Above:** *art octagonal table under construction;* **below:** *a mahogany chair by Tim Holcombe*

147

Round, rough and smooth

Three contrasting approaches to bowl-turning are shown in these exhibits at a show at the British Crafts Centre. One explores wood's texture and tone; another makes it disappear; and another even invents new forms of construction. All are innovative; one or the other — or all three — may inspire you to have a go at something new.

Jim Partridge's rough-hewn burr elm and oak bowls **(left and centre opposite)** have an almost adzed finish to them. He cuts a blank with a chainsaw, mounts it on the faceplate, then turns the top and bottom. It's sanded, then scorched with a blowtorch, and the consequent loose soot is cleaned out with wire wool. Finishing is with oil or wax.

Richard Raffan (blackwood bowl, **right**) is self-taught, and now lives in Australia. He harvests his wood personally, from either the Tasmanian forests or local merchants' offcut piles. He uses tools rather than abrasives to finish his work, arguing that the dust is hazardous to health, and that the patina should come from use.

Maria van Kesteren was an apprentice of one of the Netherland's foremost turners, Hank van Treerum. Her work (bowl, **top,** and box, **right**) is almost sculptural; grain and character of the wood becomes secondary to the form.

● The exhibition is at the British Crafts Centre, 43 Earlham Street, Covent Garden, London WC2, until Saturday 15 February. The opening hours are Monday to Friday 10am-5pm, Saturday 11am-5pm.

The grand furniture saga:2

Vic Taylor's path on the map of furniture history leads from the fall of Rome to the light side of the Dark Ages — via Byzantium

● An oak coffre strengthened with iron bands and decorated with scrolls of wrought iron in French Gothic style (c1250-1300)

'Eleven *hundred and sixty years after the foundation of Rome, the Imperial City which had subdued and civilised so considerable a part of mankind was delivered to the licentious fury of the tribes of Germany and Scythia.'*

So wrote Edward Gibbon in his *Decline and Fall of the Roman Empire*, published in 1776. The event shook the pillars of western and middle eastern civilisation and ushered in several centuries of barbaric savagery, looting, and land-grabbing.

In AD365, emperor Valentinian I of Rome gave his brother Valens sovereignty over the eastern, Greek-influenced half of his vast, unwieldy domain. A strife-torn century later, the split was complete; Byzantium (modern Istanbul) and Rome were separate capitals of separate empires.

Byzantine craftsmen were highly accomplished and in great demand in the West during the days of the Roman empire. They were particularly skilful in working and carving ivory; some small ivory chests and reliquaries (caskets containing holy relics) have survived. Some wooden examples demonstrate the principle of 'post-and-panel' framed construction; the whole exterior would be clad with carved ivory panels, usually depicting religious Biblical scenes. There would also be some decoration employing an oriental-style pattern of animals and foliage. As Byzantium was a centre of learning, there must have been bookshelves and probably cabinets as well, although few of them have survived. Some magnificent thrones have been preserved; in addition there were several kinds of chair, notably a basic design with turned legs (the Byzantines were adept at turnery) and animal-head terminals, and of course the ubiquitous X-chair.

From the fifth to ninth centuries in the West, there was a constant movement of tribes backwards and forwards, accompanied by the inevitable rapine and slaughter. The principle migrators were the Huns, the Visigoths, and the Vandals. Other excursions and incursions, particularly by the Franks, Lombards, and Saracens, continued till the ninth century when five power groups had established themselves. They were the Islamic countries: the Byzantine empire adjoining them: the Lombards in Italy: the Franks (under Charlemange) in France: and the Saracens (Moors) in Spain.

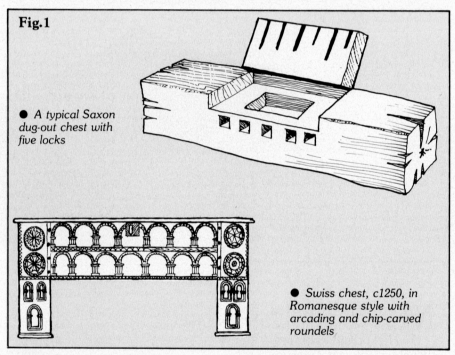

Fig.1

● A typical Saxon dug-out chest with five locks

● Swiss chest, c1250, in Romanesque style with arcading and chip-carved roundels

By the time some stability had come about in the 11th and 12th centuries, a recognisable style of furniture had emerged which has been called 'Romanesque'. Its chief characteristics were the employment of 'arcading'; the use of geometrical ornament; and coloured painted decoration. The Moors brought the first two with them into Spain together with the lancet arch, and the motifs spread throughout western Europe and even into Scandinavia. They are best seen in the ecclesiastical architecture of the time. Some of the ancient classical features were also grafted on to the style, imparting a touch of Byzantine splendour.

Arcading consisted of a continuous series of arches mounted on turned pillars. It was often carved in low relief and/or pierced, while the decoration consisted of diamond-shaped patterns and semi-circular or circular motifs scratched into the surface. By the 13th century this had been elaborated into early forms of chip carving.

Mortise-and-tenon framed construction with pegged tenons was by now standard practice, and gesso was being used on some important pieces.

Furniture was limited to chests, tables and chairs, armoires (cupboards) and beds; ownership was limited to church and nobility. Ordinary people were no better off than their predecessors in ancient Egypt! The influence of the church spread into every aspect of life; abbeys and churches were often the only places of refuge from strife, so they naturally became the storehouses of anything valuable.

The chest

The development of the chest exemplifies the growth of sophisticated styles of furniture. In its most primitive form (a 'monoxylon') it was simply a tree-trunk squared-up with an axe and a small cavity hewn out of it (fig.1). The one at Wimborne Minster in Dorset, doubtless used to

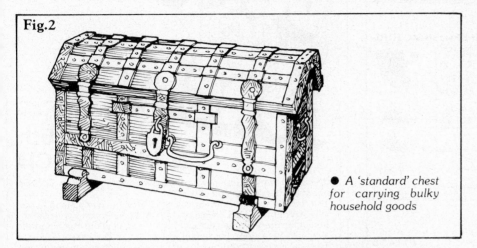

Fig.2

● A 'standard' chest for carrying bulky household goods

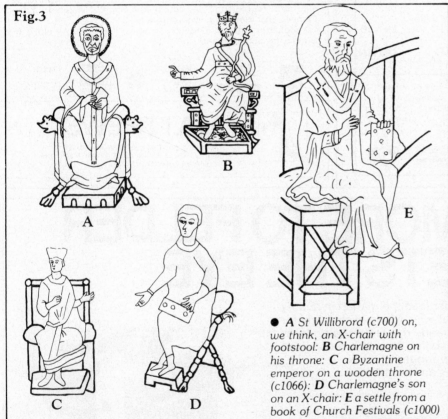

Fig.3

● A *St Willibrord* (c700) on, we think, an X-chair with footstool: **B** *Charlemagne* on his throne: **C** *a Byzantine emperor on a wooden throne (c1066):* **D** *Charlemagne's son on an X-chair:* **E** *a settle from a book of Church Festivals (c1000)*

idea of a French chest of the 13th century. Italy, too, developed its own form of dome-topped chest, called a *cassone*; the principal feature was the painted decoration on a gesso background. It was used to hold linen or clothes and in later times (the 15th century), a back was often added to form a bench seat, a *cassapanca*.

Tables

The reclining dining habits of the Greeks and Romans meant their tables were small and low. Byzantine pictures show larger, round or half-round tables in use by the seventh century, the tops of which, it seems, were supported on trestles ('horses', as the Anglo-Saxons called them). This kind of table was certainly in general use from the seventh century until medieval times, suiting as it did the life-style of a mobile nobility, constantly travelling to collect taxes and oversee their domains. It wasn't until the 14th and 15th centuries that a more permanent kind of table appeared.

Seating

Designs for seating underwent a basic change. During Greek and Roman times, couches were widely used for reclining at meals and for sleeping, but they became rare after the fall of Rome. The probable reason is that any form of seating became a matter of status, and only the highest-born classes sat on chairs to emphasise their rank. Everyone else made the best of it and often lay on cushions on the floor. Obviously, the grandest form of seating was a throne and illustrations from chronicles of the period contain many examples (figs. 3B and C). If chairs were essential — for scribes or monks writing and illuminating manuscripts for instance — they were almost always of the X-type.

There is one interesting example of a style of bench using a framed construction, which resembles the 'joyned' settles of a later period. It's shown in fig. 3E and is contained in a book of Church Festivals written about AD1000; note the way in which the under-frame rails are housed into the legs.

Beds

The need for portability applied to beds as well as other pieces. The humble slept on the floor, and only the nobility had beds, which consisted of a base of wooden boards on a framework of rails with a leg at each corner; these were called 'bed stocks'. Many lords carried a canopy of curtains around with them to be erected at each lodging place. By the 12th to 14th centuries the bed-boards had given way to a rudimentary form of springing, created by boring holes in the end- and side-rails and threading cords through them. A thin rush mattress was laid on the loose interlaced network. In Saxon times there was also the 'shut' bed, which was simply a kind of bunk (sometimes two-tier) in an alcove. ∎

keep holy relics safe, is 6½ft long, yet the cavity is only 22in long, 9in wide, and 6in deep. The lid is ponderous and secured by several iron locks. The keys were distributed to as many people as there were locks so no one could open it alone. In 1166 Henry II ordered 'trunks' (a word derived from the Latin for 'a piece cut off') to be placed in every church so the congregation could contribute to the cost of the Crusades. Similarly, it's recorded in a Chronicle of about 1173 that the keeper of St. Edmund's shrine should make a hollow trunk with a hole in the lid so that pilgrims could give money towards building a tower.

The contrast between these crude trunks and the one in fig. 1, made in Switzerland less than a century later, shows that England was behind the rest of Europe in improving cultural standards. It probably needed the

Normans (1066) to create one nation.

The Anglo-Saxon word for chest was 'cist', from which the modern term almost certainly derives; Norman-French terms were *coffre* (coffer) and *huche* (hutch). The two designs — chest and coffer — were co-existent, the difference being that a chest had a flat lid and was made by a carpenter, while a coffer had a coved or canted lid and was used for travelling. A third kind, an 'ark', had a removable, hipped lid and was used to keep grain, vegetables and stores. One also comes across a 'standard' (fig. 2), a large iron-bound chest used for storing and carrying heavy household goods.

Chest design and construction became so specialised in France that the Provost of Paris decreed in 1254 that the makers should have their own guild separate from the carpenters. The main photo gives some

152

Crossing the bar

Jim Corcoran describes how he planned his breakthrough into the specialist joinery trade — and how it turned out in practice

● **Above:** Jim's bar looks a treat, but it learnt him a few lessons – like the difference between solid oak and blockboard! **Below left,** snapping a line on a stout piece of waney-edged oak; **below right,** the basic construction on site

Until September 1984 I was a Royal Naval shipwright artificer. That meant I'd trained and gained experience in a whole range of different skills, from carpentry to plumbing — so, when I decided to move over into Civvy Street, cabinetmaking and joinery seemed a natural field.

To start the business off, I'd lined up one big job: a new 30x10ft bar for the Park Gate British Legion Club in Hampshire. I was operating out of a newly acquired 650sq ft industrial unit in nearby Stubbington, where my only piece of fixed equipment was (and is) a Lurem C260N universal machine which I bought from SAF Power Tools at Fareham.

I'd done similar jobs before, but nothing on this scale, and I was determined to get it right. So I did a lot of local research on small but important points such as the correct height for optics, the width and height of stock shelves, the lighting, the height and width of the counter, etc. I was well aware that only the right combination would make a bar that was comfortable for the customer, efficient and stress-free for the staff, and generally pleasing to the eye.

I bought no less than £5400-worth of sawn joinery-quality English oak from J. & S. Agates of Horsham, Sussex. I'd never used timber in such volume before, and my estimate of the cost eventually proved 20% short. That, however, was nothing to the 40% shortfall in my estimate of labour. If there was a failure in the job, under-estimating was it. I should have charged an awful lot more.

What's more, the timber was air-dried, and when I got it on site it shrank by a frightening amount. It was winter and the club's central heating was going full pelt, with the result that the canopy warped and actually split once it was up. I hadn't given the timber enough time to acclimatise. I know now that I'd have been commercially better off using oak-faced blockboard instead of all that solid material. If I did the job again, that's the main change I'd make — apart, of course, from a major adjustment to the price!

My first job was panelling about 60x9ft of wall, for which I used the Lurem to get out pieces up to 10in wide. I tongued, grooved and rebated them to make panels about 24x⅝x108in.

Then I made the stock bar, whose components varied from 18x1in for shelf uprights to 15x¾in for the shelves. I made up the sizeable upright widths by tonguing and grooving narrower boards on the Lurem's spindle-moulder. The bar top — 22ft long, 1½in thick and 18in wide — was cut from one piece. Bottle display units sit on top of it, and incorporate two overhead light-boxes.

As for the main bar, its principal features are a 26ft top, again 1½in thick but 22in wide. There's a small handbag shelf right along the front beneath it. The front fascia is fabricated from six tongued-and-grooved panels, screwed to the uprights and then embellished with mouldings.

The canopy consists of ½in-thick tongued-and-grooved panels secured to five hanging frames, each panel measuring about 54x24in. Its main features are internal overhead lights and the ability to fit security shutters as required.

Finally came the finishing touches — covering all the butt joints with mouldings of various sections, and giving the whole construction a protective coat of two-part polyurethane varnish.

The project had taken some three and a half months of hard work. I was single-handed (I did all the drawings and estimating) except for the occasional bit of help when it was essential in order to move something. The job was made rather more difficult by lack of co-ordination among my clients; and, although I built it to a good standard (apart from a few small sins of the kind which yield to examination on any large job), and the result looks very nice, it did not work as a promotional exercise. That kind of specialist joinery has largely been cornered by better-known firms, and I was soon forced to get down to 'grubbing': doors, windows and general carpentry.

However, since then I've also built a racing dinghy which has carried a world champion to victory, and I'm currently laying down another boat. Ideally, that will be where my future now lies . . . ■

● Jim Corcoran, Unit 3, Hammond Industrial Estate, Stubbington Lane, Stubbington, Hants PO14 2PF, tel. (0329) 667814.

154

Up to the mark

Shipping marks on softwood are a vital guide to type and quality — yet few woodworkers know one from another. Bill Brown explains

● *A forest of shipping marks hides a mountain of distinctions. It's worth knowing what they mean*

(photo Swedish Finnish Timber Council)

Most lengths of sawn timber have a shipping mark stamped on the endgrain. Not only do these marks identify the individual shippers, they also tell you what the wood's commercial grade is — and where it came from.

First, however, a word of warning. The last detail alone, the location, is a source of interest, concern and discussion to many users. The latitude and altitude of particular forests are often the subject of definite preferences when buying. But, while some of these preferences are well-founded, others are less so. Those factors do have some bearing on the type of wood likely to be produced; northern, for example, is sometimes better than southern, and western than eastern. But in a good many cases the difference is in fact one of species. Western hemlock is invariably superior to eastern, but each is a different species of the genus *Tsuga*. The same distinction could probably be made between northern and southern American oak, whose species again differ.

Again, a preference is often expressed for Swedish Upper Gulf softwood rather than South Swedish; but, while it is true that trees from near the Arctic Circle are likely to produce mild, close-grained wood because of slow growth, it doesn't always follow that trees grown nearer the Baltic at lower elevation will be fast-grown, with coarse timber.

In fact, while the wood may have a slightly coarser texture, it may also be cleaner, with knots further apart. Scots pine produces redwood which has a particular growth pattern. Each year in its early growth it throws up a leading shoot which arises from a whorl of side shoots. Obviously, if these side shoots are left unchecked by natural or artificial pruning, they eventually produce knots. In a very cold climate, particularly at high altitude, the leading shoot tends to be relatively short — which means the side whorls are produced closer together. The same trees, grown in a warmer environment and at a lower level, tend to produce much longer leading shoots, so that the eventual knot pattern is more widely spaced and gives longer clear cutting.

Much depends ultimately on the degree of good forestry practice that has been applied, and on the girth at which the trees are felled. But cleaner wood is more likely to come from the slightly faster-grown wood than the more slowly grown.

Whitewood, which is produced mainly from spruce (sometimes with a small amount of silver fir mixed in), grows like the pines — except that the side shoots tend to be staggered rather than in whorls, so the knot pattern is a little different.

GRADING

The subject of this article is European redwood and whitewood. Grading or 'bracking' of the converted timber is done according to grading rules. These vary slightly, and are interpreted by each mill according to the average material received. Thus, while the top grade is generally called Unsorted and usually means a mixture of First, Second and Third quality, sometimes with a small proportion of Fourth quality, the proportions will vary. Other and perhaps preferable grades come on the market: for example, you can occasionally get a grade referred to as Side-boards, in which the timber is taken from the outsides of relatively large logs, and which is tantamount to First quality.

The Swedish mill of Alvers & Bergenham put out the odd parcel of First quality redwood and whitewood under their **AL crown BE** mark; this reflects what I've already said about faster-growing trees, since the mill is in Gothenburg in south Sweden. It also puts out a Third quality under the mark **AL + BE.** A number of other mills in Scandinavia ship

composite Second and Third grades, but it is largely Unsorted which forms the bulk of the so-called joinery grades.

The lower or 'falling' grades of Fifths, Sixths, Wrack and Utscott are generally referred to as carcassing timber, and there is packing-case grade below that, but all vary in the defects and proportions of defects permitted.

Russia

The shipping marks applied to redwood and whitewood from the Soviet Union are probably the most easily understood, since initially they fall into three categories: Baltic ports, White Sea ports, and Kara Sea. The first letters of individual marks are E, K and KS respectively, the E signifying the state-controlled V/O Exportles.

Redwood and whitewood shipped from the Baltic areas of Riga, Leningrad, Archangel, Ventspils, etc., are marked as follows (the marking being indented on the board ends with a hammer):

E ★ RG Fourth quality from Riga
E ★★ L Unsorted; Leningrad
E ★★ VS Unsorted; Ventspils
E ★★ RG Unsorted; Riga
E ★★ AR Unsorted; Archangel.

One star signifies Fourths, two stars Unsorted; a line (as in **E — L**) usually signifies a Fifth quality, but sometimes — especially from Riga mills — it may signify Utscott or Sixths.

156

Up to the mark

The mills on the White Sea have a more northerly aspect and produce rather milder wood. They include those at Kem, Oumba and Kovda; their material, both red- and whitewood, is prefixed K:

K iv U Fourth quality; Oumba
K iv KV Fourth quality; Kovda
K iv K Fourth quality; Kem
K u/s U Unsorted; Oumba
K u KD Unsorted; Kovda
K U K Unsorted; Kem.

Kara Sea wood is shipped from Siberia — usually from Igarka, but Petchora in northeast Russia ships similar wood. The brands on the boards indicate the areas more specifically; for example, **KS iv E** is Fourth quality Kara Sea, but not necessarily Siberian wood, while **KS iv EI** is Fourth quality from Igarka in Siberia. **KS u/s E** and **KS u EI** are the corresponding marks for Unsorted. Only redwood is usually shipped from these areas. The wood marked KS is basically very mild and close-grained, as a typical result of the long, cold winters, from October to April, when mercury freezes in even the southern parts of the areas.

Sweden

Swedish redwood and whitewood fall into two categories: Upper Gulf, e.g. from Lulea, Holmsund, Pitea, etc., high up the Gulf of Bothnia, and South Swedish, e.g. from Gothenburg, Norrköping, Oskarsham, etc. Some well-known shipping marks from these areas are:

Upper Gulf redwood and whitewood; **Crown Royal Crown** (the crown is actually a graphic symbol); **Crown WIDA Crown; U Crown C;** and **U Crown R** — all Unsorted grade.

South Swedish Unsorted grade is represented by a number of marks including **ANDSJO; Crown SS Crown; Crown SIDDA Crown; GO Crown WS;** and **R Crown E.**

Finland

A popular mark for unsorted Finnish redwood and whitewood is **KEMI**, shipped from the northern port of that name. Other Unsorted marks are **Crown AKS Crown; Crown Gutzeit Crown** from Kotka; **Crown JK Crown; Crown HH Crown** and **Crown SUM Crown.** There are many more.

Norway

A Crown S is a good Unsorted mark from Norway, as are **A.U.B., B Crown L** and **BERNT.**

Poland

Shipments of redwood and whitewood are made from the Polish state mills in Gdynia and Gdansk under the marks [**L EAGLE P**] for Unsorted and [**x L EAGLE P x**] for Fifths, both in red paint.

Yugoslavia

Only whitewood is shipped from Yugoslavia, under the marks **EXPORTDRVO, JUGO-DRVO, LIGNUM, SLOVENIJALES** and **SIPAD,** all Unsorted.

There are many other marks and sources of supply in eastern, central and western Europe, but those noted here should act as a guide. Your eyes are still indispensable inspectors, particularly where you're only selecting a few boards from a yard which lets you do so.

Remember that Unsorted means 'sorted into a proportion of grades as falling', and a small stack may well have had the best taken out by previous customers. Fortunately or unfortunately, not many yards will let the customer make a selection without supervision.

When all's said and done, it's all very well to look at the front end of a stack and examine the shipping mark. If you don't note how many boards contain the pith (a bad sign), or the rate of growth, there is no point in having them turned down so you can check how many knots there are. ∎

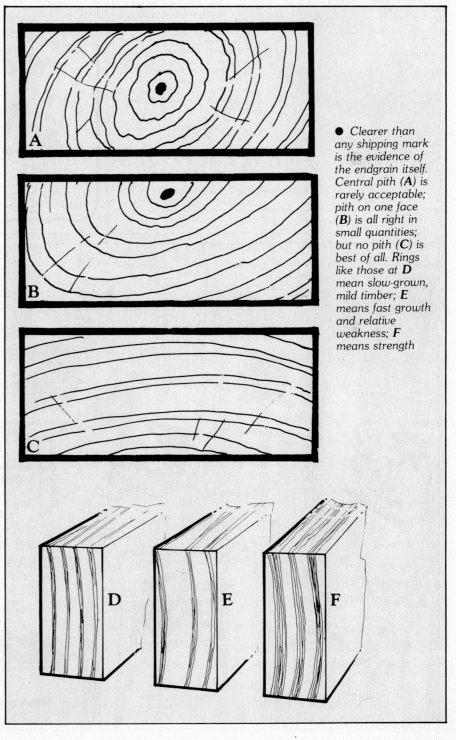

● *Clearer than any shipping mark is the evidence of the endgrain itself. Central pith (A) is rarely acceptable; pith on one face (B) is all right in small quantities; but no pith (C) is best of all. Rings like those at D mean slow-grown, mild timber; E means fast growth and relative weakness; F means strength*

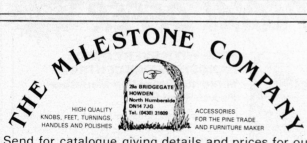

159

Making professional knobs

Bodging up knobs or handles can ruin the look of your work. Our resident expert shows you how to get results if you aren't a metalworker

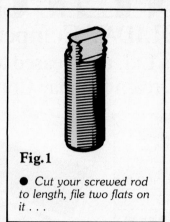

Fig.1

● Cut your screwed rod to length, file two flats on it . . .

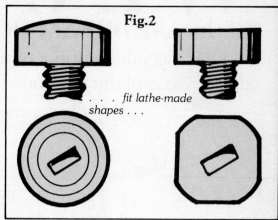

Fig.2

. . . fit lathe-made shapes . . .

Fig.3

. . . or one of a variety of bench-made ones

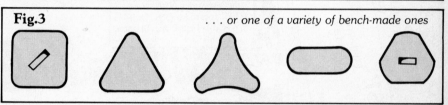

Fig.4

● Use this cam device for holding and shaping knobs; different shapes will need variations on the design

60° 90°

Many individually-made aids, tools and devices, such as gauges, require locking or adjusting knobs. On a well-made and carefully finished article nothing looks better than a nicely knurled brass knob. Alas, how many readers have the facilities for making these, or who will undertake the making of merely one or two? Rather than spoil the good looks of a tool with a brazed or welded wing-nut, I set to work making quality knobs using up those tiny offcuts of ebony, rosewood, padauk and so on that one is too mean to throw away, yet which are too small to make anything. I do not know how these knobs would stand up to a ham-fisted mob in a school or communal workshop, but if you are an owner-driver who takes a pride in your product they are perfectly satisfactory.

Start by preparing a square block slightly larger than the finished size of the knob, and somewhat thicker. Use the correct tapping drill for the chosen size of screwed rod; most of my devices work well with ¼in, ½in, 6mm or 8mm. Screwed rod is freely available in steel in 12 or 36in lengths. Brass takes a bit more finding. Readers who rely on mail order are recommended to try R. H. Whiston, in Cheshire, whose catalogue is always useful for metal oddments. Drill centrally and use the taper tap, just allowing the point to appear.

The screwed rod is now cut to length, thoroughly degreased, and two flats are filed on one end (fig. 1). The flats are well coated with an epoxy resin glue such as Araldite, and the wood block is screwed on. Make sure the two gaps are well filled and that there is a slight dome of adhesive.

If a metalwork lathe is available, face off the end, cutting through wood, glue and metal. If you can't do this, cut the flats so that when screwed up, the metal ends below the surface of the wood. In a wood-lathe the wood can be turned almost to the metal and finished by filing and sanding. Some lathe-produced shapes are shown in fig. 2, but a variety of bench-made shapes is also possible (fig. 3).

A device for holding and accurately shaping the knob is shown in fig. 4. You will no doubt be able to invent further shapes and similar aids to planing and filing accuracy.

A variety of finishes is possible — poly-urethane varnish, cellulose, oil or french polish, but not wax, which doesn't stand up to handling. My preference is for oil, which brings out the rich colours and is durable. However, polyurethane does not harden on certain woods, such as rosewood and padauk. Furniglas will supply direct a hardener for this purpose.

There is also a totally different method of making knobs, by casting. An offcut of thick hardwood will make the mould. First drill through a small pilot hole. With a large sawtooth, Forstner or flatbit, bore the main cavity to the required depth. Follow by taking the correct tapping drill right through, then tap (fig. 5). The inside of the cavity is well greased. The selected screw has its end distorted by crimping in a strong vice or by hammering. A slotted round head can have flats filed on it (fig. 6). The area inside the knob must be thoroughly degreased. Measure the length of the projecting part of the screw, and write this somewhere on the block. This will prevent cutting through to the metal later. Fig. 7 shows a routed mould with an alternative shape.

The cavity can now be filled to the top. There are several possible fillers; Cascamite

or Aerolite glues, body filler or metallic filler. Allow several days for complete hardening, then extract by splitting off the mould. Best of all is fibreglass resin, if available in small enough quantities. The hardening is very much quicker.

Now shape the knob, either in a lathe or by hand methods. I find that in the lathe a trailing cut is most successful, followed by abrasive papering. When a number of knobs is required, a split mould (fig. 8) can be used. Screw the two blocks together before drilling and tapping, then assemble with the screw in place. A very convenient mould can also be made from rigid poly-thene tubing like the stuff used by plumbers (figs. 9 and 10). Make the tube long enough to stand upright during the setting period. Turn a tight-fitting wooden plug which is suitably tapped, and adjust this to give the required thickness for the knob. Wax well, then fill to the top with the chosen filler. The casting should push out easily, leaving the mould ready for the next casting. ■

● Furniglas is manufactured by Evode Ltd, Common Road, Stafford ST16 3EH (0785 57755)
● R. H. Whiston, New Mills, Stockport, Cheshire (0663 42028)

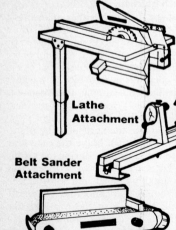

Making professional knobs

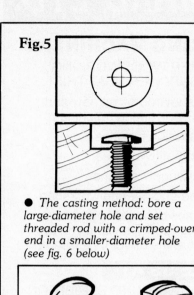

Fig.5

● The casting method: bore a large-diameter hole and set threaded rod with a crimped-over end in a smaller-diameter hole (see fig. 6 below)

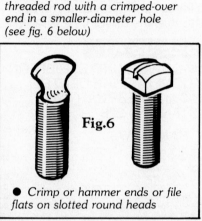

Fig.6

● Crimp or hammer ends or file flats on slotted round heads

Fig.7

● Cast a shaped knob in a routed recess

Fig.8

● Use a split mould if you want to produce more than one knob

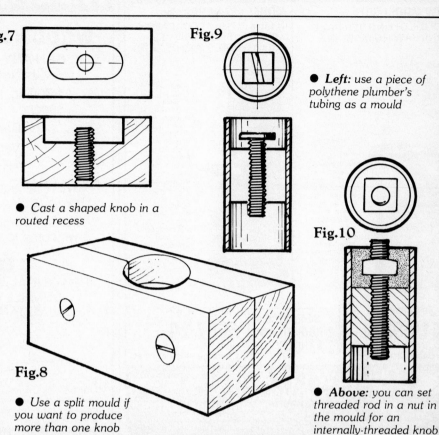

Fig.9

● **Left:** use a piece of polythene plumber's tubing as a mould

Fig.10

● **Above:** you can set threaded rod in a nut in the mould for an internally-threaded knob

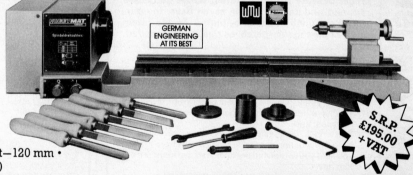

163

164

Many a strip

Noel Leach looks at some ways to make a boring chore more bearable

Mystery hangs over one of wood-working's most unpleasant processes — stripping wood. But if the removal of a hard surface film — paint, varnish, french polish or one of the various modern lacquers — is handled properly, stripping can be at least reasonably tolerable. These guidelines are really written with the amateur and semi-professional in mind, but I would also like to think there may be useful hints for professionals too.

A glance along the assorted bottles and tins in any good DIY store will give some idea of how many different types of wood-stripper there are available today. In order to choose the right product, it's necessary to understand the two types of finish you'll encounter in the journey to the 'strip section'. Basically, there are reversible and non-reversible finishes.

● **Reversible finishes:** In a nut-shell, a reversible surface film can be dissolved in its own solvent back to 'solution' form — for instance, methylated spirits will 'reverse' or dissolve standard shellac finishes such as french polish which use methylated spirits as a solvent, cellulose thinners will reverse nitro-cellulose finishes and turpentine will reverse wax or oil finishes. Shellac, nitro-cellulose, wax and oil, in fact, are all the reversible finishes with which we are concerned.

● **Non-reversible finishes:** These finishes have usually undergone chemical molecular changes during drying of the film and cannot be reversed with their own original solvent. A pre-catalysed lacquer, once dry, will not reverse even with the cellulose solvent with which it was originally mixed, and PVA glues are also a good example of non-reversibility. These non-reversible surfaces are mainly the modern branch-offshoots of cellulose lacquers, and are used extensively in modern furniture and joinery finishing. Oil paint and oil-resin varnishes are also non-reversible, because once they are dry they won't dissolve in their solvents — in this case turpentine or white spirit. In general, these finishes can be categorised as follows: Oil-resin varnish and oil paints; pre-catalysed cellulose lacquers; acid-catalysed (2-pack) cellulose lacquers; polyurethane (2-pack) cellulose lacquers; and polyester (wax-type 2-pack) lacquer. None of these will reverse or dissolve with their original solvent.

Obviously, it's necessary to identify a surface first before attempting to strip it. French polish or nitro-cellulose, wax and oil — the reversibles — are easy to recognise, but it's extremely difficult to tell whether a surface is a pre-catalysed or polyurethane film.

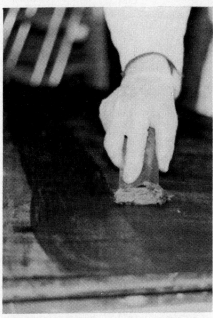

● *Rubber gloves and a blunt cabinet scraper for chemical strippers; sharp as you can get for surface preparation*

It's a great help if you know the age of the item you're working on, for you then have a general guide to the type of surface film most likely to have been used. All furniture before 1800 would have been waxed or oiled. Between 1815 and 1930, furniture was generally finished with french polish (Broadwood the piano manufacturers turned entirely to french polish in 1815), and from the 1930s onwards cellulose was greatly used by most manufacturers. Since the 1960s, sophisticated catalysed finishes have been used, and the manufacturers are still making improvements in drying times and hardness, while water-based lacquers are also being developed and perfected. These are only general guidelines, however; changes took place gradually and some manufacturers were more adventurous than others when it came to trying new finishes.

To make a more positive identification, try the following tests on an obscure part of the piece of furniture to identify:

● **French polish or shellac: a** Chip off a small piece or scratch with your finger-nail — a slight dent will be made.
   b Rub with a small amount of methylated spirits on a rag — a deposit will show on the rag.

● **Wax or Oil:** Rub with a small amount of turpentine on a rag — a deposit will show on the rag.

● **Nitro-cellulose finishes:** Rub with cellulose thinners on a rag — the surface film will soften quickly.

If you do these tests and nothing shows on your rag, you can reasonably assume that the finish is non-reversible. In this group, polyester gloss lacquer is easily identified by its glassy plastic gloss finish, and my advice to the amateur is leave well alone. Stripping this type of surface is best left to a professional.

Why strip and what to use

Any finish, whether it's varnish, paint, polish, lacquer, or emulsion, will not last for ever. Outside surfaces have to stand up to sun, rain, hail, frost, condensation, acids, salts, algae and expansion and contraction of the wood because of the weather's extremes; interior surfaces have to stand up to a range of temperatures in centrally heated homes, condensation, acids (in food), children general wear and tear, removals, storage and frequent misuse, all of which can lead to broken or chipped surfaces, blisters, burns (cigarettes), heat rings and bleach marks caused by spirits, acids and alkalis.

After identifying the surface finish, that is establishing the reversibility or non-reversibility of the surface, I would suggest the following basic procedures.

REVERSIBLE FINISHES

French polishes and shellac surfaces
If no silicone waxes have been used, then this surface can be removed by using methylated spirits or cellulose thinners. If silicone waxes have been used then a standard chemical stripper will be required, but take care with any veneers and do not use a water-washable type of stripper.

Oil or wax surfaces
These are among the easiest surfaces to remove using either white spirit (turpentine substitute) or a good turpentine with 000 steel wool to scrub it in.

Nitro-cellulose lacquers
These surfaces can be removed by using a proprietary chemical methylene-chloride non-caustic stripper. Don't use a blow-lamp or heat-gun on these finishes, or you'll have a fire on your hands!

NON-REVERSIBLE FINISHES

Paint and varnish for general joinery
This is best removed by using a blow-lamp or hot-air gun, which is quite easy and safe to use.

Paint and varnish for furniture
Use a proprietary chemical methylene-chloride non-caustic stripper, either fluid or paste, but if veneers are involved then care is required. It may be more sensible to use the dry method on these parts.

Other non-reversible finishes except polyurethane and polyester
Once again, a proprietary chemical methylene-chloride non-caustic stripper will remove the surface, but polyurethane and polyester both present special problems which are best left to the professional.

In all cases please read and follow the instructions on the container when using any chemical stripper, as they vary from one manufacturer to another. **Always** remember to neutralise afterwards using the recommended fluids.

165

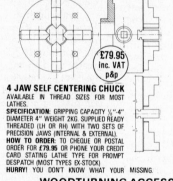

Many a strip

STRIPPING METHODS

Dry method

a With a cabinet scraper: an oblong piece of tool steel about 5x2½in, it can be sharpened on all eight edges and used in the direction of the grain to remove old varnish or french polish. It is particularly useful for removing polish from veneered surfaces which have been stuck with reversible animal glues.

b With abrasive papers: they can also be used on softer surfaces like shellac, the most suitable being 80-grit garnet or aluminium oxide. Care is needed not to 'rub into' veneers. These papers are also used with power sanders, but these machines shouldn't be used on veneered or quality furniture as they tend to cut across the grain. They are, however, useful for painted doors and coarser work.

A great deal of dust is produced with any dry method and you should always wear a face mask.

Heat method

This method has become popular recently since the introduction of electric hot-air guns which heat up the paint or varnish film, making it easy to use a scraper to remove the 'gunge'. Blow-lamps have been used for many years by professional decorators for the same purpose, and in recent years, butane gas has replaced paraffin as a fuel. The heat method is ideal for removing paint and varnish, but care must be taken to avoid burning the wood under the various layers of paint.

Chemical method

Proprietary non-caustic chemical strippers have become very popular in recent years; they come in two basic forms:
● a thin fluid — ideal for horizontal surfaces or mouldings, they are neutralised by white spirit;
● a thick paste — ideal for vertical and overhead surfaces, they are neutralised either by white spirit or water, when they are described on the tin as 'water-washable'.

These strippers usually contain methylene chloride, which is safe to use but nonetheless toxic. Instructions on the tin or bottle must be carefully read and strictly carried out. Avoid using the water-washable type on a veneered surface; too much water loosens veneers.

Procedure for chemical stripping

1 Stand the item to be stripped on various layers of old newspaper.

2 Apply stripper by brush with a dabbing action and leave for about 15 minutes. Re-apply using a liberal amount and leave for a further 15 minutes to allow the chemicals to eat into the hard surfaces.

3 Scrape off the surplus with a blunt cabinet scraper.

4 Scrub over the surface using coarse wire wool.

5 Wipe off the waste with waste cotton-wool (upholstery-type white cotton-wool is ideal for this job).

6 Use a brass wire brush to scrub out the surplus from mouldings or a sharp wooden stick like a large tooth-pick to clear corners.

7 Wash all over with water or white spirit to remove all traces of gunge from the grain.

8 When dry, sand down using 100-grit garnet abrasive paper.

9 Wash down again using methylated spirits, white spirit, cellulose thinners or water as recommended by the manufacturers.

10 Leave to dry out completely. This is very important; you should leave it for at least six and preferably 12 hours.

Caustic soda or lye (Sodium hydroxide)

This method has become very popular in recent years and therefore must be mentioned, but it is dangerous and messy, and it's best left to the professionals. Most towns have pine stripping companies who give a reasonably priced service. It is excellent for removing many layers of paint from doors and so on but can cause problems with some items of furniture because the process softens animal glues and can weaken or loosen joints. It also darkens pine. Caustic soda can be purchased in granular form from most DIY shops (usually as a drain-cleaner) and can be used either with cold water in a bath into which you dip the item for stripping, or with hot water in a more concentrated form, applied directly to the wood. Anyone attempting to use this method must remember that caustic soda is a very strong alkali which can cause serious burns to the skin, and *great care* must be taken in handling it. Strong rubber gloves, goggles and protective clothing including gumboots must be worn at all times, and the work must be done out of doors, or, if this isn't possible, in a very well-ventilated room. When stripped, the item must be washed down (a hosepipe is best) with plenty of water and left to dry.

When mixing the caustic soda, **always add the soda to water** — never the other way round, as the mixture will boil and spit. The average mixture for stripping is 1¼oz. of caustic soda to 5 litres of water.

HEALTH AND SAFETY

It must be emphasised that the following basic precautions should be taken when using any of the methods mentioned. Take particular care with chemical strippers; most are toxic.

● **Always** wear a face-mask, goggles and proper clothing.

● **Always** have plenty of ventilation in the work area, or, better still, do the work outdoors.

● Use a **barrier hand-cream** and **gloves** — thin canvas ones soaked in linseed oil are better than rubber gloves which soon deteriorate.

● **No smoking or eating** near the work area.

● After each work session, **wash your hands thoroughly** using a coaltar soap to avoid dermatitis; then apply a medicated hand-cream.

● Have a **bowl of water** handy in case of accidental spillage on the skin.

● When using a blow-lamp, it's useful to have either a **bucket of water** or a **small fire-extinguisher** handy in case you set fire to the wood! ■

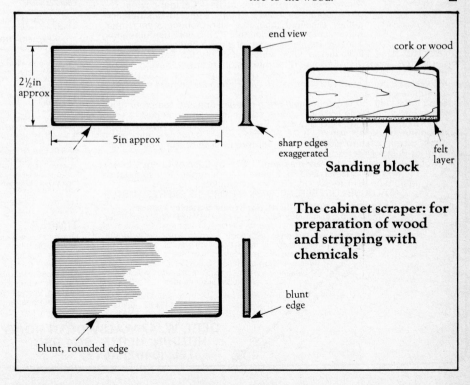

end view

cork or wood

2½in approx

5in approx

sharp edges exaggerated

felt layer

Sanding block

blunt, rounded edge

blunt edge

The cabinet scraper: for preparation of wood and stripping with chemicals

167

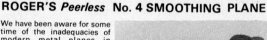

Plane speaking

Fraser Budd airs his views on production planes, states what you need in a first-class tool, and puts a new smoother to the test

The more you try to improve your skills, the more demands you make on your tools. 'A bad workman always blames his tools' goes the saying, but perhaps there are plenty of people with ability and flair hampered by poor-quality tools. Chisels which won't hold a really fine edge, saws which run off no matter how careful the cut, planes which persistently choke or tear interlocked grain. It always pays to spend more for a better tool.

I find the smoothing plane particularly interesting because it must perform to high standards of accuracy and achieve a smooth, tear-free finish at the same time. A well-tuned plane cuts both finishing time and the amount of abrasive paper you use, as well as helping to retain the sharp corners characteristic of good quality work.

I'm surprised at the poor standard of modern cast-iron planes produced by leading manufacturers. The short-cuts typical of mass production are becoming increasingly noticeable in the fine details which directly affect the functioning of the tool.

The best way to identify the problems and justify my criticism is to define what we require of a plane. What should your smoothing plane be, and what should it do?
● It should be comfortable to use, well-balanced and easy to manoeuvre on the wood, following your intended path with no other resistance than that of the cut itself.
● The sole should be dead flat and true, very finely finished and square with the sides.
● It should retain its setting, no matter how fine.
● It should have a blade which can hold a super-fine edge, even when used on hard, abrasive timber.
● It must be possible to set the blade and back-iron finely enough so even the wildest of grain can be planed smoothly and without tears. This is only possible with a really well-prepared, top-class plane.

I've spent many hours working on planes, including my own, to make them capable of these functions. In my experience it's unlikely that a new production plane would perform to these standards, no matter how sharp the edge is.

How a plane works

Planes of this type have the blade mounted bevel-downwards, resting in the tool to create a cutting angle of about 45°. Bolted to the back of the blade is the back-iron, which increases the blade's rigidity and reduces chatter. More important, it snaps

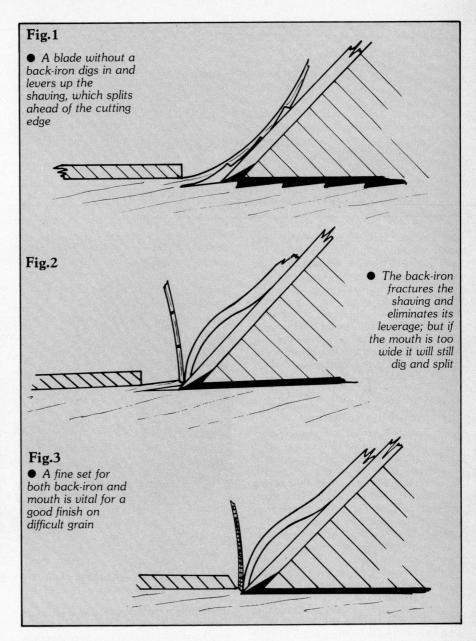

Fig.1
● A blade without a back-iron digs in and levers up the shaving, which splits ahead of the cutting edge

Fig.2

● The back-iron fractures the shaving and eliminates its leverage; but if the mouth is too wide it will still dig and split

Fig.3
● A fine set for both back-iron and mouth is vital for a good finish on difficult grain

the shaving as it is cut, reducing the leverage of the shaving which makes it split ahead of the blade-edge. Planing against the grain, this leverage makes the shaving split down into the grain and cause deep tears and chipping.

Fig. 2 shows how the distance by which the shaving can run ahead of the edge is governed by the depth of the mouth — adjustable on these planes. Obviously, where the grain is inclined to tear, a super-fine edge is required — the back-iron down as near to the edge as possible and the mouth set narrow (fig. 3).

Such a fine set often cannot be achieved in new planes because:
● The front edge of the mouth is square in cross-section, (fig. 4). As the blade and back-iron are brought forward, the gap between the casting and the iron closes to the point where even the finest shaving chokes the gap. A simple remedy is to file away the upper edge of the mouth (the dotted line in fig. 4), creating space for the

shaving to pass through even when the mouth is almost completely closed.
● The edge of the back-iron is flat and blunt (fig. 5) and fouls the cut shaving, which chokes the mouth. The back-iron should be sharp so it comes down on to the back of the blade cleanly and fits tightly. Then the shaving can be fractured as it's cut, and will be diverted out of the mouth with no fear of jamming or clogging. The simplest remedy is to file the edge sharp and polish it smooth, either on an oilstone or with fine abrasive paper.
● The back-iron often fails to make good contact with the back of the blade across its entire width. Any tiny gap soon attracts a shaving, which in turn clogs the mouth. You can correct this by working the edge on an oilstone until a perfect fit is achieved. Sometimes the iron needs slight twisting to correct it.
● New planes often seem to want to grip the wood. I first noticed this when using a student's plane during a demonstration; I

Plane speaking

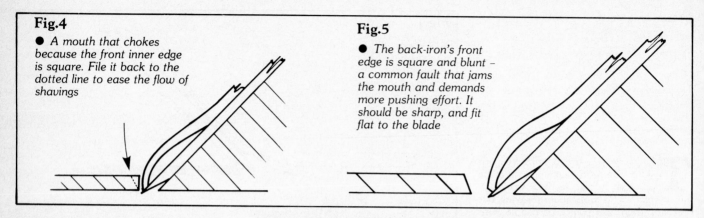

Fig.4
● A mouth that chokes because the front inner edge is square. File it back to the dotted line to ease the flow of shavings

Fig.5
● The back-iron's front edge is square and blunt – a common fault that jams the mouth and demands more pushing effort. It should be sharp, and fit flat to the blade

found it very difficult to steer the plane where I wanted, and when I used it on the skew it didn't travel at all smoothly. The reason here was the rough finish of the sole, and the only real remedy is to refinish it.
● There is generally an unnecessary amount of play between the thumbscrew and the Y-shape adjustment lever, several turns being needed to make even the smallest adjustment. I've seen planes whose Y-lever is made out of nothing but two bent pieces of metal!

Roger's 'Peerless': the smoothing solution?

Roger Buse of Roger's Tools is having some No. 4 planes produced to very high standards. At first glance the plane appears to be no different from any off-the-shelf model, but closer inspection reveals that the casting has a smooth, well-finished sole and sides, and that the handle is slightly stouter than normal. The back-iron is well made and available in standard or 'Stay-Set' patterns.

I was particularly impressed with the standard-pattern blade, produced specially for this plane using the Japanese laminating technique. An immensely hard cutting edge of about 25mm is laminated on to a softer back. Maybe you have never have used this type of laminated tool and might regard it as a bit of a gimmick. I certainly did when it was first introduced; it's far from the truth. The edge-holding qualities are quite remarkable. A finer edge can be honed at a lower angle, yet it still maintains a longer-than-normal sharp life. British plane-blades used to be made like this, with a hard-steel front section laminated on to a softer back, and this represents a revival of that tradition. The standard blade is quite satisfactory, but given the choice I'd prefer one of the new ones.

Overall the plane is well produced; the body, for instance, is left for about a year after casting to give any tension or movement in the cast a chance to settle. The depth adjustment has been refined and the only remaining slack is where the Y-lever slots into the blade. The Y-lever itself is strong and well-fitting, with a good chrome finish.

The plane I used had a one-piece back-iron, which I prefer, because I feel it helps the rigidity of the blade. The optional two-piece 'Stay-Set' iron's front section can be

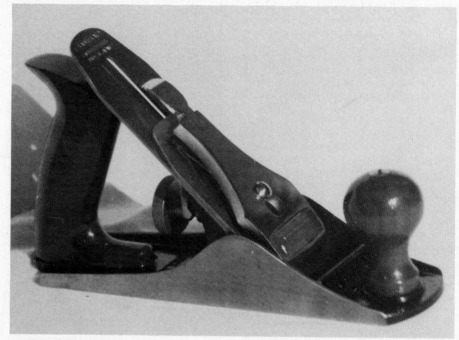

● Just an ordinary smoothing plane? No way. Roger's Peerless is just that, but it's not cheap by any standards

lifted away for quick and easy sharpening. The front edge of the back-iron needed a small amount of attention for, though it made good contact across the blade, it had a very slight flat along its edge, which was small enough to be quickly removed. The other small detail for attention was the cross-section of the front of the mouth (fig. 4), which needed some alteration. I passed these two points on to Roger, and he tells me the production models incorporate the improvements; I had a prototype.

I found this plane excellent to use. The blade was razor-sharp on arrival, and after only a couple of minutes to open the mouth-slot and sharpen the back-iron, it was ready. Once I adjusted the mouth-gap to my liking, I found it worked better than the one I've used for many years. This may sound rather remarkable, but I found the stouter handle more positive and comfortable to grip; the tool cut very smoothly, the shavings shooting up through the mouth in long streamers; and the better-fitting depth adjuster made very fine adjustments with less than the usual fuss.

The big test was, would it plane a piece of

hardwood with wild, interlocking grain? The blade, back-iron and mouth all set to the necessary ultra-fine setting very easily, and in no time at all the plane was removing the finest of shavings without even a trace of a tear. It handled well and glided smoothly, responding easily to both skew- and directional planing.

The laminated blade held its edge very well and the sharpness didn't deteriorate until long after I would have keened-up the edge on my usual blade. An inspection of the end- and side-grain pores of the wood showed them to be cleanly cut, with no fraying or crumbling.

I can only say I was most impressed with this product, and it did all I asked of it very well. It looks smart, the chrome is good quality, and it comes in its box ready to use. There can be no denying it's a good one, and it doesn't suffer from the problems of modern production planes. ■

● The Roger's Peerles No. 4 smoothing plane costs £75.95 from Roger's, 47 Walsworth Rd, Hitchin, Herts SG4 9SU, tel. (0462) 34177.

Combination curio

Bob Grant describes a
weird and wonderful tool,
and ponders on its
practical value

A friend of mine's woodworking business, started by his father last century, had accumulated more than 1000 tools. After my friend died I spent many fascinating if somewhat mournful hours going through his equipment and cataloguing it for sale. Many of the tools were in chests which belonged to craftsmen employed by his father, which had lain undisturbed for years.

Amongst them were such treasures as wooden braces, sets of moulding planes, huge Archimedean drills (which predate the now-popular geared hand-drills), and such curiosities as 1872-dated sickness-benefit contribution cards of the men who belonged to the Amalgamated Society of Carpenters and Joiners. Contributions were a shilling a week and a threepenny fine if you fell into arrears!

I came across a tool buried among these myriad and ancient items the like of which I had never seen before. For a time it had me puzzled. It looked more like a metalworker's hand-vice than a woodworking tool, but the bit-shank on top put it in the woodworker's tool-box. It was only after dismantling it that I found the solution in a 1935 Buck & Hickman's catalogue.

The Combination hand vice, made in the United States by Millers Falls, consists of 'a detachable hollow handle containing chisel, screwdriver, countersink, square reamer, bradawl, scratch awl and washer cutter'. The handle can be screwed into the vice at right-angles, and a bit-shank allows the vice to be used in a brace. Thus was the puzzle solved. It was probably bought initially on the strength of its novel promise as a universal tool, but eventually, I guess, proved too fiddly and timewasting. It's certainly still in pristine condition, and it's beautifully made; parallel jaw motion, heavy nickel-plating and a rosewood handle — all for 22 shillings!

With a mere 40 years of woodworking behind me, this is definitely a curiosity. Unless, of course, you know better? ■

● **Top:** 'The bit-shank on top put it in the woodworker's tool-box.' Working this one out would have foxed anyone without access to arcane tool catalogues: why the handle **and** the bit shank? **Middle:** the hollow handle reveals a mini-toolkit. Note the washer cutter. **Bottom:** having fixed the bit-shank in the brace and the awl in the jaws, you might find yourself wondering what was wrong with a simple bradawl...

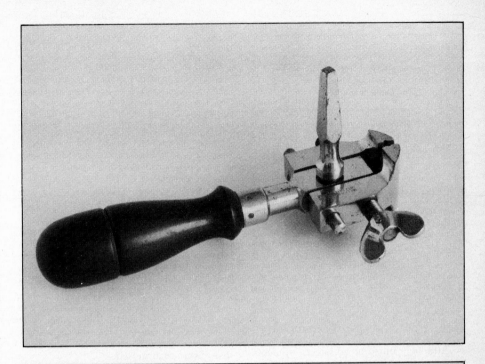

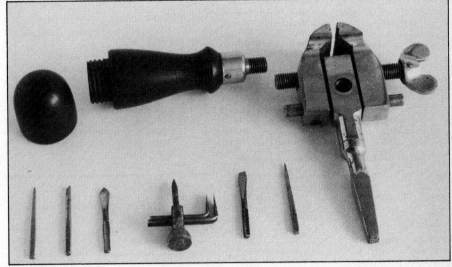

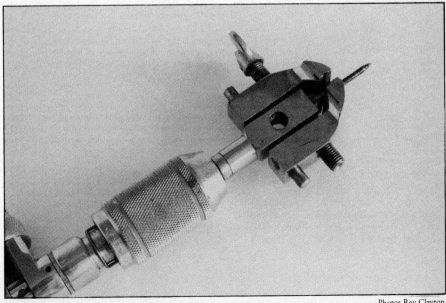

Photos Ray Clayton

Books

John Sunley and Barbara Bedding
Timber in Construction
Batsford, £14.95 hardback
Reviewed by David Savage

Timber is a remarkable natural product unsurpassed in its benefits as a material for man's use. It is strong in compression and tension, it is elastic, it is light and clean, non-toxic, non-conducting and a high insulant. It smells, feels, and does you good.

This book serves to mark the 50th anniversary of TRADA, The Timber Research and Development Association. It is a tome of considerable weight and quality, beautifully produced on high quality paper and illustrated by spectacular colour photography. It has been written by just about everyone who is anyone in timber technology and construction. As experts are very rarely comprehensible on their subject, there has been some careful editing and the book reads reasonably well.

Although aimed at architects, students and specifiers, the average woodworker can gain a lot from this very well-produced book, particularly one contemplating the construction of a house. Well done, TRADA, this book makes a fitting milestone in your history.

Tom Crabb
**Making Wooden Boxes
with a Bandsaw**
Sterling Publishing, £6.95 paperback
Reviewed by Fred Holtum

Here we have another of those 'All you have to do . . . ' books I find so infuriating, because nothing ever seems quite so easy as their authors suggest. Tom Crabb is described by the publisher as 'a master of the bandsaw', and some of his projects certainly boast an impressive dexterity. They are clearly presented in print, pictures and drawings. But, my goodness, what bizarre designs some of them are!

Making bandsaw boxes is unique, he says, 'because you begin with a solid piece of wood that you saw apart and then put back together.' Working mainly with scraps, he uses two basic techniques for making boxes with and without drawers. One involves straight cuts to fashion the conventional-shaped box. The other is to cut out shapes which result in such creations as 'Breadbox' (because it resembles a loaf) 'Footlocker' (two feet), and various animal shapes ('Whale', 'Pig', 'Turtle'). Finally comes the 'Fantasy Box' which is introduced thus: 'Once upon a time, a tower of light rose high above a faraway land of darkness. In this tower lived the Seer, a person who saw mysteries, knew secret things and made bandsaw boxes'. Oh, well!

Mr Crabb devotes a very brief chapter to the tool itself, so anyone seeking instruction on how to use a bandsaw would need to look elsewhere. One of the tools he illustrates is a 7½in Black & Decker

powered by a ⅜in drill (stockists in this country please stand up!). He stresses the need for a rip-fence for cutting straight lines. But apparently all those intricately shaped drawers he's so keen on have to be cut freehand — a task that would be made yet more difficult if the wobbly-lined figure-of-eight patterns in this book were transferred straight on to the workpiece. And is it really enough to suggest that, after such cutting and gluing, a satisfactory job can be completed simply by sanding?

The project that appealed to me most was a simple box with two drawers. Mr Crabb designed it to hold dominoes but admits that he made the domino drawer too small to hold a full set. I know the feeling! This box is made out of a single piece of poplar, so the sides of the cabinet and the drawers are ¼in endgrain. These pieces are weak, he says, and will probably break if dropped — but 'after you glue the ends back the box is structurally stable again.' I'll not take issue with an expert, but I think that method of construction should be left to someone less ham-fisted than myself.

At £6.95 I could not recommend this book to the woodworker who hasn't time to put some controversial construction methods to the test. But for the adventurous who like a challenge, may I suggest the 'Gnome-home' boxes which Mr Crabb describes as 'the backbone of the bandsaw fleet.' He doesn't explain why he calls them this, but suitably scaled up, the drawers could conceivably provide a hiding place for gaudy garden-dwellers. The only problem then remaining would be where to hide the Gnome-home!

John Trussell
**Working in Wood – Making boxes and
small chests**
Dryad, £7.95 hardback
Reviewed by Chris Yonge

The title is precise: this is a textbook of basic woodworking designed for those without the means to tackle either full-size furniture or woodturning. Mr Trussell has made the sensible decision to devote the first half of his book to descriptions of projects and the second to tools, construction, and materials.

The topics covered include all the standard joints and wooden hinges, small chests, drawers, veneering, and marquetry. As this is clearly intended to be used at the workbench, the lack of information on general design principles and history is understandable, if disappointing. However, the absence of any help to the amateur in choosing and finishing the many different woods suitable for box-making is a serious omission. Since structural and size limitations are so much less than in furniture making, existing wood textbooks are going to be unnecessarily discouraging to the box-maker.

The do-this-then-do-that style of project instructions is probably unavoidable at this level, but I found the layout and general

illustration clear and easy to follow. Some of the many photographs are indistinct, and in places one could have done with fewer but larger photos.

The box designs featured are conventional, but sound in principle and execution (though Mr Trussell should take care to ensure his dovetail keys are evenly spaced in future photographs). Enough detail is given to encourage beginners to take their first steps toward independent work and, as is to be expected from an experienced teacher, Mr Trussell is at his best in the section on woodworking technique, providing a clear and concise introduction to the appropriate methods. I would like to have seen more emphasis on safety, bearing in mind the potential readership — particularly with regard to the easily-snapped surgical blades he favours for veneer cutting — and suggestions for economic home-made alternatives to full-length sash cramps would be appropriate.

This is an expensive book for its size and content, even allowing for the hard cover and four pages of colour plates. It provides a sound introduction to one aspect of woodworking; move outside that field, or develop ambitions to craftsmanship, and you'll need a lot more information on hardwoods, finishes and design.

R. H. Farmer
The Handbook of Hardwoods
HMSO, £12.00, paperback
Reviewed by David Savage

I had to dig deep to find this book, for unlike most woodwork text and reference books, it is not publicised or freely available in craft bookshops.

Also unlike many books on wood, it does not have veneer samples and glossy photographs, both of which can be misleading. This is a large format paperback that simply tells you all about the technical properties of different species of timber.

The timbers listed cover just about every type of hardwood available in the solid form from ash to willow, abura to wanara.

For the working craftsman in wood the information given on each species is particularly valuable. When designing for a particular species, the rate of tangential movement and radial movement per foot are major considerations.

Questions on the reaction of the timber to machining, its planing and sawing characteristics, whether it takes a good polish, pins, screws and glue satisfactorily — all are answered by the HMSO with profound authority.

For the board or log purchaser, information is given on sizes, availability, weights, kilning schedules and drying peculiarities. For the chairmaker, wood bending classifications are backed up with specific data, and strength properties are clearly demonstrated.

I enjoy using this book. It supplies precise information quickly and clearly with the minimum of unnecessary guff.

Books

William J. Schnute
High Relief Wood Carving
Sterling, £8.95, paperback
Reviewed by Sid Lye

'. . . everything you need to know to produce beautiful high relief carving yourself' — so reads the publisher's notes on this new book by a very professional carver in which he relates experiences and ideas, know-how and secrets of some 30 years in his field. He describes the development of his art, from his first workshop — 'a pocket containing a three-bladed knife and a chunk of wood' — to his present studio, a veritable Aladdin's cave containing a sophisticated amalgam of hand- and power-tools — not least of which are a four-spindle duplicator and a converted hydraulic surgical table used as a workbench!

Time- and labour-saving tools and machinery abound and are obviously linked to his business acumen; many ideas for their use and the techniques involved are explained in graphic detail with fine quality colour plates, black-and-white pix and line illustrations.

In a review it is impossible to cover the many aspects of high relief wood carving which this book encompasses. Nevertheless there are chapters on the development of high relief panels, ideas, ideas into wood, perspective, lighting, wood and its conversion (felling, drying — including kiln-drying), adhesives, finishing — interior and exterior — shallow-relief, multi-layer panels and much more.

The presentation of this volume makes for easy reading. The ideas contained in its pages are a profound challenge to would-be carvers in this medium of artistic expression.

Patrick Spielman
Making Country-Rustic Furniture
Sterling, £6.95 paperback
Reviewed by Alan Bridgewater

When this book arrived, the whole rather bookish, wood-oriented Bridgewater clan became excited, and then read it from cover to cover. It's not bad, but nothing to get really excited about.

The 160 pages of text, captions, line illustrations, working drawings, plans and photographs contain a great many well-thought-out projects and ideas. If you're keen to make tables, bench-seats, chairs, duck decoys, lamps, brackets, sheds, doors, mugs, tables, weather-vanes and bird feeders, all in a country-rustic style, maybe this book is for you.

Personally, I have a partiality for New England furniture, but I don't much care for an approach that requires wood to be roughed-up or textured. Nor do I like to see a piece of so called country furniture that has been over-worked with high-tech tools. I'm sure that the author has a successful workshop, and I'm sure that for speed and economy he needs to use a whole range of time-saving tools — but is it necessary or desirable for the average woodworker to use the full range of power tools to make pieces that are actually described as 'rough-hewn rustic'?

This book is very, very American in content, approach and design, and there are a number of problems in style and word usage. When the average UK woodworker thinks of 'cottage', 'rustic' or 'country', he or she probably sees in the mind's eye images of English Victorian and Edwardian garden gazebos, quaint porch seats and trellises. This book's imagery, by contrast, has its roots in 'American homestead' and 'primitive'.

All that apart, I'm not giving it the thumbs-down, because in many ways it's sound and well put together. I just wish that the designs were a bit stronger, and the author not quite so concerned with such doubtful concepts as 'leaving nature's and man's signatures'.

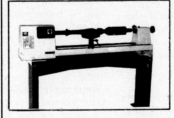
Fancy seeing your work in full colour on the pages of *Woodworker*? If you send something in, remember that *only colour transparencies* with perfect focus and a totally neutral background have half a chance!

Letters

I'D LIKE TO ADD to Stuart King's answer in 'Question Box', (WW/Oct 85) about miniature furniture-making.

First, there are excellent kits of prefabricated parts for a wide range of furniture, made by X-Acto and others. This would be an excellent way to dip one's toe in the water. If interested, contact Blackwell's of Hawkwell, 200 Main Road, Hawkwell, Essex SS5 4EH, tel. (0702) 202456/205891, for their lists.

Second, the 'Bible' is *The Miniatures Catalog*, a 1in thick 8½x11in tome, listing the products of hundreds of US suppliers and published by Boynton & Associates, Clifton House, Clifton, VA 22024, USA, tel. (703) 830-1000. This is in its seventh edition and will be shipped by surface mail For $18.95 or airmail for $27.95. I guarantee you will not regret the expense.

Third, an excellent book for beginners as well as advanced workers is *The Art of Making Furniture in Miniature* by Harry Smith, (E.P. Dutton, New York). It contains plans for some 18 projects as well as excellent illustrations and instructions about tools. It can be procured from Stobart & Son, the craftsman's bookshop, 67-73 Workship St, London EC2A 2EL, tel. 01-247 0501.

Fourth, scale timber is available from suppliers to the model-railroad hobby. A firm that offers a wide range of sizes in basswood and mahogany is Northeastern Scale Models, Inc., 99 Cross St, PO Box 425, Methuen, MA 01844, USA.

Another firm that has a comprehensive stock of sheetwood in basswood, cherry, mahogany, walnut, and maple is Midwest Products Co. Inc, PO Box 564, 400 South Indiana St, Hobart, IN 46342, USA. Sheets are available in thickness from ¹⁄₃₂ to ¾in in widths of 1, 3 and 4in, depending on the wood, and lengths of 24in.

Frank Chambers, Westport, Co. Mayo

THE *MACHINE GUIDE* (WW/Oct) is a travesty, as was the *Power Tool Guide* before it.

The introductions to each section are good and it's fair enough to accept the bumf that the makers supplied, but the answer to 'Which to Buy' never materialises. The lack of uniform information means that no effective comparison can be made.

The tables should have been for all makes, with a comprehensive breakdown in the categories. A bandsaw, for example, should have been identified by make, code number, depth of cut and throat, cutting-speeds, motor rating, table size, blade width, blade length, construction type, overall dimensions, weight; and the existence (or not) of: a brake, roller-guides, a fence, mitre-fence, 45° table cant, micro-switches on doors, and castors for mobility.

Every time I have bought a machine, I have contacted all the manufacturers I know of for technical information and spent hours drawing up this sort of table. In this way you can inspect and try out the few machines that seem suitable.

A simple matter like replacement blade-length (and your source of supply) can affect the running costs. The Guide also fails to mention the excellent machines made by Wadkin, Dominion, Viceroy, Modern, Sedgwick, Dodds, Harrison, Cookson and many others. You may consider some of them to be out of your readers' price range, but they are available second-hand and at auctions. The use of heavier and British machines should be encouraged.

I submit that the trees that went into the Guide would have been better used in a future copy of the excellent *Woodworker* — or even left standing!

Peter Whiteley, Sudbury

THE MACHINE SURVEY (WW/Oct) was all very seductive stuff, especially to anyone to whom tools in themselves are beautiful objects. I came within a hair's breadth of buying a universal myself until I began asking myself questions such as 'what else could I buy for my family with £2000?' And: 'Wouldn't I get an equal amount of pleasure using hand tools?' And: 'How do I feel about sharing a room with 1kg-pieces of finely-honed steel whizzing around at 6000 revs?' . . . However, the survey itself was a great disappointment — littl more than an advertising supplement. Truly objective comparisons were absent. Although some fairly precise statements were made (for example, under Bandsaws: 'it's rarely accurate enough for operations like picture framing') most questions went unanswered.

There seem to be too many articles (in fact, one is too many) which end with 'and our thanks to those smashing blokes at Luna/Startrite/DeWalt/Bloggs for letting us use their wonderful machine . . . ' One cannot help questioning the impartiality of it all. Surely *Woodworker* could afford to buy itself the machine in question if it wants to do an article such as this? After all, the magazine seems to assume, increasingly, that we've all got the machine ourselves! Then, if you wish to illustrate the usefulness of the machine itself you could objectively assess the work it did in comparison with the equivalent job with hand-tools or power tools. However, when I see those dreaded words at the end of an article, I know that you're not going to tell me how many hours you spent fiddling with the whatsits to cut the tenons.

Mr Sladdin, Karlsruhe, W. Germany

The Editor replies: Some points taken, gentlemen, others not. If you were misled about the nature of the *Machine Guide*, we're sorry. But if you read the introduction, you would have seen the words: 'These descriptions come from the manufacturers themselves . . . ' The truth is the *Machine Guide* was and is an advertising supplement — it brought numerous products together between two covers, and surely gave you some chance of comparison. Next time, we'll try harder to set the information out more clearly and more comprehensively.

As for *Woodworker* itself buying machinery, you don't wish half so much as we do that we could spend all our editorial time in the basement workshop! If there *was* a basement workshop . . . Few magazines are run on limitless budgets (of time or money), and we feel we can bring you information with other people's help that we wouldn't be able to do ourselves unaided. You may notice that not a word of advertisement finds its way into our wood-machining series; just words of acknowledgement and thanks. We pride ourselves on our critical independence, and believe me, if we were objectively assessing a particular machine instead of telling you what a type of machine does, you'd know the difference.

Aidan Walker

I WOULD LIKE to thank you for the excellent advice you gave concerning long hole augers (WW/June 85).

I have now successfully made one by following your instructions and have done some silver soldering for the first time. I took up woodturning two years ago, starting simply with a home-made lathe powered by a portable drill. Now I have graduated to a Sherwood lathe by James Inns (Shoptalk, WW/Jan 86), which is simple, low in price and efficient. Consequently I have adapted my long-hole-boring jig to fit the Sherwood.

Douglas Greenhall, Bromley

Letters

Bill Brown writes:

I would like to comment on Stan Thomas' reply to Mr Smith's problem (Question Box WW/Nov 85), which revolved around an external staircase made from softwood that had rotted. Oak was proposed as a replacement timber for posts, stringers and other parts of the carcase, but he wanted to keep the original softwood treads.

Mr Smith didn't say where the rot had mainly occurred, nor did he say if the posts were set direct on to a hard standing or were set in the ground. In the absence of this information, one could take the most extreme situation of risk of decay and use this as a basis for remedial action.

● The question of risk, both mechanical and by fire. External staircases are in some cases considered as fire-escapes if there is no other access from their part of the building, and local authorities are strict on this point, insisting on fire-proofing. There is nothing in the enquiry to suggest the stairs were or weren't approved by the council, but the thought should have been there, and even the smallest reference should have been made, since teak might have been a satisfactory answer if there was risk of fire. Creosote was mentioned in connection with preservation; if it had to be used at all, it should have been pointed out that it would increase fire risk.

● Emphasis was placed on oak and the difficulty in obtaining the dimension and lengths required, but this was dismissed as an alternative simply on the grounds of corrosion tendencies to non-ferrous bolts. Oak is not an ideal wood for external stairs; weathering makes it rough and splintery.

● Alternatives could have been:

a European redwood, pressure-impregnated with Tanalith or Celcure.

b Larch posts in the sizes mentioned could be obtained from most home-grown merchants. Larch is a traditional wood for posts, and in 4x4in section would have a life expectancy of 40 years or more without preservative treatment.

c Keruing would have the same life at least, while jarrah or karri would last even longer.

● There was no need to refer to sapstain as a decay hazard when preservation was already suggested. Sapwood does encourage fungi and beetles, but if redwood has developed sapstain, then it will take a better penetration of preservative because the fungi have removed much of the starch.

● There was no need to suggest that sapwood-free redwood might be available — this is virtually impossible to obtain, but there was a need to point out that if redwood was considered in 4x4in section, boxed hearts should be avoided.

● The suggestion that the posts should be jointed as shown in the sketch is poor practice. They could be jointed by other methods but why bother when there are other timbers that could be employed?

Stan Thomas replies:

● Concerning Bill Brown's first point — a fire-escape. This hadn't indeed occurred to me; simply, I suppose, because the stair *is* made of wood. Had I thought of it, I could have suggested a light concrete stair, and this would of course last a lifetime.

● The second point concerns oak as an external timber. Yes, the medullary rays *do* tend to lift in the sun, and it can also 'check' (numerous short splits). The first is a minor problem — just a glass-papering with each painting will solve it. But the second is a consequence of neglect, and it should not occur if the wood is properly maintained. After all, most of our church timbers are of oak, lych-gates for example. They may be, in some cases, rough and splintery as Bill says; but no one seems put out by this, and in some of these constructions, we are looking at work a hundred years old or more.

● About 'European redwood'. I think I'm correct in assuming that today's redwood is what in my young days was known as 'red deal' — as opposed to 'white deal' (or spruce). And we come to a moot point: 'red' was always the timber for exterior joinery, while 'white' was the timber for indoors, especially floorboards. Back in the 50s I built myself a small workshop and used 3x2in spruce for the door-jambs, with planted stops. (What an invitation to rot!) I had this material to hand; but I knew without doubt — and accepted — that in a few years they'd have to be renewed with red. Well, they are still there; while my bay window-sill (of selected red) had to be renewed in five years. The spruce took the weather too. But tradition dies hard; these could be two freak instances, and I still postulate red for exterior work. And of course, as Bill says, Celcure or Tanalith. I did say 'It doesn't *have* to be creosote nowadays.'

● Larch? Bill has a point here. This is a timber that I've never come across in joinery. Oak, ash and chestnut are almost indistinguishable side by side — elm could be included. Give them all a coat of paint, and I'll pick them out — in the dark! Larch however, I wouldn't be at all sure of; Bill says this has a life of 40 years. Keruing, yes; the market (the Cardiff yards at least) were swamped with this in the 50s. It was also called yang, and, I think, gurjun (?). But it seems to have gone out of circulation; I at least, haven't seen it for over 20 years, like pitch pine. I did get some Columbian pine (Oregon pine or douglas fir) about 10 years ago, but it had to be a special order. For this reason, I didn't think the pines were worthy of mention.

● I didn't exactly postulate the jointing of the newels, but Mr Smith asked the question about the method of jointing. There are of course other methods, splayed indent, tabling, or fish-plate, for example, but these are for tension/transverse stresses. There are no such forces in a newel-post, so if you have to joint, I stand by my butt splices here, bolted as shown.

I'VE BEEN AN AVID reader of *Woodworker* for many years and was very disappointed to find such a shambles as Vic Taylor's 'Through the Golden Gate' in the September 1985 issue.

The rot starts in line three. The basic definition is wrong: 'The first part is to the second part ... $10 \div 6.18 = 1.618$ ... as the second is to the whole, i.e. $6.18 \div 16.18 = 0.3819$'? Why is fig. 3 so big? Where is fig. 3C?

A more general gripe is that, whilst information on wood in *Woodworker* is spot-on, references to metals are sometimes misleading, and tend to reduce the magazine's status. Reginald Norris refers to die-cast steel, hand-forged (p.680). The blades probably were hand-forged cast steel; if they had been die-cast they would not have been hand-forged. Steel die-casting is a production engineer's dream — some experimental work has been done using modern refractory die materials, but it wasn't used for screwdrivers in 1934. I could go on to describe cast steel and high-speed steel and Tungsten Carbide, but perhaps you should run an article by a metallurgist on past and present cutting materials and their merits.

Could you also in a future issue make it clear why the use of a scraper in turning is almost immoral? It would first be necessary to define a scraper. Is it a negative-rake cutting tool (used largely in modern metal machining) or is it actually operating as a high-rake tool?

R. S. Read, South Woodford

EARLIER IN THE YEAR I wrote asking if you were able to provide me with some detailed information about the construction of a farthingale chair.

Vic Taylor wrote to me and in your August issue you kindly printed a most helpful and concise article from which I gleaned enough material to be able to make the set of eight dining chairs.

I have no idea how much feedback you enjoy as a result of your assistance but I felt a word of gratitude would not come amiss.

Wilfrid Pink, Fakenham

I WOULD LIKE TO EXPRESS how much I enjoyed the recent show at Alexandra Palace. The only criticism I had was the lack of attention to safety.

On several occasions fingers were within inches of moving saw-blades and I saw only one person wearing eye-protection. The worst instance of carelessness involved a demonstration with an emery disc and an electric drill. There was no protection for either demonstrator or potential buyer. In fact a small child who was watching had a stream of sparks directed (unintentionally) at his face. It only needed a Perspex screen to have made the operation safer for everyone.

A. Nichols, Billericay

WOODWORKER

style . . . craft . . . and the love of wood

March 1986 Vol. 90 No. 1108

Photo William Moorwood

● *Something's going on in the forest . . . p236*

PROJECTS
All with detailed working drawings

202 Country cousin
A cricket table — but nothing to do with bat and ball! *Alex Webb*

216 Table-top seat
The Monk's bench may or may not have been used by monks — now it's a seat, now it's a table. *Vic Taylor*

240 Nature's wooden way
Japanese *Netsuke* and Grinling Gibbons inspired these two charming carvings. *Alan and Gill Bridgewater*

244 The charm of discretion
Woodworker Show prizewinner; make this subtle and beautiful low table in oriental style. *Waring Robinson*

On the cover: Adornment and extravagance: 'Coats of many colours', p196, introduces a range of techniques and effects with paint

Photo Quill Publishing

190 The craft of cabinetmaking
Veneering: glue is spread and leaves are laid. *David Savage*

193 Shoptalk special
Saw points
A clever new tool and an updated old friend are put to the test. *Gordon Stokes*

195 Squares and rounds
WIN! A table-saw and a lathe are up for grabs in our craft competition

196 Coats of many colours
Decorative finishes: much more than a lick and a promise. *Ian Hosker*

201 Carving a career
The enterprise and skill of a professional carver. *Stan Folb*

208 Machining Wood
Your expert guide: 5
The spindle moulder gives the wood-machinist the chance to become an artist.

235 Yew turned
What happens when a canny turner discovers beauty in timber full of rusty nails . . .

236 The gleaning of the forests
Extraordinary buildings in the Devon forest are the roundwood reality of a furniture-maker's dream. *David Savage*

250 A place of your own
Workshop special: the pleasures and pitfalls of building your workspace. *Tony Matthews*

254 Up against the wall
The humble lean-to is easy to build if you want a workshop on a budget. *Peter McNiff*

257 Tales out of steel
Scenes from the street-market in pre-war Sheffield. *Ashley Iles*

REGULARS

179 This month looks at the woodworking world

181 Shoptalk takes note of products and services

184 Guild notes
If you aren't a member — read this page!

187 Question Box
Your questions answered from a wealth of woodworking experience

207 Woodworking wheeze of the month
Ways to economise on costly finishing materials. *Noel Leach*

233 Bob Wearing's Workshop
Jointing thin boards

259 Books

261 Letters
Readers' chance to talk back!

Editor Aidan Walker
Deputy editor Owen Watson
Editorial assistant Kerry Fowler
Advertisement manager Paul Holmes
Graphics Jeff Hamblin
Technical illustrator Peter Holland
Guild of Woodworkers Owen Watson, Kerry Fowler
Editorial, advertisements and Guild of Woodworkers
1 Golden Square, London W1R 3AB, telephone 01-437 0626

Subscriptions and back issues Infonet Ltd, 10-13 Times House, 179 Marlowes, Hemel Hempstead, Herts HP1 1BB; telephone Hemel Hempstead (0442) 48434

Subscriptions per year UK £16.90; overseas outside USA (accelerated surface post) £21.00, USA (accelerated surface post) $28, airmail £48

UK trade SM Distribution Ltd, 16-18 Trinity Gardens, London SW9 8DX; telephone 01-274 8611

North American trade Bill Dean Books Ltd, 151-49 7th Avenue, PO Box 69, Whitestone, New York 11357; telephone 1-718-767-6632

Printed in Great Britain by Ambassador Press Ltd, St. Albans, Herts
Mono origination Multiform Photosetting Ltd, Cardiff
Colour origination Derek Croxson Ltd, Chesham, Bucks

© Argus Specialist Publications Ltd 1986
ISSN 0043 776X

Argus Specialist Publications Ltd
1 Golden Square, London W1R 3AB; 01-437 0626

Where Craft Comes Alive..

The BRISTOL Woodworker Show '86

May 16th, 17th, 18th *It's all about wood...*

Beautiful wood... Oak, Sycamore, Ash, Walnut, Mahogany
Versatile wood... see the experts demonstrating their skills
Wonderful wood... admire the competition entries –
from marquetry to cabinet making

LOOK... at the latest woodworking machinery,
tools, supplies and accessories
LISTEN... to the advice of the demonstrators
BUY... from the many exhibition stands

All the wonder of wood at the...

Bristol Woodworker Show
Bristol Exhibition Centre
Canon's Road
Bristol

OPENING TIMES:
May 16, 17... 10 am – 6 pm
May 18... 10 am – 5 pm

For further details contact

Argus Specialist Exhibitions,
Wolsey House, Wolsey Road,
Hemel Hempstead, Herts HP2 4SS
Tel: 0442 41221

 The Bristol Woodworker Show is organised by Argus Specialist Exhibitions
and sponsored by Woodworker Magazine

Woodworker This month

Herring fishing A low-relief carving by Malcolm Jarvis, born and bred in Great Yarmouth amongst fisher-folk. Malcolm's family were curers and exporters. A piece of elm driftwood, it includes a 'cran' basket, a steam drifter and Great Yarmouth's coat-of-arms

Soon Showing!
The Bristol Woodworker Show is the jewel of May — enter your work, or just be there. Fancy winning a table-saw or lathe? See 'Squares and rounds' in this issue.
● Exhibition entry details from Elaine Rushton, A.S.E., Wolsey House, Wolsey Rd, Hemel Hempstead, Herts HP2 4SS.

Essex mouth puller from *Images of Lust*, Jerman and Weir, B.T. Basford £17.95

One of the greatest changes that has taken place of late years in workshop methods of construction (chiefly attributable to the perfecting of the twist bit) is the almost exclusive extinction of the mortise and tenon, and the substitution of the birch or other tough hardwood dowel.
October, 1906

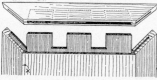
How to cut the mitred clamp: This joint was widely used for large table tops, bureau falls, and so on before the manufacture of reliable plywood and laminated board made it largely unnecessary. Now that these materials are scarce it is frequently necessary to revert to it again. It is reliable enough providing that sound, seasoned timber is used; otherwise trouble due to shrinkage is inevitable.
January, 1946

Wrong number
In January's 'Shoptalk', we inadvertently gave the wrong number for James Inns, the lathemakers. It should be (0602) 585646. Our apologies to those who wasted a call to Nottingham.

Friendly FoE
May we congratulate you, **writes Charles Secrett of Friends of the Earth,** on one of the most balanced pieces of reporting on our tropical hardwood campaign we have seen in the timber press (WW/Jan). You have succinctly, accurately and fairly summed up the different approaches that a public campaigning organisation like ourselves, and an industry body like the **Timber Trades Federation** take over an issue like tropical deforestation. More important, you point out the common ground; both sides seek the sustainable management and protection of tropical forests.

Although disappointed by other recent articles' over-emphasis on the 'sticker' aspect of our campaign we are not down-hearted. More and more retailers, manufacturers and importers are realising that our most important priority is the adoption of the Code of Conduct (or one like it) first suggested by FoE in spring 1985. The more we explain our position, and put the 'sticker' aspect in perspective (an absolute last resort when a retailer refuses even to *discuss* adopting a code) the more offers of help we get to achieve unity between the trade and environmentalists.

Let me quote one major retailer:

'I must add this company's support to such a worthy cause, since the environmental significance of deforestation is of equal worry to all. Moreover, it's true that proper and responsible management of the tropical rainforests loses no relevance in strict economic terms, since the future supply of hardwood must be safeguarded and this can be achieved by the careful 'housekeeping' provisions in the proposed Code of Conduct. As a retailer, we are not in the best position to enact such a code, and consequently wrote to our trade association, the National Association of Retail Furnishers, indicating our support for the FoE rainforest campaign (Courts Furnishers PLC).' The response is typical of many we have been getting from all levels of the trade in recent weeks.

To achieve the vital change in attitudes to own precious forests Friends of the Earth are prepared to compromise. We will gladly drop the 'sticker' aspect of our campaign if it will help negotiations with individual retailers and their Federation, and bring into being an effective, practical Code of Conduct. So far, the stickers have done one job well — to wake the industry up and to make it look long and hard at its *modus operandi*. All well and good. Now let's work together to do what we can in Britain, Europe and the other major tropical hardwood consuming nations to get sustainable management of a basic resource we all need for our future.
● The National Association of Retail Furnishers and Friends of the Earth met to discuss the Code of Conduct on Wednesday 22 January, as we went to press. Good things may come…

Diary
Guild courses are shown by an asterisk (*); for further details see the Guild pages.

March
Tuesday 4-Monday 31 **Ideal Home Exhibition,** Earls Court, London
Saturday 15 **Bob Grant: Survival metalwork***
Sunday 23-Thursday 27 **Manchester Easter School***
Thursday 27-Saturday 5 April **Making Musical Instruments** course, West Dean College, tel. (024363) 301

April
Thursday 3, Friday 4 **Charles Cliffe: French polishing***
Saturday 12 **Bob Grant: Hand veneering***
Saturday 19, Sunday 20 **Ian Hosker: French polishing***
Sunday 13 **Visit to Parnham House and the School for Woodland Industries.** See the Guild pages for details
Saturday 26 **Ken Taylor: Woodmachining***

May
Saturday 10 **Roy Sutton: Power routing***
Friday 16-Sunday 19 **Bristol Woodworker Show**
Sunday 11-Sunday 18 **London International Furniture Show,** Earls Court

October
Thursday 23-Sunday 26 **Woodworker Show,** Alexandra Palace, London

180

Shoptalk

PLANS are frequently requested by Woodworker readers; if you want to know what we've got try the **Woodworker Planbook.** The 1983 plan-prices are still being honoured, and it contains a lot of useful hints from regular Woodworker contributors.
● Woodworker Plans Service, Wolsey House, Wolsey Rd, Hemel Hempstead, Herts HP2 4SS, tel. (0442) 41221. 85p + 30p p&p.

Allowing timber to 'breathe' through whatever you coat it with seems to be all the rage. Latest with a 'microporous' finish is **Glasurit Beck,** who've produced a two-coat translucent door finishing kit. Door manufacturers Chindwell have bravely offered to exchange one of their doors finished with Lasutect if it wraps or cracks within six months of application — subject to the usual provisos of wear and tear, and correct application of the finish.
● Glasurit Beck, Slinfold, nr Horsham, West Sussex RH13 7SH, tel. (0235) 28854. Lasutect two-pack Door Finishing Kit retails at about £8 inc VAT.
● Chindwell Ltd, Hyde House, Edgware Rd, The Hyde, London NW9 6JT, tel. 01-205 6171.

ASHBY DESIGN'S PLAN-SCOPE contains details of projects from furniture to model horse-drawn vehicles.
● Ashby Design Workshop, 34a Catherine Hill, Frome, Somerset BA11 1BY, tel. (0373) 72344.

AN EXPLORATION into woodturning; courses for those 'with a sense of adventure' by Michael O'Donnell will aim at stimulating experimentation. **Charltons** the West-country timber people are also running courses on basic woodwork and carving.
● Michael O'Donnell, The Croft, Brough, Thurso, Caithness KW14 8YE, tel. (048785) 605
● Charltons, Frome Rd, Radstock, Avon BA3 3PT, tel. (0761) 36229.

A BATTERY-POWERED circular saw – the first of its type in Britain – from Bosch. It has to be handy at the tops of ladders, and should be light enough; it's got a 6in blade. 'More than 50 pieces of 2×1in timber can be cut on one charge' is the rather uninspiring claim. It takes an hour to recharge; a hefty £224 + VAT, including charger.
● Bosch, PO Box 98, Broadwater Park, North Orbital Rd, Uxbridge UB9 5HJ, tel. (0895) 833633.

SELF-TAPPING INSERTS; a possible solution to edge-fixing problems in soft boards, the Rampa range comes in a number of useful sizes and lengths. Everlasting threaded holes in Weetabix board?
● Spirol Industries, 17 Princewood Rd, Corby, Northants NN17 2ET, tel. (0536) 67634.

Last month we mentioned **Fimagen**, a new manufactured board made out of fine shavings that presents serious competition to MDF. We've had a go with it; we've routed it, tungsten-tipped sawn it, bandsawn it, hand-sawn it, handchiselled it, stapled it, screwed it and pinned it. Yes, we know manufactured board shouldn't be cut with ordinary tool steel, but have you got a tungsten-tipped chisel?

The facts of the stuff are much as you'd expect, looking at the specification, which explains the homogeneous formation between the layers of shavings. Wood particles, out of which chipboard is made, don't homogenise in layers. It's harder than MDF, the dust is coarser and smells nicer, it doesn't cut quite so easily and the finish on, say, a routed edge isn't quite so smooth. Piece for piece it's slightly heavier than MDF.

It's obviously a product to examine closely. We doubt the board would take quite such a good finish as MDF, because the particles are bigger, but we didn't spray and rub down innumerable coats of lacquer, so we'll have to wait to find out.

The major lead it has over MDF is of course the price. Buying in pallet quantities (that's around 100 sheets a time), 18mm chipboard is around £1.65 per sq. metre, 19mm Fimagen £2.27, and MDF £3.31. Maybe it just fills a gap nicely . . .

● Tafinsa Boards Ltd, 13 Bridge St, Maidenhead, Berks SL6 8PJ, tel. (0628) 783551.

Timberline

Arthur Jones' update on timber trade news

Prices change for a variety of reasons and it is often difficult to generalise. For example, shortages of logs in a producing country could herald reduced supplies for the importer and rising prices for the UK wood user. However, if demand is low, sellers may be reluctant to raise prices any further.

This has been happening with sapele. Unlike most hardwoods, the stocks are still too high for comfort in most parts of the country, so prices are highly competitive. At one time it was thought that there would be a boom in West African hardwoods, with a bigger call for such species as sipo and samba, but this has not materialised.

Generally, hardwood stocks in Britain are now getting much more into balance, except for sapele and perhaps American red oak. However, there are now regional shortages of some hardwoods because poor sales have discouraged importers from going strongly into foreign markets.

The timber market is reasonably steady and the betting is that any movement will be slightly upwards. Prices for softwood continue to show only bare possible profit margins for producers; the Poles, out with the first winter offer for shipments of seasoned wood up to April, pitched their new prices realistically at £89 per cu. m. with carriage and freight. There have been few problems selling at this figure in spite of the sluggish demand.

Whitewood prices have had a minor recovery to 7½% higher than their poorest 1985 levels. Whitewood's troubles seem to have switched to redwood, which has got cheaper in some sizes and grades. There is still too much sawn softwood being produced in Sweden and Finland, and mills will probably continue to go out of business for some time yet.

Official parana pine prices in some grades have dropped 15%, but this is hardly a cheap softwood, though it is a favourite for joinery.

Producers of both Brazilian mahogany and Philippine lauan have been reporting log supply problems and difficulties in get-ting stocks to the mills. Every hardwood importer is saying we can expect the prices for these hardwoods to go up well before the summer.

Ramin prices have risen by some 5% recently. This hardwood varies in both supply and price, largely according to what happens in Italy where it's widely used.

New quotas have been announced for EEC countries for non-EEC plywood imports. A lot of Far Eastern plywood came out of bond at the beginning of January to escape duty and this means that supplies are abundant and will stay that way for some months.

As Spain and Portugal share the overall ply quota, (which includes coniferous plywood imports from North America), there is a slightly smaller allocation, but you shouldn't find any problems. Finnish plywood prices are failing to hold the official levels, so birch plywood in cut sizes is slightly cheaper than forecast. Blockboard prices have been rising, as demand has increased in the UK.

On the subject of rising demand, prizes must go to chipboard and MDF. The recently improved Hexham chipboard plant will be offering larger supplies, especially of melamine-faced chipboard. We've passed the day when chipboard was scorned as 'not real wood'; it's quite difficult these days to find a piece of furniture in a store which isn't chipboard.

Princes Risborough Laboratory is doing test work on joinery wood primers to assess resistance to blistering and weathering in exterior applications. It's been found that some primers are unsuited to exterior work, and the findings will be incorporated in a British Standard in due course.

The new microporous coatings for exterior use allow moisture in woodwork to evaporate and at the same time prevent damp in the air getting into the wood; they also let the finish expand or contract with the wood without cracking. In these days when so much ill-seasoned timber is being sold, the new finishes can help prevent decay in timber, and also increase the time before re-painting. A real boon. ∎

Guild notes

WOODWORKERS

Shared information, advice and help are vital to good woodwork. They are also the basis of the **Guild of Woodworkers**: an international organisation which welcomes new members — whatever their skills. 1 Golden Sq, London W1R 3AB, tel. 01-437 0626.

Guild members get
- priority on our courses
- free publicity in *Woodworker*
- 15% off Woodworker Show entry
- a free display area and meeting-point at the Show
- 15% discount on our plans
- access to and inclusion in our register of members' skills and services
- the chance to contact other members for help and advice where appropriate
- specially arranged tool insurance at low rates

Please quote your Guild number when contacting us.

Owen Watson

Let's go down to the wood today...

You read the article, now see the place. If you were fascinated by David Savage's account of John Makepeace's venture in woodland industry and want to find out more, we've arranged a day at both Parnham House, his beautiful HQ, and the new School for Woodland Industry at Hooke Park. Experts will be on hand to answer your questions, and refreshments will be available. It's on Sunday 13 April, and costs £4. To book, write to the Guild, quoting your Guild number and enclosing a sae, but no money. We can only take the first 40 who write in — so hurry!

Up front

The *Woodworker* team was putting its feet up in its penthouse suite. We got to talking about promotional items for the Guild. 'Why haven't we got any badges?' said one. 'Too blatant and American,' said another. 'They're metal,' added a third. 'Why don't we have more wooden things for sale?' One of the office juniors piped up: 'Why not have wooden badges?'

'Where can you get them made?' came the discouraging reply. 'Why don't you ask Guild members whether any of them could make them?' responded this pert youth. He

● *Fed up with clearing up after an enthusiastic session with the nutcracker? Guild member John Carr Thackeray offers a solution in English elm*

was instantly made Guild President *in perpetuum*. Seriously, are any of you interested in making a badge with the Guild logo on it (either screen-printed or carved) with the appropriate fixing on the back, for an economic price?

Reaching out

Mike Cripps writes: I have to report a very negative response in respect of eager potential and actual Guild members jamming my telephone line since you published my number in the local reps list (WW/Sept 85). I feel that not enough is done at the top, and would point out that there are probably thousands of woodworkers who (dare I say it) do not read *Woodworker* or attend the Show.

In order to reach these people, surely some interesting meetings and demonstrations advertised in the local press would have people crawling out of the woodwork. Does the Guild have the funds to do this? If so, why not spend a few pounds and get this great institution off the ground? People like myself would like to make the Guild a great success. At least print some posters, membership forms and explanatory leaflets!

Changing the subject, am I correct in stating that there is no such organisation as the British Woodturners Guild, and that qualifications for this craft are now non-existent? If this is true, isn't it about time our leading woodturners got this off the ground? I would love to help — I am sure that others would as well.

●**Owen Watson replies:** I would love to spend more money and time on Guild affairs; unfortunately, both are in short supply at the moment. Our limited time is surely best spent encouraging and publicising members' local initiatives. However, a poster and membership leaflet should be here before too long.

● There is the Worshipful Company of Turners, 1 Serjeants Inn, London EC4Y 1JD, tel. 01-353 2000; turners interested in

getting an association off the ground should write to **Mike Cripps, 41 The Greenway, Ickenham, Middx UB10 8LS.**

First night

The day of the Guild's West Midlands branch first general meeting dawned bright — but would it last till evening? I had convinced **Mark Golder,** writes local rep **Bill Ferguson,** that we needed his knowledge and experience to make us (better) turners, and 11 December 1985 was the date of the momentous occasion. When Mark arrived it was with a friend — and each had his own lathe!

After a brief introduction, Mark went into action. He has an 'easy to listen to' presentation; he covered various tools and spindle work, and didn't even have much of a coffee-break, with members crowding round his lathe to ask questions and have a go. Time went very quickly, and we ran over our declared time of finishing by almost an hour.

After thanking Mark, we convinced him he was needed again for at least another session to continue with more subjects, including bowl turning. We hope that will be arranged early in the year.

I asked everyone to let me have ideas so I can arrange a programme of regular meetings, possibly monthly. There could be sessions on finishing, carving, cabinet work, machine work, marquetry, veneering, and musical instrument, toy- and clockmaking.

I would also like to see a 'Swap shop' for products, tools and small machinery, a Problem corner, and a Timber Trade for members to buy and sell timber. It might also be feasible to form a purchasing pool for small machines, tools, timber and other supplies at a discount — but we need numbers. We always need more members!

● Bill Ferguson, 40 Quinton Lane, Quinton, Birmingham B32 2TS, tel. 021-427 4571.

Guild courses

Manchester Easter School

The Guild, in association with the Manchester Central College School of Furniture, presents three courses over the Easter break. All are for 5 days, 23-27 March, 9.30-5, £125+VAT. **All bookings for these courses to the Guild office.**

Country Chairmaking — Jack Hill

Jack Hill is a well-known name in country furniture, so we are proud to get him to teach traditional country techniques using cleft and sawn wood. Many of you have seen Jack demonstrating his craft at the Show, and been impressed by his no-nonsense style and ready wit. You'll become familiar with the traditional methods, from simple three-legged and back stools, through ladder-backs to the many styles of Windsor chair. He'll be taking you through steam bending and the various jigs; you'll be using machines of **Fred Lambert's** design, and the aim is that you finish the week with a piece of furniture to take home — even beginners!

Introduction to cabinetmaking — Robert Cooksey and Keith Parry

Robert and Keith will be giving an introduction to basic machine preparation, and hand-making techniques in fine furniture. The course is aimed at the enthusiastic beginner, and those who have some experience and want to know more. At the end of the week you should have made an elegant Sheraton-style table, or be well on the way to finishing it.

Traditional upholstery — Ken Jones and John Shepherd

Can you beat 42 years combined experience in upholstery? Ken (LCG) and John will introduce you to traditional methods and materials (so don't bring your power stapler), and teach you to develop your hand-skills. They can provide a basic frame to practise on, but you can bring a piece of your own if it is stripped for action. The course has been designed for those with little or no experience.

● **Please send all enquiries and bookings to the Guild.** Richard Hill, the senior lecturer at the Central College, will be administering the courses. The College is also running a five-day course in finishing in the same week, which will include two days' demonstrations of spraying techniques. **For this course, contact them direct** at Manchester Central College School of Furniture, Lower Hardman St, Manchester M3 3ER, tel. (061) 831 7791.

GUILD COURSES

● **You must book in advance, and we must have a cheque for the full cost of the course. Make cheques payable to 'Guild of Woodworkers/ASP Ltd'. If you cancel less than two weeks before the advertised date you will forfeit 50% of the cost, unless there are exceptional circumstances.**

Survival metalwork — Bob Grant

15 March, 9.30-5, Oxford, £25+VAT. Woodworkers have always had to be able to handle steel as well as wood. Bob will show you how to grind your own cutters and tools, get that razor edge, harden steel, and silver-solder broken bandsaw blades. He'll also be covering repairing tool bodies, how to drill and tap holes, and turning the softer metals. After this course, you'll have no excuse for not getting the best out of your tools!

French polishing — Charles Cliffe

3-4 April, 9.30-5, Bexleyheath, £35+VAT. Charles Cliffe (who demonstrated his skills at last year's Show) explains all about preparation, staining, and application of this tricky finish. He'll also be dealing with using a cabinet scraper, so bring your own if you have one. If you have a piece of furniture that you want his advice on, bring it as well. This has always been a popular course, so book soon.

Hand veneering — Bob Grant

12 April, 9.30-5, Oxford, £35+VAT. Have you read David Savage's articles on veneering in this and the last issue? If you want to know more, Bob and Peter Sarac, a local harpsichord maker and cabinetmaker, will guide you through the art. He'll show you examples of cartouches, and demonstrate the scratch-stock; you'll be laying a panel with veneer, mitring a cross-banding, inlaying lines round it, and applying a balancer veneer on the back. If you have a veneer hammer, bring it; but materials will be provided.

French polishing — Ian Hosker

19-20 April, 10-5, Chester, £40+VAT. Ian is a teacher (and practising professional) who will guide you through preparation of both new and old pieces, staining and colouring techniques, grain-filling, shellac finishes, fadding, bodying in, spiriting off, and giving new life to existing polished surfaces. The fee includes course materials, and Ian will make you up a polishing kit to take away with you **if you include another £8 when you book.**

Ian is also going to do a course on **Decorative techniques** such as dragging, glazing, rag-rolling, sponging, and marbling in September. 'Coats of many colours' in this issue will give you a taste; there's more in April. Watch out for dates next month.

Wood-machining — Ken Taylor

26 April, Bletchley, £25+VAT. Ken's course on the ins and outs of machining wood is one of our most popular. Find out about table- and band-sawing, radial-arm saws, planing and thicknessing, spindle moulding, and horizontal and vertical mortising. You can also see, and try out, some good quality universals.

Power routing — Roy Sutton

10 May, Herne Bay, £25+VAT. Once you've had and used a router, you wonder how you got on without it. Not only does it cut grooves; a short list of its capabilities includes housing, rebating, straight and circular moulding, tenoning, mortising, rule-joint and template work. Roy will take you through all this, plus designing and setting out jigs; the course booked up very quickly when we did it in February, so get your booking in early!

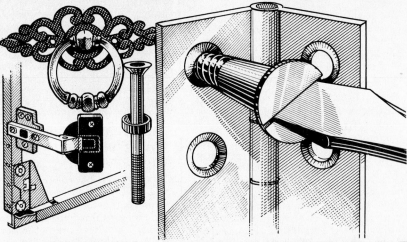

Question box

Our panel of experts solve your woodworking problems

Q *I am about to make a replica of a Charles II high-backed chair with carved back and seat, copied from one in the Geffrye Museum, Shoreditch. The problem is how to secure the seat-rails to the back legs. Working from detailed measurements and an excellent photograph, I discovered that the vertical dimension of the rails is a lot less than the horizontal dimension, and a mortise-and-tenon joint wouldn't seem practical. Could it be that it was only lightly recessed into the leg and then dowelled?*

Securing the front legs to the seat-rails also poses questions. It appears that there are blind holes in the seat-rails (the chair is painted black making examination difficult); so are the legs turned with a parallel or tapered spigot, or would they have been fox-wedged?

Would the side seat-rails be mortised to the front rail? If so, the leg spigot must pass through the tenon, so does this imply they were also dowelled?

David Hodge, Leytonstone

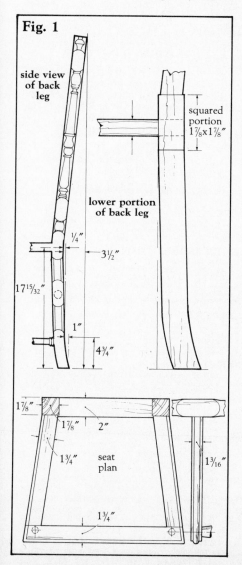

Fig. 1

side view of back leg

lower portion of back leg

squared portion 1⅞ x 1⅞"

¼"

3½"

17¹⁵⁄₃₂"

1"

4¾"

1⅞"

1⅞"

2"

1¾"

seat plan

1³⁄₁₆"

1¾"

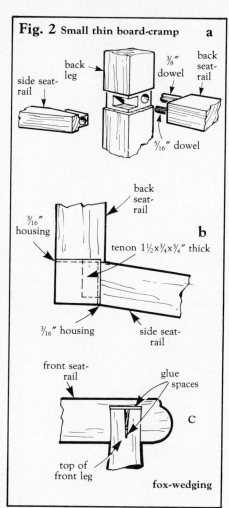

Fig. 2 Small thin board-cramp **a**

side seat-rail

back leg

⅜" dowel

back seat-rail

⁵⁄₁₆" dowel

³⁄₁₆" housing

back seat-rail

tenon 1½ x ¾ x ¾" thick **b**

³⁄₁₆" housing

side seat-rail

front seat-rail

glue spaces

c

top of front leg

fox-wedging

A Dealing with the joints between the back legs and the seat-rails first, it is necessary to make them strong enough to withstand great racking strain — particularly from people who tip chairs backwards on the back legs.

It's impossible to be certain but I agree with you that the rails were probably housed into the back legs by about ³⁄₁₆in and then dowelled. This is not a particularly strong joint and I prefer one which is 'locked' by a dowel penetrating a tenon as in fig. 2a. The details you have given indicate that the seat-rails are 1³⁄₁₆in thick which should allow you to make a tenon ¾in thick. If you look at figs 2a and b you will see that such a bare-faced tenon is cut on the end of the side seat-rail and is 1½in wide x ¾in long x ¾in thick; this rail and the back seat-rail are both housed into the back leg by ³⁄₁₆in. There are two dowels on the end of the back seat-rail; one is ⁵⁄₁₆in diameter and penetrates the tenon and the other is thicker (⅜in) and enters the leg itself.

Now for the front leg and front seat-rail joint. No doubt this follows the practice used for legs fixed to a Windsor chair-seat. This was simply to taper the end of the leg and force it tightly into the hole, leaving a small clearance gap between the end of the leg and the bottom of the hole for glue. However, there is one dodge which helps

enormously — dry the legs right down to a moisture content of 6-8% and then heat them just before driving them in. This does two things: it prevents Scotch glue from chilling if you are using it, and the end of the leg takes up moisture from the atmosphere and swells to make a tight joint, as even in warm central heating the moisture content rarely falls below about 10%.

Fox-wedging (fig. 2c) would be difficult; to do the job properly the hole would need to be undercut to accept the expansion of the leg end when the wedges go home. You could undercut the hole (after boring) with a narrow mortise-chisel which would make the joint extremely strong.

I hope these notes will help you to achieve what should turn out to be a magnificent chair.

Vic Taylor

Q *I recently bought a 24x4in sandstone grinding-wheel mounted on a spindle with bearings, and am thinking of providing treadle-power in the same sort of way as the bicycle lathe in October 1985's Woodworker.*

Is there any way of dressing this wheel and can you offer any comments on my idea?

R. Everall, Devon

A There are two distinct problems in trueing-up a 24in sandstone wheel. One is getting it to run concentrically and the other is making the working surface flat.

First check the running to see if it needs to be centred more accurately. Large natural stones do not have the same accurate hole that the small high-speed synthetic stones have. Old stones have a large square hole and are held on to a much smaller square shaft by four pairs of wooden wedges. You may be able to adjust here. However, if the wheel is very old and has been long neglected, you may need to knock out all the wedges and start again. Make sure the stone remains at right angles to the shaft in all positions when you make this adjustment. A very tedious job, but no particular skill required.

More modern stones are secured to a threaded shaft with nuts and large flanges. Here adjustments for concentricity are much easier.

A malformed edge is trued by running the wheel dry and feeding in a piece of steel water-pipe or electrical conduit at centre height in the manner of wood-turning. Keep revolving the pipe. Don't buy a 'grinding wheel dresser'. This tool is for high-speed synthetic wheels and is quite unsuitable for a slow-moving natural stone.

If there is an obstinate hard high spot, level it down locally with an old coarse file or rasp and keep an eye on it in use. It may wear down — but another may come up.

In trueing and in subsequent use, revolve the stone towards you. Arrange a draincock on the water trough and do not allow part of the stone to stand in water for long periods.

Bob Wearing

188

Question box

Q *I make a violin/viola chinrests, normally of ebony or rosewood. Ebony is getting so difficult to obtain and expensive, so I wondered if maple could be used and ebonised. It needs to be resistant to wear and body chemistry! Could you recommend a suitable ebonising process for me?*

D. Rackham, Rugby

A Although ebony is not really black, it's usual to stain woods which are intended to represent ebony to a jet-black colour. Because of the closeness of their grain, apple, pear, holly, sycamore and cherry are considered most suitable for ebonising. Maple is also close-grained and should make good chinrests.

The stain will have to penetrate to a good depth, and water stains will give the best results. The only disadvantage of water stains is that they raise the grain and make the wood feel rough. To overcome this the chinrests should be lightly sponged with warm water before staining. Allow the wood to dry thoroughly and then glasspaper it smooth. This will remove the raised grain so it won't come up rough when the stain is applied.

Black stain may be made by dissolving water-soluble black aniline dye in water and brushing it on. You will be able to obtain small quantities of these dyes from the polish suppliers listed in *Woodworker*, March 1985.

Other black stains can be made by using Indian ink or by placing a handful of rusty nails in a pint of vinegar and allowing it to stand for a few days.

Before staining the finished chinrests you should experiment with your stains on pieces of scrapwood to ensure you get the required colour. You don't say what finish you used on your ebony or rosewood chinrests, but there should be no difficulty in using the same finish on ebonised maple.

Charles Cliffe

Q *I recently acquired a Stanley four-fold 2ft boxwood rule No. 163, made in the USA. It's calibrated on the face side in ⅛th, ⅛th, and ¹⁄₁₂in; the reverse is calibrated in ¹⁄₁₆ths and has scales of ¾, ½, ¼ and ¹⁄₁₂in.*

The intriguing thing is that it is numbered to read from left to right – 1in at the right-hand end and 24in at the left. I've never seen such a rule before and am fascinated by its purpose – is it for left-handed woodworkers?

D. Bowker, S. Humberside

A The No. 163, manufactured of painted and varnished softwood during the 2nd World War, was probably a wartime expedient. It temporarily replaced the No. 63 which was discontinued in 1942 until the war ended, probably because boxwood could not be imported into America.

These rules, and most manufactured by Stanley in the USA through the years, had 'right-to-left' graduation numbering. It seems from our American archives it was customary to number boxwood rules from right to left; for example The Stanley Rule and Level Company catalogue for 1902 states: 'We are prepared to furnish boxwood rules marked in the English fashion, i.e. from left to right . . .'

A possible reason for this is that one can argue that for a right-handed person it's better to hold the rule in the left hand, leaving the right hand free to carry out more demanding manipulative tasks such as marking. The all-important numerals are, by this convention, right side up. Try it!

David Scott, Stanley Tools

Q *I have been asked to make a door and window with an arched top (fig. 1). What are the best ways to make and join the top rails to the stiles?*

Jim Webb-Jones, Dinas

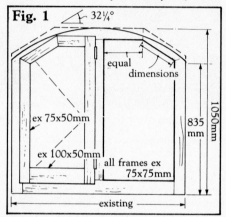

Fig. 1

A It's always good practice for any work of this kind to set out the job full-size on a sheet of ply, and fit and assemble the job on it. It's the only sure way to be certain of the accuracy of angles and overall dimensions.

You don't mention if your job is of hardwood, to be polished. If so, the neatest method of jointing the mitres would be by handrail-bolt, set in from the edges of the members and out of sight. However, a framed ledge-and-brace door and a window are more likely to be painted.

Now the top, hanging-side, of the sash shown, is at 90°; therefore, this can be jointed normally by mortise-and-tenon. The other joints, however, should be mitred, and connected either by integral tenons ('open', fig. 2), or by 'tenon inserts', fig. 3. Of the two, the inserts would be better; they should be of ply, preferably weather-proof.

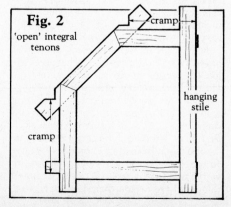

Fig. 2
'open' integral tenons

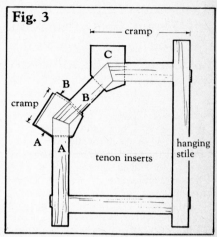

Fig. 3

Fig. 3 also shows the method of working. At the top connection, the ply (of tenon thickness) is left projecting, so that a cramp can be placed from this to the horn. But the intermediate has two, thinner, inserts; and these are staggered just a little to facilitate 'pull-up' on cramping. The method here would be: glue insert A into the stile A; insert B into the head section B; and also insert C into the head section. Allow these to set, and then assemble and cramp the whole frame on the setting-out rod. Again allow the glue to set, then trim away the surplus ply.

Stan Thomas

Q *I was very interested to read Noel Leach's article on the risks of wood finishing (WW/Aug 85). Could be recommend any particular face masks when dealing with toxic or irritant fume-producing finishes?*

Name and address supplied

A When using cellulose-based finishes like nitro-cellulose, pre-catalysed or acid-catalysed lacquers, you must take great care not to breathe any of their toxic vapour when applying them by either brush or spray gun — particularly the 'over-spray' fumes. In large finishing shops, spray-booths are used where there is a continuous running wall of water to absorb the fumes. The smaller operator has to take cheaper precautions, such as a face-mask which encloses the mouth, nose, and (in some cases) the eyes.

These are called gas and vapour respirators. They are made of rubber, and incorporate replaceable cartridges. One manufacturer who produces various types is Chapman and Smith Ltd, Safir Works, East Hoathly, nr Lewes, East Sussex BN8 6EW.

One word of warning. There must be adequate ventilation, even if you are wearing a mask. Special air-line-enclosed masks must be worn in confined spaces or in an oxygen-deficient atmosphere. Before buying a mask, make sure (by reading the manufacturer's instructions) that you have the right mask for your actual situation, and for the materials you will be using.

Noel Leach

The craft of cabinetmaking

Hand-veneering: the other half. David Savage turns his attention to the tools and techniques of the subtle art of cover-up

There's a popular prejudice against veneer — but show someone the care with which it really needs to be done, and they will see the art. Instead of superficiality and cheapness, veneering becomes a combination of aesthetic judgement, skill and dexterity.

Buying veneer is infinitely more pleasant than buying timber, as it's on show indoors and the surface figure is there to be seen rather than guessed at. Crispins in Shoreditch, one of the major London suppliers to the trade, have wonderful warren-like premises full of evocative smells and superb veneers. Don't get carried away; a few leaves of this and a bundle of that will probably set you back £50.

It's difficult stuff to store, however. It's very delicate, especially as single sheets or part-bundles that invariably get left over from a previous job. Always tape the endgrain and any splits with sellotape, not masking tape which dries on and has to be cut off after a few months. Store it in a cool and moist place — a basement is ideal.

Veneer is generally cut with a knife these days, rather than a saw. This actually tends to weaken it and create a series of minute cracks, more apparent on one side than the other; to discover which is which, bend the veneer across its width — the direction in which the bend is easier is the 'loose' side, with the cracks. With solid wood, it's common to 'book-match' boards, showing the figure like the pages of a book. With veneer it is usual to 'slip-match', or slide the veneer leaves sideways without turning them over. This allows you to keep the tight (crack-free) side upwards. In some veneers there is very little difference between tight and loose sides, but those timbers with good figure, especially a light-refracting one, do show the difference. They only disclose their secret at the very last moment when the finish is applied. Leaves that matched perfectly now look hopelessly unbalanced. Beware!

Veneers almost always need flattening before use, a process which makes the material a little more pliable. Damp the veneer with a sponge without getting it too wet, moistening it evenly on both sides. Store it in the correct order between sheets of chipboard with some heavy weights on top to aid the process. This is one of those few occasions where fire extinguishers are really useful. Try to leave the pile for several hours, but not too long because there's the possibility of mould growing after a day or two, especially on the top and bottom leaves. Mould will totally ruin a pale veneer, discolouring it irreparably.

Prepare the ground — the base — to be veneered, a purpose for which I think MDF

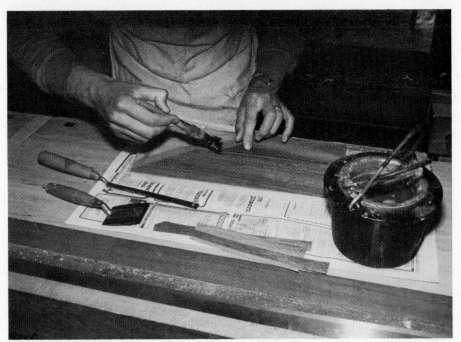

● *The tools of the trade: gluepot, brush, saw, and care. The edges need special attention*

is best. Lip the edges of the board with a solid form, using a good width to allow some edge decoration. Don't go too wide or the movement of the timber will transmit through the veneer. A tongue-and-groove is the safest method of attachment for quality work, although I'm certain that a plain buttjoint, well made, would suffice where price is a consideration.

Fit the lippings and plane them flush with the ground, then systematically tooth the entire surface. If this is a real top-class job, a counter-veneer of gaboon or Honduras mahogany is laid underneath the top leaves and at right-angles to them, before the edgelipping. I've never been entirely convinced of the necessity to do this, but I admit I always do it for safety.

With the ground prepared and well brushed, you are ready to start. Place the glue-pot on the stove nearby, and get the glue to a good temperature and consistency. Put out a bucket of hot water, and put your veneer hammer, saw and knife in it, plus a small sponge. Have a clean dry cloth nearby. Cover the bench with lots of newspaper, and see how much glue is exuded onto it as a mark of your skill. A real expert works cleanly and neatly enough to change the paper only once or twice a day, turning out first-class work. Put the electric iron on at its coolest setting, but it should only be needed to bring back areas that haven't stuck the first time. The larger the job (desk-tops or boardroom tables) the more you would have to use the iron.

Laying leaves of veneer by hand is a matter of temperature, moisture, touch and timing, and to do it cleanly is a great skill. Beginners will get quick-setting animal glue on and in walls, hair and nostrils — everywhere except where it's wanted. The entire world takes on a sticky consistency, and things adhere to you that shouldn't.

This is the procedure for veneering:

1 Cut the veneer roughly 1in larger all round than the area to be covered. A good initial practice area is about 6x18in.
2 Identify which side of the leaf is tight, the face which should go upwards. Locate the position on the groundwork by marking both veneer and board with chalk, which tells you where and on which side of the veneer to glue.
3 Brush the ground free of dust.
4 Carry the glue-pot to the bench, check the consistency, and coat the groundwork quickly and smoothly.
5 Turn the leaf so the 'up' side is down and place it on the glued area. No, I'm not mad!
6 Coat the 'down' side of the veneer with glue.
7 Put the glue-pot back on the heat.
8 Turn the leaf right side up and place or slide it into position.
9 Lightly sponge the top with a little warm water — too much will encourage the veneer to shrink on drying. The water mixes with the glue that is stuck to the 'up' side and acts as a lubricant for the hammer.
10 Begin rubbing down from the middle outwards, lightly at first. Check the veneer's position again, as it can easily slide at this stage.
11 Begin working that hammer in earnest, squeezing out the glue ahead of it. Work the hammer slowly and systematically and pay particular attention to the edges.

It's not that easy, but basically that's all there is to it. It's not about slop and glue and mess, but a little moisture, nice strong hot glue, slightly moist flat veneers and pressure at the right time in the right place in the right direction.

● *Lifting the overlap after cutting with the veneer saw and straight-edge*

It should be possible to avoid using the hot iron by working calmly, methodically, and briskly. Never hurry. If you do have an area, or more likely a corner, that hasn't stuck, try a quick dash with the iron (set the temperature to very low or 'silk'). If this fails, try putting in some new glue if this is possible. If all else fails, go back to the iron and apply more heat and more moisture. Don't overdo it, for excessive local heat can dry out and shrink the veneer quicker than anything.

You will probably want to make a joint between two leaves of veneer, which with a veneer press is done dry, before application of glue, heat and pressure. With hand-work, each leaf is laid in turn. Your first leaf will now be laid, perhaps an inch oversize. If the leaf overlaps the edges of the job, cut these off straight away, because it will lay nice and flat for a few minutes, but if it's left dangling much longer it will curl and lift the glue from round the edges. Trimming is a simple business. Invert the job onto a clean cutting-board, and use the edges as guides for your knife or veneer saw. Be careful at the end of a crossgrain cut.

Lay the second leaf overlapping the first by as much as 2in — remember the first is already an inch oversize. Lay in exactly the same way, but be careful of the seam where they change from a single to a double thickness. It's very easy for a carelessly applied veneer hammer to tear the wood at this vulnerable point. Never use the veneer hammer except with extreme precision and purpose, for it's capable of the most delicate work. With the leaves in position, place a straight-edge down the joint, and take the precaution of clamping it if the cut is long. I have a rubber-backed heavy rule for this sort of work, but don't expect an ordinary metre rule to do the job of a proper straight-edge. A rule is a measuring instrument, not a guidance system.

Now the cut. A veneer knife should have a very sharp-pointed blade with a thin kerf, a combination which makes it less inclined to stray from the line when working with

the grain. Don't lay the blade in the cut, just use the tip. The veneer saw does the job just as well. In my shop the saw has slightly more use than the knife, perhaps because it holds an edge slightly longer. If you lay veneers all day long, after a few days it will come naturally to make this cut with one pass. That is the aim, but I for one seldom hit the right consistent pressure down the entire length of the cut, severing two thicknesses of veneer but not damaging the ground. This is something that only comes with daily experience. The touch can be acquired towards the end of a long job, but it gets lost again without regular practice.

Having made the cut, lift the veneer and peel out the unwanted piece underneath the second leaf. If you've taken a tea-break between the two leaves, this piece will be well-chilled and well stuck — hard luck. For speedier workers, a crank-handled paring chisel will help ease it out of its hidey-hole. Apply a bit of hot glue and wait. Go away and cut up the veneer tape — 4in lengths every 4in across the joint and one length down the whole lot. By now the glue will be tacking; rub it down with a hammer, damp the veneer tape (or brown paper tape 1¼in wide) and rub it on. Wipe up any excess dampness, check for bubbles and blisters, then cover the whole surface with newspaper so that it will dry out slowly and evenly.

After a couple of days remove the tape with warm water and a scraper before either sanding or scraping to a fine finish. And there you have it — just don't go berserk with the belt sander! ∎

● Bob Grant will be holding a course on hand-veneering for Guild of Woodworkers members on 12 April in Oxford. See the Guild pages for further details.
● **J. Crispin and Son,** Veneer Merchants, 94 Curtain Rd, London EC2, tel. 01-739 4857; **The Art Veneers Co. Ltd,** (Mail order specialists), Industrial Estate, Mildenhall, Suffolk IP28 7AY; **R. Aaronson (Veneers) Ltd,** 45 Redchurch St, London E2, tel. 01-739 3107.

192

Shoptalk special: Saw points

Gordon Stokes looks at two new machines from the Elu stable

If you're in the market for a circular saw — and it's almost always the first serious tool to be considered when setting up a workshop for business or pleasure — you'll have to decide whether it's to be a radial-arm or a table-saw. Radial-arms are extremely versatile, but a free-standing table saw does certain jobs better, for instance dimensioning panels; so you have to think carefully about the type of work you will be doing. There are always questions of price and space, of course. I've got two radial-arms, one with a router permanently clamped to it, and I wouldn't be without either.

These two new machines from Elu — a good name for engineering and design — don't fit neatly into either category. One attractive feature which the PS 174 and the TGS 172 have in common is a high degree of portability, although they differ widely in design.

The PS 174 is described by the makers as a 'pull-over' saw, because unlike 'snipper' saws which pivot down to cut through relatively narrow stock, it works on telescopic arms. You pull it towards your body after pulling it down, so it's possible to cut wider material than with a 'snip-off', up to 250mm wide and 52mm thick.

A fence supports the work during the cut, so obviously you have to hold it firmly against the fence, and the edge of the wood must be straight. The machine should be firmly located, either on a bench or table, by bolting it through the holes provided, or better still you can bolt it to a board with a batten screwed edgewise underneath. Then you can put it on a Workmate, and the

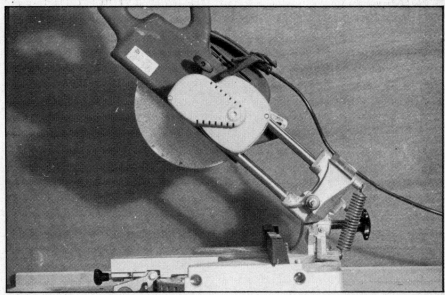

● *The PS 174's unique design is crystal-clear from the profile shot **above**. It should be pivoted down into the cut, then pulled across towards you. **Below**, the bevel cut. Pre-select notches are in the base just below the corner of the wood*

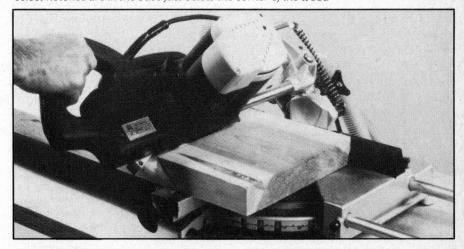

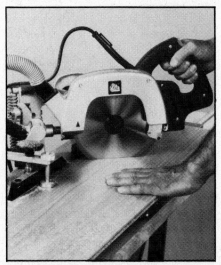

● *A straight 45° mitre can be cut in stuff up to 174mm wide – a significant improvement over an ordinary snip-off saw*

batten sits in the jaws.

It goes without saying that you must study the maker's instruction booklet carefully. The Elu booklets are clear and thorough, and set out the safety rules for machine woodwork — most of which are common sense, of course, but common sense often isn't all that common.

Safety seems to have been well to the fore of the designer's mind; the (standard) TCT blade is completely enveloped by the guard, and you have to operate two triggers on the handle to make a cut, one on top, and the other underneath. The top one rotates the guard to expose the blade, the lower one starts the machine. When you complete the cut, the saw is raised, both triggers released, and the blade and motor unit spring back up to the starting position. The guard automatically returns to its position around the blade. Cutting with this machine could hardly be simpler, and it is difficult to see how an accident could occur, but obviously hands must be kept clear of the blade's path at all times.

The PS 174 — which isn't, by the way, for ripping — is also capable of accurate

angle- and compound angle-cutting. I put it through its paces, cutting angles and measuring the result, and reckon that the accuracy is fine for general purposes. It can be used for standard 45° mitres and for various other fixed mitre angles; should 'slop' or inaccuracy develop, adjusting the settings is simple. Intermediate angles other than the pre-set ones can be selected on a scale; maximum width of crosscut in the 45° mitre position is 174mm and setting the saw for such cutting is quick and easy. Just release a locking screw and lift a latch, and you can swing the saw to the angle. If it's one of the mechanically selectable positions, the latch drops into a notch, and the locking screw is tightened. There's no notch for intermediate angles, but you just use the scale and the locking screw in the normal way.

The PS 174 also cuts bevel angles, by tilting the saw in the vertical plane as opposed to swinging it in the horizontal one. This is also a simple matter of a locking knob and scale. It can also be used with both tilt and swing to produce angled bevel cuts, or compound mitres.

Shoptalk special: Saw points

The second Elu saw — the TGS 172 — is attractive because it can be used both as a sawbench and a cut-off saw. The conversion from one to the other is quick and simple. It has a set of strong tubular legs, easily removed or fitted, or you can use it on a bench or home-built table. The unit is extremely portable, and can be moved around without fuss.

As a sawbench the machine works very well, both for ripping and crosscutting. Depth of cut is set by a handwheel; the mitre-fence provided is quite satisfactory, simply sliding on a bar at the side of the saw-table. There's an adjustable stop for 90° crosscutting, and the square of the fence to the blade should be checked with a wood-worker's square. The size of the machine's table obviously limits the size of your work-piece: if you want portability, cutting 8x4ft sheets has to take second place, though there are extensions available to turn it into a panel saw. The rip-fence is in two parts, one of which slides on the other, so the piece against which the wood rides can be moved backward or forward. This means the fence can have its forward end just past the front of the blade for most ripping, or fully forward to reach past the back of the blade when trimming the end of a wide board.

When the tool is used for ripping and crosscutting as a saw-bench, the riving-knife and guard must be in position and correctly adjusted. The saw-guard fits easily on top of the riving-knife; its forward end rests on the table, and it's lifted by the wood as it is fed forward, dropping back in place when the cut is completed. It works very well, unlike a few I've used. As with all saw-benches, it's important to check that the rip-fence is parallel to the blade, and the mitre-fence is square to it. Home-made push-sticks should always be used to complete cuts.

Depth of cut with the machine as a sawbench is up to 70mm, and up to 38mm when the saw is tilted to 45° for bevel ripping. Tilting the saw is a simple matter of undoing a locking lever and reading the tilt angle from a scale — but always test on a scrap piece if you need perfect accuracy. Tighten the clamping lever well to stop movement while you're cutting. The motor

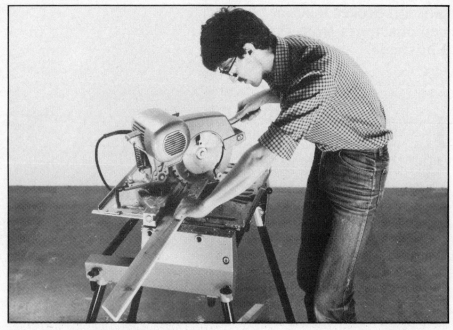

● Saws like the TGS 172 have generally been reckoned as site tools, and very handy they are too. But there's no reason why you shouldn't set one up in the workshop . . .

is a powerful 1½hp induction type, and had no trouble with the blade at full depth in hardwoods.

The change from saw-table to cut-off needs no spanners or Allen keys; set to full depth-of-cut, then remove the guard from the riving-knife. You pull out a locking pin at the front of the table, which swings on its pivot bar into the cut-off position, and the lock re-engages. If you pull the saw down slightly by its handle, the depth-of-cut adjuster can be lifted from its seating and removed; the clamping screw which holds the riving knife is slackened and the knife swings out of the way, or it can be removed. The TGS has no telescoping arms but safety has been dealt with just as efficiently as on the PS 174. At rest the saw is held over the table by a spring, and the guard fully encloses the blade. When a cut is made the handle's action retracts the guard as the blade lowers into the wood. The on-off switch is of the 'no volt overload' safety type, to prevent the motor coming on un-attended after a power failure.

The saw unit is attached to a circular plate in the table which rotates for mitre cross-cutting after a small clamping lever is released. You set the angle by a clear scale; there are positive locations for 90° and 45° angles. The depth-of-cut stop isn't set for 90° crosscuts, but follow the maker's in-structions when you use it for mitring. The saw can also be tilted to provide a bevel angle on a normal crosscut, or compound angles, but the limits won't let you do 45°x45°. Also, always check that the blade isn't going to gouge into the table, which can happen if you're not careful at these extreme limits; the manufacturers don't recommend that you try compound mitres at all in snip-off mode — it's not designed for it. Go for the more flexible (and safe!) saw-bench mode with mitre-fence and tilted blade.

There are stops for the 90° and 45° positions, and intermediate angles are set from the scale.

The PS 174 and the TGS 172 have both been subjected to exacting tests in my work-shop, and I have to say that I am consider-ably impressed by both machines. In my view it is highly unlikely that a buyer of either would have cause for dissatisfaction with the safety provisions, the accuracy, or the appearance; and as long as you treat them right, there's no reason why they shouldn't go on performing well for years. There are adjustments you can make to tighten up and re-calibrate when parts begin to wear, but it always pays to remember that however portable a machine is, it shouldn't be chucked about. ■

● The Elu PS 174 costs £295, the TGS 172 £446, both prices plus VAT. Elu Power Tools, Black & Decker Professional Products, West Point, The Grove, Slough, Berks SL1 1QQ, tel. (0753) 74277.

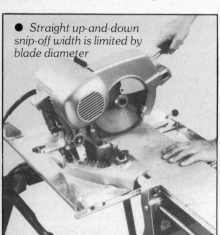

● Straight up-and-down snip-off width is limited by blade diameter

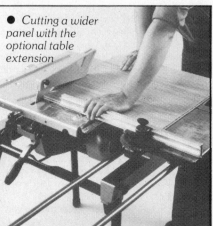

● Cutting a wider panel with the optional table extension

WIN!

● Elektra Beckum's newest precision table-saw

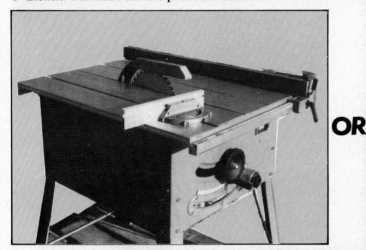

OR

● The HDM lathe, with a full metre between centres

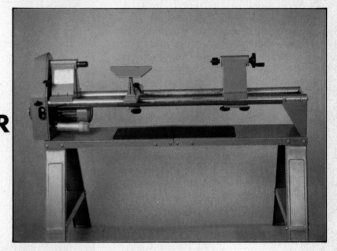

SQUARES AND ROUNDS

There are two types of woodworker — and *Woodworker*, in association with Elektra Beckum, proudly announces a competition for them both. The ones who work in squares — the joiner/cabinetmakers — can win a new table-saw; the ones who work in rounds — the woodturner/carvers — can win over £500 worth of lathe!

THE PRIZES

THE SQUARES

Elektra Beckum's PK250 precision table-saw is their latest addition to a range of serious machinery. It has a 700x900mm table, and its motor puts out 3hp at full tilt. The rip-fence is full-length, and it locks front and rear; a crosscut fence is also standard. It comes with a 10in TCT blade, 45° tilt-arbor, and rise-and-fall; it will cost at least £500 retail.

THE ROUNDS

The HDM 1000 lathe's chrome steel bed gives you 1000mm between centres. You can turn bowls up to 15in diameter; it has 4 speeds, and a faceplate and drive dog come as original equipment. The head- and live centre tailstock are both diecast, both with double bearings, and there's a spindle brake. It's worth over £500 with the stand.

Runners-up in both categories will get boxed sets of *Richard Kell's* wonderful measuring tools.

THE COMPETITION

What you have to do: make any item (out of wood, of course) that includes a chessboard. It's as simple as that. **But** we'll be judging originality and imagination, as well as craftsmanship; so you can make a chessboard on its own, or you can make something that incorporates one. It can be a chair, a chest, a table or a cabinet — anything as long as it has a built-in chessboard!

What you have to do: the woodturner/carvers are challenged to come up with an ingenious set of chessmen — or draughts, or a set of pieces for any game, ordinary or extraordinary,that can be played on a chessboard. They can be as big as you like and as fantastic as you like; what we're looking for is imagination and craftsmanship.

Final judging of both categories will be at the Bristol Woodworker Show, 16-18 May.

THE RULES

1 Entries must consist of:
● A photograph of your work
● A written description (no more than two A4 sheets) of the idea and the techniques used
● Dimensioned drawings
2 Entries must be sent to **Woodworker Squares and Rounds Competition, 1 Golden Sq, London W1R 3AB** by Monday **21 April 1986**
3 If you can't finish by 21 April but still want to enter, send a perspective drawing by the closing date instead of the photo,

along with your description and drawings
4 You can't enter both categories
5 Entries selected for final judging will be displayed at the **WOODWORKER SHOW, BRISTOL, 16-18 May,** and will be judged there by, amongst others, master-cabinetmaker **Alan Peters**
6 Decisions of the judges and *Woodworker* magazine are final in all matters concerning the competition

Coats of many colours

The beauty of a painted finish lies above and beyond concealment. Ian Hosker covers the ground

Woodworkers all share a love of wood — its infinite range of colour and texture, its temperament and capabilities. Anything that prevents us from seeing natural and structural beauty in wooden furniture makes us suspicious; little more so than paint. It covers a multitude of sins and destroys wood's natural beauty; yet some of the most exquisite furniture in the world is painted, or has painted panels, from Renaissance Italian gift cabinets garnished with precious stones, to the subtle, clean lines of 18th century English pieces. Indeed, fine furniture makers are still producing pieces painted in the manner of the 18th century.

We are put off by the image of glossy, treacly surfaces and garish colours. Properly used, however, paint can make a piece of furniture blend into a room's overall colour scheme, or provide a lively atmosphere in a child's playroom.

Paint also has a practical value. How often have you been left with offcuts of ply and other boards that are just too large to throw away but not really large enough to do anything with? Unlikely timber-marriages can be made to create furniture that is very sound in construction but wouldn't look good if it were stained or polished. Paint will hide differences between materials and homogenise the work into a coherent structure. Saleroom finds are also very good candidates for this treatment.

What does it take to produce a masterpiece? Patience, a meticulous approach to the work, the best materials and tools you can afford and a little imagination. A good colour sense is obviously very helpful. A word of caution first, though; **don't experiment on something of value!** The techniques described here are all straightforward and don't require any artistic leanings, although wherever colour is involved such leanings are always an advantage. When applying plain colour, lining, sponging, dragging or rag-rolling, plain colour is always painted onto the surface to act as a base.

As with all work, you can only expect the best result with the best tools and materials. The main materials are high quality white primer, white shellac sealer, eggshell paint, artist's oil colours, paint brushes and good artist's brushes for lining; you will also need pure turpentine and a selection of abrasive papers.

Surface preparation

To be safe, old finishes should be stripped and the surface smoothed with garnet paper (grades 2/0, 4/0 and 7/0 for ultra smooth-

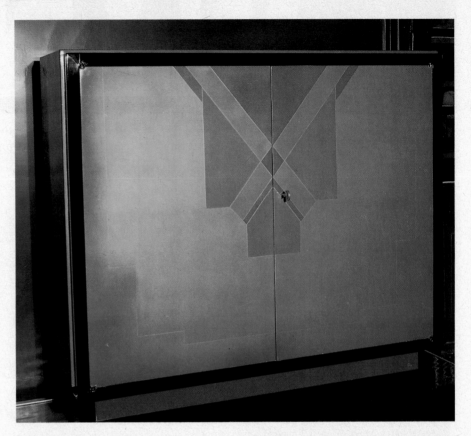

● *Paint magic; with colour sense, patience and many coats of varnish over the paint you can get a deep lacquered appearance*

ness). Do this **after** you have made any repairs. Prime the wood and allow it to dry overnight, and then stop up holes and other blemishes and smooth the whole lot again. If the timber is open-grained, a grain-filler should now be applied, taking care that there are no accumulations in mouldings or on the surface. Finally, give the work a sealing coat of white shellac sealer and allow it to dry hard. Remember a golden rule — painting furniture always requires a dust-free atmosphere.

Plain colour

The aim is to lay down a body of colour as flat and uniform as possible, and the best way to achieve it is to thin five parts paint with one part pure turpentine, and mix thoroughly. Both eggshell paint and turps can be obtained from decorator's merchants. You don't need an undercoat for eggshell; never use gloss, which doesn't look as good or make such a good base.

The normal rules for painting apply to furniture, but extra special care needs to be taken with 'laying-off' strokes — paint lightly with the bristle tips in one direction so any visible brush-marks all lie the same way. Apply the paint thinly to prevent runs and accumulations in corners. You'll need to apply at least four coats to provide a dense body; allow plenty of drying time between coats, at least overnight. Gently rub down between coats with fine wet-and-dry to remove irregularities and dust which have settled on the wet surface. The paper

● *This once-dreary dark oak table has been dragged with a pale green glaze over a white ground*

can be lubricated with water, but make sure the surface is completely dry before repainting. The last coat shouldn't be rubbed down.

Colour is obviously important. There is a very wide range available off the shelf, but the most effective ones are those you mix yourself. Take some thinned eggshell and tint it with artist's oil colour that you have

● A combination of dragging the frame, lining the mouldings, and marbling the panels. You can go over the top with these effects!

● **Above,** the top of the table shown on the other page, the moulding picked out in a contrasting colour. **Below,** dragging with a fine brush

thinned a little with turps to make it liquid. The eggshell needs to be a paler version of the final colour. For pastels the base should be white. Always make enough for the whole job because, obviously, you will never mix the exact shade again if you run out.

Lining

The plain colour on its own may be very effective, but usually a little lift is needed. Painted lines have the same effect as inlay lines and bandings in that they emphasise shape and break up large areas. On a table top, for example, a line in a contrasting colour can be painted along the edge or, more effectively, a little way in. Good judgement is needed to get the width of the line in the right proportion to the whole area. For guidance, draw faint boundaries in soft pencil — this also allows you to visualise the overall effect. They can be drawn in and rubbed out, so with a bit of trial and error you can arrive at the best width and position of line.

Eggshell can be used for the line, but you can get a better effect with a transparent colour, since this is softer. Use artists' colours for this. Mix different colours to achieve what you want, thin the mixture a little with turps to let it run smoothly from the brush, and then mix with goldsize, which acts as a binder and makes the paint dry faster. The size should be thinned with turps in equal proportions. The more size you add the more watery, soft and transparent it becomes.

Paint within your lines with a pencil brush of the right size. If you make a mistake, wipe it off with a turps-moistened rag, but dry the area completely before relining, or it may smear. The finished line may take several days to dry and harden completely because of the high oil content.

Dragging

The name may put you off, but the effect is a subtle emphasis on verticals and horizontals. A transparent colour is laid over an eggshell ground and, while it is still wet, a dry paint brush is dragged very gently over the surface leaving a series of lines of alternating base and top colours. The trick is to make the lines as straight as possible.

The colours used are important. The ground (base coat) is usually white or a paler version of the top colour, which is applied over the *dry* ground as a glaze. A glaze is simply a thinned oil-based paint and is made by adding artist's oil colour to transparent scumble glaze. This is obtainable from good decorator's merchants or art-supply shops, or if you can't get it, make your own. Mix two parts eggshell paint (or tinted undercoat) with one part white spirit — but beware; it does dry a lot faster than

shop-bought stuff. Thin the oil colour as already described and add it to enough scumble for the job in hand. The mixture can now be thinned with turps until it flows easily (possibly as much turps as there is coloured scumble).

Brush the glaze onto the work. Don't worry about brush-marks, just spread the glaze thinly and watch out for runs. Allow two or three minutes for the glaze to settle and consolidate before dragging the dry brush through it. Remember — vertical dragging for vertical members of the work; horizontal dragging for horizontal members; side-to-side on tops and shelves.

Sponging and rag-rolling

These are probably the easiest to do. In rag-rolling, glaze is painted over the base colour and a clean, lint-free rag is crumpled in the hand, pressed in the glaze, and rolled around. Repeat this in the adjacent areas until the whole work has been covered. It's most important that the rag isn't rubbed along, as this will spoil the effect. The material (crumpled newspaper or even a chamois can be used) removes some of the glaze, creating a mottled look which can resemble marble. Indeed, if the correct

Coats of many colours

colours are chosen you can successfully imitate marble. If the rag becomes soaked with glaze, change it.

There are two techniques for sponging. The first involves picking up thinned paint or glaze with a *marine* sponge and dabbing it over the ground colour using a light pecking action. Sparse or full coverage can be achieved according to the amount of dabbing you do. The second technique gives a much softer effect; the sponge is pressed into wet glaze, which has been painted over the base colour. The sponge must be softened first by soaking in water. Squeeze out all the water so that it's just damp; this will not harm the paint.

Varnishing

Coloured paint effects need to be protected against wear and tear, if they are to last, by applying at least two coats of matt or egg-shell polyurethane. This is especially important if you have used a glaze, which discolours with time. However, the paint must be allowed to dry out completely for two or three days before you do any varnishing. 'Flow' the varnish on and stroke the tips of the bristles across and along the surface to get as flat and even a finish as possible.

All this may seem a long-drawn-out process and not worth the bother, but it is no more laborious than traditional french polishing, oiling or varnishing. There is certainly greater scope for experiment, as minor blemishes are not too obvious and may, in fact, add to the charm.

The permutations are only limited by your imagination. So if you are prejudiced against paint, grit your teeth and try to convince yourself that it is a legitimate, and respectable, way of finishing furniture.

● Ian Hosker is an antique restorer who also teaches french polishing for the Guild of Woodworkers in Chester. He will be giving a Guild course on **Broken Colour** — the techniques he describes here and in next month's issue — on 6-7 September. See 'Guild Notes' for more details.

We'd like to thank Nigel Osborne of Quill Publishing for permission to use the colour transparencies, which were prepared for *Paint Finishes* by Charles Hemming, published by MacDonald at £9.95 hardback.

Photos Quill Publishing

● *A beautifully sponged pair of doors, **top**; rag-rolling with crumpled newspaper, **bottom left**, and using a rag-rolling technique to soften lines, **right***

Next month: 'Coats of many continued colours'. Ian explains graining, marbling, tortoiseshelling and some of the more advanced techniques.

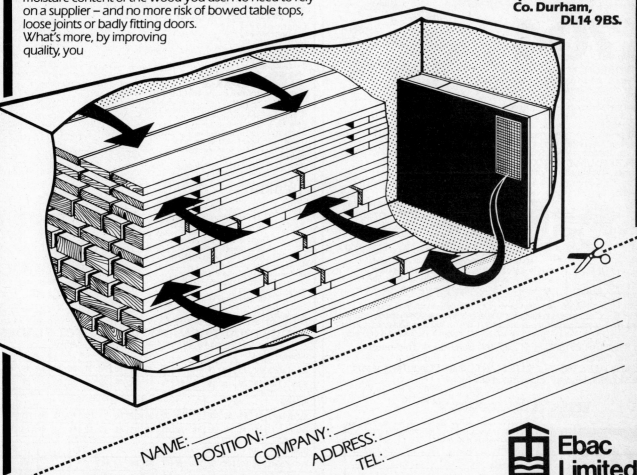
199

200

Carving a career

The life and times of
Mick Atkins, woodcarver,
as told to Stanley Folb

My apprenticeship started in 1963, and lasted almost five years. My wages started at 1/6d (8p) an hour for a 42 hour week; at the end of my first week's work I cycled home with over £3 in my pocket. I was rich! My first months were spent working with a scratch-stock and a few tools borrowed from my instructor. My job was to scratch reeds on the back feet and front legs of the Sheraton-style chairs which the firm had made for 30 years, and still make today.

I heard on the grapevine that a retired carver would sell his tools to a lad starting in the trade. The boss, my teacher and I went to see him, and after agreeing a price of £40 I became the owner of a box of tools, an oil-stone and a set of cramps. The tools had served him well for his lifetime (he was 70); he had bought them second-hand from a retired woodcarver. Some of the short tools have dates on their handles from the 1800s! The boss paid him the £40, and I paid him back at 5/- (25p) a week for a few years.

Over the five years of my apprenticeship I worked my way through the numerous chair models produced by the firm — from walnut Queen Annes through Chippendales to Regency. I never got any one-offs to

● Mick and fish,
above right: right,
willow pattern in
maple; and **below,**
one of eight window
panels in iroko for a
friend

carve, as the firm employed four carvers and I was just the apprentice. At the end of my apprenticeship I went to see the boss about my future wages. He wasn't forthcoming, so I left the firm to work on my own account.

My first customer was a manufacturer of pine mantlepieces who subcontracted the carved decorations. His work was soon mixed in with chair work from other local firms — even from my original employer. Since then I have worked on projects from chairs for palaces to carving a house-name sign for the man down the road. Now I do reproduction stuff (Adam or Chippendale style), whole sets or single chairs, and all sorts of restoration.

I find antique restoration work fascinating, though trying to work to the standards of former carvers can be daunting. I can only marvel at their design and quality of work, and try and reproduce it as best I can.

For replacement legs and spindles I use a Myford lathe, which can be a pleasant change from carving, as the motor does the work. However, I do get bored with it after turning out a dozen pieces.

Finishing is something I try to avoid, as one customer's 'great finish' is another's 'load of treacle'.   ■

● Mick Atkins, 6 Bradenham Rd, High Wycombe, Bucks, tel High Wycombe (0494) 40973.

Photos Stan Folb

Country cousin

Alex Webb describes how to make a cricket table in country style

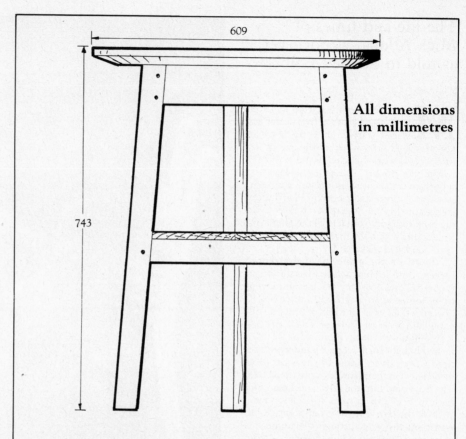

All dimensions in millimetres

609

743

● *The table is made in elm, as you can see from the colour picture **right**: but any well-seasoned hardwood would be fine. Use a dark stain for an aging effect*

N o one knows why it's called a 'cricket table', but like all such country furniture, it epitomises fitness for purpose, simple design, and well-tried and tested methods of construction. Tables like this have lasted for generations.

● The design is reproduced from *Making Country Furniture* by Alex Webb, published by B. T. Batsford, price £8.95.

Shaping the legs

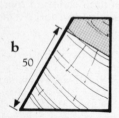

a

50
50
50
60°

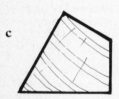

b

50

c

1 Draw a line on both ends of each leg at an angle of 60° as shown in **a**. The shaded area on the drawing must now be planed away. Working next from the side just planed, draw a 90° line across both ends of each leg at a point 50mm up from what will become the outer edge of the leg **b**, gauge a line from end to end, and once again plane away the area shaded on the drawing. The shape which remains **c** is the completed shape of the table leg.

Marking and cutting the tenons

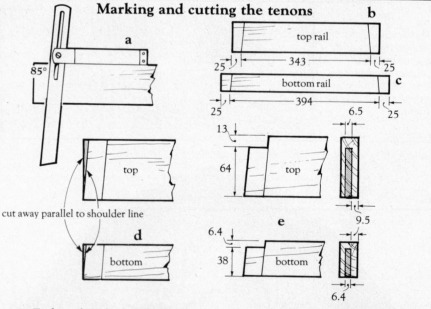

a
85°

b
top rail
25   343   25

c
bottom rail
25   394   6.5   25

d
top
cut away parallel to shoulder line
bottom

e
13
64   top   9.5
6.4
38   bottom
6.4

2 To form the splay-leg effect of this table, you have to angle the shoulders of the tenons. Set a bevel at the angle shown in **a**. This setting should be retained throughout, as it's the same on all joints for both top and bottom rails. Working with the top rails first, mark a line with the bevel in the positions shown in **b**, both on the face side and the inside of the rail. Square the lines round both top and bottom edges, thus forming a continuous line round the rail. Now do the same to the three bottom rails using the measurements shown in **c**. Now draw another line with the bevel parallel to the first on all top and bottom rails at the positions shown in **d**. The wedge-shaped piece left at the end of each rail should now be cut away. The remainder of the tenon can be marked and cut by following the measurements in **e**.

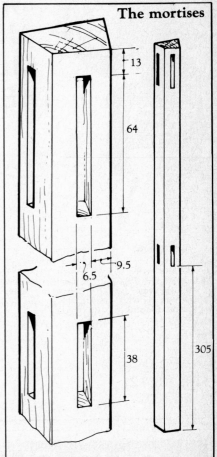

The mortises

13
64
9.5
6.5
38
305

3 The positions and sizes of the mortises are all shown above. Mark each mortise and its tenon so you know exactly which rail goes where.

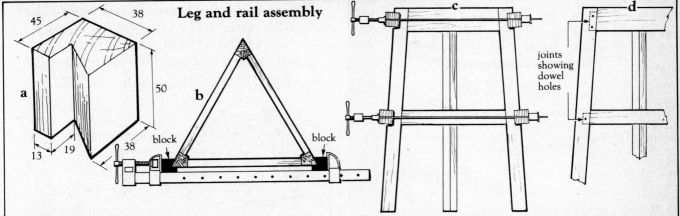

Leg and rail assembly

45
38
50
a
b
13
19
38
block
block
c
d
joints showing dowel holes

4 Triangular or other non-square frames, especially with non-square components like these legs, will need cramping blocks for easy assembly. The blocks **a** will keep the pressure angle of the sash-cramps correct, and will also stop the cramps bruising the work.

Drill a hole the same size as your dowel (6.5mm or ¼in), about 12mm from the face of the leg, through the middle of the mortise. Fit the tenon into the mortise dry and mark the hole position with a sharp pencil on to the

face of the tenon inside. Then withdraw the rail, bradawl a point about 2mm nearer the tenon shoulder than the centre of the marked hole, and drill through the tenon on that point. Chamfer the dowel-ends which will be going through the tenons.

Check all the joints dry for a good fit, and see whether the structure is true. Glue and fit one side of the frame together **b**, pulling it up with sash-cramps and blocks — making sure that the cramps don't obscure the holes

you've drilled — and drive the dowels through the holes while the cramps are up tight.

The dowels should all be overlength, and the extra can be cut off and flush-trimmed with a chisel later. Wipe off excess glue at this stage, but try not to get it into the grain if you are going to stain the wood. Fit and cramp the other sides together to make the complete frame, check it for true and set it aside to dry for 24 hours.

Country cousin

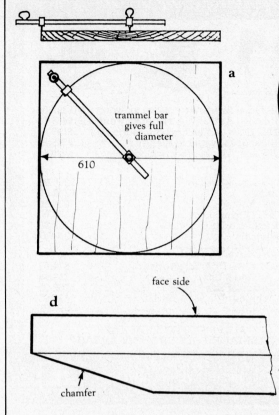

trammel bar gives full diameter

610

face side

d

chamfer

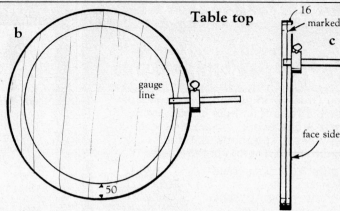

Table top

b

gauge line

50

16
marked line

c

face side

5 It will probably be necessary to join two or three boards to get the full size of the top; a single plank wouldn't be stable anyway. Glue them with the heartwood alternately up and down, let them dry and clean them up; then mark out a circle 610mm in diameter (**a**) and cut it out with a jigsaw or bandsaw. The edge should be planed and sanded before the next stage, and mark the triangle in step **6** now too. With a gauge set to 50mm, mark a line on the underside of the table-top (**b**). Reset the gauge to 16mm and, working from the face side, mark a line all the way around the table-top edge (**c**). The area between the two gauge lines can now be planed away to give a chamfer to the underside of the top (**d**). When the table is assembled you will see that the chamfer greatly reduces the heavy look a top of this thickness would normally have, without reducing strength.

Cut two pieces for the under-shelf, notch them round the legs to fit while they are separate, and mark out the triangle shape of the rails directly onto their underside while they are in position.

Fixing the top and under-shelf

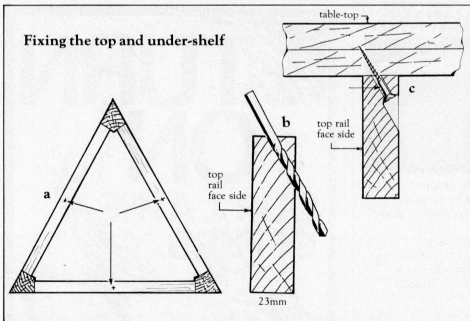

a

b

top rail face side

top rail face side

23mm

table-top

c

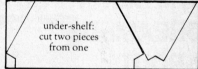

under-shelf: cut two pieces from one

6 Draw a line through the centre-point of the underside of the table-top. Set the trammel-bar or home-made compass to 305mm (the radius of the top) and with the point on the edge at one end of the diameter-line, swing it to touch both sides of the circle. The other end of the line and the two points will make a triangle which corresponds to the under-frame. Drill bigger holes in the centre of the rails (**a**) than the screws you will use, and at an angle as shown in **b**. Countersink them, line the top up on the frame on the lines you have marked, and screw up. The enlarged screw-holes allow the top to shrink and expand without splitting. L-shaped 'buttons', screwed to the underside of the top and engaging in slots in the rails, are another way of fixing a table-top to allow for movement.

Cut the triangle shape on the two pieces of the under-shelf slightly large (**d**), fit them into position and trim them to shape.

Sand the whole thing and stain and wax it, just wax it, or finish it to your taste — remembering it is country furniture! ■

Cutting list

Legs	3	711mm	x 50mm	x 50mm
Top (jointed)	1	609	609	32
Top rails	3	394	76	22
Bottom rails	3	444	45	22
Under-shelf	1	609	203	13
Dowels	18	32	6.5	

Save it!

WOODWORKING WHEEZE
of the **month**

Wood-finisher's materials are costly, **writes Noel Leach,** both traditional shellac-based products or the cellulose-based lacquer family.

A degree of wastage, as with any raw material, can't be avoided on the way to the end product — the finish — but it can be greatly reduced with care, commonsense and good housekeeping methods in the workshop.

Here are some of the ways in which you can make savings on things like pricey garnet paper, as well as liquids;

● Use absorbent paper rolls for all cleaning down, instead of expensive cloth or stockinette.

● Pour all fluids slowly and with great care when transferring them from five-litre cans to smaller containers. If air is allowed to flow into the can you will avoid blow-back spillage.

● After use, empty the spray-gun cup contents into a can or jar for further use for touching-up or other small-scale jobs. (Except, of course, acid-catalysed lacquers or polyesters, which can't be stored because their chemical make-up makes for very rapid drying.)

● Cut steel wool with (old!) scissors instead of tearing it. Fit the rolls into an easily-home-made dispenser with a pair of scissors tied to it.

● Dispense all the fluids you're using on the job in hand into small pots or containers, and put the rest back in the bottle or can. Never leave any fluids lying around overnight to evaporate or dry out hard.

● Have separate labelled boxes into which you can put ordinary abrasive papers, wet-and-dry and steel wool after you've used them. They can be used again and again! Also, keep all the used abrasive paper from portable power sanders. The ends of the sanding sheets not worn by the machine can be cut off and used by hand.

● Sweep up the workshop at the end of each day. It's surprising what sort of things end up on the floor that can be collected and re-used. This is especially true of abrasive papers, nails and screws.

● Tins, bottles and other domestic containers can be re-used to store and mix small items. For safety, remove the labels first, wash the container thoroughly and clearly label it for the new contents. For example, the plastic containers for things like peanuts and sausages make ideal storage-boxes for screws and nails, while plastic egg-boxes can be used as palettes for pigments. Mineral-water or wine bottles can be used to store liquids of all kinds, and the bottom part of plastic lemonade bottles can be cut off and used for small working liquid mixes. Be careful about this, though; white spirit melts some plastics, and glass shatters. Don't store screws in glass jars. Wooden vegetable boxes from outside the local greengrocer or supermarket can be used to hold abrasive papers, rags and so on, and will tuck away in an odd corner.

I must emphasise: **remove all food labels** and attach proper labels to show the right contents. White spirit, cellulose thinners or lemonade look exactly the same in a bottle, but could have disastrous effects on the wrong surface, whether it be timber or your insides! This is particularly true if there are likely to be children about, which of course they shouldn't be; if it's inevitable, it's best not to use drinks-bottles at all for keeping wood-finishing materials. ■

MACHINING WOOD

YOUR EXPERT GUIDE

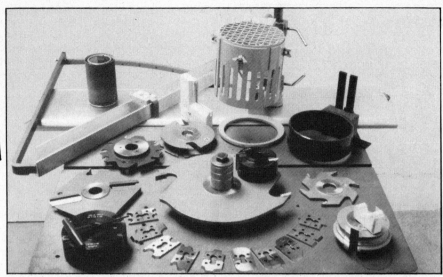

● *A bewildering but beautiful array of bits and pieces includes the angled fence and sliding table (above left), a bonnet-guard and ring fence (right) and an enormous one-piece slotting cutter on the shaft. In front are other cutter designs*

THE SPINDLE MOULDER

The simple basic design of the spindle moulder stands in marked contrast to the enormous variety of jobs it will do. Perhaps that's why it's many a machinist's favourite

Of all individual woodworking machines, the spindle moulder offers perhaps the greatest potential to the creative woodworker. It's held in great affection because it works with a special combination of power and ease; it doesn't just cut. It will make grooves, rebates, and any imaginable moulded profile; it is just about indispensable for producing and decorating curved components in quantity. It's the machine whose full use demands not just sympathy and skill, but also a touch of art. The range of work it can handle includes straight and curved moulding, tenoning, notching, corner jointing, reeding and fluting, and panel raising; rebating and grooving are just the bread-and-butter.

The basic design of the spindle moulder is very simple. A vertical spindle (the commonest size is 30mm) protrudes through a horizontal worktable, below which is a drive motor which rotates the spindle at high speed (usually in a range of 4-10,000rpm). The shaft can be raised or lowered, and extra choice of working (cutting) height from the table is given by different-sized spacer washers which fit over the shaft. An extensive range of cutters and cutter-blocks can be mounted on the spindle — straight, curved, or shaped — and as the spindle rotates and the workpiece is pushed past it along fences, the mould or cut is produced.

Cutters flew out of blocks far more often in the past than nowadays. The spindle moulder has had a rather unjustified label as the most dangerous machine in the workshop, largely because of careless setting up; the real danger area of the machine is that the work is usually hand-fed, and for a deep cut the knives have to protrude a compara-

● ***Above left:** The machine with sliding table and adjustable fence plus extraction; **above right,** a close-up of fences, guards and a home-made featherboard*

tively long way out of the fences. The safety devices that you need for each task must **always** be set up; **never** start a job without them. All woodworking machines are potentially dangerous and must be used correctly, but the spindle moulder demands more attention during setting up. The methodical approach to checking and re-checking the procedures is doubly important for safety, because there are a number of nuts and bolts you must make sure are tight.

Accidents with cutters coming out of blocks can be virtually eliminated these days thanks to various designs of safety block. Spindle moulders are usually supplied with one or several cutter-blocks in which matching pairs of cutters (or knives) can be mounted. In safety-blocks, the cutters are held in place with wedges and screws; the older designs relied on the grip of flat steel to steel, tightening an adjustable mouth on to the cutter. Your first job is to set the cutters up in the block. Work out how much projection you need — always have about two-thirds of the cutter gripped — and, most important, balance the cutters in the block. It takes care and time; you must set them up so that one edge makes

exactly the same cut as the other. They must be the same size and weight, and if you're using a proprietary safety-block, use **only** the cutters made by the manufacturer for that block.

Cutters are either solid high-speed-steel or tungsten-tipped. Straight profiles are for grooves, rebates and tenons; shaped profiles for moulded work can be bought standard, or you grind your own. The diversity and complexity of mouldings is added to by raising and lowering the block so a different part of the cutter is used, or making several passes with different cutters.

High-speed-steel cutters can be ground to give any profile you choose, but it's important to remember that rotating cutters strike the wood at an angle, which varies according to the size of the block and the projection of the cutter. For this reason, the shape ground on the cutter must always be longer than the shape you need; for a 15mm straight rebate, for instance, you'll need a cutter projection of about 17mm. For curved profiles, draw out what you want on paper, transfer the shape to the metal blank, grind it, then set it up in the block and see what you get. It's trial and error until your experience tells you how much extra to give the ins and

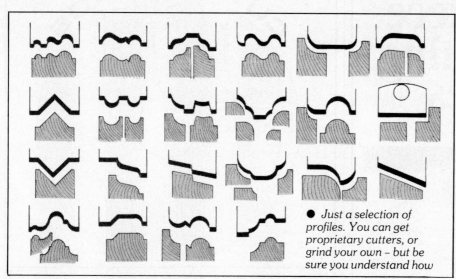

● Just a selection of profiles. You can get proprietary cutters, or grind your own – but be sure you understand how

Inca Woodworking Machinery Handbook

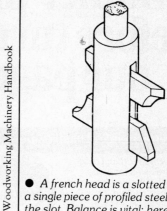

● A french head is a slotted shaft with a single piece of profiled steel through the slot. Balance is vital; here, two cutters will produce a double round-over. The cutters scrape, so a burr must be left on the face

outs. Remember too that the back of the cutting edge must be relieved — the clearance angle is usually 30°, bearing in mind that the longer the cutter-projection and the greater the cutting depth in the timber, the more clearance you need. Don't ask a HSS cutter to cut too deep.

A wide range of one-piece cutters is also available, solid steel bodies with integral knives (often tungsten-tipped), brazed permanently in position. Although they are far more costly than the block-and-replaceable-cutter system, they are always ready to use, and always perfectly balanced. The choice is extensive and includes everything from groovers to decorative moulding cutters; they do need specialist grinding, though, which is why many of them are TCT for longer useful life. Further ways to spend your money on tooling include simple rebate blocks, which come with a selection of roller-bearing ring-guides to give pre-set depths of cut, and replaceable tungsten cutters; comb-jointing and edge-joint profile blocks; two-part slotters with a selection of spacers to adjust the size of cut; the list goes on and on. Most of these are quicker to set up than the blocks which carry any cutter, but of course they're only good for one particular job, and they can be so expensive as to make commercial use the only good reason for buying them.

Cutter safety

NEVER use cutters which show signs of damage, wear or defect. To eliminate risks of accidents from faulty tools, some manufacturers advise that cutters are re-ground only twice, and should be discarded after a total of 60 hours' work.

CLEAN all the gripping and gripped surfaces with meths every time you set cutters up in a block.

ALWAYS use tools at, or below, the manufacturers' recommended speed. Most spindle moulding tasks have an optimum speed — the larger the cutting diameter, obviously, the greater the speed of the tips of the cutters. Manufacturers usually recommend maximum speeds for their blocks; don't exceed them.

Machine safety and adjustments

Cutter and block safety is only one aspect of the safe operation of a spindle moulder. As with any machine, it's vital to read the manufacturer's handbook, and to use the guards and fences provided. You'll certainly be making your own. The Shaw guard and hold-down and hold-in units (horizontal and vertical pressure-guards) should be placed to hold the workpiece and stop it kicking back. Always face the

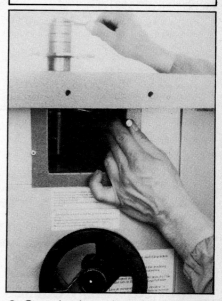

● Cutter height is adjusted by the hand wheel; here, a tommy-bar locks the shaft

'butterfly' fences — the two main ones either side of the shaft — with thick, stable ply so you can bring them closer together than the standard metal ones will go. The smaller the gap between the two sides, the better; in fact the 1974 Woodworking Machines Regulations recommend that you fit a face-board right across the gap whenever possible. Minimum exposure for the cutters is the rule. You can also pin stops and guides to the fences if they are ply-faced; and if cutters do contact them, you won't do nearly so much damage.

The two halves of the butterfly fence adjust independently, back and forward as well as in and out. This is important when the surface being fed into the machine is to be cut away; the outfeed fence will have to be adjusted to run against the cut surface.

The height of the spindle is adjusted by turning the hand-wheel on the side of the machine below the worktable. For the greatest accuracy, the spindle height should always be set on the upward movement, because the spindle and motor are being

● One design of safety-block; lugs on the screw-tightened wedges hold the cutters

● A rebate block with double-edged throwaway tungsten cutters, and wing cutters top and bottom

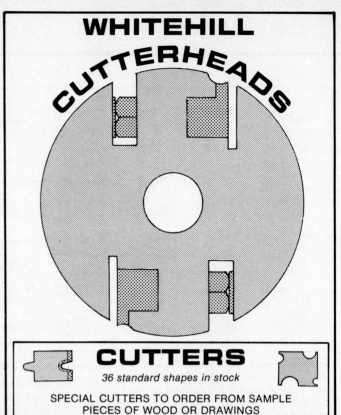

210

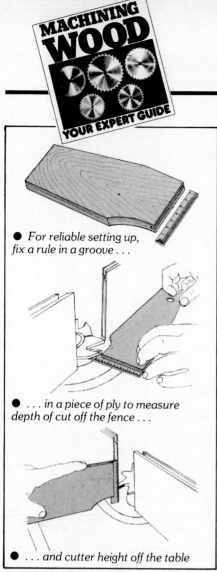

● *For reliable setting up, fix a rule in a groove . . .*

● *. . . in a piece of ply to measure depth of cut off the fence . . .*

● *. . . and cutter height off the table*

moved together, and they can settle a little on the screw-threads of the adjustment mechanism after you've locked it and turned the machine on. Always work up to a height, so you're moving the whole weight against the adjuster, and any slack is already taken up. Also, make a point of locking and interlocking the adjuster when you alter the height — some are lazy and don't do it, which eventually means you wear out your lock and then can't hold your cutters to a height. Silly, really.

When you've made and checked all the adjustments to set the cut up — to cutters, guards and fences — turn the cutter by hand to see that it doesn't foul anything. Then make a habit of checking the adjustments again, preferably with a methodically numbered mental check-list; write it out on a big board and hang it up over the machine:
● Cutters firmly fixed in block?
● Block securely fixed to spindle?
● Spindle height locked?
● Spindle brake-lock off?
● All fences adjusted and tight?
● All guards and hold-downs tight enough but not too tight?

Even if you are satisfied with the setting of the machine, it could be fatal to let your attention flag as you feed the wood into it. Spindle moulders, like circular saws, can snatch and throw out lumps of wood; feed smoothly and slowly, especially at the beginning of the cut. A power feed is an ideal solution, adding safety as well as ease, speed and smoothness to the feed operation.

The following points will help:

● Always feed against the direction of rotation. Where appropriate, clamp end-blocks in suitable positions.
● Use pushsticks whenever possible; they're essential when moulding small pieces.
● Always set up the work so that the cutters are underneath it if possible.
● Always use longer pieces of wood than you need. The ends of mouldings are not always accurate, particularly with small sections.
● Use a test piece *first*. All the machine settings are trial-and-error, and however many measuring devices you have on the set-up, you aren't going to know the cut until you cut.
● Make an anti-kickback device by cutting long, angled 'teeth' into a piece of plywood. Clamped it on to the worktable, hard against the workpiece which is against the fence, and test that you can push the work through but not pull it back. This is known as a feather-board.
● If you have some really big rebates to do, consider cutting them out with a saw, and only using the spindle moulder to clean up and get the exact size. This is just as quick, easier to set up, and you end up with useful fillet-sized pieces as offcuts rather than a whole bagful of shavings.
● Beware of curved, twisted or split timber. Unless you have a really heavy power-feed — and often not even then — the accuracy of your cut will be seriously undermined by badly prepared wood.
● Use common sense when you're thinking of machining small-section pieces, especially brittle hardwoods like oak. Cutters spinning round in a heavy block have an enormous inertia, and there is a minimum size you can safely put through a spindle

● *High narrow workpieces need high fences; push-stick at the ready*

● *Check your stock carefully. Close and straight grain (right) is best*

● *A profile from a versatile one-piece cutter. Note guards and featherboard*

moulder — depending, of course, on the size of cutter and size of cut. In the same way, power-feeds can distort small-section timber, so you might have to use a router, or even a scratch-stock!
● When planning a cornice or a moulding that will sit high up, judge how it will look at a height rather than at eye level. If you build up a moulding in several passes, make the *shallowest cut first* so that you have always got the widest running edges against fences and table. With cutters buried in the wood, this isn't always possible; often you find yourself working with the workpiece upside down.

Now you're set up, ready for ordinary straight cuts. Here are some suggestions for other operations.

Edge work on panels

Always check that the panels are flat and work to a surface you know is square and true; with the datum face on the work-table, measure from the table. Man-made boards can vary in thickness! Once the machine setting and checking is complete, rebates, grooves and slots are easy. You can get extension tables for most machines to support larger workpieces, but even so, they will need careful handling. Make sure the hold-downs are near enough the cutter to keep the cut constant, but support for a large panel towards its outside edge is also necessary.

Small, thin, or tall workpieces

Make a false fence or face-board and secure it to the fences, across the gap. Make the opening as small as possible; short or thin pieces of wood can get drawn into the machine as they pass the end of the fence. Tall pieces obviously need tall fences, and you'll need to work out ways of holding them properly vertical as well. It's quite likely that you'll be making up your own versions of pressure-guards and hold-downs for non-standard jobs.

When you fit a face-board, have a care. Say you're slotting the narrow end of a board for a tongue; the cutter height can be pre-set, but the depth setting will have to allow for the face-board. Set the cutters to the required height, then bring the fences forward away from them and lock them parallel.

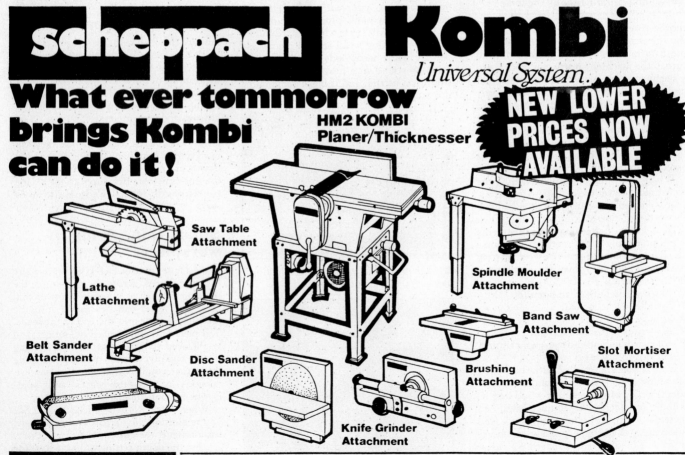

● *Fixing the all-important face-board over the gap for small work*

Fix the face-board firmly across them — screwing them is best in this case — and then start the machine and tap a long, stout block of wood held across the top of the face of both fences so that fences and face-board move back into the spinning cutters. It goes without saying you should be wearing eye-protection. You have to judge when the cutters are pushing through the faceboard to the depth you need.

Another and rather hairier way of getting this set-up is to set the height of the cutter and the depth of cut with the fences, allowing for the thickness of the face-board. Then pin a back-stop the height of the face-board to the infeed (back) fence, and hold the face-board firmly on the table with your fore-arms braced. With the back end held firmly against the backstop, slowly pivot the front end towards and against the out-feed fence with the cutters spinning. The point is that the cutters have to make their own hole for the minimum gap — and maximum effect — of the face-board. It follows that you should use stout and even-grained stuff for the face-board (½in/12mm minimum) because it takes quite a thump as you feed it into the cutters. Be careful, smooth, slow and confident. If you don't feel confident, you'll have to try and jigsaw the right size-and-shape hole out of the face-board, but this is awkward because the cutting circle means that the hole is a different shape one side of the board from the other.

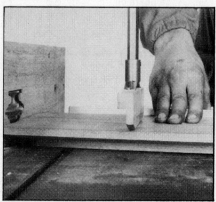

● *A panel is moulded on the back; pressure-guard, sliding table and face-board are all in use. Always measure from the table*

● *Tenoning with the workpiece firmly held and a back-up block against break-out*

Cutting and moulding across the grain

Not often called for; but when raising and fielding panels, it's best to cut the short, cross-grained section first so that any break-out at the edges will be removed by the second cut along the grain. Otherwise, back up the cross-grained cut with a piece of scrap to stop break-out.

Tenoning

You can use a single block, where the wood passes right over the cutters, and turn it over; or double-block arrangements, spaced apart the thickness of the tenon, are very efficient. With a single block, the distance between the table and the top of the cutters is critical, as this will be the depth of the tenon's shoulder. Remember your top and bottom edges are cutting the cheeks of the tenon — they need cutting-edge clearance as well as the vertical edges. This again is cross-grained cutting, so you need a hefty false fence to back the cut up and stop break-out. Make sure the clamping is good — holding the workpiece by hand against the sliding fence is not enough. Sliding tables are available for most machines, an excellent accessory for tenoning.

Dropped-in work

Grooves and rebates often have to be stopped and started before the beginning or end — or both — of furniture and joinery components. The circle made by the cutters obviously means that such cuts will not have square ends, but these can be chiselled out later if necessary. The grooves in window sashes, for instance, for the sash cords, don't even need that.

Stopped or 'dropped-in' work is easy enough on the spindle moulder as long as you take great care and set up your fences and guards properly. The principle is, as always, to feed the workpiece against the rotation of the cutters; set up a backstop to hold the rear end and stop the work from being snatched and thrown backwards. Naturally your hold-downs and pressure-guards are all in place.

Screw a hefty lump of wood to the infeed fence, in a position that puts the cutters to the work where the cut starts. Careful marking and calculating is needed in these preliminary stages. Once you are sure you have everything right do a test cut; start the machine and push the workpiece slowly and firmly under the guards and up against the fence so that the cutters are at full depth. Only when the cut is at full depth and the work hard against the fence, should you move the wood forward along the outfeed fence. A holding jig is the best way of making sure that the cut is smooth and your hands safe; small pieces can be put on a jig, or a board with handles and pins can be used for larger ones. If the cut is stopped at both ends, fix a forward stop on the outfeed fence to set the right place to finish the cut. If it's a very deep cut, set up to do it in two goes; do all your pieces at half depth, then set full depth and do them all again.

● *Dropped-in cuts should be carefully set up; **always have a backstop***

● *An unguarded ring-fence. The mark is where the cut will be deepest*

Curved work

There are two main ways to approach curved grooving, rebating and moulding — doing such work on curved pieces, that is; they involve guide-bearings on the block itself or a 'ring-fence'. The other major decision to make is whether or not to use a jig. If your workpiece has a constant, well-produced profile, it's possible to use the edge of the piece itself as a guide against which the guide-bearing of the block runs. This is where you are limited to the range of guides that come with the block, which will only allow you to get certain depths of rebate corresponding to the difference between cutting diameter and guide diameter. With a jig the exact finished shape of the

213

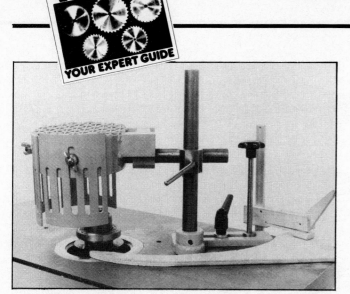

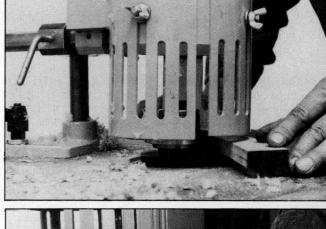

● **Above,** *a stout infeed finger, a bonnet-guard and a top bearing;* **above right** *the bearing runs against the workpiece itself.* **Right,** *ring-fence against template produces a mould on top*

component, you can use a guide the same size as the block to get the perfect shape of a roughly-sawn workpiece. Rebates and moulds on that piece, however, will involve a different guide-bearing or a ring-fence.

Before you do any curved work at all, fix up an infeed finger. There's only one point where you get maximum depth of cut, because you're presenting a wide-radius piece to a much smaller cutting diameter, so you must be exceptionally careful about feeding the work into the cut smoothly. The infeed finger is set up so you cannot dig the work in at full depth straight away; it comes in gradually. Cut a long shallow curve of stout ply and clamp it securely to the work-table so you can slide the work easily and safely into the cutter; the point of the finger should nearly touch the cutters. Always feed the wood against the rotation of the cutters; if you need to take another bite, which is quite likely since you won't get full depth at the first pass, **never move the wood backwards** on the cutters. Pull it away, and feed it in again, always against the direction of rotation.

The ring-fence gives you more flexibility than a rebate block with guide-bearings. You can use any moulding cutter with it, and set up (within reason) almost any depth of cut; if you have a really deep cut to make, it's best to set up in two goes so you never ask the cutters to go too deep in one go. The ring-fence, usually used with a 'bonnet-guard' that looks something like a helmet, is not a perfect circle, but slightly oval-shaped, so it does the job of an infeed finger. There is a mark on the ring itself which shows where maximum depth of cut comes. The advantage of this device is that you can use the same jig to produce the shape, rebate it and mould it — as you'll need to do, for instance, on a curved-top panelled door; your jig should be made with extreme precision and plenty of extra material at either end of the workpiece to fix the piece firmly on to it and leave room for your hands, and preferably jig-clamps as well. These are like mini-holdfasts which you screw to the jig, and they act as handles as well, keeping yours hands well out of the way. Have the jig on top of the workpiece and the cutters buried if possible, but it isn't always, because you will probably want to rebate

one side of the piece and mould the other. For this sort of work, components should always be made oversize so you can pin or fix to the jig through waste, and then cut to the correct size when your spindle moulding is all done; curved pieces also have awkward cross grain as well, which it's best to leave in waste areas so you can dis-card broken bits.

You won't get very far in curved spindle moulding if you don't get to grips with jigs. Remember your components are exact re-productions of the shape of the jig, so absolute precision is vital. It also pays to remember that you'll be doing several set-ups and trial-and-errors, so make a few extra components to start with as test pieces. Another aspect of testing on scrap, of course, is that with a curved fence you can cut a simple rebate on a straight piece to exactly the same depth as you can on a curved piece, so you can use ordinary scrap initially. When you get to moulding, of course, it's a different matter.

Angled cuts

Dovetail grooves, glazing rebates with angled sides or bottoms, or indeed any cut that requires to be made at an angle to the square edges of the workpiece need to be thought out carefully. Put a cutter in the block at an angle? It won't work. Imagine a square cutter set in a stationary block with a corner pointing down at the table. Now turn the block round in your mind. The lowest point of the cutter makes the complete circle at that lowest point — it would cut out a flat. So you need to make up and angled jig set against the fence, clamped and screwed, that will present the

work at an angle to the knives; or you can use a tilting spindle, if you are lucky enough to have a machine with one. This, inciden-tally, is why you should set a cutter at a very slight angle to give a flat-bottomed or -topped cut; the finish is cleaner.

Dust extraction

It's almost impossible to extract curved-work waste from a spindle moulder because the workpieces move all over the table. For straight work, extraction is imperative. Most fences include an extraction hood which doubles as a cutter guard; you can build your own out of thick ply to take your extraction system. ∎

This series was written by Judith Barker. Ken Taylor of the London College of Furniture checked it for completeness and accuracy. Aidan Walker planned it and demonstrated the techniques. Derek Wales took the pictures. But Luna Tools and Machinery made it possible. They provided vital financial support – and for photography and demon-stration they lent their machines, their space, and the help and advice of staff member Joe Wickens. So we give our warmest thanks to Luna's MD Gerry Baker for his unhesitating and generous co-operation. Luna are at 20 Denbigh Hall, Bletchley, Milton Keynes, Bucks MK3 7QT, tel. Milton Keynes (0908) 70771.

Table-top seat

When is a table not a table? When it's a settle — one you can make with the help of Vic Taylor's splendid drawings

● Having it both ways; a flick of the wrist and the table becomes a settle – and not just for monks!

The 'Monk's bench' is unusual as an early example of dual-purpose furniture. In one guise it acts as a side-table for serving food, and by re-arranging and re-fixing the top it becomes a settle.

We can tell that it is intended as a side-table because of the following two features; first, the back edge of the top lines up with the back edge of the cross-piece (fig. 2), whereas there is an overhang at the front edge; and second, there is a slot cut through each cross-piece and a peg can be pushed through to engage in a hole in the arm at each end. This allows you to slide the top towards you when sitting at the table and gives you more leg-room — quite a normal characteristic of this kind of table.

The individuality of the design, however, lies in the fact that you can withdraw the pegs, take the top off and re-position it as a settle-back by inserting each peg through its slot into a second hole bored through the back end of each arm, as shown in the end elevation, fig. 2. The result is a settle with a wooden seat and back which will need some cushions to make it comfortable.

The piece was probably made in the early or mid-17th century; it's difficult to be precise as furniture of this type was usually locally made by the village carpenter and the woodturner, and popular designs continued to be made for many years after their inception. Settles of this style are often called 'monks' benches', but there's no evidence that they were particularly favoured by monks; anyway, most monasteries had been dissolved by Henry VIII and the monks disbanded by the end of the 16th century, many years before our design came into existence.

Construction

The top couldn't be simpler. It consists of three pieces of oak, laid alongside each other and nailed to the two cross-pieces. The inevitable has happened, of course, and the pieces have shrunk across their widths with resulting gaps and splits.

If you are concerned with authenticity you can do the same, but shrinkage plates (fig. 5A) would be better. Fig. 5B shows how the plate is first screwed to the cross-piece, sunk slightly below the surface (say 1/32 in or so) which means that the cross-piece and the top will be in close contact. Use a round-head screw to fix the plate to the underside of the top; the slot will allow movement without the top splitting.

Fig. 1 shows the various joints used. You will see the framing uses mortise-and-tenon joints, all pegged; the joints on the seat rails are double tenons.

The wedged tenons on the tops and

Methods of construction

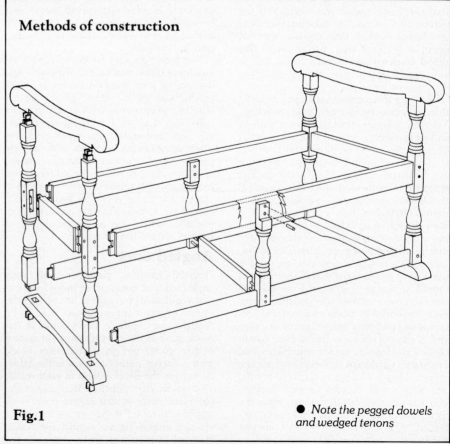

Fig.1

● Note the pegged dowels and wedged tenons

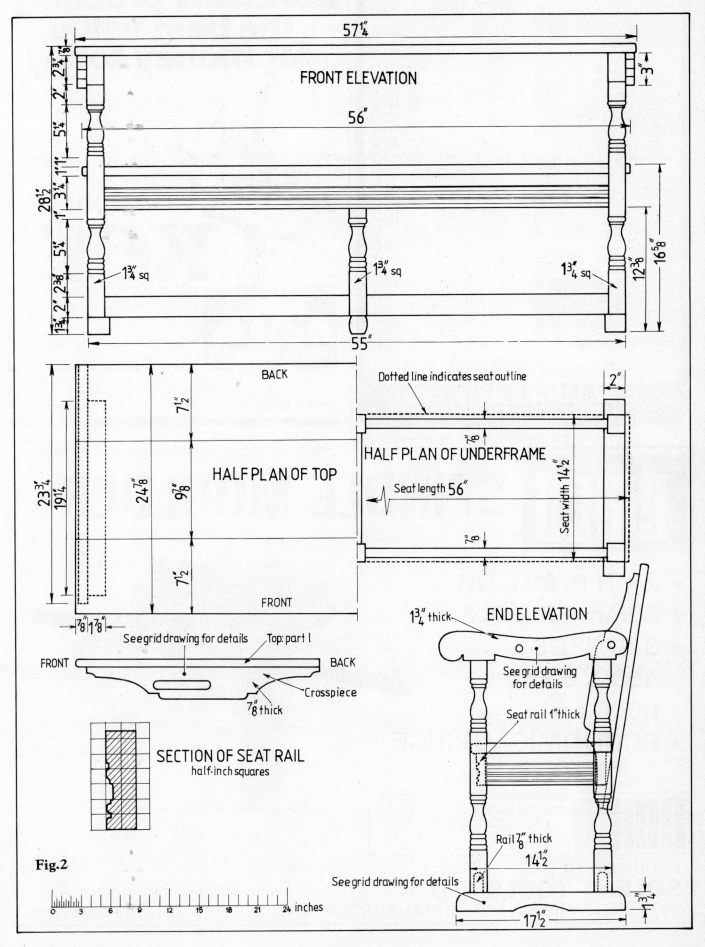

FRONT ELEVATION

$57\frac{1}{4}''$

$56''$

$28\frac{1}{2}$

$3''$

$\frac{3}{4}''\frac{7}{8}''$
$2'2\frac{3}{4}''$
$2'2\frac{3}{4}''$
$5\frac{1}{4}''$
$1'1''1''$
$3\frac{1}{4}''$
$1''$
$5\frac{1}{4}''$
$2'2\frac{3}{8}''$
$1\frac{3}{4}''2'2''$

$1\frac{3}{4}''$ sq

$1\frac{3}{4}''$ sq

$1\frac{3}{4}''$ sq

$12\frac{3}{8}''$

$16\frac{5}{8}''$

$55''$

HALF PLAN OF TOP

BACK

$7\frac{1}{2}''$

$24\frac{7}{8}''$

$9\frac{7}{8}''$

$7\frac{1}{2}''$

FRONT

$23\frac{3}{4}''$
$19\frac{1}{4}''$

$\frac{7}{8}''\frac{7}{8}''$

HALF PLAN OF UNDERFRAME

Dotted line indicates seat outline

$2''$

$\frac{7}{8}''$

Seat length $56''$

$\frac{7}{8}''$

Seat width $14\frac{1}{2}''$

FRONT

See grid drawing for details

Top: part l

BACK

Crosspiece

$\frac{7}{8}''$ thick

END ELEVATION

$1\frac{3}{4}''$ thick

See grid drawing for details

Seat rail $1''$ thick

SECTION OF SEAT RAIL
half-inch squares

Rail $\frac{7}{8}''$ thick

$14\frac{1}{2}''$

See grid drawing for details

$17\frac{1}{2}''$

$1\frac{3}{4}''$

Fig. 2

0 3 6 9 12 15 18 21 24 inches

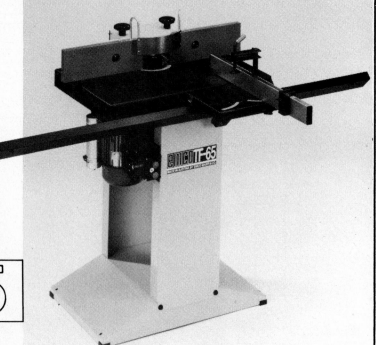
218

Table-top seat

bottoms of the legs need cutting carefully. The tenons at the top ends are blind and call for a slightly different treatment from the bottom ones which are through tenons; fig. 4 shows both kinds, B at the bottom and C at the top of the leg. Points to note are:

● The saw-cuts to accept the wedges should only extend two-thirds of the tenon length.

● The mortise should be slightly splayed as shown to allow for the expansion of the tenon when the wedges are driven home, but the splay only extends for two-thirds of the mortise depth, the same as the length of the saw cuts.

● Judge the size of the wedges nicely. They mustn't be too thin to expand the tenon properly, nor should they be too thick so they force the tenon apart prematurely and jam it before it's fully home.

The tops of the intermediate legs are cut away to accept the seat-rails, and the joints are pegged right through (fig. 1). At the bottom they are bridle-jointed over the underframe rails as shown at fig.4A, and the joints are pegged right through with dowels, which also fix the intermediate cross-rail.

Like the top, the seat consists of two pieces nailed to the end seat-rails and notched round the legs. This is obviously another case for using shrinkage plates along the end seat-rails; fixing to the front and back seat-rail can be by pocket-screwing (fig. 5C), if you don't mind a gap opening up in the middle of the seat. If you prefer comfort to authenticity, pocket-screw at the front and use shrinkage plates everywhere else.

All the seat-rails had moulded faces, the profile of which is shown in fig. 2. This would probably have been worked with a combination of moulding planes and scratch-stocks, but life is easier for us, and we can use a spindle moulder or a router to speed things up.

The only other components are the two pegs (detail, fig. 3) which call for straight-forward wood turning.

Furniture like this almost always began its life 'in the white' — free from any kind of polish. Hundreds of years' worth of wax polish would have been applied, of course, and you can do the same thing; use any good quality proprietary wax polish.

You can see from the main drawing that the piece has had some heavy wear, particularly on the front under-frame rails where the wood has been worn away to about half the original size. If you want to give your reproduction the same appearance you can use a rasp to simulate the wear, restricting it to the front under-frame rail and the edges of the legs, where feet would normally scuff the wood. The edges of the arms were also notched and bruised, and so were all the edges of the top.

● The design is reproduced by kind permission of Mrs Lyle, Barrington Court, near Ilminster, Somerset. ∎

Fig.3

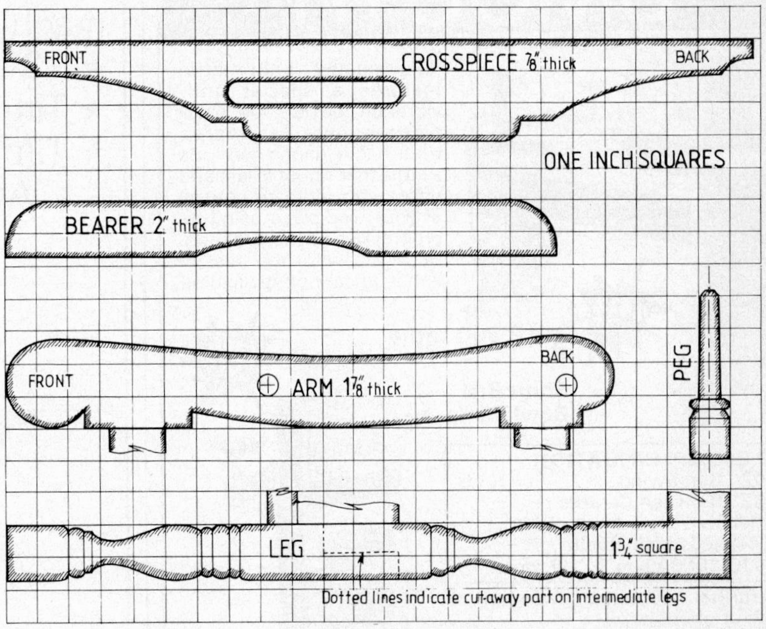

FRONT — CROSSPIECE ⅞" thick — BACK

ONE INCH SQUARES

BEARER 2" thick

FRONT — ⊕ ARM 1⅞" thick — BACK

PEG

LEG — 1¾" square

Dotted lines indicate cut-away part on intermediate legs

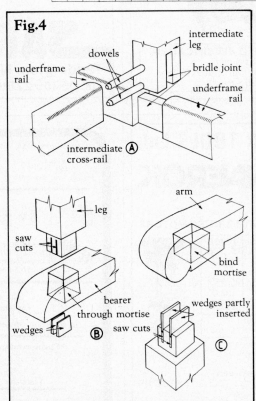

Fig.4

intermediate leg

dowels

underframe rail

bridle joint

underframe rail

intermediate Ⓐ cross-rail

leg

saw cuts

bearer
through mortise

wedges

saw cuts Ⓑ

arm

bind mortise

wedges partly inserted

Ⓒ

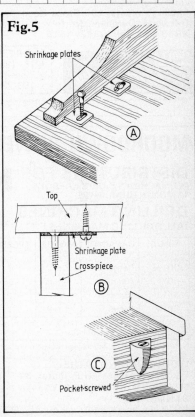

Fig.5

Shrinkage plates

Ⓐ

Top

Shrinkage plate

Cross-piece

Ⓑ

Ⓒ

Pocket-screwed

Cutting list

All components in oak: all dimensions are finished sizes

Top	1	57¼in	24⅞in	⅞in	1454mm	632mm	23mm
Crosspieces	2	23¾	3⅛	⅞	603	80	23
Seat	1	56	14½	1	1423	369	25
Arms	2	19¼	2¾	1⅞	489	70	48
Legs	4	23	1¾	1¾	584	45	45
Intermediate legs	2	13	1¾	1¾	330	45	45
Long seat-rails	2	53¼	3¼	1	1353	83	25
End seat-rails	2	13⅛	3¼	1	333	83	25
Under-frame rails	2	53¼	2	⅞	1353	51	23
Bearers	2	17½	1¾	2	445	45	51
Intermediate cross-rail	1	11	2	⅞	280	51	23

220

shopguide

AVON

BATH   Tel. Bath 64513
JOHN HALL TOOLS   ★
RAILWAY STREET

Open: Monday-Saturday
9.00 a.m.-5.30 p.m.
H.P.W.WM.D.A.BC.

BRISTOL   Tel. (0272) 741510
JOHN HALL TOOLS LIMITED   ★
CLIFTON DOWN SHOPPING CENTRE
WHITELADIES ROAD
Open: Monday-Saturday
9.00 a.m.-5.30 p.m.
H.P.W.WM.D.A.BC.

BRISTOL   Tel. (0272) 629092
TRYMWOOD SERVICES
2a DOWNS PARK EAST, (off North View)
WESTBURY PARK
Open: 8.30 a.m.-5.30 p.m. Mon. to Fri.
Closed for lunch 1.00-2.00 p.m.
P.W.WM.D.T.A.BC.

BRISTOL   Tel. (0272) 667013
FASTSET LTD
190-192 WEST STREET
BEDMINSTER
Open: Mon.-Fri. 8.30 a.m.-5.00 p.m.
Saturday 9.00 a.m.-1.00 p.m.
H.P.W.WM.D.CS.A.BC.

BRISTOL   Tel. (0272) 667013
WILLIS
157 WEST STREET
BEDMINSTER
Open Mon.-Fri. 8.30 a.m.-5.00 p.m.
Sat. 9 a.m.-4 p.m.
P.W.WM.D.CS.A.BC.

BEDFORDSHIRE

BEDFORD   Tel. (0234) 59808
BEDFORD SAW SERVICE   **K**
39 AMPTHILL ROAD

Open: Mon.-Fri. 8.30-5.30
Sat. 9.00-4.00
H.P.A.BC.W.CS.WM.D.

BERKSHIRE

COOKHAM   Tel. (06285) 20350
CHURCH'S TIMBER
STATION HILL

Open: Mon-Sat 8.30 a.m.-5.30 p.m.
Wed 8.30 a.m.-1.00 p.m.
H.P.W.T.CS.MF.A.

READING   Tel. Littlewick Green
DAVID HUNT (TOOL   2743
MERCHANTS) LTD
KNOWL HILL, NR. READING   ★
Open: Monday-Saturday
9.00 a.m.-5.30 p.m.
H.P.W.D.A.BC.

BERKSHIRE

READING   Tel. Reading 661511
WOKINGHAM TOOL CO. LTD.
99 WOKINGHAM ROAD

Open: Mon-Sat 9.00 a.m.-5.30 p.m.
Closed 1.00-2.00 p.m. for lunch
H.P.W.WM.D.CS.A.BC.

BUCKINGHAMSHIRE

SLOUGH   Tel. (06286) 5125
BRAYWOOD ESTATES LTD   ★
158 BURNHAM LANE

Open: 9.00 a.m.-5.30 p.m.
Monday-Saturday
H.P.W.WM.CS.A.

MILTON KEYNES   Tel. (0908)
POLLARD WOODWORKING   641366
CENTRE   ★
51 AYLESBURY ST., BLETCHLEY
Open: Mon-Fri 8.30-5.30
Saturday 9.00-5.00
H.P.W.WM.D.CS.A.BC.

HIGH WYCOMBE Tel. (0494)
SCOTT SAWS LTD.   24201/33788
14 BRIDGE STREET   ★

Mon.-Sat. 8.30 a.m.-6.00 p.m.

H.P.W.WM.D.T.CS.MF.A.BC.

HIGH WYCOMBE   Tel. (0494)
ISAAC LORD LTD   22221
185 DESBOROUGH ROAD   **KE**

Open: Mon-Fri 8.00 a.m.-5.00 p.m.
Saturday 9.00 a.m.-5.00 p.m.
H.P.W.D.A.

CAMBRIDGESHIRE

CAMBRIDGE   Tel. (0223) 63132
D. MACKAY LTD.   **E★**
BRITANNIA WORKS, EAST ROAD

Open: Mon.-Fri. 8.30 a.m.-1 p.m./2.00-
5.00 p.m. Sat. 8.30 a.m.-1.00 p.m.
H.P.W.D.T.CS.MF.A.BC.

CAMBRIDGE   Tel. (0223) 247386
H. B. WOODWORKING   **K**
105 CHERRY HINTON ROAD
Open: 8.30 a.m.-5.30 p.m.
Monday-Friday
8.30 a.m.-1.00 p.m. Sat.
H.P.W.WM.D.CS.A.

PETERBOROUGH   Tel. (0733)
WILLIAMS DISTRIBUTORS   64252
(TOOLS) LIMITED   **K**
108-110 BURGHLEY ROAD
Open: Monday to Friday
8.30 a.m.-5.30 p.m.
H.P.A.W.D.WH.BC.

CHESHIRE

NANTWICH   Tel. Crewe 67010
ALAN HOLTHAM   **K★**
THE OLD STORES TURNERY
WISTASON ROAD, WILLASTON
Open: Tues.-Sat. 9.00 a.m.-5.30 p.m.
Closed Monday
P.W.WM.D.T.C.CS.A.BC.

CHEADLE   Tel: 061491 1726
ERIC TOMKINSON   ★
86 STOCKPORT ROAD
Open: Mon.-Fri. 9.00 a.m.-4.00 p.m.
Saturday 9.00 a.m.-1.00 p.m.
H.P.W.D.MF.A.BC.

CLEVELAND

MIDDLESBROUGH   Tel. (0642)
CLEVELAND WOODCRAFT   813103
(M'BRO), 38-42 CRESCENT ROAD   **K**

Open: Mon-Sat 9.15 a.m.-5.30 p.m.

H.P.T.A.BC.W.WM.CS.D.

CORNWALL

HELSTON   Tel. Helston (03265) 4961
SOUTH WEST   Truro (0872) 71671
POWER TOOLS   Launceston
MONUMENT ROAD   (0566) 3555
   K
H.P.W.WM.D.CS.A.

TRURO   Tel. (0872) 71671
TRURO POWER TOOLS   **E★**
30 FERRIS TOWN

Open Mon.-Sat. 8.00 a.m.-12.30 p.m./
1.30 p.m.-5.00 p.m.
H.P.W.WM.D.CS.MF.A.BC.

CUMBRIA

CARLISLE   Tel: (0228) 36391
W. M. PLANT
ALLENBROOK ROAD
ROSEHILL, CA1 2UT
Open: Mon-Fri. 8.00 a.m.-5.15 p.m.
Sat. 8.00 a.m.-12.30 noon
P.W.WM.D.CS.A.

DERBYSHIRE

BUXTON   Tel. (0298) 871636
CRAFT SUPPLIES   **K★**
THE MILL, MILLERSDALE

Open: Mon-Sat 9.00 a.m.-5.00 p.m.

H.P.W.D.T.CS.A.BC.

DEVON

BRIXHAM   Tel. (08045) 4900
WOODCRAFT SUPPLIES   **E★**
4 HORSE POOL STREET

Open: Mon.-Sat. 9.00 a.m.-6.00 p.m.

H.P.W.A.D.MF.CS.BC.

PLYMOUTH   Tel. (0752) 330303
WESTWARD BUILDING SERVICES   ★
LTD., LISTER CLOSE, NEWNHAM
INDUSTRIAL ESTATE, PLYMPTON
Open: Mon-Fri 8.00 a.m.-5.30 p.m.
Sat. 8.30 a.m.-12.30 p.m.
H.P.W.WM.D.A.BC.

DORSET

BOURNEMOUTH Tel: (0202) 420583
POWER TOOL SERVICES
(Sales, spares, repairs)
849-851 CHRISTCHURCH ROAD
BOSCOMBE
Open: Mon.-Fri. 9.00 a.m.-5.30 p.m.
Sat: 9.00 a.m.-5.00 p.m.
H.P.W.CS.K.A.

POOLE   Tel. (0202) 686238
MACHINE SALES AND SERVICES   ★
(POOLE) LTD.
23 COWLEY ROAD
NUFFIELD INDUSTRIAL ESTATE
Open: Mon.-Fri. 8.30am-5.30pm.
H.P.W.WM.D.CS.A.BC.

ESSEX

LEIGH ON SEA   Tel. (0702)
MARSHAL & PARSONS LTD.   710404
1111 LONDON ROAD   **EK**

Open: 8.30 a.m.-5.30 p.m. Mon-Fri
9.00 a.m.-5.00 p.m. Sat.
H.P.W.WM.D.CS.A.

ILFORD   ★
CUTWELL TOOLS LTD.
774-776 HIGH ROAD

Mon.-Fri. 9.00 a.m.-5.00 p.m.
and also by appointment.
P.W.WM.A.D.CS.

GLOUCESTER

TEWKESBURY   Tel. (0684)
TEWKESBURY SAW CO. LTD.   293092
TRADING ESTATE, NEWTOWN   **K**

Open: Mon-Fri 8.00 a.m.-5.00 p.m.
Saturday 9.30 a.m.-12.00 p.m.
P.W.WM.D.CS.

HAMPSHIRE

shopguide

SHROPSHIRE

TELFORD   Tel. Telford (0952)
ASLES LTD   48054
VINEYARD ROAD, WELLINGTON   **EK★**

Open: Mon. Fri. 8.30 a.m.-5.30 p.m.
Saturday 8.30 a.m.-4.00 p.m.
H.P.W.WM.D.CS.BC.A.

SOMERSET

TAUNTON   Tel. (0823) 85431
JOHN HALL TOOLS
6 HIGH STREET   **★**

Open Monday-Saturday
9.00 a.m.-5.30 p.m.
H.P.W.WM.D.CS.A.

STAFFORDSHIRE

STOKE-ON-TRENT   Tel. 0782-48171
F.W.B. (PRODUCTS) LTD.
WHIELDON ROAD, STAFFS.
Open: Mon.-Fri. 8.30am-5.30pm
Saturday 8.30am-12.30pm
H.P.W.WM.A.D.

SUFFOLK

IPSWICH   Tel. (0473) 40456
FOX WOODWORKING   **KE★**
142-144 BRAMFORD LANE
Open: Tues., Fri., 9.00 a.m.-5.30 p.m.
Sat. 9.00 a.m.-5.00 p.m.

H.P.W.WM.D.A.B.C.

SUSSEX

ST. LEONARD'S-ON-SEA   Tel.
DOUST & MONK (MONOSAW)-(0424)
25 CASTLEHAM ROAD   52577

Open: Mon.-Fri. 8.00 a.m.-5.30 p.m.
Most Saturdays 9.00 a.m.-1.00 p.m.
H.P.W.WM.D.CS.A.

BOGNOR REGIS Tel. (0243) 863100
A. OLBY & SON (BOGNOR REGIS) LTD.
"TOOLSHOP," BUILDERS MERCHANT
HAWTHORN ROAD   **K**
Open: Mon-Thurs 8 a.m.-5.15 p.m. Fri.
8 a.m.-8 p.m. Sat 8 a.m.-12.45 p.m.
H.P.W.WM.D.T.C.A.BC.

WORTHING   Tel. (0903) 38739
W. HOSKING LTD (TOOLS &   **KE★**
MACHINERY)
28 PORTLAND RD, BN11 1QN
Open: Mon.-Sat. 8.30 a.m.-5.30 p.m.
Closed Wednesday
H.P.W.WM.D.CS.A.BC.

TYNE & WEAR

NEWCASTLE UPON TYNE   Tel.
J. W. HOYLE LTD.   (0632) 617474
CLARENCE STREET NE2 1YJ   **K★**
Open: Mon-Fri 8.00 a.m.-5.00 p.m.
Saturday 9.00 a.m.-4.30 p.m.

H.P.A.BC.W.CS.WM.D.

NEWCASTLE   Tel. (0632) 320311
HENRY OSBOURNE LTD.   **E★**
50-54 UNION STREET

Open: Mon-Fri 8.30 a.m.-5.00 p.m.

H.P.W.D.CS.MF.A.BC.

WEST MIDLANDS

BIRMINGHAM   Tel. (021-554) 5177
ROTAGRIP   **E★**
16 LODGE ROAD, HOCKLEY
Open: Mon.-Fri. 9.00 a.m.-5.00 p.m.
Sat. 9.00 a.m.-12.00 p.m.

H.P.W.CS.A.BC.T.MF.

WOLVERHAMPTON   Tel. (0902)
MANSAW SERVICES   58759
SEDGLEY STREET   **K★**

Open: Mon.-Fri. 9.00 a.m.-5.00 p.m.

H.P.W.WM.A.D.CS.

YORKSHIRE

BOROUGHBRIDGE   Tel. (09012)
JOHN BODDY TIMBER LTD   2370
FINE WOOD & TOOL STORE   **★**
RIVERSIDE SAWMILLS
Open: Mon.-Thurs. 8.00 a.m.-6.00 p.m.
Fri. 8.00am-5.00pm Sat. 8.00am-4.00pm
H.P.W.WM.D.T.CS.MF.A.BC.

SHEFFIELD   Tel. (0742) 441012
GREGORY & TAYLOR LTD   **KE**
WORKSOP ROAD
Open: 8.30 a.m.-5.30 p.m.
Monday-Friday
8.30 a.m.-12.30 p.m. Sat.
H.P.W.WM.D.

HARROGATE   Tel. (0423) 66245/
MULTI-TOOLS   55328
158 KINGS ROAD   **K★**

Open: Monday to Saturday
8.30 a.m.-6.00 p.m.
H.P.W.WM.D.A.BC.

LEEDS   Tel. (0532) 574736
D. B. KEIGHLEY MACHINERY LTD.   **★**
VICKERS PLACE, STANNINGLEY
PUDSEY LS2 86LZ
Mon.-Fri. 9.00 a.m.-5.00 p.m.
Sat. 9.00 a.m.-1.00 p.m.
P.A.W.WM.CS.BC.

HUDDERSFIELD   Tel. (0484)
NEVILLE M. OLDHAM   641219/(0484)
UNIT 1 DALE ST. MILLS   42777
DALE STREET, LONGWOOD   **★**
Open: Mon-Fri 8.00 a.m.-5.30 p.m.
Saturday 9.30 a.m.-12.00 p.m.
P.W.WM.D.A.BC.

YORKSHIRE

THIRSK   Tel. (0845) 22770
THE WOOD SHOP   **★**
TRESKE SAWMILLS LTD.
STATION WORKS
Open: Seven days a week 9.00-5.00

T.H.MF.BC.

KEIGHLEY   Tel. (0535) 663325
EUROMAIL (TOOLS)   **★**
PO BOX 13
108 EAST PARADE
Open 9.15 a.m.-5.00 p.m.
Not Tuesday but inc. Saturday
H.P.W.A.BC.

CLECKHEATON   Tel. (0274)
SKILLED CRAFTS LTD.   872861
34 BRADFORD ROAD   **★**

Open: 9.00 a.m.-5.00 p.m. Monday
Saturday Lunch 12.00 a.m.-1.00 p.m.
H.P.A.W.CS.WM.D.

LEEDS   Tel. (0532) 790507
GEORGE SPENCE & SONS LTD.
WELLINGTON ROAD
Open: Monday to Friday
8.30 a.m.-5.30 p.m.
Saturday 9.00 a.m.-5.00 p.m.
H.P.W.WM.D.T.A.

SCOTLAND

CULLEN   Tel. (0542) 40563
GRAMPIAN WOODTURNING SUPPLIES AT
BAYVIEW CRAFTS
Open Mon.-Sat. 9.00 a.m.-5.30 p.m. Sunday
10.00 a.m.-5.30 p.m. Open later July/Aug.
Sept. Demonstrations SAT/SUN or by
H.W.D.MF.BC. appointment

EDINBURGH   Tel. 031-337-5555
THE SAW CENTRE   **★**
38 HAYMARKET EH12 5JZ
Mon.-Fri. 8.30 a.m.-5.30 p.m.
Sat. 9.00 a.m.-1.00 p.m.
H.P.W.WM.D.CS.A.

PERTH   Tel. (0738) 26173
WILLIAM HUME & CO   **K**
ST. JOHN'S PLACE
Open: Monday to Saturday
8.00 a.m.-5.30 p.m.
8.00 a.m.-1.00 p.m. Wednesday
H.P.A.BC.W.CS.WM.D.

GLASGOW   Tel. 041-429-4444/
THE SAW CENTRE   4374 Telex: 777886
650 EGLINTON STREET   **E★**
GLASGOW G5 9RP
Mon.-Fri. 8.00 a.m.-5.00 p.m.
Sat. 9.00 a.m.-1.00 p.m.
H.P.W.WM.D.CS.A.

SCOTLAND

TAYSIDE   Tel. (05774) 293
WORKMASTER POWER TOOLS LTD.   **★**
DRUM, KINROSS
Open Mon.-Sat. 8.00 a.m.-8.00 p.m.
Demonstrations throughout Scotland by
appointment
P.W.WM.D.A.BC.

IRELAND

NEWTOWNARDS   Tel: 0247 819800
NORLYN MACHINERY   or 812506
UNIT 10, MALCOLMSON IND. EST.
80 BANGOR ROAD, CO. DOWN
Open: Mon.-Fri. 9.30am-5.30pm
(Closed 1-2pm for lunch)
Any other time by request.
H.W.WM.D.T.MF.A.   24 Hour Service K

WALES

CARDIFF   Tel. (0222) 595710
DATAPOWER TOOLS LTD,
MICHAELSTON ROAD,
CULVERHOUSE CROSS
Open: Mon.-Fri. 8.00 a.m.-5.00 p.m.
Sat. 9.00 a.m.-1.00 p.m.
H.P.W.WM.D.A.

CARMARTHEN   Tel. (0267) 237219
DO-IT-YOURSELF SUPPLY   **K**
BLUE STREET, DYFED
Open: Monday to Saturday
9.00 a.m.-5.30 p.m.
Thursday 9.00 a.m.-5.30 p.m.
H.P.W.WM.D.T.CS.A.BC.

CARDIFF   Tel. (0222) 396039
JOHN HALL TOOLS LIMITED   **★**
CENTRAL SQUARE

Open: Monday to Saturday
9.00 a.m.-5.30 p.m.
H.P.W.WM.D.A.BC.

SWANSEA   Tel. (0792) 55680
SWANSEA TIMBER & PLYWOOD CO. LTD.
57-59 OXFORD STREET   **★**

Open: Mon to Fri 9.00 a.m.-5.30 p.m.
Sat. 9.00 a.m.-1.00 p.m.
H.P.W.D.T.CS.A.BC.

225

Classified Advertisements

**Telephone
Andrea Smith
01-437 0699**

FOR SALE

THE FINEST SELECTION ON DISPLAY IN SCOTLAND!
WOODWORKING & METALWORKING MACHINERY POWER TOOLS HAND TOOLS
THE SAW CENTRE
HIRE OR BUY!
Visit our **NEW SHOWROOM** at **EGLINTON TOLL GLASGOW**
OPEN Mon - Fri 8am - 5pm Sat 9am - 1pm
Tel: 041-429 4444/4374, Telex: 777886 SAWCO G
Also at, 38 Haymarket Terrace, Edinburgh EH12 5JZ. Tel: 031-337 5555

Bygones

Just one item from our catalogue

MARPLES PARING GOUGES
Boxwood handles
1/4" – 6" radius
Straight or Cranked

WHILE STOCKS LAST

Special rates for quantities

Please send 50p in stamps for catalogue

TILGEAR, 20 Ladysmith Road, Enfield, Middx., EN1 3AA Tel: 01-363 8050/3080

HAND CARVED

'Adam Style' Mantle motifs in Mahogany — Example 10" × 5" centre lamp and two side pieces.
Send S.A.E. for details and quotation. Your own design quoted for if required.
SAM NICHOLSON
22 Lisnagarvey Drive, Lisburn, Co. Antrim, N. Ireland.
Phone Lisburn 3510

HARRISON GRADUATE
and **JUBILEE** Wood Turning Lathes For Sale,
Contact the specialists
L.R.E. MACHINERY & EQUIPMENT Co.
15 Upwood Road, Lowton, Warrington WA3 2RL.
Tel: (0942) 728208 day or night

FOR SALE Luna W59, with accessories £1750. ELU TGS 171 saw, with accessories £220. ELU lathe with accessories £240. Zinken router with accessories £25. Dovetailing attachment £20. Router lathe £50. Tel: 05774 461 (Kinross-shire).

LACE BOBBIN turning blanks. Extensive range of exotics, Ivory, lathes, miniature tools, sundries, lace supplies. SAE J. Ford, 5 Squirrels Hollow, Walsall WS7 8YS.

(FRESH SAWN HOLLY) Limited supply variety & sizes. Reasonable rates details 02607 282. Evenings and Weekends.

USERS AND COLLECTORS tools for sale at the Old Craft Tool Shop, 15 High Street, Whitton, Middx. Telephone 01-755 0441.

HOLMES 10" disc sander 12" × 7" table with protractor. ½ HP motor, £235.00 including VAT and carriage. Larger disc and belt sanders available. 15 Geralds Road, Terriers, High Wycombe, Bucks. HP13 6BN. Telephone 0494 33118.

CLOCKMAKERS

Extensive range of very competitively priced German quartz clock movements, (including standard quartz, pendulum, mini-pendulum, chining, striking and insertion movements). Large selection of quality dials, chapter rings, hands, bezels, clock plans and weather instruments.
Please send 25p stamps for 20 page catalogue.
Bath Clock Company (Dept. W), 13 Welton Road, Radstock, Bath.

WOOD TURNING BLANKS sealed edges. Mixed species 7"-10" diameter 1"-3" thick. Ten for £20 (including postage). Telephone 04215 67494 after 6 p.m.

ELU COMBINATION bench No. 055. Takes MH155 or MH182 including cut-off. Little used £75. Surrey 0372 52928.

WORKSHOP EQUIPMENT

WOODCARVING tools
LARGEST STOCK IN EUROPE
Ashley Iles & Henry Taylor
Arkansas Bench & Slip Stones
Strops & Strop Paste
Bench Screws, Carvers' Vices
WOODTURNING tools
Complete range of
Henry Taylor & Ashley Iles
handled or unhandled
send 40p in stamps for illustrated catalogue
ALEC TIRANTI LTD
70 High St, Theale, Reading, Berks RG7 5AR
21, Goodge Place, London W1.

The best costs less with **BIG DISCOUNTS**

off all leading brands of T.C.T. saws, router cutters, planer knives and narrow bandsaws D.I.Y. and Industrial Quality. It pays to check our prices. Same day low cost resharpening service. Visitors Welcome. Free price list on request.

**L.M. Saws, Slack Lane, Heanor, Derbyshire DE7 7GX
Telephone: 0773 715616**

Braywood Estates

Main stockists
TREND ROUTER CUTTERS, AUGERS, FORSTNER BITS
All at discount prices
Braywood Estates Ltd., Dept WW, 158 Burnham Lane, Slough SL1 6LE.
Tel. Burnham (06286) 5125.
Hrs. Mon-Sat 9am-5.30pm

FOR ALL SUPPLIES FOR THE Craft of Enamelling ON METAL Including LEAD-FREE ENAMELS
PLEASE SEND 2 × 10p STAMPS FOR FREE CATALOGUE, PRICE LIST AND WORKING INSTRUCTIONS
W. G. BALL LTD.
ENAMEL MANUFACTURERS
Dept. W. LONGTON STOKE-ON-TRENT ST3 1JW

MINIATURE COACH BOLTS Etc. LIFELIKE CHINA HORSES individually hand made Authentic scale harness kits
For new illustrated brochure and price lists send £1 in stamps or 2×1st class stamps for one price list (state materials, horse or harness) to:
Lenham Pottery (WW) 215 Wroxham Road Norwich, Norfolk NR7 8AQ

BANKRUPT STOCK
Sandvic circular saw blades tungsten tipped
O/D Sizes 5", 5½", 6" .... **£4 each**
O/D Sizes 6½", 7¼", 8¼" .... **£6 each**
All bore sizes available.
P&P £1 extra, per order.
Tel: 01 672 7776
Hannett, 1A Links Road, Tooting, London, SW17 9ED.

STANLEY COMPASS Plane £50 o.n.o. Tysock & Turner 12" Brass back Tenon Saw £25 o.n.o. Woodworkers 1951-1952 £5 each. Tel: Bristol 0272 – 556241 evenings.

SEASONED HARDWOOD oak, mahogany, Jara, including teak doors to be cleared. Offers lot Bartlett, 162 Birchwood Road, Wilmington. Phone Dartford. Tel: 62110.

STARTRITE ROBLAND 260 combination with all attachments, £1,600. Mr. Shaw 01-883-8677.

FOR SALE Major Universal Woodturning lathe, many accessories. Perfect condition. £700 o.n.o. Bill Highfield, 8 Sagar Street, Eccleston, (Nr. Chorley), Lancashire PR7 5TA.

KITY 10" × 6" planer/thicknesser, floor standing, excellent condition £350. M. Constance, 038-081-3469, Devizes.

WOODTURNERS SUPPLIES
Woodturning tools, Peppermills, Salt mills, Barometers, Thermometers, Lighters, Hourglasses, Eggtimers, Ceramic tiles and clock faces, Clock movements, Spinning wheel plans, Sealers & Polishes, etc. Fast and efficient mail order service + competitive prices. (50p in stamps deductable against first order).
ERIC TOMKINSON
86 Stockport Road, Cheadle, Cheshire, SK8 2AJ. Tel: 061-491 1726
Shop opening times:
9am-5.30pm Mon.-Sat.

227

228

229

231

Jointing thin boards

Bob Wearing's Workshop

A selection of solutions to the light edge-joint/heavy ironmongery problem

Few workshops, particularly amateur ones, are able to invest in sets of short sash-cramps; 36in capacity seems to be the shortest that people are prepared to buy. This poses gluing problems with thin pieces like drawer-bottoms, small panels and musical-instrument components. The sheer weight of ironmongery is overpowering, even if you use only the smallest cramps. Here are several solutions to the problem, which are in themselves quite satisfying projects.

Light board-cramps

Fig. 1 shows the light board-cramps described in *Woodworker*, October 1983. Make up a support board of either thin chipboard or substantial plywood, truly flat and slightly less (say ¼in) than the finished width of the jointed board. If it is to be well used, it's worth covering one face with adhesive plastic like Fablon to prevent the joint from sticking to it. You can also use thin polythene sheet or even paper. The workpiece with its support board is threaded between two or three of the light board-cramps and light pressure applied. Should there be any tendency for the joint to rise, either put a weight on top or cramp a strong batten across.

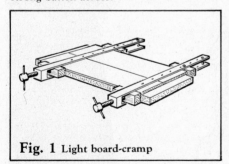

Fig. 1 Light board-cramp

Small thin board-cramp

This device, shown in fig. 2, is light, cheap and assumes the minimum of metalworking equipment. The suggested dimensions can be modified to suit the purpose or available materials. If you plan to make a number of them, it may be worthwhile making up the jig shown in fig. 3, which will guarantee complete accuracy.

I find 7in jaws ample for most small joints, and two cramps will cover quite a length of joint. The guide-rods are made from 5⁄16in bright drawn mild steel. This size is identical with 8mm, so it suits both imperial and metric workers. The screw thread, being in tension, can be very thin. However, to avoid a 'slow' thread, I settled

for ⅜in in British Standard Whitworth (BSW). The metric M10 thread is a little slower. You can see that the two fixed blocks are counterbored to take the nuts, which ensures a smooth cramping-face and also doesn't reduce the cramping capacity. The counterboring is done after the main drilling by filling the hole with a tight dowel to provide a centre. A ⅝in hole takes a 5⁄16in nut quite nicely. While the two outer holes are drilled on the centre-line, the centre hole is lowered 1⁄16in so that the cramped board doesn't rock on the higher screw.

The turned handle is drilled, tapped and the screw forced in as far as possible. There is little chance of it working loose, but if it does, a pin can be put through the handle and screw — not through the ferrule. The centre holes in the three blocks can be enlarged slightly to give easy movement of the screw. 1⁄64in or 0.5mm will be enough.

The moving jaw is fitted with a threaded plate. A forced-in countersunk nut is a poor alternative, because it's liable to be forced out again. The free end of the screw is drilled for a small split-pin and fitted with a washer.

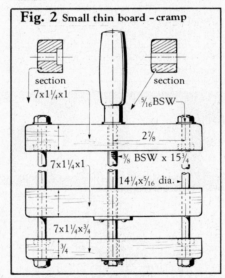

Fig. 2 Small thin board – cramp

section
7x1¼x1

section
5⁄16BSW

2⅞

7x1¼x1

⅜ BSW x 15¾

14¼x5⁄16 dia.

7x1¼x¾

¾

Try up the whole assembly and check for smooth working. The outer bars can be adjusted by their nuts to eliminate slack in the screw. Do the final shaping, then sand and finish. I prefer either linseed oil or polyurethane varnish.

Drilling without a jig

Arrange a fence on the drilling machine with a stop-block to do the six outer holes. The true edge must always be against the fence; grip the work with a cramp for perfect accuracy. Re-adjust the block and fence for the centre hole. When you've finished drilling, cramp the three pieces together with a piece of 5⁄16in rod in one end-hole. Run the appropriate drill through the other holes to ensure perfect alignment.

A drilling jig

An all-wood jig will quickly wear and lose its accuracy, so it should be fitted with guide bushes (fig. 3). These can be obtained

from good engineer's suppliers or, better still, as a spare part for the Record dowelling jig. The bushes fit tightly into a 12mm hole which for real accuracy should be drilled with a fine-point wood-drill as distinct from the metalworker's twist drill with its obtuse-angled point. A ply fence and an end-stop complete the tool. Record drill-bushes, having two flats on them, can be given a small housing to prevent rotation.

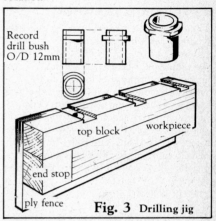

Record drill bush O/D 12mm

top block   workpiece

end stop

ply fence

Fig. 3 Drilling jig

Luthier's methods

Prepare a suitable board from ply, block- or chipboard and fit a strong vice-strip. Next, pin on the first clamping-strip of — say — ¾x½in (fig. 4a). Now lay on the pieces to be jointed with a 1x¼in strip below the joint. Press another ¾x½in strip up tightly, and pin it as in fig. 4b. Remove the ¼in strip from underneath, glue the joint and press it into place with a strip of paper or thin polythene below and above the glue. Put a weight on, or cramp a batten to prevent it springing up, as in fig. 4c.

Another luthier's method is illustrated in fig. 5 overleaf. Here the pressure is applied by tapping in a long tapered wedge. Candle wax rubbed on both edges of the wedge, and a pin driven into the baseboard, prevent the jointed boards from moving.

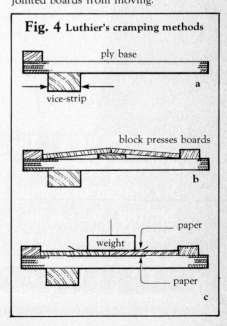

Fig. 4 Luthier's cramping methods

ply base

vice-strip   **a**

block presses boards   **b**

paper

weight

paper   **c**

Jointing thin boards

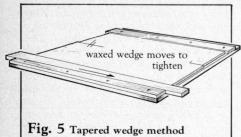

Fig. 5 Tapered wedge method

waxed wedge moves to tighten

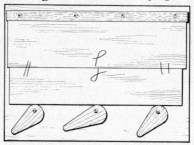

Fig. 6 Lever-cam cramping

cam-ends are spiral in plan. See Fig. 7

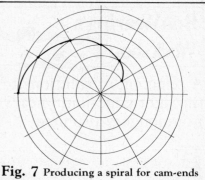

Fig. 7 Producing a spiral for cam-ends

Lever-cam method

The parts can be forced against the fixed fence by several lever cams (fig. 6), which shouldn't be too small. The shape in plan of the end should be a spiral, which you can arrive at by using the diagram in fig. 7. A poorly shaped cam won't retain the pressure, and will spring open again. Only part of the spiral is required — draw out the shape on a card then cut it out to use as a template. The cams and fixed fence can be considerably thicker than the jointed component. 12-gauge screws are recommended. A weight or batten may be needed to prevent lifting.

Planing thin joints

The pieces to be jointed are laid together, suitably marked, then folded bookwise (fig. 8a). They can be cramped together between two battens and hand-planed or, if one of the battens is made fairly wide, and woodscrews used instead of cramps, a planer may be used (fig. 8b). Working individually off the planer fence is not always so successful, but if you do, make sure that you plane one board (*Woodworker* February 1983), make if you hand-plane with a good shooting board, (*Woodworker* February 1983), make sure one piece is planed true face up and the other true face down. This guarantees a joint angle of 180°.

In all edge jointing, and particularly using thin wood, the accuracy of the joint is paramount. A poorly-fitting joint cannot be crushed together. These tools and methods aim at lightly but firmly holding the components together while the glue hardens. ∎

Fig. 8 Planing thin edges for jointing

a fold bookwise

b cramp together and plane both edges

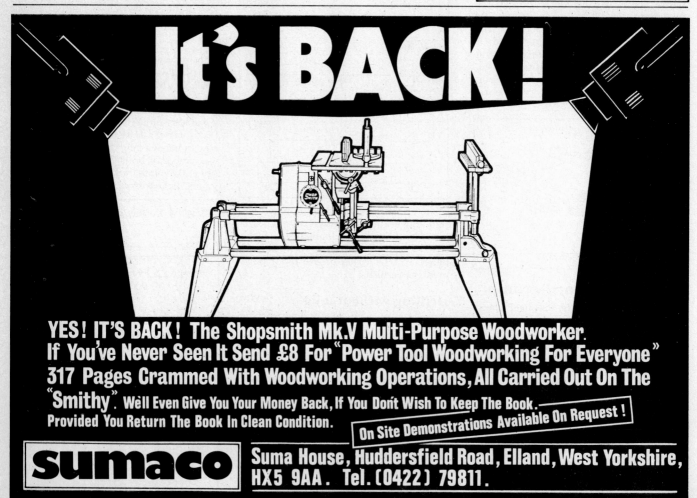

Yew turned

David Gliddon is a woodturner of more than 20 years' experience. He came across some unusual iron-stained yew . . .

I mostly work in yew, making a range from wooden fruit through thimbles to large bowls to sell in craft shops. I buy yew trees in the round and plank them myself with a chainsaw mill, or if they're clean, I get a farmer to saw them on a stenner rack saw-bench. The planks are stacked for a few weeks, then put in a wood drier for eight.

Yew is an unpredictable wood; sometimes the trees aren't worth cutting, but I can still make thimbles and small knobs out of what I salvage. There's always the possibility you'll end up with something totally different from what you set out to make — a toadstool in nail-stained yew, for example, that started out as a trinket box!

● David Gliddon, The Bungalow, High Bolham, Oakford, nr Tiverton, Devon, tel. (03985) 449.

● 'This particular tree (**above**) was full of nails – armed with a chainsaw and metal detector I cut it up and seasoned it in the kiln, nails and all.' **Below left,** the heart-shake problem; **bottom left,** thimble production, and **below right,** a vase that started as an apple!

Photos Martyn Collins

The gleaning of the forests

Will John Makepeace's Hooke Park project turn redundant forest waste into a new industrial base for Britain? David Savage paid a visit

Mega-craftsman John Makepeace must reckon himself highly vulnerable. It's one of our unpleasant national characteristics to deal our high-profile successful innovators a swift kick in the groin when they get too bumptious; and Makepeace's actions, ideas and achievements are nothing if not high-profile.

Originally intending to enter the Church, he abandoned the idea in 1957 and took up a two-year training with cabinetmaker Keith Cooper, to work with whom he paid the princely sum of £2 a week. In 1963 he moved to a broken-down group of farm-buildings in Oxfordshire that were to become home, workshops and gallery; over the next decade the set-up became a thriving furniture-making business, providing work for several craftsmen and training for apprentices and fee-paying students.

Parnham House in 1976 must have been an estate agent's nightmare. A once-beautiful Tudor house, now decidedly shabby and almost useless; Makepeace bought it, renovated it with great style and has been reaping the benefits ever since.

Makepeace recognised that no art college would or could produce designers with both the sensitivity to work in timber and the economic nous to survive self-employed. He formed the Parnham Trust to develop and administer The John Makepeace School for Craftsmen in Wood. This offers a first-class residential two-year course to students, to which much attention has been drawn by its high fees and the (former) presence of a student with royal connections.

Setting up the school, the separate workshops for his business, showrooms and a comfortable home has kept Makepeace occupied for about seven years. Lately he has become interested in forestry, forestry management and the use of small roundwood, an enthusiasm that was nurtured on a visit to Longleat where an area of woodland was offered to him totally free.

For a woodworker to be offered not just the odd stick but an entire section of forest completely free is unusual, to say the least. We're used to paying a high price for our material. Yet the offer wasn't a generous one, it was a sensible business proposition — the timber would cost more to extract than it was worth at 'rideside'.

At this time the forestry commission were selling off parcels of lowland forest, one of which, the 330-acre Hooke Park, was close to Parnham. Makepeace set about raising £250,000 to buy the forest and another £1m to finance an idea that was forming . . .

● *A deep laminated ridgeboard tops the structure – round poles wouldn't bend so much and keep strength*

● *The roof is to be covered with lightweight turf, with a goat as lawnmower! The whole structure at this stage looks just about to set sail . . .*

The reasons for such indecent energy are straightforward. As a designer and creative being Makepeace has a passion for wood, and his awareness of the use of a finite resource is particularly acute. Being offered a wood for free was an alarming experience. He is also a champion of the enterprising small business person; combine these facets and we emerge with 'The Working Woodland', and, at its centre, the 'School for Woodland Industry'.

The concept is a response to the poor condition of British forestry. Timber is our second largest import, yet our own forests produce over three million tons of small roundwood each year. The very material at Longleat that Makepeace was offered for nothing would build 30,000 homes. There are also serious transportation problems; the haulier and processor often claim 88% of the value of logs at the mill, so it becomes clear that with only 12% to cover an investment over many years, there are problems for the forest landowner. The old rural industries of hurdle making, trug and chair making, which depended largely upon coppicing, were rendered obsolete by industrial progress, so the landowner, the forester and the haulier were left in splendid

236

leafy isolation. In many instances neglect was the only economic solution to forest management.

The point, of course, is that the key to economic success lies in the integration by geographical regions of timber-growing and wood industries. But forests don't have little leggies. Burnham wood will never come to Dunsinane — industries must in their turn move to the forest. Enter John Makepeace and his idea.

First, develop a building system that uses spruce poles in the construction of buildings. Then use the buildings as a centre for developing products and woodland industries. Then, using this as a focus for public attention, develop the forestry area as a community resource for walks, recreation and education. Put in tree-top walks and paths, highlighting the ecology of the forest, its rare species and natural inhabitants.

The task of managing the 330 acres of forest at Hooke Park has fallen to Andrew Poore, an intelligent and knowledgeable young man who is also a tough business-

man. He has to demand a high price for the poles used by the Parnham Trust in the construction of the school.

The architects Ahrends, Burton and Koralek, together with German architect Frei Otto and structural engineers Buro Happold, were commissioned to design a series of buildings to house the staff, students and workshops that would become the School for Woodland Industries. The quantity surveyors are Bernard Williams Associates. Brian McPherson is chief executive, on secondment from BP, who make contributions to the community by providing management skills to projects such as this. BP is, however, only one of 20 contributing companies. Other sponsors and benefactors cover 1½ pages of close type; when you consider the problem of raising £750,000 after a first whack of £500,000, those pages look like growing considerably.

Progress to date has been considerable. The land has been purchased, designs made and models built, a beginning on forestry management has been made with the help of YTS labour, and one building, a prototype

● *Where the rafters and 'sarking-board' (a kind of soffit) meet*

● *A compression joint of the heavy-duty supports **above,** for the roof; steel cables **right** supply tension between the A-frame 'peaks'*

237

The gleaning of the forests

built with ABK architect William Moorwood on site, is nearing completion.

The buildings on the plans at first sight look rather fanciful, but models and drawings always give a distorted view. Designed to look good on site rather than at the press launch or fund-raising stage, the buildings comprise seminar rooms, workshops and offices in one hump, a visitors' centre for exhibitions, permanent displays, dining and recreation in another wooden wigwam, and terraces of rather floppy-looking staff houses. All are grouped around a moss lawn and linked by bridges or covered ways.

On site, the design becomes more than a 20th century log cabin settlement. It's an appropriate and sensitive use of location and materials. The structures will support 'PVC-coated polymer roof membranes embedded with gravel terracotta chippings and sprayed with a spore-laden growing medium to encourage the growth of moss and lichen'.

Carrying a load in tension uses less material than carrying one in compression, which is why ancient building forms such as tents, domes and arches have retained their relevance to the present day. Timber has tremendous tensile strength — have you ever tried to break a twig, not by snapping it in two, but by pulling it down its length? This inherent feature of the material has been enhanced by the development of an end-grain tensile fastening system using epoxy glues and resin wrappings designed by structural engineer Ted Happold. The strength of roundwood, which in this case varies from 5-20cm in diameter, is developed by nature. To preserve the outer capillaries from damage by gusts of wind, the tree orientates fibres diagonally around the capillaries so an element of longitudinal pre-stressing is given to the fibres, while the centre of the tree is in compression. Cut the log into boards or posts as we habitually do, and we destroy this strength element.

The team's designs employ roundwood to its best advantage. Structural A-frames were used on the prototype building, the roof members pre-stressed during construction. This encourages any additional load on the roof, such as a heavy fall of snow, to be deflected from the eaves and glass windows back into the A-frame. However, as Happold readily admits, you have to think very hard when you design in wood. The principal problem possibly stems from the use of a non-standardised material. A spruce pole in Dorset has different characteristics from one in Norway — but with research, comparative figures for stress loading should become available. Rot is also a serious problem, especially in our damp climate. In 1850, Brunel designed some fine timber structures in his trestle bridges. He designed, as the architect-team has, to allow rotted members to be removed. Brunel's designs were cheap and superb — but they rotted in 30 years and were replaced after 60. Makepeace believes that modern

● *With all the rafters in place, ropes pre-tension them to the expected curvature from the full-weight roof*

preservative methods can be used on a small scale cheaply and efficiently, and Otto, ABK and the team believe that with adequate maintenance, there is no reason why the buildings can't be long-lasting at very low cost. Only time will tell.

The School for Woodland Industry and its 'Working Woodland' looks an unlikely venture for a furniture designer, but the context of the Parnham Trust makes it seem a natural extension of Makepeace's interest

in wood. In the context of a forcing-ground for small business enterprise in wood, the School for Woodland Industry makes good economic sense, and it attempts to put forestry back in connection with the market for timber products and with the public.

Roundwood today is worth almost nothing. If the building techniques developed here are adopted for small rural building projects, the £100 per ton that Andrew Poore charges the project will seem

● More compression joints. Steel rods are cranked to go through an upright between the ends of the entering poles; the gunge is epoxy resin, injected through holes to set after fixing and adjustments

cheap — but that's the whole idea. The building technique is, however, only the first stage. The School for Woodland Industry will be just that, a school for industrial production in a forest setting. Transportation costs are reduced by placing the factory unit next to the source of raw material. Students capable of organising small manufacturing units will be trained here — a different breed from those at the existing Makepeace School. They may be slightly older people with a background in engineering, management, design or forestry. They may come sponsored by a local authority or a landowner; they may even own a small woodland.

Products using the material will be developed according to market needs. The use of forest thinnings for motorway sound screens and in the purification of metals indicates the directions in which the school will be looking. Trug making and hurdle making may have a place in 20th century woodland industry, but it is likely to be a small one. Forests in the future are more likely to echo to the buzz of the CNC router than the swish of the pole lathe and the draw-knife.

The intervention by Makepeace has very little to do with personal glory and empire-building. It is an initiative that could re-generate British forests and it has been done so far on the support of charitable trusts, public companies and individual do-nations. Britain is blessed with thousands of

charitable trusts formed on guilt and the tax-avoiding instincts of wealthy people close to death. These are organisations that generally spend the interest on capital bequests. They love novel ideas tempered by good sense and proper management, but the Parnham Trust has already carried the hat round more than once. The general public should support this initiative, and woodworkers in particular have a stake in maintaining the health and heart of British forestry. ■

● The target at the time of writing is another £750,000 — for details of how you can contribute, write to The Parnham Trust, Parnham House, Beaminster, Dorset DT8 3NA.

● Members of the **Guild of Wood-workers** are invited to a tour of both Hooke Park and Parnham House on April 13. For details, see the Guild pages.

A roundwood 'language'

'It's been very exciting,' says **Richard Burton,** the responsible partner of Ahrends Burton Koralek, 'to work with Frei Otto, Edmund Happold and Michael Dickson as part of a design team. Frei has a lot of experience in working with wood, and though I haven't worked with it in this way before, I have built in wood. This is a new tradition in an old material.'

Burton's association with Makepeace goes back a long way. He is a founder trustee of Parnham, and both his sons have studied there — his elder son Bim is making a name for himself as a furniture designer-craftsman, and is a member of the IDF (WW/Feb).

'We're craftsmen's architects,' says Burton. 'We're also fundamentally interested in the saving of resources and

energy, which is why the idea of using what would otherwise be waste as a building material is terrifically interesting for us.'

Using round components has meant a new approach to jointing, and using the flexibility of the spruce poles as a characteristic of the structure. The rafters will flex up to 200mm at the centre of their span, another 100-150 under snow. A jointing system using threaded rods with eyes, set into stepped holes in the pole-ends and then epoxied, has been developed; the strength transference between steel and wood has been tested at almost 100%, and the idea works almost as well for compression jointing as it does for tension.

● **Next month:** more technical details from job architect **William Moorwood,** who worked on site all summer . . . .

Nature's wooden way

The flowers of the field and a 'Netsuke' mouse appear under Alan and Gill Bridgewater's sympathetic chisels

Netsuke mouse

Kamakura and Kyoto were traditionally the most important centres of woodcarving in old Japan, turning out fine products for the imperial courts and palaces. Most of the carvers worked on utilitarian items like bowls, dishes, and kitchen and farm equipment, but the really skilled tended to concentrate on the uniquely Japanese, wonderfully sensitive carvings known as netsuke.

Netsuke (Net'su ka), meaning small carvings worn or attached to various articles such as a button or toggle, were primarily used to fasten boxes, pipes and tobacco pouches to a man's kimono sash. However, nineteenth-century laws banned the common people from wearing jewellery, so gradually the netsuke became an important item of adornment and prestige.

Traditional netsukes are very small, usually only an inch or so in diameter, and depict friendly animals, beasts and figures — all pierced, undercut, incised and intricately detailed. The netsuke carvers used slender, flexible-bladed chisels which they worked pen-like in one hand, while they turned and held the wood with the other.

Towards the end of the nineteenth century, Japan was opened up to the west, and in a very short time dress fashions changed and netsukes became obsolete. However, woodcarvers still work in the spirit of the netsuke tradition, and their carvings remain small, sensitive, humorous, delicate and intricate. Little figures, birds, animals and flowers; all are beautifully worked with expressive tool marks and considered, fine details.

Tools and materials

For this project you will most certainly need to use a super-fine smooth wood — what better than a piece of butter-coloured box? This wood is extremely close, even and dense in its grain, and when crisply cut, it appears to have a natural polish. You might have to search round for just the right piece, but see if you can get a 3x3x3in cube of English wood.

For tools you need a set of super-sharp miniature gouges (I use a set made by Henry Taylor), a fine-blade knife, a coping-saw, a rasp, Plasticine and, of course, scraps of paper, pencils compass and a measure.

Setting out the design

You will see that the illustrated mouse fits very snugly in a nut-shaped or ball form. Start by taking your cube of wood and the compass, and mark off all six faces with 3in diameter circles. Now, work the wood with

● *Miniature Japanese charm: a Netsuke mouse for shelves as well as kimonos*

the coping-saw and rasp until it's smooth and spherical. Making the ball is tricky. You must work the wood corner by corner and watch out for the direction of the grain. Aim to make a smooth nut of wood that fits comfortably in your hand. Of course, if you are really keen and fancy a challenge you could work a very small mouse, say 1in diameter, but think carefully about it!

Making a Plasticine maquette

Make a 3in ball of Plasticine and mark off the back, front, top and side. Look at the working drawings and photograph to see how the mouse fits the ball form. If you can't quite see how, for instance, the feet or tail work in relationship to each other, then make a little Plasticine mouse and curl him into a ball. See how the tail wraps over the shoulder and around the neck, and how the feet, ears, nose and eyes are set and detailed.

When you have made a satisfactory working model, put it out of harm's way but within easy reach; pin up as many magazine clippings and mouse studies as you can find and arrange the tools comfortably to hand.

Marking out and first cuts

Take the ball of wood and a soft pencil and carefully draw in the lines of the mouse. At this stage don't even try to detail the feet or anything else; it's much better to concentrate on the big generous curve of the tail, the hump of the spine and the other main forms. When the guide-lines have been drawn in, take the ball of wood in one hand, hold the knife as if you are going to pare an apple and then cut-in the lines of the design with a series of V-cuts. As you work, keep the ball turning and continue to pivot and control the knife with your thumb keeping a close watch on the direction of the grain.

Cutting-in and modelling

Still with the wood in one hand and the knife or miniature tool in the other, carve the wood using the V-trenches as stop-cuts. Pare and pull the knife towards you, all the time lowering the unwanted ground and cutting into the stop-cuts. Every few minutes, put the wood down alongside the Plasticine maquette and stand back to assess your progress. Is the hump of the tail standing proud? Can you see the curve of the spine? Is the head going to fit within the form? Are you cutting too deep? You must continually check and question your carving. Try not to work on a single area such as an eye or paw — it's much better to keep the wood turning and moving and carve the whole form.

With a project of this size and character, the main difficulty is not carving the individual features but keeping the overall form neatly balanced and achieving the final statement that says *mouse*.

Finishing

When you feel you have taken the carving as far as it's going to go, having carved and detailed the toes, ears, mouth, eyes and the rest, sharpen up your knife or tool, and go over the whole mouse, cutting in the fine hair texture. Make sure that the little nicks

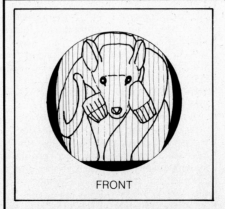

FRONT

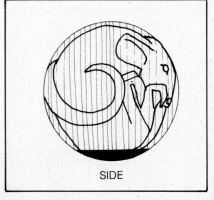

SIDE

1 After you've made a few sketch drawings and a Plasticine mock-up, take your cut and rasped ball of boxwood and draw the lines without too much detail

are organised so that they follow and emphasise the form. Finally, take a piece of the finest grade sandpaper and just touch the pad of the nose and the rims of the ears to take the wood to a smooth finish.

Hints, tips and afterthoughts
● When you are buying boxwood, take care that you buy the real thing. Avoid central American or West Indian boxwood, because it is liable to split and cut-up with a dull and off-yellow hue — go for home-grown wood.
● If you find as you work that the wood is difficult to hold, or your hands are blistered, sore or damp, wear a pair of soft chamois-leather dress gloves.

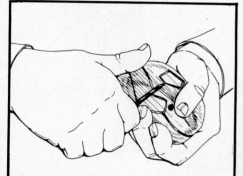

2 Cut in the lines of the design with a series of V-section cuts, using a sharp knife

3 Carve and pare the bold forms, using the V-section cuts as stop-cuts

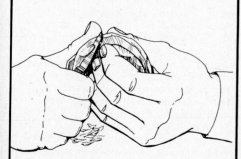

4 Continue lowering some areas of wood and modelling others

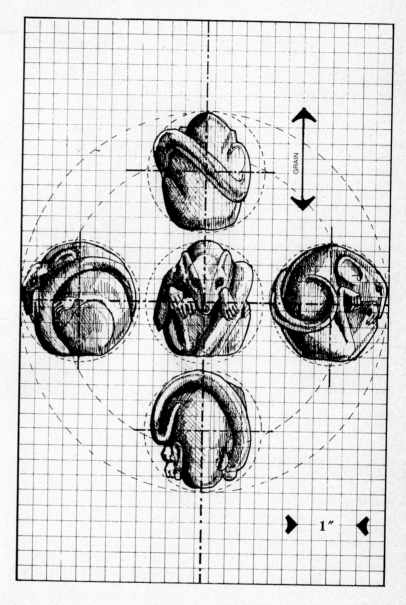

● *Five views of the mouse – note the grain direction running from base to head. The grid is four squares to the inch*

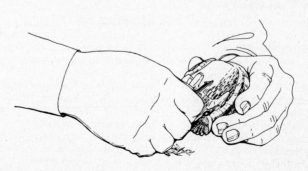

5 Go over the finished carving and cut-in the hair texture with a knife or tool

Nature's wooden way

Grinling Gibbons flower

Grinling Gibbons was born in Rotterdam, Holland, in 1648. His background is a little misty, but it is thought that his father was English and his mother Dutch. As a young man he came to England, where he was discovered by the author and diarist John Evelyn 'working in an obscure place . . . a poor solitary cottage.'

Gibbons's woodcarvings must have made a big impression on Evelyn, who had written on trees and timber usage, and was a member of the Royal Society. Within a month Sir Christopher Wren the architect, Samual Pepys the naval official and diarist, and Charles II had all seen Gibbons' work. No doubt he was soon overwhelmed with commissions — statuary for the King, swags and flowers for the Queen, carvings for Wren's great buildings, mirror frames, over-mantles, coats of arms, gifts for foreign ambassadors, cherubs, swags and much more. The Gibbons style of woodcarving was taken up by most of the important architects of the period, and worked into their decorative schemes. Birds, angels, cupids, flowers, shells, ribbons and swags, all worked in lime, were carved in a style that has variously been described as naturalistic, florid and exuberantly realistic.

Although Gibbons died in 1720, his work set the style for the next hundred years — realistic carvings from nature in lime which was built up, laminated, glued, pinned and deeply undercut.

Tools and materials

For this project you must use lime. It has smooth grain, very few knots, and best of all it can be cut and worked in just about any direction. Get yourself a small 4x4in block 1½-2in thick. You will need a couple of small spoon-bit gouges, a shallow-curved gouge, a small, shallow-curved, straight gouge, a flat spoon-bit gouge, a small knife and, of course, a bench-stop or clamp; and a pencil, sketch paper, measure, coping-saw and rifflers.

Before you start this project take a good look at the photograph and drawings and consider how the flower fits the wood and the grain.

Setting out the design

Take up your block of wood, check it over thoroughly, and make absolutely sure it's free from soft, waney wood, splits, grain-twists and orange/brown pulpy knots. Start by tracing the various views of the flower and transferring them to the top, bottom and sides of the block. If you look at the photograph and drawings you'll see I have simplified, further stylised and slightly thickened the flower petals. If you want to add more petals, or have a more complex flower centre, this is the time to re-adjust your sketches.

● *The inspiration: a Grinling*

When you have drawn in the various elevations of the flower, block them in with a pencil and make clear notes on the wood — 'top', 'side A', 'cut away', and so on.

First cuts

Take the coping-saw, clear away all the unwanted wood and establish the basic flower profile. When this has been done you'll find the little block of wood is awkward to hold and difficult to manage, so glue it to a larger piece of thick plywood, which makes for easy holding and clamping. If you decide to screw rather than glue the lime to the ply, be careful the screws don't split the wood or pierce areas to be carved as illustrated.

Shaping up

Clamp the plywood-supported, roughed-out, block of wood to the work-bench and then start chopping in with a small, shallow-curved, straight gouge. Hold the gouge in both hands and work around the flower plan, all the time cutting straight down into the wood. When you are carving, don't lever against the wood, but cut away small crisp curls and gradually work closer and closer to the outside edge of the plan view of the flower. When this is done, take the small straight chisel and cut a V-trench round the central ball of the flower.

Once you have set-in round the flower centre, take a small spoon-bit gouge, and working from the flower edge to the centre, cut away, slope and lower the ground. Continue carving in this way, cutting in and around the central area, and then gouging out and lowering the petal ground. When the centre pillar of wood stands well proud of the lowered petals, it can be rounded and undercut.

Final cuts

Take the small spoon-bit gouge and start to hollow out the centre of the flower. Work as if you were spooning into a boiled egg. That is, push the spoon-bit gouge deep into the centre of the flower and then scoop out a curl of wood. It sounds rather complicated, but, as long as you keep your tools sharp, and don't rush or be tempted to lever your tools, this project is really quite straightforward. Once you have hollowed out the flower centre, take the shallow-curved, curved gouge, and cleanly work and tool the top surface of the spread-out petals. See how the petals appear to overlap each other and gently curve and ripple at their edges.

When you have established and tooled the top surface of the petals and the flower centre, take one of the spoon-bit gouges and start to undercut the petals. Work with a light sensitive touch and only attempt to remove small parings of wood — don't lever up against the now-fragile petals or try to hack off great chunks of wood.

Nature's wooden way

Finishing

Stand back from your work and try to see it with a fresh and critical eye. Can you work the petals thinner? Are the petal overlaps convincing? Search out and correct faults, and when you feel enough is enough, take the small knife and riffler and go over the whole flower, working a delicate, tooled finish. Slide the razor-sharp knife over the wood and pare away any rough areas, clean up the undercuts, and finally cut-in the little stylised petal creases.

Hints, tips and afterthoughts

● With a rather delicate carving of this character, there are several tricky areas of short grain. For example, the tips of the petals and the fine edge of the flower centre have to be worked and carved with extra care.

● If you find your tools are cutting-up roughly and leaving a ragged finish, spend a few minutes honing them to a keen edge on the oilstone and leather strop.

● If in the final stages of carving you split a petal, don't lose your temper. Check that the break is clean and then mend it with a PVA wood glue or an epoxy resin. Bind up the mend with fine cotton, leave it for 24 hours, and then go back to work.

● These two projects are from *Step by Step Wood-carving*, by Alan and Gill Bridgewater, published by Bell and Hyman, £7.95 hardback. Our thanks to Elizabeth Sich for her help in arranging the reproduction.

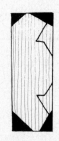

1 (above) Draw the design on the wood, marking the areas to be cut away

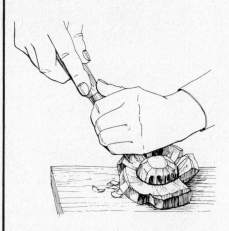

2 (above) After you've cut away the excess wood with a coping saw, take a shallow straight gouge, lower the wood round the flower centre and generally shape up the petal profile

3 (above) Undercut the flower's central ball with a fine blade knife or small chisel

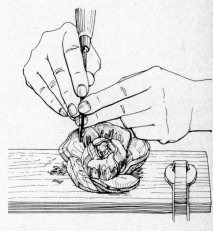

4 (above) Model the petals with a small spoon-bit gouge, carving from side to centre

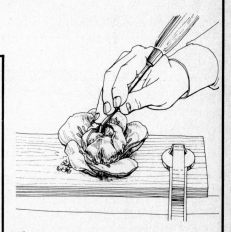

5 (above) Spoon out the flower centre with a small spoon-bit gouge. Work little by little and be careful you don't break off the delicate short grain.

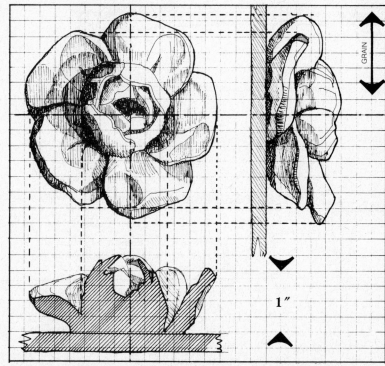

● *Three views of the flower – note the grain direction. The grid is four squares to the inch*

1″   GRAIN

6 The finished flower

243

The charm of discretion

For those with tastes towards the Oriental, this Chinese-style occasional table by Waring Robinson is a mouth-watering combination of discreet ornament and perfect proportion. Follow his inspiration — and his detailed plans

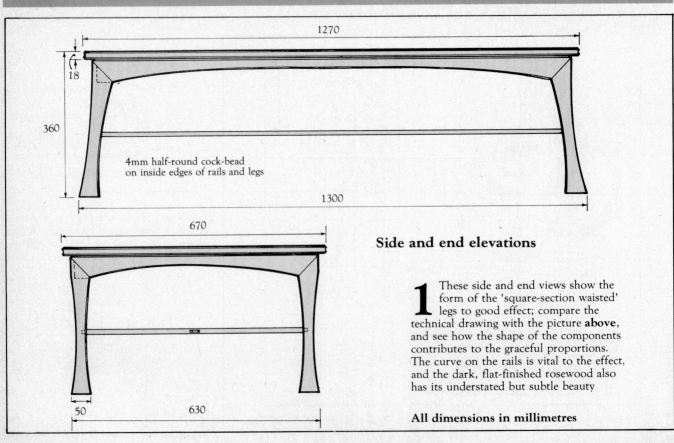

4mm half-round cock-bead
on inside edges of rails and legs

Side and end elevations

1 These side and end views show the form of the 'square-section waisted' legs to good effect; compare the technical drawing with the picture **above**, and see how the shape of the components contributes to the graceful proportions. The curve on the rails is vital to the effect, and the dark, flat-finished rosewood also has its understated but subtle beauty

All dimensions in millimetres

Our sitting room, which has gradually taken shape over a number of years, has always lacked a small table. My plan to make one occasioned much debate on the size and style. I have always favoured the use of grain, gentle curves, and decoration from joints to complement a practical shape. Carving and other embellishments, unless discreet, may give the impression of clutter, and on this point some Chinese furniture excels.

Looking through Gustav Ecke's *Chinese Domestic Furniture*, I was impressed by the proportion of the pieces drawn, their reserved ornamentation, and the strong aesthetic appeal of the mitred joints. The legs I liked less, with their inward-looking horse-hoof feet. They were apparently developed in the pre-Ming period by cutting out an oval on the sides and ends of a plain chest, which left the in-toed leg and curvilinear effect of the shaped rails with stretchers on the ground. I felt square-section waisted legs might be suitable, and a pine mock-up of a leg and rails suggested they would work. The result is a hybrid which I think looks very good.

The table has several interesting structural features. They include the mitred joints of the legs meeting the side and end rails; cock-beading on two edges of the legs, which are continuous with the same section on the rails; and the dovetailed housed rails on the undersurface of the panel which support it in the width. They are referred to as 'dovetail clamps'.

It was mostly hand-made, with assistance from a bandsaw (Minimax), an Elu MOF 96 router, and a Coronet Major Universal Tool. A scratch-stock (modified to follow a double curve) and a cabinet scraper were some of the most useful hand-tools I used.

I decided to make the table from Indian rosewood, and prepared a cutting list and patterns. The frames for the top were prepared, and the panel re-cut from 25mm thick timber — as near quarter-cut as possible. This was a moment of real pleasure, as the exposed adjacent surfaces had a lovely colour which I just didn't expect from looking at the surfaces of the rough-sawn boards. The cut pieces were then all stored in stick, weighted down.

After I finished making it, the table was oiled with raw linseed oil and white spirit in equal proportions, every day for two weeks. It was allowed to dry, and raw linseed oil was then applied over a period of several days. Finally, when this was dry, several applications of Danish (tung) oil were rubbed into the surface. To complete the finish white vaseline was applied to the surface and polished to a dull sheen — a finishing process described in Alan Peters' book *Cabinetmaking – The Professional Approach*.

The table took 140 hours to design and make. I am pleased with its light, inherent strength, and hope it will give pleasure for years.

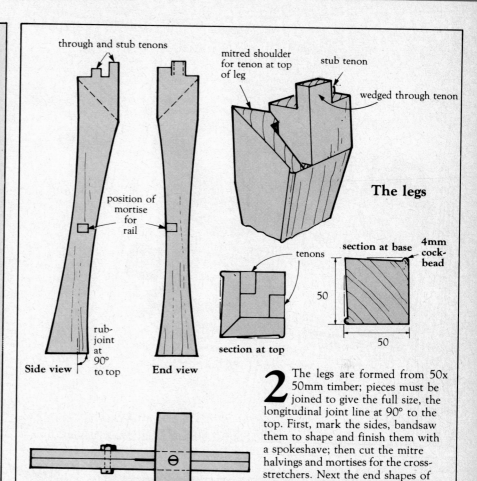

through and stub tenons

position of mortise for rail

rub-joint at 90° to top

Side view

End view

file hacksaw blade to this profile

scratch-stock with curved fence

mitred shoulder for tenon at top of leg

stub tenon

wedged through tenon

The legs

tenons

section at top

section at base

4mm cock-bead

50

50

2 The legs are formed from 50x 50mm timber; pieces must be joined to give the full size, the longitudinal joint line at 90° to the top. First, mark the sides, bandsaw them to shape and finish them with a spokeshave; then cut the mitre halvings and mortises for the cross-stretchers. Next the end shapes of the legs are marked, bandsawn and finished. The 4mm diameter cock-beads are scratched to 2mm deep, and the remaining wood to the adjacent edge worked out with shallow-sweep gouge and a scraper. The mortises in the mitre halvings are cut, and cutting the stub and through tenons completes the work on the legs.

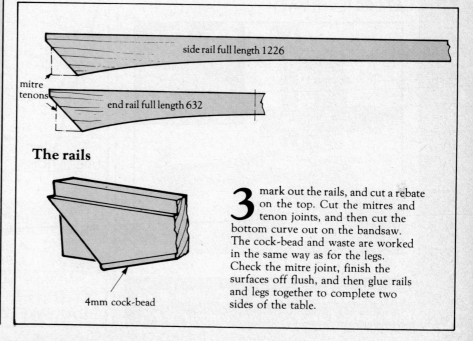

side rail full length 1226

mitre tenons

end rail full length 632

The rails

4mm cock-bead

3 mark out the rails, and cut a rebate on the top. Cut the mitres and tenon joints, and then cut the bottom curve out on the bandsaw. The cock-bead and waste are worked in the same way as for the legs. Check the mitre joint, finish the surfaces off flush, and then glue rails and legs together to complete two sides of the table.

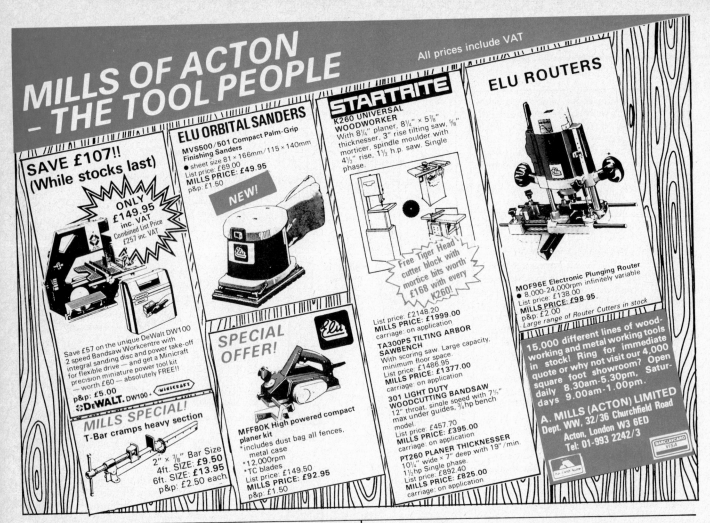
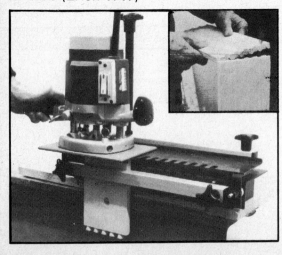
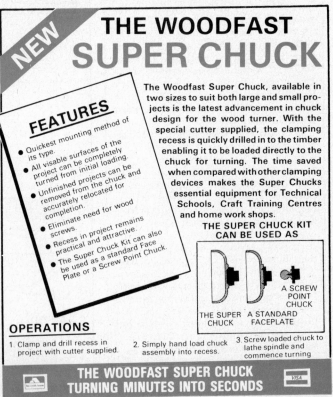
246

The charm of discretion

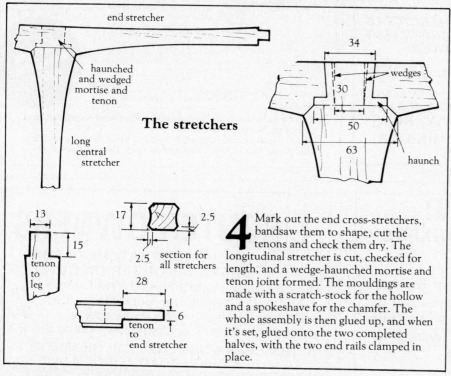

The stretchers

end stretcher

haunched and wedged mortise and tenon

long central stretcher

34

30

50

63

wedges

haunch

13

15

17

2.5

2.5

section for all stretchers

28

tenon to leg

tenon to end stretcher

6

4 Mark out the end cross-stretchers, bandsaw them to shape, cut the tenons and check them dry. The longitudinal stretcher is cut, checked for length, and a wedge-haunched mortise and tenon joint formed. The mouldings are made with a scratch-stock for the hollow and a spokeshave for the chamfer. The whole assembly is then glued up, and when it's set, glued onto the two completed halves, with the two end rails clamped in place.

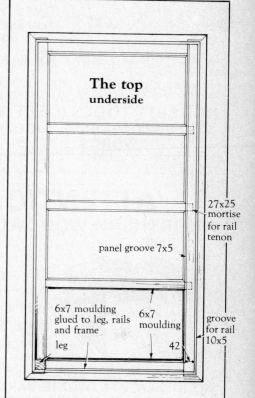

The top
underside

27x25 mortise for rail tenon

panel groove 7x5

6x7 moulding glued to leg, rails and frame

6x7 moulding

leg

42

groove for rail 10x5

Cutting list

Indian rosewood; all dimensions in mm

Frame	2	1270	x	75	x	18
Frame	2	670		75		18
Top panel	2	1134		130		10
Top panel	2	1134		137		10
Dovetail clamps	3	576		25		12
Legs	4	355		50		50
Legs	4	270		50		40
Rails	2	1226		60		15
Rails	2	626		60		15
Stretchers	2	582		45		17
Stretcher	1	1250		63		17
Mouldings	8	521		7		6
Mouldings	8	260		7		6
Mouldings	2	526		7		6
Mouldings	2	1120		7		6

5 The edge-pieces framing the top are grooved for the panel, and joined with a compromise between mortise and mitre joints, with a planted tenon in a suitable snug-fitting groove. The 10mm panel is made from four pieces, book-matched and rub-jointed. Rebate the panel to fit in the groove in the frame. Three dovetailed housings are cut on the undersurface of the panel to take the three 'dovetail clamps'. This will, of course, be a dry joint, and a good fit is quite easy with a router, guide bush and suitable templates.

Fit the panel into the frame, and glue the whole together, taking care not to let the glue get into the panel groove. The mouldings are cut on a moulding block, then mitred, glued, and sprung into position. The top is turned over, and the mortises for the leg tenons marked out and cut. The surface of the frame is protected with a piece of hardwood, glued over the point of exit of the through tenons. A groove is also cut on the underside of the frame to accept the top edge of the rebate rails. The legs and underframe are then glued and clamped into position. Finally, I used some yew to wedge the tenons, and finish them off flush with the surface.

The top: frame, panel and rail

corner

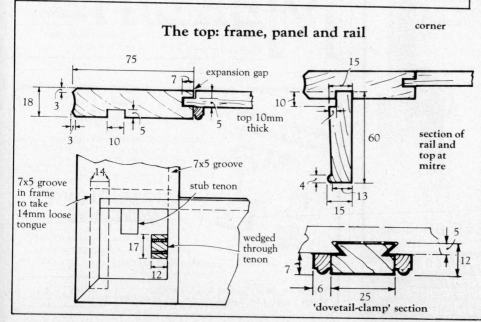

75

7

expansion gap

18

3

3

10

5

5

top 10mm thick

15

10

60

section of rail and top at mitre

4

13

15

7x5 groove

stub tenon

7x5 groove in frame to take 14mm loose tongue

14

17

12

wedged through tenon

5

7

6

25

12

'dovetail-clamp' section

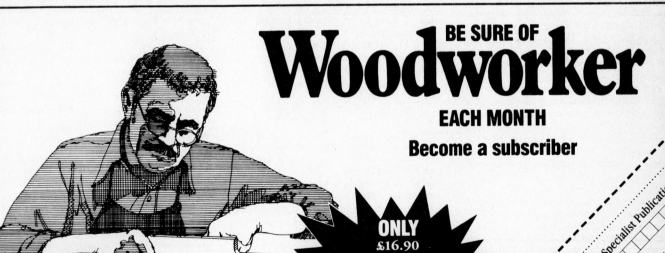

A place of your own

A serious workshop is essential if you're serious about woodworking. We present two helpful histories

Tony Matthews is now in workshop number five! Here's what he learnt from the other four

● *A veritable woodworker's palace – how many of us are set up in a place like this?*

Ever since I can remember I've been attracted to wood. At three years old I enjoyed banging nails into a large block of timber for an adoring grandfather to remove. By the age of five I was producing glorious creations from roof-batten off-cuts and two-inch nails. Now I'm middle-aged, and I'm still learning.

However, it's difficult to practise a hobby without the right environment and equipment. For this reason, I've always considered a good workshop of paramount importance, but workshops, like the tools we buy, have to be tailored to our means. Over the years I have owned five workshops, each an improvement on the last.

Number one

My first workshop, made when I was an engineering apprentice, was a light frame and asbestos sheet construction. In those days there was no concern over asbestos; the materials were cheap and (to some extent) effective. Fig. 1 shows the construction method used. The garden was small, and could only accommodate an 8x6ft base, large enough for my needs in the days when I didn't own any power tools.

A 4in thick concrete base was laid and a 2x1in batten framework made up. Joints were made with light angle-brackets from Woolworths. By careful sizing of the frame I was able to use standard cement asbestos sheets without having to cut them. Corrugated cement asbestos sheets were used for the roof, with plastic foam to fill the corrugations on the top of each wall.

This method of construction left a lot to be desired for a winter workshop. Two features are highlighted in fig. 1 which kept some of the weather out. The three inch slope on the roof, though, was inadequate for water run-off, which soaked through instead! However, it was only temporary . . . These two are the covering pieces which went over the joins of the asbestos sheets, and also the overlap of the board down the face of the concrete base.

Number two

Next house, next workshop; it was built as an extension to the back of the garage. The location was ideal — and economic — as one wall of the workshop was the rear wall of the garage. I had to get Building Regulation permission for this addition to the house.

I managed to get the house-builder to finish the brickwork and remove the window from the garage wall for relocation in the workshop, but I did all the timber framing myself. I did, however, run into trouble with the weather-proofing of the roof. Again, not wanting to spend very much, I tried using ordinary roofing felt (the type normally used under roofing tiles), but the local building inspector wasn't impressed, and stipulated heavy roof felt coated with mineral chippings.

The second workshop was not much larger than the first, but it did provide a solid wall for shelves, enough space for a home-made lathe, and room to move between them.

The construction (fig. 2) proved to be water tight, and not too cold in the winter with a fan heater running. As with the first workshop, however, condensation and rust on tools was a problem. A second car dictated the need for an extended garage, but there was no room to expand sideways so it had to be a tandem arrangement. That meant demolishing the workshop.

Number three

Building Regulation permission had been required for the garage extension, but the next workshop (fig. 3) was built at the bottom of the garden, so I didn't need it. The concrete base was there already, put down for a summerhouse which had been on the site, so that dicated the size of the building.

The use of 4½in walls in an exposed location proved disastrous. I had a builder construct the whole thing, but I didn't specify a water-proofing agent in the brickwork cement, so rain soaked through the mortar. I ended up treating the outside walls with a clear silicon sealer. Having suffered rust on my tools in earlier workshops,

and now I had a Coronet Major lathe which I didn't want to rust, I installed oil-filled radiators. A thermostat set at 46°F limited the level of electricity used; 55°F would have been preferable but I couldn't afford it. Rust was controllable on tools left in cupboards and drawers, but the lathe needed a rub down with an oily rag to protect it completely.

In all these workshops I took care to put the bench in relation to the doors so I could work long items clamped in the vice and set through the open doorway.

Number four

Moving house meant the loss of workshop number three, and the birth of number four. Moving from the country to a town was going to produce a noise problem. The houses on the new estate were built very close together, with garages set into the house fronts. No room here to build a garage extension workshop as before; no room even to build a bench in the garage. The estate was a new development and permission was required from the builders and neighbours before anything could be done.

The garden was only 35ft square and had five other gardens bordering it, so I decided to use the shed/workshop as a barrier across the end. All the required permissions were granted, but the structure couldn't be brick — too much of that around already. I opted for a prefabricated 12x6ft timber building with a ridge roof.

Four 100x50mm beams laid on house-bricks formed the under-frame for the shed floor. The beams ran lengthwise, with two under the long side walls for support.

In all prefabricated timber buildings, the outer weatherboards are fixed to a light timber frame so the framing is exposed internally. To reduce noise and make the building comfortable in winter, I insulated the walls.

The first job was to staple polythene sheeting to the inside of the outside walls, covering boards and framework (fig. 4). The polythene acts as a vapour barrier, and stops moisture penetrating into the insulation material. Then 25mm fibreglass insulation was fixed between the internal wall framing. The underside of the roof was treated in the same way, except for an additional thickness of insulation to fill up the roof void formed by the support trusses. Finally, the inside was finished off with hardboard fixed with galvanised self tapping screws. (I felt that the structure was far too light to knock in hundreds of nails, never mind what the neighbours might say.) To improve the general lighting, the walls and ceiling were coated with white emulsion paint. The outside was painted with a green wood preservative to blend with the surroundings.

The workshop was definitely warm in winter, and the tools and equipment didn't rust but the insulation was only partially effective in reducing noise. By now I had a noisy DeWalt radial-arm saw, and so it had to be used only at suitable times and as infrequently as possible.

Number five

Problems with neighbours and the children's education encouraged the next house-move to a rural spot and a property with plenty of land. The latest workshop (fig. 5), is the best. It's custom built, incorporating all the necessary features. This time planning permission was required, together with the house-builder's permission, before the workshop could be built. It was by no means certain that we would stay in the house for ever, so a design evolved which would be suitable for other uses, for example a granny annexe, playroom or studio. The workshop is therefore built to full house-building specifications and standards. The foundations are substantial, with 75mm-thick slabs of expanded foam incorporated into the concrete floor. The walls are of the cavity type, brick on the outside and thermalite aerated blocks on the inside, sandwiching 50mm thick polyurethane foam panels in the cavity.

Not being a bricklayer I subcontracted the brickwork, but did all of the carpentry and roof tiling myself. The roof is pitched at a steep angle to provide headroom in the loft above the workshop. The ceiling inside is plasterboard fixed to 175x40mm beams at 400mm centres. The loft is floored with 20mm chipboard and the rafters lined with plasterboard. The void between the plasterboard and the tiling felt is filled with mineral wool. The workshop is therefore totally cocooned in insulation material. Needless to say it is effectively warmed with a 2kw fan heater in winter, and it's cool in the summer.

Although the insulation material helps as a sound barrier, the inside of the workshop

● **Above:** view towards one end of workshop five shows everything neat and tidy

● **Right:** workshop one had its failings – not as strong or as well-insulated as it could have been. But covered joints and a damp-proof course helped

● **Left:** upstairs, the well-insulated dust-free space in the roof is excellent for finishing – and warm in winter

is noisy because the sound ricochets round the walls.

As with the workshop before this one, the walls and ceiling are white-emulsioned. General lighting is fluorescent, but it diminishes the shadow effect of turning blanks, so I have ordinary tungsten lamps by the lathe.

I had dust problems with the concrete floors of other workshops, so this one has thermoplastic floor-tiles.

Power into the workshop is connected to a four-fuse switchbox. Two 13-amp ringmains supply power to double sockets placed midway up the walls and round the skirting in the loft. The other two fuses are used for lighting circuits. Double sockets at 6ft intervals around the walls mean I never have to move far to plug something in.

The only window is on the north side and illuminates the workbench during daylight hours, but it doesn't admit direct sunlight. There is plenty of wall-space for shelves, and as in all my workshops the door is 33in wide, big enough for the largest equipment and furniture I could reasonably expect to pull in or out.

This type of construction is extremely dry, and I've had no problem with condensation or tools rusting. The building specification could well be copied for domestic use — especially the insulated floor, which carries five large pieces of equipment and the workbench.

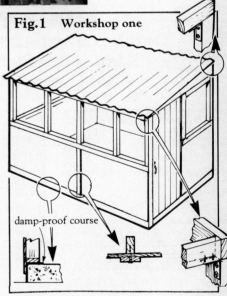

Fig.1   Workshop one

damp-proof course

Hints on building your own

● Always advise your neighbours of your workshop intentions, and be considerate when you use it.

● Talk to your local council's Chief Engineer, who will advise you whether Building Regulation or Planning approval is required. The department might also give you building advice.

● Most home-owners have garden priorities in the summer, and use the workshop more in winter. Make sure it's as warm as possible by insulating it.

A place of your own

● White walls and ceilings are helpful for general illumination.

● If you aren't familiar with wiring, it's worth the cost of sub-contracting the work to a competent electrician. The right cable-sizes, fuse-ratings and switches are important to stop circuit overloading.

● When tying brickwork into an existing building, make sure the damp courses line up. Bridging of damp courses by workshops and garden walls often causes damp in a property.

● Minimise condensation by keeping window areas to a minimum (except if you can afford double glazing) and install heating to keep the building as warm as you can afford. Don't use radiant heaters; oil-filled radiators are best.

● Extreme care is needed if you use a waste-burning stove for heating. There is usually so much dust-laden air around the workshop that combustion could be a danger.

● Inhaling dust of any kind isn't healthy. I would advocate some form of dust extraction equipment. Mobile units are ideal because they are self-contained, and don't require an external exhaust.

Finally, build the best workshop you can afford, and enjoy yourself in comfort! ■

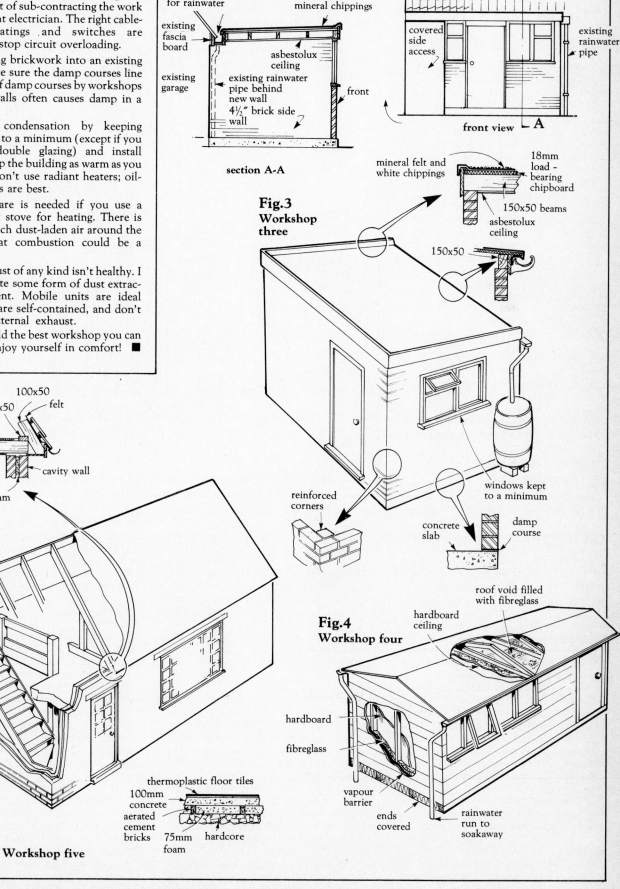

Fig.2 Workshop two

new trough formed for rainwater

board, felt and mineral chippings

existing fascia board

existing garage

asbestolux ceiling

existing rainwater pipe behind new wall

4½" brick side wall

front

section A-A

existing garage roof adjoining house

covered side access

existing rainwater pipe

front view

A

Fig.3 Workshop three

mineral felt and white chippings

18mm load-bearing chipboard

150x50 beams

asbestolux ceiling

150x50

reinforced corners

concrete slab

damp course

windows kept to a minimum

20mm chipboard floor

100x50

100x50

felt

175x40

10mm plasterboard ceiling

cavity wall

foam

Fig.5 Workshop five

thermoplastic floor tiles

100mm concrete aerated cement bricks

75mm foam

hardcore

Fig.4 Workshop four

roof void filled with fibreglass

hardboard ceiling

hardboard

fibreglass

vapour barrier

ends covered

rainwater run to soakaway

Up against the wall

Peter McNiff built one

... while a lean-to provides the low-cost solution. Peter McNiff built one

The old shed bequeathed to me by the previous owner of my house was a handy size — 10x9ft and 8ft to the eaves — but it was about 30 years old and badly ravaged by mice and timber vermin. Not only that: the inside was a shambles, cluttered up with junk of every description.

It was there (not in church) that my conscience was awakened. Here was a good workbench covered with litter; boxes of nails and screws, half-a-dozen tools rusting for lack of use; paintbrushes stuck fast to saucers. One morning in mid-April I made a New Year's resolution. This shed must come down, and a new shed be made and erected closer to the house.

The shed I built was a lean-to, 10ft long x 8ft wide, with an eaves height of 7ft, fitted into a right-angle formed by two house walls. It is essentially two frameworks, a floor and a roof. Each wall-frame was made up as a complete unit, then the two fitted together with bolts and secured to the brick walls with stout staples and screws. Apart from simplifying the construction, this made it easy to dismantle and re-erect, a big advantage if I wanted to take it away. In the event I left it there when we moved house.

Preparation and framework

A decent foundation had to be prepared first by taking off the topsoil and replacing it with hardcore, rammed well down. After marking out the site, I laid a few loose bricks equally spaced to carry the joists, then I put roofing felt over them as a damp barrier. The joists were creosoted, set down on edge 15in apart, then levelled and pegged to prevent movement when I fixed the flooring.

Next, I cut the floorboards to length and creosoted the undersides and joints. The tongue of the first board was ripped off and the edge planed smooth; it was placed flush with the joist ends, and nailed down with 2in floor brads, making sure the brads were in the centres of the joists.

Then I laid the rest of the floorboards, taking care with the fragile tongues and grooves. Some proved difficult to engage fully because of bad machining, but I managed without using a hammer, which splits the edges and would simply ruin the floor. I fit the first half-dozen boards, and then tested the back edge of the last for parallel by measuring the distance at each end from the first board. The measurements were equal, so the boards were parallel; if they hadn't been, a little give-and-take at the joints would put them right. The last board was a couple of inches too wide to

The lean-to

house-walls corner
flashing chased into mortar
roofing felt over boards
wall batten (plate)
rafter
purlin
flashing
weatherboarding
t & g floor
ledge-and-brace door
bricks carry joists

● *Cheap and cheerful it may be, but a lean-to is the solution for many of us.*

come flush with the joist edges, so I had to rip it down and plane it to the correct width.

The front and door-end frames were made up in one section each, and then I got some help to bolt them together finger-tight, standing upright on the floor. Then we got both sections aligned with their respective floor edges, their inner ends secured to the brick walls with stout staples and screws, the corner coach-bolts ($5x\frac{5}{16}$in) tightened up, and finally the frames' bottom plates fixed to the floor with no.8x4in countersunk screws.

The roof

The roof section consisted of a 10ftx2x$\frac{3}{4}$in batten (plate) for the flashing, screwed to blocks let into the back brick wall, and a similar plate 8ft long at the side brick wall to take the inside end of the purlin and the first roofing board.

Positioning these plates, I had to pay careful attention to the slope of the roofing. Their edges and lower ends were to rest on the framework; this called for careful checking of alignment for slope between plates and frame-tops before fixing the roofing. Slight deviations were adjusted with packing. I thought a single rafter and

cross-purlin would provide enough support for this type of sheltered rooftop. I cut both members at an angle to bear on the wall plates, and bird-mouthed them or notched and nailed them to the framework. Before nailing on the roofing, the shed walls had to be plumbed up true with a plumb-bob, and the angles made square; I tested everything with a large straight-edge and set-square.

Then the roofing timber ($\frac{3}{4}$in T&G match-lining) was cut to length, allowing for a 6in overlap at the two outer edges, and nailed to the plates, purlin and framework. I took care to get a good watertight connection at the brickwork junctures, with proper flashings as shown in fig. 1. A gutter and drainpipe could have been fitted, but I didn't consider them necessary.

Before I laid the roofing felt the timber was well creosoted and allowed to dry. I started at the eaves (gutter edge), and laid the felt lengthways, parallel with the gutter but overlapping at least 9in, the subsequent strips overlapping 3in up to the ridge. Here, I fixed a 6in-wide strip along the exposed edges and secured it with battens. I used bitumastic cement as adhesive, and no nails or battens at all on the felt except at the plates and the top frame-edges.

Cladding and hardware

The weatherboarding was added next, nailed horizontally to the uprights, cross-members and braces with 2in wire nails. The door was matchboard, ledged and braced with 3x1in deal, and provided with two cross-garnet hinges, a shooting-bolt and stout padlock. The five window case-ments, (bought ready-made), were fitted, the sills projecting 2in beyond the outside face of the matching and screwed down to the bottom members of the window apertures with 3½in countersunk-headed screws. When I'd fixed all the outside fittings I treated the woodwork, inside and out, with two coats of creosote.

Legal notes

With rented property, a lean-to of this type could be classed as a landlord's fixture, but if a skeleton framework is fitted at the back and inner ends of the shed where they butt to the house, and the roof is supported there by battens (as in this case), it will be a tenant's fixture and may be taken away when you move. But if the shed can't be taken down without material damage to the property, it becomes a landlord's fixture and is thus irremoveable. A conservatory, securely fixed and communicating with inner rooms, would be in this category.

It would also be wise before starting such a project to confirm that the shed will conform with local authority by-laws as to size, situation and so on, and comply with rating and insurance regulations. This would particularly apply if the property was held on a mortgage, if the shed was going to be anywhere near garage size, and if it would increase the value of the property. ■

Fig. 2

cross-halving for framing and roof

mortise and tenon
for corner-posts

stopped
bare-faced tenon
for verticals

Lean-to joints

Cutting list

All dimensions in imperial: nominal widths and thicknesses

Framework		150ft x	2in x	2in
Framework		56ft	3in	2in
Floor joists	8	10ft	3in	2in
T&G flooring		80sq ft		1in
Matchlining (roofing)		100sq ft		¾in
Batten for flashing	1	10ft	2in	¾in
Batten for flashing	1	8ft	2in	¾in
Rebated weatherboard for walls		86sq ft		
Architrave for door and windows		70ft	1in	¼in
Ledge-and-brace door	1		78in	42in

1pr cross-garnets, padlock, shooting-bolt and key
5 windows (casement) glazed, with butts, handles and casement stays
1 roll tarred roofing-felt
2in flooring brads and wire nails; staples and screws; two 5x⁵⁄₁₆in coach bolts and nuts; 3½in and 4in screws. Creosote.

Since we're on the subject of build-it-yourself, **writes Aidan Walker**, whether it be workshop or living-space, have a look at this DIY building system designed by Swiss architects Gilbert Hirt. Building with 'semi-finished' units isn't by any means a new idea — it's the pre-fab principle, after all — but they claim to have gone one better and put together a complete framing system for you.

A three-dimensional framework would consist of a series of 'building modules', special mounted frames which can be easily combined and inter-changed. They are produced to standard dimensions with standard-profile com-ponents, and they can be complemented with various-sized beams to support panel-product walls, floors, rooves and insulation, as well as windows and doors. The frames come ready for fitting joists, studs, window-and door-frames, all of which can be done without screws or nails. You can put up the load-bearing framework yourself, say the designers, and then use whatever cladding and decorative materials you like to make the structure truly a place of your own.
● Gilbert Hirt, Vieux-Canal 40, 1950 Sion, Switzerland.

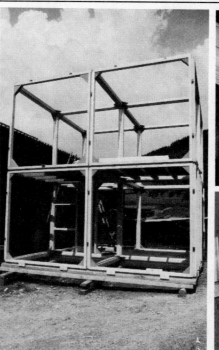

● The Hirt system in two-storey mode (**above**) – built-in buildability. One side of each member-end is a male peg, the other a female socket; three-way corners are quick and simple. Joint reinforcements **top right**, prefabricated joists **above right**

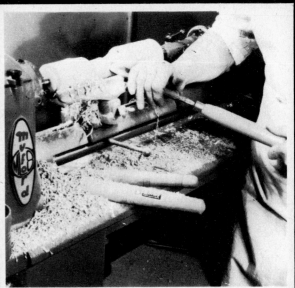

256

Tales out of steel

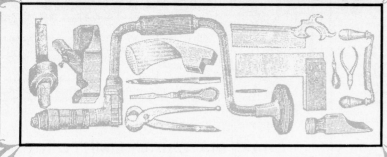

More Sheffield stories from master-storyteller and toolmaker Ashley Iles

The major events of my life have been unpredictable, but looking back on my childhood it's obvious that the foundation-stone of my life in tools was laid well before I left school.

When I was 11 (in 1934), my father bought a tool stand in Sheffield Market for £50, a lot of money in those days. My father was a patternmaker in a large Sheffield steelworks, earning just under £3 a week. As the 47-hour week was on, he had to work Saturday mornings, and it fell to me to go round the tool-houses buying stock, then get the stand ready for when my father arrived at 12.30 smelling of yellow pine. The market didn't close until 9pm — it was a long day.

I would rise early and make the rounds with a pocket full of white fivers. A ha'penny tram ride took me to C&J Hampton (Record) in Ouse Road, Darnall where I would pass an order for planes, spokeshaves, and so on through the warehouse service-hatch. It was here that I got my first smell of warehouse oil; it was all over the place. There's no describing it; you just have to smell it. A visitor I had recently was so taken with it, I gave him a little bottle to keep. Quite a few people took an interest in me at Record, chatting and asking questions. One man once took me round the factory; I don't know who he was but it was 'Morning Sir' all the way round. I can't say I was inspired but I remember some queer urges.

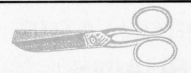

In the yard were great piles of plane castings. I didn't like to say anything, in case they were spoilt ones, but later I asked my father who was well-informed on castings. He laughed at me thinking they were scrap, and explained they were 'weathering' for several months to naturally liberate the stresses set up in casting. Years later I had first-hand experience of it. When Stanley first came to England in the early post-war years they bought out Chapman, the plane and brace people (Acorn planes), and machined a batch of unweathered planes. They had to take them all back, including three of mine, as all the bottoms distorted almost ⅛in. Moral — always take a straight-edge when buying a plane. I only remember one price in the Record range, the no.4 smooth was 8/6d (about 40p). After 2½% for cash I would leave with a heavy parcel on my shoulder. Dumping this on our stand, I would make for other firms within walking distance.

Next, Chestermans. Darned if I can remember where they were, but it was very posh, with a commissionaire on the door. Here I was called 'Sir', and not chatted up! Paying cash was a terrible embarrassment to all concerned, but it was never refused (it never is). Even so, a small boy with a fistful of fivers was quite beyond them. The last straw was 2½% for cash, but I got it.

My third call was Stringer's Scissors somewhere around the end of The Moor, Sheffield's main thoroughfare. Yes, you've guessed it, through a dark archway, up a flight of steep wooden stairs, you've heard it all before; but this time the stairs were outside and the works was a lean-to against the main wall of the yard. At the top of the stairs I would open the door and be greeted by a hell of a racket and Alice, a 14-stone Amazonian forewoman with a strong but frustrated maternal instinct. After a fuss, which only stopped short of kisses and cuddles, she would lead me past a row of 20 giggling girls working on buffing-wheels driven by noisy overhead countershafting into 'Young Stringer's' office. His father had been dead for years but the 'Young' stuck.

I wasn't to know at the time but all those girls were skilled and working 47 hours for little more than £1 a week. Quality is everything on scissors. Nothing about scissors is easy, but the really tricky bits are the finger- and thumb-holes. These were done by the 'Bow dresser'. She had a linisher belt in mid-air about an inch wide and 4ft long, running from left to right of her. For each bow the belt is taken off and pushed through the hole, then put on the drive pulley again. The inside of the bow is then polished by waggling the scissor from side to side and up and down. This has to be done for every single bow; no one has yet found a quicker way. Cheap scissors are not done on the inside of the bow, and just de-rinding a rasher of bacon will make you wish you had paid more for them, even if they will cut. Before my teens I could talk scissors like a native. Tups, long bow, tailors, black bow, nail and bent nail, side bents, hairdressers, dressmakers, and so on.

'Young Stringer' would put my order together in his little office-cum-warehouse and I would leave, trying my damndest to escape the ministrations of Alice. 2½% again of course.

On the stall my father would 'pitch' with scissors. At the end of the patter he would open a pair of hairdressers and throw the single point as hard as he could into the planking of the stand, and the crowd would see the scissors quivering violently on the fine point. Not one ever snapped off. This was the time to stand by the brown paper, as the next 15 minutes was like having a licence to print money at around 1/- a pair. So much for the first name in scissors; next time you buy a pair ask if you can drive the point into the counter.

The last port of call was R. H. Bramall & Son, Tool Factors. This firm was no more than a large shed in the back yard of a row of terrace houses, but they sold everything from gimlets to drilling machines, and did a roaring trade. There is little factoring done today; the nearest thing is a wholesale cash-and-carry, where prices are usually more than the local supermarket.

No hopes of 2½% here — there was a large notice which read 'Terms Cash Net'. Old Bramall told me that in business the first £100 was the worst, after that it was easy. By the time I got round to it the hundred had gone to a thousand, but how true I found it to be.

About 11 o'clock I would be back and getting the four-wheeled skip out of storage — commercial transport was a rarity in those days. When dad arrived all was ship-shape and Bristol-fashion.

I got threepence for going and one penny in the pound of takings, so many a Sunday morning I was quite rich. If things went very well on market day he would give me a shilling to go and have a Table-D'hote lunch at the Gambit Restaurant at the top of Commercial Street. Soup, fish, turkey, ('all you can eat'), veg, pud, and tea. Talk about how the other half live, I can afford it now but it just isn't the same.

I've no doubt that had my father stayed in the tool business, he would have made his mark. He was a born salesman and one of the very few men to grasp fully the true dimension of Fred Woolworth's original idea of the walk-round, no-obligation store. He predicted it would dominate selling for the rest of the century. However in 1938 the war drums were sounding all over Europe, and he gave up the tool business when he was promoted to foreman in a large steelworks pattern shop. He played a leading role in producing the tank armour that Churchill was desperate for. He retired at 65, and died at 84. For me, at around 14, it was the end, but the seed had been sown. Perhaps, as Churchill so aptly put it, it was 'the end of the beginning'. ∎

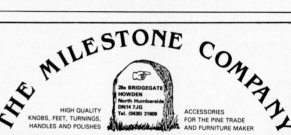

258

Books

George Buchanan
The Illustrated Handbook of Furniture Restoration
Batsford Books, £14.95
Reviewed by David Ellis

Over the past three or four years there's been a plethora of books on restoration. There's an enormous growth of interest in antiques, and people are realising that much of the furniture of the last 150 years was not only well made, but is now in vogue, and therefore worth preserving just as much as older antiques.

To say that this book is comprehensive is a major understatement. The author has covered practically every problem facing even the most skilled restorer! However, this is probably a failing for the author has set himself an almost impossible task of covering such a detailed and diverse subject in only 240 pages. He is obviously a highly skilled restorer, but I believe Mr Buchanan has tried to cover the field too broadly, and the result is that individual subjects aren't described in enough detail.

It appears that the author has produced all the line drawings himself — a formidable task, there being nearly 1000 of them! They are clear and concise in the main, although I would have liked them to be titled or numbered. I found myself looking at a drawing, not quite certain what it was telling me and having to return to the text to work it out.

Nearly a third of the book deals with setting up a workshop, safety, and preparing for work, plus excellent chapters on tools, their sharpening and use and details of all the types of joints the restorer is likely to have to repair or reproduce. Mr Buchanan then deals in detail with dismantling furniture, common faults and remedies — including light metalwork and lock repairs. I feel this latter section should have been either omitted or expanded, as it's rather inadequate.

There are interesting chapters on gluing and fastening, and also on frame furniture that should be helpful to anyone starting out in restoration, but I think the chapter on carving only scratches the surface(!), and could have been omitted. There are many specialised books on carving that cover the subject in great detail.

The chapters on carcase furniture and veneering are clear and concise, but the approach to chair restoration, excellent as far as it goes, is again far too brief. Mr Buchanan tackles the subject of wood-turning in only eight pages — including details of making a wooden-framed lathe! Everything he says is quite understandable to an experienced turner, but surely this subject is best covered by a specialised book?

There is a long and detailed chapter on finishing, dealing with almost every stain, polish and varnish that you'll ever encounter. I found this the most comprehensive part of the book, and if a beginner follows all the instructions, there should be no excuse for not getting excellent results.

I found both the chapters on upholstery proper and rush seating very informative, but I think the one on cane seating left a lot to be desired. I feel there really wasn't enough space devoted to the subject here — and why doesn't Mr Buchanan even mention the use of golf tees instead of unwieldy 'doublers'?

I'm critical of some chapters of this book, but nevertheless, I think it would prove very useful if you're starting out in the restoration field. At nearly £15, however, it isn't cheap.

● David Ellis is a professional restorer and teacher working in Wiltshire.

Aidan Walker
Craftsman's Guide to Wood Polishing and Finishing Techniques
Ebury Press, £4.95 hardback
Reviewed by Ian Hosker

A full-colour photograph of a traditional craftsman lovingly polishing a table illustrates this book's introductory page. The caption reads: 'This old-world workshop holds no inaccessible secrets; basic to all wood finishes are patience and a feel for the materials.'

The tone is set immediately and the message continues throughout the book; notably that nothing is beyond the patient, meticulous and imaginative worker.

This slim volume is one of a series of 'Craftsman's Guides' which, in the publisher's words, 'provide practical, illustrated advice'. Certainly the book fulfils that promise. It is not by any means a definitive manual of wood-finishing, but it does describe how to set about achieving the best results for a wide range of techniques, both traditional and modern.

It is superbly well turned out; after all, a book which stresses quality of finish should reflect that in its own appearance and layout. It is easy to read and comprehend; copious photographs (mostly in colour) and diagrams add to its attraction without detracting from the text. Each illustration makes a point, showing the standard or the effect which can be achieved, or clarifying detail in the text.

There are no gimmicks in the book. Even the section on 'Specials' (including marbling, glazing and antiquing) is full of sound advice.

It is ideal for the home restorer who may be a very competent woodworker but lacks the confidence or know-how to finish the piece properly. There are one or two points that need a little more explanation, but at least, the introduction points out that a book can only go so far in imparting skills.

If you need a little encouragement but are willing to learn and develop new skills, this book is a good start. The price may seem a little high for a book this size, but there are some wonderful colour plates, and it is a hardback with stitched pages. You must make up your own mind; I'm quite happy to have it on my bookshelves.

● Ian Hosker is a professional polisher, restorer, teacher and author.

William L. Sims
Two Hundred Years of History and Evolution of Woodworking Machinery
Walders Press
Reviewed by Philip Walker

It's hard to imagine that this book will prove satisfactory to the general woodworker, or even to the student of technological history.

The trouble is the lack of logical organisation of the subject. It's not simply that the book skips about in time — a description of the exhibits at the 1862 Exhibition, for example, forms a large part of the chapter on machinery *before* the middle of the 19th century, and precedes the chapter entitled 'Woodworking Machinery 1850-75' — but that the whole book is composed largely of extracts and quotations (often from trade promotional literature) without the author analysing, organising or explaining. You have to work out for yourself what are the significant features of the scores of machines described (often in tedious detail). There are, it's true, a great number of illustrations, but they have been reproduced from catalogues and the like, sometimes very poorly, and with little or no explanation.

The book would have been improved enormously by the addition of a few simple working diagrams, a comparative table or two, or even a glossary of technical terms. Indeed, the author seems to keep warning that this is a compilation — for which he himself is not taking the responsibility of adding or filtering — by peppering it with such qualifications as 'possible', 'would have been', or 'are said to have been'.

Specialists in engineering history, or anyone looking for a reference book on the subject, will have their hopes raised by the presence of a carefully prepared index. Unfortunately it is virtually limited to proper names and cannot do better than the text itself in helping us to trace the development of ideas and topics. Moreover, the sources of the illustrations are not given, and there has been a lack of care in checking the spelling of foreign names and places, as there has also been in referring to more general historical events.

Mr Sims clearly has an enormous personal knowledge of the woodworking machinery business, based on well over 50 years' practical experience. Anyone specifically concerned with the subject as a business — with markets and supplies, with trade shows and product rationalisation, will find things to interest and inspire them. And the book is right up-to-date. We are introduced to programmed automation, unmanned machining, numerical and radio control, and other exciting developments. Mr Sims points to the tempo of evolution and suggests that his book may need updating 'even before the end of the century'. It's a pity it's patchy.

● Philip Walker is a distinguished member of the Tool and Trades History Society.

Books

Henry Lanz
**Japanese Woodworking Tools – Selection,
   Care & Use**
Sterling, £9.95 paperback
Reviewed by Roger Buse

With the current rise of interest in traditional Japanese woodworking tools, there's a real need for a definitive work on the subject. Unfortunately, Mr Lanz's book does not fulfil this role.

The author takes each category of tool and explains their manufacture and methods of use but there are, to my mind, some glaring inaccuracies. One such is his explanation that tools are laminated to save scarce valuable steel. The real reason is so the toolmaker can use a much higher-carbon brittle steel by strengthening it with a soft steel, which creates a blade that is both strong and able to hold a good cutting edge for long periods. Inaccuracies like this inspire little confidence in many of Mr Lanz's other statements.

The strong chapters are those on sharpening-stones and planes. The author deals thoroughly with stones and their application to sharpening edge-tools, but because the captions to the pictures are wrong, the reader may well draw the wrong conclusions.

I could find no fault with the chapter on planes. Mr Lanz shows precisely and clearly how to condition a Japanese plane, but suggests that all Japanese planes should be conditioned before use, which could deter many would-be purchasers. The truth is that a good dealer in Japanese tools will always stock a selection of conditioned planes for those who don't want to undertake the task.

Saws are dealt with fairly comprehensively, although I can't agree with all the conclusions. I was also disappointed that yet again, a writer on Japanese tools dismisses saw sharpening in a few lines, and fails to show how to undertake this simple yet apparently daunting task.

Altogether, a disappointing book which fails to satisfy a much-needed hole in the market.
● Roger Buse is a specialist tool merchant and importer of Japanese tools.

Sharon Pierce
**Making Whirligigs and
   Other Wind Toys**
Sterling USA/Blandford UK, £6.95
Reviewed by Alan Bridgewater

Craft-related books are a most important part of my life; without them I would be lost. Over the years I've divided my library into the good, the bad, and the ugly, the little gems kept within easy reach, and the boring tomes shoved away on difficult-to-reach top shelves. So where to place *Making Whirligigs and Other Wind Toys*? Should it sit on the bottom shelf between such jewels as *The Woodmans Books* and *The Carpenter's Companion*, or should it be placed on the coldest boundaries, alongside horrors like *The Big Book Of Lampshade Making* (1939)? Problems, problems!

This book is a little treasure. It has 128 pages and 130 illustrations; it's well thought out, the material looks original, the drawings are passable and the instructions are clear. Of course it's not all roses, because the design, the photographs and the illustrations aren't all they could be — but no matter, the spirit is first class. There's a short introduction, an even shorter history, sections on general instructions, finishes, materials and equipment, and then we're taken straight to the heart of the craft with about 26 very pretty projects.

If you are interested in American folk and country crafts, and would like to make such whirligig delights as soldiers, pirates and Indians, then this book could well be for you. I reckon it's a goodish buy at £6.95.

I could moan about the short history section, the poor finish of some of the toys, and the rather thin drawings, but I won't. I'm certainly going to make the Indian whirligig, Sharon, and my boy is interested in making one for a school project — can you tell us more about the history, names of souces, books, museums and the like?
● Alan and Gill Bridgewater have written several books on toy-making and carving.

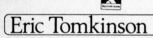

Letters

I VERY MUCH ENJOYED Jack Hill's article on the Windsor Chair (WW/April 85). However, I'm puzzled by the description and diagram that relate to the drilling of the leg-holes in the seat.

If the holes are drilled at the angles given and along the sight-lines shown (fig. 4), the chair will have a most 'off' appearance. The front legs when viewed from the front of the chair will be only about 6° from the perpendicular. I suggest that the sight-lines are incorrect.

Jack Hill also states that the holes for the stretchers are drilled at the same angles as the leg-holes. This would be the case if the sight-lines on the underside of the chair were on the same plane as the stretchers — which they're obviously not. In practice, because of the compound angles of the front and back legs, the angles would be less, about 9° and 16° respectively.

Malcolm Brown, South Glamorgan

Jack Hill replies: I am pleased to hear Mr Brown enjoyed my article on making the Smoker's Bow chair. I am equally pleased to note that his knowledge of solid geometry has provided him with two points for discussion.

In the first, the angle of the legs given in fig. 4 is correct and quite suitable. The angle of front legs should be restrained so as to avoid having too much outward splay. Too much renders them too easy to trip over. In practice Mr Brown's calculated angle of 'about 6°' gives the foot of each front leg more than 1½in of outward splay; quite adequate in my opinion.

On the second point Mr Brown's calculations and observations are correct. Yes, the compound angles of the legs do give rise to a 3° or 4° difference in drilling-angle for the stretcher-holes. Correctly, this should be allowed for. However, I find that in practice, legs can be drilled as described in the article. The stretchers can be sprung into place and in fact do their job (that of 'stretching' the chair's underframe) more effectively when this method is used.

Other careful observers may have noticed that I omitted two dimensions from fig. 4. The distance between front and back legs is given but those between each pair of back legs and each pair of front legs is not. These can be calculated from fig. 1, but should be 7in and 8in respectively each side of the centre line.

TOBIAS KAYE'S REVIEW of my book *Beginner's Guide To Woodturning* (WW/Jan), was very fair and reasonable, but I feel certain things haven't been fully understood.

Mr Kaye rightly states that I am not into 'High Design' — which Heaven forfend, if it means what I suspect it does. He goes on, again rightly, to say that my designs are mundane. Since he has had no opportunity to evaluate the articles I manufacture for sale, I assume this refers to the designs in my books, which are certainly mundane; but they are exercises carefully designed to

assist beginners who are struggling to master good tool techniques, and are therefore comparable to the scales and little jingles which one slaves over when struggling to master a musical instrument. Fugues and nocturnes are not for beginners, and neither is 'High Design'. In more than 40 years of woodturning I have obviously produced a very large number of shapes, a couple of which were, I recall, quite reasonable.

The main point is that my life is, and has been for many years, dedicated to helping those who cannot yet use a lathe effectively or with maximum safety. This has left me little time to bother about those who can.

The other point is that Mr Kaye appears to believe that I 'balance the tools on one finger' when grinding them. I don't, and I can't recall having said I do. I normally cradle the tools in three fingers and thumb, using the index finger against the grinding rest to steady my hand.

I sincerely thank Mr Kaye for the review, which I appreciated, but I felt these two points should be clarified.

Gordon Stokes, Bath

OWNERS OF WOLFCRAFT heavy-duty drill stands might welcome some further advice on how to increase its scope. Although the stand is of course for drilling, it can be used as a light press for gluing small items. When you next run out of clamps why not try making up the illustrated jig. Note that the base B is not always needed; the idea would work for any stand.

Ron White, Halstead

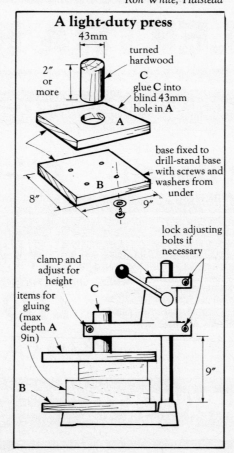

A light-duty press

43mm

2" or more

turned hardwood

C

glue C into blind 43mm hole in A

A

base fixed to drill-stand base with screws and washers from under

B

8"   9"

lock adjusting bolts if necessary

clamp and adjust for height

items for gluing (max depth A 9in)

C

B

9"

SEVERAL MEMORIES were brought back to me when I read 'The Morris men' (WW/January) which included a piece on the gifted Stanley Davies from the Romney Green stable.

I knew Davies in Windermere, my family home; and it was he who told me of Romney Green's expression, 'A gentleman shows his joints'. Apparently Green went to great lengths to devise through joints, even in tables and chairs.

Davies eventually lost his sight but kept his workshop going until his last employee found work with a Lake boat-builder. Strangely, Davies, who died comparatively recently, never sold much of his work in the South; most of his customers were local people of quite modest means.

Bob Wearing, Shropshire

READERS WHO, like me, need to economise without detracting from the quality of the work should find this woodworking 'wheezette' of interest.

Router cutters with roller-guides are expensive; those with guide-pins burr but are cheaper, so I put a thin strip of waxed masking tape along the edge to be moulded at the point where the pin will bear. This not only prevents burring but also makes for smoother operation.

P. W. Neill, Newmarket

I WOULD LIKE TO make a suggestion for holding wood to be routed to form housings for shelves and rebates. Clamps always seem to be in the way! I stick strips of double-sided carpet tape at about 12in intervals on to the bench, then apply another set of strips (at the same interval distance) on to the wood to be routed. The wood is then held so fast that it's quite difficult to dislodge from the bench at the end of the operation.

Another idea is for pulling out secret drawers in a bureau. Insert a flat magnet into the front of the drawer, and cover the whole of the inside of the drawer with baize, so the magnet can't be detected. When the drawer is pushed right back as far as it will go (there's another drawer in front of it which conceals it) it can't be removed till another magnet touches it. Attach the second magnet to a stick so it can be pushed right against the secret drawer when the first drawer is removed. It pulls the secret drawer out perfectly, and burglars will have to do some serious breaking in to detect it. The second magnet shouldn't be left in the bureau, obviously.

Lady Margaret Bullard, Melton Constable

I'M A KEEN woodworker and was extremely interested in *Woodworker's* MDF competition. It seemed to provide the answer to wide panels for furniture making and as I wanted to build a unit to match a new dining table, I wrote off to Fidor.

I was too late to enter the competition but I wanted the information anyway for my project. You said: 'The funny thing is

Remember! Any woodworking wheezes in your ever-fertile brains may just be worth money! Plans, projects, stories . . . Let us know if you have something in your workshop – or your head – that *Woodworker* can use. You may not think it's anything much–but let us decide!

Letters

that a lot of people haven't heard of it yet. But it is widely available if you know where to look.' You also said it was nearly as cheap as chipboard (WW/April 85).

I got the information and the list of stockists, then everything fell apart. It seems that MDF doesn't exist north of Watford! Stockists in Lancashire hadn't heard of it, and only stocked the plain board 'for notice-boards'.

I rang Fidor who were very helpful and said there were many places where it could be bought in London; they also gave me some possibles in the north of England. I tried a supplier in Sheffield, and one in Chorley who said they could get MDF with an oak veneer. I need mahogany. It also seemed I would have had to order a whole pack (25 sheets) to get what I want.

I appreciate that the competition was partly to publicise the material but I wonder how the competitors managed? Also during my telephone tour of the North it appeared that MDF would be considerably more expensive than chipboard unless I was manufacturing furniture for sale.

I suppose I'll have to resort to chipboard and the edging problems entailed!

K. D. Moore, Burrow Beck, Lancs

I AM THE PROUD OWNER of a Disston Morris hand-saw — it is a straight-back, 25in long, 7tpi, marked in inches and eighths along both edges. The curved brass fitting is riveted to the blade and is square to the edges and carries two spirit levels. So all you needed when you went to build your cabin was your saw, hammer and nails. You measured your timber with the edge of the saw, squared it across, cut it and plumbed it all with the same tool.

It belonged to a coachbuilder, and was given to me by his widow. I have had it for 60 years and as it was at least 40 years old when I got it, it must be well over the century mark, and good for another hundred. I would be interested to know if there are any other tools of this nature still in existence.

H. C. Saunders, Australia

● *One-tool cabin-building with Disston*

I WOULD LIKE to take issue with Charles Cliffe's 'Question Box' response to Mr Olden's query on finishing sycamore (WW/Jan). He suggests using a clear or white french polish — but this will darken over a period of time.

I use a lot of sycamore and suggest the following procedure: apply a clear cellulose

sanding sealer, leave for 48 hours and then rub down with 0000 steel wool. Follow it with bleached beeswax polish, applied with a rag well damped with pure spirit of turpentine. This will produce a very pleasing finish without excessive discoloration.

Alternatively the cellulose sealer can be replaced by ordinary egg-white! This does, however, raise the grain and will require considerably more rubbing down.

Trevor Couvelle, Isle of Wight

I WAS INTERESTED to read about the radial-arm saw in part three of 'Machining Wood', and note the attention paid to safety. There is, however, one danger not mentioned, which I would like to bring to readers' attention.

At the end of a cut, when the saw is switched off, the motor slows down, but the considerable inertia of the saw-blade (in the case of a carbide-tipped saw) tends to loosen the securing-nut. On several occasions the nut, which I had believed to be securely tightened, has come loose in this way.

It may be that this effect is peculiar to my machine, on which the stop-switch breaks contact before it has clicked into the 'off' position. If it is not fully depressed the motor will start again, and the switch has to be operated a second time. The motor then goes through a stop-start-stop sequence; it is only under these conditions that I have observed this loosening effect.

On one occasion (and one only!) matters went further, and the nut, followed by the saw-blade, came right off the end of the spindle. The saw struck the table and, still spinning rapidly, bounded forward in my direction. Fortunately, it must have landed not quite upright, since it leapt forward at a slight angle and just missed me, but when I saw the gouge it made in the wooden board it hit, I didn't use the machine again until I had fitted a safety-lock.

Fortunately there was just room for a simple and obvious arrangement consisting of a cross-hole at the very end of the motor spindle to take a $\frac{1}{16}$in split-pin. I commend this arrangement to all users of machines of this type.

H. R. Lorch, Southport

● Mr Lorch doesn't say what kind of saw he uses; some on-off switches are very much safer than this!

WHAT FUN filling in your Reader Survey — especially the column for net income! I've been a devoted reader of *Woodworker* for many years now but my income does not, and possibly never will, attain the minimum bracket on your survey. I've a sneaking suspicion that there are many others in a similar situation.

Don't worry — I'll still keep buying your excellent product. Keep up the good work! By the way, the Woodworker Show was great, but where are all the spokeshaves nowadays?

Mark Allinson, Grays

I HAVE JUST finished reading Hugh O'Neill's account of the 1985 Woodworker Show (WW/Jan). I too had a most pleasant day there, meeting the many craftsmen who were displaying their skills.

However, the section on clocks, written by Martin Bulger, gives the highest praise to N. Miller for his incredible fretworked clock. But the photograph actually shows Mr Gordon Foote's Gothic clock.

This has led some people to thinking I entered the Gothic clock; my work was in fact shown on the contents page of the January issue.

I would like to congratulate you on a fine magazine and I hope to be exhibiting at the 1986 show.

N. Miller, Colchester

● We apologise to Martin Bulger, Mr Miller and Mr Foote for this error and for any confusion caused. Both were excellent pieces of work; the mistake was ours, not Martin's.

ADVERTISERS' INDEX

Apollo Products .. 220	Moordown 220
Argus Specialist	Multistar 262
Exhibitions 178, 252	Myford Ltd 256
Asles 258	John Myland 182
Axminster 188	Naerok 214
Benmail 212	Nolanward 260
Black & Decker ... 264	The Old Stores
John Boddy Timber	Turnery 183
.... 180	A. Pollard 248
H. Case Hardware 204	Profectus 204
C.C.B. 179	Ridgway .... IFC
Charltons Timber	Roger's 192
Centre 204	Sanlin 220
Peter Child 258	Sarjents Tools 249
Craft Materials ... 258	Scott & Sarjeant . 200
Corbett Tools 248	Smiths Woodworkers
Craft Supplies 210	 186
Craft, Tools & Tackle	Solent Tools 218
.... 192	Stobart & Son 258
C Z Scientific 207	Sumaco 212, 234
Ebac Ltd 199	Tabwell Tools 246
Elektra Beckum .. 262	W. Thatcher 248
Excel Machine Tools	Tilgear .. 220, 248, 258
.... 210	Eric Tomkinson .. 260
Henry Flack 204	Tool Centre 206
Heath Saws 206	C.W. Tyzack 248, 260
David Hunt Tools 258	Treebridge 258
Ashley Iles 214	Trend Machinery 246
Kimac 214	Warren Machine
Kity 180, 200, 218	Tools 182
Lervad 206	Whitehill Spindle
E.W. Lucas 218	Tools 210
Luna Tools . 192, OBC	Woodcraft Supply 206
Magh Spa .... IBC	Woodfit 186
Matthews Bros. .. 256	Woodplan 248
Merlin Tools 248	Woodworking
The Milestone Co. 258	Machines of
A. Mills 246	Switzerland 192

Precision sawing's a push–over with our new pull–over

The **Elu** PS174 Crosscut/Mitre Saw introduces an entirely new and unique approach to precision sawing. It is designed for bench or floor-level operation and will appeal to a wide spectrum of professional users — builders, shopfitters, flooring contractors, signmakers etc., in fact any operation where timber or plastics need to be cut with accuracy using an easily transportable machine.

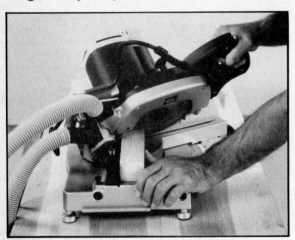

Down

The **Elu** PS174 will crosscut, mitre, bevel and cut combination mitres. On narrow workpieces, the machine is operated like a conventional mitre saw with the sawhead lowered straight down into the work and then allowed to spring-return to its upright position. The safety guard retracts only as far as is necessary to cut the material.

Across

Where the PS174 really comes into its own is on wider material, the telescoping arm giving the machine much wider cutting capacity than an ordinary mitre saw even having a much larger blade.

The whole design of the PS174 exudes quality. The extreme rigidity of its die-cast aluminium construction ensures accurate cutting of widths up to 250mm (174mm in 45° mitre setting) to a depth of 52mm (40mm in 45° bevel setting), which is ample capacity for most applications. Bevel and mitre angle adjustment is simple and quick with clear scales and the most common mitre angles have machined locations for convenience.

Up and away

Once the job is done, the PS174 weighs only 12.5kg and is therefore easily carried to the next job, even if it's up a ladder.

The **Elu** PS174 is available in both 115V and 220V AC, featuring a powerful 1200 watt low-noise universal motor. Dust extraction tubes are available as optional accessories, as are side support extensions to facilitate cutting of longer material.

The **Elu** PS174 is not like any other mitre saw you have ever seen. Check it out at your **Elu** dealer and see how it can make your cutting a real push-over.

For a colour leaflet and the address of your nearest dealer write to: Elu Power Tools, Dept. WW, Black & Decker Professional Products Division, West Point, The Grove, Slough, Berkshire SL1 1QQ. Telephone (0753) 74277

FOR SUCCESS IN WOODWORKING

WOODWORKER

design . . . craft . . . and the love of wood

April 1986   Vol. 90   No. 1109

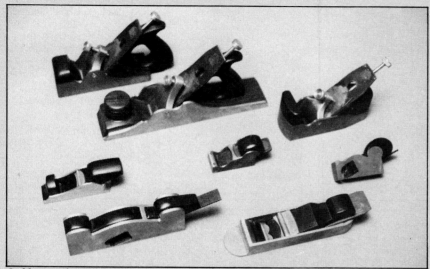

● *New tools in the old mould . . . 'Bristol fashion' p284*

283 Squares and rounds
WIN! Prize machinery and prize measuring tools await games-makers with imagination!

284 Bristol fashion
Tools ancient and modern are the stock-in-trade of a west country specialist. *Adrian Booth*

287 Collections to use
Collectors and users alike can be found drooling in London's finest old-tool shop. *David Savage*

288 Wood in the hole
History, praises, and the practical formulae of the ledge-and-brace door. *Alan Thomas*

292 Coats of many colours: 2
Marbling, graining, and other luscious effects complete our woodworker's palette. *Ian Hosker*

306 The grand furniture saga: 3
The Renaissance flowers in Europe, and touches Britain's shores. *Vic Taylor*

331 The house in the woods
A new tradition in wooden building; the architect's story of the School for Woodland Industries' green wood house. *William Moorwood*

334 JAPAN
We give Japanese tools the full treatment — starting with a specialist importer's introduction to some master makers. *Roger Buse*

338 Oire nomi
How ordinary is a humble Japanese chisel? Why it looks like it does, and what perfection means to a toolmaker. *Tony Wood*

340 Machining Wood
Your expert guide: 6
The mortiser: hollow chisel or horizontal slot. That square hole could never be easier than with this indispensable machine

345 Tales out of steel
Gas engines, forgers, strikers, and the cruel working conditions of pre-war Sheffield. *Ashley Iles*

PROJECTS
All with detailed working drawings

296 Craft afloat
Spring's here and it's time to lay out your 'Ojibwa' canoe — fun making and fun paddling! *Dennis Davis*

303 Card sharp
A cribbage box with card storage and a tricky built-up lid. *John Trussell*

325 Parlour made
A solid oak cupboard in fine country tradition. *Alex Webb*

347 Carefree coopering
A precision sanding device gets the angles just right for jointing up circles. *Roy Benfield*

On the cover: **Japanese plane-making** (p334), this month's **waterborne project** (p296), and classic tools from **Bristol Design** (p284). Four sets of the **brass measuring tools by Richard Kell** can be won by runners-up in our **'Squares and rounds'** competition, p283!

REGULARS

266 This month looks at the world of wood
268 Shoptalk an update on products and services
271 Timberline news and views for timber consumers
272 Guild notes
The Guild of Woodworkers — can you afford not to join?
275 Question box
Table-saw fences, timber drying, taper leg-flutes, shoulder yokes, warped myrtlewood . . .
281 Bob Wearing's Workshop
Ideas for light and inexpensive cramps
309 Books
349 Letters an ever-lively forum
352 Woodworking wheeze of the month
The dowel box. *Charles Cliffe*

Editor Aidan Walker
Deputy editor Owen Watson
Editorial assistant Kerry Fowler
Advertisement manager Paul Holmes
Graphics Jeff Hamblin
Technical illustrator Peter Holland
Guild of Woodworkers Owen Watson, Kerry Fowler
Editorial, advertisements and Guild of Woodworkers
1 Golden Square, London W1R 3AB, telephone 01-437 0626

Unfortunately we cannot accept responsibility for loss of or damage to unsolicited material. We reserve the right to refuse or suspend advertisements, and regret we cannot guarantee the bone fides of advertisers.

Back issues and subscriptions Infonet Ltd, 10-13 Times House, 179 Marlowes, Hemel Hempstead, Herts HP1 1BB; telephone Hemel Hempstead (0442) 48434

Subscriptions per year UK £16.90; overseas outside USA (accelerated surface post) £21.00, USA (accelerated surface post) $28, airmail £48

UK trade SM Distribution Ltd, 16-18 Trinity Gardens, London SW9 8DX; telephone 01-274 8611

North American trade Bill Dean Books Ltd, 151-49 7th Avenue, PO Box 69, Whitestone, New York 11357; telephone 1-718-767-6632

Printed in Great Britain by Ambassador Press Ltd, St. Albans, Herts
Mono origination Multiform Photosetting Ltd, Cardiff
Colour origination Derek Croxson Ltd, Chesham, Bucks
© Argus Specialist Publications Ltd 1986
ISSN 0043 776X

Argus Specialist Publications Ltd
1 Golden Square, London W1R 3AB; 01-437 0626

Master maker It's now 10 years since Alan Peters returned from his study-tour of Japan, **writes Idris Cleaver.** His current exhibition, a celebration of the influences he's absorbed, displays about 40 pieces covering most aspects of furniture making, all superbly designed and executed.

● Holborne Museum and Art Gallery, Bath, until 6 April

● *Cooper Gallery, Barnsley, 19 April-25 May*

Forest frontlines

The tropical rainforests continue to make disturbing news. **Friends of the Earth** and the **National Association of Retail Furnishers** met in January, when the latter said the former's sticker campaign was getting up their noses, but that they were basically in favour of good management of this vital resource. FoE, as Charles Secrett wrote in *Woodworker* last month, are prepared to drop those contentious stickers (WW/Jan) if they get an assurance of positive attitude from NARF and the **Timber Trades Federation.**

The TTF, whose activities are reported in terms of 'bombard press' and 'huge media campaign' (*TTJ*, 1 Feb), while claiming that 'the matter has nothing to do with the timber industry', put the blame for more than 75% of all forest destruction on the burgeoning population's search for cooking fuel. 1200 million people a day burn wood for cooking, they claim — we haven't yet been bombarded with documents quoting their sources for estimating the figure.

'In reality, but not at any retail outlet confrontation,' say the TTF, the interests of the TTF and FoE are identical.'

You bet they are. People whose money is tied up in timber are waking up to the fact (how fast?) that if the destruction goes on at the present rate, there won't **be** a means of income for them in our lifetimes. But that's small beer compared with the overall implications for the planet — Dr Tatsuro Kangi, chairman of the United Nations Conference on Tropical Timber, says: 'the sustainable development of tropical timber resources would have far-reaching beneficial effects on . . . key sectors such as agriculture, food and water supply, energy and the preservation of ecosystems.' It's our world we're talking about here.

Which is why the **International Tropical Timber Agreement** was signed by most tropical timber-producing and consuming countries in 1983. A laudable document, designed to establish a viable system of international consultation and co-operation between producing and consuming countries of tropical timber, ITTA is sadly, nearly three years later, still little more than a document. Member countries (ITTO, or the International Tropical Timber Organisation) are

allotted votes on the council according to how much timber they consume or produce; and here's an interesting thing.

Of the consumers, on whose side 650 votes are needed, France is in second place with 56 votes. First? Japan, with no less than 330! High management costs in Japan, apparently, make it uneconomic for them to harvest significant amounts of their own hardwoods, so they go round the corner to Southeast Asia, where labour and timber is cheap.

The manoeuvrings that have held up responsible management of the forests centre round two things: whose candidate will be the secretary-general of the ITTO, and where the HQ will be. For various political and diplomatic reasons, there's a stalemate — while 330,000 sq.km of forest (whether burnt for fuel or laid waste for furniture) has disappeared since the agreement was signed. Another year, claim FoE, and another 150,000 will go.

This stasis is why Friends of the Earth and the **International Institute for Environment and Development** are mounting a campaign to press the ITTO

governments to get their act together. Their letter to these governments quotes a Food and Agriculture Organisation estimate that two thirds of the tropical forest lost each year go because of agricultural expansion, the other third because of uncontrolled logging. It also points out that previously inaccessible areas of forest are opened up by logging, and the farmers and ranchers follow in on the logging roads.

'Methods do exist,' says the letter, 'to manage tropical forests sustainably, yet sadly the political will has so far been lacking to invest in these skills.' Political . . . and economic.

As always, there's arguments for being polite, and there's arguments for creating public outcry as a 'political laxative', in the words of FoE International's Des Wilson. The trade itself pushed for the international agreement to be ratified, so there's obviously some measure of responsibility in their attitude — and there's some clever media manipulation going on. It is ultimately a matter for governments; if the traders wake up, the blind social policies that cause even more devastation than logging may change.

They have to.

Obituaries

Bill Brown

It is with deep regret that we announce the death of Bill Brown after a short illness on 25 January at the age of 79.

Regular readers of *Woodworker* will have recognised and valued Bill's uncommon timber expertise, and followed his articles and 'Question Box' replies with interest.

On behalf of all *Woodworker's* readers we extend our sympathies to Bill's family, and mourn the loss of his gentlemanly erudition to our columns. We will miss him.

Peter Child

We also sadly note the death of Peter Child, author of *The Craftsman Woodturner* and pioneer of the two-day residential woodturning course. He brought turning as a hobby to the notice of thousands. His son will continue the courses.

Ear ear

New EEC legislation will require 15 million people in Europe — 2 million in the UK — to wear hearing protection. Employers will have to provide it, workers will have to wear it. Good news for manufacturers of ear protectors . . .

Shows galore

As every reading woodworker knows, our shows are the ones where you can see the finest examples of Britain's skill and talent, both professional and amateur. Naturally enough, for beautiful work to be displayed, beautiful work has to be made — and entered. So get your tools out and get to work; the categories for both the **Bristol Show, 16-18 May,** and the **London Show, 23-26 October,** are the same. They include: cabinetmaking, woodcarving, woodturning, musical instrument making, marquetry, toys and miniatures, and a host of others.

You'll have seen the craft competition that *Woodworker* is running off its own bat in association with **Elektra Beckum,** in which you can win their brand-new precision tablesaw, or their top-of-the-range lathe. It's called **Squares and rounds,** it's for both straight-line people and woodturners, and you'll find more details on our special competition page 'Squares and rounds' in this issue. There are four boxed sets of **Richard Kell's measuring tools** for runners-up — see the cover and feast your eyes.

For the London show, there are also numerous special categories, with tempting prizes donated by generous people such as **Rogers** of Hitchin. Carvers get the chance to win an award in the **Ashley Iles** carving competition; this is on a specific topic every year, and to fit in with Ashley Iles' own series in *Woodworker,* 'Tales out of steel', this year the theme to work on is **INDUSTRY.**

That's not all, of course. Our **Prize draw** at Bristol gives you the chance to win an **Emco TF65 spindle moulder,** generously donated by **Solent Tools.** It's worth £450 retail, and it's yours (you hope!) for the trouble of filling in a form.
● **All enquiries** about both shows should go to the **show organisers, Argus Specialist Exhibitions,** Wolsey House, Wolsey Rd, Hemel Hempstead, Herts HP2 4SS, tel. (0442) 41221. Get your entry forms from them, not us.
And get weaving!

Chess in Art and Society is the subject of a small exhibition at the V&A which contains delights such as the 17th century Turkish games board **above.** We hope you're inspired to enter our **Squares and Rounds** competition and win machinery or measuring tools . . .
● Victoria & Albert Museum, South Kensington, London SW7; the exhibition runs until 1 June.

Diary

Guild courses are shown by an asterisk(*); see p 272.

April

Until 5 **Wood engravings by George Tute** Bristol Museum, tel. (0272) 29771

Until 6 **Wood sculpture by Juginder Lamba** Commonwealth Institute, London, tel. 01-603 4535

6 **Visit to Parnham House and the School for Woodland Industries** see Guild pages for details

12 **Hand veneering** Bob Grant*

13-18 **Boatbuilding repairs** West Dean College, Sussex, tel. (024363) 301

19-May 25 **Alan Peters, Furniture Maker** Cooper Gallery, Barnsley

21-23 **Toymaking Symposium** John Boddy's, Boroughbridge, N. Yorks, tel. (09012) 2370

26 **Woodmachining** Ken Taylor*

26-May 21 **Modern Furniture** Aberystwyth Arts Centre, tel. (0970) 4277

Until June 1 **Chess in Art and Society** Victoria and Albert Museum, London

May

10 **Power routing** Roy Sutton*

11-18 **London International Furniture Show** Earls Court, London

16-19 **Bristol Woodworker Show**

24-31 **National Marquetry Exhibition** St Albans, details tel. (0727) 63800

June

5-6 **French polishing** Charles Cliffe*

30-July 4 **London College of Furniture Summer Show**

July

26-August 30 **Furniture from Rycotewood College** Cheltenham Art Gallery, tel. (0285) 61566

September

6-7 **Decorative techniques** Ian Hosker*

October

11-20 **Chelsea Crafts Fair**

23-26 **Woodworker Show** Alexandra Palace, London

Remember! Any woodworking wheezes in your ever-fertile brains may just be worth money! Plans, projects, stories . . . Let us know if you have something in your workshop — or your head — that *Woodworker* can use. You may not think it's anything much—but let us decide!

Shoptalk

'IN OUR VIEW THE HAND-SAW is out of date,' say **Bosch**, introducing their **reciprocating power saw**. The blade rotates to cut up or down. PFZ 550, £77; PFZ 550E (variable speed), £89.70 inc. VAT.
● Bosch, PO Box 98, Denham, Middx UB9 5HJ, tel. (0895) 833633.

MAKING MUSIC: **Merton College** are now accepting applications for their two-year course in Musical Instrument Repair and Making. It starts in September, and gives a comprehensive training in the repair and making of violins, pipe organs, guitars, woodwind and brass instruments. The course is a 'market-leader', says Phil Chambers, whose superb Martin-style guitar was a Woodworker Show 85 prizewinner.
● Merton College, Musical Instrument Technology, Morden Park, Morden, Surrey SM4 5LZ, tel 01-542 3931

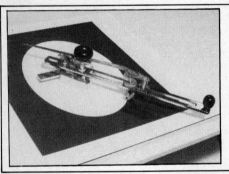

THE OVAL-ART MAT CUTTER, to mark out ovals – at a price. It also cuts circles and scollops; £310.
● Charnwood, 44 Boston Rd, Beaumont Leys, Leicester LE4 1AA, tel. (0533) 351735

So you're getting serious about marketing your work, and you want something a little more up-market than the Able Labels you've been using up to now to identify your stuff. **Branding irons** are an alternative to die-stamping or nailing on a brass plate, so your eyes light up when you see an announcement about an electric branding iron with interchangeable brands. But the fire dims when you see the price: £339.25+p&p, with an extra £59.50 for each brand.
● Express Services, 115 Stamford Rd, Kettering, Northants NN16 8QZ, tel. (0536) 81778.

Rainwater may once have done wonders for the complexion, but it's never been a great ally of wooden window frames. Trend Machinery have developed a **long-reach cutter** for routers of up to 10lb weight (with a minimum 750w at 110v) to remove wet rot-affected timber. They suggest a small framework template to cut first (⅜in depth), then you can assess damage; a hardwood insert can replace the rotted area. Trend's package of Elu MOF96 router and cutter comes in at about £100 — the cutter is available separately at £5.46.
● Trend Machinery & Cutting Tools Ltd, Unit N, Penfold Works, Imperial Way, Watford, Herts WD2 4YY, tel. (0923) 49911.

If music be the food of love, then **making instruments** must be more than fun. **West Dean College** are offering a nine day course for the less ambitious, which caters for a wide range of abilities. 27 Mar-5 Apr, £239 full board and tuition.
● West Dean College, West Dean, Chichester, West Sussex PO18 0QZ, tel. (024363) 301.

Evo-Stik's Impact 2, a **contact adhesive**, is non-toxic and solvent-free — nothing to sniff at. It's water-washable (not water-proof); works on a variety of materials including wood and laminates; and comes with a sponge applicator. It changes from white to clear when the surfaces are ready for assembly. £2.49 for 140ml, £3.49 for 210ml, inc. VAT.
● Evo-Stik, 66 Wells St, London W1, tel. 01-631 1008.

Announcing a price cut is a pleasant change for us, especially when it's for the **brushing french polish** that Charles Cliffe reviewed in 'Shoptalk' (WW/Feb). The new prices are £5.52, and £2.59 for the wax, inc. VAT. The maker, **John Myland**, are currently over the moon about being granted a Royal Warrant.
● John Myland, 80 Norwood High St, London SE27 9NW, tel. 01-670 9161.

Normally we leave **metal bending** to Superman, but we occasionally need something a little cheaper than teak in the garden. 'Tubemate' is a tube bender, plus a range of kits for things as diverse as wall partitions and outside chairs. The bender is designed for 18-gauge ¾in tube, and the tube is rust-proof and colourfast — they claim you can squeeze it in a vice and the colour doesn't flake or chip. The bender is available separately.

● M.W. Lusty, Liversage St, Derby DE1 2LL, tel. (0332) 385326. Tube bender around £38.50 inc. VAT

'**T**his will change the face of woodworking' claims the untypically immodest press release for **Fluid Wood.** The substance is used to 'marinade' wood until it's flexible and can be bent, folded, squeezed or whatever until it's dry. The instruction manual suggests you throw away your planer/thicknesser and replace it with a rolling pin. It even gives a recipe for home-made paper, although the necessary bleach isn't included.
● A.P.R. Fool Ltd, 13 Lear's Way, Nonesuch.

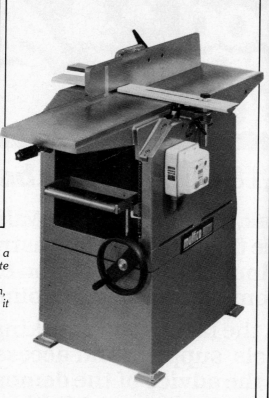

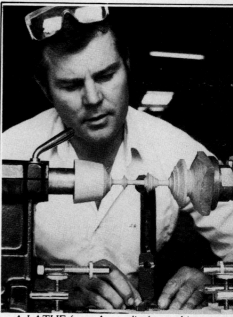

THE NEW MULTICO CPT 300/230 planer/thicknesser has a 2hp cutter motor and a separate ½hp feed motor. Maximum thicknessing capability is 12x9in, total table length 1310mm, and it can do up to 20mm rebates. Tables and fence are cast iron; £1850+VAT for a single-phase machine.
● *Multico, Brighton Rd, Salfords, Redhill, Surrey RH1 5ER, tel. (0293) 782444*

*A LATHE from Australia for making templates from a turned pattern (**above**) or copying. Its jig-mounted cutter and stylus can be used by inexperienced and handicapped people.*
● *Symtec Products, 47 Norfolk Rd, Marion, South Australia, tel. (01061) 08 296 7449*

Shoptalk special

WE THOUGHT of running a 'mystery object' competition with these abrasive photos, but we decided going through the replies would be dangerous to our mental health. **Below right** is a micro close-up of the hook-and-eye Velcro system used by **Siaco** to fix their abrasive papers to a backing plate or pad. **Centre** is a machine you'll never fit in your garage; it's a continuous buffing machine, which uses **Du Pont** abrasive monofilament brushes to sand both flat and curved surfaces, mouldings in particular. More relevant to the ordinary woodworker is the new HCAB-LL range of abrasive papers from

Hermes, which has an anti-clogging additive; and (**below left**) the Oakey Supersander drum sander from **English Abrasives,** which can be used with their new 157 range of aluminium oxide papers.
● Siaco, Saffron Walden, Essex CB10 2LA, tel. (0799) 27399
● Du Pont, PO Box, CH-1211 Geneva 24, Switzerland, tel. (01041) 22 378707
● Hermes, Greenstead Rd, Colchester, Essex CO1 2SR, tel. (0206) 867181
● English Abrasives, PO Box 85, Marsh Lane, London N17 0XA, tel. 01-808 4545

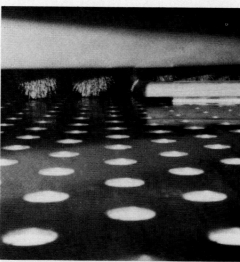

Where Craft Comes Alive..

May 16th, 17th, 18th *It's all about wood...*

Beautiful wood... Oak, Sycamore, Ash, Walnut, Mahogany
Versatile wood... see the experts demonstrating their skills
Wonderful wood... admire the competition entries –
from marquetry to cabinet making

LOOK... at the latest woodworking machinery,
tools, supplies and accessories
LISTEN... to the advice of the demonstrators
BUY... from the many exhibition stands

All the wonder of wood at the...

Bristol Woodworker Show
Bristol Exhibition Centre
Canon's Road
Bristol

OPENING TIMES:
May 16, 17... 10 am – 6 pm
May 18... 10 am – 5 pm

For further details contact

Argus Specialist Exhibitions,
Wolsey House, Wolsey Road,
Hemel Hempstead, Herts HP2 4SS
Tel: 0442 41221

 The Bristol Woodworker Show is organised by Argus Specialist Exhibitions
and sponsored by Woodworker Magazine

Timberline

Arthur Jones' update on timber trade news

Best quality, it's assumed, is what the woodworker wants. This is certainly true for the bulk of timber applications in woodworking, which is why the very best of joinery grades and clears are so frequently in demand — and always costly.

Knowledgeable timber users will stipulate the shippers when buying softwood, knowing from experience that wood from a particular shipper meets personal needs. It isn't enough to say that unsorted grade is in demand, because 'unsorted' means exactly what it says — a mixture of top grades which are no longer marketed separately.

The timber buyer may also deal with a particular mill because its wood is better quality than average, perhaps because it uses logs from more northern territories. Thus when dealing with Russian wood (here individual mill knowledge no longer applies) there is always a premium on the price of Kara Sea softwood.

At the moment the strengthening of whitewood prices has put redwood fifths and fourths under some pressure. I can hear you saying: 'Who wants to use fifths with those knots and wane, not to mention the other defects?' Let's ignore the fact that you can pick over a parcel of fifths and find quite a lot of pieces which rightfully belong in unsorted quality. Do you the woodworker *always* want the very best?

There are many jobs where some defects in timber trade terms are either not defects at all from the woodworking viewpoint, or can be overcome. Wane might not be such a serious defect if the length you need allows the wane to be cut out, or the application can disguise it.

Knots come into the same category. For most woodworkers they are anathema, but in some jobs they can be essential, giving just the character required.

Years ago the eastern Canadian lumber industry had a serious problem with white pine. It was — and still is — the most beautiful of all softwoods, easily worked and coming up to a delightful finish. But the UK importers wanted clear white pine, and there are still some magnificent examples of it in older houses. The mills burnt the pieces with knots.

Gradually the quantities of clear pine became less and less while the percentage of pine with knot blemishes (with no market value), rose alarmingly. The industry decided that drastic action was demanded. A publicity campaign was launched to praise the merits of knotty pine panelling, making the knots the main selling point. It succeeded — so much so, that knotty pine became scarce and more costly than the top grades. Even today, the producers of imitation wood panelling make a speciality of knotty pine! It's all a question of turning a defect into a plus factor.

We are seeing something similar in at least one hardwood. When an agent bravely brought the early commercial cargoes of ramin to Britain at the end of the war, there were many of his colleagues who were certain this was a hardwood which would never succeed in Britain; one importer dubbed it 'blotting paper'. Now look at the demand and price of ramin!

There is a tendency for hardwood prices to rise slightly, and it's predicted that this movement will continue into the summer. Some importers who bought cheaper cargoes last year have seen some of those contracts unshipped; the producers now want higher rates.

Devaluation of the Ghanaian currency should help to increase the demand for West African hardwoods this year. The producers have scope for being more competitive, though the total supplied from West Africa is only a small percentage of hardwoods imported.

Mention has been made of duty-free imports of plywood from Brazil, Indonesia, Korea, Malaysia, the Philippines and Singapore by Common Market countries. Each of the exporting countries has been given an allocation for this year of 84,000 cu.m., and it shows how important the UK market is to them that our duty-free allocation with each one is 64,000 cu.m., leaving 20,000cu.m to be shared between nine other Common Market countries. ∎

Guild notes

Guild of WOODWORKERS

Shared information, advice and help are vital to good woodwork. They are also the basis of the **Guild of Woodworkers**: an international organisation which welcomes new members — whatever their skills. You must be a Guild member to go on our courses or events.

Guild members get
- free publicity in *Woodworker*
- 15% off Woodworker Show entry
- 15% discount on our plans
- access to and inclusion in our register of members' skills and services
- the chance to contact other members for help and advice where appropriate
- specially arranged tool insurance at low rates

Owen Watson

● **Roy Sutton** (right) guiding a Guild member through the intricacies of power routing with a trammel bar. The photo was taken at Roy's course in February

GUILD COURSES

● Only Guild members are eligible to go on these courses — see the opposite page for details of how to join. You must book in advance, and we must have a cheque for the full cost of the course. If you cancel less than two weeks before the advertised date you will forfeit 50% of the cost, unless there are exceptional circumstances.

Hand veneering — Bob Grant

12 April, 9.30-5, Oxford, £35+VAT.
If you want to know more about this skilled (and ecologically sound!) craft, Bob and Peter Sarac, a local harpsichord maker and cabinetmaker, will guide you through the art. They'll show you examples of cartouches, and demonstrate the scratch-stock; you'll be laying a panel with veneer, mitring a cross-banding, inlaying lines round it, and applying a balancer veneer on the back. If you have a veneer hammer, bring it; but materials will be provided.

French polishing — Ian Hosker

19-20 April, 10-5, Chester, £40+VAT.
Ian is a teacher (and practising professional) who will guide you through preparation of both new and old pieces, staining and colouring techniques, grain-filling, shellac finishes, fadding, bodying in, spiriting off, and giving new life to existing polished surfaces. The fee includes course materials, and Ian will make you up a polishing kit to take away with you — **if you include another £8 when you book.**

Wood-machining — Ken Taylor

26 April, Bletchley, £25+VAT.
Ken's course on the ins and outs of machining wood is one of our most popular. Find out about (and try) table- and band-sawing, radial-arm saws, planing and thicknessing, spindle moulding, and horizontal and vertical mortising. You can also see, and try out, some good quality universals. Lunch is included.

Power routing — Roy Sutton

10 May, Herne Bay, £25+VAT.
Come and improve your expertise on the machine that almost put the moulding plane out of business. Not only does it cut grooves; a short list of its capabilities includes housing, rebating, straight and circular moulding, tenoning, mortising, rule-joint and template work. Roy will take you through all this, plus designing and setting out jigs. The course is mostly demonstrations, with some 'hands-on' at the end.

French polishing — Charles Cliffe

5-6 June, 9.30-5, Bexleyheath, £40.
Charles Cliffe, one of our 'Question Box' experts on this subject, explains all about preparation, staining, and application of this tricky (and beautiful) finish. He'll also be dealing with using a cabinet scraper, so bring your own if you have one. If you have a piece of furniture that you want his advice on, bring it as well. Charles can order supplies for you to take away if you tell him in advance. This course always fills up quickly, so **book soon!**

Decorative techniques — Ian Hosker

6-7 September, 10-5, Chester, £45.
You read the article, now do the course. Ian's feature, 'Coats of many colours' covered wonderful decorative techniques such as dragging, lining, sponging, ragrolling, marbling, spattering, and (his and my favourite) tortoiseshelling. The cost includes materials, but students should bring a few paint-brushes and jam-jars.

The working woodland

A reminder for those of you who want to visit the School for Woodland Industry (featured in this and the last issue). **The date has been changed to Sunday 6 April,** and the price to £4.50; otherwise the details are as before. There's a tour of Parnham House and the completed prototype building, together with the opportunity for a discussion with construction supervisor John Bunford, (a carpenter and joiner by training). To book, write to the Guild, quoting your Guild number and enclosing a sae, but no money. Numbers have been limited to 40, so hurry!

Duty free

Yes, you don't have to cross the Channel to dodge VAT — you can now do it in the comfort of someone else's workshop! The more financially eagle-eyed of you will have noticed that we aren't charging VAT on courses later in the year. This is because we'll be asking you to write cheques for courses to the individual tutors (who are mostly unregistered for VAT) instead of the Guild (which is registered). However, just in case Customs and Excise decide this isn't on, we reserve the right to charge VAT.

● Parnham House, the first stop on the Guild's 6 April tour of Hooke Park and the Working Woodland. Act fast if you want to go

Shipshape and . . .

Bristol readers who read the article on Charles Stirling and Bristol Design in this issue may be interested in a Guild inaugural meeting at his shop/home. It's on Wednesday 16 April, at 14 Perry Road, Bristol, starting at 8.30pm. No topics have been fixed yet, so if you have any ideas please let Charles know.

On to more commercial matters. Charles has acquired some high quality, old but unused skew-chisels and gouges, plus some 1¼ to 2in firmer-chisels in the same steel. There are also traditional laminated-steel plane-irons, unpierced irons, toothing-plane irons and rarities. He will send you a list on receipt of a sae, and give you 10% off if you quote your membership number when ordering your goods.

Joining in

All you wanted to know about joining the Guild, but never asked . . . We now have three levels of membership. **Associate** is for those who want to join in the Guild's activities but make no claim to any woodworking expertise. For **Amateur,** you must supply a photo of your work and a reference; for **Professional** two photos and references. For newly qualified woodworkers, references plus a copy of their leaving certificate will be acceptable. Rates are £3.50 (associate), £5 (amateur), and £10 (professional) a year, plus £1.50 joining fee. If you're interested in associate membership, send us your name, address, and cheque; for the other classes, please send a stamped addressed envelope for the application form.

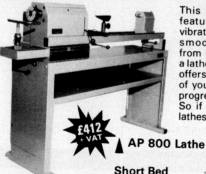

273

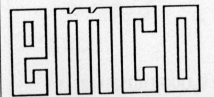

Question box

We will try to answer any questions you can throw at us, but the ones we publish are the ones of most general interest to readers.

Please type your question double-spaced with generous margins, and include a stamped self-addressed envelope. Send it to: Question Box, Woodworker, 1 Golden Sq., London W1R 3AB.

Shoulder-yokes

Q For some time I have been trying to purchase a shoulder-yoke – that indispensable part of every farm's equipment earlier this century which, alas, seems no longer to be made. A friend has offered to try and make me one if I can find any instructions for the dimensions and so on. I've been unable to trace any information; could you offer advice?

Miss B. Potter, Smallfield

A I'm intrigued! I thought milkmaids were a thing of the past. You don't say whether this yoke is to be used or just to be hung on the wall, so I'm assuming it has to 'work'.

I have noted the dimensions of an 18th century yoke to guide you, but they don't seem to vary much except that some were obviously tailored to fit individual shoulders. A few strokes with a round shave would soon sort out that problem.

The usual timbers were beech, sycamore, willow and poplar, though any suitable straight-grained stuff will do. The traditional tools of side-axe, hollow hand-adze and curved shaves may not be available, so I suggest you mark the outline on your timber and cut out with a bandsaw. A lot of 'roughing out' can be achieved with that versatile tool, and a draw-knife, followed by a spokeshave and scraper.

The hollowing-out to fit the shoulders was traditionally done using a small curved hand-adze. Amateurs today could do the same job with a good strong woodcarver's gouge.

The ends of the yokes were always turned in the lathe, but this could be dispensed with and replaced by a bit of whittling, where the forged-iron swivelling brackets are 'closed over' the yoke ends. If the lathe is used, I suggest a slowish speed, and keep an eye on the centre of the yoke. It can give you a nasty wallop on the knuckles!

As for the ironwork, look round for some old chain and get a friendly smith or engineer to make a bracket and hook, and off you go. Of course you could always dispense with the chains and use a piece of string!

Stuart King

● Stuart King is a miniaturist and expert on country craft history.

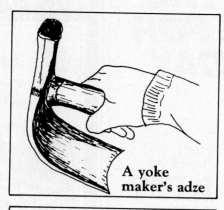

A yoke maker's adze

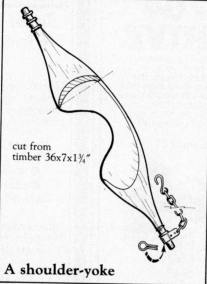

cut from timber 36x7x1¾"

A shoulder-yoke

Spraying cellulose

Q I would appreciate some advice on spraying wood with cellulose lacquer. One of my interests is making chess-boards with various coloured veneers, but I have difficulty obtaining a really good finish because of the grain-filling problem (particularly on dark veneers).

I have tried neutral cellulose filler and this shows through. Naturally I cannot use a stain. Any suggestions?

Frank Marshall, Lymington

A Give your chess-boards a first class finish by following this workshop schedule:

1 Prepare the substrate very carefully with 240-grit garnet paper and dust off.
2 Spray one liberal coating of clear gloss (if gloss is what you want) cellulose lacquer, and while the film is still wet drop extra cellulose into any grain cavity or veneer joint with a toothpick. Allow the film to dry.
3 Flat down with 120-grit lubrisil silicon-carbide abrasive paper and dust off.
6 Apply a second coat of gloss lacquer and check again for cavities.
5 Flat down again when it's dry with 400-grit wet or dry silicon carbide paper, using a little rain-water and soap. Dry off.
6 Apply a third coating of the lacquer and allow it to dry bone-hard.

7 Flat down slightly with 600-grit wet or dry paper.
8 When it's bone dry, apply pullover solution in straight-line strokes with a french-polish type rubber. This will give you a full, smooth gloss finish with no nibs.
9 After 24 hours, burnish the surface with a cellulose burnishing cream and mutton-cloth to produce a mirror-gloss finish.
10 Allow it to dry 36 hours before packing.

Thin the lacquer with, say, 10% cellulose thinners to obtain a good viscosity. Room temperature while you are spraying should be about 65°F, and there should be no draughts. The important point of the procedure is flatting at all the stages. Using the gloss lacquer as a grain-filler, you avoid the problems of standard grain-fillers. The main beauty of a nitrocellulose lacquer is that the finish film is reversible, and you can pullover and burnish without difficulty, which isn't so with pre-catalysed or acid-hardened lacquers.

Noel Leach

● Noel Leach is a professional wood-finisher and lecturer.

Taper leg-flutes

Q In Woodworker, *September '85 you carried an article on a Chippendale table. It would be most interesting to know more about how to set out and produce the diminished and taper leg-flutes with hand tools.*

H.W. Hill, Ashford

A Cutting diminished flutes on tapered legs is best done with a power router, but it's not too difficult (only time-consuming) using a hand scraper.

You don't have to make a fuss about making the holding-box; you can use odd scraps screwed together. I can't give exact dimensions, as it will vary according to the length of the leg and its thickness; however, the inside length should be an inch or two longer than the leg, and the interior of the box should be the same in depth as the widest part of the leg.

As you can see, the toe of the leg is propped up with a wedge. Its height is a matter of trial and error — the higher it is, the deeper the cut will be — and what you want to aim at is a gradual fading away of the flute until it disappears at or near the toe. It's well worth making a dummy leg out of softwood and testing on that.

The scraper is made up in two halves which are screwed together at the stop end, and the cutter is trapped and held by further screws along the stock. Make a series of screw-holes so you can move the cutter backwards and forwards and hold it with screws in the appropriate holes. You can grind the cutter from a piece of cabinet-scraper steel, an old bandsaw blade or (what I often use) a spare blade for a craft knife. I hold the blade in a pair of pliers and keep some cold water handy as you can soon draw the temper if you're not careful to dip it frequently.

276

Question box

Make the central flute first and then temporarily fix the cheek (as shown) on to one side of the box with its top exactly flush with the top edge of the box. Cut another flute which will taper towards the first one. Detach the cheek and fix it to the other side of the box and cut the last flute. You can clean the flutes up with a gouge, or glass-paper wrapped round a suitably-shaped holder.

Vic Taylor

● Vic Taylor is an internationally-known author, furniture historian, and former editor of *Woodworker*.

Bandsaw vs. table-saw

Q *I only have a small workshop, and like everyone else, only a limited budget to spend on my hobby. Ideally, I would like both a circular saw and a bandsaw, but I have neither the room nor the means to achieve this. Of the two, I would use a circular saw much more often than a bandsaw. However, I do a fair amount of woodturning, and a bandsaw is extremely useful for cutting the bowl blanks and other shapes of timber for furniture, which is my main interest. In these circumstances would it be advisable to buy a good bandsaw – the best I can afford; or are the advantages of a single machine outweighed by the inherent inaccuracies in the bandsaw's design and performance?*

J. J. Atwill, London

A Where space and/or funds are limited, and furniture-making is your chief interest the choice must be a circular saw. A bandsaw can cut curves and thicker timber than a circular saw of equal horsepower, but it doesn't compare with a circular saw for versatility. When you're equipped with the right accessories, you can perform operations such as grooving, rebating, moulding, combing, and fielding. It's also capable of more accurate work than a bandsaw, and when used with a tungsten-tipped blade (always a good investment) it can cut abrasive materials smoothly enough to need very little extra hand-work for a good finish.

As for woodturning blanks, the mitre-slide on the circular saw can be used to cut the corners off a square shape and produce an octagon suitable for mounting on the face-plate.

Ken Taylor

Rip-fence alignment

Q *In your first 'Machining Wood' article (WW/Nov '85) I read: 'Inspect the alignment of the rip fence and the saw blade – they should be fractionally out of parallel, something like 1/32in in 5ft further apart at the back of the table'. In the Woodworker's Bible by Alf Martensson I read: '. . . out of parallel by 1/32in in 5ft, with the top or back end set closer to the blade.'*

Can you adjudicate? Maybe anyone able to give an authoritative answer to this question could advise on how on earth you calculate 1 in 160 in, say, an 8in blade.

H.E. Pope, Lewes

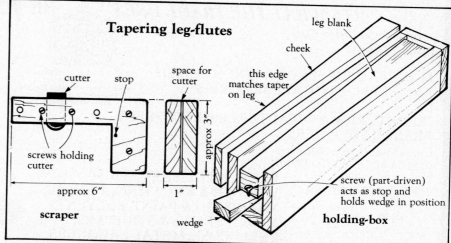

Tapering leg-flutes

cutter   stop   space for cutter

screws holding cutter

approx 6"   1"

scraper   wedge

leg blank

cheek

this edge matches taper on leg

approx 3"

screw (part-driven) acts as stop and holds wedge in position

holding-box

A1 We set the back of the fence very slightly closer to the saw-blade to keep the workpiece tight against the fence. If this setting is too close, the back of the blade will tend to bind and burn. Setting the fence away from the back of the blade may result in a slight gap between the workpiece and the fence which means the work is unsupported. We're talking about a very slight dimension which is best achieved with a paper or cardboard shim in the fence.

This whole point is fairly unimportant, and doesn't deserve all this attention. Most rip-fences, however well set, tend to go out of adjustment quickly as they are removed and put back again during the working day.

Alf Martensson

A2 To prevent overheating of some types of blade because of the material binding on the back of the saw, it's necessary to give a slight 'toe-out' or offset to the fence. Some machines are provided with set-screws at the fence to give this clearance; if not, a small piece of packing could be inserted between a false fence and the metal fence at the infeed end. As a guide, the 'toe-out' should be 3mm in 6000mm, or in more practical terms 0.15mm for a 12in saw.

Ken Taylor

● Alf Martensson is a well-known author and maker of quality furniture; Ken Taylor is a lecturer, and a wood-machinist of 40 years experience.

Straightening myrtlewood

Q *I have a well-dried 1¼x12in disc of Oregon myrtlewood. I want to make a 12in platter out of it, but it's warped – can I boil it in water and clamp it straight?*

Also, can you tell me how to turn an ellipse?

Frank Nunn, Sheffield

A My reaction to your idea of straightening out your Oregon myrtlewood is don't. It's obviously a piece of timber you regard highly, and I'd be loath to encourage you to do something you may regret. If you had several pieces around you could try out

your ideas and find a formula that worked, then give your important piece a try. You'll have to accept that the piece is distorted, and will finish less than 1½in thick. You often find, if you do manage to straighten out distorted discs, that the distortion returns when they're worked because of the wood's inherent tension.

I have been told of a lathe that does produce elliptical door knobs and the like, but surely the simplest elliptical answer is to mount your work equally off-centre on two points either side of the true centre, and blend any slight mis-match by hand.

Ray Key

● Ray Key is a well-known professional woodturner, teacher and author.

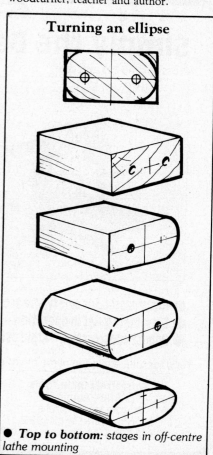

Turning an ellipse

● **Top to bottom:** *stages in off-centre lathe mounting*

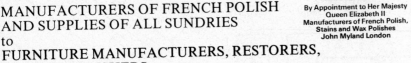

278

Question box

Blue streaks in pine

Q Can you tell me if there's any way of removing the blue streaks that sometimes occur in pine?

B. Van Ryn, Salisbury

A The short answer is no. I assume you are referring to blue sap-stain which sometimes occurs in timbers like true pine (*Pinus*). This usually penetrates well into the sapwood and needs discarding for clear finishing. Bleaching only makes matters worse, but the wood could of course be used for painting or for hidden work. Parana 'pine' (*Araucaria*) sometimes displays blue, black, or red streaks, and since you use this phrase I am wondering if this is the actual timber. If it is, then such markings cannot be removed; they are of mineral origin as opposed to sap-stain which is fungal.

Bill Brown, FIWSc

Using rotted oak

Q I recently cut down an old oak tree which wasn't entirely dead, but there was a lot of moist brown powder where the wood had rotted. Some of it is quite hard and I have it in mind to cut billets out of the hard wood and use them on my lathe. Would you advise how best to season the billets after I have cut them out? I'm thinking of pieces about 18in to 2ft long and as big as I can find in solid wood.

R.A. Hendrie, Norwich

A Your tree has suffered fungal attack, and any wood you reclaim must be sound enough to work. Test this by inserting the point of a knife into apparently sound wood, lifting a few fibres. If these break off short, then the wood, or some of it, will behave in similar fashion on the lathe. Some fungal forms which attack oak produce stringy rot, noticeable in the damaged wood in the form of white cotton-like strands. If this type of attack is present, then it's doubtful that that part of the tree is usable. However, if you can reclaim what seems to be suitable, put the pieces outside in stick with top cover, and leave them for a few months when you can bring some inside to condition in a drier and warmer atmosphere. Although fungi caused the damage, the wood, once dry, will be quite satisfactory if it's workable.

Bill Brown

Drying yew and cedar

Q A friend has been cutting down some yew and cedar trees and has given me some of the timber. I would like to know the best way to dry this wood for turning. The logs are 7in diameter x 3ft long; I don't have a drier or moisture meter, simply a dry wooden shed and a pre-cast concrete garage. How long do you think the timber would take to air-dry, and how do I know when it is dry enough to use?

R.J. Martin, Biggleswade

A Cedar dries easily and without undue difficulty. Yew also dries easily, but you must watch for end-splitting. You should leave all your pieces outdoors for a few months, placing them to allow a free air-current to get to the wood. You may find you can simply cross-pile the wood, leaving reasonable space between each piece (as long as this is safe), or you could stand the pieces on end, leaning against a substantial support with the lower ends resting on dunnage to keep them off the ground. Turning the yew pieces end-for-end every few weeks would help you to check for end-splitting — the top ends will tend to dry quicker than the lower. If you find serious splitting, the wood is drying too quickly and should therefore be moved to a more sheltered spot in the shade and out of drying winds.

After about six months, take a piece of cedar and yew, and saw out a complete disk, say ½in thick from the mid-section of each. Examine each piece and note if there are any checks; if there are one or two, mark the inner ends with a pencil. Next, weigh each piece carefully on your kitchen scales and mark the weight on the wood. Now place both pieces in any warm room with conditions like the ones where your turnery will end up. Check the pieces by both weight and appearance every few days until the weight remains constant. None of your wood will be suitable before six months and it might be expedient to do a similar test a little later purely on weight. A rough guide to dry weight can be obtained by cutting out a small, regular-sized cube, say 1in square, from both woods and placing them one at a time in a glass of water. Check the displacement, in other words, their specific gravity (s.g.). If the displacement is half, i.e. half the cube is submerged, its s.g. is 0.50. Multiply this by 62.4 to get the weight — in this case about 32lbs/cu ft. If 75% is submerged, the s.g. is 0.75 and the weight of the wood about 47lbs/cu.ft.

Cedar at 15% moisture content weighs about 36 lbs/cu.ft, and yew about 42 lbs, so with a little juggling with the values given you could get a rough idea of how much more drying, if any, is needed. You will appreciate that if the cubes sink more than mentioned, the wood is heavier; also that the value is for 15% mc, and indoor equilibrium is near 10% mc.

Bill Brown

● Bill Brown's long association with timber included posts as a trade buyer and TRADA's manager of advisory services. He was a prolific author. See 'This Month'.

Golden oak stain

Q Could you tell me how to get the deep golden colour characteristic of antique oak?

R. Pyle, Gosforth

A The colour known as golden oak is easiest to make as a water-stain; dissolve 2oz bichromate of potash in about a pint of water. When the bichromate crystals have dissolved, carefully pour the mixture into a clean bottle, leaving any sediment behind.

Before staining the workpiece, it is advisable to experiment on some large piece of waste to enable you to get the right colour. When you have arrived at the correct strength, lightly sponge the work with warm water to raise the grain. Allow the wood to thoroughly dry naturally, then paper it smooth with fine abrasive paper. After dusting off, the stain can be brushed on. You need daylight and free air circulation to allow the chemical action of the stain to take effect. When it's completely dry, lightly smooth the work again with fine abrasive paper. Brush on two or three coats of french polish (the ordinary brown polish made from orange shellac), and allow them to harden thoroughly. Smooth out any 'nibs' by lightly glasspapering, and wipe off any dust. Finally, apply wax polish evenly with a rag, allow it to stand for about 15 minutes, and then briskly polish with a soft duster. After several such waxings the wood will have a delightful warm glow.

Charles Cliffe

Staining dowels

Q I have repaired a chair with new round stretchers, which are dowels slightly shaped on the lathe. I have raised the grain with warm water, sanded and repeated the process. Then I sealed the surface with shellac, and rubbed down with fine wire wool.

My difficulty is staining before filling the grain. I have used a proprietary water-stain, applying it by dabbing with a cloth pad, and it seems impossible to get the stain to 'take' evenly on the round surfaces of the dowel rods (it is not an end-grain problem).

Can you please advise me what to do and, incidentally, on whether it's right to fill the grain after staining rather than before?

A.G. Robinson, Canterbury

A Sealing with shellac before applying your water-stain would account for uneven stain-absorption. The shellac forms a barrier, preventing the stain from entering the wood uniformly and giving this patchiness.

You are quite correct to raise the grain with warm water and then cut down the raised fibres with fine abrasive paper. When the new wood is completely dry, stain it with water-stain applied evenly with a clean rag. Don't use thick stain or apply it too liberally in an attempt to complete it in one operation — this can lead to runs and uneven colouring. Two or three light applications will give a much better result than one thick coat. When the stain is completely dry, fill the grain with a filler similar in colour to the finished piece. Allow the filler to dry overnight, then lightly sand the surface with fine paper. Dust off thoroughly before applying shellac, or whatever finish you intend to use.

Charles Cliffe

● Charles Cliffe is a professional french polisher, teacher and author.

279

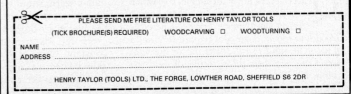

Reaching the parts...

How to make some clever and convenient cramps

Lever-cam cramps have been popular for a long time with stringed instrument makers, who need a cramp that is both light and has a long reach. Up until recently they had to be made by the user! The traditional panel cramp, on the other hand, was more common in pre-plywood days.

Traditional panel cramp

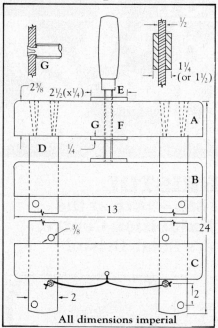

All dimensions imperial

The construction is straightforward, using through tenons, wedged but without shoulders. You can avoid having to accurately cut six deep mortises by building up as described for the lever-cam cramp. Housings can be cut to an even depth and with a fine finish by an electric or hand router. First saw carefully across the grain; if you have a radial-arm saw, you can make these cuts with great precision. The upper layer, slightly over-wide, is glued on then cleaned up. The housings in the top member **A** can be widened to take the wedges.

The arms **D** need to be made from well-seasoned old hardwood, since any warping will be transferred to the job. Cut small shoulders on the edges then cramp the two pieces together and drill the holes. Glue and wedge the arms into the fixed member **A**, with the two moving members **B** and **C** in place. Check the diagonals are equal and that there is no twist.

Traditionally the screw was wooden, but a piece of ½in. BSW screwed rod is quite a suitable alternative, operating in a steel plate **G**. This is drilled and countersunk to take a ¼in spigot, which is also drilled and countersunk. Fit this in place, then swell it out with a big centre-punch. This is quite a satisfactory arrangement since there is no strain when releasing the screw. The fixed member **A** is fitted with two steel plates **E** and **F**, one threaded and one clear. A ⁹⁄₁₆in hole in the wood avoids the screw binding here.

The handle is turned from a dense hardwood, then drilled and tapped. All the screw components are now fitted to the cramp and secured with woodscrews. The over-large hole in the fixed member **A** makes it possible to line the screw up precisely. The handle is firmly fixed when the screw is positioned. To do this, grip the thread firmly between two half-nuts while the handle is twisted on. It may be pinned, but I haven't found this necessary.

When you're cramping up a joint, protect the arms from glue with paper or polythene. A weight on top may be helpful. The tendency to rise may also be resisted by slightly angling the two gripping surfaces, but bearing in mind that minimum pressure needs to be exerted, you may not feel this refinement is worth while. The tool is completed by tying two dowel-pegs to the adjustable member **C**.

Lever-cam cramp

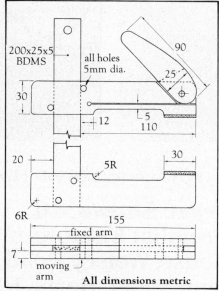

All dimensions metric

Obtain the metal bar first, a piece of 25x5mm bright drawn mild steel. Avoid black bar and any bright bar with rounded edges. The two wooden arms will create a problem if they're made from the solid; as yet there are no 5mm hand or machine mortise chisels, and there may not be sufficient depth of cut on a router cutter. It's easier to laminate the arms with the mortise in them, gluing up in odd moments.

Any good dense hardwood can be used; manufacturers use beech and hornbeam. Fruit woods, oak and ash are equally successful. Brittle timbers are to be avoided, as they tend to split along the saw-cut in the moving arm.

Thickness a length of timber to exactly the same thickness as the metal bar, then twice as much for the outer layers. Glue a long and a short inner section on to an outer layer. Hold an offcut of bar in the mortise position and cramp tightly up to it, thus making an easy and extremely accurate mortise. When it's thoroughly dry, glue on the other outer layer, taking care to clear out any glue from the mortise. The second arm is treated identically. Clean up the edges and try the bar. If the sliding arm fits too tightly, pull through a piece of bar with an end roughened from the hacksaw or tapped lightly with a hammer. The tiny hook-like edges will give just sufficient clearance — much more accurate than paring or filing.

To remove the cut-out, cramp the two arms together, then either drill two 10mm holes, sawing and paring out the waste, or remove it by routing. Drill a small terminal hole in the moving arm and make the saw-cut. Shape the ends, then drill for the 5mm steel dowels. The ones in the moving arm must be very accurately positioned.

On commercially made lever-cam cramps, a portion of the centre section of the moving arm is removed and a 5mm lever is fitted. By hand methods this slot is quite difficult to make. In the more traditional method shown here, the two outer sections can easily be pared away, while the slot in the lever presents no problem.

The shape of the cam is important. A poor shape can result in a lever which will not hold its pressure but will tend to spring open. The ideal shape derives from the spiral, only part of which is used, whose construction was illustrated last month. Draw twelve 30°/60° radii, then circles 1mm apart to suit the component to be used. Six will probably be enough. Plot the curve, moving out one circle at each radius. Transfer the useful part of the spiral to the wood and shape, a job for which a disc sander is very useful. Drill and shape the lever then hold it in place and drill through the arm. Fit the pin permanently.

Glue on the cork jaws (cut from a thin cork tile) then test the cramp out. Varnish or oil the tool and drill a small hanging hole in the bar. Remember that this is a light-duty cramp, designed mainly to hold components together while gluing. It isn't intended to crush up poorly fitting joints.

A smaller version can be made using 20x5mm bar. These jaws could also be extended a little. If the fixed arm is not riveted through, but drilled the same as the moving arm, steel bars of different lengths can be used. One cramp is never a lot of use, so while you're set up for the job, make a pair, or better still, four. ∎

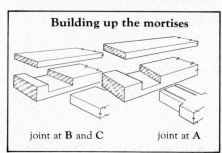

Building up the mortises

joint at **B** and **C**   joint at **A**

Win a **Woodworker Show Award** send for your entry form *today*

If it's Worth Making, it's Worth Exhibiting...

The Woodworker Shows
– where craft comes alive

Cabinet-making, woodcarving, musical instruments, marquetry, toys, woodturning, model horse drawn vehicles...there's a competition class for everyone!

LONDON
October 23rd – 26th at the
Alexandra Pavilion,
Wood Green, London

BRISTOL
May 16th – 18th at the
Bristol Exhibition Centre,
Canon's Road, Bristol

Send for your entry form for **Bristol** or **London** to:

Woodworker Shows '86,
Argus Specialist Exhibitions Ltd,
Wolsey House, Wolsey Road,
Hemel Hempstead, Herts. HP2 4SS.

Tel: 0442 41221

The London and Bristol Woodworker Shows are organised by Argus Specialist Exhibitions and sponsored by Woodworker Magazine

WIN!

● **Elektra Beckum's newest precision table-saw**

● **The HDM lathe, with a full metre between centres**

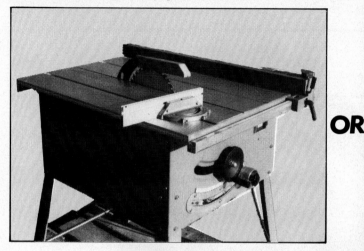

OR

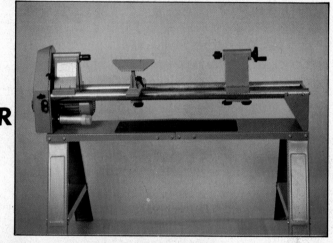

SQUARES AND ROUNDS

There are two types of woodworker — and **Woodworker**, in association with Elektra Beckum, proudly announces a competition for them both. The ones who work in squares — the joiner/cabinetmakers — can win a new table-saw; the ones who work in rounds — the woodturner/carvers — can win over £500 worth of lathe!

THE PRIZES

THE SQUARES

Elektra Beckum's PK250 precision table-saw is their latest addition to a range of serious machinery. It has a 700x900mm table, and its motor puts out 3hp at full tilt. The rip-fence is full-length, and it locks front and rear; a crosscut fence is also standard. It comes with a 10in TCT blade, 45° tilt-arbor, and rise-and-fall; it will cost at least £500 retail.

THE ROUNDS

The HDM 1000 lathe's chrome steel bed gives you 1000mm between centres. You can turn bowls up to 15in diameter; it has 4 speeds, and a faceplate and drive dog come as original equipment. The head- and live centre tailstock are both diecast, both with double bearings, and there's a spindle brake. It's worth over £500 with the stand.

Runners-up in both categories will get boxed sets of *Richard Kell's* wonderful measuring tools.

THE COMPETITION

What you have to do: make any item (out of wood, of course) that includes a chessboard. It's as simple as that. **But** we'll be judging originality and imagination, as well as craftsmanship; so you can make a chessboard on its own, or you can make something that incorporates one. It can be a chair, a chest, a table or a cabinet — anything as long as it has a built-in chessboard!

What you have to do: the woodturner/carvers are challenged to come up with an ingenious set of chessmen — or draughts, or a set of pieces for any game, ordinary or extraordinary, that can be played on a chessboard. They can be as big as you like and as fantastic as you like; what we're looking for is imagination and craftsmanship.

Final judging of both categories will be at the Bristol Woodworker Show, 16-18 May.

THE RULES

1 Entries must consist of:
● A photograph of your work
● A written description (no more than two A4 sheets) of the idea and the techniques used
● Dimensioned drawings
2 Entries must be sent to **Woodworker Squares and Rounds Competition, 1 Golden Sq, London W1R 3AB by Monday 21 April 1986**
3 If you can't finish by 21 April but still want to enter, send a perspective drawing by the closing date instead of the photo,

along with your description and drawings
4 You can't enter both categories
5 Entries selected for final judging will be displayed at the **WOODWORKER SHOW, BRISTOL, 16-18 May, and will be judged there by, amongst others, master-cabinetmaker Alan Peters**
6 Decisions of the judges and *Woodworker* magazine are final in all matters concerning the competition

OLD IS BEAUTIFUL

Apart from the fact that old tools are pretty, many people swear they're better than modern ones. We visit two emporia of the past

Bristol fashion

Bristol designer Charles Stirling sells old tools, and makes new ones in the historic tradition. Adrian Booth took a close look

Bristol Design has a window to turn a woodworker's head. It's filled with quality woodworking tools, built to last several life-times. Familiar, rare and unusual implements sit side by side; items like a chamfer-plane, made nearly 100 years ago by some forgotten cabinetmaker who carved notches into the oak body to match the position of his fingers.

Proprietor Charles Stirling (BSc, PhD) describes himself as a design consultant and woodworker. He set up Bristol Design five years ago, to combine consultancy with furniture making and the sale of quality tools through the shop and by mail-order. His scientific research background helps explain his detailed approach to problem-solving, whether it's making a piece of furniture, or advising on a tool for a specific task.

Like many new woodwork businesses, Charles Stirling's grew from a hobby. From doing small jobs for friends on a semi-commercial basis, Bristol Design developed with the idea that furniture making would be supplemented with general building work. But the work quickly moved away from site carpentry, plumbing, electrics and renovation, as Charles concentrated more and more on workshop work and making furniture.

As he did more woodwork, he noticed that the right hand-tools for special jobs were becoming increasingly hard (if not impossible) to find. This led to a particular interest in older second-hand tools, which in turn eventually led to finding tools for others with the help of local collector Graham Turner.

The next step was to start a side of the business that fills the need for the more specialist tools; manufacturing planes based on traditional British patterns. There is now a range of eight planes (with variations), made in limited numbers and bought largely by cabinetmakers and woodworking enthusiasts in Britain and abroad.

These planes are made with high quality bronze castings, traditionally sand-cast at a local foundry. They use Bristol Design's own wooden patterns, which have evolved as Stirling and Turner studied older planes

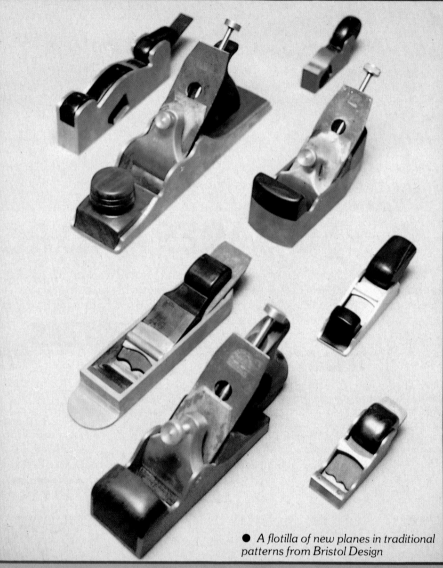

● *A flotilla of new planes in traditional patterns from Bristol Design*

and picked styles that seemed to work particularly well. The pair introduced slight modifications — putting a round bun, for example, rather than a square one, on a jack plane. The planes are not intended to be reproductions, but tools for the specialist user, built to last.

The castings are milled and surface-ground, then filled with rosewood or ebony. Many woodworkers would like to make their own unique plane, but lack metalworking facilities, so Bristol Design produce kits of machined, semi-finished metal bodies. They are ready for individual hand-detailing and filling with the pieces of ebony or rosewood that come with the kit,

roughly cut to shape. Supplied with good old irons, these kits offer the opportunity to make a truly personalised tool to fit your own hands.

Bronze is used for the castings because it is pleasing to the eye and it has the extra weight you need for use on awkward grain — plus it wears well. It doesn't corrode, or shatter if it's dropped, and it becomes dimensionally stable far earlier than cast iron. As far as they can gather from the foundry, says Charles, bronze is almost 100% stable straight after casting; they let the castings sit for six months to a year before machining anyway. Study of older planes revealed areas of possible wear, so

● *From the top: steel shoulder-plane filled with rosewood; ebony-filled old-pattern bronze plane with a steel sole; ebony-filled cast-iron plane*

some models are fitted with a steel sole-plate sweated and pinned into place, and one little chariot plane has a steel 'nose' let into the sole in front of the iron. Bristol Design occasionally supply one-off customised castings, and they also refurbish old tools.

Anyone in the business of supplying old tools will often be asked about the relative merits of old and new. 'We admit we don't always know the answers,' says Charles, 'but we do seem to find that cutting edges in old steel stay sharp longer. We put this down to economics.

'Older tools were made in relatively small numbers for professional users where a livelihood depended on them. This meant that only the best available materials were used and a great deal of care and attention went into making each tool.

'These specialist tools, for a specialist market, were very expensive in relation to wages. Even in the '20's, a Norris plane would have cost two to three weeks' wages. Mass production started changing this when Stanley, then Preston and Record, began to replace traditional lines. The new planes were capable of doing most jobs as well, and at considerably lower cost. The specialist could still buy traditional tools, but the falling demand made them uneconomic to produce. Stanley used to make 200 different types of plane, and 50-60 types of spokeshave!

'But of course there's a greater variety of router bits now than 20 or 30 years ago. Techniques have changed with the advent of power tools, and the change in the market has left some of the hand-tool work unsupported by a tool industry which must mass-produce to survive.'

Charles points out that this also applies to the steel used in cutting edges. 'The big market for chisels or planes seems to be the occasional DIY person who neither knows a good edge nor wants to pay for it. A modern plane iron, for example, has to be stamped out; better steels are more difficult to stamp, and take more expensive heat treating.'

Older tools, claim Bristol Design, are less expensive than new ones, and can provide higher quality. Some are collector's items, but in Charles' experience, collectors and users don't often clash. 'Is a user a collector if tool is bought and used only occasionally? At that level, I think it's irrelevant.

'Some older tools are also better suited to specific jobs than modern techniques. A moulding plane can be faster than a router or spindle moulder on a small job, and wet new pine needs a lot of denibbing with sandpaper after being cut with a router. Spokeshaves or draw-knives can give the user a freedom not easily achieved with a machine. A wooden brace makes sighting spindle holes (in chairmaking) easier than a metal brace. There are many examples.'

Charles says that tools evolve over time to do specific jobs, and once they work, they become standard. 'This can suggest times when a traditional tool is a better choice than a new one. If you are making a reproduction 18th century table it might not be appropriate to use a biscuit jointer.'

As far as choosing old tools goes, says Charles, 'Age by itself means very little. Age, quality and maker are all important to the collector. For most people it's quality that should be the criterion, with price a consideration. Quality isn't easy to define, and judging it only comes with experience. The best thing is to look at a number of tools. Some names are an indication of course, but I don't personally believe in just being a name-hunter. Look at catalogues of old tools, read some of the books on tools, then try them'.

Older, quality tools can be found in all sorts of places — junk shops, antique markets, flea markets, car boot sales, and of course specialist tool shops. The range is obviously greater in the tool shops, and Bristol Design claim that prices can be even lower than in junk shops. Charles had a tale to illustrate his point: 'I had a fellow in here the other day who had passed my place many times, but never came in until he had collected a lot of moulding planes from his local junk shop. He'd been told they were rare, and paid £7 each for them. When he finally came in here he found I was selling them for half the price!'

Bristol Design are always on the look-out for better quality tools, and Graham Turner covers most of the country buying. They've also built up a string of useful contacts who keep a look-out for specialised items. 'That's what makes selling second-hand tools a silly thing to do,' says Charles. They have to spend so much time looking for tools, and then keep such a range in stock, that it ties up a great deal of money. 'At least, an accountant would say we're silly!'

Charles himself uses a great variety of tools for his own woodworking, from machinery to an old Stanley smoothing plane, and a newish 12-year old Record jointer plane. 'I often try out tools from the shop. On some jobs I've only been able to get a good finish with a traditional Norris or Spiers. Usually I use a more modern plane, 10-30 years old. All my chisels are now old ones, and so are my screwdrivers. A lot of old tools have replaced my newer ones — they just feel better.' ∎

● Bristol Design, 14 Perry Road, Bristol BS1 5B6, tel. (0272) 291740. Phone first if you're coming from a distance.
SPECIAL OFFER! Bristol Design has a special deal for members of the Guild of Woodworkers . . . see the Guild pages for details.

Collections to use

When is a collector not a collector? David Savage talked to Tony Barwick at his London shop

'I've been surrounded by tools for most of my life — my father was a good carpenter, even though it wasn't his trade, and my grandfather, like his father before him, was a cabinetmaker in Hull. So I've been in the atmosphere of tools and things most of my life. However, I really began to get interested in woodworking tools about 12 years ago, and 10 years ago I set up a stall in London's Portobello Road street market, initially to dispose of the result of over-enthusiastic bidding at an auction. Business went well, and eventually led to my shop in Islington.

When I started, the aim was to sell to both users and collectors, with the emphasis on people who use tools. It still is — 85% of my sales are to users rather than collectors, although the boundary between them is often vague. The pure collector, who has nothing to do with any trade, and never touches the tools once they're safe in a display case, is a rare bird. A lot of collectors do use tools, but not to make a living. That's the real difference. What some people don't realise is that it was the early collectors who really discovered old tools before the users. There have always been people who valued good old tools, but it never really gelled until the collectors started searching them out of their hiding places in sheds and attics.

A good example is Norris planes; I bought my first only a few years ago after a few month's searching. Now you find them in most auctions because other people now realise their value. After the last war, many people thought that hand-tools would never be used again, and many were destroyed or scrapped. However, tools have been made commercially in this country for over 200 years, and there are craftsmen everywhere — so there's still a lot out there. It should be pointed out that probably less than half the tools here are practical to use. Many have suffered from the ravages of time, others have been replaced by better modern versions. Yes, some 18th century moulding planes are usable, but an awful lot are warped or misshapen. Frankly, anyone who wants to use one of the 18th or 19th century braces has got to be a masochist.

I occasionally get asked why woodworkers expect old tools to perform better than new ones. A lot depends on the individual. People prefer to use, say, an old metal plane because they get a better result than with the modern equivalent. It feels nicer to use — it handles better — because for one the steel of the blade, which is after all half a plane, is better, and, two, a lot more care went into the making. 19th century tools were very, very good, because there were a lot of manufacturers in a very competitive market during that time, and if tools weren't any good, they didn't sell.

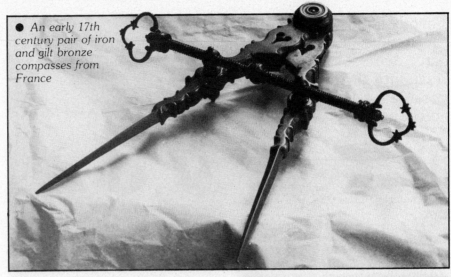

● An early 17th century pair of iron and gilt bronze compasses from France

This doesn't mean that all old tools are automatically good. You should check even a Norris plane before you buy! Put it through its paces by checking that it's square, the blade is good and still has plenty of life in it — in fact, all the things you should check when you buy any plane. There are differences between one plane-maker and another, and even between one example of a maker's product and another.

The best makes to look out for are Norris, Spiers, and Matheson. However, there are some very good — and very bad — tools that were made by users. You could buy the casing, add the wedge and bridge, and do the rest of the work yourself. Some of the people who did that made very nice planes — and some made rather nasty ones! The main advantage of these planes nowadays is that they are cheaper than the 'name' planes, but they shouldn't just be dismissed. They're the obvious starting point for a collection if you're not made of money, and want to use something as well as have it as an antique tool. Other possibilities for starting a collection are moulding planes and old chisels, but they're much harder to get. They're more for using than collecting, really; you look at an old piece of furniture and you say, now what made that?

If you've got an old wooden tool that you want to clean up, float off the dirt with linseed oil (not too much) and clean up the metal with WD40 if it's not too rusted. If the blade has had it, and you want to use the

● This basket of thumb planes could have come from an instrument maker or a ship's carpenter

tool, you'll have to get another blade. If it's 18th century or earlier, I'd suggest keeping the blade, but you'll be unlikely to want to use such a tool anyway.

It's a mistake to think that tools were ever cheap — a pre-war Norris plane cost about two week's wages. Would you pay over £200 for a plane these days? This is why many users made their own tools.'

● Old Woodworking Tools, 288 Upper St, London N1, tel. 01-359 9313.
See also 'Old planes in new hands', WW/April 1985.

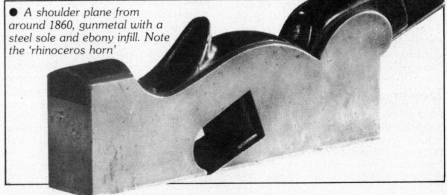

● A shoulder plane from around 1860, gunmetal with a steel sole and ebony infill. Note the 'rhinoceros horn'

Wood in the hole

There's nothing so humble or simple as ledge-and-brace doors — until you delve into their subtleties. For Alan Thomas, it's no open-and-shut case

There is more to the humble ledge-and-brace door than meets the eye. They look — and are — simple, but it is very easy to spend time and money on them and end up with a disappointing result.

Why bother anyway? There is no shortage of ready-made doors in DIY shops and builder's merchants, and very good doors they are too. Mainly imported, they are well finished in smooth, clean, knot-free timber — which, to judge from specimens in the shops, is well seasoned and shows no sign of going into winding. And, of course, demolition contractors often keep and are willing to sell any joinery they find in good condition. If there is a choice of new for those willing to pay, and secondhand for those who don't mind some work, why make doors?

A common reason is the desire to fit out old property with sympathetic joinery. The humble cottage of yesterday, today a desirable residence, usually had ledge-and-brace doors in its earlier existence which may well have been replaced by factory-made units during later rebuilding. Unfortunately door openings were often made to what are now non-standard dimensions, so factory-produced doors must be trimmed to fit and therefore look awkward. If ledge-and-brace doors are called for, professional joiners would charge a fortune for making them to a high standard that can easily be achieved at home.

My interest in ledge-and-brace doors began many years ago in what the estate agents, with a fine turn of phrase, described as a 'character-style house'. It contained a mixture of ugly doors, most of which were hardboard panelled in the fashion of 20 or so years ago. Two exceptions, both ledge-and-brace with beaded boards, looked fine; others were made to match. Then into my life came a very old cottage, still with two doors that may well have been original, made about 1800. They were at least rural 1860ish. A much-needed total rebuild meant the cottage also needed a set of doors, and they were made with very little trouble. Around the same time other minor matchboarded jobs came to hand and provided opportunities to experiment.

Design

Most people have seen a great many ledge-and-brace doors, without actually looking at them. Look carefully at some, and it soon becomes clear that there are no hard and fast rules of proportion like the ones for ordinary panelled doors. Ledges (the

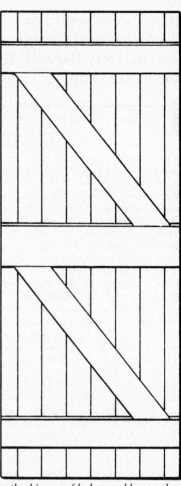

● *The correct placing of the braces in relation to the hinges of ledge-and-brace doors is vital. Where should the hinges go on the one on the right*

horizontal parts of the framing) can be two or three in number and not necessarily the same width as the braces, or diagonals. Indeed there need be no braces at all, if the ledges are wide enough. Often modern doors are made with outer framing as well, but these are more robust and better suited to a garden shed; inside doors should be simple, and even, to some degree, flexible.

What about the matchboarding that goes on the face of the door? Everyone knows the universally available kind: finishing about 3½in wide and ½in thick, tongue-and-grooved, and chamfered so you get a vee-groove when the boards go together. There's nothing very wrong with this stuff, but its narrow width is out of character with the time when 6in and 8in boards were common currency. The wider boards, of course, also reduced the amount of work to be done. And that vee-groove brings 10,000 knotty pine kitchens instantly to mind! Years ago beads were almost invariably used in simple hand-made joinery, and even in a thoroughly modern house beads look much more comfortable than the near-universal vee.

A more subtle objection to ready-for-use material is that most sawmills take timber as it comes, and machine it. Modern softwoods generally dry out after they are bought, with the result that the matchboarding cups a little across its width. The

cups produce hollows on the face of a door, and can look ugly.

The solution is to plane up the boards yourself. Not only will you save money, but delivery of both boards and finished doors will be prompt!

So far as 'design' is concerned, it's worth laying out (to a large scale) the widths of the finished boards, and also the positions of the framing members. Material thicknesses vary somewhat. My originals had boards 8in wide and only ⁹⁄₁₆in thick. The same stuff was used also for the two ledges, and the results appeared perfectly adequate despite the absence of bracing. Another specimen of uncertain age, probably made about 1880, has boards measuring 6x¾in; top and bottom ledges and both braces are 4¾x¹¹⁄₁₆in; and the centre ledge is 6½in wide. Others hover between the two.

It's most important to place the diagonals so that they are in compression not tension when the door is hanging on its hinges.

Bear in mind that the centre-line of each bead on the front does not coincide with the single joint crack on the back. This seemingly trivial detail threw me rather when positioning — from the back — a letterbox which is now off-centre on the front. At this stage some juggling with board widths will guard against the outer ones being excessively narrow.

● *125 years old, this unbraced door uses rebated boards beaded both sides*

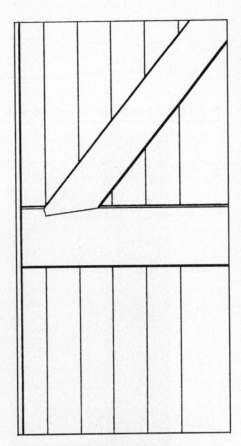

● *A toehold looks good but it's doubtful whether it makes a difference*

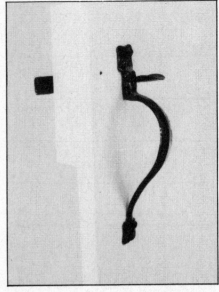

● *Rural style door furniture is best*

Door furniture

Make sure the ledges will be wide enough to accommodate the hinges, and that suitable latches or locks can be fitted. Door furniture is much a matter of taste, and some of my inherited hinges are malleable iron mock-antique. On a 'feature' door they look quite well, but really I prefer the ordinary tee-hinges, still sometimes called cross-garnets. I found a world of difference between the anaemic flimsy hinges sold in central London — all I could get — and the healthy robust things bought in a village ironmongers. The drawing top right overleaf shows the old original, undoubtedly hand-made, hinge from a cottage door. Ordinary butts not only look wrong, but also offer no support at all.

Latches are a problem. Really only Suffolk, or sneck, catches are suitable but modern offerings are nasty-looking bits of pressed metal hardly fit for a third-rate chicken coop. Not so many years ago a meatier cast-iron version called the Canadian latch was sold, but it may not be available now. Olde-worlde style fittings are usually grotesque. Anyone not daunted by the prospect of some hacksaw and file work could easily make acceptable Suffolk latches. A rim-lock screwed on to the surface looks odd, but the right one can be OK. I have come across some strange early- to mid-Victorian locks, simple, hand-made, and almost a cross between sneck and proper locks; I shall be making a couple.

Construction

Select the boards yourself. Buy them planed all round and square-edged, and avoid any with pith in them, large or loose knots, and shakes. It goes (almost!) without saying that bowed or twisted pieces should go back in the rack too. I always buy at least 10% more material than a job can need. It provides some room for manoeuvre in laying out boards, and you can always add to the come-in-useful-one-day stores. Cut the boards a trifle overlength and stack them for two or three weeks with sticks between them. Complaints about heaps of wood in lounge or bedroom must be ignored! If the design was a thorough job it will have shown the one or two boards in a door which could be made in two half-lengths. A little careful thought here can save long ends, otherwise wasted.

Begin by sorting the pieces and face-marking their convex sides — most will have a slight curve across the grain. They will also have another curve along the length; lay out the pieces so these bows counteract each other in neighbouring pieces. Put the worst in the middle, the straightest to the outsides, and number them. Take a try-plane and set-square to each edge of each board, getting them square, straight, and true — parallel too if possible, but a run-out of, say, 1/16in in a 78in board won't make a lot of difference. See if the two worst edges can be repositioned to the outer edges of the door, where they can be trimmed off during hanging.

This is not the place for a lengthy dissertation on moulding and similar planes, although anyone new to these curious and interesting tools might like to read 'Planes for re-moulding' in *Woodworker*, December 1984. Work from the 'wrong', or finishing end of the job, so shaving length is kept very short to prevent untoward splits and break-outs. At the first sign of fraying around a knot simply reduce the stroke even further. Matched tongue-and-groove planes make short work of their part in the process, and so will the beading plane once you both get going. On a five-door mass-production job I got an average over 30 boards of 25 minutes each, including tea-drinking time. Once a set is completed it should be temporarily assembled, and if possible laid flat so that the boards can begin to straighten themselves.

Failing the ideal of matched tongue-and-groove planes the correct width for the wood thickness, I have successfully machined board edges on a circular saw. All it needed was careful setting of the fence, and some trial cuts on waste wood. There would also be no objection to sawing a narrow groove in both edges of each board and using thin ply feathers — provided that a plain chamfer is used, or that the beads are proportioned accordingly. For one job it was helpful to have the tongue-and-groove offset rather than centrally placed; this worked out well using a tongue plane with a movable fence, and a modern grooving plane.

More recently a similar job in 9/16in material was handled with a pair of 3/8in planes, but working them against the back surface of the boards instead of the fronts. The object of this fiddling about was to permit the use of larger beads than was strictly suitable for the material thickness — a consideration to be borne in mind by anyone using feathers. For door boards of the usual nominal 5/8in thickness, 5/16in beads are about right, and can be cut to their full depth before the plane's built-in depth stop

Wood in the hole

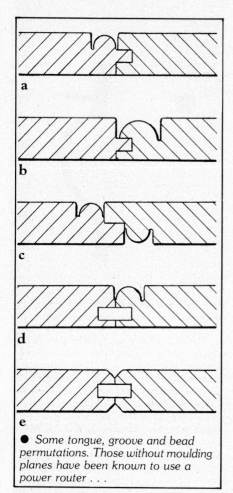

a

b

c

d

e

● *Some tongue, groove and bead permutations. Those without moulding planes have been known to use a power router . . .*

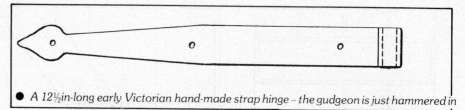

● *A 12½in-long early Victorian hand-made strap hinge – the gudgeon is just hammered in*

● *A two-part framed ledge-and-brace 'stable' door. Note the string-operated oak latch*

begins to ride the tongue. Larger beads mean deeper depth stops, so the tongue must be displaced toward the back. Quite recently some unreasonably large beads (⅝in) were successfully cut on too-thin ⅝in material (**b** above) — but on the grooved edge instead of the tongued; the bead was big enough to bridge the groove completely. If for some reason a double bead is wanted this would be the way to do it, again using narrow sawn grooves and a loose feather. For small beads in small quantities, the time-honoured scratch-stock will perform very well when a proper plane isn't available.

Assembly and hanging

Ledges and braces can be left square-edged, which looks clumsy, chamfered slightly, which was usual, or you can bead the ledges only. In any case the stuff really must be flat and true, but assess which sides will crown up if they are going to, and use them for the surfaces that will be seen.

Assembly is straightforward, but you need a large flat working surface. Work neatly, drawing faint lines to show where the nails will go, clamp lightly, and fix ledges first and braces last. One school of thought recommends that the outer boards only should be screwed, and that braces have their toe-ends let into the ledges (see previous page). Having tried both these refinements on some doors, and omitted them

from others, I can't see any difference.

For assembling most practicable thicknesses of material, 1½in or 2in oval nails are enough, provided they are punched well in. When the time comes to clench over the points it is well worth avoiding the usual practice of hammering them down across the grain. If instead, nails are bent over and punched along the grain they will create only easily filled slits, rather than a mass of woolly splintered bruising. If you are finishing a door with varnish or wax it would be worthwhile tracking down some rose-head nails.

Obviously ledge-and-brace doors can be arranged to swing in either direction, but they almost invariably have their hinges on the backs; hinges on the front just don't look right. If for some reason a door must open the 'wrong' way, then its ledges must not extend to the full width, otherwise it can't close properly against the frame rebates. Remember too that the jamb-fixed flap of the hinge sets the back of the *ledge* flush to the back of the door-frame; you can find yourself desperately moving door-stops or adding lumps to the door-frame if you haven't thought it out! ∎

290

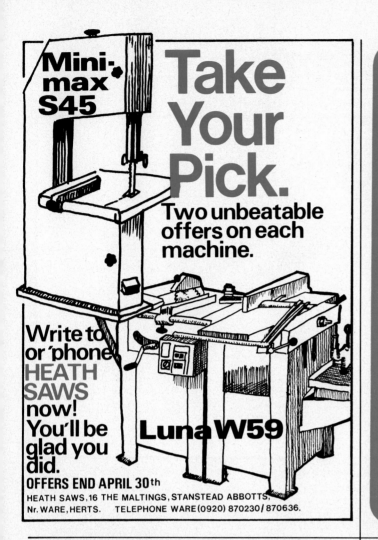

291

Coats of many colours:2

Ian Hosker's look at paint finishes concludes with some techniques that imitate nature — and may even flatter her!

Imitations may inspire the same admiration as the originals, if only in recognition of the skill required to produce a faithful copy. Last month I covered painting techniques that were decorative, pure and simple; this issue I'll be dealing with more sophisticated and adventurous effects, many of which imitate nature. They require more skill and judgement, but are't beyond anyone willing to practise and experiment.

Marbling

This technique was used in 18th century great houses because of the huge cost of using real marble on a grand scale. It was often used where it couldn't be minutely examined so the impression of grandeur was kept up and the cost down. If it's done well, only close inspection will distinguish it from the real thing.

The colour variations in marble are caused by high temperatures and pressures forcing coloured minerals into the main fabric of the calcium carbonate rock. Real marble seems to have a 'layered' quality — colour upon colour — which is stunning when imitated properly. To get something close to the original, you must keep a sample or photo of the real material to hand. What follows is a method for white marble with grey/black veins, but it can equally be applied to the multitude of other varieties, and even 'fantasy' marbles that you create yourself, relying more on

● *The glory of (painted) marble; finishing off the surface veins with a feather*

imaginative use of colour than reality.

Begin by preparing the surface in the way I described last month — briefly, repair, strip, sand, prime, fill and seal. Paint on a ground (base) colour of white eggshell or undercoat. Eggshell is preferable because its smooth and lustrous texture allows glazes to be manipulated easily. This ground can be lightly tinted with raw umber artist's oil colour to give it a greyish cast.

After the ground has dried thoroughly, draw in the deep veins. Squeeze equal quantities of black and raw umber oil colour on to an old saucer, and mix them up before thinning them to a liquid with

turpentine or white spirit. Pick up the paint on a small artist's brush, but not so much that a puddle is made on the work. The trick with veining is to apply the paint confidently and with a relaxed movement of the wrist. Hold the handle near the centre in the way a violinist grips the bow — the thumb below, the other fingers above. Now paint in the veins, with a general direction in mind, and with definite beginnings and ends. 'Fidget' the brush; that is, create slightly erratic lines with minor changes in direction, perhaps with branches (real marble doesn't have perfectly straight veins). There are no hard and fast rules about the number to draw, but remember that more veins will be added later, so you don't want a spider's web! Use a piece of marine sponge to absorb excess paint; this may smudge the veins, but it makes it more realistic. Allow it to dry for 24 hours.

Make up a paint glaze of two parts white eggshell (or undercoat) to one part turps, perhaps tinted with a little raw umber. Paint a thin coat over the work and don't worry about brush marks. Now gently pat the surface with a crumpled kitchen towel or marine sponge, which breaks up the coat and allows the deep veins to show through in some places. Paint in more veins as before on the wet glaze. They will look pretty crude and need to be softened and developed. Take a dry, soft bristled brush and gently stroke the veins along their length and then across. As if by magic, they blur and take on a more realistic look. Repeat the stroking until you are satisfied with the result; the veins should be fairly diffuse.

The drawback to all this is that is has to be done while the paint is still wet and capable of being manipulated — a relatively short time. You can increase manipulation

● *Cutting a figure with a graining comb*

time by thinning with a mixture of equal quantities of turps and boiled linseed oil rather than turps alone; however, this will increase the gloss. Paradoxically, the more you thin the paint the quicker it hardens. If you can get it, transparent oil glaze (untinted scumble glaze) tinted with white paint gives you more time and is more manoeuvrable. Large areas need to be divided up into sections, each marbled in turn. Allow 24 hours for drying.

There now remains the task of putting in surface veins, which are put in with a feather 4-6in long. Dip the tip in the veining colour and draw in the surface veins. The edge of the feather can be drawn sideways across the lines to tease out the wet colour into realistic veins.

Finally, when everything is thoroughly dry (after at least 24 hours), two or three coats of matt or eggshell polyurethane varnish will protect the work. What you should have is marble with depth — veins layered one upon the other. The method and colours should be modified to suit the work in hand or your own taste. One should experiment with different colours for each layer, but don't be too bizarre; it can destroy the effect you're trying to create.

● *Tortoiseshelling: lining separates two different coloured grounds*

Graining

At its best, wood-graining will pass for the real thing; at its worst, it's unbelievably awful! Unfortunately, we tend to see more of the bad and so it has acquired a corresponding reputation, despite its potential.

Graining relies heavily on the dragging techniques; some believe dragging itself developed from wood-graining. Scumble glaze is laid over a ground colour and manipulated to imitate grain texture and figure. Both the ground colour and glaze are normally sold ready made-up for a particular timber effect. They're usually only stocked by decorator's merchants, but a good retail outlet may be able to obtain some for you. A fantasy effect can be created using paint glazes or home-made oil glaze tinted with artists' oil colours. As with marbling, it's a good idea to have a speciment of the wood to be imitated at hand.

The undercoat is painted onto the prepared surface and allowed to dry. Thin the scumble glaze according to the manufacturer's instructions and brush it on fairly thinly. Allow a minute or two to pass for the glaze to settle before dragging a dry paint brush along the work, creating a series of alternating lines over the whole area. This forms the background grain texture upon which you will build the characteristic figure, but first soften the dragged lines by gently brushing across them.

You can buy special graining combs to create the figure; but you can also make your own from stout card by cutting a serrated edge. Look at your real wood specimen and note how its figure is formed; is it straight, angled to the general line of grain, or constantly changing direction? The way you cut the teeth will be influenced by these factors; then drag your comb through the wet glaze to simulate the figure.

Knots and certain types of figure cannot be copied with a comb. To imitate a knot, wrap a forefinger in a clean rag and place the tip on the wet glaze. Rotate your finger and then lift it away cleanly. Heartwood figure (which resembles contour lines on a map) can be simulated by using the edge of a cork and fidgeting it in. Alternatively, it can be painted in with a glaze of the appropriate colour and then softened with a dry brush along the grain. The medullary rays of oak are created by dragging across with the side of the bristles of an artist's brush, or even a feather. As with marbling, you can only get the right effect while the glaze is wet and mobile, so you must be brisk.

When you are happy with the result, allow the work to dry, then varnish it. Graining looks best under a matt or eggshell finish, but for exterior work use yacht varnish.

● *Spattering: make sure the brush isn't overloaded with this method*

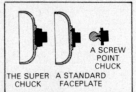

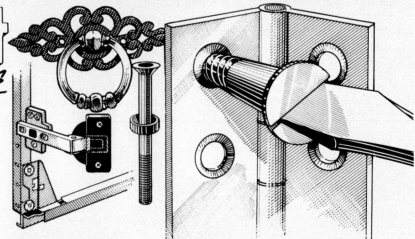
294

Coats of many colours:2

Tortoiseshelling

This spectacular effect is one of my favourites. Be warned — it can be overpowering on large areas. Nevertheless, it can be very effective on small table tops, trays or panels.

As the name implies, the idea is to imitate the carapace of the tortoise — actually, the hawks-bill turtle. Normally, natural colours are used, but there are no rules which say you must do so! Assuming that you use natural colours, what follows is the technique you should adopt.

The ground colour is a bright, strong yellow eggshell. This may seem rather bright, but what follows will darken it considerably. Paint over this a coat of dark oak polyurethane varnish. Break up the colour by zig-zagging the brush diagonally across the whole surface. Apply dabs of thinned burnt umber oil colour every two inches or so along each diagonal with a pencil brush. With a second brush, dab on thinned black oil colour between the umber — don't overdo the number of blotches or they will all blend into a uniform mess. Take your dry brush and soften the streaks by brushing along each diagonal and then across it. They will begin to blur and merge into the characteristic pattern.

Repeat the strokes along and across the diagonals until the pattern has blurred into a good imitation of tortoiseshell. The surface does not need protecting with varnish since polyurethane is already being used. However, if it's likely to take hard wear, gloss polyurethane may be used, which also gives an extra vitality to the finish.

A lighter tortoiseshell, called 'blond', is produced in exactly the same way but the ground is pale yellow, and light oak varnish is used. Leave out the black blotches, but still use the burnt umber. An amazing effect is created if the ground colour is gold or silver (either as leaf or high quality paint).

Stippling

This is easy. A paint (or oil) glaze is brushed thinly over the ground colour and the bristles of a dry brush are 'pecked' onto the surface. The glaze film is broken and the base colour shows through in a mottled pattern. Professionals use a special stippling brush which enables them to cover a large area quickly, but a 3 or 4in paint-brush will do for small areas.

Spattering

If you are sponging or stippling a surface, this technique can really liven it up. The aim is to spray a random series of (usually) dark spots on to the surface. Artists' oil colours thinned with turps may be used, although thinned dark paint will do.

Spattering may be done in a number of ways. For small areas an old toothbrush is dipped into the colour, held several inches from the work, and the surplus shaken off by running a thumb over the bristles to produce a fine spray. The spots will be quite fine, which may not suit your purposes. Another technique uses a small (½ or 1in) paint-brush loaded with colour. Take a piece of dowel in one hand, and hold it horizontal and parallel to the work. With the brush in the other hand, strike its stock against the firmly-held dowel so that spots of colour are thrown on to the work. Take care — if the brush is overloaded you will end up with a mess. Hold the dowel several inches from the surface — it's worthwhile practising on some scrap wood to judge the best distance.

Normally, spattering is done over a dry ground, but interesting patterns are formed if the paint is spattered on to a wet one. Spattering shouldn't be overdone; it's meant to highlight, not dominate.

'Porphyry' is an effect which uses spattering. Here a paint glaze is sponged on over a dry white ground. After it dries, thinned creamy white paint is sparingly spattered on to lift it. Finally, after this has dried, black is spattered on to the surface. If the paint glaze is terracotta or similar, the work will resemble ancient porphyry.

Final touches

For that added touch of class you could burnish the protective polyurethane coats to a perfectly smooth, polished finish. This is ideal for marbled work since we expect it in the real thing; however, for the others it may be just a little too perfect.

To get a good polish on varnish, you need to build up a fairly deep body, at least three or four carefully applied coats. Take a piece of felt and dip it into raw linseed oil. Pick up a little fine pumice powder on the oil and rub the surface, using a circular motion. This will grind down any irregularities such as brush-marks and adhering dust particles. Keep a wary eye on things as the grinding paste may cut through the varnish to the paint beneath. When the irregularities seem to have been removed, change the motion to straight lines along the work to eliminate the circular tracks. Finally, buff the work with a clean soft polishing rag.

You must give varnish plenty of time to harden before burnishing, because it will tear at the slightest hint of softness. 48 hours in a warm environment will probably be enough.

Wood finishing in all its forms is not a precise science. Of course there are some hard and fast rules; one of these is never say it will never work! The beauty of the techniques described in these two articles is that they are open to experiment, both in terms of colour combinations and their method of application. ∎

● For details of Ian Hosker's September course on **Decorative Techniques** see the Guild pages.

Craft afloat

If you plan to take to the water this summer, Dennis Davis' open canoe is fun to make and use

Canoeing is one of the fastest growing outdoor pastimes in Britain. The kayak, where the paddler sits on a low seat and uses a double-bladed paddle, is the most common craft; but the so-called Canadian, or open, canoe where the paddler kneels or sits on a relatively high seat and uses a single bladed paddle is becoming (in my view justifiably) more popular. It's ideal for two people, and my design, the Ojibwa, will take two adults, plus a child or touring equipment. It depends upon the weights involved and the amount of freeboard you want — I would suggest not less than 150mm between the waterline and the top of the sides.

The Ojibwa is a traditional open canoe, built with modern methods and materials. There are no woodwork joints as such, so this is really a project suitable for the woodworking beginner with a minimum of tools and expertise. There is also some scope for more experienced, or skilled, workers to exercise their talents.

You'll be able to build your Ojibwa on your own, but it will help if you can occasionally enlist an extra pair of hands. Choose a good quality plywood with three even-thickness veneers — 'stoutheart', where the centre veneer is thicker than the exterior pair, isn't recommended. Exterior-grade ply could be used to save money, but for longevity and looks, use a genuine marine grade. The gunwale strips may be of any straight-grained, knot-free timber; ash or one of the mahogany variations are suitable hardwoods, while spruce or Columbian pine are a little lighter and may be cheaper. Similarly, hardwood looks good for the end knees, thwarts or seats, but one of the better quality softwoods could be used. If you're keen to exercise your woodwork

skills, you can fit shaped thwarts or framed seats covered with woven cane or something similar. Where seats are fitted instead of, or as well as thwarts, they should be set about 100mm lower than the thwarts as shown on the general arrangement drawing. This makes for a more stable seating position — passengers should sit on the bottom of the canoe anyway, where they act as ballast.

Obtaining the glass-fibre tape and resin shouldn't present any problems; try the Yellow Pages or the supplier listed at the end of the article. When buying the resin, explain it's for a 'stitch-and-glue' canoe construction, and ask for safety recommendations. Any reputable supplier should help in this way, and will also be able to supply barrier creams, cheap plastic gloves, and other safety items. Buying this much resin and tape in High Street shops can be expensive. The monofilament nylon fishing line for the stitching is easily obtained from fishing tackle shops and some branches of Woolworths.

The Ojibwa canoe consists mainly of plywood panels 'stitched' together with nylon fishing line. The seams are sealed and reinforced by cladding them, inside and out, with a polyester resin/glass-fibre tape laminate; this is called 'taping'.

Construction

Mark out the plywood as shown in fig. 1; use an HB or softer pencil. Mark a centre-line parallel to the long side on the 'bad' side of both sheets of ply, and put one sheet aside until the other is cut out.

Starting at one end, mark lines across one sheet at 305mm intervals. Using this grid mark in the dimensions shown on the drawing; use one of the gunwale strips to join the marks. Check that all the measurements are correct and that the lines form fair curves; some of the lines are, of course, straight!

On this same sheet, draw a line across one end for the scarf joint, preferably with a lightly pressed marking gauge. This line must be set in 32mm from the end — eight

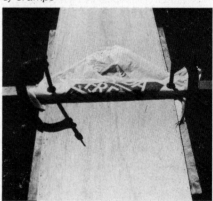

● *The ply cut out and ready for scarf jointing,* **above;** **below,** *cramping up the panel. Nuts and bolts can be used instead of cramps*

times the ply thickness. This scarf line must be marked on the second sheet of ply on the **opposite** side, so when the panels are joined the best side of each comes together.

Cut out the hull panels from the first sheet with a jigsaw, panel, or tenon saw. Use these panels as templates for marking out the second sheet. The panels are now ready for scarf-jointing together to form the full-length hull panels.

Start with the two halves of the bottom panel. Take one half and cramp it to a board — a piece of blockboard is ideal — with the scarf line on top, and the end of the panel flush with the end, or side, of the board. If you don't have a cramp, you can hold the

The Ojibwa canoe

all dimensions in mm

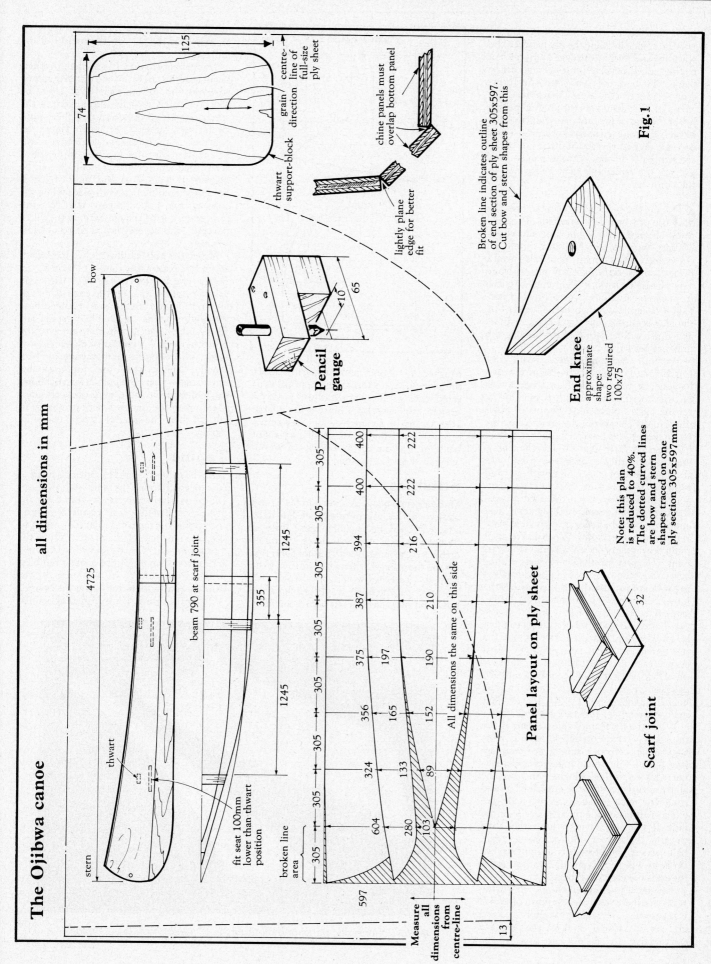

74
125

centre-line of full-size ply sheet

grain direction

thwart support-block

chine panels must overlap bottom panel

lightly plane edge for better fit

Pencil gauge

65
10

Broken line indicates outline of end section of ply sheet 305x597. Cut bow and stern shapes from this

Fig.1

End knee
approximate shape;
two required
100x75

bow

stern

thwart

4725

beam 790 at scarf joint

fit seat 100mm lower than thwart position

1245
355
1245

broken line area

305 | 305 | 305 | 305 | 305 | 305 | 305 | 305 | 305

400 | 400 | 394 | 387 | 375 | 356 | 324 | 280 | 604
222 | 222 | 216 | 197 | 165 | 133 | 103
210 | 190 | 152 | 89

All dimensions the same on this side

Panel layout on ply sheet

597

13

Measure all dimensions from centre-line

Note: this plan is reduced to 40%. The dotted curved lines are bow and stern shapes traced on one ply section 305x597mm.

32

Scarf joint

297

Craft afloat

panel perfectly well by kneeling on it on the board to plane it. Plane the ply between the scarf line and the bottom edge of the ply to a feather-edged bevel. A fine-set smoothing plane is the best tool to use, but a Surform-type plane with a new, sharp blade is adequate. It's essential that no thickness is left at the end of the hull panel, and that the bevel is flat, or even slightly concave — **not convex.** Repeat this on the other side of the second half of the bottom panel; then prepare the remaining eight half-panels in the same way.

Gluing the scarf joints also requires the use of a board — an offcut of 18mm-thick blockboard 600mm long and about 200mm wide is suitable, and should be cheap and easy to obtain. You'll also need a piece of softwood 600x50x37mm, with one side planed to form a slight convex curve from end to end. This forms a 'pressure bar' to hold the scarf joint tight to the board while the glue is curing. Two G-cramps, or bolts and nuts, will be required for holding the pressure bar to the board.

Try your scarf-jointing set-up with a dry run before you glue it. Position the two halves of the bottom panel (good side down) on the board, with the scarf joint in the centre; have a piece of newspaper or polythene under the area of the joint to stop the ply sticking to the board. Check that the two halves are correctly aligned — use the centre-line for sighting. Cover the joint with another piece of paper or polythene, and position the pressure bar on the joint, convex side down. Fix it in this position with a cramp or bolt at each end, tightened just enough to hold the paper/polythene in place at the centre (see photo). When you've got it right, repeat the process with glue in the scarf joint. To prevent the half-panels sliding apart under the pressure bar, pin both halves to the board with two panel pins through the joint. Before nailing the pins right home, snip off their heads to make it easier to get the panel off the board. The bottom panel must be glued alone, but it's better to glue the remaining panels in pairs since this will ensure each pair are identical — and save time! Place paper or polythene between each pair as well as between the lower and the board, and also check (with a dry run) that the bar is applying pressure in the centre.

While the scarf joints' glue is curing, make the six thwart support-blocks from 12 rectangular ply offcuts, using a card template (see fig. 1). Glue them together in pairs to make six 8mm-thick blocks, and when the glue has cured, round the outside edges and roughen the inside face as a key for the glue which will fasten them to the inside of the hull. If you are having seats rather than thwarts, the support-blocks may be cut in half vertically to provide end supports, but the seats will also need support strips under the ends between the blocks.

You have to roughen the ply to get the resin to adhere well, because when plywood is made the outer faces are compressed and go shiny, which makes the surface unreceptive to glues. The area to be

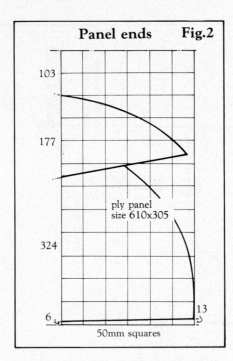

roughened is about 25mm from the edge of the plywood, and the easiest method is to scrape the surface with a short piece of broken hacksaw-blade. Since quite a large area has to be scraped — all the interior seams — you'll find it easier to fit the piece of blade into a saw-cut in a scrap of wood, which will act as a handle.

Stitching

Make a pencil gauge as shown in fig. 1, and use it to mark a line round all the edges to be stitched. Drill holes along these lines at 65mm intervals. You can make a suitable drill from a 50mm nail with the head snipped off and the point sharpened with a file; or the right-size bradawl would also work. It's essential that the holes are drilled from the same end on each panel to ensure that they

match. Roughen the area for taping as already described — on the **inside** of the hull panels.

The panels can now be stitched together. Begin near the scarf joint and fasten the chine panels to the bottom panel first. Don't be too concerned initially about getting the stitches tight; go back and pull them tight after every couple of feet. Have the continuous line on the outside where it will be cut away when the outsides of the seams are planed smooth. At the ends it will be helpful to have a second pair of hands holding the chine panels in place while the stitches are pulled tight. It's not too important if gaps remain here, as they'll be covered with several layers of resin/glass laminate.

When the hull is fully stitched together it should be reasonably rigid. Put it on a level floor, check the panels are correctly together, and block up the ends 20mm at about 380mm from the ends. To make sure the hull remains 'true' while taping the seams, place a weight in the centre of the bottom panel — a couple of plastic bags of earth, or some bricks on newspaper, will do. Finally, check that the hull remains untwisted — that both ends are vertical, and the panels at the same angle on both sides. Manipulate the panels where necessary to correct this. The interior is now ready for taping.

Taping

Tape the stitched seams by cutting a piece of tape to length to suit the seam — allow about 75mm overlap where tapes meet. Coat the ply each side of the seam liberally with resin and stipple the tape into this resin, trying to keep the tape flat against the ply. When the tape is properly wetted-out with resin it will appear transparent. Stipple out air bubbles, which are a source of weakness in the laminate, and add more resin as necessary.

225gm of resin will impregnate about half

● *Part of one side panel and all three lower panels have been stitched*

of one strip of tape — from one end to the scarf joint. Don't mix too much at once, or it will cure before you can use it all. Begin taping inside one end, and repeat for all interior seams. Apply a second layer of tape inside the ends.

Where the instructions call for a second layer of tape, it should be applied when the first layer is touch-dry rather than fully cured. The final layer may be glasspapered smooth, and for a better finish you can apply a thin coat of resin only over the smoothed tape.

Do take appropriate precautions when using the resin/fibreglass. Wear a face mask to minimise breathing or ingesting resin dust when glasspapering the cured laminate. The taping must be done in a temperature of at least 15°C (60°F) to enable the resin to cure correctly, but ventilation should be provided to allow fumes to dissipate. Working outdoors in summer shade is perhaps ideal! A few people may be allergic to resin, and glassfibre can irritate the skin, so it's sensible to take precautions by wearing barrier creams and plastic gloves to avoid skin contact as far as possible.

● *The end knee, gunwale strip fastenings, and stern thwart*

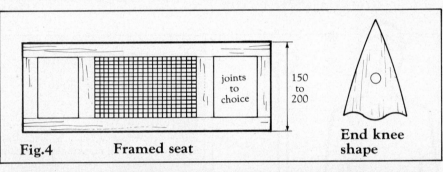

Fig.4   **Framed seat**

End knee shape

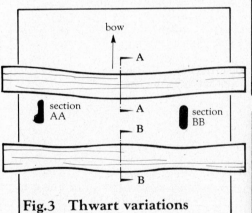

Fig.3   Thwart variations

Gunwales, knees and thwarts

When the interior taping is completed and the resin cured, the end knees and gunwale strips can be fitted. The end knees have to be planed to a reasonable fit; they are then glued and nailed into place with two Gripfast nails from each side. Mark the nail positions lightly on top of the knees with a pencil.

Begin fixing the gunwale strips at one end, where the strips are glued and screwed through the hull panels to the knees — avoid the nails when driving home the screws. Continue fixing the strips with glue and Gripfast nails at about 100mm intervals. Have the strips a little below the top edge of the ply to allow for this to be planed smooth later. Nail from the inside and hold a heavy hammer, or metal weight, against the outside to take the pressure of nailing. Cut the strips to length after fixing.

The thwarts or seats can now be fitted. Begin with the centre thwart, the front edge of which is 355mm back from the interior

● *The thwart support-block glued and pinned into position*

scarf line. Cut a little over-length to allow for fitting. When the thwart is the correct length the hull beam should be 790mm at the scarf point, **excluding** the gunwale strips. The height of the top of the thwart should be about 300mm from the bottom panel, but this may be varied to suit personal preferences. Seats should be about 200mm from the bottom panel.

The holes in the thwart support-blocks will vary a little in shape according to which thwart they are supporting. These holes are most easily cut using a jig- or coping saw, and finishing with a wood rasp. The thwarts should be rounded except at the ends, where they fit into the blocks.

To fix the thwart, slide the blocks on to the thwart, position it in the hull and glue and nail it into place, using a pair of Gripfast nails at each end. Apply glue to the inside faces of the blocks, and hold them in position against the hull using a G-cramp, or metal weight, while nailing from the outside. Clean off the glue with a damp cloth before it cures.

Craft afloat

Finishing

With all the thwarts or seats fixed, the canoe is ready for exterior tidying and taping.

Plane all the external seams smooth and rounded; fair the ends to suit, and plane the top edges of the gunwales smooth and rounded. Tape the external seams as already described — try to ensure that the tape lies neatly since it will be more apparent on the outside. The ends and bottom seams may be given two layers of tape; a 50 metre roll is enough. The external finish may be improved by glasspapering the tape/resin and applying a thin coat of resin only.

The bottom panel may be stiffened by taping **across** it on the inside at about 150mm intervals, particularly at the paddling positions. If the canoe is likely to have rough use, the bottom may be protected by cladding with a layer of thin glass cloth, or chopped strand mat, and some more resin.

Painter fixings may simply be 10mm holes in each of the end knees, or you may tape a piece of shaped wood into each end of the canoe and drill the holes through the hull and these blocks. The canoe is now ready for glasspapering and finishing.

Paddle

A single-bladed paddle may be bought or made. Making one is not difficult, but will require a spokeshave and some rubber rings obtained by cutting sections from an old — but not rotted — car inner tube. These are used to hold the two blade sections to the shaft while it is being glued together (fig. 5).

Safety

When using your canoe do take sensible precautions and wear a life-jacket or buoyancy aid at all times. The photo is of a trial in inches-deep water, I should add! Children should always wear a BSI-approved life-jacket. It's also sensible to provide the canoe with buoyancy to enable it to remain fully afloat even when loaded with equipment and water. You can get shaped inflatable bags which fit into the ends of the canoe, or small blocks taped into the hull at appropriate places.

Happy paddling! ∎

● Readers' queries should be sent to Dennis Davis, Tomain-nan-Eun, Isle of Coll, Argyll PA78 6TB; please include a s.a.e. or international reply coupon.

Suppliers

Plywood, timber, fastenings: York Marinecraft, Worthington St, Bradford BD8 8HB

Plywood: Reliable Plywood Co. Ltd, Warburton St, London E8 3RR

Resin, glassfibre tape: Trylon Ltd, Thrift St, Wollaston, Northants NN9 7QJ

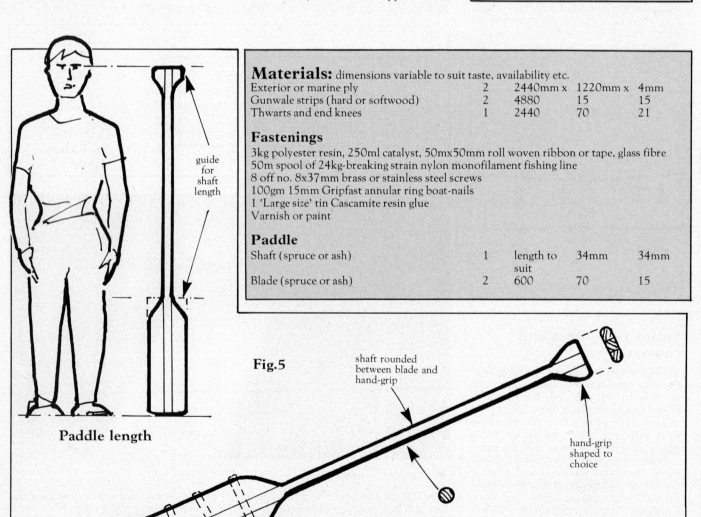

guide for shaft length

Paddle length

Materials: dimensions variable to suit taste, availability etc.

Exterior or marine ply	2	2440mm x	1220mm x	4mm
Gunwale strips (hard or softwood)	2	4880	15	15
Thwarts and end knees	1	2440	70	21

Fastenings

3kg polyester resin, 250ml catalyst, 50mx50mm roll woven ribbon or tape, glass fibre
50m spool of 24kg-breaking strain nylon monofilament fishing line
8 off no. 8x37mm brass or stainless steel screws
100gm 15mm Gripfast annular ring boat-nails
1 'Large size' tin Cascamite resin glue
Varnish or paint

Paddle

Shaft (spruce or ash)	1	length to suit	34mm	34mm
Blade (spruce or ash)	2	600	70	15

Fig.5

shaft rounded between blade and hand-grip

hand-grip shaped to choice

sections

blade held to shaft with rubber bands while glue cures

Making the paddle

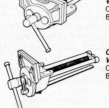

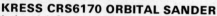

302

Card sharp

A neat and decorative cribbage board that doubles as a playing-card box, designed by John Trussell

● *Your deal – or rather, your contrasting pieces of walnut and sycamore . . .*

The box is designed to hold four packs of cards with the lid acting as a cribbage board. It's very much an exercise in accurate planing and gluing. There is no cutting list, because it's made from small pieces of walnut and sycamore, which provide an ideal contrast. Other combinations would do just as well.

The box is of conventional construction, a through-dovetail mitred at the corner with a rebate to take the plywood base. Below is an exploded view of this joint without the rebate.

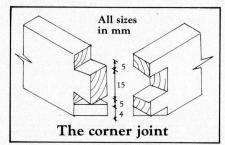

All sizes in mm

5
15
5
4

The corner joint

The interior is divided into four compartments, one of which is larger than the others to give room for peg storage. The partitions are 4mm thick, held in stopped housings and made to slide in from underneath.

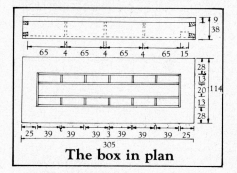

9
38

65 4 65 4 65 4 65 15

28
13
20 114
13
28

25 39 39 39 3 39 39 39 25
305

The box in plan

Make the dovetail joints, cut the housings and the rebates and glue the box together. Fit the partitions, polish them and glue them into place, followed by the plywood bottom. A 15x10mm piece of wood is glued in at the end of the widest section, with four 3mm holes drilled in it at an angle. (The angle of the holes means the pegs can be slightly longer than vertical holes would allow.) Clean up and polish the box.

The top should be made slightly larger than the box and then planed to fit. The gluing is done in stages, as shown below. In stage **a** allowance must be made for sawing into two strips and planing accurately. These pieces are very delicate at this stage and require careful handling. Cramp up carefully and make sure that the different pieces are level, or thickness will be lost at the cleaning-up stage.

Stage **b** could be done in two phases if this seems too big a step to take in one go. Stage **c** sees the end pieces glued into place. All that remains after removing the surplus wood is to glue on the side pieces slightly wider than required.

Clean up the top, planing both sides. Make it fit the box, keeping the pattern exactly in the centre. Mark lines across the width of the box to indicate the position of the holes. It's best to use a drill-stand to get all the holes exactly the same distance from each edge. Chuck up a 2.3mm drill and cramp a batten across the drill table so the

drill will make a hole the exact distance from the edge. Drill a row of holes on each side of the box, with the drill set to go only part way through the lid. Re-set the batten for the other row of holes and drill them. Drill two more single holes at each end of the centre-strip. The arrangement of the holes is shown in the photo inset.

Polish the lid with wax polish, and it's ready for hinging. It's well worth using solid drawn-brass butts and letting them into both the box sides and the lid. Be careful to choose a length of screw which won't go right through the lid.

The brass catches are designed to be held in place with brass pins, but there is room to drill a hole large enough to take a no. 1 brass screw and countersink it. Hold the box in the vice, protecting the lid, and screw the catches in position.

The pegs are made with a dowel plate. Take a strip of mild steel and drill two holes, one 3.3mm and the other 4mm. Saw strips of walnut and sycamore about 5mm square. Roughly round the strips with a chisel and tap them through the larger hole. It may be necessary to stop every now and then, remove the strip and take some more wood off with a chisel. If you try to force the wood through the hole you'll break it. Finally, pass the strips through the smaller hole — using the different-sized holes will give a better finish to the pegs. Chisel a blunt point on them, and glasspaper and polish them.

Glue some strips of ribbon on to the box base so that it will be easier to remove the packs of cards (photo). Add some baize to the bottom and the box is complete. ■

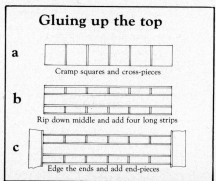

Gluing up the top

a

Cramp squares and cross-pieces

b

Rip down middle and add four long strips

c

Edge the ends and add end-pieces

WOODWORKER

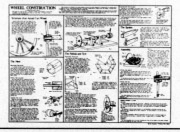

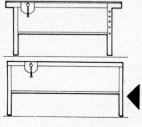

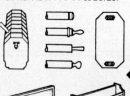
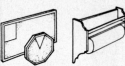

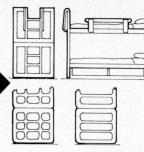

PLANS SERVICE

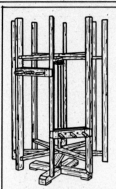

WARPING MILL
This warping mill design consists of a vertical revolving drum supported within a floor standing frame. The drum is fitted with pegs for securing the warp to, and the frame is complete with heck block for spreading warps up to 15-20 metres.
Plans No. DB 9 Price £3.20

SLOPING STYLE SPINNING WHEEL
This design is a replica of an authentic spinning wheel doem olden days, having a 486mm (19in) diameter wheel with bent wood rim. Plan is complete with mother-of-all, distaff, treadle operation etc. A feature of this wheel is its attractive turnings which make it a most decorative piece besides being functional. A design for the enthusiast woodturner. Two sheet plan.
Plan No. DB12 Price £5.40

UPRIGHT SPINNING WHEEL
In this vertical style spinning wheel the mother-of-all arrangement is situated above the main wheel. The latter is 460mm diameter and the rim is of segmented design. Simpler lines than the sloping wheel but nevertheless graceful in appearance and of course functional.
Plan No. DB 13 Price £5.40

NEW & REVISED FROM DAVID BRYANT
Full range illustrated in our Plans Handbook

DRUM CARDER
Sooner or later spinners graduate to a drum carder. This design takes the toil out of hand carding. It uses a positive gear/sprocket drive which also reduces the drag which the belt drive alternative imposes. A little metalwork as well as woodwork involved. One sheet plan.
Plan No. DB 55 Price £3.70

TABBY LOOM
A simple tabby loom having rollers, warp and cloth beams and fitted with a rigid heddle, and canvas aprons. Basic weaving width

380mm but plan can be adapted for other widths if desired. Ideal for beginners and it is surprising what can be achieved with warp and weft variations tufting etc.
Plan No. DB 2 Price £3.70

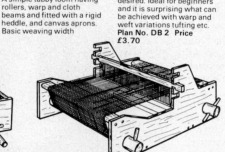

SPINNING STOOL
A spinning stool specially suited for use with the sloping bed wheel. Four legged arrangement, with richly carved seat and back. A good example of chip carving.
Plan No. DB 20 Price £3.20

DAVID BRYANT TOYS

TOYS 2
Six more exciting amusing toys, zig zag man, wobbly wheel dog, swinging monkey, woodpecker up a post and scissor toy. All drawn full size.
Plan No. DB 33 Price £3.70

TOYS
Exciting amusing toys for children. Five novelties all on one drawing including balancing clown, chinese tumbler, waddling duck, secret money box and commando climber. All drawn full size.
Plan No. DB 32 Price £3.70

TRADITIONAL ROCKING HORSE
A traditional style rocking horse. The original of this design is called Dobbin and still sees active service after many years in a doctor's surgery. Rugged construction with some scope for carving. A design to please any child. Saddle height 915mm.
Plan No. DB52 Price £3.20

85p

Woodworker PLANBOOK
1983/84
FURNITURE · MUSICAL INSTRUMENTS
MINIATURE FURNITURE · NOVELTIES
CLOCK CASES · TOYS AND MODELS

FAMOUS WOODWORKER PLANS HANDBOOK
STILL AVAILABLE

Price 85p plus 30p postage and packing (Overseas 65p)
★ Clock Cases
★ Spinning & Weaving
★ Artists Equipment
★ Kitchen Ware
★ Dolls House Furniture
★ Toys
★ Horse Drawn Vehicles
★ Furniture

The grand furniture saga: 3

From Gothic style to the birth of the re-birth: Vic Taylor's journey through the history of furniture arrives at the threshold of the Renaissance

● *A Florentine* Nerli cassone **above,** *resplendent with painted panels.* **Below,** *a late 15th century French throne-chair combines Gothic and Renaissance features*

Courtauld Institute Gallery

The Gothic style of furniture was the last before the Renaissance. It incorporated some features of the Romanesque style (WW/Feb) such as the lancet arch and arcading, and the 'foil' motif ('foil' is the Old French word for a leaf). This motif, of course, is found in trefoil, quatrefoil and cinquefoil decoration, and it was often infilled with delicate tracery. The coming Renaissance also showed itself in the use of human and animal figures, and plant and floral forms, as decoration; the point being that they were rendered naturalistically and sympathetically, not grotesquely or symbolically as they would have been in earlier times.

We must clear up the confusion about the term 'Gothic'. It's a complete misnomer when applied to architecture or furniture, as the power of the Goths was finally destroyed in 711, over 400 years before the first Gothic style church was built! The name was coined by Giorgio Vasari (1511-1574) who used it to disparage practically all the earlier styles of architecture. To him the Goths were such barbarians that it was impossible to believe they had any pretensions to culture. The term was resurrected during the 18th century, when it was usually spelt 'Gothick' and applied to a style of furniture vaguely supposed to be medieval.

Now comes the Renaissance, that re-birth of the love of knowledge for itself, and the desire to explore all avenues of human ability. It's worthwhile to sketch in the background against which the phenomenon took place in order to sharpen the contrast between 'before' and 'after'.

The before was a life in which all aspects were regulated — whether they were agrarian, economic, or industrial — and people lived and laboured as units in institutions such as manor, guild, or monastery. The shape of both social and economic activities was purely local, although some trade was carried on between country and town, or town and city. This parochialism was reinforced by the power of custom, to which all actions had to conform. Those which did not were frequently ignored. Moreover, the pursuit of wealth, the desire for material possessions, and such economic activity as there was were all rigidly controlled by the tenets of the Church.

Such an outlook was understandable in an age when ordinary people rarely travelled and communications were difficult. It's no exaggeration to say that people were more conscious of their rank or status than their nationality; they would regard themselves as knights or merchants, priests or serfs, rather than as Englishmen, Frenchmen or Germans. This view was strengthened by their common membership of the Church and their obedience to Rome; one could say that the social divisions of medieval civilisation were horizontal rather than vertical.

It is far from easy to pinpoint the beginning of the Renaissance, in either place or time. The confederation of the small Italian states into the Italian League in 1455 was an important factor, bringing a semblance of peace and stability to the area after 100 years of inter-state wars. At this time Florence emerged as a city of wealth, a focus of dynamic intellectual studies, and a centre for the production of things of beauty. Cosimo de Medici (1389-1464) and his grandson Lorenzo (1449-1492) created a Platonic-style academy where priceless manuscripts were available for study of Christian ethics and the classical philosophies, which had been amalgamated into the new 'humanism' by Petrarch (1304-1374). A new style of architecture evolved from Petrarch's combining activities, which embodied the classical precepts.

One early rediscovery was the treatise *De Architectura* by Vitruvius Pollio. He was a military engineer under Julius Caesar around 46 BC, who wrote this work on

Fig. 1

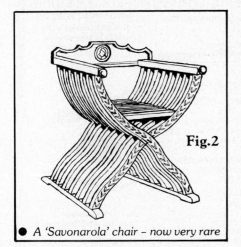

● A 'Savonarola' chair – now very rare

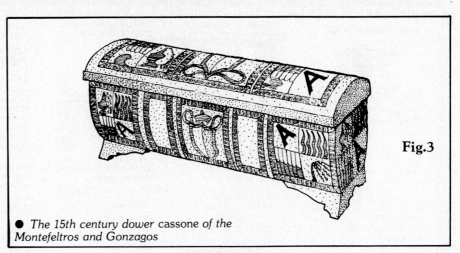

Fig.3

● The 15th century dower cassone of the Montefeltros and Gonzagos

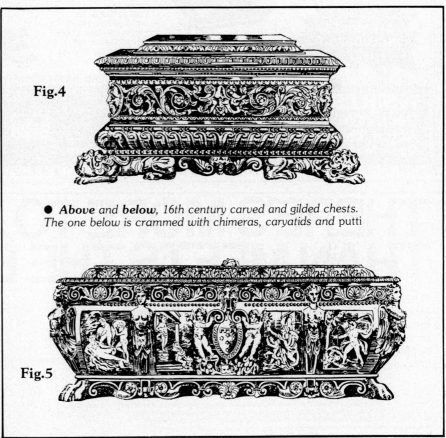

Fig.4

● **Above** and **below**, 16th century carved and gilded chests. The one below is crammed with chimeras, caryatids and putti

Fig.5

architecture in his old age and dedicated it to the Emperor Augustus. Its contents were employed by Leon Battista Alberti in *De Re Aedificatoria*, published in 1485, which set out mathematical calculations for planning and design and re-stated the ideal proportions of the four classical architectural orders — Corinthian, Doric, Ionic, and Tuscan. The result was a classical, dignified architectural style in which the combination of columns and pilasters was the dominant decorative theme.

Three years after the publication of this book, the Baths of Titus and the Golden House of Nero in Rome were unearthed. The designed of the (well-preserved) stucco decorations were adapted for ornamenting architecture, furniture, pottery and textiles — symmetrical patterns embodying human, animal and floral motifs. Raphael used them in painting stucco, and they also appear in villa designs for important families.

From the furniture history point of view, the most influential architect of all was Andrea Palladio (1518-1580), whose villas were exquisitely designed to blend with the rural surroundings yet retain superb proportions. A villa he built just outside Vincenza about 1550 served as English architect Colen Campbell's model when he built Mereworth Castle in Kent in 1723. But Palladian ideas live on in England in the work of Inigo Jones (1573-1652) and William Kent (1686-1748), both in the first rank of English furniture designers.

If it seems we have been tracing architectural rather than furniture styles, it's because architects designed and superintended the making of furniture and furnishings for their buildings. It's intriguing that both Inigo Jones and William Kent had no professional qualifications as architects, and it seems that anyone with the talent, drive, and patronage could reach the highest position in the profession. Jones was originally a painter and designer of scenery for Court entertainments, and Kent was a Yorkshire coach painter.

The spread of the Renaissance to other countries was slow at first, being confined to returning travellers' reports of the new styles. The biggest stimulus came from the unsuccessful invasion of Italy in 1495 by the French King Charles VIII — an attempt to regain his Angerin inheritance. It led to a steady and sustained Italianisation of French culture.

In England the Renaissance was slow in coming because of the issolation of the monasteries, when Henry VIII not only severed all links with Rome, but actively prevented any social or cultural intercourse with Italy. By the time the new ideas reached us they had been refined and the more extravagant onces filtered out.

It will be helpful to look at the styles which were evolving in Italy during the early Renaissance (up to 1550). As an example, one of the basic pieces of the furniture of the time was the chest or *cassone*; if we trace its development over a period of about 80 years it will give us a good idea of the immense changes that took place.

The dome-lidded *cassone* in fig. 3 is a late 15th century Italian dower chest which displays the arms of two great families, the Montefeltros and the Gonzagos, and commemorates a wedding. It is painted in tempera and the gilding is laid over gesso. The *cassone* was filled with the dowry and the bride's belongings, and carried publicly through the streets to the bridegroom's palace. Until the evolution of the chest of drawers and the cupboard at the beginning of the 16th century, the *cassone* was used to store all kinds of domestic paraphernalia such as clothes, linen and valuables. It was not uncommon to find twenty or more

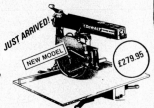

308

The grand furniture saga: 3

cassoni in one palace ranged around the walls as well as at the foot of the bed, which was the traditional place.

An even more elaborate and magnificent example is the Florentine *Nerli cassone* shown in the first photo, which dates back to about 1492. The superbly painted panels depict scenes from the Roman poet Livy: such well-known painters are Botticelli and Perugino are known to have painted similar panels.

The two pieces illustrated in figs. 4 and 5 are 16th century and are both carved and gilt in masterly fashion. It must be said that the standard of construction was distinctly shoddy on many pieces, and it seems that the energies of the craftsmen were all devoted to exterior decoration at the expense of the parts normally hidden from sight!

The example shown in fig. 5 is particularly interesting because it has some of the motifs generally associated with the Mannerist style, namely 'chimeras' (grotesque monsters), caryatids (conventionalised female figures), and *putti* (cherubs). Although the style originally referred to the *bella maniera* school of painting which appeared about 1520 in Rome and Florence, it was later applied to the designs which a Frenchman, Jacques du Cerceau, produced

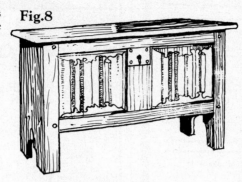

Fig.8

● *Only the panels hint at the Renaissance in England . . .*

in a book of furniture about 1550. None of his designs have ever been made in their entirety, although a table at Hardwick Hall is close. However, many of his ideas were carried over to the Baroque period.

The influence of the Renaissance was quick to reach France but it was slow to affect English designs. As you can see from fig. 6 the native style persisted well into the 16th century when this chest was made, the only 'imported' motif being the linenfold panels.

● Next: the Renaissance in England.

National Trust

● *A 17th century cabinet, highly decorated in the style of du Cerceau*

Books

Richard Raffan
Turning wood with Richard Raffan
The Taunton Press, £14.95 softback
Reviewed by Tobias Kaye

What struck me most about this book was how clear it is — clearly laid out and clearly thought out, with such details as coloured page-borders to differentiate action photos and pages with text.

The photos are well-taken and clearly reproduced, with drawings to complement them. It is the drawings, in fact, which really make the book stand out from the crowd. Much clearer than photos on their own, some exploded or cut-away, they show exactly what the text means in its descriptions of, for instance, the parts of the lathe and their function, fulcrums, arcs and hand-positions in tool control, or laying out bowls to be cut from a log.

The text takes less for granted than I would have expected, and explains clearly what to look for and what to avoid in machine and tools — how to fix and care for them, sharpening, stance, holding and cutting for spindle work, hollow and face work. Chucking, measuring, finishing and polishing, and much more are equally well defined.

Points of design are considered in a way that helps one evaluate the subject without hindering originality. Seasoning bowls in the rough, with PEG, finished, or in the microwave are all discussed, as is power sanding.

Safety is also clearly dealt with. Without making any rules to break, the subject is mentioned often in an active way, and Raffan's own various accidents are mentioned showing how they happened and when. This book is impressively comprehensive!

A gallery of Richard Raffan's own work gives inspiration and sets high targets. The whole work has a surefootedness and a marked lack of dogmatism or pedantry. Richard Raffan is internationally recognised as a master of his craft. This, his first book, makes at least as great a contribution to learning the craft as do his bowls to its advancement. I thoroughly recommend it.
● Tobias Kaye is a professional woodturner in Devon.

In brief

Design Courses in Britain 1986 *(Design Council, £3.75)*
Contains two pages of furniture courses and other assorted information on tertiary education.

Woodwork Skills *(WH Smith, Orbis, 49p)*
A short (32pp), cheap and colourful 'first steps' guide, which bears a distinct resemblance to a partwork in graphic style.

The Practical Woodwork Book *(Anthony Hontoin, John Murray, £4.95)*
A selection of increasingly difficult projects together with a summary of different joints. Aimed at schools and evening classes.

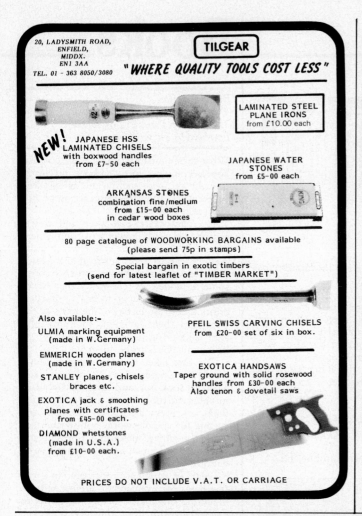

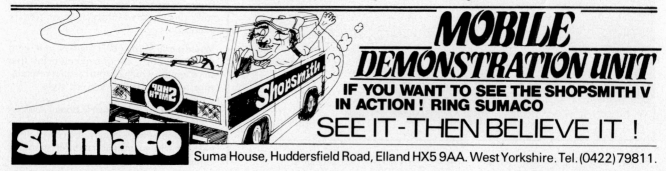

shopguide

AVON

BATH   Tel. Bath 64513
JOHN HALL TOOLS   ★
RAILWAY STREET

Open: Monday-Saturday
9.00 a.m.-5.30 p.m.
H.P.W.WM.D.A.BC.

BRISTOL   Tel. (0272) 741510
JOHN HALL TOOLS LIMITED   ★
CLIFTON DOWN SHOPPING CENTRE
WHITELADIES ROAD
Open: Monday-Saturday
9.00 a.m.-5.30 p.m.
H.P.W.WM.D.A.BC.

BRISTOL   Tel. (0272) 629092
TRYMWOOD SERVICES
2a DOWNS PARK EAST, (off North View)
WESTBURY PARK
Open: 8.30 a.m.-5.30 p.m. Mon. to Fri.
Closed for lunch 1.00-2.00 p.m.
P.W.WM.D.T.A.BC.

BRISTOL   Tel. (0272) 667013
FASTSET LTD
190-192 WEST STREET
BEDMINSTER
Open: Mon.-Fri. 8.30 a.m.-5.00 p.m.
Saturday 9.00 a.m.-1.00 p.m.
H.P.W.WM.D.CS.A.BC.

BRISTOL   Tel. (0272) 667013
WILLIS
157 WEST STREET
BEDMINSTER
Open Mon.-Fri. 8.30 a.m.-5.00 p.m.
Sat. 9 a.m.-4 p.m.
P.W.WM.D.CS.A.BC.

BEDFORDSHIRE

BEDFORD   Tel. (0234) 59808
BEDFORD SAW SERVICE   K
39 AMPTHILL ROAD

Open: Mon.-Fri. 8.30-5.30
Sat. 9.00-4.00
H.P.A.BC.W.CS.WM.D.

BERKSHIRE

**FOR ADVERTISING
DETAILS IN SHOP
GUIDE PHONE
01-437-0626
AND ASK FOR
ANDREA SMITH**

BERKSHIRE

READING   Tel. Littlewick Green
DAVID HUNT (TOOL   2743
MERCHANTS) LTD   ★
KNOWL HILL, NR. READING
Open: Monday-Saturday
9.00 a.m.-5.30 p.m.
H.P.W.D.A.BC.

READING   Tel. Reading 661511
WOKINGHAM TOOL CO. LTD.
99 WOKINGHAM ROAD

Open: Mon-Sat 9.00 a.m.-5.30 p.m.
Closed 1.00-2.00 p.m. for lunch
H.P.W.WM.D.CS.A.BC.

BUCKINGHAMSHIRE

**THIS SPACE COSTS
AS LITTLE AS
£12 PER MONTH**

MILTON KEYNES   Tel. (0908)
POLLARD WOODWORKING   641366
CENTRE   ★
51 AYLESBURY ST., BLETCHLEY
Open: Mon-Fri 8.30-5.30
Saturday 9.00-5.00
H.P.W.WM.D.CS.A.BC.

HIGH WYCOMBE   Tel. (0494)
SCOTT SAWS LTD.   24201/33788
14 BRIDGE STREET   ★

Mon.-Sat. 8.30 a.m.-6.00 p.m.

H.P.W.WM.D.T.CS.MF.A.BC.

HIGH WYCOMBE   Tel. (0494)
ISAAC LORD LTD   22221
185 DESBOROUGH ROAD   KE

Open: Mon-Fri 8.00 a.m.-5.00 p.m.
Saturday 9.00 a.m.-5.00 p.m.
H.P.W.D.A.

CAMBRIDGESHIRE

CAMBRIDGE   Tel. (0223) 63132
D. MACKAY LTD.   E★
BRITANNIA WORKS, EAST ROAD

Open: Mon.-Fri. 8.30 a.m.-1 p.m./2.00-
5.00 p.m. Sat. 8.30 a.m.-1.00 p.m.
H.P.W.D.T.CS.MF.A.BC.

CAMBRIDGE   Tel. (0223) 247386
H. B. WOODWORKING   K
105 CHERRY HINTON ROAD
Open: 8.30 a.m.-5.30 p.m.
Monday-Friday
8.30 a.m.-1.00 p.m. Sat.
H.P.W.WM.D.CS.A.

PETERBOROUGH   Tel. (0733)
WILLIAMS DISTRIBUTORS   64252
(TOOLS) LIMITED   K
108-110 BURGHLEY ROAD
Open: Monday to Friday
8.30 a.m.-5.30 p.m.
H.P.A.W.D.WH.BC.

CHESHIRE

NANTWICH   Tel. Crewe 67010
ALAN HOLTHAM   K★
THE OLD STORES TURNERY
WISTASON ROAD, WILLASTON
Open: Tues.-Sat. 9.00 a.m.-5.30 p.m.
Closed Monday
P.W.WM.D.T.C.CS.A.BC.

CHEADLE   Tel: 061491 1726
ERIC TOMKINSON   ★
86 STOCKPORT ROAD
Open: Mon.-Fri. 9.00 a.m.-4.00 p.m.
Saturday 9.00 a.m.-1.00 p.m.
H.P.W.D.MF.A.BC.

CLEVELAND

MIDDLESBROUGH   Tel. (0642)
CLEVELAND WOODCRAFT   813103
(M'BRO), 38-42 CRESCENT ROAD   K

Open: Mon-Sat 9.15 a.m.-5.30 p.m.

H.P.T.A.BC.W.WM.CS.D.

CORNWALL

**SOUTH WEST
Power Tools**

CORNWALL   Tel: Helston (03265) 4961
HELSTON AND LAUNCESTON   Launceston
  (0566) 4781
H.P.W.WM.D.CS.A.   K

**DISCUSS YOUR
ADVERTISING PLANS
WITH ANDREA SMITH
ON 01-437-0626**

CUMBRIA

CARLISLE   Tel: (0228) 36391
W. M. PLANT
ALLENBROOK ROAD
ROSEHILL, CA1 2UT
Open: Mon.-Fri. 8.00 a.m.-5.15 p.m.
Sat. 8.00 a.m.-12.30 noon
P.W.WM.D.CS.A.

DERBYSHIRE

**FILL THIS SPACE
BY PHONING
01-437-0626**

BUXTON

BUXTON   Tel. (0298) 871636
CRAFT SUPPLIES   K★
THE MILL, MILLERSDALE

Open: Mon-Sat 9.00 a.m.-5.00 p.m.

H.P.W.D.T.CS.A.BC.

DEVON

BRIXHAM   Tel. (08045) 4900
WOODCRAFT SUPPLIES   E★
4 HORSE POOL STREET

Open: Mon.-Sat. 9.00 a.m.-6.00 p.m.

H.P.W.A.D.MF.CS.BC.

**ALL THOSE SHOPS
WITH AN ASTERISK
★ HAVE A MAIL
ORDER SERVICE**

PLYMOUTH   Tel. (0752) 330303
WESTWARD BUILDING SERVICES   ★
LTD., LISTER CLOSE, NEWNHAM
INDUSTRIAL ESTATE, PLYMPTON
Open: Mon-Fri 8.00 a.m.-5.30 p.m.
Sat. 8.30 a.m.-12.30 p.m.
H.P.W.WM.D.A.BC.

DORSET

BOURNEMOUTH   Tel: (0202) 420583
POWER TOOL SERVICES
(Sales, spares, repairs)
849-851 CHRISTCHURCH ROAD
BOSCOMBE
Open: Mon.-Fri. 9.00 a.m.-5.30 p.m.
Sat: 9.00 a.m.-5.00 p.m.
H.P.W.CS.K.A.

POOLE   Tel: (0202) 686238
MACHINE SALES AND SERVICES   ★
(POOLE) LTD.
23 COWLEY ROAD
NUFFIELD INDUSTRIAL ESTATE
Open: Mon.-Fri. 8.30am-5.30pm.
H.P.W.WM.D.CS.A.BC.

ESSEX

LEIGH ON SEA   Tel. (0702)
MARSHAL & PARSONS LTD.   710404
1111 LONDON ROAD   EK

Open: 8.30 a.m.-5.30 p.m. Mon-Fri
9.00 a.m.-5.00 p.m. Sat.
H.P.W.WM.D.CS.A.

ILFORD
CUTWELL TOOLS LTD.   ★
774-776 HIGH ROAD

Mon.-Fri. 9.00 a.m.-5.00 p.m.
and also by appointment.
P.W.WM.A.D.CS.

311

shop guide

GLOUCESTER

TEWKESBURY Tel. (0684)
TEWKESBURY SAW CO. LTD. 293092
TRADING ESTATE, NEWTOWN **K**

Open: Mon-Fri 8.00 a.m.-5.00 p.m.
Saturday 9.30 a.m.-12.00 p.m.
P.W.WM.D.CS.

HAMPSHIRE

ALL THOSE SHOPS
WITH AN ASTERISK
★ PROVIDE MAIL
ORDER SERVICE

ALDERSHOT Tel. (0252) 334422
POWER TOOL CENTRE **K**
374 HIGH STREET

Open Mon-Fri. 8.30 a.m.-5.30 p.m.
Sat. 8.30 a.m.-12.30 p.m.

H.P.W.WM.D.A.BC.

SOUTHAMPTON Tel. (0703)
POWER TOOL CENTRE 332288
7 BELVIDERE ROAD **K★**
Open Mon.-Fri. 8.30-5.30

H.P.W.WM.D.A.BC.CS.MF.

WATFORD Tel. (0923) 26052
J. SIMBLE & SONS LTD.
76 QUEENS ROAD

Open 8.30 a.m.-5.30 p.m.
Mon.-Sat. Closed Wednesday.
H.P.W.WM.D.A.BC.

HUMBERSIDE

GRIMSBY Tel. Grimsby (0472)
58741 Hull (0482) 26999
J. E. SIDDLE LTD. (Tool Specialists) ★
83 VICTORIA STREET
Open: Mon-Fri 8.30 a.m.-5.30 p.m.
Sat. 8.30 a.m.-12.45 p.m. & 2 p.m.-5 p.m.
H.P.A.B.C.W.WMD.

HULL
HUMBERSIDE FACTORING/H.F.C.
SAW SERVICING LTD.
MAIN STREET
Open: Mon.-Fri. 8am-5pm.
Saturday 8am-12.00pm.
H.P.W.WM.D.CS.A.BC.K.

KENT

WYE Tel. (0233) 813144
KENT POWER TOOLS LTD.
UNIT 1, BRIAR CLOSE
WYE, Nr. ASFORD

H.P.W.WM.D.A.CS.

MAIDSTONE Tel. (0622) 50177
SOUTH EASTERN SAWS (Ind.) LTD. ★
COLDRED ROAD
PARKWOOD INDUSTRIAL ESTATE

Open: Mon.-Fri. 8.00 a.m.-6.00 p.m.
Sat. 9.00 a.m.-12.00 a.m.

B.C.W.CS.WM.PH.

LANCASHIRE

PRESTON Tel. (0772) 52951
SPEEDWELL TOOL COMPANY **E★**
62-68 MEADOW STREET PR1 1SU
Open: Mon.-Fri. 8.30 a.m.-5.30 p.m.
Sat. 8.30 a.m.-12.30 p.m.

H.P.W.WM.CS.A.MF.BC.

BURY Tel. (061 764 6769)
HOUSE OF HARBRU ★
101 CROSTONS ROAD
ELTON
Open: Mon.-Fri. 9.00 a.m.-5.00 p.m.
Send 2 × 1st class stamps for catalogue
MF.

MANCHESTER Tel. (061 789)
TIMMS TOOLS 0909
102-104 LIVERPOOL ROAD
PATRICROFT M30 0WZ
Weekdays 9.00 a.m.-5.30 p.m.
Sat. 9.00 a.m.-1.00 p.m.
H.P.A.W.

BLACKPOOL Tel. (0253) 24299
FLYDE WOODTURNING SUPPLIES ★
222 HORNBY ROAD (BASEMENT)
BLACKPOOL FY1 4HY
9.30-5.30 Monday to Saturday.
H.P.W.WM.A.MF.C.B.C.D.

ROCHDALE Tel. (0706) 342123/
C.S.M. TOOLS 342322
4-6 HEYWOOD ROAD **E★**
CASTLETON
Open: Mon-Sat 9.00 a.m.-6.00 p.m.
Sundays by appointment
W.D.CS.A.BC.

LANCASTER Tel. (0524) 32886
LILE TOOL SHOP **K**
43/45 NORTH ROAD
Open: Monday to Saturday
9.00 a.m.-5.30 p.m.
Wed 9.00 a.m.-12.30 p.m.
H.P.W.D.A.

LEICESTERSHIRE

HINCKLEY Tel. (0455) 613432
J. D. WOODWARD & CO. (POWER ★
TOOL SPECIALISTS)
THE NARROWS, HINCKLEY
Open: Monday-Saturday
8.00 a.m.-6.00 p.m.
H.P.W.WM.D.CS.A.BC.

LINCOLNSHIRE

LINCOLN Tel: (0522) 689369
SKELLINGTHORPE SAW SERVICES LTD.
OLD WOOD, SKELLINGTHORPE
Open: Mon to Fri 8 a.m.-5 p.m.
Sat 8 a.m.-12 p.m.
H.P.W.WM.D.CS.A.*.BC.
Access/Barclaycard

LONDON

ACTON Tel. (01-992) 4835
A. MILLS (ACTON) LTD ★
32/36 CHURCHFIELD ROAD W3 6ED
Open: Mon-Fri 9.00 a.m.-5.00 p.m.
Saturdays 9.00 am.-1.00 p.m.
H.P.W.WM.

LONDON

LONDON Tel. (01-567) 2922
G. D. CLEGG & SONS ★
83 UXBRIDGE ROAD, HANWELL W7 3ST
Mon-Sat 9.15 a.m.-5.30 p.m.
Closed for lunch 1.00-2.00p.m.
Early Closing 1.00 p.m. Wed.
H.P.A.W.WM.D.CS.

NORBURY Tel. (01-679) 6193
HERON TOOLS & HARDWARE LTD.
437 STREATHAM HIGH ROAD SW16
Open Mon-Fri 8.30 a.m.-5.00 p.m.
Wednesday 8.30 a.m.-1.00 p.m.
Sat. 9.00 a.m.-1.00 p.m.
H.P.W.A.

LONDON Tel. (01-636) 7475
BUCK & RYAN LTD ★
101 TOTTENHAM COURT ROAD W1P 0DY

Open: Mon.-Fri. 8.30 a.m.-5.30 p.m.
Saturday 8.30 a.m.-4.00 p.m.
H.P.W.WM.D.A..

WEMBLEY Tel. 904-1144
ROBERT SAMUEL LTD. (904-1147
7, 15 & 16 COURT PARADE after 4.00)
EAST LANE, N. WEMBLEY ★
Open Mon.-Fri. 8.45-5.15; Sat. 9-1.00
Access, Barclaycard, AM Express, & Diners
H.P.W.CS.E.A.D.

HOUNSLOW Tel. (01-570)
Q.R. TOOLS LTD 2103/5135
251-253 HANWORTH ROAD

Open: Mon-Fri 8.30 a.m.-5.30 p.m.
Sat. 9.00 a.m.-1.00 p.m.
P.W.WM.D.CS.A.

FULHAM Tel. (01-385) 5109
I. GRIZZARD LTD. **E**
84a-b LILLIE ROAD, SW6 1TL
Open: Mon-Sat 9.00-5.30 p.m.
Half day Thursday

H.P.A.BC.W.CS.WM.D.

LONDON Tel. (01-263) 1536
THOMAS BROTHERS (01-272) 2764
798-804 HOLLOWAY ROAD, N19 **E**
Open: Mon.-Fri. 8.30 a.m.-5.30 p.m. Thurs.
8.30 a.m.-1 p.m. Sat. 9 a.m.-5 p.m.

H.P.W.WM.CS.MF.BC.

LONDON Tel. 01-723 2295-6-7
LANGHAM TOOLS LIMITED
13 NORFOLK PLACE
LONDON W2 1QJ

MERSEYSIDE

LIVERPOOL Tel. (051-207) 2967
TAYLOR BROS (LIVERPOOL) LTD **K**
195-199 LONDON ROAD
LIVERPOOL L3 8JG

Open: Monday to Friday
8.30 a.m.-5.30 p.m.
H.P.W.WM.D.A.BC.

MERSEYSIDE

RUISLIP Tel. (08956) 74126
ALLMODELS ENGINEERING LTD. **E★**
91 MANOR WAY

Open: Mon-Sat 9.00 a.m.-5.30 p.m.
H.P.W.A.D.CS.MF.BC.

CROWMARSH Tel. (0491) 38653
MILL HILL SUPPLIES **E★**
66 THE STREET
Open: Mon.-Fri. 9.30 a.m.-5.00 p.m.
Thurs. 9.30 a.m.-7.00 p.m.
Sat. 9.30 a.m.-1.00 p.m.
P.W.D.CS.MF.A.BC.

FARNHAM Tel. (0252) 725427
A.B.E. CO. LTD. (Quick Hire) ★
GOODS SHED
STATION APPROACH, FARNHAM
Open Mon.-Fri. 8.00 a.m.-5.30 p.m.
Sat. 8.00 a.m.-5.30 p.m.
H.P.W.D.CS.A.BC.

NORFOLK

NORWICH Tel. (0603) 898695
NORFOLK SAW SERVICES
DOG LANE, HORSFORD
Open: Monday to Friday
8.00 a.m.-5.00 p.m.
Saturday 8.00 a.m.-12.00 p.m.
H.P.W.WM.D.CS.A.

KINGS LYNN Tel. (0553) 2443
WALKER & ANDERSON (Kings Lynn) LTD.
WINDSOR ROAD, KINGS LYNN **K**
Open: Monday to Saturday
7.45 a.m.-5.30 p.m.
Wednesday 1.00 p.m. Saturday 5.00 p.m.
H.P.W.WM.D.CS.A.

NORWICH Tel. (0603) 400933
WESTGATES WOODWORKING Tx
61 HURRICANE WAY, 975412
NORWICH AIRPORT INDUSTRIAL ESTATE
Open: 9.00 a.m.-5.00 p.m. weekdays
9.00 a.m.-12.30 Sat.
P.W.WM.D.BC. **K**

KING'S LYNN Tel: 07605 674
TONY WADDILOVE, UNIT A ★
HILL FARM WORKSHOPS
GREAT DUNHAM, (Nr. Swaffham)
Open: Tues. — Fri. 10.00 a.m. to 5.30 p.m.
Sat. 9.00 a.m. to 5.00 p.m.
H.P.W.D.T.MF.A.BC.*

NOTTINGHAMSHIRE

NOTTINGHAM Tel: (0602) 225979
POOLEWOOD and 227064/5
EQUIPMENT LTD. (06077) 2421 after hrs
5a HOLLY LANE, CHILLWELL
Open: Mon-Fri 9.00 a.m.-5.30 p.m.
Sat. 9.00 a.m. to 12.30 p.m.
P.W.WM.D.CS.A.BC.

OXON

WITNEY Tel. (0993) 3885.
TARGET TOOLS (SALES, & 72095 OXON
HIRE & REPAIRS)
SWAIN COURT
STATION INDUSTRIAL ESTATE
Open: Mon.-Sat. 8.00 a.m.-5.00 p.m.
24 hour Answerphone
BC.W.M.A.

312

shopguide

SHROPSHIRE

TELFORD   Tel. Telford (0952)
ASLES LTD   48054
VINEYARD ROAD, WELLINGTON   EK★

Open: Mon. Fri. 8.30 a.m.-5.30 p.m.
Saturday 8.30 a.m.-4.00 p.m.
H.P.W.W.M.D.CS.BC.A.

SOMERSET

TAUNTON   Tel. (0823) 85431
JOHN HALL TOOLS   ★
6 HIGH STREET

Open Monday-Saturday
9.00 a.m.-5.30 p.m.
H.P.W.WM.D.CS.A.

STAFFORDSHIRE

STOKE-ON-TRENT   Tel: 0782-48171
F.W.B. (PRODUCTS) LTD.
WHIELDON ROAD, STAFFS.
Open: Mon.-Fri. 8.30am-5.30pm
Saturday 8.30am-12.30pm
H.P.W.WM.A.D.

SUFFOLK

IPSWICH   Tel. (0473) 40456
FOX WOODWORKING   KE★
142-144 BRAMFORD LANE
Open: Tues., Fri., 9.00 a.m.-5.30 p.m.
Sat. 9.00 a.m.-5.00 p.m.

H.P.W.WM.D.A.B.C.

SUSSEX

ST. LEONARD'S-ON-SEA   Tel.
DOUST & MONK (MONOSAW)-(0424)
25 CASTLEHAM ROAD   52577

Open: Mon.-Fri. 8.00 a.m.-5.30 p.m.
Most Saturdays 9.00 a.m.-1.00 p.m.
H.P.W.WM.D.CS.A.

BOGNOR REGIS Tel. (0243) 863100
A. OLBY & SON (BOGNOR REGIS) LTD.
"TOOLSHOP," BUILDERS MERCHANT
HAWTHORN ROAD   K
Open: Mon-Thurs 8 a.m.-5.15 p.m. Fri.
8 a.m.-8 p.m. Sat 8 a.m.-12.45 p.m.
H.P.W.WM.D.T.C.A.BC.

WORTHING   Tel. (0903) 38739
W. HOSKING LTD (TOOLS &   KE★
MACHINERY)
28 PORTLAND RD, BN11 1QN
Open: Mon.-Sat. 8.30 a.m.-5.30 p.m.
Closed Wednesday
H.P.W.WM.D.CS.A.BC.

TYNE & WEAR

NEWCASTLE UPON TYNE   Tel.
J. W. HOYLE LTD.   (0632) 617474
CLARENCE STREET NE2 1YJ   K★
Open: Mon-Fri 8.00 a.m.-5.00 p.m.
Saturday 9.00 a.m.-4.30 p.m.

H.P.A.ABC.W.CS.WM.D.

NEWCASTLE   Tel. (0632) 320311
HENRY OSBOURNE LTD.   E★
50-54 UNION STREET

Open: Mon-Fri 8.30 a.m.-5.00 p.m.

H.P.W.D.CS.MF.A.BC.

WEST MIDLANDS

BIRMINGHAM   Tel. (021-554) 5177
ROTAGRIP   E★
16 LODGE ROAD, HOCKLEY
Open: Mon.-Fri. 9.00 a.m.-5.00 p.m.
Sat. 9.00 a.m.-12.00 p.m.

H.P.W.CS.A.BC.T.MF.

WOLVERHAMPTON   Tel. (0902)
MANSAW SERVICES   58759
SEDGLEY STREET   K★

Open: Mon.-Fri. 9.00 a.m.-5.00 p.m.

H.P.W.WM.A.D.CS.

YORKSHIRE

BOROUGHBRIDGE   Tel. (09012)
JOHN BODDY TIMBER LTD   2370
FINE WOOD & TOOL STORE   ★
RIVERSIDE SAWMILLS
Open: Mon.-Thurs. 8.00 a.m.-6.00 p.m.
Fri. 8.00am-5.00pm Sat. 8.00am-4.00pm
H.P.W.WM.D.T.CS.MF.A.BC.

SHEFFIELD   Tel. (0742) 441012
GREGORY & TAYLOR LTD   KE
WORKSOP ROAD
Open: 8.30 a.m.-5.30 p.m.
Monday-Friday
8.30 a.m.-12.30 p.m. Sat.
H.P.W.WM.D.

HARROGATE   Tel. (0423) 66245/
MULTI-TOOLS   55328
158 KINGS ROAD   K★

Open: Monday to Saturday
8.30 a.m.-6.00 p.m.

H.P.W.WM.D.A.BC.

LEEDS   Tel. (0532) 574736
D. B. KEIGHLEY MACHINERY LTD.   ★
VICKERS PLACE, STANNINGLEY
PUDSEY LS2 86LZ
Mon.-Fri. 9.00 a.m.-5.00 p.m.
Sat. 9.00 a.m.-1.00 p.m.
P.A.W.WM.CS.BC.

HUDDERSFIELD   Tel. (0484)
NEVILLE M. OLDHAM   641219/(0484)
UNIT 1 DALE ST. MILLS   42777
DALE STREET, LONGWOOD   ★
Open: Mon-Fri 8.00 a.m.-5.30 p.m.
Saturday 9.30 a.m.-12.00 p.m.
P.W.WM.D.A.BC.

YORKSHIRE

THIRSK   Tel. (0845) 22770
THE WOOD SHOP   ★
TRESKE SAWMILLS LTD.
STATION WORKS
Open: Seven days a week 9.00-5.00

T.H.MF.BC.

KEIGHLEY   Tel. (0535) 663325
EUROMAIL (TOOLS)   ★
PO BOX 13
108 EAST PARADE
Open 9.15 a.m.-5.00 p.m.
Not Tuesday but inc. Saturday
H.P.W.A.BC.

CLECKHEATON

CLECKHEATON   Tel. (0274)
SKILLED CRAFTS LTD.   872861
34 BRADFORD ROAD   ★

Open: 9.00 a.m.-5.00 p.m. Monday
Saturday Lunch 12.00 a.m.-1.00 p.m.
H.P.A.W.CS.WM.D.

LEEDS   Tel. (0532) 790507
GEORGE SPENCE & SONS LTD.
WELLINGTON ROAD
Open: Monday to Friday
8.30 a.m.-5.30 p.m.
Saturday 9.00 a.m.-5.00 p.m.
H.P.W.WM.D.T.A.

SCOTLAND

CULLEN   Tel. (0542) 40563
GRAMPIAN WOODTURNING SUPPLIES AT
BAYVIEW CRAFTS
Open Mon.-Sat. 9.00 a.m.-5.30 p.m. Sunday
10.00 a.m.-5.30 p.m. Open later July/Aug.
Sept. Demonstrations SAT/SUN or by
H.W.D.MF.BC. appointment

EDINBURGH   Tel. 031-337-5555
THE SAW CENTRE   ★
38 HAYMARKET EH12 5JZ
Mon.-Fri. 8.30 a.m.-5.30 p.m.
Sat. 9.00 a.m.-1.00 p.m.
H.P.W.WM.D.CS.A.

PERTH   Tel. (0738) 26173
WILLIAM HUME & CO   K
ST. JOHN'S PLACE
Open: Monday to Saturday
8.00 a.m.-5.30 p.m.
8.00 a.m.-1.00 p.m. Wednesday
H.P.A.BC.W.CS.WM.D.

GLASGOW   Tel. 041-429-4444/
THE SAW CENTRE   4374 Telex: 777886
650 EGLINTON STREET   E★
GLASGOW G5 9RP
Mon.-Fri. 8.00 a.m.-5.00 p.m.
Sat. 9.00 a.m.-1.00 p.m.
H.P.W.WM.D.CS.A.

SCOTLAND

TAYSIDE   Tel: (05774) 293
WORKMASTER POWER TOOLS LTD.   ★
DRUM, KINROSS
Open Mon.-Sat. 8.00 a.m.-8.00 p.m.
Demonstrations throughout Scotland by
appointment
P.W.WM.D.A.BC.

IRELAND

NEWTOWNARDS   Tel: 0247 819800
NORLYN MACHINERY   or 812506
UNIT 10, MALCOLMSON IND. EST.
80 BANGOR ROAD, CO. DOWN
Open: Mon.-Fri. 9.30am-5.30pm
(Closed 1-2pm for lunch)
Any other time by request.
H.W.WM.D.T.MF.A.   24 Hour Service K

WALES

CARDIFF   Tel. (0222) 595710
DATAPOWER TOOLS LTD,
MICHAELSTON ROAD,
CULVERHOUSE CROSS
Open: Mon.-Fri. 8.00 a.m.-5.00 p.m.
Sat. 9.00 a.m.-1.00 p.m.
H.P.W.WM.D.A.

CARMARTHEN   Tel. (0267) 237219
DO-IT-YOURSELF SUPPLY   K
BLUE STREET, DYFED
Open: Monday to Saturday
9.00 a.m.-5.30 p.m.
Thursday 9.00 a.m.-5.30 p.m.
H.P.W.WM.D.T.CS.A.BC.

CARDIFF   Tel. (0222) 396039
JOHN HALL TOOLS LIMITED   ★
CENTRAL SQUARE

Open: Monday to Saturday
9.00 a.m.-5.30 p.m.

H.P.W.WM.D.A.BC.

SWANSEA   Tel. (0792) 55680
SWANSEA TIMBER & PLYWOOD CO. LTD.
57-59 OXFORD STREET   ★

Open: Mon to Fri 9.00 a.m.-5.30 p.m.
Sat. 9.00 a.m.-1.00 p.m.
H.P.W.D.T.CS.A.BC.

WOOD SUPPLIERS

WOOD SUPPLIERS

315

316

Classified Advertisements

FOR SALE

FOR ALL SUPPLIES FOR THE
Craft of Enamelling
ON METAL
Including
LEAD-FREE ENAMELS
PLEASE SEND 2 × 10p STAMPS FOR FREE CATALOGUE, PRICE LIST AND WORKING INSTRUCTIONS

W. G. BALL LTD.
ENAMEL MANUFACTURERS

Dept. W. LONGTON
STOKE-ON-TRENT
ST3 1JW

THE FINEST SELECTION ON DISPLAY IN SCOTLAND!

WOODWORKING & METALWORKING MACHINERY POWER TOOLS HAND TOOLS

THE SAW CENTRE

HIRE OR BUY.

OPEN Mon - Fri 8am - 5pm Sat 9am - 1pm

Visit our NEW SHOWROOM at EGLINTON TOLL GLASGOW

Tel: 041-429 4444/4374, Telex: 777886 SAWCO G
Also at, 38 Haymarket Terrace, Edinburgh EH12 5JZ. Tel: 031-337 5555

Harrison Graduate lathe 54" bed + Ass. face plates and 11No. Sorby tools plus 6No. scrapers.
Kity 612 bandsaw on stand with motor.
Kity 635 planer/thicknesser on stand with motor. All 6 years old. *Offers invited:* Walmsley, 6 Aspels Crescent, Cop Lane, Penwortham, Preston, Lancs. PR1 9AN.

WORKSHOP EQUIPMENT

WOODCARVING tools

LARGEST STOCK IN EUROPE

Ashley Iles & Henry Taylor
Arkansas Bench & Slip Stones
Strops & Strop Paste
Bench Screws, Carvers' Vices

WOODTURNING tools

Complete range of
Henry Taylor & Ashley Iles
handled or unhandled

send 40p in stamps for illustrated catalogue

ALEC TIRANTI LTD
70 High St, Theale, Reading, Berks RG7 5AR
21 Goodge Place, London W1.

WOODTURNERS SUPPLIES
Woodturning tools, Peppermills, Salt mills, Barometers, Thermometers, Lighters, Hourglasses, Eggtimers, Ceramic tiles and clock faces, Clock movements, Spinning wheel plans, Sealers & Polishes, etc. Fast and efficient mail order service + competitive prices. (50p in stamps deductable against first order).

ERIC TOMKINSON
86 Stockport Road, Cheadle, Cheshire, SK8 2AJ. Tel: 061-491 1726
Shop opening times:
9am-5.30pm Mon.-Sat.

WOOD TURNERS SUPPLIES
Tudor Craft, Jung Hans clock movements, 20 different hands to choose from, barometers, weather stations, cutlery, jewellery box lids, pepper/salt/nutmeg mills, coffee grinders, ceramic tiles, new range which include hand painted tiles. Our service is extremely fast, friendly and competitive — give us a try. Send 30p in stamps to:
Tudorcraft, 100 Little Sutton Lane, Four Oaks. Sutton Coldfield, W. Midlands B75 6PG. Tel: 021 308 1193
For illustrated catalogue.

CLOCKMAKERS
Extensive range of very competitively priced German quartz clock movements, (including standard quartz, pendulum, mini-pendulum, chining, striking and insertion movements). Large selection of quality dials, chapter rings, hands, bezels, clock plans and weather instruments.
Please send 25p stamps for 20 page catalogue.
**Bath Clock Company (Dept. W),
13 Welton Road, Radstock, Bath.**

Byggones

Just one item from our catalogue

MARPLES PARING GOUGES
Boxwood handles
1/4" – 6" radius
Straight or Cranked

WHILE STOCKS LAST

Special rates for quantities

Please send 50p in stamps for catalogue

TILGEAR, 20 Ladysmith Road, Enfield, Middx., EN1 3AA Tel: 01-363 8050/3080

BANKRUPT STOCK
Sandvik circular saw blades tungsten tipped.
5", 5½", 6" .... **£4.00** each
6½", 8¼" .... **£6.00** each
½" to 1⅜" bore any size.
P&P £1 extra per order.
Tel: 01 672 7776
Hannett, 1A Links Road, Tooting, London SW17 9ED.

HARRISON GRADUATE and JUBILEE Wood Turning Lathes For Sale,
Contact the specialists
L.R.E. MACHINERY & EQUIPMENT Co.
15 Upwood Road, Lowton, Warrington WA3 2RL.
Tel: (0942) 728208 day or night

HAND CARVED
'Adam Style' Mantle motifs in Mahogany — Example 10" × 5" centre lamp and two side pieces.
Send S.A.E. for details and quotation. Your own design quoted for if required.
SAM NICHOLSON
22 Lisnagarvey Drive, Lisburn, Co. Antrim, N. Ireland.
Phone Lisburn 3510

The best costs less with
BIG DISCOUNTS

off all leading brands of T.C.T. saws, router cutters, planer knives and narrow bandsaws D.I.Y. and Industrial Quality. It pays to check our prices. Same day low cost resharpening service. Visitors Welcome. Free price list on request.

L.M. Saws, Slack Lane, Heanor, Derbyshire DE7 7GX
Telephone: 0773 715616

MORTICER, CHISELS, sharpening kit, for Startrite Drill. Also hand tools. Corris 629 evenings.

ARUNDEL M230 bench mounted lathe 36" between centres. Single phase 8" and 14" tool rests, faceplates, centres, £295. Telephone Lincoln 790733.

WADKIN SHERRILL 36" sander (3 phase), excellent condition, recently overhauled. Some spare belts, £700 o.n.o. Buyer to collect (Gloucestershire). Tel: 0402 813839.

WOODTURNING LATHE, Kitty 654, variable speed. Plus copying device, Child chuck, collett chuck, tailstock chuck & drills. Turning tools £500 o.n.o. Tel: 0325-480059.

LACE BOBBIN turning blanks. Extensive range of exotics, Ivory, lathes, miniature tools, sundries, lace supplies. SAE J. Ford, 5 Squirrels Hollow, Walsall WS7 8YS.

PLANER/THICKNESSER for Myford ML8. Coronet moulding block for ⅝" spindle + cutters. 4" belt sander. Tel: 061-865-3802.

CORONET MAJOR lathe, saw, planer/thicknesser, mortiser, many extras. v.g.c. £750.00 o.n.o. Pritchard Tel: 0272-873325.

(FRESH SAWN HOLLY) Limited supply variety & sizes. Reasonable rates details 02607 282. Evenings and Weekends.

USERS & COLLECTORS TOOLS for sale at the Old Craft Tool Shop, 15 High Street, Whillon, Middx. Telephone 01-755 0441.

ARUNDEL lathe, fully equipped including stand, multi-purpose chisels etc. Excellent condition £295 o.n.o. Tel: 01-567-2969.

CHAIRMAKERS spoon bits, set of 9 £40.00. Devizes (0380) 3509.

FOR SALE BLC Wood Turning lathe. Late R38 machine. Wood cabinet stand. Many extras. Immaculate condition, £725.00. No offers. Dereham 860749.

Braywood Estates

Main stockists
TREND ROUTER CUTTERS, AUGERS, FORSTNER BITS
All at discount prices
Braywood Estates Ltd., Dept WW, 158 Burnham Lane, Slough SL1 6LE.
Tel. Burnham (06286) 5125.
Hrs. Mon-Sat 9am-5.30pm

317

Profit from the use of Woodworking Machinery

A ONE DAY 'Wood Machining Course' to arm yourself with the necessary knowledge to enable you to:

- Make the correct choice of machine for YOUR purposes
- Use that particular machine to gain maximum efficiency, safely
- Open up new opportunities for you to profit from a small workshop

WARE	Heath Saw and Cutter Repairs	12th March, 1986
READING	Sarjents Tool Stores	19th March, 1986
IPSWICH	Fox Woodworking	20th March, 1986
SOUTHAMPTON	Burch and Hills Ltd.	25th March, 1986
HELSTON	South West Power Tools	9th April, 1986
LEEDS/BRADFORD	Rawdon Machine Sales Ltd.	15th April, 1986
PERTH	Wm. Hume and Co.	17th April, 1986
HULL	Humberside Factoring Co.	22nd April, 1986
WORTHING	W. Hosking	1st May, 1986
IPSWICH	Fox Woodworking	9th July, 1986
HULL	Humberside Factoring Co.	23rd September, 1986
IPSWICH	Fox Woodworking	16th October, 1986
TEWKESBURY	Tewkesbury Saw Co.	29th October, 1986

THIRTEEN VENUES TO CHOOSE FROM
One must be near to you

Telephone now for place availability and full timetable.
Rawdon Machine Sales Ltd., 6 Acorn Park,
Charlestown, Shipley, West Yorks BD17 7SW.
Telephone 0274 597826

P.S. These are *NOT* exhibitions or demonstrations of a particular manufacturer's machinery, but a general eight-hour 'HANDS ON' instruction course showing the techniques of using machinery. You will find your time well spent.

GORDON STOKES
Author of six books on woodturning, international demonstrator, and long established instructor, offers two day, one day, or hourly tuition for beginners. Maximum three students. No previous knowledge required. Benefit from forty years practical experience. More than two thousand satisfied students. Ring us on BATH (0225) 22617, or send S.A.E. (A4 size) for full details to:
202 THE HOLLOW, BATH, AVON BA2 1NG.
Act today – start a creative and lucrative hobby.

WOODCARVING AND SCULPTURE

The best short residential courses in basic sculpture, woodcarving, modelling and sketching, etc. are taught by Henry Moore's former assistant Peter Hibbard at the Old School Arts Workshop, Middleham, Leyburn, North Yorks DL8 4QG. Beginners welcome — Please send a stamp for our brochure which gives lots more information about the range of courses, the high quality of accommodation and the splendid Wensleydale surroundings.

Lower Dundridge,
Parkham,
Bideford,
N. Devon

Woodturning tuition by qualified furniture maker in rural workshop in N. Devon. 1, 2 or 3 day courses, mid-week or weekend. Local accommodation available.
Enquiries to: Kevin Richmond Price,
Horns Cross. Tel: (02375) 518 or 257

DOMINIC EXCELL
DIPLOMA: NEWARK SCHOOL OF VIOLIN MAKING
MAKER AND RESTORER OF VIOLINS, VIOLAS AND CELLOS
PART TIME COURSES IN VIOLIN MAKING
22 LANCASTER ROAD, BRIGHTON BN1 5DG
Tel: 0273 564656

KEITH ROWLEY
Demonstrator for Nolan Ward Ltd.)
Woodturning courses in the heart of D.H. Lawrence country by professional turner. Weekend courses and accommodation available. Lathes and accessories available. 1 days tuition free if you buy your lathe through me.
SAE for details to:
Keith Rowley, 68 Moorgreen, Newthorpe, Notts.   Tel: Langley 716903

WOODTURNING COURSES

2 Day courses, mid-week or weekend. Expert personal tuition in modern well equipped workshop. Comfortable accommodation available in pleasant surroundings.
SAE for details to
Cliff Willetts, Gables, Frisby On The Wreake, Melton Mowbray, Leics.
Tel: Rotherby (066 475) 246

★ WOOD FINISHING COURSE ★
"LEARN A CRAFT"
4 DAY HOLIDAY COURSE
TUITION FEE £125.00
(including all materials used during the course)
PROFESSIONAL TUITION BASED ON
40 YEARS EXPERIENCE.   *Established 1980*
20% reduced fee for groups of 2 or more, maximum 6 persons, (during March, April, May, and September, October, November.
CHOICE OF FIRST CLASS HOLIDAY
ACCOMMODATION AVAILABLE LOCALLY
(s.a.e. for brochures and further details or phone 022 877 262)
C. CAMPBELL, SUNNYTHWAITE, PENTON, CARLISLE CA6 5RZ
★ *A MEMBER OF THE GUILD OF MASTER CRAFTSMEN* ★

WOODTURNING tuition in Southampton by a professional teacher. All equipment and materials provided. Evenings or weekends. Enquire 0703-433569.

WOODTURNING COURSES. Spend a week-end picking the brains of a professional craftsman in his country cottage and enjoy some superb cooking. Accommodation available for couples. Dave Regester, Millstream Cottage, Higher Town, Sampford, Peverell, Tiverton, Devon. (0884) 820109.

CORRECTION
Previous issues of The Wood-worker contained advertise-ments for the **Eastwood Craft Centre**, advertising courses of '14 days or 4 weeks'. These advertisements were printed incorrectly and should have read **'4 days** or 4 weeks'. *We apologise for any incon-venience caused.*

FRENCH POLISHING COURSES
To suit individual needs 4 day or four weeks. Maximum 3 students; with A. V. Fry LCG, DLC,M. Coll. P. A qualified craftsman and lec-turer. SAE Midlands School of french Polishing, Eastwood Craft.

EASTWOOD CRAFT CENTRE,
18A Mansfield Road, Eastwood, Notts.
Tel: (0332) 553505 after 5 p.m.

WOODTURNING COURSES
2-day courses given by Christopher Child. £80 complete. 2 pupils maximum. We have 21 years teaching experience. 50 miles from London. Accommodation available. Send S.A.E. for details.
Tel: (0787) 237291.
The Old Hyde, Little Yeldham, Essex CO9 4QT.

PETER CHILD

GORDON PETERS
One and two day woodturning courses; weekends if desired. One student per course; husband/wife team considered. Meals and accom-modation if required.

SAE for details to:
37 Pheasant Way, Beeches Park, Cirencester, Glos. Tel: 0285 66907

CRAFT WOODTURNING
A two day residential woodturning course for beginners in a fully modernised 17th century Devon coaching inn. Teaching limited to two students per course, accommodation for families if required.
S.A.E. for brochure to:
Oliver Plant, Hartford Barton, Gittisham, Hornton, Devon, EX14 0AW or Phone Honiton 44155.

Roger Holley's Video-Workshop
teach yourself turning

This is an excellent new way to learn woodturning. The 1½ hour colour tape and booklet provides you with a comprehensive guide which covers:
1. The lathe
2. Woodturning tools
3. Tool sharpening
4. Cutting techniques
5. Chuck work
6. Finishing

Only £40

Send cheques with orders please for £40.00 (inc. p&p) and state format required (either VHS or BETA) to Roger Holley, 11 Summerleaze Park, Yeovil BA20 2BP. Tel: 0935 25521 or send SAE for full details.

FULL TIME COURSES
IN FINE CABINET MAKING
Two places exist for a one year course, leading to work of exhibition quality
David Savage FURNITURE MAKER
FOR PROSPECTUS APPLY TO:
DAVID SAVAGE CABINET MAKING
21·WESTCOMBE, BIDEFORD, DEVON EX39 3JQ

WOODTURNING COURSES
IN MID-NORFOLK
Tuition for beginners and the more experienced by professional turner, in fully equipped workshop.
Tony Waddilove, Unit A, Hill Farm Workshops, Great Dunham, King's Lynn, Norfolk. Tel: 07605 674

FURNITURE RESTORATION. Specialised weekend courses in all aspects of antique furniture restoration. Maximum of three students in well equipped Cotswold work-shops. Restorations Unlimited, Pinkney Park. Malmesbury, Wilts. Tel. Malmesbury 840888.

WOODTURNING IN NORTH WALES. Courses, beginners/intermediate, day/evening. Turning blanks, exotic/native finish-ing materials. Keith Lawrence, Old Stable Turnery, Tri-thy-centre. Mold. Tel: (0352) 771771.

WOODTURNING COURSES in mid-Norfolk. Tuition for beginners and the more ex-perienced by professional turner, in fully equipped workshop. Tony Waddilove, Unit A, Hill Farm Workshops, Great Dunham, King's Lynn, Norfolk. Tel. 07605 674.

WOODTURNING day courses, or at £5.00 per hour, with Jack Durey. Enquire: Brenchley 2465 (Kent).

A new profession for you in 1986

Learn to conserve and restore antique furniture with Bruce Luckhurst, qualified teacher and restorer for over 20 years. Applications are invited for this one-year course starting in September 1986. Previous cabinet making and polishing experience not essential for entry.

For prospectus and further details please send 9"×12" s.a.e. to Bruce Luckhurst, Little Surrenden, Bethersden, Kent TN26 3BG.

322

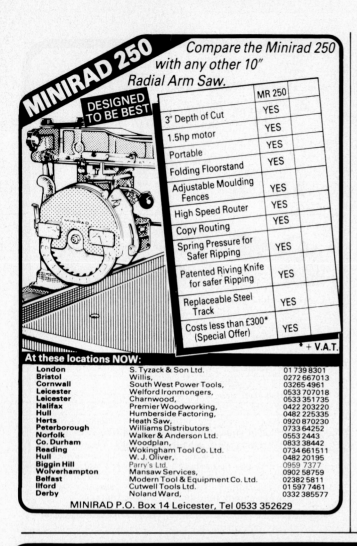

Parlour made

Alex Webb describes how to make a country-style oak cupboard

This type of cupboard first appeared during the 16th and 17th century for use in parlours and halls. They were sometimes used for storing food, and were often called livery cupboards.

● The design is reproduced from *Making Country Furniture* by Alex Webb, published by B. T. Batsford, price £10.95.

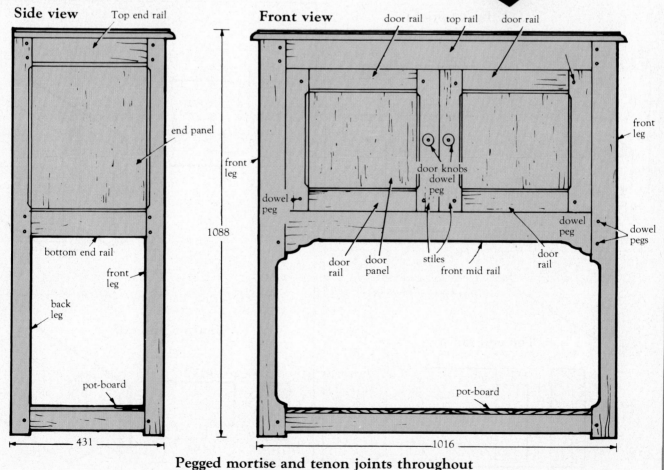

Side view
Top end rail
end panel
bottom end rail
front leg
back leg
pot-board
431

front leg
1088

Front view
door rail   top rail   door rail
door knobs
dowel peg
dowel peg
front leg
dowel peg
dowel pegs
door rail   door panel   stiles   front mid rail   door rail
pot-board
1016

Pegged mortise and tenon joints throughout

Parlour made

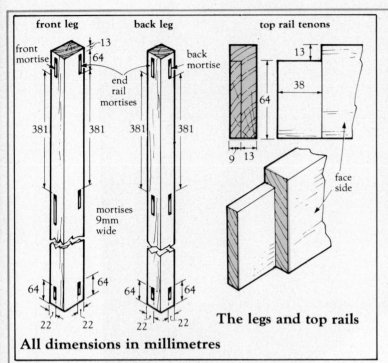

front leg **back leg** **top rail tenons**

front mortise

back mortise

end rail mortises

13
64

381 381 381 381

mortises 9mm wide

13
38
64

9 13

face side

64

64 64

64 64

22 22 22 22

9 13

The legs and top rails

All dimensions in millimetres

1 After you have prepared the timber to the cutting list, mark and cut all the mortise and tenon joints in the cupboard frame. When all these joints have been cut, run through a trial assembly to make sure all joints fit, then dismantle and proceed to the next stage.

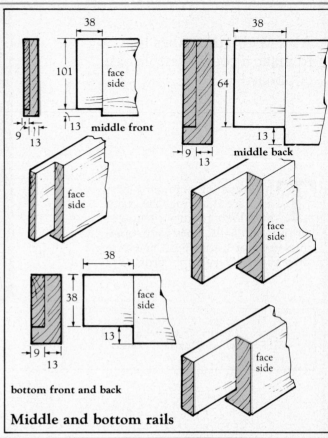

38 38

101 64

face side face side

9 13 13

middle front 9 13

middle back

face side face side

38

38 face side

13

face side

9

13

bottom front and back

Middle and bottom rails

Back upright

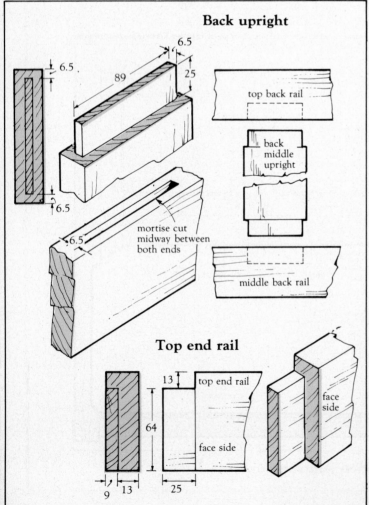

6.5

6.5 6.5 25

89

top back rail

back middle upright

6.5

mortise cut midway between both ends

6.5

middle back rail

Top end rail

13 top end rail

64

face side

face side

9 13 25

Middle end rail

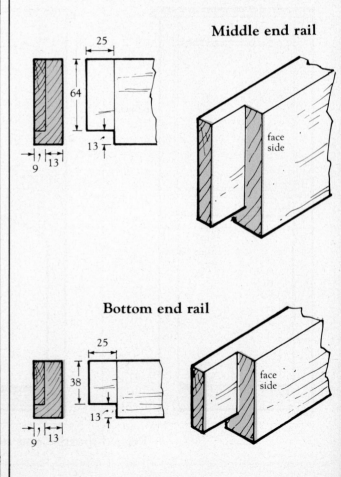

25

64 face side

13

9 13

Bottom end rail

25

38 face side

13

9 13

326

Shaping the legs and rails

2 To bring the front legs into proportion with the back legs, a shaped section has been created on the inside edges. Mark both front legs as shown in **a** then cut away the shaded area with a coping saw or jigsaw. The finished shape will then appear as shown in **b**. Any roughness made by the saw can be smoothed with medium to coarse garnet- or sandpaper, finishing off with a fine grade. To form the shaping at the ends of the middle front rail, mark out each end using the measurements shown in **c**. Use the guidelines to draw in the shape shown in **d**. The whole lower section can now be cut away with a coping saw, leaving the finished shape as shown in **e**.

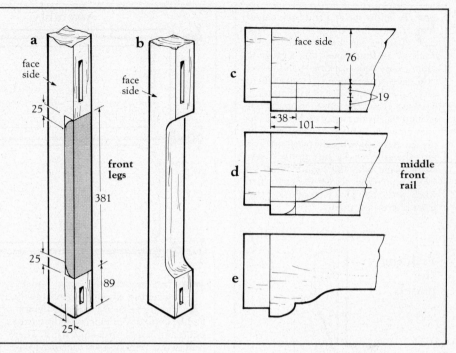

Forming the chamfers

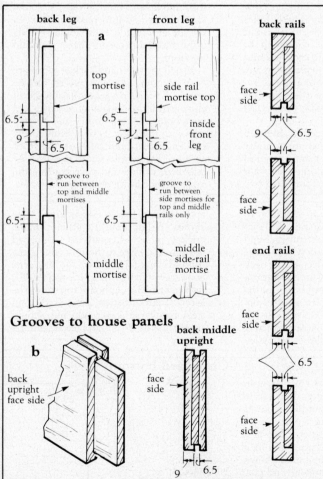

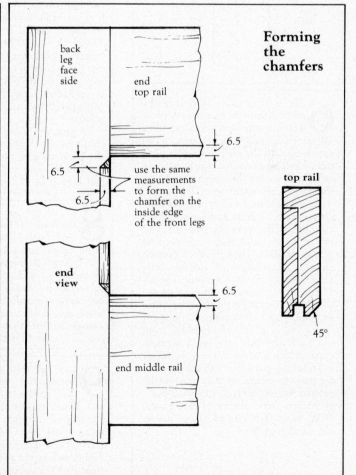

Grooves to house panels

3 Grooves in the rails and legs hold the end and back panels in the frame. They are all 6.5x6.5mm (¼x¼in), and are 9mm in from the face side of all the components. In the legs, the grooves are cut into the mortise positions by their depth, to meet the full depth of the grooves in the rails coming to meet them. The location and details of the grooves for the legs are set out in **a**, for the rails in **b**.

4 Put chamfers all round the inside edges of the end panel components to remove the sharp edges and generally improve the overall appearance. On the legs, the chamfer runs between the points where the shoulders of the top and middle end-rail tenons meet the upright; on the top and middle endrails, it runs all the way through.

Parlour made

5 To allow the end and back panels to slot into the grooves, a large chamfer has to be made on the *inside* of all four panels. Set a gauge to 3mm (⅛in) and, working from the face side, gauge a line around all four edges of each panel. Reset the gauge to 25mm and, working from the edge, gauge a line around the inside face of each panel. The area between the two lines can now be planed away, allowing the panels to drop into the grooves. Be sure to use a very sharp plane with the mouth finely set when you plane across the grain, and work with the plane held askew, going from high to low points.

Fielding the panels

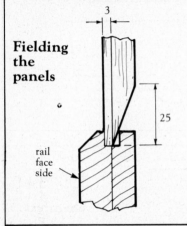

6 There are various ways to form the moulding on the top, the easiest of which is with a power router and a 19mm (¾in) radius ovolo cutter. The easiest ones to use are those with a pilot pin or guide-bearing, in which case you only have to set the depth of the top shoulder-cut to about 3mm (⅛in).

If you are using hand-tool techniques, set a gauge to 22mm and scribe a good clear line all the way round the front and two ends. A knife gauge cuts cleanest across endgrain. Then plane a 'rounded chamfer' carefully up to the line, remembering you want a radius of about 19mm down from the bottom of the shoulder. You can get the shoulder with a shoulder plane, then use it to round off the radius; or grind a 19mm radius in an old hacksaw-blade and use a scratch-stock, which is basically the same design as a marking-gauge but with a slot to hold the hacksaw-blade, set in so that just the ground radius cuts (see 'Question Box', WW/Jan, 'The charm of discretion', WW/Mar). You can, of course, use an old moulding plane!

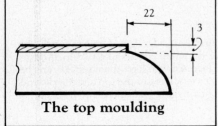

The top moulding

Assembly

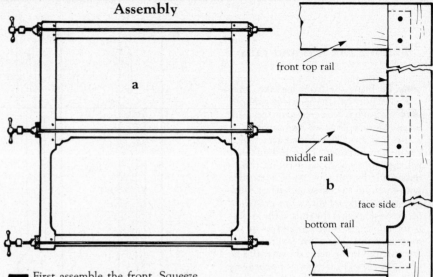

7 First assemble the front. Squeeze a generous amount of glue into the mortises that are to house the top, middle and bottom rails, push home the joints and cramp up as shown in **a.** Then drill two 6.5mm holes in each top joint, two holes in each middle joint, and one hole in each bottom joint. All holes should be drilled to a depth of about 32mm at the positions shown in **b.** Squeeze a blob of glue into each hole and tap home a dowel peg; wipe away any surplus glue, then place to one side to dry. If you wish, draw-bore the joints as explained in the cricket table project last month.

To glue up the back section, first run glue into the mortises that are to house the back upright, push it into position between the top and middle back rails and cramp up. In each joint drill two 6.5mm holes through the frame. Squeeze a blob of glue into each hole and tap home a 22mm dowel peg in each. Next, run glue into the mortises that are to house the top, middle and bottom rails, slide the two back panels into position between the top and middle rails, and assemble, using the same procedure as for gluing up the front.

When the front and back sections are perfectly dry, the end pieces can be attached. Squeeze a generous amount of glue into all the remaining mortises and push home the top, middle and bottom rails into the back section. Slide in the two end panels and push on the front section. The whole frame can now be cramped, drilled and pegged using the same method as for gluing up the front.

8 To fix the door-stop block on to the inside of the top rail, drill two 5mm holes 13mm in from each end of the block, and 13mm down from the top. Countersink one side, glue the back of the block and screw into position, using two no. 8x1in screws. To fix the cupboard top onto the frame, drill ten holes, equidistant round the top rails, of a larger diameter than the screws you will use. The angle of the holes to be drilled and further fixing instructions were shown in last month's article on the cricket table; alternatively, L-shaped 'buttons', screwed to the underside of the top and engaging in slots in the rails, are a good way of fixing a table-top to allow for movement. The cupboard top should be screwed into position using no.8x1½in steel countersunk screws, and should overhang the front and each end by 25mm.

9 Lay the four cupboard support battens flat on the bench and in each of the two long ones tap in five 38mm pins or nails until the points just appear through the wood; tap in three in the two end battens. Smear a layer of glue along each batten and fix it 13mm below the middle rail as shown in **a.** As the cupboard bottom and pot-board are made up by butting a number of boards together, the two end boards are best cut and fixed first since these notch around the leg section. Select the two boards that are to be used as end boards and cut the corners away, **b.** Then cut and fit the rest of the boards.

Cupboard bottom

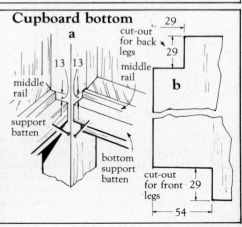

Parlour made

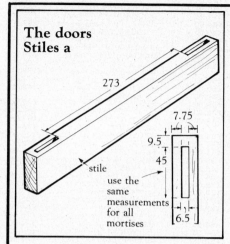

The doors
Stiles a

273

7.75

9.5

45

stile

use the same measurements for all mortises

6.5

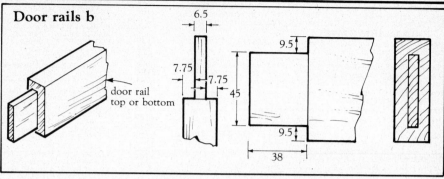

Door rails b

6.5

9.5

7.75

7.75

45

door rail top or bottom

9.5

38

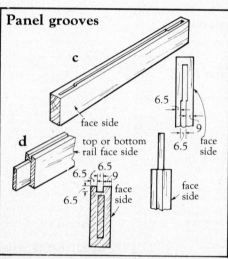

Panel grooves

c

face side

6.5

9

d

top or bottom rail face side

6.5

6.5

9

6.5

face side

6.5

face side

face side

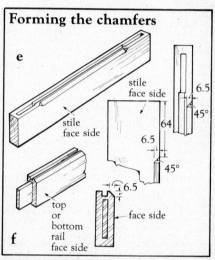

Forming the chamfers

e

stile face side

stile face side

6.5

45°

64

6.5

45°

top or bottom rail face side

6.5

face side

f

10 The first step in making the doors is to mark and cut the mortise and tenon joints. The size and location of the mortises cut into the stiles are shown in **a**, and the tenons on the top and bottom rails are shown in **b** together with all the measurements for cutting them. The grooves that are to be cut in the stiles **c**, run from the top mortise to the bottom mortise, measure 6.5x6.5mm, and are 9mm in from the face side. The grooves in the top and bottom rails run the full length of the rail **d**, the measurements being the same as those for the stiles. The chamfers into the door rails match those on the frame, and all the measurements are given in **e** and **f**. The door panels have to be chamfered on the inside to allow them to sit inside the grooves: step **5** shows the measurements and procedure.

11 To assemble the doors, squeeze a generous amount of glue into each mortise, push home the the top and bottom rail tenons into one stile, slide in the panel and then push home the other stile. Cramp up and the drill one 6.5mm hole through the middle of each joint. Squeeze a blob of glue in each hole and tap in a peg. Wipe away any surplus glue and place to one side to dry. You can draw-bore, as mentioned before.

The hinges on this cupboard are brass H-hinges, though any surface-fixing hinge would be suitable. The photo shows the position of the hinges; as they are surface fixed, little skill is needed to fix them. Simply lay them on to the frame, start a hole for the screws with a bradawl and screw them on.

Turned wooden knobs are used for handles in the cupboard illustrated, but the choice is yours.

Finally, sandpaper the completed piece to a finish, then apply the polish or wax of your choice. ∎

Cutting list

Legs, back	2	1066mm x	50mm x	50mm
Legs, front	2	1066	76	50
Top	*	1066	457	22
Top rail, front	1	940	76	22
Mid rail, front	1	940	114	22
Bottom rail, front	1	940	50	22
Top and middle rails, back	2	992	76	22
Bottom rail, back	1	992	50	22
End rails, top and middle	4	381	76	22
End rails, bottom	2	381	50	22
Pot-board	*	1016	432	13
Cupboard bottom	*	972	387	13
Cupboard bottom support battens, end	2 2	330 330	38 38	22 22
Cupboard bottom support batten, front	1	863	38	22
Cupboard bottom support	1	914	34	22
Back middle upright	1	432	101	22
End panels	2	394	343	13
Back panels	2	394	419	13
Door stiles	4	381	64	22
Door top and bottom rails	4	381	64	22
Door panels	2	317	267	13
Door knobs (if required)	2	76	38	38
Door stop-block	1	89	38	13
Dowel pegs	40	32	6.5	
Dowel pegs	12	25	6.5	

*number depends on board widths available

Wood glue; 2 pairs of hinges, 76mm, iron or brass, and screws to fix; 22 no.10x1½in steel countersunk screws; 2 no.8x1in steel countersunk screws; approximately 45 nails, 38mm, for fixing pot-board and cupboard bottom.

AXMINSTER POWER TOOL CENTRE

WOODWORKING LATHES
OUR PRICE INC. VAT

MYFORD ML8 36" centres excluding rear turning facility **£376**
MYFORD ML8B 36" crs. .... **£432** ML8C 42" crs. **£467**
HARRISON GRADUATE 30" Centres .. **£1093** 42" Centres .. **£1146** Short Bed .. **£965**
ELU DB180 38" crs. 15" dia. swing. Fully motorised **£274**
KITY 663 4 speed (Free 4 jaw chuck) **£542** KITY 664 variable speed (Free 4 jaw chuck) **£692**
MINIMAX T90 .... **£375** T100 .... **£442** T120 .... **£499**
MINIMAX COPIERS C190 .... **£431** CT100 .... **£457** CT120 .... **£499**
TYME CUB lathe 4 speed .... **£285** TYME AVON lathe 4 speed **£408**
WOODTURNING FITMENTS FOR ALL MAKES OF MACHINE (List on request)

RADIAL ARM SAWS

EUMENIA 9" 1½HP Radial Saw 15" Crosscut .... **£276** 24" Crosscut **£330**
NEW DeWALT 1251 10" 1½HP 15" Crosscut .... **POA**
NEW DeWALT DW 1501 10" Crosscut .... **POA**
NEW DeWALT 12" RADIAL SAWS 2HP 18" and 24" crosscut .... **POA**
DeWALT DW1600S 14" saw Max op. cap. 36" 2½HP 1PH .... **£979** 4HP 3PH **£940**
NEW ELU PS174 Mitre/Crosscut Saw 2" Cut 10" Crosscut **£244**
DeWALT DW1201 Folding 10" Radial Saw **£279**

SAW BENCHES

MAKITA 2708 8" Saw (will accept router and jigsaw) **£204**
ROYAL MK111B 10" Cast Iron Tilt Arbor Saw 1½HP **£599**
ROYAL MKIIIDL 10" Delux Cast Iron Tilt Arbor Saw 1½HP **£699**
WADKIN AGSP Scoring Panel Saw 10"/12" 3PH .... **£1,639** 1PH **£1,741**
ELU TGS 172 Saw Bench/Mitre Saw with TCT Blade .... **£369** ELU TGS 171 .... **£311**
LUNA L18 12" TCT Panel Saw with sliding table **£980**
SCHEPPACH TKU 12" Saw Bench 2.3kw motor Fl. Stdg. **£205**
SLIDING TABLE for TKU-TKH .... **£69** Panel Cutting Extension **£55**
WADKIN AGS 250/300 10"-12" Tilt Arbor Saw 3HP 3PH .... **£1,052** 3HP 1PH **£1,137**
New KITY 10" tilt arbor 2HP floor stdg. saw bench .... **SPECIAL PRICE**
STARTRITE TA300PS Scoring Saw c/w sliding carriage **£1,699.00**

BANDSAWS (excellent stocks of all longlife blades)

BURGESS BK3+ MkII with FREE fretsaw and jigsaw attachment .... (inc. P&P) **£115**
DeWALT DW100 2 speed. 13" throat. 4" cut. With mitre fence & disc sander **£149**
DeWALT 3401. 2 speed. 12" throat. 6" cut **£256**
KITY K613 8" cut 12" throat Bench Mtg or Floor Stdg. .... **SPECIAL PRICE**
STARTRITE 301. 12" throat. 6" cut. Steel table. Floor standing **£395**
STARTRITE 352 2 speed 14" throat 12" cut Fl. Stdg. 3PH .... **£639** 1PH **£665**
LUNA BS320 6" depth of cut. Cast table **£324**
MINIMAX P32 6" cut 14" throat Cast Tables **£367**
MINIMAX S45 10" cut 17" throat. Very solid construction. Cast Tables **£615**

PLANER/THICKNESSER

MULTICO CPT200/230 12" × 9" ¾" rebate **£1966**
DeWALT DW1150 10" × 6" 2 Speed power feed 2HP Motor .... **POA**
DeWALT DW600 Slot Morticer for DW1150 .... **£65** Stand for DW1150 .... **£25**
STARTRITE PT260. 10" × 6" Steel tables. ⅝" rebate **£820**
SHEPPACH HMO SOLO. 10" × 6". Steel tables. 2HP motor. Floor standing **£475**
STARTRITE SD310. 12" × 7". ⅝" rebate. Cast iron 3PH .... **£1,226** 1PH **£1,280**
WADKIN BAOS 12" × 7" Solid Cast. Heavy Duty 3PH .... **£2,757** 1PH **£2,930**

DRILLING AND MORTISING MACHINES

FOBCO 'STAR'. ½" capacity. 4-speed. British made precision machine **£323**
MORTICING ATTACHMENT for FOBCO M/Cs. With clamp & ⅜" chisel **£57**
WARCO 'HOBBY'. ½" capacity. 5-speed, tilting table **£125**
WARCO 2B ⅝" capacity 2MT tilt table bench mounting **£199** 2F12 floor standing **£222**
STARTRITE SP250 5-speed ½" bench drill .... **£339** Floor standing **£379**
WADKIN MORTICER 1" capacity. 1PH or 3PH **£575**
MULTICO MORTICER 240v Floor Standing **£632**
MULTICO HM MORTICER Bench Mounting ⅝" Max Capacity **£356**
RYOBI Chain Morticer 240v Portable Morticer **£344**
SMITH BCM Bench Morticer .... **£399** CM75 Floor Stdg. Model **£499**
Mortice Chisels & Bits ¼" **£14.00** ⅜" **£16.00** ½" **£18.00** ⅝" **£22.00** ¾" **£32.00**
Ridgeway chisel + bits ¼" **£19.00** ⅜" **£23.88** ½" **£23.88** ⅝" **£35.00** ¾" **£37.00**

SPINDLE MOULDERS

KITY 623 30mm Spindle 3-speed 2HP 1PH WITH SLIDING TABLE **£649**
LUNA L28 30mm spindle 3-speed 5" rise 3HP 240v **£980**
STARTRITE T30 1¼" spindle with sliding table 1PH **£889**
SCHEPPACH HF33 2 Speed 2HP 30mm **£485**
WADKIN BEL 4 Speed 5HP Spindle Moulder (3PH Only) **£1,890**
MULTICO TM1 Single Ended Tennoner 240v **£1360**

COMBINATION MACHINES

LUNA Z40 (ex Mia 6) with TCT blade **£690**
STARTRITE K260 Combination. 'FREE CUTTER SET' 1PH **£1,990**
STARTRITE K210 Combination 'FREE CUTTER SET' 1PH **£1,825**
LUNA W49 Saw Spindle Combination 12" Saw 30mm Spindle **£1,750**
LUNA W59 10" Planer 12" Saw 30mm Spindle 2HP .... **£2450** 3HP **£2690**
LUNA W64 12" Planer 12" Saw 30mm Spindle **£3050**
LUNA W69 16" Planer 12" Saw 30mm Spindle 1PH .... **£3900** 3PH **£3800**
SCHEPPACH COMBI 10" × 6" Planer. 12" Saw 30m Spindle **£860**

★ ★ ★ ★ KITY COMBINATION MACHINES ★ ★ ★ ★ ★

K5 COMBINATION K5 BASIC K704 TABLE COMBINATION K704 DIRECT DRIVE AND ACCESSORIES ALL AT SPECIAL PRICES SEND FOR LATEST PRICE LIST.
★ ★ ★ ★ *FREE DELIVERY ON ALL KITY COMBINATION MACHINES* ★ ★ ★ ★ ★

MISCELLANEOUS MACHINES & EQUIPMENT

DeWALT DW250. 10" Bevel/Mitre saw. 1HP motor **£194**
LUNA YK1500 Pad Sander 1PH .... **£1,327** 3PH **£1,300**
LUNA YKV 1200 1½ HP Face & Edge Sander. Floor Standing **£745** Wall Mounting **£725**
NOBEX 202 Mitre Saw .... **£69.96** NOBEX 303 Mitre Saw **£44**
DeWALT Twin bag dust extractor .... **£265** Multico DEA **£339**
LUNA SPS400 Dust Extractor 240v Portable Unit **£215.00**
LUNA W178 Dust Extractor Fir, Mtg. **£292**
LUNA NF259 Large Capacity Dust Extractor 1PH **£499**
LION MITRE TRIMMER excellent for accurate mitre cuts **£249**
LUNA Support Roller .... **£27** Delux Combi Support roller **£38**
MITRE CUTTERS (ORTEGUILE) ORC55 **£210** ORC80 **£260** ORC100 **£390** 100F Fl. Stdg. **POA**

SPINDLE MOULDER TOOLING

LEITZ 488 Cutter Blocks 30mm or 1¼" 92mm dia. **£44** 100mm dia. **£51** 120mm dia. **£55**
WOBBLE SAWS for Spindle Moulders 6" 3mm-21mm **£76** 10" dia. 3mm-30mm **£88**
OMAS TIGER CUTTER BLOCKS 30mm or 1¼" .... **£46** Cutter profiles .... pair **£11.50**

INDUSTRIAL QUALITY T.C.T SAWBLADES

ALL PRICES, INCLUDE V.A.T. AND P&P
GENERAL DUTY (MADE IN SHEFFIELD) PREMIUM QUALITY FOR CONTINUOUS USE (MADE IN W. GERMANY)

BLADE DIAMETER	6"				7"-7 1/4"				8"				9"-9 1/4"			
NO OF TEETH	16	24	36	48	18	30	42	56	20	36	48	64	24	40	54	72
GENERAL DUTY	£16	£17	£20	£26	£16	£17	£21	£26	£20	£25	£27	£32	£18	£23	£27	£30
PREMIUM QUALITY	-	£24	-	£31	-	-	-	-	-	-	-	-	-	£36	£40	-
BLADE DIAMETER	10"				12"				14"				16"			
NO OF TEETH	24	40	60	80	32	48	72	96	36	60	84	108	28	36	60	96
GENERAL DUTY	£23	£26	£35	£38	£25	£31	£35	£44	£34	£42	£50	£57	-	-	-	-
PREMIUM QUALITY	£29	£33	£38	£46	£33	£39	£47	£55	£38	£44	£54	£62	£43	£46	£55	£64

PLEASE STATE BORE SIZE WHEN ORDERING

ROUTERS
OUR PRICE INC. VAT

ELU MOF 96 600w ¼" **£77.95**
ELU MOF 96E 750w ¼" **£98.95**
ELU MOF 31 1200w ¼" ⅜" ½" **£123.95**
ELU MOF 77 variable speed ... **£195.00**
ELU MOF 98 1500 ¼" ⅜" ½" **£144.95**
ELU MOF 177 1600w ¼" ⅜" ½" **£156.95**
ELU MOF 177E 1800w ¼" ⅜" ½" **£181.95**
HITACHI TR8 730w ¼" **£64.00**
HITACHI TR12 1300w ¼", ⅜", ½" **£119.00**
MAKITA 3600 1500w ¼" ⅜" ½" **£141.00**
BOSCH POF5 2¼" 500w **£50.25**
RYOBI R150 ¼" 750w **£64.00**
RYOBI R500 ¼", ⅜", ½" **£113.00**

ROUTER ACCESSORIES

ELU MOF 96 Accessory Kit **£60.00**
DOVETAIL JIG c/w TCT Cutter . **£60.00**
STAIR Routing Jig **£69.00**
ELU Router Combi Bench **£89.00**
MAKITA Router Bench **£35.00**
ELU Router Bracket for DeWalt **£33.00**

BELT SANDER

ELU MHB 157 3" 600w **£85.95**
ELU MHB 157E 3" Variable Speed **£94.95**
ELU MHB 157 Stand **£21.00**
ELU MHB 157 Frame **£28.00**
ELU MHB 90 4" 850w **£143.95**
ELU MHB 90K 4" with frame . **£164.95**
HITACHI SB-75 3" 950w **£99.00**
HITACHI SB-110 4" 950w **£129.00**
MAKITA 4" 1040w **£141.50**
BOSCH 3" 620w **£69.00**

JIGSAWS

ELU ST 152 420w **£82.95**
ELU ST 152E 420w **£86.95**
BOSCH PST 50E 350w **£36.75**
BOSCH PST 55PE 380w **£61.00**
BOSCH 1581/7 Var. Speed **£102.00**

DRILL STANDS

BOSCH S7 Drill Stand **£48.00**
WOLFCRAFT Compact Drill Stand **£44.00**
WOLF Morticer Stand **£129.00**

MISCELLANEOUS POWER TOOLS

ELU DS 140 Biscuit Jointer **£156.95**
BOSCH Wet 'n' Dry Cleaner **£93.75**
HITACHI 9" Grinder 2000w **£89.00**
BOSCH Hot Air Gun 1500w **£24.00**

CIRCULAR SAWS

ELU MH151 TCT Blade **£77.95**
ELU MH65 7¼" TCT 1200w ... **£106.95**
ELU MH85 9¼" TCT 1800w ... **£152.95**
ELU MH182 8" TCT **£123.95**
HITACHI PSU-6 6" 1050w **£63.95**
HITACHI PSU-7 7¼" 1600w **£95.63**
HITACHI PSU-9 9¼" 1759w ... **£112.95**
HITACHI PSM-7 7¼" TCT 1200w **£129.95**
HITACHI PSM-9 9¼" TCT 1600w **£136.95**
WOLF 9¼ Circular Saw **£134**

WOODTURNERS "AT LAST PERFECTION"

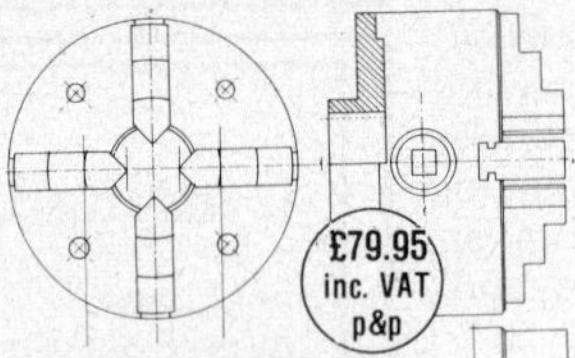

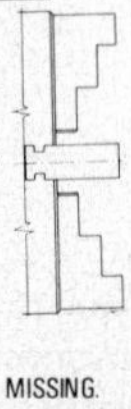

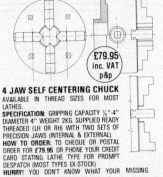

4 JAW SELF CENTERING CHUCK

AVAILABLE IN THREAD SIZES FOR MOST LATHES.
SPECIFICATION: GRIPPING CAPACITY ⅛"-4" DIAMETER 4" WEIGHT 2KG. SUPPLIED READY THREADED (LH OR RH) WITH TWO SETS OF PRECISION JAWS (INTERNAL & EXTERNAL).
HOW TO ORDER: TO CHEQUE OR POSTAL ORDER FOR **£79.95** OR PHONE YOUR CREDIT CARD STATING LATHE TYPE FOR PROMPT DESPATCH (MOST TYPES EX-STOCK)
HURRY! YOU DON'T KNOW WHAT YOUR MISSING.

BENCH GRINDERS
OUR PRICE INC. VAT

ELU EDS 163 6" DE **£56.95**
ELU EDS 164 7" DE **£61.95**
ELU MWA 149 Honer Grinder **£73.95**
LEROY SOMER 5" DE **£31.00**
LEROY SOMER 6" DE **£42.00**
LEROY SOMER 7" DE **£52.00**
LEROY SOMER Whetstone **£73.00**
LUNA 8" Whetstone Grinder **£99.00**

CORDLESS DRILLS

HITACHI Cordless DTC10 .... **£59.00**
HITACHI DV10D Hammer Drill **£99.00**
MAKITA 6012DE 2 Speed **£78.00**
MAKITA Hammer Drill 8400DW . **£99.00**
MAKITA 6" Saw in case **£168.00**
HITACHI D10DB ⅜" Var. Speed .. **£77.95**
HITACHI C6DA 6" Saw **£148.00**

HAMMER DRILL

BOSCH 400-2 400w **£29.50**
BOSCH 500-RLE 500w **£48.75**
BOSCH 7002 RLE 700w **£81.00**
HITACHI VTP1 3K ½" 460w **£74.00**
HITACHI VTP16AK ⅝" 800w ... **£103.00**
B&D P2162 ⅜" Var. Speed Rev. . **£42.00**
B&D P2264 ½" **£47.00**
B&D P2266 ½" Var. Speed Rev. . **£59.00**

FINISHING SANDERS

ELU MVS 156 1/3 Sheet **£65.95**
ELU MVS 156E Electronic **£77.95**
ELU MVS 94 Heavy Duty **£90.95**
ELU MVS 47 Heavy Duty **£98.95**
ELU Palm Sanders ¼ or ⅓ Sheet **£44.95**
HITACHI Palm Sander **£39.00**
MAKITA Palm Sander **£42.00**
B&D P6303 1/2 Sheet Ind. **£57.00**
BOSCH PSS230 1/3 Sheet **£27.00**

POWER PLANERS

ELU MFF80 850w **£88.95**
ELU MFF80K 850w **£106.95**
HITACHI FU-20 720w **£74.00**
HITACHI P20SA 720w **£84.00**

DREMEL POWER TOOLS

15" Scroll Saw Sander **£72.00**
Delux Scroll Saw Sander **£93.00**
258 Const. Speed Moto Tool **£42.95**
358 Var. Speed Moto Tool **£55.95**
359 as 358 with 35 Accs. **£68.95**
Router Base for Moto Tool **£11.95**
Drill Stand for Moto Tool **£25.95**
238 Moto Flex Tool **£78.95**
338 Var. Speed Flex Tool **£86.95**
JAPANESE HORIZONTAL WHETSTONE GRINDER **£108.00**

ELU ACCESSORIES

90% of all Elu Accessories in Stock. 10% discount on all items. Post Paid on most items. Send S.A.E. for current list.

ROUTER CUTTERS

20-25% OFF LEADING BRANDS
EXCELLENT STOCKS OF HSS & TCT ROUTER CUTTERS OVER 500 PROFILES IN STOCK. SEND NOW FOR FREE CUTTER CHART:-

LIBERON FINISHES

Sanding Sealer, French Polishes, Stains, Waxes, Wire Wool etc. All Ex Stock. Post Paid on orders over £5.00. SAE for free list.

BANDSAW BLADES

LONGLIFE QUALITY BLADES. OVER 4000 BLADES IN STOCK SEND NOW FOR CURRENT PRICE LIST.
Metal Blade Guides for DeWalt BS1310 & DW100 .... **£5.20**/set of 4

WOODTURNING ACCESSORIES (State make of Machine)

Sorby Precision Chuck **£52.70**
2½" Woodscrew Chuck **£22.00**
1½" Woodscrew Chuck **£18.50**
Drill Chuck 0-½" 1MT or 2MT .. **£15.00**
Coronet Service Kit, main brgs & belt **£37.50**
Coronet Chuck Sets **£65.00**
Collet Chuck Bodies **£28.50**
Live Centre 1MT or 2MT **£18.00**
Drive Centre Kit 5 Heads 1MT or 2MT **£39.95**
For TYME, CORONET, MYFORD, MINIMAX, HARRISON, KITY, ARUNDEL & OTHERS.

SASH CRAMPS (P&P £2.00 per order) May be mixed for quantity

RECORD 135-24" 1 off £19 5 off £17
135-36" 1 off £20 5 off £18
135-42" 1 off £21 5 off £19
135-48" 1 off £22 5 off £20
DRAPER 18" 1 off £13.50 5 off £11.50
30" 1 off £17.25 5 off £14.95
40" 1 off £18.40 5 off £16.00
60" 1 off £28.00 5 off £26.00

HAND TOOLS (P&P £1.50 per order)

STANLEY 04 Smooth Plane **£18.50**
STANLEY 04½ Smooth Plane **£20.00**
STANLEY 05 Jack Plane **£27.50**
STANLEY 05½ Jack Plane **£29.50**
STANLEY 06 Fore Plane **£36.00**
STANLEY 07 Fore Plane **£40.00**
STANLEY 10 Rebate Plane **£38.00**
STANLEY 60½ Block Plane **£18.00**
STANLEY RECORD 778 Rebate Pl. **£31.00**
RECORD 146 Hold Fast **£14.00**
Extra Collars for 146 .... **£3.00**
RECORD Cramp Heads **£12.00**
RECORD 52½E 9" Wood Vice **£62.00**
LIP & SPUR DRILL 1-13mm × 0.5 **£54.00**
CLIFTON 3 in 1 Plane **£67.00**
RECORD 04 Smooth Plane **£18.00**
RECORD 04½ Smooth Plane **£19.00**
RECORD 05 Jack Plane **£28.00**
RECORD 05½ Jack Plane **£29.00**
RECORD 06 Fore Plane **£34.00**
RECORD 07 Jointer Plane **£38.50**
RECORD 010 Rebate Plane **£38.00**
RECORD 060½ Block Plane **£15.50**
RECORD 020C Circular Plane **£66.00**
RECORD Dowelling Jig **£31.00**
RECORD 141 Corner Cramps **£21.00**
PARAMO Cramp Heads **£10.00**
RECORD 53E 10½" Wood Vice .. **£71.00**
LIP & SPUR DRILL 1/16-½ × 16ths **£39.00**
Clifton Rebate Plane 420 .... **£57.00**

CLICO SAWTOOTH CUTTERS (inc. VAT P&P) 6" long with ½" shank

⅜" .... £7.70; ½" .... £7.90; ⅝" .... £8.70; ¾" .... £9.50; ⅞" £10.20;
1" .... £10.90; 1⅛" .... £12.80; 1¼" .... £15.60; 1⅜" .... £16.20; 1½" £17.10;
1⅝" . £19.70; 1¾" . £22.40; 1⅞" . £24.80; 2" . £26.20; 2¼" . £32.90; 2½" . £43.70

IMMEDIATE DESPATCH ON CREDIT CARD PHONED ORDERS — CREDIT TERMS AVAILABLE OVER £120

CHARD STREET AXMINSTER DEVON EX13 5DZ 0297 33656 6.30-9pm 34836

BARCLAYCARD VISA

The house in the woods

On-site architect William Moorwood played a key role in building the first house of the School for Woodland Industries, featured last month. Here's his first-hand account

● *An early sketch of the school. The prototype (since changed) is on the right*

I believe that the prototype roundwood house at Hooke Park represents an important point in the evolution of a new tradition in building. As architects, Ahrends Burton and Koralek are committed both to extending the boundaries of technology for more efficient use of resources, and to being closely involved in the building process itself. Our relationship with Frei Otto and Buro Happold at Hooke (consulting architect and consulting engineers) has brought encouraging success in these aims.

We were asked to design a construction system using softwood thinnings, that could be successfully built with only basic carpentry skills. This meant all the 'high-tech' aspects of the design had to be worked out in advance to simplify work on site.

The local timber was mainly Norway spruce, with small amounts of Corsican pine, western red cedar, and Douglas fir. Spruce had the disadvantage of being the weakest timber, but there was more of it, and if we got it right with spruce, the other stronger timbers would cause fewer problems in future building. Small round-wood is very strong in tension — it resembles the structure of spun suspension wire — and the design takes advantage of this, in that the roof members all hang off the ridge cable. A cable at the eaves takes the load at the bottom of the roof members and transfers compression to the rest of the frame. Using green timber caused few problems, as shrinkage is allowed for in the design, and anyway most is across the grain rather than along it.

The key point of the whole design, and its need to be simple to work with on site, is the brilliant timber jointing system devised by Buro Happold. A conical hole is drilled in the timber, a threaded steel rod is inserted, and epoxy resin is forced into the hole. The resin penetrates the end fibres and makes a surprisingly strong bond, which is improved if the wood is green as the sap helps penetration. The resin also serves to insulate the metal from the green wood — a factor that has led to some failures in the past. The joint works very well in compression too. The resin plug binds together the central fibres, which would otherwise split apart as they do in a fence post when it's hammered into the ground.

Rot is a major problem in wood structures, and as well as allowing for it in the design it's wise to treat the wood. Our

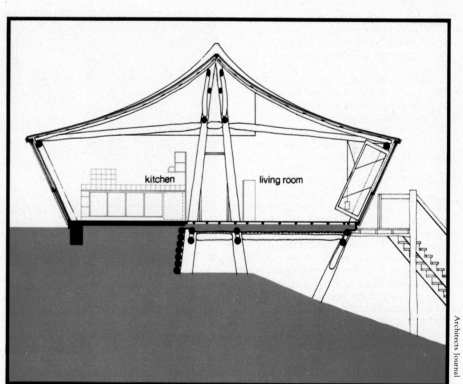

● *The section shows how compression and tension work in the structure. Tension from ridge-pole to eaves, compression from eaves to frame*

Architects Journal

solution was to dip the freshly cut and debarked roundwood in a tank on site containing concentrated 'Timbor' at 50°C. It was then stored under polythene for about two months. The advantages are that the wood doesn't have to be taken off the site for treatment and expensive pressure-impregnation is avoided.

Having dealt with the theory, we had to build a prototype to test our calculations —

something to which ABK was anyway committed as a natural part of designing a new system. Dowding and Udall, a firm in Bridport, were hired to do all the carpentry work. Before I took them on I spent a lot of time explaining the construction system and the size of timbers to be used. What impressed me was the more I explained the possible problems, the more interested and involved Tony Udall and his men became.

The house in the woods

● *The A-frames and front porch skeleton loom in a misty forest morning . . .*

● *Square to round; the outer windows caused fitting headaches*

At the same time we had arranged for a full set of fabrication drawings to be made. When we started on site there was a set of drawings itemising every element of the structural frame, which enabled us to prefabricate the entire structure in kit form. This is always done with steel-frame buildings, so the principle is well established.

One on-site design change was a modification to the resin joints. In theory the holes containing the resin and steel rods should be conical; however, we found that using a series of Forstner bits to make a stepped hole made an equally strong joint. The carpentry team were skeptical about its strength; but tests at Bath University confirmed that, in 50mm-thick roundwood, both the original and modified designs could take a 4-tonne load!

One problem was the weight of the roundwood — at five metres long and with a wet weight of up to 4 cwt, a little heavier than site carpenters were used to! We had to hire some lifters to help the carpenters, and a crane was required for the A-frames and high structural framing.

The real fun started when what had been a tolerable summer became a continuous monsoon on a steeply sloping clay site. The foundation work had been sub-contracted out, giving us a series of concrete pads on which to place the structural frame. At this stage we had our first specialist item of plant. I had only asked for a 15 tonne crane, as that would have been good enough for the job, but on our first day a 25 tonne crane arrived. This turned out to be really useful, as it could reach all over the site with ease and nothing was too heavy or too light for it. The team soon found using the crane easier than struggling in the mud on the

● *The ply acts as a 'lid' for the resin pumped in round the threaded rod while it sets*

lower side of the site! If I had been a real purist I would have tried to build the frame with a simple derrick and lots of muscle, but I saw no point in wearing out the team, and saved a lot of time and money with the big crane.

The frame was put together in the target time despite the weather, and the calculations of the timber lengths proved to have been very good. Only one spar had to have 50mm cut off it to make it fit in line — all other adjustments were minor. At this point, the great advantages of wood over a steel frame became very apparent. It isn't easy to make site adjustments, however small, to a steel frame; in timber it is very simple. With simple rope tourniquets, sections of the frame could be held together in a stable position, checked for alignment and the resin joints filled.

Our plan that no specialist tools would

be needed was also right. Everything was made with hand power-tools — even a small planer with tungsten blades was enough to take down the end of the spars, and the blades were only changed twice.

My initial role was to be the supervising architect; in the end it turned out more efficient to have me heading the building team as well. I know some carpentry, but I'm by no means qualified, so my role became to explain what I wanted and the tolerances I expected, and then to turn into a labourer and give them a hand. In the end, I became the resident expert on resin joints, as no one had had any previous experience of them.

Most of the rest of the structure was more conventional in that it used rectilinear rather than round timber. This did give problems where we had to link the two forms — you need a level surface on a round and tapered structural member. Doing this was time-consuming and therefore expensive; the answer would be a bandsaw on site to put a flat face on roundwood.

In all, it was a valuable experience to be working full-time on site. I learnt an enormous amount, even if it was nerve-racking at times. The design team found their basic ideas worked, which means that roundwood forest thinnings have a future as a building material; we also learnt lessons at the detail level that will be of benefit in later buildings. ■

● Thanks to the Architects Journal and Jill Sack of ABK for their help with this feature.

● A tour of Parnham House, John Makepeace's School for Furniture Craftsmen, and of the Hooke Park site has been arranged for **Guild of Woodworkers** members on **6 April**. See the Guild pages for details.

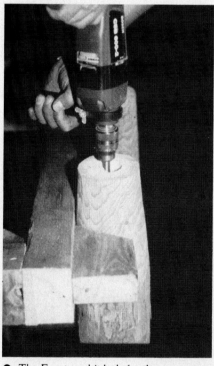

● The Forstner-bit hole for the threaded rod

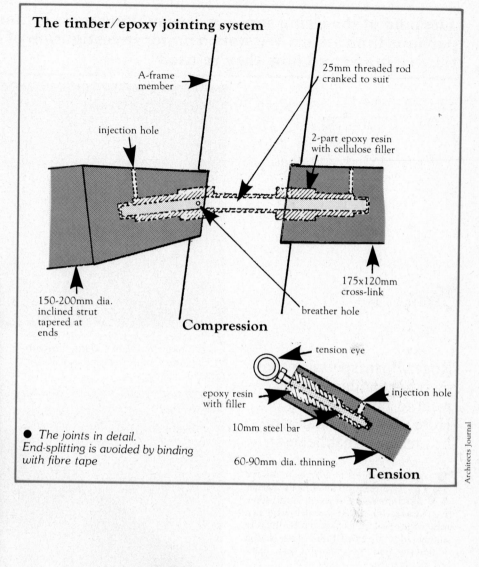

The timber/epoxy jointing system

A-frame member

injection hole

25mm threaded rod cranked to suit

2-part epoxy resin with cellulose filler

150-200mm dia. inclined strut tapered at ends

175x120mm cross-link

breather hole

Compression

● *The joints in detail. End-splitting is avoided by binding with fibre tape*

tension eye

epoxy resin with filler

injection hole

10mm steel bar

60-90mm dia. thinning

Tension

Architects Journal

● *An outline drawing of the visitors' centre containing the teaching, exhibition, and dining areas shows its startling hill-climbing shape*

ABK

JAPAN

The land of the rising sun — where making tools is more than a craft, more perhaps than an art. We start a major investigation of Japanese tools, how they're made and how they're used

● *Hand-saw maker Mr Hirota, **above**; chisel-maker Mr Nishki, **right**; **bottom**, from 'A Hundred Pictures of Daiku at Work' (Shinkenchiku-sha Co)*

Roger Buse, specialist tool merchant and importer, went to Japan last year. Here's his account of who he met and what he saw

My customers first began to ask for Japanese tools made by the master craftsmen of Honshu Island some five years ago. The interest, which has grown and continues to do so, was initially stimulated by the appearance of a selection of hand-crafted tools in American mail-order catalogues.

The tools are unconventional to Western eyes, and I was a little hesitant at first to stock a range, because of the high initial cost. From small beginnings, the trade has now increased substantially; constant enquiries and demand from my customers prompted a visit to Japan last year, to discover the secrets behind the tools' excellent quality and high reputation. I'm a compulsive traveller, so it was very much business with pleasure!

One of my first visits was to the forge of Mr Nishki, to see the production of laminated-steel chisels. The workshop looked like a conventional blacksmith's — forge (fired by charcoal), bellows and the sticky-sweet smell of hot metal on the air. Very similar, in fact, to the workshops in the alleys and back-streets of Sheffield, now disappeared and much lamented. *(See our Sheffield series, 'Tales out of steel'.)*

The chisels produced here are of superb quality, and I rather expected to see a neat pile of bar steel from a specialist mill, but Mr Nishki surprised me. He gets his soft steel from a stockpile of old second world war anchor-chain! He buys in high-quality carbon steel to laminate round the soft centre, and insists that his soft centres are

better quality than those of a nearby rival, whose raw material comes from a salvaged railway bridge!

The lamination is carried out entirely by hand and eye; dies aren't used to form the chisel blade. During the gradual shaping process, 2% straw-ash is added to the carbon steel, producing a brittle back to the blade and a hardness approaching 60-65 on the Rockwell scale. It's this arrangement which helps the blade to keep its edge longer than conventionally forged steels. During the hand beating, the tool is taken through a number of heating and quenching processes, all of which are controlled manually without thermometers, and it's finally mud-covered for annealing.

Semi-automation is introduced at the end of the hand forging in the form of a spring-hammer to produce the tang, which is an unconventional (in western terms) combination of both socket and tang. The tools are then hand-ground on a floor-mounted grindstone.

The handles are made by another specialist from a selection of timbers, including Japanese box or *gumi*, sandalwood, or the more common Japanese red oak.

When I inspected the tools I was very impressed by their razor-sharp edges, but Mr Nishki pointed out that he still expected the customer to finish the edge on a fine-grain abrasive stone, and preferably a whetstone grinder. Although Western production of alloy steels is highly sophisticated, say Mr Nishki, the Japanese still use the oldest blacksmithing techniques to hand-laminate a layer of hard and soft metal and produce one of the sharpest edges made.

A larger market exists in Japan for mass-produced saws, so there is more automation in the saw industry, but the very best saws are still hand-made. Following a 2000-year tradition in the use of steel (which occurred in Japanese river sands as a natural alloy), the master Mr Tetsonutski still handcrafts perfect saw-blades. From the 14th century on, Samurai swords were forged using this natural steel, weapons with near-surgical quality edges, and the skills have been passed down to present-day craftsmen.

Mr. Tetsonutski showed me his last remaining natural steel ingot, a fist-sized piece valued at £500. He's going to preserve it, as he now makes his blades from man-made alloys. These are produced in three grades, yellow, white and blue; the blue steel is the one for work of the highest quality.

The bar steel is hand-beaten to the basic saw-blade shape, and surface-ground to an initial thickness of .25mm, then hand-scraped to an even thinner profile tapering from the handle to the blade tip. The teeth are hand-filed, and set on one of the two edges for rip, and on the other for cross-cut. They stay sharp for five years, which may be why saw-doctoring isn't a very popular profession in Japan!

The blade is held to reflect the light and the stresses and tensions built up during hand beating are gradually removed by selective

● *Plane-body maker Mr Toda; the body is called a 'dai'*

hammer-blows. This is after the annealing process, which uses slow heating and brine quenching to bring the blade to a high degree of flexibility. Mr Tetsonutski asked me to describe the weather in the UK so he could adjust the annealing to get the right temper for our climate!

The *ryoba* (general rip-saw) and *dozuki* (dovetail saw) are most commonly used. The thin blades cut on the pull stroke, not on the forward stroke as do Western saws. This is why they can be made to such fine tolerances, and are capable of producing incredibly fine saw-cuts.

My last visit was to Mr Chiyozura Sadahide, Japan's most respected plane-blade craftsman. His skill is so well-known in Japan that he was created a national treasure by the Emperor in a personal visit to the workshop! He only accepts perfection in the articles which he produces, and his standards are virtually unattainable.

High-speed-steel, and less demanding standards with prices to match, have been accepted by other manufacturers, but Mr Sadahide still rejects 19 out of 20 of his blades. He can't satisfy demand for his beautiful masterpiece planes, which sell for about £1,000. The blades, fitted to an individually matched body which is drawn towards the user, not pushed, will split wood-cells in half.

Japanese joiners don't use abrasive paper to finish their work, and the plane is regarded as a finishing tool in its own right. Small wonder the Japanese characters for

'Evening Calm on Owaji Island', (a place of great spiritual significance) appear on each of Mr Sadahide's blades.

I was amazed at how heavy one of the planes felt and was immediately struck by how well it balanced in the hand. Once the pull technique had been mastered, keeping hand pressure on the part of the plane furthest from the user, it was very easy to remove microns-thick shavings several metres long. The finish was incredible, absolutely smooth and burnished to a shine by the body and the blade.

For me, this Japanese visit dispelled the mysticism surrounding the production of their high quality tools, and left me with the clear impression that time is of secondary importance to perfection for the blacksmith craftsmen.

Hand-crafted Japanese tools don't represent perfection simply because they're made by the people who give us Sony TVs, Yamahas and Nikons. The traditional methods of dedicated toolmakers will ensure that customers who set themselves such standards of excellence for their own work will continue to search for the products of the Oriental masters. ∎

● Poor imitations of high quality Japanese laminated chisels are finding their way on to the market, **adds Roger**, and even brand marks are being copied. *Caveat emptor!*
Roger Buse, Roger's, 47 Walsworth Rd, Hitchin, Herts SG4 9SU, tel. (0462) 34177

Oire nomi

A beautiful name for a beautiful tool — but it's just an ordinary chisel in Japan. Tony Wood explains the chisel maker's art

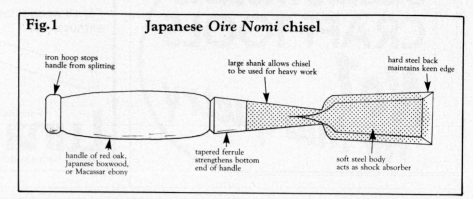

Fig.1 Japanese *Oire Nomi* chisel

iron hoop stops handle from splitting

large shank allows chisel to be used for heavy work

hard steel back maintains keen edge

handle of red oak, Japanese boxwood, or Macassar ebony

tapered ferrule strengthens bottom end of handle

soft steel body acts as shock absorber

A great deal of mystique and flowery prose has been generated about traditional Japanese woodworking tools. Roger's trip to Japan to discover some of the secrets behind their making has inspired this short series, which will deal with chisels, planes and saws; I'm starting with the *Oire Nomi*, or standard-size chisel.

As Roger explains, the blade of a Japanese chisel is two pieces of steel laminated together. The shank and tang are low-carbon, soft but very strong steel; the back, on which the cutting edge is ground, is very hard high-carbon steel. Laminating the two together gives a blade with both great strength and excellent edge-retention.

Western chisels are made from steel of only one level of carbon content, which means a compromise. A very strong blade won't take or hold a really sharp edge, and a high-carbon blade that would hone to razor-sharpness is so brittle it would shatter at the first blow of a mallet. The westerner ends up with a chisel that's quite strong, but never as sharp as a Japanese one, while the no-compromise Japanese variety has the strength for everyday use and a razor-sharp edge that holds out for an unusually (by western standards) long time.

The differences between western and Japanese chisels aren't only restricted to performance. There are several visual differences too, of which perhaps the most obvious is size. The average-sized *Oire Nomi* is only about eight inches long; not for cost-cutting to save steel, just that Japanese chisels cut so easily and maintain their edges so well, you don't need the strength of Samson and a lot of leverage. An added bonus of their short length is balance: the average Japanese chisel rests in the hand as comfortably as an expensive fountain pen.

The back is also very different from what we're used to. Turn over a Japanese chisel and you'll see one or more shallow flutes ground along the length of the blade, stopping just short of the cutting edge. If you place the back of a western chisel on a straight-edge, you'll probably find at least one high spot in its length. That high spot will probably be minute but the effect it can give to a straight cut can be alarming! Cutting a mortise for example, the back of the chisel bears against the cut face of the joint. If there is a high spot on the back of the chisel, it will push the cutting edge away from the cutting line and you end up with a stepped cut (fig. 2).

Because of its flutes the Japanese chisel has a very small area of back in contact with the cut face of the wood. Fig. 3 shows just how small on a single-flute *Oire Nomi*.

Single flutes are all very well for cutting

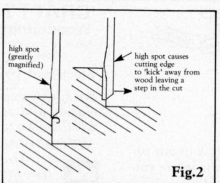

high spot (greatly magnified)

high spot causes cutting edge to 'kick' away from wood leaving a step in the cut

Fig.2

flat surfaces wider than the blade, but they aren't so convenient for paring wood narrower than the blade, because the narrow cross-section of the wood moves into the flute as you cut. The chisel isn't adequately supported on the edges of the flute, which is why many Japanese chisels have two or more narrow flutes ground into their backs. This multi-fluting offers maximum support with minimum back interference over a wide selection of material thicknesses. These chisels, perhaps the most useful to the general woodworker, are known as *San Mai Oire Nomi* (fig. 4).

The other major visual difference is that Japanese chisels don't have handles and blades running in parallel planes. In other words, if you lay a chisel back-down on a flat surface, the free end of the handle is fractionally higher than the tang end (fig. 5). Once again, there's a practical reason for this apparent quirk. The inclined handle allows the back to be rested flat on the workpiece, giving greater control for an even depth of cut as the chisel is pushed along. The cutting edge can be kept at a very low angle to the surface of the wood to make delicate paring cuts over large areas without digging in.

Japanese woodwork tools are considered as much art forms as useful implements. The toolmaker likes the look of each tool to reflect the high quality of the product, and the experience of years of perfecting the craft. It's often said of western chisels, with some pride, that the way to recognise a hand-finished tool is by the slight imperfections in it. Japanese tools that have slight imperfections never reach the door of the workshop. They are consigned to the scrap-heap, embarrassing failures.

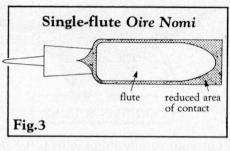

Single-flute *Oire Nomi*

flute

reduced area of contact

Fig.3

twin flutes

central web gives improved support with narrow section timber

Fig.4 *San Mai Oire Nomi*

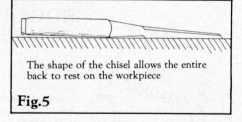

The shape of the chisel allows the entire back to rest on the workpiece

Fig.5

The workshop

The average Japanese toolmaker works alone in a relatively small and frugal workshop with a minimum of power tools, usually just a spring hammer for forging and a belt-driven grindstone for finishing. The forge, workbench and anvil are set low to the ground, and the toolmaker sits or squats to use them.

The most important item of equipment, the forge, looks very unassuming considering the valuable part it plays in the creation of each chisel. It's usually only about twelve or so inches square, the fire fanned by a foot-operated bellows. The fuel is very important, and therefore carefully selected. If a carbon-producing fuel such as coal were used, the steel would absorb some of the carbon during heating and its delicate composition would be ruined. Coke or charcoal is always used. Coke firing is for the lower-priced chisels while charcoal firing, a more time-consuming method, is reserved for the top-range tools.

Oire nomi

Chisel steels

The steel for the shank of the chisel is a general low-carbon variety. Surprisingly, many Japanese chisel makers shun virgin steel from the iron foundries in favour of 'second-hand' stuff, the theory being that old steel is superior to what's available today.. The chisel makers have many interesting sources, including old anchor chains and complete railway bridges!

Stories proliferate about the origin and composition of the high-carbon back-steel used on Japanese chisels, but for the most part there is no great secret. The steels are readily available from Japanese mills, specially formulated for high quality laminated steel tools. Of the three basic types of high-carbon steel used — yellow, white and blue — white and blue have two grades, no. 1 and no. 2.

No. 1 is the lower grade, no. 2 the higher. Each chisel maker has preferences about which steel suits a particular grade of chisel. As a rough generalisation, yellow steels are used for the cheapest chisels, white for high quality professional tools, and best blue steel for the most expensive of all. But quite often the skill of the toolmaker has more bearing on the tool quality than the steel used. Mr Nishki, for instance, heats white no. 1 steel in his forge, adds carbon in the form of straw ash, and then kneads and stretches the hot metal. This process increases the already high carbon content and changes the molecular structure for even greater strength. Mr Nishki maintains that the steel he gets from this process is even better than no. 2 blue steel! There must be some truth to this claim too, as Mr Nishki's tools have been selected by Chiyozuru Sadahide, the renowned plane-blade maker and national treasure, to be sold alongside his planes.

Making a Japanese chisel

1 The high-carbon back-steel is forged as previously described and then trimmed to size, or cut from a piece of bar steel.

2 The high-carbon steel is dipped in a descaling compound, placed on top of a bar of soft low-carbon steel and then heated in the forge. Some toolmakers lay a piece of scrap metal on top of the small piece of high-carbon steel to prevent it heating up faster than the larger mass of soft steel.

3 When it reaches a workable temperature, the work is removed from the forge and the high-carbon steel is forge-welded to the softer material. The high-carbon steel is beaten so it forms a shallow U-shape which grips the soft bar. The most important factor at this stage is to forge the high-carbon steel to a uniform thickness through its length. The result of this one operation determines how good the finished chisel will be. When the toolmaker is satisfied with the shape of the section, the tool blank is cut from the bar (fig. 6).

4 The laminated steels are then carefully forged, stretching them evenly to maintain the uniformity of the U-section.

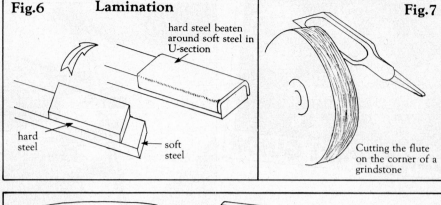

Fig.6 **Lamination** — hard steel beaten around soft steel in U-section — hard steel — soft steel

Fig.7 Cutting the flute on the corner of a grindstone

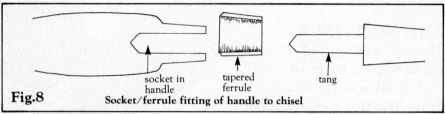

Fig.8 — socket in handle — tapered ferrule — tang — **Socket/ferrule fitting of handle to chisel**

5 After reheating the tool blank, the shank and tang are roughly fashioned from the soft steel, cooled and given a prelimary grinding.

6 The blade is reheated, forged to the approximate width and then cut to length.

7 After further beating and straightening, the side bevels are roughly formed. The entire chisel is then heated in the forge to a deep cherry-red colour, and plunged into a quenching bath of warm water. When asked what temperatures were involved in this hardening process, most craftsmen couldn't say. Like everything else, these things had been learned by experience over years, and each craftsman knew instinctively when things were just right.

8 The next operation is to grind the shank and blade to the correct width, taking care to keep the side bevels perfectly even. The quality of this grinding operation is so high that it looks as if the bevels have been ground by machine, not by hand. The flutes on the back of the chisel are then cut, using the square edge of the grinding wheel (fig. 7).

9 After all the forging operations the chisel is extremely hard and brittle, so it needs annealing to soften it slightly. Once again the techniques seem strange to western teaching. The chisel blade is covered in wet mud and then placed in the annealing fire. The mud stops the blade from getting over-hot on the outside before the steel at the core has had time to heat up; slow and even heat build-up throughout the blade gives an even temper. This annealing process really tests the skill of the chisel maker, because having the blade covered in mud means that you can't see the colour of the steel as it is heating up. The only explanation Mr Nishki could give was that when the fire was the right colour, and the mud the right consistency and thickness, he could leave the chisel heating for just the right length of time and it would be perfect. He didn't seem to think there was any problem. This annealing technique seems extremely hit-and-miss, but the proof of the

process is borne out by the consistently excellent result. One pleasing side effect of this treatment is that the mud-covered area takes on the rich matt-black colour of wrought iron.

10 The chisel blade is almost finished by now. This is the time for grinding the cutting bevel and polishing the face on ever-smoother grades of water-stone until it's mirror-smooth and bright.

11 The final operation is to fit the handle. It goes almost without saying that a Japanese chisel-handle is totally different from a western one. You won't see any ergonomic lumps of coloured plastic on Japanese chisels! Handles are made from red oak for the cheaper chisels, Japanese boxwood or *gumi* on the medium range, and fine Macassar ebony on the most expensive tools. It should be said that cheaper chisels have been known to have ebony handles — don't rely on the wood of the handle to guide you on the quality of the tool.They are fastened to the tang of the tool by a tapered ferrule, and capped with an iron hoop to stop the handle splitting.

The tapered ferrule adds strength to the bottom of the handle and also combines with the tang to give a very solid fixing. Because of the internal taper of the ferrule, the lower portion of the handle is squeezed against the tang. This means that the more the top of the handle is struck, the tighter the ferrule compresses the handle against the tang. The result is a handle that never splits or comes loose. After the handle and blade are assembled, the ferrule is ground down to follow the line of the shank, giving a long smooth taper (fig. 8).

Piecework doesn't exist in a Japanese chisel maker's workshop. Each chisel receives as much time as it needs to make it perfect; giving it any less would mean disgrace both to the toolmaker and the profession.

● **Next month:** Sharpening and using the *Oire Nomi*.

● *Horizontal and vertical: **above**, a fairly sophisticated slot-mortiser on a planer/thicknesser, and **below right** the floor-standing vertical mortiser*

THE MORTISER

There's a variety of ways to make square holes in wood — but whichever way it's done, the machine designed for the job does it best. We look at hollow-chisel and horizontal mortising

The mortise and tenon is the standard joint of quality woodwork, especially door- and window-frames (joinery) and furniture. It is strong, attractive and easy to make with the right tools (and machinery), and the right insistence on accuracy. Tenons can be cut in all sorts of different ways on a variety of machines, but machine-made mortises are best and quickest with either a specific machine or an attachment to a universal (or planer/thicknesser).

There are two principal methods of making mortises by machine; hollow-chisel and slotting. The first uses a hollow, square chisel, wider at its cutting end than at the shank, inside which a drill (an auger, as it's known) rotates. With the free-standing hollow-chisel mortiser, the tool is pulled down towards the workpiece by a hand-operated lever. As it enters the wood, the auger cuts a hole first and the chisel follows through, squaring off the corner.

It's essential that the auger enters the wood first. There's no way the chisel alone could penetrate the workpiece to any great depth, far less remove the internal section of the mortise. The chisel's work is to square off the initial round hole made by the auger, and consequently, the shape of the machine chisel with its four prominent sharp corner-points bears no resemblance to the flat face of the hand-tool.

To ensure the auger cuts first, before the chisel, the cutting edges ('ears') of the auger bit should be set 0.3mm below the corner-points of the chisel for chisel up to 12.7mm ($\frac{1}{2}$in), and 1.6mm below the chisel points for chisels larger than that. It's often tricky to get this exactly right, but a good 'rule of thumb' that old-time joiners used was to set the auger ears below the chisel points the thickness of an old penny. If you get the

auger too far away from the chisel, you'll both reduce the effectiveness of the chisel and end up with a mortise with a 'stepped' finish on the bottom of the cut; if you set the auger too close up into the chisel, both will overheat and blunt, and the auger might break off. It will certainly damage the steel of both auger and chisel.

The auger bit is also specially designed. It has no central screw-point like the augers for carpenter's braces, because the bottom of the cut needs a flat finish. It would also make it difficult to control the feed-speed and withdraw the bit from the wood. The auger's two cutting wings — 'ears' — on its outer edges cut slightly wider than the diameter of the auger body. The ears make the hole larger than the upper shank of the chisel, which also tapers; otherwise the tool would wedge in the workpiece.

The hollow chisel has a 'window' running most of its length; this is so the waste chips will be thrown out during mortising by the spiral action of the auger. It's obviously vital that you set the chisel into the machine with the window to the side so the waste can come out into the holes you've already drilled. If the window is to the face of the mortise, the chips will jam up inside the chisel, overheat, and possibly distort both steel and wood. It's worth mentioning that *cooling* is a bugbear of mortising — keep it in mind as you set up.

In the slotting method, the workpiece, mounted on a sliding table, is moved towards the revolving cutter. For the machines with which we are concerned, the cutter revolves in a set position and the workpiece moves.

The best type of horizontal mortising cutter for hand-fed machines is the 'double-edged slot-mortiser cutter', which is basically a drill with two full-length cutting

edges — not unlike a router cutter — and edges on the bottom diameter which finish the bottom of the cut. You push the workpiece into the cutters and move it from side to side with the cut at the same depth before making a second plunge cut. There are other kinds of horizontal slot-mortise cutters, but whichever ones you use, always remember that different bits require different procedures, so follow the manufacturer's instructions carefully. Most double-edged cutters these days have serrations on

Hollow-chisel mortiser parts

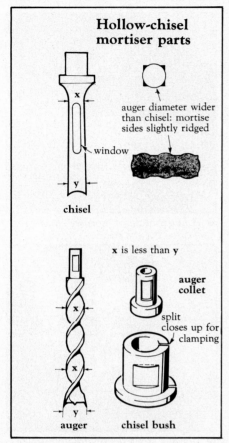

auger diameter wider
than chisel: mortise
sides slightly ridged

window

chisel

x is less than y

auger
collet

split
closes up for
clamping

x

x

y

auger   chisel bush

Horizontal slot-mortiser

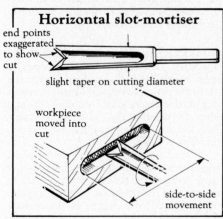

end points
exaggerated
to show
cut

slight taper on cutting diameter

workpiece
moved into
cut

side-to-side
movement

the body, which mesh up the chips and aid
waste removal — not a natural process as it is
with the auger and chisel.

Hollow-chisel mortising

The adjustments on the hollow-chisel
mortiser are to the height and back-to-front
position of the sliding table, and to the height
at which the downward movement of the
chisel stops. The clamping arrangement by
which the workpiece is held on to the table
usually slides back and forth to accommodate wide/thick pieces, but there is a
screw-up or cam-locking action on this
which will work for pieces within a common
width range, without having to reposition
the whole mechanism. This clamping block
normally comes just with a round square
pad, so you must attach a solid, larger lump

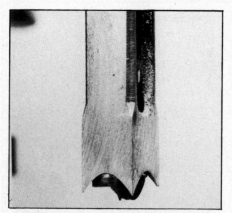

● *Set the auger just below the chisel; too
far in or out can mean disaster*

● *Upper wheel moves the table side to
side; the lower one moves it in and out*

of wood to it to extend the clamping pressure
along the length of the workpiece, and also
stop the work bruising. Don't make the extra
pressure-pad too thick, or you'll use up the
adjustment range of the block.

It's quite fiddly to set the chisel and auger
up correctly, but it must be done meticulously because you risk broken, bent or
burnt augers and chisels. There is a bush to
fit into the body of the moving part of the
mortiser, which will carry the round neck of
the chisel. Into and up through this goes the
auger, which is held in the machine by
(usually) a grub-screw that tightens through
a revolving collet on to a flat on the auger. It's
absolutely essential that you get the grub-
screw tightened up on this flat; if it doesn't
locate on the flat it won't hold the auger in
the correct vertical position, and it will travel
up into the chisel under working pressure.
Result: burnt and blunt auger (probably
broken), burnt and de-tempered chisel
(probably cracked into the bargain). At
around £20 a time for chisel, auger and
collar, getting this right is worth it!

Hand-tighten the collar and chisel, held by
a separate clamping action of the machine's
split neck, while you sort the auger out;
there's often no way of stopping the various
bits and pieces move round in relation to
each other, so the best way is to keep the
auger in one position as you move it up,
lining the grub screw-up with one of the
auger ears at the bottom.

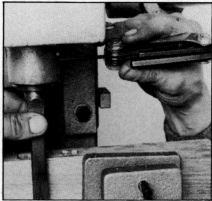

● *Allen-key tightens grub-screw for a
positive hold on the auger; the chisel is
perfectly square to the fence*

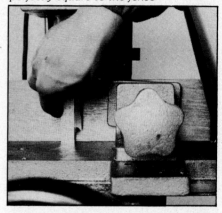

● *Measuring for mortise depth. If height
allows, block the work up on the table*

Once you're satisfied the auger is right and
at the right height in relation to the chisel, of
course (which is why you hand-tightened
the chisel at the correct height), you must
square up the chisel precisely to the fence.
This is easiest done by moving the table out
towards you until it's a hair's breadth away
from the chisel. Back-and-forth movement
of the table is either by a wheel separate from
the side-to-side one, or on some machines
you pull the wheel outwards to engage in
another set of gears. **DON'T TOUCH
THE CHISEL WITH THE FENCE!**
You'll bend or break the chisel. Get it so you
can just see light between it and the metal
face of the fence, and adjust it square so
there's exactly the same hair's-breadth
distance either side of the chisel between it
and the fence.

Most hollow-chisel mortisers don't lend
themselves to stops for side-to-side movement to regulate the length of your mortise,
because you're usually mortising both ends
of a piece, and the stops would be in different
relationship to each other for different
mortise positions. If you have a run of
constant-position mortises to do, it could be
worth setting up limiters to regulate the
movement of the table, but it means you
must put each workpiece in exactly the same
position on the table. Even for long runs, it's
usually easier to mark the ends of the
mortises on the workpieces themselves;
their position in relation to the thickness of

341

the piece is of course decided by the back-and-forth movement of the table.

The final adjustment is to the height of the chisel's stopping-point, which obviously means the depth of your mortise. You can make a mark on a workpiece, adjust the table away so the chisel misses it completely, and bring the arm down so the chisel stops at the mark. Most machines have enough stiffness in the action for the chisel to stay where it is while you adjust the depth stop — usually just a moveable block on a fixed vertical rod which bears on to a ledge on the stationary part of the machine. If you're doing stepped mortises, or, far more common, haunches out to the ends of a stile, there might be a dual-stop arrangement, or it's often easier just to cut a little hardwood block equal to the distance between the bottom of the mortise and the bottom of the cut for the haunch. In other words, if your mortise stops 10mm from the table and your haunch stops 45mm from it, you need a 35mm-thick block. Chop the mortise, then slip the block in under the stop and you effectively raise the height of the stop.

When you're set up, test on scrap as always. Check that the line of the mortise stays parallel with the work, check the auger isn't moving up into the chisel, check the depth you're getting — generally a mortise (if it isn't a through one) should be 3-5mm deeper than the length of the tenon.

You should have a wooden block of consistent thickness below the workpiece, to stop any possible disasters involving unwitting attempts to cut mortises in a solid steel table. It should naturally be thinner than the width of the workpiece, or the clamp will work on the false bedding-piece and not the workpiece. It's vital if you're doing through-mortises, for which you're unlikely to have a depth-stop set up (though this isn't a bad idea for safety). Don't cut all the way through from one side for through-mortises; mark the lines all the way round the workpieces, cut halfway one side and the other half the other. Nasty breakout can occur if you try to go all the way through from one side. If you're doing wedged through-tenons, when you turn the piece over (keeping the same face-side to the fences of course), bring the chisel down fractionally beyond the line rather than just on it or just inside it, as you have done for the tenon-shoulder side. This will widen the mortise somewhat at the back edge, and allow for the expansion that the wedges will cause.

Remember — when you're designing something with mortise and tenon joints, decide what width of mortise you're going to use very early on. Apart from the fact that it's easier to fit a tenon to a mortise than the other way round, it will affect your decisions about rebates and grooves. You should be able to match the width of grooves to the mortise-widths, so when you groove after first mortising then tenoning, the grooves give you the right depth for the haunch and the exact width of the tenon.

● A haunching cut finishes a stile-end mortise. Note the vertical depth-stop bar

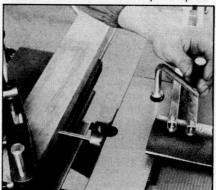

● Table-height adjustment (in this case) is by a handle connected to the machine's thicknessing table

● A horizontal slot-mortise: square the hole or round the peg?

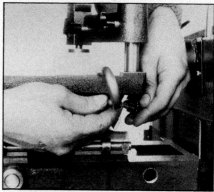

● Various stops are operated by collars, knobs and nuts. Here the end-stop for the workpiece is adjusted

Mortise thickness is based on approximately a third of workpiece thickness, and obviously relates to the standard available chisel sizes. It's possible but a pain to make mortises wider than standard-size chisels (imperial or metric), because it involves re-setting the back-to-front movement of the table, either at every mortise or after a run which must then be repeated. Also, be sure to clamp the work near the pressure-pad, but not right between it and the fence, because it will exert undue pressure on the area where the chisel is operating.

Finally, you'll find it's best to chop your square holes at both ends of the mortise first, so you can get accurately to the lines, then clear away the waste in between. This is because the chisel will deflect slightly if it's half on and half off wood to be cut, and the ends of the mortise won't be vertical. **DON'T TRAVERSE THE CHISEL FROM SIDE TO SIDE IN THE CUT AS IT CUTS!** This is the sure way to bent and broken chisels.

Horizontal slot-mortising

To all intents and purposes, the tables that fit on universal machines for slot-mortising are much the same as the ones that go on to planer/thicknessers. The bit is usually mounted in a chuck which fits on the outboard end of the cutter-block shaft, which means that the speed of cutter-rotation is much higher (between 5000 and 10,000rpm) than on hollow-chisel machines. You are also biting into wood and then moving it back and forth across the spinning cutter, so you need an understanding of what you're asking a cutter to do, and thus a sympathy. This amounts to: **don't** bite too deep in one go, and **don't** traverse the table too fast.

The adjustments on this type of machine regulate where you will put the work (end-stop clamps): the position of the mortise in relation to the thickness of the workpiece (table height): the length of the mortise (side-to-side table travel): and mortise depth (back-to-front table travel). Various machines do all these in various ways, but if you're buying, it obviously makes sense to examine closely the ease of use and potential accuracy of these stops and clamps. It's often quoted as a difficulty with horizontal mortising arrangements that although there's a stop for the side-to-side movement of the table, there's no end-stop for the position of the workpiece on the table. Some do have this, some don't; but if there isn't a facility for keeping the position of a succession of workpieces constant to the table, obviously stops to regulate the side-to-side movement of the table are little use.

So you'll have to make your own, and it could hardly be simpler. Just clamp a block on to one end of the sliding table, and make sure the workpieces are are always hard up against that. There is usually a low lip or fence on the table to keep the workpiece parallel along its length to the travel of the table. The constancy of position of the workpiece (and mortise) in relation to that end-stop block clamped to the table, of course, depends entirely on the unvarying lengths of the workpieces. It won't work if they're all different lengths!

When all the adjustments are made, run tests on scrap as usual. The in-and-out and side-to-side action of the horizontal mortiser demands a bit of concentration at first to get the right co-ordination; it's a bit like the 'pat head, rub tummy' trick. The most important thing is not to bite too deep before you go side-to-side. Start the cut, as you would with a hollow-chisel machine, by drilling to full depth at both ends, then work between the two spaces. Bite in about ¼in/6mm, cut across, then take another small bite and cut back the other way. It's better while you're unused to the action to underestimate the depth you can go rather than overestimate. If you get chatter and vibration, it's obvious you're asking the machine to do too much.

Cutter size, strength and sharpness, speed of rotation, the hardness of the wood, and numerous other factors all affect how deep you can go and how fast; some machines have one lever for both axes of table-travel, others have two, which are a little harder to co-ordinate.

Horizontal slot-mortises have round ends, which will mean either that you round off the corners of your tenons with chisel, rasp and file, or that you square up the mortises themselves with a chisel. One particular advantage of horizontal mortisers is that you can cut mortises in the edges of much wider workpieces than a hollow-chisel mortiser will take. The limits of table height and chisel height of a hollow-chisel type usually stop you making satisfactory mortises in, for instance, rails deeper than about 10in, while as long as you've got the work properly supported on a horizontal table, you could slot-mortise a 24in board if you felt the need.

Sharpening

It's vital to keep both augers and hollow chisels, and the cutting edges of double-edged slot cutters, as keen as a razor. Blunt edges heat themselves and the wood, and mortises are not air-cooled like most machined surfaces. For an auger and chisel, you need a selection of fine files and a conical reamer or grinder. The ears and flat bottom face of the auger should be dressed every time you set it up, and the four points of the hollow chisel should be of equal length and equal sharpness. When there's nothing left of an auger's ears, bin it.

The reamer, which fits in a carpenter's brace, is a common workshop accessory for hollow-chisel users. It comes with a selection of pilot pieces which fit the internal diameter of the chisel, and guide the ground edges of the reamer (which looks something like a countersink) on to the edges and corners equally. Dress the outside flat faces of the chisels, after you've reamed on the inside, using a fine oil- or water-stone to remove the burr. The long edges of double-edged slot cutters should also be dressed, but proper sharpening is best done by experts with sophisticated machinery — especially if your cutters are tungsten-edged. ■

*T*his series was written by Judith Barker. Ken Taylor of the London College of Furniture checked it for completeness and accuracy. Aidan Walker planned it and demonstrated the techniques. Derek Wales took the pictures. But Luna Tools and Machinery made it possible. They provided vital financial support – and for photography and demonstration they lent their machines, their space, and the help and advice of staff member Joe Wickens. So we give our warmest thanks to Luna's MD Gerry Baker for his unhesitating and generous co-operation. Luna are at 20 Denbigh Hall, Bletchley, Milton Keynes, Bucks MK3 7QT, tel. Milton Keynes (0908) 70771.

Sharpening a hollow chisel

end for carpenter's brace

grub screw holds pilot bit of correct size

reamer for 35° cutting edge

pilot bit

chisel held in vice with packing

filing 25° clearance bevel behind cutting edge

file section for filing clearance bevel

square fine-cut file

end view showing corners of chisel

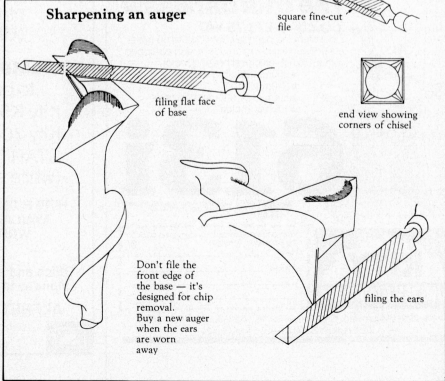

Sharpening an auger

filing flat face of base

Don't file the front edge of the base — it's designed for chip removal. Buy a new auger when the ears are worn away

filing the ears

344

Tales out of steel

Drilling, grinding and union recruitment in times (thankfully) past. Ashley Iles goes further back into Sheffield history

Spare a thought for the professional toolmaker who had to earn a living without the use of power; we are inclined to take the electric motor for granted. Up to the advent of Petter's (I think) Gas Engine, the main source of power in industry was the water-wheel. There's a fine example at the Abbeydale Works in Sheffield, now preserved as a working museum, with the wheel driving the various machines. Reading the pamphlets on the wages and conditions of the time will appal you and make you thankful for your lot — even if you are self-employed.

The gas engine had an attendant known as a 'tenter'. In frosty weather he had to get several men to help him start the engine by pulling on a rope wrapped round the flywheel. The gas engine as a main source of power would drive a factory or a mill, but in the early 19th century there was a vast army of cottage-industry outworkers working at home independently, but with the factories. Sheffield was heavily involved in this period and it is all commemorated in the presence of Vulcan, the God of Fire, presiding over the working of metals on the top of Sheffield Town Hall.

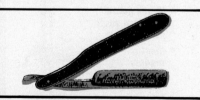

Not being around in the early 19th century I needed help from someone even older than me with a family history of the toolmaking trades. So, with the wind blowing a full gale, I found myself knocking on a door in Langsett Crescent, Sheffield. I knew the man inside was an old timer — well over 80 — but when the door opened I got a shock. I was greeted by a hearty, smiling man 6ft 3in tall, straight as a Guards officer, with a voice like a Sergeant Major and a handshake like a Record 53 without the quick-release. This was none other than

Jack Adams whom you met in the February issue: a cutler and the hardest-working man I ever met.

I sat down to tea and cake, and for the next hour or so I was transported back over 100 years by his reminiscences and information he remembered from his father and grandfather. I am very grateful to my informant; I could have gone to the archives in the Sheffield Library, but they would do well to go to him.

Boring a hole in thin steel is no problem to us, but in the mid-19th century it was a major problem and a tool called the fiddle drill was used by the scale-tang cutlers. 'The cutler put on a harness, with a leather pad on the chest to support and give pressure to the drill. The hole was bored by working a bow across from left to right like playing a fiddle; sour milk was used to lubricate the drill.'

'Graves of thousands of grinders stand in damning testimony . . .'

Cutlers then used horn extensively for handles and Chas W. Bacon, now a subsidiary of Footprint Tools, had three large vats for boiling the horn to sterilise it. Here again holes were bored with the fiddle drill.

The problems of forging without power were overcome by each forger having a striker. If a job paid 2/- a dozen, the forger got 1/2d and the striker 10d. The source of heat was a coke fire blown with hand bellows. Creating a bolster was a work of art, and before I could afford a spring hammer I had a forger called Albert Shaw, eight stones and 68 years. We took it in turns to forge and strike and we could put down six dozen, bolstered and tanged, before tea-break.

Back to my informant. 'Many of the outworkers were as far as eight miles away and men could be seen carrying scissors and other work strung together on string and flung over the shoulder. The dress of the time was frock-coat and bowler hat, and pen and pocket men went home with their coats swaying from side to side with the weight of cuttings in their pockets. Cutlers worked with treadle frames. All files were cut by hand, and if you walked down the back of the houses the file cutters could be

heard tapping away in their sheds all down the street.'

Grinding in the 19th century was an entirely different ball game to the grinding I have described in previous issues, and the premature graves of thousands of grinders stand in damning testimony to the employers of the time. Grinding-wheels were quarried stone with a high percentage of silica-hence the dread diseases of silicosis and pneumonocosis, and the maximum working life of a grinder 20 years. 'I've seen big strong men reduced to bags of bones in six years.'

Wheels were trued up and dressed with hardened bed irons from old bedsteads; clouds of dust were set in circulation for hours. Thank goodness manufactured stones put an end to it before I started. It's only inorganic dust that's harmful.

Razor grinders had grooves on their thumb nails. An open razor wasn't correct until the edge was thin enough to bend, and testing for this was done by pressing the razor edge on the thumb nail. Mr. Gillette dealt them a mortal blow, but most of them could do surgical instruments as well.

There was a trade union of sorts, with fixed piecework prices. Some men refused to join, and would undercut the prices. Union men induced them to join by entering workshops at night and putting gunpowder on top of the water in the trough (trow) under the wheel. The first spark next day . . . I leave the rest to your imagination.

'There was a sort of sanatorium on the Derbyshire side of Sheffield where the grinders were sent with "consumption". Rest and good food was the only treatment, but it was mostly a scrap-heap of skilled men.'

'Did the wheels ever break?'

'I knew a grinder have the wheel break under him. The chains holding his horsing broke and threw him through the air into a wall, smashing his face. He came back to work but he was never the same man again.

'Christmas was a big problem. The holiday was 10 days long and there was no holiday pay, so men did a lot of extra work and overtime to get the money for Christmas. The first week was calf week and the second, bull week. Some men reckoned up for work they hadn't done — they were known as "sours". After the holiday they had to clear up the sours before they were on "sweets" again.'

I was sorry to leave my informant and asked if I could call again. 'Aye, call any time lad, it all ought to be written down for all time. Let me see what tha' wrote about our Jack.'

'I will, Mr Adams. Goodbye.' ∎

Carefree coopering

If you're troubled by fast-breeding inaccuracy when you glue up segments for turning, Roy Benfield has the answer

The ever-rising cost of hardwoods has made coopering — jointing up segments for curves or circles — a necessity for most larger turning projects. When it's handled carefully, coopering can produce interesting and excellent results, but bad joints will make your work look appalling, no matter how good the turning. When making up, say, a ring of eight segments, inaccuracies of angle are exaggerated 16 times. So I decided it was worth spending a little time and effort making a simple micro-adjustment disc-sanding table.

Making the table

My design was based on a lathe able to swing a standard 10in sanding disc glued onto a homemade plywood faceplate. An extra tool-rest cross-slide is needed to provide two firm supports for as large a sanding table as practical — ¾in good-quality ply is ideal and remains stable. Two strong support rods to fit the tool-rests are needed to mount the table horizontally at a right-angle to the sanding disc.

On top of the fixed table another ply pivot-table is mounted using a ¼in bolt, nut and washers in a close-fitting hole. The centre of the pivot has to be set in line with the sanding-disc face. A permanent setting line should be scribed on the lower table for setting up the attachment by using a straight-edge across the disc face. The micro setting of the pivot table is adjusted using an eccentric cam.

A workpiece angle-setting fence is screwed onto the upper table with two woodscrews; at one end a countersunk screw in a plain hole, and a round-head screw and washer in a curved slot at the other.

With a 10in disc, only 4in of face is usable, travelling down on to the table. Three fence fixing-holes are needed across the face, with three quadrants of primary setting-holes to accommodate the numerous angle settings. A small clamp is needed for gauging the length of the components. It's also worth making a set of primary setting-gauges to suit the various angles for different numbers of segments in the rings.

Using the table

The components of each ring are cut to size by whatever means you have. Accuracy in the initial cutting can save considerable time and sawdust. Remember — every 1mm cut from an angled face multiplies itself by twice the number of component parts — that 9in fruit bowl could soon become a serviette ring!

Having prepared the ring segments, fix the cam adjuster at its halfway setting and lock the top table to the bottom table with a small G-clamp, the stop against the cam. Using your setting-gauge for the required angle, adjust the fence using the two wood-screws. Feed each component along the fence, sanding one face only. Select the smallest from the set and sand the other face. Using this as a gauge, fix a small clamp on to the fence to act as a length-stop. The top table is then released and each segment is fed onto the sander, pivoting the table.

Then place the segments on a flat surface to form the ring. Any accumulated error is brought to one point on the ring, and you can measure the gap using feeler gauges. This inaccuracy should be divided by twice the number of ring segments; for instance, a .024in error on a 6-segment ring:

$$\frac{.024}{12} = .002\text{in}$$

If the micro-setting cam is approximately double the distance from the pivot point to the workpiece, twice the movement will be needed to correct the angle. You'll have to use a .004 feeler in this case.

Depending on the way the angle needs changing, the feeler gauge is placed between the moving table and the cam. Either clamp the table and move the cam on to the feeler gauge, or insert the feeler gauge, clamp the table, remove the feeler and reset the cam.

Go through all the components methodically, sanding on one side. Reset the length stop slightly and sand the final sides. You should now have perfect angles without too many tears. I find an aluminium oxide 40-grit coarse disc gives an ideal gluing surface; you can get them from most good tool stores in packs of 10. Cleaning regularly with a rubber cleaning-block will prolong disc life and stop the wood burning. ∎

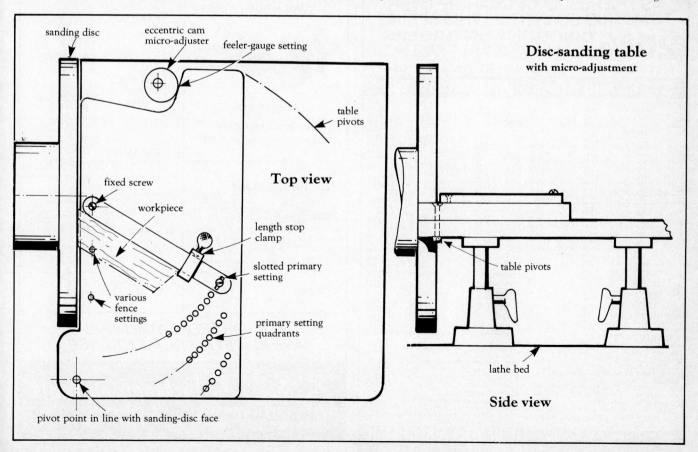

sanding disc

eccentric cam micro-adjuster

feeler-gauge setting

table pivots

Top view

fixed screw

workpiece

length stop clamp

slotted primary setting

various fence settings

primary setting quadrants

pivot point in line with sanding-disc face

Disc-sanding table
with micro-adjustment

table pivots

lathe bed

Side view

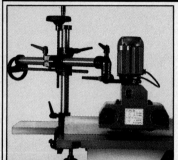

348

Letters

EDGES OF MDF soak up paint or lacquer like a sponge, and the only economic way of producing a good finish on machined edges is to seal them before finishing. 'Unibond', diluted to a thin emulsion, acts as an excellent sealant. It takes about half an hour to go off and can be sanded with a fine paper before finishing. It's also universally available and cheaper than more specialised products.

David Woodnutt, London NW6

I FAIL TO SEE the usefulness of the spring-guard shown in 'Woodworking wheeze of the month' in January's *Woodworker*. When ripping small stuff, it gets smaller with each rip and also need not be parallel.

I agree it's tricky for the last ½in, when everything chatters, but if you did use this guard it would nip the saw at the end of the cut. It would be very useful as a guide when grooving edges of boards for jointing, but to alter it after every cut would certainly become a nuisance.

W.V. Richmond, Beeston

T.F. Bernascone replies: Before making the guard I used finger-boards clamped to the bench-top, and my guard evolved from the need to use something easier to adjust and more efficient.

It doesn't matter that the stock gets smaller — the spring guard has sufficient sprung travel and you don't need to adjust it every time. The hole through which the rod travels is larger than the rod diameter — so the guard is able to take up any deviation from the parallel.

The guard doesn't nip the saw at the end of the cut — I'm not that daft! There are a series of threaded inserts in the bench-top, and if you set it up right, the guard will never touch the blade.

I would sooner adjust after every cut than have to use both hands with push-sticks.

MR THOMAS SHOULD TRY Wheelers of Suffolk before he sings their praise ('Buying Timber Wisely', WW/Jan). My experience of them was a disaster. I ordered £450 worth of iroko, which arrived 90% unusable because of terrible selection, surpassed by even worse machining. 1in nominal varied from ½in to ⅞in — after I had offered to pay extra for care in machining and selection! They had ample time, I didn't quibble on price, and I bought unseen. They didn't show any care!

The timber trade is not all roses as your magazine would have us believe. It's usually the small man who takes the brunt and has no time or resources for recourse.

R. Cohen, London

Wheelers reply: Mr Cohen favoured us with his order on 25 April 1985, and the goods were delivered to his address on 9 May 1985. Allowing for the normal practice of cheque clearance and the Easter Bank holiday, this left three working days to execute the order. As far as we are able to ascertain the customer accepted the goods from our driver without complaint, and

hasn't contacted this company since.

Most of the iroko sold by Wheelers is used for relatively low-grade joinery work. It's FAS (first and seconds), so quality complaints are few and far between from the trade, who have experience of this rather coarse and difficult timber. As far as selection goes, Mr Cohen's original order doesn't give any indication of special requirements. It's interesting to note the comments about thickness. As he specified exact lengths, we are wondering if the ends of the pieces had the usual scallops you get from a planer/thicknesser. Woodworkers are always well advised to allow at least 6in extra for crosscutting after machining.

Why does Mr Cohen think 'the small man takes the brunt and has no time or resources for recourse'? The Sale of Goods Act (implied terms) provides the individual with a wide range of protection. If a customer accepts goods and doesn't even comment at the time, there is little that we or any other timber merchant can do about it.

Objective comments from readers about dealing with the timber trade are welcomed by all of us. We always prefer customers to talk to us, and better still, come and select material for themselves. A material such as timber, with its infinite variations, can't be described in print or over a telephone.

Many of your readers are perhaps not aware of the difference between trade sawmill machinery and small domestic or workshop equipment, and the difference in results.

Stephen Goody, Managing Director

I WOULD LIKE to reply to some of the comments made by David Savage in his review of my boot *The Vaughans* (WW/Jan).

It was never part of my brief to write an account of London's East End furniture trade, and it's unreasonable for Mr Savage to complain my book is of little help comprehending it. Had he taken the trouble to read the preface, he would have seen the volume was intended by the Geffrye Museum to be the second in a series devoted to different aspects of the industry in the East End. Vaughans were chosen as typical of the larger wholesalers in the area who supplied the better class of East End store, to contrast with Sam Clarke, a small master cabinet-maker selling mainly to Whitechapel shops from his Brick Lane workshop. He was the subject of the first book. The Vaughan family was also interesting to the museum because of its origins in the silk industry (which preceded the furniture trade in the East End), and its strong connections with the Huguenot community there.

Mr Savage may not care for my style — fair enough. He may not like the system of labour which made it possible for firms like Vaughans to flourish. I have not sought to condone it and I am sure that many would agree with him. However I regard his comment that the Vaughans were merely a family 'which made its living from furniture' and that 'as piece-masters and gaffers of sometimes large concerns they

were seldom engaged at the point of production' as a gross insult to men who for many generations have devoted their lives to the furniture industry. The Vaughans were artist-craftsmen producing high quality furniture to their own designs and would hardly be in business today after 150 years had they not been actively and forcefully involved at all stages of design, production and marketing. I cannot understand how anyone reading my book impartially can have gained the impression conveyed by Mr Savage. His social views are his own affair, but he is not entitled to make false deductions from his own errors of fact.

Anthony Vaughan, Sittingbourne

I THOUGHT THAT WOODWORKER was above such things, but I see you are just like the rest of them. I refer to 'Women in woodworking' ('Shoptalk', WW/Feb). As a woman reader I take exception to the patronising tone of Kerry Fowler, assuming — well what does he assume? Is it that an attractive pack will make women buy any old rubbish, or is it that only women have an 'aesthetic' eye? Is he linking 'simple instructions' with simple women, and does he think male wood workers will cheerfully stand by and watch their offspring drink Nitromors out of a screw-top bottle?!

This latter point will surely make you realise how stupid sexism is. Child-proof caps should have people appeal, as should clear instructions, so next time you feature 'can-and-bottle pix' (can't you spell either?) please don't lower the tone of an otherwise good magazine by insulting *all* your readers. An attractive pack should appeal to anyone discerning enough to enjoy good woodwork. If a firm deserves a pat on the back for safety or design then do it, but not at the expense of women.

Lorna Dirveiks, Atherstone

Ms Kerry Fowler replies: This is a classic case of everything not being as it seems.

It might seem my tone was patronising — it was in fact ironic. I might seem I was condoning the attitude of Nitromors and Langlow — it was actually an admonition. It might seem unlikely that in the 1980's a woman is writing for *Woodworker* — but it's a matter of fact. My thanks to Mrs Dirveiks for allowing my escape from the closet and preventing any further misinterpretations.

THERE IS NO DOUBT that the ash chair by Peter Kuh has style and elegance (WW/Dec '85). However, users would be well advised not to rock backwards as the lack of stability inherent in this three-legged design would result in the sitter falling sideways.

N. Hillier, Beaminster

Peter Kuh replies: When I was working on a mock-up of the chair I opted for three legs because that gave the best appearance. In this case I chose beauty over function. Before proceeding with the rest of the job, I discussed the design with the client and pointed out that it would be less stable than a four-legged chair. She accepted the trade-off and was well aware of the disadvantage of a three-legged version.

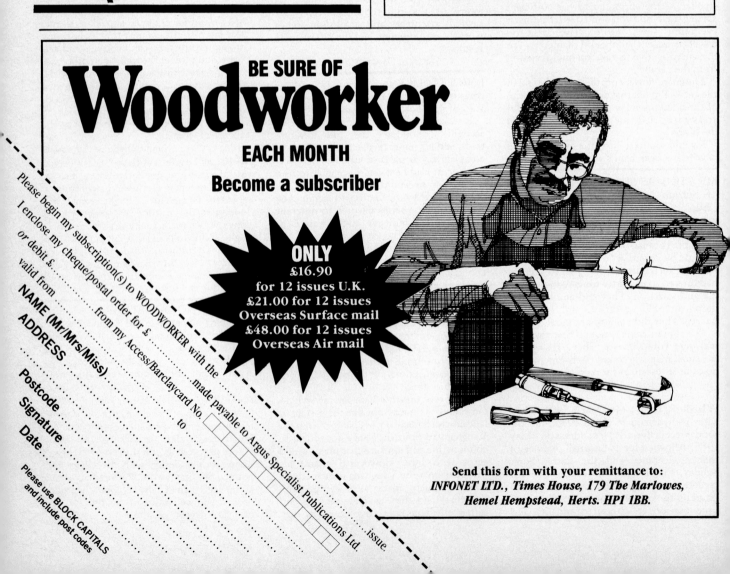

Letters

AS MY FINAL COMMENT on the right and wrongs of saw sharpening, may I say to those supporters of Bill Gates' saw-vice mount (WW/Sept 84) and in particular, but with great respect, to the elderly craftsmen who have corresponded — also to F. Seward (WW/Jan) who quotes from a handyman's book written at the turn of the century — that in the light of modern thinking and technological advance, we often have to admit we may be wrong.

I have recently been in touch with the technical expert at a leading saw manufacturer, who confirms my views. To quote from Spear and Jackson's handbook, ' . . . and keep the file perfectly horizontal.' May I also say if Mr Gates' idea was so eminently suitable as suggested by L. E. Jenner (WW/Nov 85), I wonder why the design team who produce this well-known saw-vice or clamp didn't include the tilting facility in their original design; or update present production of this most useful piece of equipment?

With regard to the ultimate test for a correctly sharpened cross-cut saw — yes, Mr Jenner, I often show my pupils how a darning needle can be made to slide between the teeth of the inclined saw.

G. Whitrick, Burton Leonard

A KIND WORD about one of your advertisers, who are subject to the bricks and whatever else you care to throw these days.

L.M. Saws of Derby are a cut above the rest (!). My recent order, which included bandsaw repairs, was delivered within six days. Not only is the price right but their quality is something special. I do think we could do ourselves a favour by passing on a mention of good products and service.

A. Whittle, Wrexham

I READ FRASER BUDD'S 'Plane Speaking' (WW/Feb) with interest. While I share his love of fine tools — I have used a Norris for decades — I feel newcomers may be put off by his criticism of 'leading manufacturers'. There has to be a compromise between cost and quality of the product — a compromise achieved by at least two plane-makers.

I would encourage the beginner to concentrate on cheaper (not cheap) tools from reputable makers. In addition be prepared to spend a little time setting a plane up yourself.
1 File a 1mm chamfer on the fore and rear ends of the sole to avoid any small burrs, made through accidental contact with metal objects, which could score the wood surface.
2 Carefully file back the front upper corner of the mouth as Mr Budd suggests and check the bottom corner is both clean and square.
3 Check the edge of the new cutter, which should be square, is parallel to the mouth — adjust the frog if it isn't.
4 Sharpen the back-iron with the rolling motion normally avoided on edge-tools, and remove any burr, so only a firm line contact is made with the surface of the cutter. Polish the top of the back-iron if you wish — anything that allows the shaving to curl over

smoothly will make life easier.
5 Check the cutter beds snugly on to the frog, especially at the lower end, and, for the same reason, don't have too thin an edge, certainly not when planing hardwoods. A delicate edge tends to vibrate, producing a ribbed surface and chatter.
6 Occasionally rub the sole on a whole piece of fine emery held on a perfectly flat surface, and give it the merest trace of oil.
7 Make sure the screws securing the knob, handle and frog are tight.

When you come across a piece of hardwood with a stripy interlocking grain which refuses to clean up, try the following.

Hone the cutter as finely as possible and put it on the strop. The edge should be dead square and straight but with slightly rounded corners. Fit the sharp back-iron as close to the cutter edge as possible and draw the corner of a sharp chisel once firmly down the angle between the face of the cutter and the convex face of the back-iron, bedding both together so that not even the finest shaving can penetrate. I can see a few eyebrows raised here, but it really doesn't harm the chisel. Adjust the frog to give the narrowest of mouth openings which still allows fine shavings to escape.

Give the cap-iron screw a slight turn, not too much or operating the cam-lever will break it. With the cutter suitably adjusted you should now be able to remove a shaving some .002in thick and produce a lustrous surface. Do keep the bright parts of your plane slightly oiled and the painted parts polished with an oily rag.

I trust Mr Budd sees my comments merely as an extension to his informative article.

J. Kenneth Jones, Llandudno

IN REPLY TO R. S. Read (WW/Feb) I think a little advice will not come amiss — 'Before you criticise someone else's work, make sure you've got your facts right.'

Nowhere in my article 'Through the golden gate' on the golden mean in September '85's *Woodworker* is there any mention of $10 \div 6.18 = 1.618$ or $6.18 \div 16.8 = 0.3819$, as he states. What I did write was $1:1.618$ and in fig. 3 I showed a line divided in the ratio of $10:6.18$. What he has done is to confuse the division sign $\div$ with that signifying a ratio, which is .

I don't know why fig. 3 is as big as it is; it's the designer's and Editor's job to decide sizes of illustrations. As for fig. 3C, the square referred to appears in fig. 4 at 'B'.

Vic Taylor

ABOUT A YEAR AGO I thought I would get some expert instruction on turning.

I attended a two-day course with an expert, and have been somewhat sore on the value of that instruction ever since. On that occasion there were three other pupils. We assembled at about 9am and finally made the workshop at 9.45, after a lengthy lecture on safety which, although I appreciate its importance, was more than a little overdone.

Then there was a discussion on sharpening; the rest of the time we watched a demonstration on beads and coves. This involved taking turns to use the tools and watching each other around one lathe which was hard against a brick wall. Imagine how difficult this made things. There was another lathe, but no attempt was made to get it going. It doesn't take a mathematician to work out how much actual practice was possible for each pupil — a 9.45 start; $1\frac{1}{2}$ hrs for a mediocre lunch, and packing up at 4.30.

It cost (in those days) £43 cash for two days; courses were run twice weekly and there was a waiting list. Not a bad return for a very poor session (the timber used would have cost about £1.50).

I am writing in the hope that my experience may be of some benefit to budding woodturners — I urge them to find exactly what the course offers and how it is scheduled.

E. Elkington, Stoke Lacy

● See 'Turning the corner' next month!

Letters

I CAN ONLY wholeheartedly agree with Tony Waddilove's letter (WW/August 85) on the cost and advice of so-called professional turners.

I should imagine the majority of your readers are, like myself, amateurs — so what's happening? I see there's now a £40 plus chisel available from one well-known tool merchant; and, even better, a £900 plus plane — whatever next?

This sort of thing is not only laughable; it is a disgrace. I'm not one for skimping on equipment (I am a plumber and heating engineer and need good reliable tools). My tube-cutter, the plumber's equivalent of a plane, cost less than a fiftieth of this £900 plane — and I bought the best.

In these days when money is tight, I feel a more realistic approach is necessary when considering equipment, timber, and most of all, design.

Your articles on the various furniture colleges were to say the least enlightening, but to what end? I know of one student who after three years' training, could not (he'd never been told how to) change the knives in a planer! 'The technicians did all that.'

This is 1986 and it's the real world, so I just hope that the survival rate of such students in employment is higher than I fear it is.

Thank you for a good magazine that has greatly improved over the last two years — it's now one of the best of its type.

Mark Figes, Holt

Dowel box

WOODWORKING WHEEZE *of the* **month**

When a length of dowel of a particular size is required but not available, it's useful to be able to make your own, **writes Charles Cliffe**. If you have a lathe, there's no great difficulty in turning a few short lengths, but what if you have no access to turning facilities? This dowel box is a very useful gadget.

Cut a piece of hardwood, usually beech, long enough to make three or four dowel lengths, and plane it up square to the size of the required dowels — for example, $\frac{3}{8}$in square for $\frac{3}{8}$in dowels. Put the square lengths in the dowel box and plane the corners off to produce an octagonal shape, then plane the remaining corners off to give the desired circular shape. Simple!

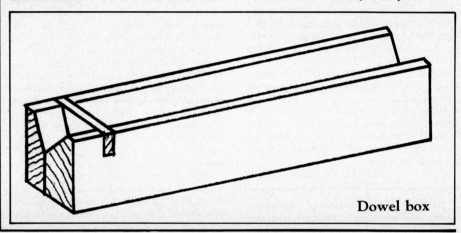

Dowel box

WOODWORKER

design . . . craft . . . and the love of wood   May 1986 Vol. 90 No. 1110

363 Turning the corner
Turning courses proliferate and the choice gets harder. We sample three of the best. *Hugh O'Neill*

371 Squares and rounds
WIN! Machinery and tools — last chance for the games makers!

372 Designs on the market
The designer/maker interface: you may be bright, but how are you at marketing? *Nick Allen*

374 Wooden wonder
The ministry pooh-poohed it, Goering hated it; but England loved the **Mosquito.** *Stuart Howe, Ken Taylor*

381 Tales out of steel
Marketing, Sheffield-style, plus the thoughts of a toolmaker on old tools. *Ashley Iles*

386 Machining Wood
Your expert guide: 7
The planer/thicknesser is the perfect machine for perfect — and vital — preparation

396 The grand furniture saga: 4
The Renaissance comes to Britain, ushered in by cherubs and chimera. *Vic Taylor*

Editor Aidan Walker
Editorial assistant Kerry Fowler
Advertisement manager Paul Holmes
Graphics Jeff Hamblin
Technical illustrator Peter Holland
Guild of Woodworkers Kerry Fowler
Editorial, advertisements and Guild of Woodworkers
1 Golden Square, London W1R 3AB, telephone 01-437 0626

Unfortunately we cannot accept responsibility for loss of or damage to unsolicited material. We reserve the right to refuse or suspend advertisements, and regret we cannot guarantee the bone fides of advertisers.

ABC

Back issues and subscriptions Infonet Ltd, 10-13 Times House, 179 Marlowes, Hemel Hempstead, Herts HP1 1BB; telephone Hemel Hempstead (0442) 48434

Subscriptions per year UK £16.90; overseas outside USA (accelerated surface post) £21.00, USA (accelerated surface post) $28, airmail £48

UK trade SM Distribution Ltd, 16-18 Trinity Gardens, London SW9 8DX; telephone 01-274 8611

North American trade Bill Dean Books Ltd, 151-49 7th Avenue, PO Box 69, Whitestone, New York 11357; telephone 1-718-767-6632

Printed in Great Britain by Ambassador Press Ltd, St. Albans, Herts
Mono origination Multiform Photosetting Ltd, Cardiff
Colour origination Derek Croxson Ltd, Chesham, Bucks
© Argus Specialist Publications Ltd 1986
ISSN 0043 776X

Argus Specialist Publications Ltd
1 Golden Square, London
W1R 3AB; 01-437 0626

● *A Tlingit Indian, resplendent in ceremonial robes. Make one of the boxes he used – p418*

412 ROCKING HORSE WINNERS
1: Harnessed in pair
Twin brothers in Kent are riding high on an international reputation. *Marc and Tony Stevenson*

414 2: Wooden thoroughbreds
A visit to the shaving-flavoured stables of horse maker Anthony Dew — with construction details. *Leonard Markham*

422 JAPAN 2
The performance chisel
Fettling, sharpening and using the **Oire Nomi.** *Tony Wood*

427 Guiding hands
Woodwork's healing powers — a charming tale from a school for the handicapped. *Eric Ingham*

432 TOOLS OF THE TRADE
The Woodworker Test: we step boldly into first-class hand-tool country, to put together the best basic kit we can find. *David Savage*

PROJECTS
All with detailed working drawings

382 Self contained
Turned boxes within boxes — a real test of skills, and some eyebrow-raising techniques. *Richard Kell*

393 Chimney chest
A far from ordinary solution to the unused space problem, in popular pine. *Graham Hewitt*

418 The watertight case
The Kwakiutl Indians had no buckets, but their boxes were just as good — steam bending with a difference! *Alan and Gill Bridgewater*

On the cover: Nick Allen's superb desk in bird's eye maple and stained veneers (p372); plus a taste of your glorious **poster!**

REGULARS

354 This month looks at the world through wooden specs

355 Shoptalk about what and where to buy

359 Timberline the tally from the trade

360 Guild notes courses and comments — are you a member?

369 Books

430 Bob Wearing's workshop
Small curved laminating

431 Woodworking wheeze of the month
An elliptical jig. *Harry Unwin*

436 Question box Finishing rosewood, bandsaw motors, workshop noise, a garden seat . . .

439 Letters you write them, you read them

BRISTOL 86 The Woodworker Show is where anyone in the west with lignin in their veins will be. Win an Emco TF 65 spindle moulder (far left), courtesy of Solent Tools; ogle the work (left) of experts; and snap up the supplies you need at the keenest prices. Is your work at the Show, or in our 'Squares and rounds' competition? It's on p371 – there might still be time!
● *16-18 May, Bristol Exhibition Centre, Canon's Rd, Bristol. Tel. (0442) 41221 for entry details*

Rolling out the barrel Gathering a cask and other feats can be seen at 'Living Crafts'. See Diary for details

The Crafts Council will be exhibiting the David Munrow Collection from 4 June-31 August. Examples of this early music fanatic's discoveries — plus contemporary instruments — will be a treat for musical woodlovers.
● Crafts Council, 12 Waterloo Place, London SW1Y 4AU

CERTIFIED!

We had a proud announcement about our UK circulation to go into this box, but had to pull it out at the last minute because of bureaucratic hold-ups. Watch this space next month . . .

Timber countries say

A meeting between government representatives of tropical timber countries Brazil, Indonesia, Ivory Coast, Malaysia and the Philippines with the Timber Trades Federation in January has produced this statement from the TTF:

'All tropical hardwood producing countries wish to point out that their most urgent concern is to maintain timber as a mainstream export and they are all involved in reforestation schemes, educational and commercial policies to that effect. All deny allegations of ecologists that the reduction is led by the timber industry.'

Massive programmes and projects have already been instituted or planned for continuing the supply of tropical hardwoods for all time, says the *Timber Trades Journal* of 15 February.

Meanwhile, 18 March saw a Birmingham rally on the rainforest problem, to be addressed by **David Bellamy** (TV treeperson), Friends of the Earth's **Charles Secrett**, the TTF's **Chris Holmes-Smith**, and a delegate from 'Survival International'. A lively evening was foretold . . .

Diary

Guild courses are shown by an asterisk (*); for further details see the Guild pages.

April
19-May 25 **Alan Peters, Furniture Maker** Cooper Gallery, Barnsley
26 **Wood-machining** Ken Taylor*
26-May 21 **Modern Furniture** Aberystwyth Arts Centre, tel. (0970) 4277
Until 30 **Musical Instrument Makers,** Parnham House, Beaminster, tel. (0308) 862204
Until June 1 **Chess in Art and Society** Victoria & Albert Museum, London

May
10 **Power routing** Roy Sutton*
8-11 **Living Crafts 86** Hatfield House, Hatfield, Herts, tel. (05827) 61235
11-18 **London International Furniture Show** Earls Court, London
16-18 **Bristol Woodworker Show**
17-June 5: **David Pye** Craft Council Shop, Victoria & Albert Museum, London
22-27 **Interbimall '86** Woodworking and Tools Exhibition, Milan, tel. (010 392) 8242101
24-31 **National Marquetry**

Exhibition St Albans School, Abbey Gateway, St Albans, details tel. (0727) 54110

June
5-6 **French polishing** Charles Cliffe*
4-Aug 31 **David Munrow Collection of Early and Folk Musical Instruments** and the **Craft Council's Second Open Exhibition of Musical Instruments** Crafts Council Gallery, 12 Waterloo Place, London SW1, tel. 01-930 4811
14 **Mosquito Aircraft Museum** visit: further details on the Guild page 360
30-July 4 **London College of Furniture Summer Show**

July
5 **Design and Workshop Drawing** Bob Grant*
26-August 30 **Furniture from Rycotewood College,** Cheltenham Art Gallery, tel. (0285) 61566

September
6-7 **Decorative techniques** Ian Hosker*
27 **Hand veneering** Bob Grant*

October
16-22 **Chelsea Crafts Fair**
23-26 **Woodworker Show** Alexandra Palace, London

Shoptalk

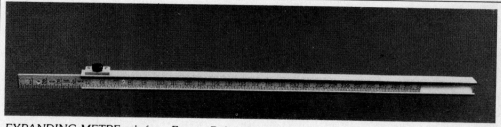

EXPANDING METRE rule from Exacta Rules, Askoy, Bryning Lane, Newton, Preston PR4 3RN

Woodworker's pin-up

And if you wanted proof that we work hard to please you (as if you did), free with this issue is (we think) one of the finest gifts *Woodworker* has ever been lucky enough to give. A full-colour, full-size poster, displaying a choice of woods from *World Woods in Colour* by William Lincoln, published by Stobart and Son. It shows 37 of the most tantalising woods we could find from the nearly 300 that the book includes — zebrano, East African camphorwood, cocobolo, purpleheart, to name a mere handful. They're chosen for their beauty, because we couldn't hope to get every wood useful to every woodworker on to a single poster; we mean it to grace your workshop (or even your living room) wall for years to come. If you want every wood in the book, of course, you'll have to buy the book! We're grateful to Stobarts for their help and co-operation, and to Wayne Wilson who designed the poster for us.

Education supplement

Our congratulations to the seven students at the London College of Furniture who won the study/tour awards offered by the Worshipful Company of Furniture Makers. Students on the LCF's Higher Diploma in Furniture Design and Production are now looking for industrial sponsorship for an exhibition of their work. Contact Martin Ryan, Furniture Dept, London College of Furniture, 41 Commercial Rd, London E1 1LA.

The College also invites early applications for its YTS training programmes. There are three new two-year programmes, the wages substantially higher than the YTS usual.
● Ian Gibson, LCF, Farrance St, London E14 7DU, tel. 01-538 2104.

Bandsaw project

John White's article on how to make a bandsaw (WW/Jan) contained some errors. If you're thinking of making it — or if you've got bits of it scattered round your workshop — please send us a large sae for the corrected drawings.

Smooth surfaces with a skew chisel? Not the simplest of tasks. The Gordon Stokes smoothing tool with cranked tang and rounded corner is designed to minimise digging and sanding problems.
● Ashley Iles (Edge Tools) Ltd, East Kirkby, Spilsby, Lincs. PE23 4DD, tel. (07903) 372

Shoptalk special

No one should need reminding, writes **Alan Thomas**, of the potential horror of fire: yet only those who have experienced fire out of control can appreciate the numbing speed at which the flames can travel.

Don't think you're safe with brick, concrete, or plaster constructions; think of the layers of decoration that have been applied over the years. Once that fire gets under way, they will all help it spread.

Ordinary plasterboard is one of the best fire-prevention building materials, but a few coats of paint will reduce it to the level of dry softwood — one of the most dangerous.

Development of 'safety paints' has followed two lines of thought. Paint systems to equal the decorative properties of conventional materials while slowing down the rate at which flame will travel; and a means of protecting vulnerable material from being heated to ignition point. **Valspar** market both kinds under their 'Timonox' label.

The *Quick Reference Guide* to hardboards, medium boards, MDF, and softboards gives technical data, main uses for the boards, application techniques, etc.
● Free from FIDOR, 1 Hanworth Rd, Feltham, Middx TW13 5AF, tel. 01-751 6107.

A new range of **small machines** from Craftsman (a division of J.J. Smith & Co.), will be at the **Bristol Woodworker Show** in May.
● J.J. Smith, David Rd, Poyle Trading Estate, Colnbrook, Slough, Berks SL3 0DQ, tel. (0753) 682743.

● *These cardboard houses show the difference; **left**, ordinary paint, and **right**, 'Timonox' protected after minutes' flame*

The paints are just that — paints. Oil-based for wood, metal, and all the usual surfaces; emulsions for the places emulsions are used, inside or out. Apply them by brush, spray, or roller (colour selection is extensive).

A chlorine polymer in the paints, when heated, produces a heavy gas which clings to a surface, absorbs elements and so interferes with the propagation of fire. It may, they say, put out a fire; it will certainly slow the rate of spread down to a third.

There's still the risk of inflammable structural materials being heated to the point at which they burn; for these Valspar is offering its intumescent coatings. Agents within the coating form gases, so that the char expands to form a thick insulating layer. However, while the paints need no extra protection, and are said to be proof against washing and condensation, the intumescent coatings need overpainting to stop their essential chemicals from leaching out.

An interesting claim of the company's is that its fire-resistant materials can be used over any existing decoration, and still be fully effective. In other words, that dangerously inflammable painted plasterboard partition, can have its previously high safety rating restored without the need to strip off the old paint first.

In workshops, there's a real risk of fire spreading across the inevitably dusty roof and walls; the intumescent coatings are recommended for such applications. Any dust and fluff will still burn, but surfaces underneath will be insulated from heat.

Because the makers are initially setting their sights on the biggest potential users of their fire resisting materials, the stuff may not be so readily available to the rest of us. Generally prices will be about 50% higher than those of otherwise similar paint systems.

There's just one snag with Timonox paints: you can't strip them with a blowlamp . . .
● Valspar Paints, Goodlass Rd, Speke, Liverpool, tel. 051-486 3950.

AXMINSTER POWER TOOL CENTRE

WOODWORKING LATHES — *OUR PRICE INC. VAT*

MYFORD ML8 36" centres excluding rear turning facility £376
MYFORD ML8B 36" crs. .... £432 ML8C 42" crs. £467
HARRISON GRADUATE 30" Centres .. £1093 42" Centres .. £1146 Short Bed .. £965
ELU DB180 38" crs. 15" dia. swing. Fully motorised £274
KITY 663 4 speed (Free 4 jaw chuck) £542 KITY 664 variable speed (Free 4 jaw chuck) £692
MINIMAX T90 .... £375 T100 .... £442 T120 .... £499
MINIMAX COPIERS C190 .... £431 CT100 .... £457 CT120 .... £499
TYME CUB lathe 4 speed .... £285 TYME AVON lathe 4 speed £408
WOODTURNING FITMENTS FOR ALL MAKES OF MACHINE (List on request)

RADIAL ARM SAWS

EUMENIA 9" 1½HP Radial Saw 15" Crosscut .... £276 24" Crosscut £330
NEW DeWALT 1251 10" 1½HP 15" Crosscut .... POA
NEW DeWALT DW 1501 10" Crosscut .... POA
NEW DeWALT 12" RADIAL SAWS 2HP 18" and 24" crosscut .... POA
DeWALT DW1600S 14" saw Max op. cap. 36" 2½HP 1PH .... £979 4HP 3PH £940
NEW ELU PS174 Mitre/Crosscut Saw 2" Cut 10" Crosscut £244
DeWALT DW1201 Folding 10" Radial Saw £279

SAW BENCHES

MAKITA 2708 8" Saw (will accept router and jigsaw) £204
ROYAL MK111B 10" Cast Iron Tilt Arbor Saw 1½HP £599
ROYAL MKIIIDL 10" Delux Cast Iron Tilt Arbor Saw 1½HP £699
WADKIN AGSP Scoring Panel Saw 10"/12" 3PH .... £1,639 1PH £1,741
ELU TGS 172 Saw Bench/Mitre Saw with TCT Blade .... £369 ELU TGS 171 .... £311
LUNA L18 12" TCT Panel Saw with sliding table £980
SCHEPPACH TKU 12" Saw Bench 2.3kw motor Fl. Stdg. £205
SLIDING TABLE for TKU-TKH .... £80 Panel Cutting Extension £75
WADKIN AGS 250/300 10"-12" Tilt Arbor Saw 3HP 3PH .... £1,052 3HP 1PH £1,137
New KITY 10" tilt arbor 2HP floor stdg. saw bench .... SPECIAL PRICE
STARTRITE TA300PS Scoring Saw c/w sliding carriage £1,699.00

BANDSAWS (excellent stocks of all longlife blades)

BURGESS BK3+ MkII with FREE fretsaw and jigsaw attachment .... (inc. P&P) £115
DeWALT DW100 2 speed. 13" throat. 4" cut. With mitre fence & disc sander £149
DeWALT 3401. 2 speed. 12" throat. 6" cut £256
KITY K613 8" cut 12" throat Bench Mtg or Floor Stdg. .... SPECIAL PRICE
STARTRITE 301. 12" throat. 6" cut. Steel table. Floor standing £395
STARTRITE 352 2 speed 14" throat 12" cut Fl. Stdg. 3PH .... £639 1PH £665
LUNA BS320 6" depth of cut. Cast table £324
MINIMAX P32 6" cut 14" throat Cast Tables £367
MINIMAX S45 10" cut 17" throat. Very solid construction. Cast Tables £615

PLANER/THICKNESSER

MULTICO CPT200/230 12" × 9" ¾" rebate £1966
DeWALT DW1150 10" × 6" 2 Speed power feed 2HP Motor .... POA
DeWALT DW600 Slot Morticer for DW1150 .... £65 Stand for DW1150 .... £25
STARTRITE PT260. 10" × 6" Steel tables. ⅝" rebate £820
SHEPPACH HMO SOLO. 10" × 6". Steel tables. 2HP motor. Floor standing £475
STARTRITE SD310. 12" × 7". ⅝" rebate. Cast iron 3PH .... £1,226 1PH £1,280
WADKIN BAOS 12" × 7" Solid Cast. Heavy Duty 3PH .... £2,757 1PH £2,930

DRILLING AND MORTISING MACHINES

FOBCO 'STAR'. ½" capacity. 4-speed. British made precision machine £323
MORTICING ATTACHMENT for FOBCO M/Cs. With clamp & ⅜" chisel £57
WARCO 'HOBBY'. ½" capacity. 5-speed, tilting table £125
WARCO 2B ⅝" capacity 2MT tilt table bench mounting £199 2F12 floor standing £222
STARTRITE SP250 5-speed ½" bench drill .... £339 Floor standing £379
WADKIN MORTICER 1" capacity. 1PH or 3PH £575
MULTICO MORTICER 240v Floor Standing £632
MULTICO HM MORTICER Bench Mounting ⅝" Max Capacity £356
RYOBI Chain Morticer 240v Portable Morticer £344
SMITH BCM Bench Morticer .... £399 CM75 Floor Stdg. Model £499
Mortice Chisels & Bits ¼" £14.00 ⅜" £16.00 ½" £18.00 ⅝" £22.00 ¾" £32.00
Ridgeway chisel + bits ¼" £19.00 ⅜" £23.88 ½" £23.88 ⅝" £35.00 ¾" £37.00

SPINDLE MOULDERS

KITY 623 30mm Spindle 3-speed 2HP 1PH WITH SLIDING TABLE £649
LUNA L28 30mm spindle 3-speed 5" rise 3HP 240v £980
STARTRITE T30 1¼" spindle with sliding table 1PH £889
SCHEPPACH HF33 2 Speed 2HP 30mm £485
WADKIN BEL 4 Speed 5HP Spindle Moulder (3PH Only) £1,890
MULTICO TM1 Single Ended Tennoner 240v £1360

COMBINATION MACHINES

LUNA Z40 (ex Mia 6) with TCT blade £690
STARTRITE K260 Combination. 'FREE CUTTER SET' 1PH £1,990
STARTRITE K210 Combination 'FREE CUTTER SET' 1PH £1,825
LUNA W49 Saw Spindle Combination 12" Saw 30mm Spindle £1,750
LUNA W59 10" Planer 12" Saw 30mm Spindle 2HP .... £2450 3HP £2690
LUNA W64 12" Planer 12" Saw 30mm Spindle £3050
LUNA W69 16" Planer 12" Saw 30mm Spindle 1PH .... £3900 3PH £3800
SCHEPPACH COMBI 10" × 6" Planer. 12" Saw 30m Spindle £860

★ ★ ★ ★ KITY COMBINATION MACHINES ★ ★ ★ ★

K5 COMBINATION K5 BASIC K704 TABLE COMBINATION K704 DIRECT DRIVE AND ACCESSORIES ALL AT SPECIAL PRICES SEND FOR LATEST PRICE LIST.
★ ★ ★ ★ *FREE DELIVERY ON ALL KITY COMBINATION MACHINES* ★ ★ ★ ★

MISCELLANEOUS MACHINES & EQUIPMENT

DeWALT DW250. 10" Bevel/Mitre saw. 1HP motor £194
LUNA YK1500 Pad Sander 1PH .... £1,327 3PH £1,300
LUNA YKV 1200 1½ HP Face & Edge Sander. Floor Standing £745 Wall Mounting £725
NOBEX 202 Mitre Saw .... £69.95 NOBEX 303 Mitre Saw .... £44 P&P £2.50
DeWALT Twin bag dust extractor .... £265 Multico DEA £339
LUNA SPS400 Dust Extractor 240v Portable Unit £215.00
LUNA W178 Dust Extractor Fir, Mtg. £292
LUNA NF259 Large Capacity Dust Extractor 1PH £555
LION MITRE TRIMMER excellent for accurate mitre cuts £249
LUNA Support Roller .... £27 Delux Combi Support roller £38
MITRE CUTTERS (ORTEGUILE) ORC55 £210 ORC80 £260 ORC100 £390 100F Fl. Stdg. POA

SPINDLE MOULDER TOOLING

LEITZ 488 Cutter Blocks 30mm or 1¼" 92mm dia. £48 100mm dia. £56 120mm dia. £60
WOBBLE SAWS for Spindle Moulders 6" 3mm-21mm £76 10" dia. 3mm-30mm £88
OMAS TIGER CUTTER BLOCKS 30mm or 1¼" .... £46 Cutter profiles .... pair £11.50

INDUSTRIAL QUALITY T.C.T SAWBLADES

ALL PRICES, INCLUDE V.A.T. AND P&P

GENERAL DUTY (MADE IN SHEFFIELD) PREMIUM QUALITY FOR CONTINUOUS USE (MADE IN W. GERMANY)

BLADE DIAMETER	6"				7"-7 1/4"				8"				9"-9 1/4"			
NO OF TEETH	16	24	36	48	18	30	42	56	20	36	48	64	24	40	54	72
GENERAL DUTY	£16	£17	£20	£26	£16	£17	£21	£26	£20	£25	£27	£32	£24	£26	£29	£36
PREMIUM QUALITY	-	£26	-	£34	-	-	-	-	-	£31	£36	£42	-	£39	£44	-

BLADE DIAMETER	10"				12"				14"				16"			
NO OF TEETH	24	40	60	80	32	48	72	96	36	60	84	108	28	36	60	96
GENERAL DUTY	£23	£26	£35	£38	£25	£31	£35	£44	£34	£42	£50	£57	-	-	-	-
PREMIUM QUALITY	£32	£36	£41	£50	£36	£42	£51	£60	£41	£48	£59	£68	£47	£50	£60	£70

PLEASE STATE BORE SIZE WHEN ORDERING

ROUTERS — OUR PRICE INC. VAT

ELU MOF 96 600w ¼" £77.95
ELU MOF 96E 750w ¼" £98.95
ELU MOF 31 1200w ¼" ⅜" ½" £123.95
ELU MOF 77 variable speed ... £195.00
ELU MOF 98 1500 ¼" ⅜" ½" £144.95
ELU MOF 177 1600w ¼" ⅜" ½" £156.95
ELU MOF 177E 1800w ¼" ⅜" ½" £181.95
HITACHI TR8 730w ¼" £64.00
HITACHI TR12 1300w ¼", ⅜", ½" £119.00
MAKITA 3600 1500w ¼" ⅜" ½" £141.00
BOSCH POF5 2¼" 500w £50.25
RYOBI R150 ¼" 750w £64.00
RYOBI R500 ¼", ⅜", ½" £113.00

ROUTER ACCESSORIES

ELU MOF 96 Accessory Kit £60.00
DOVETAIL JIG c/w TCT Cutter .. £60.00
STAIR Routing Jig £69.00
ELU Router Combi Bench £89.00
MAKITA Router Bench £35.00
ELU Router Bracket for DeWalt £33.00

BELT SANDER

ELU MHB 157 3" 600w £85.95
ELU MHB 157E 3" Variable Speed £94.95
ELU MHB 157 Stand £21.00
ELU MHB 157 Frame £28.00
ELU MHB 90 4" 850w £143.95
ELU MHB 90K 4" with frame .. £164.95
HITACHI SB-75 3" 950w £99.00
HITACHI SB-110 4" 950w £129.00
MAKITA 4" 1040w £141.50
BOSCH 3" 620w £69.00

JIGSAWS

ELU ST 152 420w £82.95
ELU ST 152E 420w £86.95
BOSCH PST 50E 350w £36.75
BOSCH PST 55PE 380w £61.00
BOSCH 1581/7 Var. Speed £95.00

DRILL STANDS

BOSCH S7 Drill Stand £48.00
WOLFCRAFT Compact Drill Stand £44.00
WOLF Morticer Stand £129.00

MISCELLANEOUS POWER TOOLS

ELU DS 140 Biscuit Jointer £156.95
BOSCH Wet 'n' Dry Cleaner £93.75
HITACHI 9" Grinder 2000w £89.00
BOSCH Hot Air Gun 1500w £24.00

CIRCULAR SAWS

ELU MH151 TCT Blade £77.95
ELU MH65 7¼" TCT 1200w ... £106.95
ELU MH85 9¼" TCT 1800w ... £152.95
ELU MH182 8" TCT £123.95
HITACHI PSU-6 6" 1050w £63.95
HITACHI PSU-7 7¼" 1600w £95.63
HITACHI PSU-9 9¼" 1759w ... £112.95
HITACHI PSM-7 7¼" TCT 1200w £129.95
HITACHI PSM-9 9¼" TCT 1600w £136.95
WOLF 9¼ Circular Saw £134

WOODTURNERS "AT LAST PERFECTION"

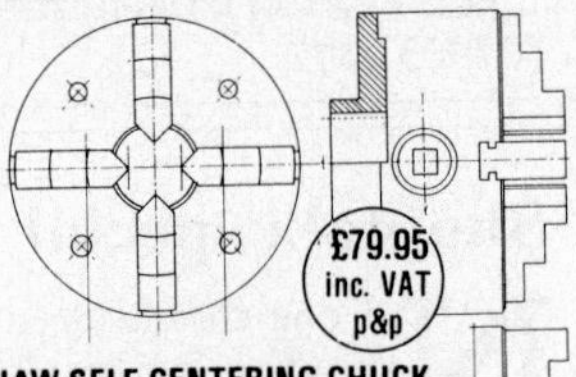

4 JAW SELF CENTERING CHUCK
AVAILABLE IN THREAD SIZES FOR MOST LATHES.
SPECIFICATION: GRIPPING CAPACITY ⅛"-4" DIAMETER 4" WEIGHT 2KG. SUPPLIED READY THREADED (LH OR RH) WITH TWO SETS OF PRECISION JAWS (INTERNAL & EXTERNAL).
HOW TO ORDER: TO CHEQUE OR POSTAL ORDER FOR £79.95 OR PHONE YOUR CREDIT CARD STATING LATHE TYPE FOR PROMPT DESPATCH (MOST TYPES EX-STOCK)
HURRY! YOU DON'T KNOW WHAT YOUR MISSING.

BENCH GRINDERS — OUR PRICE INC. VAT

ELU EDS 163 6" DE £56.95
ELU EDS 164 7" DE £61.95
ELU MWA 149 Honer Grinder £73.95
LEROY SOMER 5" DE £31.00
LEROY SOMER 6" DE £42.00
LEROY SOMER 7" DE £52.00
LEROY SOMER Whetstone £73.00
LUNA 8" Whetstone Grinder £99.00

CORDLESS DRILLS

HITACHI Cordless DTC10 .... £59.00
HITACHI DV10D Hammer Drill £99.00
MAKITA 6012DE 2 Speed £78.00
MAKITA Hammer Drill 8400DW .. £99.00
MAKITA 6" Saw in case £168.00
HITACHI D10DB ⅜" Var. Speed .. £77.95
HITACHI C6DA 6" Saw £148.00

HAMMER DRILL

BOSCH 400-2 400w £29.50
BOSCH 500-RLE 500w £48.75
BOSCH 7002 RLE 700w £81.00
HITACHI VTP1 3K ½" 460w £74.00
HITACHI VTP16AK ⅝" 800w ... £103.00
B&D P2162 ⅜" Var. Speed Rev. . £42.00
B&D P2264 ½" £47.00
B&D P2266 ½" Var. Speed Rev. . £59.00

FINISHING SANDERS

ELU MVS 156 1/3 Sheet £65.95
ELU MVS 156E Electronic £77.95
ELU MVS 94 Heavy Duty £90.95
ELU MVS 47 Heavy Duty £98.95
ELU Palm Sanders ¼ or ⅓ Sheet £44.95
HITACHI Palm Sander £39.00
MAKITA Palm Sander £42.00
B&D P6303 1/2 Sheet Ind. £57.00
BOSCH PSS230 1/3 Sheet £27.00

POWER PLANERS

ELU MFF80 850w £88.95
ELU MFF80K 850w £106.95
HITACHI FU-20 720w £74.00
HITACHI P20SA 720w £84.00

DREMEL POWER TOOLS

15" Scroll Saw Sander £72.00
Delux Scroll Saw Sander £93.00
258 Const. Speed Moto Tool £42.95
358 Var. Speed Moto Tool £55.95
359 as 358 with 35 Accs. £68.95
Router Base for Moto Tool £11.95
Drill Stand for Moto Tool £25.95
238 Moto Flex Tool £78.95
338 Var. Speed Flex Tool £86.95

JAPANESE HORIZONTAL WHETSTONE GRINDER £108.00

ELU ACCESSORIES

90% of all Elu Accessories in Stock. 10% discount on all items. Post Paid on most items. Send S.A.E. for current list.

ROUTER CUTTERS

20-25% OFF LEADING BRANDS
EXCELLENT STOCKS OF HSS & TCT ROUTER CUTTERS OVER 500 PROFILES IN STOCK. SEND NOW FOR FREE CUTTER CHART:-

LIBERON FINISHES

Sanding Sealer, French Polishes, Stains, Waxes, Wire Wool etc. All Ex Stock. Post Paid on orders over £5.00. SAE for free list.

BANDSAW BLADES

LONGLIFE QUALITY BLADES. OVER 4000 BLADES IN STOCK SEND NOW FOR CURRENT PRICE LIST.

Metal Blade Guides for DeWalt BS1310 & DW100 .... £5.20/set of 4

WOODTURNING ACCESSORIES (State make of Machine)

Sorby Precision Chuck £52.70
2½" Woodscrew Chuck £22.00
1½" Woodscrew Chuck £18.50
Drill Chuck 0-½" 1MT or 2MT .. £15.00
Coronet Service Kit, main brgs & belt £42.95
Coronet Chuck Sets £65.00
Collet Chuck Bodies £28.50
Live Centre 1MT or 2MT £18.00
Drive Centre Kit 5 Heads 1MT or 2MT £39.95
For TYME, CORONET, MYFORD, MINIMAX, HARRISON, KITY, ARUNDEL & OTHERS.

SASH CRAMPS (P&P £2.00 per order) May be mixed for quantity

RECORD 135-24" 1 off £19 5 off £17
135-36" 1 off £20 5 off £18
135-42" 1 off £21 5 off £19
135-48" 1 off £22 5 off £20
DRAPER 18" 1 off £13.50 5 off £11.50
30" 1 off £17.25 5 off £14.95
40" 1 off £18.40 5 off £16.00
60" 1 off £28.00 5 off £26.00

HAND TOOLS (P&P £1.50 per order)

STANLEY 04 Smooth Plane £18.50
STANLEY 04½ Smooth Plane £20.00
STANLEY 05 Jack Plane £27.50
STANLEY 05½ Jack Plane £29.50
STANLEY 06 Fore Plane £36.00
STANLEY 07 Fore Plane £40.00
STANLEY 10 Rebate Plane £38.00
STANLEY 60½ Block Plane £18.00
STANLEY RECORD 778 Rebate Pl. £31.00
RECORD 146 Hold Fast £14.00
Extra Collars for 146 .... £3.00
RECORD Cramp Heads £12.00
RECORD 52½E 9" Wood Vice £62.00
LIP & SPUR DRILL 1-13mm × 0.5 £54.00
CLIFTON 3 in 1 Plane £67.00
RECORD 04 Smooth Plane £18.00
RECORD 04½ Smooth Plane £19.00
RECORD 05 Jack Plane £28.00
RECORD 05½ Jack Plane £29.00
RECORD 06 Fore Plane £34.00
RECORD 07 Jointer Plane £38.50
RECORD 010 Rebate Plane £38.00
RECORD 060½ Block Plane £15.50
RECORD 020C Circular Plane £66.00
RECORD Dowelling Jig £31.00
RECORD 141 Corner Cramps £21.00
PARAMO Cramp Heads £10.00
RECORD 53E 10½" Wood Vice .. £71.00
LIP & SPUR DRILL 1/16-½ × 16ths £39.00
Clifton Rebate Plane 420 .... £57.00

CLICO SAWTOOTH CUTTERS (inc. VAT P&P) 6" long with ½" shank

⅜" .... £7.70; ½" .... £7.90; ⅝" .... £8.70; ¾" .... £9.50; ⅞" .... £10.20; 1" .... £10.90; 1⅛" .... £12.80; 1¼" .... £15.60; 1⅜" .... £16.20; 1½" .... £17.10; 1⅝" . £19.70; 1¾" . £22.40; 1⅞" . £24.80; 2" . £26.20; 2¼" . £32.90; 2½" . £43.70

IMMEDIATE DESPATCH ON CREDIT CARD PHONED ORDERS — CREDIT TERMS AVAILABLE OVER £120

CHARD STREET AXMINSTER DEVON EX13 5DZ 0297 33656 6.30-9pm 34836 BARCLAYCARD VISA

358

Timberline

Arthur Jones looks at world timber markets, and how they affect what you'll be buying and using

Pride of place this month goes to the first Russian offer of softwood for UK shipment up to September. The first offer of the season always creates a lot of interest in the timber trade because it points to the direction of prices, and this year there is a lot of encouragement for the woodworker.

Unsorted redwood is now £158 per cu. m CIF, a drop of £10 on a year ago, but redwood fourths have fallen by £18, to £103. Russian fourths are equivalent to Swedish and Finnish fifths, so the price shows quite a gap in favour of the Russian wood and it will be surprising if there aren't reductions in Scandinavian redwood fifths.

Whitewood prices have firmed up after their dramatic reductions a year ago, so it wasn't surprising to see the Russians' prices held for unsorted (£102) and fourths (£97). These are the most interesting grades to woodworrs, and we know that the importers' response was good and the offer well oversubscribed. The final contracts are likely to amount to about twice the volume of wood which the Russians put in the stocknotes, so the offer has established the softwood market firmly for 1986.

And how satisfactory this is for you! How many other woodworker's materials have dropped in price since 1985? Of course, these prices are somewhat academic, because they're the rates paid by the importer, so the wood will certainly be much dearer in the merchant's yard. But the trend is there, and you can confidently expect to pay little more for timber this year. Some will even be cheaper, especially in view of the keen competition between timber traders. So shop around for bargains.

Canadian softwood prices are solid, helped by a healthy demand in North America and comparatively low stocks in the UK.

The international value of sterling will have more effect on prices than any changes made by

the suppliers. Russian wood is priced against the Swedish currency, and automatically changes if sterling falls in value. In the same way the dollar/pound rate affects many hardwoods, panel products and softwoods round the world, so prices can change considerably simply because the pound is weak against the dollar. Strangely enough, this hasn't halted the demand for American oak over the past few months. Even though the dollar is so strong, the Americans have stayed highly competitive.

The timber trade has launched a new leaflet, *Caring for Hardwoods*. It's concerned with the external use of hardwoods, the species most suited for such applications, and how they should be treated to give an attractive long life.

Reports from world hardwood markets are almost all of firm prices, with a tendency for most species to rise. The list is long but fortunately the increases are usually quite modest and they are unlikely to affect the balance of demand between species.

The fact that so many of our hardwoods come from tropical and underdeveloped countries means that supplies are subject to all sorts of difficulties, not least the weather. But no factor is more important than politics, and upheavals in several of the main hardwood-producing countries could certainly hamper shipments. Delays, of course, inevitably produce shortages and higher prices.

Plywood prices have also shown some small increases — there are fewer examples of price-slashing now in this market. No need to go into detail about the duty-free allocations made by the EEC for the developing countries; you can safely assume the quotas won't give any supply problems over the coming months.
Briefly: Indonesia is making a determined effort to strengthen plywood selling prices from the part of the world, and there are already signs of success.
This column deals with timber and panel products, but as a footnote woodworkers will be interested to learn of the agreed link-up between Wadkin and Robinson, the country's two leading woodworking machinery manufacturers. ■

359

Guild notes

Guild of WOODWORKERS

The Guild was set up by *Woodworker* to create a meeting ground for all those involved in working wood, whether professional, amateur, or enthusiastic beginner. Guild members get:

- Access to Guild courses and events
- Free publicity in *Woodworker*
- Specially arranged tool insurance at low rates
- 15% off Woodworker Show entry
- A free display area and meeting point at the Show
- 15% discount off *Woodworker* plans
- Inclusion in our register of members' skills and services

For details, please send an sae to the Guild of Woodworkers, 1 Golden Sq, London W1R 3AB.

Work experience

Jane Cleal, a first-year student of Furniture Production and Management at Buckinghamshire College of Higher Education, wants some practical work experience with a Guild member in the Southampton/ Winchester area during the summer vacation. Please write to her direct.
- Jane Cleal, John North Hall, Marlow Hill, High Wycombe, Bucks.

Selling yourself

The Craft Centre and Design Gallery in Leeds has asked if we know of any readers who would be interested in selling their work through the Gallery. The Gallery is aided by the Crafts Council, and puts on six exhibitions a year as well as running a shop selling quality craft items.
- The Craft Centre and Design Gallery, The Headrow, Leeds LS1 3AB, tel. (0532) 462485.

Where are you now?

Renewal notices to the following members were returned marked 'Gone away'.
- Stephen Batten (London); E.G. Stannard (Ely); S.J. Croft (Blackpool); B.P. Cromwell (Bexhill); N.F. Johnston (Hexham); M.R. Cross (Poole); and J.J. Carr (London). Please let us know your new addresses if you want to remain in the Guild.

GUILD COURSES

- Only Guild members are eligible to go on these courses. You must book in advance, and we must have a cheque for the full cost of the course at the time of booking. If you cancel less than four weeks before the advertised date you will forfeit 50% of the cost, unless there are exceptional circumstances.

Wood-machining — Ken Taylor

26 April, Bletchley, £25+VAT.
Ken's course on the ins and outs of machining wood is one of our most popular. Find out about (and try for yourself) table- and band-sawing, radial-arm saws, planing and thicknessing, spindle moulding, and horizontal and vertical mortising. You can also see and try some good quality universals. Lunch is included.

Power routing — Roy Sutton

10 May, Herne Bay, £25+VAT.
Come and improve your expertise on the machine that almost put the moulding plane out of business. Not only does it cut

The Guild has arranged a **14 June tour of the Mosquito Aircraft Museum**, Salisbury Hall, London Colney, Herts. It costs the princely sum of £1, for which you get an expert guided tour, the chance to meet and talk to the people working on the aircraft, and maybe even the chance to work on one yourself! The tour starts at 10.30 am: Museum address on p377. Go straight there and you will be met. Here you see **Stuart Howe (right),** the author of our Mosquito feature in this issue, doping fresh fabric on to the Museum's TA122; **below** are six Mosquitoes of 811 squadron practising for the 1945 Victory fly-past

grooves; a short list of its capabilities includes housing, rebating, straight and circular moulding, tenoning, mortising, rule-joint and template work. Roy demonstrates all this, plus designing and setting out jigs. You'll have the chance to make something with a router during the course.

French polishing — Charles Cliffe

5-6 June, 9.30-5, Bexleyheath, £40.
Charles Cliffe, one of our 'Question Box' experts on this subject and author of *The Woodworker Manual of Finishing and Polishing*, explains all about preparation, staining, and application of this tricky (and beautiful) finish. He'll also be dealing with using a cabinet scraper, so bring your own if you have one. If you have a piece of furniture that you want his advice on, bring it as well. Charles can order supplies for you to take away if you tell him in advance.

Design and workshop drawing — Bob Grant

5 July, 9.30-5, Oxford, £25+VAT.
So you've got an idea you want to make manifest in wood? If you don't plan your work on paper, you could waste a lot of timber and effort. Bob, who is head of Craft, Design and Technology at an Oxford

comprehensive school, will guide you through putting your design on paper. Learn freehand sketching, how to use grid paper and drawing boards, tricks for laying out ellipses and other shapes, and making and using rods and templates.

Decorative techniques — Ian Hosker

6-7 September, 10-5, Chester, £45.
You read the articles, now do the course. Ian's feature, 'Coats of many colours' in the last two issues covered wonderful decorative techniques such as dragging, lining, sponging, rag-rolling, marbling, spattering, and (his and our favourite) tortoiseshelling. The cost includes materials, but students should bring a few paint-brushes and jam-jars.

Hand veneering — Bob Grant

27 September, 9.30-5, Oxford, £35+VAT.
Veneering is much more than the art of disguising chipboard. It's a skill with a long history, and can create some beautiful effects — and it saves fine and expensive wood! You'll be laying a panel with veneer, mitring a cross-banding, inlaying lines round it, and applying a balancer veneer on the back. If you have a veneer hammer, bring it; but materials will be provided.

Turning the corner

Why do most of the courses in our classifieds offer woodturning? Hugh O'Neill investigates

As a writer of articles and training manuals it hurts me to say this. You can't learn woodturning from a book.

I did try — my bedside cabinet sagged with books and magazines, and I read them all. After four months, although I did have some bowls that could be given as Christmas presents to half-blind doting aunts, I had a growing pile of irrecoverable disasters in choice hardwoods. Almost everything was scrapped. Only once had I managed to plane a spindle with a skew chisel without horrendous dig-ins.

There are two problems with trying to learn turning from books. The first is that most make extensive use of photographs. Turning has at least four dimensions (I include time), and you can't portray four-dimensional skills with two-dimensional pictures. The second problem is that most existing books are just not good enough; most miss out on the basics of tool and rest positioning, and the sweeps that the tool has to make for each cut — the real skills of woodturning.

● Jamie Wallwin at Craft Supplies

Basic skills can only be taught on the job, and by a good instructor; so most of us eventually come round to attending a course to pick up the ground work. Let's face it — without a firm grasp of the basics we can never hope to master the intricacies of fine, high quality turning.

I'm not sure whether you should start with a course, or just try a few things on your own and find out how much help you need. After four months I had acquired some useful skills; but there were also some deeply ingrained bad habits. I had also accumulated a vast range of tools — purchases, gifts, junk-shop finds, and home-mades. However, I'm certain that I had spent far more on useless books and tools than on the cost of a good course.

Potential lathe buyers often don't buy until they've been on a course. Certainly it's

● Cliff Willetts loads up the Graduate

an idea to try a number of lathes before buying, and a course where you get this facility is useful.

Having decided to take the plunge, the problem arises of choosing the most suitable course from the many available. Some are excellent, some are poor. Some suit one type of individual, some another. Unfortunately, if you choose from the adverts themselves you might as well stick in a pin. You certainly can't judge by the 'name' or the number of books that the tutor has published.

Write to two or three and ask some questions; as well as helping to make your final choice, it will provide some comeback if your chosen course doesn't live up to expectations.

Amongst the factors you should take into account are:
● The opportunity to use the lathe you're interested in.
● The range of skills covered. Some courses teach both spindle and bowl work — others spend two days on just one of the two.
● The teaching experience of the instructors.
● The amount of personal attention you expect or require; some courses have only two participants, others four or five.
● The ratio of hands-on (practical) time to watching demonstrations and listening to theory. Some courses are 5% theory, 10% demo and 85% practical; others 75% demonstration and only 25% hands-on.
● The location and environment you prefer.
● The costs — not only of the course itself, but also of extras like accommodation and travel.
● Whether or not you wish to make purchases (tools, timber, finishes, machines etc).

The factors that most influenced my choice were the skills covered, the proportion of time spent 'hands-on', and the instructors' teaching experience. I looked for instructors who had a teaching qualification, or who were employed by commercial organisations because of their teaching skills.

My final selection came down to three; two large firms and one one-man outfit. Discussions with *Woodworker* finally resulted in a decision to do all three to draw comparisons. The big ones were chosen partly because they are leaders in the field, but also on the basis of their subject coverage, their known teaching skills and the range of equipment available. The one man was chosen because of his formal teaching qualification, and his general approach. I discarded one or two 'names' becase it was obvious that they taught mainly by demonstration, and I wanted as much hands-on experience as possible.

The final list was **John Boddy's** Fine Wood and Tool Store at Boroughbridge, **Craft Supplies** in Miller's Dale, Derbyshire, and **Cliff Willetts** at Melton Mowbray.

All three turned out to be very similar in the range of skills covered and in the techniques presented. They differed in their instructional approach; Cliff Willetts' teacher training and understanding of learning theory showed through. The two big courses appeared to have identical objectives — that all students should make and take home (the same) 6 objects at least. Cliff was more concerned that you acquired the maximum skill and understanding irrespective of what finished items you took away.

It's difficult to objectively evaluate all three courses as though I were an absolute beginner on each. Few people can afford the luxury of attending three courses — a pity, because I found that **one is not enough!** Each course has its strengths; if I had to summarise, it would be 'I got quite turned on' (Boddy's); 'I understood what I was doing' (Willetts); 'I grew in skills' (Craft Supplies).

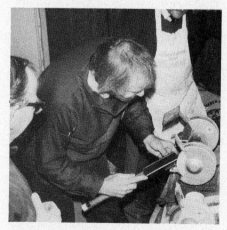

● Phil Reardon grinding a roughing gouge

John Boddy

The first course I went to was at Boddy's in Boroughbridge, Yorkshire. It should be said here that if you're doing a comparison of courses, you obviously learn more as you go along, and so things that struck me at Boddy's could have caught my attention less than the ones I went to later on. This is an inbuilt disadvantage of not being in three different places at one time, and an inevitable result of experience and understanding accumulating. At the time I was there, Allan Batty and Phil Reardon — both experienced professional woodturners of high repute — shared the teaching, but Allan has moved on.

The 'schoolroom' here was the best of all three. It was well equipped and laid out, methodical, everything to hand, light and airy and hell's cold first thing on a winter morning. Each of the six available lathes was set up with a clear space all round and was equipped with all the tools that the student would need. Communal items such as polishes, sandpaper, and bandsaw were in one central position; never once did we have to ferret for anything.

● *Skew, spindle and beading cuts on a test piece*

Phil, who led our course, starts by explaining the difference between the various lathes. Once we four students got on to the lathes it was straight into roughing out a cylinder, and then a quick practice of a series of skew-cuts on scrap wood. Almost before we had caught breath we were into an ornamental handle in white sycamore. Phil would demonstrate each cut, and then we would try it on our own piece. The handle, including beads and convex curves, was produced entirely with the skew. There was no scraping, and little sanding before the pre-catalysed cellulose lacquer finish was applied. This took us to the end of day one.

Because of the time spent earlier talking about the advantages and disadvantages of the various lathes, we were running late by the start of day two. There was therefore considerable pressure to get through the exercises, and this tended to become the objective. We did complete them all, but it took until just after 7pm!

The objects of the second project, an egg-cup, were to introduce the spindle gouge, to try hollowing out, to use measuring tools and the parting chisel, to become aware of shape and balance, and learn to work to predetermined dimensions.

Producing an egg (in rich cocobolo) using only the flat and points of a skew gave practice in shaping, showed the need for precision in form and size, and introduced parting-off with the skew and the use of wooden chucks.

Then there was a small lidded box in

pear; a scraper was allowed to get the vertical inside walls. We also now got on to alternative fillers and finishes and tried the spigot chuck.

The penultimate project was a double-ended something — to practice reproducing shapes. Most of us made corkscrew handles in kingwood.

Finally, late on the second day, we were introduced to bowl turning. Under Phil's keen eye I formed a near-perfect 7in diameter shallow bowl in brown ash.

Before I left, I splashed out on tools and timber from Boddy's themselves; there is no accommodation at the yard, but there is an arrangement with a local guest house, which must be amongst the best value B&B's in the country.

If your objective is to experience turning a wide range of items and spanning most basic techniques, then this course must be quite favoured as a starter. It did introduce me to using the skew more effectively — only two digs in two days!

Although there were a range of lathes available, we all stayed with the same one throughout. Mine was an Arundel, so I was happy; but a 'mixed' experience might have been more interesting. I ended up being very surprised at my quantity of finished work, and more than satisfied with the quality of most of it. However, I didn't feel confident that I could go away and do it all on my own. I knew 'what', but not altogether 'how'. I feel the discussion of lathes could be dropped entirely, and the time more usefully used in other ways. All that said, I wrote: 'I got quite turned on!' In the visitors book, and I meant it.

Cliff Willetts

Course number two was very different. Cliff Willetts of Frisby-on-the-Wreke, near Melton Mowbray, normally takes only two students at a time. Cliff was a qualified craft teacher before taking up commercial woodwork as a profession.

Cliff and his family live in a period farmhouse, the students stay in guest bedrooms, and the instruction studio is one of the several workshops in the converted outbuildings. The whole atmosphere is pleasant and comfortable, and a beautiful new teaching studio is almost completed; the present one is warm, methodically laid out, and each student work-place is equipped with all the tools.

I was hardly through the classroom door before I had a tool in my hand, and during the morning I consumed considerable quantities of softwood, practising increasingly complex skew- and gouge-cuts.

Cliff's teaching skill came through as he explained what was happening with each cut and each tool. Not only did he explain in words and demonstrations, he also has a number of teaching aids and models to illustrate the points.

I met the beading tool (which I don't recall from Boddy's) and did more of the convex-curve spindle work with the gouge — it had been almost entirely skew before.

● *Cliff Willetts' teaching aids*

Cliff makes you use some difficult softwoods on the basis that if you can get a good tool finish on these, you can cope with almost anything.

My take-home goodies therefore included a chisel handle, a bud holder in some tacky mahogany, a nightlight dish in parana pine, a platter in ash and a trinket box in a zebrano-like offcut from a palette rail.

Although there's only two students, Cliff doesn't stand over you all the time. You get even more personal attention. (I have absolutely no criticisms of the amount of attention on the bigger courses.) On a number of occasions he deliberately busied himself with other tasks to relieve the pressure on the student of being watched, but he was still watching, or more accurately, listening. He has a finely-tuned ear which detects the least sound of anything less than correct tool contact; I know this because he demonstrated what he had heard and explained how it had occurred (often with another plywood model). I finished feeling I had been through a fairly intense and demanding learning experience; that I had **learnt.**

I came away carrying less in my hands, but with a lot more skill in my fingertips and certainly much more understanding in my head. What I also acquired, through the additional knowledge, was confidence.

The strengths of this course must be that the smaller numbers make it easier to deal with individual needs and problems, and the teaching methods give you a better understanding of what you're doing. You may end up with fewer finished pieces, but Cliff won't tolerate second best, so they *are* finished! You get a list of recommended items of equipment for your own workshop.

Craft Supplies

It would be arrogant to suggest that I was no longer a beginner by the time that I got to the third course, but I was supposed to be writing as a complete beginner, so I was more interested in what happened to the other 'complete novice' students than to myself.

The Craft Supplies courses are held on the top floor of a beautiful old converted flour mill. The setting, in a deep gorge in Derbyshire's Peak District, is idyllic.

Jamie Wallwin is the principal tutor on

the basic courses, and special programmes are also run by Stuart Batty, Ray Key and various visitors including Dale Nish. There were five students — three men and two women.

Jamie believes in getting any nervousness out of the way as quickly as possible and it was only a matter of minutes before we were all roughing out our first spindle blank. From then through to the end Jamie was in constant attendance. He spent time with those that needed it, and gently nudged along those better able to get on with their own things. It was basic skills for one and useful wrinkles for another.

The project routine that we went through was very similar to that at Boddy's. Everybody went away with exactly the same range of items (including the same number of holed egg cups and undersized eggs). I was now much quicker however so I had, additionally, a small candlestick in a scrap of rio rosewood, and a near-completed apple.

The first item for everybody was a baton, into or on to which we applied every possible cut with a range of roughing, skew, spindle, beading, and parting tools. There followed a tool handle, an egg-cup, egg, trinket box and shallow bowl, plus various finishes.

There were six lathes, but we each stuck with the same one throughout. Jamie thinks most people have more than enough to worry about coming to terms with one lathe without having to grasp the idiosyncracies of all the different ones — he's probably right. I was on a magnificent Konig, which of all the ones I tried is now far and away my favourite.

Accommodation is available in a farmhouse adjacent to and owned by The Mill, and a good lunch is provided in the dining room of the Mill itself. This was the most sociable of the courses!

In one weekend I made enough bowls, candlesticks and egg-cups for Christmas presents for even the more discerning friends.

All three courses spend a lot of time on the skew chisel. Phill had said: 'Master the skew and you can do anything!' I'm not sure that I agree. Certainly I lost my fear of the skew at Boddy's and learnt a lot about its use. There's also no doubt that I'm now getting an external finish on my bowls with a bowl gouge infinitely better than I achieved with a scraper. I also now get a good smooth finish inside shallow bowls without too much sanding, but I still have a lot of remedial work to do inside deep bowls. In that respect none of the courses spent enough time on the use of the deep bowl gouges — but then in two days you can't hope to do everything.

In retrospect I believe I chose the courses well, but however good they are, one is still not enough. I don't think a longer course is the answer, nor would I support the idea of doing all spindle-work on one and bowls on

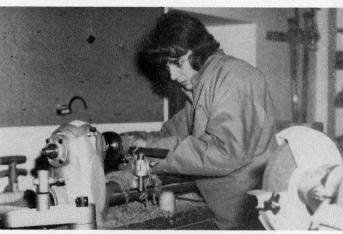

● *Jill, another Craft Supplies student*

the other. The full mix and the introduction of **all** basic techniques on one course is a good idea. What's important is to practise the whole range on your own after the course. Find out what you can and can't do, then go for a second course, where you've made sure your particular needs will be met.

There's no reason why you shouldn't start with Cliff Willetts, then go back to him for a second dose later. But starting with one of the big ones is useful to test your general level of interest, particularly if you haven't kitted up. Then, four to six months later spend a couple of days with Cliff (or one or two of the others of similar ability who have only one or two students).

But you haven't finished there! Possibly twelve months later it's back to somewhere like Miller's Dale and one of the master classes with people like Ray Key or Dale Nish. That's what I'll be doing... ▨

The courses

We sent a questionnaire to most of the courses we know; a highly edited listing is below. Do make further inquiries before booking, and do ask about whether you are insured under a public liability policy.

John Boddy Riverside Sawmills, Boroughbridge, N. Yorks YO5 9LJ, tel. (09012) 2370. 1 day £42, 2 days £70+VAT, accomm. £9.50-£37. Arundel, Tyme, Harrison lathes. Max 4 people. 25% theory, 75% hands-on. Sells tools and wood.

Peter Child The Old Hyde, Little Yeldham, Halstead, Essex CO9 4QT, tel. (0787) 237291. 2 days £80 inc. lunch, accomm. £8. Myford lathes. Max 2 people. 20% demos, 70% hands-on. Old oak barn. Sells lathes, tools, blanks etc.

Craft Tools and Tackle Unit 10, Holme Ind. Estate, Skiff Lane, Holme on Spalding Moore, York YO4 4BB, tel. (0696) 60612. 1½hrs intro £5, problem corner £10, 1 day £25+VAT. Coronet Major, Apollo Woodstyler, Tyme, Nu-Tool lathes. Sells most stuff.

Devon Woodcrafts Hartford Barton, Gittisham, Honiton, Devon EX14 0AW, tel. (0404) 44155. 2 days £60, 1 day £30, ½ day £20, accomm. £12 inc. meals. Myford and Coronet lathes. Max 2 people. Demos 5-10%, theory 5-10%, rest hands-on. Old coaching inn.

John Golder 176 Burntwood Rd, Norton Canes, Cannock, Staffs WS11 3RL, tel. (0543) 79137. £35 per day, £4.50 per hr evgs. Coronet, Tyme, two specials. 1 person, but husband and wife OK. 90% hands-on. Purpose-built workshop.

Aubrey Hammond 33 Lynch Green, Hethersett, Norwich, tel. (0603) 810571. £42 per day, accomm. £10. Apollo lathes. 80% hands-on. Large residential caravan. Sells most stuff, and own English hardwoods.

Peter Hibbard Old School Arts Workshop, Middleham, Leyburn, N. Yorks DL8 4QG, tel. (0969) 23056. 2 days £30, £65 residential, others poss. Harrison Union lathe. 1 person. Hands-on percentage depends on student. Listed building converted to study centre.

Keith Lawrence Old Stables Turnery, Coed Talon, Mold, Clwyd, tel. (0352) 771771. £30 per day, accomm. £8. Arundel, Tyme lathes. Max 2 people. 95% hands-on. Part of craft centre on Welsh farm. Sells most stuff.

Michael O'Donnell The Croft, Brough, Thurso, Caithness KW14 8YE, tel. (084785) 605. 5 days £175. Myford, Harrison lathes. Max 4 people 75% hands-on, 25% theory and demo.

G. J. Peters 37 Pheasant Way, Cirencester, Glos, tel. (0285) 66907. 1 day £45, 2 days £80, inc. lunch. Accomm. £12.50 inc. meals. Arundel lathe. 1 person or couple. 5 hrs a day hands-on. Sells tools.

K. A. Richmond Price Lower Dundridge, Parkham, Bideford, N. Devon, tel. (02375) 257. 1 day £40, 2 days £80, 3 days £100. Myford lathe. 1 person. Mostly hands-on. Workshop in countryside.

Keith Rowley 68 Moorgreen, Newthorpe, Notts NG16 2FB, tel (0773) 716903. 1 day £35, 2 days £70, accomm. £10 inc. meals. Coronet and Arundel lathes. Max 2 people, usually 1. Hands-on 85%. Annex to home. Sells most stuff.

Reg Slack Saracens Head Coaching Inn, Brailsford, Derbyshire DE6 3AS, tel. (0335) 60829. ½-3 days, £39 per day inc. lunch. Accomm. £10-£15. Coronet, Tyme lathes. 80% hands-on. Workshop attached to shop. Sells tools and finishes.

Gordon Stokes 202 The Hollow, Bath, Avon BA2 1NG, tel. (0225) 22617. 2 days £95, 3 days £145. Tyme, Mini Max lathes. Max 3 people. ⅓ each theory, demos, hands-on. Converted chapel workshop.

John Thackeray 18 Hitchin Rd, Arlesey, Beds SG15 6RP, tel. (0462) 34177. 1 day £40 inc. lunch, £5 per hour. Can travel, with or without lathe, to you. Tyme, Arundel lathes. Normally 1 person, but 2 max. 80% hands-on, 15% demos. Basement workshop at Roger's of Hitchin, who sell most stuff.

Tony Waddilove Unit A, Hill Farm Workshops, Great Dunham, King's Lynn, Norfolk, tel. (07605) 674. ½ day £27; 1 day £46, 2 days £80 inc. lunch. Tyme, Arundel, Konig lathes. Max 2 people. 7½% demos, 20% theory, rest hands-on. Self-contained craft workshop.

West Dean College West Dean, Chichester, West Sussex PO18 0QZ, tel. (024363) 301. 2 days £43 (£68 residents), 5 days £97 (£158.50 res.). Union, Coronet lathes. Max. 5 people. 80% hands-on, 20% demo. Large open-plan workshop in ex-stately home. Sells tools, finishes.

Cliff Willetts Gables, Frisby-on-the-Wreke, Melton Mowbray, Leics LE14 2NP, tel. (066475) 246. 2 days £75, accomm. £15. Harrison, Luna lathes. Max. 2 people. 98% hands-on. Purpose-built studio/workshop.

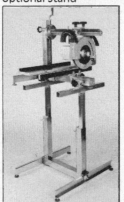

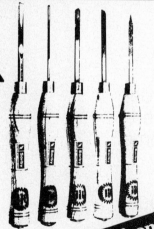

368

Books

Thomas Moser
**Measured shop drawings
    for American furniture**
Blandford Press, £20.95
Reviewed by David Woodnutt

The title of this book is at once intriguing and misleading. In over 400 drawings and photographs the anatomy of some 70 pieces of furniture is revealed; but this is not a purview of American furniture — everything here is by the same maker and bears his mark. It is more like a sophisticated catalogue advertising the products of Thomas Moser's firm. Nevertheless, it serves to show why he is among America's most respected cabinetmakers.

The genesis of the drawings is also somewhat odd. They are not workshop drawings so much as a curious kind of work-record. The pieces themselves evolved from sketches and ideas, and ten years after, the designers have inked in the lines to present us with this intimate view.

Inspecting the drawings is the next best thing to looking over the pieces themselves. The drawings bear close scrutiny and no doubt the furniture they represent will be around for many years.

The book is divided into sections — chairs, tables, desks, cases, beds and miscellaneous pieces, including clocks and a filing cabinet. Each piece is represented in a photograph, followed by a clutch of dimensioned drawings and details, with notes on the construction.

Often the photograph is accompanied by a perspective view which adds little information, and the drawings could be more elegant, but generally they are clear enough to enable a competent craftsperson to produce the pieces. The outstanding exception is in the section on chairs.

The 'continuous' armchairs which Moser seems to specialise in rely on complex bending to produce the back and arms of a Windsor-type chair in a continuous piece. The design is featured several times, yet nowhere does the author explain how to make it. It's the one technique in the book which is not likely to be familiar to most readers, and Mr Moser does nothing to enlighten us.

Most of the furniture is classically simple, allowing the forms themselves to speak without ornamentation — there is very little turning for example. A few pages of colour pictures show off some of the pieces in their full glory; using linseed oil on hardwood, spurning modern and high-tech finishes, Moser makes a glowing testament to the natural qualities of the wood.

Moser acknowledges a Shaker influence and his well-developed ideas about design are expressed in his introduction. He is at pains to point out that the drawings shouldn't be seen as definitive but rather as jumping-off points; they may be used to make the pieces as shown but they are also an inspiration to design.

As for the price, I can only say 'Ouch!'.

● David Woodnutt is a furniture designer and maker in London.

Alan Smith
Woodframe Furniture Restoration
Ebury Press, £4.95 hardback
Reviewed by David Ellis

Alan Smith's attractively small volume (8½x5in) avoids the mistake of so many recent books on restoration, namely trying to cover too wide a spectrum in one go. Alan has confined his work to woodframe furniture restoration (what I prefer to call 'restoration woodwork') rather than devoting long chapters to the use of tools — no-one in their right mind is likely to start restoring furniture unless they are reasonably competent woodworkers. By the same token, he avoids tackling other restoration crafts such as upholstery and french polishing, which are covered in great detail by specialised books.

The book opens with a few pages on the ethics of restoration, the type of furniture the reader can tackle and a basic list of useful tools and materials. By p16 Alan Smith is already dealing in clear yet simple terms with the first of seven restoration projects. Each one describes the work on one specific piece of furniture, but is applicable to a far wider range of similar items.

The first project covers the restoration of the ubiquitous Windsor chair, usually far more difficult than appears at first. But if the basic rules given here are followed there should be no problems. Project no.2 covers all the problems ever likely to be met when restoring the simple pine 'farmhouse' table, describing processes equally suitable to numerous other applications. Other projects deal with a blanket sheet, a pine chest of drawers, a Regency side-table, a sabre-leg chair and a Pennsylvania 'Dutch' dresser.

By dividing the work into projects, the author has cleverly covered a very wide range of restoration techniques and tricks of the trade. The book is well illustrated, with both colour and black-and-white photographs and excellent line drawings.

If I could find any fault in this excellent book it must be the statement made on p7: 'Do not let lack of experience in restoring put you off attempting even difficult repairs . . . Much of the finest work in this field is done by home workers.' Many valuable pieces of antique furniture can be irretrievably damaged by the budding but inexperienced restorer and, at the risk of appearing to dampen enthusiasm, I would have preferred to see readers urged to start on pieces of little value. The satisfaction of picking up a badly damaged chair or table at a sale for next to nothing and restoring it to its former glory will be just as rewarding in the early stages.

It has been a pleasure to read this book and I can unreservedly recommend it to all who want to preserve beautiful furniture for the enjoyment of future generations.

● David Ellis is an antique restorer and teacher in Wiltshire.

David Field
Projects in Wood
Mitchell Beazley, £9.95 hardback
Reviewed by David O'Connor

The first thing that struck me about David Field's book was the quality of the presentation. The beautiful colour photographs, clear informative drawings, and well laid-out text are all exceptionally easy on the eye.

The book aims to introduce the reader to the renaissance of contemporary British furniture, led by the designer-makers. Field talks lucidly and with perception about design concepts such as function, economy, anthropometrics, style and fashion, and catalogues the work of 16 designer-makers through interviews, photographs, and dozens of exploded-view drawings. The projects include tables, chairs, and storage units, and many are treated comparatively, a useful exercise which clearly shows the designers' different approaches. I found it fascinating to read about the 'low tech' environment-conscious philosophy of David Colwell; it makes his lean and economically designed work all the more interesting when you know the full logic of his method.

The last section deals with materials, finishing, and the workshop (layout and machinery), which like the rest of the book is fresh and informative. Unfortunately it isn't studied in enough depth — I would have preferred to know and see more of the work of our leading designer-makers and their philosophies. This type of technical information is better dealt with in other books — Alan Peters' *Cabinet Making; the Professional Approach* for example, which tackles similar topics. Field has chosen Peters as one of his designer-makers, and puts him firmly in the tradition of the Arts and Crafts movement, as opposed to say Floris Van den Broecke, whose work Field describes as formal, abstract and dispassionate. Because Peters works predominantly in one style, he is able to offer an in-depth study of setting up a traditional craft-based workshop, while Field is offering the student an overview of many styles and methods. Perhaps in the future each of Field's 15 other craftsmen will write their own version of *Cabinet Making; the Professional Approach* for our libraries.

This is an excellent introduction to contemporary furniture design; it's ideal for students, and especially for makers who haven't had the benefit of a design education. It would also be of interest to architects and interior designers to show the quality and confidence of the new makers, who are now a long way from the 'hanging basket' craft-show image of the past. The price of £9.95 is very reasonable, considering the time and effort that have obviously been spent, and the quality of the whole production.

● David O'Connor is a young designer-maker working in London, and has contributed to *Woodworker*.

WIN!

● **Elektra Beckum's newest precision table-saw**

● **The HDM lathe, with a full metre between centres**

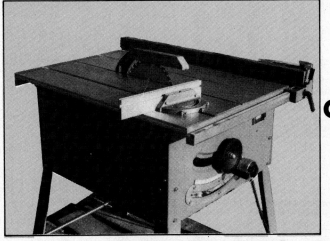

OR

SQUARES AND ROUNDS

There are two types of woodworker — and *Woodworker*, in association with Elektra Beckum, proudly announces a competition for them both. The ones who work in squares — the joiner/cabinetmakers — can win a new table-saw; the ones who work in rounds — the woodturner/carvers — can win over £500 worth of lathe!

THE SQUARES

Elektra Beckum's PK250 precision table-saw is their latest addition to a range of serious machinery. It has a 700x900mm table, and its motor puts out 3hp at full tilt. The rip-fence is full-length, and it locks front and rear; a crosscut fence is also standard. It comes with a 10in TCT blade, 45° tilt-arbor, and rise-and-fall; it will cost £500.

THE PRIZES

THE ROUNDS

The HDM 1000 lathe's chrome steel bed gives you 1000mm between centres. You can turn bowls up to 15in diameter; it has 4 speeds, and a faceplate and drive dog come as original equipment. The head- and live centre tailstock are both diecast, both with double bearings, and there's a spindle brake. It's over £500 with the stand.

Runners-up in both categories will get boxed sets of *Richard Kell's* wonderful measuring tools (below)

THE COMPETITION

What you have to do: make any item (out of wood, of course) that includes a chessboard. It's as simple as that. **But** we'll be judging originality and imagination, as well as craftsmanship; so you can make a chessboard on its own, or you can make something that incorporates one. It can be a chair, a chest, a table or a cabinet — anything as long as it has a built-in chessboard!

What you have to do: the woodturner/carvers are challenged to come up with an ingenious set of chessmen — or draughts, or a set of pieces for any game, ordinary or extraordinary, that can be played on a chessboard. They can be as big as you like and as fantastic as you like; what we're looking for is imagination and craftsmanship.

Final judging of both categories will be at the Bristol Woodworker Show, 16-18 May.

THE RULES

Entries must include the entry slip at right **plus:**
  A photograph of your work
  A written description (no more than two A4 sheets) of the idea and the techniques used
  Dimensioned drawings
  Entries must be sent to **Woodworker Squares and Rounds Competition, 1 Golden Sq, London W1R 3AB** by Monday **1 April 1986**
  If you can't finish by 21 April but still want to enter, send a perspective drawing by the closing date instead of the photo,

along with your description and drawings
4 You can't enter both categories
5 Entries selected for final judging will be displayed at the **WOODWORKER SHOW, BRISTOL, 16-18 May, and will be judged there by, amongst others, master-cabinetmaker Alan Peters**
6 Decisions of the judges and *Woodworker* magazine are final in all matters concerning the competition

Designs on the market

Nick Allen is an inventive designer with an eye for form and colour and a talent for promotion. He wanted to meet his maker . . .

Inventive Design is now just eighteen months old. We chose the name carefully, meaning to convey both originality and adaptability — our ambition is to become a major force in design, especially in Europe and the United States. We've achieved a lot in that short time, but we still have a way to go!

Our small beginnings can be traced back to when a friend asked me to make a four-poster bed. The only brief was: 'four posts, and in bamboo or whatever you like.' I accepted the job — but the piece still fills me with a mixture of pride and horror. I had made a few things before — one-offs such as curved curtain rails for a painter on silk — and some time as a stage-set painter and a fine art course at Epsom had given me machinery experience and an understanding of form and colour. During a period I spent working with a restorer I began to notice how, in comparison with the pieces he handled, modern domestic furniture was all but bereft of attention to detail, and quality in design and manufacture.

The four-poster led to other commissions, all different and each an excuse to experiment. For me, observation is a route of inspiration in the design process; I'm very interested in texture and depth, and even rusted metal or an old door with 20 layers of paint falling away can provide ideas. The 'creative jump' is rather difficult to explain. When I'm working on something difficult I often find that sleeping on the problem works, but sometimes only sheer application and a private brainstorming session will produce answers. Luckily most of my pieces so far have been designed and made to fairly loose criteria, allowing me to develop my style almost unhindered.

My aim was to use what I had learnt in producing a range of furniture for batch production; two of my early clients became friends and agreed to back me in setting up a limited company to work in the guidelines of the Business Expansion Scheme, under which part of the investors' risk is offset against tax advantages. It's not a cheap process, but it has the advantage that we are now a better investment proposition. Life, however, wasn't made easy by the fact that we started with insufficient capital to invest in stock, premises, or promotion, and far too much time was spent fighting financial fires rather than concentrating on design. Our bank manager has been understanding in our various crises!

Having made all the furniture myself before Inventive Design, I would have liked a workshop with craftsmen to make the furniture and a salesman to sell it, but we couldn't afford such a gap between invest-

● *Modern designers aren't always doing funny bendy things with found wood . . . classical chairs in mahogany*

ment and return. The only solution was to find someone else to manufacture the furniture, with me supporting, designing and selling. I set about finding the right partner, and having worked my way through a Furniture Industry Research Association list of likely manufacturers and come up with nothing, I advertised in *Cabinet Maker and Retail Furnisher*. The response to my detailed request for quality surplus capacity was overwhelming, and the net result of an exhaustive examination and elimination process was four companies, of which we are actively using two. Prototypes for new lines are being worked on by the others.

Our main manufacturer, based near Cambridge, employs about 30 people. The company had been bought out by the management, and I believe the fact that the workforce owns shares at least partly accounts for their pride in their work and the quality of their furniture. There is the usual machinery, but there's also a large amount of hand construction and finishing.

It has taken a long time, nevertheless, to establish a mutual understanding of strengths and weaknesses. At times I haven't given them enough information and supervision, so they haven't produced exactly what I wanted, and there have also been production delays, but now we iron out difficulties as we go. We discuss materials, finishes and costs at the drawing stage, which makes handing over the major part of furniture making more reasonable.

Designing a range and finding a suitable manufacturer for it, plus working on private commissions, had taken nine months. I decided to exhibit at 'Style '86', a London furniture show in October 1985; we became members of the Independent

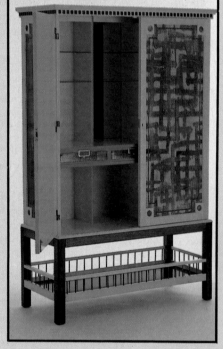

● *A dressing cabinet with full colour inside and out*

Designers Federation (WW/Feb), a co-operative set up to market British design here and abroad. The exhibition was critical. The IDF section was generally thought to have been the most interesting in the show, and our stand attracted far more attention and praise than most. The trade saw our work for the first time, we made client and retailer contacts, and the attention of the press generated more publicity than we could have afforded. One of our show 'gimmicks' had been some

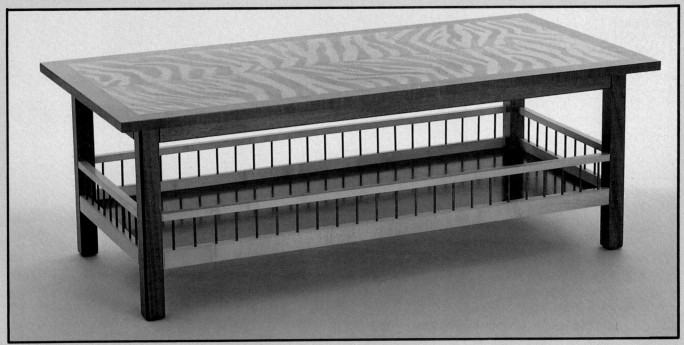

● *Colour and pattern astonish; on a simple basic form, maple and stains combine wildly!*

● *Patterned on the same theme as the coffee table and cabinet, this chest is actually traditional in shape and construction*

cardboard chairs with our company logo on them — we distributed them all round Olympia to draw attention to ourselves!

The follow-up to the exhibition has demanded more publicity material and active promotion in a style synonymous with our quality; top-class photography, as a front-line sales aid, is vital.

Blanchards of Knightsbridge are now to stock part of our range on an exclusive basis for a trial three months. We provide them with showroom samples; they display and promote them in magazines like *World of Interiors*. 'Maison' is stocking our chest exclusively, Ryman's will be handling a desk we're

designing, and we're working with Osborne and Little on a new range they will use as part of their expansion into furniture.

We are now working flat out to fulfil these commitments, from our small offices just off the Kings Road — a central location is essential. We have a full-time secretary, and are helped with planning, promotion, marketing and pricing by a business school graduate. A team with complementary skills is proving vital as we expand.

Working in a company like this is incredibly time-consuming — early mornings, late nights and weekends — exciting, but sometimes exceedingly frustrating. We believe we have designs that people want, and although we're a small

company, it's best to think big and offer the best possible service.

The last eighteen months have whizzed past, even though some days seemed as if they would never end. So much effort in so little time, but we feel we've created the foundations of what we hope and expect will be a very successful British company. But the hard work isn't over. Having clawed our way into a very competitive game, now we have to play it . . . ∎

● All designs and photographs are copyright of Inventive Design Limited, 15 Radnor Walk, London SW3 4BP, tel. 01-351 3785.

Wooden Wonder

● **Right** a T111 at Hawarden, April 1984; **bottom left**, Prototype at the Salisbury House museum; **bottom right**, a B.35 at Harlingen, Texas, October 1973

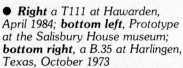

The wooden Mosquito flew in the face of convention to become an all-time classic. Stuart Howe, who lived under its flight path, tells its tale

● The FB.VI fighter-bomber

'... I turn green and yellow with envy when I see the Mosquito. The British knock together a beautiful wooden aircraft that every piano factory over there is building ... There is nothing the British do not have.'

Reichsmarshall Hermann Goering

Truly classic aircraft have often been produced in the face of official policy. As a nation we are fortunate to have had individuals and companies who have put private money and resources into a project they believed in; one such was Geoffrey de Havilland, whose foresight and determination brought us the Mosquito, so aptly nicknamed the 'Wooden wonder'.

Before WW2, the concept of an unarmed bomber was considered by officialdom as unthinkable. De Havilland's design was not only unarmed, but also made of wood, which was considered an equally retrograde step. All aircraft at that time were metal.

Design work on the Mosquito started in late 1938. The design team moved a few miles away from de Havilland headquarters, with the idea of working unhindered by officialdom and away from the main (bomb-threatened) factory. Thanks mainly to Sir Wilfred Freeman, Air Member for Development and Production at the Air Ministry (at the time virtually de Havilland's only ally in the government), a contract for 50 Mosquitoes was awarded to de Havilland on 1 March 1940 — even though construction of the aircraft hadn't started.

Why was it made of wood? Not only was there a saving in weight, but it could also be built by the semi-skilled labour employed by furniture manufacturers and coach-builders all over the country. This left the aircraft industry's own workforce to get on with vital Spitfires and Lancasters, and it also saved valuable metal. Other advantages

of using wood were that the initial design stages could be cut down and the prototype built quickly, so it went into production very quickly — less than two years from the start of design work to the aircraft entering service.

The Mosquito design had many special features, including the plywood and balsa-wood sandwich of the fuselage, a simple construction for a monococque (where frame and skin share the stresses). The fuselage was built in two halves (which simplified equipment installation), each half formed over a concrete or mahogany mould shaped to the interior. First the structural members were located in recesses in the mould to form the internal stiffening or bulkheads of the fuselage, then the inner three-ply birch skin, 1.5 and 2mm thick, was applied. Broad flexible steel bands were used to cramp the skin down over the mould.

The fuselage skin was made of a number of plywood panels scarfed and glued together, getting narrower towards the nose with its sharper double curvatures. Balsa strips were laid over the inner skin and then glued, and the steel bands applied again, after which the balsa was smoothed to the contours; the outer plywood skin was attached, and after the glue had set and the equipment was assembled in them, the two halves were bonded together on special jigs with wooden cramps.

The Mosquito wing was made in one piece with a front and rear spar and stressed skin covering. The top surface was of two birch plywood skins, interspaced by

square-section stringers which ran the length of the wing. On the undersurface, the outboard panels were of only one ply skin, while the centre section of the wing (which housed the fuel tanks) was made of stressed balsa-plywood panels which formed the tank doors. Both main spars were box construction, separated by interspar ribs made of spruce laminations.

The tailplane had two spars separated by inter-spar ribs and covered with plywood, while the flaps consisted of a nose section formed by the leading edge end spar, connected by ribs to the trailing edge. The fin was also of two-spar construction with inter-spar ribs. All the surfaces were given a covering of Madapolam (fabric) using red dope, and then the camouflage was painted.

By November 1940, the hastily-constructed prototype was ready and made its maiden flight on 25 November, piloted by Geoffrey de Havilland Jnr. Three more Mosquitoes were constructed before production moved to the main factory at Hatfield.

Once the Mosquito had proved its worth, Hatfield couldn't cope with the demand, so de Havilland's factory at Leavesden, near Watford, went over to Mosquito production, followed by Standard Motors at Coventry, Percival Aircraft at Luton and Airspeed at Portsmouth; after the war another line was set up at Chester.

Before the end of 1942, a production line had been set up in de Havilland's Toronto factory, and in 1944 one started in Australia, in the company's Sydney works.

Wooden Wonder

A total of 7,781 of all models of Mosquito were built before 1950, when production finished.

There were nearly 50 different models of Mosquito, used in every role imaginable. 'Multi-role combat' is a modern military term, but the Mosquito's flexibility pre-dated it by 40 years. As a bomber with just two crew, the plane could carry as great a bomb load faster, farther and higher than some of the four-engined bombers with crews of up to 11. It was equally successful as a 'pathfinder', and the night-fighter version protected Britain by night, virtually stopping enemy activity. It was also successful against the V-1 flying bomb. Our heavy bombers on their raids over Europe were protected by the Mosquito day and night, and by November 1944 Mosquitoes had claimed 659 enemy aircraft and over 500 flying bombs. Fighter bombers, land-based marine combat aircraft, photo reconnaissance planes, even mail planes, training and torpedo bombers — the Mosquito played all the roles. They went to many post-war foreign air forces, and even the Russians got at least one!

It wasn't until 1953 that the weary planes were phased out of front-line service; however, they still operated in secondary roles and a number were towing targets as late as 1963.

In the 1940s and 50s many surplus Mosquitoes were bought up by civilian operators for survey and experimental work, where they ranged the world carrying out their tasks. Indeed, there were cases of civilian Mosquitoes carrying out clandestine work for the CIA over South-East Asia in the early 1950s!

Thanks to its wooden construction, some 28 examples of the Mosquito still exist today — a healthy number, when you think that not one example of many other famous designs now exist. It's partly due, of course, to the fact that a wooden airframe was no use to the scrap metal man.

Today, many of these 28 are now being rebuilt, and currently two are airworthy, while a third is due to fly in Canada in the very near future. On 15 May, 1959, the unofficially preserved prototype was officially enshrined in its own little hangar at Salisbury Hall, its original Hertfordshire birthplace, as a memorial to all those that had built, flown and maintained it. It now forms the centrepiece of the Mosquito Aircraft Museum.

The Mosquito rebuild

I recovered the fuselage of a Mosquito FB.VI (the widely-used fighter-bomber version) from Delft Technical University in Holland in 1978. This particular plane served with nos. 605 and 4 Squadrons, entering service in 1945 and seeing at least one operational mission before the war ended. Although some components were missing, and some parts carefully sectioned out of the fuselage to show construction, the fuselage was in very good condition. I

● After 20 years in Israel, the wing is resurrected. A bit of work to do!

● The wing comes to the Mosquito Aircraft Museum. Some of the fuselage still remains

decided to try and make up a complete plane — its serial number was TA122 — but with components now like gold dust, this was clearly going to be no easy task!

The biggest missing component was the one-piece wing, which I found in Israel, and which was generously flown back to England free by El Al in July 1980. It remained in the Museum's workshops while we concentrated on our second Mosquito, but in spring 1985 work began on rebuilding the wing under the direction of Colin Ewer, who had helped build Mosquitoes after the war at Hatfield. This rebuild is probably the most ambitious restoration task undertaken by a private,

voluntary aviation museum in the UK.

Colin's task isn't an easy one. All the plywood skins have rotted away, as have all the trailing and leading edges. The spars also need repairs in several places and almost all of the 32 ribs will either need repair or replacement. Several feet of the starboard wing and the port wing-tip are missing altogether, while all four of the underwing tank doors require major repair work. The spruce stringers, which run outwards, dividing the two top wing-skins, had become exposed when the skins rotted away, but are still attached to the ribs and most of them are good enough to be used again.

The first task was to remove the old plywood facings on both spars, which were in good condition. Colin decided to start rebuilding the centre section, and then work his way out on both sides, the best way to retain the shape of the wing. First of all, the stringers were removed and both rib no. 1s, which were in poor shape, were taken out. The front and rear spars were then repaired as far as 'rib no. 2' on either side, and new plywood facings were attached to the inside and outside of both spars. Two unused rib 1s, which had been donated to the Museum many years ago, were then fitted in place of the damaged ones, and at the time of writing both rib 2s were almost repaired. The metal undercarriage brackets have all been refurbished and re-attached to the wing.

The material being used in the rebuild follows the original specifications laid down by de Havilland. The most expensive part of the project is the aero-grade Canadian birch plywood, a top-quality 8x4ft sheet of which costs about £300! Finnish birch to a similar specification isn't quite so expensive. It's estimated that the wing rebuild will need some 60 sheets of birch plywood of various thicknesses, so we were grateful when British Plywood Manufacturers Ltd of Enfield, Middlesex (suppliers of the original plywood) generously offered us a substantial discount. We are also indebted to Humbrol Ltd for the Cascamite glue, much of which will be needed before the project is completed!

And of course we need help. Please get in touch if you want to be involved in the rebuild of one of the classic aeroplanes of all time!

Making Mosquitoes

Ken Taylor writes: When I joined F. Wrighton & Sons as a 16 year-old apprentice in 1942, production of the Mosquito fuselage was already well established and was followed a few months later by the wing. Considering the all-wood construction of the aircraft, the mill was quite small and the machinery very basic — a hand-fed rip saw, a surfacer, a thicknesser, two small dimension benches, a bandsaw, a spindle, a router and two bobbin sanders.

The spruce, balsa and ply were inspected and check-weighed on delivery to determine moisture content and any material not up to spec would be rejected. The spruce was of superb quality and was a pleasure to cut, but as there wasn't dust extraction on the saw the machinist soon began to look like a snowman. Because of the sharp taper of the wing, every wing rib was a different size, so many settings were required on the dimension bench to produce a batch of components. Each batch was inspected, and if it was within the specified tolerances, it was given the AID (Aircraft Inspection Department) stamp and sent for assembly.

The ply for the skins was cut oversize on the bandsaw and then brought to size on the router using very accurate jigs supplied by

● *The fuselage of TA122 is offloaded at the MAM, February 1978*

British Aerospace

● *The inner skin and between-skin structural members being fitted; in the former behind, numbered steel bands are set on for bonding*

de Havillands. There were no tungsten-tipped cutters in those days, so frequent regrinding was necessary because the ply was bonded with resin glue. The edges of the skins were then scarfed on the bobbin sander, marked with a serial number and identified with the fuselage assembly position.

The balsa was machined into planks ⅜in thick, but left quite random in width and length — generally they were 3-4in wide and from 2-5ft in length.

The next shop contained the jigs for the fuselage shells. They were made of mahogany, and well polished to prevent the ply or balsa sticking to the jig. The turnbuckles which secured the band clamps were attached to the jig supports and were placed edge-to-edge across the shell, running the whole length of the fuselage. The bands had holes punched over their entire length to let out surplus glue when

the balsa planking was being clamped down on the shell. Large bradawls were pushed through the holes into the balsa so the excess glue could squeeze out and be washed off. The bands were applied three times; first when the inner skin was being fixed to the formers and longerons (which fitted into slots in the jig); second when the balsa planking was being glued down, and third when fixing the outer skin. The completed shell would be lifted off the jig bodily by the jig crew, and the two half-shells would then be joined temporarily with special clamps so no misalignment or twisting could occur. They were then taken to de Havilland's for finishing and fitting out into finished aircraft.

The one-piece wings were assembled in vertical steel jigs with the trailing edge upwards. The main spars were delivered pre-fabricated, and the ribs were attached by gluing and screwing plus hundreds of

Wooden Wonder

hand-cramps. The ply skins (the upper one was reinforced by douglas-fir strips) were then glued and screwed to the ribs and spars with brass screws. The screws were close together and it was all hands to the 'Yankee' pump screwdrivers — no electric or air-operated drivers then! After our work on them, the wings were taken to the finishing department for covering in Madapolam (a fine linen-type fabric) which was stuck in place with red cellulose dope applied by brush.

Special mention should be made of the adhesive, which was known as 'Beetle Cement', a type of urea formaldehyde manufactured by B.I.P. Ltd. This adhesive was used in the furniture trade just before the war. Two types of Beetle cement were used; type 'W' for bonding the plywood laminations and type 'A' for gluing the balsa to plywood and for general assembly work. Cement 'W' used a special hot hardener so the glue-line could stand the three-hour boil test which was required for aircraft use. Cement 'A' was a special gap-filling type where joints might not be in close contact while the glue cured. As heat could not be applied, it had to set properly at normal shop temperature.

As far as I know, things went as the designers intended; large numbers of inspectors made sure they did! At the end of the war, F. Wrighton's went back to making furniture. ■

● The Mosquito Aircraft Museum, Salisbury Hall, London Colney, St Albans, Herts, tel. (61)23274. Open Sundays 10.30-5.30 from Easter to the end of October plus Bank Holiday Mondays, and Thursdays from July-September 2-5.30. Groups by arrangement. The Museum has a Supporters' Society, which welcomes members with an interest in aviation history. They also welcome any help in restoring the wing — contact Stuart Howe or Colin Ewer for details at the above address.

● The Guild of Woodworkers is organising a tour of the Museum with talks by the restorers; for details see the Guild pages.

British Aerospace

● **Above:** The two-halved construction of the Mosquito fuselage; **left:** fitting out FB.V1s at Hatfield

Tales out of steel

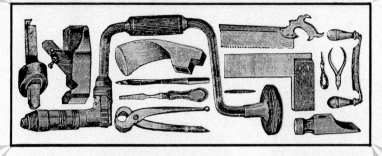

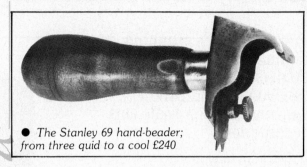

● *The Stanley 69 hand-beader;
from three quid to a cool £240*

Ashley Iles introduces the
Sheffield tool industry's
first marketing man, and
reflects on the attraction
of old tools

It's a fact that confidence tricksters have sold the Eiffel Tower four times. In a court of law this is known as fraud, in certain areas of business it's called marketing, and we're all prey to it in one way or another. Hence the saying 'Buyer beware'. Let me hasten to add that the marketing man's is a difficult and honourable profession, quite distinct from the representative who sells. The marketing man unifies the workforce and management to produce the consumer's needs as revealed from market research.

Disreputable marketing men do exist, and it's well known that an article worth 10p (this one perhaps) can be sold for £5 with a plausible tale (copywriter) and fancy box (presentation). The customers are not only those legendary types whose births are at one minute intervals, but you and me.

Fortunately for us the first marketing man in the tool business was of the highest integrity, Mr Stormont Archer. (Personally I dislike unusual Christian names. I've spent my life in envy of the Bobs, Jacks and Toms of the world, rubbing out hyphens between Ashley and Iles.) He was an edge-tool manufacturer in Fitzwilliam Street, Sheffield. In the late 40s he produced the first tools in fancy display boxes, and literally cleaned up — with a rep who was reported to have worked for a firm selling ultra-violet lamps in the Bahamas. The big firms keep a close eye on the little firms as their only source of ideas, and I've never seen them sit up so quickly. Box firms popped up all over the place, but Stormont Archer had a season's lead and it made him. Men of vision and conviction are as scarce as parsons in Heaven.

Mr Archer was much my senior and had we met I'm sure we would have had a lot to talk about, both of us having started from scratch. After all, setting up on your own account manufacturing is not without its pitfalls. Looking back, I'm glad I started with very little capital. If I had had it, I'd have spent it on the wrong things. Anyway, money is secondary to skill and technical training, and having acquired a skill it's comparatively easy to apply it in another direction. To make tools myself as a one

man band I had to learn three extra trades.

Fortunately I learn very quickly. I am good at some things but not so good at others; there've been times when I needed expert advice but in the early days I couldn't afford it, so I had to use the back door. I'm not a mason, but somehow or other I managed to acquire quite a background of accomplished friends. Once when things weren't going very well I managed to get an interview with Mr Sidney Osborn, a director of dozens of companies. I washed behind my ears very carefully and arrived at his office on Paternoster Row dead on time. I explained my problems in detail while he looked straight through me with his fearless steel blue eyes. When I finished he said: 'You have either too much going out or not enough coming in.' I waited for him to go on but that was it. But what wonderful advice it was! I couldn't believe it could be so simple, but it was. 30 years later I sought his advice again when a firm wanted to buy me out. I drove with my sons to his house on the top of a Derbyshire mountain, and received a warm welcome. His advice was even shorter than the first time — just the one word: 'No'. I've always found people very helpful, but I'm cautious of those who give advice not asked for.

Just for once I have an overpowering urge to divert from the 'narrative line'. When Arthur Negus said a piece of furniture was 'right' we all knew exactly what he meant. In the tool trade the comparable word is 'feel'. My father often spoke of tools having feel, it's something quite distinct from patina. Technically it could be a combination of design, material, finish and balance. Aesthetically my father again comes to my rescue. 'It's like putting out your hand and having a tool built inside your fingers and palm.' Close? But how can we experience this enigma first-hand?

Once in the Medina, the ancient centre of Valletta in Malta, I felt an atmosphere so utterly timeless and overpowering that returning to the normal world was like travelling through 1000 years in time. I felt exactly the same as I walked into Chelsea Old Town Hall in January, the venue of the first London auction of antique tools by David Stanley (no relation). The hall itself is a masterpiece of architecture and craftsmanship, I've seen worse ceilings in Florence. But far above anything else was the vast tapestry of 1300 specimens of tool-making from AD1600 on, every one an

individual credit to its time in history.

Some were in mint condition, others 'F' (fine) then 'G+' to 'G' to 'G—' and fair. Some were damaged or incomplete, some showed the wear of centuries of use. Many had great antique value, others were valuable because of rarity, but mostly the value was in quality and sheer craftsmanship. All made you wish you were rich.

Quality. I picked up a Norris A5 coffin smooth-plane made of steel, the curved sides dovetailed into the base so neatly the dovetails couldn't be seen. The infill was solid polished rosewood and the iron rested against a gunmetal lever bar. The enclosed handle (also of rosewood) flattered my hand, and the long-handled spur curled between my finger and thumb. The iron was adjustable both ways, hence the A in A5. Price £300-£400, 'G+'. I put it down very carefully and bought it later.

Antiquity. I picked up a moulding plane by I Cogdell 1750, estimated value £70-100, and was brought to mind of the War of Independence; a surgeon's saw preceding anaesthetic by 400 years made me wince and think of teeth-marks on bullets. In all these tools, the past was never so present.

Rarity. With a Stanley 69 hand-beader in my hand, I thought of the days when if anybody had offered me three quid for mine I would have snatched their hands off. It went for £240, with only one of the six cutters it should have had, and when bidding for a 'Unique Mitre Plane' passed £2000 I was glad I didn't itch anywhere where scratching could be taken as a bid.

Regret; I looked at an array of brass-framed braces (£250-£600) that had bored their last holes, and thought of the days when my father would walk in having got one at half a crown and be berated for buying rubbish. I did something I had always wanted to do, I bought a Stanley no. 1, the no. 4's little brother. Being TT and a non-smoker has its compensations. I saw one sold early last year in London for £1075 plus VAT. Price? Have a guess, for a prize of six 'unexpurgated' manuscripts of these articles.

Where was the true value of these tools? What were dealers and experts from all over the world bidding for? What on earth could raise the value in 50 years of a Norris A1 jointer from £7.50 to an 'opening' bid of £900? Quality, rarity, antiquity, yes; but above all they were buying 'feel', the sheer perfection from when making tools was an art as inscrutable as the Sphinx. ∎

Self contained

Richard Kell's stunning container-and-tray set uses African blackwood and boxwood — and some unusual turning tools and techniques

● *Beautiful blackwood and box: the stalk will bend, if you dare to tweak it!*

My first lathe-based interest was in ornamental turning. Just about all my instruction came from Holtzapfel's *Turning and Mechanical Manipulation*, which I thoroughly recommend to anyone interested in the lathe or its products.

My principal machine for the past 10 years has been a Victorian treadle-driven ornamental turning lathe. I use other more modern equipment for toolmaking, but I much prefer the directness and satisfaction of treadling the old lathe — and it's also good exercise! It's quite surprising to the unpractised how quick and easy treadle operation can be for small work like the pieces featured here; it's also a very good tutor, as it shows up any bluntness of the tools or inefficient practices.

I have deliberately kept away from any 20th-century books on woodturning, as I believe the best way of doing things reveals itself sooner or later, and more importantly, I wanted to develop my own sense of design. I was able to develop my own feeling and sensibility for outline and form by gradually working through various periods of design and ornamentation, looking at particular styles and why objects were produced as they were. The thoroughly enjoyable aspect of original design is that a solution always fits the time when it was schemed. As I never care to see my past early efforts, and I never repeat old designs, I was lucky to sell most of my 'speculative' work.

Since 1979 I have been interested in producing various forms of small container, none of them absolute solutions but each with some interesting feature. The container described here is fitted with two stacking trays which were initially designed to keep fine gold chains separate, but they can be used as ring trays in larger sizes. All my containers have African blackwood bodies and boxwood trays. These woods are my favourite; I like their subtlety, the ease with which they hold small details and fine edges, and (when they are turned correctly) they work to a beautiful finish straight from the tool. I particularly abhor abrasive papers for this class of work; old John Oakey has his place elsewhere. Occasionally I use a fine 600 grade 'wet-and-dry' paper to regulate and even out the reflected light from the component in the lathe, but it's certainly not a substitute for good technique.

The tools

The two main tools I use are a graver and a general-purpose internal tool. You can make them by softening an old file, filing it to shape, then hardening and tempering it to light straw. Heat the tool gradually against a firebrick for hardening, and allow the metal to soak at red heat (in a subdued indoor light) at 1 minute for every $\frac{1}{16}$in of cross-section. Then quench it vertically in a jam-jar of tepid water, stirring it moderately while it's held by pliers. To temper it, brighten the metal (keeping all fingerprints and grease or oil from the brightened surface) and apply heat at the tang end of the tool, keeping the flame off the working end. Watch the temper colours travel slowly up the shank and when you have about $\frac{1}{2}$in of light straw at the tip, plunge it into warm oil. Hone up the cutting edges on an oilstone, smooth the rubbing edges which bear on the top surface of the lathe tool-rest, and slightly radius the corners to avoid the tool snagging on the rest. A popular misconception is that high-speed-steel tools are harder than hardened 'straight' carbon-steel, but this isn't neces-

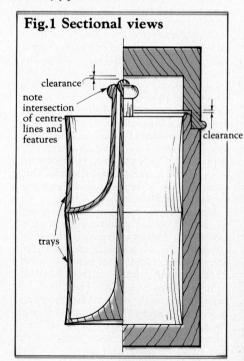

Fig.1 Sectional views

clearance

note intersection of centre-lines and features

clearance

trays

sarily the case. The real advantage of HSS is
that it has added elements which allow it to
retain its hard cutting edge even at red heat,
whereas the relatively unsophisticated
carbon tool will lose its cutting edge at
approximately 200°C — an essential point
for a production turner.

The advantage of a 'straight' high-carbon
steel tool such as an old file with say, 1.2%
carbon, is that the tool is easily formed to
shape and heat-treated. The superior honed
edge of an unsophisticated but correctly
heat-treated 'straight' carbon-steel tool is
best, for low-speed small-diameter work —
say 800rpm on the treadle lathe.

The techniques

I use the hand-turning techniques of the
brass finisher or ivory turner for this type of
work on African blackwood and dense
boxwood — holding the tool on the radius
rather than at a tangent to the workpiece, as
in conventional softwood/home-grown
hardwood techniques. Do I hear cries of
'that's scraping not cutting'? When done
correctly it's quick, safe and accurate and
produces the most perfectly-cut translucent
shavings. When you're working to within
$\frac{1}{1000}$in to fit the lid to the body, and not
resorting to 'filling' polishes or abrasives
it's the only way. Another seldom-seen
practice of mine — particularly suited to
this small and accurate work — is the way
the tool and hand-rest are gripped to
provide total control, which is helped by
having a smooth flat top surface to the
hand-rest. (If you want to quickly sum up a
hand turner, check the top surface of the
tool-rest — is it in good shape?) Curl the
left hand round the column of the hand-
rest support and bring the thumb round
the near side of the hand-rest to bear downwards, holding the tool on to the hand-
rest's top surface. Keep the tool handle
in a comfortable but firm grip with the
right hand, with both elbows close to your
sides.

The tool should be approximately horizontal — tipping the tool too far is unsafe
with these particular tools. Clamp the tool-
rest firmly in the correct position, and keep
the gap between tool-rest and work as small
as possible.

All my tool handles are different; when
working fast you have to be able to
recognise which tool to pick up without
searching, and using different woods and
profiles for tool handles is a great help.
Most trade turners would knock up their
own handles in bygone days; bought ones
are a dubious luxury in their uniformity of
appearance. Fit a strong ferrule and burn
the tang into its housing.

The job

The first step before any turning begins is to
fully understand the design, construction
and way of working. The experienced
worker will always have the desired result
fixed in their mind's eye. Even extremely
complex work is easily complete when the
job is broken down and planned in

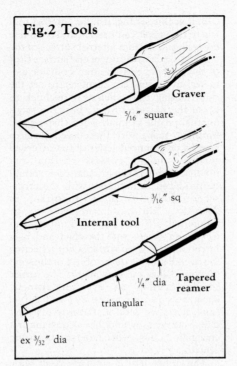

Fig.2 Tools

Graver
$\frac{5}{16}$" square

Internal tool
$\frac{3}{16}$" sq

Tapered reamer
$\frac{1}{4}$" dia
triangular
ex $\frac{3}{32}$" dia

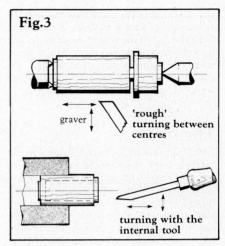

Fig.3

graver

'rough' turning between centres

turning with the internal tool

individual stages.

To turn the body blank, first prepare a
suitable piece of material to an octagonal
section, mount it between centres and turn
all exterior surfaces using the graver (fig. 2).
Determine the size of bead you want to use,
so you'll know the correct diameters to
turn. Aim only for a quick but adequate
finish at this 'roughing out' stage. Gently
grip the blank in the vice and saw down the
split-line, giving the two halves; chuck each
half in turn and rough turn their internal
surfaces with the internal tool (fig. 2).

The top surface of the tool is tapered
downward so the sharpened edge doesn't
catch or drag itself into the workpiece. All
dimensions at this stage should allow, say,
no more than $\frac{1}{16}$in for finish-turning after
the work has been allowed to season and
relieve itself of all stresses. Over a five year
period I produced approximately 400
containers, many of them with quite
complex hinges and internal trays, and I was
able to develop the ability to judge by feel
when a container was ready to be finish-
turned. For this container, three months
indoors should serve, though only trial and
error will tell. To chuck, I use either old-
fashioned wooden cup-chucks or an
engineer's three-jaw self-centring chuck.
The cup-chucks are quite effective in batch
work if the container-body sizes are graded
so the smallest ones are turned first; one
chuck body lasts longer this way.

When you're ready to finish-turn, first
chuck the lid by the upper end and turn the
inner internal cavity to finished size, giving
it a smooth and regular surface finish. Face
the joint outer end surface, and work the
bead using the graver, then turn the joint
diameter with the internal tool. Use its
shank as a sighting-rod against the lathe bed
so that (by previous experience or trials)
you'll get a parallel bore. If you do get a
slight taper, it's better that the bore is

smaller at the mouth so that by working
onto a parallel male spigot you get a
uniform sliding fit. I find it easier to
produce a parallel external diameter than an
internal one.

Don't apply any wax to the internal
surface at this stage, as a dry friction-fit is
needed for when the lid is 'wrung' onto the
body for finish-turning. All my containers
have a parallel sliding fit between the two
halves, as I want them to slide shut
precisely. A taper fit doesn't seem precise
enough for me and doesn't befit this quality
of work.

Chuck the body, set it running true and
finish-turn the internal cavity; a parallel
bore is easiest for fitting the internal trays.
Next, turn the joint spigot using the graver;
all surfaces must be flat, parallel and true.
The radius on the lip of the spigot serves
two purposes. It allows a correctly-sized
register diameter to be turned, to help turn
the full length of the spigot accurately, and
also, when it's formed, it aids the fitting
action of the two halves. I find an engineer's
vernier caliper of great help, as an interference fit of about two or three
thousandths of an inch is required between
the two joint diameters. When all surfaces
have been waxed the two halves should still
need gentle pressure to assemble — wax will
greatly ease a previously tight fit. At this
setting, 'wring' on the lid, ensuring the body
isn't knocked from true, and turn the
remaining outer surfaces of the lid. Remove
from the chuck, separate the two halves,
and with either an engineer's three-jaw
chuck (something like an old business card
will protect the previously finish-turned
surface under the chuck jaws) or a slightly
tapered push-on mandrel, turn the bottom
surface and lower diameter to the finished
size.

In practice a batch of half-a-dozen
containers is enough to allow flexibility and
development of the design, though those
who don't have to make a living at the lathe
need only go for one or two at a time!

All the container needs now is an inlay of
sterling silver. Clean off some 28-gauge
silver wire with emery paper. Mark where
you want the inlay to go with small pin-
pricks, then mount a small twist-drill in the

Self contained

chuck and bore the holes freehand into the container — but not through to the inside. Coat the end of the wire in Araldite, push it into the hole and snip it off. File it down when the glue is dry, then mount the container on a mandrel and smooth it off with 600-grade wet-and-dry paper.

The trays

The good quality boxwood I use for the internal trays is becoming ever harder to get, so it's worth finding and hanging on to a good source. The trays should be rough turned at the same time as the bodies, and allowed to season and settle before finishing; it's also wise to include one or two spare trays in case something goes wrong!

Having roughed them out and allowed them to dry and settle, make a note of the length of tray side and height of stalk. Chuck and turn the bottom surface using the internal tool (fig. 2). Halfway along, use the graver to turn a parallel diameter that allows a 1/32 in between the tray and the internal wall of the body. Reverse the tray in the chuck, set it running true, face the end of the stalk and turn it to size. Turn the stalk profile to shape (fig. 5) a little at a time, using the thumb and forefinger of the left hand at the rear of the hand-rest as a support; do secure any loose clothing such as cuffs and ties. Aim to get a good finish straight off the tool, honing as and when worsening surface finish and cutting noise indicate.

Still at this setting, use the internal tool where the graver can't reach, and complete the stalk and bottom internal surface of the tray (fig. 6). Face the upper end surface (lip) of the tray and turn the tray's outside diameter, using this last diameter to set the tray running true when you re-chuck to finish the outside surface. Bear the tray's internal profile in mind when shaping and finishing; make sure the curved surfaces aren't a pronounced series of flats. Curved surfaces should possess rhythm and fluidity, and in this particular case, should be produced in harmony with the cross-section. This is most important as distortion and movement have to be minimised. Work that is lumpen and lacking in grace, with botched and ugly intentionally curved surfaces not reflecting the overall scheme of the object or the solid section, makes me very angry. The turner should develop an eye for flatness, squareness (where necessary) and curve. Look at a curve, seek out flat areas in it, and define curves as with either a constant or a changing radius, with fixed or changing centres.

The upper tray is similarly dealt with. In addition, the tapered hole is produced (fig. 7) by a home-made reamer at the first setting when turning the undersurface (which rests on the top of the lower tray). Ensure concentricity, both when forming the internal taper and rec-chucking. When turning the outside surface of the stalk (fig. 8) the lengths are such that the inner stalk 'ball' projects an amount equal to half its

diameter, and diametrical clearance should be no more than to allow assembly.

The reamer (fig. 2) is not really necessary, but I made it to provide some basic tooling to increase speed and accuracy. It is made from a length of 1/4in dia. silver steel; file the tapering flats until their surfaces meet sharply on the diameter, and originate at 3/32in diameter; then harden, temper and hone.

Mount the trays on a gently tapered scrap-wood mandrel, and very gently finish the tray's outside diameter to the curved profile (fig. 9). The wall thickness should change gradually — I find a pair of small double-ended calipers tremendously useful for checking this. The calipers I make and sell were specifically developed for this purpose. Thousandths of an inch may sound frightening; but with a little practice on the vernier caliper, they should become second nature!

The finish is generally a light beeswax polish. Several well-known specialist wood importers/merchants stock ready-cut blocks of suitable wood about 1½in. sq.x3in) which should keep down the expense. ∎

● Richard has a stock of finished graver blanks that he has hardened, ground, and honed. Prices are £4.60 (3/16in) and £5.75 (3/8in), which includes VAT, postage, a heavy gauge brass ferrule, and an instruction sheet. Available from Richard Kell, 67 Newbiggin Rd, Ashington, Northumberland NE63 0TB.

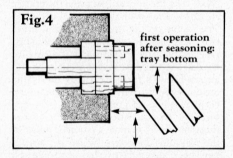

Fig.4

first operation after seasoning: tray bottom

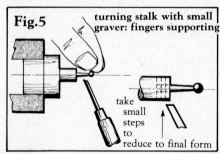

Fig.5

turning stalk with small graver: fingers supporting

take small steps to reduce to final form

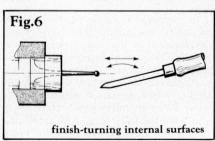

Fig.6

finish-turning internal surfaces

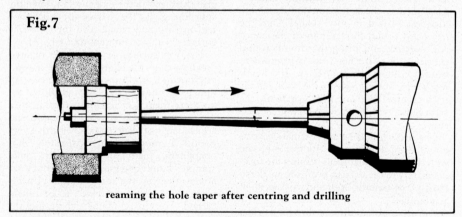

Fig.7

reaming the hole taper after centring and drilling

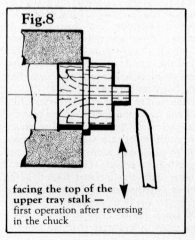

Fig.8

facing the top of the upper tray stalk — first operation after reversing in the chuck

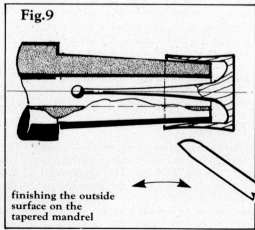

Fig.9

finishing the outside surface on the tapered mandrel

MACHINING WOOD
YOUR EXPERT GUIDE

PART 7

THE PLANER/ THICKNESSER

Fine woodwork needs fine skills, fine tools and (if you're lucky) fine machinery. But you can't do a thing if the wood isn't flat and straight. For that, you need a planer and a thicknesser

G etting the most out of your tools and machines to create the desired effect is what this series is all about, and preparation of the raw material is a vital part of quality in the finished article. Cutting, shaping and joining with machines all depend for accuracy and speed on perfectly straight, flat and square-edged stock.

Planing and thicknessing sawn timber produces straight working stock of consistent width and thickness. Both processes are handled by individual machines, but here we are looking at a single machine that combines them. The planer part (the overhand planer or surfacer) comprises a single cutter-block, usually with two knives, set between two tables, the infeed and the outfeed. A vertical fence sits across both tables longitudinally, and can be moved across the width of the tables. Bridge-guards or cutter-guards cover the cutter-block both sides of the fence.

Below the two top tables is the thicknessing table, which is adjustable up and down to set a distance between itself and the cutters spinning above it. This distance is the thickness the machine will give the material. Access to the thicknesser part of such machines varies from model to model; sometimes both tables hinge back, sometimes the outfeed table only hinges up and back, sometimes the surfacing tables both lift off. On the machine in the photographs, the outfeed table hinges away to give you room to feed into the powered feed rollers of the thicknessing end.

It's worth bearing in mind that accurate surfacing is an *absolute prerequisite* of accurate thicknessing, and if tables lift and/or hinge, carefully-adjusted settings

● *A combined planer/thicknesser, the outfeed table hinged back for thicknessing. Vital dust extraction is also set up*

● *Calibration for the thicknessing table is adjustable – but always check the workpiece thickness too*

can go out. Sawdust and general crud can also collect on the surfaces on to which the locating lugs of the tables bear; so make sure all the hinging parts are perfectly clean whenever you change function from planing to thicknessing and vice versa.

Machine settings are all-important. The infeed and outfeed tables should be perfectly aligned and flat, individually and together, across and lengthways. This must be checked with a straight-edge as soon as you take delivery of the machine. The tables can be adjusted separately, so discrepancies can soon be corrected. If there is a dish or bow in the surface itself, however, send the machine straight back!

Adjustments

If face and edge of the workpiece are to be square to each other, the fence must stand at a perfect right angle to the table. Use a steel engineer's square to check, remembering that sawdust can get in the way and that fences usually move a little when you tighten the knobs.

The cutters need to be adjusted perfectly in line with the outfeed table at the top of the cutting arc. Putting new knives in is where you'll come across this with a bump, but you must check the alignment before you start using a new machine. Most modern blocks have spring-loaded cutters, so you can finger-tighten the nuts and push the knives down into the block, then let them come back up into the right position. Place a perfectly straight piece of wood on

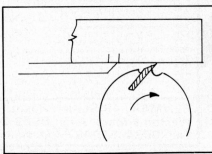

● *Knives are in the right position when the straightedge moves 2-3mm forward*

the outfeed table, projecting over the cutters. Turn the block by hand to check that the highest point of the knives' rotation is at precisely the same level as the outfeed table. The straight-edge should move forward about 2mm as each knife kisses it; more and they're too high, less means they're too low. If the blades are set lower than the outfeed table, the wood will hit the near end of the outfeed table because the cut isn't deep enough; if they're set higher, the wood will end up with a concave cut over the length, and a 'snipe' at the end where the last few inches leave the lower infeed table as it passes over the cutters.

The depth of cut is set by lowering the infeed table by the required amount. Most machines are calibrated in millimetres, and the maximum depth of cut depends on the machine, the thickness of the workpiece and the type of wood. Generally, the finer the grain and the sharper the knives, the slower the rate of feed and the smaller the depth of cut, the finer the finish. You will probably find yourself setting a hefty cut first, where big irregularities in the surface mean only some areas touch the cutters, and as the timber gets flatter, you use finer cuts. Obviously, you can't set too deep a cut with a wide board — you're asking the cutters to do too much work and risking 'throwback' of the board.

Surfacing

Before you start work on the planer/thicknesser, carefully examine the piece of wood to be planed. There are three things to look

Surfacing

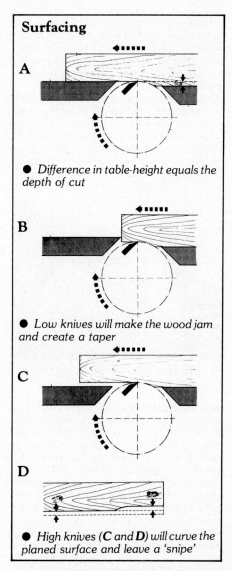

A

● *Difference in table-height equals the depth of cut*

B

● *Low knives will make the wood jam and create a taper*

C

D

● *High knives (**C** and **D**) will curve the planed surface and leave a 'snipe'*

Faces and directions

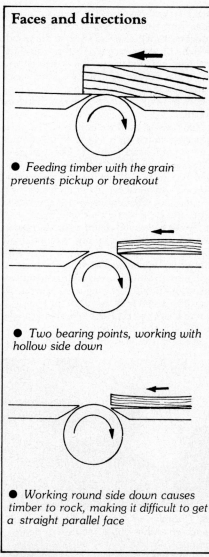

● *Feeding timber with the grain prevents pickup or breakout*

● *Two bearing points, working with hollow side down*

● *Working round side down causes timber to rock, making it difficult to get a straight parallel face*

● *The guards cover the cutters both sides of the fence*

● *For edging, the bridge guard is moved slightly back, but remains within 10mm of the workpiece*

● ***Surfacing: top,** press hard on the infeed table; **middle,** transfer pressure; **bottom,** the outfeed table gives the trued surface*

for. First, remove any foreign bodies in the workpiece; stones, nails, grit — even dust from the floor — can damage and blunt the cutters. Second, look at the grain of the wood. Most grain runs thrugh timber on a diagonal, and the workpiece should be fed into the knives *with the grain sloping in the same direction as the blade movement,* so the cutting action smooths the grain. Otherwise the cutters will pick up and tear the grain. Thirdly, look down the length of the piece to identify the concave face and edge. Start with the concave surface down on the tables so the highest parts of the workpiece are removed first, and the ends are cut first. If you work the convex side first, there is nothing to stop the wood rocking back and forth as it goes from table to table, and you'll never get a flat face. Few pieces of wood, of course, are regularly convex or concave; you have to judge, and often juggle a bit to get the parts you want to cut first.

For maximum safety, as on all woodworking machines, only the minimum amount possible of the cutting blades should be left exposed to prevent accidents to the hands. This means that all the guards should *always* be used. When surface

planing, the bridge guard should always be in position over the cutter block and at a height which allows just sufficient space for the wood to pass underneath. The Woodworking Machinery Safety Regulations state 10mm between workpiece and guard. It's often sensible to move the fence as close as possible to the near edge of the infeed table so you don't have to lean over cutters, but they should be guarded anyway. If you do this all the time, you'll wear the cutters unevenly.

For planing edges, the workpiece passes between the fence and the guard, so the bridge guard should be set as close as possible to the cutters while allowing a gap no more than 10mm bigger than the width of the wood between fence and guard.
Protection for eyes and ears: it's essential to wear safety glasses or goggles, and ear protectors are strongly recommended, since these machines are noisy, and often kept running for long periods.

Surfacing demands a surprisingly skilful

technique. Adopt three positions while feeding a workpiece through: first, both hands should press the wood down firmly on to the infeed table as you push; second, one hand should go over the guard to transfer pressure on to the part of the wood that is now on the outfeed table, while the other hand stays behind, pushing but not pressing down; thirdly, both hands go on the outfeed side, holding the (now flatter) forward end of the work on the outfeed table and pulling through. Edging requires a somewhat different technique: the forward hand particularly must press in towards the fence as well as down on the outfeed table. You need sensitive fingers because you must register the machined and therefore flatter parts of the work on the datum surfaces of outfeed table and outfeed side of the fence. The aim is always to get the pressure on to the outfeed table as soon as possible, because the outfeed side of the piece on each pass is the 'truer' side. If you press down on the infeed table, the forward end (if it gets over the cutters) will lift away from the outfeed table, and you'll end up with a tapered workpiece. You almost always have to

make several passes of the same surface or edge over the cutters, according to the roughness, of curve and twist of the wood. When you eye your piece before you start, estimate how much you'll lose before you get it flat and straight full length; if your cutting list allows it, you can cross-cut long pieces to minimise curvature and therefore waste.

Having said all this, think about it again if you're planing thin wood which bends under your hand pressure. Don't press it down at all on the infeed table; it will bend and be cut, then spring back to its original shape. You must let it cut under its own weight, not pressing down on the infeed side, and only gently on the outfeed.

To cut bevels and chamfers on the planer, the fence can be set at any required angle between 45° and 90°. Remember that with the workpiece being planed at an angle, you will have to set the infeed table rather lower than for simple surfacing work. Again, set the guard carefully to allow just enough room for the workpiece to pass between the guard and the tilted fence.

Rebates can also be cut on the planer,

nessing a number of pieces of wood, it is good practice to stack the wood methodically according to a system so you know which pieces have been done and which haven't at a particular setting. If you're preparing a series of workpieces of different sizes, it's best to do the biggest first and keep re-setting the machine in sequence from larger to smaller dimensions. Planning work like this is particularly useful in relation to thicknessing; re-setting will simply mean winding the table up underneath the cutter block. Having a system will save a lot of machine-setting time, and you

● A holding block must always be used for short pieces

will also be able to identify very quickly all the pieces to be thicknessed to the same depth. Also, once you've got true faces and edges and are ready to go to thicknessing, mark all your true surfaces! Be sure to check everything carefully before you change settings or functions; having to go back on yourself wastes time, and it's often impossible to get a setting exactly the same as it was.

Working with short pieces of wood on this machine presents a number of dangers:

● Chamfering. Careful with the guards, and remember you'll need extra depth of cut

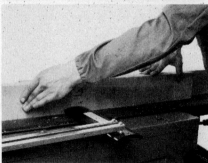

● Edging: top, the fence is the datum surface – keep the trued face hard against it. Middle, pushing in and along; bottom, forward hand presses the work against fence and outfeed table

388

● Thicknessing goes quicker when there's two of you!

width and depth depending on size and power of machine. Set the fence to give the required width of the rebate, adjust the infeed table to the correct depth and feed the wood through, pressing continuously against the fence. Make more than one pass at different setting if you have to take big bites.

As you will often be planing and thick-

apart from the threat to fingers getting very close to the cutters, the cutters will tend to draw short pieces into the works and chuck them out again at high speed. To plane short pieces, always use a jig or pushblock which covers the workpiece and applies forward as well as downward pressure. On the thicknesser, never use workpieces shorter than the distance between the infeed and outfeed

● *Only good thick pieces should be thicknessed to width*

This series was written by Judith Barker. Ken Taylor of the London College of Furniture checked it for completeness and accuracy. Aidan Walker planned it and demonstrated the techniques. Derek Wales took the pictures. But Luna Tools and Machinery made it possible. They provided vital financial support – and for photography and demonstration they lent their machines, their space, and the help and advice of staff member Joe Wickens. So we give our warmest thanks to Luna's MD Gerry Baker for his unhesitating and generous co-operation. Luna are at 20 Denbigh Hall, Bletchley, Milton Keynes, Bucks MK3 7QT, tel. Milton Keynes (0908) 70771.

rollers. You must establish this when you get your machine, and always add a few safety inches to the minimum workpiece length.

Thicknessing

Like the planer, the thicknesser needs to be set carefully to get accurate results. In front of the cutter block, the serrated feed rollers grab the wood and feed it steadily under the cutter-block; as with surfacing, you mustn't make too deep a cut in one pass, but there are also drawbacks to making too shallow a cut. Feed rollers can leave their impression on the surface of the wood, which won't be cut away if the cut is too shallow — experiment to establish your minimum — plus sometimes the cut will be so shallow that

even the feed rollers don't grab, and the wood stays in the machine. You have to lower the table to extricate it.

Thicknessing timber obviously needs an established datum surface. The true face you have planed is invariably run on the feed table, and the cutters cut the unplaned side to the set thickness, perfectly parallel to that planed face. You can use a thicknesser to give you width — passing the pieces through on edge — but you must be sure the timber is sturdy enough not to bend under the pressure of the rollers. If you do thickness to width, do it first because you will then be moving the table up at every re-adjustment.

There is a limit to how close the table can go towards the cutters, and for thicknessing

very thin pieces of wood (say, 4mm or less) you must make a false bed out of strong plywood, preferably formica covered. These materials have a guaranteed consistent thickness and will therefore maintain the accuracy of the machine while stopping the workpiece bending, cracking and exploding under the pressure of the rollers and cutters.

Polygonal workpieces can be planed and thicknessed, with accurate (and safe!) jigs and V-groove beds. Jigs must fit exactly over the thicknessing table so they don't move as well.

Machine sympathy is very important on the planer/thicknesser. Hard woods and wide workpieces give the cutters a lot of work, so don't try to take off too much wood in one pass. Experience will also show you your minimum depth of cut. Don't push a whole clutch of pieces through the thicknesser at one go; they can jam or ride up over each other. If the differences in size are too great, you'll also get some uncut ones while others are being damaged because the cut is too much.

Feed speed is important, and also needs a sympathetic approach; the slower you push it through, the finer the finish. Thicknessing feed rollers may have adjustable speeds; machines have two, three or four-knife blocks, and obviously the more knives, the finer the finish. More time-consuming to set up, though. Always keep the knives in pairs (or threes) so they're reground at the same time and stay in balance. The cutter-block takes a lot of weight at a high speed — it needs balance!

Extraction is a necessity with planer/thicknessers. There is usually a hood that comes with the machine, but you must make one if not. The works will jam up very quickly if the large volumes of waste these machines produce aren't removed — and chips can find their way on to pieces being thicknessed and damage the surface, pressed in by the rollers.

● *A holding-jig for thicknessing polygonal shapes. It must be firmly held on to the table*

MACHINING WOOD *YOUR EXPERT GUIDE*

SETTING THE KNIVES

● *The dial gauge – answer to the knife-setter's prayer?*

There is a notice on my planer, **writes Graham Hewitt**, which warns that the performance of the machine depends on the correct setting of the knives. After quite a few weeks' use I realised I was about to discover the truth of that statement, since it was obvious that their keen edge had begun to dull. The planed surfaces on my pieces of pine were looking woolly, and it needed a belt sander to cure it. Clearly I had to change the cutters.

Taking them out and posting them off to a saw doctor was no problem, but setting the spare pair according to the instructions in the manual took me about four hours. Subsequent efforts reduced the time to about an hour or so, but that's the sort of practice I can do without.

The manual said to press the knives level with the exit table using two battens, then test the setting at each end of each knife using a small batten with pencilled marks, indicating how far the batten is moved by the knife when the cutter block is rotated. If the setting is correct the batten should be moved forward about 2-3mm on each occasion. But how far the batten will move when picked up by the cutter depends on such things as the mass of the batten and the speed at which the cutter block is rotated. There had to be another way, as the heat generated by this frustrating business was creating a fire hazard.

After several more fruitless hours spent knife changing, I sent off post-haste for a dial gauge.

The gauge has a large, clearly marked scale reading from 0-10mm in .01mm graduations. Each complete revolution of the needle represents 1mm, and this is accumulated on a smaller dial. The instrument has a spring-loaded contact probe projecting from the bottom of the gauge, which when depressed causes the needle to travel round the dial. On the back is a lug by which it can be attached to a stand.

I had two sizeable offcuts of mahogany which I thought would be ideal for a stand. I comb-jointed and glued them at right angles, and reinforced the joint with a dowel covered with a wooden plug. Then I cut two slots in the stand as shown in the diagram, and countersunk them to the diameter of the bolt head which would secure the gauge to the stand. The slot on the short arm enables the gauge to be mounted vertically on the stand for setting planer knives, while the slot on the long arm allows the gauge and stand to be mounted horizontally on a sliding carriage or mitre-protractor — for setting cutters on the spindle moulder or for checking the alignment of the saw-bench table.

This is how I use the gauge: first, I place the stand on the outfeed table with the gauge mounted so the dial is set at a convenient datum, say 2mm. Then I check the height of the outfeed table in relation to the cutter-block, and adjust it if necessary to 1mm above the cutter block: thus the dial should read 1mm when the table is correctly adjusted. Then, with the first knife in position and the holding screws slack enough to allow some movement, I adjust the knife until the dial reads the same as the datum 2mm at both ends. This should be done with the knives aligned with the top-dead-centre (TDC) marks on the block housing, but sometimes it's easier to align the contact point of knife and gauge with the TDC mark and rotate the block minutely to find the highest reading. Once the knives are adjusted and the screws tightened I double check the setting with each knife aligned at TDC.

All this is done, of course, with the **machine isolated** from the mains, and in line with recommended safety practice the whole operation is **completed in one session** without interruption.

I've found the instrument is also useful for setting up cutters on the spindle moulder. The slotting disc, for example, has two cutters mounted opposite each other, which must project to exactly the same arc to give a clean cut. The Whitehill block also takes pairs of knives of various profiles which must be set correctly for optimum results. At first I adjusted the knives by trial and error, a procedure that can take only a couple of minutes or much longer, usually longer. But with the dial gauge mounted horizontally on the sliding carriage, the knives can be set virtually first time to produce a crisp clean cut and save time, temper and timber. ■

● Dial gauges are about £20 from suppliers such as J. Simble & Son, or Graham Engineering, both of whom advertise in *Woodworker*.

Chimney chest

An empty fireplace and a need for storage? Graham Hewitt explains how to solve both problems at the same time

Older houses seem to have been built with the minimum aid of level and plumb-bob, and my 200-year-old cottage is no exception to this rule. In two of the cottage's three far-from-square recesses I have made a simple cupboard and a revolving bookcase, and for the third and largest, we decided a built-in chest of drawers would be most appropriate.

Site preparation

The first essential when converting an old fireplace is to deal with the flue. It must be cleaned — if you have a small son you could send him up it with a brush — and you must put a ventilated cap on top of the chimney to prevent rain from entering, while allowing it to breathe and therefore keep damp out. When you close off the flue at the hearth end, you should allow for ventilation by, for example, drilling holes in the blocking-off board.

If your recess is like mine — rough unrendered boulders — then you'll have to render it square with some form of lining. I used chipboard to create a five-sided box to which the frame of drawer-rails and runners could be attached.

First I hammered into the mortar between the stonework a number of wedge-shaped plugs which should have been 'chopped with an axe, twisted, but of parallel thickness (not tapered)' (K. Austen, *Site Carpentry*). I used a plumb-bob and square to shorten them as necessary, and nailed wooden battens to them for the chipboard lining. It's a fiddly and uncomfortable job grovelling round in an old fireplace, but it helps the later stages to get this lining as near square as possible, otherwise you might feel inclined to return the recess to its former use, and use your carpentry as kindling.

One important dimension to bear in mind at this stage is the position of the front 'gate-frame' in relation to the wall, for this will govern the depth of the lining. Whether the gate-frame finishes flush or projects depends on how you detail the joint between the frame and the room wall. In my case I wanted the front frame to stick out from the wall enough to attach a surround to mask the gap (large in my case) between the wall panelling and the chest in the chimney.

Once the site work was completed the next job was to accurately measure the internal dimensions of the lined recess, apply them to my drawing, and work out the sizes of the various chest components.

Not quite the designer-craftsman, I'd forgotten to work out how to attach the gate-

● *A solution to the storage problem in Scots pine*

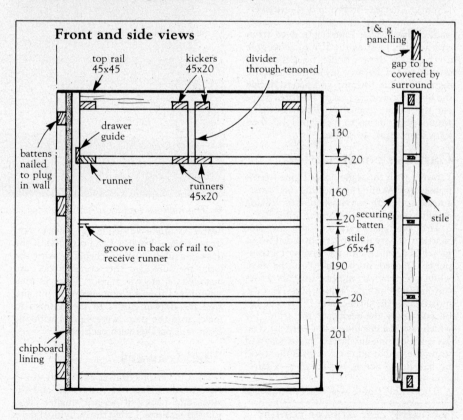

Front and side views

t & g panelling

gap to be covered by surround

top rail 45x45

kickers 45x20

divider through-tenoned

drawer guide

battens nailed to plug in wall

runner

runners 45x20

130

20

160

20 securing batten

stile 65x45

stile

groove in back of rail to receive runner

190

20

201

chipboard lining

frame to the lining. In the best work, as it says in the woodwork books, the lining would fit into the grooves in the rear of the gate frame. This seemed rather difficult, er, unnecessarily complicated, so I opted for another equally effective method which would allow me to adjust the frame for plumb. Three battens were screwed to the rear of the frame stiles and top rail to butt tightly against the external faces of the lining when the frame was in position. Having offered the frame up, checked it for

plumb and ensured it was parallel with the room wall, I could then screw through the lining into the battens.

When wood is expensive and money scarce, it's well worth spending some time working out the most economical way of using timber you already have. This means not over-designing component size, while of course keeping in mind the amount you're likely to lose in machining or from timber defects. I had some 200x50mm pieces of Scots pine which went into the

Chimney chest

● *Note the size of the gap between chest and wall, plus how the drawer-rails attach at the back*

drawer-runners and carcases (I re-thought the thickness of sides and backs from 15 to 12mm). The gate-frame and the drawer-fronts came out of some good quality waney-edged pine I had left over from another job. Cutting the 50mm Scots pine down for the drawer bodies needed a bit of serious maths, because my saw's maximum depth of cut is 140mm, so I had to decide the optimum widths to rip to before I deep-cut the 16mm (approx) thicknesses that would plane down to a finished 12, then joint them back up again.

Carcase construction

I started with the waney-edged pine for the frame, ripping and thicknessing then cross-cutting to length for finished sizes, leaving an allowance for horns on the stiles.

The mortises were cut on the slot mortiser. These devices are intended to cut mortises parallel with the length of a component placed horizontally on the bed, while a lever slides the bed on rails across the cutter — quite a rapid process. But the mortises for the three centre-rails needed to be cut *across* the width of the stiles, for which task the machine is less efficient. You do it by locking any lateral movement and using the height adjuster to pass the wood up and down across the cutter — a fairly slow process.

Before the frame was assembled I cut

Locating rear drawer-runners

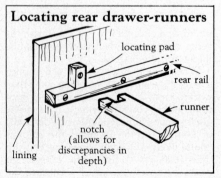

grooves in the rails for the tongues of the drawer-runners, another operation for the mortiser. Finally, the frame was glued and clamped, and checked for square and winding.

Once the front frame was fitted to the lining, I could fix the internal components in position. The drawer-runners were to be tongued into the front rails and rest on horizontal bearers at the rear, notched over a vertical locating piece as shown in the drawing below left.

Although it's not critical that the lining be absolutely true, it's essential for the drawers to operate smoothly that the runners are parallel with each other and the guides square to the front frame. So I drew a line, carefully with a spirit level, on the back lining level with the underside of each drawer-rail, to mark the top of the back

bearer. Similarly, using a square and straight-edge, I marked the position of the drawer-guides; further checking with the tape measure as the components are installed is always a good idea. During assembly, I found it convenient to pin and glue the drawer-guides to the runners to make sure the pairs were square with the front and parallel with each other.

The drawers

Next, the various drawer parts were cut to size, whole pieces for the fronts and the sides and backs of several smaller edge-jointed sections. I tried the individual parts in the openings and planed them to fit smoothly before assembling the drawers with a rebate joint at the front and grooves at the back.

The front joint was reinforced with panel pins, and here a loss of concentration brought forth a naughty word as I realised I had just hammered the pins home through my prime pine front. The slip reminded me that I need to be continually asking myself questions about what I am doing. 'Am I nailing through the side into the front?'

The drawers

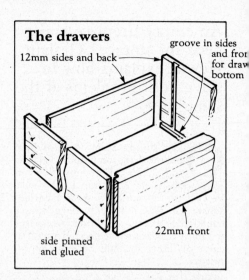

● *The kickers and location pieces for drawer-rail ends*

'Yes, sir.'

'Then proceed.' And when I don't, I tend to make a mistake. Woodworking is quite a cerebral activity, and there are few tasks where you can safely switch to auto-pilot.

While the drawers were in the cramps I glued the slips on to give a larger wearing surface for them to run on. When they were dry, I cleaned the drawers up with the plane, waxed the runners, and, plane in hip-pocket, took them to meet their apertures.

Architraving

The final job was to make the surround to mask the gap between the frame and panelling. The gap was quite large, and required an architrave about 130mm wide at the top and 200mm at the sides. It would obviously have to be made up of several edge-jointed pieces. I also wanted to edge it with a moulding to relieve the large expanse of flat wood, so I experimented with my quarter-rod cutter on the French head of the spindle moulder till I was satisfied. The moulding on both edges was in two parts. First I ran the quarter-rod profile along one edge of each of the outer boards, then profiled a small section to glue to the moulding on the outer boards to produce the profile shown in the diagram. With the boards and mouldings glued, it was time to cut the mitres on the table-saw, using the sliding mitre-square. This has two faces ground at right-angles which enables an angle up to 45° and its reciprocal to be cut using alternate faces. This way you are sure of getting a 90° joint. But, as every school-boy knows, when mitring two boards of unequal width the angle cannot be 45°. A full-size drawing, corroborated by trig-onometry on the calculator, established the correct angle and avoided embarrassment.

I decided to glue the sides and top *in situ*, as I thought that would be easier and would put less stress on the structure. In the event it put more stress on me and my vocabulary, as I struggled with recalcitrant sash-cramps which needed to be shown who was boss. With a few judiciously placed panel pins I managed to glue the surround to the frame and at the same time keep the mitres tight, which have so far managed to stay that way.

Eventually, I will stain the whole con-struction dark oak to match the bedroom suite, but so far I have not found a formula which meets the approval of the resident artistic director. Admittedly a mixture of black and brown boot polish gave a nice deep stain, but since no expert has mentioned the method in any of the books I've read, it can't possibly be tried. Mean-while, the nearest approach consisted of a spirit stain on top of a water-stain, but I don't think the experts are too keen on that either.

Adding up the time taken to construct and fit the chest of drawers and multiplying by the hourly rate charged by the local garage, I find the piece is way beyond my means — but then, one-offs are always dearer . . . ∎

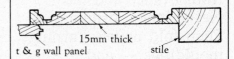

Profile of surround

15mm thick
t & g wall panel   stile

● *Remember – mitre-joining different widths needs careful maths!*

Cutting list

Good quality pine for visible parts

Front frame

		mm	mm	mm
Stiles	2	831	65	45
Rails	2	708	45	45
Centre Rails	3	708	45	20
Front Divider	1	171	45	20

Internal

Front/back divider	1	520	45	20
Top kickers	4	520	45	20
Runners	10	520	45	20
Guides	8	515	45	20
Rear frame-rails	3	668	45	20

Drawers

Fronts	2	304	130	22
	1	626	160	22
	1	626	160	22
	1	626	200	22
Sides	4	535	130	12
	2	535	160	12
	2	535	190	12
	2	535	200	12
Backs	2	290	105	12
	1	612	135	12
	1	612	165	12
	1	612	175	12
Drawer slips	10	500	25	9
Drawer bottoms (ply)	2	288	510	6
	3	610	510	6

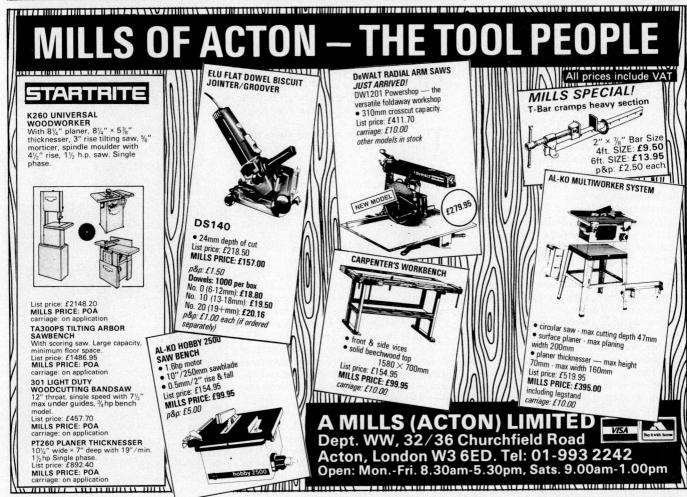

The grand furniture saga:4

The Renaissance flows across the English channel from France and the Netherlands, bringing linen-fold panels, turnings, mouldings — and grotesqueries like the Great Bed of Ware.
Vic Taylor is your guide

The Italianisation of French culture followed the Franco-Italian wars of 1495-1559, and changed the style of French furniture from simple medieval to luxurious Classical. The latter formed the basis for the ensuing Baroque, and the later magnificence of the Sun King Louis XIV (1643-1715). The arrival from Italy of Catherine de Medici gave more impetus to the desire to imitate the sumptuous lifestyles of the Italian aristocratic King François I, who built a superb palace at Fontainebleau which became a cultural centre for all things Italian. It was here, too, that the fusion of French and Italian ideas became what is now known as the First Renaissance.

Two Italian designers, Giovanni Batista Rosso (1495-1540) and Francesco Primaticcio (1504-1570) introduced the 'Mannerist' features mentioned last month in part 3. Primaticcio in particular gloried in exotic motifs like mythological figures, harpies, sphinxes, nymphs, swags of flowers and fruit, helmeted heads, and all kinds of strapwork and Arabesques.

Many of these were adopted by the French designer, du Cerceau (WW/Apr). He lived from 1520 to 1584 and was one of the best-known designers from Fontainebleau who set out to create a French national style. Although the general appearance of his furniture was French, the basis of the ornament was still Italian. In 1563 he published *Livre contenant Passement de Moresques*, a book which contained patterns of Arabesques and strapwork.

During the reign of the French King Charles VIII (1483-1498), Domenico da Cortona and Bernadino da Brescia, two Italian 'marqueters' (workers in marquetry) were invited to practise their craft. They worked in France for many years, introducing marquetry and inlaying, much of it in exotic woods.

Around 1520 there were several important changes. Walnut replaced oak, the timber universally used for medieval-style furniture; the mitre joint was introduced; and turning became popular for legs and stretchers of chairs and tables. Mouldings assumed greater importance as design motifs, and were displayed in various geometric shapes such as triangles, lozenges, and squares.

Despite all this, furniture was still relatively scarce in France, and had to be readily portable for transporting from one

● *Above:* The Great Bed of Ware – Tudor excess par excellence; *right*, a late 16th century Caquetoire or gossip chair

palace or castle to another. The Renaissance reached the Netherlands before arriving in Britain, the styles coming mainly from neighbouring France and from a royal marriage link with the Habsburgh Empire, which had a common frontier with Italy.

The change from medieval styles took some 50 years — Gothic designs were still in use even at the end of the 16th century. A noteworthy decorative motif by Flemish craftsmen at this time was 'linenfold' carving. Opinions differ as to whether it represents fold of linen or parchment, as one type is called *parchemin* — French for parchment.

Other Flemish designers of the time were Lucas vay Leyden, who published sheets of Renaissance ornament, and Johann Vredeman (1527-1604) who also published furniture designs about 1580. The inspiration for these came from du Cerceau's book, but there was another — *Livre de la Diversite des Termes* published by Hugues Sambin (1520-1600). It contained designs for *termes* (pedestals) decorated with a grotesque mixture of foliage, reptiles, and insects. It was from these sources that the Renaissance styles reached Britain, where they were eagerly taken up.

During the Elizabethan era (1558-1603) religious, cultural, and commercial ties with the Netherlands were far greater than with any other country, and these links were reinforced with the flight of Huguenots to

● A joyned panel-back chair from the late 16th century

England to escape religious persecution. Elizabeth I's strong and stable government was intent on pursuing prosperity at home and trade overseas, so it's no surprise to find William Harrison writing in his 1580's *Description of England:* 'The furniture of our houses also exceedeth and is grown in manner even to passing delicacy; and herein I do not speak of nobility and gentry only, but likewise of the lowest sort'.

Oak was the principal timber for Tudor-style furniture, although imported soft-woods and native hardwoods such as ash, chestnut, and elm were also used. Some walnut was imported too, but it wasn't until the Restoration (1660) that it supplanted oak. Tudor construction techniques were limited to 'post and panel', using pegged mortise-and-tenon joints. Such furniture was made by joiners; the real craftsmen were the 'cofferers', permanently employed at Court to make coffers (chests for storage and travelling, often covered with rich fabrics and decoration). Their skills brought them commissions to make tables, chairs, screens, and other furniture.

Renaissance influences gradually apeared in decorative motifs such as linen-fold panels, bulbous legs and 'cup and cover'-type supports, acanthus leaf carving, inlay-ing, and strapwork, which it's reasonable to assume derived from the pattern books I've mentioned. Two more features are worthy

of special note; the 'Romayne' panel, a carving of a human head in profile (the original was probably a portrait of Erasmus); and the 'Nonsuch' chest design, with architectural-style decoration in coloured woods on the front panels.

Furniture was not only valuable in Tudor times but also a status symbol. Beds, dining tables, panel-back chairs, stools, chests, and cupboards were in general use, and becoming more numerous; the master bed often reached gigantic proportions, and carried such a heavy tester that it needed the support of massive posts at the foot end, and an inlaid and highly decorated head-end. The Great Bed of Ware (c1596) takes the design to its limits!

The 'joyned' panel-back chair was a status symbol, and was reserved for the use of the master of the house while the rest of the family sat on stools or benches. Towards the end of the 16th century a chair called a *caquetoire* or 'gossip' chair became popular, based on a French chair designed to accommodate the voluminous skirts of the time.

Other Renaissance developments in Britain were the draw-leaf extending dining table, which has survived almost unaltered to the present day, and the 'court cupboard' — whose ancestry will be explored in the next instalment of our Grand Furniture Saga. ∎

shopguide

AVON

BATH   Tel. Bath 64513
JOHN HALL TOOLS   ★
RAILWAY STREET

Open: Monday-Saturday
9.00 a.m.-5.30 p.m.
H.P.W.WM.D.A.BC.

BRISTOL   Tel. (0272) 741510
JOHN HALL TOOLS LIMITED   ★
CLIFTON DOWN SHOPPING CENTRE
WHITELADIES ROAD
Open: Monday-Saturday
9.00 a.m.-5.30 p.m.
H.P.W.WM.D.A.BC.

BRISTOL   Tel. (0272) 629092
TRYMWOOD SERVICES
2a DOWNS PARK EAST, (off North View)
WESTBURY PARK
Open: 8.30 a.m.-5.30 p.m. Mon. to Fri.
Closed for lunch 1.00-2.00 p.m.
P.W.WM.D.T.A.BC.

BRISTOL   Tel. (0272) 667013
FASTSET LTD
190-192 WEST STREET
BEDMINSTER
Open: Mon.-Fri. 8.30 a.m.-5.00 p.m.
Saturday 9.00 a.m.-1.00 p.m.
H.P.W.WM.D.CS.A.BC.

BRISTOL   Tel. (0272) 667013
WILLIS
157 WEST STREET
BEDMINSTER
Open Mon.-Fri. 8.30 a.m.-5.00 p.m.
Sat. 9 a.m.-4 p.m.
P.W.WM.D.CS.A.BC.

BEDFORDSHIRE

BEDFORD   Tel. (0234) 59808
BEDFORD SAW SERVICE   K
39 AMPTHILL ROAD

Open: Mon.-Fri. 8.30-5.30
Sat. 9.00-4.00
H.P.A.BC.W.CS.WM.D.

BERKSHIRE

BERKSHIRE

READING   Tel. Littlewick Green
DAVID HUNT (TOOL   2743
MERCHANTS) LTD   ★
KNOWL HILL, NR. READING
Open: Monday-Saturday
9.00 a.m.-5.30 p.m.
H.P.W.D.A.BC.

READING   Tel. Reading 661511
WOKINGHAM TOOL CO. LTD   ★
99 WOKINGHAM ROAD

Open: Mon.-Sat. 9.00 a.m.-5.30 p.m.
Closed 1.00-2.00 p.m. for lunch
H.P.W.WM.D.CS.A.BC.

BUCKINGHAMSHIRE

MILTON KEYNES   Tel. (0908)
POLLARD WOODWORKING   641366
CENTRE   ★
51 AYLESBURY ST., BLETCHLEY
Open: Mon-Fri 8.30-5.30
Saturday 9.00-5.00
H.P.W.WM.D.CS.A.BC.

HIGH WYCOMBE Tel. (0494)
SCOTT SAWS LTD   24201/33788
14 BRIDGE STREET   ★

Mon.-Sat. 8.30 a.m.-6.00 p.m.

H.P.W.WM.D.T.CS.MF.A.BC.

HIGH WYCOMBE   Tel. (0494)
ISAAC LORD LTD   22221
185 DESBOROUGH ROAD   KE

Open: Mon-Fri 8.00 a.m.-5.00 p.m.
Saturday 9.00 a.m.-5.00 p.m.
H.P.W.D.A.

CAMBRIDGESHIRE

CAMBRIDGE   Tel. (0223) 63132
D. MACKAY LTD   E★
BRITANNIA WORKS, EAST ROAD

Open: Mon.-Fri. 8.30 a.m.-1 p.m./2.00-
5.00 p.m. Sat. 8.30 a.m.-1.00 p.m.
H.P.W.D.T.CS.MF.A.BC.

CAMBRIDGE   Tel. (0223) 247386
H. B. WOODWORKING   K
105 CHERRY HINTON ROAD
Open: 8.30 a.m.-5.30 p.m.
Monday-Friday
8.30 a.m.-1.00 p.m. Sat.
H.P.W.WM.D.CS.A.

PETERBOROUGH   Tel. (0733)
WILLIAMS DISTRIBUTORS   64252
(TOOLS) LIMITED   K
108-110 BURGHLEY ROAD
Open: Monday to Friday
8.30 a.m.-5.30 p.m.
H.P.A.W.D.WH.BC.

CHESHIRE

NANTWICH   Tel. Crewe 67010
ALAN HOLTHAM   K★
THE OLD STORES TURNERY
WISTASON ROAD, WILLASTON
Open: Tues.-Sat. 9.00 a.m.-5.30 p.m.
Closed Monday
P.W.WM.D.T.C.CS.A.BC.

CLEVELAND

MIDDLESBROUGH   Tel. (0642)
CLEVELAND WOODCRAFT   813103
(M'BRO), 38-42 CRESCENT ROAD   K

Open: Mon-Sat 9.15 a.m.-5.30 p.m.

H.P.T.A.BC.W.WM.CS.D.

CORNWALL

SOUTH WEST
Power Tools
CORNWALL   Tel: Helston (03265) 4961
HELSTON AND LAUNCESTON   Launceston
(0566) 4781
H.P.W.WM.D.CS.A.   K

CUMBRIA

CARLISLE   Tel: (0228) 36391
W. M. PLANT
ALLENBROOK ROAD
ROSEHILL, CA1 2UT
Open: Mon.-Fri. 8.00 a.m.-5.15 p.m.
Sat. 8.00 a.m.-12.30 noon
P.W.WM.D.CS.A.

DERBYSHIRE

BUXTON   Tel. (0298) 871636
CRAFT SUPPLIES   K★
THE MILL, MILLERSDALE

Open: Mon-Sat 9.00 a.m.-5.00 p.m.

H.P.W.D.T.CS.A.BC.

DEVON

BRIXHAM   Tel. (08045) 4900
WOODCRAFT SUPPLIES   E★
4 HORSE POOL STREET

Open: Mon.-Sat. 9.00 a.m.-6.00 p.m.

H.P.W.A.D.MF.CS.BC.

PLYMOUTH   Tel. (0752) 330303
WESTWARD BUILDING SERVICES   ★
LTD., LISTER CLOSE, NEWNHAM
INDUSTRIAL ESTATE, PLYMPTON
Open: Mon-Fri 8.00 a.m.-5.30 p.m.
Sat. 8.30 a.m.-12.30 p.m.
H.P.W.WM.D.A.BC.

DORSET

BOURNEMOUTH Tel: (0202) 420583
POWER TOOL SERVICES
(Sales, spares, repairs)
849-851 CHRISTCHURCH ROAD
BOSCOMBE
Open: Mon.-Fri. 9.00 a.m.-5.30 p.m.
Sat. 9.00 a.m.-5.00 p.m.
H.P.W.CS.K.A.

POOLE   Tel: (0202) 686238
MACHINE SALES AND SERVICES   ★
(POOLE) LTD.
23 COWLEY ROAD
NUFFIELD INDUSTRIAL ESTATE
Open: Mon.-Fri. 8.30am-5.30pm.
H.P.W.WM.D.CS.A.BC.

ESSEX

LEIGH ON SEA   Tel. (0702)
MARSHAL & PARSONS LTD.   710404
1111 LONDON ROAD   EK

Open: 8.30 a.m.-5.30 p.m. Mon-Fri
9.00 a.m.-5.00 p.m. Sat.
H.P.W.WM.D.CS.A.

ILFORD
CUTWELL TOOLS LTD.   ★
774-776 HIGH ROAD

Mon.-Fri. 9.00 a.m.-5.00 p.m.
and also by appointment.
P.W.WM.A.D.CS.

398

shop guide

GLOUCESTER

TEWKESBURY Tel. (0684)
TEWKESBURY SAW CO. LTD. 293092
TRADING ESTATE, NEWTOWN **K**

Open: Mon-Fri 8.00 a.m.-5.00 p.m.
Saturday 9.30 a.m.-12.00 p.m.
P.W.WM.D.CS.

HAMPSHIRE

**ALL THOSE SHOPS
WITH AN ASTERISK
★ PROVIDE MAIL
ORDER SERVICE**

ALDERSHOT Tel. (0252) 334422
POWER TOOL CENTRE **K**
374 HIGH STREET

Open Mon.-Fri. 8.30 a.m.-5.30 p.m.
Sat. 8.30 a.m.-12.30 p.m.

H.P.W.WM.D.A.BC.

SOUTHAMPTON Tel: (0703)
POWER TOOL CENTRE 332288
7 BELVIDERE ROAD **K★**
Open Mon.-Fri. 8.30-5.30

H.P.W.WM.D.A.BC.CS.MF.

HUMBERSIDE

GRIMSBY Tel. Grimsby (0472)
58741 Hull (0482) 26999
J. E. SIDDLE LTD. (Tool Specialists) **★**
83 VICTORIA STREET
Open: Mon-Fri 8.30 a.m.-5.30 p.m.
Sat. 8.30 a.m.-12.45 p.m. & 2 p.m.-5 p.m.
H.P.A.BC.W.WMD.

HULL
HUMBERSIDE FACTORING/H.F.C.
SAW SERVICING LTD.
MAIN STREET
Open: Mon.-Fri. 8am-5pm.
Saturday 8am-12.00pm.
H.P.W.WM.D.CS.A.BC.K.

KENT

WYE Tel. (0233) 813144
KENT POWER TOOLS LTD.
UNIT 1, BRIAR CLOSE
WYE, Nr. ASFORD

H.P.W.WM.D.A.CS.

MAIDSTONE Tel. (0622) 50177
SOUTH EASTERN SAWS (Ind.) LTD. **★**
COLDRED ROAD
PARKWOOD INDUSTRIAL ESTATE
Open: Mon.-Fri. 8.00 a.m.-6.00 p.m.
Sat. 9.00 a.m.-12.00 a.m.
B.C.W.CS.WM.PH.

LANCASHIRE

PRESTON Tel. (0772) 52951
SPEEDWELL TOOL COMPANY **E★**
62-68 MEADOW STREET PR1 1SU
Open: Mon.-Fri. 8.30 a.m.-5.30 p.m.
Sat. 8.30 a.m.-12.30 p.m.

H.P.W.WM.CS.A.MF.BC.

LANCASHIRE

MANCHESTER Tel. (061 789)
TIMMS TOOLS 0909
102-104 LIVERPOOL ROAD **★**
PATRICROFT M30 0WZ
Weekdays 9.00 a.m.-5.30 p.m.
Sat. 9.00 a.m.-1.00 p.m.
H.P.A.W.

BLACKPOOL Tel: (0253) 24299
FLYDE WOODTURNING SUPPLIES **★**
222 HORNBY ROAD (BASEMENT)
BLACKPOOL FY1 4HY
9.30-5.30 Monday to Saturday.
H.P.W.WM.A.MF.C.B.C.D.

ROCHDALE Tel. (0706) 342123/
C.S.M. TOOLS 342322
4-6 HEYWOOD ROAD **E★**
CASTLETON
Open: Mon-Sat 9.00 a.m.-6.00 p.m.
Sundays by appointment
W.D.CS.A.BC.

LANCASTER Tel. (0524) 32886
LILE TOOL SHOP **K**
43/45 NORTH ROAD
Open: Monday to Saturday
9.00 a.m.-5.30 p.m.
Wed 9.00 a.m.-12.30 p.m.
H.P.W.D.A.

LEICESTERSHIRE

HINCKLEY Tel. (0455) 613432
J. D. WOODWARD & CO. (POWER **★**
TOOL SPECIALISTS)
THE NARROWS, HINCKLEY
Open: Monday-Saturday
8.00 a.m.-6.00 p.m.
H.P.W.WM.D.CS.A.BC.

LINCOLNSHIRE

LINCOLN Tel: (0522) 689369
SKELLINGTHORPE SAW SERVICES LTD.
OLD WOOD, SKELLINGTHORPE
Open: Mon to Fri 8 a.m.-5 p.m.
Sat 8 a.m.-12 p.m.
H.P.W.WM.D.CS.A.*.BC.
Access/Barclaycard

LONDON

ACTON Tel. (01-992) 4835
A. MILLS (ACTON) LTD **★**
32/36 CHURCHFIELD ROAD W3 6ED
Open: Mon-Fri 9.00 a.m.-5.00 p.m.
Saturdays 9.00 am.-1.00 p.m.
H.P.W.WM.

LONDON

LONDON Tel. (01-567) 2922
G. D. CLEGG & SONS **★**
83 UXBRIDGE ROAD, HANWELL W7 3ST
Mon-Sat 9.15 a.m.-5.30 p.m.
Closed for lunch 1.00-2.00p.m.
Early Closing 1.00 p.m. Wed.
H.P.A.W.WM.D.CS.

LONDON Tel. 01-723 2295-6-7
LANGHAM TOOLS LIMITED
13 NORFOLK PLACE
LONDON W2 1QJ

LONDON Tel. (01-636) 7475
BUCK & RYAN LTD **★**
101 TOTTENHAM COURT ROAD W1P 0DY
Open: Mon.-Fri. 8.30 a.m.-5.30 p.m.
Saturday 8.30 a.m.-4.00 p.m.
H.P.W.WM.D.A..

WEMBLEY Tel. 904-1144
ROBERT SAMUEL LTD. (904-1147
7, 15 & 16 COURT PARADE after 4.00)
EAST LANE, N. WEMBLEY **★**
Open Mon.-Fri. 8.45-5.15; Sat. 9-1.00
Access, Barclaycard, AM Express, & Diners
H.P.W.CS.E.A.D.

HOUNSLOW Tel. (01-570)
Q.R. TOOLS LTD 2103/5135
251-253 HANWORTH ROAD
Open: Mon-Fri 8.30 a.m.-5.30 p.m.
Sat. 9.00 a.m.-1.00 p.m.
P.W.WM.D.CS.A.

FULHAM Tel. (01-385) 5109
I. GRIZZARD LTD. **E**
84a-b LILLIE ROAD, SW6 1TL
Open: Mon-Sat 9.00-5.30 p.m.
Half day Thursday
H.P.A.BC.W.CS.WM.D.

MERSEYSIDE

LIVERPOOL Tel. (051-207) 2967
TAYLOR BROS (LIVERPOOL) LTD **K**
195-199 LONDON ROAD
LIVERPOOL L3 8JG
Open: Monday to Friday
8.30 a.m.-5.30 p.m.
H.P.W.WM.D.A.BC.

**WELCOME TO THE
SHOP GUIDE!**
THE SERIOUS WOODWORKERS
GUIDE TO LOCAL SHOPS AND
SERVICES. IF YOU WISH YOUR
NAME TO APPEAR IN THESE
PAGES PHONE 01-437-0699 AND
ASK FOR ANDREA SMITH.

MERSEYSIDE

RUISLIP Tel. (08956) 74126
ALLMODELS ENGINEERING LTD. **E★**
91 MANOR WAY
Open: Mon-Sat 9.00 a.m.-5.30 p.m.
H.P.W.A.D.CS.MF.BC.

CROWMARSH Tel. (0491) 38653
MILL HILL SUPPLIES **E★**
66 THE STREET
Open: Mon.-Fri. 9.30 a.m.-5.00 p.m.
Thurs. 9.30 a.m.-7.00 p.m.
Sat. 9.30 a.m.-1.00 p.m.
P.W.D.CS.MF.A.BC.

**THIS SPACE COULD
BE YOURS**

NORFOLK

NORWICH Tel. (0603) 898695
NORFOLK SAW SERVICES
DOG LANE, HORSFORD
Open: Monday to Friday
8.00 a.m.-5.00 p.m.
Saturday 8.00 a.m.-12.00 p.m.
H.P.W.WM.D.CS.A.

KINGS LYNN Tel. (0553) 2443
WALKER & ANDERSON (Kings Lynn) LTD.
WINDSOR ROAD, KINGS LYNN **K**
Open: Monday to Saturday
7.45 a.m.-5.30 p.m.
Wednesday 1.00 p.m. Saturday 5.00 p.m.
H.P.W.WM.D.CS.A.

NORWICH Tel. (0603) 400933
WESTGATES WOODWORKING Tx
61 HURRICANE WAY, 975412
NORWICH AIRPORT INDUSTRIAL ESTATE
Open: 9.00 a.m.-5.00 p.m. weekdays
9.00 a.m.-12.30 Sat.
P.W.WM.D.BC. **K**

KING'S LYNN Tel: 07605 674
TONY WADDILOVE, UNIT A
HILL FARM WORKSHOPS
GREAT DUNHAM, (Nr. Swaffham)
Open: Tues. — Fri. 10.00 a.m. to 5.30 p.m.
Sat. 9.00 a.m. to 5.00 p.m.
H.P.W.D.T.MF.A.BC.*

NOTTINGHAMSHIRE

NOTTINGHAM Tel: (0602) 225979
POOLEWOOD and 227064/5
EQUIPMENT LTD. (06077) 2421 after hrs
5a HOLLY LANE, CHILLWELL
Open: Mon-Fri 9.00 a.m.-5.30 p.m.
Sat. 9.00 a.m. to 12.30 p.m.
P.W.WM.D.CS.A.BC.

OXON

WITNEY Tel. (0993) 3885
TARGET TOOLS (SALES, & 72095 OXON
TARGET HIRE & REPAIRS) **★**
TOOLS SWAIN COURT
STATION INDUSTRIAL ESTATE
Open: Mon.-Sat. 8.00 a.m.-5.00 p.m.
24 hour Answerphone
BC.W.M.A.

399

shop guide

SHROPSHIRE

TELFORD   Tel. Telford (0952)
ASLES LTD.   48054
VINEYARD ROAD, WELLINGTON   EK★
Open: Mon. Fri. 8.30 a.m.-5.30 p.m.
Saturday 8.30 a.m.-4.00 p.m.
H.P.W.WM.D.CS.BC.A.

SOMERSET

TAUNTON   Tel. (0823) 85431
JOHN HALL TOOLS   ★
6 HIGH STREET
Open Monday-Saturday
9.00 a.m.-5.30 p.m.
H.P.W.WM.D.CS.A.

STAFFORDSHIRE

STOKE-ON-TRENT   Tel. 0782-48171
F.W.B. (PRODUCTS) LTD.
WHIELDON ROAD, STAFFS.
Open: Mon.-Fri. 8.30am-5.30pm
Saturday 8.30am-12.30pm
H.P.W.WM.A.D.

SUFFOLK

IPSWICH   Tel. (0473) 40456
FOX WOODWORKING   KE★
142-144 BRAMFORD LANE
Open: Tues., Fri., 9.00 a.m.-5.30 p.m.
Sat. 9.00 a.m.-5.00 p.m.
H.P.W.WM.D.A.B.C.

SUSSEX

ST. LEONARD'S-ON-SEA   Tel.
DOUST & MONK (MONOSAW)-(0424)
25 CASTLEHAM ROAD   52577
Open: Mon.-Fri. 8.00 a.m.-5.30 p.m.
Most Saturdays 9.00 a.m.-1.00 p.m.
H.P.W.WM.D.CS.A.

BOGNOR REGIS Tel. (0243) 863100
A. OLBY & SON (BOGNOR REGIS) LTD.
"TOOLSHOP," BUILDERS MERCHANT
HAWTHORN ROAD   K
Open: Mon-Thurs 8 a.m.-5.15 p.m. Fri.
8 a.m.-8 p.m Sat 8 a.m.-12.45 p.m.
H.P.W.WM.D.T.C.A.BC.

WORTHING   Tel. (0903) 38739
W. HOSKING LTD (TOOLS &   KE★
MACHINERY)
28 PORTLAND RD, BN11 1QN
Open: Mon.-Sat. 8.30 a.m.-5.30 p.m.
Closed Wednesday
H.P.W.WM.D.CS.A.BC.

TYNE & WEAR

NEWCASTLE UPON TYNE   Tel.
J. W. HOYLE LTD.   (0632) 617474
CLARENCE STREET NE2 1YJ   K★
Open: Mon-Fri 8.00 a.m.-5.00 p.m.
Saturday 9.00 a.m.-4.30 p.m.
H.P.A.BC.W.CS.WM.D.

NEWCASTLE   Tel. (0632) 320311
HENRY OSBOURNE LTD.   E★
50-54 UNION STREET
Open: Mon-Fri 8.30 a.m.-5.00 p.m.
H.P.W.D.CS.MF.A.BC.

WEST MIDLANDS

FOR THE REGIONAL GUIDE — LOOK NO FURTHER

WOLVERHAMPTON   Tel. (0902)
MANSAW SERVICES   58759
SEDGLEY STREET   K★
Open: Mon.-Fri. 9.00 a.m.-5.00 p.m.
H.P.W.WM.A.D.CS.

YORKSHIRE

BOROUGHBRIDGE   Tel. (09012)
JOHN BODDY TIMBER LTD   2370
FINE WOOD & TOOL STORE   ★
RIVERSIDE SAWMILLS
Open: Mon.-Thurs. 8.00 a.m.-6.00 p.m.
Fri. 8.00am-5.00pm Sat. 8.00am-4.00pm
H.P.W.WM.D.T.CS.MF.A.BC.

SHEFFIELD   Tel. (0742) 441012
GREGORY & TAYLOR LTD   KE
WORKSOP ROAD
Open: 8.30 a.m.-5.30 p.m.
Monday-Friday
8.30 a.m.-12.30 p.m. Sat.
H.P.W.WM.D.

HARROGATE   Tel. (0423) 66245/
MULTI-TOOLS   55328
158 KINGS ROAD   K★
Open: Monday to Saturday
8.30 a.m.-6.00 p.m.
H.P.W.WM.D.A.BC.

LEEDS   Tel. (0532) 574736
D. B. KEIGHLEY MACHINERY LTD.   ★
VICKERS PLACE, STANNINGLEY
PUDSEY LS2 86LZ
Mon.-Fri. 9.00 a.m.-5.00 p.m.
Sat. 9.00 a.m.-1.00 p.m.
P.A.W.WM.CS.BC.

HUDDERSFIELD   Tel. (0484)
NEVILLE M. OLDHAM   641219/(0484)
UNIT 1 DALE ST. MILLS   42777
DALE STREET, LONGWOOD
Open: Mon-Fri 8.00 a.m.-5.30 p.m.   ★
Saturday 9.30 a.m.-12.00 p.m.
P.W.WM.D.A.BC.

YORKSHIRE

THIRSK   Tel. (0845) 22770
THE WOOD SHOP   ★
TRESKE SAWMILLS LTD.
STATION WORKS
Open: Seven days a week 9.00-5.00
T.H.MF.BC.

FILL THIS SPACE FOR ONLY £10.00

CLECKHEATON   Tel. (0274)
SKILLED CRAFTS LTD.   872861
34 BRADFORD ROAD   ★
Open: 9.00 a.m.-5.00 p.m. Monday
Saturday Lunch 12.00 a.m.-1.00 p.m.
H.P.A.W.CS.WM.D.

LEEDS   Tel. (0532) 790507
GEORGE SPENCE & SONS LTD.
WELLINGTON ROAD
Open: Monday to Friday
8.30 a.m.-5.30 p.m.
Saturday 9.00 a.m.-5.00 p.m.
H.P.W.WM.D.T.A.

SCOTLAND

CULLEN   Tel. (0542) 40563
GRAMPIAN WOODTURNING SUPPLIES AT
BAYVIEW CRAFTS
Open Mon.-Sat. 9.00 a.m.-5.30 p.m. Sunday
10.00 a.m.-5.30 p.m. Open later July/Aug.
Sept. Demonstrations SAT/SUN or by
H.W.D.MF.BC. appointment

EDINBURGH   Tel. 031-337-5555
THE SAW CENTRE   ★
38 HAYMARKET EH12 5JZ
Mon.-Fri. 8.30 a.m.-5.30 p.m.
Sat. 9.00 a.m.-1.00 p.m.
H.P.W.WM.D.CS.A.

PERTH   Tel. (0738) 26173
WILLIAM HUME & CO   K
ST. JOHN'S PLACE
Open: Monday to Saturday
8.00 a.m.-5.30 p.m.
8.00 a.m.-1.00 p.m. Wednesday
H.P.A.BC.W.CS.WM.D.

GLASGOW   Tel. 041-429-4444/
THE SAW CENTRE   4374 Telex: 777886
650 EGLINTON STREET   E★
GLASGOW G5 9RP
Mon.-Fri. 8.00 a.m.-5.00 p.m.
Sat. 9.00 a.m.-1.00 p.m.
H.P.W.WM.D.CS.A.

SCOTLAND

TAYSIDE   Tel: (05774) 293
WORKMASTER POWER TOOLS LTD.   ★
DRUM, KINROSS
Open Mon.-Sat. 8.00 a.m.-8.00 p.m.
Demonstrations throughout Scotland by
appointment
P.W.WM.D.A.BC.

IRELAND

NEWTOWNARDS   Tel: 0247 819800
NORLYN MACHINERY   or 812506
UNIT 10, MALCOLMSON IND. EST.
80 BANGOR ROAD, CO. DOWN
Open: Mon.-Fri. 9.30am-5.30pm
(Closed 1-2pm for lunch)
Any other time by request.
H.W.WM.D.T.MF.A.   24 Hour Service K

WALES

CARDIFF   Tel. (0222) 595710
DATAPOWER TOOLS LTD,
MICHAELSTON ROAD,
CULVERHOUSE CROSS
Open: Mon.-Fri. 8.00 a.m.-5.00 p.m.
Sat. 9.00 a.m.-1.00 p.m.
H.P.W.WM.D.A.

CARMARTHEN Tel. (0267) 237219
DO-IT-YOURSELF SUPPLY   K
BLUE STREET, DYFED
Open: Monday to Saturday
9.00 a.m.-5.30 p.m.
Thursday 9.00 a.m.-5.30 p.m.
H.P.W.WM.D.T.CS.A.BC.

CARDIFF   Tel. (0222) 396039
JOHN HALL TOOLS LIMITED   ★
CENTRAL SQUARE
Open: Monday to Saturday
9.00 a.m.-5.30 p.m.
H.P.W.WM.D.A.BC.

SWANSEA   Tel. (0792) 55680
SWANSEA TIMBER & PLYWOOD CO. LTD.
57-59 OXFORD STREET   ★
Open: Mon to Fri 9.00 a.m.-5.30 p.m.
Sat. 9.00 a.m.-1.00 p.m.
H.P.W.D.T.CS.A.BC.

PUT YOUR BUSINESS ON THE MAP — WITH WOODWORKER SHOP GUIDE!
FOR ADVERTISING DETAILS PHONE ANDREA SMITH ON 01-437-0626

WOOD SUPPLIERS

NORTH HEIGHAM SAWMILLS

Good, Kiln-Dried stocks of most Home-Grown timbers, and exotic, Imported Hardwoods.

Stocks include: Apple, ash, beech, blackwood, box, cedar, cherry, cocobolo, ebony, elm, holly, lemonwood, lignum, lime, mahogany, maple, oak, padauk, pear, plane, rosewood, satinwood, sycamore, walnut, yew, zelkova.

Please send S.A.E. for priced stock list to:

North Heigham Sawmills, Paddock St. (off Barker St.), NORWICH NR2 4TW. Tel: Norwich 622978.

THE WOOD SHOP

Our Cabinetmaker and Woodturners sawmill specialises in **homegrown**, imported and exotic timbers for the small user.

We can **machine** to your cutting list and **deliver** to your home.

Open 7 days a week, 9 to 5.

Send for new brochure to Treske Sawmills, Station Works Thirsk YO7 4NY Tel (0845) 22770

Treske Sawmills

THE WOODSTORE

Suppliers of Native Hardwoods

MOST HOMEGROWN SPECIES IN STOCK LARGE AND SMALL QUANTITIES SUPPLIED FRESH SAWN, AIR DRIED AND KILN DRIED

MACHINING FACILITIES AVAILABLE

Send sae for Price List to

TREEWORK SERVICES LTD

CHESTON COOMBE, CHURCH TOWN, BACKWELL, Nr. BRISTOL OR PHONE FLAX BOURTON (027583) 3917 OR 3078

We also offer a tree milling service

WOOD VENEERS

Come and select your own from our extensive range of exotic timbers — from 0.6mm to 3mm thick.

C. B. VENEERS LTD., River Pinn Works, Yiewsley High Street, West Drayton, Middx. UB7 7TA.

Telephone: (0895) 441986

SEASONED NORTH AMERICAN LONG LEAF PITCH PINE AVAILABLE

Converted from timber beams to your specification or in our standard sizes. From timber originally imported circa 1880.

Traditional and modern mouldings available.

Largest sixes section 14" × 12".

Architraving and Skirting all in stock

FOR A LIMITED PERIOD SPECIAL SUPPLY WITCH ELM.

J. R. NELSON & CO

"The Saw Mill,"
Wills Farm,
Newchurch, Kent.

Tel: Hamstreet (023373) 3361

HARDWOOD blanks for turning. SAE for lists. G. W. Monk Pantllidiart W, Brynafnan, Llanafan, Aberystwyth, Dyfed, Wales.

FOR ADVERTISING DETAILS PHONE 01-437-0626

OAK
ASH
ELM

We specialise in producing top quality fresh sawn and kiln dried English hardwoods at very competitive prices. Also oak beams up to 24′ long. Send S.A.E. for price list.

This months special offer.

Kiln dried Lebanon Cedar in boards up to 4′ wide only £8/cu.

MICK JONES TIMBER
Caebardd, Guilsfield, Welshpool, Powys, Mid. Wales.
Tel: 093884 283

Hardwoods for the Craftsman

Send for a FREE CATALOGUE

Fitchett and Woollacott Ltd.

Willow Road, Lenton Lane, Nottingham NG7 2PR
Telephone: (0602) 700691. Telex 377401

Wood Supplies Advertisement Coupon

Send to: **Classified Ad Dept. A.S.P. Ltd., 1 Golden Square, London, W.1.**
Tel: 01-437-0262

FROM _____

_____

_____

I enclose remittance to the value of _____ to cover _____ inset or retain.

Private & Trade Rate, 46p per word. (VAT inclusive) minimum £6.90. Display Box rates s.c.c. £8, (minimum 2.5cm (+ VAT)

Classified Advertisements

FOR SALE

WORKSHOP EQUIPMENT

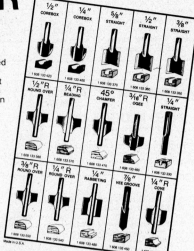

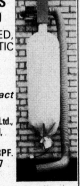

405

406

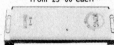

410

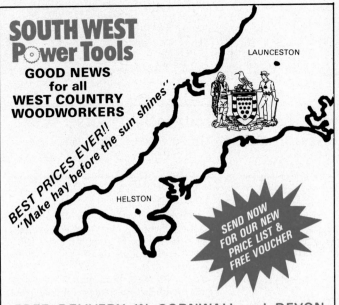

411

The undisputed king of moving wooden toys is the magnificent rocking horse. We look at two internationally successful businesses producing these fine creatures, and give you the facts to make your own.

Harnessed in pair

The Stevenson Brothers' horses are rocking all over the world. They introduce themselves and their business

● *Marc Stevenson checks the quality of finish on a reproduction pine horse, mounted on a 'safety' stand. Steeds in background racks await colour . . .*

Children's Christmas dreams these days conjure up a computer or a BMX. Such modern toys have none of the enchantment that the Victorian child found in a superb wooden rocking horse, a companion on journeys of imagination into a world of fantasy.

To bring a little Victorian pleasure to the 20th century child, twin brothers Marc and Tony Stevenson began making their range of rocking horses in October 1982. Marc has a design degree from Bristol Art College, with special interest in toys for physically and mentally handicapped children, while Tony had served an apprenticeship with Uncle James Bosworthick, a Suffolk rocking-horse maker of over 40 years' experience.

'We began working from a farm near Ashford, Kent, with help from our bank manager and a small grant from CoSIRA. As our confidence grew, we took on two staff and in December 1983 moved into our present workshop in Bethersden, where a full-sized rocking horse on the roof announces our trade. We were determined to export and, after several meetings with the British Overseas Trade Board, attended the 1984 International Toy Fairs in London, Nürnberg, New York and Sydney. This was the turning point; our 1984 turnover was double that of the previous two years.

The 1985 New York and Sydney Toy Fairs established us internationally, the small pile of paperwork became a mountain, and the bank statements a jungle. We needed an administrator and another craftsperson. From then on we have continued to expand; it's still hard work, like most small businesses, but we believe in letting the staff develop their talents, and all six members practise more than one skill at the workshop.

The horses are made in a variety of woods and a number of finishes. The selected timber is marked up with templates based on Victorian designs, then roughly cut to shape and thickness. The six pieces which make up the body of the horse, together with the head, neck and muscle-blocks, are glued together and the legs fitted with glued mortise-and-tenons and dowels. The 'blocked-up' horse is then hand carved to the basic shape with mallet and gouge, after which attention is paid to the finer details such as the head, ears and legs, complete with colt-like gait.

After carving, smoothing with rasps and various grades of glasspaper can take up to three days to complete. The saddle block is fitted at this stage and the mane-slot and tail-hole cut. Great attention is paid to final details; the leather tack is made by a local saddler and a brass plaque with the maker's name, date and number of the horse engraved is attached to the stand.

We aso run an extensive restoration department, which deals with matters as small as fitting a new mane with real horsehair, up to a complete overhaul. The sickbay also cares for horses from museums and film hire companies. Collection and estimation is free, and horses have arrived from as far away as Cornwall, Scotland and Germany. The price of restoration varies considerably, the average repair costing around £250. One complete restoration, an 1840's 'Georgian bow' horse, arrived at the workshop in two plastic bin-liners, and cost almost as much as a new horse to do — but worth it to the owner, who had his family horse revived. Owners are often very attached to their horses, so we take great care to find out exactly how the restoration job should be carried out. Most people don't want their horses to look brand spanking new, and prefer the old, muchloved, dappled look.

In three and a half years, we can say we

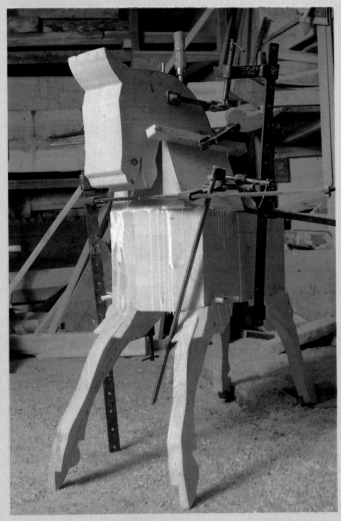

● **Above**, a 'blocked-up' animal in cramps ready for the carver's touch. Note the leg dowels. **Above right**, a 'palomino' pine horse on bow rockers; **below right**, gouging starts in the foreground, finishing touches behind
Photos Jacqui Hurst

have achieved our aim of selling our horses world-wide. We are exporting now to Hong Kong, Australia and the U.S., and the last Nürnberg Toy Fair has brought orders for Europe and Japan. But Bethersden is a craft workshop, where six people work in a friendly atmosphere, enjoying what they do — we believe the quality of the animals is a testament to that. At the back of the workshop stands evidence of our next move — a huge carousel horse, inspired by the American carousel carvers Stein and Goldstein, is taking shape. We're already thinking about a full-size steam-driven carousel, where this one and numerous **'** fellows will proudly prance . . .

● Stevenson Brothers, Ashford Rd, Bethersden, Ashford, Kent TN26 3AP, tel. (0233 82) 363.

Wooden thoroughbreds

Anthony Dew is an
ex-merchant seaman
spreading the rocking-horse
message from a converted
abattoir. Leonard Markham
sought him out

photos Hugh Mayfield

● *A champion mahogany steed in Anthony's display area, ready for the nursery*

The rocking horse is making a come-back. Once firm family favourites, bowing more recently to the fashion for electronic family playthings, these traditional and attractive toys are re-emerging — largely because of the work of craftspeople like Anthony Dew.

Anthony was originally a merchant seaman, but his fast-developing international reputation for thoroughbreds in wood has grown from the time when he started making rocking horses after taking a carving and sculpture course. Several commissions followed and business flourished, allowing Anthony to develop his rocking-horse passion full time. Two years ago he move to a former abattoir and butcher's shop in Holme-on-Spalding Moor, and set to on his own conversions and extensions; now he has fully-equipped workshops and an eye-catching retail outlet — a popular tourist attraction.

Anthony sells self-assembly kits and accessories as well as completed horses, and has also written a book for home horse makers, *Making Rocking Horses*, which carries full constructional details and scale drawings.

Although hobby horses and simple plywood kits are a commercial essential of his business, the manufacture of fully-carved traditional rocking horses is Anthony's chief delight. He makes three sizes of horse to suit individual requirements, all displaying the impeccable pedigree of an acknowledged craftsman's precision and excellence.

Selecting the timber for horse heads and bodies, Anthony looks for stability and sympathy to the chisel. Yellow pine has always been ideal, but increasing rareness and price have pushed him towards Malayan jelutong. It has the visual drawback of surface latex ducts, but such blemishes can always be filled and hidden with paint. Anthony crafts high-prestige steeds from the finest Brazilian mahogany, finished to enhance the inherent richness of grain and colour which particularly appeal to adult buyers. Ash is chosen for horse legs because of its resilience to shock and stress; Anthony prefers Douglas fir for stands. All the timber is bought kiln-dried.

Constructionally, each horse consists of 12 main pieces: head, neck and legs sections, upper and lower body-blocks, and two sets of middle side-blocks enclosing an inner cavity. Equestrian features and musculature are carved from eye- and ear-pieces, and neck and leg muscle-blocks.

Using patterns for each size of horse, Anthony scribes each piece on timber of the right type and thickness before cutting it on a heavy-duty bandsaw. He keeps 'horns' on both the neck section and the upper body-block to assist cramping. He creates a degree of animation by cutting the head section ½in over-size and bevelling its joint-face before gluing the head to the neck; the resulting angle of the head produces an impression of life. After roughing the surfaces to be jointed, Anthony spreads Cascamite glue and cramps the head and neck sections together using the neck cramping-horn and the horse's forehead, protected by an offcut. Two headless 1in panel pins, tapped into the area to be joined, help gluing and prevent slipping when the cramp is tightened.

When the glue is dry the ears of the horse are roughly separated with a coping saw and the facial cuts outlined in pencil. Then the delicate process of evolving the features — unique to every horse — can begin. Anthony uses a variety of chisels and gouges; he urges those with limited carving experience to avoid disaster by practising with clay or Plasticene models.

After gluing the neck muscle-blocks into position, the carved head and neck is fixed to the upper body-block. The surfaces are glued and joint strength is augmented by tapping ½in glued pegs into ½in holes,

drilled from the underside of the upper body-block.

Mortise joints were preferred by many old rocking-horse makers to fix the legs, but Anthony uses glued and dowelled butt-joints, strong and simple to construct. The lower ends of the legs are carved before fixing, then the splays of the upper legs are marked on the lower body-block, and their housings cut. The legs are glued and cramped into position, with nails to assist cramping (unsightly nail-holes will be hidden by the muscle-blocks). After joining, two ½in holes are drilled through each leg into the lower body-block, and glued dowels tapped in as before. The leg muscle-blocks are glued at the top of each leg, their tops planed flush with the top of the lower body-block when they're dry. The four middle blocks are glued and dowelled to the lower body-block, and finally the head and upper body-block are fixed the same way. Then the carving of the body begins.

Equine contours are sculpted with, in sequence, a draw-knife, progressively smaller sizes of gouge, and a spokeshave. A power sander completes the shaping. Among the numerous and varied tools of the rocking-horse maker's multi-faceted trade — Anthony is carver, joiner, gessoer, leather worker and blacksmith all in one — the carver's chops take an essential role. Their narrow jaws, which hold almost any shape at almost any angle, are ideally suited

414

to the carving and shaping processes. The construction stages finish with fitting the saddle block, cutting a groove for the mane, and drilling the tail-hole. Two cross-struts are fixed to the hooves for mounting on the stand.

Then the surface of the horse must be covered with gesso, a mixture of whiting and animal glue derived from rendered-down rabbit skins. It is worked while it's hot to a thin, smooth cream, which is brushed on to the horse in successive coats for a blemish-free painting surface. The traditional dappled grey finish requires several coats of undercoat and up to three coats of gloss; the surface is then dabbed with a paint-dipped latex rubber pad, held in a cover of mutton-cloth. A pattern of roughly circular dappling is extended to head, neck and body until Anthony gets the desired random effect; hooves, eyelashes and eye-rims are painted in a matching colour. After the genuine horse-hair mane and tail have been fitted, glass eyes are installed, ear, nose and mouth cavities are picked out in red paint, and finally a coat of shellac varnish seals the surface.

Anthony uses only tried and tested techniques and materials to create something that is both an item of fantasy for a thousand headlong rides, and a piece of furniture of enduring appeal. Such thoroughbreds deserve only the best accoutrements — only finest-quality tack is used to ready the horse for its final mounting.

The frames are of two types, the well-known bow rocker, and the increasingly preferred swing-iron. The swing-iron frame, patented in 1880, requires less room

than its rival, but the chief appeal to parents is that it's inherently safer — for both rider and spectator!

The douglas fir swing-iron stand consists of a top rail from which the brass swing-irons hang; a long bottom rail; cross-pieces for stability, and two lathe-turned stand-posts. Once the hoof cross-struts are fitted, the horse is ready for the nursery.

It's a fortunate child indeed who receives one of Anthony's incomparable steeds (they cost several hundred pounds), but

many connoisseurs of quality from as far away as Saudia Arabia and the US have willingly paid the price. Less wealthy admirers may only dream of ownership, but Anthony's book is there to encourage even those with modest wood-working skills to build these treasured toys. ∎

● The drawings are reproduced with Anthoy Dew's permission from his book *Making Rocking Horses*, published by David & Charles at £7.95.

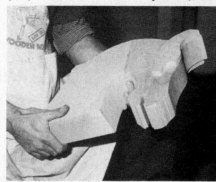

● *Head and neck, glued ready for carving; note the grain directions*

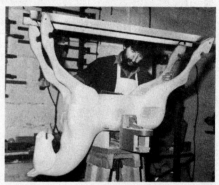

● *Hand finishing, the horse held in the carver's chops*

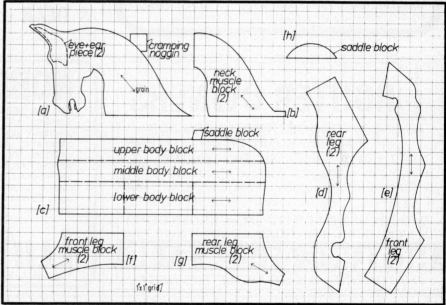

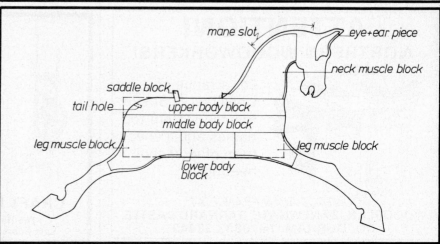

● *Anthony marks out a head from a template*

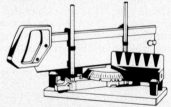

416

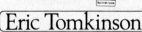

The watertight case

A box made from two pieces of wood? The North-west American Indians did it, so why shouldn't you — guided by Alan and Gill Bridgewater

● *The painted designs on four sides of a Kwakiutl Indian food tray – before bending!*

● *Your finished project. Motifs, of course, are up to you*

● **The bending process:** *the cut and kerfed plank is bent to box form . . .*

. . . joined at the rebated corner 'seam' and held with rope twist-stick clamps and wedges . . .

. . . drilled at the corner and fixed with glued hand-whittled wedge-pegs

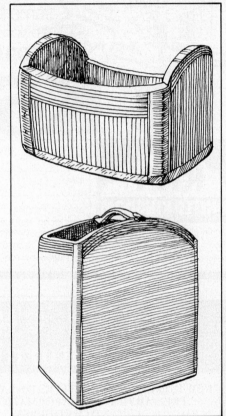

● *A Kwakiutl food-tray and water-box, with characteristic curved-rim profile*

How was this possible? It was clear enough: 'The Kwakiutl Indians were superb carpenters. They made boxes, the sides constructed from a single piece of wood.... The craftsmanship was of such perfection that they were watertight and used by the women for cooking...'

I knew the Indian tribes that live on the north-west coast of British Columbia were uniquely skilled in wood crafts — building, carving and painting, everything from gigantic totem poles to masks, bowls and canoes. But watertight boxes and chests? I wonder. The *Encyclopedia Britannica* rumbles on about the Canadian Indians for page after page, until you come to this little gem: 'The even-grained cedar was split into planks with which the larger communal, rectangular houses were built; smaller boards were steamed and bent into serviceable watertight boxes . . . ' Aha! Our scratchings about in libraries, museums and old book shops led to the British Museum in London, The Pitt Rivers Museum in Oxford, a museum in Cambridge, and to the books of Franz Boas. We eventually saw some 19th century Indian boxes and trays, and sure enough, the sides of the boxes appeared to be made from a single plank bent three times along its length, rebated, pegged, sometimes sewn at one corner, then let into and fixed to a massive slab-cut base. I would have liked to have pulled the boxes apart and discover just how they had been made . . . but you know museums. Thanks to Franz Boas' books, and some Canadian sources, we soon had the answers.

The original method

The Indian craftsmen consulted the spirits when it was decided that a box was needed, and then set about selecting a suitable standing tree. The lower branches and spurs were lopped off flush with the trunk, then the tree was felled. Then the Indians drove lines of wedges along the length of the trunk, converting it into planks. The centre plank was checked for flaws, and then worked with an elbow-adze, crooked knife and gouge until it was 1½-2in thick.

The smooth tool-textured plank was then measured for width, adze-trimmed to size, and marked out for the box required. Knife-cuts were made across the grain and width of the plank at the inside corner positions, then worked until they became crisp-sided V- or U-trenches. Next the plank was turned over, and the wood pared and thinned opposite each of the kerf-cut trenches. The ends of the plank were then rebated and cut so that when it was steamed and bent, they would come together and form the fourth corner of the box. A shallow trench was dug on the waterlogged beach, a fire lit, and then the plank was soaked, heated, and steamed using hot stones, with sea-grass as insulation. The box maker would put rope stick-twist clamps across the width of the board, place the plank face-down, then, standing on the plank and the clamp, heave the sides of the box over and in. The rebated ends were brought together when the box corners were all at 90°, the whole box held true with more rope stick-twist clamps. Then the 'seam' corner was drilled, glued and pegged. When the whole clamped and pegged box was cool, the bottom edge was thinned and then let into a slab-cut and rebated baseboard. Finally, the corners were trimmed and the box carved and painted.

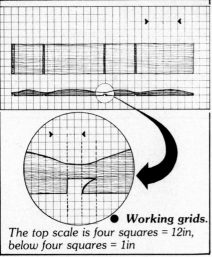

● **Working grids**.
The top scale is four squares = 12in,
below four squares = 1in

Making a kerf-cut steam bent chest

You will see we used a 2in-thick plank of rough-sawn seasoned cedar, and made a box about 12in wide, 24in long and 12in deep; also see from the drawing above how we marked out and measured the kerf-cuts.

You can (up to a point) change the overall size of the box, but **you must adjust the size of the kerf-cuts to fit.** For example, if you look at our kerf details top far right, you will see we reduced the 2in plank thickness to about 1in; see how the depth and width of the kerf and the depth of the kerf undercut all relate. It might also be a good idea to have a trial run on a piece of scrap wood, and see if you can successfully work a couple of corners. Our researches have come up with a dozen or so kerf types (above right); everthing from a simple V-cut, almost like a folded mitre, to a very complicated, deeply worked and undercut double 'swallow-tail' type. There is room for experiment! The Northwest Coast Indians usually made their boxes out of straight-grained, knot-free cedar, but no doubt you could try woods like maple, pine or even parana pine.

Look for a piece of rough-sawn straight-grained wood that seems sound and a good colour. Avoid stains, twists, knots, splits and all the other nasties that might cause problems, and most important of all, go for a piece of 'tree centre' wood that has its grain at 90° to the plank face. Set it out along its length (above). Allow 1in for the fourth corner rebate, 12in for the first side, ½in for the first kerf, 24in for the second side, ½in for the second kerf, 12in for the third side, ½in for the third kerf, and finally 24in for the fourth side. The board should come to a blunt end finish. Mark the inside

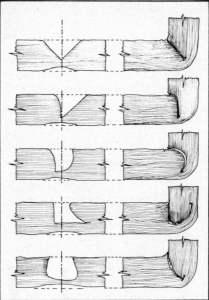

● A selection of kerf types the Indians used. The fibres are stressed and compressed at the joint

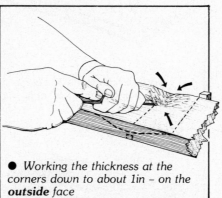

● Working the thickness at the corners down to about 1in – on the **outside** face

and outside of the board and all the kerf channels.

Place your marked-out wood outside up, then work with an adze or gouge along its length so the wood comes to a series of 2in hills — the box sides — and 1in hollows — the kerf corners (above).

Flip your plank over so that it's inside up, then cut in the ½in-wide corner kerf channels with saw and chisel to a depth of ½in. Chop out and rebate the channels, leaving them straight-sided and crisply worked. Work away at the channel sides with a sharp long-bladed knife and a ½in chisel; the side undercuts should go ½in into the wood. Cut a 1in-wide, ½in-deep rebate at one end of the plank, then work the other end of the plank to fit.

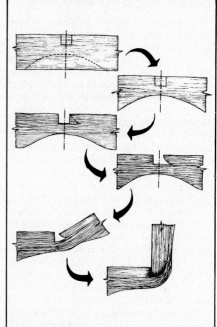

Kerf details
● The order of working the kerf-cut and steam-bent corners

● Support the plank on a sandbag to work the corner rebate and ½x½ kerfs

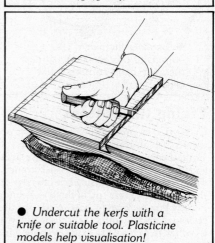

● Undercut the kerfs with a knife or suitable tool. Plasticine models help visualisation!

The watertight case

Steaming and Bending

The equipment options go from a sophisticated steamer with a long plywood steam-
box and a purpose-built gas or electric
boiler, through an Indian-style metal tank
and raw fuel fire, to a knocked-up electric-
kettle-hose-and-plastic-bag! This part of
the project is tremendously exciting, so all
the more reason to be completely
organised. Set yourself up with heat/fire-
proof gloves, non-inflammable protective
clothing and a tidy work area, together with
someone to give a hand. It may be worth
having a trial run with a scrap of wood.

Steam the plank for 45-70 minutes, or
until you can flex and bend it at the kerfs.
Now work with what I would describe as
considered and controlled haste. Take the
steamed wood, make sure the stick-clamp is
in place, and bend the wood a corner at a
time. Hold the box sides down with the
weight of your feet, then heave the wood
up, so that the box angles are at 90°. Work
the corner kerfs in order 1 — 3 — 2. The
wood should eventually wrap round so the
blunt end of the plank comes to rest in the
1x½in rebate. When this stage is reached,
quickly get the strap or rope twist-stick
clamps in place, then quickly drill, glue and
peg the rebated corner seam. Drill from
both faces, and vary the peg angles for more
strength. Wait at least 48 hours for the glue
and wood to rest, then take the knife and
gouge and trim back the fourth pegged
corner so that it matches the other three.

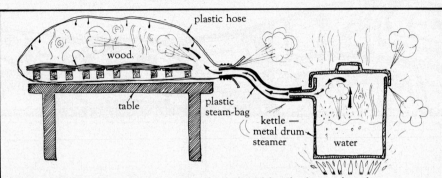

● *The steamer apparatus: a heavy duty plastic for the bag, a length
of hose, a kettle or drum and a couple of hose clips. Support the wood
off the surface of the table, and steam it until the kerfs are pliable –
about an hour*

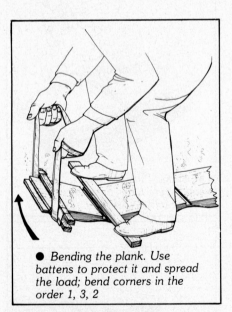

● *Bending the plank. Use
battens to protect it and spread
the load; bend corners in the
order 1, 3, 2*

Fixing the bottom

Place your steam-bent box on the base so
there's an all-round base-to-box lip of
1½in, then mark each of the box/base sides
and the position of the base/slab trench.
Then trim back the outside bottom edge of
the box with a knife to 1in thick all round.
Put the box back on its base, mark out the
revised trench width, then clean out the
trench with a chisel to a depth of about ½in.
Go easy on this channel or trench —

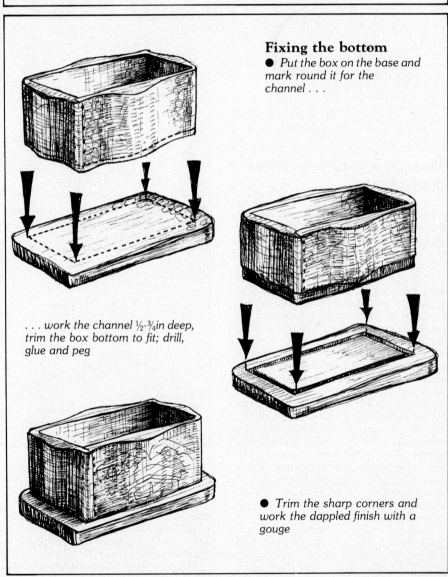

*. . . work the channel ½-¾in deep,
trim the box bottom to fit; drill,
glue and peg*

Fixing the bottom
● *Put the box on the base and
mark round it for the
channel . . .*

● *Trim the sharp corners and
work the dappled finish with a
gouge*

especially when you come to the round
corners, where you might have to use a
knife and gouge. When the box-to-base is a
good fit, drill, glue and peg, as with the box
corner-seam. Finally take a sharp knife,
trim off the kerf-bend whiskers or sprung
wood fibres, and go over the whole box
giving it a nicely scalloped and tooled finish.

Painting the Motifs

Look at our design ideas, then decide just
how you want your motifs. Make a good
master design of how the motifs will fit the
box sides, then take a tracing and press-
transfer the lines of the design on to the
wood with a pencil — you could use carbon

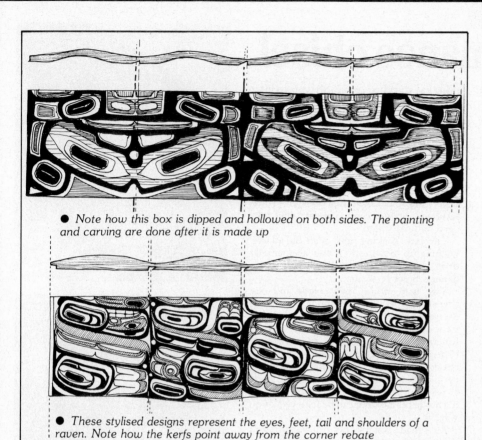

● *Note how this box is dipped and hollowed on both sides. The painting and carving are done after it is made up*

● *These stylised designs represent the eyes, feet, tail and shoulders of a raven. Note how the kerfs point away from the corner rebate*

paper. Now lightly cut in the drawn lines with a craft knife, which will stop the colours bleeding. Block in the design areas with watercolours — don't try to work solid, heavy, vibrant colours, but rather limit your palette to basic earth colours like red ochre, black, and yellow ochre, with maybe just a touch of blue and green. When the paint has dried go over the whole box with a scrap of sandpaper and just break the colours at box corners, edges and pattern high-spots. Finally, give the box a couple of coats of wax inside and out — and the job's done!

Afterthoughts

If you like the idea of this project, but consider our methods and techniques just too primitive, there's no reason at all why you shouldn't, say, work the end-plank rebate and the initial kerf-cut with a power tool. Shape the project to suit your own needs and aims.

It really needs to be approached with as few preconceived ideas as possible. You might ruin a length or two of wood, but along the way you will extend your wood-working skills — and have a lot of fun! ■

Cutting list *All rough sawn cedar*
Sides   74½in x 12in   x   2in
Bottom   27   15   2
12 ¼in cedar pegs; PVA glue; watercolours.

The performance chisel

Tony Wood explains how to tune and use the *Oire Nomi* — a chisel for the connoisseur

When you get your nice new Japanese chisel home, don't be in too much of a hurry to start using it. There are several things you will need to do before it touches any timber. The preparation should only take about 45 minutes, and when you make that first scalpel-like cut, you'll congratulate yourself on having taken the time.

The basic chisel preparation 'kit' consists of two waterstones (one 800-grit coarse and one 6000-grit fine), a flattening plate, honing grit (coarse, medium and fine), a sharp knife, a hammer and some thin oil. 'Chamelia' is the recommended oil, which is so thin it makes conventional 'thin oils' look like treacle. Another useful though not essential piece of equipment is a Nagura stone, which will save a lot of hard work in sharpening, and will also protect your waterstones from excessive wear.

Waterstones

There are two basic types of waterstones: natural and man-made. Natural stones, although superior to man-made ones, are incredibly expensive and difficult to find, so I will concentrate on the more popular and accessible man-made ones.

As their name suggests, waterstones use water as the cutting medium. They are also very absorbent; it's no use just trickling a few drops of water on to the surface of a waterstone and hoping it will do. They're thirsty, and should be totally immersed in water until air bubbles stop escaping. Don't worry about the wooden bases that some of them are mounted on — they can be safely immersed too. A good test to see if a water-

stone has absorbed enough water is to lift it out of the water and look carefully at the surface. If pools remain on the surface, it is saturated and ready for use. If the water 'disappears' into the stone, it needs a longer soaking. Coarse stones take up more water than fine ones, and need longer soaking times because there are larger air gaps between the cutting particles. Also, most waterstones double their weight when saturated, so you can appreciate why they need a lot of water.

The best soaking tank is an old plastic washing-up bowl, so if you accidentally drop the stone in the bowl you won't damage bowl or stone.

Two waterstones, one coarse and one fine are the practical minimum, but there's no reason why you shouldn't have more in various grades. Japanese craftspeople generally have 15-20 stones, and no correct order of use. They use one stone, then check the cutting edge with a jeweller's eyeglass before deciding on the next grade to use. This is perfection taken to extremes; it's not necessary, but can be achieved if you want it.

Man-made waterstones can be stored in water so they're always ready for use, but natural ones must be thoroughly dried out after use or they'll disintegrate. If you keep your man-made waterstones permanently in water, it's a good idea to add a small amount of bleach to stop it stagnating. If you don't want a bowl full of water standing round all the time, the stones can be stored in polythene bags or airtight plastic containers. However, with these non-immersion wet storage methods you'll probably need to soak the stones for a few minutes before use to 'top them up'.

If the faces start to get worn, true them up by rubbing two stones together, but remember to keep wetting them!

Preparing the chisel

The first preparation job is to fit the hoop on top of the handle properly. When you buy a Japanese chisel, the hoop isn't firmly fitted, just wedged on to stop it getting lost in transit. Remove it and trim the end of the handle with a sharp knife until the hoop sits firmly about $\frac{1}{16}$in. below the handle top. Now hammer the top fibres of the handle over to form a mushroomed end that sits comfortably in your hand.

● **Above:** *the handle hoop ready for the fibres to be turned over.* **Top:** *From* 100 *pictures of Daiku at work*

If you want to make your chisel truly authentic, you'll have to remove the lacquer from the handle, which is applied to make the chisels more acceptable to Western tastes; it's definitely not the done thing in Japan! The best way is to scrape it off carefully with a sharp knife. It's a messy job, but the natural finish is worth the effort. The true Japanese-style finish is achieved by wiping the stripped handle with a cloth impregnated with chamelia oil. It's not a bad idea, in fact, to periodically wipe the whole chisel with the impregnated cloth to prevent corrosion of the blade. Chamelia is such a light oil, you can safely leave a thin trace on the chisel without it transferring to you or your timber.

● *A finished chisel, the handle stripped awaiting chamelia oil*

At last it's time to get down to sharpening. Make sure you've immersed your waterstones in the tank and left them there so they'll be ready when you need them — there's nothing more frustrating than starting at a waterstone waiting for the bubbles to stop because you forgot to immerse it before you started!

First of all, the back (the flat cutting-edge surface) of the chisel needs to be flattened to remove any high spots left by the hand forging. Not that Japanese chisels are poorly finished — all chisels have high spots. With a Western tool, it would take much longer to do than with a Japanese chisel, because there's less back to flatten; the hollow-ground flute makes it a relatively quick operation. Flattening also removes the protective clear lacquer on the blade back.

You'll need a flattening plate, some chamelia oil and honing grit. Apply a few drops of chamelia oil to the flattening plate and sprinkle on a small amount of the coarse grit. Work the back of the chisel up and down the plate, maintaining a steady pressure on the centre of the blade. The handle should only be supported by your other hand; if you grip it too tightly you'll find the back of the chisel tends to lift away from the flattening plate as you work, resulting in an uneven finish. After a few passes up and down the flattening plate, stop and check progress. You should be able to see where the high and low spots are by the difference in appearance. The high spots will be scraped where the honing grit has been cutting them, and the low spots will still retain the initial polish. The effect you are trying to achieve is an overall uniformity of appearance to the back of the cutting edge and the supports on the side of the hollow-ground flute. (fig. 1).

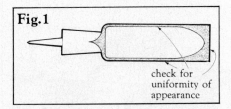

Fig.1

check for uniformity of appearance

When there are no more high or low spots, wipe the grit mixture off the flattening plate and chisel and repeat the process with successively finer grades of grit. Now take your coarse waterstone out of the soaking tank and work the Nagura stone up and down the face quite hard until you get a thick creamy paste. If the paste starts to dry out, add a few drops of water to keep the texture correct. Using the same action as in the flattening process, work the back of the chisel along the stone until the scratches caused by the honing grit are removed. Finally change stones and use the fine stone until you get a mirror finish. All this may sound like hard work, but it's surprising just how quickly waterstones cut — so make sure you check the back of the chisel frequently, or you may remove more steel than you need to.

● *The kit: plate, grit, Nagura, chamelia, stones*

● *Working up a paste with the Nagura stone*

● *Flattening the chisel-back on a coarse waterstone*

The next stage is to hone the bevel on the front of the chisel. Because of the characteristic single long bevel, it's easier to maintain the honing angle without having to use a honing guide. Work up a creamy paste as before, using the Nagura stone on the coarse waterstone. There's no mystery about finding the correct honing angle; simply rest the bevel on the stone, supporting the handle in one hand. Then, using the index finger of the other hand, press down on the back of the chisel just behind the cutting edge. The bevel will automatically seat itself along its whole length. Now, maintaining the bevel angle, work the chisel along the stone until an even finish is achieved along the cutting edge. Don't worry too much if the rest of the bevel isn't uniform; the purpose of this

● *Finding the correct bevel: note the finger position*

operation is just to hone that important cutting edge while maintaining the bevel angle. Once again, make frequent checks or you may work harder than you need to. When you are satisfied with the finish, change to the fine stone and repeat the process until you have an even mirror finish along the cutting-edge.

Lightly hone the back of the chisel on the fine stone to remove the wire edge and dress the cutting edge. The action here is slightly different to the front honing. Support the handle of the chisel in one hand, and with the back of the chisel resting flat on the stone, apply quite heavy pressure with the fingers of the other hand to a point just behind the cutting edge. This action removes a wedge of metal from the length of the blade, with more metal being taken from the cutting end of the blade than the handle end. This wedge-shaped cut maintains the $\frac{1}{32}$-$\frac{1}{16}$in distance between the cutting edge and the hollow-ground flute on the back of the chisel.

This final honing is probably the most critical operation of all. If it's omitted or done incorrectly, the cutting edge will begin to encroach into the hollow ground flute until it finally breaks away. But back honing is nothing to be afraid of; just maintain good pressure at the cutting edge and make frequent checks to monitor progress.

You should now have a very sharp chisel, and it goes without saying that great care should be taken when handling it.

Using the chisel

Now the moment you've been waiting for! But before you start cutting away, a word of caution. When paring timber with a Japanese chisel, keep your fingers well clear of its sides. Never use a finger along the side of the chisel as a guide; all the careful work you've just put in to flatten and hone the back has turned the thin supporting edges at the side of the blade into highly efficient finger-slicers. The only consolation is that if you forget you won't feel any pain — and you won't forget again!

The technique of holding a Japanese

JAPAN 2

chisel is to support the back of the blade carefully quite high up with one hand, then push with the palm of the other hand. Don't worry if this feels rather awkward and unstable at first — it soon becomes second nature. Providing the chisel is kept sharp, most cutting operations can be made by pushing like this. However, when cutting mortises or making any deep cuts, a mallet or *ryoguti genno etuki* (chisel hammer) should be used carefully. Even the lightest of taps with a mallet can send it horrifyingly deep into your precious timber.

The one thing you shouldn't do with a Japanese chisel is use it like a crowbar. You know what happens when you're cutting a mortise — whack the chisel with a mallet, then lever it backwards and forwards to break out the waste timber. Well, try that with a Japanese chisel and you'll end up with a blade the shape of a banana, or worse still, with two pieces of chisel! Japanese chisels are precision tools and require techniques to match.

The technique for cutting mortises or making any deep cuts with Japanese chisels is to make a series of opposing angled cuts across the area to pare out the wood (fig. 2). When the required depth has been reached, the last remaining pieces of waste are removed with a special hook chisel (fig. 3), which has a cutting edge set at 90° to an ordinary chisel's cutting edge.

As I've said, it all may seem strange and awkward at first — but learning these techniques of preparation and use is well worth it. You won't really understand what the fuss is about until you really get the feel of these tools; and perform they do! ■

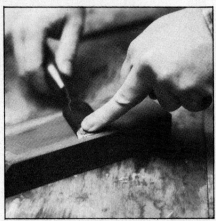

● *Removing the wire edge from the cutting edge; note the finger position*

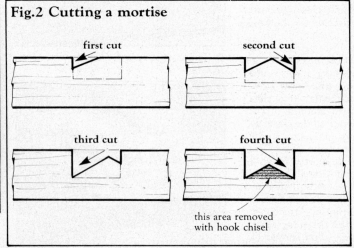

Fig.2 Cutting a mortise

first cut

second cut

third cut

fourth cut

this area removed with hook chisel

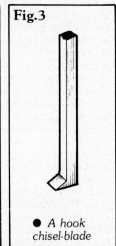

Fig.3

● *A hook chisel-blade*

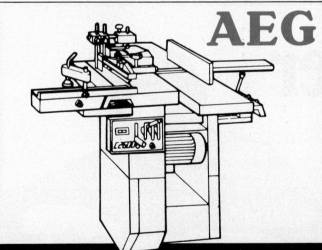

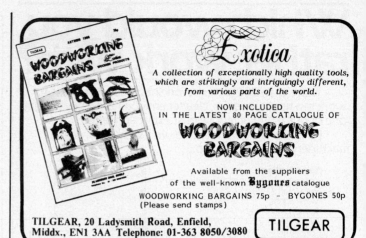

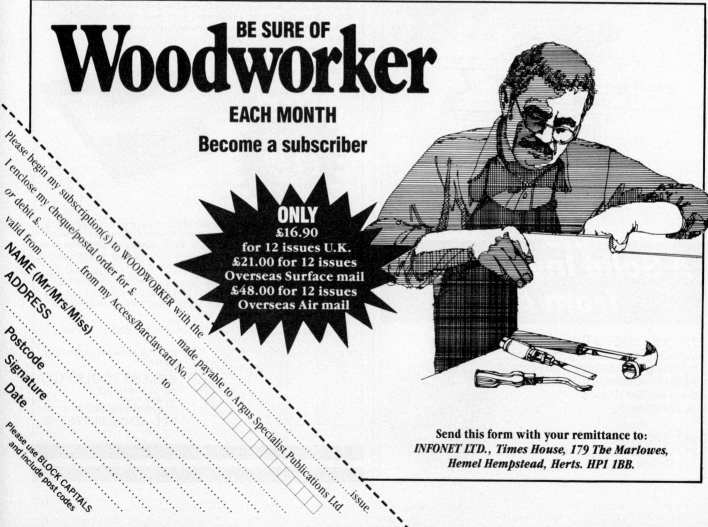

Guiding hands

Woodwork for disabled children means more than making something, as teacher Eric Ingham explains

● *Marking out a menu/duty board for the dining hall; the children's abilities differ widely*

Ian's face was alive with excitement and pride when his parents came to the place where his woodwork was displayed during Open Week at school. The pleasure he obviously felt when his small occasional table was admired by Mum and Dad is a feeling many of us have enjoyed — when a finished item of our own work has been the centre of attention. In Ian's case, however, there is a slight difference; he is mentally and physically handicapped with a degenerative form of epilepsy. He has seldom enjoyed success at any level during his short life, and his table has given him a sense of achievement and a new-found and rarely experienced self-esteem.

Ian and about 65 other children attend a special school for children with severe learning difficulties in the north of England, where small groups of five or six, (boys and girls) have a woodwork lesson each week. They start woodwork when they reach 11 or 12, when they have acquired most of the manipulative skills needed to use tools. The main aims of the lessons are to teach the basic skills of using tools, the care and safety aspects, and of course, to produce a finished article — from kitchen-roll holders to stools and small tables.

We have also found that even the more profoundly handicapped children who can't move their limbs can participate in woodwork at a purely sensory level — the smells of sawdust, resin, and varnish, the feel of sawdust on their hands and arms, of fine and a coarse sandpapers, and the sounds of saws and hammers.

The equipment consists of an old centre-well bench with a huge vice at either side, much too high for some of our younger pupils. We have recently acquired a child-size bench at an exorbitant price from an educational supplier. (A possible opening here for individual craftsmen?) We also have a Workmate, which is invaluable.

We suffer as do most schools from an acute shortage of money, so we have to beg or scrounge our wood supplies. Fortunately, we know two carpenters, one of whom keeps telling me he'll be out of business soon if he uses any more men and machine-time cutting boards for us; we're still getting them! The other provides us with all the offcuts from each job, which can sometimes result in a nice piece of mahogany mouldings, and veneered ply from a shop-fitting job, suitable for tea-trays, fire-screens, and so on.

It's essential in this type of practical work with handicapped children to have some adult assistance. This is because of safety, and also because of the method of teaching, which is quite different from the woodwork room at an ordinary school.

We do occasionally demonstrate to the group, but most teaching is done one to one by 'precision teaching' methods. This involves breaking a task down into very small steps to ensure that the child can achieve the step successfully and each tiny achievement is rewarded, usually by verbal praise. If necessary the child is prompted through each step, either verbally ('put your other hand here'), gesturally (pointing or otherwise indicating), or physically (actually taking the child's hand a moving it or shaping it with your own in the desired action).

Sometimes if a task is particularly difficult (assembling several pieces to make a finished article for instance), it may be necessary to use a method called 'back-chaining'. The teacher assembles all the pieces except the final one and allows the child to fit this, then the process is repeated leaving out that piece and the penultimate piece, and so on, with praise for each successful stage until the child itself can complete the full assembly.

All our tools are normal hand-tools because although power tools would save time and labour, they are too dangerous for handicapped children, even with close supervision. We occasionally use an orbital sander, but at least one adult hand is required to stop the sander taking the young operator for a walk off the workpiece and even off the bench!

For ease of use and safety, we use Surform-type shapers instead of planes, and small hand-saws of the Eclipse type rather than large panel-saws.

427

Guiding hands

Wherever possible we avoid using adaptations to the standard tools in an effort to keep everything as 'normal' as possible, but occasionally a slight modification is necessary to give a child better control over, or easier manipulation of a tool (below).

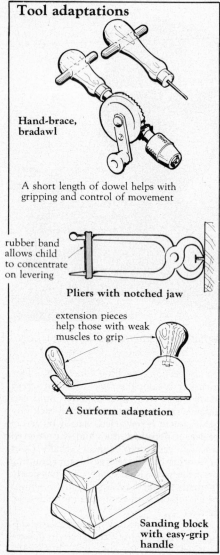

Tool adaptations

Hand-brace, bradawl

A short length of dowel helps with gripping and control of movement

rubber band allows child to concentrate on levering

Pliers with notched jaw

extension pieces help those with weak muscles to grip

A Surform adaptation

Sanding block with easy-grip handle

We avoid jigs because we aren't trying to mass-produce, but aim to make individual pieces of work at the child's own competence level. However, the children do have difficulty in using rules and measuring tapes with any accuracy, so we make aids when they're needed. A recent job, for instance, required the cutting of numerous equal lengths of dowelling, so the arrangement below was fixed in the Workmate jaws.

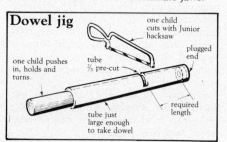

Dowel jig

one child cuts with Junior hacksaw

one child pushes in, holds and turns

tube ⅔ pre-cut

plugged end

required length

tube just large enough to take dowel

In addition to actual woodwork, some time is spent with each group developing the language and concepts involved. Language development is generally a vital part of their education, so expressive and receptive speech and memory skills are as integral to the woodwork lesson as they are to every other facet of the child's school life.

Part of each lesson is specifically set aside for learning to recognise and name tools, and this is usually carried out in the form of a game using the actual tools as well as charts, drawings and pictures.

The children particularly enjoy finishing given instructions such as: 'Who can tell me which tool is behind the saw?'

'What colour is the handle on the round shaper?'

'Put the small saw away in the cupboard.'

'Which is the heaviest hammer?'

'Did the nail go through the wood?' — Thus with just a few questions and instructions we would have covered quite a complex language involving colour, prepositions, weight, size, recognition and naming.

When all the tools are away in the bench cupboard we begin the important job of

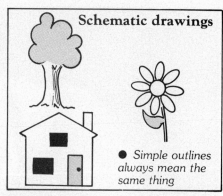

Schematic drawings

● Simple outlines always mean the same thing

cleaning up the workshop area, which again gives our children new sensory experiences whilst clearing away sawdust, shavings and all the excess glue and varnish!

The children particularly enjoy finishing, with various grades of sandpaper, and assembling the pieces to (we hope!) look like the isometric drawing I did at the beginning that gives them an idea of the finished product.

The children are only at an early 'schematic' stage of art development and relate extremely well to simple line drawings like those above. It helps them

● A pupil sands her work with intense concentration and care

tremendously to assimilate what it is they are making and what it will be used for.

Visual information, as we all know, is more easily absorbed and has a greater impact than merely listening to spoken words or even reading. Try it for yourself by imagining that the steam-bent box article in this month's *Woodworker* was devoid of illustrations and all you had to work from were written instructions!

The drawings are used not only to give the children an idea of what the finished item should(!) look like but also, accompanied by sketches of associated items, they are invaluable in demonstrating what the item is used for and in extending language skills. Having been very impressed with one of my better temporal-sequence drawing explanations of how the bench we were using started life as a tree (below), one young lady airs her new-found knowledge almost

● *Where a bench comes from*

every time I see her!

Conventional woodwork joints are too difficult for our children, so we get through large quantities of glue, screws and dowels, and sometimes — I suspect simply for the sheer pleasure of hitting it — the odd nail.

Finishing is usually clear gloss varnish, or if we have more than the average number of blemishes to hide, a colour stain varnish.

We have moments to remember. Neil, for instance, was told to glue (with PVA) and then hold a joint together 'for a while' until it set. He was discovered half an hour later still holding it because the workpiece, Neil's fingers and the bench-top were all set in one congealed joint! Other fond memories include the occasion when one of our pupils, a degree of maladjustment exacerbating his other handicaps, suddenly decided that working with wood was not for him and that the teacher (me) was in the way of something intensely expressive he had to do with the hammer!

Although our children get a great deal of satisfaction and pleasure out of making something for themselves, we do try to engender a feeling for others — a group or community awareness. To foster this we have worked together as a group on several projects with each child doing a part. These have included a large menu/duty roster board for the dining hall, and a ninepins

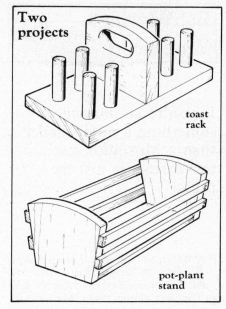

toast rack

pot-plant stand

game and hoopla board for the school's lunchtime social club. We're beginning on some plant troughs for a local old people's home, but they're are more likely to be ready in time for Christmas roses rather than spring bulbs!

● Eric Ingham is Deputy Head of Woodlands Schools, Blackpool.

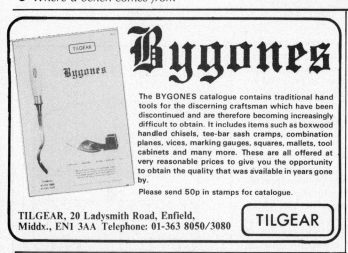

Small curved lamination

If you're laminating something a mite smaller than a Mosquito fuselage, this former is just the thing

● Strong canvas and threaded rod are the starting points for the miniature curved laminator . . .

This method derives from a technique used by those guitar makers who favour steaming or boiling the sides of their instruments rather than using the bending iron.

Prepare two blocks slightly longer and wider than the finished sizes you need. They should be of ample thickness — if they're too thin they'll bend or snap under pressure. Layers of plywood would be very strong but good hardwood is quite satisfactory and it certainly works better. The two pieces are cramped together (with register marks on them) and two small pilot holes, say ⅛in, are drilled through the plain block and just into the shaped one.

On these centres, two 1in holes are bored about ¼in into the shaped block. Set two ¼in-thick specially-made washers into the holes. They should be a tight enough fit, but two small screws will fix them if they're loose. Drill a further ¼in into the wood through the washers.

Now for the fixed block. Enlarge the pilot holes to ½in. Now you need two rectangular nuts; ½in Whitworth is a strong, quick-acting thread, but a metric 12mm is quite satisfactory. Use a piece of screwed rod to locate the nuts, scribe round them and cut cavities to receive them. Four no.6x½in screws secure them. Two housings are ploughed or routed on the reverse side of the block, the corners only slightly rounded. Readers without much equipment can let in two squares or hexagon nuts, but this is not such a good solution.

Accurately plane the shaped block to the required curve — there is virtually no spring-back. The corners are generously rounded. A variety of shaped blocks can be fitted to one device.

The woodwork can now be varnished with a number of coats to bring it to a good finish and to discourage any surplus glue from sticking.

Making the screws from threaded rod should present no problems; while short-cuts are possible at the handle end, don't omit the stubby pointed spigots. The two hardwood strips, which are fixed with five no.8x1in screws, should be a tight fit with the fabric round them. The fabric should be

● Which would be ideal for tops of small boxes. Different shapes to suit your ideas can be used on the same base

a strong canvas, cut as an accurate rectangle and fixed very precisely to the block. A thin coating of PVA adhesive prevents the edges fraying. Mark the centres at each end on both the canvas and the shaped block.

Laminating with the former

Make a hardboard pattern for the veneer laminates. Veneer is commonly 0.6mm thick, so five layers make 3mm or approximately ⅛in; seven (including the glue layers) is about 3/16in. Successive layers have the grain at right angles to each other, as in plywood, so you need an odd number of laminations. The top lamination may be quartered, but you'll have to be more careful with it, and the four quarters should be held very firmly together with strong tape.

Cover the shaped block with clean paper (not newsprint), taping it on to the underside. Stack your veneers, mark the centre line on the top one, then glue them together. I prefer 'Aerolite' or 'Cascamite' to PVA, as the latter hardens too quickly and may not allow the layers the necessary movement to take up the curve. Lay the stack on the shaped block, line up the centre-marks and fix at the centres with plastic tape. Cover with clean paper.

Insert this assembly into the canvas and locate the screw spigots in the washers. Take up the slack, checking the centre marks on the canvas. Cramp a small batten along the centre-line, then tighten the screws, after which the batten can be removed. Getting

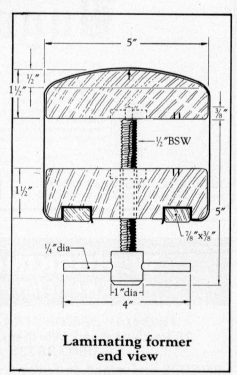

Laminating former end view

enough pressure without tearing out the canvas requires judgement; this is aided by feeling the canvas and inspecting the ends, although generally the canvas is quite robust. The 'owner driver' should find no difficulty, but supervision will be essential in a school or communal workshop. ■

An elliptical jig

WOODWORKING WHEEZE

of the **month**

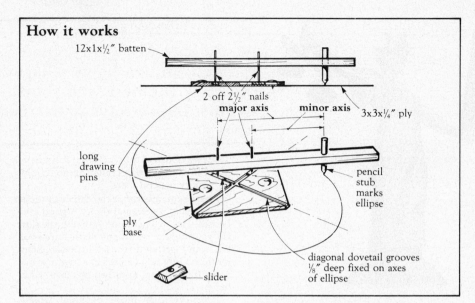

How it works

12x1x½" batten

2 off 2½" nails

major axis — **minor axis**

3x3x¼" ply

long drawing pins

pencil stub marks ellipse

ply base

slider

diagonal dovetail grooves ⅛" deep fixed on axes of ellipse

During WW2 I worked on moulds for the fuel tanks on the wing-ends of Mosquitoes, writes **Harry Unwin**. I also devised a natty little drawing instrument — an elliptical compass — for the fairing under a Beaufort Bomber's 200-gallon tank; it's a simple device which should prove equally handy for the workshop.

The best way is to aim to make a template that you will be using for your given size. You must know the major and minor dimensions of the ellipse. Start with a 3in square of ¼in-thick ply, a 12x1x½in batten, two 2½in nails and a pencil stub. Cut two tapered grooves ⅛in deep across the diagonals of the ply — hence the term

'Maltese cross' — and cut two small sliding pieces to fit firm and slide smooth in the grooves. Rub a pencil in the grooves for graphite lubrication.

Drill two holes for the nail points to fit tight in the sliders and another two in the batten for their shanks, 1in apart at one end of the batten. The distances between the two nails and the pencil are the major and minor axes of the ellipse, so drill the batten

for the pencil at the precise point you need. Draw two lines at right angles on the board from which you will cut your template, forming the major and minor axes of the ellipse, then pin the grooved base-piece to the board, the grooves lining up with the right-angled lines. Move the pencil round; slide the sliders; and hey presto, your ellipse! If you need a smaller ellipse, make a smaller base-piece.

Tools of the trade

WOODWORKER INVESTIGATES. The only way you'll ever know how good is a hand-tool is to use it. So how do you know what to buy? The most expensive must be the best, you think — but all may not be as it seems. David Savage has been testing the bench tools that go to make a cabinetmaker's basic kit

These articles will assess something absolutely basic to all cabinetmaking — the tools. The young apprentice (or for that matter the enthusiastic amateur) will be looking for hand-tools that will last literally a lifetime without paying more than necessary. I have approached every reputable toolmaker I could think of, plus others recommended by Roger Buse of tool merchants Roger's of Hitchin, with this proposal: 'We wish to assemble a basic kit of bench tools for a young apprentice entering the cabinetmaking trade. May we test the best of your products and compare them with the best of your competitors?'

The bench tool-kit would comprise marking and measuring tools, a set of chisels, a couple of saws and a couple of planes. In a commercial workshop these are the bench tools everyone has. I distinguish them from 'shop' tools, which are more exotic and less frequently used but are there in the shop for everybody. An apprentice or enthusiast would probably acquire a full complement of these as time went on.

Each article in this test series will examine one area of the basic tool kit, compare the products offered for testing and discuss how to use the tool and how to adjust or tune it for the best performance.

Praises and a warning

I must say a word of commendation for the British tool industry. With very few exceptions, the people I approached responded to my rather cheeky idea with remarkable enthusiasm. I found that most tool makers are very interested in how the user responds to their products.

This isn't an attempt to copy a *Which* report on hand-tools. I have neither the laboratory equipment nor the scientific aptitude to provide so-called objective comparisons. My comments are based on **entirely subjective experience.** I use tools like these every day to earn my keep and like other craftspeople, I understand how a well-made tool should perform. To counter my personal peccadilloes, the tools

were passed round the workshop and where possible used by other craftsmen, so I could get a more general view.

Please remember that the choice of tools is essentially a personal thing. A good saw becomes an extension of yourself; the saw isn't cutting the board and neither are you, but both together do the job in one efficient motion. Only you can select a saw that fits your frame, and comfortably into your hand.

I believe that more potential woodworkers are put off the craft by hand-tools that can't perform than by any other single factor. Tools should be completely on your side, no aspect or facet of their manufacture a discouragement to you from producing the job. But so many people buy tools in good faith, expecting them to perform straight from the box, or at best with a little honing. Usually this isn't the case. Planes need several hours of fettling to cut a fine shaving, chisels need polishing, gauges need adjusting. What has really prompted these articles is the fact that how to fettle tools is the most useful thing I can tell a beginner. With tools that are working for you not against you, the chance of producing fine work is high; otherwise I wouldn't give you a cat in hell's chance.

Having got that off my chest and warned you of the fireworks to come, let's get to the subject of this month's examination — marking and measuring tools. With many practical activities, the end result is often determined right at the beginning. If the job isn't marked out correctly (from a properly made cutting list) with clear, accurately scribed lines, you might as well pack up and go home. The tools are: two rules, one marking knife, two marking gauges (one doubling as a pencil gauge), one cutting gauge, one mortise gauge and two squares.

Rules

Rabone Chesterman seem to have this market pretty well to themselves. I think everyone should have a small 150mm rule, easily found in the apron pocket, most used for setting up machines and measuring out joints. A second 600mm rule will cover almost all larger cabinet measurement work. We have a metre rule and tape measures as shop tools, but these are seldom needed. The Rabone Chesterman 64R (marked both sides) and 47R (single-side marking) ranges are well-marked with engraved graduations in metric and imperial and they have a rustless satin face that doesn't damage with use. I can't see any reason to spend quite a lot more money for

the very heavy engineering-quality rules. The 64FR range of small rules is also useful to measure the circumference of curves — it's narrower and bends more easily.

Marking knives

These are less easy to recommend, in fact you're lucky to find one nowadays, so few manufacturers admit to making them. Footprint are a rather surprising outfit; they market their chisels quite widely in the UK, but also do a complete range of hand-tools that I'd never heard of. One of them is a marking knife which was nice to handle, small and light — as a good knife should be. Clay (Paramo's brand-name) make a marking knife whose cutting edge was at completely the wrong angle to the sides and much more crudely made, but it was a harder-grade steel than the Footprint equivalent. Now we get into the swamp. How hard is hard and how do we measure it? Isn't *really* hard steel just too hard and brittle? I really don't know. The way I tell harder steel from softer is on the grindstone. We use a very slow-cutting horizontal whetstone — softer tool steel comes to an edge very quickly with a large corrugated burr, whereas finer hard steel is considerably slower to reach an edge, the bevel has a finer mirror shine and the burr is small and fragile.

The marking knife should be ground at 25° like an edge tool, but unlike an edge tool, also honed at that angle. The point of the knife should be acute and the face side dead flat. With any knife you will have to spend some time grinding then honing to an edge so that the point is sharp and clean. Test it on close-grained hardwood across the grain. It should cut a thin clear line, with one shoulder at 90° to the surface. To use the knife with a rule, place the rule on the job with the measured distance ending where the rule ends, and run the face side of the marking knife against the end of the rule. When squaring a line across a job, place the knife in the measured mark and bring the square up to the face side of the knife. Always hold the marking knife upright, even if it means turning the job around to get the 90° shoulder on the right side. Used correctly, a marking knife is absolutely accurate — that 90° shoulder marks the end of the job with inflexible precision. It's an important tool and I wouldn't care to recommend either of the products tested. The Footprint knife would have been suitable had the blade been of harder steel, and the Clay knife would eventually have been made into a decent knife, but not without some effort.

● *The Stanley 5061, a marking gauge 'revolution' at £4.49; refined Marples 2050 behind, £5.69*

Marking gauges

Unlike the marking knife, which is usually used across the grain, a marking gauge is used along the grain to mark a line parallel to a straight edge. This essentially simple tool comes in three forms. The ones I used by Footprint, Rabone Chesterman and Marples have a simple square stock and square fence. The Marples MR2050 is slightly more refined, with an easily-used brass knob. All were good, serviceable tools, the Marples possibly a little less angular and uncomfortable to use.

Clay and Sarjents market a similar tool with a fence rounded to the hand. The Sarjent's marking gauge was particularly nicely made, with brass strips inlaid in the fence to prevent wear. I must admit to being doubtful about the value of these brass strips. I have used such a gauge for many years, and the natural expansion and contraction of timber has loosened the strips so they stand proud of the fence, giving a false reading. This may just be my bad luck, and it was not a Sarjent's gauge. The final form is the Stanley 5061, which revolutionises the marking gauge by putting the pin across the diagonal of the stock. This allows you to see exactly where the pin is marking, a considerable advantage. I had never used this type of gauge before, and was very impressed. Most people file the marking pin to a knife-edge or point; some angle the blade so the fence is pulled on to the edge of the job. Another idea is to put an edge on the marking pin similar to the marking knife. This seems a good idea except you have to turn the pin around for different tasks. As long as the pin leaves a clear scribe line along the grain, it's doing its job.

Using the tool is a one handed operation. Set the fence to roughly the right place and give the adjustment knob a preliminary tighten. Usually a gauge is adjusted precisely to a mark on the job or against a rule held in the left hand. This is always done at eye level, against a source of light. Adjust the gauge by tapping the stock against the bench, either one end or t'other according to the reading, and once you're

certain it's right, make sure the knob is turned up tight. It's no use having fancy gauges with built-in rules. A simple tool used one-handed is fast, efficient and accurate.

Pencil gauges, I suppose, should be mentioned. Generally, I like to keep tools around the bench down to a minimum — that way I save time. It's amazing how much of a day can be wasted rummaging around trying to find this or that. My marking knife can get from one end of the workshop to the

other quicker than I can! Don't buy a pencil gauge — you'll only use it once a year. Drill a hole in the other end of the marking-gauge stock and stick in one of those clutch pencils when you need it. (I'm very much in favour of clutch pencils with replaceable leads.) Cutting gauges should really be abandoned if you're following the policy of minimum bench tools. They do have a use for scribing across the grain in certain timbers that marking gauges tend to tear, and perhaps on very fine, small jobs like jewellery boxes. But if my marking gauges are sharp they should do the job just as well. Clay and Sarjents make good cutting gauges similar to their marking ones, the Sarjents' product slightly better finished.

Mortise gauges

The minimum tool policy should really also apply to mortise gauges, which are more shop than bench tools, but have been included because weekend woodworkers who work alone all need mortise gauges at some stage. There is a type of mortise gauge whose sliding pin is operated by a sliding knob, not by an adjusting-screw at the end of the stock; these are usually the economy models, and Rabone Chesterman were the only people who submitted one for testing. Made of rosewood with brass fittings, it looks superb — but it's annoyingly difficult

● *Marples 2154 combination mortise and marking – £21.59's worth*

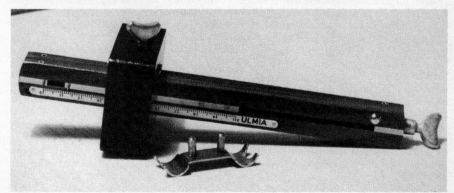

● *The Ulmia rosewood 315K mortise gauge, plus gizmo for marking off curved edges: £25.86*

Tools of the trade

to use. The screw that tightens the rear pin also tightens the fence, making it very hard to set up. This screw is also threaded directly into the timber rather than a metal sleeve, another attempt to cut costs.

Four models of mortise gauge with an independent screw adjustment for the rear marking pin were submitted — Ulmia, Marples, Sarjents and Clay. Sarjents' was the only one that isn't a combination mortise/marking tool. The Clay and Sarjents' mortise gauge seem to use the same brand of rear screw mechanism. This is an accurate method of moving the rear pin, but both of the ones I tested were unpleasantly sticky to use because of the coarseness of the thread. Both were in exotic hardwoods with pretty decorative brass fittings; the fence locking-screw on the Sarjents' tool threaded into steel, on the Clay gauge into wood.

Rather different was the Marples M2154 mortise gauge — much less flashy, with a finely-pitched rear pin screw-adjustment. This is better made than the ones Sarjents or Clay submitted. Ulmia produce what seems to be the ultimate mortise gauge — beautifully crafted in rosewood, with a light delicate action to the rear pin and positive independent locking of the stock. There is also a built-in scale and a gizmo that plugs in to allow you to gauge on a convex or concave edge. I liked this gauge until I discovered the design error. For all general framework less than 60mm, it will be great. There may, however, be occasions when you need to mark a mortise well into the middle of a job, such as a carcase division. Then you see that the stock of the Ulmia gauge is in two parts, which may distort if the fence is pulled back and tightened hard. I demand reliability in tools over the entire range of adjustments, so I would recommend the Marples.

Squares

Here Ulmia get their own back! I'm very fussy about squares, believing that a square is either just that, exactly square, or it's fit only for the bin. However, there are squares sold that are damn near square, and they're perfectly useful for all kinds of other jobs — site carpentry, DIY and fiddling about the house. For cabinetmaking we get so prissy and precious about it that only an exact square is acceptable.

So how do we know what we are buying or using is square, when the only way of checking is to put it against another (possibly inaccurate) square? The method of turning a square over against an edge, thus doubling the possible inaccuracy, is itself clumsy and open to error. I have one large all-metal square in my workshop, the 'shop standard' against which all the others are judged. This square is periodically checked by a local engineer using what he calls a 'bottle gauge', which is a steel cylinder about 300mm high and 100mm in diameter. The sides are perfectly parallel and its ends square to the sides. You sit this gauge on a surface plate and offer your

● **Above:** mortise gauge by Sarjents' (£15.95) behind the Clay combination tool at £20.99. **Right:** 50mm and 150mm no.9 Rabone squares sit in front of Ulmia 250mm, Sandvik and Footprint – the no.9 Rabones are to engineer's standards

square up to it, measuring any inaccuracy visually. Be careful to clean all the surfaces, and, if the square is old, check for bumps and dings that can give a false reading. My 'shop standard' nearly ended in the rubbish bin because of almost invisible pimples of glue which caused it to read 'a bit off'.

Because our work is judged by our senses of touch, smell and sight, a square that's visually accurate is enough for our purposes. Equally, one that is 'just off' is an ever-present menace undermining all your attempts at fine work. Go through the checking ritual carefully — don't just bang one square down against another, willing it to fit. Hold the 'standard' — a steel square — up to the light and bring the inside angle of the one you're testing up to it. Press the stock down hard, then slide the blade against the blade of the steel standard, looking as it arrives for that even glimmer of light. Don't do it in the dark either — look against a strong source of light.

There are two main types of square; the ones with a brass-faced wooden stock and a steel blade most common in the woodwork trades, and the all-steel ones more common in engineering. I suggest you look for a 150mm square as your main weapon, with possibly a smaller 50mm or 75mm square to carry about in your apron pocket.

Until I began the research for this article I didn't realise there are two standards for squares; BSS 939, an engineer's square specification, and BSS 3322. All-metal squares to BSS 939 are very good tools — accurate, square and probably expensive.

Footprint, Clay, Marples, Rabone Chesterman and Stanley all submitted 150mm squares, with wooden stocks faced with brass attached to a blued steel blade by three fixing points. All but the Footprint were 'just off'. Only Stanley claimed BSS 3322 on the tool, which was the least inaccurate of the others.

Though I suspect that most squares of this type conform to the BSS 3322 guidelines, it is possible to find an accurate 90° square in this specification, which Footprint proved by providing such a marvel for test. Don't expect an all-steel square to be accurate just because it is all steel — the Rabone Chesterman no.1909 is really a carpenter's tool, doesn't claim the BSS 939 standard on the tool, and this one wasn't square. It does have a 45° measure on the stock and metric scale on the blade, both of which would be useful to a site chippy. Sandvik provided a very similar all-steel square that offered the same features; despite having a blade that wasn't milled exactly straight, it gave a reading very close

● *Try your try-square before you buy!*

to 90°. With all these squares, 90° accuracy is something you may or may not get. Those that were chosen by the companies and submitted for test were less than accurate except for Footprint and Sandvik.

By pestering the owner of your tool shop, and checking the ones you're trying against another more expensive square, you may get a good 'un. However, the chances are that the conditions won't allow you to check squares with enough accuracy. I wouldn't advise anyone to buy an ordinary BSS 3322 square from a mail-order firm and expect it to be spot on.

The next grade up in price and quality is BSS 939. It should be stamped on the stock, and assure you of a tool as accurate as a woodworker, however pernickety, would need. Rabone Chesterman produce a range of engineer's squares of this type in their no.9 range. These are superb — no qualification. They are available up to 600mm long (at a massive price), and the smaller 50mm, 75mm, 100 and 150mm sizes — the ones of interest to the cabinetmaker — are quite within the pocket range of anyone serious about the craft.

Finally, Ulmia's 250mm try-square is large, light and absolutely accurate. Weight is often a problem with large squares, but the Ulmia is delicate and nice to handle and use. I was rather taken. It didn't come under BSS 939, but then it's made in Germany so it's not surprising.

If I seem unnecessarily fussy about marking and measuring tools, I make no apology for it. Good marking-out is the beginning of quality cabinetmaking — but only the beginning! ■

Next month: bench planes

● David and *Woodworker* would like to thank the following tool manufacturers and distributors for the loan of tools, their co-operation and assistance, without which the test series would have been impossible:
Footprint Tools, PO Box 19, Hollis Croft, Sheffield S1 3HY, tel. (0742) 753200
Paramo (Clay) Hallamshire Works, Rockingham St, Sheffield S1 3NW, tel. (0742) 25262/3
Rabone Chesterman, Camden St, Birmingham B1 3DB, tel. 021-233 3300
Record Ridgway (Marples), Parkway Works, Sheffield S9 3BL, tel. (0742) 449066
Sandvik, Manor Way, Halesowen B62 8QZ, tel. 021-550 4700
Sarjents Tools, 44 Oxford Rd, Reading RG1 7LH, tel. (0734) 586522
Stanley Tools, Woodside, Sheffield S3 9PD, tel. (0742) 78678
Tilgear (Ulmia supplier), 20 Ladysmith Rd, Enfield EN1 3AA, tel. 01-363 8050

Getting what you pay for?

These are the recommended retail prices including VAT, in £p, and all are for the tools that David tested. Model numbers are not quoted because some of the tools are not marketed with them; except in the case of the Clay marking gauge, the manufacturers sent the tools they considered top of their ranges. Clay sell a brass-faced gauge for £6.84. All the squares were 150mm except where otherwise stated. You should be able to get discounts!

	Rule	Marking knife	Marking gauge	Mortise (c = combination)	Square
Footprint		2.73			6.62
Clay/Paramo		3.74	3.74	20.99c	7.53
Rabone	150mm 64R/3.68		4.80	9.89c	1909/14.10
	150mm 47R/2.51				no.9/10.07
Marples			5.69	21.59c	5.78
Sandvik					200mm/9.19
Sarjents			3.95	15.95	
Stanley		4.40			8.30
Ulmia				25.86c	250mm/11.50

Responsible testing

A test like this is a difficult one to do scientifically, and that hasn't been the aim. Using tools is a matter of personal as well as inorganic chemistry. We feel that the personal opinion of a respected cabinetmaker like David Savage will help guide prospective buyers, and that's what we want to do. David's letter to the manufacturers states in no uncertain terms: **'I do not advise manufacturers to submit products that they do not believe will stand comparison with the best in the field.'** It turns out that in some cases lower-quality tools have in fact been submitted.

We sent a copy of David's article to all the manufacturers and asked them for comments; here are the replies we've had.

Paramo/Clay

I was somewhat disappointed by the response to our own products. Mr Savage falls into the trap of comparing a high quality professional product from one manufacturer's range with a medium quality tradesman/DIY product from another range. He should, in doing comparative tests, do manufacturers the justice of comparing like with like.
Marking knives. Mr Savage comments that the Clay marking knife is ground at 'completely the wrong angle'. This we cannot accept; the Clay marking knife is ground to approximately 30°, as we find that it's common for the user to hone an angle on to it. We find that a 30° angle with a slight touch on an oilstone produces a long-lasting edge. He is quite correct that our product is made from the finest hard-grade quality steel.
Gauges. This is a typical example of comparing products of vastly different price and coming to a subjective comment as regards their relative worth. The Sarjents' marking gauge with brass strip inlays to the wearing face is compared with our own basic product. We also make a brass-faced gauge which would have been a fair comparison with the other product.
Mortise gauges. It is our impression that the Marples adjusting screw mechanism was, in fact, manufactured by the same company who manufactures both our own and most other gauge manufacturers' adjustments.
Squares. As one of the largest manufacturers of carpenters' squares in the UK, we manufac-

ture squares for many other reputed manufacturers. Although our ethics of confidentiality preclude us from elaborating further on various points, suffice it to say some of Mr Savage's views cannot be correct. All our squares, manufactured both for our own and for other brands, are manufactured to BSS 3322; this is a fairly close tolerance and allows for one thou per inch out of square on the finished product. BSS 939 is an engineer's square specification and covers squares from much the same tolerance as the BSS 3322 up to the precision squares which we ourselves use for setting our testing equipment to ensure that our product complies to BS standard.

I feel that many of Mr Savage's opinions are highly subjective and the result of his own personal preferences, and would stress that my comments apply to his views on many of our competitors' products, not merely those relating to our own products.
J.M.W. Pridham, MD Paramo Tools Group

Footprint

Marking knives. We are looking into the matter of the type of steel, which is a carbon steel, and also the hardening, but could you please return the knife for us to examine.
Marking gauge. Insufficient information given to enable us to comment.
Square. We are pleased the Footprint square passed the test described. All Footprint squares are tested against jigs before despatch to ensure accuracy.

Rabone Chesterman

Mortise gauges. We have been manufacturing several thousand 1924 marking and mortise gauges a year for the past 16 years, and our Service Dept assures me that we have not received a single complaint about the operation of the gauge or its effectiveness in use. As for the implication that the thread will wear due to it being cut directly into a wood fence, our Service Manager cannot recall one complaint of this nature.
Squares. When Mr Savage refers to our 1909 pattern as not being square, there is no indication of the amount of inaccuracy and your reader will be left to ponder. Our tolerance for this type of square is 0.001in per inch ($\frac{1}{1000}$in per in) of blade. Therefore a 6in blade has a tolerance for out-of-squareness of 0.006in ($\frac{6}{1000}$in).

B.T. Fagan, Associate Director, Advertising and PR

435

Question box

Our panel of experts solve your woodworking problems

Turning books

Q *I'm a relative newcomer to lathe work, and am in search of some really good literature on the more advanced aspects of turning. I'd be grateful if you could point me in the right direction.*

Stephen Bristow, Ledbury

A I can appreciate your difficulty. For many years the most commonly available book was F. Pain's *The Practical Woodturner*, which remains far better value than many subsequent books not written by people with Pain's mastery. Perhaps ironically, I recommend familiarising yourself with *all* the books available via the local library, in an attempt to gain a general impression. I also recommend Ray Key's *Woodturning and Design* for good value, and I hope the improvement in standards will continue with Richard Raffan's *Turning Wood*.

Woodturning can't just be learnt from a book, one has simply got to do it. The best way of learning, is to attend one of the better residential courses (see 'Turning the corner' in this issue.) A few days with a seasoned professional gives one a unique insight into the subject which no book can match.

Anthony Bryant
● Anthony Bryant is a professional turner in Cornwall.

Finishing rosewood

Q *I make musical instruments, mainly guitars, dulcimers and mandolins. I use Honduras mahogany, Indian rosewood, American black walnut and German maple for the back and sides and either Alpine or Sitka spruce for the soundboards.*

With rosewood, the finish never seems to harden. I have used spirit varnish and polyurethane, the final coat cut back and then burnished with tripoli powder and a little oil, then buffed to a mirror finish.

On my last acoustic guitar, in Honduras mahogany and Sitka, I tried a brush-on cellulose lacquer. The mahogany has turned out fine, but the sitka front has haze patches over it. I never varnish in the cold, keeping the temperature round about 65°. Could the problem be damp, and why has the mahogany not gone the same way?

Ted Cawley, Munlochy

A Rosewood is a difficult wood to finish. The problems come when you use modern finishing materials; the wood is chemically active, particularly with some cellulose-based products such as acid-catalysed and polyester lacquer. First wash the surface with methylated spirit, using a clean rag. When it's dry, apply a liberal coating of a dewaxed shellac sealer, specially formulated for use under the cellulose

you're using, and allow it to dry bone hard. Lightly sand down with 320 grade lubrisil paper and dust of with a talk-rag. Apply your cellulose lacquer over this surface film and you'll have no further trouble. It's far better to spray on your cellulose lacquer than use a brush-on type.

Your haze patch problem on spruce could be due to a draught on your surface film while it's drying; the wood being slightly damp before coating; faulty or out-of-date lacquer; thinners wrong for your lacquer; mixing incompatible materials from different manufacturers; or moisture in your spray-gun air-line. Perhaps the mahogany didn't haze up because these factors don't apply in the same way.

Some haze can be removed with an anti-haze cream when the surface is bone-dry. A formula for an anti-haze cream is equal parts of french chalk, methylated spirits, white vinegar, raw linseed oil, water, and white spirit. Shake it well and burnish with mutton cloth. Don't use it on open-grain finishes. Not all haze can be eradicated with an anti-haze cream; it's a matter of trial and error.

Noel J. Leach
● Noel Leach is a professional woodfinisher and lecturer

Timber marks

Q *I am an industrial archaeologist conducting a survey of 19th century silk mills and dyehouses in Macclesfield. Frequently I come across marks like those below, but am unable to decode them. It's been suggested they might be an old-established timber supplier's marks, or those of an importer; they seem too complicated for carpenters' assembly marks. Any suggestions?*

Mark Handscomb, Macclesfield

Mystery markings

● *Top to bottom: on a purlin, rafter and tie-beam*

A I think we can rule out the possibility of the marks being carpenter's marks, which indicate joint assembly, and are normally found at the ends of timbers or near mortises. These marks seem to be near the centre of a timber. Also, carpenter's marks show a logical sequence.

The next possibility would be merchant's or importer's marks. However, merchants and importers handle timber in large quantities and each piece is marked in the only place where it can be seen as it lies, without having to turn over a whole stack — on the endgrain, in other words. Moreover, the same mark is used for each merchant, load or quality, so it was painted, stencilled or struck in.

So it seems that woodsmen or converters are the most likely authors. Richard Harris, Research Director of the Weald and Downland Open Air Museum, says such marks are normally found on the **hewn** surfaces, not the **sawn** ones. They were made when the tree was first squared into a balk with axes, before it was sawn into dimensions. Since this method of converting hasn't been used for 200 years or so, such timber would have been imported, and I surmise your timbers are in fact imported pitch pine. It was favoured in the last century for buildings such as mills, churches and schools where strength and length were required. It was regularly available in hewn 18in square sections about 45ft long, ideal for beams or resawing into purlins, rafters, and so on. In fact as I was writing this in what used to be a hayloft over the coach-house of an 1843 house, I looked up and saw similar marks on the hewn under-surface of a pitch pine rafter directly over my head!

This helps me dismiss one other possibility; that the marks were made by the users of the buildings. (For example, to indicate the various areas of an industrial process, or as tallies of some sort.) Apart from the fact that they have been observed in too many different situations for this to be plausible, there is the question of how they were made. The marks on my rafter and, as far as I can judge, the ones on the Macclesfield timbers, appear to have been made with a timber-scribe or race-knife. They are shallow grooves, about ⅛in across, with perfectly clean edges. Yet it's been pointed out that it is extremely difficult to scribe a clean groove across the grain of a softwood — at least if the wood is reasonably dry. However, if these marks were made by the men who hewed the newly felled trees, dense with moisture and sap, the knife would cut cleanly.

I feel that any further research into the precise meaning of these marks would need to be done in the areas where the timber grew, and into the customs by which the woodsmen claimed their piecework rate for the baulks they had hewn.

Philip Walker
● Philip Walker is a member of the Tools and Trades History Society.

Bandsaw motors

Q I recently obtained a bandsaw made by Whitehead Junior Tools Ltd of Halifax, Yorkshire. The machine is stamped no. 8867 type BJ, tested 15.3.50. It has a 12in throat, 6in depth of cut, and the saw pulleys are 12in diameter. The machine has no motor. Could you advise on a suitably-sized single phase motor and the gearing on the pulleys?
R.A. Law, Droitwich

A Short of reverting to technical data and formulae, the best course I can suggest is to use the pulley arrangement I used when building my bandsaw (WW/Jan). A 2¾in dia. A-section pulley on the motor and 5in dia. on the drive-shaft should do it, assuming a motor speed on 1425rpm; this would result in 800rpm at the drive-shaft.

I find it difficult to advise on motor size. The bandsaw would probably be heavier than today's models, but I don't know enough facts about the machine. If it's slightly larger than my design, a ¾hp, 1425rpm motor should be adequate.
John White
● John White wrote 'A bandsaw you can build' (WW/Jan). Write for amendments to the drawings, enclosing an A4-sized sae.

Tensioning wide bandsaws

Q Are there any books on tensioning 5in-wide bandsaws? I recently bought a Stenner band rack, and have a problem with blades cracking at the gullet, and sometimes at the back. The Swedish saws we use sometimes crack after only a week's use; my two 3in British saws have never cracked. I have an old tensioner, but I don't know how to use it, as it has a curved metal gauge rather than a dial.
John Sheehan, Fethard

A The tensioning of bandsaws is not easily learnt from a book, no matter how well written. Cracks: check your machine first. If it's new the wheels on the head-rig should be in good condition, if it's second-hand, you should have it checked by an expert or by Stenners. The wheels may need regrinding. Badly-worn wheels can cause cracks; a symptom of this is sawdust clinging quickly to the front edge.

You could fill a book with possible reasons for cracks in bandsaws. Are you running them too long? Even if the saw is cutting well, don't use it for more than four hours. On some woods, the saw won't even last as long as that. Is the set equal either side? A saw should carry 2-3 gauges of set — if a saw is 13 gauge the swaged tip should measure 16 gauge or 3mm across the tip. The round in the bottom of gullet shouldn't be too sharp or burnt (blue) which will cause case-hardening, when it will crack under strain. Are you using the correct amount of weights on the straining arm? Use as little weight as possible, providing the saw runs straight. Does the saw oscillate? This is generally because of poor tensioning. It could be lack of tension,

uneven tension, or the back of the saw could be uneven.

Grinding and swageing is reasonably straightforward, but to tension a saw properly takes skill and a lot of experience. Tension rolls don't have gauges to note the poundage; it's done purely by feel and practice. There is a book by A. Simmons, *Wide bandsaws*; Robinsons also have a small book which has a lot of very good advice.

If you are having trouble with new saws it's probably nothing to do with the steel or who makes them, but far more likely to be one of the above reasons.
E. Doubleday
● Mr Doubleday is a lecturer at the London College of Furniture, and was a saw doctor for 25 years. Thomas Robinson & Son Plc, Railway Works, Rochdale, Lancs OL16 5NB, tel. (0706) 47811.

Workshop noise

Q I'm hoping to buy a terraced house in the near future and would like my own small workshop, but I'm concerned about the noise of hand power-tools, especially the plunging router. I don't want to disturb neighbours so is it possible to insulate a room to absorb sound – or even sound-proof it properly – without spending huge amounts of money? Would it be better if the workshop was below ground level – in a cellar for example?

Are there certain makes of hand power-tools quieter than others (in particular routers)?
David Muff, Norwich

A It's difficult to sound-insulate a room in a terraced house cheaply and effectively, but one fairly economic method is to cover the party wall with papier-maché egg-boxes which are in turn covered with ½in insulation board. Batten the wall to the thickness of the egg-box material and secure the insulation board to the battens. I have installed removeable secondary glazing with a 4in gap in one window of my workshop, which has silenced an irate neighbour and satisfied the local council.

These methods can also be applied to a garden shed, but of course there can be problems of dust and lack of ventilation, so you'll need a small extractor fan.

Although a cellar workshop would be quietest, there are the pitfalls of dampness, difficulty of access, and again, ventilation. A reasonably insulated garden shed is what I'd opt for and provided you show reasonable consideration by using machines at sensible times (routers at midnight are not on!) there should be no problems.

The router is a noisy beast, but I have compared the Elu MOF 96 with the 96E, and find the electronic version marginally quieter. A bandsaw is, of course, a great deal quieter than a circular saw.

One last point: make sure that all your electrical equipment is properly suppressed. You neighbours may well forgive you for a noisy machine, but never for ruining their favourite TV programme!
Roy Sutton
● Roy Sutton is a professional woodworker and teacher of wood-machining.

Warped doors; collapsible tables

Q I have two small problems. The first is a corner cupboard door. It is antique, mahogany and with a small amount of inlay. There is one rather large single panel in a frame, the members about 2¾x¾in cross-section. The corners are through tenoned and wedged. The door frame appears to have warped, so when it's closed, the hinge side is accurately lined up and fixed (three hinges) and the outer edge is correct at the bottom but ⅜-½in proud at the top.

Second is a small card table. It's very plain, and I'm unsure how it was used. It's merely a simple baize top with legs at one end that fold inwards, so it can be carried by a side handle. Obviously it can't be used free-standing and my customer has asked if the present folding legs on one side can be repeated on the other, so they both fold inwards and it can still be carried. What do you suggest?
H.K. Kitchen, Leamington Spa

A It would be undesirable to remake the whole door as the item is antique; remedial action on the existing door is preferable. A certain amount of interference with the frame will have to be tolerated and you could try either of the following techniques — the first of which means operating on the front of the door.

1 Determine the length of the part of the frame member which is cast; it may be that the stile and top rail are affected. Cramp the door flat to the bench and make a number of saw-cuts to a third of the thickness of the frame at about ½in intervals (below). Tap slightly wedge-shaped pieces of matching wood into these saw-kerfs and release the cramps. If the structure remains flat, go ahead and glue in the pieces. If the error is still apparent, tap the wedges in further and/or increase the number of cuts until the door is flat. This method will leave you with the problem of masking your remedial work, so you may prefer to try:

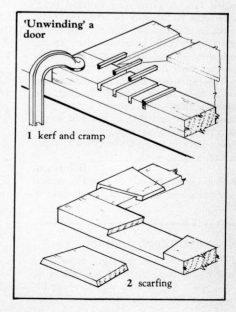

'Unwinding' a door

1 kerf and cramp

2 scarfing

Question box

2 The second method entails scarfing in a piece on the back of the door. As before, determine the length of the cast and cramp the structure flat. Cut a wedge shaped piece away to half-depth which is driven home until the member is straightened. This can now be glued and cramped in and the surplus cleaned off afterwards.

Your curious card table may well have been originally used when travelling and the free end propped or laid on a coach-seat or possibly on the traveller's knee. As you don't give specific sizes I can only advise you on a general approach to converting

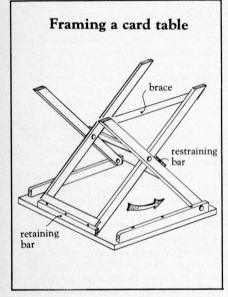

Framing a card table

brace

restraining
bar

retaining
bar

your table to a suitable fold-away type. As the sketch shows this is basically made from two frames, one inside the other. One is anchored to pivots on the side bars whilst the other is pivoted to it at the centrepoint, and rests against a retaining bar when assembled. A small turn button (not shown) could be usefully fixed here as the table will fold if lifted up. The inner frame stows inside the outer one when both are folded flat. A restraining bar and brace piece must be fitted to the anchored frame to hold and stiffen the whole structure. The metal pivots could be either bolts or rivets, and they should have a nylon or steel spacer-washer between the surfaces. For a light table not over 2ft sq., 2x⅝in hardwood could be used for the underframing. The diagram shows the general arrangement viewed from underneath, but you would have to make a measured drawing of the piece to obtain necessary lengths and angles before starting work.

Bob Grant

● Bob Grant is head of Craft, Design and Technology at an Oxford comprehensive school.

Restoring teak colour

Q *I have a garden seat made from Burma teak. After 14 summers in the open, 14 sandings and 14 re-varnishings, it has lost its lovely red colour. I would like* to get right down to basics, strip, bleach, colour and protect. It has a presentation plaque which I can remake. How do I go about it?

Brian Cook, Builth Wells

A It should be possible to strip the old varnish from your garden seat, glasspaper it smooth and re-finish it in a couple of weeks, provided you spend an hour or two a day on it. If the seat has been outside all winter, it will need to be brought into the workshop and allowed to dry naturally. Removal of the old varnish will help drying; stripping is best with a proprietary stripper such as Nitromors. Once the old varnish has been completely removed, all traces of the stripper must be washed off, using white spirit for 'original' and clean water for 'water washable' stripper.

If the seat has been badly stained, (say by the weather) it can be bleached with a two-part bleach from a polish supply house. This will be easier to use and give better results than oxalic acid.

The wood is smoothed by using progressively finer grades of abrasive paper; the less accessible parts may be more easily reached with steel wool. After thoroughly dusting off, the seat can be stained with ready-for-use stain as sold in DIY shops, or you may prefer to make your own water stain. Dissolve some burnt umber in a jar of water and some burnt sienna in another. You can arrive at the colour you want by mixing the two stains together in a third jar and adjusting the proportions. Experiment on an inconspicuous part, such as the under-side of the seat rails. Always make more stain than you think you will need because it can be disastrous to run out of stain before the job is complete; the next mix might have a slightly different colour.

Allow the stain at least 24 hours to dry thoroughly before applying three or four coats of Spar varnish. Use a clean, new, good quality varnish brush, and after each coat has hardened lightly glasspaper it smooth before the next coat. See 'Wood finishes: what and where?' WW/Mar 85, for suppliers.

Charles Cliffe

● Charles Cliffe is a professional french polisher, teacher and author.

Garden seats

Q *I want to make a garden seat which is to be fairly elaborate – cabriole legs, some carving to the main members and also some applied carving. Is elm suitable or would you recommend another wood other than (very expensive) oak or teak? How should I ask that the legs (4x4in) and other frame members (2in thick) be cut from, say, an 18in trunk? Should the wood be air-dried or kiln-dried? What glue would you recommend for the joints, which I also intend to peg? Should the same glue be used for the applied carving?*

I intend to use clear Cuprinol as a finish. Is there a better finish? If I use Cuprinol, can it be applied to the joints before gluing?

The seating struts are to be fixed by screws, counter-bored and plugged. Should these screws be ordinary metal, brass, or some other metal?

How do I work the square areas of the cabriole legs with rasp, file and scraper?

G. Milliner, Poole

A Use elm — other hardwoods are so expensive. However, it would be a very unusual piece of elm that didn't distort when dried. But dry elm isn't as durable as wet. In my young days, we occasionally made bacon-curing vats of wet elm — and it really was wet; the shavings rusted our vices and tools. It also gave off an overpowering odour of horse urine! A good air drying should do, which would bring the MC down to about 20%. The trunk should be cut into the required sections, and stacked with free air-circulation around each piece, with just a roof over to shield from sun and rain. If the ends are covered with mastic, this will prevent too rapid drying out at the end grain, and prevent 'checking' (splits). The time usually allowed for air drying was one year per inch, so 4in material would take four years! Having said all this, I'd cut the trunk, stack for, say, three to six months for a superficial drying, and then use the material, and let the drying continue *in situ*. This is for out-door work only, of course; let the distortion, which will almost certainly occur, add character to the seat.

Use Aerolite waterproof glue for such out-of-doors woodwork; this or something similar, is what is used in all-weather plywood, and water doesn't affect it at all.

I couldn't suggest a better preservative than Cuprinol. As for gluing of 'preservative' timber — as an experiment, I treated two bits of timber with 'Protim' preservative, let them dry for a few days, and then rub-jointed and glued them. When the glue had set, I tried breaking the joint but as usual, it was the wood that failed, not the glue. Then I repeated the experiment, applying the glue directly on the wet preservative; and the result was the same — no glue failure. But I wouldn't say this would always happen; these might have been two freak occasions!

Cutting the trunk depends on how much waste is to be permitted. The best way is to cut 'radially'; this reduces warp to a minimum. However, your sections are mainly square, so to avoid excessive waste, I'd 'slash-saw' (tangential).

I'd suggest galvanised or anodised iron-mongery; brass screws would shear. Iron screw first, and then brass? It doesn't work, I'm afraid; it's the final turn that tightens, and this is where the brass will always shear. When brass screws are used without shear, it simply means that the jointing — or whatever — hasn't the tightness that an iron screw would give.

To clean-up the flats of the cabrioles, a finely-set shoulder plane should be used across the grain; a cabinet scraper along the grain; then glasspaper both ways. No rasps; no files!

Stan Thomas

● Stan Thomas is a joiner and cabinet-maker of great experience.

Letters

IF THE BIRDS illustrated in 'Carver's Garden' (W/W Feb) are *Aegithalos caudatus* then my *Parus* are bloaters!

I respectfully suggest the author of the caption subscribes to the RSPB who produce very informative magazines twice yearly.

R. Wolstenholme, Harrogate

● Perhaps the funniest thing about this mistake was that only one reader both noticed it and wrote in about it. Our apologies, especially to Andrew Armitage, for naming his goldfinches as long-tailed tits, and his apple blossoms as almond. *Editor.*

THE LOWER OF THE TWO steadies in Ray Key's 'Question box' reply to N. A. Howarth (WW/Feb) doesn't appear to be a practical design. Initially, the steady could be positioned in the bed to ensure that the wedge was in contact at centre-line height, but the least wear or reduction in diameter of the workpiece would free the wedge. It could not move down the inclined face to take up wear because of the V-notch, and even if it were able to do so, the notch and lower in relation to the spindle centre.

A steady whose notch moves forward horizontally under pressure from a spring-loaded wedge is better, in my opinion.

W.J. Wooldridge, Bexhill-on-Sea

THANKYOU FOR PUBLISHING 'The Gripping Story' (WW/Jan). I have patented the chuck-plate system, but have not even received a reply from the chuck manufacturers that I have written to, notably Pratt-Burnerd in England and Emco in Austria. If readers wish to have the system made available, then I suggest they badger scroll makers or suppliers, who might thus be persuaded the system isn't merely some crackpot idea.

Mike Darlow, Australia

YOUR BANDSAW article (WW/Feb) claims hardened blades are unsharpenable. I take my blades to a local engineer's merchants, who send them to Dentons of Bolton. According to Dentons this type of blade has been sharpened for many years, using the same type of wheel as they would use to sharpen a conventional blade.

Michael Foden, Stockport

I WOULD LIKE to contest two points in the Bandsaw article (WW/Jan). I don't understand why you suggest the guides should be set off the body of the blade. If you wish to control the blade rather than have it follow the grain or some other whim, it's essential to have the guides against the blade.

Secondly, when you talk about 'other causes of poor cuts from wandering blades . . . ' there is no mention of the actual bearing surface of the blade guide which must be flat and perpendicular to its sides. This, and leaving the guides too far off the blade, are the major causes of the bandsaw's reputation for not cutting straight lines.

The remedy for the problem, if you have those plastic blade guides often supplied with smaller machines, is to discard them and use hardwood planed to fit — cut into short lengths and sanded square across the ends which should be soaked in oil. These should be dressed square regularly, but will do a fine job compared to the plastic variety which can wear off square in literally seconds.

If you have the large steel blocks such as Startrite use, they should be inspected every 6-12 months. This is the secret of good straight cutting on a bandsaw.

T. Kaye, Devon

SEVERAL YEARS AGO I invested in a Sjöberg bench, one of the special features of which was said to be the ball-jointed nylon vice — supposed to grip even tapered objects. But this vice is the weakest point of the design in my opinion.

It clamps the workpiece against the bench front, but the ball joint allows the workpiece to rotate unless it's held in place with

Letters

an ancillary steadying device. I have devised a number of ideas for modifying this vice, but believe the real answer is to replace it with a good old-fashioned British model — but it isn't easy to see how — or if — this could be done. I'd be pleased to hear from anyone who has made this conversion, because I believe it would greatly improve the usefulness of the bench.

Jack Saxon, Caithness

Sjöberg's UK agent replies: We were interested to hear of the problem Mr Saxon has with his Sjöberg workbench.

The front vice is fitted with the swivelling nylon pressure pad, as Mr Saxon points out, in order to provide a soft but firm grip on uneven surfaces. This is in addition to the normal functions of the vice. This Swedish design has the added advantage of being free from guide rods, which can interfere with the working area.

Any rotation of the workpiece during tightening is normally prevented by holding the workpiece with your free hand — which would be necessary even with the traditional British vice.

We have passed Mr Saxon' comments on to the manufacturer and we too would be interested to hear from any reader who has found it necessary to fabricate any special device.

Geoff Brown,
Managing Director, BriMarc

THERE SEEMS to be a lot of fuss about Japanese laminated irons. The scythes, sickles, hedge hooks and slashers in the Abbeydale Hamlet Museum near Sheffield were all made by hammer-welding tool steel to a backing of iron. All my older tools are made this way.

The £995 Japanese plane is a dear bit of metal if you discount the wooden stock. You mention two weeks' wages for a Norris. In 1935, wages on a normal week were £3.50. A Norris Malleable, not dovetailed, with rosewood fillings and all adjusting and locking gear was £1.75.

W.V. Richmond, Beeston

I TOO ENCOUNTERED ebonising problems (Question Box WW/March) when working on antique long-case clocks and plinths.

I used beech from old bits of furniture and finished with six coats of black paint, then a final rub down with metal polish to lose the surface shine. This is very effective but requires patience — make sure every coat is dry before applying the final finish.

Harry Unwin, Exmouth

RE: R.S. Read's letter (WW/Feb) my screwdriver blades from George Buck (Tottenham Court Road) were made from cast steel rod. They were hand-forged. Also note: John Hall Tools Ltd have **not** merged.

R. Norris, Mountain Ash, Mid Glam

ADVERTISERS' INDEX

A.E.G.	425	Old Stores Turnery	359
Apollo Products	410	Plans Service	370
Argus Exhibitions	357,390	Rogers of Hitchin	361
A.V.F.S.	425	Sanlin	424
Axminster	356	Sarjents Tools	368
Benmail	385	Scott and Sarjeant	358
Black & Decker	IFC, 379	Solent Tools	425
John Boddy	358	J.J. Smith	426
H. Case	380	Southwest P. Tools	411
C.C.B.	431	Stobart and Son	417
Charltons Timber	380	Sumaco	385
Charnwood	397	Tabwell Tools	421
Peter Child	417	Taylor Bros	411
Craft Materials	416	Henry Taylor	440
Craft Supplies	367	W. Thatcher	416
Data P. Tools	440	Thomas & Willis	417
Elektra Beckum	367	Tilgear	410, 416, 426, 429
Excel	420	Eric Tomkinson	417
Heath Saws	379	Tool Centre	421
Heward & Dean	416	Toolmail	380
David Hunt Tools	417	Treebridge	417
Ashley Iles	380	Trend	411
Kity	362, 379, 417	Tyme Machines	362
E.W. Lucas	410	Cecil W. Tyzack	410
Luna	OBC, 416	Warren M. Tools	366
Magh Spa	IBC	Whitehill	411
A. Mills	395	Woodfit	397
John Myland	366	Woodplan	416
Naerok	392	Woodworking Mach. Switz.	
National Marquetry Exhib.			426
	392		

WOODWORKER

design . . . craft . . . and the love of wood

June 1986   Vol. 90   No. 1111

453 The grand furniture saga: 5
Buffets, aumbries, and when is a court cupboard not a court cupboard? Storage furniture starts here. *Vic Taylor*

455 WORKBENCH OF THE FUTURE
A brilliant idea for a competition for brilliant ideas — design a workbench and win one of Sweden's finest!

456 Resurrection
A first for UK woodwork journalism — the story of the restoration of York Minster's soaring timbers. *Leonard Markham*

464 JAPAN 3 Twisted mystery
An intricate twisted dovetail that just won't pull apart, whichever way you try. *Alan Peters*

467 Tools of the trade 2
Bench planes: the *Woodworker* test department gets stuck into good, better and best. *David Savage*

480 Machining Wood Your expert guide: 8
Sanding machines — tables, belts, discs and drums show the quick way to the fine finish

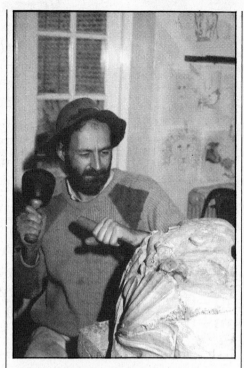

● *One of 68 carved bosses takes shape for the vault of York Minster – p456*

485 Tales out of steel
Not a lot of people know about these facts from metal history; a wry toolmaker's individual viewpoint. *Ashley Iles*

491 Buying timber wisely: 5
Continuing our visits to specialised merchants supplying the specialists. *Alan Thomas*

494 Ornament for all
An expert introduces the fascinating 'art and mysterie' of **Ornamental turning** — plus a project for enthusiasts! *Tubal Cain*

503 Powerful people
Some large-as-life sculptures in a Cheltenham gallery, and their strange and unsettling effect. *Tim Ashby*

509 Winning willows
Growing and processing the timber for one of England's expanding exports — the game of cricket. *George Jaffa*

512 Bowled over
The gargantuan bowls of Ed Moulthrop, woodturner extraordinaire, demand some outlandish tools and techniques. *Ray Key*

Editor Aidan Walker
Editorial assistant Kerry Fowler
Senior advertisement manager Paul Holmes
Advertisement manager Trevor Pryor
Graphics Jeff Hamblin
Technical illustrator Peter Holland
Guild of Woodworkers Kerry Fowler

Editorial, advertisements and Guild of Woodworkers
1 Golden Square, London W1R 3AB, telephone 01-437 0626

Unfortunately we cannot accept responsibility for loss of or damage to unsolicited material. We reserve the right to refuse or suspend advertisements, and regret we cannot guarantee the bone fides of advertisers.

ABC
UK circulation
Jan-Dec 85
28,051

Back issues and subscriptions Infonet Ltd, 10-13 Times House, 179 Marlowes, Hemel Hempstead, Herts HP1 1BB; telephone Hemel Hempstead (0442) 48434

Subscriptions per year UK £16.90; overseas outside USA (accelerated surface post) £21.00, USA (accelerated surface post) $28, airmail £48

UK trade SM Distribution Ltd, 16-18 Trinity Gardens, London SW9 8DX; telephone 01-274 8611

North American trade Bill Dean Books Ltd, 151-49 7th Avenue, PO Box 69, Whitestone, New York 11357; telephone 1-718-767-6632

Printed in Great Britain by Ambassador Press Ltd, St. Albans, Herts
Mono origination Multiform Photosetting Ltd, Cardiff
Colour origination Derek Croxson Ltd, Chesham, Bucks
© Argus Specialist Publications Ltd 1986
ISSN 0043 776X

Argus Specialist Publications Ltd

1 Golden Square, London
W1R 3AB; 01-437 0626

PROJECTS
All with detailed working drawings

460 Woodcut craft
An age-old method of turning carvings into pictures, and it's not essential to be a carver! *Tim Ashby*

474 Window on the world
Joinery classics: we start an occasional series on constructional woodwork with a quality sliding sash window. *Graham Hewitt*

497 Ornamental ivory
An intricate box in a superb material for those with patience and imagination. *Tubal Cain*

504 Hinged in the middle
An extending dining table with ingenious folding beams solves the problems of length and flex. *David Applegate*

On the cover:
Ed Moulthrop's bowls are giant-sized for some (p512), plus dramatic work on **York Minster** (p456); and a free gift of a deep and beautiful finish, courtesy of Briwax!

REGULARS

443 This month casts an eye on the world of wood

445 Shoptalk keeps you abreast of the market

447 Timberline Market movements in the trade

449 Question box Yellow oak, weatherproofing windows, cabriole legs . . .

479 Guild notes courses, activities — have you joined?

511 Bob Wearing's workshop
Unwinding with winding strips

493 Woodworking wheeze of the month
Drilling holes in tight corners. *Alan Thomas, Michael O'Hara*

515 Letters Readers write and readers read

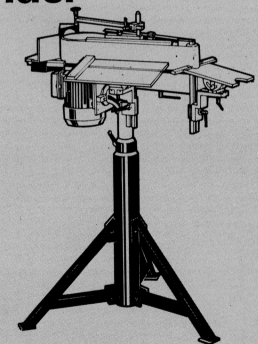
442

Woodworker
This month

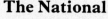

Wax works!

A special free gift this month — a sachet of **Briwax**, the best-known wax name in the country. A blend of beeswax and carnauba — it's perfect for a beautiful warm, natural glow. If you've never tried a wax finish before, here's your chance!
● Our thanks to Henry Flack, PO Box 78, Beckenham, Kent, tel. 01-658 2299

Small talk

The Mulberry Bush, the specialist miniaturist suppliers, will be presenting their awards at the **National Miniature Fair** in Dorking.

The event, which is organised by the *Home Miniaturist* magazine, takes place on 15th June; see diary for details.

The National

To many people 'The National' means horses, Aintree and jumps **writes Polly Curds**. To thousands of other people, however, it's the national annual marquetry exhibition. This year it's the 34th.

From 24-31 May inclusive about 350 marquetry exhibits will be on display at St Albans School, Abbey Gateway, St Albans, representing the work of marquetarians at all levels of expertise, from all over the country. Leading marquetarians will be exhibiting their work from over 20 local groups. Some of their work may be familiar through the Woodworker Show, some will be new and made exclusively for the competitions at the National.
● Contact Julian Duggan, 44 Ardens Way, St Albans, Herts, tel. (0727) 54110. Admission free.

Obituary:
Max Burrough

We sorrowfully record the death of Max Burrough, one of *Woodworker's* favourite contributors ('Then', WWs/1984 and 85), at the age of 72.

He was an authority on the furniture of the Arts and Crafts movement: a 'Max Burrough archive' is to be set up at Cheltenham Museum where many pieces of the period are kept.

Rewarding designs

Student furniture designers wishing to attend the 'Design for Profit' conference held at the RIBA on 17th July should act quickly — and **through their colleges** — as places are now very limited.

The conference is part of a business-backed exhibition for manufacturers, featuring the work of successful participants from *House & Garden's* 'Young Designer of the Year' Award.

● Tutors or students should contact Deborah Jones at Arthur Young, Rolls House, 7 Rolls Buildings, London EC4 1NH, for availability of places (free for students) and further details.

● *College link: Students from the City Literary Centre for the Hearing Impaired learn at the London College of Furniture. Here, a jumping jack*

Wanted!

Voluntary Service Overseas need skilled woodworking volunteers; 9 Belgrave Square, SW1X 8PW, tel. 01-235 5191.

Forest forward

After the 18 March rally where the Timber Trade Federation and Friends of the Earth met publicly over the rainforest issue — David Bellamy stated that a mere 2% of timber felled in the tropical rainforests goes into the world timber trade — another TTF/FoE meeting on 8 April has created very positive noises. Both organisations, very happy with the meeting, are jointly mailing internationally influential bodies connected with the forests to persuade them to work for genuine progress on decisions by the **International Tropical Timber Organisation** (WW/Apr). ITTO meets 12 June; here's hoping.

Diary

Guild courses are shown by an asterisk (*); for further details see the Guild pages.

May

Until 25 **Alan Peters, Furniture Maker** Cooper Gallery, Barnsley
Until June 1 **Chess in Art and Society** Victoria & Albert Museum, London
4-28 **Small Carved and Turned Wood: Exhibition** Parnham House, Beaminster, tel. (0308) 862204
16-18 **Bristol Woodworker Show**, Bristol Exhibition Centre
17-June 5: **David Pye** Craft Council Shop, Victoria & Albert Museum, London
22-27 **Interbimall '86** Woodworking and Tools Exhibition, Milan, tel. (010 392) 8242101
24-31 **National Marquetry Exhibition** St Albans School, Abbey Gateway, St Albans, details tel. (0727) 54110
23-25 **Furniture and clockcase design** (course) West Dean College, Sussex, tel. (024363) 301

June

5-6 **French polishing** Charles Cliffe*
4-Aug 31 **David Munrow Collection** of Early and Folk **Musical Instruments** and the **Craft Council's Second Open Exhibition of Musical Instruments** Crafts Council Gallery, 12 Waterloo Place, London SW1, tel. 01-930 4811
6-15 **Retrospective Exhibition** Rycotewood College, Oxon. tel. (084 421) 2501
14 **Mosquito Aircraft Museum** visit: further details on the Guild page
15 **The National Miniature Fair** details The Home Miniaturist, 18 Calvert Rd, Dorking, Surrey
24-26 **Shrewsbury College Exhibition** Town Hall, Shrewsbury
30-July 4 **London College of Furniture Summer Show**

July

5 **Design and Workshop Drawing** Bob Grant*
26-August 30 **Furniture from Rycotewood College,** Cheltenham Art Gallery, tel. (0285) 61566
27 **E. W. Godwin Centenary** 20th century Furniture Designs, V&A Museum, London
28-29 **Crafts at Whatton House** Loughborough

September

6-7 **Decorative techniques** Ian Hosker*
27 **Hand veneering** Bob Grant*

443

444

Shoptalk

Sorry — the frame clamp in 'Shoptalk', WW/Feb comes from JEM marketing and has nothing to do with Vitrex as we said.
● JEM Marketing, 180 Princes Avenue, Palmers Green, London N13 6HL.

The new improved Sanko **saw-bench** is now available from Elektra Beckum. The table tilts to 45%, it has 3in depth of cut and an adjustable rip-fence. 3500rpm under load; it's portable, it's light and it's £149+VAT.
● Elektra Beckum, 10 Willment Way, Avonmouth, Bristol BS11 8DJ, tel. (0272) 821171.

Vidal Sassoon has a lot to answer for with his three-stage approach to hair-care. Cuprinol have just launched a Garden Furniture **Colour Restoration System** that is claimed to restore colour *and* preserve. It consists of pre-treatment gel, conditioning gel and colour application. You'll be pleased/horrified to know that it's unscented, and will cost under £10.
● Cuprinol, Adderwell, Frome, Somerset BA11 1NL, tel. (0373) 65151.

Woodturner and teacher Don White has set up in a new workshop. He hopes to expand his courses:
● Don White, The Old School, Tytherington, Glos, tel. (eves) (0272) 564931.

The Coronet Lathe and Tool Co. has been acquired by Record Ridgway: enquiries to
● Parkway Works, Sheffield S9 3BL, tel. (0742) 434370

TRITON WORKCENTRE MK3 will turn any router or jigsaw and portable circular saws 165-265mm into table machines; £189.75+VAT.
● M&M Distributors, PO Box 128, Bexhill on Sea TN40 2QT, tel. (0424) 216897

Bosch have got a new 'budget' **plunging router** out — the POF 400 has a fixed motor speed of 27,000rpm and plunges to 54mm. It comes with ¼in collett, parallel guide, circle guide and a ¼in two-flute bit: £57+VAT. They are also adding an orbital sander (**below**) to their cordless range; it takes 115x140mm sheets, runs at 20,000opm, and takes an hour to re-charge. £105+VAT.
● Bosch, PO Box 98, Broadwater Park, North Orbital Rd, Denham, Middx UB9 5HJ, tel. (0895) 833 633.

EVERY DIYer becomes a professional joiner, claim Al-Ko, with their new ADH150 150x100mm planer/thicknesser. H'mm ... £297+VAT.
● AL-KO, 1 Ind. Est., Medomsley Rd, Consett DH8 6SZ, tel. (0207) 590295

BUY 1000 Siafast 1923 150mm sanding discs and you get this £107 ARO orbital sander thrown in — can't be bad. Siaco are giving away other sanders to bulk buyers of their abrasives range:
● Siaco Ltd, Saffron Walden, Essex CB10 2LA, tel. (0799) 27399

WELL-KNOWN NAME in radial-arm saws reappears on the UK market; the Sears Craftsman Heavy Duty 10in has a 2½hp motor, 3in depth of cut, 16½in crosscut width, and extra cutters galore. £549+VAT.
● A-Z Tool Sales, 7/8 Union Close, Kettlebrook Rd, Tamworth B77 1BB, tel. (0827) 56767

SLOT'N'DOT is a dust-free sanding-disc backing pad; slots and dots don't have to match the holes in your disc. £8.95+VAT.
● Super Stork, Queensbury Station Parade, Edgware, Middx HA8 5NN, tel. 01-952 5151

WORKSHOP RANGE new from Burgess includes 5 and 6in bench grinders (£58 and £65 inc. VAT), and a £109 fretsaw; the BK3 bandsaw is well known. The 7in disc sander costs £100 inc. VAT.
● Burgess Ltd, Leicester Rd, Sapcote, Leicester LE9 6JW, tel. (0455 27) 2292

JOEY'S THE NAME of this leather tool pouch; £40.90+VAT.
● H. Fine & Sons Ltd, 93 Manor Farm Rd, Wembley, Middx HA0 1XB, tel. 01-997 5055

Timberline

Arthur Jones on what's happening in the timber trade

Quality is more important to the woodworker than price. Not, of course, that you want to pay through the nose for your wood supplies; but certainly, quality can go alongside competitive pricing.

The general guide in timber buying is the grading of the wood. But this is only a guide and there can quite properly be wide variations in quality within the grading rules. This is why importers place such great value on the products of known mills. Their timber will be marked according to the grading rules, but the quality can be quite different.

Experienced woodworkers know this is the case, and while few have the knowledge to ask for timber from specific mills, they know they can deal with a particular importer or merchant who has this knowledge and so get the benefit of the timber man's experience. It's a case of finding the reliable timber firm dealing with the reliable shipper.

There's a strong movement in the timber trade to establish a quality assurance scheme. Most consumers favour such schemes, and they provide some safeguards, but the woodworker can't expect a quality assurance plan to replace the confidence which comes from buying from a shipper who guards a reputation for quality.

Most of the problems associated with using wood come from careless processing. There has been a spate of complaints to the Timber Research & Development Association about troubles with wooden doors, and these can often be traced back either to faulty design or to the use of improperly seasoned wood.

The softwood market continues steadily on its path towards a year of stability, with stocks much more in line with demand and prices showing a slight strengthening, especially whitewood. The Czechs have sold for this year at the same prices as were paid last autumn. All signs of the forward market point to firmness and possible slight price increases, which means we will surely soon come to the end of cheap offers. The trade will soon have to pay more attention to higher replacement costs and put up selling prices in readiness on our home market. It shouldn't cause any panic buying, as the movement will be marginal and after all, you have enjoyed many months of falling timber prices at a time of inflation!

The political troubles in the Philippines naturally created a serious interruption to work in the forests and the mills, so it will take a little while for the market in woods from that region to settle into a new pattern. Lauan must be among the main species affected. Many contracts for hardwoods from the Far East have been running late, and with the stronger prices now applying, it's probable that those cheaper earlier contracts will never be shipped.

The Americans have donated $10,000 to our National Hardwood Campaign, joining several overseas hardwood-supplying countries in giving financial aid to the scheme. At least it makes more information on hardwoods available to the general public, which must be good for woodworkers.

Turners have been buying more sycamore according to some reports, and this has been followed by higher prices. Increase the demand and the prices go up, but it's often hard to pinpoint what has caused the change in demand.

More interest is being shown in southern pine plywood from America, to take the place of the more expensive Canadian plywood. Finnish birch plywood prices have risen by some 5%. New Russian birch plywood prices are up by 4% for sanded grades.

Woodworkers are using a lot more particleboard these days. Trade in these panel products set a new record last year, following a rise of 10%. Britain reached record output of home-produced chipboard, but imported boards still form the bulk of trade and there were sharp increases from Portugal and Spain. And now that Spain is in the Common Market we can expect to import even more from them. ∎

447

Question box

Laburnum veneer

Q *I want to turn a freshly-cut laburnum tree into oyster veneer for decorative boxes. I would be grateful for any information you can give me.*

Fred Cooper, Halesowen
F.W. Shackleton of Preston asks a similar question.

A I know of no contemporary book that deals with the subject; even Charles Hayward's excellent *Practical Veneering* only mentions the topic in passing. However, in brief:

1 Dry the timber carefully to around 12% moisture content; splits must be avoided. Suitable methods include

a Conventional in-the-round air/natural drying; remember to paint the ends and leave on the bark. This can take up a few years, depending on the diameter of the log.

b A variation on the above is to bury the whole log in builder's sharp sand which is marginally drier than the log. The two can be allowed to dry out together, perhaps with water occasionally sprinkled on the sand to retard the process. However, it's rather hit or miss.

c PEG treatment, which is expensive but effective. The polyethylene glycol (PEG) solution stabilises the wood immediately from the green state.

d Slice the veneers off the green log and re-stack them interleaved with thick absorbent paper, then hold it all flat in a press. Change the wet paper for dry as needed.

2 The conversion procedure depends on the pattern you require. For squares and rectangles trim the dried log throughout its length and slice the veneers off on a dimension saw using the mitre slide; veneer thickness should be a bare ⅛in. To cut round pieces, make up a vee-cradle to support the wood against the mitre slide. If you used the stack method and the pieces still have their natural configuration, you will have to make up a template, say from a piece of plywood and perspex, and trim each piece using vertical cuts with a chisel.

3 Flatten the veneer with coarse glasspaper on the underside; the top surface can be levelled after laying. Don't use a machine sander as it will generate heat cracks.

4 Oyster veneers can't be laid by the hammer method; they must be pressed individually into the ground, which should be toothed and sized as in conventional veneering. The veneer absorbs the moisture present in most glues; this causes problems when it dries out. However, I have found that aliphatic resin glues with a fast grab time (such as those made by Humbrol) are effective. Even so, it would be wise to tape all joints as you go, and remember that the veneers will tend to pull unsupported work hollow.

Bob Grant

A 'Oysters' can be cut to the required thinness only by a very fine-toothed saw. If you have one, start at a 45° angle and vary it till you get the figure you want. Laburnum is highly valued as a turnery wood but is difficult to season in large cross-sections without cracks forming. If you wish to convert and dry it yourself, it would be prudent to saw it into thin planks to reduce the possibility of seasoning degrade, but then it would be suitable only for small turned items such as lace bobbins. If you prefer to provide material for larger items such as bowls, it might be wisest to find a buyer who will purchase the standing tree so that it can be dimensioned to their needs.

Michael White M.A.

● Bob Grant is head of Craft Design and Technology at an Oxford comprehensive school, and teaches courses for the Guild of Woodworkers; Michael White, a consultant on timber and trees is an ex-Scientific Officer at the Forest Products Research Laboratory.

An arched pergola

Q *I saw a design for a pergola with curved overhead arches. How do you make such arches, and what is the best timber?*

G.J. Hill, Oadby

A Oak would have been the solution 25 years ago, but now it's as expensive as the other common hardwoods. Elm would be a good alternative, but where would one obtain 3x3in elm for the upright posts?

Second-hand pitch pine or larch is equally elusive so we're left with stock softwood — say 3x3in red deal; well treated but not with creosote which might damage plant life. Pour the preservative into a bucket and leave the ends of the posts in it for a week. Sink the posts in concrete, but bring the concrete above ground level, and slope it away from the post so rainwater can run off easily.

If the main posts were about 3x3in, the head timbers could be of lighter section — say 3x1½in, jointed as in fig. 1. Whether these are cut in one piece or segmented depends on curvature; assuming a width of say, 36in and a rise of 6in, these could be cut in one piece, as there wouldn't be much short grain (fig. 2). A pronounced circle, would have to be segmented (fig. 3). This is

semi-circular; **A** is made up of two segments, **B** is of one piece from crown to base — which, while it is workable, is not advisable because of the very short grain and waste. Both fig. 2 and fig. 3 **A** joins are at about 70°; fig. 3 **B** shows that 45° produces too much short grain; so 60° would be about the point to decide upon two pieces. There is no hard-and-fast rule concerning this; it's just a guide, as some timbers are far more split-resistant than others. Iroko and mahogany, for example, could take far more short grain with their two-way grain than walnut or Douglas fir.

The end-to-end jointings are plain open tenons, well glued (waterproof glue) and dowelled. But distortion can occur in assembly; draw the full-size curve out on a sheet of hardboard and assemble each curved section on it.

The longitudinal curves can be fixed to the surfaces of the posts, using galvanised or anodised nails. In its early days, the pergola won't offer much wind-resistance; but as foliage increases, diagonal wind-braces should be added which can then be hidden under the greenery.

Stan Thomas

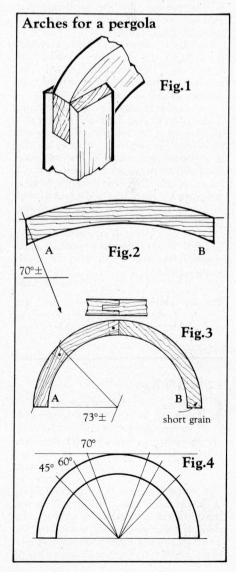

Arches for a pergola

Fig.1

Fig.2

70°±

Fig.3

73°±

short grain

70°
45° 60°

Fig.4

Question box

Weatherproofing windows

Q I am renovating an old cottage and want to use hardwood (oak, elm or chestnut) windows, but I'm tempted by trouble-free modern UPVC windows, despite their appearance. I've seen some softwood windows with a plastic insert in the rebate to keep the casement shut tight – is it possible to buy this and fit it to hand-made frames? Would a clear weatherproofing finish alone be enough? What is the best form of weatherproofing for hardwood to keep its natural colour? Is there any book on the design and manufacture of windows?

Ken Rhodes, Welwyn Garden City

A The big disadvantage of wood is, of course, its instability. Decay and insect attack have been virtually eliminated with modern preservatives. UPVC isn't affected by any of these, but would such windows look out of character in an old cottage? I think so. Also, if you get any 'settlement' after your renovation work, these windows can't be 'eased' by planing.

Thousands of old cottages still have their original wooden windows, which had no preservative treatment in their day. I would in this instance, use the hardwood you mention, well treated with a modern (not creosote) preservative.

I think the 'plastic inserts' you mention are ordinary draught-strip — available at any reputable DIY store. But it wouldn't be for 'keeping the casement shut tight'; the fastener would do this.

For weatherproofing to retain the natural colour of hardwood, I can only suggest two or three coats of yacht varnish. There are numerous 'microporous' finishes on the market now, with, as far as I can tell, very good performance. As for books, I don't know of one that deals exclusively with windows, but there are standard texts (used in City and Guilds courses) by Ken Austin (*Contract Joinery*) Peter Brett (*Carpentry and Joinery*) Frank Hilton (*Purpose-made joinery*) and A. B. Emary (*Site carpentry and advanced joinery*). (Also see 'Window on the world' in this issue.)

Stan Thomas

● Stan Thomas is a joiner of vast experience who holds a live 'Question box' and 'tool hospital' at Woodworker Shows.

Cabriole legs

Q I would like to know the correct proportions and profiles for a cabriole leg with a ball-and-claw foot. Do you have any tips on carving it, together with a rope edge moulding for a table top?

A. Reynolds, Braintree

A The first stage in making a cabriole leg with a ball-and-claw foot is draw out the outline on squared paper and cut out a thin plywood template from this (fig. 1). The foot is much larger than the foot of a plain cabriole leg, because allowance has to be made for carving the claws. Use the template to mark the shape on one face of the leg, then bandsaw it out. Then pin the waste pieces back in their original positions while you mark and bandsaw the adjacent face. Shape the upper part of the leg with a spokeshave and file, then turn the leg upside down to mark out the foot. Draw in the diagonals, and draw two circles with the compass point on the intersection. The outer one, which is the size of the ball at its centre, touches the sides of the foot. The inner circle is the size of the ball where it runs into the flat base of the foot. Draw in the claws as shown in fig. 2, remembering the outer claw is the largest, the two side claws slightly smaller and the inner claw the smallest. The lower half of the foot is radiused as in fig. 2. Carve away the wood between the toes on the upper half of the ball with a half-round gouge. Remember that nothing is carved from the centre of the ball, because it extends to the outer face of the leg at this point. Cut to the outline of the claws, but don't carve the knuckles till later. Round the ball at its centre-line, then work down towards the inner circle at the base of the foot, using a gouge of slightly greater curvature than the ball. Having carved the ball, shape the claws and smooth the leg with a file and fine glasspaper.

As all four legs will have to match I suggest you take the work in stages. The four legs should be squared up together, marked out, the claws cut together and the balls rounded.

The rope edge should first be drawn out on paper to ensure that the twists fall in the right places. It will then be simpler to mark the design on the table-top for carving.

Charles Cliffe

● Charles Cliffe is a professional polisher, author and teacher.

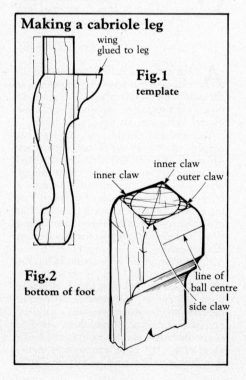

Making a cabriole leg

wing glued to leg

Fig.1
template

inner claw

inner claw

outer claw

Fig.2
bottom of foot

line of ball centre

side claw

Drying mahogany

Q I use 2x1in sapele mahogany for table frames. This timber is very attractive and finishes at the right colour for my purposes, but tends to move in the legs. Is this due to moisture drying out? Would a moisture meter be helpful? I have never seen one advertised, so I have no idea of the price. I have a multimeter – could I adapt it for this purpose, and if so, how would I make connections and calibrate it?

M. Marshall

A Unfortunately I don't have the complete design of your tables, but a stretcher bar to tie the legs together might help. The original method of converting timber is an important factor; quarter-sawn is inherently more stable than flat-sawn material, so you could select this for the legs. The moisture of the timber while the piece is being made and when it's in service (particularly if the two are different) will lead to movement problems. You should try and ensure your timber is dry when you buy and kept dry during working and in use. As a rough guide, timber for house furniture should be around 12%m.c.

Electric moisture meters are a handy and quick method of establishing the moisture content of timber, but they have their limitations and unless a number of readings throughout the moisture gradient of a sample are taken, the results are likely to be inaccurate and unreliable. The problem is usually getting the spikes deep enough into the specimen; a surface-only reading may be markedly different from one near the centre of the stock.

Most electric moisture meters measure the electrical resistance of the wood, and the majority of these machines are built to indicate between 6 and 28% m.c. (which is the fibre saturation point). Protimeter make an excellent range.

Making your own meter from the normal electrician's ohm-meter would be possible, but there may be difficulties in obtaining one that has enough range. The principal problem would be in calibrating it.

Basically you would have to set the meter readings to known moisture content samples (the oven drying method is the most reliable) to say, 8, 15 and 28% to give dry, medium and high-reading bands. But then the meter would only be useful for the species that was used for the control samples. A correction factor would have to be applied for other woods as the electrical resistance of wood varies with the species and this could only be done by more experiment. Commercial machines have this factor built in. If you with to pursue this interesting subject further, contact the Timber Research and Development Association, Hughenden Valley, High Wycombe, Bucks HP14 4ND.

Bob Grant

● Protimeter, Meter House, Fieldhouse Lane, Marlow, Bucks SL7 1LY.

Yellow marks in oak

Q *I recently bought some rough-sawn English oak, which showed yellow stains after I had machined it. The supplier assured me the stains were caused by a fungus which produced a form of acid, that the acid was unstable and that it would disappear after a month or so's exposure to light – even if a finish had been applied. Was this correct?*

Kenneth May, Chester

A These yellow stains could well be caused by a fungus. A mould of the *Penicillium divaricatum* group is usually responsible for 'golden oak'. The hyphae of the fungus exude a persistent yellow pigment. It would be unwise to proceed on the assumption that the stains will disappear on exposure to light; better delay your project for a few weeks while you expose the bare surfaces to direct sunlight. I would be surprised if the stains do indeed disappear, but would very much like to hear if this does prove to be the case.

Michael White

Child-safe Danish oil

Q *I want a satin-like lustrous finish on a drop-side cot I have made in American redwood pine. Would Danish oil be suitable, especially as teething children may bite it? If I wanted to darken it slightly, what should I do?*

J. Borkett, Port Talbot

A You didn't state which brand of Danish oil you intended to use on the cot; if you use Rustins it will be OK, as our product is lead-free.

You will find the Danish oil will darken the pine slightly, which may be enough for you. If not, you can add some of our wood dye to the Danish oil to obtain a darker finish. But it would be wise to test the mixture of oil and dye on the underneath of the cot to make sure it's the correct shade. You should also remember that when oiling wood for the first time, you should make two to three applications and that if you have added dye to the Danish oil, each application will make the finish slightly darker.

Ronald E. Rustin

● Ronald Rustin is the director of Rustins!

Plane identification

Q *I read with interest the letter from Peter Tonks (WW/Jan) about the plane he inherited from his father. I was also left a plane which is almost identical to the one in the diagram, except mine is 16in long. The name on the blade is Charles Taylor. Any information you could give would be appreciated.*

R. Ryan, Burnley

A I'm afraid it isn't possible to give an absolutely definite answer to your question without seeing your plane.

However, I feel fairly confident it was a one-off job, made by a craftsman for individual use. Perhaps that craftsman was your father, or one of your forefathers?

If the tool had been made by one of the professional planemaking firms, such as Spiers or Norris, I think the firm's name would be prominently visible, usually across the bronze lever-cap, although the lettering on the earlier Spiers of Ayr planes is rather small. Another clue is the length in this case 16in. The range of planes offered by the well-known plane makers usually went up in ½in increments (I have no idea why!), so a similar Spiers or Norris would almost certainly be 15½ or 16½ inches long.

Of course these firms were quite small, and there was a lot of individual hand work, so most of them would do any special job to order. So we can't absolutely rule them out, but this is much more likely to be a one-off, home-made job. Thousands were made like it, and it may be of interest that the periodical *Work* printed detailed instructions for making a closely similar plane in one of its 1889 issues. So it is probably a Ryan family heirloom! Charles Taylor has been noted as a maker of plane cutters, but his details are not known.

Philip Walker

● Philip Walker is ex-secretary of the Tool and Trades History Society.

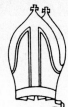

The grand furniture saga:5

Vic Taylor draws the portraits of some ancestors of modern furniture with a look at the misnamed 'court cupboard' and other storage pieces

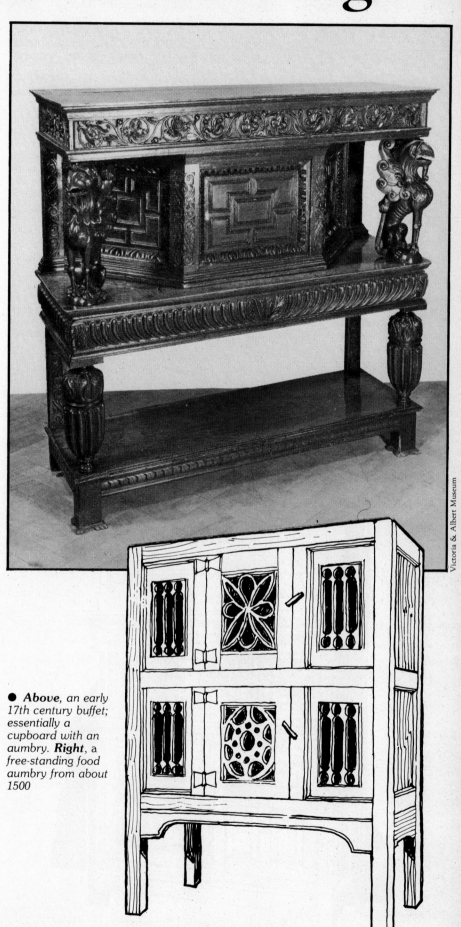

The fascinating history of what might loosely be called 'Renaissance storage furniture' covers at least 200 years, starting in the 14th century. Several of the designs persisted until after 1600.

We begin with two ancestral pieces, the 'aumbry' and the 'cupboard'. The aumbry was originally a kind of hollowed-out space enclosed by doors, usually set into the wall of a church or a castle, although free-standing designs were being made by the later Middle Ages. Aumbries served as storage for a wide variety of articles such as clothes, books, ecclesiastical vestments, ornaments, and food, and the name seems to have derived from their use for storing alms in the form of food left over from banquets. There is, for instance, a record in 1483 of a 'litell olde almery in the logge at the gate' at Marshalsea prison. And Henry VIII ordered that all the relics and fragments of a meal should be gathered by the officers of the almery and be given to the poor at the outer gate under the scrutiny of the almoner. There is an even earlier reference, quoted by Ivan Sparkes in *English Domestic Furniture 1100-1837* that in 1256, one Godfrey de Lyston made 'an almariolum in the middle of the turret in the upper bailey to keep the Queen's clothes'. This quotation also illustrates yet another of the several names for the piece; *aumbrie, armoire, almerys, arombry* and *ambry*, were all used as well as those already mentioned.

The earliest cupboards were a literal interpretation of the word — sets of boards (shelves) arranged one above the other on which flagons, cups, plate and ornaments were displayed. Sparkes has it that it was recommended at the French court that the cupboard for the Queen should have five shelves; for Isabella of Portugal, four; three for countesses, two for wives of bannerets, and one shelf for less noble women. It's obvious that cupboards and the articles displayed on them were very much status symbols, and to emphasise the point, Henry VIII had a cupboard of nine or 10 shelves at a banquet at Richmond! The shelves were usually covered with drapery or carpet, and the piece had no back. In fact, it was frequently made so it could be dismantled for easy transport.

During the second half of the 15th century, cupboards with aumbries began to appear, which meant that part of the space between two shelves was enclosed by doors and fitted with a back. An inventory reports that Cardinal Wolsey had 21 cupboards of 'waynscote' (oak), of which five were 'close' (enclosed).

● **Above**, an early 17th century buffet; essentially a cupboard with an aumbry. **Right**, a free-standing food aumbry from about 1500

The grand furniture saga:5

Another piece of dining-hall furniture of this period was the 'buffet', a kind of sideboard from which drinks were served, and on which valuable drinking vessels were displayed. A typical example was slightly more than 4ft wide and about 4ft high, with three open shelves, the lowest of which was supported on block feet and covered by a carpet. The middle and uppermost shelves were often inlaid. The back supports were plain, presumably because they were hidden by the plate and ornaments displayed, while the front ones were richly carved and usually of the 'cup-and-cover' design. The rails were also decorated with inlay and/or strapwork. The top and middle shelves had drawers underneath, the one on the middle shelf often conspicuously deeper. By the beginning of the 17th century many examples were constructed with aumbries between the two uppermost shelves.

In Shakespeare's *Romeo and Juliet*, when the hall is to be cleared for revels, the servants are told to remove 'the court cupboard and look to the plate'. That court cupboard would be practically identical with the buffet just described; the adjective 'court' (French for 'short') is appropriate because such pieces were generally less than 4ft high.

So it's plain that what we call a 'court cupboard' today is misnamed. It should, in fact, be known as a 'hall' or 'parlour' cupboard, a design widely used throughout the 17th century. The canopied upper part was probably developed from the buffet-cum-aumbry design which appeared around the turn of the 16/17th centuries, and the lower enclosed part was a variation of a press, probably for eating and drinking utensils.

The hall cupboard design was used in Wales as a basis for the *Cwpwrdd deuddarn* and the *Cwpwrdd tridarn*. The first is a press cupboard about 57in high, surmounted by an upper cupboard with a heavy canopy carrying pendant knobs or bosses. The *tridarn*, which appeared about the middle of the 17th century, has a third stage added to the top for the display of pewter, earthenware, and so on.

Livery cupboards are often mentioned in inventories of the 16th and 17th centuries, but there are several contenders for the title, so it's difficult to describe a typical style. The most likely design appears to have been a free-standing aumbry supported on legs; the doors were pierced, or contained balusters with spaces between so air could circulate freely and food would stay fresh.

'Livery' was an allowance of bread, beer, and candles put in each guest's bedroom for use in the night, the word deriving from the old French *livre*, meaning 'free'. The practice continued until the days of the Commonwealth in 1649.

The food aumbry was a relation of the livery cupboard, and this too could be

● *Predecessor to the wardrobe – the 17th century press cupboard*

either free-standing or hung on a wall. It also had pierced panels for ventilation, which were often lined with cloth or sheets of pierced tin (like American 'pie safes'). They are sometimes identified in contemporary inventories as a 'drinke aumbry', a 'mylke aumbry', or even an *'aumbry pro candelis'* (for candles).

Press cupboards, based on the French *armoire* (meaning a closet or cupboard), were confined to the houses of the wealthy, a means of storing clothes and linen. We could call them wardrobes, as they were enclosed by doors and contained an assortment of shelves and pegs; we must be careful, however, as Chaucer uses the word 'wardrobe' to describe a privy! In the 16th century, 'press' also referred to a small room fitted for storing clothes (also called a *garde-robe*).

The earliest designs of press, in the 14th century, were simply large cupboards with shelves and plain doors, but by the 16th century the doors were often panelled and fitted with a lock and key. By 1600 they contained sliding drawers or shelves at the top which were enclosed by doors, while the bottom part consisted of a row of long drawers. The largest presses could be 6ft 9in tall by 4ft wide, although smaller ones about 4ft tall by 4ft wide were also made. Not such a long way from the designs of today — although 'press', as far as cupboards are concerned, has much more to do with the process of manufacturing cheap board carcase-material than with the job of the piece itself! ■

● *A splendid* cwpwrdd tridarn *from the Welsh Folk Museum; it is based on a hall cupboard. Dated 1695*

● Ivan Sparkes, *English Domestic Furniture 1100-1837*, Spur Books.

WORKBENCH OF THE FUTURE!

A **WOODWORKER** and **SJÖBERG**
COMPETITION to test your SKILL!

WIN

1 A magnificent Sjöberg 2000 workbench, with a 2000mm-long laminated beech top and two vices — worth £700 (if you could buy it in the UK)
PLUS
2 A long weekend in a luxury hotel in Sweden, with a visit to Sjöbergs

The total value of these enticing prizes?

£1500!

WHAT YOU HAVE TO DO The traditional workbench design is hundreds of years old — no special provision for power tools or modern equipment. But Sjöberg are committed to constant improvement: SO

DESIGN THE WORKBENCH OF THE FUTURE — OR FEATURES FOR A WORKBENCH — OR BENCH ACCESSORIES — that make benchwork more flexible, comfortable and easier with today's tools and materials

---

THE WINNER will be the entry (judged by *Woodworker* and Sjöberg) which makes the greatest overall contribution to workbench design

ENTRIES must be in the form of detailed drawings and/or photos, plus explanatory notes on no more than two A4 sheets for each item. Send to **'Workbench of the Future'**, Woodworker, 1 Golden Sq, London W1R 3AB.

CLOSING DATE 31 AUGUST

- Prizewinning designs will become the property of Sjöberg, who reserve the right to put them into production.
- Sjöberg will pay £100 to any entrant other than the winner whose idea is put into production
- Similar ideas will be judged on quality of presentation
- All decisions about the competition are final, and no correspondence will be

held. Employees of ASP Ltd, Sjöberg Ltd, Brimarc Ltd or their advertising agents are excluded from entry
- SJÖBERG WILL MAKE UP THE WINNING DESIGN TO BE EXHIBITED AT THE WOODWORKER SHOW, ALEXANDRA PAVILION, LONDON, 23-26 OCTOBER
- An entry is automatically taken as agreement to abide by the rules of the competition, and take (within reason) the offered dates for the holiday

---

SPECIAL OFFER! £100 off!

If you want to make sure of a SJÖBERG bench, have a look at this. The 1900 has a 1900mm-long laminated birch top, two vices, and storage underneath. With a Sjöberg Holdfast, it's worth £520 retail. *Woodworker* and Sjöberg are offering it to you for just £420! That's a clear £100 off!

- Make cheques payable to Argus Specialist Publications Ltd

To: Reader Services, Wolsey House, Wolsey Rd, Hemel Hempstead, Herts HP2 4SS
Please send me ☐ Sjöberg 1900 benches with ST82 Holdfast at £420 each. I enclose
a cheque for ....
Name...
Address ....
.... Post Code..............

Resurrection

● *Almost as dramatic as the soaring roof itself! The 'tent' expands on the blue rails; the vault below takes shape*

Reconstruction and research

To get an idea of the work that the Minster team took on, the first thing to understand is that roof and vault are two entirely separate structures. The vault is (was) 15th century, the roof as it existed before the fire was built in the 1770s and strengthened in the 1880s. No properly detailed drawings of either existed; in the late 1960s, Mr David Green, son of the Minster's Clerk of Works at the time, made drawings from a detailed inspection, but was severely hampered by the difficulty of actually getting into the narrow space (18in in some parts) between roof and vault. So when the roof fell in, says Derek Phillips, Director of the Minster's Archaeology Office with a major responsibility for planning and overseeing the reconstruction drawings of the original roof and vault, they could put the bits together on the ground and see how they all went together. Hundreds of charred and broken joints were painstakingly reassembled, photographed from the air, and then detailed drawings were prepared with the help of the 1960s versions. Architect Charles Brown and structural engineers Ove Arup are the design and building firms with the contract, but of course a task like this is an enormous and diverse research challenge — which the Minster's Archaeology Office was ideally equipped to meet.

The roof structure

The principal timbers of the new roof are the 40ft rafters which form A-frames. In normal roof construction, horizontal tie-beams cross between the lower extremities or feet of the angled rafters to form triangular sections, but the marked upward rise of the vaults into the roof space means that the position of these beams has to be

● *English oak meets English stone . . .*

Whatever the reasons the pundits suggest for the York Minster fire, the effect was devastating. We asked Leonard Markham to look at the restoration work

When York Minster's south transept burnt in July 1984, the craft of centuries went up in flames. The conflagration might have been seen by some as a divine reprimand, but for others it was a unique opportunity to commit themselves and their skills to restoring one of the finest structures in Europe. Nearly two years into the restoration programme, re-roofing is well advanced, and already a triumphant framework is taking shape high above the ground. Some of the timber has been donated by well-wishers, who like the

Minster's army of craftsmen are proud to contribute to one of the most envied jobs in building.

Restoration of the 13th century south transept to its former glory, the responsibility of the Minster's Dean and Chapter, is supervised by superintendent of works Bob Littlewood, whose family have served the Minster for four generations. Bob served his apprenticeship under the eye of his carpenter grandfather, and was particularly involved with the renovation of the beetle-ravaged north transept vault. Today he heads 53 permanent employees, a workforce whose diverse but complementary skills make them almost entirely self-sufficient.

The Minster's 12 carpenters are currently erecting the south transept roof and inner vault of English oak. Their experience and expertise in working and maintaining the traditional material influenced the decision to reject steel for the job, because of uncertainty about the metal's longevity and the likelihood of contortion in a fire.

halving and mortise-and-tenon joints, so jointing has generally been abandoned in the new structure in favour of direct fixing. Stainless steel bolts with dog-toothed shear-plates are sandwiched between the flushed and bolted members. The A-frames, the secondary rafters and purlins, and the vaulting sections are all assembled in this way, with no loss in strength or stability.

In days of old, construction of the vault would have been lengthy and laborious, each solid curved rib cut by hand. But today, the 130 ribs (some over 20ft long and weighing half a ton or more) are quickly assembled from 3-3½in laminations cut on a spindle moulder. The laminated sections are glued first with Cascamite, then clamped together and put in a heated polythene tent to cure overnight. Bonding is augmented by bolting at 8in staggered intervals, and the completed ribs are finally mortise-and-tenoned into the vertical boss backing-sections.

The carving

Boss carving — a delicate and unhurried task — goes on in a small workshop off the stonemason's yard. The four phlegmatic carvers, under the direction of master craftsman Geoff Butler, have been given artistic licence to produce a number of the 68 bosses, based on their personal selections on the theme of the *Benedicite*, a canticle celebrating the earth's physical

unusually high. The resulting inherent outward dynamic tendency is counteracted by fixing cross scissor-braces, tying the feet of the rafters to points below the frames' apex.

Traditional ribbed vaulting is being built below the roof. The vaulting will be a suspended structure tied at its extremities to projecting corbelling, and it offers unlimited scope for master craft. 68 carved and gilded bosses will embellish each set of converging ribs, a massive job of neck-straining artistry!

All constructional timber is prime English oak. A-frame specifications dictated the use of only specimen trees, which needed to be straight, comparatively branchless along a 40ft length, and without too much heart- and sapwood. Most of the trees were donated from large estates, but because of the exacting quality requirements, some were rejected and more had to be bought. Hedgerow oaks go for the vaulting timbers, whose specification isn't quite so high. They are large-diameter butts — ideal for sawing the curved vault planking.

A-frame timber, surprisingly, is used unseasoned. It matures *in situ*, and suffers no ill effects, but the oak for the vaulting is air-dried for six to nine months, then kiln dried for another six. Moisture content must be below 20%.

All the wood is sawn and planed in the Minster's own workshops, deliberately oversize to allow charring from up to one hour of exposure to full flame without collapsing. The fire threat is acknowledged!

The massive A-frames are assembled on the ground, using a radically different fixing system from traditional jointing. It's been established that the most fire-vulnerable parts of previous structures have been the

● **Above:** *view from above of work on the vault. The diagonals in the further half are yet to be fit.* **Below:** *you can get a clear idea of the relationship between the A-frame rafters and the vault inside*

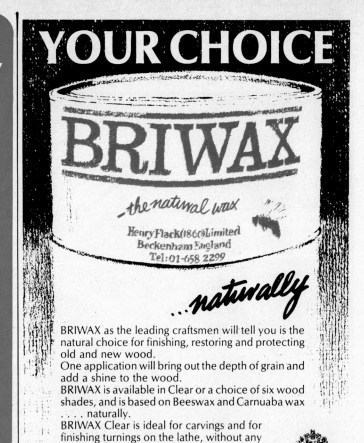
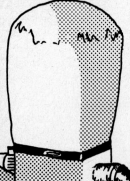

458

Resurrection

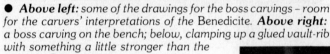

● **Above left:** *some of the drawings for the boss carvings – room for the carvers' interpretations of the* Benedicite. **Above right:** *a boss carving on the bench; below, clamping up a glued vault-rib with something a little stronger than the average G-cramp!*

wonders. The outer rows of bosses will all be the traditional foliage pattern, except for six very small ones, designed by children in a BBC 'Blue Peter' competition.

The bosses are made up of glued oak laminations, like the rib vaulting. They may be up to 42in square, and can take up to three weeks each to carve. Each carver works from drawings by the bench; after carving, the bosses are glued and bolted into position ready for painting and gilding.

The future

The need both to prevent and restrict future fires is a paramount consideration in the design. Dimensions have been increased to prolong stability, conventional jointing has been rejected in favour of bolting, and several other additional measures are proposed. Instead of using the traditional oak matchwood planking between the vaulting ribs and bosses, plaster will be applied to metal laths to inhibit flame spread, while the roof space will be compartmented to contain fire. But perhaps the most innovatory precautionary features will be the bottom-hinged roof trapdoors, devised to vent fire. They will be built under the sheet-lead roof covering at intervals along each pitch, and will be fitted with heat-sensitive catches designed to trigger if the temperature rises quickly. The low melting-point of lead should ensure unimpeded venting, but if the covering does remain intact, the positions of the open trapdoors can be determined from the outside by locating roof studding put there for the purpose. Firemen's axes would do the rest. New internal, heat- and smoke-detectors will be installed, and modern lightning conductors on the external pin-

nacles will be connected to an earthing tape which girdles the Minster.

Many months of dogged and dedicated slog remain, before the south transept is re-dedicated in three or four years' time. Then the workforce will revert to their more prosaic duties of repair and maintenance;

knowing every time they look up the satisfaction of involvement in such a task. ■

● Our warmest thanks to Derek and Margaret Phillips at the Minster for their exertions in helping us prepare the first woodworking article on the restoration of the Minster to be published.

Woodcut craft

Tim Ashby introduces a popular and enjoyable method of putting your carving talents to graphic use

The art of producing prints from illustrations cut into wood blocks stretches back to the days of the Chinese Empire. This craft has since developed, both in the European and Oriental traditions, to encompass many techniques, styles and a rich diversity of images.

Compared with other forms of printing such as etching, screen printing and lithography, woodcut printmaking is a very direct method for creating original 'plates' or blocks. For those who love working in wood there is the twin fascination of producing a 'carved' object and a resulting printed picture. Here I want to introduce the newcomer to the art, a step-by-step approach to producing apparently complex yet attractive woodcut prints. The main ingredients of success are an understanding of the process, sharp tools, good timber — and, of course, patience and a steady hand.

One of the joys of producing woodcuts and woodcut prints is the diversity of their uses. The blocks themselves can make attractive plaques; the prints can be used for pictures, posters, frontispieces for books, or in groups as attractive murals. Also, consider photocopying your original prints, which can then be enlarged or reduced for greeting cards, letterheads and postcards; you might even like to experiment with printing on a variety of papers, cards and fabrics.

Timbers for woodcuts

It's important to differentiate between 'woodcuts' and 'wood engraving'. Essentially, woodcuts are created by carving reliefs in long-grained timber ('plankwood') with gouges, chisels and knives, while wood engravings are cut on composite blocks of endgrain with special engraving tools (fig.1).

● *The techniques aren't difficult, but you must be a bit of an artist. This design was drawn by Juan Wijngaard and cut by Tim Ashby*

Different results are achieved from both processes: Woodcuts are often bold and direct, while you can get incredibly fine detail from wood engravings. Different timbers are used for the two processes: I recommend cherry, pear, lime, maple and sycamore for woodcuts for their ease of working and smooth texture.

When purchasing your timber, make sure it's well seasoned and defect-free.

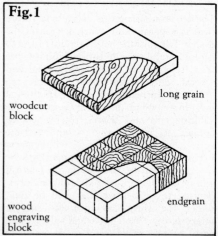

Fig.1

woodcut block

long grain

wood engraving block

endgrain

Preparing the block

Whether you buy timber in the rough or machined and cut to size, you need to check that it is planed *flat* on both main surfaces; that both main surfaces are *parallel* to each other; and that the surface on which you

● *Left: the block which made the print above. Note the specially designed handles on the tools*

will be cutting is sanded smooth. Wet and dry paper (180 and 240-grit) is ideal for this. The board needs stiffening to keep it flat, for which a simple, direct method is shown in fig. 2.

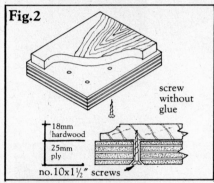

Fig.2

screw without glue

18mm hardwood
25mm ply

no.10x1½″ screws

Tracing

Once you have prepared your block, trace your chosen illustration on to the sanded block as follows:
● Fix carbon paper to the block with masking tape so the carbon is in contact with the timber.
● Position the tracing-paper illustration over the carbon *to allow a good inch of* timber outside all four borders of the illustration. Fix the tracing paper in position with masking tape, though remember that whichever way the illustration is fixed, the final print will be a reverse image.
● Trace all the black areas of the illustration, *including the borders*, on to the blocks so that an identical illustration will be transferred to it.
● Remove the tracing and carbon papers.

Tools

The tools for the various processes in producing woodcut prints are:

Preparing the block Jack and smoothing planes, straight-edge, marking gauge (for making sure both main surfaces of your board are marked parallel during planing), sanding block, drills, screwdrivers, drawing instruments.
Cutting the block Gouges, chisels, contour carver (or similar knife), mallet, oilstones, grinding wheel, sturdy bench or drawing board, good lighting, comfortable chair/stool.
Printing Roller, palette-knife, inking plate, burnisher (a wooden spoon can work well for this).

The tools for preparing the block are standard, but it's worth considering further the tools for cutting the block.

You can create a pattern on timber ready for printing with almost any metal implement — a sharp fork can produce interesting results! However, woodcut techniques (compared with engraving), generally need gouges, chisels and knives. These tools are easily available in their traditional carving and cabinetmaking profiles, and can all be used to good effect, though they do have certain drawbacks: because of the shape of the handles and the length of steel used, they don't sit comfortably in the hand for long periods and they prevent close contact with your material. Special woodcutting tools have evolved which are available from good hand-tool dealers; a number of different handle patterns and cutting profiles are also available. The woodcutting tools in fig. 3 comprise a useful range of profiles.

Sharp tools play an essential role in the success, fun and quality of your woodcut project. Every mark you make on the timber reflects the cutting action of the tool, and blunt instruments will produce blunt results. Be in tune with your tools, and make sure they're sharp.

The tools for printing are straightforward if you are producing hand-burnished prints

Fig.4

smooth cut with grain   cut tears against grain

(a technique used frequently by the Japanese). The roller and palette-knife are fairly standard art-shop materials; the inking plate can be made of sheet metal or thick glass. Wooden spoons can be used as burnishers. It isn't really worth considering a small printing press unless you intend to produce large volumes of prints.

Cutting the block

Once you have prepared your block, illustration and tools, start cutting the relief surface. But before you start, you must become acquainted with the cutting action of your tools — experiment on a sample of the timber you are using to see how both the tools and timber work.

When cutting your timber, avoid working against the grain, especially where it slopes sharply through the block, as this will tend to lift and tear the printing surface (fig. 4).

There are occasions, however, when you'll have to work against the grain. In this case, it's advisable to take shallow cuts with a **sharp** gouge, chisel or knife and then to gradually deepen the cut once you know the printing surface hasn't been damaged (it's wise to use shallow cuts initially anyway, as your tools will be easier to control).

Every cut you make on the block will represent a white area on your final print and the uncut areas will show black. It will be obvious from your traced illustration which are the white and black areas. Your main role is to remove the white areas cleanly with your tools in a direct, spontaneous and sensitive manner.

As you work the illustration, you'll need to see how your picture is progressing, which can be done by taking proofs. There are a number of ways to do this, and perhaps the most trouble-free method is with carbon paper. Tape it to the block the carbon facing *upwards*, lay a piece of white paper over the carbon and tape this to the block, then rub over the white paper with your burnisher and a carbon image of your relief will be transferred.

Should you make any mistakes with your tools, it's possible to repair the damaged area by inlaying a new piece of timber in that area. You can rework it later when the glue has set. In some cases, plastic wood can be used for minor repairs.

When you've finished cutting your picture, you'll need to remove waste wood outside the borders. Cut lines on the edge of the borders with a straight edge and sharp knife or scalpel; remove the waste timber, first with a gouge and mallet, then close to the border with a chisel.

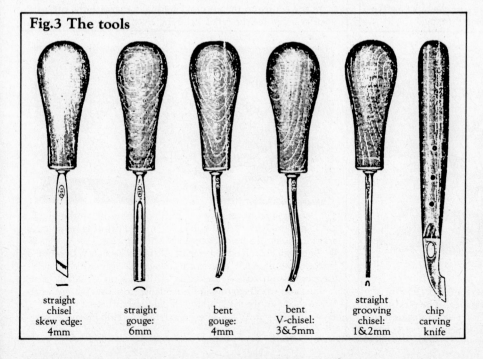

Fig.3 The tools

| straight chisel skew edge: 4mm | straight gouge: 6mm | bent gouge: 4mm | bent V-chisel: 3&5mm | straight grooving chisel: 1&2mm | chip carving knife |

Woodcut craft

Printing without a press

1 Spread enough ink on the inking plate with a palette knife (practice and experience will tell you how much is enough — according to the size of your block, the number of prints you are creating and the absorbency of your paper). Spread the ink evenly in all directions with the roller on the plate.

2 Spread an even coating of ink on to the block with the roller. A light touch with an easy rhythmic action is required — don't overload with ink, and avoid excessive pressure. Again, practice makes perfect. (You should make sure the block is free of dust and woodchips before commencing this stage.)

3 Carefully place the paper in position on the block (it's worth experimenting with different types of paper). The tackiness of the ink will 'grab' the paper, though it's best to position it quickly and cleanly without excessive movement.

4 Press the paper *lightly* with the palm of your hand, working from the centre out to the corners — avoid wrinkles in the paper. With your burnisher, work in small circular movements from the centre to the corners; gradually increase the pressure until you can see the relief 'grinning' evenly through the paper.

5 Working from one corner, peel your print from the block. Leave it to dry. When you have finished printing, your tools and block should be cleaned with white spirit. ■
● This article is an edited version of Ashby Design Workshop's Woodcut Foliopack *Woodcraft through the ages*; we're grateful for permission to use the material. Books on woodcut print making and wood engraving are available from the Ashby Design Workshop, as are ink, roller and palette-knife sets.
● Ashby Design Workshop, 34a Catherine Hill, Frome, Somerset BA11 1BY.

463

JAPAN 3
Twisted mystery

Alan Peters explains how to cut *Nejiri Arigata*, a Japanese 'twisted dovetail' to puzzle the brain and test the eye

Nejiri Arigata was taught to me by Kintaro Yazawa, a Japanese furniture maker — not in Japan but here in my workshop in Devon. Kintaro is not an elderly master of his craft, but a young university-educated craftsman working in an efficient, modern workshop in a quiet part of Kyushu Island. I never saw this joint while I was in Japan in 1975, nor on my later visits East to Korea or China, so I know nothing of its original uses, only that it's traditional and not new.

Kintaro arrived virtually on my doorstep with his wife Yoshiko and young son Ryohei during the cold winter of 1981/2. They were on a pilgrimage to England to study the British Arts and Crafts Movement, and the work of Gimson and the Barnsleys in particular. In the week or so Kintaro spent as my guest, he generously passed on the technique and mysteries of the joint, but it has taken four years and a major one-man exhibition to provide the excuse, time and incentive to build it into a piece of furniture!

The design of the low table is a nothing,

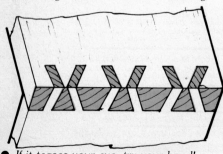

● *If it teases your eye, try your hand!*

● *A traditional joint from Japan, translated into distinctly English idiom, in downright English yew.* **Below,** *the table attracted much attention at Alan's exhibition*

in the sense that the very simple solution of one board cut into three and jointed at the corners has been exploited many times before. It is the mystery and intricacy of this joint and its fascinating visual appeal, plus a rather lovely slab of Devon-grown yew, which caused the table to attract the attention of visitors — particularly woodworkers — at my exhibition.

The joint is tremendously strong, and unlike a conventional dovetail, it can't be driven apart in a straight pull in either direction once it's assembled. But in many ways it's not actually a difficult joint to cut, as all the angles are a constant 75° which is merely reversed to 105°, and all the endgrain shoulders are at a normal 90°. The chief problem is that the joints can't be scribed from one piece to the other as can normal dovetails and pins, so each piece has to be accurately marked out and cuts made to the line without reference to each other. I also encountered difficulty assembling and gluing the 20in-wide table, so I'd strongly recommend a shorter trial joint than my arrogant first attempt!

Here is the procedure I adopted, which I would recommend:

1 Materials I chose yew for its decorative qualities, but it was an unwise choice because of the wildness of the grain. Choose a clean, mild-grained hardwood which saws and chisels cleanly and which will allow you to see your marking out clearly.

2 Preparation The timber should be machined or hand-finished to accurate width and thickness, and then accurately cross-cut into the three pieces.

3 Setting out I didn't allow for any joint projections to be flushed off afterwards, but gauged my shoulder lines exactly to the thickness of the material — 1¼in. The gauge lines were heavily incised on the inside surfaces, but lightly cut on the outside.

4 Positioning of joints As with decorative dovetailing, it takes trial and error with dividers, plus some judgement, to arrive at a well-proportioned and aesthetically pleasing row of joints purpose-measured for the width of your board. End and top have to be marked out at the same time; your point of reference is the shoulder-line on top of the top surface (**A**, fig. 2) and the inside top corner of the ends (**B**). At these points the setting out should be identical on all pieces. Accurately mark it all out with a pencil, a single bevel and dividers for accurate positioning, and *do carefully mark in all the waste* in bold colour. Whether you feel the need to mark out on the inside surfaces is a matter of experience. I never do in dovetailing, and I didn't here either, but you may feel more confident if every surface is completed.

5 Cutting the top You'll discover that what you are actually doing is cutting a series of identical parallel slots, and I see no reason why with a little ingenuity, this part at any rate couldn't be cut with machinery. I decided not to risk it on that lovely expanse of yew, and cut them as a row of dovetails, aiming to leave the cut surfaces direct from the saw with no paring. I consider it bad practice to adjust the workpiece in the vice to get a cut at 90° to the bench — far better to perfect the technique of following any angle required without having to remove it from the vice.

6 Removing the waste I used a coping saw, and pared back to the shoulder-lines with a chisel as normal. Check the rows of slots carefully; if you are unlucky you may have to pare back to your pencil lines, but do this and any other tidying up *before* attempting to cut the two end pieces.

It's also possible that you have had to increase the width of the odd slot or recess because of inaccurate sawing. If so, ensure that you alter the corresponding marking-out on the appropriate end.

7 Cutting the ends Here your aim is two series of parallel tenons all identical in angle and thickness, unless they've

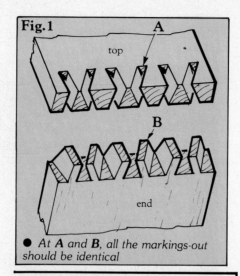

● At **A** and **B**, all the markings-out should be identical

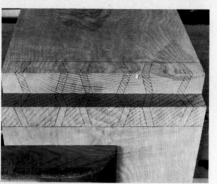

Marking out – see above

Slots on the top: 'tails are straight from the saw

Finishing the ends – the 'open socket' goes

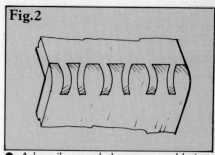

● A heavily rounded corner would give this effect

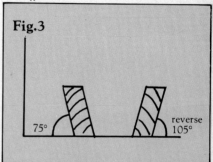

● Simply a matter of one angle and its reverse!

'Pins' on the ends – a series of identical angled tenons

The end; 'pins' should have been adjusted according to 'tails'

Twisted mystery

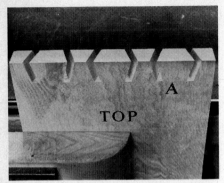

The top cleaned up and ready for fitting

Fitting the joint one way . . .

And fitting it the other

Start fitting from here. Top and end must be moved into each other little by little from alternate directions

Simple: a perfect fit first time out! Now for the glue and final finish

been modified for previous errors. The problem is that they are all at a compound angle, and therefore require extra care in sawing to the line. The waste is once again removed with a coping saw, and pared back to the shoulder-lines. The aim as before, and as in all hand dovetailing, is a fit direct from the saw cut. Anything short of that is a failure. But of course we all fall short of the ideal at times, and you may have to pare the odd one or two back to your pencil lines.

8 Fitting up dry This is the most difficult part and calls for a not-too-tight fit. The point of entry is at **B** in fig. 1, and it's advisable to lay the top upside down on the bench and drive the ends on to it. I used a club hammer and a large hardwood block,

driving partly downwards but more from the outside inwards, and in fact I ended up clamping the top down to the bench itself.

As this was only a dry run, I didn't drive it completely home, but drove it off again, eased the odd spot that bruising showed to be obviously too tight, and then sanded up my interior surfaces ready for the final assembly.

9 Final assembly I covered some stout hardwood blocks with leather, to allow me to exert clamping pressure both downwards and along the length of the top. I also concentrated on only one end at a time. As with good dovetails, I think cramps probably need not be used, but I was pleased that I had taken the precaution of preparing them because I simply couldn't drive my second end down to the shoulder-lines.

I used a PVA-based adhesive sparingly on the side grain, and not at all on the endgrain except on the four outside shoulders. The leather on the blocks is obviously to avoid damage to the workpiece, but it also absorbs any discrepancies on the surface where the joints are, enabling pressure to be exerted on each individual portion of the joint.

I didn't have to maintain the cramps in position, but merely used them to force up the joints. ∎

● Alan's exhibition is at the Cooper Gallery, Barnsley until 25 May, where it has come from Cheltenham and Bath. Colin Wilson took the colour pictures.

● Our warm thanks to Paul Bertorelli, editor of *Fine Woodworking* magazine, Newtown, CT 06470, USA, for whom Alan originally prepared the article.

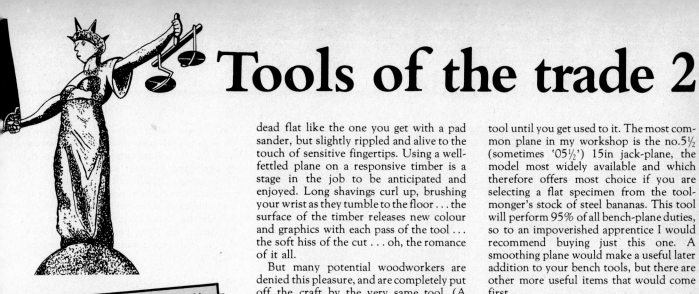

Tools of the trade 2

'We propose a major series assembling a basic kit of hand-tools for the young apprentice cabinetmaker or serious amateur woodworker. The object will be to locate the very best saws, planes, chisels, gauges, etc. currently available.

'Each tool will be tested by a skilled cabinetmaker in my workshop, who uses similar tools every day in his work. Chisels will be polished, honed and checked for hardness of steel. Planes will be examined for flatness, smoothness of adjustment and accuracy of casting. Gauges will be checked for accuracy and fitness for purpose.

'All tools will be put to the most critical examination and tested within the bounds of the normal activity of the professional workshop. I do not advise manufacturers to submit products that they do not believe will stand comparison with the best in the field.'

BENCH PLANES

David Savage continues his close look at the basic bench tools on the market, and explains the art of tuning a plane

Our forefathers wouldn't have looked on the hand plane with the same affection that we do today. Their material was probably prepared entirely by hand planing — very exacting, backbreaking work; but, nowadays machines gobble our rough boards, spitting out dimensioned timber ready for jointing and fitting. The hand plane now often comes second to the power sander as a finishing tool, and I know many workshops have almost completely dispensed with it. Nevertheless, there are many of us who still enjoy using a plane for delicate fitting and, where the job demands it, for putting a final finish on surfaces.

We are blessed in this country with native hardwoods that generally react well to hand-tools. Oak, ash, chestnut, beech and sycamore will all take a fine polished surface straight from the plane. The hand plane will also leave a 'tooled' surface, not dead flat like the one you get with a pad sander, but slightly rippled and alive to the touch of sensitive fingertips. Using a well-fettled plane on a responsive timber is a stage in the job to be anticipated and enjoyed. Long shavings curl up, brushing your wrist as they tumble to the floor . . . the surface of the timber releases new colour and graphics with each pass of the tool . . . the soft hiss of the cut . . . oh, the romance of it all.

But many potential woodworkers are denied this pleasure, and are completely put off the craft by the very same tool. (A certain well-known power tool manufacturer promotes an electric plane with a visual display of hand planing at its most unpleasant!) It's easy to understand the predicament; you buy a plane — it should work, after all it's new — there isn't much to it, is there? So the instructions go into the bin along with the box. Boyhood memories of my frustration with this bloody implement (no matter how I tinkered, it still wouldn't get the same results as the school planes) still give me every sympathy with the owners of recalcitrant smoothers and truculent try-planes.

tool until you get used to it. The most common plane in my workshop is the no.5½ (sometimes '05½') 15in jack-plane, the model most widely available and which therefore offers most choice if you are selecting a flat specimen from the toolmonger's stock of steel bananas. This tool will perform 95% of all bench-plane duties, so to an impoverished apprentice I would recommend buying just this one. A smoothing plane would make a useful later addition to your bench tools, but there are other more useful items that would come first.

Fettling a plane may take as much as two days' solid work; Fraser Budd's excellent article 'Plane speaking' (WW/Feb), tells you a great deal, and illustrates the functions of the mouth, cutter, frog and back-iron clearly.

Checking the tools

Amongst the weapons selected by the manufacturers as examples of the best of their product lines, Stanley and Record Marples each presented a no.5½ and a no.4 smoother for examination. Footprint only

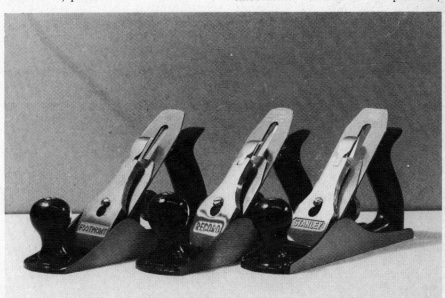

● All in a row . . . no.4 smoothers from Footprint, Record and Stanley. Where is the new plane that needs no fettling?

It must be said I have also considerable sympathy with plane manufacturers, who are trying to produce what should be a very exact instrument in a material that's almost as dimensionally unstable as timber. Cost factors and the various applications of the hand plane mean plane makers have the problem of mass-producing to a price a very personal product which must be modified later by the user.

The bench-plane chosen for general cabinet work would be between 15 and 22in long, either a 'jack', a 'fore' or a 'jointer'; the choice is largely a personal one. Many cabinetmakers argue that the longer the plane the more accurate and flatter the work but a 22in jointer is a cumbersome

presented a no.4, although they do a no.5 as well. Paramo presented the PM10 Planemaster, a disposable-cutter plane, and Bristol Design, one of the smallest plane makers and a welcome addition to the market, produced a gunmetal-bodied no.A5 panel plane and a no.A3 'coffin shaped' smoothing plane. It's rather sad that no wooden-bodied planes were available for testing. I believe the wish to have a plane with easy adjustment of the blade has made wooden planes almost obsolete, which is a pity since they are generally nice to handle and much lighter to use; they're more slippery on the work.

I'll start with Bristol Design, since their products are so different from the others.

467

Tools of the trade 2

● *David's own 14in Norris panel plane lined up in front of the Bristol Design version. Note the difference in handle and 'bun' shapes*

Their A5, which seems to be based on the Norris 14in panel plane, is made from a cast gunmetal channel fitted with rosewood filling and screw adjustment. It's very attractively priced at £150, so it isn't directly comparable with either the cheaper standard bench planes or the genuine Norris, which would cost considerably more. The image presented is one of quality, but the reality was rather disappointing. The plane had a sole that arched from toe to heel with a gap at the centre of about 0.3mm — about the same as the other jack-planes in the test. It would take some hours to flatten. The sides were out of square to the sole by an amount I would find unacceptable, and which would inhibit the tool's use on a shooting-board. Although correction for square could be made by adjusting the iron, this shouldn't be necessary.

Bristol Design use old Marples irons in their new planes, which must be a good idea because these heavy, thick blades were laminated and could hold a keen edge for many work hours. The iron and back-iron could have done with some attention; both were somewhat old and pitted. The blade is located by a very positive and smooth-acting adjustment and fixed by a screw lever-cap, which is attached to the body by steel set-screws that protrude crudely beyond the sides, again making the plane difficult to use on the shooting-board.

The mouth has a great effect in determining the performance of a plane. I checked every bench plane in my workshop, and found the mouth of every one was set at about 0.5mm. The mouth gap can be set on models with a moveable frog, but on 'fixed mouth' planes such as this, the way the maker has mouthed the tool is of paramount importance. This plane had a mouth (the gap ahead of the blade when it's set to cut) of 1.5mm. It was out of square with the sides by 1mm, and wasn't filed straight but in a slight curve. Thomas Norris would be sucking his teeth; but there's more to come. The plane was passed around three other woodworkers, all of whom found the enclosed handle very uncomfortable. The problem seems to be the size of opening and its closeness to the iron,

which prevents long-fingered people from extending a guide finger behind the blade, as a Norris A1 would allow. Short-fingered users seem to have a similar complaint, wanting the aperture less upright and further back.

The coffin-shaped smoother based on a Slater plane was considerably better, I'm pleased to report. It had a sole, as usual, that needed flattening, and the sides were out of square, but as a smoother is almost never used on its side this isn't important. The adjustment was again good and smooth, this time with a more easily gripped knurled knob. The lever-cap was again attached by those crude set-screws, but everything else was rather good. The set of the mouth on this plane was good at 0.75mm, which suggests that handmade planes vary as much today as they have always done. The gunmetal and rosewood are finished very nicely on both planes.

I'm sorry to sound so critical of detail and design, because really I support Bristol Design's initiative without reserve. The products, when detail problems have been resolved, should represent very good value. Planes can also be purchased in kit form at approximately 50% of the finished price, but if you add an extra £30 for the nice adjustment mechanism it's still costly for an apprentice.

I didn't spend any time with the Paramo

PM10 Planemaster, which is a throwaway-blade plane. I would regard this as more a tool for the home maintenance market, though there are reports that with a bit of fettling a good result can be achieved.

The bench plane in general use today is cast iron, examples of which were provided for test by Record Marples, Stanley and Footprint. All these planes are similar in design and performance, so I'll discuss them as a group.

Sole and sides

None of them were flat, although the Stanley 5½ and the Footprint no.4 would have needed the least work to get them so. The no.4 Footprint smoother had the best finish to the sole. The best solution to the 'banana syndrome' is to go to your friendly (patient!) toolmonger equipped to find a flat plane. When you have looked at the entire stock, choose the next best thing — a plane that's nearly flat. In my workshop we work the plane across a 100-grit sanding belt which has been stretched along the bed of the jointer. (The machine is electrically isolated and we take care to keep the dust out of the machine bearings.) It may take several hours of patient rubbing to get a good result, so do it a bit at a time; a plane may also go out of true once it's flattened, so check periodically. It may take quite a time to make sure the thing is stone dead.

The sides of a jack should be at 90° to the sole, to enable it to be used on the shooting-board. Here again the Stanley 5½ came nearest, with the right side, (used most) at exactly 90°. If you were left-handed, the Record 5½ I had would have suited you, as the left side was pretty near 90°. The sides can be trued up with a file if you're good at

● *No.5½s from Stanley and Record. Right angles on the right and left respectively!*

metalwork, but it's best to take your plane to a small engineering shop to do it. Once the sole is either ground or machined flat, and square, polish it with a honing stone; this will help the tool slip more easily across the job. Fussing round flattening the sole like this may seem a lot of bother, but if you think of a plane as a chisel in a flat-bed jig, taking a shaving of one hair-thickness, it becomes clear why that jig should guide so accurately.

Blade and back-iron

Next examine the blade and back-iron. The blade (sometimes called an iron) should have a flat back, which you should check with a straight-edge against the light. All the planes' irons were good except the one on the Record 5½, which would have taken a great deal of honing to get flat. Even if it is dead flat, all the marks on the blade should be polished out by rubbing the back on a honing stone, held flat.

We use Japanese water-stones, which give a better result faster than even the best natural oil-stone. Once the back of the blade is brought up to an even mirror-polish for the first 10mm or so, you can start on the other side, on which the cutting bevel is ground. The back of your iron should now only ever be honed on your finest stone; the mirror-polish, which shows that scratches in the steel have been removed, guarantees you will have no jagged serrations at the cutting edge which do nothing for the quality of cut.

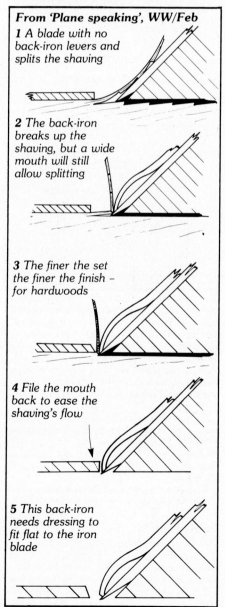

From 'Plane speaking', WW/Feb

1 *A blade with no back-iron levers and splits the shaving*

2 *The back-iron breaks up the shaving, but a wide mouth will still allow splitting*

3 *The finer the set the finer the finish – for hardwoods*

4 *File the mouth back to ease the shaving's flow*

5 *This back-iron needs dressing to fit flat to the iron blade*

The bevel on the blade should be ground at 25°, to a slight curve. This may sound mad — a plane's job is flattening things, and a curved iron goes against this idea — but think of the advantages. If the cutting edge of the iron is straight, or even straight across with rounded corners, you are pushing that entire width through the job, and a 50mm-wide shaving takes a lot of push. Also, if your blade isn't set exactly square to the sole, one corner or the other will dig in and you will end up ploughing furrows down that table-top. If the blade is slight curved, three things happen. **1** the blade only cuts in the centre of the plane, eliminating the ploughed-field problem; **2** the ribbon of shaving is narrow and therefore lighter to cut and more under control, and **3** the shavings feather out to nothing towards the edges. A fingertip run across a planed surface will detect slight parallel hollows and ridges, invisible to the eye. It's difficult to say how much of a curve to put on a plane iron. A jack-plane may take a 1mm curve across the width, a smoother much less. The curve is so slight, it's almost not there. Remember also that with honing, the carefully-put-in curve is gradually flattened out, and the ribbon of shaving becomes un-comfortably wide.

Honing a curve takes a bit of 'touch'. Find the 25° grinding angle, slightly lift the blade so the tip is touching, then pull back. The entire top half of your body should rock back and forth, your arms, wrists and fingers locked, holding that angle. After two or three pulls on a water-stone, you'll see a tiny burr develop on the edge. There's no short cut to honing; that burr must be formed and then removed, and the way in which it's removed will determine the quality of the edge. We do it on a 'Gold' polishing water-stone, wiping the burr first on the back then the front until it falls away. No stropping on the hand or bits of leather, that burr must be polished off, not broken. Test it on the hairs of your forearm — it should shave them with a dry crackling sound.

The back-iron should be fitted until no light can be seen between it and the blade (see Fraser Budd, WW/Feb, for details). Of the planes tested, Record back-irons seemed to fit slightly better than Stanley, but there was very little in it. Footprint use a back-iron similar to the Stanley type, but it fitted well. All would need some gentle rubbing on the water-stone to ensure a perfect fit. The back-iron should sit tightly against the cutting-iron, about 1mm (or less) back from the edge depending on the wood you're planing.

Frog and adjuster

Next adjust the frog, the block of steel on which the cutting-iron sits. This is moved back and forth to adjust the gap in front of the cutting-iron as it protrudes through the sole, and this mouth, as I mentioned earlier, should be very narrow. We are generally working dry hardwood to remove fine

shavings, so a narrow mouth is important to hold the timber down ahead of the blade — particularly important when working wild-grained material. With softwood or if you want to take a lot off a narrow edge, the mouth obviously needs to be wider.

The Footprint and Stanley planes I had were well-mouthed, a straight gap at 90° to the plane sides. The Record Marples' mouths weren't quite so straight and true. Any inaccuracy here could be solved by gentle file work to relieve the metal at the front of the mouth (see Fraser Budd for details).

The seating of the blade on the frog could be checked with engineer's blue, if you were really obsessional, but a quick check with a square for flatness should be all that's necessary.

Most problems with planes can be overcome with time and careful attention, but the adjustment mechanism has very little scope for improvement as far as I know. The knurled-knob-and-Y-lever design of adjustment is slow to operate, with as much as two full turns of slack between forward and reverse actions. Stanley are the worst offenders. Record Marples are a bit better with one turn of lost motion, despite a less substantial-looking mechanism. The little Footprint smoother really came out well; the adjustment mechanism has a substantial yoke with only quarter-turn of lost motion, which makes the adjustment on this tool considerably easier and faster.

All the planes presented were nicely finished with very few rough edges. Record Marples still use stained beech handles, as do Footprint. Footprint handles are slightly larger than most and very comfortable. The knurling to the brass adjustment knob on the Footprint smoother was rather crude, and the finish on the cutting-iron rather coarse.

Does all this fiddling about seem an unending bore? To get a £40 plane to perform as well as a £400 Norris is a fiddle, I'm afraid — it can be hard work and it will take you some time, but it's possible. Apart from differences in the quality of steel for the cutting-iron, I believe a well-fettled production plane can be as effective a precision instrument as the very best of the Norrises.

Comment and conclusion

These articles on tools may give the false impression that the tools are fundamentally important. Nothing is further from the truth; the work — and only the work — is of fundamental importance. Everything else is only a matter of the means of achieving the standards we set ourselves. The *activity* of removing long ribbons of silk-like shaving is the attraction, not the ownership of the instrument that produced them.

Adjust a plane slowly; sight down the sole to see the blade just emerging, and do it in good light so the contrast between blade and sole is greatest. Run a dab of candle-wax down the plane sole and draw two or three chalk-lines across the job. Now begin

Tools of the trade 2

● *The Paramo PM10; a useful mouth the width of the body, but should we rely on disposable blades?*

— with the grain. Press down, keeping your nose above the frog, and watch how the ribbons are emerging. Don't let the plane run away from you, go with it. It should be possible to stop in mid-stroke, change your stance, then carry on with the same shaving. The chalk-lines will tell you where you have removed material and where you haven't. Clean up a board slowly and systematically, one shave all over.

What can we say or do to prevent people buying hand-planes in good faith, finding they don't perform well, and blaming themselves? Stanley provide a miserable booklet that explains in several languages how to fiddle about with every plane in their product range. Record only do two languages, but fare rather worse. Neither document is going to win a design award. Stanley hop around from page to page, language to language, but generally somewhere have most of the information. Record Marples' guidance for users is more sketchy and even less clear. I didn't get Footprint's leaflet, which describes their range and includes 'hints and tips on use, care and maintenance'; I don't think Bristol Design do one.

How did the planes compare? I hope Bristol Design get their act together and produce some nice tools; Paramo have at least attempted to solve the problem of the plane that doesn't work straight from the box, but in doing so have sacrificed some 'personal potential', notably the chance of fettling blade and back-iron as well as body and sole. Record Marples and Stanley produce such similar products that it's difficult to recommend one — especially when your local shop may have better or worse examples than the ones we tested. If pressed, I'd probably select the Stanley products and get used to the very poor adjustment mechanism. Footprint produced what is for me the most interesting product. It's well made, and the one I got

required the minimum of fettling.

I believe it is unreasonable to expect manufacturers to make precision instru-

ments at production prices. But planes as they're sold today won't plane wood straight from the box — full stop. The techniques for upgrading the products, to whatever degree of tune you demand, should be more clearly set out. A wood-worker's equivalent of the Government Health Warning should be attached to every new plane — 'This tool can damage you self-esteem — read the enclosed leaflet'! ■

● **Next month:** block and shoulder planes.

● David and *Woodworker* would like to thank the following tool manufacturers and distributors for the loan of tools, their co-operation and assistance, without which the test series would have been impossible:
Bristol Design, 14 Perry Rd, Bristol BS1 5BG, tel. (0272) 291740
Footprint Tools, PO Box 19, Hollis Croft, Sheffield S1 3HY, tel. (0742) 753200
Lester-Brown Machine Tools (Ulmia importer), Coventry Rd, Fillongley CV7 8DZ, tel. (0676) 40456
Paramo (Clay) Hallamshire Works, Rockingham St, Sheffield S1 3NW, tel. (0742) 25262/3
Rabone Chesterman, Camden St, Birmingham B1 3DB, tel. 021-233 3300
Record Marples, Parkway Works, Sheffield S9 3BL, tel. (0742) 449066
Sandvik, Manor Way, Halesowen B62 8QZ, tel. 021-550 4700
Sarjents Tools, 44 Oxford Rd, Reading RG1 7LH, tel. (0734) 586522
Stanley Tools, Woodside, Sheffield S3 9PD, tel. (0742) 78678
Tilgear (Ulmia supplier), 20 Ladysmith Rd, Enfield EN1 3AA, tel. 01-363 8050

Recommended retail prices

Maker	Model	Price inc. VAT
Bristol Design	A5	£150 with adjuster
		£80 kit
	A3	£110 with adjuster
		£55 kit
Footprint	no. 4 smoother	£21.56
Paramo	PM10 Planemaster	£21.56
Record Marples	no. 5½ jack	£40.09
	no. 4 smoother	£25.36
Stanley	no. 5½ jack	£39.30
	no. 4 smoother	£24.80

● We asked manufacturers for their replies:

Bristol Design

We are indeed a small (very small!) manufacturer, and initially intended producing traditional British planes to fill a supply problem — not enough good-condition older planes.

We wanted to produce planes similar to older ones, not replicas but user's tools. We tried staying traditional with some items, such as screws holding caps in place, but experimented in other areas such as a round front fub (handle) on the panel plane and a non-knurled knob on the adjustment mechanism.

David Savage's comments on such things as knurling and screws were partly preceded by design changes in the making. On our smaller planes, the pins holding lever caps are already being ground off on the surface grinder, and both of the smoothing, the mitre and the panel planes should have this by May. Flatness and squareness of sides is a problem now solved on most of our models; the panel plane is ground with a larger surface grinder.

The handle holes in the parallel-sided smoothing plane (not covered in the test) and

the panel plane are too small. The original idea was that a user could open this up and shape it exactly to fit his/her hand, but we must accept that this isn't on (except in kit form of course), and produce a 'universal' larger handle, in the panel plane with more room in front of it as well. Most of our planes do have very fine mouths (some only as wide as the thickness of paper) and the wide mouth is being corrected in the panel plane.

We now have secured a large stock of unused older irons of very high quality (British ones, probably comparable to the best current Japanese laminated ones) and are supplying these in all our finished planes, the kits and separately.

We will be closed from 21 May-25 June except for limited service in the shop on Saturdays.
Charles Stirling

Footprint

Though we were by and large pleased with the results of the test, it's obvious there is still scope for improvement, and to this end we have taken steps to attain a finer finish on the cutting iron and better knurling on the brass adjustment-knob.
C. J. Jewitt

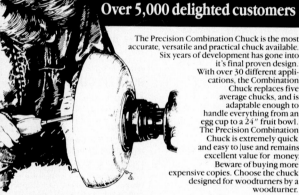
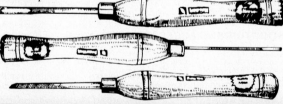

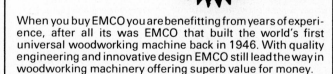

471

473

Window on the world

JOINERY CLASSICS

Woodworker opens an occasional series on the major tasks in building and constructional woodwork. Where better to start than the double-hung sliding sash window, as made by Graham Hewitt?

W indows have two functions: they admit light and they ventilate. They must also, of course, keep the worst of the weather firmly outside. My windows let in light, and they also ventilated, even when they were closed and air was unwanted! Riddled with woodworm and slowly rotting, they would have to go.

A quick visit to the local depot of a large national joinery firm revealed ill-fitting joints and rough and bruised surfaces. I also realised my non-standard openings would require awkward rebuilding of the standard frames, all of which convinced me I should make my own.

I hoped Ken Austin would throw some light on double-hung vertically sliding sash windows. His *Contract Joinery* illustrates a construction using solid jambs and spring balances housed in grooves; it gives appropriate dimensions for the sash sections and shows jointing methods. The solid jamb design seemed more straightforward than the traditional cased (box) construction, and never one to opt for a difficult course when an easy one presents itself, I chose this method. The naming of parts is in fig. 1.

Preliminaries

Before my next step — scale drawings and a cutting list — I had to think about how to locate the window in the opening, for this would determine its overall dimensions. My window opening in this case is in a stone wall about 30in thick, formed by a brickwork lip built out from the stone against which the window-frame butts (fig. 2). The frame sits quite well back in the reveal of a south-facing wall, which gives a double advantage — the worst of the weather (when it's not raining, it's about to rain) sweeps past the window not on to it, and the inset position gives it even more protection.

Careful measuring from the outside and various nervous remeasurings determined the overall size of the frame, from which I calculated a cutting list for a timber merchant to produce my sawn Brazilian mahogany boards. The British Woodworking Federation booklet *A Specifier's Guide to Wood Windows* specifies an average moisture content for exterior joinery of 16%±3%, which should fall within the range of most kiln-dried timber sold by commercial yards.

But before my final scale drawings I had to make one further decision — whether to install single or double glazing. The public's conversion to the merits of double glazing has no doubt warmed many a salesman's heart, to say nothing of insulating his bank balance, but as Barry Richardson points out in *Remedial Treatment of Buildings*, close fitting curtains can be almost as effective. Since sealed units eventually fail and trap condensation, I decided that single glazing plus thick curtains, shutters in the splayed reveals and full draught-stripping, would provide more than adequate insulation. Shutters and curtains may not prevent condensation on the glass, so if this is a problem, sealed units with the optimum 20mm air-gap may be a better solution.

The final sizes of the various components are shown in the horizontal and vertical sections (fig. 3) and may be modified within the overall relationship of the parts. Two critical measurements, however, are the size of the opening and the external dimensions of the frame, for the window must sit in the opening so the external finishing — brickwork, render or whatever — makes it weathertight.

● *From the inside looking out; a solid joinery job, but not so simple*

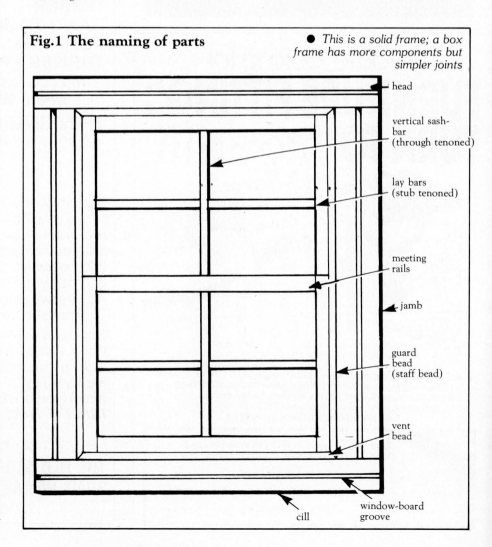

Fig.1 The naming of parts

● *This is a solid frame; a box frame has more components but simpler joints*

- head
- vertical sash-bar (through tenoned)
- lay bars (stub tenoned)
- meeting rails
- jamb
- guard bead (staff bead)
- vent bead
- cill
- window-board groove

Fig.2 Window reveal

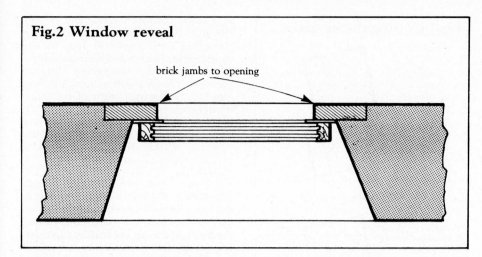

brick jambs to opening

Fig.3 Vertical and horizontal sections

All dimensions metric

spiral balances

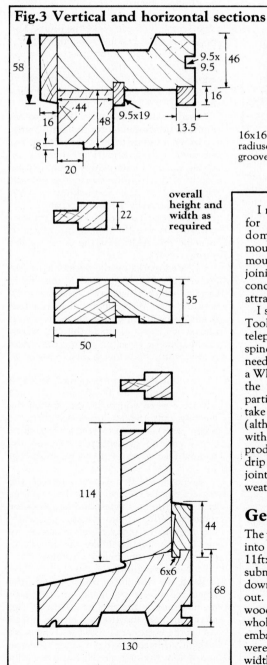

9.5x 9.5

46

58

16

44

48

9.5x19

16

13.5

8

20

16x16 radiused groove

44

22

overall height and width as required

35

50

114

44

6x6

68

130

had soon decided how to cut the parts out economically. Then I transferred the plan to each individual board with adhesive freezer labels, making sure that what I had decided on paper was feasible in practice, allowing for saw-kerfs, planing and cross-cutting.

Needless to say, the first board presented the first problem. It had to be crosscut in the middle in a sort of 'Z'. A jig-saw would have proved useful, but as it was, I crosscut the two legs of the Z with a handsaw and then scraped away with the blade of a coping-saw until I had made enough start on the parallel-grain cut to insert a padsaw. Absurd, but I would know better next time. I crosscut each board according to the plan with a portable circular saw, and then ripped the pieces to width on the table-saw ready for planing. I labelled them on the endgrain and stacked them in neat piles to avoid confusion before planing and thicknessing. It's also a good idea to write the finished dimensions on the ends for easy reference: pink chalk or a contrasting-coloured wax crayon is ideal for this.

The frames

The frame is the first part to do. It consists of:
- head and jambs 114x44mm   from 2in stuff
- cill   130x68mm   from 3in;
- outer lining   58x16mm   from 1in;
- parting bead   9.5x19mm   from 1in;
- guard bead   13.5x16mm   from 1in;
- vent bead   13.5x44mm.

The guard bead is screwed into a shallow rebate for positive location, and forms a channel with the parting bead, which is a hand-tight dry fit in its groove. This channel is 45.5mm wide and contains the bottom sash, which is 44mm thick. The extra 1.5mm is for clearance and to allow seasonal movements. The outer channel is identical and is formed on the outside by the outer lining, which is screwed to the head and jambs.

With all the frame members dimensioned and crosscut oversize, work can begin on the various grooves and rebates. First the cill. This has a 12° bevel in two steps, a 9.5x9.5mm window-board groove, a 6x6mm groove for the vent bead, and a mortar channel and drip mould on the underside. I cut the bevels on the circular

I made the sash members square, partly for simplicity and partly because my domestic specifier considered that mouldings only trap dust. Traditional mouldings would have slightly complicated joining methods, but as far as appearance is concerned, square sections seem quite attractive to us.

I sent my drawings to Whitehill Spindle Tools in Luton who very obligingly telephoned me to explain what special spindle-moulder cutters they thought I needed, which I subsequently ordered. I got a Whitehill block, cutters for the groove for the balances, the glazing rebates, the parting-bead housing and the grooves to take the window-boards or plasterboard (although these could have been formed with a router). I also needed a cutter to produce the mortar channel, one for the drip mould, also a slotting disc for the comb joints and a groover for the router to cut the weatherstripping slot.

Getting out the stock

The preliminaries over, I strode confidently into the 'machine shop' and wrestled an 11ftx9in board of mahogany, which finally submitted after two falls and a knock-down, on to the Workmate for marking out. After several more humiliations from wooden opponents I finally twigged that the whole thing could be done with less embarrassment on paper, since the boards were square-edged and pretty regular in width for their whole length. A few rectangles on the back of a large envelope, and I

● *The deep walls meant a wide cill and extra cladding – plus a useful shelf*

saw with the table (or arbor) tilted, and finished them off with a plane and belt sander. Set the tilt on the saw to 12°, adjust the rip-fence to the right of the blade, and make a deep cut for the large bevel with the blade height not quite up to a mark 59mm from what will be the inside edge. This 59mm is the thickness of the vent bead plus the sash thickness and clearance allowance. The second bevel is cut with the rip-fence on the left of the blade to a mark 13.5mm from the inside edge. This manoeuvre requires care as the cill must be held tight to the fence against the slope of the table (if your table tilts), while the blade remains unguarded. It is also, I must emphasise, **not** to be attempted without assistance, and is anyway in contravention of the 1974 Woodworking Machinery regulations. Alternatively, with the table level, a wedge-shaped batten could be clamped to the table with the fence on the right, and the cill passed over the shaped batten. If your blade tilts rather than the table, you will work differently — but it's a dicey operation either way. You can always make the bevel with a hand-plane! Finally, with the blade set low and the table level (or blade vertical) a cut is made on the top face of the cill to remove waste. My method of cutting bevels is shown in fig. 4.

Next you cut a series of grooves and rebates on the jambs, head and cill, for which some offcuts of the same dimensions are useful to mark out the positions of the parting bead, balance grooves, guard-bead rebate, and window-board groove. I used a vernier caliper and scriber to mark the end-grain, and scored the waste parts in pencil, to avoid lapses into the vernacular. Then you juggle with the spindle moulder till you get the correct cut for each pass, using the offcuts to test the settings. Any spindle moulder work, you'll find, is far quicker and more efficient if you remember to machine enough dimensioned sizes for test-offcuts.

Crosscut the frame members for jointing. I used twin mortise-and-tenon joints for the frame, cutting a recess on the cill to avoid complicated sloping shoulders (fig. 5). A comb joint would also have been possible. Doing the mortises and tenons in this way allowed me to dowel through the endgrain of the head and cill to lock the joints. I finished the dowel-holes with plugs and 'painted' the ends with Cascamite.

The rest of the (straightforward) work on the frame consists of fitting the beads and outer lining. The latter can be mitred at the head and screwed to the frame so the screwheads are hidden when the frame is fitted in the opening; or they can be plugged. The parting bead (that hand-tight dry fit in its groove for future ease of removal) can be butt-jointed at the head, or if you're clever, mitred. The best way to fit it is thickness a piece of scrap until it's a good friction-fit in the groove, then thickness the bead (which should have been pre-machined close to the final dimension) at the same setting.

My method of jointing the frame — cutting the tenons on the spindle moulder

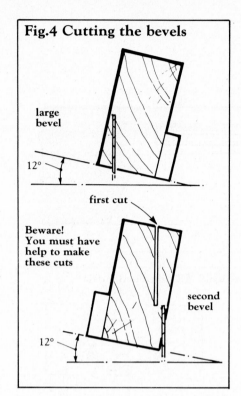

Fig.4 Cutting the bevels

large bevel

12°

first cut

Beware! You must have help to make these cuts

second bevel

12°

— left cill/jamb and head/jamb gaps corresponding to the depth of the guard-bead rebates. This error, er, unique detail should be filled by a small tenon on the ends of the guard beads, which are secured to the frame by screws. Finally, the vent bead can be fitted and then you can start work on the sashes.

The sashes

At this stage it's as well to take direct measurements from the frame, to check the exact width of the sash channels and the internal height and width of the frame in which the sashes should fit. Apparently it has been known for these actual dimensions to differ from those on the drawings, or so I have read.

Once you have dimensioned the sash components, the bottom rail can be bevelled to match the cill. Then work the glazing rebates on the rails, stiles and bars, followed by the ones on the meeting rails. Finally, crosscut the pieces to exact length before making the joints on the spindle moulder.

Calculate the exact lengths of the pieces

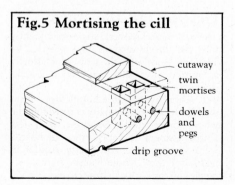

Fig.5 Mortising the cill

cutaway

twin mortises

dowels and pegs

drip groove

as follows: the top, meeting and bottom rails are the same as the internal width of the frame, less an allowance of 3mm for the weatherstrip. The top and bottom stiles are calculated on the assumption that the *glazing* sizes in each sash are identical. First measure the internal height of the frame from the *bottom* of the sash bevel on the cill, not the top. This latter error would cause some amusement and a permanently ventilated window, since the sashes would be too short. Then deduct from this measurement a 3mm allowance for the weatherstrip, plus the height of the top rail, meeting rail and bottom rail. Then divide this figure by two to give the glazed height of each sash excluding the sash bars. To find the length of the top and bottom sash stiles, add the height of the respective sash rails to the previous figure.

Once the pieces have been crosscut to exact length, you can make the joints. The top sash is entirely comb jointed, while my bottom sash had comb joints between meeting rail and stiles, and mortise-and-tenons between stiles and bottom rail. I dowelled and plugged all the joints for reinforcement.

I used a slotting disc with 10mm cutters on the spindle moulder for the comb joints, for which a sliding table or tenoning jig is a necessity. A few offcuts are needed for setting up the joints, which really consist chiefly of two 10mm-wide tenons on each part (fig. 6). Since the thickness of each piece is reduced by the glazing rebate, one of the slots is equal to the thickness of the sash stuff (in this case 48mm) and the other slot must be this width less the depth of the glazing rebates.

I aligned marks on the backs of the test pieces with a backing piece on the sliding carriage which I had previously cut flush with the disc. With the test piece clamped firmly in position, I brought the fence up against its end and made the cut, which could then be repeated on the other test pieces simply by bringing them hard up to the fence.

Make the shallower passes first, so if you make a mistake, all is not lost. It's also advisable when you make the cuts on the meeting rails (which are wider than the other parts), to ensure you leave a thick tenon and not a feathered edge on the rebated face when the two rails meet (fig. 7).

Having made two 10mm passes at the correct depths you can mark the positions of the slot on the corresponding pieces for removal. With 10mm cutters, the waste will have to be removed in two passes by moving the spindle. Make the cut on all parts at one setting before altering the set-up for completion of the cut.

With the trial joints up to scratch, the actual cuts can be made on the sash members using the trial pieces to set up, after which the mortise and tenons can be cut on the bottom rail and stiles. This joint is slightly different — in the joiner's mortise and tenon, the mortise piece is cut with a spur and the tenon with a franking, a sort of

Fig.6 Sash: top rail and stile

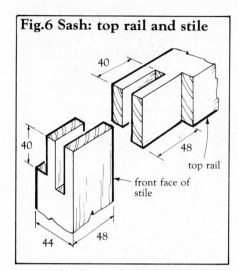

40

40

48

top rail

front face of stile

44   48

reverse haunch. This is to conserve strength in small-section sash material which is usually moulded as well (fig. 8).

Finally, make the joints for the sash bars, the vertical bar through-tenoned to each rail and the lay bars stub-tenoned between.

I glued the sashes with Cascamite and drilled and dowelled each joint from the outside face while they were in the cramps, finishing with a matching plug. Checks for square and winding, of course, should have been made before gluing up an irreversible boomerang!

Once the glue has set the joints can be cleaned up, the ends of the meeting rails which fit over the faces of the stiles trimmed to clear the parting bead, and the sashes tried in the frame to ensure all is well. It's quite satisfying to slide them up and down in their channels and discover that they are a good fit, and once the draught-stripping is fitted, any lateral movement disappears.

● *The comb-jointing set up on the spindle moulder. Guards removed for clarity*

Fig.7 Meeting rail joint

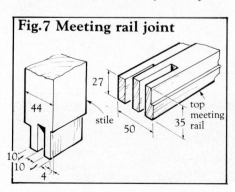

27

44

stile   50

top meeting rail

35

10
10
4

I fitted weatherstrip specially designed for sliding sashes, which fits neatly into a 2mm router-cut groove and is quite unobtrusive in operation. Schlegel, who supplied the strip were most helpful, providing technical data and taking my order direct — I couldn't locate a company to sell the small quantities I needed.

I dislike putty and my wife dislikes my puttying, so I opted for glazing fixed with screws and dry glazing tape for the seal. This method is essential if you intend to use a natural finish. The outside of my windows were finished with mahogany 'Butinox', a semi-transparent water-repellent preservative from Norway, which I applied with a cloth. The inside was sealed and waxed.

The final task is to fit and adjust the balances. Write down the number of turns

● *Comb joints on the meeting rails; note how the stile runs through at the front*

● *Bottom rail detail; pinned tenons and carefully matched plugs*

Fig.8 The franked joint

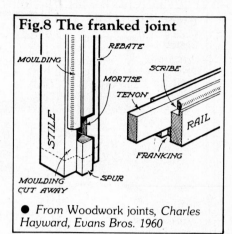

MOULDING   REBATE   SCRIBE
STILE   MORTISE   TENON   RAIL
FRANKING
MOULDING CUT AWAY   SPUR

● *From* Woodwork joints, *Charles Hayward, Evans Bros. 1960*

you give to the springs before you disassemble the whole contraption for building-in and find out it's too big for the opening! ■

Books and suppliers

Ken Austin, *Contract Joinery*, International Thompson £7.95

Barry Richardson, *Remedial Treatment of Buildings*, Longmans, £21.00

British Woodworking Federation, *A Specifier's Guide to Wood Windows*, £1.50. BWF, 82 New Cavendish St, London W1M 8AD

Woodworking and building books from **Stobart and Son**, 67-72 Worship St, London EC2A 2EL, or **The Building Centre Bookshop**, 26 Store St, London WC1.

Spindle tooling: Whitehill Spindle Tools Ltd, 16 Union St, Luton, Beds LU1 3AS

Weather stripping and glazing tape: Schlegel Engineering, Henlow Industrial Estate, Henlow Camp, Beds SG16 6DS

Spiral balances: Westland Engineers Ltd, PO Box 5, Yeovil, Somerset BA20 2YA.

● **Joinery Classics.** If you have recently done or are about to do a first-class job of first-class joinery — windows, doors, staircases, arches, vaulted roofs, whatever — how about submitting it for our series? We need typed (double-spaced) copy, good photographs and line drawings. Write and tell us what you want to do — there's fame and fortune in it!

Cutting list

Frame

Jambs	2	114mm	x	44mm	x	length required	ex 2in
Head	1	114		44			ex 2in
Cill	1	130		68			ex 3in
Vent bead	1	13.5		44			ex 2in
Parting bead	3	9.5		19			ex 1in
Guard bead	3	13.5		16			ex 1in
Outer lining	3	58		16			ex 1in

Sashes

Stiles	4	48	44	ex 2in
Meeting rails	2	50	35	ex 2in
Top rail	1	48	44	ex 2in
Bottom rail	1	114	44	ex 2in
Sash bars	2	44	22	ex 1¼in
Lay bars	4	44	22	ex 1¼in

Guild notes

Guild of WOODWORKERS

The Guild was set up by *Woodworker* to create a meeting ground for all those involved in working wood, whether professional, amateur, or enthusiastic beginner. Guild members get:

- Access to Guild courses and events
- Free publicity in *Woodworker*
- Specially arranged tool insurance at low rates
- 15% off Woodworker Show entry
- A free display area and meeting point at the Show
- 15% discount off *Woodworker* plans
- Inclusion in our register of members' skills and services

For details, please send an sae to the Guild of Woodworkers, 1 Golden Sq, London W1R 3AB.

Working visit

I teach English in a technical school in Paris, **writes Mlle F. Dubost.** One of my pupils, an 18-year old woodwork trainee, would like to spend August with a British joiner/cabinetmaker, preferably in London but not necessarily. If anyone wants an extra pair of willing hands for August, please write to me at:

- Lycée Technique St Nicholas, 92 Rue Vaugirard, 75006, Paris, France.

Mosquito visit 14 June

Below is the all-conquering Wooden Wonder, the centrepiece of the Mosquito Aircraft Museum. The Guild visit to the Museum is on **Sunday 14 June at 2pm.** Mosquito fanatics, themselves heavily involved in the rebuilding of the TA122 aircraft featured in last month's article, will be there to meet you, take you round, and show you what's going on. Last month we said it costs £1 — it's actually **75p!** The whole family is very welcome. Sweets and biscuits are available there, but no capacity for hot drinks, so take your own Thermos!

- Mosquito Aircraft Museum, Salisbury Hall, London Colney, Nr St Albans, Herts AL2 1BU.

Decorative techniques — Ian Hosker

6-7 September, 10-5, Chester, £45.
You read the articles, now do the course. Ian's feature, 'Coats of many colours' in the March and April issues covered wonderful decorative techniques such as dragging, lining, sponging, rag-rolling, marbling, spattering, and (his and our favourite) tortoiseshelling. The cost includes materials, but students should bring a few paint-brushes and jam-jars.

Hand veneering — Bob Grant

27 September, 9.30-5, Oxford, £35+VAT. Veneering is much more than the art of disguising chipboard. It's a skill with a long history, and can create some beautiful effects — and it saves fine and expensive wood! You'll be laying a panel with veneer, mitring a cross-banding, inlaying lines round it, and applying a balancer veneer on the back. If you have a veneer hammer, bring it; but materials will be provided.

French polishing — Charles Cliffe

5-6 June, 9.30-5, Bexleyheath, £40.
Charles Cliffe, one of our 'Question Box' experts on this subject and author of *The Woodworker Manual of Finishing and Polishing*, explains all about preparation, staining, and application of this tricky and beautiful finish. He'll also be dealing with using a cabinet scraper, so bring your own if you have one. If you have a piece of furniture that you want his advice on, bring it as well. Charles can order supplies for you to take away if you tell him in advance.

Design and workshop drawing — Bob Grant

5 July, 9.30-5, Oxford, £25+VAT.
So you've got an idea you want to make manifest in wood? If you don't plan your work on paper, you could waste a lot of timber and effort. Bob, who is head of Craft, Design and Technology at an Oxford comprehensive school, will guide you through putting your design on paper. Learn freehand sketching, how to use grid paper and drawing boards, tricks for laying out ellipses and other shapes, and making and using rods and templates.

MACHINING WOOD

YOUR EXPERT GUIDE

● *A 6ft sliding-table belt sander. Note enclosed drums and the captive pad on the bar; the fence for top sanding is at the right-hand end*

SANDING MACHINES AND ABRASIVES

The finishing touches to our major series — the quickest and easiest way to get the finest feel to your work. Next month: how to get rid of the dust!

Don't ever let anyone tell you that sanding by machine is a complete substitute for sanding by hand. By sanding, of course, we really mean 'abrading', because even average standards of finish on furniture are best achieved with garnet and silicon papers, not the familiar 'sandpaper' (which is in fact glasspaper). Hand sanding is hard, boring work, but it is satisfying. The virtue of patience is rewarded as you watch and feel the wood responding to your hands (or block), coming up smooth and silky, with a warmth that only hand-work seems to give.

But there's no hyperbole to get you round the fact it's a chore; which is why there are sanding machines. We aren't interested in rotary discs on power drills here, or even the hand-held belt sanders, much more powerful and capable of getting a far finer finish. We are looking at workshop-size machines, and featured here are two versatile versions of standard models; the sliding-table belt sander, and a drum-and-belt combination. A small stationary belt sander (12-18in useable length) is often called a linisher. Look at catalogues and manufacturers' ranges for the wide variety of types — they will almost certainly be disc, belt, drum or a combination of any or all. The huge automatic-feed 'wide belt' (36in) sanders also need not concern us here; they are for volume production.

Abrasives

You must know your tools before you start working with them, and the abrasive belts and discs that sanding machines use are as important as are cutters to a router. Not quite as expensive, perhaps, but getting that way. Most machines use aluminium oxide grit material, with a strong cloth or paper backing; for belt sanders, be careful to mount the belts the right way round (indicated by arrows) because the seam is joined diagonally across the belt, and you can rip it apart as soon as it touches your work if you've got it wrong. The abrasives (open- or closed-coat) come in stepped grades from 80 grit (particles per sq cm) up to 320 grit or more, but the most useful workshop range is 100 (really coarse), 150 (medium finishing) and 240 (fine). Open coat for resinous timbers, old finishes and paint.

With the long belts for sliding-table machines (the one here has a 6ft table), it's important to remember that atmosphere has an effect on shape. Never leave the machine with the tension on the belt, or it will curve across the width; this is OK if it curves towards the worktable, but sometimes damp can make the edges curve down and the middle up, and you can very easily dig a sharp, high-speed edge into your precious work. Keeping the workshop warm and dry is always a good idea, of course, and this will minimise the problem, but that's not always possible so it's best to take the precaution of slacking off the tension at the end of every day. The edges are tough, like the rest of the belt, but even the slightest nick or tear in the edge will turn into a great rip under working loads, and the belt will shear, fly off the wheels and flap round the workshop, if it hasn't already wrapped itself round your head. So store and handle the rolled belts very carefully. A new 150-grit cloth-backed belt for a 6ft sliding-table sander can cost the best part of £10! Make these tough abrasives — belts, discs, pads, sheets, whatever form they come in — last longer by de-clogging them occasionally with a wire brush. This works well when you're using resinous timber like pitch pine, but it can obviously only be done so often before renewal. Don't hold the wire brush against a belt or disc running under power!

Drum sanding

One of the simplest routes to machine sanding is to fit a sanding drum attachment on to a spindle moulder in place of the cutter-block. The 3 or 6in-diameter drum, which will be rubber-faced or even inflatable to take 6in-deep (average) tubes of abrasive paper, is ideal for curved workpieces, which should be fed through freehand and *carefully*. Several passes are often needed to get the right finish. The sanding drum attachment can also be used for flat surfaces with the two halves of the guide fence lined up to support the workpiece. This vertical drum also comes as part of a 'disc-and-bobbin' sander, where the same motor drives a large disc on one side and an 8in-high (approx.) 4in-diameter abrasive cylinder on the other. The bobbin rises and falls to spread wear on the abrasive. The key to successful drum or bobbin sanding is smooth feeding-in towards the rotating drum, *always against the direction of rotation*. Danger doesn't lie so much in cutting your fingers to pieces — although you can do a great deal of damage to flesh in a very short time with high-speed abrasives — as in the drum snatching the work out of your hands and spinning it off the table at an extremely uncomfortable height. Hold the work firmly down to the table, hands either end well away from the drum, and bring it in smoothly, walking round the machine with the curve.

Although you can get excellent results on a drum (independent, bobbin, or mounted

● *Drum sanding on a spindle moulder; the drum has a soft rubber surface*

● *Another version of a drum, this time a hard one on a combined drum/belt machine*

on a spindle moulder), its usefulness is limited because sanding depth is restricted by the height of the shaft and some workpieces are just too large or too awkward to handle on a small worktable.

Table belt sanding

So what most small workshops really need is a sliding-table belt sander — or 'pad sander', which comes in a variety of types and sizes. Some have a wide range of height adjustment on the table, some have two positions, some are designed so both table and belt can turn through 90° for edge sanding. All operate on the same principle of a long, continuous abrasive belt running horizontally round two wide wheels or drums, one of which is connected to a motor. The driven wheel has a fixed position on the machine, the idler wheel is adjustable to control the tracking and tension of the belt. Between the wheel/drums, in the space between upper and lower belt positions, a captive pressure-pad slides back and forth on a fixed horizontal bar, moving up and down to press the belt on to the work. The drum-and-belt assembly is mounted over the table, which as well as adjusting vertically, also slides backwards and forwards (ie across the long axis of the machine) beneath the belt. You should also have a hand-held pad, a 6x10in ply block with a comfortable handle and a ¼in felt base.

● *Keep the table moving back and forth and the pad going from side to side. Make sure the stop on the table is the right height for thin pieces*

All the adjustments to the belt are made on the idler drum. To load a belt, make sure the machine is off and isolated, then slacken off the drum-to-drum length and slip the belt on at both ends (right way round!). Then tighten the tension until downward pressure of your hand meets with a springy resistance that stops your downward movement about a hand's breadth below the straight and level. Tension is important — too tight and you'll ruin the belt and the machine's bearings, too loose and it'll flap and tear. Atmosphere, age and condition of belt, size and hardness of work — all these and other things affect your decision on how tight the belt will be. Belts stretch, obviously; check and renew settings every day. When you're satisfied the tension is right, check the tracking very carefully. The last thing you want is the belt creeping across the drums and carving a groove in the metal of the drum housings until it can take no more and has to tear. Making sure the machine is isolated, give the belt a manual turn with a wide sweep of your arm so it spins, at least momentarily, at something like operating speed. See which way it creeps across the drum, and make minute adjustments accordingly, waiting for the effect of the wheel's altered position to show up. Little by little is best — it's too easy to make too big a difference, so the damn thing starts going off the drum the other side. When you reckon everything is as it should be, turn the machine very quickly on-off and you'll get an idea of how accurate your 'manual' estimate has been.

Put the work on the table and adjust the height so the belt is 5-10mm (about ½in) above it. There should be a restraining bar across the table, whose position has to be adjusted according to the length of the workpiece; also beware very thin pieces of

● *Slipping a new belt over the adjustable, undriven wheel. Left hand holds the tension lever*

● *Tracking adjustment; the spanner moves the plunger which aligns the wheel's axle*

ply, hardboard and so on, being snatched off the table, shooting over the bar and into the other end of the shop. Thin pieces are best held on a separate board with a wooden batten across it (pins out of the belt's way)

482

so you can sand the batten to the exact thickness of the work.

Sanding wide panels calls for good co-ordination, because these machines are so powerful that surfaces quickly become uneven if the pressure-pad stays in one place for more than a moment. You can soon remove a veneer completely! The secret is to *keep pressure pad and table moving continually*, the pressure pad sliding from left to right along the fixed bar and the table sliding backwards and forwards. Rather the same 'pat head, rub tummy' kind of co-ordination as the horizontal mortiser, in fact. A good trick with valuable veneered boards is to pin hardwood lips all round the edges at exactly the same height as the veneer. They will protect the vulnerable edges from snagging or wearing right through. With a hand-held pad, never let it

● *Adjust belt height at between 5-10mm above the work*

go off the edges of the work, which will undoubtedly round over or 'dub'.

Most sliding-table belt sanders have a vertical fence above, and a flat surface under, the top run of the belt, where it's easiest and safest to do small pieces. Make sure the stop is in the right position to retain the work, which you should lay down gently but with a firm grip. When you're sure you can feel what sort of pull the belt is giving you to work against, you can push the timber down on the belt. Keep your fingers out of the belt's way! *Always* put the work hard up against the stop as you lay it on the belt. If you're lucky enough to have a machine with edge-sanding facilities then you must also make sure that the stops are set up right and the work properly held against them. The speed and power of these machines — the belts move at around 15m a second — makes it tempting to use coarse belts to take quite large lumps off small pieces, instead of using a plane or saw. Your own hand-pressure allows a fine touch. It doesn't mean don't be careful, though — the only safe woodworking machine is one completely unconnected to any power, with no human in sight!

Disc sanding

Not the drill attachment, but an independent machine with a disc (anything up to 24in diameter) with a table and fence hard up to it. Like belts, discs of various sizes and

grits are available; the smaller ones are extremely useful for trimming endgrain and other small-section work that needs a lot taken off in a short time. But remember that even with the fine-grit discs, you won't get anything like a 'finish finish' — the circular path of the grit will inevitably show up on long grain, and even endgrain if it is close and hard. Always bear in mind that half the disc is travelling up, half of it down, so *put the work on the 'down' side without fail.* This means, of course, that the maximum area you can sand in one go is limited by the size of the disc — half its diameter, in fact. Jigs, stops and adjustable fences can be devised to get a variety of angles and bevels (*see 'Carefree Coopering', WW/April*), but if you are concerned only about getting exact right angles to a face or edge, you must meticulously check the accuracy of your

● *Edge sanding on the top run of a long belt, end hard against the stop*

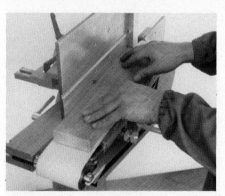

● *Flat sanding on a small drum/belt combination machine. The vertical fence turns round to act as a table*

● *Another version of edge sanding, this time on a large machine with the belt/drums turned through 90°*

● *A high vertical fence is essential for accurate endgrain trimming; you can make your own*

fence to the face of the disc. The combination machine shown has a range of adjustments to the table for angle-sanding, a drum at one end for curved work, and on top of that the tables and drums move through 90°. Adjustable table height will allow you to work on different parts of the belt on this sort of machine; don't turn it over to use the other half, you'll be running the belt the wrong way round. All the safety considerations apply with machines like this; remember to hold the work firmly, always use stops and fences, and watch the tips of your fingers!

Extraction

The large belt sanders, because of the speed of the belt, tend to carry a lot of the dust along the belt to where it's collected in one of the drum housings and taken away through a mobile or built-in extraction system (*see 'Waste away' in this issue*). It's out of the question to use these machines without some form of dust control, for the sake of your own lungs, and also because

● *Adjusting height on the same 6ft sliding-table. Some machines have an electric motor for this!*

accumulations of hot dust are potentially explosive. Wear a mask if you'll be working on a belt sander for more than a minute or two; dust collection cannot by the very nature of the machine be particularly efficient. The smaller disc and belt sanders are even more difficult to extract, and perversely it's often on these machines that you want to take large lumps off small pieces — and make huge quantities of dust. The only answer is a good mask, and clothing tight at the wrists and neck. ∎

Now all you have to do is read 'Waste away' in next month's issue, the Health and Safety notes in August's, and then sit back and think about all the wood-machining information you've gleaned over the months of our series. If you haven't got it all, don't worry — we're putting it together in book form so you can have it without ripping your *Woodworkers* apart; the main thing, of course, is that like everything else in woodwork, you can't learn wood-machining by reading alone. You've just barely started! ∎

Some abrasives manufacturers

3M UK, 3M House, PO Box 1, Bracknell, Berks RG12 1JU, tel. (0344) 26726

Baxter and Fraulo Ltd, 4-8 Minerva St, London E2 9EH, tel. 01-739 7091

Carborundum Abrasives GB Ltd, PO Box 55, Trafford Park, Manchester M17 1HP, tel. 061-872 2381

Draper Tools Ltd, Hursley Rd, Chandlers Ford, Hants SO5 5YF, tel. (0421) 566355

English Abrasives Ltd, Marsh Lane, London N17 0XA, tel. 01-883 4514

Hermes Abrasives Ltd, Hermes Works, Greenstead Rd, Colchester, Essex CO1 2SR, tel. (0206) 867181

Klingspor Abrasives (UK) Ltd, Dukeries Close, Claylands Ind. Estate, Worksop, Notts SB1 7DN, tel. (0909) 476261

RJH Tool and Equipment Ltd, Artillery St, Heckmondwike, W. Yorks WF16 0NR, tel. (0924) 402490

Siaco Ltd, Radwinter Rd, Saffron Walden, Essex CB10 2LA, tel. (0799) 27 399

Specialised Abrasive and Tape Co. Ltd, Satco House, Winchester Rd, Bishops Waltham, Hants SO3 1BA, tel. (048 93) 4666

Wadkin plc, Green Lane Works, Leicester LE5 4PF, tel. (0533) 769111

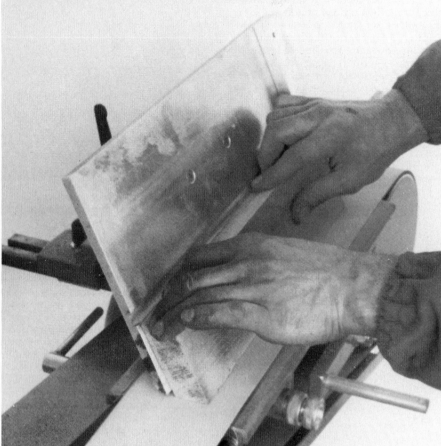

● **Above:** *This particular machine has a bevel-sanding facility. Set the angle carefully and test it.* **Below,** *a dust-mask is essential when you've a lot to do*

This series was written by Judith Barker. Ken Taylor of the London College of Furniture checked it for completeness and accuracy. Aidan Walker planned it and demonstrated the techniques. Derek Wales took the pictures. But Luna Tools and Machinery made it possible. They provided vital financial support – and for photography and demonstration they lent their machines, their space, and the help and advice of staff member Joe Wickens. So we give our warmest thanks to Luna's MD Gerry Baker for his unhesitating and generous co-operation. Luna are at 20 Denbigh Hall, Bletchley, Milton Keynes, Bucks MK3 7QT, tel. Milton Keynes (0908) 70771.

Tales out of steel

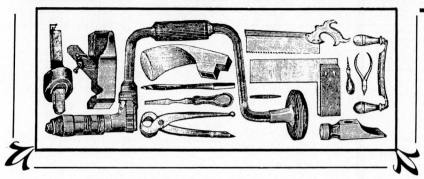

Meet Messrs Brierley, Mushet and Bessemer — men whose mistakes and ideas made landmarks in the history of metal. Ashley Iles takes an individual view

I was bashing away on the anvil one day when Tommy Merrill walked in. (You remember Tommy, I mentioned him in my first article in December 85; the surgical instrument maker with the hairy ears.) Putting a piece of 1¼in square stainless steel on the anvil, he said: 'Look wot them silly buggers at Wostenholme's 'ave gid me to mek a pie neef art of.'

'A pie knife?' I exploded. The hairs on his ears bristled as he explained further. 'It's fo' that theer Denby Dale Pie wot they 'ave in Derbyshire. They use ten cows an' six oxos to mek it.'

He came back later when my son had spent most of the day knocking it down on a ½cwt hammer to 3½x⅜in. 'That's moor like it,' he beamed. A lesser man would have said 'Now what do I owe you?' Not Sir Thomas. Ignoring me, he turned to my son and said — 'Na' lad, come in tomorra mornin and ah'll show thi' 'ow to mek that Mallay Chris tha'rt after.' The Mallay Chris (a Malay Kris) is a diamond-section double-edge dagger with waves in the length, which makes a wider wound than an ordinary dagger. They're extremely difficult to forge and Tommy claimed that he was the only forger who knew how. However next day he imparted the secrets and my son later made one. It is now one of his proudest possessions.

Most outworkers got their steel from Hale & Penningtons, who had an infinite variety of steel in all sizes for all trades. Sizes were available in sections where the minimum of work was required in forging. If the right size wasn't available the forger had to 'make the steel' first to the right size before forging it to shape — and many a battle ensued on pay-day.

Steel for knives and cutlery was only 0.55% carbon and not suitable for edge tools. I remember some steel I got from Geo. Senior on Pond Street called Virgin Bessemer — 1.15% carbon. As I walked out of the warehouse with the steel on my shoulder a voice behind me called — 'Tha'll

'ave to 'arden thi' 'ammer for that.' How true, it was the toughest, hardest steel I have ever worked and it reeked of phosphorous. To harden a hammer, by the way, you get the head white hot, then put it under a water tap and let the water run on the face. Then and only then is the face hardened.

Professor Bronowski in his *Ascent of Man* claims that two million years ago when *Homo Erectus* first split a piece of stone and used the sharp edge as a tool he broke from his environment for the first time and started the chain of events leading to the technology of today. So much for the birth of the tool business. It's equally incredible that after two million years most major industrial advances have happened in the last 200 years, sometimes by accident and sometimes through men of immense stature. Sheffield playing a prominent part, of course.

Not long ago I had a bill for £375 for ten small grinding wheels. It should have been £37.50, some stupid clot had got the decimal point wrong. But the greatest decimal point error in the history of the steel trade was made by Mr Brierley working for Firth Vickers. He was making some steel with an alloy content of 1.15% chromium, but he got it wrong somehow and put in 15%. Well, they chucked the steel into the yard and Mr Brierley after it. They didn't know what to do with the steel, but a custom-made dog-house was built for Mr Brierley; which he occupied until some months later, when some bright spark noticed that in spite of the atrocious weather the steel hadn't gone rusty. Now this was success too good to be true, the best brains in the city had been trying to produce rustless steel for years. The mongrel in the dog-house became Supreme Champion overnight. Champagne corks popped and the whole city celebrated the birth of Stainless Steel. Mr Brierley was elevated to the management. How true is the old Italian proverb: 'To succeed one must not be too good!'

Ever heard of Robert Mushet? A very interesting chap indeed, he had the gambling instinct, wild abandon and faith in all mankind of an astronaut. In 1867 (exactly 100 years before my move from Sheffield to Lincolnshire), just for the sheer hell of it he chucked a lump of wolfram into a pot of pig iron. Let me explain that wolfram is tungsten ore, not a new name in pet foods. The effect was so dramatic it changed the whole course of industry; he had made the very first alloy steel. Even

today the quality of High Speed Steel is determined by the percentage of tungsten.

In 1852 Samuel Osborn, destined to become a leading Sheffield industrialist, started making steel in a small way. In 1868 he took over the Clyde Iron and Steel Works in the centre of Sheffield. This works had converters (not missionaries), crucible melting furnaces, steam hammers and rolling mills for both sheets and sections. Sam knew a bright lad when he saw one. He was quick to acquire the sole rights of Robert Mushet's self-hardening alloy steel, and went to town in a big way. Just imagine being a marketing man at that time with a product that would cut harder metals faster, deeper and at higher speeds (HSS). So tool steel was born. When mass production came along, tool steel had been waiting for it — or had created it.

Perhaps the greatest name in the Industrial Revolution was Abraham Darby. The Darbys came like the Rocky movies, I, II and III. About 1750, number one started melting iron in a blast furnace or cupola at or near Coalbrookdale in Shropshire. In a cupola, the tall chimney-shape furnace is charged with layers of iron ore, coke or charcoal and limestone which acts as a flux. The whole thing is then fired with an air blast; the slag is tapped off at the top and the iron at the bottom, into a ladle from which it is poured into sand moulds.

In 1947 I was the 'Technical Superintendent' at the Coalbrookdale Company at £570 a year. I was living at Dale House, which had been built for Abraham Darby III. My task — I was 24 — was to stop the 40% scrap on castings and double production of the Rayburn Cooker in three months. After that everything else in my life has been a piece of cake. The Darbys were Quakers, but more like earthquakers.

The curse that plagued all the Darbys was the limitations of their product. Cast iron, having 5% carbon, is brittle and weak in tension. Various messy methods of reducing the carbon existed like puddling (wrought iron) but it fell to Mr Bessemer to make it a commercial proposition and produce the first real steel.

I admire a chap who has an idea and gets on with it against all odds but Mr Bessemer takes the biscuit — a sort of Einstein with spanners. There is a static Bessemer converter at the Kelham Island Museum in Sheffield, a massive, awe-inspiring sight. Seeing one go off is like all the outer space movies you have ever seen. When I worked at Edgar Allen's Steel Works in Sheffield I frequently saw them going off and it is a truly terrifying sight. The converter stands like a space rocket in the centre of the foundry, filled with 400 tons of molten iron. The valves are opened, and compressed air is blown through the bottom making the metal boil. The oxygen in the air burns out 4% of the carbon, and escapes through the top with a deafening roar. It's tapped out into ingots, and iron has been transformed into steel in a matter of minutes. ∎

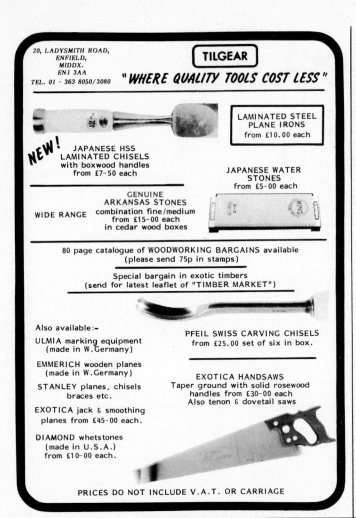
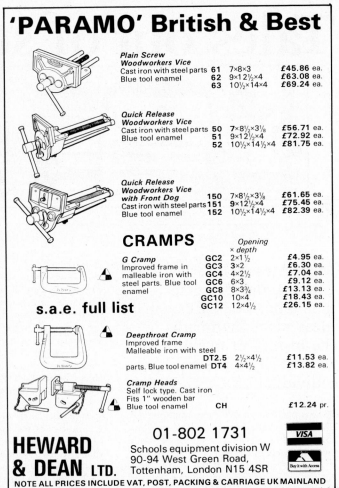

486

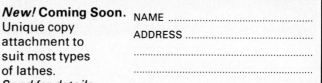

487

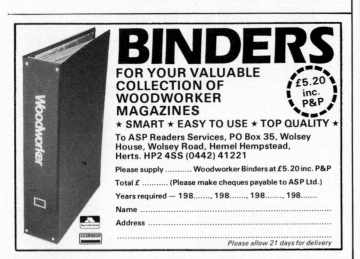
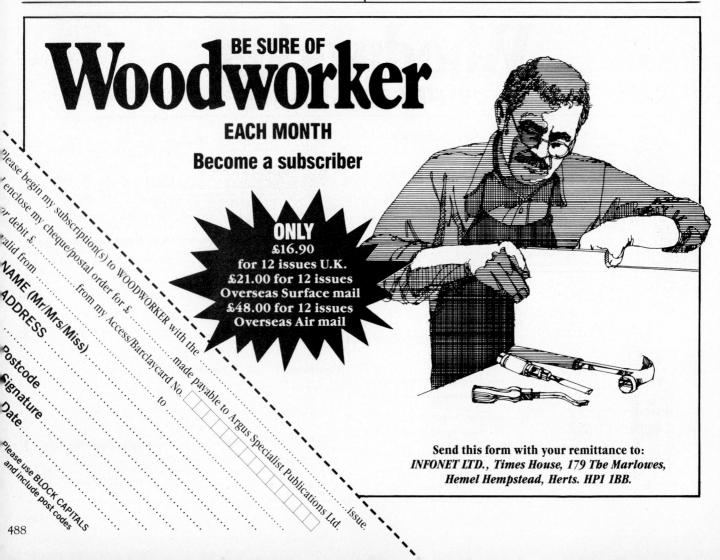

489

Buying timber wisely:5

Alan Thomas' tour of timber merchants who cater for small buyers with high standards takes him to north London

Seek and ye shall find might well be the motto over the portals of **General Woodwork Supplies.** Standing listening in the shop leaves a strong impression that it's a point of honour with General Woodwork to have whatever is wanted, no matter how obscure or obsolete, on a shelf, hanging on a nail, or lying in a bin or basement ready for a chance enquiry. While other merchants have thoroughly destocked in recent years, these people seem to have gone quite the other way.

And among the dustbins and plastic guttering, the sink plungers, paint, boxes of nails, pickaxe heads and lavatory pans, is one of the best stocks in London of rare and exotic woods.

It's only to be expected that the London area should be well served by timber suppliers, especially as cabinetmaking is a traditional London industry. General Woodwork began in a thoroughly traditional way, supplying the thriving proliferation of little masters of the furniture trade in the East End. The 1940s and 50s saw this district languish as bigger firms moved to more convenient trading estates and new towns, and smaller ones disappeared; General Woodwork emigrated three miles up the road to Stoke Newington, which must have seemed like the suburbs after seedy Shoreditch.

It's emphatically a family business. Grandfather Cohen founded it, his son Harry carried it on; and *his* sons Dave and Michael shoulder most of the burden now. A reminder (if they ever need one) of their origins is Grandfather's bench in a back room, with enough hand-tools round it to reassure anyone who wonders if the family really knows about wood.

The premises now occupy four adjoining shops in a busy shopping street, the traditional hardware display outside on the pavement. So far, not much sign of covetable timber. Inside, some racks of fairly ordinary planed-all-round softwood, leavened with ready-made doors, melamine-surfaced chipboard, and the like. But locate Dave Cohen among the groves of overflowing shelves, and accept his invitation to look round the cellar, and you're in a dusty wonderland.

'Can customers walk round? Of course customers can walk round! There's no trouble supplying — we can supply anything to anyone, if they will adapt their wants to our way of business,' says Dave, trotting past sledgehammers stored on the staircase and shelves of paint cans. 'We can't stock everything, every size; if you

● *Extensive and exotic timber at General Woodwork Supplies*

must have a particular sized piece of rosewood, say, by Saturday, perhaps it's not possible. But we can supply anything given time.' How much time? 'Oh, give it seven days.'

The basement store runs underneath all four properties, and some of the rooms can't be negotiated for stock. 'That's oak in there, all oak; here's a nice piece of walnut — there's American black and there's African cherry (what do you think of that piece of cherry?); I chalk the date on every piece — well, most of them — so I know how dry they are. Some of this has been in stock for years — years. That's all teak in there; I know it all down here, every piece.

'What you have to remember, I tell the customers, is that timber doesn't grow on trees! It comes from an importer, a supplier. Our secret is we've got every importer at our fingertips, and we know just where to go to get what a customer wants. So we don't need to carry big stocks of what you might call the ordinary hardwoods.'

Behind the shops is a separate building which contains a variety of milling machinery. There are the usual saws for converting, plus a four-cutter Wadkin moulder with racks behind it holding literally dozens of sets of cutters. All manner of mouldings and skirtings can be supplied, including obsolete patterns now coming into fashion again. The Cohens keep all the offcuts, and during spare moments turn them into strip mouldings. A belt sander 4ft long ('It was 8ft, we had to cut it down to get it in!') puts a finish on flat work after the planer has finished with it.

For customers who lack facilities or inclination to do all their preparatory work

themselves, the machine shop is a boon: it's quite willing, for example, to make up extra-wide boards for table tops and the like. Dovetailing, rebating, fretsawing, turning, and carving can also be supplied to order.

Mail order is a valued source of trade: 'We never turn a mail order enquiry away unless it looks like trouble,' says Dave enigmatically. 'I'll show you what I mean later. I base my mail order on high quality planed, ready-for-sanding timber that is dry and in good condition, with any exchange if the customer isn't satisfied.'

In common with most retail suppliers he feels that many customers, whatever their other skills may be, are distinctly amateur when it comes to buying their raw material. His point was underlined by a buyer in the shop who had difficulty comprehending the impossibility of getting three 4in-wide pieces out of a 12in utile board. That incident prompted the unearthing of a recent postal enquiry — one that 'looked like trouble.' The writer had taken three closely-typed pages to detail his requirements, with a bewildering variety of alternatives in timber species, dimensions to engineering standards, and ending with the stipulation that none of the many pieces show any sign of planer ripple. 'What I'll do with that one,' said Dave philosophically, 'is give him a ring and see what he really wants.' Customers range from the obviously commercial — builders and shopfitters who want serving yesterday — to local amateurs, by way of a shadowy in-between territory which includes sheltered workshops and local authorities. A steady demand comes from evening-class pupils; years ago, explains Dave, father Harry made it his business to become friendly with evening-class teachers.

Dave Cohen would like to publish a really comprehensive catalogue of his wares, but says the task defeats him; it would run into hundreds of pages and be permanently out of date. Because the stock has accumulated over so many years, and because much of it is so scarce it's hardly worth listing, the standard stock-list looks positively humdrum, with its afrormosia, box, elm, lime, mahoganies, oaks and walnuts. But anyone wanting anything for carpentry, joinery, or cabinetmaking is more than welcome to give Dave a ring and ask. To help minimise misunderstanding, prices quoted include carriage and VAT. *General Woodwork Supplies, 76-80 Stoke Newington High St, London N16, tel. 01-254 6052. Mon-Sat 8-6, Thur 8-1. The High Street is one-way from the central London direction.*

If you're a casual customer, there really isn't much point in calling at the Tottenham HQ of **Abrams and Mundy**. All you'd find is an unpretentious office building with some excellent panelling, but apart from samples — no wood.

This old-established north London firm is something of a rarity in that although it's

Buying timber wisely: 5

one of the larger hardwood importers, supplying many very large users, it's also prepared to handle small orders from the general public. It wasn't always so: 'Years ago,' Roger Douglas, group sales manager, admits, 'if we got a request for just a few pounds worth of timber, we'd probably suggest they went round to the yard and slipped old so and so a quid for a drink. It wasn't worth our while to put small orders through the books when the paperwork in every transaction cost us maybe £20.'

In those days gone by staple customers included shipbuilding yards (all those beautifully panelled cabins and state-rooms), Government departments (now persuaded to use less expensive materials) and British Railways. Now, of course, that kind of bulk demand hardly exists.

Less obvious but just as profound changes have come to other sections of the woodworking industry, he points out. 'Ten years ago every joiner kept some timber in stock against future orders, and a small shop might easily have 20 or 30cu.ft racked. Now any stockholding is an accident. Users just can't afford to have money tied up any more.'

So the company has had to rethink its business methods; for example, tripling the variety of items in its catalogue has increased trade two and a half times. This has benefited small consumers, but the 8am–4pm (Monday to Friday only) working hours are a potential drawback for the strictly amateur buyer. There are at least some Saturday mornings when collections can be made for an hour or two. Timber is supplied sawn only, not finished; indeed, the company still tends to think of itself as primarily a supplier of log-sawn timber, for that was virtually its sole trade until three years ago, and it was also the way in which shipyards and the like wanted to buy. Why? 'Because in that kind of really high-class joinery log-sawn gives the advantage of continuity of colour and texture.' Teak of course is different in that it's sold in dimensioned stock, 'from the size of toothpicks up.' Buying teak without working out the cutting list very carefully could make the price three times higher than necessary.

Setting out to meet the needs of smaller users, Roger Douglas has discovered that ignorance — all right, unfamiliarity — is the main cause of perplexity and unreasonableness in customers, and puts much of it down to the different ways in which softwoods and hardwoods are marketed. 'Anyone can walk into any shop selling wood and sees racks of planed-all-round stuff, in a great variety of dimensions, and the assistant is willing to saw off just what you want. Hardwoods aren't sold like that. We have to import timber according to standard specifications: each one is different, but take, for example, Brazilian mahogany. Parcels are offered to us with board widths from 6 to 20in and lengths from 6 to 16ft, but with an average of 9in wide and 9ft long. So in that sense it's a lucky dip for us. We haven't got any machinery (except very large), so our

● General Woodwork again: pear, lime, black walnut – and what can't be found can be ordered

customers' wants must be governed by the sizes of the boards available at the time.'

But what about the standard injunction to send detailed cutting lists with every order?

'I'm coming to that. We aggregate customers' cutting lists into the most economic size of board, and that, of course, helps to match colour and texture.' He quotes the example of a superb chest he saw recently made from spalted, that is fungus-stained, beech. At much the same time he had had to give an allowance to a furniture mass-producer who had inadvertently taken delivery of some similarly affected material.

A subtle assistance Abrams and Mundy can offer is a 'lump-sum price.' The company will calculate how much timber will be called for in a job, allowing for wastage, and for making sure there's enough. It comes no cheaper, but it obviates the risk of running out of material and makes it easier to quote a firm price in the knowledge that margins won't be squeezed through quantity misjudgement.

Roger Douglas sees no real disadvantage to customers, even those in home garage workshops, in buying his sawn-only supplies. 'These days the readily-available power hand-planers and routers mean that it's no longer necessary to buy timber ready-finished.'

Of the two timber yards owned by Abrams and Mundy, one is really a warehouse holding something like 25,000cu ft of square-edged material. This huge quantity has to be stacked, and stacked high, so the buyer who insists on the stock being turned over until a particular grain and colour is found can expect a dusty answer. In the logs and log-sawn yard buyers are welcome to try; however, planks there can weigh up to a quarter-ton each! Better by far (indeed, the company almost insists on it) to telephone at least the day before to explain what you want and why.

'We have a skilled staff that really know wood. If, say, you wanted to make that table-top in 1in mahogany, a nice piece with twirly grain would be just right. But if

you're making a door, straight grain and stability would be far more important. And if we know all the order is for one piece or a suite of furniture and you tell us if you want a light or dark colour, we will sort out matching timber to suit.'

Roger Douglas has a theory that user choice is sometimes based on standard text-books about timber, and that people are misled by out-of-date illustrations — particularly, he thinks, of ex-colonial timbers. He also has his share of breath-taking demands for quotes by return of post. 'We have just received a very long cutting list, all for small sizes, and fully machined. It asks for three different timbers, each re-selected into light, medium and dark. It's not impossible, but it does sound more like his quotation to his customer — not from me to mine!'

Although postal enquiries are welcomed, mail order isn't possible. Transport can be arranged and the whole country is covered.

Afrormosia, iroko, utile, Japanese and north American oak, sapele, and Brazilian mahogany figure large in Abrams and Mundy's catalogue; several others are held in bulk, and Roger Douglas draws attention to their rock maple, American ash, and Douglas fir. Softwoods proper are also kept for general building, but the fir is, in his opinion, commercially on a par with the hardwoods.

None of the conventional carving or turning woods are kept — at least, not in the forms in which amateur users would expect to buy them. Exotics are not likely to be in stock either, but it's always worth asking: Abrams and Mundy supplied some black-bean to repair the Speaker's chair in the House of Commons.

Prices are hard to assess in that the company sells its material in a different form from most other suppliers; but Roger Douglas points out that he supplies many of the conventional retail timber outlets. Why not, he asks reasonably, buy from him and cut out the middlemen?

Abrams and Mundy, 286-288 High Rd, Tottenham, London N15, tel. 01-808 8384. The yards are not very far away in Edmonton. Mon-Fri 8-4. No mail order. ∎

Holes in corners

WOODWORKING WHEEZE of the month

1 Sooner or later, **writes Alan Thomas,** it's necessary to drill holes in positions where there isn't enough headroom to use a brace, (wheel or ordinary) and where a power drill won't go either. The holes needed are usually larger than a gimlet or awl can manage, on top of that.

I've just had to drill pilot holes for no.10 screws in the top framing of a window, where the available space is just 9in. Short-tempered fiddling about got me nowhere — and then the penny dropped. What it needed was a tap wrench; then the only space restriction would come from the length of the drill.

The picture shows how the job was done. Tap wrench on twist drill; press down with one hand; rotate drill with the other. Each of eight holes, all 1¼in deep, took less than a minute.

As a refinement, it might be worth slipping a short piece of loose-fitting tube over the drill in order to guard against the possibility of sore fingers, but it's hardly necessary.

● *Getting into tight corners with the tap wrench*

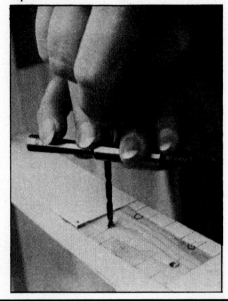

2 If you own a socket set, **adds Michael O'Hara,** here's another answer: get a mild steel nut, ⅝in AF or thereabouts, checking you have a socket to fit it. With an old saw file, alter the hole in the nut to a square shape, slightly tapered, to fit the shank of a Jennings-type bit; then simply put the socket on its ratchet, the nut in the socket, and a bit of the required size into the nut. Using the ratchet to turn the bit, holes can be drilled quite easily in an overall space of little longer than the bit. ■

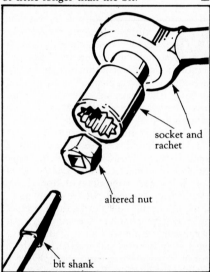

socket and rachet

altered nut

bit shank

Ornament for all

Ornamental turning —
a mysterious art very
different, you think, from
'plain' lathe work. Tubal
Cain reveals the ideas
behind the mystery, and
explains how to make your
own beautiful ivory box

Most turners decorate their work, so why is ornamental turning something different? The definition is easy. Look at the drawing on this page. At **a** we have a piece of 'plain' turning — true, it's decorated, but it has been turned between centres. Now look at **b**. No decoration at all, but it's classed as 'Ornamental'. Why? Because there's *no way* it could be turned between centres in a normal lathe. One end is elliptical, the other circular. In technical terms, 'plain' turned work is *always* a 'solid of revolution', however highly decorated, while 'ornamental' turning may be completely undecorated, but it's *never* a 'solid of revolution'. All ornamental turning is done in a lathe with a few special features and accessories, which enable it to produce forms and shapes a normal lathe can't. So why use such a misleading name for the art?

In the 16th and 17th centuries, many courts employed a 'Court Turner' along with the court artists, architects, and landscape designers, and they vied with each other to produce more and more exciting artefacts for their royal masters. The more ingenious modified the ordinary lathe to extend its capabilities — headstock mandrels which could rock sideways or move endways, controlled by cams, attachments which could turn off-centre ('eccentric chucks') or produce ellipses, and some even more exotic. Photo 1 is an example of such a machine from about 1760, with examples of some of the work it could do shown in photo 2.

In 1795 an Alsatian named Charles Holtzapffel emigraged to London and set up as a maker of lathes and scientific instruments. His machines were notable for soundness of design, and even more for quality of workmanship. In effect he introduced ornamental turning to this country, plus many new and revolutionary devices — particularly the rotating cutter-frame, applied to work held stationary in the chuck. This hobby became very popular, and other makes became available; it was known variously as 'Eccentric', 'Complex', or 'Ornamental' turning.

Towards the end of the 19th century OT diminished somewhat, and the last 'Ornamental' lathe was made in 1914. The First World War practically killed it, and between the wars comparatively very few practitioners carried on, whose number was diminished even more during the Second War. In 1948 a group who met occasionally

Photo 1 *An ornamental turner's lathe of about 1760. Accessories include eccentric and elliptical chucks, swash-plate mandrel movement, and a simple cycloidal chuck*

Photo 2 *Examples of the sort of work done on the lathe above. Full instructions in* Manuel de Tourner, *Bergeron, 1796*

Ornamental and plain turning

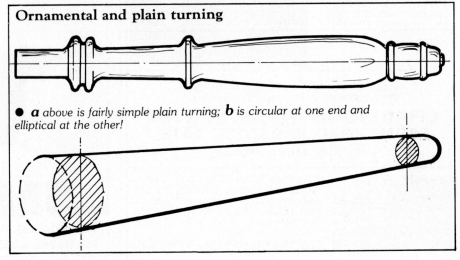

● **a** *above is fairly simple plain turning;* **b** *is circular at one end and elliptical at the other!*

Photo 3 *The author's Holtzapffel lathe. Most of the hand-tools are 100 years old*

decided to form a society to promote the study and practice of the art. It went ahead under the leadership of the late Fred Howe, perhaps one of this century's most versatile and expert craftsmen, but the question of a name caused problems. A 'Society of Eccentric Turners' might lead to misunderstanding, and a 'Society of Complex Turners' even more so — yet to include all the descriptions would be unwieldy. So, for good or ill, the name 'Society of Ornamental Turners' was adopted. The 20 original members' efforts bore fruit, and today there are several hundred expert practitioners all over the world.

The lathe

This can be very elaborate (photo 3), and a complete outfit even more so, but complexity is by no means essential. In fact, provided the bed is rigid and the headstock bearings substantial, the only essential feature is the set of **dividing circles** on the headstock pulley and their associated **detent** (photo 4). These allow the mandrel to be indexed round and stopped at suitable points when ornamentation is applied with the rotary cutting-frames. The one in the photo has three circles of 96, 120 and 144 holes, which will meet all ordinary needs (96 is, perhaps, the most used) but some have as many as six. The detent must be really rigid and will preferably, have a calibrated adjusting screw at the bed end so the pattern can be aligned exactly.

The sliderest

This is another essential, and means the lathe bed must allow the rest to be correctly aligned to the lathe centre wherever it sits along the length. The one on my Holtzapffel no.2456 is shown in photo 5. It is 13in long, and is carried on a large peg in a socket on the **cradle A** which is registered in the

longitudinal slot between the lathe-bed bearers. An adjusting **ring-nut B** allows the height of the rest, and hence the tool or cutting-frame to be set very precisely. This method of support allows the rest to be set at any angle, and a **degree scale** is provided at **C**, together with two adjustable stops which are normally adjusted so one sets the traverse exactly parallel to the lathe centre, and the other sets it exactly at right angles. They can be removed when not needed. The **mainslide D** travels on the vee-flat **slideways F** controlled by a 10tpi feed-screw and the indexed hand-wheel **E**. Adjustable **fluting stops** can be used to set precise limits to the travel — one can be seen at **F**.

The **topslide** and toolholder **J** is carried in vee-flat ways on the mainslide, moved forwards or backwards by the lever **H**. The *rate* at which the slide is moved inwards is controlled by the **square-headed screw L**, which resists the force applied to the hand-lever. It's normally operated by the socket-knob seen on top of the tool holder in this photograph. There is a second similar screw on the other side at **M**, which is calibrated and used as a depth-stop; it can be locked once it's set. The lever **H** can be set on either side of the slide (a very useful feature); the second pivot pillar is seen at **K**. The mainslide and topslide screws are calibrated so cuts can be repeated to within about 0.001in. Incidentally, this photo also shows the dividing circles on the brass driving pulley at **O** (six rows) and the **detent adjusting-device** at **N**. The motor on the backboard (it just stands on rubber feet) is used to drive the cutting-frames.

The **tool-holder** is known as a 'tool receptacle', for it's rather more than a mere holder. It is in the form of a $\frac{9}{16}$in-wide trough, and all accessories have shanks which are $\frac{9}{16}$in square and a good slide-fit in

Photo 4 *Division circles on the pulley of a Fenn ornamental lathe*

the trough. They and the tool-holders proper are held down by two square-headed screws. One can be seen at **P** in photo 5. To change a tool or appliance these two screws are slightly relaxed, the tool or frame is slid out, the new one put in, and the screws nipped up again. Very quick. Most important, all the sliderest cutting tools are of uniform section, carried in a sort of 'boat' which fits the receptacle, so we can change tools and always be sure the point lies exactly at lathe centre-height. No messing about with packing. The same applies to the cutting-frames.

The tools themselves are ground with zero top rake (ie the top is flat) and no more than 20°-30° front clearance, except for elliptical workpieces. That is, the cutting angle runs from 60°-70°. Many turners are contemptuous of such tools, deriding them as scrapers, but believe me, they cut. I've made swarf many feet long cutting boxwood, blackwood and the like, and longer still with ivory. They're really sharp, with a lapped and polished edge, and you never insult them by proffering them to a grindstone. An ornamental turner will *never* use abrasive finishing papers; the fine polish is a matter of 'tool finish' only, though it

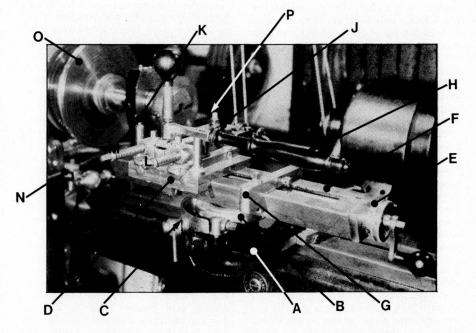

Photo 5 *The sliderest and its parts, all of which are explained in the text*

Ornament for all

may occasionally be OK to polish with the parent material's shavings.

The position is even more rigorous for the smaller cutting tools used for the cutting-frames. There's no way the incised patterns can be polished, and the highly reflective facets characteristic of cutting-frame work can *only* have a tool finish. So these cutters (again of uniform section though rather smaller than those of the sliderest, with similar cutting angles) must be really sharp. Also, that cutting edge must last right through the generation of the pattern; I've cut one rather special pattern which involved no less than 296 different settings of the work and cutter, and where the cutter ran nearly half a mile! It would be impossible during this period to take out and re-sharpen the edge. Such cutters are rough- (yes, rough) sharpened on a hard Arkansas stone, then honed with flour abrasive on a brass lapping-plate, and finally polished with rouge on an iron lap. The resulting edge is razor sharp, of high polish, and very durable. Incidentally, all the tools are carbon steel (HSS will not take the high polish needed, and is too soft) and most of mine are well over 100 years old — a few are 160!

Cutting-frames

The use of 'drills' as miniature routers for cutting flutes was common even in earlier days, but it fell to Holtzapffel to introduce the 'flycutting' types, perhaps 150 years ago. The simplest is the 'vertical' cutting-frame (the cutter revolves in the vertical plane, the axis horizontal) seen in photo 6. It can be used to produce large flutes or a 'basketwork' pattern, but it has a few disadvantages, especially with the endless ropes which I use — so the more elaborate 'universal' cutting-frame (photo 7) is the one I favour. The one shown is relatively modern (about 1905). You can see that the whole head can be set at any angle; there's a scale of degrees on the large-diameter boss at the base. It's geared, so it's possible to keep the drive-rope well out of the way and, equally useful, to use larger pulleys.

The 'eccentric cutting-frame' (or ECF) is perhaps Holtzapffel's most brilliant contribution to OT. Photo 8 shows the idea. The $\%_{16}$in-square shank carries a through-spindle on opposed hardened-steel cone bearings, with a pulley at the back and the cutter-head at the front. The cutter itself is carried in a holder which can be traversed along the head (and locked) allowing a circle of swept diameter from zero to about 3in. Photo 9 shows the device in detail. Each mark on the index knob represents a movement of 0.005in, so it's literally possible to 'work to a thou'.

Tool shapes

Many are special-form tools, but there is a range of basic shapes for both sliderest and cutting-frame tools, shown in photo 10. They are always referred to by their number; two numbers, in fact — one is the

Photo 6 *The vertical cutting-frame. Tubes are for lubrication at 2000rpm*

Photo 7 *The Birch 'Universal' cutting-frame, set up to cut horizontally. It will work at any angle*

shape, and the other gives either the angle, radius, or width. Thus a '91-90°' will have a 90° angle; '94-10' will be a flat tool, $^{10}\!/_{100}$in (0.1) wide, and a '96-5' will have a radius of .05in. 120 sliderest tools make a complete set, and a similar set of cutting-frame tools would be 144 or more, plus any 'specials'. But for many years I managed with about a dozen sliderest tools and only the three small ones in photo 9.

Overhead drives

The presence of an 'overhead' characterises the ornamental lathe to many, but this isn't the case by a long chalk. Many small engineer's lathes in the 19th century were fitted with one, and almost all watch and clock-maker's lathes had them. Clearly there must be some means of driving the cutting-frames; one form of overhead is seen in photo 3. These were all devised for treadle drive, and many very elaborate systems can be found. But things are much simpler with motor drives. Most practitioners today use a very simple jockey and set a motor on the backboard of the lathe. If the motor has rubber feet it won't walk about, and tension can be adjusted by pushing the motor about. Often the drive can be taken direct, with no jockeys. My own motor develops $\frac{1}{6}$hp (more than adequate) and is a shunt-wound DC machine arranged for variable speeds from almost zero up to 2000rpm.

The final essential accessory is a good magnifying glass! It's needed for tool-setting, examining the tool for sharpness, and looking at the intersection of cuts when making trial pieces. Mine is a 1½in-diameter objective glass from an old telescope, mounted in a frame made from scrap ivory fragments.

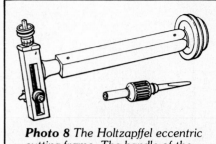

Photo 8 *The Holtzapffel eccentric cutting-frame. The handle of the key/drift is ornamentally turned*

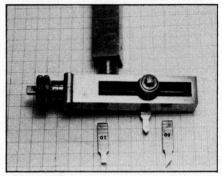

Photo 9 *The author's eccentric cutting-frame with three tools. The squares are ¼in*

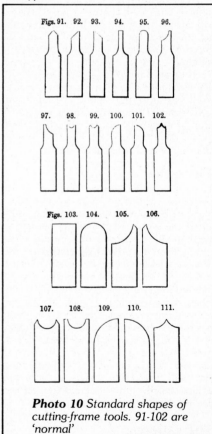

Photo 10 *Standard shapes of cutting-frame tools. 91-102 are 'normal'*

● For a fuller account of the 'Art and Mysterie', *Woodworker* April 1973, March 1974 and following provide great detail.
● The Society of Ornamental Turners: The Secretary, 17 Chichester Drive, East Saltdean, Brighton BN2 8LD.

Ornamental ivory

Try your hand at the mysterious art of OT with this superb decorated box

Photo 11 top: this is what to aim for!
Photo 12 above: the lid, with its 'fish'
pattern surrounded by shells

A special occasion called for a more than usually special gift, and also provided the impetus for me to 'open' the very large piece of ivory which I had for long been too timid to show to a saw! So preliminary sketches were made of the design. It's always prudent to leave some flexibility with ivory, as it isn't possible to ascertain the 'nature' of the material until the skin has been removed. Sometimes the natural pattern can make it a crime to decorate ivory at all. In the final design (photo 11), the body is 3¾in diameter, and the whole thing about 2¾in tall. The lid (photo 12) carries a centre pattern known as the 'Fish' — four fishes facing inwards — surrounded by a ring of 12 sea-shells. Naturally, fishes need a basket, so the body of the box is decorated like that, with 11 rows of 24 'weaves', an odd number of rows to get the first and last in line. The extremes of the basket carry a 'bead' of architectural form. To get the essential element of surprise needed in such a work, there is another pattern cut on the inside of the lid (photo 13), one I developed

from a classical design (Holtzapffel no.222) by stopping it off before all the cuts are complete. I call it my 'Wave' or 'Flow' pattern, as it vaguely resembles the ripples formed by a stream passing an obstruction.

Both the fish and the wave are let into the main body of the lid, which is African blackwood (just for contrast, you understand). All ivory starts off as a hollow at the root, the hole gradually diminishing until it disappears about one-third up the length, but there is what is often called a 'nerve' right through the length. It may be no more than an unobtrusive dot, but on large pieces it can be quite large. This was so with this piece, and as it wasn't exactly central, it would have spoiled the appearance (at least on the lid). So it was only sensible to inlay these two patterns.

Preliminary work

Fig. 1 shows the stages in preparing the ivory. Opening it up always releases stresses, so do this well before you start the job proper. It is cut from the tusk radial to the curve (fig. 1a), and the first step is to set

Photo 13 The inlaid pattern on the underside of the box lid

it in the four-jaw chuck and face the two ends, either by parting-off or plain machining (fig. 1b). See fig. 1 for details.

Had it been wood, the core could have been chewed out by coarse drilling and even coarser boring, but for ivory trepanning is more economical. This is in effect 'axial

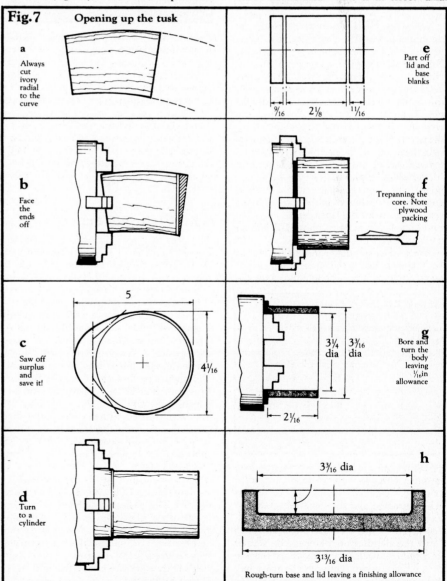

Fig.7 **Opening up the tusk**

a Always cut ivory radial to the curve

b Face the ends off

c Saw off surplus and save it!   5   4¹/₁₆

d Turn to a cylinder

e Part off lid and base blanks   ⁹/₁₆   2⅛   ¹¹/₁₆

f Trepanning the core. Note plywood packing

g Bore and turn the body leaving ¹/₁₆in allowance   3¼ dia   3³/₁₆ dia   2¹/₁₆

h Rough-turn base and lid leaving a finishing allowance   3³/₁₆ dia   3¹³/₁₆ dia

All dimensions in imperial

497

Ornamental ivory

parting-off'. I have some proper trepanning tools (photo 14) with a curved blade so the kerf can be kept very narrow. The piece is set in the four-jaw with a thin layer of plywood behind (fig. 1f), though it may sometimes be necessary to trepan part-way and then reverse the workpiece. The resulting hollow cylinder is then machined to within $\frac{1}{16}$in or so of finished size inside and out (fig. 1g) and finally the lid and base are roughly hollowed (fig. 1h). They leave the pieces as long as possible to recover from this rather drastic change in shape. Only at this stage can you make a final decision on the diameter of the finished box, as until now you don't know how much would have to come off completely to clear the 'bark' on the tusk.

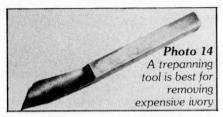

Photo 14
A trepanning tool is best for removing expensive ivory

While the body was resting I made the two inlay pieces. The ivory for the fish was roughed out to the shape in fig. 2 and also left to rest; this piece came from another chunk, trepanned out of a smaller box some years ago and very nearly the same colour as the larger pieces. Meanwhile I made the blackwood pattern. Fig. 3 shows the settings. I turned the piece to $1\frac{1}{2}$in diameter, faced the end, and cut a semicircular bead round the periphery. The actual pattern was cut using the eccentric cutting-frame (photo 9), set to 0.3in on the micrometer, the sliderest square across the bed and adjusted so the axis of the cutting-frame was 0.25in from the lathe centre-line. The tool I used was no.91 of photo 10, with an included angle of 90°.

With the spindle running at about 1800rpm I slowly advanced the cutter, using the depth screw **M** in photo 5 for the

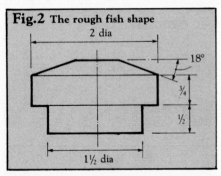

Fig.2 The rough fish shape

present, until I judged the groove was deep enough. This was with the detent in hole 69 of the 96-hole division plate. The cutter was then retracted and the mandrel rotated to engage with index hole 71. Using control-screw **L** this time, the cutter was again fed in until the depth stop **M** engaged. Then I stopped the machine and examined the two cuts under a magnifying glass to make sure the depth was right so the crest between the

two cuts met at a sharp point with no flat. It wasn't quite deep enough so stop **M** was re-adjusted a little and the two cuts repeated under the control of the screw **L**. This time all was well, so the lockscrew on **M** could be tightened and the whole series of 16 successive cuts could be made, arresting the mandrel at the division numbers shown on the drawing. The piece was then parted off to a shade over 0.1in thick — actually 0.115in — so it would stand proud by a smal amount from the level of the ivory surface.

The Fish pattern

The previous operation was dead simple, but not so the Fish! This calls for some very deep cutting indeed, extreme precision in the settings, and manipulation with great care so the cutter can retain its edge through the whole operation; it would be fatal if it were necessary to remove the cutter while making the actual scales on the fish bodies. The eccentric cutting frame is used throughout, with a no. 93 tool of 45° angle. The edge was honed on an Arkansas stone, and then lapped with oilstone dust on a brass lap, after which I formed a secondary cutting angle with rouge on an iron lap. It's also wise to use a rather wider cutter than usual, and to ensure that the sides (ac and bd in fig. 4) are given clearance and sharpened, otherwise some rubbing may occur during the deep cuts.

The task can best be understood by studying photo 12 in conjunction with figs. 4 and 5. The 'scales' are formed by cutting a series of circular grooves, each of smaller radius than its predecessor, struck from a centre nearer the middle of the pattern, and to a reduced depth. A cross-section of the fish's body is shown in fig. 4 though this is a sketch rather than a scale drawing, and at

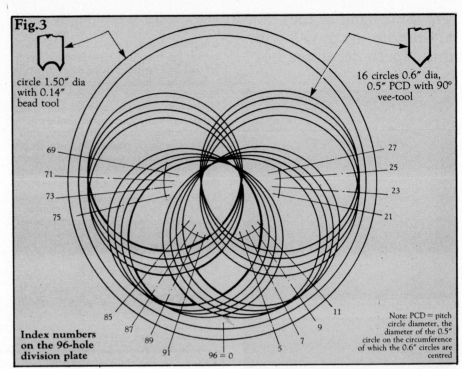

Fig.3

circle 1.50" dia with 0.14" bead tool

16 circles 0.6" dia, 0.5" PCD with 90° vee-tool

69
71
73
75

27
25
23
21

85
87
89
91

11
9
7
5

$96 = 0$

Index numbers on the 96-hole division plate

Note: PCD = pitch circle diameter, the diameter of the 0.5" circle on the circumference of which the 0.6" circles are centred

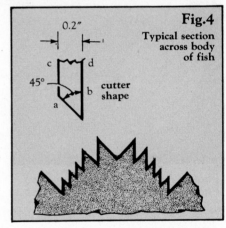

Fig.4

Typical section across body of fish

0.2"

45°

c   d
     b   **cutter shape**
a

this point the second and later cuts seem to be fairly shallow. However, fig. 5 tells another story. Here, C_0 is the centre of the pattern; C_1 is the centre of rotation of the first cut, made at radius R_1; and C_7, R_7 the corresponding positions at the seventh cut. (There are eight cuts in all for each fish). Though cut seven penetrates very little into the workpiece at the centre, the depth at the

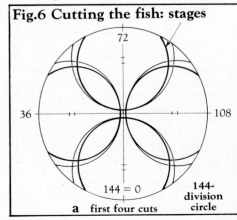

Fig.6 Cutting the fish: stages

72

36

108

$144 = 0$

144-division circle

a   first four cuts

498

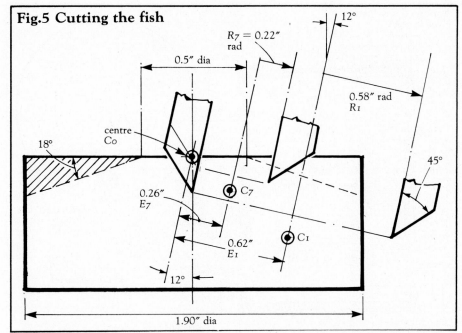

Fig.5 Cutting the fish

$R_7 = 0.22''$ rad

$0.5''$ dia

$12°$

$0.58''$ rad R_1

$18°$

centre C_0

$45°$

$0.26''$ E_7

C_7

$0.62''$ E_1

C_1

$12°$

$1.90''$ dia

edges of the workpiece is considerable — the tool is almost completely immersed. This problem can be eased by machining the top of the blank at an angle; this was 18°, as shown, and could perhaps have been greater with no harm. Most practitioners would normally make a sample from boxwood to establish the optimum settings, cutting speeds and so on, but in this case I worked directly into the ivory and had to estimate the angle.

Fig. 6 shows the procedure. The blank was first turned as shown in fig. 2, and gripped in a three-jaw chuck; a wood spring-chuck would have been better (or a brass cup-chuck) for not getting so much in the way, but with a pattern like this any slip would have been fatal. I also took care to start the work at a time when I knew that I could work right through and complete it, so there was little risk of the jaws biting into the work and losing their grip over time. I skimmed the blank over, and brought it to about 1.93in OD.

I set the sliderest at 12° and adjusted the eccentric cutting-frame to zero radius. Then the position of the topslide was set so the point of the cutter spun at a mere point exactly at the centre of the blank, after

which I moved the tool to a radius of 0.58in; and the sliderest to move the centre of rotation to 0.62in away from the work's centre.

The detent was set in the 144 (= zero) hole of the 144-hole dividing circle and the cutter, making about 900rpm, was *very* carefully advanced until the depth of cut at the centre was about 0.2in. The depth-stop was locked at this setting. I withdrew the cutter, rotated the work to engage the no. 36 hole of the dividing circle, and repeated the process. Then again at holes 72 and 108, thus producing the four cuts seen at **a** in fig. 6. After the first cut, it's clear that the tool-point will pass over grooves already machined. This can lead to snatchings, and it's imperative that a very firm hold be kept on the feed lever **H** and that the rate of infeed (controlled by **L**) be steady and slow.

After making the first four cuts, I stopped the machine and made three adjustments; the radius R, fig. 5, is reduced by 0.06in; the eccentricity E is reduced by 0.06in; and the depth stop **M** (photo 5) is set to reduce the depth of cut by 0.02in. Then four more circles are cut at the same division holes as before, producing what you see in fig. 6b. The radius, eccentricity

and depth were then adjusted again by the same amounts, and the process repeated six more times to make eight sets altogether. It then looks like fig. 6c, though these diagrams show only the line of the very point of the tool; the actual appearance is of a multiplicity of facets.

At this stage there are literally grooves all over the work, and the next step is to remove some of them! The usual procedure is to remove the tool, resharpen it, and hone a very small flat on the point, but I don't like spoiling a specially prepared cutter. Instead, I keep an identical half-vee-point cutter which already has a flat, 0.01in wide, at the tip. This is set in the holder of the ECF and adjusted to about 0.33in radius. Then the sliderest is set so the cutter clears the work altogether. The dividing index is set at the same initial figure as before (144 = 0) and the cutter traversed inwards on the sliderest very carefully, to remove the incisions over the 'plateau'. In fact the first cut wasn't deep enough, so I tried a second which just cleared off all evidence of previous work. The fluting stop was brought into play (**G**, photo 5) and carefully adjusted until the amount removed appeared as you see in the photo (12) of the lid. I was fortunate, for the radius I chose was just about right, but on other occasions I've had to increase it gradually after the first cut to get the shape. (This shows the merit of making a trial on boxwood!) Once the first plateau had been formed, the mandrel was indexed round, using the same holes as before, to machine all four. The appearance was now as in fig. 6d.

The next step was to form the fishes' tails. the ECF is reset at radius 0.2in (after an initial trial of 0.18) and the depth stop adjusted to about 0.03 greater depth. The tool was fed in radially far enough to form a proper 'tail', and the fluting stop locked up. Then the four tails were cut at division plate settings of 13 +23, 49 + 59, 85 + 95, and 121 +131. The pattern was inspected to ensure no improvement could be made, and then I cut the remaining scollops at divisions 4-32-40-etc, to fill the gaps. The result was fig. 6 — or better, photo 12! Then I took a final skim off the overall diameter to reduce it to 1.90in, and parted the disc off 0.16in thick at the edge. Time for a pipe and a cuppa!

b second four cuts

c cuts 1-32 fish scales formed

d cuts 33-36 shaded areas deep to remove unwanted cuts

cutter fed across thus

e cuts 37-52 shaded areas form fishes' tails

Ornamental Ivory

Base and lid

I find it easier to machine a spigot to fit a socket than vice versa, so these two parts were tackled next. The base presents no problems. Gripped in the four-jaw independent chuck and set running true, machine the roughed-out cavity to size, using a vernier gauge to measure the bore. Treat the lid likewise, but in addition, the 1.51in cavity must be excavated to fit the blackwood disc. Now, it isn't easy to offer up such a disc to a hole during boring, but fortunately we have a gauge — the body of the piece from which it was parted off. So I used this to get an easy gluing fit. As far as practicable, I made the two bores of lid and base identical, but so that any error would make the base the larger of the two.

A piece of boxwood was set in the four-jaw chuck and machined to a good fit to the cavity of the base. Then the base was machined on the outside to the dimensions shown in fig. 7, and the boxwood spigot re-machined to fit the lid. In this case, as a pattern was to be cut, I set small pieces of double-sided tape on the shoulder of the chucking-block to give added security. After machining to profile, I excavated the cavity for the fish, again using the stub of the blank as a gauge. For a glue-fit like this I usually allow a radial gap of between 0.001 and 0.002in. Then the machine was set up to cut the 12 shell patterns.

The basis of this pattern is shown in fig. 8. It is generated from a series of circles of diminishing diameter, the centre of each circle displaced by an amount which superimposes the incisions at the 'root' of the shell. The pattern is usually cut using a double vee tool, no.91 (photo 10), but I prefer to use a no.92 with a shallow angle, the sloping face pointing towards the centre of the circle. This gives a profile nearer to a natural shell's.

The sliderest was set at the angle (11.75°) used to form the lid and a fine polishing skim cut across. Then I set the ECF up with a radius of 0.275in and made careful trials so the cut circle lay in the centre of the sloping face of the lid. The sliderest index was then set to zero, and 12 circles cut at this setting, using 0-8-16-24 etc holes in the 96-hole division plate. The radius was diminished by 0.025in and the topslide moved by the same amount. The depth of the circles was, of course, limited by the topslide depth-stop, and after cutting the first circle at the new setting it was carefully examined under a glass to ensure the apex between the grooves was at a sharp point and that it lay somewhat below the sloping surface. When this was established, I cut the second row of circles and repeated the process until, at the final cut, a simple cone was produced. Experience has shown me it's often difficult to remove spigotted workpieces when they're double-sided taped as well; I had made four chisel cuts on the shoulder of the block-chuck so narrow chisels could be used as levers. I put a slip of postcard between chisel and ivory for protection.

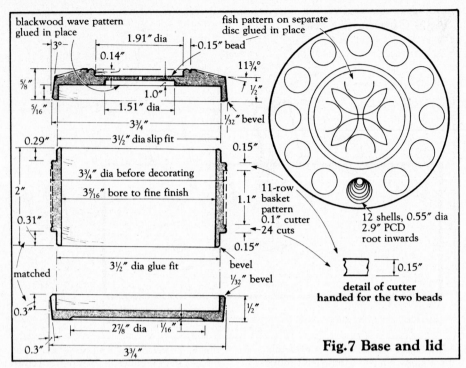

Fig.7 Base and lid

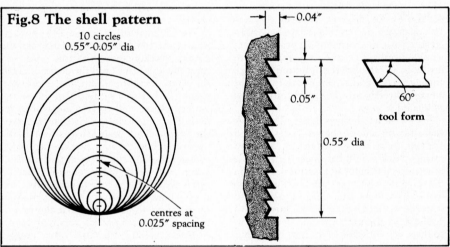

Fig.8 The shell pattern

10 circles
0.55″-0.05″ dia

centres at 0.025″ spacing

0.04″

0.05″

0.55″ dia

60°

tool form

Body

The dimensions are shown on fig. 7, and the first step was to finish-bore the inside. This was done in the four-jaw independent chuck gripping very lightly, setting the blank true with a dial indicator. This showed me the blank had gone oval by about ±0.006in since the roughing out — well within the machining allowance I had left on it. After boring, I faced one end up true while it was still in the chuck, and made two 'chucking plugs'. The first was ⅝in thick and had a shallow spigot to fit the ivory bore and a shoulder about ¼in wide. A centre-hole was very carefully made in this piece. The second piece had a longer spigot, and this one was left in the chuck after machining. I set the ivory blank on this with the previously-machined face set against the shoulder and the far end also faced to the correct overall length. Then it was removed and replaced with a few slips of double-sided tape on the shoulder, like

the lid; the second, centred, block was fitted to the outboard end and the tailstock poppet engaged. I designated the tailstock end 'bottom', and machined the spigot to a glue-fit (0.002in clearance) to the base. More important, the height of the spigot was matched exactly to the depth of the recess in the base. The outside diameter was then machined to overall finished size.

The geometry of the 'Basketwork' decoration is shown in fig. 9. It consists of 11 rows of 24 circular incisions, cut with a no.94 cutter 0.10in wide. Each row is cut exactly 0.10in from the previous one, and is displaced circumferentially by two divisions of the 96-hole circle; thus alternate rows lie exactly in line with each other, but are displaced from their neighbours to form the 'basket'. I applied two 'handed' decorative beads to finish the pattern.

In this case I did use a preliminary set-up with boxwood, but this was only to make sure the cutting-frame had been set with the

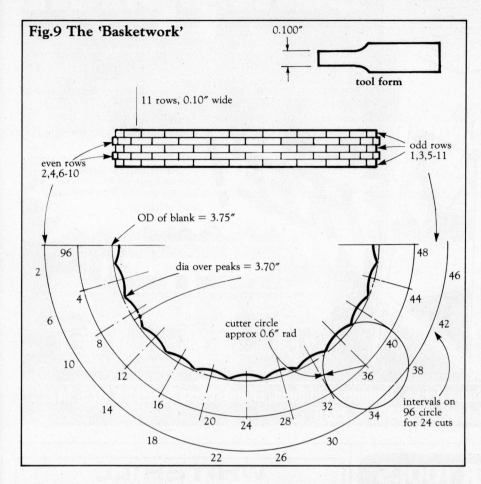

Fig.9 The 'Basketwork'

0.100"

tool form

11 rows, 0.10" wide

even rows
2,4,6-10

odd rows
1,3,5-11

OD of blank = 3.75"

dia over peaks = 3.70"

cutter circle
approx 0.6" rad

intervals on
96 circle
for 24 cuts

96 48
2 46
4 44
6 42
8 40
10 38
12 36
14 34
16 32
18 30
20 28
22 24 26

cutter rotating true in the vertical plane. If it wasn't, there would be little ridges on the sides of the incisions where the cuts had overlapped. I cut the first decorative bead at the tailstock end, using a low mandrel speed to reduce any risk of chatter. The cutting-frame was set up so the right-hand side of the cutter just cleared the edge of the moulded bead, the dividing index set at zero. I advanced the cutter, using the depth-stop **M** initially, until I judged it was nearly deep enough. The mandrel was then in-dexed over four holes and a second cut made to the same depth. This process was repeated, each time with a slightly deeper cut, until I could see the two cuts met at a point, and that point was slightly below the surface of the ivory. The depth-stop was then locked up, and the next operation used only the feed-control screw **L** (photo 5). The cuts were made at every four divisions of the index circle, then the sliderest was adjusted to carry the topslide across a distance exactly equal to its width. I keep a few cutters specially for this type of pattern, the widths established by micrometer as exactly those given by the divisions on the sliderest micrometer-screw.

The second circle was then cut using exactly the same depth but at the second set of divisions (fig. 9). This process was continued until all 11 were cut. Photo 15 shows the work in a similar box in African blackwood; which photographs rather better than ivory. Once all the basket was cut, I formed the decorative bead using the

opposite-hand cutter to that at the other end. This basketwork pattern is not at all difficult, but it can be tedious — there are 264 different settings and cuts, and it's easy to lose count — or worse, forget to retract the feed-control screw so the next cut goes in with a rush. You have to get an automatic — but careful and vigilant! — rhythm to the manipulation.

Finally, the piece is reversed on the block-chuck and the spigot machined to fit the lid. I first turn the spigot parallel to a fairly stiff push-fit using the sliderest, and

then use hand-tools to form a very slight taper — this is easier done by hand, as one can shave off as little as a tenth of a thousandth of an inch with care. I usually leave the lid just a trifle tight on the last ⅛in of the taper, and just a trifle slack on the first ⅛in. Then after a few days, if the ivory has moved to make the lid too tight, it can be eased with a hand-scraper inside the lid. (Unfortunately little can be done with a lid that grows loose!)

The final job, after brushing all over with a very fine (and *very* clean) silver-polishing brush to remove ivory dust, is to glue up. Many people use Araldite, and there's no doubt it's wholly compatible with ivory. However, I prefer old-fashioned Seccotine, the Lepages Glue so highly praised by ornamental turners 120 years ago. It has two advantages; first, if any spreads where it shouldn't it's very easily removed with warm water and a clean cloth, and second, the glued joint can be taken apart if necessary. If, on the other hand, the glue gives way, no harm is done and the pieces can be re-glued without difficulty. The base presents no problems at all — the merest smear on the spigot will suffice. But the two discs do need some care. I drilled a small hole (seen in fig. 7) and then applied a little glue on the underside of the ivory fish first, and pressed this in. A little glue emerged from the hole, so I removed the disc, wiped off some of the glue and tried again. I now had a measure of the amount of glue to apply to the blackwood. The problem here arises from the fact that though the machined recesses will have dead flat bottoms, this cannot be guaranteed with a parted-off surface.

The only remaining job (after leaving the whole thing for a day or so to ensure the lid still fits; for the record, it went just a trifle slack) was to find a suitable presentation box and an appropriate card to go with it. The gift was indeed reckoned to be a special one! ∎

● **Next month:** adapting an ordinary lathe for ornamental turning.

Photo 15 The basketwork pattern cut on an African blackwood box

Powerful people

Seven strange sculptures have been living in a Cheltenham Gallery. Love them or hate them, you couldn't ignore them; Tim Ashby came under their spell

Tom Dagnall is a sculptor who trained at Liverpool, Brighton and Chelsea art colleges and who now lives and works near Preston in Lancashire. These are pictures from his recent exhibition at Cheltenham's Park Gallery.

The setting — two bare rooms devoid of furniture — seemed at first a spartan backdrop for just seven pieces. But the effect was to draw you into the rooms and focus your eye and mind; the strangely powerful figures not only occupied their own space, but also seemed to capture the space round them.

The seven human-size carvings initially appeared larger than life. All carved in ash or elm, they were obviously meant to occupy a large space, not to sit decoratively on somebody's sideboard. They demanded your immediate attention and wiped out the need for analytical words.

Anyway, putting the impact and mood of these pieces into words would not only give a false impression, it would also negate one of the sculptor's main intentions. Tom wants his work to be experienced first hand without any intermediary to cloud the view, and though it isn't a new approach — the visual arts convey *visual* messages — it's a refreshing attitude. Modern sculpture only too frequently requires verbal explanation for the artist's abstract intentions to be understood. Tom's sculptures speak for themselves — to the informed or uninformed — in a language that needs no explanation.

Yet though this type of work speaks to many, not just the informed few, there's a basic dilemma for the artist trying to address the market as opposed to the mind. The sculptures' prices range (justifiably)

● An uncomfortable, uncompromising vision of humanity: a strangely moving exhibition. If these figures talked what would they say?

from £2-4000, so only select private individuals with fairly large houses can afford them. I suggested they be scaled down to reduce the price and make them more available to people with smaller incomes and dwellings, but Tom rightly argued that this would reduce the sculptures' power and impact. I also doubt whether this sort of work is suited to production runs! The pieces need space, so should be in large dwellings — or, even better, in public places.

Woodworkers would also raise their eyebrows to hear Tom uses no drawings when he creates his sculptures. 'Direct from mind to tool to log' is his method; a comment on the power of his creativity which speaks so uncompromisingly from the pieces themselves. Such power should be felt by wide audiences. ■

● Park Gallery, College of St Paul and St Mary, The Park, Cheltenham.

Hinged in the middle

David Applegate's unusual solution to an unusual brief for an extending table — six legs and folding beams!

● *An ingenious hinging mechanism . . .*

● *. . . and some delicate detail*

I was asked to make a table to seat 12 people, which would close up to a comfortable size for four. The table undercarriage, which could consist of up to six legs on castors, shouldn't get in the way of sitters' feet and legs; timber and its colour should match existing furniture as closely as possible. Access for a finished piece of this size was difficult, so the table had to be delivered in pieces and assembled on site. It was OK to store two loose leaves elsewhere, but the client wanted to be able fit only one if necessary. After some discussion, my client and I chose solid Brazilian mahogany for the material, with an extended size of 7ft 6in and a closed size of 3ft 6in, 4ft wide.

Normal High Street dining tables only extend to about another third of their closed length, with the extension piece concealed under outer leaves; or they use a rising pair of half-size leaves in the centre which cunningly open to form the extra surface. In this case the closed length requirement of 42in precluded the use of full-length bearer beams to carry the additional leaves, because if the beams had enough overlap to give the length to support the centre, they would stick out at each end when the table was closed up. That clearly wouldn't do!

Feasibility and design

It seemed to me at the design stage that although six legs were allowed, the foremost requirement was strength — 12 pairs of elbows might well be bearing down on the top at any one time, not to mention occasional use as staging to change a lamp bulb! I considered the idea of a set of telescoping beams with interlocking stopped dovetail tongues and grooves, including a controlled differential sliding movement of intermediate beams carrying the centre legs; but it filled me with horror! I just could not visualise success with such a system which depended so much on inherent stability of the material, so I turned my attention to the possibilities of folding beams, supported at their centres in the extended position by the centre legs, which would arrive more or less in the middle of the table when it was closed up. The centre legs would also be well out of the way of sitters (fig. 1).

This configuration attracted me, but its success obviously depended on the rigidity, strength and accuracy of the hinges. The requirements for the hinges emerged:
● Maximum length to resist horizontal bending loads.
● Good running fit between pins and bushes, with maximum bearing area for long life.
● Accurate location of hinge fingers on folding beams.
● Good appearance.
At first I considered a metal hinge like the ones on the edges of wallpaper pasting tables, fitted in pairs at each break-point. But I could see the screws getting loose, the hinge-pins wearing, and they probably wouldn't be pretty anyway. So I fastened on the idea of a knuckle type made of ½in birch

Plan and dimensions — all in imperial

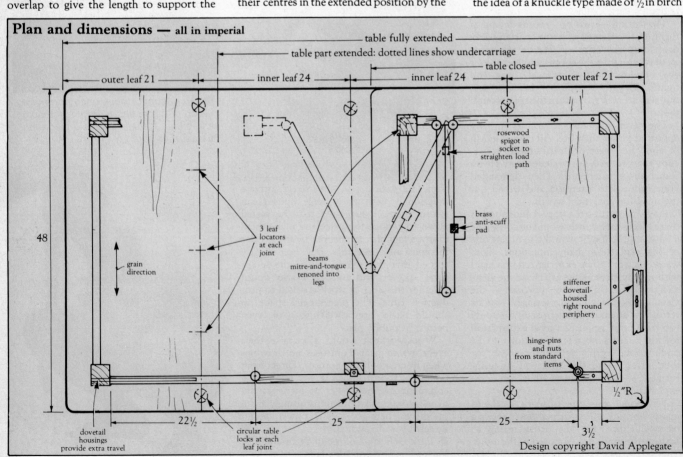

table fully extended
table part extended: dotted lines show undercarriage
table closed
outer leaf 21 — inner leaf 24 — inner leaf 24 — outer leaf 21

48

grain direction

3 leaf locators at each joint

beams mitre-and-tongue tenoned into legs

rosewood spigot in socket to straighten load path

brass anti-scuff pad

stiffener dovetail-housed right round periphery

hinge-pins and nuts from standard items

½ "R

dovetail housings provide extra travel

22½

circular table locks at each leaf joint

25

25

3½

Design copyright David Applegate

Fig.1

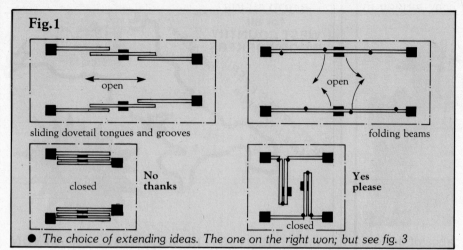

open

sliding dovetail tongues and grooves

open

folding beams

closed

No thanks

closed

Yes please

● *The choice of extending ideas. The one on the right won; but see fig. 3*

multiply, with brass bushes secured by epoxy resin, and turning on a steel pin. This multi-fingered hinge would (I hoped) ensure rigidity, with its extensive gluing bearing areas. The leaf-bearing beams were decided at 4x1½in; this would allow seven hinge fingers at each break-point, giving ¼in clearance top and bottom for bolt heads and nuts (fig. 2).

But a problem with this idea became apparent. When the table was closed, loads at the centre of the table-top would be resisted only by the folded beam's resistance to twisting about its hinge — it would rotate round the centre leg, as in fig. 3a.

Fig.2 Multi-finger hinges

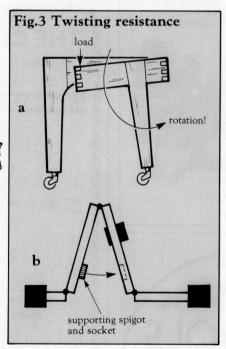

multi-ply hinge fingers

⅝

1½

beam

5

So it seemed a lock between the two folded arms was necessary, which would be achieved by a block on one beam locating (endgrain first) into the other as they came together. This would provide a virtually straight load path between the two corner legs (fig. 3b).

It was also clear that without the leaves fitted, the assembled undercarriage would float round like a demented concertina; to

prevent this, the leaves would have to locate — and lock — accurately together. Only the two outer leaves could be fixed to the undercarriage, so both they and the removable leaves had to be fixed to each other both laterally and longitudinally. Across the width, the usual method of pegs and holes was obvious; but having seen so many wooden stumps floating sadly in jagged craters, I resolved to use tapered steel pins entering brass bushes, three on each leaf (fig. 4). Locking along the length would be by commercially available circular table locks, fitted on the underside of each leaf.

With the undercarriage fully extended,

Fig.3 Twisting resistance

load

a

rotation!

b

supporting spigot and socket

both intermediate leaves could be inserted. But to lock all the leaves together, the undercarriage would have to be pulled together again slightly, so the last set of leaf locators actually entered and the leaves closed up. But: this would push the centre legs inwards — very unsightly — and would also introduce a dog-leg in the load path. So it was clear that one of the outer leaves would have to slide relative to the under-

Fig.4 Leaf locators

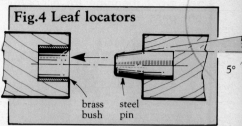

5°

brass bush   steel pin

Fig.5 Sliding dovetail slip

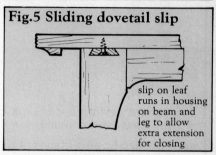

slip on leaf runs in housing on beam and leg to allow extra extension for closing

Fig.6 Tenon details

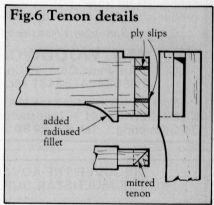

ply slips

added radiused fillet

mitred tenon

carriage to achieve final locking. I decided to do this by mounting the leaf on a dovetail slip running in a matching housing in the top edge of the undercarriage (fig. 5).

As for the structure itself, the mortise and tenon joints at each corner leg had to be capable of taking the varying bending moments applied during extension and retraction, as well as those of normal use. The nominal 4in depth of the beams was increased on the lower edge by adding a radius fillet (fig. 6). The tenon ends were cut at 45°, and ply slips added.

Construction

I carefully laid out the boards for the table-top to decided the best combination of figuring commensurate with endgrain direction; hand-planed the sides with a jointer until they were straight and square, routed them for loose ¼in ply stopped tongues, and glued them together under clamp pressure. While these set and settled, I cut the beams to length, and cut the appropriate radii at the hinge points. These radii must allow clearance for the hinge fingers to rotate without rubbing. The slots for the fingers were then routed out, and the ends chiselled square. Only when I was sure that this pioneer work on the hinge housings was right and the beam lengths correct did I start on the more familiar task of forming tenons for the leg joints. The format for these is shown in fig. 6.

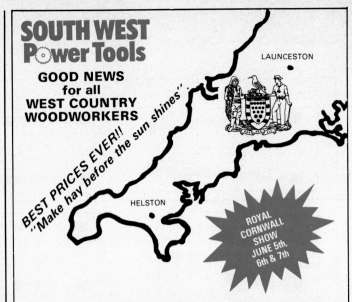

506

Hinged in the middle

After gluing the beams to the legs, I considered the business of making and fitting the hinge fingers in detail. The need to keep all the beams horizontal — and the legs vertical — meant they had to be made and fitted with the utmost accuracy. I quickly found that the only possible datum on the fingers had to be the hole drilled for the brass bush; all the other cuts had to be relevant to that hole. As 42 fingers were needed, I devised a simple jig to profile the outer radius, the rear edge and the overall length. Assembly was done with the bushes and hinge pins in position, and I ensured alignment by folding the associated beams back on themselves and clamping them with polythene sheet between them to stop them sticking together.

The hinge-pins and bushes were made from standard ½ in UNF steel bolts and ½ in I.D. drawn brass tube respectively; the bolt-heads and nuts were reduced in thickness and polished by a friendly neighbourhood turner, who also made the leaf locators shown in fig. 4.

The undercarriage less the centre legs could now be assembled dry and given a preliminary functional test. Obligingly, it worked! I extended the assembly gingerly, and established the centre-point of each side to find the correct place for the centre legs — under the middle joint of the two inner table leaves. The centre legs, which were tapered on all four faces as opposed to the corner legs' two, were fitted to the appropriate beams with open mortise joints, and that finally completed the undercarriage structure. I cut the leaves to size, and drilled holes for the leaf locators; these had to be dead accurate, because all the leaf pins had to enter all the leaf bushes with a gentle whoosh of escaping air. So, with blocks and rods and a load of sticky tape, I took the plunge with the router. The undersides of the leaves were dovetail-grooved to receive dovetailed stiffeners: these were slot-screwed to the leaves, and mitred at the corners. Then I reeded the exposed edges of the leaves with the router; tricky at the corners, necessitating more blocks and tape. Lastly, the top surface was sanded using successively finer grades of aluminium oxide paper.

I had done some finishing before assembly. All the visible surfaces were pigmented, brushed with sanding sealer and lightly sanded, so at least some excess glue could be peeled off. After assembly, a coat of button polish finally brought up the colour match. The moisture-resistant layers of polyurethane were then brushed on, lightly sanded between coats, and the whole thing was finished with several applications of wax polish.

All the brasswork — the hinge bushes, castors, leaf locators, the anti-scuff pads at the top of the centre legs, the circular table leaf locks — were fitted using Araldite and screw attachments. The glue I used was PVA throughout: with a 'dynamic' article like a folding, extending, mobile, elbow-supporting dining table, PVA's elasticity is essential to complement that of the timber.

My client, a member of the Church, wanted some Biblical symbols on the table, and these were produced in low relief on the tops of the main legs, subtly shaded by the table-top. The entire table was pigmented to match the colour of existing mahogany dining chairs, and the reeding on the table edge was to echo a feature on the chairs. Delivery and assembly was very simple — by withdrawing two hinge-pins, the whole thing is instantly converted to two easily managed sections (and the two loose leaves, of course).

I admit the hinge design, with its load-spreading characteristics, owes more to naval aircraft wingfold and helicopter bladefold hinges than to traditional cabinet-work. Also, the idea that the locked table-top should give stability to the assembled structure possibly derives from the aero-nautical idea of stressed-skin construction. But since making this table, I've seen a photograph of a card-table treated on similar lines in the 19th century. So perhaps my thoughts of an aerospace relationship are pure fancy!

At all events, this table worked very well. I was able to give it a dummy run before final delivery, lending it to the client for a formal lunch with the new Bishop of Taunton. Some problems came to light (unconnected with the Church!) and were rectified quite easily. I found this exercise extremely valuable, as it confirmed before final delivery that the table fulfilled all the requirements of the brief. ∎

Fig. 7 Edge detail

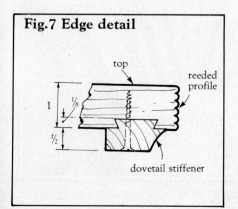

top
reeded profile
1
⅛
½
dovetail stiffener

Fig. 8 Corner

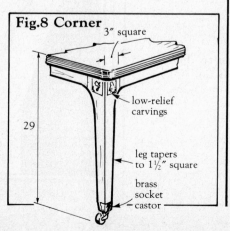

3″ square
low-relief carvings
29
leg tapers to 1½″ square
brass socket
castor

Winning willows

The month is June, so the game must be cricket. George Jaffa looks at the trees and the skills that go to make a first-class bat

Frangibility, or the noticeable modern tendency of things to break, doesn't extend to cricket bats. The beginnings of cricket are lost in the mists of time, but the few firms that make bats have plied their trade with little change since the sport stabilised its image in the first half of the last century.

Bats used in the 13th century were probably just sticks with heavy heads, roughly carved from tree timber to suit the individual, but by the mid-18th century, today's blade shape was already in use — against underarm bowling. Overarm delivery would have sent the batsman screaming back to the pavilion; bats then were solid with springless handles! The separate shock-absorbing handle didn't make its appearance for another century, although maximum overall dimensions (4½x38in) were laid down as long ago as 1835.

Today's cricket bats are works of art in wood, despite the numbers in which they are made. Mechanisation helps at various stages, but the final shaping is down to the flair of the craftsman, who in turn is dependent on exemplary choice of wood — and that falls to experts with a lifetime's experience in assessing *Salix alba spp. caerulae*. This willow is almost the only timber used, and trees more than 12 years old are seldom chosen. What they got up to a century ago is another matter. I suspect the older trees tend to early decline because they take such a buffeting from pollution, plus hybridisation makes choice much more difficult. In 1888 a 111ft 53-year old willow, (near the end of its life) made an incredible 1179 sound bats!

The playable cricket bat is a far cry from one of the willow clefts stacked for seasoning in open-sided sheds for up to a year. It's even further from a crude 28in trunk length waxed at both ends to prevent splitting and warping. All that can be said of that stage is that the cleft approximates in size to the finished article. During its long drying period, the wood loses more than half its weight (air-dried bat willow weighs about 25lb per cu ft).

The drying session ends with clefts being rough cut, planed to final shape and size and fed into a specially shaped rolling machine. With a pressure of around 2,000lb per sq ft to compress the wood fibres, it reduces the cleft size by about 1/16in. Rolling also ensures strength in edges particularly vulnerable to the impact of a hard cricket ball. The process used to be carried out by hand with skilful use of a hammer; there's no saying

● *Splitting willow clefts at Wright and Sons of Great Leighs, Essex – the country's leading willow grower*

● *Gray-Nicols use a species of eccentric copy lathe for the bat blades. Blade below, template above*

whether the bats were better, but the roller is certainly quicker.

Splice cutting and handle fitting are akin to carpentry joints in some ways, except that a carpenter's skill doesn't have to withstand constant blows. These days splices and handles are machine-cut for accuracy and convenience. Handles, which are responsible for most of the resilience in the blade, are made from best East Indian 'Sarawak' cane, very carefully selected. The

process of creating the intriguing seriate cross-section of the handle head starts when the cane is split vertically by machine and the pieces planed both sides for gluing. 12-16 lengths of cork, rubber gutta percha or whalebone are inserted, and the finished article is shaped slightly oval, one end wedge-shaped to splice into the blade. This splice joint really sums up the bat maker's skill. Although powerful glue is used, the bat relies for its strength on nothing more

● *Blades are carried under rollers which exert great pressure to compact the fibres*

than a perfect fit! If the handle wedge is a fraction too small, the bat comes apart under pressure: too wide a wedge, and the blade splits in play. Fitting the joint to perfection is done entirely by eye. During the process, the maker first gets a feel of the fit by gently tapping the wedge into the splice, then bit by bit takes minute shavings from the handle. The fit is usually so good that handle and blade can only be separated by a sharp blow on the bat's shoulder. Animal glue is used for the final fixing, which single job demands considerable skill in itself, because the handle is at a slight angle from the blade to achieve a good balance.

The final preparation demands super-lative craftsmanship. If you've ever wondered whether a mould or matrix is needed to get the bat's shape, the answer is that it's entirely down to the craftsman's skill and eye. He sculpts. He gauges the flat front, straight sides and humped back using a draw-knife pulled towards him (the back is known as the 'meat'), with the bat strung between vice and a special belted apron holding the handle. The draw-knife gives way to a small plane to get out the knife marks, and then to a spokeshave. The handle is shaped in the same way with a draw-knife, but the final finish is put on with rasp and file. Towards the end, the finisher periodically tests the bat at an imaginary crease for balance and feel. When he's satisfied, it is sanded.

Today, cricket bats are bleached in three applications at 24 hour intervals — it doesn't necessarily improve them, but it's a matter of popular demand. Then the bat has to be rolled again to compress the fibres raised by the bleach, and given another sanding. Final burnishing is with a white

● *Right: a stack of glued handles ready for shaping. Note the different sorts of lamination*

wax compound, which gives the blade its satin smooth finish.

The handle is bound (linen thread in animal glue) on a lathe and topped with the ubiquitous rubber grip, also glued on. Then it's up to the proud owner to lovingly apply regular doses of raw linseed oil. The small hole at the bottom of the bat, incidentally, is made by the lathe — it's not an 'oil hole' as some people think.

Although demand for bats is on the increase, other old manual skills of this calibre are notably on the wane. So is the electronically made bat just round the corner? The answer is probably no, as long as this country hogs the trade. Britain grows 90% of the world's cricket bat willows and the remainder (of indifferent quality) come from India and Pakistan. The tree favours marshy areas like East Anglia and the Thames Valley, but individual specimens can be found dotted about the countryside elsewhere.

Plantations for the trade demand rigorous management, usually a task for specialists only. G.S. Wright & Sons Ltd of Great Leighs, Essex, who have been at the game for several generations, have plantations which run to about 30 trees per acre. The young sets are planted some 3-

40ft apart to accommodate the massive crowns achieved at maturity. Growth is fast: 10-12ft in the first three years. Faster growth is possible if rooted plants are used — up to 15ft. The rate of success in mature growth terms is relatively high (90%), but as many as half of rooted plant-grown trees might be indifferent for bats.

The bat cleft comes solely from the trunk, while the remaining timber is ideal for chip baskets and artificial limbs. To ensure perfect stems, the young trees are regularly disbudded (an expert's painstaking task), but cultivation is not without problems. The cricket-bat willow is resilient and remarkably tolerant of cold weather, but it dislikes salt-laden winds, and its chief predator is the bacterial 'water mark' disease. The bright orange 'butterfly' stain which sometimes appears in bat fibres could easily be mistaken for disease, but strangely enough, it's normally taken to indicate the best wood obtainable. So if you're at deep cover when someone with a lurid orange bat comes to the crease — wake up! ■

● Thanks to Wright and Sons, Great Leighs, Essex for the first photo, and to Gray-Nicols of Robertsbridge, Sussex, where the others were taken.

● *The art of shaping the bat by hand – balance is all*

● *Not more fibre compression, but testing the finished bat for soundness*

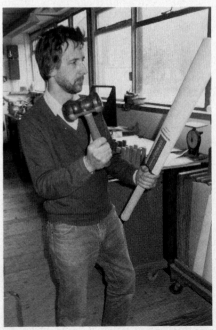

Unwinding

A twist in a frame or board is a maddening thing, and there's no proper tool to tell you it's there — which is why you should make your own winding strips

The Oxford Dictionary states: 'Wind — go in a circular, spiral, curved or crooked course, meander. (Path, river winds; "herd winds o'er the lea")'.

Winding strips are among that small collection of vital tools which no money can buy. They are magnifiers of twist and are essential for testing the truth of a board, frame, box, drawer or carcase. So essential, in fact, that I seriously wonder how anyone can do quality work without them; but many try, and surprisingly, many have never heard of them.

If you fall into this category, don't delay — make a pair of winding strips right away. Or better still, make two pairs, a long and a short.

Ideally, you should use old well-seasoned wood, possibly salvaged from old furniture. Winding strips that warp are worse than useless. A wedge-shaped section gives greater stability, though this isn't essential. The dimensions given are only suggestions, dependent mainly on the material available.

Face and edge the two pieces, saw them to length and get them to width and thickness, **A**. Gauge and plane the taper (**B** and **C**); the strips can, of course, be produced using the planer and thicknesser. **E** shows how it can easily be arranged on the planer; fix a piece of hardboard or thin ply to the planer table with double-sided tape, and run the strip at an angle over that and against the fence. A heavy cut will give a good angled face, then finish off with a fine cut with the hardboard removed and the piece running on the face of the taper.

For a quality version, apply a dark veneer to the front face of one strip and let in two dark sights to the other. If the timber itself is dark, apply light-coloured veneer. A quicker and more workaday model can be made by using sprayed matt black paint. The front strip is simply sprayed on one face, and the rear one taped up with sticky tape which is then cut true with a cutting gauge, knife and square (**D**). Then spray on the sights. Sticky tape works better than masking tape, as the latter's rough texture lets paint creep under it.

When you're using winding strips, make sure the surface to be tested is flat, position the two strips at its extreme ends and sight across their tops. Slowly lower your head, watching the light area between the dark front strip and the dark sights on the back

one disappear. Remember winding strips are magnifiers of twist, so don't be too discouraged by the error revealed (**F** and **G**).

When you're testing glued-up frames or box constructions, take particular care to keep the winding strips free from glue — a blob of glue will magnify a possibly non-existent error! ∎

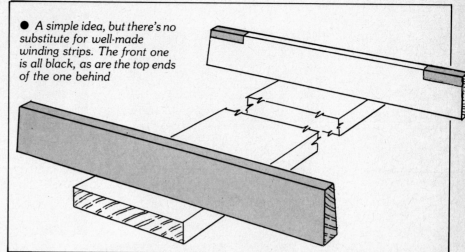

● *A simple idea, but there's no substitute for well-made winding strips. The front one is all black, as are the top ends of the one behind*

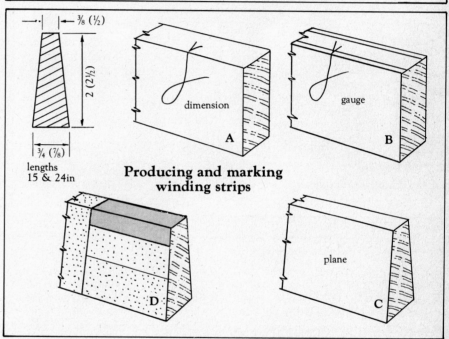

lengths 15 & 24in

⅜ (½)
2 (2½)
¾ (⅞)

dimension **A**

gauge **B**

Producing and marking winding strips

plane **C**

D

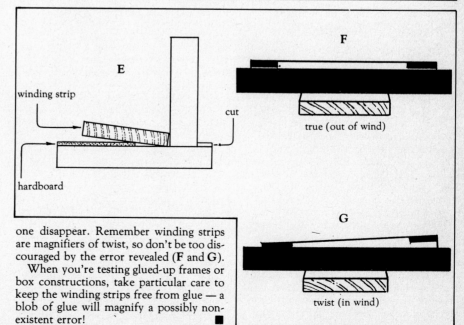

winding strip

hardboard

E

cut

F

true (out of wind)

G

twist (in wind)

Bowled over

● *Final shaping with the lance. Tool handles are shovel or hay-fork size*

● *Get an idea of the scale of these pieces from the cover shot! Ed works 20in-diameter bowls to a thickness of about ⅓in...*

'Big is beautiful' is undoubtedly the theme of Ed Moulthrop's work. Ray Key introduces the dynamic American turner and his grand-scale techniques

My trip last October to the US for the 'Woodturning — Vision and Concept' Exhibition/Seminar at the idyllic Arrowmont School for the Arts, presented the ideal opportunity to spend a few days with Ed Moulthrop — the turner renowned for his giant creations. After the Arrowmont event and lectures (five days with America's best: Ellesworth, Osolnik Hogbin, Stirt and Stubbs) I met Ed in the sweltering heat of Atlanta. With mid-October humidity at 60% and temperatures well into the 80s, it's worlds apart from our woodworking conditions!

Ed Moulthrop's work can be somewhat awe-inspiring in its size and scale, but its pure simplicity always shows off the beauty of the materials he uses. He's a multi-talented individual who seems to make a success of everything. After establishing himself as a leading architect, he taught architecture and physics at the Georgia Institute of Technology; served as the chairman of the Georgia State Arts Commission for eleven years, and — in his spare time — became an accomplished wood sculptor and water-colour artist. A man of great talent and much energy.

His passion for turning goes back to when he was 15. He started with conventional lathe and tools, but about 25 years ago he gave them away and made his own. As an engineer and toolmaker, he has developed his own unique versions of both lathe and tools; his working methods are equally unique. Everything he makes is from endgrain, the main reason why he uses PEG (not my personal favourite), which allows for a much wider use of his timber. It's log to lathe — no cutting discs on a bandsaw — so the heart is present in all his work. There's an abundant supply of local timber and he has two tame tree-surgeons (a rare commodity) who contact him when something of interest turns up.

Trunks and limbs are delivered in short lengths (felling a complete trunk is usually impossible in crowded forests, so trees are cut down in sections) and stored on poly-thene sheets to trap water and keep the base permanently moist. This induces spalting which adds character to the timber, but any more than two years' wet-storage would cause too much decay. The sections of trunk are stood on end and covered with shaving mulch to slow down drying and reduce radial cracking; they are protected from the intense sun by the foliage of the trees round Ed's stock area. Most of the wood is worked within 12-18 months, depending on species and size.

The simple trick of storing the logs on high ground means that they can be rolled downhill when they're needed. Ed's wife Mae has to help with the larger ones — they can weigh up to 1600lbs — by nudging up to them with the car and then reversing slowly down the slope as Ed 'shepherds' from the other side!

Before it's mounted on the lathe, each end of a log is trued up with an electric chainsaw. Loose bark, decay and stones are removed, and the baulk is mounted on an appropriate-sized face-plate with long woodscrews and coach screws. Two-ton capacity overhead lifting gear, its electrical controls allowing precise positioning, is brought into play to bring the baulk actually on to the lathe.

Tools and machinery

Ed's lathes are something special. His roughing machine, apart from the mechanics and the tool-rest, is entirely wooden — a ¾in birch ply structure with a 2in pine door on top, a 2in square timber corner support to the ground, and the whole thing bolted to the floor. A nearby scrapyard supplied the 3½in-diameter shaft and the 5hp 80rpm geared motor, which supplies the virtually unstoppable power. The tool-rest is supported by an arm like a railway sleeper; it draws out from the lathe and can pivot according to the size of the enormous bowls, fixed with two G-cramps.

There are ³⁄₁₆in holes drilled along the top of the rest, into which Ed puts hardened pins (masonry nails) to pivot his tools. He moves the pivot point along as the work takes shape. His finishing lathe is built along the same lines, only smaller, with a 1½hp motor and a smaller shaft; he never turns faster than 800rpm.

Ed has three basic tools in various sizes; a loop for removing bowl interiors, a lance for outside shaping, and a cut-off tool. They're all made from old reamers (bought from a favourite scrapyard) which he forges into the shapes he wants; they're extremely hard and chip easily if they're knocked — not how a manufacturer would do it, says Ed. All are epoxy-resined into long shovel or hay-fork type handles. His latest monster is 10ft long, weighs 75lb and has a 2½in drill-rod handle. It was so difficult to control that it needed a 1cwt castered tool-support for the end of the handle, to run on the floor; Ed manipulates it in the middle.

The work

The lance which is used for all the outside shapes looks like a round-nosed scraper, but the underside is round, with a long bevel, which rubs and supports the cut in the same way as a gouge. It always cuts, never scrapes. Once the work has a pleasing outside shape in rough, a slight depression is made in the centre. Ed mounts a long twist spur-bit in a hand-brace, marks it for depth of cut, then as the lathe moves at low speed, he presents the threaded drill-tip to the work, horizontal and parallel to the shaft. The tip pulls the bit into the wood and the hollow core is created. Sometimes he can get the bit out while the lathe is running, but if not it's let go of the brace, step back and turn the lathe off! The mass is rapidly hollowed out with the loop tool, opening up the core as it's pivoted against the pin in the rest. It's super-efficient on endgrain, leaving giant spaghetti shavings.

All Ed's work is rough-turned wet, the sap and surface water still present, which makes bulk removal easier and allows the

● Ed's timber store in the leafy Atlanta humidity; mulch on top of the logs, polythene below to retain moisture

roughed items to be soaked in PEG. Ed's 'PEG farm' consists of 12 250-gallon vats, each containing 150 gallons of the solution! The discrepancy, of course, allows for displacement of the bowls when they go into the vats. Ed has long experience with PEG, and he now has the process down to a fine art. After the objects are removed from the lathe and date-stamped, they are soaked in PEG for a minimum of three months (five during the mild winter when osmosis takes longer in the unheated vats), then removed and left to drain on racks, preferably outside. Then they are put into a dehumidifying room to remove the last moisture, and taken for finishing.

The finishing workshop is also dehumidified (to combat the persistent

humidity), and it's here that the bowls are re-mounted on face-plates, and hand- and power-sanding (a flexible drive shaft connects directly to a ½hp motor) completes the shaping. Cracks and flaws are filled with epoxy resin and wood dust for a perfect match, then sanded to finish.

Ed is a little cagey about the applied finish. Coat upon coat of whatever it is is applied, sanded, buffed, oiled and waxed — but he's still seeking the ideal finish to go over PEG. The cut-off tool concludes the finish at the base, which is made concave by power sanding after the last surplus material is taken off and the work removed from the lathe. Finally the pieces are engraved with Ed's mark and dated.

All this is what I saw and was told by Ed, but I also had the chance to use his tools and rough out a large bowl. The tools (of course!) are like nothing I've ever used before; I felt I would have been happier using a conventional gouge for the outside form, but the loop tool for internal hollowing was quite something. Used on endgrain, it removed bulk quicker than any tool I've used.

Perhaps the most commercially successful turner in the US — his pieces range in price from $250-1500, $5000 for the biggest — Ed works eight or nine hours a day six days a week to produce about 250 items a year. They vary in size from 8-40in diameter, and the biggest so far stands 48in high! Its finished diameter is 30in; the blank started on the lathe weighing 1600lb, and ended up weighing 70. He sells through a selection of galleries across the States, and usually mounts two exhibitions a year of around 40 pieces, which almost always sell out.

Despite his phenomenal success, Ed is a modest, easy-going man with a dry wit and a warm line in hospitality. It's his talent and work that are larger than life. ∎

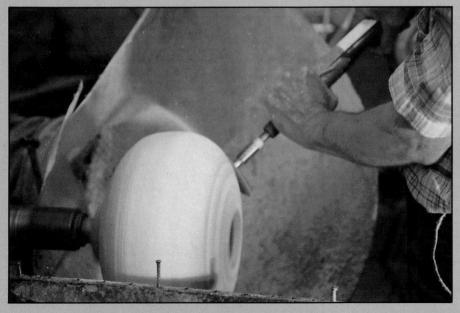

● Power sanding with the flexible shaft before filling, matching and applying that secret finish

514

Letters

AS A PROFESSIONAL carver, I was interested in 'Carving a Career' (WW/Mar). I found it interesting, but I felt Mick Atkins hadn't really enjoyed his apprenticeship or life as a carver. He gave the impression that pay and conditions were very poor. I agree they were never grand, but my own experience shows they were far better for some of us.

My diary for 1963 (the year Mick Atkins started) shows a good carver in a high-class firm in London earning 9/- (45p) per hour, and a journeyman a little less. This means that an apprentice starting at 30% of a man's rate would receive nearly 3/- per hour; almost what Mick Atkins quotes. It's only in recent years that carver's wages have been devalued. I know of one man who left his job as a bus driver in 1948 and found his wages doubled as a carver. This wouldn't be the case in 1986!

Mick did very well to get a kit of tools for £40; that certainly wouldn't have bought the 350 tools I need.

He makes no mention of the fun and competition to be had with other apprentices, nor does he mention the day release at school where you met apprentices from other firms, each claiming their firm had the best work.

We had plenty of opportunity of working on 'one-offs', as it was common practice for an apprentice to finish a piece started by a top craftsman. This is the best and only way to learn your craft. We were also lucky in that the firm employed up to 25 carvers at a time, so there was always plenty of interesting carving going on. I think everyone remembers the excitement of carving their first coat of arms or large figure.

We didn't have the problem of going to see the boss about our wages that Mick had at the end of his apprenticeship. This was controlled by the rating committee, which was a panel of journeymen and employers which fixed a rate according to ability.

Anthony Webb,
Master carver at St Paul's Cathedral

ANNE MCBRIDE ('Old and yew', WW/Feb) is wrong on two counts. Firstly, English yew is *second* best; and to the words 'most highly prized was slow-growing mountain yew' should be added 'from the high Italian mountains', a piece of information from Roger Ascham's *Toxophilus*, dated 1545. *Master of Game* by the Duke of York, dating from 1410, is undoubtedly a plagiarism of a work by a Gaston de Foix, indicating that the French had the knowhow in bow making, and access to finer yew than the English variety, very early on. The bow is thought to have arrived with the Danes, so Englishmen would have been looking for home-grown material to make them. In the 1500s, bow staves were imported as duty on wine, so many staves per barrel as a tax. The *Hatfield Papers* (1574), give four districts as sources of good bow-staves: Salzburg, Austria; above

Basel; Revel, Dansk, Polonia, and all countries east of the Sound; and Italy. The most important factor is the need for the yew to grow slowly (which it does only in a cold climate), for the close grain.

'Sawing' the staves defeats the whole purpose of using yew, for its very structure, and thus its springiness, depend on leaving the fibres as a continuous thread. Alas it isn't possible to plane off the bumps and lumps — if you do, the bow will collapse at these points when drawn. This is the reason why nearly all, barring the very best and most expensive, yew bows have distortions in their length, for it isn't easy to get straight grain for a continuous two metres.

Those interested in the fascinating subject of bows and bow-making should read the superb book by A. E. Hodgkin, *The Archers Craft* (Faber & Faber, about 1953). Quite the finest book on the subject.
David Crump, Launceston

I WOULD JUST LIKE to clear up a small error in my letter on the Vaughans (WW/Apr). It should have referred to West End stores, not East End, as the main market area for the Vaughans' furniture.
Anthony Vaughan, Lynsted

READERS MAY REMEMBER one of our folk toys on *Woodworker*'s front cover (Dec 85) to illustrate the extract from *Making Wooden Toys* (David & Charles). We are now researching an encyclopaedia of moving traditional folk toys and would be glad to hear from readers who have any knowledge of the subject.

What we're looking for is anyone who remembers, has in their possession, or knows where to find, old moving toys, ingenious mechanisms, books — and anything at all on the subject. Anyone who gives us any help will of course have full accreditation.

The idea is to prevent the art of making traditional folk moving toys from dying out, so we'd be more than pleased to hear from anyone with an interest in it.
Anthony and Judy Peduzzi, Southernwood, Predannack, Mullion, Cornwall TR12 7HA

HAVING READ Mr Elkington's letter in April's *Woodworker*, I feel I must reply because it could deter would-be participants from going on woodturning courses. It's important from the safety angle that people don't adapt the DIY trial-and-error attitude and operate powerful lathes without first receiving professional tuition.

I've just returned from a two-day course on woodturning at Craft Supplies Ltd, near Buxton. The course only took four pupils, each of whom had the use of a lathe with a complete set of tools. Apart from about the first half an hour, when the instructor explained the operation of each chisel, we spent the two days woodturning ourselves.

We each had our own room in the hostelry which was comfortable, warm and quite adequate. Vast quantities of good wholesome plain country foods were supplied by Jane who runs the hostel.

When we eventually set off for home we had each made a chisel handle, an egg, an egg-cup, a jewel box with lid, a bowl and a lace bobbin; all the materials for which *and* full board were included in the price of £105. This was much more expensive than the course which Mr. Elkington attended, but we got great value, thanks to Jamie Wallwin's first-class instruction.

Mr Elkington's advice is to shop around to see what you're going to get. I didn't, but I was lucky.
Bryan Orchard

● See also 'Turning the corner', WW/May.

● **Correction** Mr Elkington has written to say that the woodturning course he wrote about in 'Letters', WW/April, was *nine* years ago, not one. This was a handwriting matter; please type your letters if you can!

I AM A FURNITURE RESTORER working in Australia and have difficulty finding good antique reproduction brass handles, knobs (wooden and china), and general fittings. I'd be grateful if any readers who specialise in such items would get in touch with me at this address.
J. Burchhardt, 29 Blackhall St, Woombye 4559, Queensland, Australia

Letters

I LEARNT THE HARD way (there are now 10 stitches in my index finger) about a very dangerous practice on the small bandsaw ('Machining wood', WW/Feb). My bandsaw is fairly typical: two wheels, 6in depth-of-cut — but without a groove in the table like the one in your article. The combination of a jig and holding-block running in a groove might have prevented my accident. I was cutting ½in-thick 'wheels' from a 2in-diameter cylinder, running the cylinder end along the ordinary fence. I've done this many times before, and all was well until I tried to cut the last wheel with just over 1in of stock left. The blade grabbed the wood with a bang, twisting it violently and dragging my knuckle on to the blade below the top guide, which was well down.

I can only emphasise that bandsaws are only 'comparatively' safe, and feel that retailers should supply short instruction courses to all buyers. I'll take more care in future but I was lucky not to have lost my whole finger.

P. R. Quelch, Argyll

RECENT LETTERS on sharpening handsaws (WW/Sep, Nov 85, Jan, Apr 86) made me think of an alternative practice which, I was told, is called the Australian method. You can see why if you examine the two approaches:

English: if you call the 'direction' of the file that of the handle, the leading edge of the saw tooth leans in that direction, and the tooth vibrates so the point and edge are not smooth.

Australian: the 'direction' of the file is away from the handle, and the leading edge and point of the saw-tooth lean away, so you get a smoother point and edge (and longer-lasting when cutting hardwoods).

It's good to keep an open mind on different practices; and interesting to know that Indian carpenters sharpen to cut on the 'full stroke', and the Swedish 'Bushman' saw cuts in both directions!

L. Turner, Dudley

I WONDER IF any of your readers can help with a bit of detective work. In the collection of photographs left by my father, I found two pictures labelled '1932' — but nothing else (*see right*). They appear to be pictures of carved bed-heads and I'd like to know who carved them and where they are now. If any reader has an idea of their origins I'd be glad to hear from them.

J. Baldwin, 107 Cleveland Ave, Darlington, DL3 7BD

Searching for flamingoes . . .

● . . . *does anyone know where this one of two bedheads came from or where they went?*

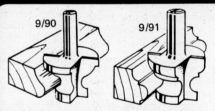

shopguide

AVON

BATH   Tel. Bath 64513
JOHN HALL TOOLS   ★
RAILWAY STREET

Open: Monday-Saturday
9.00 a.m.-5.30 p.m.
H.P.W.WM.D.A.BC.

BRISTOL   Tel. (0272) 741510
JOHN HALL TOOLS LIMITED   ★
CLIFTON DOWN SHOPPING CENTRE
WHITELADIES ROAD
Open: Monday-Saturday
9.00 a.m.-5.30 p.m.
H.P.W.WM.D.A.BC.

BRISTOL   Tel. (0272) 629092
TRYMWOOD SERVICES
2a DOWNS PARK EAST, (off North View)
WESTBURY PARK
Open: 8.30 a.m.-5.30 p.m. Mon. to Fri.
Closed for lunch 1.00-2.00 p.m.
P.W.WM.D.T.A.BC.

BRISTOL   Tel. (0272) 667013
FASTSET LTD
190-192 WEST STREET
BEDMINSTER
Open: Mon.-Fri. 8.30 a.m.-5.00 p.m.
Saturday 9.00 a.m.-1.00 p.m.
H.P.W.WM.D.CS.A.BC.

BRISTOL   Tel. (0272) 667013
WILLIS
157 WEST STREET
BEDMINSTER
Open Mon.-Fri. 8.30 a.m.-5.00 p.m.
Sat. 9 a.m.-4 p.m.
P.W.WM.D.CS.A.BC.

BEDFORDSHIRE

BEDFORD   Tel. (0234) 59808
BEDFORD SAW SERVICE   K
39 AMPTHILL ROAD

Open: Mon.-Fri. 8.30-5.30
Sat. 9.00-4.00
H.P.A.BC.W.CS.WM.D.

BERKSHIRE

READING   Tel. Littlewick Green
DAVID HUNT (TOOL   2743
MERCHANTS) LTD   ★
KNOWL HILL, NR. READING
Open: Monday-Saturday
9.00 a.m.-5.30 p.m.
H.P.W.D.A.BC.

READING   Tel. Reading 661511
WOKINGHAM TOOL CO. LTD.
99 WOKINGHAM ROAD

Open: Mon-Sat 9.00 a.m.-5.30 p.m.
Closed 1.00-2.00 p.m. for lunch
H.P.W.WM.D.CS.A.BC.

BUCKINGHAMSHIRE

MILTON KEYNES   Tel. (0908)
POLLARD WOODWORKING   641366
CENTRE   ★
51 AYLESBURY ST., BLETCHLEY
Open: Mon-Fri 8.30-5.30
Saturday 9.00-5.00
H.P.W.WM.D.CS.A.BC.

HIGH WYCOMBE   Tel. (0494)
SCOTT SAWS LTD.   24201/33788
14 BRIDGE STREET   ★

Mon.-Sat. 8.30 a.m.-6.00 p.m.

H.P.W.WM.D.T.CS.MF.A.BC.

HIGH WYCOMBE   Tel. (0494)
ISAAC LORD LTD   22221
185 DESBOROUGH ROAD   KE

Open: Mon-Fri 8.00 a.m.-5.00 p.m.
Saturday 9.00 a.m.-5.00 p.m.
H.P.W.D.A.

CAMBRIDGESHIRE

CAMBRIDGE   Tel. (0223) 63132
D. MACKAY LTD.   E★
BRITANNIA WORKS, EAST ROAD

Open: Mon.-Fri. 8.30 a.m.-1 p.m./2.00-
5.00 p.m. Sat. 8.30 a.m.-1.00 p.m.
H.P.W.D.T.CS.MF.A.BC.

CAMBRIDGE   Tel. (0223) 247386
H. B. WOODWORKING   K
105 CHERRY HINTON ROAD
Open: 8.30 a.m.-5.30 p.m.
Monday-Friday
8.30 a.m.-1.00 p.m. Sat.
H.P.W.WM.D.CS.A.

PETERBOROUGH   Tel. (0733)
WILLIAMS DISTRIBUTORS   64252
(TOOLS) LIMITED   K
108-110 BURGHLEY ROAD
Open: Monday to Friday
8.30 a.m.-5.30 p.m.
H.P.A.W.D.WH.BC.

CHESHIRE

NANTWICH   Tel. Crewe 67010
ALAN HOLTHAM   K★
THE OLD STORES TURNERY
WISTASON ROAD, WILLASTON
Open: Tues.-Sat. 9.00 a.m.-5.30 p.m.
Closed Monday
P.W.WM.D.T.C.CS.A.BC.

CLEVELAND

MIDDLESBROUGH   Tel. (0642)
CLEVELAND WOODCRAFT   813103
(M'BRO), 38-42 CRESCENT ROAD   K

Open: Mon-Sat 9.15 a.m.-5.30 p.m.

H.P.T.A.BC.W.WM.CS.D.

CORNWALL

SOUTH WEST Power Tools

CORNWALL   Tel: Helston (03265) 4961
HELSTON AND LAUNCESTON   Launceston
(0566) 4781
H.P.W.WM.D.CS.A.   K

CUMBRIA

CARLISLE   Tel: (0228) 36391
W. M. PLANT
ALLENBROOK ROAD
ROSEHILL, CA1 2UT
Open: Mon.-Fri. 8.00 a.m.-5.15 p.m.
Sat. 8.00 a.m.-12.30 noon
P.W.WM.D.CS.A.

DEVON

BRIXHAM   Tel. (08045) 4900
WOODCRAFT SUPPLIES   E★
4 HORSE POOL STREET

Open: Mon.-Sat. 9.00 a.m.-6.00 p.m.

H.P.W.A.D.MF.CS.BC.

PLYMOUTH   Tel. (0752) 330303
WESTWARD BUILDING SERVICES   ★
LTD., LISTER CLOSE, NEWNHAM
INDUSTRIAL ESTATE, PLYMPTON
Open: Mon-Fri 8.00 a.m.-5.30 p.m.
Sat. 8.30 a.m.-12.30 p.m.
H.P.W.WM.D.A.BC.

DORSET

BOURNEMOUTH Tel. (0202) 420583
POWER TOOL SERVICES
(Sales, spares, repairs)
849-851 CHRISTCHURCH ROAD
BOSCOMBE
Open: Mon.-Fri. 9.00 a.m.-5.30 p.m.
Sat. 9.00 a.m.-5.00 p.m.
H.P.W.CS.K.A.

POOLE   Tel. (0202) 686238
MACHINE SALES AND SERVICES   ★
(POOLE) LTD.
23 COWLEY ROAD
NUFFIELD INDUSTRIAL ESTATE
Open: Mon.-Fri. 8.30am-5.30pm.
H.P.W.WM.D.CS.A.BC.

ESSEX

LEIGH ON SEA   Tel. (0702)
MARSHAL & PARSONS LTD.   710404
1111 LONDON ROAD   EK

Open: 8.30 a.m.-5.30 p.m. Mon-Fri
9.00 a.m.-5.00 p.m. Sat.
H.P.W.WM.D.CS.A.

ALL THOSE SHOPS WITH AN ASTERISK HAVE A MAIL ORDER SERVICE ★

GLOUCESTER

TEWKESBURY   Tel. (0684)
TEWKESBURY SAW CO. LTD.   293092
TRADING ESTATE, NEWTOWN   K

Open: Mon-Fri 8.00 a.m.-5.00 p.m.
Saturday 9.30 a.m.-12.00 p.m.
P.W.WM.D.CS.

HAMPSHIRE

ALDERSHOT   Tel. (0252) 334422
POWER TOOL CENTRE   K
374 HIGH STREET

Open Mon.-Fri. 8.30 a.m.-5.30 p.m.
Sat. 8.30 a.m.-12.30 p.m.
H.P.W.WM.D.A.BC.

SOUTHAMPTON   Tel: (0703)
POWER TOOL CENTRE   332288
7 BELVIDERE ROAD   K★
Open Mon.-Fri. 8.30-5.30

H.P.W.WM.D.A.BC.CS.MF.

HERTFORDSHIRE

WARE   K★
HEATH SAWS
16 MALTINGS
STANSTEAD ABBOTTS (near Ware) HERTS.
Open: Mon.-Fri. 8.30am-5.30pm
Sat. 8.30am-1pm. Sunday by appointment.
P.W.WM.D.CS.A.

HUMBERSIDE

GRIMSBY   Tel. Grimsby (0472)
58741 Hull (0482) 26999
J. E. SIDDLE LTD. (Tool Specialists)   ★
83 VICTORIA STREET
Open: Mon-Fri 8.30 a.m.-5.30 p.m.
Sat. 8.30 a.m.-12.45 p.m. & 2 p.m.-5 p.m.
H.P.A.BC.W.WMD.

HULL
HUMBERSIDE FACTORING/H.F.C.
SAW SERVICING LTD.
MAIN STREET
Open: Mon.-Fri. 8am-5pm.
Saturday 8am-12.00pm.
H.P.W.WM.D.CS.A.BC.K.

KENT

WYE   Tel. (0233) 813144
KENT POWER TOOLS LTD.
UNIT 1, BRIAR CLOSE
WYE, Nr. ASFORD

H.P.W.WM.D.A.CS.

MAIDSTONE   Tel. (0622) 50177
SOUTH EASTERN SAWS (Ind.) LTD.   ★
COLDRED ROAD
PARKWOOD INDUSTRIAL ESTATE
Open: Mon.-Fri. 8.00 a.m.-6.00 p.m.
Sat. 9.00 a.m.-12.00 a.m.
B.C.W.CS.WM.PH.

517

shop guide

LANCASHIRE

PRESTON   Tel. (0772) 52951
SPEEDWELL TOOL COMPANY E★
62-68 MEADOW STREET PR1 1SU
  Open: Mon.-Fri. 8.30 a.m.-5.30 p.m.
    Sat. 8.30 a.m.-12.30 p.m.

H.P.W.WM.CS.A.MF.BC.

MANCHESTER Tel. (061 789)
TIMMS TOOLS   0909
102-104 LIVERPOOL ROAD ★
PATRICROFT M30 0WZ
  Weekdays 9.00 a.m.-5.30 p.m.
    Sat. 9.00 a.m.-1.00 p.m.
H.P.A.W.

BLACKPOOL Tel. (0253) 24299
FLYDE WOODTURNING SUPPLIES ★
222 HORNBY ROAD (BASEMENT)
BLACKPOOL FY1 4HY
   9.30-5.30 Monday to Saturday.

H.P.W.WM.A.MF.C.B.C.D.

ROCHDALE Tel. (0706) 342123/
C.S.M. TOOLS   342322
4-6 HEYWOOD ROAD E★
CASTLETON
   Open: Mon-Sat 9.00 a.m.-6.00 p.m.
    Sundays by appointment
W.D.CS.A.BC.

LANCASTER Tel. (0524) 32886
LILE TOOL SHOP K
43/45 NORTH ROAD
  Open: Monday to Saturday
    9.00 a.m.-5.30 p.m.
   Wed 9.00 a.m.-12.30 p.m.

H.P.W.D.A.

LEICESTERSHIRE

HINCKLEY Tel. (0455) 613432
J. D. WOODWARD & CO. (POWER ★
TOOL SPECIALISTS)
THE NARROWS, HINCKLEY
  Open: Monday-Saturday
    8.00 a.m.-6.00 p.m.
H.P.W.WM.D.CS.A.BC.

LINCOLNSHIRE

LINCOLN Tel. (0522) 689369
SKELLINGTHORPE SAW SERVICES LTD.
OLD WOOD, SKELLINGTHORPE
  Open: Mon to Fri 8 a.m.-5 p.m.
    Sat 8 a.m.-12 p.m.
H.P.W.WM.D.CS.A.*.BC.
    Access/Barclaycard

LONDON

ACTON Tel. (01-992) 4835
A. MILLS (ACTON) LTD ★
32/36 CHURCHFIELD ROAD W3 6ED
  Open: Mon-Fri 9.00 a.m.-5.00 p.m.
    Saturdays 9.00 am-1.00 p.m.

H.P.W.WM.

LONDON Tel. (01-567) 2922
G. D. CLEGG & SONS ★
83 UXBRIDGE ROAD, HANWELL W7 3ST
  Mon-Sat 9.15 a.m.-5.30 p.m.
   Closed for lunch 1.00-2.00p.m.
   Early Closing 1.00 p.m. Wed.
H.P.A.W.WM.D.CS.

LONDON

LONDON Tel. 01-723 2295-6-7
LANGHAM TOOLS LIMITED
13 NORFOLK PLACE
LONDON W2 1QJ

LONDON Tel. (01-636) 7475
BUCK & RYAN LTD
101 TOTTENHAM COURT ROAD W1P 0DY

  Open: Mon.-Fri. 8.30 a.m.-5.30 p.m.
    Saturday 8.30 a.m.-4.00 p.m.
H.P.W.WM.D.A..

WEMBLEY Tel. 904-1144
ROBERT SAMUEL LTD. (904-1147
7, 15 & 16 COURT PARADE after 4.00)
EAST LANE, N. WEMBLEY ★
  Open Mon.-Fri. 8.45-5.15; Sat. 9-1.00
  Access, Barclaycard, AM Express, & Diners
H.P.W.CS.E.A.D.

HOUNSLOW Tel. (01-570)
Q.R. TOOLS LTD 2103/5135
251-253 HANWORTH ROAD

  Open: Mon-Fri 8.30 a.m.-5.30 p.m.
    Sat. 9.00 a.m.-1.00 p.m.
P.W.WM.D.CS.A.

FULHAM Tel. (01-385) 5109
I. GRIZZARD LTD. E
84a-b LILLIE ROAD, SW6 1TL
  Open: Mon-Sat 9.00-5.30 p.m.
    Half day Thursday

H.P.A.BC.W.CS.WM.D.

MERSEYSIDE

LIVERPOOL Tel. (051-207) 2967
TAYLOR BROS (LIVERPOOL) LTD K
195-199 LONDON ROAD
LIVERPOOL L3 8JG
    Open: Monday to Friday
     8.30 a.m.-5.30 p.m.
H.P.W.WM.D.A.BC.

MIDDLESEX

RUISLIP Tel. (08956) 74126
ALLMODELS ENGINEERING LTD. E★
91 MANOR WAY

   Open: Mon-Sat 9.00 a.m.-5.30 p.m.
H.P.W.A.D.CS.MF.BC.

SOMERSET

CROWMARSH Tel. (0491) 38653
MILL HILL SUPPLIES E★
66 THE STREET
  Open: Mon.-Fri. 9.30 a.m.-5.00 p.m.
    Thurs. 9.30 a.m.-7.00 p.m.
    Sat. 9.30 a.m.-1.00 p.m.
P.W.D.CS.MF.A.BC.

NORFOLK

NORWICH Tel. (0603) 898695
NORFOLK SAW SERVICES
DOG LANE, HORSFORD
  Open: Monday to Friday
    8.00 a.m.-5.00 p.m.
   Saturday 8.00 a.m.-12.00 p.m.
H.P.W.WM.D.CS.A.

KINGS LYNN Tel. (0553) 2443
WALKER & ANDERSON (Kings Lynn) LTD.
WINDSOR ROAD, KINGS LYNN K
  Open: Monday to Saturday
    7.45 a.m.-5.30 p.m.
  Wednesday 1.00 p.m. Saturday 5.00 p.m.
H.P.W.WM.D.CS.A.

NORWICH Tel. (0603) 400933
WESTGATES WOODWORKING Tx
61 HURRICANE WAY, 975412
NORWICH AIRPORT INDUSTRIAL ESTATE
  Open: 9.00 a.m.-5.00 p.m. weekdays
    9.00 a.m.-12.30 Sat.
P.W.WM.D.BC. K

KING'S LYNN Tel: 07605 674
TONY WADDILOVE, UNIT A ★
HILL FARM WORKSHOPS
GREAT DUNHAM, (Nr. Swaffham)
  Open: Tues. — Fri. 10.00 a.m. to 5.30 p.m.
    Sat. 9.00 a.m. to 5.00 p.m.
H.P.W.D.T.MF.A.BC.*

NOTTINGHAMSHIRE

NOTTINGHAM Tel: (0602) 225979
POOLEWOOD and 227064/5
EQUIPMENT LTD. (06077) 2421 after hrs
5a HOLLY LANE, CHILLWELL
  Open: Mon-Fri 9.00 a.m.-5.30 p.m.
    Sat. 9.00 a.m. to 12.30 p.m.
P.W.WM.D.CS.A.BC.

OXON

WITNEY Tel. (0993) 3885.
TARGET TOOLS (SALES, & 72095 OXON
TARGET HIRE & REPAIRS)
TOOLS SWAIN COURT
  STATION INDUSTRIAL ESTATE
  Open: Mon.-Sat. 8.00 a.m.-5.00 p.m.
    24 hour Answerphone
BC.W.M.A.

SHROPSHIRE

TELFORD Tel. Telford (0952)
ASLES LTD 48054
VINEYARD ROAD, WELLINGTON EK★

  Open: Mon. Fri. 8.30 a.m.-5.30 p.m.
   Saturday 8.30 a.m.-4.00 p.m.
H.P.W WM.D.CS.BC.A.

SOMERSET

TAUNTON Tel. (0823) 85431
JOHN HALL TOOLS ★
6 HIGH STREET

    Open Monday-Saturday
    9.00 a.m.-5.30 p.m.

H.P.W.WM.D.CS.A.

TAUNTON Tel. 0823 443766
CUTWELL TOOLS LTD. ★
CREECH HEATHFIELD
SOMERSET TA3 5EQ
Mon-Fri 9 a.m.-5 p.m. and also by appointment.
P.W.WM.A.D.CS.

STAFFORDSHIRE

STOKE-ON-TRENT Tel: 0782-48171
F.W.B. (PRODUCTS) LTD.
WHIELDON ROAD, STAFFS.
  Open: Mon.-Fri. 8.30am-5.30pm
    Saturday 8.30am-12.30pm
H.P.W.WM.A.D.

SUFFOLK

IPSWICH Tel. (0473) 40456
FOX WOODWORKING KE★
142-144 BRAMFORD LANE
  Open: Tues., Fri., 9.00 a.m.-5.30 p.m.
    Sat. 9.00 a.m.-5.00 p.m.

H.P.W.WM.D.A.B.C.

SUSSEX

ST. LEONARD'S-ON-SEA Tel.
DOUST & MONK (MONOSAW)-(0424)
25 CASTLEHAM ROAD 52577

  Open: Mon.-Fri. 8.00 a.m.-5.30 p.m.
   Most Saturdays 9.00 a.m.-1.00 p.m.
H.P.W.WM.D.CS.A.

BOGNOR REGIS Tel. (0243) 863100
A. OLBY & SON (BOGNOR REGIS) LTD.
''TOOLSHOP,'' BUILDERS MERCHANT
HAWTHORN ROAD K
  Open: Mon-Thurs 8 a.m.-5.15 p.m. Fri.
   8 a.m.-8 p.m. Sat 8 a.m.-12.45 p.m.
H.P.W.WM.D.T.C.A.BC.

WORTHING Tel. (0903) 38739
W. HOSKING LTD (TOOLS & KE★
MACHINERY)
28 PORTLAND RD, BN11 1QN
  Open: Mon.-Sat. 8.30 a.m.-5.30 p.m.
    Closed Wednesday
H.P.W.WM.D.CS.A.BC.

TYNE & WEAR

NEWCASTLE Tel. (0632) 320311
HENRY OSBOURNE LTD. E★
50-54 UNION STREET

    Open: Mon-Fri 8.30 a.m.-5.00 p.m.

H.P.W.D.CS.MF.A.BC.

TO ADVERTISE PHONE ANDREA SMITH ON 01-437-0626

YORKSHIRE

BOROUGHBRIDGE Tel. (09012)
JOHN BODDY TIMBER LTD 2370
FINE WOOD & TOOL STORE ★
RIVERSIDE SAWMILLS
  Open: Mon.-Thurs. 8.00 a.m.-6.00 p.m.
  Fri. 8.00am-5.00pm Sat. 8.00am-4.00pm
H.P.W.WM.D.T.CS.MF.A.BC.

SHEFFIELD Tel. (0742) 441012
GREGORY & TAYLOR LTD KE
WORKSOP ROAD
  Open: 8.30 a.m.-5.30 p.m.
    Monday-Friday
   8.30 a.m.-12.30 p.m. Sat.
H.P.W.WM.D.

HARROGATE Tel. (0423) 66245/
MULTI-TOOLS 55328
158 KINGS ROAD K★

    Open: Monday to Saturday
    8.30 a.m.-6.00 p.m.

H.P.W.WM.D.A.BC.

shopguide

WOOD SUPPLIERS

WOOD SUPPLIERS

OAK ASH ELM

We specialise in producing top quality fresh sawn and kiln dried English hardwoods at very competitive prices. Also oak beams up to 24' long. Send S.A.E. for price list.

This months special offer.
Kiln dried Lebanon Cedar in boards up to 4' wide only £8/cu.

MICK JONES TIMBER
Caebardd, Guilsfield, Welshpool, Powys, Mid. Wales.
Tel: 093884 283

NORTH HEIGHAM SAWMILLS

Good, Kiln-Dried stocks of most Home-Grown timbers, and exotic, Imported Hardwoods.
Stocks include: Apple, ash, beech, blackwood, box, cedar, cherry, cocobolo, ebony, elm, holly, lemonwood, lignum, lime, mahogany, maple, oak, padauk, pear, plane, rosewood, satinwood, sycamore, walnut, yew, zelkova.

Please send S.A.E. for priced stock list to:

North Heigham Sawmills, Paddock St. (off Barker St.), NORWICH NR2 4TW. Tel: Norwich 622978.

THE WOOD SHOP

Our Cabinetmaker and Woodturners sawmill specialises in **homegrown**, imported and exotic timbers for the small user.
We can **machine** to your cutting list and **deliver** to your home.
Open 7 days a week, 9 to 5.
Send for new brochure to Treske Sawmills, Station Works
Thirsk YO7 4NY
Tel (0845) 22770

Treske Sawmills

TOP QUALITY BRITISH HARDWOODS

Kiln and Air-dried
Sold waney-edged at trade prices, or machined to your cutting list.

James Fraser-Harris, Culmhead, Taunton.
Tel: (082342) 395

WELSH OAK and ASH

Kiln dried, small — medium quantities. Deliveries arranged.

Valley Timber Company,
Cwm Cych near Newcastle Emlyn, Dyfed. Tel: (023977) 200

BERKSHIRE HARDWOODS Suppliers of kiln dried English Hardwoods Oak, Ash, Beech, Chestnut, Cherry and Yew available in planks and turning blanks. Tel: Crowthorne (0344) 773586 or 772157.

VENEERS, all types. SAE list. S. Gould (Veneers), 22 Spencer Road, N. Wembley, Middx. HA0 3SF. 01-904-7954. T/C

LIMEHOUSE TIMBER

See the wood from the trees!

Select from our stock of English and imported hardwoods, Russian redwoods, veneers and exotics. Send 17p stamp for stock list.

A unique source in London for all wood users.

Machining facilities available

Open 9-5 Mon.-Fri., 9-3 Sat.

5 Grenade Street, London E14 8HL. 01-987 6289

Broughton-Head Timber Ltd

Parva Stud, Church Row,
Hinton Parva, Swindon,
Wilts. Tel: Swindon 0793 790552

Kiln dried and air dried stocks including Acacia, Amazakoue, Apple, Ash, Beech, Bubinga, Cedar, Cherry, Chestnut, Burr Elm and Oak, Mahogany, English Oak, Pau Rosa, Pear, Sycamore, English and American Black Walnut, Wenge.

Please telephone or send stamp for details
We specialise in small quantities — Minimum one plank
Opening hours: Anytime subject to confirmation by telephone. Excluding Sundays.

H. G. MILDENHALL AND SONS JOINERY AND TIMBER

Over sixty species of timber available, small quantities our speciality. From Bobbin blanks, Turning and Carving blanks. Full machining facilities available. Send s.a.e. with cutting list for quote by return. To:

H. G. Mildenhall and Sons,
Joinery and Timber, 11 Oxford Street,
Lambourn, Nr. Newbury, Berks. RG16 7XS. Tel. 0488 71481

Hexhamshire Hardwoods

KILN DRIED HARDWOODS FOR THE CABINETMAKER, WOODTURNER & CARVER IN NORTH EAST ENGLAND & SCOTLAND
Exotic Hardwoods

Telephone Slaley (043473) 585 *any time*

THE WOODSTORE
Suppliers of Native Hardwoods

MOST HOMEGROWN SPECIES IN STOCK
LARGE AND SMALL QUANTITIES
SUPPLIED FRESH SAWN, AIR DRIED
AND KILN DRIED
MACHINING FACILITIES AVAILABLE
Send sae for Price List to

TREEWORK SERVICES LTD
CHESTON COOMBE, CHURCH TOWN, BACKWELL, Nr. BRISTOL
OR PHONE FLAX BOURTON
(027583) 3917 OR 3078
We also offer a tree milling service

HARDWOODS

Afromosia, Ash, Beech, Cherry, Iroko, Jelvtong, Lavan, Mahogany, Oak, Obeche, Ramin, Sapele, Serayah, Teak, Utile, Walnut etc. Also veneered Plywood & Blockboard. Available from:

F.H. Bleasdale (Timber) Ltd.,
(Established 1968), Unit 43,
Highfield Industrial Estate,
Chorley, Lancs.
Tel: Chorley 71102.
Send your cutting list for quotation.

HAMPSHIRE HARDWOODS Turning, Carving, etc. Come and choose from 24 English or 34 foreign/exotic timbers. All air dried 3-10 years. Liss 892750 after 7.00 p.m. or weekends.

SEASONED NORTH AMERICAN LONG LEAF PITCH PINE AVAILABLE

Converted from timber beams to your specification or in our standard sizes. From timber originally imported circa 1880.

Traditional and modern mouldings available.

Largest sixes section 14" × 12".

Architraving and Skirting all in stock
FOR A LIMITED PERIOD SPECIAL SUPPLY WITCH ELM.

J. R. NELSON & CO

"The Saw Mill,"
Wills Farm,
Newchurch, Kent.

Tel: Hamstreet (023373) 3361

SPECIAL MODELMAKER'S PACKAGE

A random selection of English and foreign seasoned hardwood boards and scantlings, mostly 18" lengths, suitable for model making. ONLY £12 plus VAT (£1.80). Includes delivery. (UK Mainland).
British Gates, Dept. WWM, Biddenden, Nr. Ashford, Kent.

Hardwoods for the Craftsman

Send for a FREE CATALOGUE

Fitchett and Woollacott Ltd.
Willow Road, Lenton Lane, Nottingham NG7 2PR
Telephone: (0602) 700691. Telex 377401

TIMBERLINE

In addition to our much improved range of over 50 species of fine imported and home grown hardwoods we would like to announce that we now carry comprehensive stocks of the following:

Veneers, decorative lines and bandings, polishes, waxes, stains, adhesives, abrasives and woodwork construction plans. You are always assured of good service and a friendly welcome.

Business hours
Tues.-Sat. 9.30am-5.30pm
Please send large sae for free catalogue quoting ref. WW.

TIMBERLINE,
Unit 7, Munday Works,
58-66 Morley Road,
Tonbridge, Kent TN9 1RP.
Tel: (0732) 355626

REMEMBER!
CRAFTWOODS OF DEVON

Have increased stocks of Tropical and Home grown hardwoods, for Woodturners, Carvers, Cabinet makers, Bobbin and Jewellery makers. Also available, a large selection of Veneers, for Restoration work, and packs for Marquetry.
Please send S.A.E. for catalogue to:
Thatchways, Thurlestone, Kingsbridge,
S. Devon TQ7 3NJ. Phone 0548 560721

SAWN TIMBER Oak £5 per cu/ft. Ash £3.50, Macracarpa £4, Beech £3.50, Corsican Pine £3.50 (no VAT). Phone Richard Lewis after dark. Rackenford (088488) 385.

520

521

Classified Advertisements

FOR SALE

THE FINEST SELECTION ON DISPLAY IN SCOTLAND!
WOODWORKING & METALWORKING MACHINERY POWER TOOLS HAND TOOLS
THE SAW CENTRE
HIRE OR BUY
Visit our NEW SHOWROOM at EGLINTON TOLL GLASGOW
Tel: 041-429 4444/4374, Telex: 777886 SAWCO G
Also at, 38 Haymarket Terrace, Edinburgh EH12 5JZ. Tel: 031-337 5555
OPEN Mon - Fri 8am - 5pm Sat 9am - 1pm

PLOUGH AND MULTI-PLANES
All planes in good condition, many unused and original boxes. **Record** 043 3 blades £12. 044 8 blades £18. 044C 10 blades £29. 050 15 blades £29. 450 23 blades £65. **Stanley** 13. 052 10 blades £29. 13 050 18 blades £39. 45. 23 blades £69. 55 52 blades £110.
The Tool Box, Umbourne Bridge, Colyton, Devon. Tel: (0297) 52868

HAND CARVED
'Adam Style' Mantle motifs in Mahogany — Example 10″ × 5″ centre lamp and two side pieces.
Send S.A.E. for details and quotation. Your own design quoted for if required.
SAM NICHOLSON
22 Lisnagarvey Drive, Lisburn, Co. Antrim, N. Ireland.
Phone Lisburn 3510

HARRISON GRADUATE and JUBILEE Wood Turning Lathes For Sale,
Contact the specialists
L.R.E. MACHINERY & EQUIPMENT Co.
15 Upwood Road, Lowton, Warrington WA3 2RL.
Tel: (0942) 728208 day or night

**FOR ALL SUPPLIES FOR THE
Craft of Enamelling
ON METAL
Including
LEAD-FREE ENAMELS**
PLEASE SEND 2 × 10p STAMPS FOR FREE CATALOGUE, PRICE LIST AND WORKING INSTRUCTIONS
W. G. BALL LTD.
ENAMEL MANUFACTURERS
Dept. W. LONGTON
STOKE-ON-TRENT
ST3 1JW

BANKRUPT STOCK
Sandvik circular saw blades tungsten tipped.
5″, 5½″, 6″ .... **£4.00** each
6½″, 8¼″ .... **£6.00** each
½″ to 1⅜″ bore any size.
P&P £1 extra per order.
Tel: 01 672 7776
Hannett, 1A Links Road, Tooting, London SW17 9ED.

WOOD TURNERS SUPPLIES
Tudor Craft, Jung Hans clock movements, 20 different hands to choose from, barometers, weather stations, cutlery, jewellery box lids, pepper/salt/nutmeg mills, coffee grinders, ceramic tiles, new range which include hand painted tiles. Our service is extremely fast, friendly and competitive — give us a try. Send 30p in stamps to:
Tudorcraft, 100 Little Sutton Lane, Four Oaks. Sutton Coldfield, W. Midlands B75 6PG. Tel: 021 308 1193
For illustrated catalogue.

Braywood Estates
Main stockists
TREND ROUTER CUTTERS, AUGERS, FORSTNER BITS
All at discount prices
Braywood Estates Ltd., Dept WW, 158 Burnham Lane, Slough SL1 6LE.
Tel. Burnham (06286) 5125.
Hrs. Mon-Sat 9am-5.30pm

CLOCKMAKERS
Extensive range of very competitively priced German quartz clock movements, (including standard quartz, pendulum, mini-pendulum, chining, striking and insertion movements). Large selection of quality dials, chapter rings, hands, bezels, clock plans and weather instruments.
Please send 25p stamps for 20 page catalogue.
Bath Clock Company (Dept. W), 13 Welton Road, Radstock, Bath.

Eric Tomkinson Woodturner
Lathes, Bandsaws, Grinders, Woodturning tools & chucks, screw boxes, peppermills, saltmills, coffee grinders, barometers, lighters, hourglasses, quartz clock movements, circular tiles & clock faces, cheese domes, sealers & polishes, fast and efficient mail order service + competitive prices. S.A.E. for catalogue.
Shop Open: 9-5 Mon.-Sat.
BARCLAYCARD VISA
ERIC TOMKINSON, 86 Stockport Road, Cheadle, Cheshire SK8 2AT. Tel: 061-491-1726.

FOR SALE 3 rolls carving tools (65), mint condition 9″, 10″, 11″ £150 the lot. 78 Queens Road, Sedgley, Dudley, West Midlands. Tel: Sedgley 64168.

LACE BOBBIN turning blanks. Extensive range of exotics, Ivory, lathes, miniature tools, sundries, lace supplies. SAE J. Ford, 5 Squirrels Hollow, Walsall WS7 8YS.

WOODTURNING LATHE Coronet on bench with tools and accessories. Excellent condition, £450 o.n.o. Phone 041-9430681 (after 6pm).

(FRESH SAWN HOLLY) Limited supply variety & sizes. Reasonable rates details 02607 282. Evenings and Weekends.

USERS AND COLLECTORS tools for sale at the Old Craft Tool Shop, 15 High Street, Whitton, Middx. Telephone 01-755 0441.

TURNERS 10 tea chests full seasoned mahogany pieces (space needed) £12 each. Tel: Southborne (0202) 421785.

AMERICAN Readers, Woodworker magazine volume 80 to 986 Jan. 1976 through volume 88 to 1087 June 1984. 102 issues in 9 easibinders, mint condition $200.00. Phone (215) 33 — 2506.

SAWBENCH British built, 12″ diameter, 4″ max depth of cut, 2HP single phase, rolling table, rip & cross cut fences, all guards, purchased new 1983, £350. Tel: (0844) 237068.

DE WALT DW50 Planer/Thicknesser with stand & spare cutters, £300. Caldbeck (06998) 325.

WOODCARVING tools

LARGEST STOCK IN EUROPE

Ashley Iles & Henry Taylor
Arkansas Bench & Slip Stones
Strops & Strop Paste
Bench Screws, Carvers' Vices

WOODTURNING tools
Complete range of
Henry Taylor & Ashley Iles
handled or unhandled

send 40p in stamps for illustrated catalogue
ALEC TIRANTI LTD
70 High St, Theale, Reading, Berks RG7 5AR
21 Goodge Place, London W1.

LINCOLN 10″ sawbench cast iron 24″ × 27″ complete motor etc. v.g.c. 6 blades, £230 o.n.o. Worthing 210980.

INCA 7½″ saw including morticer — 8⅝″ planer, both on motorised stand, £400. Telephone 074488 4729.

CORONET Major 500, circular saw, planer, morticer, etc. £800 o.n.o. Tel: Chalfont St. Giles 2250.

FOR SALE Major Universal lathe, 5 speed, reversing switch, saw table, TCT blade, planer, thicknesser, hold-down spring, morticer, moulding block and cutters, centres and ejector, £850 o.n.o. Tel: Southbourne (0202) 421785.

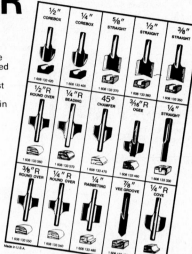

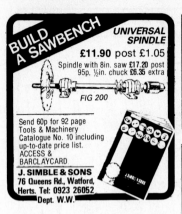

524

FIND THE RIGHT COURSE IN WOODWORKER!

DAVID STANLEY AUCTIONS

6th consignment sale of 1200 lots of ANTIQUE WOODWORKING AND ALLIED TRADES TOOLS on TUESDAY 24th JUNE, 1986

Viewing MONDAY 23rd JUNE and morning of sale at CHELSEA TOWN HALL, KINGS ROAD, CHELSEA, LONDON

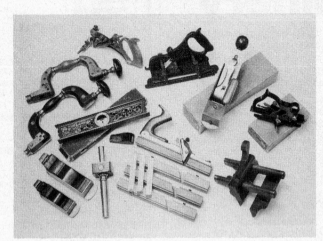

Our much improved catalogue includes 1100 illustrations, more colour photographs, estimated prices, full postal bidding instructions and a prices realised list to follow.

To include:
A rare and important 16C iron plane (similar to P-TAMPIA p.12 fig. 3). *A unique pattern makers, patent removable sole plane by D. Kimberley. Ultimatum braces in boxwood, rosewood, ebony and beech and a rare Sims type brace. A rare "Triptych" by HOLTZAPFFEL.
17C moulding planes and three coachbuilders ploughs Boxwood miniatures and ivory and boxwood rules NORRIS, SPIERS, MATHIESON, SLATER and PRESTON tools.
*Two miniature mitre planes by BUCK
STANLEY No's: *gunmetal 42, 43, 52, 62, 67, 72, 95, 100½, *101½, 140, *196, *278 and 444, and a fine unused *STANLEY No. 9 with (genuine) side handle in original box.

* *as illustrated*

Many fine carving tools, chisels and gouges, trammels, levels, squares, plumb bobs etc.

100 page catalogue (SAE for prices realised list to follow) £5 from:
DAVID STANLY AUCTIONS
Stordon Grange, Osgathorpe, Loughborough, Leicestershire, England LE12 9SR.
Tel: 0530 222320

AUCTION SALE

At Unit 1, Manton Road, Rushden, Northants. On Saturday 7th June at 10.30 a.m. Viewing Thursday 5th & Friday 6th June 9 a.m. to 7 p.m. and all day Saturday from 7 a.m. Under Instructions From Pilgrim Pattern Makers, P & D Engineers, Contents of Model Engineering Workshop, Contents of Wheelwrights/Blacksmiths Workshop, Qty of Carriers Lost Goods, Local Authorities Etc. Contents of Motor Rewind Workshop.

5 Old Handcarts, Qty Wheels Etc. Rigid Pipe Threading Machine, Wadkin EKA 4 Headed Tenoner, JTA Disc/Bobbin Sander, JV Double Disc Sander, RS Wood Lathe, BRA Cross Cut Saw, Spindle Moulder, Chisel Mortiser, BT500 Thicknesser, Pad Belt Sander, LS Router, BGP Panel Saw, Hydrovane Compressor, Bench Grinders, Sash Cramps, G Clamps, Work Benches, Myford Super 7 Lathe, Myford Woodturning Lathe, Dominion P/Thicknesser, Dominion Spindle Moulder, Boxford Lathe, Super Brown Cut Off Saw, Surface Grinder, Fell Variety Wood Lathe, Industrial Woodburning Stove, Universal Woodworking Machine, Bandsaw, Jig Saw, Dust Extractor, Pillar Drill, Bench Grinders, Fobco 7/8" Drill, Various Sheet Metal Machinery, Qty Electric Tools, Large Qty Inspection Equipment, Bridgeport Turret Mill, Qty R8 Tooling, Colchester 2000, Colchester Master, Colchester Student Lathes, Tom Sernior Milling Machine, SCM Spindle Moulder, Multico Tenoner, Qty Office Equipment. Collection Old Railway Lamps & Signs, Including 'Rushden Station' Sign, Scale Model Traction Engine, 1984 Diesel Safari Landrover.

All Items to be sold without reserve. Approx 700 Lots.
For Catalogue Send Five 12p Stamps To:
The Auction Dept. Warner Auctions, 155 High Street, Irthlingborough, Northants.

BUSINESS OPPORTUNITIES

BUSINESS FOR SALE

Established and thriving one-man furniture making business for sale in N.W. Eire. Large, equipped workshop adjacent to spacious carefully renovated 4 bedroomed farmhouse (part furnished). Breathtaking coastal views; 2 miles from beach. Also garage, timber store, fuel store, Cow byre. Stands on 10½ acres.
£49,000 sterling.
Phone Donegal 36115 for details.

BUSINESS FOR SALE

Wood Turnery established 1977 producing gift ware. Well established range of products and outlets throughout U.K. and exporting to wholesalers in U.S. and Australia. Scope for expansion.
Enquiries to: **Box No. 3486**, Woodworker Magazine Classified, ASP Ltd, 1 Golden Square, London W1R 3AB.

PHONE NOW ON 01-437-0626 FOR ADVERTISING DETAILS.

528

WOODWORKER

design . . . craft . . . and the love of wood

July 1986   Vol. 90   No. 1112

541 **WORKBENCH OF THE FUTURE**
Win a deluxe bench and a Swedish holiday in our original design competition — or just go for the fantastic reader offer!

546 **The best medicine**
Portrait of an unusual medical man with a passion for fine furniture, and details of his equally unusual table. *Stan Folb*

548 **Built in the Balkans**
Joinery and house carpentry, Transylvania style — a rural ride in full colour. *Tony Deane*

550 **Shoptalk special**
Headstand
Wm. Ridgway's new multi-purpose drill-stand is causing a buzz, so we put it through its paces. *Simon Mathews*

553 **The grand furniture saga: 6**
The mid-16th century brings a new design of table to English society, but the gate-leg is as popular now as ever. Our furniture history unfolds. *Vic Taylor*

565 **Tools of the trade 3**
Low-angle planes: there are highs and lows among block and shoulder-planes too. We get an angle on the best for the money. *David Savage*

photo Stan Folb

● *Trevor Roberts assembles one of his elegant ash chairs. See more of his work on p546*

583 **Waste away**
A fitting end to the story of **Machining Wood** — gathering the gunge, and what to do with it next. *Steven Hurrell*

587 **WHEELSPIN**
A two-sided look at spinning wheels begins with an old German model's revitalisation. *Frank Lapworth.* See also **Projects**

596 **Sitting ducks**
Some ducks are decoys and some are real. We challenge you to tell the difference in Peter Mallinson's work. *Neil McAllister*

598 **The King's makers**
Vile & Cobb are not famous names in 18th century furniture, but George III rated them better than Chippendale! *Leslie Syson*

600 **Tales out of steel**
Exporting tools from Sheffield in its 50's heyday was no picnic, especially when your factory was 13ft sq! *Ashley Iles*

601 **Ornament for all 2**
If you got hooked on Ornamental Turning last month and can't get a Holtzappfel lathe, try adapting your own. *Michael Foden*

604 **JAPAN 4**
Ryoba noko giri
Where do they use a combined crosscut and ripsaw with a .25mm-thick blade? *Tony Wood*

PROJECTS
All with detailed working drawings

542 **Matching the apple**
Richly figured fruitwood and secret mitred dovetails are just some of the ingredients in this demanding and delicate piece. *Edward Thom*

556 **Designer DIY**
While at the simpler end of the spectrum, we have a modern dining suite, as stylish as it's easy to make. *Richard Entwistle*

590 **The flat spin**
The other half of our spinning wheels feature, in which new ideas improve an old design. Make it and learn to spin with it! *Roger Sear*

On the cover
Larch tiles on the roof of a tiny Transylvanian church — see p548 for more joinery behind traditional joinery behind the Iron Curtain. Plus an unbeatable offer (p541) on a superb **Sjöberg** bench!

REGULARS

530 **This month** What's on, what's been, what's ahead

531 **Shoptalk** All the product news you need

535 **Timberline** Update on the ways of the world wood markets

537 **Question box** Bagpipe turning, fruit-stained ash, double-glazed bow windows, a TV snack-table . . .

563 **Guild notes** News, ideas and courses for enthusiasts

569 **Letters** and Advertisers' index

573 **Books** Careers, toys and a new range from the USA

575 **Bob Wearing's workshop** Make your own scratch-tool

581 **Woodworking wheeze of the month**
A versatile dowelling jig. *Herbert Beckett*

Editor Aidan Walker
Editorial assistant Kerry Fowler
Senior advertisement manager Paul Holmes
Advertisement manager Trevor Pryer
Graphics Jeff Hamblin
Technical illustrator Peter Holland
Guild of Woodworkers Kerry Fowler

Editorial, advertisements and Guild of Woodworkers
1 Golden Square, London W1R 3AB, telephone 01-437 0626

Unfortunately we cannot accept responsibility for loss of or damage to unsolicited material. We reserve the right to refuse or suspend advertisements, and regret we cannot guarantee the bone fides of advertisers.

ABC
UK circulation
Jan-Dec 85
28,051

Back issues and subscriptions Infonet Ltd, 10-13 Times House, 179 Marlowes, Hemel Hempstead, Herts HP1 1BB; telephone Hemel Hempstead (0442) 48434

Subscriptions per year UK £16.90; overseas outside USA (accelerated surface post) £21.00, USA (accelerated surface post) £28, airmail £48

UK trade SM Distribution Ltd, 16-18 Trinity Gardens, London SW9 8DX; telephone 01-274 8611

North American trade Bill Dean Books Ltd, 151-49 7th Avenue, PO Box 69, Whitestone, New York 11357; telephone 1-718-767-6632

Printed in Great Britain by Ambassador Press Ltd, St. Albans, Herts
Mono origination Multiform Photosetting Ltd, Cardiff
Colour origination Derek Croxson Ltd, Chesham, Bucks
© Argus Specialist Publications Ltd 1986
ISSN 0043 776X

Argus Specialist Publications Ltd
1 Golden Square, London
W1R 3AB; 01-437 0626

Woodworker
This month

Letters

Matter of courses

E. Elkington's letter (WW/Apr) and Hugh O'Neill's 'Turning the corner' (WW/May) on woodturning courses together illustrate the top and bottom ends of the woodturning instructional spectrum. I believe, writes **Brian Cox,** it would be useful to expand on the brief descriptions of the courses given at the end of Hugh O'Neill's piece in the May issue. Budding woodturners contemplating a course feel they need some unbiased views about what's on offer before they sign a cheque, and it's clearly impractical to send a group of anonymous novices to each and every course to obtain the data for a balanced comparative report.

However, I think it should be possible to compile, from the opinions of ex-students, some sort of table which would give other potential woodturners some guidance.

All readers who have attended a woodturning course in the last few years — let me know what you thought of it. I need: **1** the course attended/instructor's name, **2** the approximate date, and **3** whether you thought the course was excellent value, useful, not as good as expected, or a waste of money. All replies will be in total confidence; names will not be released to anybody in any circumstances — not even the Editor. The data will be extracted, collated and printed in *Woodworker* in due course.

● Brian Cox, Seven Bells, Woodland Ave, Cranleigh, Surrey GU6 7HZ, (0483) 274783.

● **Craft Supplies** was one of the venues where Hugh O'Neill took his courses for the comparative feature in the May issue. We're sorry we omitted their address: The Mill, Millers Dale 41, Buxton, Derbys. SK17 8SN, (0298) 871636.

● **Matthews of Tamworth** have also asked us to point out they do one-day woodturning courses: Kettlebrook Rd, Kettlebrook, Tamworth, Staffs, (0827) 56188.

Copyright appeal

Argus Books are planning a book of reproduction furniture designs that have appeared in *Woodworker*, and are appealing to these authors listed below to get in touch with Phil Chapman (Publishing Director) Argus Books, 1 Golden Square, London W1R 3AB. Please write to him as soon as possible — many thanks!

P. Chillingworth	Serpentine-front sideboard	Apr '74
Dr Justis	Huntboard	Jul '74
W. L. Rowson	Child's arm chair	Feb '72
G. M. Guest	Jacobean box stool	May '72
J. L. Ford	Period cupboard	Jan '70
J. M. Gorman	Windsor chair	Apr '66
A. R. Bishop	Grandmother clock	Apr '73
Unknown	Memorial book rest	Jun '57
Unknown	Sofa dressing table	Nov '57
Unknown	Shield mirror	Jul '58
Unknown	Bureau bookcase	Aug '53

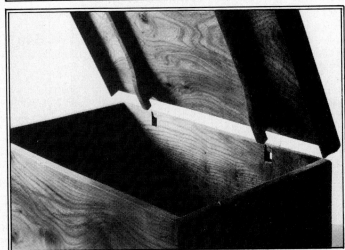

Flying lid? No, the 'Wooden Hinge' exhibition at Bloomsbury Joinery in London's Covent Garden, 2-13 June. How can a box lid stay open without visible support? **Luke Hughes,** designer of the pieces on display, has the answers. 01-404 5995

Flying school? Not this one, writes **G. Williams.** The oldest wooden schoolhouse in the USA (St. Augustine, Florida) is chained down against the storms . . .

David Jones was one of the joiners from **Erddig,** the National Trust's Wrexham 'working community', making traditional garden furniture at the Chelsea Flower Show, 20-23 May

LIFS-ers

Congratulations to **Oliver Peake** and **Kate George** of Middlesex and Leicester Polytechnics on jointly winning the London International Furniture Show College Trophy. Oliver's entry was a rocking-chair for modern times, laminated ply on a tubular steel backbone frame; Kate's dressing table is in moulded resin. A good start and lots of publicity for these bright sparks — now let's see what they do with it.

Co-op Show

17 and 18 June were the dates of the third Exhibition of Worker Co-operatives at the Kensington Exhibition Centre in west London. All sorts of people working in all sorts of co-ops were there; if you want to know more, phone Mayerlene Frow, 01-403 0300.

Diary

Guild courses are shown by an asterisk (*); for further details see the Guild pages.

June
4-Aug 31 **David Munrow Collection of Early and Folk Musical Instruments** and the **Craft Council's Second Open Exhibition of Musical Instruments** Crafts Council Gallery, 12 Waterloo Place, London SW1, 01-930 4811
24-26 **Shrewsbury College Exhibition** Town Hall, Shrewsbury
30-July 4 **London College of Furniture Summer Show**

July
5 **Design and Workshop Drawing** Bob Grant*
5 **Solent Guild Carvers and Sculptors' Annual Exhibition,** All Saints Church, Commercial Rd, Portsmouth
26-August 30 **Furniture from Rycotewood College,** Cheltenham Art Gallery, (0285) 61566
27 **E. W. Godwin Centenary** 20th century Furniture Designs, V&A Museum, London
28-29 **Crafts at Whatton House** Loughborough

August
31-September 21 **Furniture and Screens** Exhibition: Lucinda Leech, Charles Wickham, Michael Dunwell. Old Town Hall, Bampton, Oxon

September
6-7 **Decorative techniques** Ian Hosker*
27 **Hand Veneering** Bob Grant*

October
13-18 **International Creative Marquetry Show** The Corn Exchange, Ipswich. Contact 63 Church Lane, Sproughton, Ipswich IP8 3AY
16-22 **Chelsea Crafts Fair,** Old Town Hall, London SW3
23-26 **London Woodworker Show** Alexandra Pavilion, London N22

November
Woodmex 86 Woodworking equipment exhibition, NEC Birmingham, contact 01-486 1951

Shoptalk

Best of Britain 20-year old Colin Ashman is the 'Skill-Build' joinery gold medal winner. The competitions were held in Portsmouth in April

Forest push

On 1 May the Timber Trade Federation, Earthlife, the Friends of the Earth, the Green Alliance, the International Institute of Environment and Development and the World Wildlife Fund sent a joint letter to MPs, MEPs and members of the House of Lords urging them to encourage the government to work to break the deadlock over the International Tropical Timber Organisation (WW/Apr). It's great news for all, and a triumph of common sense.

Meanwhile, another voice is to be heard coming from Brian Johnson, an associate of the environmental group **Earthlife** who produced a magnificent (and commercially sponsored) supplement on the vexed rainforest question for the *Observer*'s 2 Feb issue. In a well-argued if slightly self-congratulatory article in the *Timber Trades Journal* of 3 May, Johnson examines the dynamic of environmental groups who need to show their subscribing and donating public that they're actually doing something, and pinpoints 'a misunderstanding within the tropical timber trade, both of the scale of environmental concern among the public in many countries, and — equally important — of the convenience of the timber trade as a tool in the hands of the Green publicists'. He doesn't let the Greens pull any wool over his eyes, but neither is he an uncritical fan of the timber trade, in which he sees evidence of a certain sloth, and blindness to the importance of being seen to *want* to co-operate. That's all changed now, of course.

His own group work on a different premise from either the trade or the regular Green groups; 'Earthlife were established to show *by example* that environmentally sensitive and sustainable development can actually work and be financially rewarding'. It is not as yet revealed how good are relationships between the environmentally committed groups; Earthlife could represent a threat in some measure to anti-capitalism.

Still, it looks like they go for positive action; Earthlife are campaigning for the sponsorship of a genuine stretch of rainforest in the Cameroon, where public donation will save and sustain the trees. Give £20 and you get a colour poster with a computerised square on it showing the 1000 trees that owe their continuing existence to your money. They have T-shirts, publications, (you can get the *Paradise Lost?* supplement for £1), a schools' pack, rainforest prints — good solid fund-raising ideas.

Earthlife's commercialism and professionalism are fine, but it seems they rather want to emphasise the contrast with other environmental groups. Perhaps there's more work yet to be done on the general atmosphere of *bonhomie* that appears to be enfolding the participants in the discussion.
● Earthlife, 10 Belgrave Sq, London SW1X 8PH, 01-237 7055.

Show gold

Lucky (and skilled) winners at the **Bristol Woodworker Show**: A. Collins gets the Emco spindle moulder, thanks to **Solent Tools:** gold medals went to G. Evans (cabinetmaking), T. Moss (carving), R. Smith (carving), J. Shepherd (turning), M. Trainos (turning), J. Wilmut (musical instruments), T. Howell (toys), I. Fobbester (clocks), and C. Anderson (juniors).
Squares and Rounds winners were N. Short and N. Packer — thanks, **Elektra Beckum** and **Richard Kell.**

For those who aren't satisfied with glossing over the surface, the Art Veneer Co. have just produced the latest edition of their *Veneering Manual and Catalogue* — which is much more than a catalogue.

It includes details on veneer production and veneering history, hints on marquetry, parquetry and polishing, a step-by-step practical guide, and details of tools and products. Yours for £1.30 inc. p&p.
● The Art Veneers Co, Ind. Est., Mildenhall, Suffolk IP28 7AY, (0638) 712 550.

Buy any Makita **cordless** industrial power tool and you get £7.50 worth of ratchet screwdriver and bits free. A spring promotion from the makers of one of the largest cordless power-tool ranges — so act now!
● Makita Electric UK Ltd, 8 Finway, Dallow Rd, Luton, Beds LU1 1TR.

The *Woodworker* 1985 Index has had a few production problems, now sorted out. Apologies for the wait; also for the extra 25p we have to charge for the new ones we've had printed. It's now £1.75 inc. p&p.
● Woodworker Reader Services, Wolsey House, Wolsey Rd, Hemel Hempstead, Herts HP2 4SS

Clockmakers — have you such a yen for the real reproduction thing that you can't bear to use mass-produced mechanical or quartz **movements**? Then take note — Samuel Coulton are making hand-crafted clock movements with a 10-year guarantee.
● Samuel Coulton, Lower Damgate Farm, Stanhope, Derbyshire, (033527) 367.

Ebac, major name in dry-it-yourself, are introducing their TR3000 **wood dryer** — an improved version of the model previously only available in the US — to replace their ageing Minor-Plus in the UK. The unit is designed to dry 250cu ft of 1in hardwood per run, and has a slim profile so it will take up little room mounted high on the wall. It comes with a control system for £1,125+VAT.
● Ebac Ltd, St Helen Ind. Est., Bishop Auckland, Co. Durham DL14 9AD, (0388) 66191.

Putting wood in t'hole might once have been the answer for those awkward little gaps and fissures — but with such products as Rota-Fix's **'Resi Wood'** things are a little simpler.

It consists of two lumps of doughy material which you mix together and form on to damaged timber. Shades of compo? It can be planed and screwed after curing and comes in mahogany or natural, starting at £5.00 (plus p&p) for 370cc.
● Rota-Fix (Northern), Rota-Fix House, Heol Rheolau, Abercrave, Swansea SA9 1TB, (0639) 730481.

The address of Anthony Dew, the **rocking-horse maker** featured in the May issue, is: The Rocking Horse Shop, Old Rd, Holme upon Spalding Moor, York YO44AB, (0696) 60563. His book *Making Rocking Horses* costs £8.95, not £7.95 as we said. Anthony also runs woodcarving courses and sells rocking-horse makers' accessories from the shop.

NO USER FATIGUE with the Siaco rigid **hand-sanding tool**? That's the claim. It's light, and uses the unique velcro-backed Siafast abrasive papers. £7.75+VAT for the 250x70mm size.
● Siaco Ltd, Saffron Walden, Essex, (0799) 27399

VARIOTEC is Wolfcraft's new **machining table** which takes *any* portable power saw, jigsaw or router. Accessories include no-volt switch and extension tables. A very good price: £80 the table, £28 the switch, inc. VAT.
● Brimarc Ltd, Kineton Rd, Southam, Warks. CV33 0DR, (0926 81) 2044

 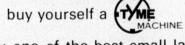

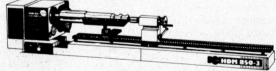
532

Shoptalk

21 April found me at the **Wooden Toymaking Symposium** at John Boddy's in Boroughbridge, Yorkshire, writes **Alan Wills,** for three days of the company of people who share a common interest and joy in handling, working and talking about wood.

The event was the first of a series, so the syllabus was informal, letting the participants decide the format, swap ideas and knowledge, and be able to take something home that had been fun in the making. Peter Longthorne, a successful Leeds toymaker, also gave a talk.

Pencils, rulers, saws, lathes, sanders — a hive of enthusiastic activity. By lunchtime on the second day, we could see each other's work taking shape and were wondering if we hadn't chosen something a little too ambitious. But Phil is a professional teacher, and knows exactly when to give encouragement and advice. Seven-and-a-half hours wasn't enough for us on the second day; after dinner we were back for another two-hour evening session, and tiredness was something we didn't even consider.

Three days of enjoyment in the most pleasant surroundings, the best of Yorkshire hospitality and a notebook full of ideas for our own workshops.
● Phil Reardon's Toymaking Symposia run at regular intervals; the next one is 10-12 October. They cost £75+VAT for tuition, timber, notes and lunch, but not accommodation, which can be arranged nearby. Write for a booking form to John Boddy's, Boroughbridge, N. Yorks YO5 9LJ, (09012) 2370.

RECORD MARPLES/ RIDGWAY launch a new range of **combination augers** that you can use in a brace or a power drill. Sizes range from 5x¼in to 8x1½in; there's a metric range too. An 8x¾in costs £6.08+VAT.
● Record Marples Ltd, Parkway Works, Sheffield S9 3BL, (0742) 449066

Startrite's new 351 vertical **bandsaw** is based on the 352 but has fewer smart (and pricey) features and a smaller throat (8in). It comes in at a substantially lower price than its brother — £484+VAT.
● Startrite Machine Tool Co., Waterside Works, Gads Hill, Gillingham, Kent, (0634) 55122

The *Woodworker* Plans Service deals in **plans** by all sorts of luminaries, as well as our own designs; Ashby Design Workshop and David Bryant to name but two. Write for a catalogue, which costs £1.15 inc. p&p.
● Woodworker Plans Service, Wolsey House, Wolsey Rd, Hemel Hempstead, Herts HP2 4SS, (0422) 41221.

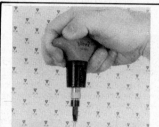

CHUBBY T-GRIP **ratchet screwdriver** by Vitrex comes with two double-ended bits; good for the site worker's toolbox at £5.99 in.c VAT.
● Vitrex, 457-463 Caledonian Rd, London N7 9BB, 01-609 0011

SCANTOOL have a **wet grinder** and a range of combination wet and dry wheel machines. The 150 is £69, the 'Combi 150' £80, both + VAT.
● Luna, 20 Denbigh Hall, Milton Keynes MK3 7QT, (0908) 70771

Skil 'Twist' is the name of a new small **rechargeable screwdriver**, writes **Aidan Walker**, which, the manufacturers claim, is a 'breakthrough in the rechargeable tool market'. It's light — 400gm — and designed in 'in-line' format rather than pistol-grip, which means you use it more or less like an ordinary screwdriver. It comes with a recharger/toolholder that you're supposed to keep the tool plugged into all the time you're not using it.

Woodworker test dept. had a good solid go with the thing, using it for two short periods over two days. It was fully charged when we started but we didn't plug it back into the charger after the first session, to see how long it took to run down completely with fairly hard use. There's a cut-out on the charger so it won't overcharge if you keep it plugged in all the time — which is handy, since the one we had was just plain too weak to work after about half an hour.

We used it for screwing and unscrewing into wall-plugs, and putting no.8x1½ and 1¼in screws into softwood and chipboard with and without clearance and pilot holes; and we found the strength a long way short of impressive. A light touch on the trigger keeps up the speed, which is what you need, because it's quite slow; but not variable, so once it's turning there's not a lot of control over the driving of the screw. You can't turn the bit by hand to line it up with a slot on a screw you've set into the hole already — you have to trigger the driver or re-align the screw. The speed is 130rpm, which the makers say gives high torque; the short

HAMMER DRILL from Black & Decker Professional with pneumatic action. The 115v version's box has a built-in transformer! £125+VAT, £220 the lot.
● B&D Professional, Westpoint, The Grove, Slough SL1 1QQ, (0753) 74277

FOUR SIDES at a time with Wadkin's new **planer/sizer.** Feed and cutters adjust automatically; for £7000+VAT, a worthy investment.
● Wadkin plc, Green Lane Works, Leicester LE5 4PF, (0533) 769111

answer to that is, not as much torque as my wrist. After about 20 minutes' work, it wouldn't put a no.8x1¼in chipboard screw right home in piloted 18mm dense chipboard.

The bit it came with is double-ended, but the slot wouldn't fit no.6s or 4s. There's a range of bits available from Skil, but you can't use your Stanley Yankee or any other screwdriver bits in it. On really tough drives you end up helping it along with your wrist, working it much like an electrified ratchet screwdriver. With the right size bits, it'd be ideal for hanging a row of cabinet doors — you don't need elbow-room to get elbow-power; but if you were hanging a lot of room doors, you'd need to keep it on charge while you cut each set of hinge recesses, or it'd be more trouble than it was worth after three or four dozen no.8x1¼s. So how far are you from the elecritricity, after all that? Handy to have, but no substitute for a Yankee or ordinary ratchet — or for the more powerful and expensive cordless pistol-grip screwdrivers. It costs around £20.
● Skil (GB), Fairacres Ind. Est., Dedworth Rd, Windsor, Berks, (07535) 69525.

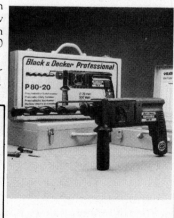

Timberline

Arthur Jones on what's happening in the timber trade

Native hardwoods are important to most woodworkers. The process of bringing suitable logs to the sawmill, however, is relatively haphazard and costly because of the fragmented nature of the supply.

Many farmers or landowners in need of cash approach a timber merchant to offer hardwoods on their land. This might consist of a single tree, or just a few trees scattered about; what might appear to the farmer to be a magnificent oak can actually be damaged or diseased, and in any case, the buyer will look entirely from the viewpoint of what can be produced in the mill from the felled log.

Sometimes the cost of felling, getting the log to a roadside and transporting it to the mill is more than the tree is worth. Much time can be wasted chasing offers of this kind from all parts of the country — and time is money.

Now a firm of auctioneers specialising in native timber sales is to launch an auction for British hardwoods. The first (of standing timber) will be in the autumn and another, perhaps next spring, will be felled wood.

The scheme has the support of timber growers and it's hoped that these auctions will lead to a steady supply of good quality native hardwoods on the market. They will save buyers' travelling time, for the auctioneers will inspect lots and give careful descriptions at auction. This marketing improvement will also, we hope, lead to native timbers taking a bigger share of UK hardwood sales. Could be a brighter prospect for woodworkers.

As far as today's market is concerned, you must expect to pay rising prices for fresh softwood supplies over the coming months. There is a sense of market optimism among timber importers at the moment, bred from a knowledge that forward prices on the world market are firm and showing few (if any) signs of weakness. Both redwood and whitewood prices are steady among the main world suppliers, and demand in the UK has been increasing marginally at a time when stocks are at a low level. The worst period for variety in stocks is the early summer, before the new season's wood gets into the yards, and

you might find you have to search round for what you want. This doesn't signify a softwood shortage, merely a seasonal patchiness among stocks.

Overseas producers, after a couple of barren years when profits have been difficult — impossible in some cases — to make, are pressing hard for higher prices. They could achieve modest success, though at home the lower rate of inflation should limit price rises. Dropping interest rates will also help the woodworker, for the timber stockist works on a bank overdraft and this cost will fall.

On the world market, the devaluation of the French franc could give a boost to sales of some African hardwoods.

Hardboard prices have risen, helped by enforced price increases imposed by the EEC on a Swedish mill and four Finnish producers as a result of an anti-dumping enquiry. The investigation showed that the firms involved were selling hardboard to the UK at prices 5%-25% below what they were charging on their own markets for the same hardboard. To protect producers in the Common Market, all those involved have been forced to lift their prices, though the difference for you is probably a matter of pence per sheet.

Some new hardboards are coming into the UK from new markets, mainly in the southern hemisphere, and quality has been questioned in some cases. Take care; the cheapest is not necessarily the best buy, and as the difference is literally measured in pence the risk of spoiling the end product for small savings can't be justified. Leave those risks to the bulk buyer for mass production.

Sales of particleboard and MDF are soaring, the furniture trade leading the rush. There's also a lot more interest from UK woodworkers in the modern versions of these panel products, much improved from earlier days.

Many hardwoods are now dearer than they were at the beginning of the year. There are a few exceptions, such as keruing, but most of the tropical hardwoods are up in price and stocks are now less well-balanced. ■
● **Auctioneers:** Bidwells, Forestry Chartered Surveyors, Trumpington Rd, Cambridge, (0223) 841841.

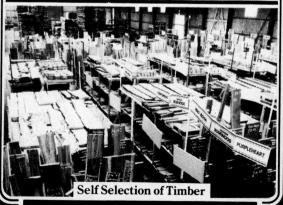

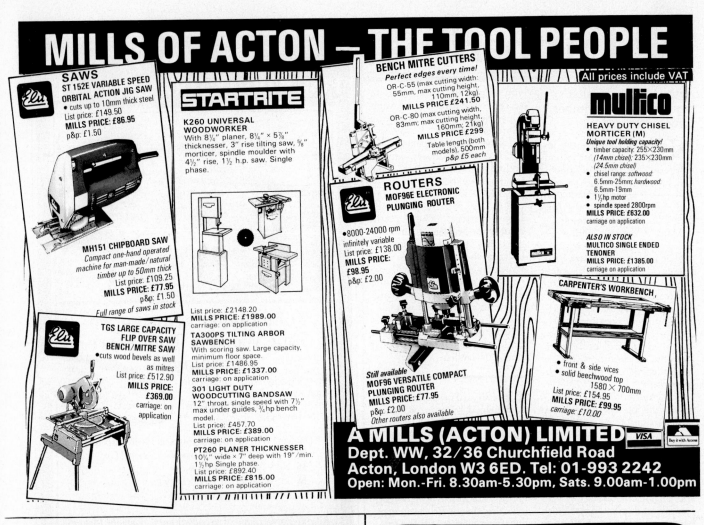
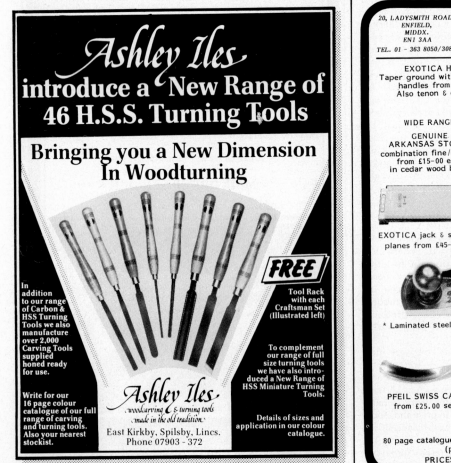
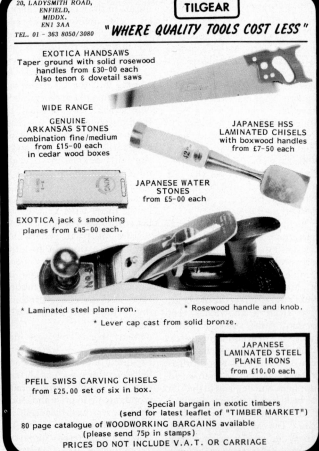
536

Question box

Our panel of experts solve your woodworking problems

We will try to answer any questions you can throw at us, but the ones we publish are the ones of most general interest to readers.

Please type your question double-spaced with generous margins, and include a stamped self-addressed envelope. Send it to: Question Box, Woodworker, 1 Golden Sq., London W1R 3AB.

Grey staining

Q *I want to make a small piece of hardwood furniture with a colour as close to grey as possible. I don't want to use paint. Which wood should I use? How should I get the grey colour?*

J. F. Dye, Amersham

A It isn't possible to stain wood grey with a wood dye. Grey is a mixture of black and white, and although there are black wood dyes, there are no white. If you dilute black wood dye and apply it to white or bleached wood, you get a weak unattractive black.

To make a grey, therefore, you must use pigments. Tint a white undercoat paint to grey with a black paint and thin it with teak oil or an oil varnish which has been thinned with an equal volume of white spirit. You get a grey wash coat which will leave white or bleached wood with a grey finish, through which the grain can still be seen. Trial and error will tell you your shade of grey. When it's dry, the wood can be clear finished or waxed.

Ronald E. Rustin

Fruit-stained ash

Q *Some ash bowls which I turned and oil-finished have been badly stained by strawberry juice.*

Since then I have tried a variety of finishes to avoid staining – polyurethane, Craftlac (with melamine) – but with only limited success. Any advice?

F. G. Endersby, Malvern

A There are certain fruits which will stain even plastic laminates such as Formica! The type of finish that would have the most resistance to staining would be a two-part cold-cure lacquer such as Rustins Plastic Coating, which has a base of butylated urea-formaldehyde and melamine. But even this may stain slightly with fruits like blackberries. Stains in the finish can normally be removed by wiping over with a dilute solution of household bleach. You'll probably find that the stains can also be removed in this way from the bowls which you have oil-finished.

Ronald E. Rustin
● Ronald Rustin is the director of Rustin's Ltd, stain and finish manufacturers.

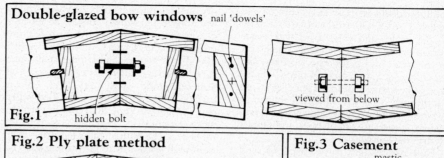

Double-glazed bow windows nail 'dowels'

Fig.1 hidden bolt · viewed from below

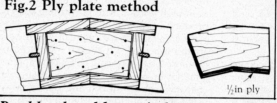

Fig.2 Ply plate method ½in ply

Fig.3 Casement mastic · rebate · short tenon

Double-glazed bow windows

Q *I want to make new bow windows in Brazilian mahogany, double-glazed, but with the double-glazing units going in from the inside, held in by a fillet much like a door stop. I'm trying to get away from glazing bars on the outside which tend to weather and work loose. There's a weakness round the joints because of the 10° angle – what's your opinion of the idea?*

Mr Young, Spennymoor

A Assuming your job is a box window, the classic connection at the frame cills is by handrail bolt and dowels (fig. 1). (See WW/April 77.) If you can't get handrail bolts, they can be improvised by threading the head end of an ordinary bolt, and using a castellated nut for a 'live'. A washer is essential under the live nut, which is then punch-tightened. The cill of a box window would require a 4in-long bolt. A simpler method of connecting the cills at the mitres is to cut shaped pieces of ½in ply, and glue/nail (round wires) these on the (flattened) cill's top surface (fig. 2). This is the method for the head anyway.

For a casement construction, the corners can be connected simply by screws in the rebates (fig. 3). Let the jambs run through from head to base, but before final assembly chop away the tenons (endgrain) to about ¹⁄₁₆in below the surface, so the mitre won't open up in the event of shrinkage. Also, on final assembly, a bead of mastic should be put along each mitre, about ½in in from the outer surface.

Stan Thomas
● Stan Thomas is a joiner of vast experience who holds a live 'Question box' and 'tool hospital' at Woodworker Shows.

Bagpipe turning

Q *What sort of lathe is needed to turn bagpipe drones? Would it be easy to set up a jig? Are there any publications on making bagpipes?*

W. Scarah, East Looe

A Bagpipe drones are basically cylindrically bored interconnecting tubes. Normally these have a single reed fitted at the bag end, and the other end is open.

Although almost any lathe can be used to make drones, the job can be simplified if the one you use has the following features:
● The lathe must be big enough to hold the work. Drones are made in several sections, so this shouldn't be a problem.
● As with all tools, the lathe should be good quality. It's *essential* that the lathe doesn't vibrate excessively when it's running, because the effect would be transferred to the job. Very smooth bores are required for wind instruments.
● A three-leg steady is necessary to hold the free end of the work when machining the bore. If this isn't available a fixture can be made with a ball bearing assembly to hold the work. (See Peter Tomlin on wind instruments, WWs/1971 and 72.)

Although you don't say, I presume you are referring to the machining of the bore when you ask about a jig. There are several publications on making bagpipes, but as many of the techniques of drone-making are similar to those in other wind instruments, these would be most useful:
Trevor Robinson, *The Amateur Wind Instrument maker*, John Murray;
W. A. Cocks and J. F. Bryan, *Northumbrian Bagpipes*, The Northumbrian Pipers Society;
W. Garvin, *The Irish Bagpipes*, Blackstaff Press.

Steve McCordick
● Steve McCordick makes bellows-blown Uillean and Northumbrian bagpipes.

Renovating oak panelling

Q *My house has a large oak-panelled inglenook, the frames of solid oak and the panels of oak-faced plywood. The panelling is french polished and showing signs of wear and tear. How should I restore it? What treatments are available and which would you recommend? I would like a wax-polished finish.*

John Paton, Sutton Coldfield

A The preparation of your oak panelling is of paramount importance. You must take great care to remove all traces of old polish. Apply a water-washable chemical stripper, a paste type ideal for vertical surfaces, with an old brush using a 'stipple', not a brushing, action, and allow 15-20 minutes for the stripper to eat into the old polish. Use OOOO steel wool to 'scrub in' to the gunge, and wipe it off with waste cotton and cellulose thinners. Use a soft brass wire brush for the corners and mouldings; a 'quirk stick' (a piece of hardwood like a large tooth-pick) or even an old toothbrush is handy. When all the gunge has been removed, wash down with warm water to neutralise the stripper, and allow it to dry out bone-dry.

Now use 240-grit garnet paper to sand down every inch, and dust it down — a vacuum cleaner with a brush attachment is helpful here.

You are now ready for re-finishing. Stain the oak with an oil stain such as Colron, which is easy to apply; use a small soft mop or brush to get into the corners. Wipe it down with a rag and allow it to get bone-dry (24 hours), then apply one coat of a dewaxed shellac sealer or french polish thinned with 25% methylated spirits, with a brush or mop. Allow it to dry for three to four hours at about 65°F.

Don't sand it down now, but apply two or three coats of an interior matt polyurethane varnish (as you don't like shellac), allowing each coat to dry bone-hard. When the final coating has been applied, leave it for seven days. Go all over it with Lubrisil 320 grit paper (every inch!) and dust off.

Now for the nice part. Liberally apply a good standard beeswax furniture polish (no silicones) using OOOO steel wool to scrub it into every inch of your oak. Simply polish off surplus wax with mutton-cloth and re-wax in the normal way from time to time. This will give you a first-class antique finish which will look as though it has been there 50 years or more.

Precautions: Wear rubber gloves and a face-mask when applying chemical strippers, and don't smoke. Have plenty of ventilation when using both chemical strippers and polyurethane varnish, or you'll have a sick headache for days.

Noel Leach

Refinishing a car dash

Q *I have been asked to renovate the dashboard of a rebuilt Triumph TR4A. The dash is mahogany-faced 7-ply, walnut veneered, with an unidentified clear plastic protective coating of measurable thickness, and a painted back. I intend to strip to the basic ply, re-veneer in walnut using the 'Glu-film' method, re-paint the back and apply several coats of exterior varnish all over.*

Is my proposed technique adequate for the purpose or can you suggest something better? Are there any special precautions I need to take? And can you identify the current plastic protection applied to the dash?

D. R. Lowe, Newark

A First, after re-veneering you must make sure the pre-staining preparation is meticulously done, making sure the slightest hole, dent or veneered joint is filled and sanded. Use 240-grade garnet paper to a fine smooth finish. I would use a spirit stain, as the area is so small; this will

dry out in minutes at 65°F. As you intend to use a varnish I would suggest an interior polyurethane high-quality varnish because of its speed in drying. Apply four or five liberal coatings, and most important, take care in flatting down between coats. Use 400/600-grade (wet and dry) silicon carbide paper with rain or distilled water and a little soap. The final coat of varnish, when it's bone-dry and after you have denibbed, can be burnished by hand or power mop used with a little burnishing soap to produce a fine mirror-gloss.

As an alternative to varnish and to save application time, I'd suggest a gloss nitrocellulose lacquer finish. This can be applied either by brush or spray-gun, and again each coat must be de-nibbed and flatted down using the techniques I have described for varnishing. With nitrocellulose, use a pull-over solution on top of all coats, applied with a rubber and then let it dry hard. Then burnish it to a mirror-gloss finish.

Your second question about precautions: they are the basic workshop ones. Good ventilation when applying polyurethane varnish, don't smoke or work near a naked flame, and keep the temperature at approximately 65°F or your varnish won't dry.

I can't identify the current finish without seeing it. My guess is that it would be either polyester lacquer (looks like glass) or a gloss cellulose finish.

Noel Leach

● Noel Leach is a professional wood-finisher and lecturer.

TV snack-tables

Q *I want to make a pair of small folding tables suitable for TV snacks. My prototype had the legs pivoted at the centre of the 'X' and at one top end, the dowels capped at each end. The dowels at the other end were removable for folding. I found this somewhat cumbersome, not rigid enough, and eventually the dowels snapped.*

I would prefer an all-wood mechanism, unless it isn't practical.

E. P. Monahan, Maidstone

A Your design probably failed for want of effective bracing and strength of stock. The simple alternative shown is essentially two braced frames, one moving inside the other. The wider frame is pivoted at the top end to the side runners which are fixed to the underside of the table-top. The inner frame rests against the restraining bar **A** when in the open position. The illustration shows the top underside up for clarity.

Assuming that the table is roughly 2ft sq, the legs can be made from 1¼x⅞in stuff, sound and straight-grained. The brace pieces can be 1½x½in, fixed with dovetailed halvings or bare-faced mortice-and-tenons. The pivots can be made from rivets or nuts and bolts, with a spacing washer between the members.

The diagram isn't to scale, and I advise

you to make an accurate drawing of the whole table before starting work.

Bob Grant

● Bob Grant is head of Craft, Design and Technology at an Oxford comprehensive school.

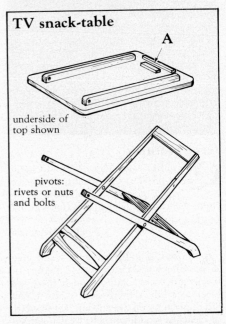

TV snack-table

underside of top shown

pivots: rivets or nuts and bolts

Drying for carving

Q *I have some air-dried yew, about 48x14x 3in, which I have stacked with spacers in the garage, and some elm burr, about 24x14x4in, which appears to be reasonably dry, despite being freshly sawn. As my finished carvings will no doubt end up in centrally-heated homes, is it safe to leave the yew in the garage until it's used? Or should I bring it inside my centrally-heated house? The garage doors are open during the day. As the elm has been standing in a 'dead' state or been felled for a few years, will it be all right for carving? I am hoping to carve two bowls, the finished walls about ½in thick.*

D. J. Shale, Sutton Coldfield

A No matter how thoroughly these timbers have been air-dried, they will certainly lose more moisture in centrally-heated surroundings and either distort or crack, or both. It would be wise to reduce them to near the final dimensions or to rough blanks and gradually condition them as such indoors.

Michael White

● Michael White is a timber consultant and ex-Scientific Officer at the Forest Products Research Laboratory.

Matching stains

Q *I was asked to match a deal door with some existing furniture for a customer. After applying a single coat of Cuprinol Redwood stain and one of Colron Yellow Pine (wiping each coat off before it could be totally absorbed) and then a couple of*

Question box

Ronseal Satincote plus wax, I found that, in clear daylight, I had achieved a very good match. The customer now complains that in situ the door doesn't match up; could this be because he has small windows, and has to use electric light most of the time? How can I kill the 'too red' effect, assuming he's correct?

H. K. Kitchen, Leamington Spa

A It may very well be that in artificial light the deal doors appear redder than they really are. If this is the case you only have to decide whether the customer wants a colour for electric or for artificial light.

It's quite possible that the yellow pine stain wasn't light-fast, and the redwood stain is now showing through more. You could strip off the Ronseal, apply a yellow stain to bring the doors back to their matching colour and then re-varnish. The trouble is that this would entail a great deal of hard work with no guarantee of success, as the second application of yellow might fade.

Before embarking on such a major task it's worth experimenting on some pieces of deal like the door stuff. Stain it with redwood stain, wipe off and allow it to dry as you did. Get some light-fast yellow oil powder and mix it thoroughly in white spirit, then introduce a little of this yellow stain into a small quantity of the varnish. Blend it in by stirring well, then varnish over the stained deal samples. It may be that one or two such varnishings will reduce the red tone and bring back the colour you're after. If so, lightly glasspaper the doors to provide a key, dust them off and varnish them with your yellow tinted varnish. As the yellow stain is light-fast you should have no further trouble. Light-fast yellow oil powder can be obtained from the suppliers listed in 'Wood finishes — what and where?', WW/Mar 85.

Charles Cliffe

Sharpening a scraper

Q *How do you sharpen a cabinetmaker's scraper, and what method do you use for getting the scraping burr edge?*

D. Latimer, Langholm

A First grip the scraper in the vice and file the two long edges straight and square. Then remove the file marks by holding the scraper upright on the face of the oilstone and rubbing it back and forth. To remove any burr formed at this stage, lay the scraper flat on the stone and rub it along three or four times. Wipe off the oil, place the scraper flat on the bench, and burnish it by pressing the back of a gouge (or spring-steel burnisher) firmly on the top surface and making several strokes of the gouge from one end to the other.

Now hold the scraper upright on the bench, gripping it securely, covering the top edge with your apron or a cloth to protect your hand. Place the gouge against the scraper's edge, held at about 80° to the face.

Apply a fair amount of pressure to the gouge and bring it smartly upwards. Repeat this three or four times to produce a burr, which will remove very fine shavings. Sharpen all four long edges of the scraper like this at the same time.

Sharpening and using the cabinet scraper are fully illustrated and described in my *Woodworker Manual of Finishing and Polishing*, available from Argus Books Ltd, at 1 Golden Sq, London W1R 3AB, £2.50 plus p&p.

Charles Cliffe

● Charles Cliffe is a professional wood-finisher, teacher for our Guild and author.

Easy seasoning

Q *I can get cuttings of local timber (apple, ash, beech, etc) for turning fairly easily. Is there any quick way I can mature the timber using only domestic appliances? If I work the timber when green, how can I subsequently preserve it?*

E. J. Heckels, Horsted Keynes

A An ordinary microwave oven can be used very successfully for drying small pieces of timber, and partly or fully turned wooden bowls. The drying period can be very short indeed — in some cases, green to fully dry in minutes.

A model with low power-settings and a timer is essential, and a turntable is desirable to help spread the heat evenly, especially when drying irregular-shaped pieces. Wood must be dried slowly with the oven set at 'defrost'; after five minutes or more, the piece should be allowed to cool, so the moisture can escape. More heating and cooling will be needed till the piece is dried. Drying times can vary greatly, depending on the species and the thickness of the wood.

Remember: the greater the bulk in a microwave oven, the longer it must be heated. Excessive heating can cause internal burning before you are aware of it. See 'Oven-ready timber', WW/June 85.

Wood turned green should be dried and then treated in the normal way with your favourite finish.

Bert Marsh

● Bert Marsh is one of the country's leading professional woodturners.

Using rhododendron

Q *I can get some common rhododendron logs 2-6in diameter, in lengths of up to 6ft. Can you tell me if it's suitable for turning and carving, and what properties the timber has in terms of strength and grain?*

C. C. Fort, Co. Kerry

A The wood of the common rhododendron is somewhat variable, usually a pale pink on cutting which turns pale yellowish brown after exposure. Density is like European birch, with a strength somewhere between elm and beech. Grain, which is often wild, plus other growth characteristics, may cause considerable warping on drying and break-out on cutting.

For turning or carving, the wood should be converted from one side of the log as far away from the centre as possible. Don't try to use the entire log section, as this is likely to result in cracking along the grain, so your maximum available 6in diameters will only produce turnings of about 2in diameter.

It's inevitable that such small-diameter logs will suffer from high differentials in shrinkage, and turnings or carvings may distort or crack after you've finished them.

The close texture of the wood produces a pleasing finish.

Ron Hooks

● Ron Hooks is a professional timber consultant.

Cabinetmakers' files

Q *Some plan instructions I'm working on mention 'cabinetmaker's files'. What are they?*

H. Hussey, Cheadle

A The woodworker's file is slightly different from the metalworker's file in that the cut is coarser and the teeth are rather differently shaped so it doesn't choke easily. The half-round shape is slightly flatter than the engineer's file. Cabinet files were freely available pre-war in fine, medium and coarse cuts, but certainly by 1962 they had disappeared from the catalogues.

Engineer's files, half round and round in 'bastard' and 'second cut' are a tolerable substitute. A parallel file with a 'safe edge' is also useful at times. Buy new files and keep them for wood and they will perform well for a long time.

Rasps, however are still available from good dealers. They come round and half round, in various lengths, as wood rasps and cabinet rasps, the latter with finer teeth. Cabinet rasps were made in regular (second cut) and 'smooth', and wood rasps in 'bastard', 'second cut' and 'smooth'. It's doubtful if more than one grade now exists.

Rifflers are rather spoon-shaped fine rasps, used by sculptors for three dimensional shapes. They are quite readily available.

The range from a good supplier should be like this:

Wood rasps		
Parallel hand	Bastard cut	10, 8 and 6in
Round	Bastard cut	10, 8 and 6in
Half round	Bastard cut	12, 10, 8 and 6in
Cabinet rasps		
Half round	Second cut	12, 10 and 8in
Rifflers	16 various shapes	

Bob Wearing

● Bob Wearing is a lecturer and regular *Woodworker* contributor of great knowledge and experience.

AXMINSTER POWER TOOL CENTRE

WOODWORKING LATHES — *OUR PRICE INC. VAT*

MYFORD ML8 36" centres excluding rear turning facility £376
MYFORD ML8B 36" crs. ..... £432 ML8C 42" 42" crs. £467
HARRISON GRADUATE 30" Centres £1175 42" Centres £1232 Short Bed £1037
ELU DB180 38" crs. 15" dia. swing. Fully motorised £274
KITY Lathes 663-664 & Copiers ..... SPECIAL PRICE
MINIMAX T90 ..... £375 T100 ..... £442 T120 ..... £499
MINIMAX COPIERS C190 ..... £431 CT100 ..... £457 CT120 ..... £499
TYME CUB lathe 4 speed ..... £285 TYME AVON lathe 4 speed £408
WOODTURNING FITMENTS FOR ALL MAKES OF MACHINE (List on request)

RADIAL ARM SAWS

ELUMENIA 9" 1½HP Radial Saw 15" Crosscut ..... £276 24" Crosscut £330
DeWALT DW1251, 1501, 1751, 8001, 8101 ..... SPECIAL PRICES
DeWALT DW1600S 14" saw Max op. cap. 36" 2½HP 1PH ..... £979 4HP 3PH £940
NEW ELU PS174 Mitre/Crosscut Saw 2" Cut 10" Crosscut £244
DeWALT DW1201 Folding 10" Radial Saw £279

SAW BENCHES

MAKITA 2708 8" Saw (will accept router and jigsaw) £204
ROYAL MK111B 10" Cast Iron Tilt Arbor Saw 1½HP £599
ROYAL MKIIIDL 10" Deluxe Cast Iron Tilt Arbor Saw 1½HP £699
WADKIN AGSP Scoring Panel Saw 10"/12" 3PH ..... £1,639 1PH £1,741
ELU TGS 172 Saw Bench/Mitre Saw with TCT Blade ..... £369 ELU TGS 171 ..... £311
LUNA L18 12" 3HP Basic Saw ..... £840 With sliding table £980
SCHEPPACH TKU 12" Tilt arbor saw bench 2.3HP TCT Blade £205
SLIDING TABLE for TKU-TKH ..... £80 Panel Cutting Extension £75
WADKIN AGS 250/300 10"-12" Tilt Arbor Saw 3HP 3PH ..... £1,052 3HP 1PH £1,137
New KITY 10" tilt arbor 2HP floor standing saw bench ..... SPECIAL PRICE
STARTRITE TA300PS Scoring Saw c/w sliding carriage £1,699

BANDSAWS (excellent stocks of all longlife blades)

BURGESS BK3+ MkII with FREE fretsaw and jigsaw attachment ..... (inc. P&P) £115
DeWALT DW100 2 speed. 13" throat. 4" cut. With mitre fence & disc sander £149
DeWALT 3401. 2 speed. 12" throat. 6" cut £256
KITY K613 8" cut 12" throat Bench Mtg or Floor Standing ..... SPECIAL PRICE
STARTRITE 301. 12" throat. 6" cut. Steel table. Floor Standing £395
STARTRITE 351 8" Cut Floor Stdg. £495
STARTRITE 352 2 speed 14" throat 12" cut Fl. Stdg. 3PH ..... £694 1PH £699
LUNA BS320 6" depth of cut. Cast table £324
MINIMAX P32 6" cut 14" throat Cast Tables £367
MINIMAX S45 10" cut 17" throat. Very solid construction. Cast Tables £615

PLANER/THICKNESSER

MULTICO CPT200/230 12" × 9" ¾" rebate £1966
DeWALT DW1150 10" × 6" 2 Speed power feed 2HP Motor ..... POA
ELEKTRA 10" × 6" Power Feed £495
STARTRITE PT260. 10" × 6" Steel tables. ⅝" rebate £834
SHEPPACH HMO SOLO 10" × 6" 2HP with Adjustable Fence £495
STARTRITE SD310. 12" × 7". ⅝" rebate. Cast iron 3PH ..... £1,317 1PH £1,388
WADKIN BAOS 12" × 7" Solid Cast. Heavy Duty 3PH ..... £2,757 1PH £2,930
LUNA 12" × 9" 3HP ..... £1350 WADKIN RM300 12" × 8" £1390

DRILLING AND MORTISING MACHINES

FOBCO STAR ½" Cap 4 Speed ..... £335 Mortising Attachment £63
WARCO 'HOBBY'. ½" capacity. 5-speed, tilting table £125
WARCO 2B ⅝" capacity 2MT tilt table bench mounting £199 2F12 floor standing £235
STARTRITE SP250 5-speed ½" bench drill ..... £339 Floor standing £379
WADKIN MORTISER 1" capacity. 1PH or 3PH £575
MULTICO MORTISER 240v Floor Standing £632
MULTICO HM MORTICER Bench Mounting ⅝" Max Capacity £356
RYOBI Portable Chain Mortiser ..... £365 Chisel Mortiser £396
SMITH BCM Bench Mortiser ..... £399 CM75 Floor Stdg. Model £499
Mortice Chisels & Bits ¼" £16.00 ⅜" £17.50 ½" £20.00 ⅝" £25.00 ¾" £37.00
Ridgeway chisel + bits ¼" £19.00 ⅜" £23.88 ½" £23.88 ⅝" £35.00 ¾" £37.00

SPINDLE MOULDERS

KITY 623 30mm Spindle 3-speed 2HP 1PH WITH SLIDING TABLE £649
LUNA L28 30mm spindle 3-speed 5" rise 3HP 240v £980
STARTRITE T30 1¼" spindle with sliding table 1PH £943
SCHEPPACH HF33 2 Speed 2HP 30mm £485
WADKIN BEL 4 Speed 5HP Spindle Moulder (3PH Only) £1,890
MULTICO TM1 Single Ended Tennoner 240v £1,360

COMBINATION MACHINES

STARTRITE K260 Combination. 'FREE CUTTER SET' 1PH £1,990
LUNA W59 10" Planer 12" Saw 30mm Spindle ..... £2450 3HP £2690
LUNA W64 12" Planer 12" Saw 30mm Spindle £3050
LUNA W69 16" Planer 12" Saw 30mm Spindle 1PH ..... £3900 3PH £3800
SCHEPPACH COMBI 10" × 6" Planer. 12" Saw 30m Spindle £949

★★★★ KITY COMBINATION MACHINES ★★★★

K5 COMBINATION K5 BASIC K704 TABLE COMBINATION K704 DIRECT DRIVE AND ACCESSORIES ALL AT SPECIAL PRICES SEND FOR LATEST PRICE LIST.
★★★★ *FREE DELIVERY ON ALL KITY COMBINATION MACHINES* ★★★★

MISCELLANEOUS MACHINES & EQUIPMENT

KEW Hobby Pressure Washer £239
DeWALT DW250. 10" Bevel/Mitre saw. 1HP motor £194
LUNA YK1500 Pad Sander 1PH ..... £1,327 3PH £1,300
LUNA YKV 1200 1½ HP Face & Edge Sander. Floor Standing £777 Wall Mounting £752
NOBEX 202 Mitre Saw ..... £69.95 NOBEX 303 Mitre Saw ..... £44 P&P £2.50
DeWALT Twin bag dust extractor ..... £265 Multico DEA £339
STARTRITE Dust Extractor CYCLAIR 55 ..... £395 CYCLAIR 75 ..... £509
LUNA SPS400 Dust Extractor 240v Portable Unit £215
LUNA W178 Dust Extractor Floor Mounted £299
LUNA NF259 Large Capacity Dust Extractor 1Ph £555
LION MITRE TRIMMER excellent for accurate mitre cuts £249
LUNA Support Roller ..... £28 Deluxe Combi Support roller £39
MITRE CUTTERS (ORTEGUILE) ORC55 £210 ORC80 £260 ORC100 £390 100F Fl. Stdg. POA

SPINDLE MOULDER TOOLING

LEITZ 488 Cutter Blocks 30mm or 1¼" 92mm dia. £48 100mm dia. £56 120mm dia. £60
WOBBLE SAWS for Spindle Moulders 6" 3mm-21mm £76 10" dia. 3mm-30mm £88
OMAS TIGER CUTTER BLOCKS 30mm or 1¼" ..... £46 Cutter profiles ..... pair £11.50
WHITEHILL CUTTER BLOCKS 4⅞" × 15/16" ..... £48 5⅜" × 15/16" £66

INDUSTRIAL QUALITY T.C.T SAWBLADES

ALL PRICES, INCLUDE V.A.T. AND P&P

GENERAL DUTY (MADE IN SHEFFIELD) PREMIUM QUALITY FOR CONTINUOUS USE (MADE IN W. GERMANY)

BLADE DIAMETER	6"				7"-7 1/4"				8"				9"-9 1/4"			
NO OF TEETH	16	24	36	48	18	30	42	56	20	36	48	64	24	40	54	72
GENERAL DUTY	£16	£17	£20	£26	£16	£17	£21	£26	£20	£25	£27	£32	£24	£26	£29	£36
PREMIUM QUALITY	-	£26	-	£34	-	-	-	-	-	£31	£36	£42	-	£39	£44	-
BLADE DIAMETER	10"				12"				14"				16"			
NO OF TEETH	24	40	60	80	32	48	72	96	36	60	84	108	28	36	60	96
GENERAL DUTY	£23	£26	£35	£38	£25	£31	£35	£44	£34	£42	£50	£57	-	-	-	-
PREMIUM QUALITY	£32	£36	£41	£50	£36	£42	£51	£60	£41	£48	£59	£68	£47	£50	£60	£70

PLEASE STATE BORE SIZE WHEN ORDERING

ROUTERS — OUR PRICE INC. VAT

ELU MOF 96 600w ¼" £77.95
ELU MOF 96E 750w ¼" £98.95
ELU MOF 31 1200w ¼" ⅜" ½" £123.95
ELU MOF 77 variable speed £195.00
ELU MOF 98 1500 ¼" ⅜" ½" £144.95
ELU MOF 177 1600w ¼" ⅜" ½" £156.95
ELU MOF 177E 1800w ¼" ⅜" ½" £181.95
HITACHI TR8 730w ¼" £76.00
HITACHI TR12 1300w ¼", ⅜", ½" £119.00
MAKITA 3600 1500w ¼" ⅜" ½" £149.95
BOSCH POF5 2¼" 500w £49.00
RYOBI R150 ¼" 750w £64.00
RYOBI R500 ¼", ⅜", ½" £113.00

ROUTER ACCESSORIES

ELU MOF 96 Accessory Kit £60.00
DOVETAIL JIG c/w TCT Cutter £60.00
STAIR Routing Jig £69.00
ELU Router Combi Bench £89.00
MAKITA Router Bench £39.00
ELU Router Bracket for DeWalt £36.00

BELT SANDER

ELU MHB 157 3" 600w £85.95
ELU MHB 157E 3" Variable Speed £94.95
ELU MHB 157 Stand £21.00
ELU MHB 157 Frame £28.00
ELU MHB 90 4" 850w £143.95
ELU MHB 90K 4" with frame £164.95
HITACHI SB-75 3" 950w £99.00
HITACHI SB-110 4" 950w £129.00
MAKITA 4" 1040w £155.00
BOSCH 3" 620w £69.00

JIGSAWS

ELU ST 152 420w £82.95
ELU ST 152E 420w £86.95
BOSCH PST 50E 350w £36.75
BOSCH PST 55PE 380w £61.00
BOSCH 1581/7 Var. Speed £95.00

DRILL STANDS

BOSCH S7 Drill Stand £48.00
WOLFCRAFT Compact Drill Stand £44.00
WOLF Morticer Stand £129.00

MISCELLANEOUS POWER TOOLS

ELU DS 140 Biscuit Jointer £156.95
BOSCH Wet 'n' Dry Cleaner £93.75
HITACHI 9" Grinder 2000w £89.00
BOSCH Hot Air Gun 1500w £24.00

CIRCULAR SAWS

ELU MH151 TCT Blade £77.95
ELU MH65 7¼" TCT 1200w £106.95
ELU MH85 9¼" TCT 1800w £152.95
ELU MH182 8" TCT £123.95
HITACHI PSU-6 6" 1050w £63.95
HITACHI PSU-7 7¼" 1600w £95.63
HITACHI PSU-9 9¼" 1759w £112.95
HITACHI PSM-7 7¼" TCT 1200w £129.95
HITACHI PSM-9 9¼" TCT 1600w £136.95
WOLF 9¼ Circular Saw £134

WOODTURNERS "AT LAST PERFECTION"

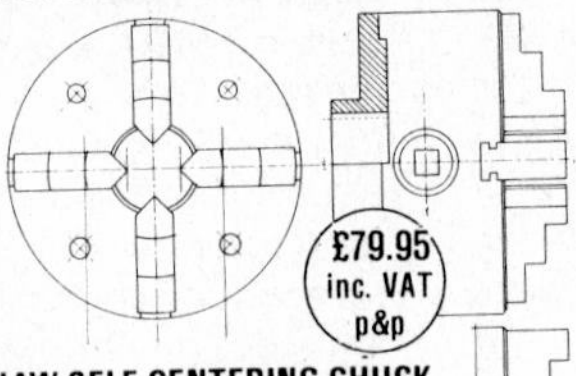

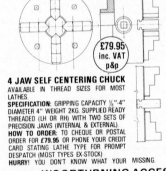

4 JAW SELF CENTERING CHUCK
AVAILABLE IN THREAD SIZES FOR MOST LATHES.
SPECIFICATION: GRIPPING CAPACITY ⅛"-4" DIAMETER 4" WEIGHT 2KG. SUPPLIED READY THREADED (LH OR RH) WITH TWO SETS OF PRECISION JAWS (INTERNAL & EXTERNAL).
HOW TO ORDER: TO CHEQUE OR POSTAL ORDER FOR £79.95 OR PHONE YOUR CREDIT CARD STATING LATHE TYPE FOR PROMPT DESPATCH (MOST TYPES EX-STOCK)
HURRY! YOU DON'T KNOW WHAT YOUR MISSING.

BENCH GRINDERS — OUR PRICE INC. VAT

ELU EDS 163 6" DE £56.95
ELU EDS 164 7" DE £61.95
ELU MWA 149 Honer Grinder £73.95
LEROY SOMER 5" DE £31.00
LEROY SOMER 6" DE £42.00
LEROY SOMER 7" DE £52.00
LEROY SOMER Whetstone £73.00
LUNA 8" Whetstone Grinder £108.00

CORDLESS DRILLS

HITACHI Cordless DTC10 ..... £59.00
HITACHI DV10D Hammer Drill £99.00
MAKITA 6012DE 2 Speed £78.00
MAKITA Hammer Drill 8400DW £99.00
MAKITA 6" Saw in case £168.00
HITACHI D10DB ⅜" Var. Speed £77.95
HITACHI C6DA 6" Saw £148.00

HAMMER DRILL

BOSCH 400-2 400w £29.50
BOSCH 500-RLE 500w £48.75
BOSCH 7002 RLE 700w £81.00
HITACHI VTP1 3K ½" 460w £74.00
HITACHI VTP16AK ⅝" 800w £103.00
B&D P2162 ⅜" Var. Speed Rev. £42.00
B&D P2264 ½" £47.00
B&D P2266 ½" Var. Speed Rev. £69.95

FINISHING SANDERS

ELU MVS 156 1/3 Sheet £65.95
ELU MVS 156E Electronic £77.95
ELU MVS 94 Heavy Duty £90.95
ELU MVS 47 Heavy Duty £98.95
ELU Palm Sanders ¼ or ⅓ Sheet £44.95
HITACHI Palm Sander £39.00
MAKITA Palm Sander £42.00
B&D P6303 1/2 Sheet Ind. £57.00
BOSCH PSS230 1/3 Sheet £27.00

POWER PLANERS

ELU MFF80 850w £88.95
ELU MFF80K 850w £106.95
HITACHI FU-20 720w £74.00
HITACHI P20SA 720w £84.00

DREMEL POWER TOOLS

15" Scroll Saw Sander £72.00
Delux Scroll Saw Sander £93.00
258 Const. Speed Moto Tool £42.95
358 Var. Speed Moto Tool £55.95
359 as 358 with 35 Accs. £68.95
Router Base for Moto Tool £11.95
Drill Stand for Moto Tool £25.95
238 Moto Flex Tool £78.95
338 Var. Speed Flex Tool £86.95

JAPANESE HORIZONTAL WHETSTONE GRINDER £129.00

ELU ACCESSORIES

90% of all Elu Accessories in Stock. 10% discount on all items. Post Paid on most items. Send S.A.E. for current list.

ROUTER CUTTERS

20-25% OFF LEADING BRANDS EXCELLENT STOCKS OF HSS & TCT ROUTER CUTTERS OVER 500 PROFILES IN STOCK. SEND NOW FOR FREE CUTTER CHART:-
TECHNIQUES OF ROUTING £6.95 (inc. P&P)

LIBERON FINISHES

Sanding Sealer, French Polishes, Stains, Waxes, Wire Wool etc. All Ex Stock. Post Paid on orders over £5.00 SAE for free list.

BANDSAW BLADES

LONGLIFE QUALITY BLADES. OVER 4000 BLADES IN STOCK SEND NOW FOR CURRENT PRICE LIST.
Metal Blade Guides for DeWalt BS1310 & DW100 ..... £5.20/set of 4

WOODTURNING ACCESSORIES (State make of Machine)

Sorby Precision Chuck £52.70
2½" Woodscrew Chuck £22.00
1½" Woodscrew Chuck £18.50
Drill Chuck 0-½" 1MT or 2MT £15.00
Coronet Service Kit, main brgs & belt £42.95
Coronet Chuck Sets £65.00
Collet Chuck Bodies £28.50
Long Hole Boring Kit £32.00
State ¼, 5/16, ⅜ & Machine.
Live Centre 1MT or 2MT £39.95
For TYME, CORONET, MYFORD, MINIMAX, HARRISON, KITY, ARUNDEL & OTHERS.

SASH CRAMPS (P&P £2.00 per order) May be mixed for quantity

RECORD 135-24" 1 off £19 5 off £17
135-36" 1 off £20 5 off £18
135-42" 1 off £21 5 off £19
135-48" 1 off £22 5 off £20
DRAPER 18" 1 off £13.50 5 off £11.50
30" 1 off £17.25 5 off £14.95
40" 1 off £18.40 5 off £16.00
60" 1 off £28.00 5 off £26.00

HAND TOOLS (P&P £1.50 per order)

STANLEY 04 Smooth Plane £18.50
STANLEY 04½ Smooth Plane £20.00
STANLEY 05 Jack Plane £27.50
STANLEY 05½ Jack Plane £29.50
STANLEY 06 Fore Plane £36.00
STANLEY 07 Fore Plane £40.00
STANLEY 10 Rebate Plane £38.00
STANLEY 60½ Block Plane £18.00
STANLEY RECORD 778 Rebate Pl. £31.00
RECORD 146 Hold Fast £14.00
Extra Collars for 146 ..... £3.00
RECORD Cramp Heads £12.00
RECORD 52½E 9" Wood Vice £62.00
LIP & SPUR DRILL 1-13mm × 0.5 £54.00
CLIFTON 3 in 1 Plane £67.00
RECORD 04 Smooth Plane £18.00
RECORD 04½ Smooth Plane £19.00
RECORD 05 Jack Plane £28.00
RECORD 05½ Jack Plane £29.00
RECORD 06 Fore Plane £34.00
RECORD 07 Jointer Plane £38.50
RECORD 010 Rebate Plane £38.00
RECORD 060½ Block Plane £15.50
RECORD 020C Circular Plane £66.00
RECORD Dowelling Jig £31.00
RECORD 141 Corner Cramps £21.00
PARAMO Cramp Heads £10.00
RECORD 53E 10½" Wood Vice £71.00
LIP & SPUR DRILL 1/16-½ × 16ths £39.00
Clifton Rebate Plane 420 ..... £18.00

CLICO SAWTOOTH CUTTERS (inc. VAT P&P) 6" long with ½" shank

⅜" ..... £7.70; ½" ..... £7.90; ⅝" ..... £8.70; ¾" ..... £9.50; ⅞" £10.20;
1" ..... £10.90; 1⅛" ..... £12.80; 1¼" ..... £15.60; 1⅜" ..... £16.20; 1½" £17.10;
1⅝" £19.70; 1¾" £22.40; 1⅞" £24.80; 2" £26.20; 2¼" £32.90; 2½" £43.70

IMMEDIATE DESPATCH ON CREDIT CARD PHONED ORDERS — CREDIT TERMS AVAILABLE OVER £120

CHARD STREET AXMINSTER DEVON EX13 5DZ 0297 33656 6.30-9pm 34836

BARCLAYCARD VISA

WORKBENCH OF THE FUTURE!

A *WOODWORKER* and **SJÖBERG** COMPETITION to test your SKILL!

WIN

1 A magnificent Sjöberg 2000 workbench, with a 2000mm-long laminated beech top and two vices — worth £700 (if you could buy it in the UK)
PLUS
2 A long weekend in a luxury hotel in Sweden, with a visit to Sjöbergs

The total value of these enticing prizes?

£1500!

WHAT YOU HAVE TO DO The traditional workbench design is hundreds of years old — no special provision for power tools or modern equipment. But Sjöberg are committed to constant improvement: SO **DESIGN THE WORKBENCH OF THE FUTURE — OR FEATURES FOR A WORKBENCH — OR BENCH ACCESSORIES — that make benchwork more flexible, comfortable and easier with today's tools and materials**

THE WINNER will be the entry (judged by *Woodworker* and Sjöberg) which makes the greatest overall contribution to workbench design

ENTRIES must be in the form of detailed drawings and/or photos, plus explanatory notes on no more than two A4 sheets for each item. Send to '**Workbench of the Future**', Woodworker, 1 Golden Sq, London W1R 3AB.

CLOSING DATE 31 AUGUST

● Prizewinning designs will become the property of Sjöberg, who reserve the right to put them into production
● Sjöberg will pay £100 to any entrant other than the winner whose idea is put into production
● Similar ideas will be judged on quality of presentation
● All decisions about the competition are final, and no correspondence will be

held. Employees of ASP Ltd, Sjöberg Ltd, Brimarc Ltd or their advertising agents are excluded from entry
● SJÖBERG WILL MAKE UP THE WINNING DESIGN TO BE EXHIBITED AT THE WOODWORKER SHOW, ALEXANDRA PAVILION, LONDON, 23-26 OCTOBER
● An entry is automatically taken as agreement to abide by the rules of the competition, and take (within reason) the offered dates for the holiday

---

SPECIAL OFFER! £100 off!

If you want to make sure of a SJÖBERG bench, have a look at this. The 1900 has a 1900mm-long laminated birch top, two vices, and storage underneath. With a Sjöberg Holdfast, it's worth £520 retail. *Woodworker* and Sjöberg are offering it to you for just £420! That's a clear £100 off!

● Make cheques payable to Argus Specialist Publications Ltd

To: Reader Services, Wolsey House, Wolsey Rd, Hemel Hempstead, Herts HP2 4SS
Please send me ☐ Sjöberg 1900 benches with ST82 Holdfast at £420 each. I enclose

a cheque for ....

Name..

Address..

Post Code..

Matching the apple

● *A dainty marvel that demonstrates the importance of sensitive selection for grain and colour*

Edward Thom's secretaire is carefully book-matched and lovingly made — from a fruitwood that carried its own inspiration

This design started with a few preliminary sketches, and I did detailed construction drawings during the development. Rather than work from preconceived and fixed ideas, I was led by the feelings that the apple inspired. Its distinctive dark/light colour contrast told me that book-matching should be used to the full, and this became the predominant stimulus for the whole piece. The drawings here were done after I completed the construction.

The carcase

This is made from a single piece of apple, carefully selected for its beauty of grain and colour, and for the balance between dark heartwood and light sapwood. You must make absolutely sure that you lay the pieces

out in this sequence: side, top, side, base (fig. 2). This way the grain flows all the way round the secretaire, the only break in continuity coming at one corner, which naturally should be at the base.

Having decided that the darker heartwood should go towards the back, I planed the rear edge of the single piece from which the four sides were cut, and used that as my face edge. Dimension it with a thicknesser or try-plane to 150x12mm; if dimensioning a piece this size by hand daunts you, cut it in two to get side/top and side/base.

Decide which side you want to use as the face side, and once you've made this choice, it's sensible to mark out the groove in the back edge to take the back panel, since ploughing a groove in one piece is a lot easier than doing it in four. The groove is 4x4mm, set 4mm in from the back edge, so you can set a mortise gauge to get both marks, or use a marking gauge set separately to 4mm and 8mm.

Secret mitred dovetails

This joint, it need hardly be said, requires absolute accuracy. The detail drawings show the dimensions for the base joints (fig. 3); you must adjust the size of the dovetails to suit the narrower top, where two tails will be ample. On both top and bottom, use exactly the same sizes for the width of the meeting faces of the mitres — 7mm front, 8mm back.

Set a cutting gauge to 12mm and gauge the shoulder lines, and use a mitre-square or sliding bevel as a guide to knife the lines of the mitres. Now set the cutting gauge to 2mm and gauge the lap to mark the rabbets — the long mitred meeting faces of the joint.

Now change to a marking gauge set to 2mm, to gauge the lap on the endgrain. With all the rabbets marked out, use a fine dovetail saw to cut them out.

Mark out the pins, for which the rake is 1:6, and the mitres with knife-lines. Cut the side mitres first with a fine dovetail saw, and then cut the lap mitre with a sharp bevel chisel. Give the edges a final trim with a shoulder-plane.

Cut the pins out by sawing first on the inside of the knife-lines, then working carefully with a chisel. Use the completed and cut-out pins as a template to trace the tails out, then cut them in the same way as the pins with saw and chisel.

The shelf and partitions

The shelf is 12mm thick, held in the carcase sides with stopped housing joints. The rear edge of the shelf is set 8mm in from the back edge of carcase, which brings the back edge of the shelf flush with the inner surface of the back panels.

Match the three vertical partitions and plane them to 4mm thick; they range in height from front to back 60, 80 and 100mm. They are set into stopped grooves in the carcase sides.

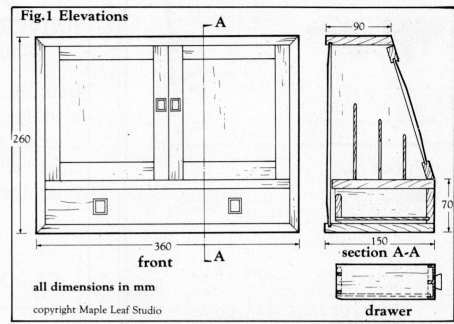

Fig.1 Elevations

260

360

front

A

A

all dimensions in mm

copyright Maple Leaf Studio

90

section A-A

150

70

drawer

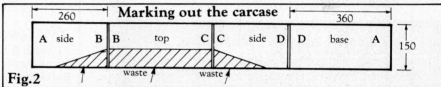

Marking out the carcase

260

360

A   side   B B   top   C C   side   D D   base   A

150

waste   waste

Fig.2

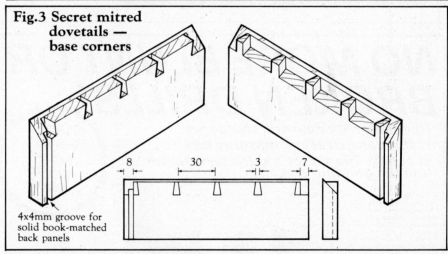

Fig.3 Secret mitred dovetails — base corners

8   30   3   7

4x4mm groove for solid book-matched back panels

Fig.4 Section through vertical divide/back panels

back panel   vertical divide   back panel

70

5

The back panels and vertical divide

I gave special attention to grain and colour when selecting the ideal piece for the back panels, because not only are they themselves book-matched, but they must also match the door panels. Book-matching isn't possible with wood with flat annual rings, so choose a piece with the endgrain ring markings as near vertical through the thickness as possible.

The finished thickness of the panels is 5mm; I used a quarter-sawn piece 15mm thick to make both panels. Use a marking gauge set to half the thickness, and scribe all the way round the edge, then use this line as a guide for sawing. Cut through the depth with a hand-saw or bandsaw to reveal matching surfaces, although the saw kerf and plane work will change the pattern slightly. This is why you must work with the minimum sawing and planing. The result will be two matching panels, beauti-

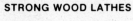

544

Matching the apple

fully harmonious in grain and colour.

The sectional view (fig. 4) shows the shaping on the panels and the method of holding them in position. The vertical divide is a piece of sapwood with a pattern similar to the sapwood sections of the back panels. The edges are rebated with a 4x4mm step.

Cut a tenon to hold the vertical divide in position, to fit exactly in the panel groove. Thus it has the same dimensions as the groove — 4x4mm in section and 62mm wide.

The book-matched doors

The door panels are made the same way as the back panels, and the frames use square-haunched stopped mortise-and-tenon joints (fig. 5).

The frame members are 9mm thick, the stiles and top rails 20mm wide and the bottom rails 24mm. The panels are 5mm thick and the grooves to hold them 3mm wide and 4mm deep.

Prepare the panels and frames for both doors at the same time, then mark the grooves out with a mortise gauge. Plough all the grooves and then mark out all the mortises and tenons with a knife. Cut the tenons and haunches with a dovetail saw, and remove the waste in the mortises with a ⅛in mortise chisel.

When you have completed all the joints and panels, dry-cramp them with two sash-cramps aligned across the joints. Make all the standard checks for squareness across the diagonals, and make sure the whole door and panel assembly is perfectly flat.

Fig.5 Doors — joint detail

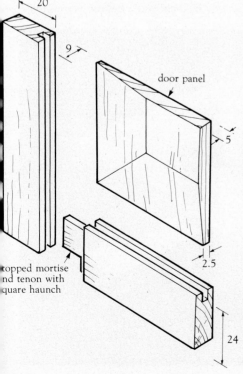

20

9

door panel

5

2.5

24

stopped mortise
and tenon with
square haunch

The hinges

Glue the doors up, plane the surfaces flush, and then get ready for the hinges. Use 25mm solid drawn brass butts and matching brass screws, and note that the positioning and method of fitting is *very important*. The top edge of the uppermost hinge is on a line with the lower edge of the top door rail, and for the lower hinge, align the bottom edge with the upper edge of the bottom door rail.

Set the hinges into the door stile by first measuring the *overall* thickness of the knuckle with a marking gauge. This measurement is marked on to the stile, and represents the depth of the housing. The width of the housing, also measured with a marking gauge, is the distance between the edge of the flange and the centre of the hinge-pin.

The door slopes at 72° to the vertical, and you will have to plane the bottom rail to the same angle to fit into the carcase.

The doors are completed with book-matched handles in perfect harmony with the whole secretaire. They are held by a single brass countersunk screw from the inside of the stile, but once you're happy with the positioning of the handles you can glue them as well.

The drawer

The drawer-front is made from a heart-wood section, and the handles are made from a single piece of apple, book-matched the same as the door-handles.

The drawer-front is 10mm thick and the sides 8mm; a 4mm groove is ploughed in the drawer-front and sides to hold the 4mm-thick solid bottom. If you decide to have the sides less than 8mm thick, you'll have to put drawer-slips inside the carcase.

Assembly

The carcase, shelf, three partitions, two back panels and vertical divide all have to be glued up at the same time. Spend plenty of time dry-cramping all the parts together and making sure every part fits perfectly, using clear identification marks to avoid confusion. For parts such as the panels and the partitions, which have to be polished before gluing up, it's a good idea to use letters marked on masking tape; lettered labels can easily be removed after gluing up without any damage to the wood. Whatever you do, *never* rely on memory when assembling!

Once you're happy with all the joints, prepare for gluing up, with all the sash cramps already set to length from dry cramping. Glue up, make all the standard checks for square, and remove excess glue from all the inside surfaces.

For a finish I chose teak oil, which is entirely natural and allows the wood to speak for itself. I think you'll agree it was well worth giving the particular character of the apple a voice! ∎

● Maple Leaf Studio, Rhosybol, Anglesey, (0407) 831 145.

The best medicine

Trevor Roberts is a medical man with a furniture-making business and a liking for tricky tasks. He talked to Stan Folb, who took the pictures

I started my working life as a doctor, but have been making furniture now for about three years. I was never really inspire by the practice of medicine, and after 13 years in various specialities and general practice, I decided to call it a day. I'd always had a strong interest in music and theatre, so I looked for something in those areas and was lucky to find a job as technical manager of the (then) new Roundhouse Studio Theatre. Various posts as stage manager or technician followed, leading to a spell of four years as carpenter in the Theatre Department of the Central School of Art and Design, where I built scenery designed by the students. Their designs were usually very imaginative and interesting, but they needed a fair bit of technical ingenuity to make them practical!

During this period, I developed an interest in the finer aspects of woodworking, and managed to get a day release to attend the City and Guilds 564 course in furniture making at the London College of Furniture. Bob Thornhill is an enthusiastic and inspiring teacher — *Woodworker* ran a 'diary' series last year by one of his students ('Starters', WWs/Jan-Aug 85) which gives an idea of the atmosphere of intense creativity.

I would like to have done a full-time course, but I couldn't do it and survive financially, so I settled for a TOPS course in carpentry and joinery, followed by another in wood-machining under Frank Whitehouse, another excellent teacher and a bit of a machinery genius. The machinery experience on this course made me very safety-conscious, and I'm concerned about the number of woodworkers who buy and use machines without professional instruction.

Having got so far I felt like going it alone, and so started my own full-time business with the help of the Enterprise Allowance scheme and a friendly bank manager. It meant a move out of the garden shed into local premises — a decent workshop space rented from a small engineering firm.

Work came in all right; slow but steady. I must admit I found it difficult to work fast and efficiently enough to make a profit, so when the Enterprise Allowance scheme ran out, I decided to subsidise my furniture business by going back to medical practice. Now I do a number of sessions per week for the National Blood Transfusion Service; I find the hypodermic syringe demands the same sort of manual dexterity as a dovetail saw!

In theory at any rate, having some regular income should enable me to spend some of my time making speculative pieces to my own designs. I don't rate myself particularly highly as an original designer, and prefer to concentrate on simple designs in solid wood.

Among the various woodworking themes that enthuse me, I could quote my favourite maker as Alan Peters, and my particular interest lies in applying machining methods and engineering principles to jointing. There are plenty of ideas, but I despair of living long enough to try them all out!

The circular table

This table is in English cherry, a pedestal design that I saw as a challenge, because although you often see the inverted bell shape in metal or fibreglass, I've never seen it in wood. It's coopered — a bit like an inside-out barrel in constructional technique, even down to the radius edge-planing system I devised with my jointer. It's reminiscent of the old cooper's planing method — running down a huge baulk with a mouth and blade set in it, curving and giving an angled edge to the staves at the same time. The tolerances for coopering barrels are somewhat forgiving, however!

The basic structure consists of a circular base, a central hexagonal pillar for which I used a good straight-grained softwood (nice and dry), and six radial supports for the top. There are six vertical ply 'webs', one under each bearer, which curve to the sectional shape of the pedestal and provide stability. The bearers are haunch-tenoned into the central hexagonal post, and glued and screwed through to a ply disc biscuit-jointed on top of the webs; the webs are biscuited to the base (another disc of 18mm

● **Above,** the load-bearing properties of Trevor's 'Rietveld' chair; **below,** a chess table detail

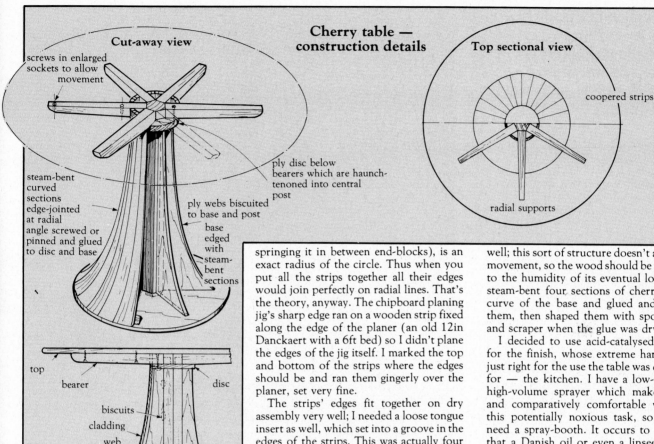

Cherry table — construction details

Cut-away view

screws in enlarged sockets to allow movement

steam-bent curved sections edge-jointed at radial angle screwed or pinned and glued to disc and base

ply webs biscuited to base and post

ply disc below bearers which are haunch-tenoned into central post

base edged with steam-bent sections

Top sectional view

coopered strips

radial supports

top

bearer

disc

biscuits

cladding

web

post

glue-block

edge section

ply base

Vertical section

---

ply) and central post. The top is a straight-forward selection and edge-jointing job, the edge radiused the full thickness.

The 'cladding' is 24 coopered cherry strips 10mm thick, tapering from about 90mm wide at the bottom to around 25 at the top. They are glued and pinned (with glue-blocks) to the base, and glued and screwed (screw-holes plugged) to the top disc.

I made a template for the face shape of strips after some serious geometry to work out their width at various heights so I could get a smooth curve. I cut and shaped them oversize to the template (oversize for planing), then steam-bent them to a jig. It's vital to (a) overbend a little to allow for spring-back, and (b) leave the strips to dry properly on the jig — at least a day, and pre-ferably more if you have the time.

The planing operation was interesting, though I wouldn't care to repeat it. It involved a piece of chipboard cut to exactly the shape formed between the central axis of the central post and the inside face of the curved strips. The chipboard was cham-fered to a point at the straight edge; when this planing jig is laid on its side, the line between the chipboard's 'sharp edge' and the desired edge of the cherry strip (held centrally on the jig's curved edge by

springing it in between end-blocks), is an exact radius of the circle. Thus when you put all the strips together all their edges would join perfectly on radial lines. That's the theory, anyway. The chipboard planing jig's sharp edge ran on a wooden strip fixed along the edge of the planer (an old 12in Danckaert with a 6ft bed) so I didn't plane the edges of the jig itself. I marked the top and bottom of the strips where the edges should be and ran them gingerly over the planer, set very fine.

The strips' edges fit together on dry assembly very well; I needed a loose tongue insert as well, which set into a groove in the edges of the strips. This was actually four slots rather than one all the way up; I cut them with an $\frac{1}{8}$in bit in the table router and a 'single point of contact' curved fence. It needed a bit of juggling to get the right angle of cut into the sides so the tongues would line up across the edges of the strips.

All the strips finally went in and fit very

well; this sort of structure doesn't allow for movement, so the wood should be matched to the humidity of its eventual location. I steam-bent four sections of cherry to the curve of the base and glued and pinned them, then shaped them with spokeshave and scraper when the glue was dry.

I decided to use acid-catalysed lacquer for the finish, whose extreme hardness is just right for the use the table was designed for — the kitchen. I have a low-pressure high-volume sprayer which makes short and comparatively comfortable work of this potentially noxious task, so I don't need a spray-booth. It occurs to me now that a Danish oil or even a linseed/poly-urethane/ Danish combination might be better because of the 'renewability factor' — there are some scratches appearing in the AC lacquer now, and there's no reviver for that! ∎

● Trevor Roberts, 25 Nottingham Rd, Isleworth TW7 6PD.

● *Curving, coopered cherry; an elegant and difficult design for a kitchen table!*

Built in the Balkans

Transylvanian traditions
include startling
rough-hewn joinery as well
as the odd vampire.
Tony Deane was there with
his camera

It's hardly surprising to find a country with a name like Transylvania filled with wooden buildings and artefacts. This is a place where the way of life flirts with the 20th century, yet retains the serenity of an older age; where wooden farm carts pulled by buffaloes or cows creak along the roads, carrying rosy-cheeked children peeping out of mounds of newly mown hay. Across the fields, lines of peasants scythe into knee-high grass, while shepherds down from the summer mountain pastures catch the latest gossip, chatting to vividly dressed women with faces like Russian dolls.

As you go north across the Carpathian mountains towards the Russian border, the villages show an ever-richer variety of medieval wooden buildings with carved façades. Farmhouse entrances are guarded by beautifully proportioned lychgates, sometimes thatched, but usually tiled with larch pantiles. Where gates have been recently repaired or replaced, traditional designs have been perpetuated by the use of the old symbolic carved characters — but occasionally the hammer-and-sickle of the Communist Party appears as a contemporary feature. An Egyptian-looking 'shaduf' stands just beyond the farm gate; tapped water isn't common in the remote areas, so the well is the usual source of water in the villages. Frequently the whole bole of a tree — generally elm — hollowed and about a metre high, forms the surround at the well-head instead of brick or concrete. Hen-houses, pigsties and hazel-stick panelled maize stores on stilts bear testimony to the endurance of everyday wooden buildings whose design has evolved to the optimum over the years. Water-mills crudely hewn out of elm and chestnut can be seen still grinding the village corn.

But the slender spires of the village churches, standing over the farms and orchards, represent the pinnacle of rural wood craftsmanship. Built up of entire tree-trunks, the church walls are joined at the corners by giant dovetails, some of the pins half a metre across! Inside, the walls have been trimmed flat with adzes and hung with crudely embroidered vestments that seem somehow to diminish rather than enhance the purity of the building's atmosphere. Most churches have a bell hung in the base of the larch-clad spire, which may also contain a jettied gallery; hardly more than chapel size, they are used each day for mass, filled almost to bursting by a congregation

Wood is put to a multitude of practical

● A magnificent galleried wooden spire rises into the blue Rumanian sky . . . but the church is hardly larger than a chapel

uses in this part of the world, but village carvers express their deep feeling and attachment for the trees by carving tree trunks *in situ*. Instead of (say) a storm-killed tree being cut down for firewood, it will be turned by a sculptor into some fantastic figure of local folklore. In the middle of nowhere, I came across several dozen such carvings on a wooded hillside; some were conservatively fashioned like Michelangelo's *Pieta*, others would have gladdened the heart of Picasso.

In Transylvania as in most places, traditional features and characteristics are disappearing, and the Rumanian government encourages local councils to preserve an-

cient buildings of their district wherever possible. It might even mean dismantling a farmhouse and outbuildings and moving them to an open-air museum! As the use of modern materials and techniques grows, the skills that produced the lovely homes and barns of Transylvania will vanish.

As I travelled south, I left Transylvania through a giant carved archway covered in good luck symbols. I couldn't help feeling that woodworkers from any country at all would identify immediately with the people who still live by the axe and adze in this lovely, remote part of the Balkans; where love of wood is the language, there's no doubt you'll be made to feel at home! ∎

● *Vasil Salajan is this local hero's name – the date is 1978*

● *No job for a dovetail saw, this!*

● *Well-weathered carved screens and larch tiles on rural farm buildings*

Shoptalk special
Head stand

● **Above, left to right:** *the Universal Woodworking Stand demonstrates reasonable claims to its name – drilling, mortising, mitring. Note the mortise clamping system.* **Below,** *the 'Power Expansive' bits and their pieces*

Drill-stands are essential equipment for the vertical-minded, and mortisers are (arguably) indispensable. Simon Mathews took a close look at a new product that's both in one — plus it mitres!

The speciality of Wm. Ridgway and Sons, one of the UK's renowned quality tool manufacturers, has always been wood-boring bits and mortising bits and chisels. They do a wide range of these and similar cutting tools — not surprising since the firm's founder was a skilled hand-forger (primarily of auger bits) before he set up on his own in 1878.

Boring bits and similar tools can't be used on their own, of course; they need a drill to turn them round. Power drills are often used hand-held, but if you need accuracy there's no substitute for a drill-stand, and Ridgways have recently launched one that seemed to me to be of outstanding quality.One from the first production batch is already in my workshop, and I've had a chance to assess its potential.

The Ridgway Universal Woodworking Stand is a substantial piece of equipment in every sense. Robustly made and designed for hard use to professional standards, it's almost all iron castings and mild steel bar. The reason behind the 'Universal' name is that it is designed for drilling and boring, but also takes a mortising attachment, and another which converts the stand into a

mitre-trimmer. This really is something new; I'm not aware of a similar piece of equipment that converts to give you mitring as well.

Drilling

The stand accepts all power drills with a now-standard 43mm collar, which is very firmly held in the headstock casting by the clamp, tightened with a couple of screws. The headstock itself can be raised and lowered on the main column for different sizes of workpiece to go under it, and it can also be rotated round the column and used in any position away from the central. A lever on the left locks it in any location, and the main lever on the right is long enough to give good leverage for normal purposes.

The lowering-and-raising mechanism is a very smooth rack and pinion, and you can adjust the headstock's sliding action if you should ever need to. A stout spring on the main column raises the drill after each lowering. A stop is built into the top of the headstock to limit the down-reach of the drill, useful for both drilling and mortising, but it isn't calibrated so you have to set depth with a rule.

If the mortising fork is fitted, it needs to be swung out of the way for normal drilling and boring. The workpiece is then supported on the base, though it's always good practice on a drill-stand or drilling machine to have a piece of scrap between workpiece and base or table — accidental wood-boring bit-to-metal contact can cause havoc to the bit. With everything set up, I bored various sizes of holes in different kinds of timber using different types of bit, and I found the

action sweet and smooth. Everything stayed rock-steady.

You must take note of the power of the drill when you need to bore large holes. The drill I was using is 500w, with a wood-boring capacity of 30mm. Using the drill in the stand doesn't increase the capacity, so if you try to bore larger holes, you can harm and possibly burn out your drill. You won't of course, damage the stand.

Most of us need to drill something other than wood occasionally — usually metal. As I expected, the stand worked fine. Always hold pieces of metal smaller than about 24in in a drill-vice or Mole wrench for drilling, and wear safety goggles.

Mortising

Many small planer/thicknessers and most combination machines have provision for a slot-mortiser, which produces round-end mortises rather than the square-ended ones cut by hollow-chisel machines. Most people prefer square ends, and usually trim the round ends of a slot-mortise square with a chisel. The Ridgway Universal stand's mortising attachment accepts square chisels up to ¾in, although you could cut larger mortises by re-setting for a second pass.

The mortise-chisel holder is gripped in the same clamp as the drill collar, along with a set-screw which passes directly from the holder into the headstock. I had reservations about this arrangement, figuring maybe drill and chisel-holder would be securely held, but not both when the clamping-screws were tightened. My anxiety proved totally groundless; chisel-holder and drill were both very positively held even with the set-screws only moderately tightened.

The clamping-fork holds two fences, lengths of angle steel held by a couple of wing-nuts; height of the fork and position of the fences are set to straddle the workpiece from above. They must of course be set to allow minimum clearance with the wood freely movable, and it's also essential that the chisel itself is correctly aligned with the mortise you're cutting. It's wise to set the depth-stop, whether the mortise is to be through or stopped. With all the adjustments made, I found actually cutting the mortises was perfectly straightforward; the main handle provides adequate leverage.

Mitring

The mitring attachment makes this drill-stand different from anything else like it, and its ability to cope with this operation especially excited me. There are two parts to the attachment, the cutter-block and the mitre table/fence. The cutters are tungsten vanadium, one of the best materials there is for a keen, tough cutting edge which will retain sharpness for long periods. There are two cutters in the block, pre-set at 90° to each other. The table/fence bolts to the base, and although the bolts go at the extreme ends of the base slots, the anchorage is very secure. It's important to follow the instructions for setting the relative positions of block and table/fence, because it's essential to get the headstock at the correct height and the clearance of the blades in the vee of the table/fence precisely adjusted. When the apparatus is correctly attached to the stand, mitring performance is impressive, although as you'd expect, it's not for heavy cuts. Look at it as more for trimming; it won't slice through the middle of a largish section. This is best done with a saw, and then the attachment can be used for precise trimming to exact length. I tested its limits by trimming a piece of hardwood about 1½in square, about the equipment's full capacity, and it sliced through the end of this with ease. The cut surface was clean, and two cuts butted together were a perfect fit and exactly 90°.

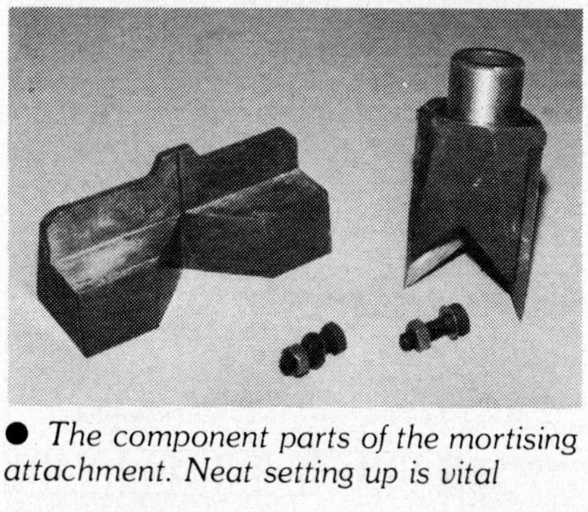

● *The component parts of the mortising attachment. Neat setting up is vital*

I think I also discovered a use of the drill-stand which the makers may not be aware of — at least it's not mentioned in their literature. One of my assortment of routers has a 43mm collar, which could be held very firmly in the collar-clamp of the stand, and opens up the possibility of using the stand as a small overhead router. An assortment of cutters and a measure of ingenuity widens this item's scope considerably.

Overall, I was most impressed with this stand and what it and its attachments could do, all made to quality standards rather than price limitations.

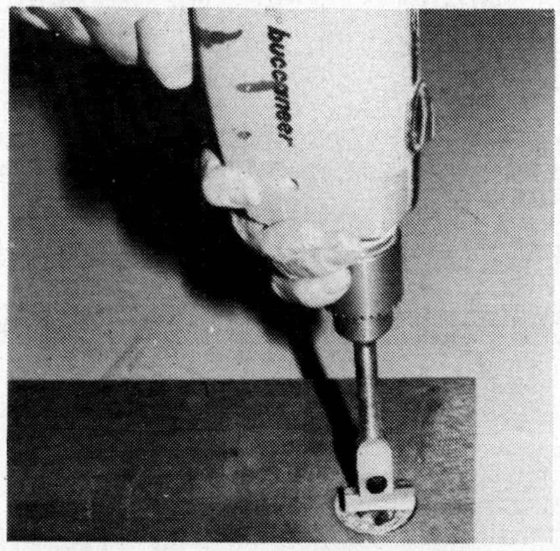

● *Drilling veneered chipboard with a medium-duty bit. Heavy-duty hole-bottoms are flatter*

Expansive bits

Launched about the same time as the drill-stand is a range of power expansive bits, two 'medium duty' and two heavy duty. Their cutting diameters are infinitely adjustable in the ½-1¾in and ⅞-3in ranges for the medium duty, and ⅞-2in and 1⅜-3⅛in for the heavy duty. Two different-size cutters come with each bit for a wide cutting range; on the medium-duty bits these are secured by a slotted screw, and on the heavy-duty bits by a recessed set-screw for which an Allen key is provided. All the bits are basically the same pattern; the medium ones offer shank diameters of ¼ and ⅜in, and the heavy-duty ones ⅜ and ½in.

I tried the medium-duty bits in a hand-held power drill and in the drill-stand. Performance was good, although a fair amount of pressure was needed to make sure cutting was maintained — the points of the bit are plain rather than screw-nosed. I found the real limitation was the power of the drill, in fact — even the 600w drill lost its appetite for work at little over half the maximum potential diameter of 3in.

The holes the medium-duty bits make if you stop part-way through the wood aren't flat-bottomed but stepped, the point making an indentation in the centre. This

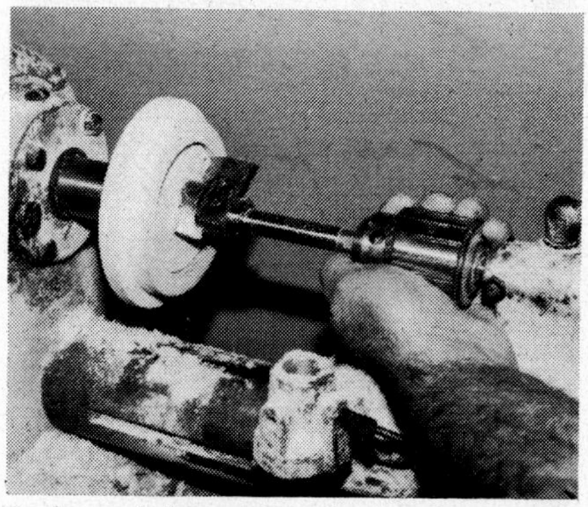

● *A good clean cut with a heavy-duty bit mounted in the lathe tailstock*

must be kept in mind if you need a flat-bottomed hole, especially where you're drilling in thinnish material. These bits would be unsuitable, for instance, for blind holes for the barrel bodies of concealed hinges; the bottom finish on a heavy-duty bit hole, however, is quite flat enough for this job.

With the larger of the two heavy-duty bits opened up to maximum, I mounted it in the tailstock of my lathe, and set up a turned oddment of wood for boring. Cutting was reasonably good; lathe speed had to be dropped to its lowest to comply with the recommended rpm.

Next I tried the smaller heavy-duty bit, again using the lathe to ensure I had the power. I set the bit to around 1¾in, but this time mounted the wood to bore into endgrain. The piece of hard elm I selected had a slight tendency to scorch during boring, and the cutting was a little slow. Endgrain always offers greater resistance to cutting tools than side-grain, the very reason I tried this test.

More sample drilling on a drilling machine gave very acceptable results, including through-holes from one and both sides. Large holes need care because of the projection of the cutter from the body.

Although I hadn't by any means blunted the bits during my trials, I thought I'd see how they responded to sharpening. I found the fixed cutter (a part of the body) filed quite well, but the adjustable cutter proved much harder, and would only respond to a small oilstone.

I scored these bits just short of full marks. They would be welcomed in most workshops, especially where there is a particular need for large holes, and wood-turners are likely to find them especially useful; but whether they can be regarded as a complete alternative to fixed-size bits depends to some extent on the work. For special sizes they'd be excellent.

● The basic stand costs £175.89, or with mortising attachments £201.59; chisels aren't included in this price. The mitre attachment costs £109.59, and the price of stand with attachments is £306.98. All prices inc. VAT.

● The bits range from £16.49 to £37.66.

● Wm. Ridgway and Sons Ltd, Oscar Works, Meadow Street, Sheffield S3 7BQ, (0742) 756385.

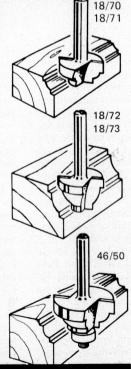

552

The grand furniture saga: 6

Furniture for the
Elizabethans: Vic Taylor
traces some of the designs
for eating, seating, and
sleeping in the late
16th century

● An oak gate-leg table with falling leaves and ball-and-ring baluster turning, circa 1670

From Henry VIII's reign, the nobility created a surge in the building of country houses — but it isn't generally appreciated that from about 1560 onwards the urge to build or rebuild spread down to the wealthier yeomen. The net result was that houses contained more rooms, and the old custom of the whole household living, eating, and sleeping in one or two rooms gradually disappeared.

The new arrangement usually consisted of a hall and separate dining parlour, and in 1547 we find a writer advising readers to 'make the hall of such a fashion that the parlour be annexed to the head of the hall, and the buttrye and pantry at the lower end thereof.'

Such dining parlours demanded smaller dining tables than the monolithic 'joyned' or trestle tables which were still being used. Two solutions to the problem emerged: a cut-down version of the joyned table, and the draw-leaf extending table, which appeared about 1552. It's often claimed that this design was of purely British origin, but it's almost certain that it was imported from the Continent, like so many other designs of the time. The construction, wherever it originated, has survived unaltered until the present day (fig. 1).

The first of these table designs had comparatively plain and square legs, mainly decorated with chamfers which make their appearance lighter. By 1575 the familiar 'cup-and-cover' bulbous legs had become fashionable, reaching their most exaggerated proportions about 1600; by 1650 the design had virtually disappeared.

Some of the most popular chair designs

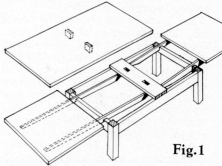

Fig. 1

● **Above,** extension draw-leaves for expandable dining capacity; note the blocks which fit in the cross-rail. **Left,** an oak folding side-table, early 17th century; the gate-leg supports the fold-back semi-circular top

are shown in fig. 2 overleaf — the turned (sometimes called the 'thrown') chair, the Glastonbury chair, the wainscot chair, and the X-chair.

Turned chairs might be called primitive or 'vernacular' designs, as they can be traced back beyond the 13th century from illustrations in manuscripts of that time. They were made for ordinary folk by the local turner, who was probably the wheelwright as well. In Elizabethan times they were in the form of a triangular armchair with a triangular seat which could be left as bare wood, upholstered with a thin stuffing, or fitted with a loose cushion. The component turned parts had pins turned on their ends which fitted and pegged into sockets. The designs persisted into the 18th century, when they were supplanted by 'Brewster' and carver armchairs, also built from turned parts.

553

The grand furniture saga: 6

The Glastonbury folding chair is supposed to have originated with the Abbot of Glastonbury (executed by Henry VIII in 1539), but it's more likely that it was based on an Italian design. The construction used wooden planks joined together with wooden pins, the back with a pronounced rake, while the shaped arms pivoted on a wooden rod passing through the tops of the legs and the sides of the seat. Decorative motifs in the back usually consisted of round-headed arches ornamented with *guilloche* patterns, together with conventionalised flower designs set in lozenges in the back panel.

Wainscot chairs were a development of the earlier 'joyned' chairs (part 4, WW/May), except that the box-like compartment beneath the seat was replaced by underframing, and the arms lost their side-panels, becoming open and also shaped. The legs and arm stumps were baluster-turned, intricately carved crest-rails with supporting scroll-shaped brackets were added, and the back panels were ornamented with inlays of stylised floral sprays or chequered patterns. 'Wainscot' in this context carries its original meaning of figured oak, particularly from Baltic ports, and it has no connection with the modern description of panelling. A variation of the wainscot, the 'caquetoire' chair (part 4) became popular about 1550.

The X-shaped seat probably has one of the oldest ancestries of any furniture design, as the basic style can be found throughout the ancient civilisations. Roman magistrates used such seats (made of bronze and called *curules*), and their association with authority continued through the centuries in which they were used only by royalty or nobility. In 1590 an inventory of Lord Lumley's possessions included 76 chairs of 'clothe of gold, velvet and sylke' and 80 stools to match; none has survived, but it's probable many of them were the X-shape.

Settles were widely used in ordinary homes, as the tall backs and ends kept out draughts, and two or three settles drawn up around a roaring fire made a warm and cosy corner in the kitchen. Another item of seating for poorer folk was the 'back stool'; it appeared about 1600 and was simply a joined stool in which the back legs were extended upwards and joined with back rails. It had no rake in the back legs and so could be pushed against the wall when not in use. This design of seat was the first to be made without arms, so it could be considered the forerunner of the dining chair.

Beds have always been costly, and Elizabethan ones were no exception. Often lavishly appointed, they were regarded as status symbols and were frequently mentioned specifically in wills. This has been a great help establishing where, when and for whom specific examples were made.

One of the most popular beds among the rich in the 15th century was the 'sparver', which had a large metal ring suspended from the ceiling from which draperies hung

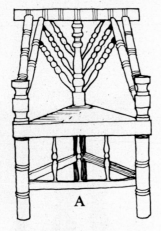

A

Turned or 'thrown' chair

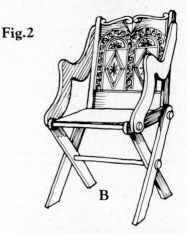

Fig.2

B

Glastonbury chair

C

Wainscot chair

D

X-chair

tent-fashion. A basically similar design is still used today under the name of a 'corona' bed. The precursors of the enormous Elizabethan beds such as the Great Bed of Ware (part 4) were the 'hung' beds of the 13th century, fitted with canopies. They developed into what we loosely call 'four-posters', correctly referred to as 'sealed' beds, with richly carved panelling at the head-ends ('celours'), which could be seven or eight feet high. There were two 'tail-posts' at each foot-end, and the two ends supported a heavy 'tester', a wooden canopy panelled on the underside and bounded by a frieze of heavy moulding. The tester also supported the draperies which drew together to make a draught-free and private space. It was quite common for secret compartments to be built into the head-ends, and some even had small religious shrines! Swans' down was used for the rich man's bed, while the poor made do with mattresses of wool, straw, rushes, or animal wool (washed to remove grease). Until the 17th century, mattresses were supported on strong cords laced through holes in the bed rails; wooden slats later replaced the cords.

As trade with the Far East opened up during the 17th century, new methods of furniture finishing using shellac and japanning became fashionable.

From medieval times, when furniture was finished at all it was usually painted, but this practice gradually died out during the 16th century. Two other techniques — oil polishing and wax polishing — took its place. The oils used at the time were nut oils (probably hazel or walnut), poppy oil, and linseed, which oxidised and darkened with exposure to the air. Wax polishing with beeswax, however, imparted a warm brown colour to the wood which only darkened if dust settled and was ingrained into the surface with repeated rubbing.

Although I can't prove it, I feel sure the timber was often stained with animal blood. It was certainly common practice among the early settlers in North America to use a milk-paint composed of milk and animal blood, and it's possible they were continuing the tradition of their mother countries.

The timber the Elizabethans used was mainly oak, although for unimportant furniture local timbers such as ash, chestnut, beech, or elm occasionally appeared. Such were the demands on home-grown oak that as early as 1233 there were complaints of shortages of good timber; Henry VIII had to pass an act to preserve the oak forests from the depredations of carpenters and charcoal burners so the timber could be used for building ships. We could go with Drake towards the Armada, but that is another story . . . ■

555

Designer DIY

Simple but stylish — that's the theme of Richard Entwistle's new book of designs for the keen beginner

Professional furniture designers owe much to the Italians, who have been the strongest influence on commercial furniture design since the 1970s. And much has been done to bring Italian designers to the forefront by Italian manufacturers, who have appreciated what design can do for them commercially. This has earned Italy worldwide respect, although it has been left to the retailers to discover this style and import it to other countries. For me, 'designer' to a great extent means 'Italian', because the Italians have led the world during the last 20 years.

I have always been aware, however, that few books on making furniture at home reflect the current styles and trends seen in shops and magazines. Many DIY magazines and books would not inspire those interested in modern design, and so discourage us from making our own furniture. I believe that, given a fashionable and stylish design and an easy way of making it, DIY furniture transforms itself into an attractive proposition.

My purpose is to provide others with the know-how to produce furniture that is modern in design, inexpensive and created in materials that are readily available from ordinary suppliers. I hope to appeal to those who want to achieve good results quickly – certainly not just to DIY buffs or repressed cabinetmakers!

Points to note

- The materials for these projects have been carefully chose so that the final cost is always less than the price of an equivalent article in a shop.

- Most of the joints in the pieces are dowels, the most commonly used joint in industry, and the simplest and easiest, though not perhaps the strongest, if you are not interested (yet!) in hand-cut dovetails or mortise-and-tenons. See this month's 'Woodworking Wheeze' for a simple home-made dowelling jig.

- The methods are designed to be simple and fast; don't compromise on the details, because I have already simplified the processes as far as possible. The aim is for you to make accessible, achievable and well-designed furniture quickly.

DIY Designer Furniture by Richard Entwistle is published by Ebury Press, price £9.95. We are grateful for permission to use this extract.

● *Contrasting colours and simple construction make these pieces an attractive introduction to making your own furniture*

The table

It's the use of black in this range that gives the group such a strong graphic image. The suite would, in my opinion, work less well in any other colour, and would also lose the contrast of the coloured panels. If you feel unable to live with black, however, a mid-grey would be a good second choice. The three designs aren't difficult to make; the table and sideboard are straightforward enough, the design and detailing following strongly the characteristics of the chair, which itself has been strongly influenced by the difficulty in making shaped piece parts. To solve the problem I have eliminated shaped parts completely. The comfort and support afforded by a correctly curved back

is here achieved by carefully defining the seat and back angles. An upholstery cushion may also be fitted if you want.

Table cutting list
Pre-veneered chipboard

A top	1	2000mm x 900mm x 18 or 16mm		

Hardwood

B long rails	2	1490	67	26
C end rails	2	639	67	26
D legs	4	721	35	26
E inner legs	4	696	35	26
F floor rails	2	630	35	26
G short floor rails	4	125	35	26
Dowels	48		50	10
Screws	8	no.8x1½in countersunk steel		
	24	no.6x⅝in chipboard		
Mahogany edging strip		8mx19mm		

The table

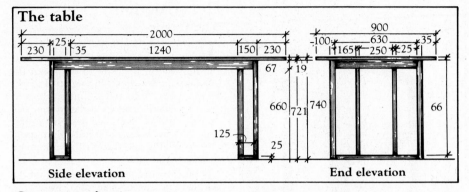

Side elevation

End elevation

Construction

1 Take the two long underrails **B** and mark out the ends for three equally spaced holes. Drill to the correct depth. Note that where a long end joins a thickness — ie where the long underrails **B** and short floor rails **G** meet end rails **C** and legs **D** — the holes should be about 30mm deep in the long ends and 20mm in the faces of **C** and **D**. It's best to go a millimetre or two deeper than the overall dowel length to allow for glue — but not too deep!

Dowel-spacing guide for rails and legs

leg parts **D-G**

rail parts **B-C**

2 Repeat the marking and drilling process with the two end rails **C**, then take the two long underrails **B** and transfer the dowel-hole positions to their reciprocal positions on **C**, 140mm from the ends. A dowel-marking 'point', which you just slip into your drilled hole, is good for this.

3 Continue round the frames; taking the outer legs **D** next, mark out at their tops to take the three dowels from **C** on the narrower edges. Again, use **C** to mark out reciprocal hole positions.

4 Carry on from the outer legs **D** to the short floor rail **G** and on to the long floor rail **F**. The joint between **F** and the inner leg **E** is 165mm in from the end of **F**.

5 Take the inner legs **E** and drill two 4.5mm clearance holes at the top of the legs (ie, not the dowel hole end). These should be marked out on the 35mm face and equally spaced.

6 Take the inner legs **E** and position their tops on the long underrail **B** 100mm in from each end. Pilot drill through the legs with a 3mm (⅛in) drill.

7 Try a dry assembly to make sure all the joints have been correctly drilled and that the holes are deep enough.

8 Glue up in the following order:

Frame assembly

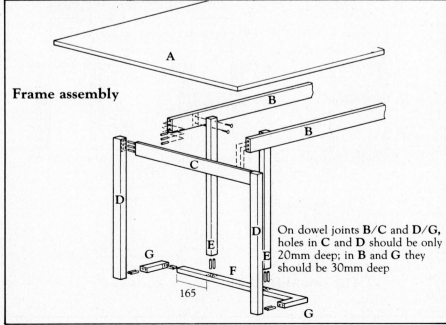

On dowel joints **B/C** and **D/G**, holes in **C** and **D** should be only 20mm deep; in **B** and **G** they should be 30mm deep

Clamping order

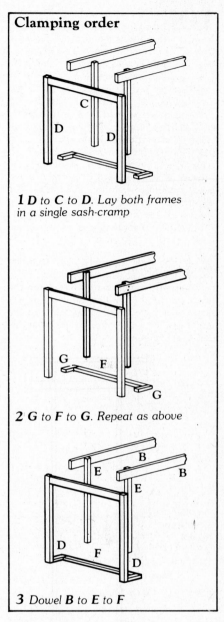

1 *D* to *C* to *D. Lay both frames in a single sash-cramp*

2 *G* to *F* to *G. Repeat as above*

3 *Dowel B to E to F*

1 legs **D** to end rails **C**; lay the two frames in a single sash cramp, keeping them separate with paper.
2 Short floor rails **G** to floor rails **F**. Cramp them like the leg frames.

Stand the frames upright for final assembly. Clamp the short floor rails **G** to the legs **D**, and screw the inner legs **E** to the long underrails **B**; then drop them into position on the floor rails **F**, dowelled and glued. Clamp across from the inner face of the inner legs **E** to the end rail **C** to hold the long underrails to the end-frame. Wipe all the glue off with a damp rag and leave the assembly to dry.

9 Take the top **A** and edge it with the self-adhesive edging strip, using a hot iron to make it stick. Any burn marks will be covered later by black paint. After you have finished one edge, trim it with a sharp craft knife or a wide, sharp chisel and sandpaper before you start the next one. When trimming, work in the same direction as if you were planing; try a small section first.

557

10 Finish the frame and top separately. Sand all the surfaces with 100- then 150-grit abrasive paper (garnet is best), then apply primer or undercoat with a good quality brush; spread the paint evenly with brush-strokes in all directions, then stroke the surfaces with the bristle-tips in the 'long' directions. When the base coat is thoroughly dry, cut back with fine garnet (240-grit) to remove all the nibs and high spots; clean with a 'tack rag' (a cloth dampened with turps and varnish) and put on a 10% thinned first coat of the final colour. When it's hard dry, rub it down gently with fine 'wet'n'dry' silicone carbide paper (220- or 240-grit). Clean off again, apply a second thicker coat, and repeat the rubbing-down/applying paint for the final coat.

11 For final assembly, lay the table-top upside down on the carpet and centralise the frame on top of it. Screw the frame to the top with six table shrinkage-plates that have been pre-attached to the under-frame in the appropriate positions (see drawing below).

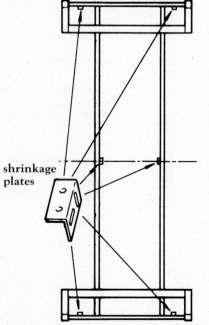

shrinkage plates

The chairs

The design employs hardwood because softwood sections of timber would be much thicker, and therefore visually more clumsy. Because there are so many joints to complete, I suggest the use of a dowel jig. Always choose a 10mm dowel where you can for strength; if you aren't making your own dowel jig, there are a number of proprietary designs you can buy.

If you are making four or six chairs, treat the process like a production line. Carry out each operation on every piece of wood, and label each part with a letter of the alphabet — 24 off part **A** and so on. If you are preparing them from scratch it helps to tick them off on your cutting list as you go through the processes; also you'll find stacking and moving the pieces methodically is very important. Confusion can easily reign!

Construction
The frame

1 Take all the hardwood parts and mark out the positions of the dowels. Use the illustration opposite to work out the positions and a dowelling jig to drill the holes. Also drill and countersink four 4.5mm ($\frac{3}{16}$in) clearance holes in the back rail **B**. Where the thickness of a part prevents you drilling to a full 25mm deep, drill to 20mm and then drill to 30mm on the reciprocal part.

2 Take the two arms **F** and mark out the curve to the outside edge, which has been defined by the position of the dowels. If you are making six chairs, it's best to make a template from cardboard and draw round it. Jigsaw to the line then finish the shape with a Surform or rasp and a plane, or you can roughly take a triangular shape off both ends with a saw and finish to the line with a smoothing plane. Finish-sand with 80-grit sandpaper and block.

3 Practise a dry assembly before gluing, making sure you have enough packing pieces for cramping.

4 Glue up in the following order:

1 Side seat rails **D** to back seat rail **E**; cramp them.
2 Front seat rail **C** to side and back rail assembly. Cramp.
3 Legs **A** to the seat frame; cramp them in position and use your eye to line up the legs so they are parallel. Take care to get the rear joint to the *inside* of the back legs **A** (see drawing above, opposite).
4 Fit arms **F** and back seat rail **B** to the completed frame. The fronts of the arms can be weighted down, while a sash cramp is spanned across the arms at their widest

Chair cutting list

(one chair only)
Hardwood

A legs	4	625mm	x 35mm	x	25mm
B back rail	1	450	35		25
C front seat rail	1	450	70		25
D side seat rails	2	400	50		25
E back seat rail	1	320	50		25
F arm pieces	2	450	85		25

Birch ply

G seat disc		480mm diameter x 12mm		
H back panel		650	300	12
Dowels	34	50	10	
Screws	6	no.6x¾in countersunk steel		
	8	no.6x½in csk steel		
	2	no.8x1½in csk steel		

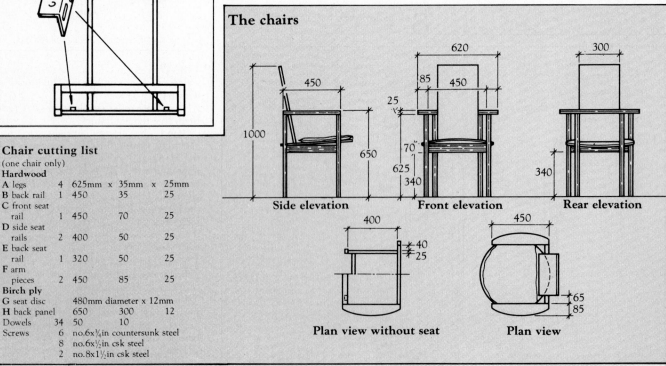

The chairs

Side elevation — 1000, 450, 650

Front elevation — 620, 85, 450, 25, 70, 625, 340

Rear elevation — 300, 340

Plan view without seat — 400, 40, 25

Plan view — 450, 65, 85

Chair assembly

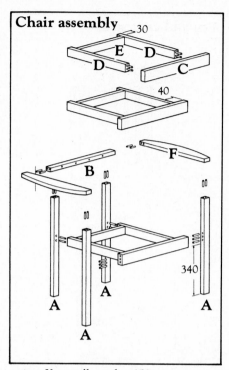

point. You will need a 450mm spacer to prevent the fronts of the arms being forced inwards.

NB: Leave the sub-frames to dry between each step.

The seat

5 Mark out the 480mm-diameter seat with a compass or trammel-bar arrangement; it's a simple matter to put two nails in a straight piece of (say) 1x1in softwood 240mm apart. An adjustable version will be more sophisticated! The easiest way to cut out the disc is with a jigsaw, but otherwise cut it with a coping saw or padsaw and finish to the line with a Surform or plane. Finish with sandpaper and block, adding a shallow radius to the front edge, and putting a crisp edge with a sharp plane on the rest of the circle.

The seat

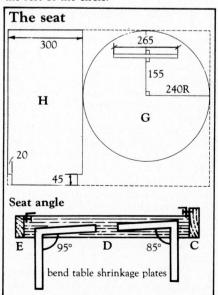

Arm rests

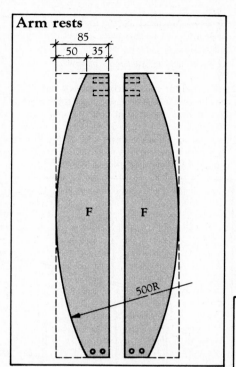

6 Mark out the slot in the seat, as shown in the drawing below left; it will be at right angles to a line drawn through the centre of the disc.

7 Cut the slot by drilling a 10mm (³⁄₈in) hole at one end to start and then cut out the hole with a jigsaw. Otherwise drill as many holes as possible then break through them with a padsaw, file and chisel. A jigsaw is much easier and neater!

8 Take the back panel **H** and cut out the two notches (see drawing below left) before you finish sanding.

9 Paint the frame and the two panels separately. (See the instructions for the table for a good paint finish.)

10 Final assembly: bend table shrinkage plates to the angles shown, then screw them to the seat frame and fix the seat in position with 12mm (½in) screws.

11 Secure the back panel from the outside face of the back rail with two no.8x½in screws. Pilot drill through the clearance holes, taking care not to break through. Fill the countersinks with filler, and paint them black to conceal them.

Seat cushion

It's a simple matter to make a cushion with two pieces of fabric and a piece of foam. Mark out two circles, 257 and 242mm radius, on the two bits of fabric laid one on top of the other; cut out round the larger one, pin the pieces together and sew them along the smaller circumference. Cut off a tangent of the circle to fit the seat, notch round the circumference to help it turn flat inside out, and put your foam inside. Sew along the flat seam with two tapes sewn into it; they will go through the slot in the ply seat where the back panel meets it and hold the cushion in position.

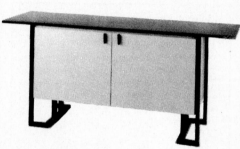

The sideboard

This sideboard completes the dining-room suite. As you see, the under-frame reflects that of the dining table and is designed to provide a serving surface for the table as well as allow storage of crockery and cutlery. Inside there are two compartments (you may wish to put in a shelf on adjustable sockets here). The back is finished as well as the front so the sideboard doesn't necessarily need to stand against a wall. For

The sideboard

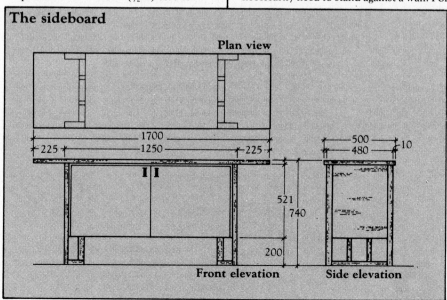

this piece of furniture, I have used a gap round the doors as a feature, both as a visual detail and also as a device to minimise the effect of the tolerances you need to adjust the hinges for the lay-on doors.

Construction

Top

1 Edge the top panel **A** with self-adhesive edging strip and a hot iron. Any burn marks will be covered by black paint. After you have finished one edge, trim it with a sharp craft knife and sandpaper before you move on to the next. When trimming with the knife, work in the same direction as if you were planing. Finish all edges with sandpaper and put to one side.

The frame

2 Mark out and drill the dowel joints in exactly the same way as for the dining table; see the drawing below.

Sideboard cutting list				
Pre-veneered chipboard				
A top	1	1700mm x 500mm x 18 or 16mm		
Medium density fibreboard (MDF)				
B doors	2	590	500	16
C centre panel	1	505	448	16
D end panels	2	521	448	16
E top front rail	1	1168	70	16
F bottom panel	1	1168	448	16
G back panel	1	1200	500	16
Hardwood				
H outer legs	4	721	35	26
J inner legs	4	175	35	26
K long floor rails	2	410	35	26
L short floor rails	4	125	35	26
M door handles	2	60	20	10
Dowels	20	50	10	
Screws	30	no.8x1¼in countersunk steel		
	24	no.6x¾in csk steel		
	4	no.6x1in csk steel		
Mahogany edging strip		4.5mx19mm		

Leg frame assembly

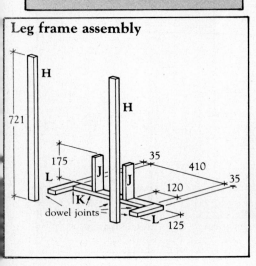

3 Try a dry assembly to make sure both frames fit together well. Label the joints and re-drill deeper if necessary.

4 Glue up the frames as follows:

1 Short floor rails **L** to long floor rails **K**. Lie the two assemblies as a pair in a single sash-cramp, separating with newspaper. Wipe off the glue with a hot damp rag and leave all the under-frame parts to one side. Don't fix the long legs to the floor frames yet; they go on to the cabinet side first.

Leg and carcase assembly

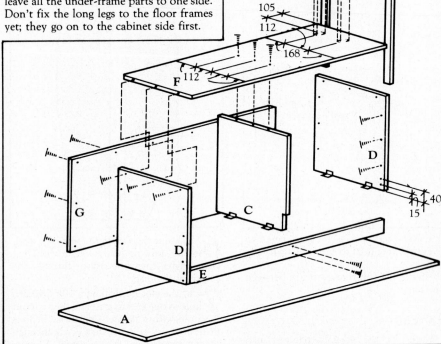

The carcase

5 The MDF carcase is now to be screwed together, so mark out all the parts — end panels **D**, top front rail **E**, bottom panel **F** and back panel **G** for 4.5mm (³⁄₁₆in) clearance holes to be drilled on centres 8mm in from the outside edges.

See the construction drawing above for details: on the end panels **D**, mark out three equally-spaced holes on each side and three on the bottom only. Mark two more at the top front corner.

On the back panel **G**, drill three equally-spaced holes along either end, a total of seven along one long edge only, and three more in the middle.

On the bottom panel **F**, drill seven holes on the bottom panel. Make sure that the three in the centre are accurately positioned.

On the top front rail **E**, drill two holes centrally marked.

6 Countersink these holes from the direction in which they are to be screwed.

7 Notch out the centre panel **C** to take the top front rail **E** as shown in the drawings above.

8 Hold the centre panel **C** upside down in the vice so the bottom edge is flush with the bench top. Squeeze some PVA glue along the exposed edge and place the bottom panel **F** in position with the three countersinks uppermost. Holding the two panels flush and in position, drill through

with a 3mm (⅛in) pilot drill. Fix it with screws and wipe off any excess glue.

9 Place this assembly front downwards on the floor and screw on the back panel **G** in the same fashion, lining up the flush edge at all times. Leave 16mm at each end for the end panels.

10 Do the same for the end panels **D** and finally the front horizontal rail **E**. Wipe off all excess glue and leave it to dry.

11 All the screw heads and countersinks on the outside of the cabinet must now be filled with filler.

12 Take the two door panels **B** and mark them out for the hinge positions. Use 25mm-diameter socket hinges, and drill the 25mm hole so that its edge is 2mm from the edge of the door and its depth is 13mm.

You must check when buying these hinges how far you have to drill to set them into the door — some types require a depth of 15mm, which in a 16mm door is a bit dicey! Fit the hinges to the door and then offer the door and hinge up to the cabinet to see if you need to space the mounting plate out on the inside of the cabinet wall; the doors need enough room to open inside the set-forward legs (see the section on these hinges).

13 Drill 3mm (⅛in) clearance holes for the handles in the top inside corners of the doors.

14 Paint the cabinet light blue inside and out, including the doors (see the table section for finishing).

15 The legs **H** should now be screwed to the carcase. Taking a scrap piece of 16mm MDF, line up the legs at the front of the carcase so the edge of the leg extends beyond the side panel by 16mm. In this way it will eventually end up flush with the door front. Pilot drill (3mm/⅛in) and screw the legs on. Work round the cabinet; the back legs should line up flush with the outside of the back panel.

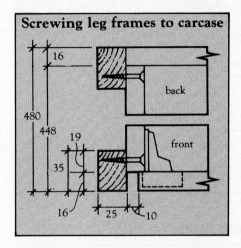

Screwing leg frames to carcase

16 Turn the cupboard over and glue the dowel joints to the underframe, **L/K/L** (see step 4), completing the leg frame with the inner legs **J**. Clamp and leave to dry. Wipe off excess glue with a damp rag.

17 Turn the cupboard back the right way up and screw through the bottom panel into the inner legs **J**, making sure they are correctly positioned.

18 Sand down the leg frames and paint them black, taking care to keep a good sharp edge where the legs meet the cabinet. Use masking tape for this. Paint the top and handles also.

19 Hang the doors, measuring up from the bottom of the cabinet.

20 Screw the top down on to the carcase with table shrinkage plates and apply the black wooden door handles **M**.

Adjustable hinges

An adjustable hinge allows you to manoeuvre a door into perfect alignment, thus overcoming problems of inaccurate manufacture or bad assembly.

It has also allowed designers to plant doors on the front of cabinets, without exposing any part of the hinge mechanism. Manufacturers and cabinetmakers are also now able to position a run of several doors with no more than 2mm between them. This is because adjustable hinges have an essentially different movement from ordinary hinges, allowing the door to open within its own thickness.

The hinges come (usually) in two sizes and several types; the most common ones are designed for 18mm material and have a 35mm-diameter round base, off which the sprung arm pivots. The other part of the hinge is the metal mounting plate, which goes on to the cabinet side; in most cases, doors are hung so the outside edge of the door lines up with the outside edge of the cabinet side. Where there is a run of doors, however, or, as in the case of the sideboard, a projection on the line of the outside edge of the cabinet, you need to give the door a few millimetres for the outside corner to swing through its opening arc. This is why you occasionally need to space the mounting plate out on the inside of the cabinet; you can gauge the thickness of this spacer by offering up the door itself with the hinge already fit, (or a scrap of door-thickness with a hinge in it) to the position where the door should lie, and measuring off. If you do make spacers, be sure to drill a sensible clearance hole for the screws that hold the mouting plate.

The mounting plates hold the arm of the hinge in such a way that the hinge itself can be adjusted in and out in the cabinet's back-to-front dimension and also its side-to-side one. This means you can close or open gaps at top and bottom of the doors, get them absolutely parallel, adjust the action of the door itself, and get the opening space right too. The more expensive adjustable hinges often have a vertical slot in the mounting plate which allows you to raise and lower the whole door — the in-and-out movement has something of a height-altering effect, but it's only limited and in some cases it can be the opposite of what you want. There are also (even more expensive) hinges which allow the door to open through 170°, so that it comes back more or less flat against its neighbour. ■

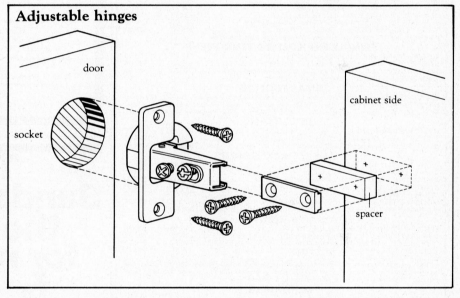

Adjustable hinges

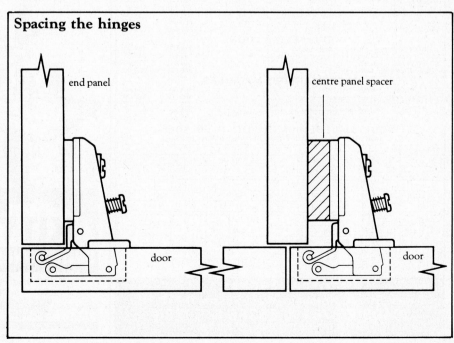

Spacing the hinges

561

Guild notes

Guild of WOODWORKERS

The Guild was set up by *Woodworker* to create a meeting ground for all those involved in working wood, whether professional, amateur, or enthusiastic beginner. Guild members get:
- Access to Guild courses and events
- Free publicity in *Woodworker*
- Specially arranged tool insurance at low rates
- 15% off Woodworker Show entry
- A free display area and meeting point at the Show
- 15% discount off *Woodworker* plans
- Inclusion in our register of members' skills and services

For details, please send an sae to the Guild of Woodworkers, 1 Golden Sq, London W1R 3AB.

GUILD COURSES

● Only Guild members are eligible to go on these courses. You must book in advance, and we must have a cheque for the full cost of the course at the time of booking. If you cancel less than four weeks before the advertised date you will forfeit 50% of the cost, unless there are exceptional circumstances.

BOOKING FORM

I wish to book for the following course(s).
- ☐ **Design and workshop drawing** 5 July, £25+VAT = £28.75
- ☐ **Decorative techniques** 6-7 September, £45: make cheque payable to Ian Hosker
- ☐ **Hand veneering** 27 September, £35 +VAT = £40.25

Please make cheques payable to 'The Guild of Woodworkers/ASP Ltd' unless otherwise stated.

Name ....

Address ....

....

....

Guild no. ....
Send to: The Guild of Woodworkers, 1 Golden Square, London W1R 3AB. The Guild reserves the right to cancel any course.

Design and workshop drawing — Bob Grant

5 July, 9.30-5, Oxford, £25+VAT.
So you've got an idea you want to make manifest in wood? If you don't plan your work on paper, you could waste a lot of timber and effort. Bob, who is head of Craft, Design and Technology at an Oxford comprehensive school, will guide you through putting your design on paper. Learn freehand sketching, how to use grid paper and drawing boards, tricks for laying out ellipses and other shapes, and making and using rods and templates.

Decorative techniques — Ian Hosker

6-7 September, 10-5, Chester, £45.
You read the articles, now do the course. Ian's feature, 'Coats of many colours' in the March and April issues covered wonderful decorative techniques such as dragging, lining, sponging, rag-rolling, marbling, spattering, and (his and our favourite) tortoiseshelling. The cost includes materials, but students should bring a few paint-brushes and jam-jars.

Hand veneering — Bob Grant

27 September, 9.30-5, Oxford, £35+VAT.
Veneering is much more than the art of disguising chipboard. It's a skill with a long history, and can create some beautiful effects — and it saves fine and expensive wood! You'll be laying a panel with veneer, mitring a cross-banding, inlaying lines round it, and applying a balancer veneer on the back. If you have a veneer hammer, bring it; but materials will be provided.

Second time lucky

The second meeting of the Guild's West Midlands branch took place in March, and as local rep **Bill Ferguson** reports, proved constructive.

Mark Golder again gave a working demonstration, this time of bowl-turning and his various finishing processes. Everyone was duly impressed; a question-and-answer session was only interrupted to recruit a number of 'volunteers' to the newly formed committee. Guild West Midlands hopes to plan a short programme of events for now and a complete winter programme for 86/7.

Bill is always happy to hear from other members but **please send an SAE** if you write to him at: 40 Quinton Lane, Quinton, Birmingham B32 2TS, 021-427 4571.

Crafty moves

The Crafts Council, the body set up to assist craftspeople in England and Wales, has produced a very useful 1986 Crafts Map.

It shows the positions of selected shops and galleries on the 'Crafts Council List' where you can display your work (if you're lucky) or view examples of the huge range of crafts being developed today. Fabrics, glass, ceramics, jewellery — craft doesn't mean just wood!

The map is available free from the Crafts Council, 12 Waterloo Place, London SW1Y 4AU.

Things to do . . .

Is the name of Edgar Lawrence's new craft shop in Brixham. He was the local rep for West Yorkshire, so now we need someone else. Come forward, please, new local rep for W. Yorks!

Edgar has taken over a retail business which covers all types of craft for all members of the family — tapestry starter-kits, candle-making kits, marquetry supplies, and so on. And, of course the woodcraft side — *de rigeur* — most of which will be supplied by Edgar himself. He will also be giving woodturning demonstrations and making gifts for visitors: **plus** — Edgar will also be taking care of the direct sales part of Allen Young's **Woodcraft Supplies** business, which is now concentrating on mail order and has closed its retail shop.

Edgar offers a warm welcome to any Guild members who find themselves in that area on holiday, or indeed who live thereabouts. Look in on him and his wife at Things To Do, 42 Bolton St, Brixham, Devon TQ5 9DH.

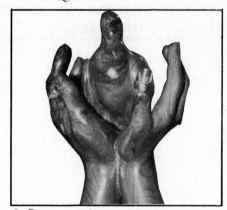

● *Prayers or doves might help your Gallery entry!*

London Gallery

For the exhibitionists amongst you, here's a timely reminder that Guild members have the opportunity to display their work **free** at the **London Woodworker Show** (Alexandra Pavilion, 23-26 October).

It operates on a first-come-first-served basis; so send us photos of your work **now**: small pieces of furniture, carvings, in fact anything wonderful and wooden — but we won't have room for four-poster beds!

Please limit your entries to two or three items, depending on the size. We want as wide a variety as possible to show just what you all get up to.

Mark your envelopes clearly for the 'London Gallery' and send to the Guild of Woodworkers, 1 Golden Square, London W1R 3AB.

564

'We propose a major series assembling a basic kit of hand-tools for the young apprentice cabinetmaker or serious amateur woodworker. The object will be to locate the very best saws, planes, chisels, gauges, etc. currently available.

'Each tool will be tested by a skilled cabinetmaker in my workshop, who uses similar tools every day in his work. Chisels will be polished, honed and checked for hardness of steel. Planes will be examined for flatness, smoothness of adjustment and accuracy of casting. Gauges will be checked for accuracy and fitness for purpose.

'All tools will be put to the most critical examination and tested within the bounds of the normal activity of the professional workshop. I do not advise manufacturers to submit products that they do not believe will stand comparison with the best in the field.'

Low-angle planes

David Savage continues his hand-tool test with an explanation of low-angle cutting and a serious look at what's on the market

The bench planes we discussed last month all have a blade and back-iron assembly, set in the body with the bevel of the iron down. The effective cutting angle is thus determined by the designer of the plane, and there's little we can do to change it and little point fiddling about with it.

Low-angle planes, however, have a single blade or iron set in the body of the plane with the bevel up. Closer examination will show that the pitch (the angle between blade and sole) is set a good deal lower than the bench plane's usual 45° — hence 'low angle'. Different makers' different ideas on 'useful pitch' vary from 12° to 20°, but the pitch of the blade only *contributes* to forming the all-important cutting angle — it *doesn't determine* it. The cutting angle on low-angle planes can be varied by you the user, by simply changing the grinding angle; if you use a plane with 12° pitch for fine endgrain work, you can get a low cutting

angle of 37° without grinding the blade at an angle lower than 25°, while for work with the grain, it's possible to increase the cutting angle to 50-55° without a great deal of effort. This is all, however, in the realm of theoretical possibility; by and large my planes stay on the same setting from one year to another, but it's comforting to know the choice is there. For this reason of choice alone it would be worth considering planes in this category with a very low pitch of 12° or so, for the lower the pitch, the greater your choice of cutting angles.

The planes in this low-angled category are the block, the shoulder- and the bull-nosed. There are many other kinds such as chariot, mitre or rebate plane, but these are either old types which are no longer made, or derivations from the three main classes. The one exception is the rebate plane, similar to a shoulder-plane but with a greater pitch for (generally) use with the grain. The advent of the router has made this primarily a joiner's tool, almost but not quite redundant.

Cutting angles

bench plane with back-iron: bevel below

back-iron

45° cutting angle

45° pitch

shaving aperture or mouth

grind different bevels for different cutting angles

adjustment

blade supported close to edge

15°, 20° or 25° pitch

low-angle plane: blade bevel above

Block planes should be small and comfortable to hold in one hand. They are quite commonly used for trimming endgrain, though it is often a mistake when a bench plane with more heft would do the job better. Chamfering and removing arrises are the jobs for which these little planes are most useful; a little block plane can be made to work where a bench plane would be clumsy and unwieldy. The essence of the tool's function is the trimming and cleaning of surfaces, not the removal of a great deal of stock.

The shoulder-plane can also be made to work as well with the grain as a rebate plane — indeed, in most situations, a similar setting can be used. This tool is designed for endgrain work, with a lowish pitch of perhaps 15-17° and sides accurately machined square to the sole. The squareness is important, because it allows the side of the plane to be used as a jig or guide. The blade of a shoulder-plane extends the full width of the sole, and should just protrude beyond the side of the body to cut a clean corner. A shoulder-plane is also a 'trim-and-fit' tool, and must sooner or later be included in the tool-kit of anyone serious about joinery or cabinetmaking.

The tools: block planes

Five block planes were presented for test — a sixth, very serious, contender from Bristol Design will be considered separately, because it's not strictly comparable to mass-produced products. Three makers produced five planes — Record their 09½ and O60½, Stanley their 9½ and 60½, and Footprint their 9½b. To add to the confusion of digits, cutting angles and pitches, all these so-and-so's look pretty much alike!

Things in common to begin with. None of the planes could conceivably be called flat, but 30 minutes' hard work would set most to rights. Stanley were the worst offenders, followed closely by Footprint. The finish on the tools ranges from the rather poor Records to the very well-finished Stanleys, the same good finish evident on the sole of the Footprint. Their polish was very impressive, but it's a pity the casting had cupped after the polishing

● *The Record 09½ – a 'high' low-angle block plane with a blade pitch of 20°*

process. A good finish usually indicates attention to detail throughout the production process, so it isn't surprising that the blade seating was at its best in the Stanley 9½ and 60½. It's not difficult when you get a new plane gently to file off any high spots and blobs of paint that prevent the iron from seating well.

All the block planes had adjustable front portions in the sole that could close the mouth right up to the blade, a valuable feature that makes the tool more precise in use. A tiny mouth isn't essential on endgrain, but it is very useful in general work. (A word on terminology: most people, including myself, refer to the mouth of a plane as the opening ahead of the cutter with the plane set up for a shaving. This is technically wrong — the mouth is the entire opening in the sole of the plane, and the gap ahead of the cutter should be called the 'shaving aperture'. But what the hell!)

The block planes were generally the same size, 150-160mm long and all (except the Stanley 60½) with a cutter-width of 42mm. This is a comfortable size to use in one hand. The Stanley 60½ is a full 7mm narrower, with a correspondingly narrow cutter.

These block planes divide into two distinct groups. The Record 09½, the Stanley 9½ and the Footprint 9½b have a blade pitch of 20°, and the blades of the others are pitched lower at 12½-13½°.

'High' low-angle

The Record 09½ and the Footprint 9½b are of almost identical design, and quite why copies of this nature are made is beyond me. The blades adjust with a wheel moving vertically on a threaded rod, the action of which was smooth and positive on both planes. Lateral adjustment is by a lever engaging in a slot in the blade. The Record 09½'s blade was ground out of square, which might make setting up difficult, and the Footprint 9½b's front knob is small, and made even more fiddly by an upturned front-sole adjustment lever right in front of it.

The Stanley 9½ is a very similar plane, set with a pitch of 21°. The blade is adjusted by a block-plane version of the conventional bench-plane rear knob. Both Stanley planes have nice comfortable brass adjustment knobs, but although the 9½'s lateral adjustment works well, it would soon be dumped in the bin. The problem is it rattles — or it did on the plane I had. Put the thing down, ting-a-ling, pick it up, ting-a-ling; no, Mr Stanley, never ting-a-ling.

'Low' low-angle

The second category is the lower than low-angle planes. The Record O60½ has a traditional rear knob adjustment with an unnecessary amount of free play — no real excuse for this sloppy engineering. There is no lateral adjustment mechanism, but then one isn't needed because you can easily push the blade left and right by hand. The Stanley is 7mm narrower, with a blade set at

● *The 'low' low-angle Record 060½ had good support for the cutting edge*

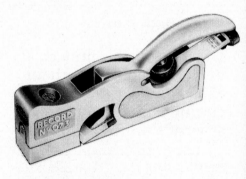

● **Right:** *Bristol Design's A10b thumb-plane and the A6 shoulder-plane in front of their Norris-type big brothers, and* **below right** *the Record 073 shoulder-plane, more affordable at £50*

13°. The conventional rear-screw adjustment had less free travel, but ting-a-ling, the lateral ting-a-ling adjustment was there again. The other difference that might convince me to buy the Record O60½ rather than the Stanley is the support for the cutting edge. At cutting height the blade on the Stanley 60½ extends 3.5mm into the mouth beyond the body of the plane, where on the equivalent Record it was 2mm. The effect may well be that the Record blade has more support nearer to the cutting edge, reducing the possibility of chatter.

Bristol Design

The sixth block plane, or, as they call it, the A10b 'thumb-plane' was offered by Bristol Design. It's cast in gunmetal with a steel sole, and infilled with ebony. The length is 130mm excluding the blade, which is made extra long to allow for repeated changes of angle, and is of heavy-gauge tool steel with a polished back. It would take and hold a fine edge. The mouth or cutting aperture is dead right at 0.5mm with good seating to the cutter, and support to within 1.5mm of the cutting edge. Blade adjustment is old-fashioned 'tap and try', but with a blade pitched at 15° in this case, adjustment is far easier than on bench planes with 45°-pitch blades. I really liked this Bristol Design product, but because of the price I doubt it would form part of an apprentice tool kit. However, at £82 it is exceptional value; it's as well-made as the Norris 31, upon which it is modelled.

Shoulder-planes

If you wanted to buy a shoulder-plane until very recently, your choice was limited to two. Now, with the growth of companies like Bristol Design and Clico (Sheffield) Tooling the selection has widened.

The prime choice for many would have been, and perhaps still is, the Record 073. It is 230mm long, with a cutter width of 33mm, and as shoulder-planes go, it's a heavyweight. Sooner or later, there will come a task that only a hefty, wide-bladed plane of this type can accomplish, but it might be regarded as a little too clumsy for general cabinetmaking. The blade has a pitch of approximately 20°, adjusted by a conventional rear screw, but the knob is too small for comfortable use, and rather stiff when the blade is tensioned. The blade seems to be designed to be seated well only at the mouth, so as the mechanism tightens down on the blade, it bends down to the bed. The blade is supported at the sole to within 1.5mm of the cutting edge, and the mouth is reduced to a working shaving aperture by adjusting the front section. Some patient work with a file would be necessary to get this down from its smallest opening of 2mm to the 0.5mm I'd use.

The 073 I tested was flat and square. It seems that castings of this type stay where they're put much better than other plane bodies, and as this tool is often either guided by one side or used on its side, this is a valuable asset. Detailing on the plane was very poor indeed. Edges were left sharp and uncomfortable to the hand, and when the adjustable front sole is pulled back it exposes two unpleasant sharp points of steel, well capable of making a nice job of denting this and that.

The Bristol Design A6 shoulder-plane is almost exactly the same length and weight as the Record with a slight increase in cutting width. Like the thumb-plane, it's cast gunmetal with an ebony infill and a steel sole, and the plane I tested was flat and as square as I would hope to find. The blade is pitched at approximately 18°, secured by an ebony wedge. It's Bristol Design's policy to use, when possible, second-hand cutting irons and this plane had one, but unfortunately it was too narrow for the plane so it didn't protrude slightly from the sides as a good iron should. Adjustment is 'tap and try'. The tool had a cutting aperture of a very creditable 0.75mm, and the seating of the blade was flat and gave support to within 1mm of the cutting edge. The finish

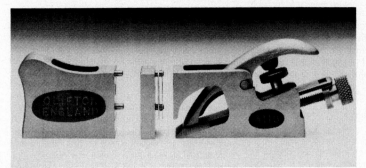

● The Clico 3110's three-in-one design makes for good flexibility in use – £75

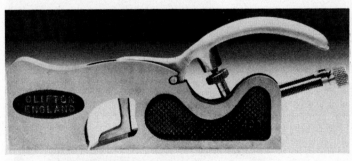

● The answer to your shoulder-plane dreams? The Clico 420 is full length but half width (20mm)

on the ebony infill was very good, and the metalwork had all the unpleasant arrises removed. The finish to the gunmetal was a little coarse compared with the thumb-plane. In all, a very nice product. At £80, it may not fit the pocket of an apprentice, but like the thumb-plane, it represents good value for money.

Both these shoulder-planes are rather large, but Stanley's 93 is smaller, with a body length of 150mm and a cutter width of 26mm. It's finished in nickel plating, and most of the arrises on my example had been removed, but any flattening or extra attention to the rather coarse surface finish might remove parts of the nickel plate. The casting was generally square and flat, but the two-part body could mis-align, giving an out-of-square reading — something that occurred on one side of the test plane. The blade is low-slung at approximately 15°, and it's seated only at the mouth and

towards the rear of the plane. There was a gap of about 1mm between the blade and the bed at the point pressure is put on the iron, which may well be a valid design feature, but it does encourage the user to tighten the blade down hard and so make the (conventional rear knob) adjustment very stiff. The blade is supported to within 2mm of the cutting edge, and some work would be needed to narrow down the adjustable mouth from its rather wide 2mm.

When Record Ridgway was taken over by Bahco, who subsequently rationalised the wide product range, a small toolmaking company was formed separately and took staff, machines and products abandoned by Bahco. Clico Tooling Ltd have attempted to cover the gap in the market created by the withdrawal of many of Bahco's 'less profitable' lines, although after Record's own more recent management buy-out, that company's own

policy has moved on. More and more woodworkers are finding once-discontinued products now being made again to high engineering standards, which is what Clico is all about. The planes I tested are the Clifton 3110 and the 420.

The 3110 is (to my memory) the Record three-in-one plane, once discontinued and now reborn. It is 150mm long and has a 30mm-wide cutter, falling very neatly into a 'middle-weight' bracket. The blade is set at about 18° pitch, adjusted by the conventional rear knob which has rather coarse knurling and isn't comfortable to use. The screw thread is rather coarse, which gives a very rapid adjustment rather lacking in refinement, but the blade is well seated for a good 20mm behind the cutting edge, unlike both the Record and Stanley tools, and it is supported to within 1mm of the cutting edge. The plane body was very well finished, with most of the unpleasant

arrises removed, and the casting was square and had remained stable after machining. The front of the plane is removable, which allows adjustment of the mouth; at 0.75mm it was already very good. It would be possible to use this as a chisel-plane with the front removed, and even more useful, a short bull-nosed section can be fitted. The two shims that come with it also increase the cutting aperture; with both in and the long fore-end fitted I'm told you can use the 3110 as a narrow smoothing plane. This is one instance where an adaptable implement can fulfil at least two roles without compromising the quality of either. Nice one Clico.

The Clifton 420 shoulder-plane is a tool that cabinetmakers especially have been wanting for years. It's 207mm long with a 20mm-wide cutter, on a similar scale to the full-size heavyweight shoulder plane but exactly half the thickness and half the weight. The 420 has the same 18° pitch with the same unpleasant adjustment knob and coarse thread. I wonder: couldn't this adjustment be tucked in behind the plane more neatly and the handle shortened accordingly? Both Clifton planes have these sticky-out bits that catch on things and get knocked off in an accident, but then the Record 073 has had sticky-out bits for donkey's years and nobody has thought to improve it. The 420 has a malleable cap-iron that shouldn't snap at the weak point, because it doesn't have one, or so they say. The blade is well seated along its length, and supported to within 1.5mm of the cutting edge. On first inspection, the mouth looked a shade too large, but at 0.75mm, it's as good as one could hope for in a mass-produced plane. It's not adjustable.

Mr Alan Reid of Clico tells me the delicate point of the casting immediately behind the blade's cutting edge, where mouth and sole of the plane meet, is of 'metallurgically sound construction' on Clico planes. This apparently means the castings are made 50mm larger to allow for removal of unsound metal created in the casting process.

So I must try and choose tools upon which an impoverished apprentice might spend his or her hard-earned crack. Of the block planes, the lower-angle tools offer more versatility. I would probably (very reluctantly) accept the rather crude finish and poor adjustment of the Record O60½ in exchange for support for the blade at the point behind the cutting edge. The Bristol

Design A10b thumb-plane is, however, a superior tool by a considerable margin, and if price wasn't as important as quality that's where we would turn. One shoulder-plane for all tasks would probably be the Clifton 3110. I'm delighted that Clico have produced this excellent medium-weight shoulder-plane, but why in the age of microtechnology have they copied a design developed in the late 19th century? The entire Sheffield tool industry act as if industrial designers didn't live north of Watford. I know woodworkers are conservative by nature and no Yorkshire steelmaster is going to have a fancy-pants designer telling him how to make tools. But surely it isn't beyond human wit to improve things — just a little? ∎

● **We asked the makers for comments:**
Clico
a The coarse knurling and 'lack of refinement' in the adjustment screw have been taken care of by a re-design.
b On both the Clifton 3110 and 420 planes we have thickened the cutter considerably to eliminate the 'bowing' of the blade referred to in the review of the Record 073. Perhaps more importantly, the thicker blade has the effect of narrowing the mouth, so the 'shaving aperture' becomes significantly finer than the open mouth. The thickness of the cutter also permits the user to hone the blade to a secondary angle and overcome some of the problems with 'pitch' explained earlier in the article.
c Both Clifton planes are modelled on Preston originals from the turn of the century. We decided to sidestep some of the 'improvements'

introduced by subsequent manufacturers to suit volume production, which, we believe, tended to 'throw out the baby with the bath water'.
d I'm amused by Mr Savage's severe judgement on Sheffield's manufacturers for not originating new designs (after all, wood and hands haven't changed that much in the last 1000 years or so!) when a fair portion of his article dwells on the considerable merits of Bristol Design's beautiful reproductions of Norris planes. Perhaps no industrial designers live west of Watford either!
Alan Reid, Chairman

● David and *Woodworker* would like to thank the following tool manufacturers and distributors for the loan of tools, their co-operation and assistance, without which the test series would have been impossible:
Bristol Design, 14 Perry Rd, Bristol BS1 5BG, (0272) 291740
Clico (Sheffield) Tooling Ltd, Unit 7, Fell Rd Ind. Est., Sheffield S9 2AL, (0742) 433007
Footprint Tools, PO Box 19, Hollis Croft, Sheffield S1 3HY, (0742) 753200
Lester-Brown Machine Tools (Ulmia importer), Coventry Rd, Fillongley CV7 8DZ, (0676) 40456
Paramo (Clay) Hallamshire Works, Rockingham St, Sheffield S1 3NW, (0742) 25262/3
Rabone Chesterman, Camden St, Birmingham B1 3DB, 021-233 3300
Record Marples, Parkway Works, Sheffield S9 3BL, (0742) 449066
Sandvik, Manor Way, Halesowen B62 8QZ, 021-550 4700
Sarjents Tools, 44 Oxford Rd, Reading RG1 7LH, (0734) 586522
Stanley Tools, Woodside, Sheffield S3 9PD, (0742) 78678
Tilgear (Ulmia supplier), 20 Ladysmith Rd, Enfield EN1 3AA, 01-363 8050

Recommended retail prices

Maker	Model	Price inc. VAT
Record Marples	09½ block	£21.13
	060½ block	£19.04
	073 shoulder	£50.22
Stanley	9½ block	£24.15
	60½ block	£24.15
	93 shoulder	£30.91
Footprint	9½b block	£21.34
Bristol Design	A10b thumb	£82.00
	A6 shoulder	£80.00
Clifton (Clico)	3110 3-in-one	£75.03
	420 shoulder	£64.95

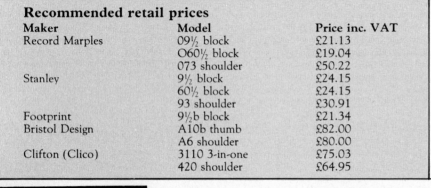

Letters

I FEEL I MUST COMMENT on David Savage's hand veneering articles ('Craft of cabinetmaking', WWs/Feb, Mar), and I make no apologies should my criticisms seem harsh. The photos in the February issue showing him 'hammering' down a minute piece of veneer give the impression he has never seen or been shown how the veneer hammer should be held. It looks unprofessional and untutored; if that's what he teaches, his pupils have my sympathy.

There are two ways of holding the 'hammer'. In both cases it is gripped by the *head*, usually with one hand; even on the rare occasions when both hands are needed, they are placed one above the other, *on the head*. The handle is purely to steady the grip. The photo shows a miniscule piece of veneer being 'hammered', so is the groundwork nailed down to prevent it slipping and sliding all over the place while he is waggling the handle like an indecisive crab? What rubbish!

In the March issue, the statement: 'With solid wood, it's common to "bookmatch" boards . . . With veneers it is usual to "slipmatch" . . . ' must be a printer's error, because the reverse is true, especially on fronts and tops.

Cover your bench with paper by all means, as Mr Savage suggests, but raise the panel on two clean sticks, particularly if both sides are to be done (almost always), otherwise you will be forever picking bits of paper off the panel your fingers, the gluepot and all over the place.

I do hope Mr Savage doesn't carry his glue-pot to and fro each time he applies glue to a panel. I would suggest that in the same way he advises (correctly) to have all tools to hand, he also arranges to have the glue-pot to hand too, saving wear and tear on limbs, shoes, and time.

It's entirely unnecessary (except perhaps for the very difficult veneers such as burrs and curls) to apply glue to both the groundwork and the veneers. It's a waste of glue and time, extremely messy, and smelly when the hot iron is applied. It's also very difficult to clean off later, because no matter how much you wash down, a thin glue-layer will remain, forming a hard glaze. Soul-destroying work to clean off with a scraper, the only tool that can do this job. The plane can't be used for obvious reasons, and if you use any sort of electric sander on a hand-veneered panel with glue on the surface, the heat generated will melt it, churn it up and clog the paper. If you continue, the glue beneath will soften and horribly blister the veneer, even if it doesn't tear chunks off. Don't even think of using a belt sander on hand-veneered panels, even if the glue has been scraped off.

It's quite sufficient to spread glue on the groundwork leaving no bare spots, place the veneer in position, rub a wet rag over it, dab a spot of glue in it here and there if you must, run the hot iron over the surface, and — if the hammer is used correctly (not as in the photo) — you will get the desired result. Some of the glue squeezed out will unavoidably get on to the hammer and be transferred to the veneer surface, lubricating it even more. There is much more to it; the skill can only be acquire by constant practice, and above all, being shown the correct way at the outset.

I couldn't believe it when I read Mr Savage's advice about laying joins. Put glue under the join and walk away from it? Surely he isn't confusing patching a bicycle inner-tube with laying veneers with Scotch glue? It shouldn't normally be necessary to add glue to a join, but if it is, hammer it down as quickly as possible. Use the hot iron if need be, but don't under any circumstances walk away leaving it to congeal, because it would then be impossible to hammer down without a very hot iron and plenty of water. I must say this is the silliest advice I have read in many a long year.

Mark Kenning, Evesham

David Savage replies: Belt sanders generate heat, and in clumsy hands can be destructive tools. However, modern small belt sanders with guide frames can be used, (with care) without danger of melting the glue. Pad-sanding machines have been a common feature of professional workshops, including my own, for many years, and I'm surprised Mr Kenning is unaware of their advantages.

Of course, bookmatching is widely used by everyone, but it doesn't change the problem. Some veneers refract light, and this light-catching property is changed by laying one leaf of the two upside down. Now to more serious matters.

Mr Kenning's abrasive and arrogant attacks on fellow professionals (this is not the first) lead me to an important point. His cloak of concern for the craft conceals a destructive and dogmatic attitude to any practice differing from his own.

Workshop practice must, in a healthy enquiring situation, develop in different ways. Our answers to solutions are partly determined by individual conditions and materials. Mr Kenning's dogmatism states that it's impossible for anyone to solve problems in a way different from Mr Kenning's. It is possible to argue endlessly and fruitlessly about the angle a saw might be sharpened or a veneer-hammer held. The quality of result is of paramount importance, not the method by which it is attained. The Japanese woodworker would smile at our workbenches, and suggest we hold wood with our feet. What rubbish!

I COULDN'T HELP but smile at the reply by Stephen Goody of Wheeler's to one of his customers complaining about 'the usual scallops'(Letters, WW/Apr).

After 20 years as a wood-machinist, and having heard the cry 'It's the machine!' many a time, I can say that unless the machine is really old and worn, problems are usually the operator's fault, not the machine's, or, of course, the firm's for not allowing enough maintenance time. If the problem was scalloping, it was almost certainly because the thicknesser rollers and/or the outfeed table of the surfacer were wrongy adjusted. The latter usually magnifies the effect of the former.

As to Mr Goody's suggestion of allowing 6in extra for crosscutting the faults out (exact measurements were specified) — what waste! Surely if the problems of these machines are insurmountable (age, wear, ineptitude?) then maybe the pieces could be crosscut *after* machining and the cost could be passed on to the customers (although how many would stand for this for long, I leave to imagination).

Maybe Mr Goody could pass on his 6in pieces to me; I'm sure I could make good use of them!

D. Galley, Gloucester

TWO ITEMS in May's 'Question Box' caught our attention:

For John Sheehan and tensioning wide bandsaws, Arthur Simmonds' book *Wide Bandsaws – The Art of Saw Doctoring* extensively covers tensioning, levelling, brazing, welding and all general maintenance for saw-blades. It costs £9.75 paperback or £17.00 hardcover inc. p&p.

Secondly, on the subject of Charles Horsefield's letter about spindle moulder safety, this summer we are publishing a *Spindle Moulder Handbook* by Eric Stephenson at £10.95 plus p&p. It will be a large, fully illustrated, book devoted entirely to this machine. The very points that Mr Horsefield makes about the emphasis on safe working are a special feature of this new work.

Brian Davies, Director,
Stobart & Son, 67-73 Worship St,
London EC2A 2EL, 01-247 0501.

YOUR MACHINING WOOD article on mortising (WW/Apr) shows a chair mortise two-wing bit, but a different, stronger pattern of mortise bit is recommended for most general-purpose slot-mortising, particularly in hardwoods. The slot-mortise miller bit has a double action; the teeth mill out of the chippings, and the relieved cutting edge follows on to smooth the finish and shave the slot to final accuracy. This pattern is better for general use because it is stronger, faster and less vulnerable to point breakage. It also requires less sharpening.

A. D. B. Reid, Chairman
Clico (Sheffield) Tooling

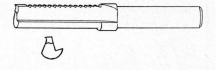

I OWN AN EDISON router. The base and base-plate are broken; Edison have moved from their old address. Does anyone know where they are or where I can get spares?

B. J. Northcott
65 Southbrook Rd,
Countess Wear,
Exeter, Devon EX2 6JF

Letters

YOUR LONG PIECE ABOUT THE MOSQUITO (WW/May) was very nicely put together. I was an RAF flight-sergeant working on the aircraft, and it reminded me of the love-hate relationship one was bound to develop for one's subject. There was another side to the brilliance of the Mosquito concept; they who made it didn't have the agonies of mending it when someone broke it. Once it was put together, the Mozzie could be a formidable jigsaw puzzle to work on in a draughty hangar or windy corner of an airfield. The write-up didn't reveal that Aerolite 306 was developed especially for these repair tasks, along with alternative grades of hardener and a fairly complex set of techniques for applying makeshift accelerated setting devices in the field. Nor did we learn of the terrors of take-off and landing; sitting in the fuselage at such times was akin to being shut in a packing-case while someone on the outside tried to break in with a sledgehammer. Having endured the uncertainties of airtests after repairing Mosquitoes, where one strained the ears for sounds of rending timbers above the general resonating din, it's perhaps understandable that one should set some store by the adhesiveness of Aerolite 306. There were times when one truly believed one's life depended upon it.

John Bull, Sheffield

I'D LIKE TO COMMENT on Roy Sutton's 'Question Box' advice to Mr Muff on his workshop noise problem (WW/May).

I totally agree with Mr Sutton that it's difficult to insulate anything effectively *and* cheaply. But Mr Sutton's suggestion, although cheap, will not be effective in terms of sound insulation. There is no such thing as a lightweight high-insulation structure, and whatever method is finally adopted must involve the use of a relatively heavy material. The Building Research Station produce a number of useful digests which could help Mr Muff understand the basic principles involved.

It must always be remembered that the treatment is limited to what is practical in each circumstance, taking account of the existing structure and the level of sound generated in the room. The Environmental Health Officer at the local authority could well give Mr Muff some very valuable advice.

The best method for a party wall is to put fibreglass insulation against the wall then build a stud wall 125mm in from that, clad with two 13mm sheets of plasterboard. It would reduce the sound transmitted, but it's not cheap.

in Pollution Studies,
Tottenham College of Technology

ADVERTISERS' INDEX

AEG	579
Air Plants	586
Apollo Products	579
Axminster	540
A-Z Tool Sales	IBC
Benmail	572
Black & Decker	570
John Boddy Timber	535
Builders Direct Mail	552
H. Case Hardware	555
Charltons Timber Centre	586
Peter Child	581
Chronos	594
Craft Materials	580
Craft Supplies	534
Cutwell Tools	555
Data Power Tools	574
DIY Supply	594
Early Music Shop	570
Elektra Beckum	563
Excel Machine Tools	544
Government Supplies	544
Heath Saws	589
J. W. Hoyle	578
David Hunt Tools	589
Ashley Iles	536
Kity	534, 562
Kraft Kabin	574
Ledbury Craft Supplies	532
E. W. Lucas	564
Luna Tools	580, OBC
Matthew Bros	595
A. Mills	536, 570
Multistar	580
John Myland	552
Old Stores Turnery	532
A. Pollard	578

P & J Dust Extraction	582
Plans Service	577
W. M. Plant	555
Profectus	579
Wm. Ridgway	IFC
Rocking Horse Shop	580
Rogers	571
Sanlin	532
Sarjents	574
Scott & Sarjeant	562
J. J. Smith	544
Solent Tools	582
Stobart & Son	572
Sumaco	578
Swann Morton	564
S.W. Power Tools	589
Tabwell Tools	555
Taylor Bros	595
Henry Taylor	574
W. Thatcher & Sons	594
Thomas & Willis	581
Tilgear	536, 562, 572, 580, 594
Tool Centre	589
Tool Mail	589, 595
Treebridge	580
Trend Machinery	552
C. W. Tyzack	571
Warren Machine Tools	564
West bromwich College	595
Whitehill Spindle Tools	579
Woodfit	571
Woodworking Mach. Switz.	572
XR Machines	580

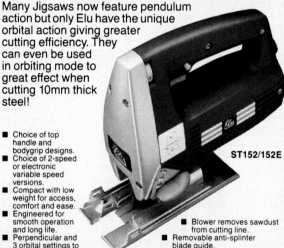

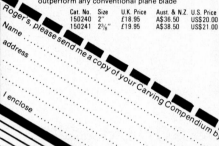

571

Books

Paul Greer
Jobs in Carpentry and Joinery
Kogan Page, £2.90 softback
Reviewed by Aidan Walker

This is a useful little book, competently written and presented for the school leaver. It explains in simple language the sorts of jobs in the woodworking trades, the kind of qualities an applicant (aspirant?) will need, some basic stuff on tools and materials, categories of employment, types of training, and the ways that a young person can prepare him/herself for jobs and courses.

It's intended to go straight into the careers rooms of secondary schools, and will fill an undoubted gap on the shelves; Paul Greer is a careers officer, so the presentation of the information is informed with that point of view rather than a professional woodworker's. Mr Greer obviously knows how far to go with a subject before a 16-year old's attention will flag, which — along with the fact that he's limited to 100 small pages — means that there could be more details about the jobs he describes. It's an introduction; if the reader is really interested, she/he will go on to more reading.

The treatment of training is definitely biased to YTS. City & Guilds courses and others run by colleges themselves get rather brief mention, while YTS seems to get more than it deserves. Perhaps this is because that particular form of training is most likely to be considered by the average school leaver, though I can't help feeling that a mention, at least, of some of the disadvantages of YTS from the trainee's point of view should be offered to help decision-making.

I liked the idea of the 'What qualities will I need?' chapter, and was pleased to see that mathematical ability is a sub-section all on its own. The sub-section on 'speed' should certainly have mentioned the paramount importance of an organised, methodical approach in the workshop or on site. Jobs in carpentry and joinery are what the book is about, and as far as it goes it serves the purpose very well. Most suitable for that gap on the careers-room shelves, but not a comprehensive run-down of every way you can make a living in woodwork.

Numerous authors
Fine Woodworking on . . . series
Taunton Press, £6.95 each, softback
Reviewed by Aidan Walker

The only question you could have about these books is: should I buy them all at once or one at a time? They are compilations of selected articles from the first nine years of the leading American journal *Fine Woodworking*, and they are a mine of information to lose yourself in for weeks and months. The same as looking through back issues? No, because the books are arranged to cover specific subjects — *Bending Wood, Woodworking machines, Boxes, carcases and drawers, Planes and chisels, Making period furniture, Joinery, Tables and desks, Chairs and beds, Finishing and refinishing, Making and modifying machines,* and — two that will be especially popular with *Woodworker* readers — *The small workshop* and *Proven shop tips.*

FWW is a serious and scholarly magazine, with a circulation in the US of a paltry quarter of a million! Out of all those readers, you're fairly certain to amass a huge body of experience, expertise and ingenuity, and that's what the journal's editors have most successfully done. The selection of the articles to go into the books must have been a difficult job — between 30 and 40 in each one — and they're well edited, well drawn and well presented. There's no colour photography, but the illustrations use tints, and for £6.95 who can complain? The only minor gripe I could raise is that *Proven shop tips* carries a number of column-width blank spaces, presumably where the ads appeared in the original magazine format. They could have sorted this out, but the book would have been more expensive to produce, and it really doesn't detract from the value of the information you get.

Some of the articles will inspire you to get working on something straight away, some of them are more generally interesting and informative pieces that you file in the back of your brain for later, and some are just downright entertaining. Not in a humorous sense — if anything, *FWW* tends to take itself rather too seriously — but in the fascinating and absorbing sense, the sort of reading that woodworkers love because it widens and deepens our own understanding and enthusiasm for the craft, the materials and the tools. Much the same reasons why you read *Woodworker*, in fact!

● At the time of writing, the books are available from Sarjents Tools, 44-52 Oxford Rd, Reading RG1 7LH, (0734) 586522, John Boddy's Riverside Sawmills, Boroughbridge, N. Yorks YO5 9LJ, (09012) 2370, and The Old Stores Turnery, Wistaston Rd, Willaston, Cheshire, (0270) 67010.
● Aidan Walker is an ex-professional joiner and cabinetmaker and the editor of *Woodworker*.

Alan and Gill Bridgewater
Guide to Making Wooden Toys that Move
Argus Books, £6.95 hardback
Reviewed by Brian Coombes

There is a long history of toys. They have been found interred in children's tombs 3000 years old; Indians carved dolls and rattles for their children hundreds of years ago. The basic requirements haven't really altered — movement and colour still excite any child. These ideas form the basis of Alan and Gill Bridgewater's new book.

While you don't, as Alan Bridgewater says, need to be a woodworking guru, it helps to have a basic knowledge of woodwork and woodworking tools to be able to make full use of the book.

The guide lists 10 projects, ranging from designs that pivot or counter-balance to ones that pull along, and is well illustrated. Each project has step-by-step instructions and paragraphs on 'considering the project' — giving some thought to what is involved; 'materials' — vital to have all these to hand before you start; and 'tools' — again, make sure you have all the necessary gear before you start. Other sections for each project include information on setting out the design, cutting/gluing and drilling, and finally painting. The diagrams for each project are self-explanatory, as long as you have a basic appreciation of line drawings.

An extremely useful book for all potential toymakers, and indeed for those who have already made a start.
● Brian Coombes is a miniaturist and dolls' house maker.

In brief

Design Courses in Britain 1986 *(Design Council, £3.75)*
Contains two pages of furniture courses and other assorted information on tertiary education.

Woodwork Skills *(WH Smith; Orbis, 49p)*
A short (32pp), cheap and colourful 'first steps' guide, which bears a distinct resemblance to a partwork in graphic style.

The Practical Woodwork Book *(Anthony Hontoin; John Murray, £4.95)*
A selection of increasingly difficult projects together with a summary of different joints. Aimed at schools and evening classes.

Collins Complete Do It Yourself Manual *(Albert Jackson, David Day; Collins, £25 hardback)*
500 big colour pages and a comprehensive indexing and cross-referencing system suggest that the 'complete' claim is well founded. Obviously an enormous amout of thought has gone into the design of the book to make it easy to use and find the bits you want. Could well be worth the fantastic price for the serious DIYer, and even the

woodworker who wants to sort out the plumbing.

Practical Carpentry *(Percy Blandford; McDonald Books, £5.95 softback)*
A reprint of a straightforward, solidly written and presented basic introductory text. The usual stuff, neatly illustrated; photos are out of fashion for giving practical information these days, and a good thing too. A good line drawing is much clearer. If not everything you need to know, then everything you need to know about what you need to know. Good value.

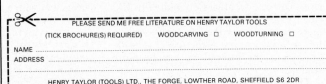

A metal scratch-tool

This home-made version of a defunct but desirable hand beader is just the thing to hone your skills with metal and wood

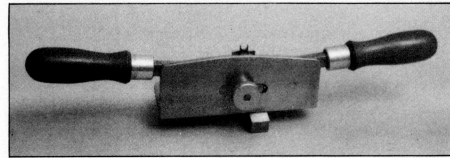

● *From this side, you can see the top of the two-ended cutter above the backplate. One fence is fitted; one either side of the workpiece is better*

In the late 19th century, the American tool company Stanley were producing a lot of wooden tool designs in metal, many of which are now extremely rare — like my no.66 Universal Two Handed Beader. The decline in demand for such tools seems to have been caused not by declining standards in hand-work — it's as good or better than it ever was — but by the declining volume of hand-work and hand-workers. My beader, patented in 1886, is 11½in long, of cast iron and nickel-plated over copper. It was sold with 14 double-ended cutters, two fences (one for curved edges), and two blanks for the owner to grind special shapes. People who have seen and used my example are envious and enthusiastic, so I worked out a design that

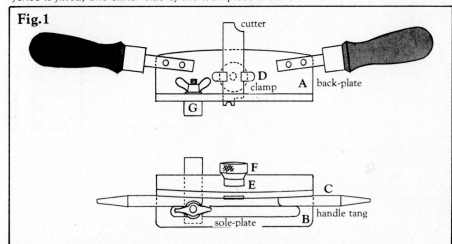

Fig.1

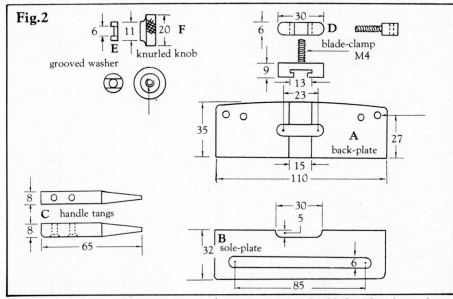

Fig.2

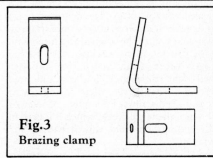

Fig.3
Brazing clamp

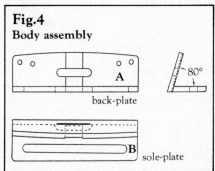

Fig.4
Body assembly

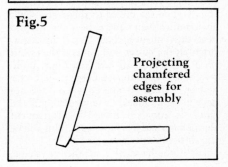

Fig.5

Projecting chamfered edges for assembly

could be made with the minimum of metalworking equipment and an average woodworker's metalworking skills.

Small mouldings, beads, small corner rebates, narrow grooves for inlay stringings, small routings — these are just some of the applications of the tool, which I think is well worth making.

The back-plate **A** (figs 1 and 2) is cut to size and a shallow 15mm central groove formed. Use a milling or shaping machine if one is available, otherwise it's a rather tedious and cautious filing job. The depth isn't critical — 1 or 1.5mm is enough. As an alternative, four small pins can be inserted

to position the blade. The clamp slot is simply drilled with a number of 5mm holes between the 6mm end holes and then filed out, and the small handle holes can now be drilled and countersunk on the flat face.

The sole-plate **B** (figs 1 and 2) is easier. The long slot is drilled, sawn, and filed out, after which you can cut the mouth. File the joining edge accurately to 80° to braze the back-plate on. Hold the two pieces together for brazing or silver soldering with two simple clamps (figs 3 and 4), and suitable screws, nuts and washers. If you don't have brazing facilities, ask a garage or small engineering firm to do the job — it's

A metal scratch-tool

elementary. Use brazing rod of the lowest melting point available; notice in fig. 5 that the two parts are assembled with a marked projection and that three corners should be slightly chamfered.

Clean the assembly well with increasingly fine grades of emery cloth, and note that the front bottom edge of the sole-plate is rounded slightly (fig. 4).

The handle tangs **C** (figs 1 and 2) are quite straightforward; they are drilled then countersunk on the outer side only. Saw the rod for the rivets to the total thickness of the two components, plus $1\frac{1}{2}$ times the rivet diameter. Rivet on the handles then file it all flush.

The blade-clamp **D** (figs 1 and 2) can be made in two ways. The whole thing can be cut from one piece, the stem filed round and then threaded, or a preformed screw can be fitted to a threaded hole and fixed with a touch of brazing or silver solder. This latter is much the easier but as with all heat methods, some later cleaning up is required. The clamp must not be too thin and therefore weak, so it protrudes slightly through the back-plate. This calls for a grooved washer **E**, fig. 2. The clamp is held either with a nicely turned and knurled knob **F** (fig. 2) or a wing-nut, which does the job just as well.

The fence **G** (fig. 6) is a simple filing or milling job. Make two, for working with a fence both sides of an edge ensures accuracy and makes it unnecessary to concentrate on avoiding a slip. The original was fitted with a shaped fence for working from curved edges, but it's easier to drill the fence with two holes through which you can hold specially-shaped wooden facings with round-head screws. Fix a piece of screwed rod into the fence block, which is locked in the setting you want with a washer and wing-nut.

As $\frac{5}{8}$x$\frac{1}{16}$ ground flat stock (tool steel) is increasingly difficult to find, it's best to settle for 15x1.5mm, which a good tool dealer will stock in 18in or 330mm lengths. Excellent cutters can be made from worn-out and broken power-hacksaw blades, but avoid the 'all hard' type, which aren't workable. The type you need has a high-speed steel teeth-strip of about $\frac{1}{4}$in wide, and the rest is fine for sawing, filing and hardening.

File the double-ended router cutters to shape, heat them to red then bend them over (fig. 7). Make other cutters as you need them, one at each end of 2in lengths (fig. 8). File the pieces to shape at a slight angle rather than square, heat them to red heat then quench them in oil or water. Brighten the cutter with emery, then lay it on a larger piece of metal and heat both, watching the colours emerge. The cutter will be correctly tempered when it reaches dark brown. Quench it immediately; if the cutter is too soft it will want frequent sharpening, and if it's too hard, filing will be too difficult.

Lastly the handles. Turn them to shape,

fit suitable ferrules, and drill a hole about 7mm. Heat the tips of the handle tangs to dull red (a small propane torch is fine), push on the handle to almost the final position, remove it, wait for the metal to cool then tap the handle on permanently.

There may be a bad spot in your timber which doesn't scratch well. This can be left oversize, and when you've done all the other work, move the fence across and push the tool in the opposite direction. Naturally this can only be done when the cutter shape is symmetrical, and to reverse the tool when you're using an asymmetrical cutter, the cutter needs to be turned over. To make this possible, sharpen the cutter at 90° and not at a slight angle. ∎

● Small amounts of mail-order metal from K. R. Whiston Ltd, New Mills, Stockport, Cheshire Sk12 4PT.

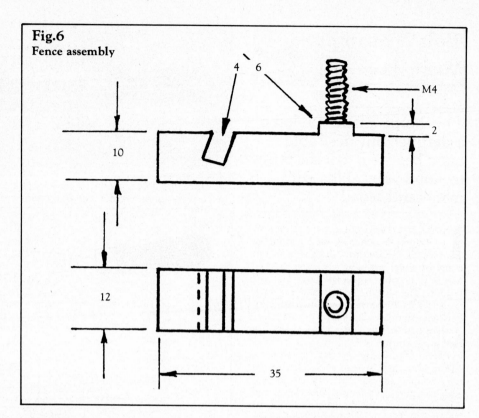

Fig.6
Fence assembly

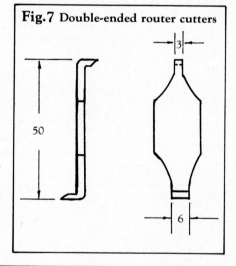

Fig.7 Double-ended router cutters

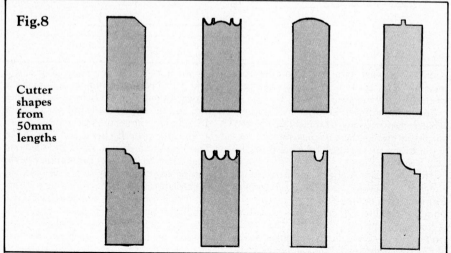

Fig.8

Cutter shapes from 50mm lengths

Woodworker
PLANS SERVICE

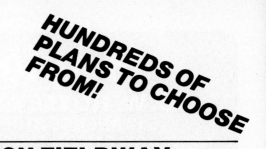

JOHN THOMPSON FIELDWAY COLLECTION — OVER 40 DESIGNS

ALL ILLUSTRATED IN THE WOODWORKER PLANS HANDBOOK

YORKSHIRE WAGON
This example is of the Vale of Pickering type, very robustly built, a handsome vehicle. Model is 16in. long.
Plan JT/40　　　4 Sheets　　　**Price £3.30**

HEREFORD WAGON
A small size plank sided wagon, it is now in the reserve collection at the Museum of Rural Life at Reading. Model is 15in. long.
Plan JT/14　　1/8 scale, 2 large sheets　　**Price £2.95**

HOP TUG
The high ladders fore and aft are a feature of this unusual wagon. Model is 19in. long.
Plan JT/15　　1/8 scale, 2 large sheets　　**Price £2.95**

HAMPSHIRE WAGGON
Constructed about 1900, this is an unusual wagon with double shafts. A superb subject for someone who wants a wealth of detail. Model is 17in. long.
Plan JT/10　　1/8 scale, 2 large sheets　　**Price £2.95**

1850 EAST ANGLIAN WAGON
This massive and stately vehicle dates from 1850, now in the reserve collection at the Reading museum of Rural Life. Model is 19ins. long.
Plan JT/20　　1/8 scale, 5 sheets plus sheet of photos
Price £4.50

HOW TO MAKE WHEELS
The chart MODEL WHEEL CONSTRUCTION gives step-by-step instructions to enable the average handyman to produce excellent scale wheels Available only with one other plan order.
Plan No. JT/001　Price 80p

OXFORDSHIRE WAGON
To many people this is the epitome of the English farm wagon. Used on Blackwood farm, the original is now in the Oxford County Museum this 1/8 scale model is 18ins. long.
Plan No. JT/18　1/8 scale 4 sheets plus photo sheet **£3.60**

GLAMORGAN WAGON
A most elegant wagon. This wagon was built around 1870, now renovated and on display at St. Fagans.
Plan JT/38　　1/8 scale　　**Price £3.30**

ASHBY DESIGN WORKSHOP — TRADITIONAL FURNITURE FOR HOUSE & GARDEN
FULL LIST SENT WITH EVERY ORDER OR ON RECEIPT OF AN SAE.

NEW!

NURSERY PLAY TABLE
This versatile table has a number of features that make it ideal for the nursery. The working height of the table which varies with the height of the blackboard, will suit children between three and ten years old. There is a storage space for large and small toys and an optional posting box may be built into the system. A simple screw and glue construction is used needing less than two sheets of plywood & 4.5 metres of softwood batten.
Plan ADW110　　　**Price £4.00**

TAPA SYSTEM PLAN PACKS
Each Pack comprises:
A1 size Plan	2 Frameworks
3 A3 Plans	4 Chair designs
Full-size profiles	Cutting List
Joint details	Schedules

Featuring a series of modern furniture designs for the home, the TAPA system of plan-packs is a new concept in woodworking projects. Each plan-pack focusses on a specific object and explores many alternatives to the original model. The Dining Chair is the first in the series, featuring ideas based on the simple halving joint prototype.
Plan ADW134　　　**Price £5.75**

DAVID BRYANT CRAFT DESIGN PLANS
HOME & LEISURE, TOYS, SPINNING WEAVING
ALL ILLUSTRATED IN THE WOODWORKER PLANS HANDBOOK

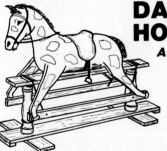

DRUM CARDER
Sooner or later spinners graduate to a drum carder. This design takes the toil out of hand carding. It uses a positive gear/sprocket drive which also reduces the drag which the belt drive alternative imposes. A little metalwork as well as woodwork involved. One sheet plan.
Plan No. DB54　　　**Price £3.70**

TABBY LOOM
A simple tabby loom having rollers, warp and cloth beams and fitted with a rigid heddle, and canvas aprons. Basic weaving width 380mm but plan can be adapted for other widths if desired. Ideal for beginners and it is surprising what can be achieved with warp and weft variations tufting etc.
Plan No. DB 2　　　**Price £3.20**

SLOPING STYLE SPINNING WHEEL
This design is a replica of an authentic spinning wheel doem olden days, having a 486mm (19in.) diameter wheel with bent

WARPING MILL
This warping mill design consists of a vertical revolving drum supported within a floor standing frame. The drum is fitted with pegs for securing the warp to, and the frame is complete with heck block for spreading warps up to 15-20 metres.
Plan No. DB9　　　**Price £3.20**

wood rim. Plan is complete with mother-of-all, distaff, treadle operation etc. A feature of this wheel is its attractive turnings which make it a most decorative piece besides being functional. A design for the enthusiast woodturner. Two sheet plan.
Plan No. DB12　Price £5.40

UPRIGHT SPINNING WHEEL
In this vertical style spinning wheel the mother-of-all arrangement is situated above the main wheel. The latter is 460mm diameter and the rim is of segmented design. Simpler lines than the sloping wheel but nevertheless graceful in appearance and of course functional.
Plan No. DB13　　　**Price £5.40**

SPINNING STOOL
A spinning stool specially suited for use with the sloping bed wheel. Four legged arrangement, with richly carved seat and back. A good example of chip carving.
Plan No. DB20　　　**Price £2.20**

FAMOUS WOODWORKER PLANS HANDBOOK
STILL AVAILABLE

Price 85p plus 30p postage and packing (Overseas 65p)
★ Clock Cases
★ Spinning & Weaving
★ Artists Equipment
★ Kitchen Ware
★ Dolls House Furniture
★ Toys
★ Horse Drawn Vehicles
★ Furniture

CUTS EVERYTHING

Except corners

The EMCO BS-3 is a three pulley bandsaw with outstanding performance, at an unbeatable price. A comprehensive range of accessories are available making the EMCO BS-3 a machine capable of disc sanding, drum sanding, belt sanding, cutting with the circular cutter device and mitre cuts, making this machine an invaluable aid in the workshop.

‡ *steel construction*

ONLY £315 + VAT

The EMCO TS-5 is a robust workhorse bristling with features. Made of steel with welded machine housing and stand the EMCO TS-5 deals with large workpieces with ease by simply adding the optional extension tables which more than double the working area. The EMCO TS-5 can be used for longitudinal cuts, diagonal cuts, combing, grooving, coving and even disc sanding.

ONLY £225 + VAT

When you buy EMCO you are benefiting from years of experience, after all it was EMCO that built the worlds first universal woodworking machine, back in 1946. With quality engineering and innovative design EMCO still lead the way in woodworking machinery offering superb value for money.

The BS-3 and TS-5 are just two specialist machines in the EMCO woodworking range, which includes spindle moulders, planer-thicknessers, lathes and combination machines, each specifically designed for todays woodworker.

Send now for your FREE colour brochures on the EMCO range.

emco

FOR FURTHER INFORMATION WRITE TO
SOLENT TOOLS LTD.
267 LONDON RD,
NORTH END,
PORTSMOUTH, PO2 9HA
TEL: (0705) 667652/3

THE PERFECT START TO A BETTER FINISH

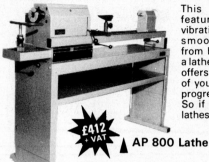

579

A dowelling jig

This is an idea for a jig which must be made up for the size and thickness of the job in hand, writes **Herbert Beckett**. It is easy and accurate to use, can be applied to any size of work, and can even be altered for drilling angled holes.

You need a piece of hardwood, a piece of ¼in ply, and two ¾in screws; plus a drill-stand for vertical accuracy. I am using an example of ⅝in chipboard, but the measurements based on board thickness can be adjusted for metric.

Say you want to join ⅝in chipboard with 1½x⅜in dowels, 1½in apart. The hardwood **guideplate** should be about ⅞in thick, 4in long and 2¼in wide — this latter determined by a suggested 3in maximum drilling depth less the ¾in depth of the dowel holes. Square the guideplate up and scribe a line all round ⁵⁄₁₆in (half the board thickness) from the face. Drill two ⅜in holes on the edge 1½in apart, spaced equally from the centre-line, through the 2¼in dimension of the plate — from edge to edge. You'll need the drill-stand for this, because it requires absolute accuracy on quite a deep hole. Drill another hole on the centre-line 2in deep, big enough to carry a screw-head, and take that hole right through at a clearance diameter for the screws you're using.

The ¼in ply **faceplate** is 4in square, scribed with centre-lines both ways. Drill a small 'spyhole' ¼in down from the centre and countersink it almost right through; also drill two screw-clearance holes 1¼in up from the centre, 1½in away from the line on each side.

Screw the faceplate to the guideplate, overlapping 2in and perfectly square with it. Now you have the jig; pencil a line on the face of the chipboard to be joined marking the centre between the two dowel positions. Put the faceplate hard on the face of the board and slide it along until the line appears through the spyhole. Clamp the jig hard down, the edge of the guideplate hard against the edge of the board, and drill your perfectly positioned and depth-regulated holes through the guideplate holes. Transfer marks and holes to the other piece of board.

For using the jig on a broad face, draw the line of the holes and the centre-point of the joint. Drill a pilot hole for the screw you're using where the two lines intersect. Take the faceplate off the guide-plate and drop a screw down the central hole in the edge; now screw that into your pilot hole, and line up the guideplate, standing on its edge on the board, the scribed lines matching the pencilled joint line. Tighten the screw and drill the first hole, wedging or clamping the guideplate so it doesn't wander. Drop an undersize dowel through the drill hole into the first hole in the board to hold the guide-plate square when you do the other hole.

For angled dowel joints, the edge of the guideplate can be planed to the right bevel; one hole will be longer than the corresponding one in the joining piece, but this isn't critical unless the angle is really steep. In that case, use longer dowels. ■

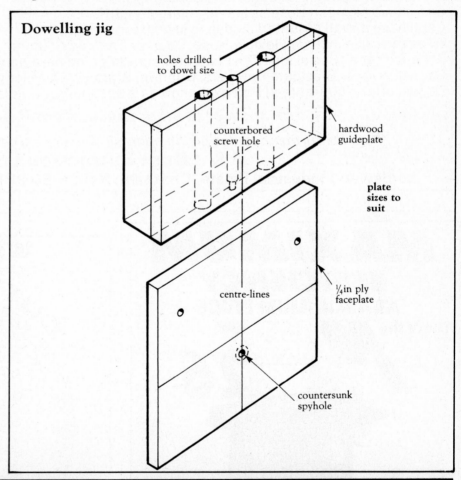

Dowelling jig

holes drilled to dowel size

counterbored screw hole

hardwood guideplate

plate sizes to suit

centre-lines

¼in ply faceplate

countersunk spyhole

Waste away

Wood waste — nuisance or asset? Steven Hurrell's 'Machining Wood' endpiece on what you and your equipment need to stop the rising tide

Dust has been the woodworker's bane since the first meeting between steel and wood. Progress, in the form of machinery, has made us more efficient in producing chips and dust as well as saving time and energy in just about every woodworking operation. Long-term effects on health are very worrying, but difficult to gauge; however, every woodworker must be familiar with that blocked-up feeling after a day's sanding. Dust also creates a major safety issue in the workshop. (See 'Not so dusty', WW/Feb.)

Dust, shavings and offcuts on the floor and around machines not only present an obstacle course, but can create a serious fire risk. Most workshop insurance policies require 'all shavings, sawdust and other refuse to be swept up daily and removed weekly'.

One of the greatest dangers is when chips fall onto the machine table. Any misjudgement in clearing them away with your hands can lead to an accident with revolving cutters or blades. The short answer, of course, is — don't use flesh, use wood to push bits and pieces away.

Power tools

Portable routers, planers, sanders, jigsaws and drills all produce dust which is very difficult to extract. Where large or continuous amounts of waste are being produced or vision is interfered with by flying particles, you should wear some form of mask and eye protection.

Some manufacturers of portable power tools have been quick to realise the dust problem and have made planers and sanders with integral collection bags, jigsaws with built-in air jets that allow a clear view of the cutting line, and other additions; but the problem remains with many tools.

Machinery

Planing machines are the worst offenders, producing large volumes of waste. Surfacing waste is deposited in the base of the machine, which when it isn't extracted can soon build up to a level where the revolving cutter-block picks up the chips and spits them out into the tables. Pity the machinist in the firing line!

The better surfacing machines have a slope built in below the cutter-block, which allows the waste to fall away. Even so, regular clearance at floor level is necessary. Machines with cabinet bases that trap the waste and offer little access should be avoided if you don't have or aren't planning to have good extraction equipment. This

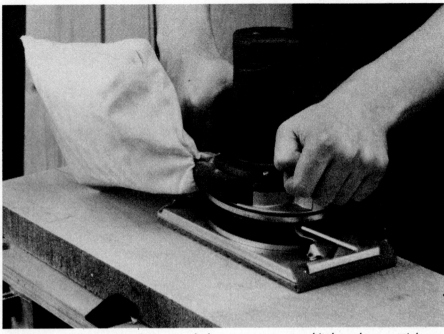

● No portable power tool is particularly easy to extract; orbital sanders certainly need it!

problem is magnified on combined planing machines, because the thicknessing table (which in any case should be fully lowered) prevents the waste from clearing, making frequent stoppages necessary.

Thicknessing machines produce waste thick and fast, and in their bare form deposit heaps of chips on the floor in front of the machine, as well as a haze in the air. Prolonged use becomes very uncomfortable, not only for operators but anyone working nearby. With this type of machine the main objective is to prevent the dust becoming airborne by fitting hoods that deflect the waste downwards.

Machinery equipped with mechanical feeds (thicknessers, moulders, automatic lathes and so on) should ideally be connected to an extractor, not only because of the large and continuous volume of waste, but also to prevent a build-up of chips in the machine itself. If feed rollers are not kept clear of loose chips, surface finish can be marred when they're pressed into the face of the work. With resinous woods such as pine, the problem is increased because the goo tends to get permanently stuck to the rollers, and frequent machine stops are inevitable to remove the build-up.

With circular saws, the main problem is again one of build-up of waste in the base of the machine. When the saw is used illegally (with crown guard and riving-knife removed) for grooving, rebating, or tenoning, the machinist is exposed to a continuous stream of dust that is picked up by the revolving blade and thrown over head and shoulders. The drawing shows an idea for overcoming the build-up inside machines.

As the spindle moulder is such an adaptable and variable machine, dust extraction is usually omitted for much the same reasons as proper guarding is also neglected — it's time-consuming to set up for a small

amount of work. Extraction is essential when involved in long runs of moulding, or permanent spindling set-ups. For straight-forward moulding operations using the standard fences, it's easy to fit an extraction hood behind the fences, but with curved work where a ring fence, ball-bearing guide or similar set-up is in operation, 100% extraction can be difficult. Because of the way in which curved components are presented to the machine, the direction of the chips isn't always controllable. Hoods can be fitted, but they often interfere with the work.

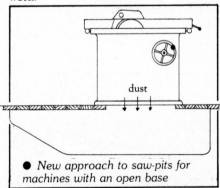

● New approach to saw-pits for machines with an open base

The overhead router is similar to the spindle in that the upredictability of the flow of chips makes extraction difficult. There are combined extraction hoods and guards that overcome this, and with a certain amount of ingenuity you can make your own.

If you have a separate tenoning machine, it's likely that you're in a workshop that puts a large volume of work through it, and extraction is already there. Tenoning removes a large amount of waste material, so permanent connection to an extractor is best if constant stoppages for clearances are to be avoided.

Waste away

Dust does not present a great problem with bandsaws, except with continuous use or deep cutting. The main problem is that dust tends to be carried round by the blade and deposited over the machine table, work and operator. Brushes are fitted to the bigger machines to prevent this: the drawing opposite below shows an efficient bandsaw extraction system.

Sanding machines produce probably the most offensive, and also highly combustible, dust. Most manufacturers of mobile cyclone-type extraction units advise against using their products with sanding machines. Belt, drum, bobbin, disc sanding and linishing machines should be 'plumbed' into a separate ducting system employing spark arresters, high efficiency filters, and a cabinet collector that offers some explosion relief. Even this is not enough when toxic fumes are also present — in this case, take expert advice.

Machines like chisel mortisers and pillar drills aren't generally worth connection to an extractor. Here the problem is not one of volume of waste, but its inevitable obstruction of pencil lines or centres on the work piece. A constant or controllable jet of compressed air is an efficient method of clearance, and even hooking up a good vacuum-cleaner on 'blow' over the work is worth doing.

Hoods

Until fairly recently dust extraction as we know it today was a mere dream — so on older, used or reconditioned machines, there will almost certainly be no obvious means of extractor connection.

Most dust extraction engineers are able to fabricate one-off hoods, ducting, or even design combined hoods and guarding. For many machines though, it should be possible for the resourceful woodworker to construct simple hoods from thin plywood. The main requirement is the smooth passage of waste. Hoods should be positioned in line with the main stream of chips so their initial momentum assists the extraction process, and be as close to the blade or cutter as practicable.

● If they're well made, home-made hoods can be extremely efficient – especially on planer/thicknessers

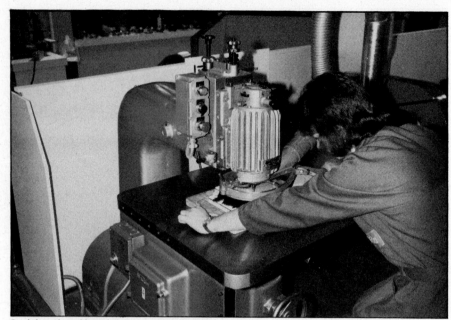

● A hood and brush 'skirt' is best for overhead routers, notoriously difficult to extract

Hoods fitted over cutter-blocks should be securely fixed in place and not allowed to rattle round. Some form of ventilation may also be necessary, as noise levels can be increased by badly designed or constructed hoods which become a sort of trumpet.

Extraction hoods often also guard the unused or exposed parts of blades or cutters. When designing or constructing such fittings, you must consider the possibilities of flying cutters, and use material strong enough to retain them.

Industrial regulations concerning dust extraction largely revolve round the length of time that individual machines are at work. For those who come under the jurisdiction of the Health and Safety Executive, a copy of *The Woodworking Machinery Regulations 1974* makes a worthwhile read.

Mobile extractors

For the majority of small or medium-sized workshops, where the thicknesser is the main offender and other machines only present an occasional problem, the popular mobile single-bag unit is the obvious choice. Mobile extractors are available in all sorts of shapes, sizes and wattages. Although there are exceptions, the mobile single-bag unit is only really capable (at its best) of handling one machine at a time.

Not only are mobile units ideal for all machinery as and when the need arises, they can also be fitted with various attachments that turn them into giant vacuum cleaners for the once-a-year workshop spring-clean. They work on the cyclone principle — waste material is drawn into the unit by the fan, where the heavier wood particles are separated from the air and fall into the collection bag. The air then returns to the workshop through the linen filter.

Machine-planing and sawing often mix larger pieces of waste with the usual saw-dust (when planing wild boards, for example, an explosion inside the machine reveals troublesome grain or a loose knot). Although most extractors can cope with pieces of this size, they aren't really suited to handling 'solids'. Rags and large pieces of paper should also be avoided, as the motor could overheat if they get into the fan.

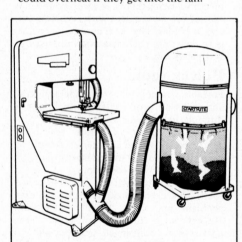

● Special duct-kits for a mobile extractor may be necessary if you do a lot of bandsawing

What to look for

The power of any extractor must be considered first. Power is usually rated in cubic feet per minute (cfm), or its metric equivalent. Different manufacturers have their own ideas and opinions on power, but as examples, the average circular saw, small spindle moulder or 10-12in planer will require around 550 cfm, and 18in planers or tenoning machines around 750 cfm.

The size of ducting will usually be dictated by the inlet diameter on the extractor unit, and should be in proportion to the power of the motor, but again the average 12in saw or planer needs 5in, and 19in planers need 6in-diameter ducting.

Obviously, when considering the power of a given extraction unit, a lot depends on the type of work your machines do. Although you may only ever feed narrow strips through your 30in thicknesser, it's wise to cover its maximum capability. If your unit is some distance from the machinery it will serve, or a branch is to be fitted, then some power drop will be inevitable and power must be increased proportionally.

The capacity of the collection bag or bags on multiple machines is also important. Although a one-bag unit may well have adequate power to handle the output of a large planing machine, if it's continuously running at anything near its maximum capacity, stoppages for bag changing will be so frequent that a multi-bag unit would make much more sense.

A system

The next step up is permanent ducting to each individual machine feeding a central extraction unit, often housed outside the main building. Although not outside the scope of the resourceful woodworker, this really requires the services of an extraction specialist. Permanent extraction systems demand a large, and (you hope!) one-off investment, so it is essential that you take every consideration into account. Most extraction engineers offer a complete planning and technical service, and are able to solve most dust problems.

The power needed for permanent extraction systems is dictated by the number and size of machines, the distance from each machine to the point of collection, and the number of branches or junctions. In most small workshops, machines (although often running together) are not often cutting at their full power, so the size of motor, and therefore cost, can be kept down by the fitting of dampers in the system that direct the air-flow to come only from the machines actually producing waste.

A useful addition when planning an extraction system is the fitting of a sweep-up point. This is a duct opening at floor level where workshop sweepings can be directed.

The majority of extractors use medium gauge see-through polythene collection bags-which can usually be obtained from the manufacturer or supplier of the unit. There are alternatives — for storage and re-usability, heavy gauge polythene bags are ideal, although expensive. If you dump your waste and don't want the inconvenience or discomfort of emptying lots of bags of sawdust, then rolls of light-gauge polythene tubing of the right circumference for your machine can be used. This is cut off and knotted at one end to seal it for use.

Some extractors are of a size that allows you to use an average refuse sack, but these are really no cheaper than other ones generally available, and you can't see the sawdust level. It may be worth getting a quote from a specialist supplier if you are buying more than a few hundred bags each time.

● Before and after extraction. Where once (left) flew dust and shavings (which also pile up in the machine and bruise the work) there is now (above) a clean-as-a-whistle workshop

When choosing an extractor, check the way in which the collection bags are held in place. On some units the arrangements are very poor, both in quality and design of fasteners, and ease of operation. Over a long period, quick and easy bag changing will be much appreciated!

Using wood waste

When the next piece of mahogany passes through the planer and the dust falls to the floor, the story should be far from over. Not only are there ways to save money from using wood waste; in some cases a handsome profit can be made.

What you do with your wood waste largely depends upon the volume. Small and inconsistent quantities may have to be dumped, and you may even have to pay for their removal. On the other hand, large and regular producers of wood waste (especially softwood shavings) may well be able to sell it to specialist companies. Offcuts can easily be sold or given away as firewood.

The obvious choice for most workshops is to use wood waste for winter-time heat. However, do check that your insurance allows this. The type of sawdust that most woodworkers produce will usually be dry and therefore a valuable fuel. Wet wood waste, such as that produced by sawmills, can also be burnt, but has a lower heat value — it may be necessary to mix wet and dry to allow it to burn. However, a very cold December can soon erode your summer-time stock. There are in fact many wood users (sawmills, joinery shops) who are only too glad to get rid of the stuff. Transporting it can be another matter, as it doesn't take many bags of sawdust to fill the average car boot or van. If you have to make lots of trips, the petrol costs can easily cancel out your fuel savings.

Wood waste heaters

One of the most popular small workshop sawdust burners is the 'dustbin' type, which generates heat by slow combustion of the fuel material packed inside. Output can be regulated by simple adjustment of the air vents to give a comfortable working temperature. It also cooks some of the best toasted sandwiches you ever tasted!

In larger workshops wood waste heaters can be either free-standing self-contained units, just requiring a flue connection, or they can be housed outside the main workshop area with heat delivered by ducting.

Heating output is rated in BTUs. Your requirements can be roughly calculated by multiplying workshop volume (cubic feet) by five; thus a 1000sq ft workshop, with a ceiling height of 10ft, requires a heater rated at 50,000BTUs. Obviously, efficiency depends to a large degree on the type and construction of the building and its level of insulation.

This type of unit will not only burn the usual offcuts, sawdust and shavings, but also straw, paper and any other combustible material. They usually burn solid fuel (coal and coke) as back-up alternatives. Stoking can be done manually or by an

Waste away

automatic fuel-delivery line (usually fed by a manually filled hopper). Connecting this to the extraction system proper offers total automation. For those working in smokeless zones, afterburners can be fitted to comply with the requirements of the Clean Air Act. During warm weather, hot air can be 'dumped' or used for timber drying.

Whatever system you choose to suit your individual needs, the saving on oil, gas or electric heating usually means that the initial investment is easily recovered over a very short period (within 12 months in some cases), resulting in almost-free heat for ever after.

Briquetting

If you have many machines at work all day, a briquette press may be the answer to your waste problem. Although requiring a high initial investment, it could create a profitable offshoot of the main business. However, you need to be producing at least 15 tonnes of waste a week; the type of company that would install such a machine probably spends more on this single installation than you, I or the average small woodworking set-up ever considers spending on machinery or tools. ■

● Many machinery manufacturers also make dust extraction equipment. Suppliers are listed here:

● 'Dustbin' wood waste heaters *(above left)* also do shaving-flavoured toasted sandwiches; for the volume producers, a briquetting machine *(above right)* is worth it

Startrite Machine Tool Co, Gads Hill, Gillingham, Kent ME7 2SF

Black & Decker, West Point, The Grove, Slough, Berkshire SL1 1QQ

Clean Air Systems, Unit 2, Bunny Trading Estate, Gotham Lane, Bunny, Notts NG11 6QJ

Fulgora Stoves, 167 Battersea Rise, London SW11

Air Plants Ltd, 295 Aylestone Road, Leicester LE2 7PB

Ashcraft Engineers Ltd, Unit 1, Griffin Industrial Mall, Griffin Lane, Aylesbury, Bucks HP19 3BP

P&J Dust Extraction, Unit 1 Revenge Rd, Lordswood Ind. Est., Chatham, Kent ME5 9PF

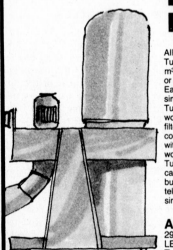

Wheelspin

● **Above left,** *the 'flyer drag' spinning wheel before and,* **right,** *after restoration*

Spinning old and new — we look at two variations on the endless theme of spinning wheels. First, Frank Lapworth explains how he restored the form and function of a mid-European 19th century model

When some friends of mine bought an old spinning wheel in very poor condition about a year ago, I was asked to have a look at it because of my interest in spinning. (My wife and I are both fanatical spinners, and we give demonstrations at craft fairs and lectures to local groups and colleges.)

As soon as I saw the wheel I offered to restore it. It is of the 'flyer drag' or 'bobbin lead' type, where the bobbin is driven continually by the drive-band round the wheel. The flyer — the U-shaped piece through the centre of which wool is twisted, and then distributed along the bobbin by the hooks — is dragged round by the yarn itself as it is wound on to the bobbin. Both bobbin and flyer have to turn of course, but at different rates. The twist of the yarn — loose or tight — is controlled by a leather strap which acts as a brake on the flyer's rotation; the drag on the flyer is controlled by turning a knob to adjust tension on the

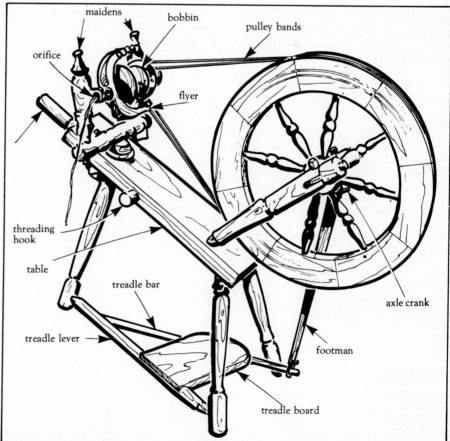

● **Above:** *Naming of parts. The wheel imparts twist to a supply of fibre fed through the orifice, turning it into yarn which is wound on to the bobbin. From* Woodworker, *Jan 85*

Wheelspin

strap, tightening or slackening it.

The overall design of the wheel is typical of the kind used in southern Germany, Austria, and the Tyrol, and my ideas about its origins were verified by some German printed on the underside of the treadle. It's impossible to read clearly, but the word Wien (Vienna) is just legible, a hint at the address of the maker. One can tell the wheel had been used long and hard from the wear in the parts of the mechanism — notably the flyer and wheel-bearings, and particularly where the brake-band goes over the flyer. There were also minute grooves worn in the flyer-hooks, which suggest it was probably used for spinning flax. If it had been used for wool, the grooves would have been larger. It's difficult to tell, but the sort of use it had obviously had and the way it was made would date it at between 1830 and 1850.

It's made from a variety of woods. The legs, uprights, the crosshead 'mother-of-all' on which the flyer assembly is mounted, the maidens — turned pieces that project from the mother-of-all to carry the flyer itself — and drive-band tensioner are all walnut or some similar hardwood. The flyer also has a walnut boss, into which oak arms of the 'U' are dovetailed. The rest of the wheel is of a close-grained softwood, probably pine, and it's all stained a dark walnut-brown.

When I first saw it, the wheel was in generally pretty poor shape, although the parts were almost 100% original, and I could see where it had been repaired over the years to keep it going. Repaired not restored — a confirmation of my idea that it was a worker's wheel and not a piece of decorative furniture. It had also suffered from the ravages of woodworm, which had damaged every part. The wheel itself was well eaten away, the surface particularly so.

Preparation

First I took the spinning wheel apart and thoroughly cleaned it with white spirit to rid it of years of accumulated grime and grease. This also gave me a chance to inspect it more closely and see what needed to be done.

Although there was now no evidence of active woodworm, I treated all the timber several times with Cuprinol woodworm killer, and injected the flight-holes with the fluid. I reamed out the flight-holes to a slight taper with a Swiss needle-file, sanded hardwood cocktail-sticks to fit the taper, and glued and tapped them into place. Then I cut the ends off slightly proud of the surface, and when the glue had set sanded them flush to match the contours of the wood.

The job

Restoration proper could now begin. Here is a list of the things that were wrong with it and what I did, in the order I dealt with them.

The footman — the driving member which connects the treadle to the cranked axle of the driving bar — was split at the upper end, and on the rear side (the side away from you

● **Left**, *the spinning head showing worm-damaged flyer and extinct brake-band*

● **Right**, *the wheel, badly pock-marked, awaits cocktail-stick treatment*

as you sit and spin) a piece of the timber had decayed away next to the crank slot. The split at the top had been repaired by driving an iron staple into the top end to bridge the split and hold the two halves together. This driving member is also sometimes called the 'pitman'.

I removed the staple and glued the split together. The decaying timber at the rear was cut away, and I cut a piece of mahogany to fit and glued it into place.

The wheel, which is made in two asymmetrical halves, had also been repaired with staples, four in all, to hold the joints together; the side of the rim was badly worm-eaten across its surface, and there were deep, irregular channels in the wood. The metal crank-arm was bent and out of line with the spindle.

I straightened the crank arm and removed the staples, whereupon the wheel sprang apart at the joints. In order to make it fit together again, I had to slightly trim the ends of two of the spokes in the shorter piece of the wheel. Only then would it go together properly. I repaired the surface damage by making some walnut wood-dust, mixing it with a little PVA glue and rubbing this paste into the damaged area. When it was thoroughly dry I sanded it smooth. There was also a decorative short finial missing from the inside edge of the wheel-rim, so I turned one up to match and fitted it.

The flyer arms, which are compound-dovetailed into the boss, were loose, and the hole in the rear maiden (towards the footman and crank) that carries the flyer spindle or 'quill' was badly worn. I don't think the leather brake-band and tensioning knob were original; the brake-band itself was fixed to the maiden with a tin tack!

I reglued the flyer arms back into the boss, and made a new tensioning-knob and shaft. I made a new brake-band, and secured it with a buttonhole fixing over the knob at the outer end of the maiden. The spindle bearing in the rear maiden was comparatively simple to plug and re-drill.

The front upright was cracked and in danger of coming apart; the **stool** or **saddle**, the flat 'base' which carries the legs and wheel uprights, was cracked across the centre, and the legs were loose.

I glued and cramped the upright together, and filled other cracks which wouldn't cramp up tight with pieces of walnut, which I stained to match as near as possible. I reglued the stool and filled the wood where necessary, but it was impossible to remove the legs for re-pegging because nails had been driven in to hold them. To get those nails out might have done more damage than I wanted to risk — I had no wish to turn up new legs, or get into boring out the old wood for new spigots. The answer was to re-peg the legs from underneath, instead of through the sides of the stool where it had been done originally.

Finally I stained over the whole spinning wheel with walnut stain, and repolished it with clear Briwax. I replaced the drive-band, as the one that came with the wheel was too thick to get sensitive tension adjustments, and put a leather thong in place of the piece of string which attached the treadle to the footman.

To complete the outfit and make it into a practical spinning wheel, I made a threading-hook, a 'Lazy Kate' bobbin rack, and two spare bobbins. I have tried it — it works fine, within the limitations of the design — and my friends were delighted! ∎

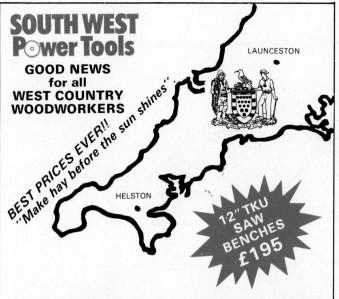

589

The flat spin

Roger Sear's Kingston spinning wheels look traditional, but they boast some subtle modifications. Here's how to make one — with spinning tips included!

The traditional image conjured by the words 'spinning wheel' is a charming old lady in voluminous clothes sitting outside a rose-entwined cottage behind some romantic contraption. The image persists, but it's nostalgic romance, not fact.

The old-time spinner lived on the lower breadline; part of a tenuous worker chain in which a break could spell disaster for many. The shepherd — the supplier — was the first in line, followed by the comber who prepared the fleece by lashing it through heated combs to enable the spinner to make the fine worsted yarn for the weaver's loom. Each link in this chain had to hold. As many as nine or 10 spinners could just manage to keep one weaver supplied with yarn, but improvements to looms like the flying shuttle speeded weaving up more and more, and hard-pressed spinners simply couldn't keep up. Despite the extra capacity of the 'Great wheel', or 'Walking wheel', it was not until the 'Flyer wheel' was introduced in the 15th century that spinning was speeded up, and until the 18th-century invention of the spinning jenny, the flyer was the only wheel that gave the weaver enough yarn in enough time.

The two major types of wheel that evolved are the Saxony with a sloping bed, and the upright Hebridean or Shetland wheel. Most serious spinners who spin the gossamer-fine yarns favour the Saxony, more stable than the Shetland which was used where space was really at a premium.

My first introduction to spinning came in 1923 when I was five. One of my duties was to rotate a 48in great wheel for my lace-maker great-aunt. Years later I still retained an interest in spinning, but nowhere could I find the wheel that I really wanted, so I resolved to make one. I went the rounds of museums with steel tape and camera, and visited hundreds of hand spinners, many of whom expressed decided views on the shortcomings of available wheels. Poor adjustment, heavy action, a tiring treadle action and too-low gear ratios were the main faults they listed. Though they didn't regard the appearance of the machine as important, they all thought a wheel should look fairly traditional. Most preferred the Saxony to the Shetland, the main reason being stability. All wanted doubled-band systems (where one belt round the large driving wheel runs both the bobbin and the flyer) and a standard flyer system as distinct from overhung types. An improved belt-tension system rated very highly amongst desirable improvements.

● *Above: a Saxony wheel. Roger himself has tried and tested many variations, as you can see from the box-mounted version* **right**

I was surprised at so much criticism, yet realised as a spinner that I had never really been happy with the antiquated, coarse, wooden-threaded sliding block system for adjusting the driving-belt tension. The obvious answer was a hinged block (damsel) that would allow very sensitive adjustment with a 26tpi screwdown wheel; this solved the problem most effectively. Fig. 1 and the photo above right illustrate the idea, and confirm my motto in the workshop — KISS (keep it simple, stupid!).

The heavy action necessitated much research. It seemed that friction had to be reduced and the stroke of the crank connecting treadle to wheel should be modified. I tried an adjustable crank out on a number of skilled spinners, who all set it up within $\frac{1}{16}$in of each other, so that was another to cross off the list. A 3in stroke, $1\frac{1}{2}$in cranking has proved ideal, and operator fatigue is almost eliminated.

A $\frac{1}{4}$in axle diameter means the bearings can be made of bronze, Oilite, PTFE or even epoxy resin. I know these materials aren't traditional, but b . . . . . r tradition — I want to spin, not struggle. The axle will bend cold if you use mild steel.

Now came the real crunch — speed. Most spinners treadle at about the speed of a Viennese waltz, and to obtain acceptable spinning speed meant a wheel to flyer-pulley ratio of about 7 or 8:1. To get the

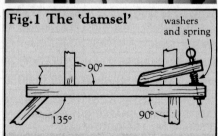

Fig.1 The 'damsel'   washers and spring

belt in contact on 40% of the whorl that drives the flyer (whorl = pulley), you would need a driving wheel with a minimum diameter of 26in, which would allow a flyer whorl of 3in diameter, ample for controlled slip. The extremely critical bobbin whorl-to-flyer whorl ratio *must* be 13:19 at the circumference measured at the

● *The hinged block or 'damsel' allows adjustment of the drive-belt tension with a sprung threaded bar*

bottom of the V-groove, a steep, deep 'V' of about ¼in. I have found these dimensions give the best results, but many will say 'but my wheel spins OK.' Well, it might, and Bleriot's plane flew. So does Concorde!

Making a wheel

First you need to set out the rim shape; a quarter segment will do for a felloe mould. For a 26in wheel, a 26in external and 20in internal diameter will do. Cut four segments from 1¼in material; leave about ¼in waste on the outside, but cut internal as finely as possible. Form the circle and shoot the ends of the felloes to fit and either tongue or dowel them together. Try a dry run with blocks nailed on a board and wedges to act as cramps. When the joints satisfy you, glue them up and put aside flat to set.

Now forget the rim while you cut a 7in diameter disc from the same stuff as the felloes and clean it up. This is the hub or nave. Centralise the hub in the rim and measure the spoke length between hub and rim. Now add 1in to this length to get the full length of your spokes. Decide how many spokes you wish to have — 12 or 16 is the best number — and cut and turn them; but 1in of each end must be parallel turned to ½in diameter, and I mean dead ½in! Finish the spokes off at this stage or prepare to swear later!

Clean up the inside — only the inside — of the rim with a flap-wheel. With dividers or a large protractor, set out the spoke positions round the inside of the rim and drill a ¼in-diameter hole 1in deep at each spot. Lay the rim on a flat board and position the hub spot on, then strike a line from each spoke point on the rim to the centre-point of the hub. Mark these lines over to the edge of the hub and drill a ½in hole 1¼in deep at each point. Dry-fit the spokes, and check when they're pressed

right home that you have a ⅜in minimum gap at the rim end. Now drill the rim end of each spoke and insert a ¼in dowel protruding ⁵⁄₁₆in. By now you will have tumbled the method! Squirt glue into the hub holes and insert the spokes. Lay the spoke/hub assembly inside the rim, spot-glue the dowel ends and slide them home into the rim, ensuring that both rim and hub are cramped down to avoid twisting. The wheel is now assembled and, after wiping off any surplus glue, it should be left to dry.

When the glue has set, drill a ¼in hole at the hub centre for the axle, lay the wheel flat on a scrap board and drive a 4in nail through the axle hole. Leave 1in standing up, and cut off the head. With this as a centre, use a trammel to strike the outer circumference of the rim, then bandsaw off and clean up the whole wheel. With a half-round cutter in the router, form the belt groove, working from both sides, and clean it up. The flat of the rim can now be carved, inlaid or just polished — the choice is yours.

If you don't work metal on your lathe, you'll have to find someone to make two flanged collars from brass or alloy as shown in fig. 2. Form the axle as in fig. 3 from ¼in bright mild steel. Screw the collar on to the wheel and cut a 3in-diameter disc from matching timber about ⅜in thick with a ¼in central hole. Set the axle vertically in the vice and slide on the wheel, followed by the disc. Fix the disc to get the wheel true, or at least within ⅛in. That's the wheel finished; now for the rest.

The structure

The next stage is the saddle, or base, and the legs, or columns. For the saddle you need 26in of 7x1¼, cut to the shape shown in fig. 4 and cleaned up. Put the saddle aside and concentrate on the three legs which should be around 1½in square, two 14in long and one 20in long. Rough-turn these to 1in diameter along 2in on one end, then bore 1in-diameter holes in the saddle as shown and fit the legs. When the legs have been tried in position and trimmed to a firm

Fig.4 The saddle

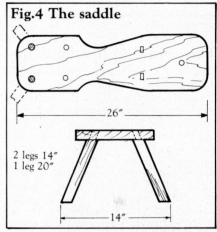

2 legs 14"
1 leg 20"

stand, turn them to any shape that pleases you but leave the bottom 2in fairly plain. You'll see why later on. With the legs now ready to be fitted, make a saw-cut about 1in vertically down in the top end of each leg. Glue the legs in with the sawcut *across* the saddle and wedge them home.

Use 1½in stock for the columns holding the wheel, about 20in long and rough-turned with the same 1in parallel portion as the legs. Bore the 1in holes in the saddle as shown in fig. 4, dry fit the columns and offer up the wheel. Allow the rim to run about 1in clear above the saddle and mark off the axle holes. Carefully drill a ¼in hole at your marks and try the axle, checking it's true with the saddle and square across. Turn the two columns to your choice of shape, then screw two threaded ¼in-bore lampholder bushes in on the inner faces for bearings. Flush off the larger portion. The columns are fitted like the legs, but glue them in with the axle slid into position for true running.

Fig.2 Drive collars

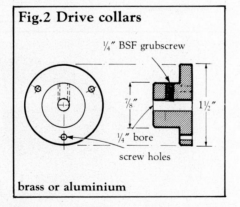

¼" BSF grubscrew

⅞"   1½"

¼" bore

screw holes

brass or aluminium

Fig.3 The axle

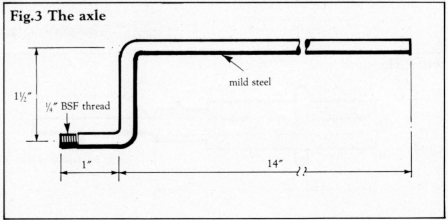

1½"

¼" BSF thread

mild steel

1"   14"

The flat spin

The damsel

The damsel block is the next task. Cut it out as shown in the photo and fig. 1, then let in the butts and screw it into position. Drill a ⅜in hole for the adjuster, which you can make from ¼in BSF studding. Turn a 2in-diameter knob, and set a ¼in nut in on the underside with Araldite. Screw in the studding, with Loctite or Araldite on the thread, and then thread it through the hole with washers and a spring between the damsel block and the saddle. Solder a nut on to a piece of brass and fit it underneath the saddle to allow the damsel a degree of controlled tilt.

The spinning mechanisms

Now the complication really starts! 'Mother-of-all' is the name given to the T-shaped contraption that actually carries the spinning mechanism. It is made of two 1½in cylinders, one with a 1in spigot turned on one end and a ¾in spigot on the other. It's about 12in overall length. The 1in end of this lower cylinder fits vertically into the damsel and is glued and wedged. Next comes the crossbar, the other cylinder about 15in long. Set the wheel up in its bearings and rest the crossbar on the ¾in turned end of the vertical cylinder, about two-thirds of the length to the driving side. Sight the belt groove, mark the feed-line point on the crossbar about 2in from the back (the connecting-rod side) and drill a ¾in vertical hole right through the crossbar at the point where the crossbar and lower cylinder meet. Now fit the crossbar on dry and mark the rope line position. Measure back from this point 2in and drill a vertical ½in-diameter hole. Measure 8in forward from the centre of this hole, and drill another. These two holes will carry the maidens which carry the flyer 'quill'. You will need two pieces 1¼in square and about 7in long for the maidens; turn these to your fancy, the bottom 1½in further reduced to ½in to be a fairly tight push-fit in the holes on the crossbar (to be known as the mother-of-all from now on).

Next you need two pieces of ¼in-thick leather, 2x1in, for the bearings which fit into mortises cut 4in above the turned shoulders of the maidens that bear against the mother-of-all. These will look like little flags when glued and pinned into position.

Get a metalworking friend to make up the quill from fig. 5, and you can be getting on with the treadle section. With all your work set up, stand on one side of the machine with the wheel on your right — to be known as the 'driving side' from now on. Mark off and drill a ¼in hole through the two driving-side legs 2in above the floor. These holes must be aligned, as they carry the pivot-pins for the treadle crossbar. Now cut a piece of 1in square stock to fit between the two legs, and drive a 4in nail through the leg and into the crossbar at each end. Cut off the nail heads and you have your pivots.

The footplate is ⅜in thick, 5 or 6in wide and long enough to project 1in over the crossbar on the driving side. It reaches on the other side to a point exactly below the crank point. The footplate may be shaped as you wish but should almost form a point at the crank end. Drill a ¼in-diameter hole near this point.

The connecting rod or 'pitman' should be ¾x¼in section with a ¼in hole drilled at the bottom for the thong which laces it to the footplate. The length of rod may be determined after a trial run. Pack underneath the footplate to bring it up to dead level with the floor and, with the crank at the bottom of its stroke, mark and then drill the hole at the top of the rod to receive the crank. Tighten the grubscrew on the collar to hold the axle to the driving wheel, and try it for running. Sod's Law will undoubtedly apply at this stage, and the wheel will have a heavy spot, but this will be to your advantage later on, so worry not and don't try to adjust the lateral movement of the wheel between its columns at this stage.

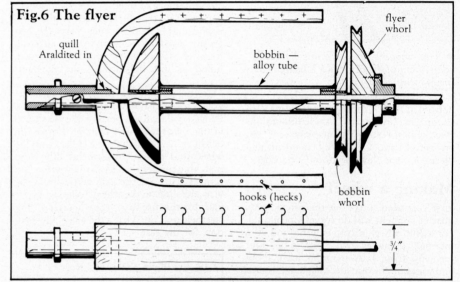

Fig.6 The flyer

flyer whorl

quill Araldited in

bobbin — alloy tube

hooks (hecks)

bobbin whorl

¾"

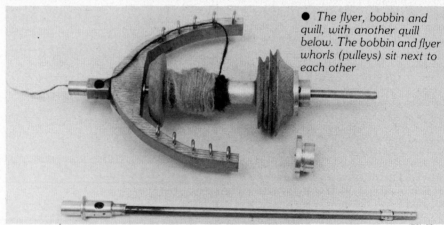

● *The flyer, bobbin and quill, with another quill below. The bobbin and flyer whorls (pulleys) sit next to each other*

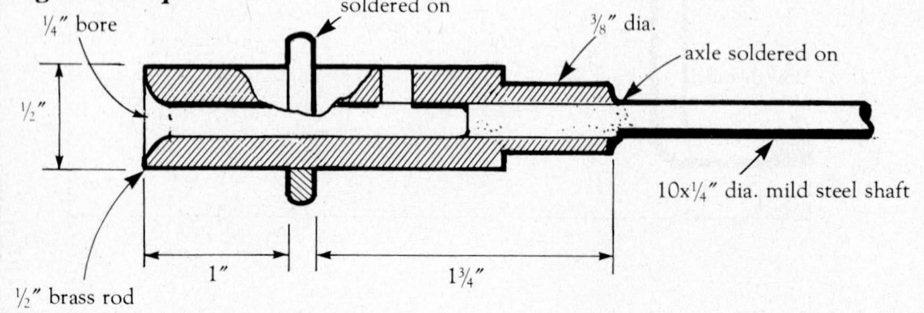

The flyer/bobbin

The flyer/bobbin assembly is rather complicated, so if I seem pedantic please bear with me. To begin with you will need:
- ● Three discs of 3in diameter, 1¼in thick with a ¼in central hole.
- ● 7in of 5x1in hardwood.
- ● 7 or 8in of ¾in-diameter aluminium tubing (try a piece of curtain rod for this).
- ● 15 small screw-hooks ⅜in long.
- ● A spool of medium whipping twine (get it from a yacht chandler).

Fig.5 The quill

¼" bore

brass washer soldered on

⅜" dia.

axle soldered on

½"

10x¼" dia. mild steel shaft

½" brass rod

1"

1¾"

- A short length of ¼in studding.
- Two nuts with washers to suit.

The flyer itself is U-shaped with the bottom (curved) portion 1in across, blending into the ⅜in sides fairly rapidly. Clean it up and remove the arrises. Now hold the flyer in the vice and drill a ¼in hole centrally through the 1in end. Slide the flyer along the quill shaft so that it resembles a trident, check it for truth, remove it and counterbore for the ⅜in quill section. Glue it on with Araldite so that when laid flat the quill hole faces upwards.

Fit a Jacob's chuck on the lathe and thread one of the 3in discs on the piece of studding as a mandrel. Turn one face to fit the loop of the flyer when slid on the quill shaft, making sure you have a clearance of ¹⁄₁₆in. Replace the disc on the mandrel with the curved side to the chuck, and turn a spigot to fit the aluminium tube about ⅝in long. Sand and remove.

Turn the second disc with a similar spigot but just leave a ⅜in section untouched on the edge. This will be turned later.

Take the third disc, fit the flanged collar like the one on the driving wheel, mount it on the mandrel and tighten the grubscrew in the collar. Just clean up the diameter, and turn a sweep up on the collar side to leave a ⅜in flat portion. Now sink a ¼x¼in V-groove in which to run the cord drive, and run a length of *soft* wire round the base of the V-groove to measure the *exact* circumference. Divide this measurement on your calculator by 19 and multiply the result by 13. Cut the wire to this new length to give you the circumference of the V-groove bottom on the second disc. Tricky, but reduce it slowly until it comes right.

Drill a ½in hole in the leather bearing on the driving side, insert the quill up to the flange, sight the quill with the main axle and mark and drill a ¼in hole in the other leather.

Now comes the moment of truth! Thread the discs on to the quill with the spigots facing each other and the collared pulley (whorl) flat to the no.2 disc. Now ease the big driver over to the back and slide the pulleys along the quill to run fair to the wheel groove. Lock the grubscrew and set the loose pulley about ¹⁄₁₆in away; caliper the distance between the faces of the spigoted pulley and the feed end of the bobbin. Cut the aluminium tube to this length and Araldite it on to the spigots to make the bobbin. When it's set, ease it to a light running fit. You will only need one bobbin with the Kingston system.

Slightly oil the quill spindle and slide the bobbin on. Check for a very easy fit, then feed the flyer whorl on so the bobbin turns freely. Lock the flyer whorl grubscrew and fit the assembly in the two leather maiden bearings (the horizontal mother-of-all can still turn on its ¾in spigot) and sight the V-grooves with the groove on the driver. A spacer may be needed at the back.

Set the damsel to half position and tie one end of the whipping-twine belt to a maiden. Pass it round the driver and over the bobbin whorl and round the driver once more. Tie

a slip knot (tight) so the same belt drives both bobbin and flyer whorls, pull just tight, lock up the knot and carefully seal it with a match. If the belt fouls the ends of the flyer, cut back the arms to clear it. Try the run of the wheel, turning it anti-clockwise from the driving side: adjust side 'float' in the driver with packing, and watch the bottom run of the belt. Swing the mother-of-all to get a fair feed with both lines. Oil the leathers and run the wheel for a while. When it runs smoothly and the belt is running fair, put a screw through the ¾in spigot to lock it.

Now make a pencil mark on the flyer (the quill-hole side) just on the aluminium side of the bobbin end, remove the flyer assembly and strip off the whorls and bobbin. Hold the flyer arms in the vice and, from the pencil mark (quill-hole side of flyer) screw in the small hooks. These are known as 'hecks'; you will need to space seven equally along each arm of the flyer to distribute the yarn along the bobbin. Remember to screw them in on the same side of both arms and open to the outside face. Now reassemble and test.

Treadle the wheel over and adjust the belt tension so that it just spins the flyer, but when the flyer is held with a finger touch the bobbin spins and the belt slips on the flyer whorl. Now cut off the spare axle, leaving 2in projecting to carry the hanker. Fig. 6 shows the hanker, so make it as you will need it. Push the hanker on the axle and screw a heck into the mother-of-all to give a fair lead to the yarn, and you are ready to spin.

Fig.7 The hanker

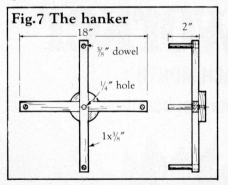

I haven't attempted to tell you any turning patterns, as you're probably a better turner than I am — you couldn't be worse. My wish was just to tell you how I build my own wheels, and they are perfect spinners. My lathe is an 1886 Britannia screwcutter swinging an 8in chuck, and by reversing the gear train and hand-turning the lead screw with a router clamped to the compound slide, I can cut a multiple-start spiral of one turn in 4in — so I have fun!

Happy spinning! ∎

- Roger Sear is very happy to answer queries about making the wheel or spinning, and can supply the axles and quills: please send a s.a.e. to him at 30 Brighton Rd, Shoreham by Sea, Sussex, (0273) 591053.

Spinning on a Kingston system Wheel

You will need fleece to use your wheel, preferably carded. This can usually be obtained from a local craft shop or one of the specialist suppliers. Fleece with a reasonably long staple (fibre length) is needed, and we would suggest Romney Marsh or Cheviot to start off with.

Tie a 2ft length of commercial yarn on to the bobbin and thread it round a hook, through the hole in the top of the quill, and out through the aperture (a bent hairpin works well). Now check the drive belt is just tight enough to spin the bobbin whilst the flyer is held with one finger. The belt must be able to slip on the flyer whorl. Hold the end of this leader about 6in from the quill between thumb and forefinger of the right hand, the rest in the left about 4in back. Now start to treadle the wheel anti-clockwise, and the yarn in front of the right hand will start to store twist. The yarn will be drawn in and on to the bobbin, but keep the pinch on and move your hands towards the wheel. But slide the left hand back about 6in and *slide* the right pinch back to the left . . . the twist will follow it, but it *mustn't* be allowed to pass the pinch . . . feed both hands forward to allow wind-on, and repeat the operation till it gets easy, then unwind and do it again . . . and again . . . and again.

When you have mastered the wind-on (tighten the belt to increase pull if it's not enough), pull out from your fleece a small handful and make a 'roving'; a sausage about a finger's diameter. With about 12in of leader out, hold a *few* wool fibres against the leader in the right hand and pinch the rest gently in the left about 3in back . . . Start the wheel and the leader will grip the wool, so then slide the right hand back towards the left, moving the left back, which allows a few fibres to slide through. *Both* hands move forward in unison to allow wind-on. The yarn will form in front of the right hand and wind on, the thickness being controlled by the amount fed through from the left. Practice but don't worry if it's a bit lumpy; this is why I said practice. As the bobbin fills, move the yarn along to the next hook till the bobbin fills that. When the bobbin is full, lift the belt from the bobbin whorl over on to the flyer whorl, put the hanker on the axle and wind off. Tie off the hank with tape, remove it from the hanker and wash it with detergent; rinse it and hang it up with a heavy weight on it to dry. When it's dry, ball up and make another hank; same treament. The yarn must be plied for knitting, so place both balls in a bowl and tie both ends to a leader as if you were spinning. Tighten the belt a little and treadle the wheel *clockwise*, holding the twin yarns between your fingers . . . it will ply and wind on fast. You can do it . . . now practice!

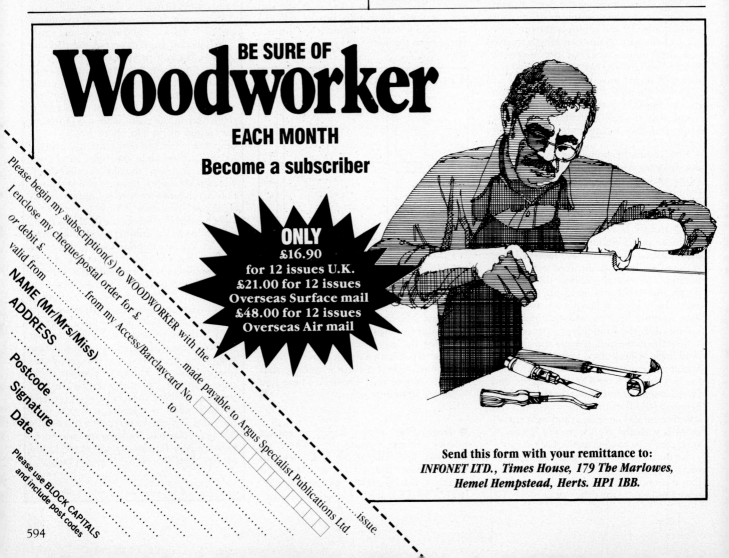
594

Sitting ducks

Peter Mallinson's carved wildfowl are a great deal more than decoys — almost more birdlike than the birds themselves! Neil McAllister talked to him and took the photographs

What separates the average from the exceptional? Carving technique can be taught, it's true, but without the vital love of the subject matter, inert wood will never be transformed into art.

Tighnabruaich is a tiny village at the end of a road to nowhere, sitting alongside the strikingly beautiful Kyles of Bute. Not an exceptional place, but the home of an exceptional woodcarver. Peter Mallinson is a 31 year-old salmon farmer who started carving only two years ago, but is rapidly making his name as a prodigious wildfowl carving talent. He started carving as a result of 'The need to express the artistic side of my interest in bird life', and learning by trial and error, developed his own style to produce exquisite life-size birds. He particularly favours the teal and widgeon that surround him during his working hours; not to be categorised with the roughly carved and painted decoys so fashionable at the moment, these birds' truth as works of art depends on a creative drive that wells from a deep affinity with the subject.

Peter prefers to carve in jelutong, which he finds responsive. He marks out the rough shape on a rectangular block, then bandsaws out the basic form, which is rounded and smoothed to the correct shape with Surforms. Feather detail and texture are then drawn on and carved in; the final texture is burnt in with a tool like a soldering iron. The head is made separately, and attached to the body block when it's nearly finished, then the carved and textured creation is sealed and painted with oil paints. The final result is uncannily close to the real bird.

As the photographs show, Peter's standard of work is nothing short of superb, especially considering the short time he has taken to refine his skills. A problem that comes with such ability has already arisen; keeping up with orders. Demand for his work has been mounting as the word has spread about his talent, and each piece takes a minimum of six weeks to carve in his spare time — about 40-50 hours of full-time work. This investment of hours is reflected in his prices, although he's not expensive by some standards; life-sized heads are around £35, while a full-sized harlequin or drake mallard might cost £200. Birds that demand a lot less work — and, some might say, a lot less skill — have been known to go for twice as much! ■

*At first glance, you might wonder what these creatures are doing in Woodworker anyway – they aren't made of wood are they? **Left** and **below**, a female pintail in jelutong; **above**, a male harlequin in jelutong and lime. **Top right**, the two of them get together*

The King's makers

Vile & Cobb were household names in the 1760s — for George III. Leslie Syson looks at the work of these undeservedly little-known craftsmen

Much has been written about the work of furniture designers such as Chippendale and Sheraton, and perhaps one reason why they are better known than others is the effect of Chippendale's *Gentleman and Cabinet-Maker's Director* of 1754 and Sheraton's *Cabinet-Maker and Upholsterer's Drawing Book* of 1791. These and other publications helped popularise their furniture styles, but they have also created some confusion. How much furniture described as 'Chippendale' is the actual work of the man himself? Some earlier cabinetmakers signed their work, but Chippendale doesn't appear to have considered marking even his finest pieces in any way — unlike some of our contemporaries with their mice and other creatures crawling round the furniture. Only signed invoices still in the possession of owners of furniture can really show authenticity.

Once he was established in his London workshops, Chippendale's own time at the bench must have been very limited. The story of a disastrous fire at his workshops in St Martin's Lane in 1755 gives an indication of the size of his business; the tool-chests of 22 journeymen were destroyed, and there could well have been others that escaped damage and weren't recorded. Further confusion about what is a genuine Chippendale arises from the fact that many other craftsmen could use the *Director* for reference to produce their own versions of 'Chippendale' furniture.

Chippendale had to realise he couldn't please all the clients all the time; he wasn't without a few dissatisfied customers. He had a disagreement with the architect Sir William Chambers about the furnishing for Melbourne House in Piccadilly, during which Chambers claimed Chippendale's drawings could be improved! Sir Rowland Winn was perhaps even harder on the unfortunate cabinetmaker in 1767, when he told Chippendale he would make sure he advised friends previously recommended to go to the craftsman, that he would prefer them to employ some other person! A little later Sir Rowland was in contact with Chippendale about slow delivery, a correspondence that supplies us with some of the limited information about Chippendale's work for royalty — his explanation of that delay was that he was busy with work for the Royal family. It was about that time that eight arm-chairs and two sofas were made

● *The jewel cabinet for Queen Charlotte, made in 1761; a far cry from 'wretched low rooms'. Even given the prices of those days, £138.10s doesn't seem a lot to pay!*

by Chippendale for that pinnacle of patrons.

There have been many other craftsmen, not only during Chippendale's time, who are at least equally deserving as he is of our attention and respect. Since Chippendale wasn't favoured with much work for royalty, it seems worth looking at the other craftsmen who worked for the Royal family, amongst whom we discover Vile and Cobb — cabinetmakers to the Crown under George III.

George II had shown little interest in furniture, especially after the Queen's death in 1737. According to Horace Walpole's *Journals*, he slept in a room on the ground floor and dined in a 'wretched low room' next to it. 'There is nothing but a green damask bed, a buroe and two or three chairs and a green couch and some chairs in these two rooms which are not even hung', was Walpole's comment. So, on the acces-

sion of George III in 1760 and his marriage to Queen Charlotte shortly afterwards, there was no doubt much scope for refurbishing. Vile and Cobb didn't have long to wait. In 1761 they produced 'a very handsome jewel cabinet' for the Queen, made in mahogany and veneered in many different timbers including padouk, amboyna, tulip, olive and rosewood. The top, front and ends were inlaid with ivory, and both front and back were a beautiful serpentine shape. The sides are concave. It contained eight half-width drawers with a full-width drawer at the bottom, all lined with black velvet and enclosed by cabinet doors. Four carved cabriole legs with whorl feet supported the cabinet, which stood 42in high. Vile and Cobb charged £138.10s. for supplying it, which seems a fairly high price compared to other contemporary pieces; but it's an exquisite piece of work by the finest cabinetmakers of the time. Lord Folkestone is known to have complained about Vile's high prices, but the partnership's standard of work and reputation seem to have allowed them to command such charges. The break-front bookcase in the photo cost £107.14s, and the bureau-secretaire for the King (photo), which had a crown carved on its pediment since it was made soon after the Coronation, cost £71. How ridiculous that sounds by today's prices!

William Vile was the senior member and the cabinetmaker of the partnership with John Cobb. Vile had worked with William Hallett, a successful cabinetmaker working in Long Acre in London in the 1730s, who had established something of a reputation with his own style of furniture. He had financial support, which must have been a good foundation for Vile, and it's possible that Hallett provided him with support in different ways later in his life. John Cobb, on the other hand, had been apprenticed to Tim Money, an upholsterer in Norwich. The partnership doesn't appear to be recorded until 1751, and even at that time, it only appears as William Vile & Co. By 1755 Cobb had moved to a house in St Martin's Lane which had been occupied by Hallett, next door to Vile & Co; it made them near neighbours of Chippendale, a situation in which interchange of influence was highly likely.

Although Vile was probably the more expert cabinetmaker and Cobb the upholsterer, the division could hardly have been rigid; neither was regarded as a chairmaker. Cobb, probably about 15 years younger then Vile, gained a reputation for being very self-opinionated, and apparently used to dress in the most expensive and fashionable clothes — even, at times, in the workshop where he would strut about like a peacock giving orders to the men. There is a story about how his pomposity was deflated by George III at Buckingham House, recorded by J. T. Smith in 1828: working in His Majesty's library, Cobb was giving instructions to a workman who had placed a ladder against a book which the King wanted. Cobb was asked to hand the book to the King, but instead of doing so he called to the workman — 'Fellow, give me that book.' The King heard this and asked Cobb what was his man's name. 'Jenkins', said Cobb. 'Then, Jenkins, you shall hand me the book,' replied the King; we aren't told how shamefaced Cobb was, if at all. (*Nollekens and his times*, 1828, vol II.)

Cobb may well have been the more innovatory partner, and indeed, his name is associated with what became a fashionable and very convenient table which Smith describes as drawing 'out in front with upper and inward rising desks, so healthy for those who stand to write, read or draw'. Vile's name, on the other hand, is more strongly associated with, for example, the 1760 bureau-cabinet in the Terry collection in Fairfax House in York. It is elaborately fretted in a basically geometric pattern, though it is also decorated with festoons and leaf-pattern carvings. One might see a connection between this and the Chinese

● **Above:** a mahogany break-front bookcase for the Royal family; the size of the windows bestows elegant proportions without heaviness. **Right**, for £71 George III got this bureau-secretaire with its finely fretted top sections and a bombé-shaped base. Note the crown on top

Chippendale style, but Vile must surely be allowed a claim to greater refinement and accuracy of pattern-design. His name is also predominant in furniture produced for the Crown; after all, he was the senior partner, 61 years old when the Royal patronage was established. Among the first pieces the partners supplied were a coin cabinet for the King and the bureau-secretaire mentioned earlier, the top of which consisted of finely fretted panels and doors and the bottom of which had a *bombé* shape. It had five drawers, three full width, with the top drawer-space divided into two. All were fitted with ornate brass loop handles.

Among the larger pieces made for the Royal family is a break-front bookcase, again in mahogany as was much of the fashionable furniture of the time. Contributing to its impressive appearance are four Corinthian pilasters and a broken pediment. Although these may suggest heaviness, nothing detracts from the display of books inside, because the doors are proportioned more like windows in relation to the whole piece. Laurel-wreath carving adorns the solid doors of the base.

It's possible that much of the carving done for Vile & Cobb was supervised by John Bradburn (Bradborn according to some records). When Vile retired in 1765, Bradburn took over the royal patronage. Cobb continued in business and apparently did quite well, particularly in producing very attractive inlaid commodes. A notable example is at Corsham Court in Wiltshire.

Vile lived only two years after his retirement and Cobb died in 1778. What is remarkable is that Vile & Cobb, although obviously successful in building up a high reputation over many years, had to wait until the accession of George III before having any hope of receiving royal attention — and then, that it only lasted four years. In that time however, the quality and quantity of work produced enhanced their reputation so much that, as Percy Macquoid acknowledges in his *Dictionary of Furniture*, 'It is to them that pride of place among contemporary cabinetmakers must be assigned'. ■

Books

● Thomas Chippendale, *Gentleman and Cabinet-maker's Director*, 3rd edition 1762, and Thomas Sheraton, *Cabinet-maker and Upholsterer's Drawing Book*, 1791: Dover reprints from Constable & Co Ltd, 10 Orange St, London WC2H 7EG, 01-930 0801, or Stobart and Son, 67-73 Worship St, London WC2A 2EL, 01-247 0501

● Geoffrey Beard, *National Trust Book of English Furniture*, National Trust, 36 Queen Anne's Gate, London SW1, 01-222 9251

● Anthony Bird, *English Furniture for the Private Collector*, Batsford, 1961

● Ralph Fastnedge, *English Furniture Styles*, Pelican Books, 1955

Tales out of steel

Humorist and toolmaker Ashley Iles remembers the trials of exporting from Sheffield in the post-war period, and conjures the frantic atmosphere of a boom town

'Laurel Blades for Hardy Beards' was the slogan of the Laurel Razor Blade Co., Sheffield, the proprietor of which had his finger in so many pies it's a wonder he ever made any razor blades at all. He came to see me about 1953 to ask if I could make him some cheese tasters, a thing like a hollow reamer which is pushed into a cheese, turned half circle, and pulled out with a sample of the cheese for tasting in the hollow. Next time he came it was for ham-boning gouges, which for me was a new departure. They resembled a curved paring gouge about 1in wide with a scale tang. He ordered two gross a time at 2/4d. each, and paid cash — which made my wife blissfully happy.

He exported to an atlas-full of countries, and not only accurately assessed my export potential but showed me how to go about it through the Board of Trade Export Services. The fact I'm writing this today — or in business at all — is entirely down to exporting in the early days.

My capacity at that time was a single room 13ft square, 4ft below ground, in which I had a ¼cwt power hammer, a cutler's frame, a 24in wet grinding wheel, a gas furnace, an anvil, a no.5 fly press and a warehouse-cum-workbench. No caravan designer could have done better. Such is youth; with this manufacturing capacity, I embarked on an export programme!

The Board of Trade (now the Department of Industry) had an office in Sheffield then, where my contact was Mr Featonby — straight as a gun barrel and patriotic as St George himself. I was naive to a fault at the time, and during our first meeting said: 'Can I be sure that what we discuss will not go any further?' His reply should go down in the annals of the Civil Service. 'Mr Iles, I can assure you that the gentlemen of the Board of Trade are beyond reproach.'

The mysteries of exporting unfold like a pack of fortune-telling cards. One never knows what's round the next corner, anything can happen and usually does. I had

read an American book on mail order, and had a go both in the UK and the USA — my slogan: 'Tools to Your Home from the Home of Tools'. But for the USA there was one almighty snag. Each parcel had to have a completed form CD3 (four pages). Forms are the curse of bureaucracy but CD3s were a nightmare. It was almost impossible to get parcels out of the country.

However, the freight side started to develop. My first export order was from Harris Scarf, a department store in Adelaide, Australia. Their resident UK buyer came to see me bringing the order. What he thought of my set-up I don't know, he had just been to Footprint Tools. I sent the order off in a tea-chest tied with electric wire.

● *Ashley at 29, bashing out a living from his 13x13ft workshop*

Some time later the postman called with a big fat registered letter. I opened it with trembling fingers and drew out $1000 in cash from Custom Woodcraft, Springfield, Illinois. Payment in advance. My capital troubles were over — I even paid my income tax. A few months later an order came from New Zealand, covering the Maori trade and the islands of the South Pacific. At the time Gracie Fields was singing the old Maori song 'Now is the hour' — and so was I.

Exporting has its moments. At first I couldn't afford a banding machine for packing-cases, and had to borrow one from a warehouse woman I knew in Calver St. When the boss' car wasn't there I would dash in and grab the machine and a coil of

banding fixed on a wire stand. One day I was taking the machine and coil back, and as I hurried across West St the coil slipped off the reel. Hundreds of yards of banding uncoiled in the road in one great mess, and stopped the traffic in one direction. Dashing into a workshop next to the Saddle Inn, I grabbed a wheelbarrow and two shovels, and returning to the scene, got a passer-by to take the other shovel. Between us we got the lot on the barrow and I wheeled it to the nearest rubbish bay. When I got back to the firm where I borrowed it, 'Don't explain,' said the woman, in between shrieks of laughter. 'I saw it all through the window, it was better than the Keystone Cops.' So I became a one-man-band exporter.

The production quantities in the Sheffield of that time were enormous. There was a grinder, about 20 years old, outworking for John Petty doing nothing but the tin-opener blade of a Scout knife. He ground thousands of them so quickly you just couldn't see anything. There was a man called Jack Ball who hired a room in Bailey lane on a first floor and started a brass foundry — on a wooden floor! He was a good moulder but the business side licked him, not the wooden floor. Ernie Gregg set up on his own in Petty's yard as a hammer man. He did anything that came along, but he had a continuous order for rubber-tapping knives for plantations. He made hundreds of thousands of them. He's still on the go, and very choosy about who he works for.

The city-centre pubs were full day and night. A man in West Street anticipated the post-war leisure boom and made a fortune — I never saw him sober. He would walk into a crowded pub and buy drinks all round, and the brandy he himself drank would supply all the St Bernards in Switzerland. He ran a van with 'Jesus Saves' emblazoned on both sides in 6in letters.

The juke box had just been introduced, but the characters in the pubs provided all the entertainment you could wish for. I particularly remember 'The Duke of Dornall'; what a man! He arrived straight out of Burton's window, in evening dress, bowler hat and cane. He was deaf and dumb and always broke. To watch him mime drinks out of people was out of this world, Chaplin couldn't have done better. Under no circumstances would he buy a drink for himself or anyone else.

Russian Edna made the rounds of the pubs every night. Her profession was the oldest one; she wore a coat, nothing else, just a coat. When negotiations reached the crucial stage she would open the coat and invariably clinch the deal.

The city was alive and buzzing like a beehive, the atmosphere thick with enterprise and challenge. When we were in Hong Kong in 1981, my wife was complaining of the hubbub, on the verge of hysteria. I got her out of it quickly by taxi to the Star Ferry to Kowloon. 'Didn't it bother you?' she asked. 'No,' I replied, 'it was just like old Sheffield.' ∎

Ornament for all 2

Fascinated but foxed by
last month's treatise on
Ornamental Turning?
Michael Foden explains
how to turn a plain lathe
to ornamental use

● *The division-plate is turned from a piece of aluminium; the indexing numbers come
from a stationer's!*

It's probably 100 years since an Ornamental Turning lathe as built by Holtzapffel, Birch and others has been made in England. They were masterpieces of engineering, but extremely cumbersome because of bulk and the treadle-operated overhead drive; most owners today have adapted their machines for electric power. You need a lot of workshop space for such a lathe, and I was anxious to devise an alternative that would get similar results, but use a much smaller overhead drive and accessories.

My design (the culmination of many months' thought) relates specifically to Coronet lathes, but all you need to adapt it for other woodturning lathes is a different motor mounting. Turners have adapted metal-turning lathes like the Myford for this type of work, but I don't know of woodturning lathe adaptations, though I wouldn't be surprised if it all hadn't been done before. An engineer's machine already has cross-slides, so it only requires an overhead drive; a much simpler conversion. Other OT-type modifications include routers or flexible drives attached to and sliding along a tool-rest, but I wanted to duplicate the cutting action of the original OT lathes, so have used cutting-frames. I feel they get better results than routers anyway.

What you need
1 — The division-plate

Once you have set this 'conversion kit' up, it's only a matter of minutes to change from ornamenting plain turnings to plain turning itself and back again.

The first ornamental essential is a dividing head and index pointer, which enables plain-threaded work to be ornamented by dividing it into equal segments. I could only find one commercially produced division-plate for woodturning lathes — it cost almost £20 and has only a dozen divisions, so as it's a simple matter to make an accurate divider on the lathe for almost nothing, I decided to make this job my first metal-turning attempt.

Cut a 6in-diameter disc out of a piece of perfectly flat ⅛in aluminium plate. Use contact glue to fix the plate as centrally as possible to a 7in plywood 'faceplate', and turn it to a perfect disc; having no metal-turning tools, I soon discovered that a HSS bowl-gouge used on its side did the job fine. Using the lathe so you can centre accurately, bore a hole for your lathe-spindle (¾in for the Coronet Elf) in the

plate with a flat bit. Make sure the central hole is correct before marking and drilling the division holes — if you ruin the spindle hole after drilling the divisions, you'll have wasted a great deal of time. Make a well-fitting wooden plug for the spindle hole you've just drilled, and use the centre of this to *very accurately* mark out with a protractor as many divisions as you want. I've found a row of 36 holes (every 10°) and a row of 24 (every 15°) give a wide choice of segment groupings. Use a drill-press if you can to drill the 8in holes on your marks. If you're really careful at this stage, it's possible to make a division-plate as accurate as a commercially made one. Attach the small self-adhesive numbered stickers you can get from stationers to the plate close to the holes for easy working, and spray it all with clear lacquer to protect the stickers in use.

The plate is fixed on the mandrel by the chuck used to turn the work, and a pointer stops the plate at the positions you want. My index pointer is a piece of spring steel drilled at one end for a 1x⅛in brass bolt, which is tapered slightly and has had the threads filed off half its length (do this on the lathe), fixed through the spring steel with a nut. The other end of the steel piece has an elongated slot for adjustment (see photo), and is held on the end-turning tool-rest with a hexagonal Allen-type screw in the tommy-bar position. Used this way, the pointer has unlimited adjustment in all directions. Tyme lathe owners can also use this method, which can easily be adopted for other makes of machine.

2 — The cross-slides

The second essential is two dovetail slides with tool-holders which can be mounted at right angles to each other. Emco make a top-slide for their Unimat 3 metal lathe and I use two of these, but there are other types on the market. If the slide has a protractor, grind it off. Drill a 2in length of round steel

bar that fits your lathe's tool-post holder, tap it down one end, and fit the slide to this through the pre-drilled hole in its base. The little necessary countersinking in the steel bar should present no problems. The top half of this lower slide's tool-holder is cut and ground away, and the remaining part drilled and tapped so the second slide can be mounted securely on it. Each slide is fixed by a single bolt so it is completely adjustable, and with this arrangement plus the available movement on the tool-post holder you will get an almost unlimited range of positions.

It's *essential* that these slides are mounted *securely* to each other and to the post. If you aren't capable of this work, get an engineer to do it for you. As a final touch, a narrow collar can be fitted over the post and adjusted so the cutter will always operate at centre height when the apparatus is placed in the tool-rest holder. It's preferable to grind a little off the top of the Coronet tool-rest holder to be sure of enough adjustment, but this may not be necessary on other machines.

3 — The cutting-frame

First I tried a Dremel drill fixed to the cross-slides to rout the ornamentation, but the results were very poor. High-speed steel fluted cutters, router bits and burrs were all tried without success. The cutting principle was incorrect for such small-scale apparatus, and eventually, I bought a watchmaker's 4in cutting frame from Chronos Ltd in St Albans. This has a ⅜in square shank, which enables it to be used horizontally or vertically. The spindle incorporates a pulley groove, and is drilled to accept a ¼in-diameter round cutter which is set at 90° to the spindle and secured by a small grub set-screw. The frame is held in the tool-holder of the upper slide and the depth and length of cut is determined by moving the two dovetail slides. A stop has

Ornament for all 2

● *The cross-slide assembly mounted on the tool-post holder, the cutting-frame held in the top slide*

to be fixed to the slide to make sure each cut is made at the same depth; a small square of brass with a channel slightly larger than the thickness of the base of the slide filed in it fits over the base, and one of the narrow edges is tapped through for a pointed-end grub set-screw. The screw tightens on to the cross-slide base and limits its movement; a small square of shim material is slipped under the set-screw before tightening to avoid marking the slide.

4 — The drive

Finally, to complete the apparatus you need a motor and overhead drive. The highly elaborate series of pulleys and counterbalance weights used by traditional OT lathes to get the correct tension on the drive belt won't be attractive to most turners, who have neither the space, the inclination nor the knowledge to set up such a system, however successful. My simple solution is a small motor fixed on a universal joint which drives the cutting-frame. My own motor is the Dremel Mototool held in the Mototool holder, which is welded on to the end of a 12x⅜in dia. steel rod. This passes at 90° through the top of a 15x¾in dia. rod, held in position by a bolt threaded into the top of the larger rod. The latter fits in the split collar on the Coronet's saddle which normally holds a back-steady. The rods are round and adjustable in two planes, so we have in effect a simple universal joint; as the saddle moves along the lathe bed, the motor moves with it, always close to the cutting frame. The Dremel chuck holds a ³⁄₃₂in spindle incorporating a ½in-diameter pulley. Finding a drive belt was difficult, and I finally settled on one made by Mamod. It's a continuous loop of finely coiled steel wire, 4in in diameter and ¹⁄₁₆in thick, and has just the right amount of stretch. These belts can be repaired if necessary by ordinary electrician's solder, though they'll last a long while if they aren't

abused; pulleys and belts are readily available from any good hobby shop. Although this belt gives a good positive drive under medium tension, it shouldn't be overstretched because it could wear the motor bearings. This lightweight drive also makes sure you keep your cutters sharp, as the belt slips and cutting stops at the slightest hint of bluntness.

If you don't have a Coronet you'll need to devise a mounting of the universal joint near to the lathe bed, and a collar welded or bolted on to the lathe saddle seems a good solution. You could use another motor than the Dremel, mounted according to its shape, but it should be very compact or you'll have operating difficulties. The cutter-frame bearings won't tolerate very high speeds; 3000 or 4000rpm is adequate. If you use a constant-speed Dremel Mototool you must regulate it with an electronic control.

This completes the set-up apart from the actual cutters. The main attraction of this unit is its compactness and versatility; although the slides are very small, they have enough travel to allow the top of a 4in-diameter box lid to be completely decorated. Furthermore, all the work is done on one lathe, using the same chuck or faceplate; simply fit the division-plate and replace the tool-rest with the slide unit.

Cutters

Originally, cutters were made from cast steel, but this is now impossible to get and unless you're prepared to buy antique tools and grind, harden and temper the steel, you can forget it. Silver steel is available in suitable sizes, but requires hardening and tempering and I have had good results with high-speed steel.

High-speed steel offcuts are often available at reasonable prices from firms specialising in router cutters and as these are already hardened and tempered, they

only require grinding to shape. Choose the right wheel or you'll find it hard going. Try the ceramic wheel which is standard on Leroy Somer bench grinders and there should be no problems. Always remember that the bench grinder is a cutting tool and the wheel should be kept sharp with a dressing stone. A grinder can be lethal if it's used carelessly, and it's imperative that the steel pieces are *well secured* before starting work.

Drill a bar down its axis to take the ¼in-diameter high-speed steel piece, cut to length. A grub-screw holds the piece firmly, or you can use a small drill chuck. Exact sizes aren't critical, but I usually start with a 1in-long piece and first grind half the diameter away to a depth of ½in. Aim to produce a perfectly flat face at the diameter line — this does require some practice! The next stage is to grind a taper along the back in line with the first grinding, which should finish about ¹⁄₂₀in thick at the tip of the cutter. Then grind each side away at an angle to ensure clearance round every edge. The final rough shaping is at the end of the cutter, which is ground to the outline you want. It's difficult not to overheat the steel when producing thin sections, but it's unlikely this will have an ill effect on the high speed steel.

The 'Goniostat'

This is a device that enables exact levels to be ground and polished. Your cutters won't be satisfactory if the levels and chamfers aren't ground accurately, and a special jig is needed as the process is impossible to complete freehand. Get hold of an alloy or Tufnol plate 4½x5½x¼in, and attach it to a metal post that fits the lathe banjo. (This is basically a miniature sanding table, not difficult to make.) Square up the sides, and

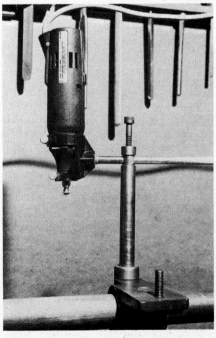

● *The Dremel Mototool held in the 'universal joint' mounting*

using the $4\frac{1}{2}$in side as a base line, mark a line in the middle at 90° and two at 30°, one either side of it. Use a $\frac{3}{8}$in-square length of brass for a pointer and cutter-holder, drilled for the high-speed steel piece and tapped for a securing grub-screw. If you fix the pointer-bar to the plate with a 3mm bolt in an elongated hole and let a nut in underneath, it's possible to adjust the cutter to the desired angle and projection. In practice, you'll only really need 30° and 90° angles, 30° for side-cutting tools and 90° for the flat-ended ones. Set a plywood sanding disc up on the lathe, faced with a good abrasive (about 150-grit); silicon carbide Liberty Green paper is excellent and is available in discs. If the table is set so it meets the sanding disc at 120°, the correct bevel will be produced. Fix small blocks to the table from the underside to keep this angle when you transfer the plate-and-bar jig and cutter to the oilstone. Fix the stone with its face in line with a flat surface, and move the jig to and fro over this surface to take the grinding marks out of the cutter on the stone. When you have a keen edge, polish the cutter on a slab of brass with flour-emery and oil, and finally on cast-iron and crocus powder. It's *essential* that the bevels are polished to perfection, not so difficult with the jig.

Materials and ideas

There isn't a large range of materials that can be successfully cut, but fortunately boxwood is ideal (and cheap enough) for trial runs. The ideal material is ivory; not many of us can afford to buy it at current prices, but it's sometimes possible to get second-hand stuff. African blackwood is the only real substitute, not cheap but within reach. Try purpleheart, partridge wood and ebony, but results aren't usually so good; when it comes down to it, you can experiment on any hard, fine-grained timber.

● *A view of the whole works. The drive-belt is a coiled steel wire loop; everything is adjustable in all directions*

Small lidded boxes are a good starting point, and I suggest you experiment on boxwood pieces before cutting expensive timbers. This will let you judge the effects of the different-shaped cutters, and get the feel of cutting speeds, rates of feed and so on. As far as trying your first patterns is concerned, common sense should prevail, and don't attempt anything too elaborate until you feel at ease with the apparatus. You'll have to compute most patterns on paper before cutting, but this should brush up your maths if nothing else!

As you become more involved in OT, you'll soon realise that engineering rather than woodworking plays an ever-increasing role, and it's important not to let this become an overriding factor and lose sight of the objective. As woodworkers, we seek the finished product, and if we have to become engineers along the way that's all to the good — it will add to our knowledge and skills. I say this because I know many people 'into' OT have become so obsessed with the mechanics of the apparatus that the finished work becomes irrelevant. There's no doubt it's a fascinating diversion from plain turning, and if you really get bitten by the bug, plain turning will become only a means to an end. I have only scratched the surface of this very complex subject, and it's up to enthusiasts to follow these leads and find out more for themselves. All the apparatus described is only basic — I leave it to you to improve on it! ∎

Addresses

● **Books** J. J. Holtzapffel, *The principles and practice of ornamental or complex turning*: Stobart & Son, 67-72 Worship St, London EC2A 2EL, 01-247 0501, or Dover reprint of 1894 edition from Constable & Co. Ltd, 10 Orange St, London WC2H 7EG, 01-930 0801/7
● **Society** of Ornamental Turners, Secretary, 17 Chichester Drive, E. Saltdean, Brighton BN2 8LD
● **Chronos** Ltd, 95 Victoria St, St Albans, Herts
● **Metal** supplies: K. R. Whiston Ltd, New Mills, Stockport, Cheshire (mail order and small orders OK)
● **Dremel** Mototool from Skil (GB) Ltd, Fairacres Ind. Est., Dedworth Rd, Windsor, Berks, (07535) 69525.

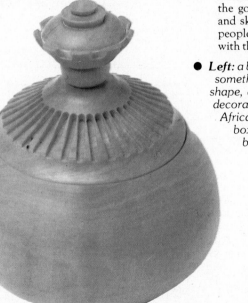

● *Left: a boxwood box, something of a vase shape, and delicately decorated; **right,** an African blackwood box with central boxwood inlay*

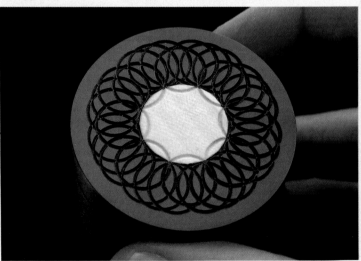

Ryoba Noko Giri

● *Oriental style for excellence in craft –* the Ryoba Noko Giri

Just about the only similarity between a regular Japanese saw and a western one is that they both cut. Tony Wood explains the difference

there are several very good reasons for it. The blade of a western saw is pushed along to make the cut, an action which imparts quite strong compression forces to the blade and hence the teeth. For this reason, a medium-hard steel has to be used, a compromise between hard steel for good edge retention and soft steel for strength. As in all compromises, the best features of each extreme are sacrificed. If a western saw were made of hard steel, it could be sharpened to perfection but the compression forces exerted on the blade during cutting would shatter it. If the blade were made from soft steel, on the other hand, it would absorb sawing shocks but go blunt very quickly. This is where the pull-stroke cutting action of Japanese saws wins hands down; because the cut is made by pulling through the wood, there are no compression forces on the blade, which in fact, is held under tension through the cutting stroke, rather like a hacksaw blade in a frame. This means there's no need for a saw-blade that can resist compression shocks, so a much harder steel can be used, which gives three major benefits:

● The blade can be made thinner for a narrower cut and greater accuracy;
● the teeth remain sharp for a very long time;
● the saw is less tiring to use, as less energy is required.

so they don't slip in the kerf, while the hardwood rip teeth have a larger angle which gives extra strength and prevents the points from digging into the wood, so the saw is easier to pull (fig. 2).

Similarly, there are softwood and hardwood versions of the crosscut teeth, which basically are shaped like tiny single-edged knives. The points score the wood, severing the tough fibres, and the remaining parts of the teeth clear away the waste from the cut. The difference this time is the angle of the bevel on the cutting edge of each tooth (fig. 3). Blade lengths of the Ryoba Noko Giri vary from 7½ to 14in, and the number of teeth per inch depends on the length of the blade. In other words, all 7½in saws have the same number of teeth per inch, whoever

L ike western woodworkers the Japanese use many different saws, each one designed for a specific purpose. The commonest Japanese saw available is probably the *Ryoba Noko Giri* (fig. 1).

The most noticeable peculiarity about the *Ryoba Noko Giri* is its shape, which reminds you of a toothed fish-slice. It hardly seems worthy of a second glance, but don't let the strange appearance put you off. Used properly, this saw will outperform any western counterpart. Another oddity about this saw is that there are teeth on both of the long edges of the blade: no, it isn't a cunning Oriental economy measure that lets you flip from one side of the blade to the other when one set wears out. A closer look reveals that the teeth on one side of the blade are different from the ones on the other. In fact, the *Ryoba Noko Giri* is the answer to many a woodworker's dream: one side is a ripsaw, the other a crosscut saw. Owning a *Ryoba Noko Giri* means that the right tool is always to hand for general sawing — no more cutting along the grain with a crosscut saw because you couldn't find the ripsaw!

The final major difference between this and a western saw is that the teeth slope backwards towards the handle, which means that the cutting stroke is the pull, not the push. This may sound a bit daft, but

The teeth

Once we've seen the *Ryoba Noko Giri*'s teeth slope in a different direction from western saws, it's worth looking at a few other interesting differences. A novel but very useful feature of the ripsaw teeth is that they are graduated in size along the length of the blade; short teeth at the heel, longer at the toe. The short teeth are used in a rapid action to start the cut (definitely safer than using your thumb). Once the cut has been started, the full length of the blade is used, the large teeth at the toe cutting extremely quickly.

Two different types of *Ryoba Noko Giri* are made, one with rip teeth for cutting softwoods and one with rip teeth for hardwoods. The softwood version has sharply angled teeth that bite deeply into the timber

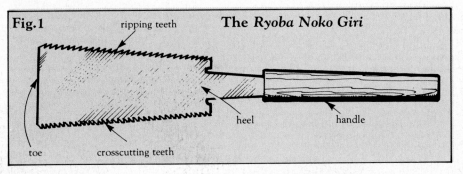

Fig.1   ripping teeth   **The *Ryoba Noko Giri***

heel   handle

toe   crosscutting teeth

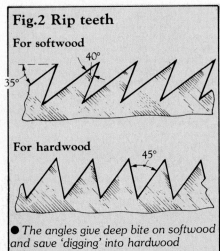

Fig.2 Rip teeth

For softwood

40°

35°

For hardwood

45°

● *The angles give deep bite on softwood and save 'digging' into hardwood*

the manufacturer. The smaller saws have finer teeth and are used for delicate cabinet work, while the larger ones' coarser teeth are more suited for joinery and general carpentry.

Saw construction

The *Ryoba Noko Giri* consists of two main parts: the blade and the handle. However, unlike western saws, the blade has a tang to which the handle is attached (fig. 4).

There are two categories of Japanese saws: machine-made and handmade. Machine-made saws are relatively cheap, costing anything up to around £35; but a good handmade saw can cost up to £200. Obviously the difference in price relates directly to the quality. The machine-made saw is made from good quality hard steel just like the handmade one, but nearly all the production processes are mechanised. A blade blank is stamped out of a sheet of forged steel and surface-ground to the correct thickness; the teeth are then stamped out and sharpened and a relatively cheap handle is attached. The only non-mechanised operation is the fixing of the handle. As you can imagine, all this is done rather quickly and so the results are good rather than brilliant.

Handmade tools, though, are a completely different story. The sawmaker takes a bar of hard steel and forges it to the rough shape and size of the blade. The width and length of the blade are arrived at in two different ways depending on the quality of the saw; on medium priced saws (between £85 and £100), a guillotine is used to crop out the shape. On higher quality tools, the sides and toe of the blade are hand-ground with water-stones to get perfect perpendicular edges for the teeth. When the blade is the correct length and width, the thickness is reduced with a very hard double-handed scraper that pares away tiny particles of metal from the surface. The blade is worked so the body of the blade is thinner than the area in which the teeth are cut, which gives a 'hollow-ground' effect and prevents the blade jamming in a cut (fig. 5).

The scraping pattern is highly critical, because as the change in thickness has to be very gradual, particularly in the region where the tang starts. Removing too much metal here would mean a saw-blade could easily snap off at the handle, but removing too little would mean the blade would bind in the cut. Achieving the correct balance between the two extremes is where the sawmaker's skill pays dividends.

After scraping, the teeth are cut and the blade is hardened. Then it is tempered by gradually raising its temperature to soften it very slightly. If this stage were omitted, the saw-blade would be too brittle for practical use. The speed of tempering controls the quality: the slower it's done, the finer the blade can be 'tuned' and the better the finished quality will be, because it's only the molecules *on the surface* of the steel that need to be softened. The steel at the core of

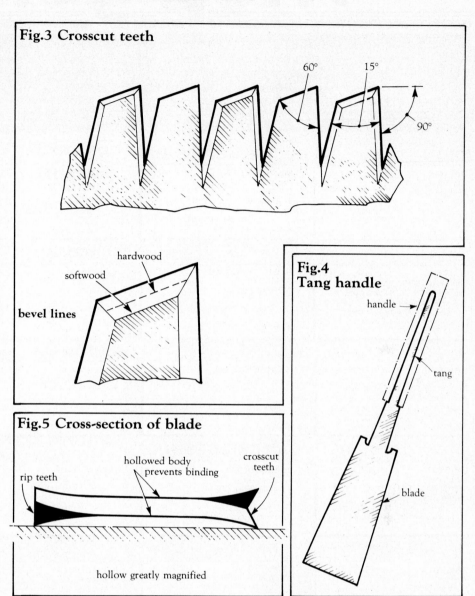

Fig.3 Crosscut teeth

60° 15° 90°

hardwood
softwood
bevel lines

Fig.4 Tang handle

handle
tang
blade

Fig.5 Cross-section of blade

rip teeth
hollowed body prevents binding
crosscut teeth

hollow greatly magnified

the blade remains as hard as the original forged bar. This mild tempering gives the blade a certain amount of flexibility because the outer steel is softer and allows the teeth to retain a good cutting edge because of the harder core-steel. Only one blade is worked at a time, the maker turning it carefully in the heat to get an even temper — for a high quality saw, this can take up to three hours. Traditionally, blades were tempered in a bath of hot sand, dipping them dozens of times until the required temper was reached. Nowadays, however, electric heating elements have taken over. There's no 'correct' temperature for tempering; the sawmakers develop an eye for the right signs, and they seldom make mistakes.

All these forging and heating operations build up considerable stresses in the blade, which could make it weak and unstable — so they're carefully removed. Stress-relieving, to give it its proper name, is a matter of delicately tapping the blade with specially designed hammers. The process is an art in itself; hit the blade too hard and you cause new stresses somewhere else, hit it too lightly and the stress doesn't go. The

actual stress-points are located by holding the blade at eye level and looking along it for different colours of refracted light. Stress-relieving can either make or ruin an expensive saw-blade, so for the high quality saws several hours can be spent just getting it right.

Sharpening comes next, and finally a handle is fitted. Handles are generally made of *Hinoki* (Japanese cypress) or *Sugi* (Japanese cedar) and are bound with rattan cane along their length. No glues are used to fit the handles; they rely on a tight push fit to stay on.

A final word. A sawmaker of high quality *Ryoba Noko Giri* comments on his products: 'Even if you use a saw every hour of every working day for five years it will still be sharp'. There's no proof to back this up, but from first impressions, it's not an idle boast.

● **Next in the series:** sharpening and using the *Ryoba Noko Giri*.

● **Woodworker** and Tony would like to thank **Roger Buse** of Roger's of Hitchin for his inspiration and help in preparing this series. Roger's, 47 Walsworth Rd, Hitchin, Herts SG4 9SU, (0462) 34177.

AVON

BATH Tel. Bath 64513
JOHN HALL TOOLS ★
RAILWAY STREET

Open: Monday-Saturday
9.00 a.m.-5.30 p.m.
H.P.W.WM.D.A.BC.

BRISTOL Tel. (0272) 741510
JOHN HALL TOOLS LIMITED ★
CLIFTON DOWN SHOPPING CENTRE
WHITELADIES ROAD
Open: Monday-Saturday
9.00 a.m.-5.30 p.m.
H.P.W.WM.D.A.BC.

BRISTOL Tel. (0272) 629092
TRYMWOOD SERVICES
2a DOWNS PARK EAST, (off North View)
WESTBURY PARK
Open: 8.30 a.m.-5.30 p.m. Mon. to Fri.
Closed for lunch 1.00-2.00 p.m.
P.W.WM.D.T.A.BC.

BRISTOL Tel. (0272) 667013
FASTSET LTD
190-192 WEST STREET
BEDMINSTER
Open: Mon.-Fri. 8.30 a.m.-5.00 p.m.
Saturday 9.00 a.m.-1.00 p.m.
H.P.W.WM.D.CS.A.BC.

BRISTOL Tel. (0272) 667013
WILLIS
157 WEST STREET
BEDMINSTER
Open: Mon.-Fri. 8.30 a.m.-5.00 p.m.
Sat. 9 a.m.-4 p.m.
P.W.WM.D.CS.A.BC.

BEDFORDSHIRE

BEDFORD Tel. (0234) 59808
BEDFORD SAW SERVICE K
39 AMPTHILL ROAD

Open: Mon.-Fri. 8.30-5.30
Sat. 9.00-4.00
H.P.A.BC.W.CS.WM.D.

BERKSHIRE

READING Tel. Littlewick Green
DAVID HUNT (TOOL 2743
MERCHANTS) LTD
KNOWL HILL, NR. READING
Open: Monday-Saturday
9.00 a.m.-5.30 p.m.
H.P.W.D.A.BC.

READING Tel. Reading 661511
WOKINGHAM TOOL CO. LTD.
99 WOKINGHAM ROAD

Open: Mon-Sat 9.00 a.m.-5.30 p.m.
Closed 1.00-2.00 p.m. for lunch
H.P.W.WM.D.CS.A.BC.

BUCKINGHAMSHIRE

MILTON KEYNES Tel. (0908)
POLLARD WOODWORKING 641366
CENTRE ★
51 AYLESBURY ST., BLETCHLEY
Open: Mon-Fri 8.30-5.30
Saturday 9.00-5.00
H.P.W.WM.D.CS.A.BC.

HIGH WYCOMBE Tel. (0494)
SCOTT SAWS LTD. 24201/33788
14 BRIDGE STREET ★

Mon.-Sat. 8.30 a.m.-6.00 p.m.

H.P.W.WM.D.T.CS.MF.A.BC.

HIGH WYCOMBE Tel. (0494)
ISAAC LORD LTD 22221
185 DESBOROUGH ROAD KE

Open: Mon-Fri 8.00 a.m.-5.00 p.m.
Saturday 9.00 a.m.-5.00 p.m.
H.P.W.D.A.

CAMBRIDGESHIRE

CAMBRIDGE Tel. (0223) 63132
D. MACKAY LTD. ★
BRITANNIA WORKS, EAST ROAD

Open: Mon.-Fri. 8.30 a.m.-1 p.m./2.00-
5.00 p.m. Sat. 8.30 a.m.-1.00 p.m.
H.P.W.D.T.CS.MF.A.BC.

CAMBRIDGE Tel. (0223) 247386
H. B. WOODWORKING K
105 CHERRY HINTON ROAD
Open: 8.30 a.m.-5.30 p.m.
Monday-Friday
8.30 a.m.-1.00 p.m. Sat.
H.P.W.WM.D.CS.A.

PETERBOROUGH Tel. (0733)
WILLIAMS DISTRIBUTORS 64252
(TOOLS) LIMITED K
108-110 BURGHLEY ROAD
Open: Monday to Friday
8.30 a.m.-5.30 p.m.
H.P.A.W.D.WH.BC.

CHESHIRE

NANTWICH Tel. Crewe 67010
ALAN HOLTHAM K★
THE OLD STORES TURNERY
WISTASTON ROAD, WILLASTON
Open: Tues.-Sat. 9.00 a.m.-5.30 p.m.
Closed Monday
P.W.WM.D.T.CS.A.BC.

CLEVELAND

MIDDLESBROUGH Tel. (0642)
CLEVELAND WOODCRAFT 813103
(M'BRO), 38-42 CRESCENT ROAD K

Open: Mon-Sat 9.15 a.m.-5.30 p.m.

H.P.T.A.BC.W.WM.CS.D.

CORNWALL

SOUTH WEST Power Tools
CORNWALL Tel. Helston (03265) 4961
HELSTON AND LAUNCESTON Launceston
(0566) 4781
H.P.W.WM.D.CS.A. K

CUMBRIA

CARLISLE Tel. (0228) 36391
W. M. PLANT
ALLENBROOK ROAD
ROSEHILL, CA1 2UT
Open: Mon.-Fri. 8.00 a.m.-5.15 p.m.
Sat. 8.00 a.m.-12.30 noon
P.W.WM.D.CS.A.

DEVON

BRIXHAM Tel. (08045) 4900
WOODCRAFT SUPPLIES E★
4 HORSE POOL STREET

Open: Mon.-Sat. 9.00 a.m.-6.00 p.m.

H.P.W.A.D.MF.CS.BC.

PLYMOUTH Tel. (0752) 330303
WESTWARD BUILDING SERVICES ★
LTD., LISTER CLOSE, NEWNHAM
INDUSTRIAL ESTATE, PLYMPTON
Open: Mon-Fri 8.00 a.m.-5.30 p.m.
Sat. 8.30 a.m.-12.30 p.m.
H.P.W.WM.D.A.BC.

PLYMOUTH Tel. (0752) 665363
F.T.B. LAWSON LTD.
71 NEW GEORGE STREET
PLYMOUTH PL1 1RB
Open: Mon.-Sat. 8.30 am-5.30 pm
H.P.W.CS.MF.A

DORSET

BOURNEMOUTH Tel. (0202) 420583
POWER TOOL SERVICES
(Sales, spares, repairs)
849-851 CHRISTCHURCH ROAD
BOSCOMBE
Open: Mon.-Fri. 9.00 a.m.-5.30 p.m.
Sat. 9.00 a.m.-5.00 p.m.
H.P.W.CS.K.A.

POOLE Tel. (0202) 686238
MACHINE SALES AND SERVICES ★
(POOLE) LTD.
23 COWLEY ROAD
NUFFIELD INDUSTRIAL ESTATE
Open: Mon.-Fri. 8.30am-5.30pm
H.P.W.WM.D.CS.A.BC.

ESSEX

LEIGH ON SEA Tel. (0702)
MARSHAL & PARSONS LTD. 710404
1111 LONDON ROAD EK

Open: 8.30 a.m.-5.30 p.m. Mon-Fri
9.00 a.m.-5.00 p.m. Sat.
H.P.W.WM.D.CS.A.

GLOUCESTER

TEWKESBURY Tel. (0684)
TEWKESBURY SAW CO. LTD. 293092
TRADING ESTATE, NEWTOWN K

Open: Mon-Fri 8.00 a.m.-5.00 p.m.
Saturday 9.30 a.m.-12.00 p.m.
P.W.WM.D.CS.

HAMPSHIRE

ALDERSHOT Tel. (0252) 334422
POWER TOOL CENTRE K
374 HIGH STREET

Open Mon-Fri 8.30 a.m.-5.30 p.m.
Sat. 8.30 a.m.-12.30 p.m.

H.P.W.WM.D.A.BC.

SOUTHAMPTON Tel. (0703)
POWER TOOL CENTRE 332288
7 BELVIDERE ROAD K★
Open Mon.-Fri. 8.30-5.30

H.P.W.WM.D.A.BC.CS.MF.

HERTFORDSHIRE

WARE K★
HEATH SAWS
16 MALTINGS
STANSTEAD ABBOTTS (near Ware) HERTS.
Open: Mon.-Fri. 8.30am-5.30pm
Sat. 8.30am-1pm. Sunday by appointment.
P.W.WM.D.CS.A.

HUMBERSIDE

GRIMSBY Tel. Grimsby (0472)
58741 Hull (0482) 26999
J. E. SIDDLE LTD. (Tool Specialists) ★
83 VICTORIA STREET
Open: Mon-Fri 8.30 a.m.-5.30 p.m.
Sat. 8.30 a.m.-12.45 p.m. & 2 p.m.-5 p.m.
H.P.A.BC.W.WMD.

HULL
HUMBERSIDE FACTORING/H.F.C.
SAW SERVICING LTD.
MAIN STREET
Open: Mon.-Fri. 8am-5pm.
Saturday 8am-12.00pm.
H.P.W.WM.D.CS.A.BC.K.

KENT

WYE Tel. (0233) 813144
KENT POWER TOOLS LTD.
UNIT 1, BRIAR CLOSE
WYE, Nr. ASFORD

H.P.W.WM.D.A.CS.

MAIDSTONE Tel. (0622) 50177
SOUTH EASTERN SAWS (Ind.) LTD. ★
COLDRED ROAD
PARKWOOD INDUSTRIAL ESTATE
Open: Mon.-Fri. 8.00 a.m.-6.00 p.m.
Sat. 9.00 a.m.-12.00 a.m.
B.C.W.CS.WM.PH.

shopguide

LANCASHIRE

PRESTON   Tel. (0772) 52951
SPEEDWELL TOOL COMPANY   **E★**
62-68 MEADOW STREET PR1 1SU
Open: Mon.-Fri. 8.30 a.m.-5.30 p.m.
Sat. 8.30 a.m.-12.30 p.m.

H.P.W.WM.CS.A.MF.BC.

MANCHESTER   Tel. (061 789)
TIMMS TOOLS   0909
102-104 LIVERPOOL ROAD   ★
PATRICROFT M30 0WZ
Weekdays 8.30 a.m.-5.30 p.m.
Sat. 9.00 a.m.-1.00 p.m.
H.P.A.W.

BLACKPOOL   Tel. (0253) 24299
FYLDE WOODTURNING SUPPLIES
222 HORNBY ROAD (BASEMENT)
BLACKPOOL FY1 4HY
9.30-5.30 Monday to Saturday.
H.P.W.WM.A.MF.C.B.C.D.

ROCHDALE   Tel. (0706) 342123/
C.S.M. TOOLS   342322
4-6 HEYWOOD ROAD   **E★**
CASTLETON
Open: Mon-Sat 9.00 a.m.-6.00 p.m.
Sundays by appointment
W.D.CS.A.BC.

LANCASHIRE   Tel. (070 681) 4931
'TODMORDEN'   ★
TOWNLEY TIMES, HAREHILL STREET
OFF BURNLEY ROAD
Open: Mon., Fri. 8.30 am-5.30 pm.
Sat. 9.00 am-1.00 pm
H.P.W.D.A.BC.

LEICESTERSHIRE

LANCASTER   Tel. (0524) 32886
LILE TOOL SHOP   **K**
43/45 NORTH ROAD
Open: Monday to Saturday
9.00 a.m.-5.30 p.m.
Wed. 9.00 a.m.-12.30 p.m.
H.P.W.D.A.

HINCKLEY   Tel. (0455) 613432
J. D. WOODWARD & CO. (POWER
TOOL SPECIALISTS)   ★
THE NARROWS, HINCKLEY
Open: Monday-Saturday
8.00 a.m.-6.00 p.m.
H.P.W.WM.D.CS.A.BC.

LINCOLNSHIRE

LINCOLN   Tel. (0522) 689369
SKELLINGTHORPE SAW SERVICES LTD.
OLD WOOD, SKELLINGTHORPE
Open: Mon to Fri 8 a.m.-5 p.m.
Sat 8 a.m.-12 p.m.
H.P.W.WM.D.CS.A.*.BC.
Access/Barclaycard

LONDON

ACTON   Tel. (01-992) 4835
A. MILLS (ACTON) LTD   ★
32/36 CHURCHFIELD ROAD W3 6ED
Open: Mon-Fri 9.00 a.m.-5.00 p.m.
Saturdays 9.00 am-1.00 p.m.
H.P.W.WM.

LONDON

LONDON   Tel. 01-723 2295-6-7
LANGHAM TOOLS LIMITED
13 NORFOLK PLACE
LONDON W2 1QJ

LONDON   Tel. (01-636) 7475
BUCK & RYAN LTD   ★
101 TOTTENHAM COURT ROAD W1P 0DY

Open: Mon.-Fri. 8.30 a.m.-5.30 p.m.
Saturday 8.30 a.m.-4.00 p.m.
H.P.W.WM.D.A.

WEMBLEY   Tel. 904-1144
ROBERT SAMUEL LTD.   (904-1147
7, 15 & 16 COURT PARADE   after 4.00)
EAST LANE, N. WEMBLEY   ★
Open Mon.-Fri. 8.45-5.15; Sat. 9-1.00
Access, Barclaycard, AM Express, & Diners
H.P.W.CS.E.A.D.

HOUNSLOW   Tel. (01-570)
Q.R. TOOLS LTD   2103/5135
251-253 HANWORTH ROAD

Open: Mon-Fri 8.30 a.m.-5.30 p.m.
Sat. 9.00 a.m.-1.00 p.m.
P.W.WM.D.CS.A.

FULHAM   Tel. (01-385) 5109
I. GRIZZARD LTD.   **E**
84a-b LILLIE ROAD, SW6 1TL
Open: Mon-Sat 9.00-5.30 p.m.
Half day Thursday

H.P.A.BC.W.CS.WM.D.

MERSEYSIDE

LIVERPOOL   Tel. (051-207) 2967
TAYLOR BROS (LIVERPOOL) LTD   **K**
195-199 LONDON ROAD
LIVERPOOL L3 8JG
Open: Monday to Friday
8.30 a.m.-5.30 p.m.
H.P.W.WM.D.A.BC.

MIDDLESEX

RUISLIP   Tel. (08956) 74126
ALLMODELS ENGINEERING LTD.   **E★**
91 MANOR WAY

Open: Mon-Sat 9.00 a.m.-5.30 p.m.

H.P.W.A.D.CS.MF.BC.

SOMERSET

CROWMARSH   Tel. (0491) 38653
MILL HILL SUPPLIES   **E★**
66 THE STREET
Open: Mon.-Fri. 9.30 a.m.-5.00 p.m.
Thurs. 9.30 a.m.-7.00 p.m.
Sat. 9.30 a.m.-1.00 p.m.
P.W.D.CS.MF.A.BC.

NORFOLK

NORWICH   Tel. (0603) 898695
NORFOLK SAW SERVICES
DOG LANE, HORSFORD
Open: Monday to Friday
8.00 a.m.-5.00 p.m.
Saturday 8.00 a.m.-12.00 p.m.
H.P.W.WM.D.CS.A.

KINGS LYNN   Tel. (0553) 2443
WALKER & ANDERSON (Kings Lynn) LTD.   **K**
WINDSOR ROAD, KINGS LYNN
Open: Monday to Saturday
7.45 a.m.-5.30 p.m.
Wednesday 1.00 p.m. Saturday 5.00 p.m.
H.P.W.WM.D.CS.A.

NORWICH   Tel. (0603) 400933
WESTGATES WOODWORKING   Tx
61 HURRICANE WAY,   975412
NORWICH AIRPORT INDUSTRIAL ESTATE
Open: 9.00 a.m.-5.00 p.m. weekdays
9.00 a.m.-12.30 Sat.
P.W.WM.D.BC.   **K**

KING'S LYNN   Tel. 07605 674
TONY WADDILOVE, UNIT A   ★
HILL FARM WORKSHOPS
GREAT DUNHAM, (Nr. Swaffham)
Open: Tues. — Fri. 10.00 a.m. to 5.30 p.m.
Sat. 9.00 a.m. to 5.00 p.m.
H.P.W.D.T.MF.A.BC.*

NOTTINGHAMSHIRE

NOTTINGHAM   Tel. (0602) 225979
POOLEWOOD   and 227064/5
EQUIPMENT LTD.   (06077) 2421 after hrs
5a HOLLY LANE, CHILLWELL
Open: Mon-Fri 9.00 a.m.-5.30 p.m.
Sat. 9.00 a.m. to 12.30 p.m.
P.W.WM.D.CS.A.BC.

OXON

WITNEY   Tel. (0993) 3885,
TARGET TOOLS (SALES, & 72095 OXON
TARGET HIRE & REPAIRS)   ★
TOOLS SWAIN COURT
STATION INDUSTRIAL ESTATE
Open: Mon.-Sat. 8.00 a.m.-5.00 p.m.
24 hour Answerphone
BC.W.M.A.

SHROPSHIRE

TELFORD   Tel. Telford (0952)
ASLES LTD   48054
VINEYARD ROAD, WELLINGTON   **EK★**

Open: Mon. Fri. 8.30 a.m.-5.30 p.m.
Saturday 8.30 a.m.-4.00 p.m.
H.P.W.WM.D.CS.BC.A.

SOMERSET

TAUNTON   Tel. (0823) 85431
JOHN HALL TOOLS   ★
6 HIGH STREET

Open Monday-Saturday
9.00 a.m.-5.30 p.m.
H.P.W.WM.D.CS.A.

TAUNTON   Tel. 0823 443766
CUTWELL TOOLS LTD.   ★
CREECH HEATHFIELD
SOMERSET TA3 5EQ
Mon-Fri 9 a.m.-5 p.m. and also by appointment.
P.W.WM.A.D.CS.

STAFFORDSHIRE

STOKE-ON-TRENT   Tel: 0782-48171
F.W.B. (PRODUCTS) LTD.
WHELDON ROAD, STAFFS.
Open: Mon.-Fri. 8.30am-5.30pm
Saturday 8.30am-12.30pm
H.P.W.WM.A.D.

SUFFOLK

IPSWICH   Tel. (0473) 40456
FOX WOODWORKING   **KE★**
142-144 BRAMFORD LANE
Open: Tues., Fri., 9.00 a.m.-5.30 p.m.
Sat. 9.00 a.m.-5.00 p.m.

H.P.W.WM.D.A.B.C.

SUFFOLK
LOCKWOOD WOODWORKING MACHINERY
WHITE GATES BUNGALOWS
THE COMMON, MELLIS
NEAR EYE/DISS IP23 8DY Tel: (037983) 8126
Open: Mon., Wed., Thurs. Fri. 8am-8pm.
Tues. & Sat. 8 am-5pm.
Lathe demos every Saturday morning.
We cover both Norfolk and Suffolk.
H.P.W.D.A.

SUSSEX

ST. LEONARD'S-ON-SEA   Tel.
DOUST & MONK (MONOSAW)-(0424)
25 CASTLEHAM ROAD   52577

Open: Mon.-Fri. 8.00 a.m.-5.30 p.m.
Most Saturdays 9.00 a.m.-1.00 p.m.
H.P.W.WM.D.CS.A.

BOGNOR REGIS   Tel. (0243) 863100
A. OLBY & SON (BOGNOR REGIS) LTD.
"TOOLSHOP," BUILDERS MERCHANT
HAWTHORN ROAD   **K**
Open: Mon-Thurs 8 a.m.-5.15 p.m. Fri.
8 a.m.-8 p.m. Sat 8 a.m.-12.45 p.m.
H.P.W.WM.D.T.C.A.BC.

WORTHING   Tel. (0903) 38739
W. HOSKING LTD (TOOLS &   **KE★**
MACHINERY)
28 PORTLAND RD, BN11 1QN
Open: Mon.-Sat. 8.30 a.m.-5.30 p.m.
Closed Wednesday
H.P.W.WM.D.CS.A.BC.

TYNE & WEAR

NEWCASTLE   Tel. (0632) 320311
HENRY OSBOURNE LTD.   **E★**
50-54 UNION STREET

Open: Mon-Fri 8.30 a.m.-5.00 p.m.

H.P.W.D.CS.MF.A.BC.

YORKSHIRE

BOROUGHBRIDGE   Tel. (09012)
JOHN BODDY LTD   2370
FINE WOOD & TOOL STORE   ★
RIVERSIDE SAWMILLS
Open: Mon.-Thurs. 8.00 a.m.-6.00 p.m.
Fri. 8.00am-5.00pm Sat. 8.00am-4.00pm
H.P.W.WM.D.T.CS.MF.A.BC.

SHEFFIELD   Tel. (0742) 441012
GREGORY & TAYLOR LTD   **KE**
WORKSOP ROAD
Open: 8.30 a.m.-5.30 p.m.
Monday-Friday
8.30 a.m.-12.30 p.m. Sat.
H.P.W.WM.D.

HARROGATE   Tel. (0423) 66245/
MULTI-TOOLS   55328
158 KINGS ROAD   **K★**

Open: Monday to Saturday
8.30 a.m.-6.00 p.m.
H.P.W.WM.D.A.BC.

shopguide

WOOD SUPPLIERS

WOOD SUPPLIERS

610

Classified Advertisements

All classified advertisements under £25.00 must be pre-paid: Cheques/PO made payable to A.S.P. Ltd. (WW). **Private and trade rate** *46p per word (VAT inclusive) minimum £6.90.* **Display box rates s.c.c. £8 (minimum 2.5×1).** *All advertisements are inserted in the first available issue.*
Copy to Classified Dept. (W.W.), A.S.P. Ltd., 1 Golden Square, London W.1. There are no re-imbursements for cancellations.

Telephone Andrea Smith 01-437 0626

FOR SALE

WOODCARVING tools

LARGEST STOCK IN EUROPE

Ashley Iles & Henry Taylor
Arkansas Bench & Slip Stones
Strops & Strop Paste
Bench Screws, Carvers' Vices

WOODTURNING tools

Complete range of
Henry Taylor & Ashley Iles
handled or unhandled

send 40p in stamps for illustrated catalogue

ALEC TIRANTI LTD
70 High St, Theale, Reading, Berks RG7 5AR
21. Goodge Place, London W1.

Eric Tomkinson Woodturner

Lathes, Bandsaws, Grinders, Woodturning tools & chucks, screw boxes, peppermills, saltmills, coffee grinders, barometers, lighters, hourglasses, quartz clock movements, circular tiles & clock faces, cheese domes, sealers & polishes, fast and efficient mail order service + competitive prices. S.A.E. for catalogue.
Shop Open: 9-5 Mon.-Sat.

BARCLAYCARD VISA

ERIC TOMKINSON, 86 Stockport Road, Cheadle, Cheshire SK8 2AT. Tel: 061-491-1726.

THE FINEST SELECTION ON DISPLAY IN SCOTLAND!

WOODWORKING & METALWORKING MACHINERY POWER TOOLS HAND TOOLS

THE SAW CENTRE

HIRE OR BUY!

OPEN
Mon - Fri
8am - 5pm
Sat 9am - 1pm

Visit our NEW SHOWROOM at EGLINTON TOLL GLASGOW
Tel: 041-429 4444/4374, Telex: 777886 SAWCO G
Also at, 38 Haymarket Terrace, Edinburgh EH12 5JZ. Tel: 031-337 5555

SAMUEL COULTON
fine hand made clocks
High quality hand made pendulum clock movements
Designed to complement the work of those fellow craftsmen for whom only the best will do. Individually made to order. Send £2.00 for detailed colour brochure.
Samuel Coulton Clocks, Lower Damgate Farm, Stanshope, Nr. Ashbourne, Derbyshire.
Tel: (033527) 367.

THE WHISTON CATALOGUE
Nuts, bolts, screws, washers, bar materials. In brass, alloy, steel, stainless steel, P.T.F.E., nylon, Tufnol, sheet material, electrical and mechanical items. We could go on and on! Better to send for free catalogue No. 114 and see for yourself.
K. R. Whiston Ltd., Dept. WW, New Mills, Stockport, Cheshire. Phone: 0663 42028.

LERVARD WORKBENCH £130, Ebac mini seasoner £375. Sperber chainsaw mill £700. Tel: Dorking 886933 (Evenings).

ARUNDEL LATHE 33" bed K450. Accessories, tools, timber and extras £390. Tel: Stevenage 62829.

£50 MINIMUM Norris/Spiers planer, unusual Stanley models, quality braces. Free comprehensive list (0492) 49019.

EBAC kilns Mini and Minor. Also timber stock. Tel: 0222 861584.

CORONET LATHE with bowl rest and faceplate. New, unused, £120. Stanger 096-93 594 (North Yorkshire).

FOR SALE: Kity, planer/thicknesser 636 £480. DeWalt bandsaw BS1310 £130. Mr. André Chasterman, 69 Madley Road, London W5.

PRIVATE COLLECTION books, carpentry, joinery, many antiquarian. SAE list. Reeves, Quarry Road, Burniston, Scarborough. 0723 870267.

STARTRITE 12" TA sawbench £475. DeWalt 6" bandsaw £160. 16 boxwood chisels and gouges £35. 12 carving tools £15. 6 gravers and 4 stones £20. Dorking (0306) 888456.

WOODWORKER JAN. 1950 Oct. 1971 inclusive. Feb. 1976 May 1986 plus 20 pre-1950. All perfect. Offers. Phone 0985 215288. After 6pm.

INDIAN ROSEWOOD, 100 pieces, 19" × 1½" × 1½", £150, collected. Tel: 0246 — 74608. Evenings. Also some Partridgewood.

FOR ALL SUPPLIES FOR THE
Craft of Enamelling
ON METAL
Including
LEAD-FREE ENAMELS
PLEASE SEND 2 × 10p STAMPS FOR FREE CATALOGUE, PRICE LIST AND WORKING INSTRUCTIONS

W. G. BALL LTD.
ENAMEL MANUFACTURERS

Dept. W. LONGTON
STOKE-ON-TRENT
ST3 1JW

CLOCKMAKERS
Extensive range of very competitively priced German quartz clock movements, (including standard quartz, pendulum, mini-pendulum, chining, striking and insertion movements). Large selection of quality dials, chapter rings, hands, bezels, clock plans and weather instruments. *Please send 25p stamps for 20 page catalogue.*
Bath Clock Company (Dept. W), 13 Welton Road, Radstock, Bath.

WOOD TURNERS SUPPLIES
Tudor Craft, Jung Hans clock movements, 20 different hands to choose from, barometers, weather stations, cutlery, jewellery box lids, pepper/salt/nutmeg mills, coffee grinders, ceramic tiles, new range which include hand painted tiles. Our service is extremely fast, friendly and competitive — give us a try. Send 30p in stamps to:
Tudorcraft, 100 Little Sutton Lane, Four Oaks. Sutton Coldfield, W. Midlands B75 6PG. Tel: 021 308 1193
For illustrated catalogue.

HARRISON GRADUATE and JUBILEE Wood Turning Lathes For Sale,
Contact the specialists
L.R.E. MACHINERY & EQUIPMENT Co.
15 Upwood Road, Lowton, Warrington WA3 2RL.
Tel: (0942) 728208 day or night

TO FILL THIS SPACE - PHONE 01-437-0626 COME AND JOIN THE CROWD

BANKRUPT STOCK
Sandvik circular saw blades tungsten tipped.
5", 5½", 6" .... £4.00 each
6½", 8¼" .... £6.00 each
½" to 1⅜" bore any size.
P&P £1 extra per order.
Tel: 01 672 7776
Hannett, 1A Links Road, Tooting, London SW17 9ED.

LACE BOBBIN turning blanks. Extensive range of exotics, Ivory, lathes, miniature tools, sundries, lace supplies. SAE J. Ford, 5 Squirrels Hollow, Walsall WS7 8YS.

USERS AND COLLECTORS tools for sale at the Old Craft Tool Shop, 15 High Street, Whitton, Middx. Telephone 01-755 0441.

CORONET UNIVERSAL LATHE, end turning root, child chuck, longhole borer, grindstone, planer, heavy tool kit. £650. Wilmot 098985 — 233.

READ ON FOR MORE CLASSIFIED IN WOODWORKER

611

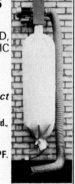
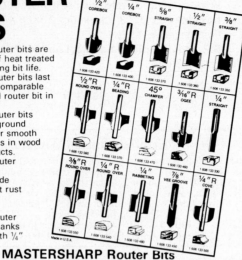

612

614

616

WOODWORKER

design . . . craft . . . and the love of wood
August 1986   Vol. 90   No. 1113

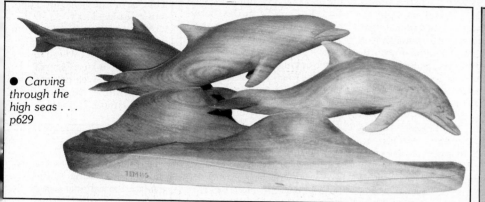

● Carving through the high seas . . . p629

PROJECTS

Make them 'off the page'

626 Jacobean hi-fi
A solid oak cabinet for an up-to-date function. *Ron Hicks*

629 Dolphin School
A chance to reproduce a Show gold prizewinner. *Terry Moss*

672 Table portable
Turning your hand-held saw into an accurate table tool. *John Kitto*

680 Turning green
Natural-edge bowls in unseasoned wood with step-by-step colour pictures. *Lech Zielinski*

685 Art ducko 2
Decoys in the spirit of the American folk tradition. *Alan and Gill Bridgewater*

690 The garden workshop
This '*Bonsai* centre' is excellent for any garden task. *Richard Blizzard*

On the cover: Bristol beauties by **G. Evans, Edward Hopkins, Nigel Short, Nicholas Packer** and **Alan Fell**; pp632 and 639. **Photos Colin Wilson**

REGULARS

618 This month News and views

619 Shoptalk products, services

623 Timberline Timber market movements

648 Books Toymaking, turning . . .

655 Guild notes Courses, news, and a special offer

661 Letters Get your own back

669 Advertiser's index

674 Bob Wearing's workshop Pulley trouble

674 Woodworking wheeze A cabinet-scraper holder. *Glyn Condick*

675 Question box Oxford frames, cutting saw teeth, bleaching . . .

631 Workbench of the future
Time's running out — 31 August's the closing date for our enticing competition!

632 Bristol 86
The Show which matters most went to the West Country, and this is (some of) what was there. *Adrian Booth*

639 Bristol 86 — Squares and Rounds
The entries to our chess-board competition were such a high standard, we just couldn't help giving you a few inside stories.

644 The grand furniture saga: 7
Flemish and Baroque influences spread through Europe, and the 'auricular' style skirts the edges of grotesquerie. *Vic Taylor*

649 Course fishing
What's a weekend course got to offer the restorer with more enthusiasm than experience? *Kerry Fowler*

650 JAPAN 5 Double time
Looking after two-edged Japanese saws, including sharpening: yes, you can do it! *Tony Wood*

653 Far-flung craft
Sensible, quality woodwork is alive and thriving on the Atlantic coast of Donegal. One man's account of his life and business. *Phil Townsend*

656 Tools of the trade 4
Chisels: workshop testing the best on the market, and seeing which ones really rate. *David Savage*

665 Tales out of steel
Making your mark was something the Sheffield toolmakers never did — they got a skilled marksmaker! *Ashley Iles*

667 Machining wood — safely
A Health & Safety officer spells out the letter and the spirit of the safety laws — the last (and first!) word in our series. *Charles Horsefield*

682 Art ducko 1
We take a two-sided look at the burgeoning art of decoy carving, starting with the man who's taking a lead in making it grow. *Michael Foden. See also Projects*

Editor Aidan Walker
Deputy editor John Hemsley
Editorial assistant Kerry Fowler
Senior advertisement manager Paul Holmes
Advertisement manager Trevor Pryer
Graphics Jeff Hamblin
Technical illustrator Peter Holland
Guild of Woodworkers John Hemsley, Kerry Fowler

Editorial, advertisements and Guild of Woodworkers
Golden Square, London W1R 3AB, telephone 01-437 0626

Unfortunately we cannot accept responsibility for loss of or damage to unsolicited material. We reserve the right to refuse or amend advertisements, and regret we cannot guarantee the bone fides of advertisers.

ABC
UK circulation
Jan-Dec 85
28,051

Back issues and subscriptions Infonet Ltd, 10-13 Times House, 9 Marlowes, Hemel Hempstead, Herts HP1 1BB; telephone Hemel Hempstead (0442) 48434

Subscriptions per year UK £16.90; overseas outside USA (accelerated surface post) £21.00, USA (accelerated surface post) £38, airmail £48

UK trade SM Distribution Ltd, 16-18 Trinity Gardens, London SW9 8DX; telephone 01-274 8611

North American trade Bill Dean Books Ltd, 151-49 7th Avenue, PO Box 69, Whitestone, New York 11357; telephone 1-718-767-6632

Printed in Great Britain by Ambassador Press Ltd, St. Albans, Herts
Mono origination Multiform Photosetting Ltd, Cardiff
Colour origination Derek Croxson Ltd, Chesham, Bucks
© Argus Specialist Publications Ltd 1986
ISSN 0043 776X

Argus Specialist Publications Ltd
Golden Square, London
W1R 3AB; 01-437 0626

Woodworker This month

The designer salesperson

Summertime is the time when students of furniture design and making rear their heads and show their work. It looks like an interesting summer this time round; we'll have detailed reports about what's been going on in the next two issues.

But meanwhile, there are some interesting developments we can trace, mainly in the business orientation of college students, and of college teaching. **Rycotewood College**, one of the acknowledged leaders in furniture craft and design education, mounted a Retrospective exhibition from 6-15 June, showing the work of some of the more successful designer/makers who have been at Rycotewood since 1974; and very fine work it was too, most of it.

Even more interesting was the 6 June one-day seminar, grandly entitled 'The furniture designer/maker in a modern industrial society', to which many of the well-known names in this surprisingly small world had brought their faces.

'You're either a furniture maker or a businessman', said **Sandy Mackilligin**, ex-Edward Barnsley apprentice and head of Wood, Metal and Plastics at Brighton Polytechnic; 'I don't think the two cohabit in one person.' That was his opinion, and it was clearly not shared by many of the assembled company; despite his later qualification and modification of the statement, Mr Mackilligin's position still holds some sway, in

or out of Rycotewood. The teachers of that college, to their credit, are keen to promote the idea that you can make money (not just a living), and still be fresh, creative, and enthusiastic; but there are many makers of stunningly beautiful furniture who are still struggling for their crust after all these years.

'I'm not a furniture maker,' said **Rupert Williamson**, whose work is outstanding in its luminous and elegant beauty (WW/Apr 85); 'I'm just an artist who happens to make furniture.' That wasn't an arrogant statement, because Rupert isn't an arrogant person — it was more self-deprecating than anything. But the idea showed through — if you have an art, you mustn't prostitute it by making any money out of it, or worse still, to be seen to *want* to make money out of it, or worse yet, to actually *enjoy* making money out of it!

Meanwhile, *Woodworker* contributor **Luke Hughes**, ('Woodworkers making a living', WWs/1984 & 85), is getting set to make a very decent living, and very nice furniture, and a name for himself on top of it all. Why? Because he's got a good business head, and he doesn't think money is a dirty word. He's chock-full of ideas for beautiful pieces, and he's at the point where he can use the systems he's set up to keep some ready cash coming in while he and his colleagues (they all earn the same) make the furniture they want to make.

He's not alone, of course; there's hundreds of you out there, grafting away making

lovely stuff, and many of you with wizard commercial wheezes on top. Much of what you do and the way you do it must be down to luck (**David Lindley** Furniture's production manager. **Tony Milsom**, described one of their 'moneyspinners' — a water-coloured stationery range that's selling like hot cakes at a handsome profit), because where you can get your capital often depends on who you know.

But that is still no excuse for you to sit in your freezing workshop and complain you can't make a living because no one buys your stuff. How can they buy it if they don't know who and where you are and what you make?

Which brings us back to Colleges. It's interesting that some put great emphasis on photographing students' work, and others barely seem to recognise the fact that it may be useful to some outside people to have pictures . . . which in turn would help the students themselves . . . like the magazines of this world, for instance?

So if you're making quality furniture that isn't selling and you're wondering why, take a close look at your operation. How much are you *really* considering the business angle? How good is your photography, your stationery, your awareness of what the press can do for you? Getting hard-headed doesn't mean getting thick-headed; it may just make the difference between whether the world gets the benefit of your creativity or not. Yes?

Tip-off

'Home Cash' is a new BBC2 series starting in the autumn. They're on the cadge for 'good, money-saving ideas'.

Any parsimonious tips, from putting up shelves to total face-lifts; or how and where to buy tools and materials, will be gratefully received by producer Erica Griffiths, Rm 902, BBC, Villiers House, Ealing, London W5 2PA.

School report

The Certificate of Pre-Vocational Education (CPVE) is the latest in national awards, introduced by the Business & Technician Education Council and the City and Guilds of London Institute.

It is designed for students after secondary education, to 'develop the skills, knowledge and attitudes . . . essential for adult life' like using lathes and computer keyboards.

CPVE is already being piloted with Youth Training Schemes, and prospective employers are urged to work with local schools to ensure skills right for the area are taught.

We would like to know your opinions on the CPVE and the new GCSE (General Certificate of Secondary Education); if you're involved in woodworking education, or if you're a woodworking employer, tell us what you think.
● Please mark letters 'Education', *Woodworker*, 1 Golden Square, London W1R 3AB.
● A free leaflet on the CPVE is available from Sales, City and Guilds, 76 Portland Place, London W1N 4AA.

Showtime!

We're approaching those mystical dates in the woodworkers' calendar when tools are abandoned, chairs left legless and doors unhinged . . .

The **London Woodworker Show**, 23-26 Oct, is at Alexandra Pavilion where you'll see the best in machinery and products.

Have you entered the competition categories yet? There's special prizes to be won too . . .
● **Argus Specialist Exhibitions, Wolsey House, Wolsey Road, Hemel Hempstead, Herts HP2 4SS, (0422) 41221.**

● *Luke Hughes' console table and 'bull's-eye mirror*

● *One of Luke's range of blanketchests with luscious veneered panels*

Diary

Guild courses are shown by an asterisk (*); for further details see the Guild pages.

June

21-Aug 31 The Forest of Dean sculptures plus photographic exhibition at the Arnolfini Gallery, Bristol. **See This Month**

July

5-Aug 2 Endgrain exhibition Peter Kuh, Arts Centre, Exeter, (0392) 21971

26-Aug 30 Furniture from Rycotewood College Cheltenham Art Gallery (0285) 61566

27 E. W. Godwin Centenary 20th century Furniture Designs, V&A Museum, London SW7

28-29 Crafts at Whatton House Loughborough

August

14-Sept 10 Mike Scott Wood-Works Exhibition, The Craft Centre and Design Gallery, The Headrow, Leeds LS1 3AB (0532) 462485

31-Sept 21 Furniture and Screens Exhibition Lucinda Leech, Charles Wickham, Michael Dunwell; Old Town Hall, Bampton, Oxon

September

5-Oct 4 Guy Taplin carved birds exhibition British Crafts Centre, 43 Earlham St, London WC2H 9LD, 01-836 6993

6-19 Oct The Forest, exhibition, Southampton Gallery

6-7 Decorative techniques Ian Hosker*

7-9 DIY '86 Novotel Exhibition Centre, London W6

23-25 Timber Build '86 Westminster Exhibition Centre, Royal Horticultural Halls, London SW1

27 Hand Veneering Bob Grant*

October

2-3 French polishing Charles Cliffe*

5-9 Building '86 Earls Court, London

11 Wood-machining Ken Taylor*

13-18 International Creative Marquetry Show The Corn Exchange, Ipswich. Contact 63 Church Lane, Sproughton, Ipswich IP8 3AY

16-22 Chelsea Crafts Fair Old Town Hall, London SW3

23-26 London Woodworker Show Alexandra Pavilion, London N22

November

Woodmex 86 Woodworking equipment exhibition, NEC Birmingham, contact 01-486 1951

Erratum

In March's Shoptalk we gave the wrong telephone number for Mick O'Donnell's woodturning courses. The correct number is **084 785 605**; apologies.

Art in the raw

If you go down to the woods today — more precisely to the Forest of Dean — there'll be surprises in the shape of Sound Sculptures and the occasional Cathedral Window. These are just some of the fruits of the six sculptors commissioned to contribute to the landscape.

The project not only includes the *in situ* sculptures and workshops, but an exhibition entitled 'The Forest' at Southampton Gallery, 6 Sept-19 Oct. It's complemented by an **Earthlife** exhibition and screening of the film *The Emerald Forest*, 1-6 July and 5-10 August.

The sculptures will be photographed, and the pictures will be at the Arnolfini Gallery, Bristol, 21 June-31 August.
● Martin Orrom (0272) 713471 or Louise Cogman (0272) 299191

Striking lucky Happy **Mike Collins**, between Mike Warner and Jim Wilson of **Solent Tools**, receives the Emco spindle moulder he won in the Bristol Woodworker Show prize draw. He was at the Show looking for some machinery! Many thanks, Solent . . .

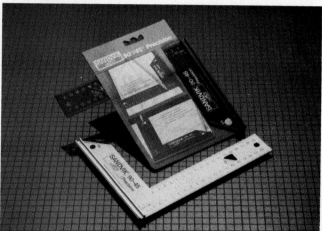

Sandvik are trying hard in the UK, with a whole range of up-rated and improved products. **Top**, the 'tool-box saw' has a 14in blade with 8ppi, the teeth designed for both crosscut and rip. Depends what sort of toolbox you use, of course, but it looks like a handy little site-tool, and no one could complain at £5.91. **Middle**, the 9045 all-steel squares are new to the UK, made of *one piece* of steel and marked in both imperial and metric. Three sizes and two finishes; from £7.49 to £9.99. **Above**, a new version of their sliding-jaw steel cramps — these 'F' cramps use one piece of steel for the main arm, and the claim is they're lighter and stronger than ever. Six sizes, from £9.76 for the 80x160mm to £22.98 for the 100x600mm.
● Sandvik UK, Manor Way, Halesowen, W. Midlands B62 8QZ, 021-550 4700

Shoptalk

The *Woodworker Manual of Finishing and Polishing* by Charles Cliffe — our own Guild teacher and 'Question box' expert — is available in a new edition. It sold like hot cakes last time round, so don't delay; a highly useful little handbook at £2.50.
● Argus Books, Wolsey House, Wolsey Rd, Hemel Hempstead, Herts HP2 4SS, (0422) 41221

Ronseal is now available in aerosol spray cans, designed for tricky jobs like wicker furniture, mouldings, louvre doors or for touching up damage. Available in gloss or satin, each can covers about 1½ sq m and costs £2.99 in.c VAT.
●Sterling Roncraft, Chapeltown, Sheffield S3D 4YP, (0742) 467171

Buy a Sjöberg 1422 workbench and get a **free holdfast** worth £25. That's the limited-period offer from BriMarc to promote this model, costing £199.95 inc. VAT.
● BriMarc, Kineton Rd, Southam, Warwicks CV33 0DR, (0926 81) 2044

A wide range of **cordless tools** has just been launched by Black & Decker Professional, who see them being most useful in non-plug-in situations! The nine-tool range runs from a 6-cell 10mm single speed reversing drill at £80+VAT to an 8-cell 10mm reversing adjustable clutch Scrudrill at £140+VAT, and includes a cordless jigsaw at £135+VAT (each with charger and kit box).
● B&D Professional, Westpoint, The Grove, Slough, Berks. SL1 1QQ, (0753) 74277

In our June issue a mistake crept into the advertisement for Alan Holtham's **Old Stores Turnery**. We apologise for the wrong address that somehow got in there; the correct one is The Old Stores Turnery, Wistaston Road, Willaston, Nantwich, Cheshire, (0270) 67010

What Workmate did for manual DIY, Powermate could do for power tools. It's a diecast aluminium **workstation** for holding a range of portable power tools, from circular saw to drill-stand. Recommended price is £69.99; fittings and accessories are extra.
● Meritcraft, Martindale Industrial Estate, Hawks Green, Cannock, Staffs, WS11 2XN, (05435) 73462

An inexpensive mobile ½hp **dust extraction** unit. Neat and compact, it's mounted on castors and costs £199.70 inc. VAT; carriage £14. Ring for local stockists.
● Fercell Engineering Ltd, Unit 60, Swaislands Dve, Crayford Industrial Est, Crayford, Kent, DA1 4HU, Crayford 53131

Those awkward 8x4s will be easier to carry with this new gadget; the Carrymate will also be good for doors. Made in sheet steel, it has a **carrying lip** with non-slip lining, so the 25mm lip will hold a 2in door (it's not U-shaped) or up to five sheets of 4mm ply; £14.50 inc. VAT and p&p.
● Williams Mastercraft, The Workshop, Viney Rd, Lymington, Hants SO41 8FF, (0590) 76059

More accurate electric drilling is promised by a novel range of **power bits** with brad points from A. Levermore & Co. The company's Irwin range, heat-treated the full length, is available in 13 sizes from 6-25mm. Levermore don't recommend retail prices, but say their quality products are in the upper-middle to top bracket.
● A. Levermore, 24 Endeavour Way, London SW19 8UH, 01-946 9882

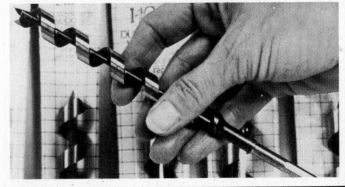

A novel **carving machine** that will easily repeat complicated patterns has just been launched by its British designer Peter Booker. A Makita router in a steel tube box frame is hand-controlled to follow horizontal and vertical contours of the original pattern.

Peter, who has a keen interest in musical instruments, claims violin fronts and backs can be completed in a quarter of the conventional time and to very fine limits. The machine cuts in any direction, and will carve shapes up to a maximum of 30x21in and 9in deep. So it can be used for repeat carving of three-dimensional statues and decoy ducks, or for decorative chairbacks and guitar fronts. It will also cut mortises and tenons, and dovetails.

Peter Booker has a long career in pattern-making, and developed his machine when he had difficulty buying a suitable repeat carver.

● The 'Re-Peter Machine' costs £1254 ex-works; Freepost NC 774, Wortham Woodcraft, Union Lane, Wortham Ling, Diss, Norfolk IP22 1BR

A EG claim their new rechargeable **battery screwdriver** will drive at least 120 no. 5x¾in screws on one charge. Lightweight and reversible, the AS6RL costs £69.50+VAT, and takes an hour to charge.

● AEG (UK) Ltd, 217 Bath Rd, Slough, Berks SL1 4AW, (0753) 872101

D ominion has upped the specification on its heavy duty 12x7in ES combined **planer/thicknesser**; it now has a three-knife cutter-block. Price at £2792+VAT ex-works remains the same as the two-knife model.

● Dominion Machinery Co. Ltd, Denholmgate Rd, Hipperholme, Halifax, West Yorkshire HX3 8JG, (0422) 202258

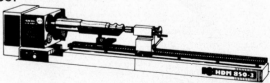

UNRIVALLED POWER AT UNBEATABLE PRICES

WITH EMCO'S SUMMER MADNESS SPECIAL OFFERS

Machine room versatility is valuable time and money as you know, so EMCO have made it possible for you to satisfy your machining needs at a fraction of the normal cost. Our special summer madness offer means you get a super value machine stand or sliding table or circular saw attachment — free when you buy a woodlathe, Rex 2000 or Spindle Moulder. Buy an EMCO Star 2000 woodworker and you're entitled to a Planer/thicknesser attachment at only half price — yes half price. You pay only £240 inc. VAT.

When you buy EMCO, the best cost less. You'll benefit from years of quality EMCO Engineering and innovative design. EMCO still lead the way in woodworking machinery offering superb value for money.

Emco Rex 2000
Basic Model

DB6 Woodlathe £475 + VAT
FREE MACHINE STAND WORTH £112.70

Star 2000 Universal Woodworker £735 + VAT.
Half price planer/thicknesser

TF65 Spindle Moulder £450 + VAT
FREE SLIDING TABLE WORTH £112.70

Illustrated above
FREE
Circular saw attachment inc. rip fence sawblade extension set + additional bearing worth £256.45 inc. VAT

To find out more about the EMCO range and special offers, just clip the coupon for your free colour brochure.

emco

FOR FURTHER INFORMATION WRITE TO

SOLENT TOOLS LTD.
267 LONDON ROAD,
NORTH END,
PORTSMOUTH, PO2 9HA
TEL: (0705) 667652/3

A PERFECT START TO A BETTER FINISH

622

Timberline

Arthur Jones on what's happening in the timber trade

Fashions are as much a feature in the timber trade as in the rag trade. Commercial wood users making consumer products, especially furniture manufacturers, switch timbers to give the flavour-of-the-year in colour and appearance, and the current vogue is for lighter colour.

This has led to more sales of American white rather than red oak, and the fact that white oak has been slightly cheaper is just a coincidence. Lighter colour has been the main attraction, and the similar appearance of ash has led to more interest in this wood as well. Incidentally, the high value of the yen has made Japanese oak expensive.

Changes of fashion like this can have effects on your pocket. If the major users of hardwoods suddenly switch to a particular species, inevitably prices rise. This is happening with beech, for a lot has been bought recently by furniture firms who seem to be switching from some tropical hardwoods. So prices have been lifting by at least 5% and by 10% or more in the South East of England.

Region and season can also affect prices. Prices for many goods are higher in the South-East than in other parts of the country and hardwoods are no exception. So prices for imported hardwoods, especially from North America and the tropics, can be lower in Liverpool (a major port for receiving these supplies) than in the North-East of Scotland; transport can add considerably to costs.

Prices are also affected by seasons. Many large users of hardwoods buy on a seasonal basis and this leads to fluctuations in price, just as you expect to pay more for your cream tea in Devon during August than in January.

With home-grown hardwoods proximity of supply is usually more important. Some areas of Britain are strong in deci-duous woodlands whereas in others where softwoods predominate (like Scotland) you'll have to pay more for hardwoods.

You'll usually find no problem in getting dried native hardwoods even in the rural areas, for many small craft firms now run their own kilns, and wood merchants generally have dried hardwoods.

In urban areas some timber firms are starting counter sales of hardwoods. Most offer only a limited range but it's a trend which many of you will appreciate.

Tropical hardwoods have been in abundant supply for many years but in some parts of Britain stocks of some *shoreas* are scarce.

Political problems continue in the Philippines and the logging ban was extended recently, but the trade is confident that business will soon be back to usual for this major source of hardwoods.

Ramin is costing more at the moment, but the price of Brazilian mahogany seems to have passed its peak and could even come down before the end of the year.

Supplies of native softwoods have become far more plentiful. In recent log auctions prices have increased sharply for quality material, part of the move to sell better quality English softwood and win a better image for the timber. This means you'll have to pay more in future.

With imported softwoods price rises will be well within the rate of inflation. You might even pick up a bargain if you want fifth quality imported softwood, for trade prices have actually dropped slightly.

You may grumble even more about retail wood prices when you learn that stockbrokers have forecast a profit rise of 27% among timber firms this year. To be fair, this comes after a long spell when profits have been unsatisfactory; stronger demand has enabled timber companies to reduce the cut-price competition.

Meanwhile, the sheet materials and panel products side has shown various price increases but most have been small and supplies have been good in all areas. ∎

Jacobean hi-fi

If, like Ron Hicks, you dream of wall-to-wall oak furniture, make a start with his 'traditional' hi-fi cabinet, deservedly commended at the Bristol Show

● *If spinets and clavichords had been on disc or tape, this might be a genuine antique! Note the sliding/folding door arrangement, the hinged top, and the base/plinth/leg-frame detail. You should cut holes in the back for ventilation*

My ambition to fill a room with oak furniture has started coming to fruition in the last few months. First a Welsh dresser, then a corner cabinet, a round occasional table, and most recently, a hi-fi cabinet. They are all loosely styled along Jacobean lines. The cabinet may appear difficult to make, but I think you will find it easier than it looks, because I spent a lot of time thinking the project out.

All the timber for the top and framework came from 25mm boards (roughly 1½-2cu ft) and the legs from 50x50mm timber. After picking my timber I had both sides of the boards planed up with minimum waste; the final thickness was 23mm.

Preparing the timber

I selected the best parts of the timber for the top, trimmed them off a little oversize, shot the edges, rub-jointed them together and then put them to one side. Turning the legs presented no real problems, but the timber must be dead square and perfectly centred as with all square-ended turning.

Most of the framework timber is 45mm wide so I cut a few lengths at 48mm. I ripped them on the bandsaw, since I don't own a circular saw, cut them a little over-length, and prepared them with a jointer, using vernier calipers for accuracy. I also shot the front and back of each piece to remove any planer marks; using a very sharp plane all round in this way, little cleaning up was needed. I brought the lengths to size and squared up the ends at the same time using my home-made disc sander.

Then I set up the router table (also home-made) and started on the mouldings. The bottom outside edge of the leg frame was shaped with an ovolo cutter, using the round only; then I took a second cut after moving the fence the same amount as the diameter of the cutter. After disc sanding the legs to length I assembled the leg frame. All the joints are dowelled, as this gives ample strength and I find them more convenient for the home workshop than the mortise and tenon. I checked the frame for square and kept it under cramp pressure till it was dry. I set my leg-frame rails 12mm back from the face of the legs.

The base

I made the base with 45x23mm front and side rails, their front edges ovolo moulded top and bottom. I mitred the corners, setting the mitre forward off the front and side by 16mm. I screwed the front and side rails down from the top; the screws are concealed by the side frames and front bottom rail. The front and rear corner-posts form part of the side frames, so I routed these next. I rounded the outside edges of the rear posts and cut a rebate to take the ply back, stopping it at the point where the top back stretcher runs into the post. I rounded the three outside corners of the front post, and then moved the cutter in as I did with the plinth rail, but cutting from both edges. What I call the 'chocolate bar' effect I achieved by working across the centre portion with a ply pattern and a collar in the router. Top, bottom and middle rails I set back from the corner posts by 9mm. Then I completed the panels by dowelling all joints; I dry-assembled top, bottom and middle rails, cleaned them up, and added the front and back posts. If you mark all internal corners it will give you stopping points for the panel grooves; mine were made to accept 4mm oak faced ply.

After gluing up I fixed this to the leg frame by screwing up through the plinth side rails. The back should be flush to the back leg and the front directly over the front leg.

The bottom front rail is cut round the corner posts, but the top one is cut *between* the posts, and later fixed to the lid's underside. The bottom one has a rebate to take the ply bottom. I produced the stopped V-cuts on these rails on the router table using a straight cutter and a ply pattern set up on the table at 45° to give the 'V'. With the back top rail cut to size and rebated, I had completed the main carcase. I ran the back panel down to the plinth and grooved it to the bottom panel.

Inside the carcase

Shelves and divisions can be put in to suit your own equipment. My side and back top rails were made wide enough for my shelf to be screwed and glued to them. Most equipment needs airflow, and cables need to be fed through, so holes are needed. I cut the top to the same size as the capping on the leg frame, with the same moulding as on the sides and front. Now with the top hinged and the front rail glued and cramped, the only major job left is the doors.

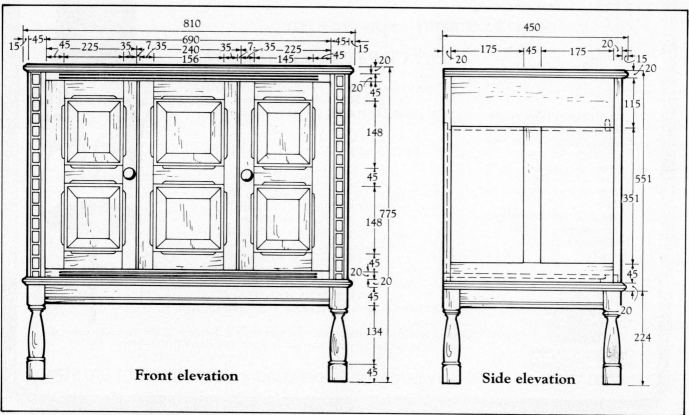

Front elevation

Side elevation

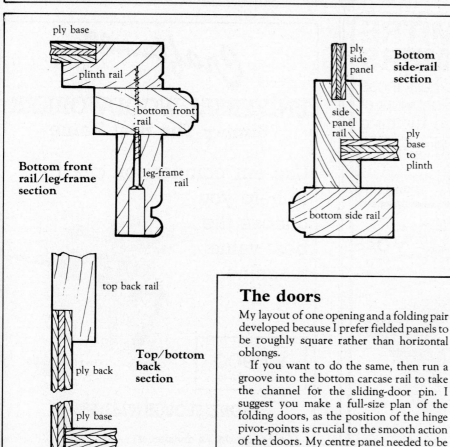

ply base

plinth rail

bottom front rail

Bottom front rail/leg-frame section

leg-frame rail

ply side panel

Bottom side-rail section

side panel rail

ply base to plinth

bottom side rail

top back rail

Top/bottom back section

ply back

ply base

The doors

My layout of one opening and a folding pair developed because I prefer fielded panels to be roughly square rather than horizontal oblongs.

If you want to do the same, then run a groove into the bottom carcase rail to take the channel for the sliding-door pin. I suggest you make a full-size plan of the folding doors, as the position of the hinge pivot-points is crucial to the smooth action of the doors. My centre panel needed to be 6mm longer than the two outside ones. I made the door frames similar to the end panels, with top, middle, bottom and outside stiles 45mm wide and the meeting

stiles 35mm and 40mm; the larger ones to the middle door have a small 'V' cut into them 6mm from the outside edge. All internal edges have an ovolo moulding stopped 25mm from the corner. I suggest you make them up dry and clean them up before moulding or putting the panelling in; cleaning up after the ovolo is put on tends to lose the small quirk in the ovolo, and also the panels stand proud of the frames, making cleaning up with a power sander impossible.

The thought of making the fielded panels hurt my brain and the cost of a fielded-panel cutter hurt my pocket! Anyway, I couldn't find a cutter large enough with the angle I needed. So I came up with the idea of letting the two router-guide rods into a piece of thick ply at the angle I needed and the correct distance apart, so the router slid up and down at the correct angle. Rebating the panels first and using a fence under the router, I pushed the panels through, moving the router up or down the guide rails to widen the fielding. I needed two cuts using a 16mm cutter but you can't see the line because I waxed the ply router-base to make the going easy. I stained the cabinet, sprayed on three coats of cellulose sanding sealer, and rubbed it down well with fine wire wool. After leaving it to harden off for a day or two, I waxed the unit, paying special attention to nooks and crannies.

Overall dimensions of my cabinet are: 810mm wide, 730mm high and 440mm deep, with 225mm legs.

Now this project is finished, I'm off to buy more oak to make a home for the video. Then, perhaps the microwave? ∎

Dolphin school

Terry Moss' evocative figure carvings won a gold medal at the Bristol Woodworker Show. Here's his step-by-step account of how they came to life

● *Above and **below**, the winning team, front and top views, wonderfully fluid in form*

Many carvers have a love/hate relationship with their craft. Talking to fellow carvers I am fascinated to hear the different things that give joy — and those that definitely don't. Some enjoy cutting the wood with chisels and gouges, others the design and sanding: but I think we all enjoy that concluding moment, the final application of beeswax, or the last cut with the chisel or gouge if the piece is to be left tooled and unpolished.

I enjoy the design and planning of the project, I have my moments with the mallet and gouge but my greatest thrill is to see the end product. It means you can start another and you have the enjoyment of achievement. I like to vary the finish between tooled and sanded carving which adds to the interest — but I refuse to enter the controversy about the type of finish that should be used.

I conceived this carving as a single group originally, but as I worked the design I realised it could be split into different components and combinations (fig. 1); this would require slight modification to the base. Whatever the combination you choose, your personal interpretation of the wave forms on the base will give the carving your distinctive touch. I used plum, a soft fruitwood, but the grain was very good and its figure, suggesting sea and water movement, enhanced the design.

Techniques

I have developed my own techniques to design a carving and transfer it to the material ready for working. I usually start by drawing the design in my sketch book (figs. 2 & 3). I use many sources for designs

but with a subject like the dolphins you are mostly reliant on photographs or line drawings from wildlife books — unless you have a dophinarium in your back garden! Illustrations are fine but foreshortening caused by perspective in photographs can distort proportions on a finished carving; your drawings should help solve this problem.

Then I use Plasticene to make a model of the design to highlight some of the carving problems and get a good three-dimensional reference. I use this continually when carving, checking shapes are not running away when the frenzy hits, for the gouge and mallet take on lives of their own, removing great lumps of wood; nothing looks worse than a flattened shape.

After these two preliminary stages the drawing is enlarged by squaring up to the required size. In this case the 100mm (95mm finished) thickness governed the amount of enlargement — I had to be sure the design fitted into this dimension. Then I make card templates (figs 4, 5 & 6) which are laid on the wood and traced around with felt-tip pen for bandsawing. Once the shapes are cut out, the bottom and edges are planed and trued up and the next step is to

remove as much waste as required from the dolphins. I use ½in and ¾in no.7 gouges for this, avoiding damage to the base and leaving edges square.

When gluing the three parts together I used a Pelidon Dowlitt jig, as the dowels give extra strength and the jig is very accurate.

Gouging the waste

I removed more of the waste with gouges; as well as shallow section tools, ⅜in no.6 and ⅜in no.4 fishtails and skew chisels, I use a big 1¼in and a small ½in and two V-shape tools, a ¼in and a ¼in bent. The holes and hollows in the waves are made by drilling into the wood from both sides. I use a long ⅜in twist-drill as the distances are quite considerable on the full-size carving. When I have drilled a few holes I enlarge them with a gouge and finally a round Surform. You have to watch the direction of the grain; I had to reverse the Surform and cut with a pulling action, in the way Japanese tools are used. As the carving developed I used a back bent tool, ¼in no.5, to cope with the undercut areas. The biggest difficulty was in carving the dolphin curving over the side, as

Dolphin school

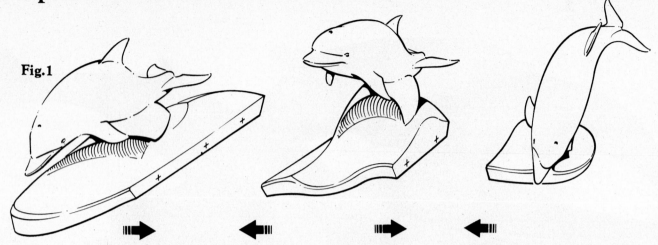

Fig.1

● **Above**, *the interlocking design allows a variety of display patterns*

this required cutting against the grain.

I find a flexible drive router very useful for the undercutting here. You have to be very careful cutting against the grain with a gouge as it is easy to split the wood and the damage does not show up until polishing.

Finishing

For a smooth finish I use rifflers and various grades of sandpaper. I finished the dolphins smoother than the waves to give contrast between them, but I found access difficult in the areas beneath the waves so I left these tooled. I could have done more carving before joining the pieces together, but I wanted to make sure the wave forms blended together, and with the resulting thin edges it would have been difficult to keep the sections square when clamping them together. So I decided to join them after roughing out the dolphin shapes.

If you want to carve the dolphins yourself, the drawn shapes should help with the basic layout. They certainly look good when finished and polished, but the photographs show the carving immediately before polishing. To finish I usually wipe the wood with methylated spirits and then finally sand with fine-grade sandpaper. I use one or two coats of home-made beeswax polish to seal the wood. Elbow-grease brings the polish to a fine look but it takes several applications. Why not try this project yourself? I think you'll be very pleased with the design, and get a great feeling of achievement and satisfaction when it's finished. ∎

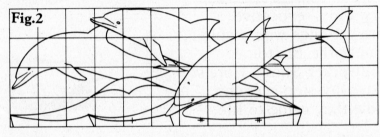

Fig.2

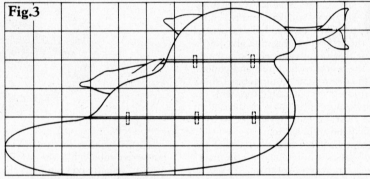

Fig.3

● **Top** and **above**, *sketch-book drawings, here on a 50mm grid; squares can be enlarged or reduced to suit material*

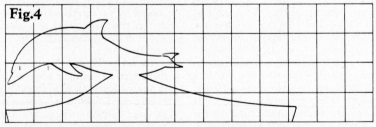

Fig.4

● **Above**, *templates are drawn using a Plasticene model for guidance*

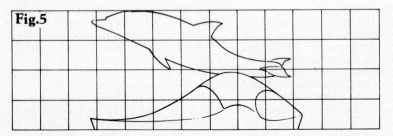

Fig.5

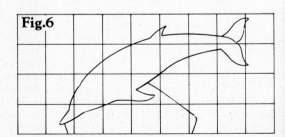

Fig.6

● **Above right** and **left**, *the dipping and diving templates ready to be traced on to wood and bandsawn to shape*

WORKBENCH OF THE FUTURE!

WOODWORKER and **SJÖBERG**
COMPETITION to test your SKILL!
WIN

1 A magnificent Sjöberg 2000 workbench, with a 2000mm-long laminated beech top and two vices — worth £700 (if you could buy it in the UK)
PLUS
2 A long weekend in a luxury hotel in Sweden, with a visit to Sjöbergs
The total value of these enticing prizes?

£1500!

WHAT YOU HAVE TO DO The traditional workbench design is hundreds of years old — no special provision for power tools or modern equipment. But Sjöberg are committed to constant improvement: SO
DESIGN THE WORKBENCH OF THE FUTURE — OR FEATURES FOR A WORKBENCH — OR BENCH ACCESSORIES — that make benchwork more flexible, comfortable and easier with today's tools and materials

---

THE WINNER will be the entry (judged by *Woodworker* and Sjöberg) which makes the greatest overall contribution to workbench design

ENTRIES must be in the form of detailed drawings and/or photos, plus explanatory notes on no more than two A4 sheets for each item. Send to 'Workbench of the Future', Woodworker, 1 Golden Sq, London W1R 3AB.

CLOSING DATE 31 AUGUST

● Prizewinning designs will become the property of Sjöberg, who reserve the right to put them into production.
● Sjöberg will pay £100 to any entrant other than the winner whose idea is put into production
● Similar ideas will be judged on quality of presentation
● All decisions about the competition are final, and no correspondence will be

held. Employees of ASP Ltd, Sjöberg Ltd, Brimarc Ltd or their advertising agents are excluded from entry
● SJÖBERG WILL MAKE UP THE WINNING DESIGN TO BE EXHIBITED AT THE WOODWORKER SHOW, ALEXANDRA PAVILION, LONDON, 23-26 OCTOBER
● An entry is automatically taken as agreement to abide by the rules of the competition, and take (within reason) the offered dates for the holiday

---

SPECIAL OFFER!   £100 off!
If you want to make sure of a SJÖBERG bench, have a look at this. The 1900 has a 1900mm-long laminated birch top, two vices, and storage underneath. With a Sjöberg Holdfast, it's worth £520 retail. *Woodworker* and Sjöberg are offering it to you for just £420! That's a clear £100 off!

● Make cheques payable to Argus Specialist Publications Ltd

To: Reader Services, Wolsey House, Wolsey Rd, Hemel Hempstead, Herts HP2 4SS
Please send me ☐ Sjöberg 1900 benches with ST82 Holdfast at £420 each. I enclose

a cheque for ....

Name...

Address ....

.... Post Code...........

Bristol 86

Craft is growing all over the country, especially wood craft and especially in the West. That's why the Bristol Woodworker Show was there in May, and that's why we asked Adrian Booth to look it over

Bodgers, coopers, cabinetmakers, turners, chippies, marquetarians, DIYers — woodworkers of all shapes, sizes, and ages turned out in force to May's Bristol Woodworker Show '86.

It's the second year that the three-day event has been held in Bristol, and people came from all over the West Country, pushing attendance figures up by 30% on last year. Growing *Woodworker* sales also reflect the same upsurge of interest in woodworking, and the great increase in numbers of craftspeople turning their skills to making a living. Significantly, Friday was almost as busy as Saturday and Sunday and many traders reported that day's take as their best.

The appeal of the Show for the woodworker is obvious. Where else can you see the latest machinery and tools, pick up new tips and bargains, see high quality work, and meet so many like-minded individuals — all under one roof? At times it was difficult to get near the competition displays. Amid the hubbub of the Show, visitors studied the entries in silence, calculating the hundreds of hours that went into some of the finest competition pieces you're likely to see.

Judging can't be an enviable task. When each piece must be considered for its individuality, craftsmanship and flair, no two pieces can truly be considered in the same light. However, none could dispute the elegance of the 'sold to me as pearwood' carved plum dolphins by **Terry Moss** from Charfield in Gloucestershire. A technical illustrator by trade, he worked out the design first in Plasticene, which helped him identify where the problems would occur. As he pointed out just after receiving his medal, 'There's not a lot of point spending 2-300 hours on a piece of carving if you haven't got your design properly worked out!'

John Shepherd from Huntington in Yorkshire had a nice surprise when he visited the Show while he was staying with relatives in the area — he found he'd won the gold medal for his American rocking chair. John has never seen an original, but liked the design after seeing a photograph, and did some research on it. The award was particularly gratifying for him because he has just turned self-employed as a furniture maker.

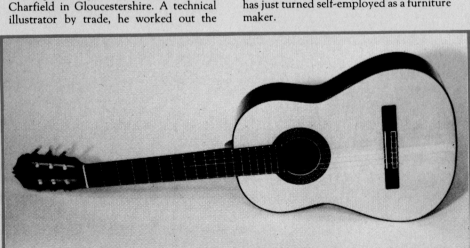

● Opposite, *above left: John Shepherd*'s rocking chair got a gold, as did *Mr G. Evans*' superb oval table *right. Below left, Mr I. Fobbester*'s magnificent yew and rosewood clock and *John Wilmut*'s classical guitar were both gold winners. *This page, top: Mr E. Presley*'s monk's bench; *right, Edward Hopkins*' amazing Squares and Rounds entry. *Above, Trevor Howell*'s gold loco

The Juniors' gold was won by **Craig Anderson** (18) from Milford Haven for his jewellery box, made at school as part of his A-level course. Winning the medal should provide encouragement for him; he's off to Bucks College in High Wycombe soon, to study furniture design and management.

Among the exhibits were two antique mahogany pieces on loan from Longleat House, used to advertise reproduction plans available from **Ashby Design Workshop.** This company had good reasón to be pleased with the weekend — they picked up a commission to produce a replica of the elegant Spanish 18th century Universal Desk during the weekend, 'for a four-figure sum'.

There was a good selection of timber suppliers, amongst whom Avon-based **Treework Services** were displaying their selection of native hardwoods, demonstrating some surprising variations in the most recognisable timbers. This company obtain most of their timber from woodland renovation schemes, and are committed to working for the survival of threatened woodland. ('Buying timber wisely', WW/Jan).

The expansion of the craftsman/professional market hasn't gone unrecognised by manufacturers of tools and equipment. Several top names were demonstrating universals at the show, aimed at those of us forced to work with confined space and confined budgets! **AEG** unveiled their new Maxi 26 universal, a six-function compact design offering 90mm depth of saw-cut and 45° of blade tilt. The planer cuts up to 260mm wide; there are high safety specifications, easy belt changing and lots of add-ons. It retails at £1349+VAT.

Elsewhere you could see the **Craftsman** range from **J.J. Smith.** Traditionally suppliers of heavy-duty machinery, they bring industrial features to the small workshop; micro-switches that cut the motors out when the tables and doors are open, three-bladed cutter-blocks to improve quality of cut, and noise-reducing teeth to the cutter gap on the tables. Craftsman make four

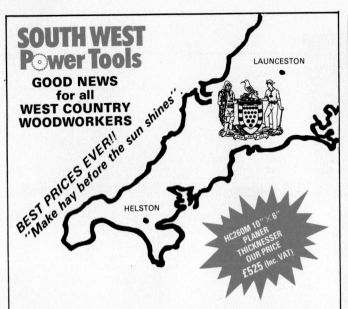

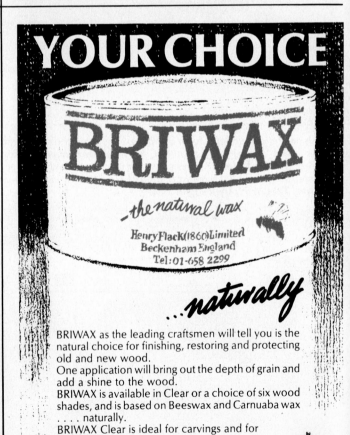
634

'Fine Craft and Fine Design'

* Seminars and courses
* Comprehensive tool insurance
* Central skills register
* Information and advice
* Show entry discounts

Professional and amateur

Write for application forms to: Guild of Woodworkers, 1 Golden Sq. London W1R 3AB

Guild of Woodworkers
~Identify Yourself

* Window stickers 120×60mm)	50p
* Envelope stickers (38×25mm) 50	£1.00
100	£1.75
200	£3.25
500	£7.50
1000	£15.00
Woodworker apron (state S, M, L)	£4.00

STILL AVAILABLE IN THE OLD LOGO
Ties | £4.50
Window and envelope stickers
SPECIAL OFFER
Tie and apron | £7.50

PO/Cheque with order to: Guild of Woodworkers, 1 Golden Square, London W1R 3AB

635

types of universal, but they say they sell more two- and three-function units for those with more space, because there's little difference in price.

And the **Shopsmith** — a multi-function American lathe-based system, first on the market in 1953 — is making a comeback. Squeezed out until recently by the strength of the dollar, the Shopsmith is again on sale in the UK. Regular demonstrations gave a good indication of this reliable machine's capabilities, and one visitor revealed that he bought a Shopsmith in 1956, only complaining that he recently had to replace the motor!

Quality hand-tools from names like **Sarjents** and **Roger's** caught many a discerning eye, and there was a great deal of talk about Japanese chisels and saws. Among the small manufacturers, **Clico** attracted a great deal of interest with their planes. Formed three and a half years ago by refugees from the Swedish takeover of **Record Ridgway**, this 14-man outfit bought stock, machinery and jigs from their

● *Talking about Eumenia radial-arm saws is work that* **Craig Warren** *of Warco enjoys*

former employers and began producing a range of router cutters for the aerospace industry. Record Ridgway's plane department manager recently joined them, and they started from scratch to produce a range of specialist planes discontinued by Record Ridgway, based on the original Preston designs ('Tools of the trade', WW/Jul). These include the Clifton multi-plane and the 3110 and 420 shoulder-planes. Improvements to the latter are typical; the handle is now made from malleable iron, rather than the more brittle grey metal. Webs have been thickened, the cutter's thickness doubled, and the cutter-pad is now twice the original length. The pointed tip that supports the cutter — traditionally vulnerable to knots and nails — has been

● *Left,* AEG's new 'Maxi' universal made its first public appearance amidst great interest; **right**, Squares and Rounds winner **Nicholas Packer** gets the glad hand and a fine lathe from Elektra Beckum's **Peter Simpson**

strengthened by adding $\frac{3}{8}$in to the casting, allowing it to cool at an even temperature, and machining it back.

And for the really serious woodworker, the £850, 6ft 'Bristol Workbench' from **Iori — Fine Woodworking** looked suitably impressive. It has facilities for clamping numerous and varied workpieces, and the top is made of nearly 4in-thick stack-laminated kiln-dried beech, with birch ply tongues and five steel tie-rods. With its warm oiled finish, this bench had many an appreciative hand passed over it in three days — as nice to look at as it would be solid to use.

O ne of the best things about the Woodworker Shows is the people you meet. Woodworking can be a lonely occupation,

● *Above,* Chair bodger **Mike Abbott;** *top right,* **Nigel Short,** *Squares and Rounds the winner, with Elektra Beckum table-saw an* **Peter Simpson. Right,** *Jim Wilson of Solent Tools dips lucky for the Emco spindle-moulder winner*

but I saw and heard complete strangers strike up healthy conversations about timber, joints, tools, machinery, and the finer points of craft. Salesmen can have a tough time, too — a canny carpenter won't be taken in by smooth talk when it's a matter of increased production for reduced cost. Machinery representatives really earn their keep!

The well-oiled conversation about old tools *vs* new continued, particularly around the **Tool And Trades History Society**'s stand. TATHS members have plenty to talk about; their motto is 'The history of tools is the history of man'. On their stall reposed a selection of strange-looking tools, over which hung the notice 'Wotsit?' The range included a drawer-lock chisel (easy), a cork-borer sharpener (not so easy), and

even items the society itself couldn't identify. Not me, alas.

Then there were the experts. Always glad to have a serious natter, over the three days they entertained those gathered round their stalls by giving practical demonstrations of how they tackle their daily technical problems. They included the familiar face of **Zach Taylor**, a colourful character who makes and plays lutes and teaches their construction. He also had a number of other unusual wooden musical instruments, including a Celtic harp. Regular *Woodworker* contributor **Stan Thomas** was there to give advice on general benchwork, the correct way to sharpen tools, how to work out joints and angles on jobs like panelled spiral staircases, and just about any other teaser you could try on him. Stan's tools are well used — some of his chisels are now into their last half inch!

Manchester chairmaker **Jack Hill** fascinated onlookers with regular displays of his traditional craft. Jack, an ex-wood-

work teacher who now lectures at Manchester Central College and also teaches for our **Guild of Woodworkers**, likes his timber green, and believes in using the eye and the rule of the thumb for measuring. I watched him make a chair 'stick'. First splitting the log to size with an axe, commenting 'if it grows straight, it'll cleave straight', then he moves to his rustic looking foot operated shaving horse, and uses a draw-knife to shape it roughly. One of his tools, much like a giant pencil-sharpener, was designed and made by chairmaking authority **Fred Lambert**. The 'rounder' is a tapered tube with handles, and a blade on the inside. With the stick in the lathe his rounder could take off the finest of shavings, several yards long.

Meanwhile, another chair maker was amazing everyone downstairs with his pole lathe. **Mike Abbott** is pleased to be called a bodger, because that's what he is. His pole lathe, weighed down at one end by a heavy trunk, was on the **Living Wood** training stand, and Mike will be giving green woodworking courses in the North by the time

● *Top: scrutiny for the Squares and Rounds entries; **above left**, the finer points of fine instruments from **Zach Taylor**. Above right, Michael Trainos' gold-winning bowls; **right, Iori** and his crème de la crème of benches. **Below right**, woodworking wisdom and **Stan Thomas** are one and the same*

you read this. Mike went through a preliminary process similar to Jack Hill's, using a side axe to split his ash chair-legs. 'I like my timber as green as I can get it.'

All in all, the 86 Bristol Woodworker Show did it did in 85, but with a bevy of new faces and new ideas. Bigger and better than last year, but not yet as big as the October Show in London. See you there!

● London Woodworker Show, Alexandra Pavilion, London N22, 23-26 October. **Enter the competitions:** details from **Argus Specialist Exhibitions**, Wolsey House, Wolsey Rd, Hemel Hempstead, Herts HP2 4SS, (0442) 41221.

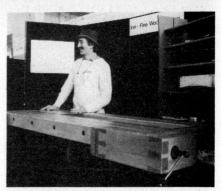

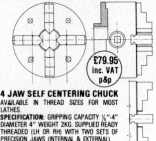

Bristol 86
Squares and Rounds

The entries for our Squares and Rounds competition were as varied in ideas and imagination as they were numerous. More than 40 people dreamed up variations on the theme of chess — furniture with an inbuilt chessboard, or a set of chess pieces. The preliminary judging, weeding out the ones to go to Bristol for final assessment, was hard enough; the judging at Bristol itself even harder. Imagination, skill, and meticulous attention to detail are not easy criteria when all the entrants have more than their fair share of each!

We thought it would be useful to pass on some of the judges' comments. Imagination was an important element in the competition, and the entries in the 'Squares' — the furniture section — were indeed brimming with it. But very few people indeed had stretched their imaginations beyond tables. Surely there are other pieces of furniture which suit the proportion and function of the chessboard? And then there was the question of finish, that old chestnut. It still seems that hardworking and highly skilled craftspeople graft away at their labour of love, and when they've completed the construction and (perhaps) sanded it down, they've finished. Oh yes, and then what shall I put on it? A couple of coats of polyurethane? In this as in any competition, the winners are those who know that finishing is part of the job. Just as joints are integral to construction, so finish is integral to appearance, and joints alone won't make your piece gold-worthy!

Here are the winners' pieces, drawings and design thoughts, with some of the other outstanding designs. Thank you, everyone who entered, and better luck next time; and thank you, **Elektra Beckum UK** and **Richard Kell** for your generosity.

THE SQUARES
Nigel Short
won an **Elektra Beckum** tablesaw

The table is designed on an organic, *Art Nouveau* theme, which might seem to give some freedom in the shaping, but in fact puts a lot of constraints on the form. The piece is dual-function, with a reversible and removable games top which could be replaced with a plain one in oak or any other material. The dimensions are thus not those of a traditional games table, but a cross between that and a low side-table.

To convey the image/impression I wanted, I needed to carefully co-ordinate the four side elevations, the plan view and both games boards to eliminate all straight lines and symmetry. Wild-grained English oak helped the organic appearance.

All photos Colin Wilson

Nigel Short's drawings overleaf

The main framework is 100x20mm boards laminated into 100x100mm pieces for legs and rails, which are joined with mitred twin mortise-and-tenons. I partly shaped and drilled the corner supports for fixing, then took the frame apart and cut the inside symmetrical shape away.

If the top was to be reversible, it had to be symmetrical, but I made a diagonal the centre-line of symmetry, and disguised the balance by varying the thickness on the outside of the frame. Even though all the curves look random, they had to be worked

out to avoid hitting the tenons and screws at the joints. I bandsawed, rasped, filed and glasspapered the shapes.

Continuing the 'no straight lines' theme on the chess and backgammon boards posed major problems! Eventually I evolved a method; all the joints are on random curves. The timbers are 5mm-thick sycamore and Indian laurel. Both boards were glued either side of 18mm chipboard and edged with 100mm oak with tongued mitres. I put in a 2mm Indian laurel string to define the board edge, and wax finished it.

Squares and Rounds

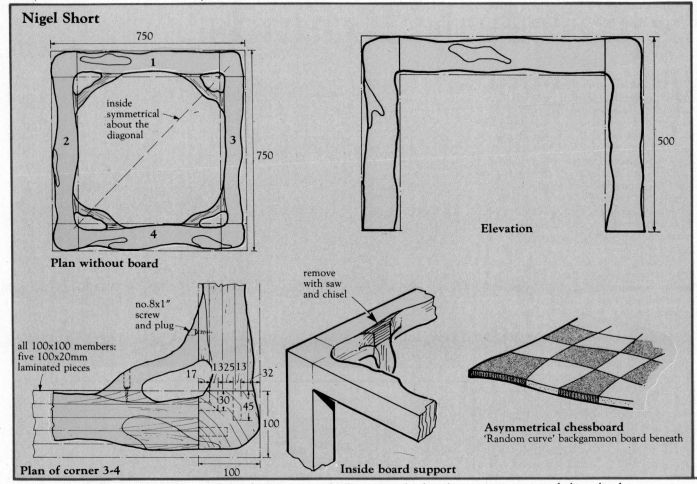

Nigel Short

750

1

inside symmetrical about the diagonal

2   3

750

4

Plan without board

Elevation

500

no.8x1″ screw and plug

remove with saw and chisel

all 100x100 members: five 100x20mm laminated pieces

17   13 25 13   32

30   45

100

Plan of corner 3-4   100

Inside board support

Asymmetrical chessboard
'Random curve' backgammon board beneath

Aubrey Gill

won a boxed set of **Richard Kell's** measuring tools

Two pieces of weathered sycamore, left over from a larger table, were halved in thickness, opened book-fashion and jointed with loose tongues to give a table-top. The elliptical shape was dictated by the size of the wood — there wasn't enough for an adequate rectangle. Because dark figuring appeared only at one end, I thought I should fill part of the remaining space with further dark tone; a chessboard chequer would provide use as well as interest.

A side of 42mm for the individual squares gave a reasonable overall size to the board, with enough room for the chessmen. Plain-grained wood seemed not very interesting, and endgrain in one piece not much more so, so I went for endgrain in an arrangement of 14x28mm rectangles and 14x14mm squares.

I thought the base should echo some part of the top, and a scheme of vertical segments of alternating dark and light woods seemed to have possibilities. The arrangement of these members in an S-shape gave a degree of interest plus a challenge in the making. The S-shape was then mirror-imaged to allow the players to slip one foot under the table if they wished. I chose wengé for the dark, and field maple for the light segments.

The table-top without the chess board meant jointing the four pieces with loose tongues and bandsawing to the shape of a cardboard template on which the pure ellipse had been generated.

To make the chessboard, lengths of about 300mm of holly and wengé were accurately sized to 14x14mm and 14x28mm and glued up with Aerolite 306 in a simple L-shaped jig to give a bundle of four squares. I checked and adjusted it for squareness and then sliced it into pieces about 2.5mm thick — only 16 pieces to insert instead of 64!

The overall size of the chess board was marked out on the table-top, and guides set up on the four sides for routing out the recess; these were secured with double-sided adhesive tape, and I fixed up two movable pieces to support the router away from the edge guides.

I designed the base with all segments the same width (52mm) and angled to give the right spread. A straight section of 80mm in the centre, set at approximately 15° to the minor diameter of the ellipse, is followed on each side by eight segments of 20° included angle and then by four segments of 16½°. The segments, all 23mm thick, were chamfered to 10° and 8¼°, leaving their widest sides accurately at 52mm. Then I jointed them with loose tongues; I couldn't cramp these joints, so planed the tongues to an easy fit in the 5mm-wide grooves (cut undersize on the circular saw and finished on the router as spindle moulder). The tongues were made slightly narrower than the combined depth of the grooves to prevent hold-off; I filled the slight gaps on the bottom edge of the base with wax beaumontage for the sake of appearance.

I set up a vertical member perpendicular to the saw-bench and cramped the 80mm centre-section to it, checking with an engineer's square for perpendicular.

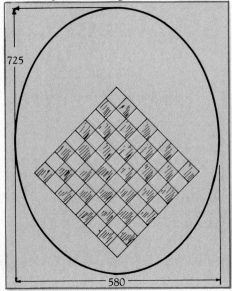

725

580

Bill Morley

won a boxed set of Richard Kell's measuring tools

A table is ideal for a chessboard, but an unfinished game can be disturbed, so I designed this chess table with a removable board that can be hung on the wall for added decorative effect. The table is compatible with modern or more traditional furniture, and is rigid and heavy for good stability.

Both table-top and board are laminated to eliminate warping, the outer laminations ¼in thick. The top laminae are canary whitewood, the dark squares and lippings utile; I inlaid black lines in the board for a nice detail, and was careful to use grain direction as a feature.

The legs are utile, mortised into the thick, stable top, into the top surface of which I let endgrain utile squares to give the appearance of the legs coming right through. They also tie in with the chess-board.

The board is mounted on polished brass brackets, which give a gap for fingers underneath to pick it up, and also allow the board to be hung on the wall.

The construction is unconventional but appropriate to the job, and the table should last well because all the outside edges are of hard, dark wood. The edge-lippings are pre-stressed to guard against shrinkage.

Bill Morley's drawings overleaf

● We wanted to print many more pictures and drawings, but just didn't have the space. Well done also to **John Ashworth, Alan Fell, Kim Gyr, George Hendrie, Chris Storey, G. Nicol**, and all the others!

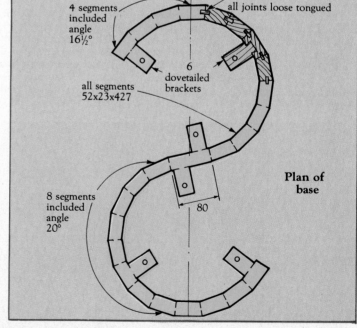

4 segments included angle 16½°

all joints loose tongued

all segments 52x23x427

6 dovetailed brackets

8 segments included angle 20°

80

Plan of base

Working from the middle, I glued the segments of one end into position one at a time, checking each for squareness to the saw-table and allowing it to set before adding the next. Then I repeated the process the other end, and the result came out within 5mm of the drawing.

I cut the dovetailed sockets for the fixing brackets before assembly, but the brackets were not inserted until the whole S-shape had been glued up and given its first two applications of wax. The sockets were masked out with drafting tape.

The table-top is fixed to the base by six

M6 brass screws passing through the wood brackets into 32x8mm light-alloy metal inserts fixed in the table-top. This allows the table to be partially dismantled. I sanded to 600-grit silicon carbide, and finished the whole thing with Fiddes' 'Robjo' light wax.

Squares and Rounds

Bill Morley

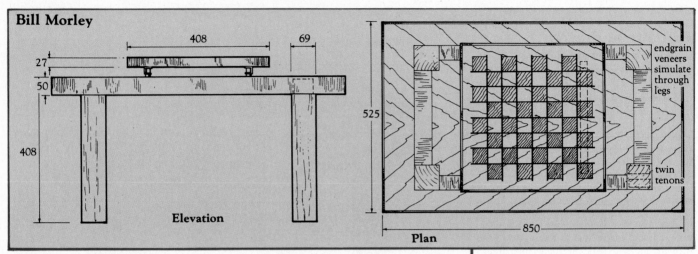

Elevation

Plan

endgrain veneers simulate through legs

twin tenons

408, 69, 27, 50, 408, 525, 850

Edward Hopkins

The idea of a box which vanishes in a simple movement appeals to me. It is an illusion and a fitting start to a game of chess.

The arrangement is austere and economical. A seemingly complicated temple-like structure turns inside-out and becomes a flat square table, chequered in sycamore and ebony. The table stands on an octagonal shaft braced to the ground by quartered mahogany legs, which are intended to appear of an entirely different nature to the temple — they are rounded and red like roots. The column rises and seems to pierce the box, which is shaped on top to form finger-grips for the flaps. These unfold, and the column segments become pendant at the table corners.

The column is from 2in oak, halved and tongued. It is tenoned and wedged into the table-top, which is made of quartered stuff; chamfers add complication and increase the scale. On some squares inside, the chamfers prevent the hinged flaps collapsing beyond 90° in the closed position. The box on the shaft assumes a crystalline quality in

marked contrast to the legs; it is almost organic.

The piece intends to entice the players through the triangular doorways to where the chessmen safely wait; and while they wait, it should be an object as stimulating, unusual and as varied as the game itself.

Andrew Cuningham

The attraction for me in this piece was the variety of different processes involved. I decided to make a miniature, and found that ¼ was the smallest practical scale in which everything could be made correctly — joints, lock, key, hinges and drawers. I decided on English walnut.

I sawed the pedestal to shape and glued the foot blocks on, which I sawed and carved to shape. The hexagonal columns were turned to the right silhouette, then I cut the facets, guided by hexagons marked top and bottom. The moulding at the base

of the column is a segment cut from a shaped cylinder.

The U-shape supporting the table-top is three laminated pieces (glued round a former), joined to the sides of the top with stub tenons. The U-drawer presented bending and gluing problems; I used the front and back pieces as formers to steam and glue the single piece that forms the basket. The top drawer is conventional — lap-dovetailed at the front and through-dovetailed at the back.

'continuation' of octagonal shaft as handles

oak shaft halved and tongued

4 rounded mahogany legs

28"
33"
10"
24½"

1" quarter-sawn oak

ebony and sycamore parquetry blocks

2" brass butts

18"

flap forms lid

flap becomes vertical side

shaded area stays flat

wedged tenon on octagonal shaft

squares chamfered to allow hinging to 90°

The castle folds flat to make the chessboard

The key is made in three parts, the shaft turned and drilled and the ring and pin brazed on to it. The lock, a ¼-scale version of the full-size one, is all brass apart from the pin and spring.

The moulding round the top section was turned in short lengths then planed to the right section, held in a V-trough. I tried split turning, but the pieces were too delicate.

The folding top was very troublesome. First I tried solid walnut with the ebony and box squares cut (for convenience) from endgrain and let in, but both parts warped badly after a few days. Then I tried cross-grained squares, but the stresses proved too much. Eventually I made a walnut and ¹⁄₁₆in aluminium sandwich, gluing the walnut with epoxy.

The polished steel scissors, cotton reels, ivory thimble and needle case, darning mushroom and draughts counters seemed essential to complete the piece!

Diane Ratchford

Why not incorporate a chessboard into a table which could also be used as a coffee table? The height is correct ergonomically for a coffee table, and the actual dimensions of the table-top were governed by the probable use of a sculptured chess set.

In keeping with the overall design, the legs' stepped outline reflects the chessboard squares. The stepped table-top surround is again in keeping with the theme.

The wood for the base and top surround is solid sycamore, and the paler squares in the chessboard are sycamore veneers. The contrasting squares are 2mm laburnum oysters, and the sycamore veneers (and obeche backing veneer) had to be laminated to the same thickness to prevent any warping. The squares for the chessboard were cut to size and sanded to the exact dimensions. Once the squares were taped together, I glued them on to a chipboard base which I cut to exact size after the glue was dry. A simple tongue and groove joint holds the surround to the top. The surround has mitred edges and a spindle-moulded stepped edge. The decorative stringing was inlaid in a groove cut into the surround after the top and surround were joined.

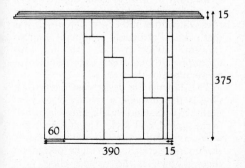

THE ROUNDS
Nicholas Packer
won an **Elektra Beckum** lathe

Living in the West Country, I have always been fascinated by the mystical legends of mediaeval kings, so I chose to picture chess as a war-game set in the time of Camelot. This chess set leans towards fantasy and the legendary King Arthur and his knights. The King and Queen are shown recognisably as King Arthur and Queen Guinevere. The castles, in typical fairytale style, represent powerful landowning barons in their castles, and the pawns the smaller provinces with lesser individual power but collective strength. The Church, often the power behind the Crown, is represented by a simple figure in mitre and plain cloaked dress. The knights, the King's champions, wear their armour showing their readiness to fight, and carry their shields displaying their King's coat of arms.

The pieces are made of deal, all whittled with a knife (including those which appear to be turned) with the definite idea of keeping the shapes simple yet readily identifiable and a suitable size.

The set was sanded then stained (with a bottle of un-named stain inherited from my grandfather!) then lacquered with walnut-stained varnish. The white pieces were finished with clear varnish.

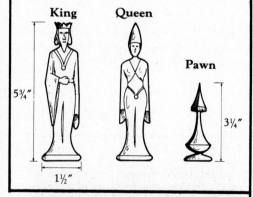

The legs were made up of individual strips of sycamore, each cut to size with the edges chamfered to 45°. The lengths were glued and dowelled, and the corner fixing is again a tongue and groove joint.

Kim Gowney
won a boxed set of **Richard Kell's** measuring tools

This chess set is designed on the theme 'The Age of Chivalry', and is intended to capture the essence of mediaeval Britain while recognisably retaining the essential characteristics of the individual chessmen's authority and power.

The pawns have a soldierly appearance, their heads shaped like old tin helmets. The rook is both a keep and a battlefield tent. The knight with his lance is, along with the Queen, perhaps the piece most closely connected to the era and general atmosphere. The friar, with his tonsure and belt, was a common feature of old-time Britain. The Queen is like a damsel, obviously feminine compared to the other pieces, but still carrying full authority. The King, with his helmet and circlet crown over it — as worn by kings in battle — is definitely the general of the scenario.

The pieces are made of flowering cherry and mahogany (stained to get a better contrast 'twixt black and white). I used a ¼in parting tool, a ½in bowl gouge, ⅜, ¼ and ⅛in spindle gouges and a ¹⁄₁₆in parting tool. I sanded them all down to 800-grit wet and dry and finished them with Fiddes' 'Robjo' light wax. All the darkened areas were friction-burned.

The entire set can be made with just a lathe and its tools, apart from drilling for the knights' lances and Queens' veils.

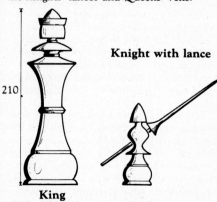

The grand furniture saga: 7___

Our latest episode in furniture history outlines the background to Baroque and tells how a royal wedding helped export English design. Vic Taylor explains

● *A Spanish fall-front desk or bargueno in walnut, mounted on a chest of drawers; trestle stands were sometimes used*

Spanish furniture during the 15th century owed a great deal to designs from the Netherlands. Flemish wood-carvers introduced the linenfold pattern of carving and the 'romayne' medallion during the 15th century, but by 1500 Netherlands influence had greatly diminished, even though Spanish kings were now their rulers. Spain grew steadily poorer both economically and politically, but the Spanish aristocracy seemed determined to maintain its standards, and popular furniture showed this.

The earlier Flemish influence was replaced by the *Mudejar* styles. The *Mudejares* were Moorish refugees who, after the fall of Granada in 1492 and the expulsion of the Moorish rulers, were allowed to stay in Spain if they renounced Islam. Many of them were skilled furniture makers and leather workers.

Furniture of this kind was decorated with geometrical designs in carving or inlays of wood, ivory, or bone, or with 'plateresque' motifs, curvilinear abstract patterns which were sometimes developed into conventionalised flower-heads. Another feature was the use of tooled, stamped leather called *guadamecil* on chest and chairs — it is sometimes called 'Cordovan leatherwork' because the town of Cordova was the centre of the craft.

Two designs were peculiarly Spanish and both were writing cabinets, the *bargueno* and the *papeleira*. Both consisted of a chest standing on its side with nests of drawers and cupboards; the lid of the *bargueno* dropped down to form a writing surface, while the smaller *papeleira* was left open. Both had strong loop handles, usually iron, at each end. The interiors became more and more elaborate and intricate, and by the end of the 17th century they had many of the exaggerated motifs favoured by the Spanish designer Don José Churriguera who died in 1725. He was an exponent of the Spanish Baroque style, whose grotesque architectural motifs and weird human figures often outrivalled the excesses of the Italian version.

The *bargueno* was often decorated with pierced ironwork (sometimes gilt) on the front of the fall, frequently backed with crimson velvet — a favourite device of Spanish makers — and occasionally silver was used instead of iron. The piece was supported in one of three ways — a trestle-stand with runners resting on the floor (*pie de puente*), a chest of four deep drawers (a *taquillón*) or a side table.

Spanish tables of the period generally had either trestle ends which were connected to the top by decorative iron brackets, or straight, heavily turned or twisted legs and deep drawers, the fronts of which were often carved with roundels or conventionalised foliage and fitted with iron ring handles. In each case the edges of the tops were left square and never moulded.

The most typical Spanish chair was the *sillón de fraileros* or monk's chair. Both its seat and back were leather, with deep front and back stretchers, the front one usually pierced and carved. The design was the basis of several similar styles, and contemporary versions can be seen today in restaurants and clubs. The ubiquitous X-chair was also popular (called the *sillón de cadera*) and it was often upholstered with fringed braid on the back and seat and decorated with *mudejar* inlay.

Walnut was most frequently used for furniture, as it was (and is) plentiful in Spain, but cypress, oak, and pine were among other timbers popular with makers and buyers.

Portugal expelled the Moors in 1249, but the *mudejar* influence of geometrical design and curvilinear patterns lingered on together with fine decorative leatherwork. By the 16th century, however, Portugal had developed strong trading links with China and India and the influence became apparent. Unfortunately, wars and other hazards have destroyed almost all of the furniture, porcelain, and other artefacts of the period.

The marriage of the Portuguese princess Catharine de Braganza to Charles II of England, and English aid to the Portuguese to prevent a Spanish invasion, created a strong friendship between the two countries which they still enjoy. One result was that the Portuguese adopted English furniture styles in the 17th and 18th centuries, although they added embellishments more to their tastes.

Two Portuguese designs are interesting. One is the *contador*, a cabinet of drawers mounted on a stand with legs heavily turned in the typical 'reel' style. The drawer-fronts were moulded geometrically to give a shimmering effect when light played on them, known as the *tremidos* effect. It is almost identical with the Wellenschrank effect found on the large cupboards (called *schranks*) which were mainly produced in Frankfurt in the late 17th century.

The second design was a chair with both seat and the tall medallion-shaped back upholstered in embossed leather. The legs were turned and terminated in fluted scrolled feet called 'Braganza' feet which frequently appear on late 17th century English furniture. Also, the front stretcher was very deep and pierced with the interlaced scrolls which were a favourite Portuguese motif.

This love of turned and twisted work shows in other types of furniture. The Spanish *sillón de fraileros*, for instance, was slimmer and more elegant, with turned legs, stretchers, and feet; it was also sometimes adorned with an arched top and brasswork. On the *cama de bilros*, a bed with four posts and open head- and foot-ends, the posts were elaborately turned or twisted and the open ends were filled with a tracery of turned pillars and rails.

The next important style in Europe was the Baroque, which began in Italy and reached its zenith there during the first quarter of the 17th century. But before moving on, we ought to consider a style

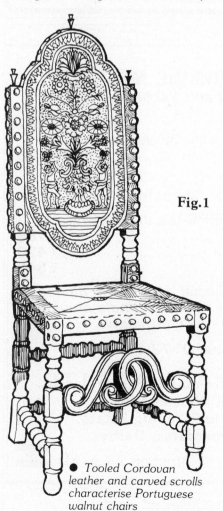

● *Tooled Cordovan leather and carved scrolls characterise Portuguese walnut chairs*

Fig.1

Fig.2

● *A rosewood cabinet or contador with geometric mouldings; extravagant turnings and pierced friezes were hallmarks of Portuguese furniture at that time*

which linked the late Renaissance designs with the Baroque, the 'auricular' or 'lobate' style. Its originator was a Dutch silversmith, Paulus van Vianen (1568-1613).

Characteristic of this style are the contorted and convoluted motifs which vaguely resemble human ears or ear lobes (hence the name) with grotesque human faces, sea shells and sea monsters. The fashion was short-lived and commonest in southern Germany and Switzerland.

In French the word 'baroque' means irregular, strange or grotesque, but it derives from an Italian word describing an irregular pearl — the connection with oyster shells is obvious and they were favourite motifs in Baroque designs. Other decoration included mermaids, mermen, Tritons, sea-horses, leafy swags and garlands, animal legs and feet, and *putti* (cherubs). Inlays of ebony, or wood stained to resemble it, were applied as backgrounds for elaborate gilt mounts and mouldings, and copper sheeting was used as a base for painted panels.

Later in the 17th century recurrent wars between Italian states led to a drop in lifestyle and paint was applied to disguise cheap timber (such as pine) and poor construction. The wood was coated with glue size and fine gauze laid over it to conceal cracks and other imperfections. Over this a background coat of paint was embellished with painted designs of flowers, arabesques or small classical scenes before lacquering. Gilding was still used for mounts and mouldings.

The most spectacular feature of the period was the decorative use of marble inlay. The craft had been a traditional Italian skill and was boosted when the Grand Duke of Tuscany founded the *Opificio delle Pietre Dure*, a specialist workshop in Florence. It produced both flat and raised work and became so famous that much of its production was exported, especially to France. Later *scagliola* was developed with powdered selenium made into a paste and interspersed with marble chips.

Ownership of such Baroque designs was largely confined to the aristocracy, the wealthy and dignitaries of the Church as status symbols. Much humbler furniture was used in the living quarters for everyday life.

In the next article we will see how the Baroque style influenced the rest of Europe. ■

Books

Some of these books are out of print so we haven't included publishers' names, but you should be able to find them in a library.

John Gloag, *A Social History of Furniture*, 1966

Hugh Honour, *Cabinetmakers and Furniture Designers*, 1969

Ivan Sparkes, *English Domestic Furniture*, 1980

Margaret MacDonald Taylor, *English Furniture*, 1965

Andrew Brunt, *Illustrated Guide to Furniture*, 1978

Ralph Edwards, *Shorter Dictionary of English Furniture*, 1964

World Furniture, 1965 and 1980, Helena Hayward and Noel Riley, editors

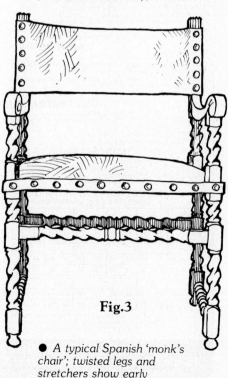

Fig.3

● *A typical Spanish 'monk's chair'; twisted legs and stretchers show early Baroque influence*

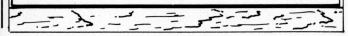
646

647

Books

William Wells
Performing Wooden Toys
Batsford, £7.95
Reviewed by Alan Bridgewater

Yet another book on making wooden toys, which, at the last count, makes the fourth this year — could we be in for a 70s-style book boom?

In our collection of books on toys and toymaking we have everything from Lesley Gordon's delightful work *Peepshow into Paradise* (1953), through to a smashing little title called *The Junior Craftsman* (1926 or thereabouts). The traditional British toymaking book is solid, well-written and beautifully illustrated — note the emphasis on beautifully illustrated! So how does William Well's *Performing Wooden Toys* compare?

Well, for all its 88 pages, 137 line illustrations, and eight colour photographs, it's good only in parts. There are 17 beautifully considered and well-thought out projects — who wouldn't be excited about such delights as making a Hook trick, a Magic propeller, or an Exploding destroyer? The text is nicely organised and clearly written, the eight colour plates of completed projects very good, but the rest is a letdown. The main project illustrations, line and working drawings, are a badly-worked mish-mash. The working drawings, for example, are a confusion of imperial measurements, their approximate metric equivalents, plus lines, sections and arrowheads. The few hand-on-tool illustrations are so weak, they could have been left out. As for the project drawings — the detailed drawings which should describe how the toys work — I'm still trying to figure some of those out.

The index is also weak, which is a shame; not necessarily the author's fault, this one, but it is such details that make or break a book.

Even taking into account the modest cover price of £7.95, the book is but a poor-to-middling buy. Interesting? Inspirational? — Certainly. But the drawings! . . .

Mike Darlow
The Practice of Woodturning
Melaleuca Press, £15 (approx)
Reviewed by Michael O'Donnell

Not enough professional turners take to the pen. There was a big gap from Frank Pain to the recent Key and Raffan books — and now Darlow, a step which, in theory, must be good for woodturning.

Mike Darlow is a professional, and this is obvious from the content of the book. I would say that the majority of his turning is spindle work, and his favourite tool (he uses it almost continuously) the skew chisel. To make a living spindle turning you have to be very fast, accurate, and able to produce a finish from the tool without sanding which requires a thorough understanding of the skew. Mike has described the tool, its sharpening and use, in detail, making it possible to follow the instructions directly from the book and use the tool in exactly the way he does. It certainly works because I tried it; this must be the best, almost definitive writing on the skew.

The spindle turning section is good, with lots of professional tips. All the drawings are clear and well-drawn, and in the main, the photographs make their point. Many of them are printed full-page size, and are easy to study.

Unfortunately the rest of the book falls far below this standard. Mike has tried to cover all aspects of turning, resulting in a book which is heavy in both weight and reading; many of the sections don't fulfil a function or come to any definite conclusion. Terminology is also a problem, more because of the terms he doesn't use rather than the ones he does.

The section on design is mainly about antique legs, which could more accurately be described as reproduction rather than new designs. He lists far too many design rules; if you followed them precisely you'd probably produce the same leg each time.

The information on chucks and holding devices is very dated, although his method of using the three-jaw chuck is interesting and certainly safer than conventional ones. His turning theory, as he says, is extrapolated from metal turning textbooks. It falls far short of being any help to the woodturner, and indeed would leave you somewhat confused; it doesn't explain how the tools work or the importance of the bevel in stability or form control. A form of tool theory also appears in a number of other sections — again mainly irrelevant.

As with the rest of the book, the workshop procedure section has some good tips, but it should be read as his methods rather than the best or correct method of working. The bowl-turning section really shows up a total lack of understanding of how gouges work, how to use the bevel and where to stand for complete control. The photographs show very poor results from the gouge, and procedures which would be slow and imprecise.

I would be rather sceptical about learning to fell trees from a woodturning book — a good reference for further reading would be much safer. I'm not saying he's wrong, just not an acknowledged expert! Felling, particularly near property, is a risky business.

What little he had to say on 'green' turning would not have been missed if it was omitted, and the work in the gallery section I found really quite depressing.

It's a great pity that Mike didn't stick to what he knows, and produce a smaller, less expensive book which would have been a must for all spindle turners. While it isn't cheap, and there are sections best left unread, I would certainly recommend it just for the skew chisel and spindle turning sections.

It is, after all, only the price of a gouge.

● Alan Bridgewater is a multi-skilled craftsman and co-author with his wife Gill.

● Mick O'Donnell is a professional woodturner and teacher.

Course fishing

Fresh start or busman's holiday — the weekend course should be fun. Kerry Fowler went to West Dean College to investigate

● *West Dean's benefactor, the late Edward James, accompanied by Dali's* Le Sommeil

West Dean, a huge flint mansion deep in Sussex, is simply ripe as a film location. It's a glorious old place with shrubberies and gravel paths perfect for a Margaret Rutherford afternoon constitutional, and the greying resplendence of the interior would make an ideal back-drop for the frenetic bumblings of Will Hay.

The house is simply stacked high with antiques and works of art; so much so that Sotheby's are holding a five-day auction just for back-room stock. Edward James was the man responsible for this cornucopia; an art patron extraordinaire (Dali, Magritte and Tchelitchew all received his attentions), he became an enigmatic tax-exile who donated his mansion and grounds to the college foundation. The college runs one-day to year-long residential courses ranging from designer knitting to boat-building, but top rung is the antique restoration year's course, which is run in conjunction with the British Antique Dealers Association. It produces the *crème de la crème* of restorers. The students handle extremely valuable pieces of furniture from museums such as the Victoria & Albert, and tackle total rebuilds to the most intricate of repairs — I witnessed one student painstakingly bring colour back to an enormous marquetry chest, each tiny segment having to be colour-coded like the ultimate in painting-by-numbers.

Going from the sublime to the ridiculous, the dilapidated sewing-box on stilts which constituted my rather feeble offering for the 'Caring for Antiques' weekend seemed beyond redemption. The job was to repair and re-finish it; in two days, course-tutor Mick Paul managed a transformation second only to Cinderella's. The warp was unwarped and the 'fine English ply lid' had acquired a recognisable, if not delicate, grain.

The other course participants had more savvy and respect and brought such pieces as an Edwardian yew table, a mock Tudor bench and an assortment of antique boxes, all in dire need of resuscitation. Mick Paul is one of those terribly reassuring people who gently oversees your work with suggestions, not orders — a sort of wry Arthur Negus. The course is interspersed with mini-lectures and the first dealt, rather conveniently for the Edwardian table, with stain-removal. Oxalic acid was preferred to a two-part bleach solution, but it was firmly stressed that it is a poison, available only from chemists, to be treated with care, and never to be used with wire wool. It's a simple process: soak the crystals in warm water; apply first to stained areas with rag or brush (wear gloves), wash off with water after 15 minutes and then re-apply to the entire surface (again leave for no more than 15 minutes and wash off).

This treatment worked wonders on the yew table but by now I was more concerned with clamping my lid, which had been in soak for longer than was healthy. Leaving it groaning under a ton of weights, I attacked the meths and stripped the carcase of my beast in preparation for some french polishing tricks.

Whether it was the fumes or genuine enthusiasm, I was totally hooked. The notion of a sedate weekend and gentle instruction evaporated in the general haze — I was even dreaming shellac and abrasives! Fortunately the non-course activities of eating, drinking and socialising were all so pleasant (the meals a real delight and the bedrooms fodder for Jane Austen-type reflections) that total obsession never took hold.

Mick is an old West Deanian. He completed the antique restoration course a few moons ago and is a professional restorer (now semi-retired) and a dab-hand at french polishing. It's a long but totally rewarding process. The first stage is making the 'rubber' with which to apply the shellac; Mick whipped one together, from lint wadding and lint-free cotton as the outer, in a matter of seconds. The wadding is then soaked with equal parts of transparent polish and meths and applied with exactitude in even sweeps across the surface; wait until it's minimally dry (touch with the back of hand to check) and then re-apply up to seven coats depending on the condition of the wood. Then comes the fun task of adding colour, in my case Vandyke water stain, a gungy tar-like mixture; the problem being that the polish is oil-based and so it usually takes a couple of attempts to secure the water colouring.

Once the desired hue is achieved, more layers of polish are added to give the finish a final fix. By this time I was more than a little fond of the box on legs; it was positively radiant. Once its legs were filed and the warpless lid replaced, it was ready to do my bedroom what the rejuvenated Eros has done to Piccadilly.

By Sunday afternoon the workshop, which was converted from the massive stable area and is exceptionally airy and clean, was full of proud owners of re-glossed, virtually unmarked tables; boxes which had been furbished with new inlay; an old wind-up gramophone now fit to have a dog ear-holing its trumpet; and a totally defunct (but re-veneered) dismembered chair. Plans for its re-assembly had to be shelved — the time factor does limit really ambitious renovation. The important elements of the course were those of interest and learning through your own, (and others') mistakes and achievements; naturally your own piece is the most crucial but it's fascinating to watch the range of techniques required for the variety of ailments. One of the most beneficial tips was Mick's magic cleaning potion — equal parts of boiled linseed oil, liquid paraffin, vinegar, water and meths — which cleans even the filthiest of woods splendidly.

If you're thinking of taking the course — both an education and a pleasure — then take either something you loathe which has potential, or something of value which has distinct defects. Otherwise you'll be left with too much time on your polish-stained hands. Of course there is plenty to occupy your eye both in and out of doors; there's a fascinating arboretum (where Edward James is buried) and the grounds house some wonderful tree specimens, in particular the Cypress cedars. But the 'Caring for Antiques' weekend is essentially about learning, appreciation, and sharing in the experiences of like-minded woodaholics. ■

● Details of the extensive range of courses are available from: West Dean College, Chichester, West Sussex PO18 0QZ, tel. (024363) 301.

Double time

You can use a double-edged *Ryoba Noko Giri* double-handed, but it's not doubly difficult to sharpen — as Tony Wood reveals

● *Short strokes and a pulling action get the Japanese saw into action*

When you get a new Japanese saw, the blade will have a lacquer coating to prevent corrosion during transit. The first thing to do is get rid of it with methylated spirits, but be warned, it takes a fair amount of elbow-grease and time. After the blade has been cleaned, lightly oil it with some chamelia oil. While you're at it, you might as well give the handle a quick wipe too. Chamelia oil is extremely light, and won't transfer to your timber so don't worry. In fact it's a good idea to clean and oil the blade regularly to remove any resin stuck to it. This is especially relevant if you're cutting a lot of softwood.

Using the *Ryoba Noko Giri*

Because a *Ryoba Noko Giri*'s blade is thin and brittle, you must use it with great care. The saws are so sharp that very little force is required to keep them cutting rapidly and smoothly.

Probably the best way to experience the 'pull' cutting action for the first time is to use the saw holding the end of the handle only between your forefinger and thumb. This way, you won't be tempted — or able — to put too much pressure on the blade, and you'll soon establish a natural cutting rhythm. If you give yourself time to develop the slightly different techniques, you'll be rewarded by quick, clean cutting and a saw

that stays sharp for a long time. The traditional way to hold the *Ryoba Noko Giri* is to grip the handle as you would a hammer; larger saws have larger handles, for which a double-handed grip is often used, one hand at each end of the handle. But the most important thing is to be comfortable when using the saw, which is why you'll probably end up developing your own way of holding it.

Start each cut on the small teeth nearest the handle, using short cutting-strokes with the handle held low down to the work. Then when a kerf has been made, slowly increase the length of the cutting-stroke until the full length of the blade is working.

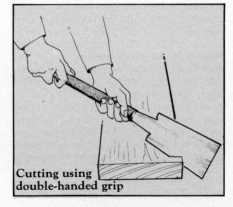

Cutting using double-handed grip

Don't be tempted to try increasing the pressure on the handle to get a faster cut, just let the saw do the work.

Many people experience difficulty using the full length of the rip blade. If this is so, try cutting with the saw almost perpendicular to the work. The reason for this is quite simple; the *Ryoba Noko Giri* is a Japanese saw, developed for Japanese woodworking techniques, not western ones. Japanese woodworkers don't use waist-high benches for sawing, they use low wooden trestles, generally no more than 12in off the ground. This enables them to stand directly over the work and keep the saw precisely on the line, even for very long cuts. Not to say, of course, that the Japanese have a monopoly on sawing straight! This stance increases the angle of the blade to the wood, so the teeth are designed to cut most efficiently in this position (fig. 1). You'll soon develop the method that works best for you.

Maintenance

Saw maintenance is generally thought of as resetting and resharpening, but for practical reasons, the only recommended maintenance apart from regular cleaning is resharpening. Setting the teeth on a Japanese saw is as much an art as a science because of the hardness of the blade-steel. Bend the tooth too little, and it will spring back to its

Fig.1

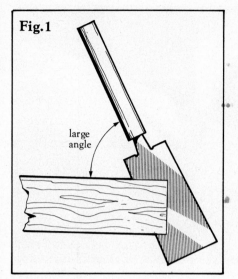

previous position; bend it too far, and it will snap off when it is moved back to the correct position.

The teeth on Japanese saws are individually set, either by bending them with a special tool called a *mafuri*, or by striking them with a saw-setting hammer called an *asari-tsuchi*. There shouldn't really be any need even to consider resetting. The only things that can affect the set of the *Ryoba Noko Giri* are bad working techniques and carelessness, so if you avoid both of these sins, resetting won't be a problem.

Probably the biggest hurdle to get over will be whether or not to have a go at sharpening your own saws, but look at it this way; if your saws are blunt they're not much use, so any sharpening you give them must be an improvement. As long as you take care there's no fear of damaging them.

The tool for sharpening Japanese saws is the *yasuri* (saw-file). It's about 6in long including the tang, about ¾in wide, and it has a shallow diamond cross-section (fig. 2). The traditional method of holding the saw is in a wooden saw-vice which looks a bit like a very large clothes peg, except that instead of a spring to shut the jaws, a

● A saw in a Japanese vice. The teeth should be about ¼in above the jaws

Fig.2 The *Yasuri* saw-file

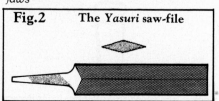

Fig.3 Saw-vice

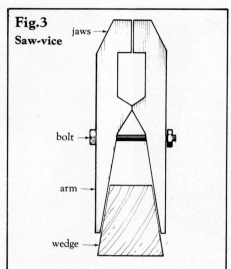

wooden wedge is banged between the arms, forcing the jaws closed (fig. 3).

The high price — £100 — of a genuine saw-vice will put most people of, but needless to say, there's a very cheap and simple alternative; two softwood battens and a bench-vice. Watch you don't make the pieces of wood so wide they grip and damage the teeth on the other edge of the blade, and make the 'jaws' long enough to support the length of the blade (fig. 4). The

Fig.4

Fig.5

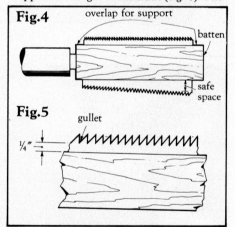

blade should be gripped so the gullets of the teeth are about ¼in above the wooden battens (fig. 5).

Before you use the saw-file, you should fit a handle for safety and blunt the cutting teeth along one of the 'sharp' edges (fig. 6). This is to prevent untold damage during sharpening to the crosscut teeth, each of which has three distinct cutting surfaces: the trailing edge (*uwa-ba*), the leading edge (*shita-ba*) and the top (*uwa-me*). See fig. 7 for how this works. When you're sharpening the top of the tooth, it's very easy to strike the leading edge of the one next to it and put a nasty nick in it. If you use the file with its blunted edge towards the leading edge of the next-door tooth, the tops can be sharpened without problems (fig. 8).

The best way of blunting the file's teeth is to work it on a coarse oil- or water-stone, preferably the edge in case you dig the

Fig.6

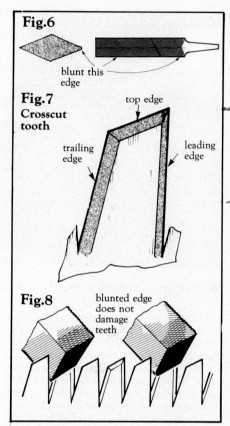

Fig.7 Crosscut tooth

Fig.8

corner of the file in. Try to get a slightly rounded profile on that edge of the file for maximum protection; no need for a perfectly smooth finish, just remove the sharpness. When you've done this, mark the handle on the blunted-edge side so you know which edge is which.

Sharpening the crosscut teeth

Clamp the saw-blade in either your very expensive genuine saw-vice or very cheap wooden battens so the gullets are about ¼in proud of the jaws. The file is held in two hands, one gripping the handle and providing the motion, the other gripping and steering the blade.

Before you start, lay the file in the gullet between two teeth and move it slightly to one side. Now you can see why the file has such a strange diamond shape. If you've moved it to the correct side, the file fits perfectly against the leading edge of one tooth and the trailing edge of the next. This is the cutting position, sharpening two cutting surfaces at a time.

More saws are ruined by over-caution than by over-confidence. Use the full length of the file and an even pressure, following the existing bevel of the cutting surfaces. It only needs one pass of the file per gullet, and if you use any more, you won't make the saw any sharper, you'll just cut more metal away and reduce the blade's life. Don't be tempted to use several light strokes of the file to give a better finish, because all that's likely to happen is the bevel of the cutting surface will be damaged.

Double time

● *Filing crosscut teeth edges,* **above left,** *and then their tops,* **right**

Crosscut teeth are sharpened alternately, so the pattern is; sharpen one pair of cutting surfaces (back of one tooth and front of the next), miss a pair, then sharpen a pair and so on (fig. 9). Follow this pattern for one side of the blade, then turn the saw round in the vice and sharpen the rest of the leading and trailing edges. At the end of the second pass down the blade, they should all be sharp, because one stroke cuts two surfaces.

The next step is to sharpen the top cutting edges. This is where the careful blunting of the file will pay dividends; no matter how careful you try to be, you're bound to touch an adjacent tooth occasionally during this process. The technique is the same as for the *uwa-ba* and *shita-ba*: use an even pressure, an even length of stroke and most important of all maintain the original bevel angle. Once again, sharpen alternate teeth, turning the saw round in the vice when you have finished one side.

Sharpening the rip teeth

The rip teeth of the *Ryoba Noko Giri* are sharpened in much the same way as the crosscut teeth, but this time there are only two cutting edges to worry about, and no bevels on them (fig. 10). So for sharpening the rip teeth, hold the file at right angles to the face of the blade, which guarantees the required square profile of each tooth is maintained (fig. 11). That square-on feature means the cutting edges don't alternate, so you can start at one end of the blade and sharpen every tooth without missing, or turning the blade. ■

● Tony and *Woodworker* would like to thank Roger Buse of Roger's of Hitchin for his inspiration and assistance in preparing this series. Roger will persuade reluctant Japanese saw-sharpeners to try it themselves, or he will do it for you; there is no one else in the UK at the moment who is offering this service.

Roger's, 47 Walsworth Rd, Hitchin, Herts SG4 9SU, (0462) 34177.

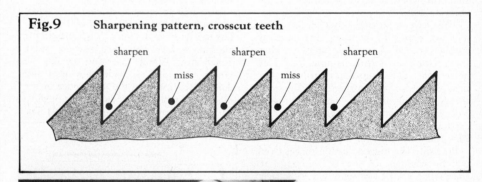

Fig.9 Sharpening pattern, crosscut teeth

sharpen   sharpen   sharpen

miss   miss

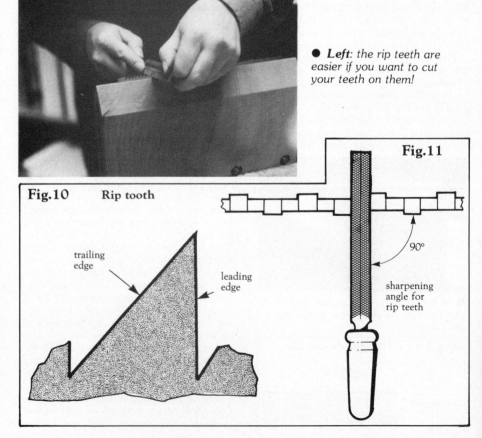

● **Left:** *the rip teeth are easier if you want to cut your teeth on them!*

Fig.10 Rip tooth

trailing edge

leading edge

Fig.11

90°

sharpening angle for rip teeth

Far-flung craft

Phil Townsend lives and works on the north-west Irish coast. He describes his life making furniture about as far from the madding crowd as you can get

Compared to today's generation of designer/makers I'm a very late starter. I suppose I really began with a course in three-dimensional design in the early 70s, but after graduating I drifted into other, mostly non-related work. My ideal in those days was the self-sufficient jack-of-all-trades.

Some seven years ago my wife, daughter and I moved here with the intention of living the 'good life', keeping a mixture of livestock and growing our own food on a 10-acre smallholding, earning an income from some craft enterprise.

I had been using a smallish timber garage for a workshop, so the first thing we did over here was put up a substantial concrete block building designed to accommodate all forseeable craftwork contingencies. All we knew at the time was the work would be likely to involve wood. Priorities were plenty of natural light, adequate power points, solid fuel heating and versatile access. Having experienced the annoyance of moving lengths of timber round in a tight space I made sure there was plenty of headroom and a storage loft. One end of the workshop was partitioned off as a rough-and-ready temporary kitchen and living room while we demolished most of the old thatched house on the property and rebuilt it with a second storey.

We did all the work (apart from the plumbing), entirely on our own out of economic necessity. I'd done a confidence-building TOPS course in carpentry and joinery some years before, so after tackling all the construction woodwork in the house I turned my hand to furnishing it.

Cottage-style pine furniture was a natural choice — hard-wearing, in keeping with the rural lifestyle and easy to make without sophisticated equipment. I think I made just about every stick in the place, and when our two sons arrived in 81 and 82, I decided to try my hand at making a living making furniture to sell.

I took photographs of all the pieces I'd made and then made a dozen samples ranging from a rocking cradle to a corner dresser. I put them into my future showroom, a small room at one end of the house with direct access from outdoors. Then I made an eye-catching sign to hang in a field opposite our lane, put an ad in the local newspaper and crossed my fingers.

That first year was both exciting and instructive. In the beginning I was very machinery under-equipped, though I'd more than enough hand-tools.

I had a lightweight panel saw, a small surface planer and a few DIY-grade power tools, managing for more than six months with little drill-attached drum sanders.

From the outset I was never without work, and I also had an MSC Enterprise Allowance. It wasn't long before I invested in a Startrite K260 universal, a heavy-duty drill-press, a second-hand lathe, compressor and spray equipment and some professional quality power tools, mostly Elu. For the price the universal is ideal for my one-man band business though at times I could use a wider planer/thicknesser. Apart from what I started out with I've spent about £4500 on equipment. The items I most need are a kiln, a decent bandsaw for deep-cutting and curved work and a pad sander to take some of the tedium out of sanding.

I've converted one of my several good-sized outbuildings into a timber store, knocking out the top of one gable end to allow lengths up to 18ft to be slid in and out, and I've put up a rack inside for 8x4ft sheets.

I work mostly in Scandinavian pine, readily available and good quality if you're willing to spend a while sorting through a bale or two. Not only is it far cheaper than commonly imported hardwoods like iroko and mahogany it also has the vigorous visual quality associated with country-style furniture. Every so often the local sawmill will have something interesting which is often sold for little more than its normal raw material — the ubiquitous Sitka spruce. The mill has supplied us with

Douglas fir, larch, ash, oak, and recently a large amount of Spanish chestnut for stock. The only sources of kiln-dried native hardwoods are in Dublin or across the border in the North, so transport costs can be substantial — I was recently quoted £60 delivery for 30 cu ft of ash from Dublin. So far I've managed to confine manufactured board to bedroom furniture, usually block-board with a heavy veneer of, say, parana pine. This is edged with a solid wood strip, either matching or strongly contrasting, and will accept stain well; there's no need for furniture made from such board to look monotonous.

These days I do fewer free-standing pieces and more fitted kitchens and bathrooms. I find the general view of fitted furniture as a poor relation of 'genuine' furniture both shortsighted and unrealistic,

● *Top, Phil and Douglas-fir sewing desk; left, the house and workshop were built almost from scratch!*

when so many space-restricted modern homes use it. Where fitted furniture does go wrong is when it's done to a set pattern with little imagination. I try to upgrade the quality of fitted work by considering the function of the room as a whole, not just plonking down so many 'units' along a wall. This manipulation of available space calls for the interior design approach especially where space is at a premium.

Because there's no cabinetmaking tradition on this western seaboard of Ireland, there's almost nothing in the way of direct competition for a radius of 40 or 50 miles. Whereas in England I would consider my present standard of craftsmanship only a good average, here I am spoken of as a master craftsman ('Ah, the wonderful hands ye have on ye') which is good for the ego but makes for complacency. Living out here, there's little opportunity to gain knowledge and improve my craft at first hand, so I rely heavily on reading. I regard books as similar to tools, vital both for extending the scope of my production and increasing efficiency. The monthly magazine is also of course indispensable for woodworking stimulation! Especially in the beginning I often felt the lack of contact with other furniture makers. The three I know personally live between 50 and 180 miles away, and when we do meet we tend to talk shop until one or the other's wife calls a halt!

One of the nice things about rural Ireland is that there is little class structure here. The people who come to me range from local

● *Phil's biggest challenge so far – the bureau/bookcase in yellow pine*

fishermen to the TD (MP). You quickly get on to Christian name terms and when I know someone well and perhaps done several jobs for them, I sometimes suggest a specially designed piece of furniture for a specific function. I will charge for materials and labour with a profit margin in the normal way, but don't feel able to charge for design time because I am in effect being paid to teach (and enjoy) myself.

Early this year I made my most demanding piece to date — a bureau/bookcase with a fall-flap front in yellow pine. The basic design is derived from the traditional bureau but I endeavoured to give it simple lines, and a lightness of feel which — I hope — is unmistakably modern. The brief demanded a drawer large enough for A2 size paper, plus deep drawers for documents.

This was almost immediately followed by a desk for sewing. The brief called for storage for the sewing machine (it goes in the kneehole cupboard), large drawers to contain fabric, and small drawers for buttons, pins, scissors, and so on. I also made a gallery at the back on to which a lamp can be clamped. This piece is made from Douglas fir, and like the bureau/bookcase uses a canted-in front to take away any possible square, heavy feel. It also gives improved toe-room and creates a

more visually stimulating surface.

My enthusiasm for designing and making is unfortunately not matched in another very important area — book-keeping. I know it's important not to look on book-keeping as a chore, but I seem to have a mental block when confronted with standard business-management practices. Because I make to order and sell direct, with no rent or rates on the business buildings, and no time or money spent travelling, I've never found it a problem to earn a decent income without working overtime. On average there's enough work ahead to keep me going for six to eight weeks (this seems to be the limit most people are prepared to wait) and most of it comes via personal recommendation — I think I've put three small ads in the paper in as many years.

All in all, I've a lot to be grateful for in the start this location's afforded me, however 'late' it may be! But now I feel I need to move closer to a larger centre of population, if I'm to realise a growing ambition to be more deeply involved in my work and share this participation with like-minded souls. Maybe the hurly-burly of the harsh world of competition will send me scurrying back here! ■

● Phil is selling his property and business. If you're interested, write to Phil Townsend, Pine Design, Inver PO, Co. Donegal, Eire.

Guild notes

Guild of WOODWORKERS

The Guild was set up by *Woodworker* to create a meeting ground for all those involved in working wood, whether professional, amateur, or enthusiastic beginner. Guild members get:

- Access to Guild courses and events
- Free publicity in *Woodworker*
- Specially arranged tool insurance at low rates
- 15% off Woodworker Show entry
- A free display area and meeting point at the Show
- 15% discount off *Woodworker* plans
- Inclusion in our register of members' skills and services

For details, please send an sae to the Guild of Woodworkers, 1 Golden Sq, London W1R 3AB.

GUILD COURSES

● **Only Guild members are eligible to go on these courses. You must book in advance, and we must have a cheque for the full cost of the course at the time of booking. If you cancel less than four weeks before the advertised date you will forfeit 50% of the cost, unless there are exceptional circumstances.**

Decorative techniques — Ian Hosker

6-7 September, 10-5, Chester, £45.
You read the articles, now do the course. Ian's feature, 'Coats of many colours' in the March and April issues covered wonderful decorative techniques such as dragging, lining, sponging, rag-rolling, marbling, spattering, and (his and our favourite) tortoise-shelling. The cost includes materials, but students should bring a few paint-brushes and jam-jars.

Hand veneering — Bob Grant

27 September, 9.30-5, Oxford, £35+VAT.
Veneering is much more than the art of disguising chipboard. It's a skill with a long history, and can create some beautiful effects — and it saves fine and expensive wood! You'll be laying a panel with veneer, mitring a cross-banding, inlaying lines round it, and applying a balancer veneer on the back. If you have a veneer hammer, bring it; but materials will be provided.

From the past . . .

Guild member **Laurence O'Carroll** who lives near Huntingdon, Cambridgeshire, has a large number of back copies of *Woodworker* going back to 1963 which he is offering to a fellow member. No charge, says Laurence, who is reluctantly parting with the issues because he won't have room in his new house. But he would like the recipient to make a donation to a deserving charity of his or her own choice.

Please write directly to Laurence at 3 Grainger Avenue, Godmanchester, Huntingdon, Cambridgeshire PE18 8JT.

Nice one, Ian

Ian Hosker, one of our regular tutors on finishing techniques, has offered to organise a local group based on South Wirral, Cheshire. The suggestion came from some students in one of his night classes, so naturally he stepped forward. If you live in the area please drop a line to Ian Hosker at 1 Spring Avenue, Little Sutton, South Wirral, Cheshire L66 3SH.

Your man

John Hemsley is my name; I'm the new deputy editor of *Woodworker*, and I shall be administering the Guild from now on. I'm very keen to make the Guild even more useful to you the members, with more courses and development of stronger links between you all.

To do this I need your help. Please send me your ideas, and suggest new courses you would be interested in. I also want to build up more local groups, where you can meet regularly with others involved with wood; why don't you volunteer as a local rep?

French polishing — Charles Cliffe

2-3 October, 9.30-5, Bexleyheath, £40.
Charles Cliffe, one of our 'Question box' experts and author of *The Woodworker Manual of Finishing and Polishing*, explains preparation, staining, and application of this tricky (and beautiful) finish. He'll also be dealing with using a cabinet scraper, so bring your own, plus any small piece of furniture that you want advice on. Charles can order supplies for you to take away if you tell him in advance.

Wood-machining — Ken Taylor

11 October, 9.30-5.30, Bletchley, Bucks, £25+VAT.
Ken's course on the ins and outs of machining wood is one of our most popular. Find out about (and try for yourself) table- and band-saws, radial-arm saws, planers and thicknessers, spindle moulders, mortisers and universals. Lunch is included in the price.

. . . towards the future

Here's your chance to get your name on a national register organised by the **Crafts Council** to promote professional craftspeople. It might get you more business.

The Register is run on a cardfile system, and you have to complete three sets of cards, which can then be looked at in the Crafts Council Information Centre. The Register is regularly used by members of the public, the media, researchers, exhibition organisers, shops and galleries.
● Emma Routh, Crafts Council, 12 Waterloo Place, London SW1Y 4AU, 01-930 4811.

And another chance

Don't forget you have a chance to display your work at the **London Woodworker Show**, Alexandra Pavilion, 23-26 October.

But it operates on a first-come-first-served basis, so **send us photos of your work now:** carvings, turnings, small furniture — but no large items.

Mark your envelopes clearly 'London Gallery'.

Gilding the lily

As reward for belonging to the prestigious Guild of Woodworkers you will soon be offered a very special deal.

A subscription to *Woodworker*, (delivered to your door each month) could be yours — at a price planed to perfection!

So keep your eyes on the letter-box, and we'll be revealing the facts no-one else can . .

BOOKING FORM

I wish to book for the following course(s).
☐ **Decorative techniques** 6-7 September, £45: make cheque payable to Ian Hosker
☐ **Hand veneering** 27 September, £35 +VAT = £40.25
☐ **French polishing** 2-3 October, £40; make cheques payable to Charles Cliffe
☐ **Wood-machining** 11 October, £25 +VAT = £28.75

Please make cheques payable to 'The Guild of Woodworkers/ASP Ltd' unless otherwise stated.

Name..

Address..

....

....

Guild no...
Send to: The Guild of Woodworkers, 1 Golden Square, London, W1R 3AB. The Guild reserves the right to cancel any course.

Chisels

David Savage's careful tests of what's what for discerning hand-tool users bring some challenging results . . .

And so we come to chisels. Up to now I have studiously avoided discussion of blade sharpness, or the relative hardness of different plane irons, but this is by no means for lack of concern.

A keen edge on a tool enables a skilled worker to exercise touch and control. A chisel slices through endgrain, a plane hisses over board. Work becomes a pleasure. With a fine cutting edge, all manner of things are possible and without one, everything is a struggle. First to go are lightness, sensitivity and control, disappearing as the edge dulls. This isn't an instant transition, and the inexperienced worker may not notice it happening; what was a gentle pleasure is now more of a fight. It's soon obvious, as the fibres tear, that the tool has lost its edge — but this has really happened long before.

The view is now common amongst woodworkers that today's steels don't hold this keen edge long enough. I say steels sold today aren't capable of holding a keen edge as long as steels used by our forefathers, and that in this respect some toolmaking has regressed, not progressed.

The steels in today's chisel- or plane-blades have what their makers describe as 'greater toughness'. This resistance to shock and abuse may be of value to the site carpenter or to someone doing home maintenance, where tools might be abused, but joiners and cabinetmakers are generally workshop-based, and can treat tools with greater care. So — do modern edge-tools hold this keen edge, or do they not?

Testing edges

The idea had to be put to some kind of strict and fair test. In a perfect world, we would have a machine cutting a paring of precise thickness at a given pressure, and we'd then measure the amount cut before the edge dulled and have a basis for comparison. Unfortunately, chisels are used by fallible human beings, and this fallible human being was the one who had to do the test.

It was very simple. I prepared each chisel to the best of my ability to hold a keen edge, the backs mirror-polished, the bevels ground to 25° then honed to 30°. Each edge was a good shaving edge, which is important, for the sharper the cutting edge, the longer it should last.

I clamped a good-length batten of 60x10mm ash on edge to an MDF cutting-board on my bench. The batten was on edge because I aimed to test vertical paring of the 60x10mm endgrain; the length of the batten was carefully measured before and after each chisel had done its stuff.

Paring this section of tough timber like ash is a demanding test for both tool and operator. It took the best part of two days to test and re-test five modern European chisels, three Japanese chisels and an old-fashioned paring chisel. At the end of this, I had ash parings up to the ankles and was suffering from chiseller's elbow. Each chisel was generally propelled by hand-paring, but about 25% of the stuff was removed with gentle taps from a small nylon-faced ½lb hammer, with which I wanted to give some simulation of shock without abusing the tool. This also gave me some relief, and to be fair, I must say the chisels that kept their edge longest got more than their fair share of taps. Boredom is a terrible enemy.

Tool preparation

Before the test began, each chisel was very carefully prepared. I advise anyone nowadays to treat each new hand-tool they purchase with the gravest suspicion, and at present my workshop seems to be filled with card-carrying members of the Flat Earth Society. They seek the absolutely flat plane sole with a grim, glazed determination; the once-adequate Japanese water-stone has been worn to a shadow of its former self and been replaced by something resembling a large house-brick. It's not absolutely necessary to have every chisel-back dead flat for its entire length, but it does help, especially when making a deep paring cut as in the test. I should state here, having noticed that some say 'face' and some say 'back', that when I say 'back' I mean the part of the blade that runs flat all the way down to the cutting edge. Certainly, the backs of all the European chisels tested, measuring from tip to handle, were concave. This varied from .25mm to .75mm, and it also varied from chisel to chisel as well as from brand to brand. Generally, Stanley presented the flattest chisels.

There seems to be no easy way to get a decent length of blade flat than to tape a piece of silicon-carbide paper to a flat steel machine-table, sit down and rub. The next

● *The Paramo/Clay 4003 range, whose 'ergonomic' handles were more comfortable for some than others*

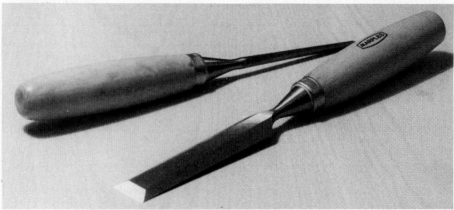

● *Marples' boxwood handles on blades the same as the 'Blue Chip' range. Boxwood handle size doesn't alter with blade size*

stage is the water-stone. It took me a long time to accept this Japanese intrusion into the workshop, but I suppose prejudice is the corrupter of all wisdom. Japanese water-stones are just superb. They give a faster cut than any India, carborundum or Arkansas stone I have used, and the polishing stone can bring up a mirror-shine in seconds. I invested a lot of money in a good set of Arkansas stones and slips, all of which now sit redundant at the back of the sharpening bench, gathering dust. The Japanese stones sit in plastic trays of water; they're remarkably soft and need great care in use. We flatten them on a sheet of wet-and-dry paper that lives beneath the water-tray, a process which only takes a minute or so and should be done regularly. If we didn't have the Flat Earth Society in the workshop, I would expect a stone to last several years.

The 1000-grit red stone will take out abrasion marks and show a uniform grey surface very quickly, and the 6000-grit finishing stone will polish up a mirror-shine in 10 seconds if blade and stone are both flat. A mirror-finish on a chisel-back is essential if you want a really keen shaving edge. Machine marks will form serrations at the cutting edge, jagged teeth that chew the rather than slice through the wood fibres. Getting a mirror-finish is simply removing these coarse scratches and polishing the surface with finer and finer abrasives. So, follow the steps — flatten the chisel-back with silicon-carbide paper, hone on the 1000 grit red stone, then on the 6000 grit polishing stone. Once that chisel-back has been polished it only ever touches your finest stone.

The bevel of most bench chisels is ground to an angle of 25°, with a secondary 30° bevel honed on the cutting edge. We have a sharpening system that makes honing tools fast and easy. To save time and maintain accuracy, the secondary bevel is kept as narrow as possible by frequent touching-up on the grinder, and I don't mean an engineer's dry grinder. They are a menace to fine edge-tools — one slip or a moment's loss of concentration and you have a blued blade that will never hold a keen edge. The blued area must be ground back, wasting years of good steel. If I only had to recommend one machine for a hand workshop, I think it would be Sharpenset's horizontal water-cooled grindstone. It grinds tool steel to a mirror-finish with great control and accuracy. The cut is slow, but as long as the water runs over the cutting edge, it's very difficult to draw the temper of a cutting tool.

The final stage of preparation is to dub off lightly any sharp edges down the length of the blade. A light rub with silicon-carbide paper will remove the arrises, but don't go too near the cutting edge, as you want the corners of the chisel square.

Honing an edge takes a bit of practice. Place the bevel-side down on the red stone, pressing hard on the extreme tip of the chisel. This will establish the 25° angle you

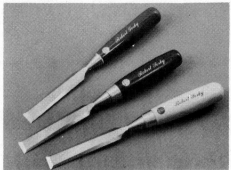

● *New Sorby 'Gilt Edge' chisels* **above** *come with plastic, boxwood or rosewood handles.* **Right**, *the Marples 'Blue Chip'*

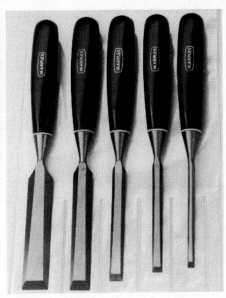

have ground and checked. Now lock your elbows into your sides, and lock your wrists, holding that angle constant. As you rock back on the balls of your feet, the chisel is pulled back across the stone, and as it travels the length of the surface, the angle increases beyond 25° to hone just the tip. No figures of eight, no forward pushes or the stone ends up looking like a ploughed field. Two pulls or at the most three will turn a burr, and now go to the finishing stone and polish the bevel you have just created. Again two or three pulls will do the job.

This business of burrs needs some explaining. There is no short-cut to getting a keen edge; a burr or 'wire edge' must be turned up, and for the best edge it should be *polished* off on the stone. If it's broken off, the breaking action will leave the edge that much duller. A Japanese stone produces a smaller burr than does an oilstone, but it can still be felt on the back of the chisel as a slight ridge at the very tip. Turn the chisel over and pull the back across the polishing stone. If the stone is clean you may see the burr fall away. If you don't, give it a couple more pulls, then polish first the bevel side and then the back once again. Good daylight and keen eyesight are useful! I was very careful in the way I prepared the chisels loaned for the test, because I felt it was important we had all the edges absolutely as keen as possible.

The tools

Five European makers presented chisels for test. They were all the traditional bevel-edged pattern much favoured by cabinet-makers, lighter in section than 'firmer' or square-sided chisels, and designed to make working against dado sides and dovetails easier. Their lightness means that you should use a light hammer or mallet prudently — a very small nylon-faced hammer, in fact, is a common bench-tool in my shop.

The blades of all the test tools were beautifully forged and finely ground; Robert Sorby Ltd have brought out a new 'Gilt-edge' chisel that was especially attractive. The bevels were nicely placed and sweetly ground, leaving narrow sides down the entire length of the tool. The Stanley 5001 chisel had a finely polished blade; Marples chisels have had high quality machining for many years now, and the examples I tested were finely formed with nice thin sides.

All the chisels had blades about 110mm long. Modern chisels all seem to have a

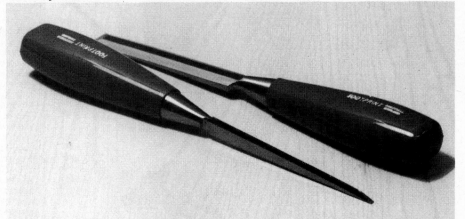

● *Footprint 6 and 16mm, with non-roll-around handles. Note the depth of the smaller blade*

Woodworker

Titles from ARGUS BOOKS

NEW!

Woodworker Manual of Finishing and Polishing

CHARLES DEREK CLIFFE   0 85242 882 0

Many woodworkers produce excellent work but find difficulty in applying a high quality finish. This book will enable woodworkers to impart to their work a polish that will stand up to a close and critical examination. The various types of finish and their processes are described simply and fully. By following the steps set out in this manual the best results will be obtained with the most economic use of time.

210 x 148mm., 96 pages, 2nd edition. Product code 70163.
☐ Please tick if this title chosen.   **£2.50**

Also available:

Woodworker Annual Volume 89   0 85242 864 2

This volume runs to 976 pages comprising all the 1985 issues of this popular magazine. A wide range of subjects includes developments in tools, techniques and design, examples of work by experts and students, how-to-do-it articles and many projects – chairs, cabinets, dressers, tables, bathroom furniture, games and toys, even a kayak and a pole lathe.

298 x 216mm., 976 pages copiously illustrated. Hardback 1985. Product code 70147.
☐ Please tick if this title chosen.   **£18.50**

NOTE: Argus Books will be publishing a series of books in association with WOODWORKER MAGAZINE in the Autumn. Please send me details ☐

HOW TO ORDER By Post

Indicate titles required, complete the details below and return the whole form to:

**Argus Books Ltd Freepost
Hemel Hempstead, Herts, HP2 4SS**

(Please add 10% part postage & packing min 50p)

I enclose my remittance for £ ....

* Please charge my Access/Mastercard/Barclaycard/Visa

* Delete as appropriate

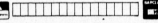

By Phone Telephone (0442) 41221 Ext 262
Quote Access/Mastercard/
Barclaycard/Visa No.

Allow up to 21 days for delivery

Signature ....

Name ....

Address ....

....

....

tapering section where the handle and blade meet, the idea apparently being to blend the two together. Stanley 5001 handles are simple, round plastic jobs, comfortable, hard-wearing and quite attractive. The Marples Blue Chip has a similar handle, but with flattish sides that hinder it from rolling from the bench. The new Sorby tool's handle comes in plastic, boxwood or rosewood, all of which were attractive and well finished. The Footprint handle, similar in shape to the Marples Blue Chip, also stays where you put it and is very comfortable to use.

Many makers offer a choice of plastic, boxwood, ash or beech handles fitted to the same blade. Marples presented chisels with both plastic and boxwood handles, and I think they also do an ash variation, but the problem is they put the same-size handle on 1in blades as they do on ¼in ones. The balance and feel of a hand-tool are of great importance, and nobody who had a go with the Marples boxwood chisels liked the balance of the smaller tools. Many preferred the Blue Chip range. Sorby seem to be making the same mistake by attempting to make one handle-size fit every chisel.

Paramo produce the Clay 4003 chisel, exotically handled in black plastic. Some hated the styling, but I quite got on with the various humps and bumps. Here someone had at least attempted to design a handle to fit the activity. The cold and slippery touch of plastic isn't to my taste, but I can see the value of using it for some chisel-handles.

Three Japanese chisels were tested; 'Samurai' bronze and silver seal chisels from Roger's, and a boxwood handle butt-chisel from Tilgear. I have had a couple of Japanese chisels sitting in a drawer for about four years now because I couldn't get on with them, finding them heavy and cumbersome to use. This test has gone a long way to changing my mind about Japanese chisels.

They are shorter than European tools, with about half the effective blade-length. The handles, like those on Western chisels, blend into the steel of the blade, fitting to a socket; simple wood cylinders with an annoying steel hoop at the top. I had no intention of battering the things to death, so I took the steel hoop off all three and improved their feel by a good margin.

The blades of both Roger's 'Samurai' chisels are of forged laminated construction, a hard carbon-steel cutting edge laminated to a softer steel backing (see 'Oire Nomi', WW/Apr). The Tilgear chisel was different in that a high-speed-steel cutting edge was brazed to the soft backing, extending half the length of the chisel-blade. The backs of Japanese chisels have a curious hollow ground in them, which has two very useful functions. It makes flattening of the blades a simple matter, for only the edges need to be trued, and it's also meant to make paring more controllable. The blades of these chisels are much thicker than those of the European tools. They are designed for use with a hammer and can take quite a battering. This heaviness isn't

necessary for delicate work; the sides of the tools I had were up to 2mm thick near the cutting edge, making them more like firmer- than bevel-edged chisels.

The test
And so the test began. I was very careful to check the edge of each tool as I progressed, and stopped once I detected dullness along more than two-thirds of the chisel's edge. Seeing this needs good eyesight, because it's no more than a glimmer of light on the edge of the tool. A sharp cutting edge won't catch light, a dull one will. Use sunlight if possible and a magnifying glass if in any doubt, but look damn hard at that edge. The bare results of the test shown in the table are the product of two days' pretty intensive work. The results were very surprising to me, and rather distressing. I went to considerable lengths to make the test fair

● **Left,** the Footprint 12mm with beech handle and brass collar; **right,** Stanley 5001 and Marples 'Blue Chip' respectively

and accurate, and each chisel was tested at least twice. If two consistent results weren't achieved, I made a third or fourth test.

I had expected there to be a difference between old and new, between Japanese and European, but the extent of that difference is a shock and worry. Much that I believed about European tools in general and Japanese chisels in particular will clearly have to be reviewed.

The Ward paring chisel was put into the comparison as an indication of the standard set by old-fashioned tool makers. It's interesting that the results from this tool are similar to that given by the best and most expensive Japanese chisel.

Clearly, there's a difference of opinion among toolmakers about what properties are of greatest value to the woodworker. European makers seem to believe a softer, more forgiving steel has more use (or a larger market) than the harder laminated steels.

Without doubt there's a price to pay for the keen, long-lasting edge. These Japanese tools are expensive thoroughbreds, with all the fickle sensitivity of a highly-strung racehorse. The hard steel is brittle; abuse it, use it as a lever, and you'll chip the edge. A careless 'chink', one chisel-edge to another, and you could have wiped out 40 quid's worth of tool. Scammelling round in the bottoms of mortises could even chip an edge; these tools must be handled with great respect.

Honing an edge on a Japanese chisel isn't more difficult than on a Western one, but it does need a great deal more care because the burr hangs on that bit longer. Honing the high-speed-steel chisel from Tilgear was especially difficult. The final consideration is the form of the Japanese chisel itself. Each one was beautifully balanced, with different handle-sizes for different blade-widths and weights. The chisels I had were designed for temple joiners, whose work is frequently complex but seldom small. European cabinetmakers use very little else but thin-sided bevel-edged chisels. Apart from trying a Japanese cabinetmaker's version which I understand is available, the answer must be to fettle a Japanese chisel in the same way we fettle any other tool. The grindstone and a small jig has already served

Bevel-edged chisel	Length of 60x10mm ash piece pared down end-grain before first dulling perceived	Recommended retail price inc. VAT
Stanley 5001 12mm	7mm	£6.50
Footprint ½in	8mm	£4.67
Marples Blue Chip ½in	8mm	£5.63
Paramo/Clay 4003 ½in	13mm	£5.23
Sorby Gilt-Edge 12mm (plastic handle)	7mm	£6.61
Tilgear HSS 12mm	23mm	£9.76
Roger's Samurai Bronze Seal 12mm	33mm	£6.87
Roger's Samurai Silver Seal 12mm	66mm	£16.08
Ward paring chisel	57mm	n/a

to make a lightweight racing model from one of Roger's test chisels, and research is still in progress . . .

As for the European chisels, I really don't know what to say. I have used and recommended this type of tool to people kind enough to ask my opinion. To find out they hold an edge for so short a time is a worry. It would be possible to accept the situation. We have a fast and slick way to put an edge on tools, so down-time isn't great. We could look at this positively, and treat frequent chisel-sharpening as a natural break in a job demanding extreme concentration, but we would really be kidding ourselves. If Japanese chisels can be adapted to my needs, then they will slowly replace most European chisels in my workshop.

The European chisels can't really be treated as a whole, although the test results were very similar. The Paramo/Clay tool with the sculptured handle held its edge marginally better than its competitors. For the home maintenance market, the site chippy and the jobbing builder, the forgiving nature of the European tool will be an important asset.

Perhaps we'll see the names of fine English toolmakers disappear from British workshops, but somehow I doubt it. For the person seeking to buy the very best edge tools — if you have the will to care for them, and the pocket to pay for them, you must be looking at Japanese products. I don't believe that putting flashy, oversize, boxwood handles to standard blades will sell European edge-tools at the top end of the market. We're just not that daft. ∎

● David and *Woodworker* would like to thank the following tool manufacturers and distributors for the loan of tools, their co-operation and assistance, without which the test series would have been impossible:
Bristol Design, 14 Perry Rd, Bristol BS1 5BG, (0272) 291740
Clico (Sheffield) Tooling Ltd, Unit 7, Fell Rd Ind. Est., Sheffield S9 2AL, (0742) 433007
Footprint Tools, PO Box 19, Hollis Croft, Sheffield S1 3HY, (0742) 753200
Lester-Brown Machine Tools (Ulmia importer), Coventry Rd, Fillongley CV7 8DZ, (0676) 40456
Paramo (Clay) Hallamshire Works, Rockingham St, Sheffield S1 3NW, (0742) 25262/3
Rabone Chesterman, Camden St, Birmingham B1 3DB, 021-233 3300
Record Marples, Parkway Works, Sheffield S9 3BL, (0742) 449066
Roger's, 47 Walsworth Rd, Hitchin, Herts SG4 9SU, (0462) 34177
Robert Sorby Ltd, Athol Rd, Woodseats Rd, Sheffield S8 0PA, (0742) 554231
Sandvik, Manor Way, Halesowen B62 8QZ, 021-550 4700
Sarjents Tools, 44 Oxford Rd, Reading RG1 7LH, (0734) 586522
Stanley Tools, Woodside, Sheffield S3 9PD, (0742) 78678
Tilgear, 20 Ladysmith Rd, Enfield EN1 3AA, 01-363 8050

● We recommend an article which appeared in *Fine Woodworking*, Mar/Apr 1985, by Bill Stankus on the scientific testing of chisel steels. *Fine Woodworking*, Taunton Press, Newtown CT 06470, USA.

We asked for the makers' comments:

Footprint

A very interesting article, particularly in respect of sharpening on Japanese water-stones. Mr Savage obviously comments as a professional, and for him the expensive Japanese chisels are obviously ideal. The average purchaser, however, is unlikely to appreciate the finer details and merely wants a functional tool which will do the job and is good value for money. At Footprint this is what we offer the purchasing public.

It's not necessarily a bad fault for a chisel-blade to be slightly concave, particularly in the case of a paring chisel. In years gone by, when chisels were ground by hand, they were always very slightly concave.

Christopher Jewitt

Roger's

I obviously have little criticism to make when Mr Savage concludes that our Samurai chisels are superior to the other brands he tested, and confirms that our more expensive Japanese Silver Seal range is superior to the Bronze Seal range, as the price would imply. As for the thickness of Japanese chisels and their suitability for paring, the Japanese do make paring chisels as thin as ours, and these are fitted with long handles without top rings. The tool is extremely light and easy to use.

Roger Buse

Sorby

I read Mr Savage's report with a degree of concern, because comparative tests we have done would lead me to question some of the results. We shall conduct our own more scientific tests to come up with an accurate comparison.

There are various points I would like to add to the report. The myth that old steel is better than new is rubbish. In any process where the human factor is involved, there will obviously be differences in tools, especially tools made some 50 years ago where a lot of hand-work was involved. The old tools around today are only the very best ones that have stood the passage of time. Those too soft will long since have been discarded, those too brittle would have failed even quicker.

Modern technology has improved the quality of steel; it is more consistent, and improved techniques of heat-treatment should make hardness more precise. However I must qualify this by saying human error can also foul up the process, but we do have at our disposal steels and technology to produce the best chisels in the world.

An area in particular that has improved in recent years is the grinding: old hand-grinding techniques were not only expensive but fraught with human error. Even the most skilled craftsman could not approach the quality produced on a specialist chisel-grinding machine, which produces a slight hollow grind on the undersurface. This allows a perfectly flat surface to be honed in seconds. Sorby Gilt-Edge chisels are

lapped and honed using a brand new diamond-lap process. This means the tools are ready for use.

A further point on hardness. Some years ago Sorby upgraded their steel from that adopted by most of the other chisel manufacturers. This more expensive grade gives a far more consistent hardness and at the same time improves toughness — a feature particularly important with harder timbers, or when the chisel gets the occasional less sympathetic blow. The hardness of a Sorby Gilt-Edge chisel is consistent to the last inch. Furthermore, every single Sorby chisel is hardness-tested, which protects the customer from human error in production. (I believe Sorby are the only manufacturer doing this.)

Mr Savage's article goes into great depth about how he produces a 'honed finish'. I would have expected an article on chisel testing to have considered: **1** The significance of hardness further back than the first $\frac{1}{16}$in; **2** The metallurgy of the tool; **3** The effect on the chisel of harder woods and less sympathetic blows.

I would like to stress that in designing Gilt-Edge, we spent a lot of time to ensure that the discerning craftsman got the best chisel at an affordable price. The following further features distance it from other chisels made, especially Japanese chisels:

1 A slender blade, with bevels ground to produce a fine parallel edge to assist the delicate cutting of dovetails.
2 A well-balanced handle that not only feels but also looks good, and a tapered brass ferrule that blends the high quality handle into the ground bolster (which itself has a machined back surface for positive handle seating).
3 The chisel has a 2in tang for strength, security and improved balance.

These features, in addition to superior steel, diamond honing and lapping, give Sorby the 'edge' over other chisels.

The mystique of Japanese chisels has been exposed in the United States, where they were in vogue some years ago. I have been advised by a major US wholesaler who deals in quality tools, both Japanese and European, 'that the American craftsman is returning to the British chisel with its improved design, ease of sharpening and lack of brittleness. The Japanese chisels only made a small impact on the US market, and would appear to be a curiosity rather than a serious substitute to the British or European bevel-edge chisel.'

Maybe Japanese chisels will replace British chisels in Mr Savage's workshop, but I am confident that the vast majority of British craftsmen will appreciate the toughness, the consistency of hardness, the feel, the balance, the appearance and value for money that they will get with some brands of British chisels.

Nick Davidson

Tilgear

We're pleased that our mid-range HSS boxwood chisel performed well. However, we were disappointed that our top-of-the-range forged laminated 'Exotica' Ebony Chisel wasn't available for test; we were sold out, which speaks for itself.

J. Lewis

Letters

Japanese tools

THOUGH NOT EXACTLY inundated with irate letters about the fuss we've been making about Japanese tools lately, we have had a number of points made to us by our valued correspondents — yourselves. Many old British chisels and plane-irons are of laminated steel, you say; it's not as if the Japanese were the only ones to do it. There is also a hint that we might be saying Japanese is better because it's Japanese — but this just isn't the case. If something's good, we'll say it is, and we'll let you know. We asked Roger Buse, who has helped us with our Japan series, to answer some of the arguments, and we're printing one of the letters we've received as a sample.

RE RECENT articles about Japanese tools in *Woodworker*. The latest on chisels describes the elaborate preparation that is necessary before use, and warns that sharp side-edges are a hazard to fingers. Finally we are told that this superb tool needs careful handling or it may bend like a banana or snap in two. At this point I checked that it wasn't April 1st!

Another article praises Japanese tool-makers who secure pieces of old chains and bridges to make what we are told are superb chisels and plane irons. So much so that one Japanese plane is priced at an unbelievable £995!

Let us have some response from British toolmakers telling us about the virtues of British steel and quality control in manufacturing tools. That might balance the image conveyed by some writers that because it's Japanese it's better than British.

In case you think I'm ultra-conservative, I do have some Japanese water-stones; they are extremely good. But why hasn't any British firm made a similar product?
Dr R. W. Page, Guildford

Roger Buse of Roger's of Hitchin replies: I think it's possible that readers have not digested the articles on Japanese tools, and they are emotionally charged with the idea that we are knocking British products. Would their reaction have been so strong if we had praised chisels from, say, Sweden?

Tools handed down from one's father will certainly be of excellent quality, but few woodworkers have the good fortune to acquire tools in this way; if everybody did, there would be no British toolmaking industry and I would be a dealer in antique tools.

Unfortunately toolmakers today look for a wider general market rather than just skilled professional and keen amateurs; they have to produce a tool which will take a lot of punishment from uncaring hands, and the resulting quality is but a shadow of what was made 50 years ago. If British manufacturers produced a high quality laminated tool I would be first in line for the privilege of selling it.

I will answer Dr Page's criticism by pointing out that there is no amateur market in Japan, and skilled craftsmen like to do all the final tool preparation themselves. Quality Japanese tool manufacturers don't have their sights on exports, but aim to satisfy the demand for high quality tools among their own craftsmen. Unfortunately some Japanese manufacturers are now producing inferior tools for the construction industry; these are commonly exported and are difficult to distinguish from the genuine article.

As for handling, these chisels require only the respect which I would expect any *Woodworker* reader to give tools; the warning was included as a cautionary point.

The use of old bridge steel for the fronts of the finest tools is not really strange, as many other manufacturers are now scouring the world for what is known as 'pre-atomic' steel; such steel is considered superior to that produced since the atomic age began, and I am told that the combined action of age, moisture and air changes the nature of the steel.

Regarding the £995 plane, I can only reiterate that Mr Sadahide is held in awe by all Japanese wood craftsmen; his blades are acknowledged as the ultimate in perfection. No-one queries the price of a Rolls-Royce compared with a Mini, and this is a perfect analogy.

In case you think I am a Japonophile, let me assure you I try to supply only the finest tools available from any part of the world and I would be a very happy man if I could claim a totally British range. This, however, is impossible, and regretfully I buy about 60% of my stock from foreign sources.

Gas power

I WAS INTRIGUED by Ashley Iles' mention (WW/Apr) of the use of gas engines for driving machines in the Sheffield works, after water-wheels and before the DC electric motor of the time.

I actually saw a Crossley gas engine working in 1936 in the basement of the Methodist Great Assembly Hall in the Mile End Road, London. I went with a London tuner for Rushworth and Dreaper, who were responsible for maintaining a three-manual Bevington organ there. It had a central position on the end gallery, and the engine was four floors below — put in at the same time as the organ in the 1880s.

The caretaker would start the engine before we arrived; it could be rather nasty and kick back, throwing the starter-man, and needed the knack of getting hands and arms away from the flywheel spokes as quickly as possible!

This early machine was the 'Hot tube start'. A 15in metal tube was detached from the cylinder side socket, pre-heated to red hot on a gas ring and quickly pushed back into the cylinder socket. The gas was turned on from a wall-fitting to inflate the rubber diaphragm, and then the flywheel was thrown. As Mr Iles says, in frosty weather the 'tenter' would have men pull a rope wrapped round the wheel for starting.

The flywheel was connected by belts to a shaft, which passed to the basement bellows-feeder room, from where a two-throw crankshaft was connected by 'pitman' rods to the huge double-acting French vertical feeder bellows. The engine was cooled with a water-jacket with a large funnel-top for topping up.

A marvellous ingenious apparatus, if somewhat noisy — it could still be heard four floors up!
R. C. Norris, Mid-Glamorgan

Non-U turning

I KNOW MANY woodturners will criticise the novel approach I recently used but I thought readers might be interested in an alternative to the straight-across chisel that gives beginners so much trouble.

I am a competent woodworker, but seldom use a lathe. Recently I needed to produce a batch of turned legs — a simple tapering shape bowed halfway down the length. With a bit of practice I managed to get fairly close to the finished shape with a roughing gouge.

The I wanted that smooth polished look obtainable with the straight-across chisel. I tried it out, but it was soon obvious I would not master the technique in time to complete the job. So I looked for an alternative.

First I tried a block plane, with the tool rest up high and the lathe in operation; this was surprisingly successful, and would be quite adequate for long straight cylindrical pieces.

Then I used a spokeshave and this was completely satisfactory. The full bevel rubs and polishes beautifully. Intricate curves are produced with ease, wood removal was fast, effective and controlled, and not once did I get a dig-in. The process felt quite safe.

There are limitations with this method, such as cutting right up to the corner of beads. But for this one job and the level of my skills it worked very well. As a bonus I got the feel of slicing on the lathe that subsequently helped me to cope with the straight-across chisel.
Cliff Moore, Fulwood, Preston

Letters

Bandsaw motor

IN THE MAY 'Question box' Mr R. A. Law of Droitwich asked about a motor suitable for a Whitehead Junior tools bandsaw. The original machine was fitted with a 1hp, 1450rpm, single-phase motor, with a 6in main drive pulley and a 1½in motor pulley. This gives a higher drive shaft speed than that recommended by John White, who answered the query. He may have been misled by the reference to 12in wheels; the wheel rim is indeed 12in diameter, but the tyre takes this to about 12⅜in.

These machines are very serviceable. The blade-guides can be made from standard ¼in-diameter brass rod (medium to hard) and the blade back bearings are available at most bearings stockists; (RHP bearings code 6203 ZYJW; Hoffman and R & M also make them).

The blades are 86in long and are no longer available off the shelf, but Tyzacks will make them up. Alternatively Mr Law could buy a bandsaw-blade repair kit (£13.80) and lengths of blade (45p per foot) from someone like Simbles of Watford; jointing the lengths with a gas blow lamp and silver solder is then relatively simple.

Hugh O'Neill, Ruislip

● S. Tyzack & Son, 341 Old Street, London EC1
● Simble & Sons, The Broadway, Queens Road, Watford, Herts

Repairs to a winding door

I HAVE DOUBTS about Bob Grant's solution to the problem of repairing winding doors ('Question box', WW/May, from Mr H. H. Kitchen).

This is a common problem and many remedies have been tried, with various degrees of success. But no professional would ever dream of mutilating a frame by kerfing or scarfing — not even a painted door, let alone an antique. In any case, the result would be either to bend the stile or straighten it a bit if it were bent, and it certainly would not remove a warp.

I can offer two methods commonly used in the trade and which I have used many times over the past 60 years; but I won't guarantee a permanent 100% cure.

Method one has only a 50/50 chance of success but is worth trying because it costs nothing and takes little effort. If it fails you can use my second more drastic method, which has a 95% success rate.

1 Remove the panel if it is beaded in, but don't remove the frame from the carcase. Pack out the diagonal 'correct' corner, in this case the bottom corner, to about three times the amount of warp or even a bit more; in this case about 1¼-1¾in. Then cramp or wedge the proud corner back to its stop; if you can't use cramps then a batten can be wedged between the frame and a suitable wall. The surface of the frame must be protected. Leave this cramping in

Unwinding drastically

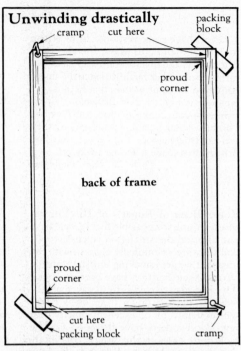

cramp — cut here — packing block
proud corner
back of frame
proud corner
cut here — packing block — cramp

position for at least three days, a week if it is not inconvenient, before removing the cramps and packing. Don't be alarmed if you find the frame is now warped in the opposite direction, that's just how it should be. The frame should slowly start returning to its original condition, but (you hope) not revert all the way.

After a few days you can replace the panel, but check that this is not warped; a raised and fielded panel of nominal 1in thickness in wind will pull the frame. You can try straightening the panel in a similar way by forcing in the opposite direction.

A final touch to help keep the door straight is to fit catches to top and bottom of the door, rather than just the middle.

2 Remove the door from the carcase and the panel from the frame, if beaded. Lay the frame face down on a clean surface — a table-top or workbench is ideal. Using packing material to protect the surface, place a 1in block of wood under each of the diagonally opposite corners and cramp the other two corners (you could use props to the ceiling) to force the frame in the opposite direction by at least the same amount as the original wind.

With a dovetail or fine saw, cut partly through the join of the stile to the rail at the raised corners at both ends; go as far as the mortise and about a quarter of its thickness, but no more. Cut long-grain wedges of a matching wood, or you could use several pieces of veneer. Glue these in and immediately release the pressure, allowing the frame to spring back in a non-winding condition. Leave to dry and carefully clean off the inserts; colour out the thin glue-line to leave an almost invisible join.

You could dry-test, but I wouldn't recommend it, as a weakened dry joint won't stand much pulling about. Instead, if the initial insert doesn't do the job, repeat the

process using thicker inserts so the frame is forced further back; do it carefully and you should have no problem.

I have used this method to force out of wind doors with 4x2in stiles and 8x2in bottom rails. Just one last point; make sure you are forcing the right corners, or you will make the warping even worse!

Mark Kenning, Evesham

Multi-Plane spares

I RECENTLY TRIED to order all the special bases and cutters for the Record 405 Multi-Plane from Roger's of Hitchin, but was told it takes about a year to get them from the manufacturers. I contacted Record directly and received all the special bases apart from the no. 10 hollow-and-round which they apparently did not have in stock.

It would be helpful to woodworkers if manufacturers had a policy of non-obsolescence of spare parts as there must be several hundred (or thousands?) of 405 Multi-Plane owners who might want special bases and cutters, as well as the extra cutters over and above the 26 supplied as standard. With the Multi-Plane costing more than £300, it's vital to have some spares available.

J. McLauchlan, Edinburgh

Mr A. A. Taberner, Managing Director of Record Marples Ltd, replies: Our policy when withdrawing a product from the range is to try and calculate the demand over a five-year period. We then produce and put into stock at least five year's normal requirements for spare parts. This system has worked very well, and today we still repair and service products that are over 50 years old.

In recent years someone decided to copy the original Record Multi-Plane, and we were slow to recognise that there was a sudden surge in very large orders for genuine Record spare parts from the UK and the USA. The result was that our stock suddenly depleted. We started production of certain spare parts in economically viable production batches.

The only comment I can make on the purported quote 'that it would take a year to get them from Record' is to confirm that deliveries for spares for the Multi-Plane were extended for the above reasons; this is not the norm.

Record Marples stocks in Sheffield about £500,000 worth of spare parts. The majority of parts for our current range of products are included in our price list. Over 300 Record Marples Supercentre tool outlets carry a selection of these parts. To carry the full range in any tool outlet would be prohibitive in terms of space, stockholding value and stock turn rate. We therefore offer a hotline service which enables a Supercentre to get spares from our Customer Service Departments in Sheffield.

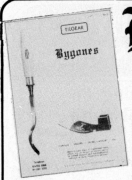

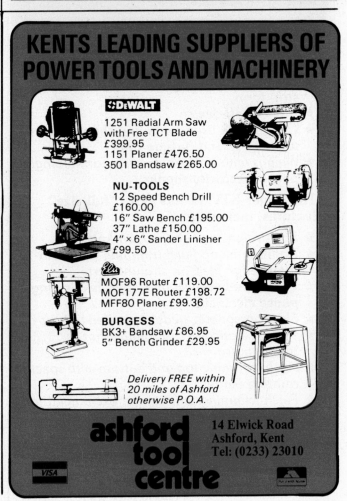

Tales out of steel

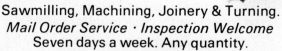

There's tools and there's trademarks. Ashley Iles scours Sheffield on the trail of the elusive marksmakers, a dwindling elite of highly skilled craftsmen

What's in a name, asks Shakespeare. In Sheffield the name was everything; manufacturers built up world-famous reputations by producing an incredible range of tools — each stamped with their marks.

No matter how big a manufacturer or what range he produced he would never dream of making his own name stamps. These are known in the trade as marks, and so you have the highly skilled trade of the marksmaker, where the craftsman is elevated to the artist. The expertise was passed down from father to son and trade secrets were jealously guarded.

I used to know a marksmaker, F. Atkin in Calver Street who was the nicest man you could ever wish to meet; I often went to him for marks. His workshop was on the first floor with an outside flight of stairs. By the time I walked to his bench he had put away tools, files, punches and his work; everything bar the vice and magnifying glass had disappeared. On one of my visits I had the temerity to ask him how he made marks, and with the polished evasion of a politician he told me his life story.

He had been apprenticed to his father till the latter died, then had had his fling, going to the USA and playing the piano for silent movies. All went well until talkies came along. So he came back to Sheffield and resumed his trade. An interesting story but he never told me or showed me anything about marksmaking.

That same day I also went to see Mr Basil Walker, trading as Geo. Bonsor and possibly the only surviving master marksmaker in Sheffield. First I had to find him.

Sheffield's northern rampart is the Wicker with the Wicker Arches over which the LNER railway came into Victoria Station. West of the Wicker is an area of narrow lanes with buildings and workshops unchanged in 200 years. The atmosphere grew thicker as I sought and found Nursery Lane, and the name-plate on a door which Emily Brontë would have called the postern gate. At the top of the stairs Basil greeted me and we immediately got down to business.

He was making a mark — BEL AIR — and apologised for having to use 3x magnifying spectacles, blaming his 57 years. 'In the old days I could do $\frac{1}{32}$ letters without them', he said. The mark he was making was to have $\frac{1}{16}$in letters. Putting a 2in-long piece of $1\frac{1}{4}$x$1\frac{1}{4}$in steel upright in the vice he filed the end dead flat and marked a centre line both ways with scriber and rule.

Then he reached for an old tobacco tin containing the master marks for that size that he had made 30 years before. Using these he punched in the cavities of the letters, producing two holes for the B and one hole each for the A and the R; each letter and its order is in reverse. At each hammer blow he gave a grunt of satisfaction, confident that the hole was the right depth and the spacing was dead in line for the letters still to be created.

Next he used a rough file to chamfer the edges down to the exact size of the letters. Finally he picked up a small three-cornered file and attacked the actual letters in earnest. They came alive as if by magic. Using a briar striking block he tested the mark on a piece of card. Basil pointed out that BEL AIR was plain lettering but it would be more difficult if the letters had serifs (little feet or tails). The process is similar for all letters from $\frac{1}{64}$in to 3in and Basil pointed out that once the outline of an H had been cut it could equally made into an E or F by filing away across the lines.

He took me over to a pantograph machine worth about £6000, used for cutting trade marks. This machine has two arms, one for going round the outline and the other for cutting, which also increases or decreases the size of the design. It's complicated, but basically the marksmaker draws an enlargement of the design cutting a groove all round the outline. He puts it on the machine and a brass reverse is cut, reduced by the machine to the actual size. A Bakelite (as it then was) mould is made from the brass reverse; this is the actual master with the design raised and is used in another machine to cut the actual steel mark. Basil could, of course, cut all trade marks by hand but the advantage of the pantograph was the time saved in producing a number of identical marks.

I believe that woodworkers and anyone who makes anything should have a personal mark of some sort. A distinctive tiny mouse used by a Yorkshire cabinetmaking firm has helped make them world-famous.

In the tool trade two types of marks were used; an indenting mark for finished tools and a black mark for forgings. The hand forger would just pick up the mark and thump it in. The power-hammer driver for obvious reasons had the mark fixed to the end of a steel bar and applied a light blow into the warm steel.

No doubt Basil will retire in the next few years, leaving yet another void in the annals of the tool trade. It was a privilege for me to watch a master marksman at work. ■

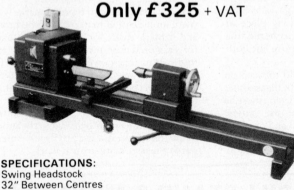
666

Machining wood — safely

Charles Horsefield is an HM Inspector of Factories at the Health and Safety Executive's National Industry Group in Luton, which has specific responsibility for the woodworking industries. Who better to have the last, crucial word on **Machining Wood?**

Throughout the 'Machining Wood' series, references have been made to safety aspects of the various operations. It's been pointed out that some methods of work are more hazardous than others, and that regulations which apply in commercial workshops actually prohibit some of the arrangements commonly used in home workshops.

My aim here is to highlight safety aspects of basic machine woodworking, and to clarify the legal position on matters raised in the series. So it will be mainly useful to readers engaged in woodworking '. . . by way of trade or for the purposes of gain' in premises where the 1961 Factories Act and hence the 1974 Woodworking Machines Regulations apply. On the other hand, the Regulations are derived from accident experience. They aren't intended to act as an obstruction to efficient working, they are the codification of experience gained in the prevention of injuries and ill health at work. So they should be of more than passing interest to anyone who uses woodworking machinery.

The 1974 Woodworking Machines Regulations

This isn't an attempt to provide a guide to the Regulations, because one is available from HM Stationery Office, but it's important to note the main guarding premise upon which they are based. This is expressed in Regulation 5, which states: **Without prejudice to the other provisions of these Regulations, the cutters of every woodworking machine shall be enclosed by a guard or guards to the greatest extent that is practicable having regard to the work being done thereat, unless the cutters are in such a position as to be safe to every person employed as they would be if so enclosed.** The term 'woodworking machine' is defined by a schedule listing 12 basic machine types.

The 'other provisions' include the specific requirements for crown-guards at circular sawing machines and bridge-guards at overhand planing machines, for example, but the underlying principle of enclosure 'to the greatest extent practicable' should lead to guarding which *does not allow a hand to reach the cutter*. Regulations 34 and 36, which specifically refer to vertical spindle-moulding machines, (including high-speed routing machines) take the matter two stages further. Regulation 34 states where it is impracticable to provide a guard enclosing the cutters to such an extent 'that they are effectively guarded', but it is practicable to provide a jig or holder, the machine should not be used unless **a jig or holder of such a design and so constructed as to hold firmly the material being machined and having suitable hand-tools which afford the operator a firm grip . . . is provided'.** Regulation 36 goes on to require that, in stopped work, where it is impracticable to provide a jig or holder in pursuance of Regulation 34, a suitable backstop must be provided.

The other fundamental component in the Regulations is training. Concessions are

made to the need to approach dangerous, partially guarded cutters in a way not generally permitted in industrial safety legislation, but only with the proviso that the woodworker must be trained to avoid danger. The training requirements laid down in Regulation 13 include, not surprisingly, a knowledge of the specific safeguarding Regulations, and this is the area in which employees in small workshops are most often deficient. They just don't know what the legal requirements are. There is also a limitation imposed on the use of the more dangerous hand-fed machines by young people under 18.

Suitable training isn't always easy to arrange, but machinery suppliers should be able to assist. Certificates of Approval relevant to young people's training, issued under the 1974 Regulations, are currently being amended, but many colleges and some industry associations provide training which can be specific to particular businesses or even industrial machines. You can get advice from the local offices of the Health and Safety Executive.

The accident picture

There are far too many accidents in the woodworking industries (WW/Feb), and an extensive survey is currently under way to try to establish where and why accidents happen and what more can be done in terms of published guidance and Regulations to reduce them. This detailed survey has been arranged because earlier work shows an increase in woodworking accidents against a background of decreasing employment and decreasing accidents in other comparable industries.

The first 600 reports by HM Inspectors of Factories to be analysed show a familiar pattern. The majority of accidents have occurred at the three basic categories of hand-fed machines:

Fig.1

● *Rebating, grooving and similar work on a circular saw must be guarded with Shaw-type pressure-pads or tunnel-guards like the one below*

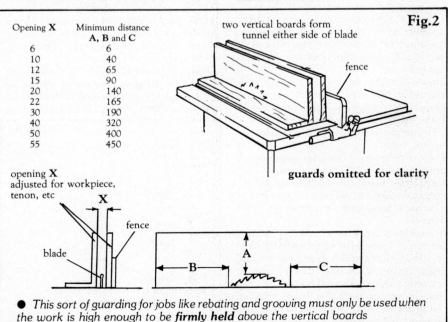

Opening **X**	Minimum distance **A, B and C**
6	6
10	40
12	65
15	90
20	140
22	165
30	190
40	320
50	400
55	450

two vertical boards form tunnel either side of blade

fence

Fig.2

opening **X** adjusted for workpiece, tenon, etc

X

fence

blade

guards omitted for clarity

A

B

C

● *This sort of guarding for jobs like rebating and grooving must only be used when the work is high enough to be **firmly held** above the vertical boards*

Machining wood — safely

Machine	% of total accidents
Circular saws	37
Planers and thicknessers	23
Vertical spindle moulders and routers	16
	76

The same three basic categories are, of course, those most likely to be in small workshops. Indeed, many of the automated machines in larger factories now move the worker away from the acute danger you're very close to at a hand-fed machine. It's also worth noting that, if the list above was adjusted to allow for the relative number of saws, planers and spindle moulders in use and their respective working hours, the hierarchy would probably be reversed to show that spindle moulders (including routers) have the worst accident record.

Injuries from woodworking machines tend to be permanent. Occasionally, inspectors hear a finger cut off cleanly by a saw or guillotine-blade has been replaced by micro-surgery and at least some function preserved, but more usually, by the very nature of the cutting, the damage is irreparable and the victim permanently disabled. Not a lot can be done with bone which has been routed away. While finger injuries don't stop you working completely — many older woodworkers have less than their full ration of digits — there's no question of denying some disablement. 14% disablement is sometimes quoted for a single lost finger. If an unfortunate woodworker touches a moving cutter with almost any other part of the anatomy, the outcome is likely to be much worse, and more extensive amputations are frequent.

Safety issues in the series

Circular saws
Riving knives should be kept adjusted so they are as close as practicable to the saw-blade. It is important that they are the right thickness to be effective, and this means they must be thicker than the plate of a parallel-plate blade but, obviously, thinner than the kerf.

Crown-guards must be strong, and adjusted so they extend from the top of the riving-knife to a point as close as practicable to the surface of the material being cut.

Putting these requirements together, it's evident that:
a A satisfactory riving-knife-mounted crown-guard is difficult to design, and many on the market are both flimsy and inadequate. Care is necessary in machine selection if good safety standards are to be observed.
b Accidents involving a hand contacting a bench-saw blade where thin material such as 16mm chipboard is being cut should never occur as, if the crown-guard is correctly adjusted, there shouldn't be a big enough gap to reach the blade without contacting the nose of the guard first. The often-quoted necessity to 'see the cut' can't

be justified if the work is fed against a fence.

Some requirements of the Regulations relating to special operations on circular saws are not as well known as they should be. For example:

Ripping heavy timber The use of a bench saw for a ripping operation where the teeth of the saw-blade do not project throughout the operation through the upper surface of the material being cut is prohibited.

Rebating, tenoning, moulding and grooving may not be carried out unless the saw-blade is effectively guarded. Proprietary tenoning jigs, for example, must therefore always be supplemented by some form of guarding. Two arrangements are illustrated (figs. 1 & 2). Such operations involving breaking into or out of the timber should **not** be carried out on a bench-saw, **irrespective of the depth of cut.**

Narrow bandsaws
The friction disc or rollers must be kept adjusted so they are as close to the surface of the machine table as is practicable having regard to the nature of the work. Further, the part of the blade above the friction-disc or rollers and below the top wheel must be guarded by a flanged frontal plate.

Spindle moulders
Cutters should be suitable for the blocks in which they are mounted, to avoid detachment. Increasingly manufacturers are introducing cutters with positive location features like grooves or pins, and although these may reduce the extent you can re-grind, remember that horrible (sometimes fatal) injuries have been caused by flying cutters. *The manufacturers' instructions on cutter projection and peripheral speed should be strictly observed.* (Calculations derive from spindle speed and cutter diameter.)

Cutter-guards must be strong enough to contain flying cutter parts. The home-made thin ply boxes we often see are inadequate. Timber guards (including false fences where they form part of the enclosure) must be substantial; all guards should be fitted before any cutting operation commences.

Straight-through work It should be practicable to guard the cutter effectively when straight work is being processed and the cut extends for the full length of the

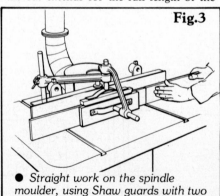

● *Straight work on the spindle moulder, using Shaw guards with two pressure-pads*

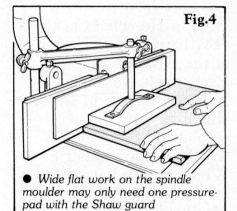

Fig.4

● *Wide flat work on the spindle moulder may only need one pressure-pad with the Shaw guard*

workpiece. Attempts are often only nominal, using standard equipment which would allow hand/cutter contact on kickback. The extension of Shaw-type pads can ensure effective enclosure. (figs 3 & 4).

Face-boards/false fences or some other means *must* be used to reduce the gap between straight fences as far as practicable. This can both greatly reduce the exposure of dangerous parts, and also provide essential support for the workpiece very close to

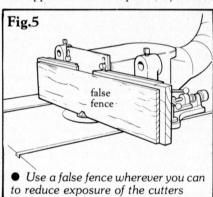

Fig.5

false fence

● *Use a false fence wherever you can to reduce exposure of the cutters*

the cutter (fig. 5). On some machines the false fence cut-out can be achieved safely and accurately by winding back the fence adjustment so the cutter breaks through to where you need it.

Fig.6 handle clamp
bonnet guard
hand shield block blank jig base

● *Make sure your jigs have good hand-guards and workpiece-holding clamps*

Jigs or holders should be used, if practicable, whenever effective guarding is not practicable. Suitable hand-holds should be provided (fig. 6).

Stopped work has been found to lead to a large proportion of spindle-moulder accidents. If using a jig or holder is not

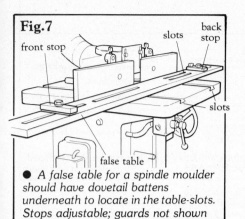

Fig.7

front stop · slots · back stop · slots · false table

● *A false table for a spindle moulder should have dovetail battens underneath to locate in the table-slots. Stops adjustable; guards not shown*

practicable, a backstop is mandatory — but a combination of the two is usually both possible and desirable. Back- and front-stops can be conveniently fixed on a false table (fig. 7).

Mortisers

Mortisers are 'woodworking machines' as defined in the Regulations and, although the hand-operated hollow-chisel machine creates few safety problems, other types require guarding.
Chain mortisers require enclosure of those parts of the chain not in contact with the timber.
Horizontal slot-mortisers if provided with a reciprocating table, can be used with a false fence to minimise cutter exposure.
Swinging-chisel or reciprocating mortisers require cutter enclosure which may have to be tailored to the job in hand.

Planing machines

Surface and edging without re-setting the bridge-guard between operations is permitted under Regulation 27, provided that 10mm clearances to the workpiece under and beyond the end of the guard aren't exceeded. Many accidents occur when the right hand drops from the back of the workpiece into the gap between the end of the bridge-guard and the fence.
Chamfering is safer using a second fence fitted to the infeed table to prevent the workpiece sliding sideways under the bridge-guard.
Recessing, rebating, tenoning and moulding are prohibited unless either the cutter is effectively guarded (e.g. by Shaw-type guards) or an attachment for which a Certificate of Exemption has been issued is provided. Such attachments incorporate a sliding-feed carriage arrangement.
Combined Planer/thicknessers when used for thicknessing, require complete above-table cutter-block guarding, usually in the form of an extraction duct and, also, at least a 'nip-bar' to prevent fingers being taken in between the feed-roller and the timber. Unless either divided feed-rollers or anti-kickback fingers are provided (they may not be on older machines) workpieces can only be fed singly.

Wood waste and sanding
Chip removal

Effective exhaust appliances are *mandatory* at thicknessing machines and spindle moulders (if the latter are in use more than six hours a week) as well as at certain larger machines. In the case of high-speed routers, some means of blowing away the chips and particles may be substituted. This is a *safety requirement*, not just a matter of good house-keeping.

Health hazards

These arise from exposure to wood dust, and permissible limits of exposure have recently been lowered to take account of concern — particularly over the risk of nasal cancer. This should be borne in mind when extraction arrangements are made, especially if hardwoods are being used.

Fire and explosion hazards

These are particularly relevant where wood dust which will pass a 500μ sieve is produced. (Particles of less than $5/1000$mm.) Such dust is generally considered explosible, and if a significant proportion of the material passing into a waste collection system is dust (10% is the figure usually quoted), explosibility should be taken into account. Modern board materials such as MDF have been found to produce a high proportion of explosible dust from sawing, routing and boring, so it shouldn't be assumed that the problem won't arise if sander dust is separated from general waste.

Collectors handling explosible waste are best located in safe positions outside the workroom and they require careful design. Small units inside the workroom require some form of protective enclosure, but this is a matter for a competent ventilating engineer. The local office of the Health and Safety Executive will advise you.

One point worth noting is that serious injuries sometimes occur when flammable dust is hand fed to waste boilers — the dust can flash back. The practice is highly disapproved of; don't do it.

Finally, it's worth mentioning a recent incident in which a self-employed cabinet-maker died in a fire in his workshop. The Coroner could only point to the accumulation of waste materials in an old building, and some unspecified source of ignition. *Fire hazards should not be underestimated*, particularly by those who work alone.

Published guidance

Authoritative guidance will shortly be available in a **British Standard Code of Practice on the Safeguarding of Woodworking Machines**, which sould be ready for publication in 1987.

It is divided into four sections and the first, a general one, will shortly be released for public comment. Further parts to come cover circular saws, vertical spindle moulders (including high-speed routers,

hand-held routers, shaping machines and CNC routers), planing machines (including thicknessers), and narrow bandsaws. ■

Other useful publications

The Woodworking Machines Regulations 1974 — Statutory Instrument 1974, no. 903
Safety in the use of woodworking machines, Guidance Note PM 21
Guards for planing machines, Guidance Note PM 2
Safety in the Use of Woodworking Machines, HSW Booklet no. 41
Furniture and Woodworking, Health and Safety 1977
A guide to the Woodworking Machines Regulations 1974, Health and Safety Series Booklet HS (R) 9
All the above are available from HM Stationery Office or Government Bookshops, plus:
Wood Dust: Hazards and Precautions – A Guide for Employers, Free leaflet available from local offices of the Health and Safety Executive

● **The Health and Safety Executive** has local offices throughout the country. They are in the phone book under 'Health and Safety'.
● HMSO, 48 High Holborn, London WC1V 6HB.

Woodworker
PLANS SERVICE

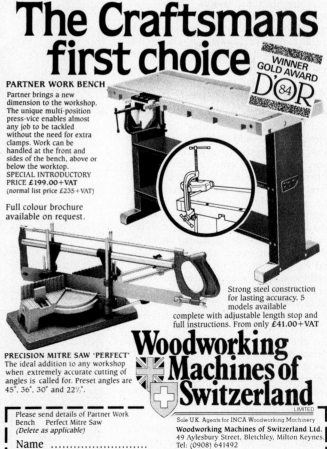

Table portable

Your hand-held circular saw will take on a new workshop identity if you make this neat and sturdy bench for it. Just follow John Kitto's instructions

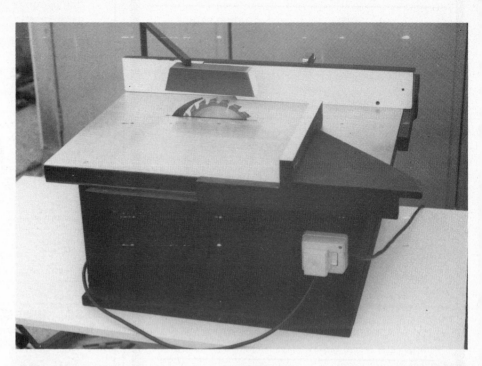

Portable power circular saws are useful tools, but their portability can be a disadvantage when you want the precision and flexibility of a table-saw. Which is why I extended the usefulness of my portable saw by mounting it in a sawbench. With a good-size table, a panel fence, a rip-fence and a crosscutting facility, I can tackle many more operations.

The saw-bench is of the right size for use on the workbench or trestles, built from 1¾x¾in softwood, ¼in plywood, ¾in plywood and — one luxury — ⅛in aluminium sheet for the table surface. If you aim to do this, use a saw with a riving-knife and flick-back guard, and make sure you can use the tilt, and rise-and-fall. A top guard is essential for safety. I've found it's worthwhile buying a 24-tooth TCT saw for chip-free cutting in melamine board, and other manufactured boards. There should be easy access for adjustments in height and tilt, and for dust collection, and you should be able to remove the saw easily and use it as a portable saw. I made a pull-out dust tray to go underneath.

Making the sawbench

Start by notching the two 20x11in base sides and gluing and screwing the 1¾x¾in softwood rails. Add strips on to the long sides for cramping to a workbench, and short pieces in the base for clamping in a Workmate. Mitre the 1¾x¾in softwood to form the top frame, and glue and pin the ¼in ply to this. Cut the saw slot and position the saw-blade in it; the flick-back guard can be carefully kept in the 'use' position to provide guarding under the table. Build up round the saw base-plate and fix turn-buttons on ¼in countersunk machine screws, wing-nuts and washers so the saw can be removed without fuss. With the saw switch in the 'on' position, wire in an on/off switch and fix it on the left-hand side of the base in a convenient position. Cut the saw-slot in the aluminium top surface and countersink four ⅝x³⁄₁₆in slots, one at each corner. Fix the plate to the top surface. Secure the top to the base with four woodscrews, two from the front and two from the rear.

The panel fence is made from ¾in plywood, faced with plastic laminate and secured to the softwood and ply bracing. Make sure this is aligned exactly with the saw-blade. I have permanently fixed a small G-cramp at the operator's end to position

● A good-looking and efficient solution for the hand-held saw user. The time it takes to make is time well spent. Note the switch and sturdy crosscut fence (**top**), adjustable guard and access beneath (**above**), and clamp-on mitre fence (**left**)

the fence for width, with a small cramp position at the back end as well. The rip-fence, again of ¾in ply faced with plastic laminate, can be cramped on to the panel fence and adjusted forward to suit the cut.

The crosscut fence is made from a plywood brace and the 1¾x¾in softwood, and the runner guide is from ¾in aluminium angle or something like it. The top guard is made from suitable hardwood faced with plywood, and some ½in square metal tube with two weld joints.

For simplicity, the 'paint system' is two coats of blackboard paint on all the exterior parts, with black cellulose on the guard metalwork and red or yellow paint on the actual saw guard.

Using the saw-bench

A 7¼in saw copes with softwoods and hardwoods up to 1½in. I've found it works well on ⅝in melamine board, having made two fitted kitchens, two fitted wardrobes, some office units and some 9ft storage units. Remember to have the blade at optimum cutting height, not too high to cause break-out under the material and not too low to cause the material to ride up and flake the melamine on the top surface. About ½in above the work is right for a saw of this diameter. I recommend you wear goggles, especially when cutting melamine as the fine dust given off pervades the air for a while. Always use a push-stick on smaller pieces and enlist help when cutting longer, heavier pieces.

Tilting the blade is by the usual adjustments to the saw, and also by moving the aluminium table surface across on its slots. This means the saw gap is kept to a minimum, providing good support for the material you're cutting. Grooving and rebating are possible, and should be done safely; pay attention to the guarding and use a push-stick at all times. Crosscutting at 90° works well with the crosscut fence, and an additional 45° fence can be cramped on for mitres. ■

● *View from underneath shows the fit of the sole-plate and the hefty turn-button fixings*

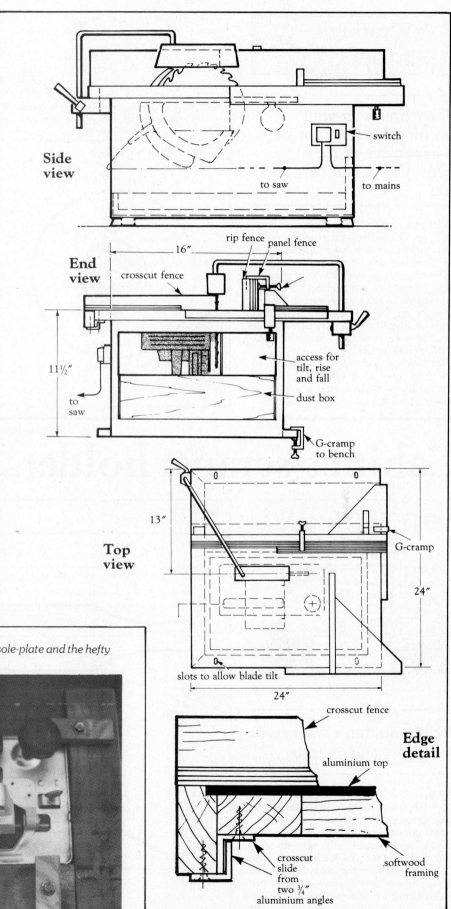

Side view

switch

to saw — to mains

End view

rip fence — panel fence

crosscut fence

16″

11½″

to saw

access for tilt, rise and fall

dust box

G-cramp to bench

Top view

13″

G-cramp

24″

slots to allow blade tilt

24″

Edge detail

crosscut fence

aluminium top

softwood framing

crosscut slide from two ¾″ aluminium angles

Pulley trouble

Nasty noises in your machinery might not be as expensive as they seem. Check the bore first . . .

There seems to be an outbreak of pulley trouble in my part of the world. Several friends have experienced it, but my first contact concerned my planer.

The original symptom was an unpleasant noise. I immediately thought of the trouble and expense of replacing a bearing, but had to press on for the moment. The next symptom quickly followed; considerable loss of power. Certainly the motor had gone — even more expense!

But before I had become reconciled to this, there was a clang as the pulley fell off into the guard. What a relief — a moment with an Allen key and no further costs.

Unfortunately, the symptoms were chronic. After two more repeats, investigation was necessary.

When a pulley has run loose for a while, possibly scoring the shaft with its grub-screw, the bore has become slightly oversize. When the grub-screw is tightened, the shaft is gripped at two points; **A** on the circumference and **B**, the grub-screw. This allows the pulley to flutter slightly, and the

vibration loosens the screw once again.

The answer is to drill, tap and fit a second screw at 120° from the first. The shaft is now gripped at three points like a three-jaw chuck; **A** on the circumference, **B**, the original grub-screw, and **C** the new one. There will now be no flutter or vibration and the pulley won't work loose again. As an added precaution, two small dimples can be drilled into the shaft. ∎

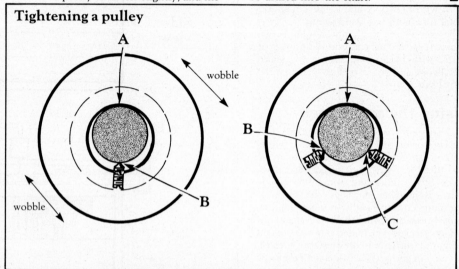

Tightening a pulley

Cabinet-scraper holder

When you don't want to be all fingers and thumbs . . .

Tired of blistered thumbs, **writes Glyn Condick**, from scraping large surfaces? Too mean to buy a scraper plane? I use this little tool on big jobs where the old thumbs might suffer severely.

Simply turn a piece of beech (fig. 1), cut a slot (fig. 2) and fix the blade in position with a round-headed screw. Adjust the length of the blade to obtain a good scraping action. ∎

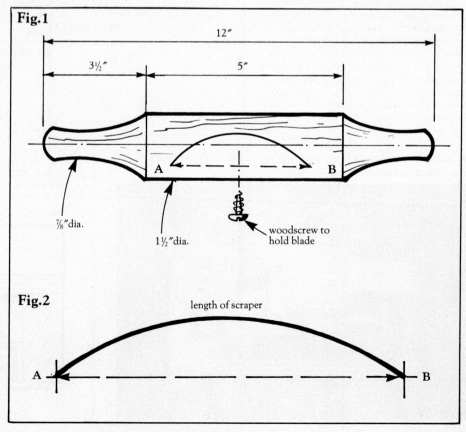

Fig.1

12″

3½″ 5″

⅞″dia.

1½″dia.

woodscrew to hold blade

Fig.2

length of scraper

A B

Question box

Our panel of experts solve your woodworking problems

Turning alder

Q *I have it in mind to make some small (3½in dia.) mazers in alder, and decorate them with silver edging. Can you advise on the suitability of alder? Will it turn, and can I use it in the round?*

F. G. Allen, Norwich

A Alder will withstand constant wetting and drying, which is why it was used for mill clogs and lock gates. It turns relatively easily, especially green, but turning endgrain, shaking will be impossible to prevent and the piece will be ruined.

I imagine the silver edging has to fit very snug, and if (almost certain) the timber moves just a little, the piece is likely to split and distort.

I wouldn't recommend attaching silver edging to alder until you're familiar with its working idiosyncracies. Shaking and movement is certain in any drying.

Anthony Bryant
● Anthony Bryant is a professional wood-turner in Cornwall.

Oxford frames

Q *I've made a picture-frame with the sort of simple halving joint you see in church hymn-number boards. How do you make the groove at the back with traditional hand methods? If you run the groove through to the ends with a plough plane there are eight ugly cut-outs to be made good, or if you stop them it means a lot of chisel work which is hard to keep neat. I also found the large groove made one of the end horns very weak.*

A. G. Jacobs, London N21

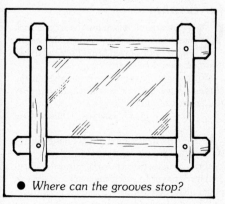

● *Where can the grooves stop?*

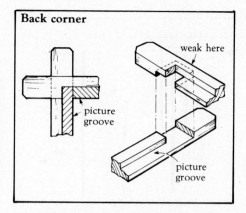

Back corner

weak here

picture groove

picture groove

A This type of frame was known as an 'Oxford' frame, and very popular they were too. You have made it correctly; there are 'eight ugly cut-outs to be made good at the ends'. These cut-outs were not usually filled in, but formed part of the feature of the frame. The mouldings, however, were worked round the outside of the frame as well as inside; the easiest way of doing this would be with a plunge router, jointing up the four corners, working the mouldings right round the outside and inside, then turning the frame over to rout the rebate. But should you prefer to work by hand, then make a simple halving joint; 'plant' the mouldings (fig. 1), then take the joint apart. This will show exactly how the joint has to be cut. Round the perimeter, the mouldings (finished) can of course go full depth if preferred (fig. 2), or the four short rebates (**R**, fig. 1) can be filled in.

Stan Thomas

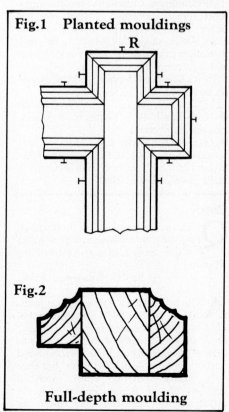

Fig.1 Planted mouldings

R

Fig.2

Full-depth moulding

Cutting saw teeth

Q *I want to know how to cut new teeth in a very badly worn saw, and how to put a set on a tenon saw with very small teeth.*

J. Struthers, Greenock

A A saw should never be sharpened without first being 'topped', running a flat file (one stroke, lengthwise) along the tops of the teeth (fig. 1). But note how the file must be held at 90° to the face of the saw; if you don't take this precaution, the saw won't cut straight. A simple way of making sure is to fit the file into a piece of wood about 4in long (fig. 2).

The first thing you have to do is bring the edge back to shape, and this could well entail the complete removal of many teeth for subsequent re-filing. Now this can be a tedious job, so before deciding, is the saw *worth* the trouble? If there are kinks or buckles in the blade, it isn't worth it, for a kinked saw-blade will never cut true.

Having trued-up the edge, lay a steel rule along the blade upright in the 'chops' and with a Junior hacksaw, make a very light mark upon the edge, at, say every ¹⁄₁₀in for 10ppi. Now place the saw-file between these cuts, and file notches until the cuts are reached, not worrying at this stage about angles or 'every other tooth'. Having done this along the blade, all the teeth should now be set and filed 'double-rake' and 'hook' as you want them. (fig. 3), filing 'every other' now, of course.

No angles are given in fig. 3, for while the rip should be at 90°, the crosscuts (panel, hand and tenon saws) go by personal preference. The less the hook the slower the cut, but it's also cleaner across the grain. The rip with 'full hook', will not cut across the grain of course, and very little set is needed, for you can put a wedge into the cut to open it out. But the set on crosscuts depends on the work — workshop, minimum; site, more — and wet or dry

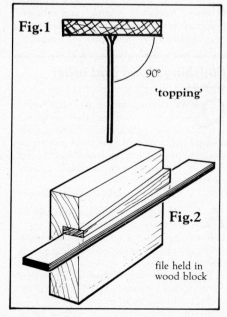

Fig.1

90°

'topping'

Fig.2

file held in wood block

Question box

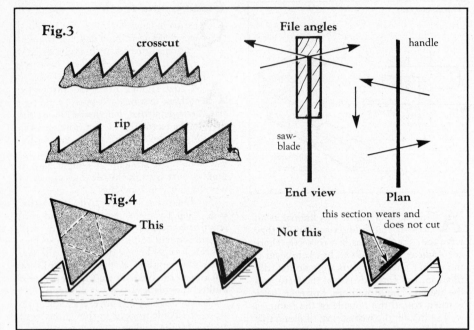

Fig.3 crosscut

rip

Fig.4 This

Not this

File angles

handle

saw-blade

End view

Plan

this section wears and does not cut

material — wet needs more set than dry. With an Eclipse set, I set 'one up' for shop work; 'on the figure' for site work, and 'one down' for wet material, that is, for my 10ppi panel saw (workshop), I set the anvil to 11. Setting must of course be done 'every other', and from each face.

The size of file is important, not for results, but for file life. One face of the file should be just over twice the tooth depth (fig. 4). This gives us virtually three files, but if the file is less than double the tooth, you can see the consequences.

Your tenon saw with very small teeth that can't be set is a dovetail saw, which shouldn't be set. In fact it's a miniature rip saw, and in sharpening this, 'double rake' is ignored, as with the full rip. These saws should be sharpened 'square both ways', but still 'every other', and from each face.

Stan Thomas

● Stan Thomas is a joiner and cabinet-maker of great experience who advises on tools and work at Woodworker Shows.

Finishing wood and other things

Q *Why is it necessary to wet wood before sanding it for finishing? Can you tell me where to get Lubrisil silicon-carbide abrasive paper? Would a polyurethane varnish give me a professional finish on a piano? Is my Black & Decker 5550 orbital sander suitable for fine sanding the piano?*

John Riddell, Glasgow

A Wood is damped down — not soaked — for three main reasons:
1 If you're using a water-stain the grain swells up; pre-damping and sanding avoids this.
2 With stains other than NGR types, damping down releases soft fibres in grain cavities, causing them to swell up.
3 If you have stripped a surface using

chemical fluids or pastes, damping down lifts and pushes out 'gunge' from the grain — useful for open-grained woods like elm and oak.

Lubrisil, made by English Abrasives Ltd, is sold in many stores but if you have difficulty try J. Myland and Co. Ltd who advertise regularly in *Woodworker*.

You won't get a professional finish to your piano using varnish. You'll get best results by french polishing or spraying nitro-cellulose, if you are experienced in these techniques. Otherwise I recommend a good quality interior oil-resin varnish rather than polyurethane. Apply three coats, flatting down well between coats, and then allow to harden for three weeks. Finish with a furniture burnishing paste or cream.

Please don't use a power orbital sander on exotic woods!

Noel Leach

● Noel Leach is a professional wood-finisher and lecturer.
● English Abrasives Ltd, Marsh Lane, London N17 0XA, 01-808 4545; John Myland Ltd, 80 Norwood High St, London SE27 9NW, 01-670 9161

Plane . . .

Q *I have just acquired a plane iron and cap-iron made by an American firm called Millers Falls. Can you tell me anything about it?*

Andrew G. Robinson, Ayrshire

A The Millers Falls Company was founded at Millers Falls, Massachusetts, USA in 1969. Reputed makers of quality tools, they sold many of their products in Britain, mainly hand-drills, braces, hand boring machines and hand-vices. But they only started making planes, modified versions of the Bailey/Stanley type, in 1929, so this cap-iron and cutter are presumably no earlier than that date. The

Millers Falls trade mark is used by the Ingersoll Rand Corporation who took over the firm about 10 years ago; a reprint of their 1887 catalogue is available from Ken Roberts Publishing Co., Fitzwilliam, NH 03447, USA.

Philip Walker

. . . and fancy

Q *I have a saw which appears to be a 14in tenon, but the back is hinged just in front of the handle. It can be tapped off the blade and the cut continued. It is stamped 'The Hinge Back Saw Co., 95 Queens St, Cheapside, E.C. Patent 1911.' Can you tell me anything about it?*

George Taylor, Petersfield

A The Hinge Back Saw Co. must have been formed purely to exploit this invention, and the address was probably an accommodation address with a solicitor or agent, although there was once an ironmongery/tool dealer near the junction of Queen St with Cheapside, which may have been no. 95. The patentee's name and other details could be obtained from the Patent Office. I don't think the saw can have been in production for very long, because in a lifetime of investigating old tools, I have never heard of another like it. There is no trace of the company or address in the 1920 Kelly's Directory.

It was evidently one of the endless series of inventions to combine more than one function in a single tool — in this case the stiffness of a tenon-saw with a bandsaw's ability to pass right through a piece of wood. Other designs to the same end existed, for example, the Melhuish New Pattern Combination Saw — 'Can be used as hand, back, pruning and general purpose saw' — on offer in 1912 at 3s. 6d. However, such tools seldom do any one of their jobs entirely satisfactorily, so they were usually shunned by workmen. Nevertheless, the rare Hinge Back Saw would now no doubt be an interesting curiosity for collectors of old tools.

Philip Walker

● Philip Walker is former secretary of the Tool and Trades History Society.

Sharpening scrapers for turning

Q *Is it enough simply to grind a scraper each time at about 80°, leaving the burr on the upper side of the chisel? Presumably, no oil-stone should be used?*

What about trying to turn an edge on the blade with a burnisher as if it was an ordinary flat cabinet scraper?

H. H. Lawson, Johannesburg

A As a professional turner I have always ground my scrapers much as you describe. I use a 60-grit carborundum wheel and have never found it necessary to turn an edge, although I know some turners do.

I have always found an edge from the

676

wheel perfectly satisfactory, being able to take shavings with each cut. If you get dust, regrind. High-speed steel tools keep their edge much longer; I recommend them.

Ray Key

● Ray Key is one of the country's leading professional woodturners.

Period finish for mahogany

Q *I have completed a reproduction 18th century stool in Brazilian mahogany and would like some advice on the best finish to use. If I opt for raw linseed oil, as opposed to wax polish, how should I apply it?*
S. W. Reeve, Epsom

A The finishes used in the 18th century were varnish, paint and japan; oil or wax finishes belong to the preceding century but you could use either.

Both finishes are straightforward to make up and apply, but the oil finish tends to be rather sticky initially and to collect dust unless each application is well rubbed in. It also darkens the colour of the wood.

To prepare the oil (raw linseed for preference) warm it for about 15 minutes to simmering heat, but don't boil it. Watch out; because oil is inflammable, it's best to use a double-boiler. Then remove it from the heat and add one part in eight turps substitute, and about one teaspoon of terebene driers per half pint.

Rub the oil on generously while it is still warm and scrub it in with a stiff-bristled brush. Then polish it with a piece of flannel or lint-free cloth wrapped round a heavy weight like a brick until the surface is dry. Repeat the rubbing process daily for a few weeks, for the surface will continue to absorb more oil.

For wax polishing, use a stiff-bristled brush to apply it, rubbing it hard into the grain. The main disadvantage is that it shows marks, particularly those caused by water.

If wax interests you I recommend you find out about Black Bison staining wax from John Myland. They can supply two mahogany colours, Georgian and Victorian, and the wax both colours and finishes the wood.

Vic Taylor

● Vic Taylor is an internationally known author, a furniture historian and a former editor of *Woodworker*.

Turning chipboard

Q *I am experimenting with turning chipboard and want to know where to get 1½-2in sheets. Secondly, how do I prevent the cutter chipping (which occurs as the pressed edges of the board hit it)?*
C. Lockwood, Cirencester

A My experience of turning chipboard is that it's poor stuff for the purpose. It's an industrial material, and not really suited to craft processes and tools. Standard-grade

chipboard is commonly available up to 1in thick, but it can be stack-glued for deeper thickness, although this practice is generally frowned upon for turning.

It's widely available from timber and builder merchants; a large stockist is Porters (Selby), Station Rd, Selby, Yorks YO8 0NP, Selby 703577.

The problem of chipping tool edges is a working characteristic and is because of the hardness and graniform nature of the glues.

But there is a marginal difference and improvement in cutter life if the true woodturner's cutting action of gouges and chisels is followed, rather than a mere scraping action. If scrapers must be used, reduce the underside clearance angle to a minimum, say 4°, just enough to clear the revolving work. A reduction in turning speed will help.

It occurs to me that Medium Density Fibreboard (MDF) may well suit your purpose.

Bob Grant

● Bob Grant is head of Craft Design and Technology at an Oxford comprehensive school and teaches courses for the Guild of Woodworkers.

Bleaching oak

Q *I'm fitting kitchen cupboards, framed in Burma teak and panelled in light figured oak. I have bleached the oak with household bleach, but the effect has been to darken not lighten it. Can you bleach light oak, and if so, how? What finish will prevent it darkening with age? Can I use a two-part polyurethane on the oily teak, or should I just oil it?*
B. Shaw, Rickmansworth

A Household bleach is often used to lighten wood, but your oak has reacted adversely with the chemicals in the bleach. One of the most commonly used bleaches is 2oz oxalic acid dissolved in a pint of hot water, applied with a mop made by tying a piece of rag to the end of a stick. Wear rubber gloves and protective clothing as oxalic acid is poisonous.

After the acid has dried for about two hours, wash the panels with vinegar to neutralise the acid. Let the panels dry overnight and then fill the open pores of the grain with a neutral grain filler. This will provide a better surface for the lacquer finish and will add to the light appearance, though there's no method of preventing oak slowly darkening with age.

You'll probably find a two-part bleach easier to use and more effective than oxalic acid.

The oil should be removed from the surface of your teak door-frames by wiping them with a rag liberally sprinkled with white spirit. The doors can now be assembled and lacquered as you suggest with polyurethane. No matter how clear the lacquer may be, it will have a slight darkening effect.

Charles Cliffe

● Charles Cliffe is a professional wood finisher, teacher and author.

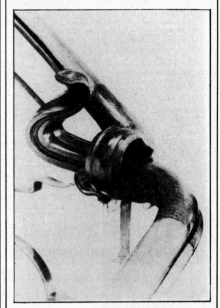

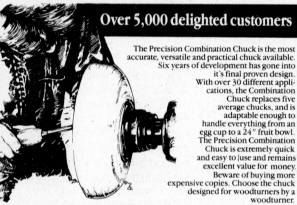
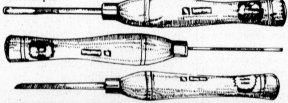

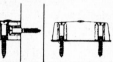

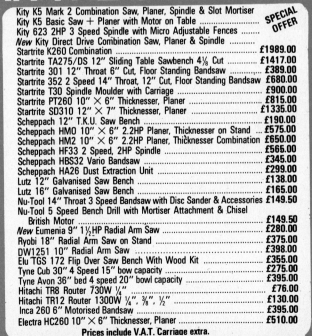

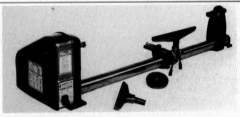

Turning green

You don't have to be famous — or even a supremely skilled turner — to produce beautiful natural-edge bowls in green wood. Lech Zielinski explains how he does it

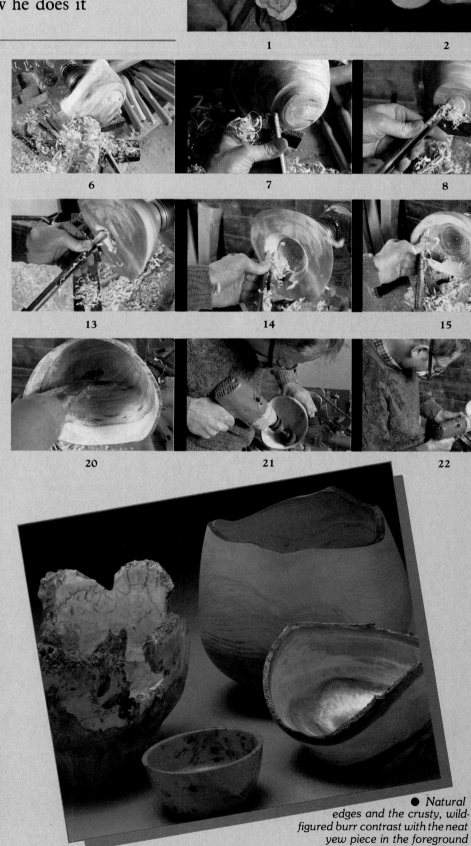

'**G**reen' or 'wet' turning has been around for quite a long time, but despite its advantages only a relatively small number of woodturners do it. As for public awareness, one of the most common questions you get when you explain a bowl is turned straight from the log is: '. . . but isn't it going to crack or warp when it dries?' Well . . .

Wet-turned bowls are made by rough-turning the blank to your design, leaving the walls thicker than the final dimension. Then the bowl is seasoned in controlled conditions before dry-turning to final size and finishing. If the bowl has dried to the moisture content of the surrounding air (10-15%) there will be no change in its final shape.

Recently I took part in a woodturning seminar 'From tree to finished wood' in Letterfrack, Co. Galway, organised by The Irish Woodturners' Guild. Some of the best Irish woodturners demonstrated their excellent skills there, most of them working green wood.

One advantage of this method is that if you want to produce, say, a large salad bowl, only the size of the tree and your skills are the limiting factors — as long as you have a heavy industrial lathe. One woodturner, Keith Mosse, brought some of his giant elm turnings with him, which must have been 600-700mm across. If you wanted to turn a bowl of similar size from dry wood, just think of the time it would take for such a log to dry; you'd grow grey waiting.

Another aspect of wet turning was brilliantly demonstrated by the well-known American turner Del Stubbs, with his translucent bowls. He used freshly cut holly to illustrate how versatile, confident and imaginative use of tools can lead you to a piece of turning no more than 1mm thick — I measured it myself.

As the walls became thinner and translucent and the wood began to dry, Stubbs kept the bowl wet with a sponge to prevent changes in shape and to allow for fine shearing cuts. These fine cuts largely avoided the need for sanding, but he used some wet-and-dry for a really smooth finish. When the bowl dries — it can be a matter of a few hours under a bulb or seconds in the microwave oven — some unpredictably beautiful changes in shape occur that make his work look like a papadam, a butterfly or a dried leaf. You are unlikely to eat from such a bowl.

● *Natural edges and the crusty, wild-figured burr contrast with the neat yew piece in the foreground*

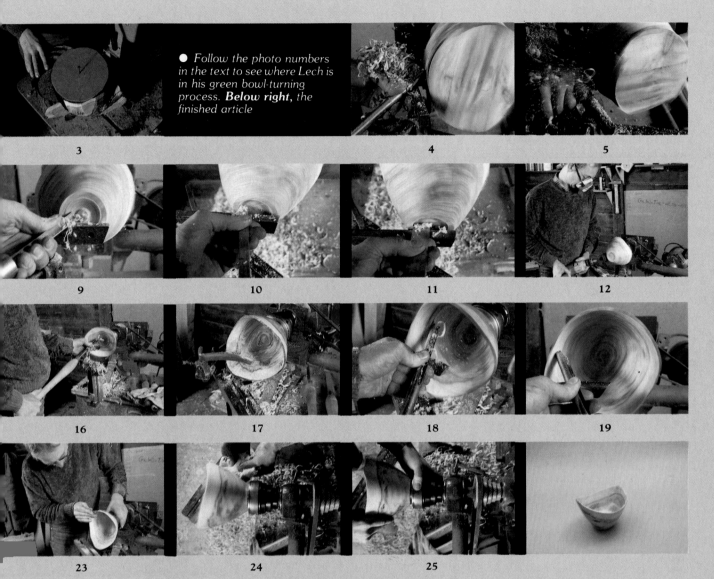

● Follow the photo numbers in the text to see where Lech is in his green bowl-turning process. **Below right,** the finished article

3   4   5

9   10   11   12

16   17   18   19

23   24   25

The natural-edge bowl

I make bowls from yew, walnut, elm, laburnum, and particularly oak and elm burrs when I can find them; they are rare, but fascinating to turn because of their mysterious beauty. Here's how to turn a chunk of log into a 'natural-edge bowl', where the top of the bowl retains the bark or at least the outline of the log.

For this bowl I selected a yew log about 300-400mm across and cut a 300mm-thick slice from it with a chainsaw before examining it for the best possible yield (photo 1). I decided that four bowls could be made and sketched them on the surface (photo 2). I cut the piece in half along the centre-line with a chainsaw first, then in half again on the bandsaw. Avoid using a bandsaw for the first cut, as the tension in the wood maybe released and jam the blade.

I cut off the tree pith to provide a flat base for the next cut before nailing a hardboard disc to the bark, about the size of the opening of my planned bowl. I bandsawed round this template (photo 3) standing the wood steadily on the flat surface which was going to be the bottom of the bowl. The more precise the cut, the less vibration

there will be when the blank is mounted on the lathe and turned, especially important with some large blanks weighing 3-4kg.

Mounting the blank

I removed the hardboard and used the nail mark to locate a 1in saw-tooth machine bit for a neat hole for the pin-chuck. Mounting the blank on the chuck and using the slowest speed — about 450rpm — I started roughing out the outside of the blank with a high-speed-steel gouge (photos 4 and 5). This tool has its top edges cut back so there is less risk of catching, especially when it's deep inside the bowl; I also find it more versatile than the traditionally ground gouge, and it can shear and scrape too. I use the tool rolled on its left side, cutting from the bottom in the direction of the bark. At this point you need to use some pressure to hold the gouge steady. I use my right hand to control the movement, and change the depth of cut by varying the force. My left hand restrains the gouge on the tool-rest while I keep the extra-long handle tightly against the body for extra stability.

I continued shaping the bowl with cuts about 6mm wide towards the top (photos 6

and 7). When a sharp tool is used correctly the gouge feels sweet and a steady stream of shavings will tell you you're doing fine. But if you hear rattling and there is more dust than shavings, try changing the angle of the cut, remembering the bevel should still rub behind the cut. I resharpen the tool for the final cuts which are some 2-3mm deep. A good cut leaves a better finish than any scraper would.

Next I prepared the bottom of the bowl for the 2in expanding-collet chuck. I trued up the base with a gouge rolled on its right side and moving towards the centre (photo 8). I used a ½in fingernail gouge to continue making the recess (photo 9), a small skew scraper to make the dovetail cut-out (photo 10) and finally a square-end scraper to smooth the recess (photo 11).

Hollowing out

The bowl was securely fixed in the expanding-collet chuck ready for the hollowing, and I switched on the motor to check the centring. Although this method of chucking should give good results, you may have to readjust the work a few times before it's spinning perfectly. I made the recess flange about 8mm wide and 5mm deep. The

Turning green

bowl must be secured tightly, for the flange can't take unlimited pressure; the centrifugal forces are working against it and so is the gouge. If the flange splits you won't be able to remount the bowl.

I started to hollow the inside, rolling the cut-back gouge on to its back with the flute up and the bevel rubbing just behind the cut to provide stability (photo 13).

On stability generally, it's important to have a good stance while turning. You need to stand centrally so that as you make a cut you don't need to move your feet to follow the cut. You need to sway the weight of your body to left or right in fluid movement with a relaxed but firm stance; training in T'ai Chi is invaluable.

I gradually hollowed out the bowl with cuts about 6mm wide and the lathe running at 850rpm (photos 14 and 15). With this kind of bowl the gouge is hitting and missing the wood as the high and low points of the bowl pass by, so the lathe should not be run at too low a speed. For even smoother cuts or if the walls are very irregular, as with burrs, I run the lathe at 1100rpm.

The final cuts

As the walls got thinner I made smaller cuts, about 2-3mm (photos 17, 18 and 19). Perfect entries into the bowl at the beginning of each cut are essential as mistakes could split the walls. I held the gouge securely against the body with good pressure on the tool-rest, and continued making light cuts until I reduced wall thickness to 8mm.

For the bottom part of the bowl I used a bowl gouge ground more obtusely to about 60-65°, which is good for cutting at nearly 90° to the bottom. Finally I removed any ridges with a 1in round-nose scraper and the turning was complete (photo 20).

I sanded the outside and the inside at this stage, using an electric drill and abrasive discs attached with Velcro to foam pads (photo 21). I find this method far more efficient than hand-sanding, and I recommend it. The foam provides a cushion that shapes itself snugly to the bowl contours and allows a large area to be sanded at once. At the same time, as the lathe and the drill are both spinning, there is much less danger of overheating, and of scratching with coarse grit (it's important that the lathe doesn't run faster than the pad). I start with 80 or 100-grit aluminium oxide, go through 180, 240 and then to 400 and 600-grit wet-and-dry silicon carbide. If the bark on the edge of the bowl falls off during turning I hand finish the edges to give a smooth feel to the fingers (photo 23).

When the bowl is purely decorative I apply Craftlac Melamine sealer to the whole surface. When it is dry I spin the bowl and apply soft paste wax, buffing it to a light sheen. Once the bowl is completely dry I repeat the process, the bowl either on or off the lathe. For functional items I use domestic cooking oil with a sanding sealer as a base. ∎

682

Art ducko 1

There are decoy ducks and decoy ducks; some are more lifelike than the real thing, some are workaday hunters' lures, and some are rough-hewn sculptures inspired by both. We visit the country's major exponent of the 'finely detailed' school of decoy art, and present a down-to-earth practical project

Bob Ridges is playing a leading role in the upsurge of interest in decoy carving in the UK. Michael Edwards went to one of his courses

All photographs Michael Edwards

● **Top**, this graceful pintail drake was carved in American sugar pine. **Middle**, a flotilla of bandsawn blanks; **above**, the textured feather effect from the special hot tool

If you marvel at decorative duck decoys like the ones featured here and in last month's *Woodworker*, don't struggle on scarcely knowing a bill from a parson's nose. Take some advice from Britain's leading decoy carver, Bob Ridges, who runs the Decoy Art studio at Farrington Gurney near Bristol.

After a successful career as a master mariner with the Merchant Navy, Bob took a lecturing post with the Bristol Nautical College in 1980, a career which enabled him to concentrate on decoy carving in his spare time. The next move came a couple of years later; taking the self-employment plunge, Bob was quietly confident that his decoys would stand him in good stead. He could find no one else in Britain carving, or teaching others how to carve, the finely detailed birds for which he had developed such a passion. But he didn't just want to carve ducks; as a former lecturer, he made education a major part of his plan. Before he could teach others, however, he had to be taught, and sought experience and expertise in New Orleans where the cream of American decoy carvers worked. That extra knowledge made all the difference. Bob mounted an exhibition of his work in Bath, and soon after was asked to contribute to a

woodcarving exhibition at Parnham House.

Bob arranged and taught a successful three-day course in Wells in 1983, which made him realise that public interest was taking off. He approached the Wildfowl Trust with the idea of taking decoy courses in weekend carving schools at their reserves, and they booked him several lecture/demonstrations at their Gloucestershire headquarters and several other sites. In December 1984, Bob organised the first British duck carvers' convention at the Slimbridge Wildfowl Trust.

Each year Bob runs several crash courses in this originally American art, where all you'll need to bring besides yourself is an apron. Everything from the wood to a sharp Stanley knife and a tin of standby Elastoplast is included.

The two day weekend courses (it normally takes two weeks to complete a decorative decoy) are often appropriately held at Wildfowl Trust centres. I eavesdropped on a course at Lancashire's Martin Mere, where 22 budding decoy carvers were preparing to blossom.

The course began on the Friday evening with Bob's excellent lecture about the history of the craft. The use of decoys seems to have started amongst the Egyptians along the River Nile, but ancient evidence of their existence in America was found in 1924 when 11 almost perfectly preserved canvasback decoys were discovered in Lovelock Cave, Nevada. They were dated from more than 1000 years ago, made from bundles of reeds and bound with raffia-like string.

'We don't really know what happened between those early Red Indian days and the settlers starting to use wooden decoys. I'd like to think they found the Indians using decoys and learned the tricks from them — and perhaps because they had better tools, they fashioned their decoys from wood.'

Using decoys to hunt duck grew steadily, reaching a crescendo in the late 19th century when professional wildfowlers known as 'market hunters' first appeared. They sought wildfowl on the Atlantic flyway from Canada right down to the Carolinas, to supply the restaurants and hotels in the growing cities of Boston, Baltimore, New York and Washington. They relied heavily on decoys, employing rigs of up to 100.

At that time the decoy carver producing functional, rather than decorative decoys, was as familiar along the east coast of the United States as the village blacksmith was in rural England. Every village or township had its resident decoy man.

'These men were chopping 25¢ decoys from whatever wood was available,' says Bob. 'Sometimes the wood came from the masts of wrecked ships, and towards the end of World War II, balsa from ships' rafts was washed ashore and eagerly collected. As long as it served the purpose, the type of wood was immaterial.'

In the first part of this century, carvers were sticking to the stylised or plain form of the original hunting decoy. Thrown about in boats, left up to several months out on the water and buffeted by wind, rain and storm water, they had to be robust. A superficial resemblance to the relevant species was all that was needed.

You can always tell an authentic duck-hunter's decoy by a tethering ring beneath

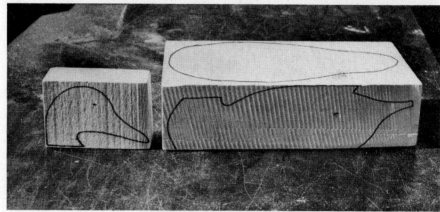

● **Top**, *the duck inside every block of wood, waiting to come out!* **Middle**, *shapes drawn in three dimensions on the blocks;* **right**, *these bandsawn blanks are what the students get*

the front, but even more indicative was the owner's name under the back. There was always the chance that the anchor-line would break in bad weather, letting the decoy drift away. Unless it was claimed in six months it went to the finder.

Following the 1918 Congress ban on commercial duck-hunting triggered by the extermination of the Labrador duck, professional carvers turned to decoration in an attempt to attract new, more fastidious buyers.

Cutting out decoys for practical, hunting uses, many carvers expressed a great deal of art in their work, adding little refinements to present aesthetic appeal, but it was the post-World War II folk-art boom that gave the decoy makers. Now the emphasis was decorative rather than utilitarian. Here was something uniquely American, true native art.

'When I first became interested in the craft, you could pick up quite attractive decoys for $500 — about six years ago,' says Bob. 'Today it's difficult to find a worthwhile decoy at a price you can afford. This year in America it's expected that a single decoy will break the $100,000 barrier at auction.'

Collecting decoys as an art form increased steadily in the mid-1940s-50s, and progressed slowly through the 60s and 70s. Interest was aroused, and as more and more amateur carvers took to the craft, small, regional competitions were held throughout the United States.

Then in 1970, the first World Championship Wildfowl Carving Competition was held at Ocean City, Maryland. Entries came from all over the US and Canada, and it was there that an aptly-named carver, Rev. Jack Drake,

● **Above:** *two heads better than one? Textured heads before (left) and after painting.* **Left,** *Peter Maidstone puts the finishing touches to his drake*

caused a sensation. After carving his duck in the conventional way he had used a hot tool — a cross between an electric pyrograph poker and a soldering iron — to add individual feather detail. The effect by today's standards was rather crude, but the idea was there. The gauntlet had been thrown. From then on realism became increasingly important.

Today, the work is so precise and life-like that it's difficult to tell the decoy from the real thing. What started off on the East coast went across the States and into Canada, and now it has crossed the Atlantic.

In December 1984, Britain's first decoy contest was held at Slimbridge in Gloucestershire, attracting competitors from as far as Ireland and Scotland. 'Although the standard in Britain is so much lower than in America,' Bob comments, 'we're on the way, and within a few years we'll have people capable of competing at world level. Perhaps one day we'll bring the coveted Blue Ribbon back with us!'

A good exercise for any would-be decoy carver is to carve an egg from a piece of two-by-two, using only a knife and fine glass-paper. If you can do that, you can carve a duck.

Some of Bob Ridges' ducks are stylised — streamlined and elegant. Others display every feather in such startling reality that I was almost tempted to blow into the plumage and expect it to ripple. There's no magic wood involved. Use lime, pine, spruce, even mahogany; there's a duck inside every block of wood. The best for beginners is jelutong, the wood of the chewing-gum tree — soft and easily worked. It isn't readily available in this country, but Bob sells everything that the aspiring decoy carver might need, from bandsawn blanks of jelutong to artificial ducks' eyes.

Before you can carve a duck you have to know something about the bird. Bob's early days would see him out with binoculars on ponds, lakes and nature reserves, simply watching ducks. Noting how they moved was vital to be able to transfer the creature's character to wood. How is the tail held? Does the drake hold his head high or low when in repose? Is his neck straight, or does it have a sinuous curve? Does he sit high or low in the water? Bob meticulously documented all the answers and observations for each species, taking photographs of the birds for reference to ensure correct proportions.

Making a decoy

Decoys are made from two pieces of wood, one for the head and neck and the other for the body — not for economic reasons, but to make the best use of grain direction, since the head is usually turned slightly to one side on the finished bird.

Having obtained your two rectangular blocks, you must draw the outline of the head and the neck and body on their respective pieces. The dorsal part of the body should also be indicated.

The next operation is bandsawing the blocks to more easily workable pieces. Cut cautiously, to retain an exact profile of the completed decoy. You can always buy the blocks ready bandsawn from Bob so you don't begin with a mistake.

Then use a craft knife to round the duck's back over in a gentle arch rather than a distinct hump. With enough wood removed, sand the back as smooth as possible, making the back contours flow naturally. We aren't concerned here with feather detail; it's more for the specialist with the specialist feathering tool. Be careful not to make the tail too long; ideally it should be thin and narrow rather than broad and chunky.

The head is the most difficult part of the whole exercise.

'Most people have a common misconception about the shape of a duck's head,' says Bob. 'Donald Duck has a lot to answer for; blown cheeks, pointed heads, sharp beaks and popping eyes. One point I try to hammer home is the one of correct proportions.'

Your decoy should have grace and poise, be alert and alive. Don't make the common mistake of putting the forehead too high, and flat cheeks are out. A duck's bill is in two parts, which should be evident in the finished piece. Nostrils should be correctly placed and not over-enlarged, and the neck should flow beautifully into the body, fixed with epoxy putty when all the carving is complete. When the putty is set, sand it smooth to follow the neck, avoiding bulges in the join.

Painting will depend on the species of your duck. You are as well to start with something simple art-wise, like the tricoloured pochard which Bob's first students make. Oils or acrylics are best.

Fortunately, everyone on the course I watched made the same mistakes, cutting the wood in chips rather than slices — faults quickly made good by the teacher and a few well-placed strokes of the blade.

Eyes were a problem for most of the students. The sockets have to be larger than the eye, but the eyes themselves must also be set at the correct depth in the recess with epoxy putty. Don't set them too deeply, or your bird might take on a sleepy look!

The atmosphere of the course, though hectic, was friendly and thoroughly happy. When the finely glassed particles of jelutong had settled, everyone had a drake pochard hewn with their own hands to take home. Packing two weeks into two days was pushing it, but Bob Ridges is a tutor who teaches rather than tells, and he has a knack of making his knowledge easily digestible.

He publishes *Decoy Art Review*, a quarterly magazine which goes as far afield as Israel, Iceland, Norway, Germany, Australia, South Africa and even America.

'Quite a number of our students are selling their work now. The whole thing is blossoming very nicely, and I can see it sweeping Britain as it did America.' ■

● Bob Ridges, Decoy Art Studio, Farrington Gurney, Avon BS19 5TX, (0761) 52075. Bob teaches courses and sells everything you need for decorative decoy carving.

Art ducko 2

Taste the spirit of the
American folk tradition in
decoy carving, as
explained by Alan and
Gill Bridgewater

For me the whole joy of decoy making
lies in the fact that the craft is open
to personal interpretation. I refuse to
get involved in the confusing debate about
how decoy ducks should be described, what
tools are used or how they are worked.

Decoy ducks, as far as I am concerned,
are no more or less than three-dimensional,
duck-inspired woodcarvings that can be
painted, varnished, burnt or otherwise
textured to create a decorative sculptural
form. They can be painted realistically with
each feather in accurate detail; or you can
use big bold blocks of colour to give a semi-
abstract naive art effect. The same applies to
tools. Axe, knife, bandsaw, bowsaw,
crooked knife, rasp or gouge — if one or all
of these work for you, then that's what's
right for the job.

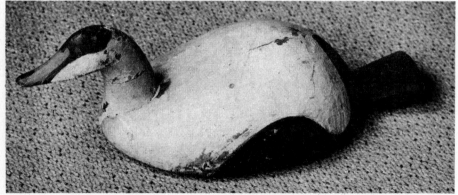

● An American Eider decoy, perhaps 19th century. Simple form and bold colour

The craft of decoy making has evolved
over hundreds of years and is the coming
together of many ethnic, folk and tribal
traditions. So it follows that there are very
few hard-and-fast rules as to form,
decoration or technique.

The word 'decoy' has several possible
roots, but it probably came from the Dutch
words, *kooj, koye* or *de kooi* meaning to lure,
entice or snare. When the first European
settlers saw the Indians using stick and mud
decoys, they copied and developed the
decoy idea using western woodcarving
methods and techniques.

The point of decoys is simple enough;
Alexander Wilson's book *American Orni-
thology*, published in the early 19th century
and now re-published by Dover Books,
describes how they were used. Five or six
wooden figures, cut and painted to
represent ducks, and weighted by lead to
float at the appropriate depth on the
surface, were anchored in a likely position.
These attracted passing flocks of ducks,

which alighted and were shot. Not very
sporting, but an efficient way of hunting.
Large-scale duck shooting was banned in
1918 and these hunting decoys or gunner
ducks have since been called decorative
decoys.

The decoys were traditionally made by
the hunters themselves, the bodies worked
with axe and knife and the heads sawn and
whittled. Some decoys were made of slats of
wood and canvas.

So there you have it, no mystique, and
certainly no high-art duck carvers — just a
simple country craft with naive duck-like
forms being made by ordinary folk.

Carving a duck

Before you rush out to buy your tools and
materials, consider just how you want your
decoy to be worked. Do you want to make a
very detailed duck study? Will you use non-
traditional tools like a bandsaw? Are you
going to glue-fix the head to the body or use
dowels and copper pins? Decisions like
these need careful consideration. Try to
pick up background information by visiting
relevant craft centres and museums (such as
the American Museum in Bath and the
Craft Centre, London) and notice how the

decoys are worked, formed, painted and
put together. If possible, get to handle
decoys, feeling their weight and evaluating
their simple bold lines.

Now you are ready to use a sketchbook
(grid paper is best) and make a series of
drawings to show the views, elevations,
profiles, colours and fixings. Finally, make
a full-size working drawing, complete with
measurements and colour details.

Shaping the body

You can use a piece of pine, a lump of lime,
(an easy wood to carve), cedar, mahogany
or a length of found wood — any timber
that is straight-grained and relatively free
from knots, splits, stains and other nasties.
Set out your sketches and working
drawings, and decide what size you want
your finished decoy to be (our scale is one
grid-square to ¾ in). Now trace your design
and transfer the profiles to the wood faces.
Check at this stage that you have the grain
running correctly from head to tail, and
from the tip of the beak to the back of the
head crest. Label the various drawn profiles
and then clear your working area of all
clutter, pin up your drawings and set out
your chosen tools.

Start by cutting out the body profile
quickly, removing the areas of waste with a
band- or bow-saw. Don't try to achieve
anything like a finished form at this stage —
do no more than knock off the corners.
Then working with a good knife — I use a
North West Canadian Indian crooked knife
— begin to carve and work the body,
cutting with the grain from centre to end
and referring to your drawings until the
duck body becomes sharp-ended and
begins to take on duck characteristics. Your
sketches should have revealed that the
forms have a very low centre of gravity, so
the body bulge is well below the centre or
water line. Continue cutting, taking caliper
readings from the drawings, and gradually
carving closer and closer to the required
duck form.

1 Trace outlines on to blocks

2 Saw main waste, then carve with small
scalloped cuts

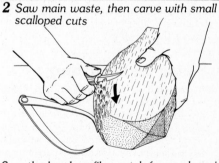

3 Chop the head mortise with the body
in a padded vice

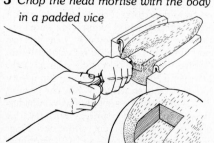

4 Saw the head profile; watch for weak grain

Art ducko 2

The head

If you go back to your museum studies, you will see how the heads are variously nailed, spiked, screwed and dowelled into the duck bodies. In this project we have slotted the neck tenon into a deep body mortise. If you would prefer to use a dowel, have copper nails as a decorative feature and such like, just modify the project accordingly.

Secure the duck body in the jaws of a muffled vice, note the depth, width and length of the neck tenon and then work the mortise as illustrated. Hold the chisel with one hand, and guide, push and control with the other, ensuring that the tool doesn't run too deeply into the wood. Work the head-to-body joint cautiously, and trial fit repeatedly.

Whittling

Clamp the head wood in the vice and then cut out the side profile. Our design is inspired by an American merganser decoy that was made by Lothrop Holmes in about 1860, and the neck is longer and more delicate than the modern English type of squat mallard decoys. So there are areas down the length of the neck that are short-grained and fragile: this shouldn't be a problem as long as you work with appropriate care, but if you think it necessary, you can strengthen the neck with a drilled and glued through-grain dowel.

When you have cut out the head profile, look again at the working drawings and then start the very relaxing business of whittling the duck's head. I usually settle down in the garden with a selection of razor-sharp knives. It's a beautiful feeling to have a chunk of choice wood in one hand, cutting and carving with co-ordinated eye and blade, and watching the wood curl away in quiet crinkles and crisps . . . pure poetry. Using your thumb as a pivotal lever, draw the blade through the wood; don't try to hack off great slabs or force the blade into the grain, but let the blade slice off delicate, dappled and scooped curls. From time to time use calipers to check your whittling against the drawings.

Fixing and finishing

When you have carved and worked a good head — a head that says all you want it to say — it can be glue-fixed into the body using PVA. Brush and wipe with a damp cloth the areas to be glued, have a last check that the angle of head to body is correct, and then put the whole thing together as shown. After about 24 hours or so when the glue is dry, stand back and view the decoy from all angles. If it looks right you can now use a range of graded glasspapers to bring the whole form to a good finish. However, some decoy makers prefer to leave their work with a dappled tooled finish, while others really go wild with a variety of small knives, burning tools and dentist's burrs.

Virtually every decoy maker I've ever

● *A simple modern decoy form by Alan. A through dowel secures the head to the mortised body; the eyes are hardwood plugs*

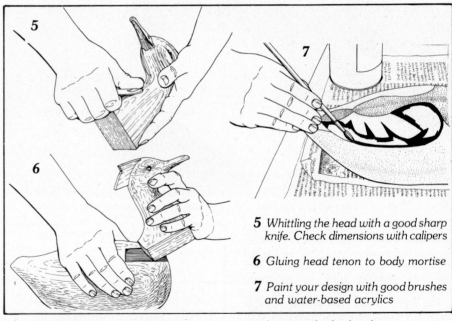

5 *Whittling the head with a good sharp knife. Check dimensions with calipers*

6 *Gluing head tenon to body mortise*

7 *Paint your design with good brushes and water-based acrylics*

met, English or American, has his or her own particular preferred materials and techniques. Some use gloss-type household paints, others prefer water-based emulsions and acrylics, and there are those who stick to wax and lacquers. For this decoy we used Pebeo acrylic wood paints marketed by Artemis of Croydon, which is easy to use and comes in a very good range of colours.

Wipe the decoy over with a damp cloth, then use a soft flat brush to lay on a very thin coat of base white. While the ground paint is drying, take a scrap of wood that has already been base painted, and try out techniques with various short and long-haired brushes. You can use dappling,

smudging and dry-brush printing, try working with thick colours to achieve a flat graphic effect, or experiment with masses of swirling pattern in the American dower-chest tradition. Carry on until you know how you want your decoy to be painted. In general, don't heap the paint on, but use many thin coats.

Don't worry if the first decoy is a mess, and above all don't pay too much attention to the 'my way is best' duck gurus. Go your own way — and the best of luck! ■
● Artemis, 684 Mitcham Rd, Croydon, Surrey CR9 3AB, 01-684 1330.
● Dover Publications, Constable & Co. Ltd, 10 Orange St, London WC2H 7EG.

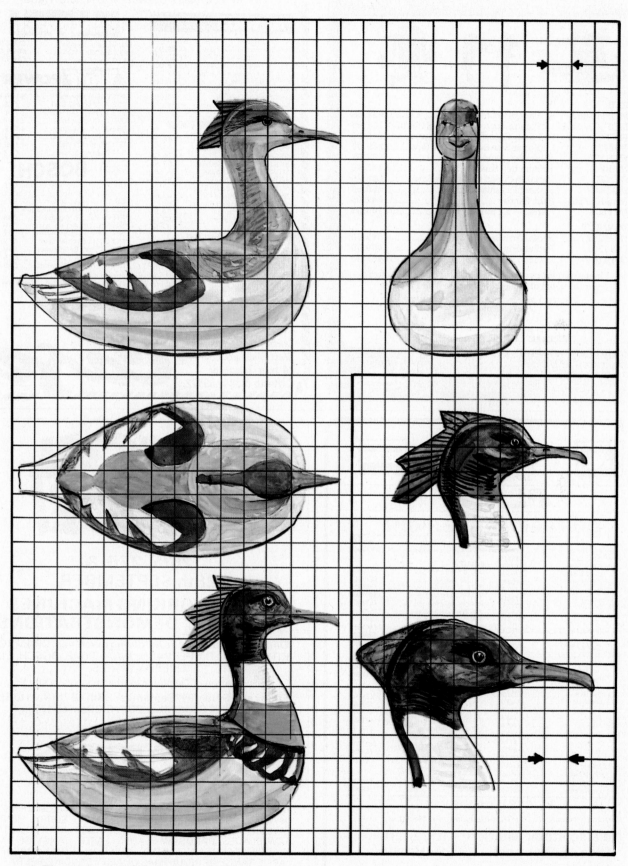

● *The coloured working-drawing grid is based on one square to ¾in. Breast to tail about 9in, base to top of head about 8½in. Note the head variations*

688

The garden workshop

Richard Blizzard's versatile,
easy-to-make work-centre
for the green-fingered
will add attraction and
efficiency to your garden

The Japanese word *Bonsai* simply
means a plant grown in a tray or a
pot. It's thought it was the Chinese
who first started planting small wild trees in
pots, but there's no doubt that it's the
Japanese who have perfected the gentle art
of miniaturising trees.

This garden work-centre has provision
not only for potting plants and pruning
miniature trees, but also for displaying
them on the rack shelving. The work area of
the centre has a slatted roof to give shade to
the gardener and the plants, while the front
area has a corrugated PVC roof which
provides a valuable collecting area for rainwater. The work-centre is self-contained
and makes a useful and attractive addition
to the garden.

The project

1 Start by cutting the two legs and feet to
length. A recess must then be cut in the
feet to take the legs, and the two then glued
and screwed together.

2 Now cut all the cross-pieces that support the slatted shelves. These cross-
pieces, unlike the feet, will only be bolted in
position, allowing the whole centre to be
dismantled.

3 Cut recesses in the cross-pieces to fit
the width of the legs.

4 Clamp the cross-pieces to the legs and
drill through for the coach-bolts.

Slatted shelving

Once all the joints have been cut and all
cross-pieces bolted to the legs, the next
stage is the slatted shelving. I find roofing
batten is very useful for this, especially if
you don't have a power ripsaw. Check the
bundles over carefully before you buy, as
quality varies hugely in each bundle.

1 Build one shelf unit at a time by fixing
the battens on to the cross-pieces with
rustproof screws and waterproof glue. As
you work towards the top shelves, the
whole unit becomes increasingly rigid and
stable.

2 The work-shelf is the only one which
requires extra support, so you can slide
a wooden framework in between the
bottom shelf and the work-shelf. This gives
extra rigidity and eliminates any 'bounce'
when you're working.

Roof sections

The roof is in two sections, a wooden
slatted one at the back and a corrugated
PVC one at the front. The rainwater gutter
and downpipe provide you with your own
water supply, very handy for daily watering.

● *Just right for potting or pruning bonsai – or anything else!*

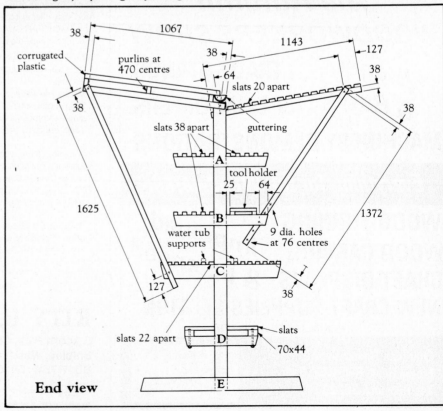

End view

1 Glue and screw the frameworks together for the two roof sections.

2 Fix the slats on to one framework in the same way as for the slatted shelves.

3 Cut the PVC for the other roof framework to size with a fine-toothed tenon saw. Cramp it to the bench or a solid surface, as it tends to wave about. Don't apply too much pressure while cutting.

4 Screw the PVC to the framework with corrugated-sheet fixing screws or 'screw-nails' and plastic cups. Fix the screws at the top of the corrugation, supporting it underneath with some hefty dowel — a broom handle is ideal. Fix the screws with the plastic cup in place and then snap on the top which prevents the rain getting in.

5 Now bolt the two roof sections onto the top of the uprights.

6 The guttering and downpipe should be fixed on to the centre with clips, available from builder's merchants. Then fix a small plastic tub on a shelf next to the work-shelf to collect the rainwater.

7 As with all garden furniture, the garden centre should be finished with wood preservative. Allow a few days for it to dry thoroughly before putting plants on it, unless you use one of the new 'plant-friendly' products. ∎

●This is an extract from Richard Blizzard's book *Blizzard's Wizard Woodwork*, published by BBC Publications at £8.95 hardback, which accompanied his BBC TV series first broadcast in spring 1985 on BBC1. We are grateful to BBC Enterprises Ltd for permission to use the piece. The colour photograph is by David Brittain and the line illustrations by William Giles.

Cutting list

Vertical legs	2	2135mm	x	95mm	x	44mm
Horizontal support **A**	2	717		70		44
Horizontal support **B**	2	717		70		44
Horizontal support **C**	2	914		95		44
Horizontal support **D**	2	546		70		44
Feet **E**	2	1220		95		44
Longitudinals	2	1511		70		44
Glazed roof purlins	3	1727		44		32
end pieces	2	1067		44		44
supports	2	1625		44		32
Slatted roof rafters	3	1143		38		35
supports	2	1372		44		44
slats	16	1727		44		22
Deck **A**, **B** and **C** slats	31	1511		32		22
Deck **D** slats	20	546		32		22
Water tub support rails	2	457		32		22
slats	3	267		32		22
Main decking support	1	864		44		44
frame horizontal	1	546		44		44
verticals	2	470		44		38

Extras

Corrugated plastic sheeting
Assorted 9mm coach-bolts
No.8 and no.10 galvanised woodscrews
76mm dia. rainwater guttering and downpipe
Water tub
Wood preservative
Waterproof wood glue
Corrugated plastic sheet-fixing screws and sealing caps and washers

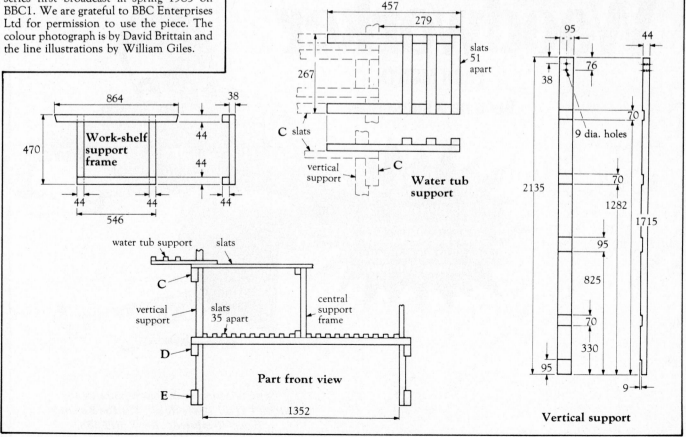

Work-shelf support frame

Water tub support

Part front view

Vertical support

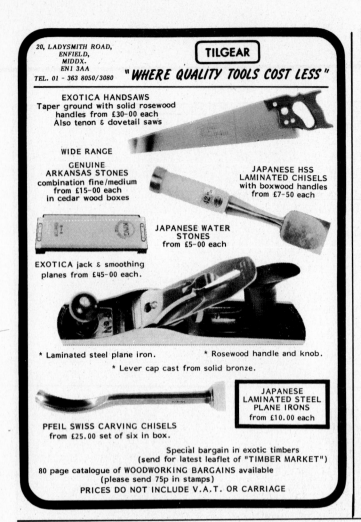

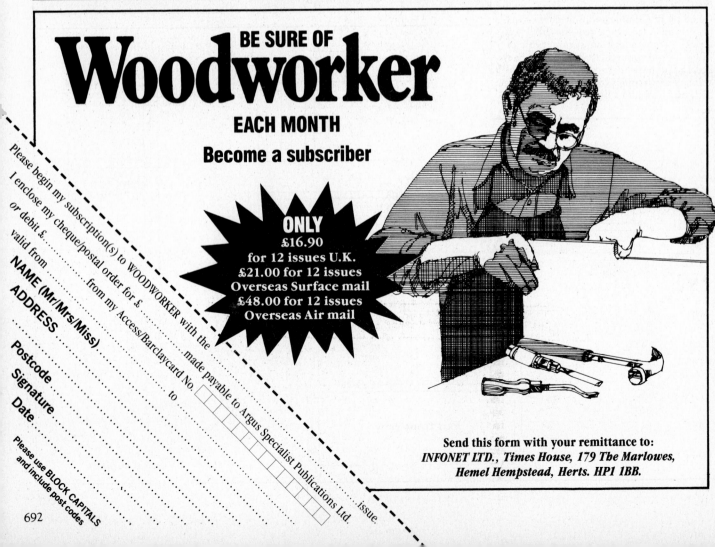

shopguide

AVON

BATH Tel. Bath 64513
JOHN HALL TOOLS ★
RAILWAY STREET

Open: Monday-Saturday
9.00 a.m.-5.30 p.m.
H.P.W.WM.D.A.BC.

BRISTOL Tel. (0272) 741510
JOHN HALL TOOLS LIMITED ★
CLIFTON DOWN SHOPPING CENTRE
WHITELADIES ROAD
Open: Monday-Saturday
9.00 a.m.-5.30 p.m.
H.P.W.WM.D.A.BC.

BRISTOL Tel. (0272) 629092
TRYMWOOD SERVICES
2a DOWNS PARK EAST, (off North View)
WESTBURY PARK
Open: 8.30 a.m.-5.30 p.m. Mon. to Fri.
Closed for lunch 1.00-2.00 p.m.
P.W.WM.D.T.A.BC.

BRISTOL Tel. (0272) 667013
FASTSET LTD
190-192 WEST STREET
BEDMINSTER
Open: Mon.-Fri. 8.30 a.m.-5.00 p.m.
Saturday 9.00 a.m.-1.00 p.m.
H.P.W.WM.D.CS.A.BC.

BRISTOL Tel. (0272) 667013
WILLIS
157 WEST STREET
BEDMINSTER
Open: Mon.-Fri. 8.30 a.m.-5.00 p.m.
Sat. 9 a.m.-4 p.m.
P.W.WM.D.CS.A.BC.

BEDFORDSHIRE

BEDFORD Tel. (0234) 59808
BEDFORD SAW SERVICE K
39 AMPTHILL ROAD

Open: Mon.-Fri. 8.30-5.30
Sat. 9.00-4.00
H.P.A.BC.W.CS.WM.D.

BERKSHIRE

READING Tel. Littlewick Green
DAVID HUNT (TOOL 2743
MERCHANTS) LTD ★
KNOWL HILL, NR. READING
Open: Monday-Saturday
9.00 a.m.-5.30 p.m.
H.P.W.D.A.BC.

READING Tel. Reading 661511
WOKINGHAM TOOL CO. LTD.
99 WOKINGHAM ROAD

Open: Mon-Sat 9.00 a.m.-5.30 p.m.
Closed 1.00-2.00 p.m. for lunch
H.P.W.WM.D.CS.A.BC.

BUCKINGHAMSHIRE

MILTON KEYNES Tel. (0908)
POLLARD WOODWORKING 641366
CENTRE ★
51 AYLESBURY ST., BLETCHLEY
Open: Mon-Fri 8.30-5.30
Saturday 9.00-5.00
H.P.W.WM.D.CS.A.BC.

HIGH WYCOMBE Tel. (0494)
SCOTT SAWS LTD. 24201/33788
14 BRIDGE STREET ★

Mon.-Sat. 8.30 a.m.-6.00 p.m.

H.P.W.WM.D.T.CS.MF.A.BC.

HIGH WYCOMBE Tel. (0494)
ISAAC LORD LTD 22221
185 DESBOROUGH ROAD KE

Open: Mon-Fri 8.00 a.m.-5.00 p.m.
Saturday 9.00 a.m.-5.00 p.m.
H.P.W.D.A.

CAMBRIDGESHIRE

CAMBRIDGE Tel. (0223) 63132
D. MACKAY LTD. ★
BRITANNIA WORKS, EAST ROAD

Open: Mon.-Fri. 8.30 a.m.-1 p.m./2.00-
5.00 p.m. Sat. 8.30 a.m.-1.00 p.m.
H.P.W.D.T.CS.MF.A.BC.

CAMBRIDGE Tel. (0223) 247386
H. B. WOODWORKING K
105 CHERRY HINTON ROAD
Open: 8.30 a.m.-5.30 p.m.
Monday-Friday
8.30 a.m.-1.00 p.m. Sat.
H.P.W.WM.D.CS.A.

CHESHIRE

NANTWICH Tel. Crewe 67010
ALAN HOLTHAM K★
THE OLD STORES TURNERY
WISTASON ROAD, WILLASTON
Open: Tues.-Sat. 9.00 a.m.-5.30 p.m.
Closed Monday
P.W.WM.D.T.C.CS.A.BC.

CLEVELAND

MIDDLESBROUGH Tel. (0642)
CLEVELAND WOODCRAFT 813103
(M'BRO), 38-42 CRESCENT ROAD K

Open: Mon-Sat 9.15 a.m.-5.30 p.m.

H.P.T.A.BC.W.WM.CS.D.

CORNWALL

**SOUTH WEST
Power Tools**
CORNWALL Tel: Helston (03265) 4961
HELSTON AND LAUNCESTON Launceston
(0566) 4781
H.P.W.WM.D.CS.A. K

CUMBRIA

CARLISLE Tel: (0228) 36391
W. M. PLANT
ALLENBROOK ROAD
ROSEHILL, CA1 2UT
Open: Mon.-Fri. 8.00 a.m.-5.15 p.m.
Sat. 8.00 a.m.-12.30 noon
P.W.WM.D.CS.A.

DEVON

BRIXHAM Tel. (08045) 4900
WOODCRAFT SUPPLIES E★
4 HORSE POOL STREET

Open: Mon.-Sat. 9.00 a.m.-6.00 p.m.

H.P.W.A.D.MF.CS.BC.

PLYMOUTH Tel. (0752) 330303
WESTWARD BUILDING SERVICES ★
LTD., LISTER CLOSE, NEWNHAM
INDUSTRIAL ESTATE, PLYMPTON
Open: Mon-Fri 8.00 a.m.-5.30 p.m.
Sat. 8.30 a.m.-12.30 p.m.
H.P.W.WM.D.A.BC.

ESSEX

LEIGH ON SEA Tel. (0702)
MARSHAL & PARSONS LTD. 710404
1111 LONDON ROAD EK

Open: 8.30 a.m.-5.30 p.m. Mon-Fri
9.00 a.m.-5.00 p.m. Sat.
H.P.W.WM.D.CS.A.

GLOUCESTER

TEWKESBURY Tel. (0684)
TEWKESBURY SAW CO. LTD. 293092
TRADING ESTATE, NEWTOWN K

Open: Mon-Fri 8.00 a.m.-5.00 p.m.
Saturday 9.30 a.m.-12.00 p.m.
P.W.WM.D.CS.

HAMPSHIRE

ALDERSHOT Tel. (0252) 334422
POWER TOOL CENTRE K
374 HIGH STREET

Open Mon.-Fri. 8.30 a.m.-5.30 p.m.
Sat. 8.30 a.m.-12.30 p.m.

H.P.W.WM.D.A.BC.

SOUTHAMPTON Tel: (0703)
POWER TOOL CENTRE 332288
7 BELVIDERE ROAD K★
Open Mon.-Fri. 8.30-5.30

H.P.W.WM.D.A.BC.CS.MF.

HERTFORDSHIRE

WARE K★
HEATH SAWS
16 MALTINGS
STANSTEAD ABBOTTS (near Ware) HERTS.
Open: Mon.-Fri. 8.30am-5.30pm
Sat. 8.30am-1pm. Sunday by appointment.
P.W.WM.D.CS.A.

HUMBERSIDE

GRIMSBY Tel. Grimsby (0472)
58741 Hull (0482) 26999
J. E. SIDDLE LTD. (Tool Specialists) ★
83 VICTORIA STREET
Open: Mon-Fri 8.30 a.m.-5.30 p.m.
Sat. 8.30 a.m.-12.45 p.m. & 2 p.m.-5 p.m.
H.P.A.BC.W.WMD.

HULL
HUMBERSIDE FACTORING/H.F.C.
SAW SERVICING LTD.
MAIN STREET
Open: Mon.-Fri. 8am-5pm.
Saturday 8am-12.00pm.
H.P.W.WM.D.CS.A.BC.K.

KENT

WYE Tel. (0233) 813144
KENT POWER TOOLS LTD.
UNIT 1, BRIAR CLOSE
WYE, Nr. ASFORD

H.P.W.WM.D.A.CS.

MAIDSTONE Tel. (0622) 50177
SOUTH EASTERN SAWS (Ind.) LTD. ★
COLDRED ROAD
PARKWOOD INDUSTRIAL ESTATE
Open: Mon.-Fri. 8.00 a.m.-6.00 p.m.
Sat. 9.00 a.m.-12.00 a.m.
B.C.W.CS.WM.PH.

LANCASHIRE

PRESTON Tel. (0772) 52951
SPEEDWELL TOOL COMPANY E★
62-68 MEADOW STREET PR1 1SU
Open: Mon.-Fri. 8.30 a.m.-5.30 p.m.
Sat. 8.30 a.m.-12.30 p.m.

H.P.W.WM.CS.A.MF.BC.

MANCHESTER Tel. (061 789)
TIMMS TOOLS 0909
102-104 LIVERPOOL ROAD ★
PATRICROFT M30 0WZ
Weekdays 9.00 a.m.-5.30 p.m.
Sat. 9.00 a.m.-1.00 p.m.
H.P.A.W.

ROCHDALE Tel. (0706) 342123/
C.S.M. TOOLS 342322
4-6 HEYWOOD ROAD E★
CASTLETON
Open: Mon-Sat 9.00 a.m.-6.00 p.m.
Sundays by appointment
W.D.CS.A.BC.

shop guide

LANCASHIRE

LANCASTER   Tel: (0524) 32886
LILE TOOL SHOP   **K**
43/45 NORTH ROAD
Open: Monday to Saturday
9.00 a.m.-5.30 p.m.
Wed. 9.00 a.m.-12.30 p.m.
H.P.W.D.A.

LEICESTERSHIRE

HINCKLEY   Tel. (0455) 613432
J. D. WOODWARD & CO. (POWER   ★
TOOL SPECIALISTS)
THE NARROWS, HINCKLEY
Open: Monday-Saturday
8.00 a.m.-6.00 p.m.
H.P.W.WM.D.CS.A.BC.

LINCOLNSHIRE

LINCOLN   Tel: (0522) 689369
SKELLINGTHORPE SAW SERVICES LTD.
OLD WOOD, SKELLINGTHORPE
Open: Mon to Fri 8 a.m.-5 p.m.
Sat 8 a.m.-12 p.m.
H.P.W.WM.D.CS.A.*.BC.
Access/Barclaycard

LONDON

ACTON   Tel. (01-992) 4835
A. MILLS (ACTON) LTD   ★
32/36 CHURCHFIELD ROAD W3 6ED
Open: Mon-Fri 9.00 a.m.-5.00 p.m.
Saturdays 9.00 am.-1.00 p.m.
H.P.W.WM.

LONDON   Tel. 01-723 2295-6-7
LANGHAM TOOLS LIMITED
13 NORFOLK PLACE
LONDON W2 1QJ

LONDON   Tel. (01-636) 7475
BUCK & RYAN LTD
101 TOTTENHAM COURT ROAD W1P ODY
Open: Mon.-Fri. 8.30 a.m.-5.30 p.m.
Saturday 8.30 a.m.-4.00 p.m.
H.P.W.WM.D.A..

WEMBLEY   Tel. 904-1144
ROBERT SAMUEL LTD.   (904-1147
7, 15 & 16 COURT PARADE   after 4.00)
EAST LANE, N. WEMBLEY   ★
Open Mon.-Fri. 8.45-5.15; Sat. 9-1.00
Access, Barclaycard, AM Express, & Diners
H.P.W.CS.E.A.D.

HOUNSLOW   Tel. (01-570)
Q.R. TOOLS LTD   2103/5135
251-253 HANWORTH ROAD
Open: Mon-Fri 8.30 a.m.-5.30 p.m.
Sat. 9.00 a.m.-1.00 p.m.
P.W.WM.D.CS.A.

FULHAM   Tel. (01-385) 5109
I. GRIZZARD LTD.   **E**
84a-b LILLIE ROAD, SW6 1TL
Open: Mon-Sat 9.00-5.30 p.m.
Half day Thursday

H.P.A.BC.W.CS.WM.D.

MERSEYSIDE

LIVERPOOL   Tel. (051-207) 2967
TAYLOR BROS (LIVERPOOL) LTD   **K**
195-199 LONDON ROAD
LIVERPOOL L3 8JG
Open: Monday to Friday
8.30 a.m.-5.30 p.m.
H.P.W.WM.D.A.BC.

MIDDLESEX

RUISLIP   Tel. (08956) 74126
ALLMODELS ENGINEERING LTD.   **E**★
91 MANOR WAY

Open: Mon-Sat 9.00 a.m.-5.30 p.m.
H.P.W.A.D.CS.MF.BC.

ENFIELD   Tel: 01-363 2935
GILL & HOXBY LTD.
131-137 ST. MARKS ROAD ADJ.
BUSH HILL PARK STATION, EN1 1BA
Mon.-Sat. 8-5.30
Early closing Wed. 1 p.m.
H.P.A.M.MC.T.S.W.

NORWICH   Tel. (0603) 898695
NORFOLK SAW SERVICES
DOG LANE, HORSFORD
Open: Monday to Friday
8.00 a.m.-5.00 p.m.
Saturday 8.00 a.m.-12.00 p.m.
H.P.W.WM.D.CS.A.

KINGS LYNN   Tel. (0553) 2443
WALKER & ANDERSON (Kings Lynn) LTD.
WINDSOR ROAD, KINGS LYNN   **K**
Open: Monday to Saturday
7.45 a.m.-5.30 p.m.
Wednesday 1.00 p.m. Saturday 5.00 p.m.
H.P.W.WM.D.CS.A.

NORFOLK

NORWICH   Tel. (0603) 400933
WESTGATES WOODWORKING   Tx
61 HURRICANE WAY,   975412
NORWICH AIRPORT INDUSTRIAL ESTATE
Open: 9.00 a.m.-5.00 p.m. weekdays
9.00 a.m.-12.30 Sat.
P.W.WM.D.BC.   **K**

KING'S LYNN   Tel. 07605 674
TONY WADDILOVE, UNIT A   ★
HILL FARM WORKSHOPS
GREAT DUNHAM, (Nr. Swaffham)
Open: Tues. — Fri. 10.00 a.m. to 5.30 p.m.
Sat. 9.00 to 5.00 p.m.
H.P.W.D.T.MF.A.BC.*

NOTTINGHAMSHIRE

NOTTINGHAM   Tel: (0602) 225979
POOLEWOOD   and 227064/5
EQUIPMENT LTD.   (06077) 2421 after hrs
5a HOLLY LANE, CHILLWELL
Open: Mon-Fri 9.00 a.m.-5.30 p.m.
Sat. 9.00 a.m. to 12.30 p.m.
P.W.WM.D.CS.A.BC.

OXON

WITNEY   Tel. (0993) 3885,
TARGET TOOLS (SALES,   & 72095 OXON
TARGET HIRE & REPAIRS)   ★
TOOLS SWAIN COURT
STATION INDUSTRIAL ESTATE
Open: Mon.-Sat. 8.00 a.m.-5.00 p.m.
24 hour Answerphone
BC.W.M.A.

SHROPSHIRE

TELFORD   Tel. Telford (0952)
ASLES LTD   48054
VINEYARD ROAD, WELLINGTON   **EK**★
Open: Mon. Fri. 8.30 a.m.-5.30 p.m.
Saturday 8.30 a.m.-4.00 p.m.
H.P.W.WM.D.CS.BC.A.

SOMERSET

TAUNTON   Tel. (0823) 85431
JOHN HALL TOOLS   ★
6 HIGH STREET

Open Monday-Saturday
9.00 a.m.-5.30 p.m.
H.P.W.WM.D.CS.A.

TAUNTON   Tel. 0823 443766
CUTWELL TOOLS LTD.   ★
CREECH HEATHFIELD
SOMERSET TA3 5EQ
Mon-Fri 9 a.m.-5 p.m. and also by appointment.
P.W.WM.A.D.CS.

STAFFORDSHIRE

CROWMARSH   Tel. (0491) 38653
MILL HILL SUPPLIES   **E**★
66 THE STREET
Open: Mon.-Fri. 9.30 a.m.-5.00 p.m.
Thurs. 9.30 a.m.-7.00 p.m.
Sat. 9.30 a.m.-1.00 p.m.
P.W.D.CS.MF.A.BC.

TAMWORTH   Tel: (0827) 56188
MATTHEWS BROTHERS LTD.   **K**
KETTLEBROOK ROAD
Open: Mon-Sat 8.30 a.m.-6.00 p.m.
Demonstrations Sunday mornings by
appointment only
H.P.WM.D.T.CS.A.BC.

SUFFOLK

IPSWICH   Tel. (0473) 40456
FOX WOODWORKING   **KE**★
142-144 BRAMFORD LANE
Open: Tues., Fri., 9.00 a.m.-5.30 p.m.
Sat. 9.00 a.m.-5.00 p.m.

H.P.W.WM.D.A.B.C.

SUSSEX

ST. LEONARD'S-ON-SEA   Tel.
DOUST & MONK (MONOSAW)-(0424)
25 CASTLEHAM ROAD   52577

Open: Mon.-Fri. 8.00 a.m.-5.30 p.m.
Most Saturdays 9.00 a.m.-1.00 p.m.
H.P.W.WM.D.CS.A.

BOGNOR REGIS Tel. (0243) 863100
A. OLBY & SON (BOGNOR REGIS) LTD.
"TOOLSHOP," BUILDERS MERCHANT
HAWTHORN ROAD   **K**
Open: Mon-Thurs 8 a.m.-5.15 p.m. Fri.
8 a.m.-8 p.m. Sat 8 a.m.-12.45 p.m.
H.P.W.WM.D.T.C.A.BC.

WORTHING   Tel. (0903) 38739
W. HOSKING LTD (TOOLS &   **KE**★
MACHINERY)
28 PORTLAND RD, BN11 1QN
Open: Mon.-Sat. 8.30 a.m.-5.30 p.m.
Closed Wednesday
H.P.W.WM.D.CS.A.BC.

TYNE & WEAR

NEWCASTLE   Tel. (0632) 320311
HENRY OSBOURNE LTD.   **E**★
50-54 UNION STREET

Open: Mon-Fri 8.30 a.m.-5.00 p.m.

H.P.W.D.CS.MF.A.BC.

W. MIDLANDS

WOLVERHAMPTON   Tel. (0902)
MANSAW SERVICES   58759
SEDGLEY STREET   **K**★

Open: Mon.-Fri. 9.00 a.m.-5.00 p.m.

H.P.W.WM.A.D.CS.

YORKSHIRE

BOROUGHBRIDGE   Tel. (09012)
JOHN BODDY TIMBER LTD   2370
FINE WOOD & TOOL STORE   ★
RIVERSIDE SAWMILLS
Open: Mon.-Thurs. 8.00 a.m.-6.00 p.m.
Fri. 8.00am-5.00pm Sat. 8.00am-4.00pm
H.P.W.WM.D.T.CS.MF.A.BC.

SHEFFIELD   Tel. (0742) 441012
GREGORY & TAYLOR LTD   **KE**
WORKSOP ROAD
Open: 8.30 a.m.-5.30 p.m.
Monday-Friday
8.30 a.m.-12.30 p.m. Sat.
H.P.W.WM.D.

HARROGATE   Tel. (0423) 66245/
MULTI-TOOLS   55328
158 KINGS ROAD   **K**★

Open: Monday to Saturday
8.30 a.m.-6.00 p.m.
H.P.W.WM.D.A.BC.

THIRSK   Tel. (0845) 22770
THE WOOD SHOP   ★
TRESKE SAWMILLS LTD.
STATION WORKS
Open: Seven days a week 9.00-5.00

T.H.MF.BC.

LEEDS   Tel. (0532) 574736
D. B. KEIGHLEY MACHINERY LTD.   ★
VICKERS PLACE, STANNINGLEY
PUDSEY LS2 86LZ
Mon.-Fri. 9.00 a.m.-5.00 p.m.
Sat. 9.00 a.m.-1.00 p.m.
P.A.W.WM.CS.BC.

HUDDERSFIELD   Tel. (0484)
NEVILLE M. OLDHAM   641219/(0484)
UNIT 1 DALE ST. MILLS   42777
DALE STREET, LONGWOOD   ★
Open: Mon-Fri 8.00 a.m.-5.30 p.m.
Saturday 9.30 a.m.-12.00 p.m.
P.W.WM.D.A.BC.

CLECKHEATON   Tel. (0274)
SKILLED CRAFTS LTD.   872861
34 BRADFORD ROAD   ★

Open: 9.00 a.m.-5.00 p.m. Monday
Saturday Lunch 12.00 a.m.-1.00 p.m.

H.P.A.W.CS.WM.D.

695

696

WOOD SUPPLIERS

697

Classified Advertisements

FOR SALE

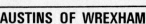

701

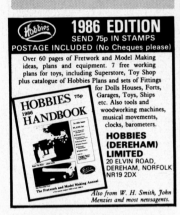

WOODWORKER

design . . . craft . . . and the love of wood   September 1986   Vol. 90   No. 1114

711 Shoptalk special
Universal acclaim
The *Woodworker* test: a new universal machine from AEG looks hard to beat at the price. *Gordon Stokes*

717 Tools of the trade 5
Handsaws: Panel and back-saws come under our eagle eye for the last in the 'best hand-tool you can buy' series. *David Savage*

721 The Midas touch
The art, science and challenge to your skills in laying the visual luxury of gold leaf — explained by professionals. *Peter and Frances Binnington*

725 WORKBENCH OF THE FUTURE
There's still time to win a bench **and** a holiday in our testing competition if you move fast!

726 JAPAN 6
Hira-kanna
We look at those 'back-to-front' wooden-bodied planes with custom-made irons that cut a micron's thickness. *Tony Wood*

Editor Aidan Walker
Deputy editor John Hemsley
Editorial assistant Kerry Fowler
Senior advertisement manager Paul Holmes
Advertisement manager Trevor Pryer
Graphics Jeff Hamblin
Technical illustrator Peter Holland
Guild of Woodworkers John Hemsley, Kerry Fowler
Editorial, advertisements and Guild of Woodworkers
1 Golden Square, London W1R 3AB, telephone 01-437 0626

Unfortunately we cannot accept responsibility for loss of or damage to unsolicited material. We reserve the right to refuse or suspend advertisements, and regret we cannot guarantee the bone fides of advertisers.

ABC
UK circulation
Jan-Dec 85
28,051

Back issues and subscriptions Infonet Ltd, 10-13 Times House, 179 Marlowes, Hemel Hempstead, Herts HP1 1BB; telephone Hemel Hempstead (0442) 48434

Subscriptions per year UK £16.90; overseas outside USA (accelerated surface post) £21.00, USA (accelerated surface post) $28, airmail £48

UK trade SM Distribution Ltd, 16-18 Trinity Gardens, London SW9 8DX; telephone 01-274 8611

North American trade Bill Dean Books Ltd, 151-49 7th Avenue, PO Box 69, Whitestone, New York 11357; telephone 1-718-767-6632

Printed in Great Britain by Ambassador Press Ltd, St. Albans, Herts
Mono origination Multiform Photosetting Ltd, Cardiff
Colour origination Derek Croxson Ltd, Chesham, Bucks
® Argus Specialist Publications Ltd 1986
ISSN 0043 776X

Argus Specialist Publications Ltd
1 Golden Square, London W1R 3AB; 01-437 0626

730 Art attack
The first crop of College shows gives us a chance to air some views on design and experiment. *Friedbert Meinert*

734 86 degrees!
But how hot are these furniture makers of the future? Work from the RCA, Ipswich, Manchester, Middlesex and Parnham. *Luke Hughes, Peter Howlett, Jack Hill*

740 Past defence
On the other hand . . . we stick our necks out over the design-and-make values taught in Colleges and bought by the public. *Peter Howlett*

743 Which way to turn
Need to make a major machine-buying decision? Try this systematic approach, applied here to a lathe. *Hugh O'Neill*

757 Tales out of steel
You can practically hear the drop-hammers ring as Sheffield cold chisels are 'mooded'. *Ashley Iles*

759 The grand furniture saga: 8
Baroque reaches its peak in Europe, and chairs begin to get comfortable. Good news for 17th century sit-upons! *Vic Taylor*

772 French lesson:1
We proudly present two colourful insights into the world of French woodwork, looking first at the lives of country clogmakers and coopers. *Marie-Laure de Montesquieu*

780 French lesson: 2
But where does the designer/craftsman fit in? An inside view of the business, training, tools and trades in France. *Paul Davis*

● *Parnham graduate Oliver Darlington's rock maple bar stool; more student work p734ff*

PROJECTS
with detailed drawings

714 Treasured chest
The drawings of this period Zeeland jewel chest are themselves almost art, show how should your finished item turn out! *René Coolen*

750 Doubled-up
A dressing table/desk of ingenuity and elegance — and it saves space! *Leslie Stuttle*

761 Sit and spin
You don't need a spinning wheel to use this neat little traditional seat, but you need a good eye for angles to make it. *Arthur Wood*

On the cover: M. Claude Gozard at work on his barrel staves — p772.
Photo Marie-Laure de Montesquieu

REGULARS
706 This month News of note

707 Shoptalk Win a saw with a Shoptalk tip

709 Timberline Timber trade topics

747 Guild notes Courses and chances

755 Bob Wearing's workshop A table-saw tapering jig

767 Question box Bowling woods, a puzzle bench, removing acrylics . . .

777 Woodworking wheeze of the month A jigsaw sander. *Glyn Condick*

799 Letters Readers write

800 Advertisers' index

Woodworker
This month

Safe timber

Nuclear radiation from the disaster in Chernobyl *will not* endanger timber in the short or long term. This assurance came from the National Radiological Protection Board after public concern at contamination affecting lambs in North Wales.

Mr Roger Gelder, principal scientific officer for the NRPB, in an exclusive interview with *Woodworker*, said no timber was grown in the Chernobyl area, and very little in the Ukraine generally.

Tool appeal

We've discovered an organisation that collects and refurbishes unwanted hand-tools and ships them to Third World craftsmen. We'll have a feature on **Tools for Self Reliance** next month.

Meanwhile, start putting aside old hand-tools for TFSR — condition is irrelevant, since they're used to refurbishing rusty, chipped and toothless tools. **Bring them to the London Woodworker Show**, where we'll have a reception area for your unwanted items.

Star of the Show?

Could you be a prize-winner at the **London Woodworker Show**? Here is your chance to have your handiwork displayed before 10,000 visitors to the Alexandra Pavilion, 23-26 October, and win a medal!
● Entry forms from the show organisers, **Argus Specialist Exhibitions, Wolsey House, Wolsey Road, Hemel Hempstead, Herts HP2 4SS, (0442) 41221.**

Stick it!

The Woodworker Show and **Theo Fossel**, co-founder of the British Stickmaker's Guild, announce a new competition for the Show — Walking sticks! Your entry should be an all-wood stick, can be decorated with carving but not paint, and can be stained. It can be ordinary length or a long 'hill stick', but it should be useable; if it's jointed, you can't cover the join with a metal collar.

The prize — an £80 specially engraved glass tankard, yours to keep. Many thanks to The . . .
● Entry forms from the Show organisers, address above.

Afore ye go . . .

We have decided we should take out **Dantomuro Furniture's** classified ad for skilled tradesmen to go and work in New York because of complaints from readers who have gone to the US to 'start a new life' and been bitterly disappointed. All we can say is, if you are considering such a major move, make sure of several things **before you go:**
● Get an official written contract on the pay, terms and conditions of employment
● Make sure you have all the correct visas and immigration documents
● Find out as much as you can about your prospective employer — discover trade associations via the embassy, and check on reputations and bona fides.

Basically, covering yourself and informing yourself in every way you can think of sounds like common sense, but you'd be surprised . . . .

Turned green!

A mistake occurred in **Lech Zielinski's** article 'Turning green' in last month's *Woodworker*. The second paragraph explains how some wet-turned bowls are rough-turned, seasoned and they dry-turned to the final dimension. This refers, for example, to large and/or functional bowls of the kind made by Keith Mosse, mentioned in the fourth paragraph. The bowl which Lech himself turns in the article does not undergo this seasoning process half-way through, and is wet-turned from blank to finished in 1½ hours without a break. We are sorry for this confusion, and apologise to Lech for the mistake.

The colour photos of Lech in action were by professional photographer **James Edmonds,** and the pictures of the bowls are by Lech himself.

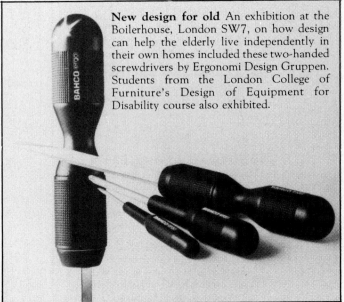

New design for old An exhibition at the Boilerhouse, London SW7, on how design can help the elderly live independently in their own homes included these two-handed screwdrivers by Ergonomi Design Gruppen. Students from the London College of Furniture's Design of Equipment for Disability course also exhibited.

Sculptured wood

A wood sculpture symposium is being held in September in Letterfrack, Co. Galway. The works being made will be left as a permanent public exhibition, in line with the symposium's aim of bringing art out of the gallery into the community.

The symposium, jointly organised by the Regional Arts Officer Helen Bygrove, the Sculpture Society of Ireland and Connemara West (a community-based development company) gives sculptors the chance to work on a large scale, and in partnership with others. It lasts for four weeks; all places have now been filled.
● Kieran O'Donohue, Connemara West Centre, Letterfrack, Co. Galway.

Diary

Guild courses are shown by an asterisk (*); for further details see the Guild pages.

August
14-Sept 10 **Mike Scott Wood-Works**; The Craft Centre and Gallery, The Headrow, Leeds LS1 3AB (0532) 462485
29-31 **Cabinetmaking for beginners** West Dean College, Chichester, W. Sussex PO18 0QZ (024363) 301
31-Sept 21 **Furniture and Screens**; Exhibition Lucinda Leech, Charles Wickham, Michael Dunwell, Old Town Hall, Bampton, Oxon

September
5-Oct 4 **Guy Taplin, Carved Birds**; Exhibition, British Crafts Centre, 43 Earlham St, London WC2H 9LD, 01-836 6993
6-7 **Decorative techniques** Ian Hosker*
7-9 **DIY 86** Novotel Exhibition Centre, London W6
9-Oct 19 **Pure Music**; musical instruments, Rufford Craft Centre, Ollerton, Newark, Notts NG22 9DF (0623) 822944
23-25 **Timber Build 86** Westminster Exhibition Centre, Royal Horticultural Halls, London SW1

October
2-3 **French polishing** Charles Cliffe*
5-9 **Building 86** Earls Court, London
11 **Wood-machining** Ken Taylor*
13-18 **International Creative Marquetry Show** The Corn Exchange, Ipswich. Contact 63 Church Lane, Sproughton, Ipswich IP8 3AY
16-22 **Chelsea Crafts Fair** Old Town Hall, London SW3
25-Nov 22 **Painted Wood**; carved/painted birds, bowls and furniture, Cleveland Crafts Centre, 57 Gilkes St, Middlesbrough TS1 5EC (0642) 226351
23-26 **London Woodworker Show** Alexandra Pavilion, London N22
25 **Rough Wood 2**; Forestry and architecture seminar, Parnham House, Beaminster, Dorset DT8 3NA

November
Woodmex 86 Woodworking equipment exhibition, NEC Birmingham, contact 01-486 1951

Shoptalk

If you read David Savage's personal tests on saws in this issue and want to know more, Argus Books are publishing a paperback which is the first specific book on the subject. Author Ian Bradley gives detailed guidance on the use and maintenance of all types of saws, from handsaws onwards. *Saws and Sawing* costs £4.95 and is available from woodworking and hardware suppliers and specialist bookshops.

● Argus Books Ltd, Wolsey House, Wolsey Road, Hemel Hempstead, Herts HP2 4SS, (0442) 41221

Shoptalking points is a special name for a special deal that Sandvik are offering *Woodworker* readers. For the next four issues, a Centenary edition Sandvik 100 **universal handsaw** — 22in, 8ppi — awaits the contributor of the **most original time- and labour-saving workshop or site tip** for hand-tool users! Write to 'Shoptalking points', Woodworker, 1 Golden Sq, London W1R 3AB — now!

Sharpening blunt and broken drills could be 'as easy as sharpening a pencil' with a new device from Bondseal Products. The **drill sharpener** incorporates two grinding wheels — green silicone carbide and white aluminium oxide — for steel and masonry bits up to ½in diameter. A built-in depth setter guards against over-grinding. A dressing stone is provided to maintain the wheels. The device costs £26+VAT.

● Bondseal Products, Station House, Billingshurst, West Sussex, RH14 9SE, (0403) 814841

Shopsmith's back! Popular US **universal** with a high reputation re-appears on our shores; £895+VAT for the basic saw/drill/lathe/sander, add-ons extra.

● Sumaco, Huddersfield Rd, Elland, W. Yorks HX5 9AA, (0422) 79811

A spindle moulder **cutter block** offering 36 different profiles is now available from Trend. The cutter-block is in light alloy, profile knives in tool steel, HSS and TC grades, each pair held securely by wedges and pins.

A set of block with 15 blades costs £148+VAT. Blades from £8.60+VAT per pair, blocks £39+VAT.

● Trend Ltd, Unit N, Penfold Works, Imperial Way, Watford, Herts WD2 4YY, (0923) 49911

AEG's £70 AS6RL **cordless screwdriver** is quality gear. An hour to charge for an hour's use means that with an extra battery (£17.50+VAT), you've got continuous use. It 'hinges' in the middle for a choice of pistol-shape or straight fore-and-aft.

The 180rpm no-load speed alters under load, giving easy control; the two supplied bits (others optional) are hardened steel and locate positively in the chuck.

One of the nicest things about the tool is the adjustable torque; on maximum, it drives sharp-threaded no.8x1¼s right into unpiloted softwood and block-board with only an awl-hole as a starter.

The only niggle is that the driving switch, the on-off/lock switch and the release to turn the handle to 'pistol' are all a bit close together.

Do you need the AS6RL at this price? It rates only a few quid less than the bigger cordless tools' recommended prices, and is no real substitute for them; but for specialised jobs where you need lightness, compactness and cordlessness, this has to be the one.

● AEG, 217 Bath Rd, Slough, Berks SL1 4AW, (0753) 872101

Power tool **table attachment** for the fancy Workmate 2 from Black & Decker carries any make of router (max 750w), circular saw or jigsaw; table £40, W/M 2 £55, legs if you want the table but not the W/M, £15.

● B&D, Westpoint, The Grove, Slough, Berks SL1 1QQ, (0753) 74277

Timberline

Arthur Jones on what's
happening in the timber
trade

It's a relief to hear that nuclear radiation from the Chernobyl disaster will not effect imported timber, as reported in 'This Month'. To put our minds even more at rest, Polish authorities are checking radiation levels of all exported timber to make sure they are clear of contamination.

Which leaves me feeling happier about the main timber news of the month, which is the second Russian offer of softwood. Shipment of the wood will be made from September through to next January, so you won't be seeing some of this timber until next spring.

But at least we know the prices now. All these prices are based on the CIF (carriage, insurance and freight) quotations per cu. m. Unsorted redwood has increased by just £1 to £159, but redwood fourths have stayed at £103.

Whitewood prices have shown a larger gain of £2 for both unsorted and fourths, making the new prices £104 and £99. The Russians also added £2 to the price of fifths (representing the lower grade sixths in Swedish and Finnish wood) which is a grade not selling too well this year.

Importers found the new prices quite acceptable, the small increases being well within inflation levels. New price lists from other East European sources all closely follow the pattern set by the Russians.

How will this affect woodworkers? Current trends indicate that softwood prices are a firming market, with no sign of any weakness. You'll probably find some price rises at retail level over coming months, but nothing horrific. And there will be no shortages.

Swedish and Finnish mills are also trying to push up their prices, but they are being forced to stay close to the Russian level,

knowing that there will be no further Soviet price schedule until 1987. The Finns were helped by a recent small 2% devaluation of their currency.

In hardwoods the conditions are not quite so good. There are delays with some shipments from the Far East for a variety of reasons — heavy rains, political upheaval and logging restrictions.

The new Philippines government, determined to stamp out corruption, has banned logging over quite a large area while investigations are carried out into timber practices under the old regime. Whole areas have been closed and there will be delays in arrivals of such species as lauan. And political problems aren't confined to the Philippines; they are creating supply problems for *shoreas* from Sabah, and heavy rains hampered logging in Indonesia.

This means arrivals of sawn hardwoods from the Far East will be delayed this summer, leading to some price increases. I doubt if there will be any actual shortages of hardwoods available, though stocks could become patchy in some areas.

You might consider switching to a different timber for a lower price or easier availability. You may not welcome this if you have found a particular timber to your liking and want to avoid change, but it could be a bonus; a switch may overcome your prejudice and introduce you to the values of other woods on the market.

I don't want to give you the impression that there are shortages building up in all hardwoods; there is still too much sapele on the market for the health of hardwood importer profits, and American species are readily available and not too expensive at the moment.

Home timber prices are rising at least as much as imported values. With elm, for example, we are now paying the price for the ravages of Dutch elm disease. ∎

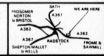
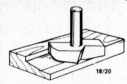 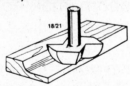
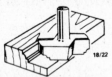 
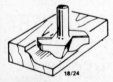 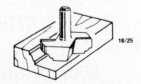

710

Shoptalk special

Universal acclaim

AEG's Maxi 26 universal sets new standards in what you get for the money — but how does it perform? Gordon Stokes checked it out

U niversals *vs* individual machines — the argument will long be with us. I think individual free-standing machines are the better bet, but only if there is ample room to set them up safely and effectively, and enough money to pay for them. That remains a daydream for most amateur woodworkers.

So we've all been waiting for a universal of good quality at a reasonable price, and I think the Maxi 26 made by Lurem and marketed by AEG will interest many hobby woodworkers and one-man businesses.

I've been testing the machine which was displayed at the Bristol Woodworker Show. I was impressed by what I saw there, and trying it out in my own workshop has confirmed my opinion.

Now keeping the price low does involve sacrifices, and in this case it's principally the use of sheet steel for the tables. Many people decry this type of construction, but I find cast tables today are rather variable. The pressed steel tables on the Maxi 26 will be good enough for general use if production models are made to the same high standards as the prototype I tried.

Normally I make allowances for small snags in prototypes, which will be sorted out before production. I found no such problems with the Maxi 26, however, which performed very well. Its two-speed 1500w motor had power to spare in all the tests; the motor wasn't strained even with full depth of cut on planer or saw, which is unusual. I found changing speed quite simple, by moving the motor on its mounting to select either of the two pulleys. The motor has a very efficient braking system to ensure that cutters and blades don't run on when you switch off.

The general high safety standards also show in the well designed guards, and there are three separate 'off' switches round the casing. Additionally, a micro-switch ensures you can't start the machine with the belt-access door open; you can even lock the on-off switch so nobody can operate it when you're out.

The low price of the machine also means there is no central control for changing from one operation to another. But I found belt-changing simple, by opening the access door, releasing the tension and changing the drive before re-tensioning and closing the door. I tried hard to make the belts slip, but

they wouldn't — and if you are sceptical about how long they will last, the supplier says the calculated life of a belt is more than 5,000 hours of work — that's two years of using them eight hours a day!

Four belts are used; retail price when they need replacing ranges from £2.35 to £10.05 + VAT.

Planer/thicknesser

In this really compact machine I particularly like the working position when planing. You can stand at the side of the feed-table, rather than behind it — easier and safer than on some comparable machinery. The planer runs at 6200rpm, giving just over the conventional 12,000 cuts per minute through its two-bladed cutter-blocks. It produced an excellent finish on both hard and soft woods, using sharp and correctly set cutters; setting these isn't difficult with the special device that comes with it. The knives are spring-loaded in the cutter-block, which simplifies things.

● **Above**, a very pretty bit of kit for £1350+VAT – and a performer too. **Left**, the belts clip away when not in use; fears that they'd slip under full load were unfounded. **Below**, the saw is well guarded, but the plastic bench insert (taken out here) is a bit flimsy

As with all 'over-and-under' machines, the thicknesser table should be wound down to its lowest point for surface planing, and shavings which accumulate must be removed by a dust extractor, or by switching off and then pushing them clear with a piece of wood. The planer fence is also the saw-fence, and has an ingenious guard for the planer cutter-block. On the model I tested the fence wouldn't tilt, but it will on future models.

The thicknesser performed very well, and I was surprised the central pillar rise-and-fall system for the table moved so smoothly; on some machines this mechanism can be jerky and inaccurate. A lever engages the roller for the power feed, and the machine operates with both surface planing tables down, not raised as with other combination machines. A combined guard and chip-deflector is provided, which is fitted quickly and neatly by raising the feed table to its limit. 10x6in, and nothing to be ashamed of.

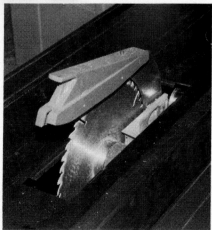

Circular saw

The circular saw has a 10in blade, giving a 3½in cut, with ample power. The blade can be tilted to 45°, but as is normal on cheaper machines you must be careful to return it to exactly 90° after angled ripping to achieve

Shoptalk special

accuracy. The normal steel blade supplied works well when it's sharp, but TCT blades are available, and would be best if you're cutting manufactured boards regularly.

The saw is very easy to adjust for depth of cut and angle. The blade is fully retractable below the table when using the spindle moulder, but with an unusual safety factor; the blade retracts with the guard attached, so you can't forget to replace it. Although there's no mitre guide-slot in the table surface, there's a sliding table mounted on a rail, to which material can be clamped when crosscutting, or when working endgrain with the spindle moulder, as you would when tenoning. Some sawing depth of cut is lost, but usually not significantly. The sliding carriage can be reversed for cross-cutting wider boards. Incidentally, a length of flexible piping is provided to duct sawdust to floor level, and you could fit a dust extractor to this.

Mortiser

The mortiser is above average partly because most slot-mortisers run too slowly. The Maxi gives 6200rpm for mortising, or 3800 if large cutters are used. The most appealing feature is the single lever control which works like a joystick and gives perfect control while leaving one hand free to steady the timber.

If you do large amounts of mortising you will find the machine frustrating, but for occasional home workshop use it does a fair job. The mortiser chuck has a very efficient safety guard; but mortise cutters must be removed after use, not left in the chuck. They're razor-sharp and can be very dangerous.

Spindle moulder

The spindle moulder has no unusual features, but it does operate very nicely. The whole machine runs smoothly with little vibration and I had no problems making a full-depth cut with ovolo cutters, with the wood clamped firmly to the sliding carriage. Normally I wouldn't make cuts as heavy as this, but I was testing to extremes.

I was pleased with the efficient guarding, since I am not sure it is wise to let loose untrained operators on spindle moulders, and there have been serious accidents. The machine has micro-adjustment for the spindle-moulder fence; more expensive machines sometimes don't have this, which can be irritating. A ring-fence is an optional extra for moulding curved work, but I recommend you leave this until you've got

● *Above, crosscutting with the sliding carriage; right, the spindle moulder handled full depth of cut with ease*

some training behind you, perhaps through one of the machining courses you'll find in *Woodworker*.

Conclusion

My verdict is that the Maxi 26 is excellent value for money; you'll be well pleased if you choose this as your first combination machine. The dark green livery is attractive, and it's a pleasure to use, which is more than can be said of some machines. I have reservations about the 'anti-corrosive coating' withstanding workshop wear and tear for very long. The black paint is baked on and the manufacturers are confident, so we'll just have to wait and see. The machine is well priced and should produce some shock waves in the market place.
● AEG Maxi 26 retails at £1349+VAT.
● AEG (UK) Ltd, 217 Bath Rd, Slough, Berkshire SL1 4AW, (0753) 872101.

● *Full-depth thicknessing with no problem*

● *The mortiser is easy to operate – a one-handed 'joystick'*

Treasured chest

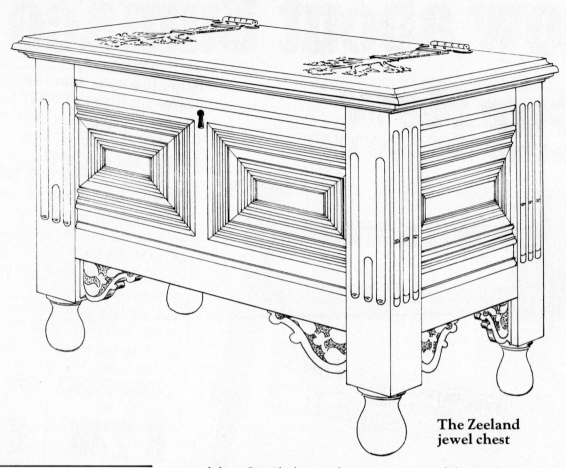

The Zeeland jewel chest

René Coolen presents his magnificent drawings of a delicate period piece — a 17th century Dutch jewel cabinet

T his chest, made of oak with ebony marquetry, is an exquisite example of furniture from the most southern province, Zeeland. In the first half of the 17th century the southern section of the Netherlands was occupied by Spanish forces, and furniture design was extravagant compared with the more restrained Protestant culture of the north.

Dutch craftsmen also made full use of exotic veneers imported by the Dutch East India Company, which had been formed in 1602.

In this tiny chest — it measures about 20in long, 13in high and 13 deep — the influence of neighbouring Flanders shows in the laid-in mouldings on the panels.

Inside the chest a small compartment to the right would have held jewels or gold coins. It had a lift-up lid which supported the top when it was raised.

The chest is supported on bun feet,

copied from Spanish designs; these were usually made from fruit-wood, with an ebonised finish. The oak is finished with a dark wax.

Construction is with mortise and tenon joints secured with wooden pegs.

Between the bottom of the stiles and the bottom rails are fixed sawn-out consoles or brackets, with floral carving against a back-ground decorated with a nail punch.

The elaborate hinges, reaching almost to the front of the chest top, clearly show their Gothic derivation.

From a design point of view, the back construction is not strong enough for the heavy hinges, and a panelled frame would have been better. But it has survived 350 years! ∎

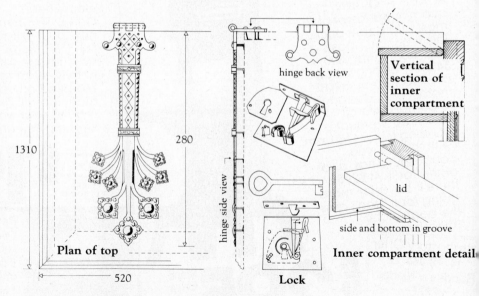

Plan of top

1310

520

280

hinge side view

hinge back view

Vertical section of inner compartment

lid

side and bottom in groove

Inner compartment detail

Lock

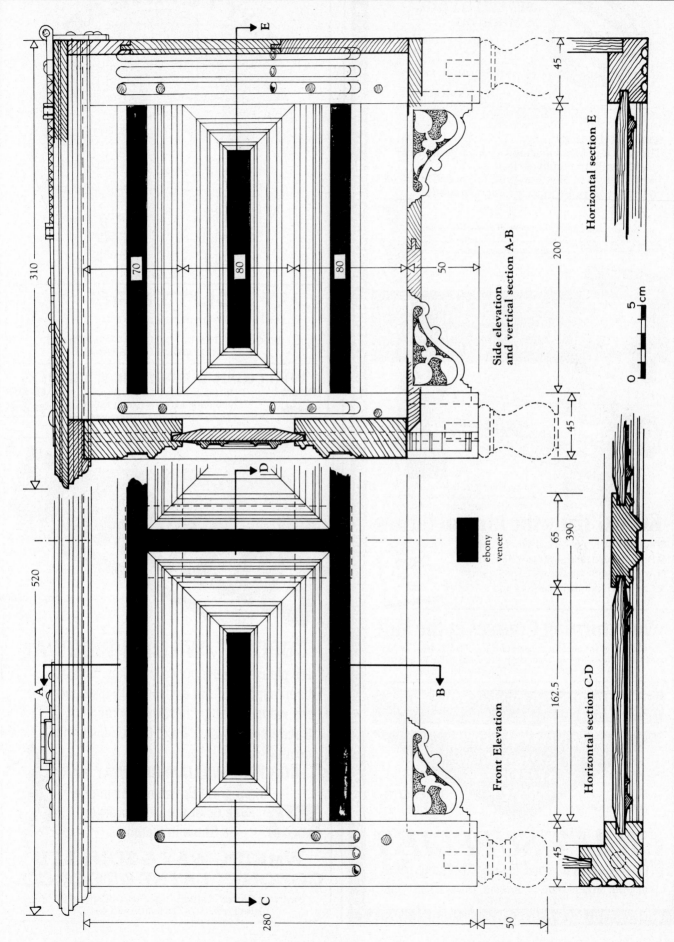

Side elevation
and vertical section A-B

Horizontal section E

ebony
veneer

Front Elevation

Horizontal section C-D

5 cm

0

Tools of the trade 5

'We propose a major series assembling a basic kit of hand-tools for the young apprentice cabinetmaker or serious amateur woodworker. The object will be to locate the very best saws, planes, chisels, gauges, etc. currently available.

'Each tool will be tested by a skilled cabinetmaker in my workshop, who uses similar tools every day in his work. Chisels will be polished, honed and checked for hardness of steel. Planes will be examined for flatness, smoothness of adjustment and accuracy of casting. Gauges will be checked for accuracy and fitness for purpose.

'All tools will be put to the most critical examination and tested within the bounds of the normal activity of the professional workshop. I do not advise manufacturers to submit products that they do not believe will stand comparison with the best in the field.'

Handsaws and back-saws

The last episode:
David Savage's testing
test of the best hand-tools
you can buy cuts no corners

Some people go potty about saws. They fill page after page with dreary argument upon the exact angle at which a fleam saw should be sharpened, whatever that may be. But most garden-shed workshops hum and buzz with band-and table-saws — it really is a shame. There are still people who insist on doing it all by hand — a 28in 4½-point full ripsaw, followed by a 26in 7-point crosscut, finishing off with a fine-cutting 22in 10-point panel saw. Such people must rank as woodworking heroes of our age and I will do or say nothing to dissuade them. I envy the peaceful silence of their workshops and

the sense of purpose that enables such unnecessary exertions to take place.

The modern shop, however, whizzes and whirrs, sucks and chops so efficiently that it's difficult to find a place for handsaws except as a back-up. Perhaps, for example, to crosscut the occasional board when untangling the lead of a jigsaw would be too much fuss. Around the bench the dovetail saw is still in regular use for precision work, whilst a small tenon saw serves for occasional general sawing when the table-saws are occupied, or (more likely), it's not worth taking the job to the saw.

The only person in my workshop to gain regular daily experience with handsaws is Neil, the hapless apprentice, who is of tender years and not allowed to use the most useful machines. Until his 18th birthday, the law quite rightly sentences him to two years' hard labour. But after two years he'll be able to go to a machine with the confidence that he doesn't need to use it. He could get the same perfect accuracy of result using good hand-tools combined with practised skill.

These days, the handsaw has far greater use on site than in the shop. To examine the saws submitted for test and to teach me a thing or two I sought the advice of Roger Shantz, who served his time in a London joinery firm specialising in hand-railing. Roger's work is almost all on site, fitting high quality specialist joinery. To watch him testing the saws, as one would in a tool shop, was to watch a real performance, a cross between a fencing master bending and flashing a rapier and sighting along it for perfect recoil, and a concert violinist tuning up for a concerto. First he bent the blade to a half circle and examined the regularity of curve, then he let it spring back to what should, when sighted from the top, be a perfect straight line. Any inclination on the part of the saw to retain a curve after this mistreatment would have condemned it to the scrap heap, but fortunately all passed.

The second, more aesthetic, test entailed gripping the saw horizontally, its toe in the left hand. The blade was put under tension by twisting it to a shallow 'S' configuration, and with the blade held thus Roger struck it next to the handle hard with the tip of his thumb. All the blades gave different notes. What we were listening for was a clear sustained ringing tone that would rise as the tension was changed.

Then you examine the handle for a snug fit with the blade, for comfort and for balance. The heel or butt of the saw should project well below the handle; a mean depth of blade warns that there won't be enough for a lifetime of resharpening. Bear in mind that if a tooth is damaged it may take 10mm of blade depth to re-establish the line of the teeth.

An eye for a saw

The length of a saw is measured from toe to heel (or toe to butt) excluding the handle. The blade should be made of a high-grade

alloy steel, tempered for toughness. A good surface finish with the maker's name engraved rather than painted on is an indication of quality. The top edge of the blade could be either straight, or have an elegant curve — a skew back — which is traditionally supposed to help balance in the hand. It's also very elegant.

A convex curve on the toothed edge of the blade, however, is of considerable advantage. This is the 'breasted' blade and is another sign of high quality. The slight curve or breasting fits the action of the saw better than a straight blade. The sawyer's arm pivots round a fixed shoulder point, acting in a slight curve, so the breasted tooth (theoretically) has the capacity to stay on the job just that bit better.

The teeth of a saw are counted in points per inch, while the other system of teeth per inch (TPI) gives one less per inch. Saw-makers are trying to standardise on one system, so we should help them by ignoring the old one. Points per inch are just that — how many points including the first and last in one inch of saw-blade.

I haven't included ripsaws, but they should be sharpened straight through with the rear of the gullet more upright than the crosscut saw (figs 1 and 2). A good ripsaw has teeth that diminish in size towards the toe of the blade.

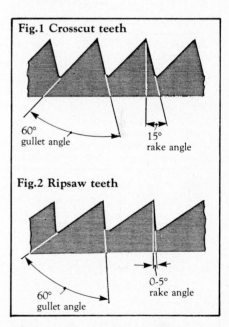

Fig.1 Crosscut teeth

60° gullet angle

15° rake angle

Fig.2 Ripsaw teeth

60° gullet angle

0-5° rake angle

Crosscuts made up the full range of test saws. Some were described as 'universal' to suggest they would also rip as well as crosscut, but the teeth were still sharpened in the crosscut manner (fig. 3).

The 'set' is the amount each tooth is bent left or right, which gives clearance so the blade won't trap in poorly supported or seasoned timber. The more set to the blade, the more work needed to push it through the job. For this reason top-quality saws have minimal set, and their blades are taper-ground, that is thinner on the top edge, or

Fig.3 Cross-sharpening

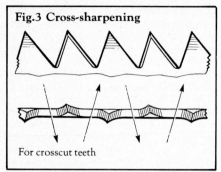

For crosscut teeth

back, than near the teeth to discourage binding. To be able to claim a saw is taper-ground it's only necessary to grind 'one thin to back', or give a tapering thickness of just one grinding pass, but a better system proposed by one maker involves several thinning grinding operations, moving along the blade from heel to toe. This doesn't make the saw look any different from other taper-ground saws, but it's interesting that the ones in question — the Pax — performed very well compared with their competitors (fig. 4).

Fig.4

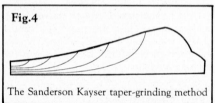

The Sanderson Kayser taper-grinding method

The setting of any saw is important; the correct set should rarely extend below half the depth of the saw tooth. Top-quality saws have very hard teeth that can be broken off with careless setting, so it's better to send the saw to a good saw-doctor. You can use setting tools (they look a bit like pliers) called saw sets to do it yourself, but you must know what you're doing.

Choosing a handsaw is a very subjective

Fig.5 Setting

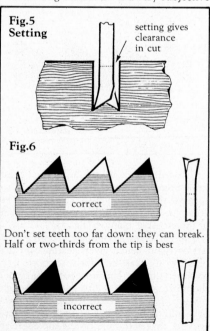

setting gives clearance in cut

Fig.6

correct

Don't set teeth too far down: they can break. Half or two-thirds from the tip is best

incorrect

matter which has much to do with your own build, size of hands, length of arm and length of leg. Sawing is a balancing act — a good sawyer makes it look as if very little effort is needed and the job could go twice as fast. To gain the full work from the saw rather than the sawyer, it should be a controlled motion, with directional adjustments not made consciously. The sawyer 'thinks' the saw down the line. The cliché is that you let the saw do the work, but with no human effort at all, of course, there'll be no work done. You the sawyer provide steady controlled motion without pressure into the cut. Force the saw into the cut rather than let its own weight do the work, and you're asking for wobbly saw cuts and aching limbs.

There is also the question of stiffs and floppies — blades, that is. I have a definite floppy; my old Disston wiggle-waggles about, causing me to sniff at modern saws as the crude products of industrial accountancy, but Roger Shantz set me straight. Floppies, or saws with a thin blade, are most useful when the job is stiff, like dry hardwood. A floppy can have minimal set and cut a fine kerf with minimal effort, but when the job itself is floppy, like board material, then a thin saw-blade will be more difficult to get out of the kerf. A stiff saw will pull out easily; so it's floppies for stiff and stiffs for floppy.

Testing handsaws

The saws we had for test were used by virtually everyone in the workshop. There are now seven of us, all different ages, builds and experience. I also got Roger to put the saws to test, and lent a couple to my neighbour who was sawing up railway sleepers — poor devil, he wanted to borrow a chainsaw.

The least popular, in my view rather undeservingly, was the Stanley Eagle 26in 6-point, a taper-ground, skew backed tool, but without breasted teeth. The blade isn't very deep, and faint milling marks were still

● *Sandvik Disston D95, Sandvik 288 and Roberts & Lee Dorchester handsaws*

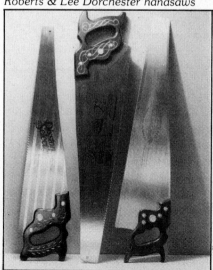

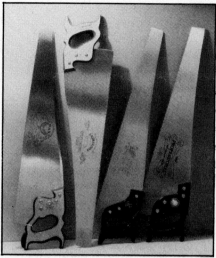

● *Sanderson Kayser Pax, Footprint, Stanley Eagle and Spear & Jackson Professional*

visible on the blade. The handle was comfortable, well attached to the blade and the balance was good, but it's plastic, which nobody really liked.

The Footprint 26in 6-point is a well-made saw without any frills. Again it's taper-ground and skew-backed, with a straight tooth line. The blade is somewhat deeper that the Stanley Eagle, giving a good life expectancy, and the handle is beech, set high on the blade. It is attached by three rather than the usual four or five brass screws. Most users were surprised by how well this very unpretentious saw performed.

Next in popularity came the Spear and Jackson Professional 26in 6-point, which has a larger handle of stained beech, fixed at five points. The slot into which the blade fits closes above the blade, always a good sign of care in manufacture, and the rear of the handle is also reinforced with a dowel across the grain. The rather florid maker's name and logo are painted rather than etched on to the blade, but the blade itself is protected by lacquer that must be removed for the tool to show its potential. If we'd taken it off earlier in the tests, I'm sure this would have been one of the more popular stiff saws. It's well made, beautifully balanced and tough.

Another stiffy was the Disston Select D95 26in 8-point. I was really put off this saw by the marketing and packaging of the product. 'The Ultimate Handsaw — The carved, comfort grip, balanced handle has a rich walnut finish accented by a brass anodized medallion and screws, and wheat carving highlighted in gold.' As they say in the States, bulls..t! This stained beech handle is nowhere near as well fitted as the one on the Spear and Jackson saw. The blade is skew-backed and taper-ground, but not breasted. It's the shallowest of the saws offered for test — only 15mm of sharpenable blade below the handle. Despite all this, we all enjoyed using the flashy Disston. The handle is large and heavy, and the blade small so effort was greatly reduced. Sad to compare it to an old pre-war Disston, but still a decent saw for man-made boards.

One of the old British saw-makers, Roberts and Lee, produced a first-class floppy. The Dorchester 26in 10-point is a super saw. The handle is solid walnut with the slot closed above the blade in the best manner; five solid brass screws hold the blade neatly and purposefully, and the handle is a joy to hold, again fully taper-ground and skew-backed with a straight tooth-line. The depth of blade ensures a long usable life. The name and logo are etched in to the blade and protected by a thin coat of lacquer, which should really be removed before use to prevent stickiness. But it still sawed a fine clean kerf.

The Sandvik 288 26in 8-point is another saw on similar lines to the Disston, covered in gold scroll work and florid lettering, with a really enormous handle. It would be possible to wear gloves and use this saw, which may be the thinking behind it. The slot on the handle top where the blade fits is open, and the handle is fixed with rather crude cross-head screws — it lacked the sophistication of the Roberts and Lee. The blade was skew-backed and taper-ground as usual, but also breasted, and the saw really cut well. I particularly enjoyed using it; I'm a big chap and I like a decent-sized saw. The breasting seemed to make all the difference in keeping the cut on the tooth for the full sweep of my arm. The larger-than-usual handle again seemed to make the work go easier.

The most popular saw was the Pax 26in 10-point, made by Sanderson Kayser, another old-established British saw-makers who really know their business. This saw has everything. The handle is well fitted and finished, with a closed slot and five brass screws. The painted and lacquered beech handle sits well into the blade, with an opening for the hand only just above the heel, but it's well shaped to fit the hand. The 26in blade is skew-backed and taper-ground in six stages — Sanderson Kayser are the only manufacturers to claim this advantage. The saw-tooth line is also breasted to a slight convex curve. Neil decided that if he was to do two years' hard labour, he needed the best saw in the workshop, so he hogged this one. The little blighter can only be commended for his good taste.

Of the saws offered (I'm sorry that W. Tyzacks Ltd didn't see fit to let us compare their 'Nonpareil' brand), the Pax by Sanderson Kayser, the Sandvik 288 and the Roberts and Lee Dorchester all showed first-class qualities in different ways. The breasted saws would be my choice every time, but the Spear and Jackson Professional would also be a very sound decision. Choosing a saw is very personal, play tunes on it, swish it around in the shop, but get one that sits well in your hand.

Back-saws

And so to back-saws. The tenon saw used to be the general bench saw as its name indicates, but nowadays we use a small 9in table-saw in the bench shop for most of our joint cutting. Sometimes, however, it is easier to just do it by hand, for which we use a tenon or large dovetail saw. The only tenon saw presented for test was quite a nice one from Spear and Jackson. The sticky goo they use to protect the blade needed removing with meths. This one, like many back-saws, came with too much set for precise work; either clamp the saw-teeth between two steel rules in the vice, or tap some of the set out on an anvil.

The most-used back-saw, I find, is the dovetail saw. This is very similar to a tenon saw, but with a small eight or 10in blade and 18-20 points per inch. The dovetail saw is commonly sharpened 'in house' by the owner, and it can be done straight across like a ripsaw without too much difficulty. Fix up a good light, and don't do this job too late in the day.

Dovetail saws also usually come with more set than necessary. I have one saw with almost no set at all that I use exclusively for very fine small work. It needs a spot of candle wax to prevent it binding in the job, but the cut is as fine as you will get. It's useful to have a second saw for larger work with a shade more set.

Dovetail saws are very delicate tools — the blades are thin and easily buckled, the teeth small and sharp. To cut straight with a dovetail saw, it helps to treat it with a little respect. Beginners invariably saw too fast, squeeze the handle too tight and press down too much. The handle should be comfortable, and the brass back solid and heavy, for it's this mass that provides downward pressure. The blade should be very thin, but capable of remaining straight in use.

The Spear and Jackson Professional Dovetail saw, 8in 20-point, is a very good tool. The handle, in common with the Professional Handsaw, is a rather plain, stained beech affair, which didn't detract from its comfortable fit to the hand. The Pax 8in 20-point has an open handle with their two-tone colour scheme, but as they make such fine saws it may pay Sanderson Kayser to make cosmetic changes to their handles so they not only were the best, they also looked the best. The Roberts and Lee Dorchester Dovetail is an example; it has a closed handle, beautifully detailed and polished in solid black walnut. All the saws were comfortable to use, the Pax possibly the least. All use good heavy brass backs with a good two-point fixing between blade-back and handles. The blades of the

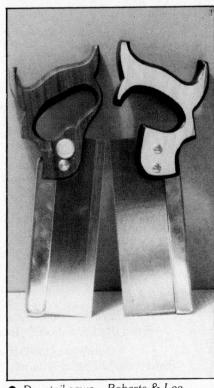

● Dovetail saws – Roberts & Lee Dorchester **left** and Sanderson Kayser Pax

Saw	RRP excluding VAT
Sanderson Kayser Pax 26in 10-point	£28.00
Roberts and Lee Dorchester 26in 10-point	£33.81
Sandvik 288 26in 8-point	£40.92
Spear and Jackson Professional 26in 6-point	£40.77
Sandvik Disston D95 26in 8-point	£44.37
Footprint 26in 6-point	£15.83
Stanley Eagle 26in 6-point	£30.15
Sanderson Kayser Pax Dovetail 8in 20-point	£23.46
Roberts and Lee Dorchester Dovetail 8in 20-point	£27.14
Spear and Jackson Professional Dovetail 8in 20-point	£29.75

● David and *Woodworker* would like to thank the following tool manufacturers and distributors for the loan of tools, their co-operation and assistance, without which the test series would have been impossible:
Bristol Design, 14 Perry Rd, Bristol BS1 5BG, (0272) 291740
Clico (Sheffield) Tooling Ltd, Unit 7, Fell Rd Ind. Est., Sheffield S9 2AL, (0742) 433007
Footprint Tools, PO Box 19, Hollis Croft, Sheffield S1 3HY, (0742) 753200
Lester-Brown Machine Tools (Ulmia importer), Coventry Rd, Fillongley CV7 8DZ, (0676) 40456
Neills Tools (Spear & Jackson), Handsworth Rd, Sheffield S13 9BR, (0742) 449911
Paramo (Clay) Hallamshire Works, Rockingham St, Sheffield S1 3NW, (0742) 25262/3
Rabone Chesterman, Camden St, Birmingham B1 3DB, 021-233 3300
Record Marples, Parkway Works, Sheffield S9 3BL, (0742) 449066
Roger's, 47 Walsworth Rd, Hitchin, Herts SG4 9SU, (0462) 34177
E. T. Roberts & Lee, Northumberland Pk, London N17 (01) 808 2486
Robert Sorby Ltd, Athol Rd, Woodseats Rd, Sheffield S8 0PA, (0742) 554231
Sanderson Kayser, PO Box 6, Newhall Rd, Sheffield S9 2SD (0742) 44994
Sandvik, Manor Way, Halesowen B62 8QZ, 021-550 4700
Sarjents Tools, 44 Oxford Rd, Reading RG1 7LH, (0734) 586522
Stanley Tools, Woodside, Sheffield S3 9PD, (0742) 78678
Tilgear 20 Ladysmith Rd, Enfield EN1 3AA, 01-363 8050

Tools of the trade 5

Pax and Dorchester saws were almost identical in thickness, depth and cut. The Spear and Jackson was perhaps a gauge thicker and a good ten years shallower. All three saws could be made to do super work once the varnish was removed from the blade and some of the set tapped back. My preference would be the Roberts and Lee — a beautiful, well balanced tool.

The end

During the past months we have examined hand-tools with the object of selecting the best tools for a young cabinetmaker. The results of the series has been both encouraging and distressing. Fine saws and marking and measuring tools are still being made, planes that had been discontinued are being made again with care and concern for quality. Steel bananas are still being sold as bench planes, and rubber chisels abound.

The past months have necessarily placed undue emphasis on the importance of the tools to fine workmanship. Good tools do matter, but it's the use to which they're put that's our only real concern.

A new generation of woodworkers are seeking to produce work of supreme quality and demanding the best tools. To an extent the tool industry in Sheffield and elsewhere is not recognising this market shift. Those companies that have retained a high quality product line against the market trend through the 60s and 70s will now prosper, and those that have traded down won't sell inferior products in this 'up' market by adding boxwood handles.

I am delighted and relieved to reach the end of this series; I shall enjoy getting back to making furniture. ∎

We asked for the makers' comments:
Sanderson Kayser

Congratulations on the depth and quality of the article. We were pleased our 'Pax' saws stood up well against the competition, though some comments on the dovetail saw have made us think.

We produce dovetail saws with both open and closed handles; at the London Woodworker Show we sold twice as many dovetail saws as any other type — and all with open handles.

We are now looking at the cosmetic aspects of the handles, as David Savage suggests.

W. Harper

Sandvik

Engraving the maker's name on the blade has nothing to do with the quality of the steel or its cutting ability. Anyone can engrave anything on a saw-blade!

Universal teeth have a different angle of rake, shape and ground-edge angle from crosscut.

The Sandvik 288 and 277 handsaws are both correctly taper-ground on both faces.

The Disston D95 Select is hand-made and filed. It is not a standard tool, but a traditional saw for the traditional craftsman who can file its teeth to specific requirements. Definitely not a saw for a trainee cabinetmaker — try the Sandvik 277 instead.

We disagree about companies trade down. All the big UK companies still produce good quality, traditional handsaws for professional craftsmen; but this market has declined by 30% since 1979, while the DIY market has boomed. All manufacturers have done is change the mix. The average DIY user expects to use a handsaw on only a few occasions a year, and wants to pay under £10 — not £30-40. Yet the £7 saw must perform almost as well as the £40 saw, at least over short periods.

Nowhere in the article does Mr Savage refer to tooth technology. Sandvik is proud to be world leader in producing ground-tooth handsaws. Tests confirm our belief that ground teeth perform better and keep their sharpness longer than the traditional filed-teeth saws.

Neither does he mention hardpoint teeth. When time is money, many professional saw-users find it more economical to buy a hardpoint (long life) saw and throw it away when blunted, rather than spend time and money re-sharpening teeth. We produce both hand- and tenon saws with hardpoint teeth.

Richard Frost

The Midas touch

Fancy trying your hand at restoring a gilded picture frame? Peter and Frances Binnington introduce the basics of this specialised craft

Craftsmen were embellishing carved wooden objects with gold leaf a thousand years before Tutankhamun, and the methods and materials used have hardly changed to this day.

The unique fascination of gold arises from a simple chemical property. Gold cannot combine with oxygen and so doesn't corrode or even tarnish. Its enduring brilliance had a particular religious and magical significance for the ancient Egyptians, sunworshippers with aspirations to eternal life. In strife-torn medieval Europe, alchemists sought to transmute base metal into gold, the symbol of incorruptible purity, the chivalric ideal.

Gold is so malleable you can beat it as thin as $\frac{1}{250,000}$in; thinner than a lightwave, its third dimension virtually disappears.

In the old days when raw materials were expensive and labour was cheap this thin gold leaf was applied to wooden objects to transform them apparently into solid gold. Methods of matting and burnishing the gilding, and of tooling and punching were developed to compound the illusion.

Gilding was the fashionable finish throughout Europe from the Renaissance to the French revolution. It was a perfect decorative medium to display effectively but economically the wealth and power of Church and nobility; in the Baroque period entire decorative schemes were created solely for the extravagant use of gold leaf. Today, who but the oil rich can afford such ostentation? High labour costs limit gold leaf to more modest schemes; social pressures dictate gold may be used for the restoration of old palaces, but not in the creation of new ones.

Despite this, the mystique of gold lives on; though restraint is fashionable, decorators prize gold's aesthetic appeal.

You'll have noticed that on antique and venerated objects that have been handled and used the gold surface has worn thin. You may see a soft 'feathering' away through the layers of coloured clay and creamy white gesso, sometimes through to the now burnished wood on the arrises; or the surface may break and map, revealing the red or ochre earth colours below.

What you are looking at is the clay or bole originally under the thin gold. It is made of clay mixed with dilute rabbitskin size. Applied thinly and evenly bole provides a cushion and a colour for the gold

● *Standing the test of time; gilding methods remain virtually unchanged*

● *Cutting gold leaf on the gilder's cushion, screened by an old parchment legal document*

Photos Peter Binnington

— the warm red counteracting the cool of the metal.

Traditionally a thin coat of yellow bole was applied to reach every crevice, followed by several coats of an earth red on the higher areas. If the gold leaf then missed any part of the hollows, the cracks in the gold would only reveal yellow. Other colours of clay were also used: the Victorians liked to blacken their bole by adding graphite; this burnished especially well, and was reserved for the most prominent areas of a carving or moulding.

Clays used in Italy tended to be hot in colour, reflecting the climate or simply what was available locally; in Britain taste and availability both led to cooler colours.

In modern gilding, bole colours vary from the traditional to deep colours such as green, which can be very effective on a frame for a modern painting. Under silver gilding a cream/white bole is often used, though sometimes it's black or blue according to the effect required.

In restoration work, the new gilding must blend with the old, in colour-matching the bole, getting the right colour gold, and in the distressing or toning.

Tiny cracks in the surface, *craquelure*, occur naturally in old pieces because of movement of the timber and groundwork below. These effects must be replicated in restoration work, but they are also used by modern gilders to give fashionable subtlety.

Toning or distressing tests the real skill of the gilders as they invisibly match an existing piece or age a brand-new piece. Rather more skill is needed than for the fairly mechanical laying and burnishing of gold.

Ageing is imitated in various ways, from crude to sophisticated techniques; many workshops have their own secret recipes for getting good results.

In modern furniture design gilding is largely underexploited. The tradition of gilt picture and mirror frames continues, with new mouldings and new textures, but few craftsmen show originality. One innovator is Sebastian Wakefield, who is combining gold and silver leaf with new materials such as MDF board and synthetic lacquer, to produce original furniture of great presence and beauty.

What is gilding?

Gilding is attaching gold leaf to a wooden surface. The metal is beaten extremely thin, cut and laid as leaves between sheets of tissue paper and sold in book form; the leaves are $3\frac{1}{4}$in square, and each book has 25 leaves.

Two kinds of gilding are used, oil and water gilding, named after the method of attaching the gold leaf to the surface. A high burnish is only achieved by water gilding, but being water soluble it can only be used indoors and for pieces not handled much, such as picture and mirror frames and display furniture.

Oil gilding gives a bright and durable finish, for exterior work such as pub signs, iron railings and wrought ironwork, as well as for interior decoration of churches, theatres and palaces. Oil gilding is also often used as a cheaper alternative on furniture and frames, with water gilding highlights where a burnish is required.

With either technique careful surface preparation is vital. For oil gilding, the wood is prepared with varnish, paint or french polish, and sometimes filled and smoothed with gesso. Oil size — boiled linseed oil and resin — is then applied and when it's tacky the gold or other leaf can be laid down.

With water gilding gesso is always necessary to get the extremely smooth, marble-like surface, and a dark brilliance that can't be achieved by oil gilding.

The Midas touch

Gilding should not be confused with using 'gold' paste or paint, whose sole virtue is speed. It looks nothing like the real thing.

Gesso

Gesso, used to fill the grain and soften the contours, is made from chalk and animal glue. You carefully mix fine-grade whiting into warm melted rabbitskin size or runny glue. When the liquid can absorb no more chalk you stir the mixture and then sieve several times to remove lumps.

You start with a hot primer coat of rabbitskin size alone, then apply several coats of warm gesso. Some gilders use many coats of thin gesso, others use a few thick coats. Some prefer to use parchment clippings instead of rabbitskin which makes an even finer glue. Gesso can be shaped and cut with special cutting tools to open up fine areas of carving that might have become clogged, such as the veins of leaves.

Bole

The next stage depends on what type of gilding or decoration is being used. If you want to use oil gilding apply a primer coat of well thinned paint, let it dry and repeat with further thinned coats, rubbing smooth in between for best results.

For water gilding you use several coats of clay on top of the gesso. This clay, or bole, is a little greasy and provides a cushion between the porous gesso and the gold.

Hard clay is reduced to a paste with water and mixed with animal size to a thin cream. Apply four or five coats of clay, smoothing between coats, with progressively finer papers. Now gild as soon as possible, as dust causes problems when burnishing.

Gilding tools

The gilder's cushion, or cutch, is a board covered in calf or chamois leather with loops beneath for holding the left thumb, and for tucking the knife away when not in use; a parchment screen at one end cuts down draughts and prevents the leaves of gold flying away.

A special brush or 'tip' is used to pick up and position the gold, typically 3in wide, very thin, and with 1½in long badger, squirrel or camel hair in a card handle. It is just wider than the leaves of gold.

It takes some practice to learn to handle the tools and get into effective routines. When you're not using the gilder's knife, either balance it between the small and ring finger of the left hand or tuck it away in the strap of leather provided underneath the cushion. You also hold the gilder's tip in the left hand, when you're not using it to pick up or lay the gold, using your first and middle fingers to hold it steady. At the same time the large loop of the cushion is around the left thumb (reverse if left handed).

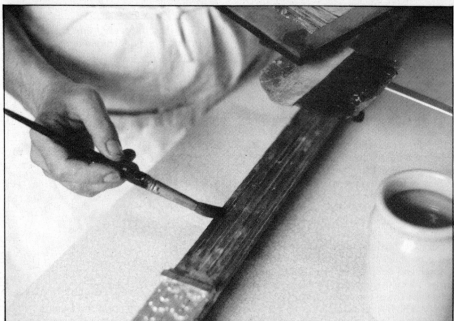

Handling techniques

You transfer leaves of gold from the book to the back of the gilder's cushion by blowing gently, opening one page at a time so the leaf lands on the leather. You blow out up to half a book at a time. Then you bring forward single leaves using the knife and laying each flat against the cushion square with the edge. This takes a little practice as the leaf will fly up and away with the slightest breath of wind. Breathing has to be controlled; try to develop a habit of breathing out of the side of the mouth using the Bogart technique!

Gold will inevitably be wasted during this practice period, and you'll have to reconcile yourself to this if you want to pass the apprenticeship stage and maybe eventually master the craft.

● **Top**, *laying out the leaf on the cushion; **middle**, applying a water base to a frame; **bottom**, the gilder's tip, the gold leaf and the frame*

Now you are ready to cut the gold leaf into strips, squares or rectangles to suit the work. The knife must be sharp enough to cut without tearing the gold — but not so sharp as to cut the leather of the cushion. Lay the edge of the blade flat on the gold, push forward and then draw back right through the gold; don't use the point as though you were cutting a cake, or you will damage the leather.

Once you've cut the leaf transfer the knife back to its position in the left hand. Now, taking the tip or brush in your right hand draw it across your face or hair to pick up some natural oils. You'll find this is sufficient to pick up a piece of gold, and you then swap tip plus gold back into the resting position in the left hand.

Water gilding

You should have a pot of cold water with a good soft brush standing on the bench to your right. Holding the brush in your right hand, use plenty of water to coat the area to be gilded. Put the brush back in the pot, transfer the tip back to the right hand and quickly lay the gold on the wet surface. You'll find the gold is strongly attracted to the water and will be almost pulled off the tip. Avoid wetting the leaf surface or you'll mark it.

As the gold is so very light the slightest draught will blow one or all the leaves away. Shut all windows and doors during gilding, and move gently around the room.

Once the gold leaf is in position, you can start burnishing.

Frequently, particular areas are picked out for burnishing, and the rest left matt, giving a beautiful contrast. Matt areas can be toned and protected with a lacquer, but burnished areas are usually left alone, as it is difficult to key on to such a highly polished surface.

● **Above**, *single-stem flower vases by Sebastian Wakefield*

● **Left**, *cutting a rectangle of gold leaf for frame members*

● *Below left, bits and pieces ready to gild and fit, and* **right** *a variety of gilding effects*

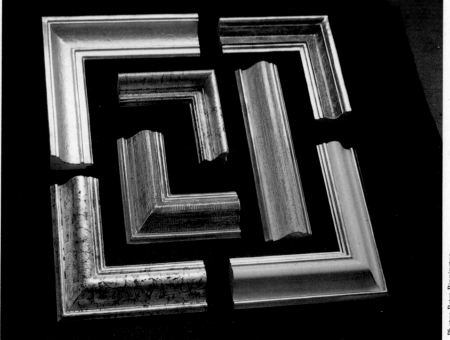

723

The Midas touch

Burnishing depends on weather conditions; you get a better burnish while the ground is still a little soft and moist so the wetter the atmosphere the better. Traditionally a dog's tooth was used for this purpose, but today we use an agate stone. Stones, with handles attached, are available in various shapes, and you should choose a shape to suit the particular moulding or carving. Work the stone backwards and forwards, first in one direction and then another, gradually harder and harder until a fine, deep and even burnish is achieved.

Oil gilding

Oil gilding is much quicker and simpler. Briefly, you apply gold size very thinly to the prepared surface with a stiff, short bristle brush. If the surface is painted, check it is dry and dust-free. If the surface is gesso a thin coat of shellac will seal it. Areas you don't want gilded can be dusted with whiting or French chalk to prevent the gold sticking.

When the size is almost dry — to the point where it will 'squeak' under the knuckle — the gold leaf can be laid; experience counts in telling whether the size is ready. Gold size has varying drying times, 20 minutes to two or three days. For exterior work a quick drying size is often chosen to prevent too much dust and dirt settling, but generally the longer the size has to dry, the better the results. Loose leaf gold, laid as in water gilding gives brighter results; in many cases, however, it's more convenient to lay with transfer gold — leaf that has been lightly attached to waxed tissue paper of slightly larger size than the leaf. Laying the leaf this way is much easier

● **Above,** *spot the patches in an antique carved oak picture frame ready for matching;* **below,** *a black burnish and silver frame with a silver-leaf mirror*

● *A combed and burnished finish on a new frame; see preceding page for other special effects such as the 'Dutch metal broken'*

as it is cut with a pair of scissors. It can be handled with the fingers, laid down and pressed from behind and the tissue discarded. For exterior work transfer gold is used.

These are the basic principles of gilding, but this is only an introduction to the subject. If you want to know more we recommend *Practical Gilding* by P. & A. MacTaggart, published by Mac & Me, Welwyn, Herts.

Fine work is only achieved after years of practice and experience. Please don't attempt restoration work on any valuable piece without good training and extensive

practice; give it to a member of the British Antique Restorers' Association!

● We run courses suitable for beginners. They last five days and cover water and oil gilding and restoration, with 4-6 students at a time. Send an SAE to Frances Binnington, 65 St John's Hill, London SW11 1SX, 01-223 9192. ■

British Antique Furniture Restorers' Association (BAFRA), Chairman, Peter Brazier, Nash Court Farmhouse, Marnhull, Sturminster Newton DT10 1JZ, (0258) 820 255

WORKBENCH OF THE FUTURE!

SJÖBERGS OF SWEDEN

A *WOODWORKER* and SJÖBERG
COMPETITION to test your SKILL!
WIN

1 A magnificent Sjöberg 2000 workbench, with a 2000mm-long laminated
   beech top and two vices — worth £700 (if you could buy it in the UK)
   PLUS
2 A long weekend in a luxury hotel in Sweden, with a visit to Sjöbergs
   The total value of these enticing prizes?

£1500!

WHAT YOU HAVE TO DO The traditional workbench design is hundreds of years old — no special
provision for power tools or modern equipment. But Sjöberg are committed to constant improvement: SO
**DESIGN THE WORKBENCH OF THE FUTURE — OR FEATURES FOR A
WORKBENCH — OR BENCH ACCESSORIES — that make benchwork more flexible,
comfortable and easier with today's tools and materials**

THE WINNER will be the entry
(judged by *Woodworker* and Sjöberg)
which makes the greatest overall contribution to workbench design

ENTRIES must be in the form of detailed drawings and/or photos, plus
explanatory notes on no more than two
A4 sheets for each item. Send to **'Workbench of the Future'**, Woodworker,
1 Golden Sq, London W1R 3AB.

CLOSING DATE 31 AUGUST

● Prizewinning designs will become the
property of Sjöberg, who reserve the right
to put them into production.
● Sjöberg will pay £100 to any entrant
other than the winner whose idea is put
into production
● Similar ideas will be judged on quality of
presentation
● All decisions about the competition
are final, and no correspondence will be

held. Employees of ASP Ltd, Sjöberg Ltd,
Brimarc Ltd or their advertising agents
are excluded from entry
● SJÖBERG WILL MAKE UP THE
WINNING DESIGN TO BE EXHIBITED
AT THE WOODWORKER SHOW,
ALEXANDRA PAVILION, LONDON,
23-26 OCTOBER
● An entry is automatically taken as agree-
ment to abide by the rules of the com-
petition, and take (within reason) the
offered dates for the holiday

SPECIAL OFFER!   £100 off!

If you want to make sure of a SJÖBERG bench, have a look at this.
The 1900 has a 1900mm-long laminated birch top, two vices, and
storage underneath. With a Sjöberg Holdfast, it's worth £520
retail. *Woodworker* and Sjöberg are offering it to you for just £420!
That's a clear £100 off!

● Make cheques payable to Argus Specialist Publications Ltd

To: Reader Services, Wolsey House, Wolsey Rd, Hemel Hempstead, Herts HP2 4SS
Please send me ☐ Sjöberg 1900 benches with ST82 Holdfast at £420 each. I enclose

a cheque for ....

Name...

Address ....

.... Post Code.................

Hira-kanna

At first glance you'd think a Japanese wooden plane is like one of our own block planes — but pulling gives you more push. Tony Wood explains how they're made

● *Components of the Japanese plane – body, chip-breaker and blade – and how it looks when assembled*

The plane is the most recent hand-tool developed for Japanese woodworking, popular as a finishing tool since glasspaper is very rarely used. Japanese wooden planes look very similar to simple western block planes, but the two things likely to give them away are the thinner body and shallower blade angle. The major difference is in the use; Japanese planes are pulled towards you, not pushed away.

The earliest Japanese planes were called *Yari-kanna*. These looked a bit like a small spear with a slightly turned-up blade, and were used double-handed to smooth boards that had been hewn with an adze. *Yari-kanna* were first used in the 14th century and identical tools are still used today.

Wooden-bodied planes first came to Japan from China in the mid-15th century. They looked very much like modern-day Japanese planes but had a handle on both sides of the body and were used with a push action.

This method wasn't favoured by the Japanese, because it was difficult in the traditional sitting position. So the basic design was refined; the handles were removed, the body turned round, and the pull-action plane of today had evolved.

The modern Japanese wooden plane *Hira-kanna* has three separate components: the body, the chip-breaker and the blade. The blade is the most important. The body of the plane is rather like the handle of a chisel; it's there to make the blade comfortable in use, nothing more, which is why plane bodies are made to suit blades and not vice-versa. Because each body is individually crafted to suit one blade and one only, if the blade is ever damaged beyond repair, the body will have to be reworked to suit a new blade or discarded altogether — a frightening thought when a plane could cost up to £1000.

The chip-breaker

It's a common misconception that the chip-breaker acts as a wedge to hold the blade in position. In fact, the chip-breaker is really a second blade, held in place by a steel pin, controlling the shavings and reducing tear-out of the fibres by severing them as the main blade lifts them. Without the chip-breaker, the blade would dig deeply into the grain when removing large amounts of timber, tearing out the fibres.

The blade

Plane blades and chip-breakers are made of laminated steel in much the same way as chisels (WW/Apr) having a relatively soft back and an extremely hard cutting edge.

Each blade takes hours, sometimes days, to complete, depending on the quality and hence the price. Not every blade is destined for sale. Many reach the final stages of completion but never leave the workshop, so high is the blademakers' quality control; most of these 'rejects' would still outperform a 'perfect' western plane blade, if you could ever persuade the blademaker to release one.

The body

Although the blade is the most important part of the plane, the body (*dai*) is more

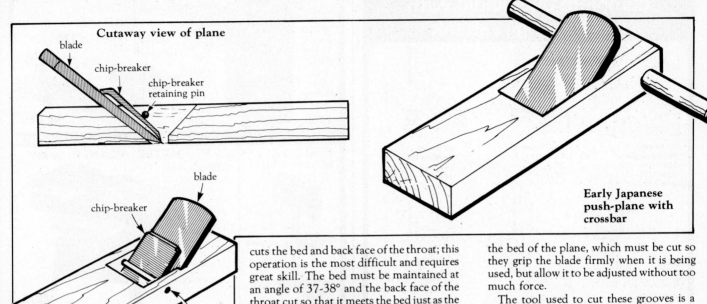

Cutaway view of plane

blade

chip-breaker

chip-breaker
retaining pin

blade

chip-breaker

retaining pin

pull from this end

**Early Japanese
push-plane with
crossbar**

intricate and exacting in construction. After all, it is the body that must fit the blade and not the other way around.

In olden times, a Japanese joiner would have gone to a blademaker for a blade, and then take it to the *dai* maker to have the body made. Nowadays, however, a plane-blade maker usually commissions a body maker to craft a number of bodies for his blades, and it's not uncommon for batches of 20 or more blades to be sent to the *dai* maker at one time. So a blademaker tends to develop a very close working relationship with a particular *dai* maker. In this way, good *dai* makers, who were once looked down on as 'just another carpenter', are becoming highly sought-after.

Oak, either white or red, is the traditional material for the *dai*, but now some plane bodies are being made from Macassar ebony because of Western demand for expensive exotic-looking tools. These planes are for export only, mainly to the USA. The problem with Macassar ebony is that in the large bulk required for a plane body, it's a fairly unstable timber, difficult to work and prone to splitting. That's why in Japan you will only find small finger-planes made from this attractive wood. No self-respecting Japanese woodworker would use a full-size Macassar ebony-bodied plane; it's a fancy tool for non-serious Western woodworkers!

Making the body

The body blank is first planed square to the finished size and the throat marked out. The throat is then carved out with a chisel, and the inner sides carefully pared down to leave a smooth surface. The *dai* maker next

cuts the bed and back face of the throat; this operation is the most difficult and requires great skill. The bed must be maintained at an angle of 37-38° and the back face of the throat cut so that it meets the bed just as the chisel starts to break through the sole of the plane. If this single operation is done wrongly the body will have to be scrapped. The work of opening out the mouth of the plane is done with a very thin and flexible backless saw called an *Anahiki-nokogiri*. All through the work, constant reference is made to the blade destined to fit the body.

Unlike western plane-blades, Japanese blades are self-wedging, the blade held in position by friction. This is why oak is used for the *dai*. Dense and hard, oak is also flexible and so it grips the blade. The sides of the blade run in grooves cut parallel to

the bed of the plane, which must be cut so they grip the blade firmly when it is being used, but allow it to be adjusted without too much force.

The tool used to cut these grooves is a saw called an *Osaehiki-nokogiri*, the blade about 5in long with 22 to 28 teeth per in, and no set to them. This is because a perfectly clean cut is required, as there isn't enough clearance inside the throat for cleaning up with a chisel. Finally the pin is fitted to hold the chip-breaker in place. This is generally steel, a tight fit in the body. On more expensive planes, the pin is narrower than the body so that small wooden plugs can be inserted into each of the pin holes to conceal the metal. ■

● Thanks to Roger Buse of Roger's of Hitchin; (0462) 34177.

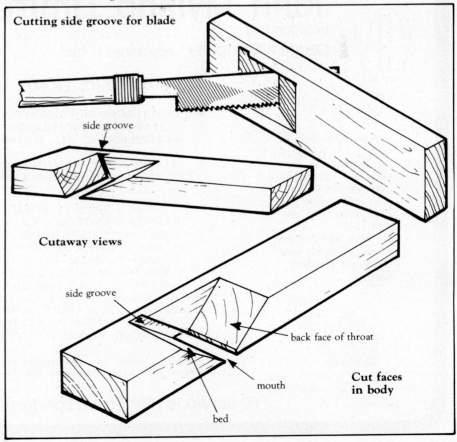

Cutting side groove for blade

side groove

Cutaway views

side groove

back face of throat

mouth

bed

**Cut faces
in body**

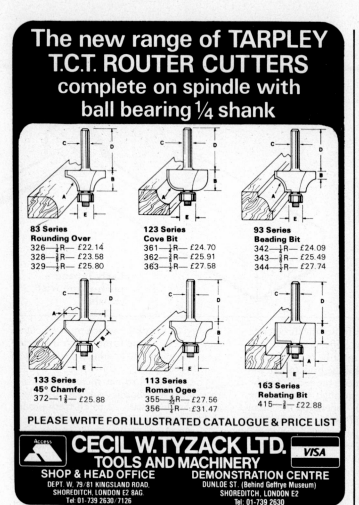

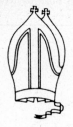

728

Art attack

College showtime is arguing time, especially when it comes to the old is-it-furniture-or-is-it-art? chestnut. Friedbert Meinert raises his voice for experiment . . .

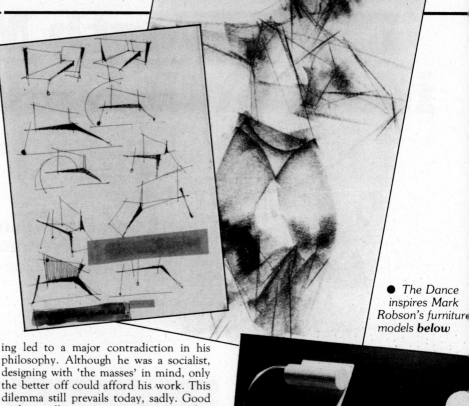

● *The Dance inspires Mark Robson's furniture models **below***

Why do students from Middlesex Poly *spend their time making things that most other people hate? That was former editor Peter Collenette's question last autumn after he'd visited their furniture degree show (WW/Nov 85).*

'From spiky, spidery metal things to flimsy Wendy houses in cloth and gaudily painted plywood, the 18 students exhibiting offered almost nothing at all for the visitor's pleasure or comfort,' wrote a belligerent and bemused Peter.

Peter Collenette's article on the Middlesex Polytechnic furniture degree show ('Nothing to show', WW/Nov 1985) highlighted how design colleges can be misunderstood, and some of their work, as in Peter's review, misrepresented. The confusion that arises may have many reasons; one factor is that colleges don't explain their approach.

I cannot speak for the colleges. But since I am a student at this subversive institution, enjoying the apparent anarchy of the furniture department, I would like to explain how I see it by looking at the way some designers, past and present, have developed their ideas.

How has art infiltrated craft and design — and vice versa — and in particular, how has art affected the design of furniture?

Art and craft are perfect partners. Craft has the techniques; art has, dare I say it, 'vision.' Art without craft has no substance, no permanence. Craft without art is empty, repetitive and regressive.

Over the centuries craftspeople and artists of all kinds have been openly 'stealing' each others' ideas, but until the late 1900s a strict divide kept the craftsman in a subservient role to the grand artist.

The unique contribution of the Arts and Crafts movement was to unite the craftsman and the artist, rather than point out their differences. The movement influenced the taste of entire nations, inspired other movements of design and, most importantly, let loose the chains of excessive ornamentation.

William Morris's liking for the medieval led to designs which were pure, simple and above all, hand-made. He hated the machine, fearing that we would become its slaves and that it would lead to shoddy products. His obsession with manufactur-ing led to a major contradiction in his philosophy. Although he was a socialist, designing with 'the masses' in mind, only the better off could afford his work. This dilemma still prevails today, sadly. Good craft, as well as art, is not a mass commodity and can't be afforded by everyone.

John Ruskin expressed the beliefs of many of the movement's followers in *Stones of Venice*: 'The workman has not done his duty, and is not working on safe principles, unless he so far honours the materials in which he is working as to set himself to bring out their beauty, and to recommend and exalt as far as he can, their peculiar qualities.'

The Arts and Crafts pioneers recognised the need to draw together the resources of all creative people — painters, writers, architects, cabinetmakers, silversmiths and others. The talents of all these disciplines together contributed to the success of the movement.

Ironically the movement inspired one pioneer of the industrial application of design. In Germany during the 1920s art and craft joined forces under one roof. The celebrated Bauhaus school was the great melting pot of ideas for those involved in two- and three-dimensional work — painters and printers, architects, cabinet-makers, potters, weavers, silversmiths, bookbinders and many others.

The school zealously believed in the fusion of the traditional, rigorous training of the craftsman and the more experimental education of the artist. Bauhaus members were called apprentices, journeymen and masters, paying respect to the craft tradition. The philosophy, like Morris's, was socialist. The crucial difference, however, was the school's interest in co-operation with industry, recognising that it could mean good design for everybody, affordable to all.

Many Bauhaus designs were taken up by industry and were successfully produced. The educational principles were adopted by many schools of art and design and are still an inspiration in many parts of the world today.

Sadly, the liberal and progressive art practises of the school were branded as degenerate by the Nazis and the school was closed in 1933. The Bauhaus is now re-opened and operating in East Germany.

Design — the product

We drive it, we eat it, we wear it, we sleep in it, we live in it and we'll probably die in it. With the help of machines and modern technology 'design' is mass-produced and neatly packaged. The design consciousness of an entire nation is raised, carefully monitored and engineered. Whether this is a good or a bad thing I don't wish to discuss here; the fact is it affects us all.

I believe that this relatively new phenomenon of 'design' has emerged as a focus for discussion, and it needs continual reassessment to clarify its aims and objectives.

The study of pure design — by which I mean learning about proportion, structure, movement, colour, function, aesthetics and so on — is today the major part of the design student's work. With this in mind I would like to show how imaginative and realistic products can result.

Confusion and horror met Stephen Horner's comment in 'Nothing to show': 'I approach each design anew, divorced from preconceptions.' Peter's keen reply was: 'That's an extraordinary thing to say. The idea that it is possible, let alone desirable, to make something without reference to the past is a peculiar product of the last mad 100 years or so.'

I must point out that to design does not necessarily mean to make, though it is a process that will hopefully lead to making. Designing, particularly when it's free from the constraints of making, can be of great importance and might look at times like a rather playful activity. But this freedom has ensured, especially in the 'last mad 100 years or so' some exciting developments in woodwork and furniture making. These achievements are not threatened by students experimenting with new forms and structures, however imperfect they might be on occasions. Given the right environment and guidance, experimentation can be a constructive avenue for new ideas and genuine innovation.

This attitude to design is nothing new. Time and time again designers have tried to break from tradition, particularly in the last decade, achieving startling results and constant controversy.

Art Nouveau

On a recent trip to Brussels I visited a building designed by the famous Art Nouveau architect Victor Horta (1861-1947). It is a monument dedicated to that movement, and an extremely fine one. The entire house, the façade, all the woodwork, metalwork and glass was designed in the style, right down to the doormat. Its richness demonstrates clearly what can emerge from design restrictions. Many of

● *Three design classics: a Horta doorway detail **below left**, a Mackintosh chair **right**, and Keler's cradle **above***

the motifs come from plants and flowers and, apart from the actual techniques of building, reference to past styles is deliberately avoided. Plant forms, carefully observed, simplified and abstracted, are reproduced; a twisting liana becomes a handrail growing up massive marble staircase. The slender trunk and branches of a tree become the architraves and door lining.

You might think taking plants as an inspiration for your work is innocent enough and uncontroversial. Not so, as Stephen Madsen vividly describes the ensuing struggle of the Art Nouveau masters in his book *Sources of Art Nouveau*. It was a struggle between decoration and structure or the flower and the stem. Should the latter be disguised by the former or stand in its own right? Victor Horta expresses his own attitude towards decoration rather poetically: 'I leave the flower and the leaf and take the stalk.'

The most revolutionary change in design at the turn of the century occurred in Scotland. Charles Rennie Mackintosh (1886-1928) and the Glasgow School gained fame and popularity, though at first mainly on the Continent. The English craft fraternity received him with cynicism, first because they didn't like Art Nouveau (not that I blame them for that) and then they accused him of being, in the words of May Morris, 'needlessly spartan.'

Mackintosh's most important achievement was to go well beyond Art Nouveau and create a pure language of architectural design that manifests beautifully in his furniture. Fortunately his achievements were eventually recognised, and furniture design became virtually unthinkable without reference to Mackintosh.

The interior of the Glasgow School of Art, designed by Mackintosh, is an example of his radical language crying for change and

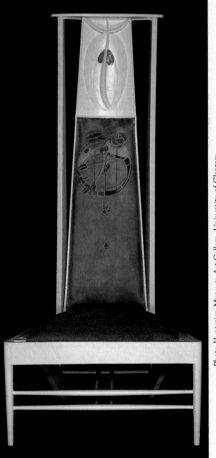

Photo Hunterian Museum Art Gallery, University of Glasgow

achieving it. It is ruthlessly spartan; pillars are simply square and only taper towards the ceiling. Much of the woodwork is coarsely finished and stained black or brown, set against white- or cream-coloured walls. Mackintosh's work is bursting with that vitality and power which finely finished woodwork can rarely achieve. What became known as the 'Modern Movement' was uncompromisingly described in a nutshell by C. F. A. Voysey: 'The natural forms have to be reduced to mere symbols.'

Art attack

Creative quest

The quest of the designer for inspiration has taken him or her to the extremes of many creative fields and can become an obsession. When such people are hungry for ideas, nothing is safe; architecture, the plant and animal world, the human body, our man-made surroundings, even abstract geometric shapes are dissected on the drawing-board. An example of such a quest and a favourite of mine is Peter Keler's cradle, shown on the preceding page. A member of the Bauhaus school, he attended a colour seminar by the painter Wassily Kandinsky, who believed that certain colours go with certain shapes; for example blue, the colour of eternity, belongs to the circle, yellow is for stability and goes with the triangle. It's quite mystical and rather beyond me, but we are used to certain colours for temperatures — blue for cold, red for hot. Keler merely grabbed the idea, radically simplified it and the cradle was the result.

In those days before design schools as we know them developed, the only way into design was to study architecture. It's not surprising, then, that the most influential modern furniture designers were architects — Phillip Webb, Mackintosh, Marcel Breuer, Mies van der Rohe. Now that design schools exist, the field is much more open to other views and influences, ensuring diverse results and maintaining the ability to shock, please and serve.

Divided responsibilities

Designers vary in their approaches. Some prefer to do the whole job themselves; others merely draw, experiment and make models, leaving the actual making to somebody else; and there are those who stick to the drawing-board.

Should a furniture designer also be able to make his/her own furniture? Ideally yes, but with mass-production and industrial design, this is no longer always possible. Very different demands are made on the designer now. Students today can choose which path to take, and the design colleges which aspect to teach. Some do a bit of each, which is no bad thing.

There are plenty of reasons for acquiring some practical experience without trying to become an expert craftsperson; getting to know materials and how they behave, learning methods of construction and the appropriate use of materials and techniques. We have to accept that designing and making depend on each other and are both complex. Deciding which one to emphasise can be an agonising choice. Apart from the colleges' role in research into styles, the function of furniture and its role in the surroundings, there is great pressure on the design student to develop his or her individual style and personal techniques.

For many of us it comes back to the question of what source material we want to

● *The table in Cézanne's* The Card Players *above, recreated* **below** *in three dimensions by Howard Raybould*

use; maybe the sails of windmills to develop a screening system, the image of coloured building blocks as an idea for seating, the geometry of traditional forms, or some personal fascination. Mark Robson, a student at the Middlesex Polytechnic, has based his furniture designs on the figures of the dancer. His fascination with the human form in motion has led him to simplify the shapes and turn them into structures. Capturing the movement in drawings, sculpture and photography, he builds models of the simplified positions and goes to a prototype. The illustrations on the preceding page show a progression of Mark's work from the fleshy sketch to numerous configurations to suggest possible constructions.

Finally I want to draw your attention to a book recently published which highlights the lengths to which furniture designers will go to develop variety. When I first saw the book, *Masterpieces – Making Furniture from Paintings*, I was horror-struck. The pieces seemed banal and I thought it was a joke.

There was Van Gogh's painting of the rush-seated chair, carefully re-constructed minus pipe and tobacco pouch. 'Is the designer taking the mickey?' I thought. I kept an open mind however — John Makepeace is one of the contributors — and some of the pieces work well. Though the idea of making a piece of furniture depicted in a painting still makes me shudder and some of the examples brought tears to my eyes, it was when the designers interpreted rather than copied what they saw in the painting that the results were successful.

Howard Raybould's Card Table, based on Cézanne's *The Card Players* is humorous and beautifully made. It must have been frustrating to recreate the obviously flowing lines of a table cloth from a two-dimensional painting and perhaps it would have been better to set up a similar still-life and work from that.

The book also gives detailed plans and instructions, just in case anybody is mad enough to want to have a go. It's worth having a look at and it advises readers to

seek their own furniture inspiration in painting. It will raise a smile and a chuckle, I am sure.

The designer's job is to interpret what he or she sees and then to translate that into a workable reality. Good design results from study of art and craft, not a carbon copy of one or an ignorance of the other. ■

Books

Stephen Madsen, *Sources of Art Nouveau*, Da Capo, £8.95.

Thomas Howarth, *Charles Rennie Mackintosh and the Modern Movement*, Routledge and Kegan Paul, £26.

Frank Whitford, *The Bauhaus*, Thames and Hudson, £4.50.

Richard Ball and Peter Campbell, *Masterpieces – Making Furniture from Paintings*, Blandford, £11.95.

Coronet are Back!

With the perfect blend of the established Major and the exciting new Coronet No. 1

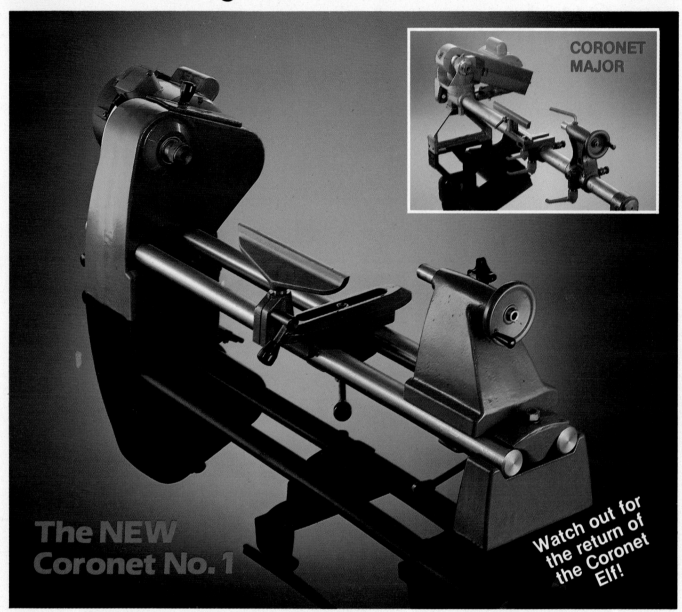

CORONET MAJOR

The NEW Coronet No. 1

Watch out for the return of the Coronet Elf!

The NEW Coronet No. 1

- The first Coronet Twin Bed Bar Lathe
- Made of solid cast iron construction
- Compatible with all Coronet wood turning aids and fitments
- Competitively priced — yet retains the hallmark of Coronet quality — to give a lifetime of usefulness

- Turning between centres 24″
- Diameter over bed 12″
- 3 speed "poly V" drive system
- Speed range 450 — 2000 rpm

Coronet Major

- Return of the well used, well proven flagship of the Coronet range
- Solid, robust and reliable
- The "standard" of the industry
- Turning between centres 33″
- Diameter over bed 9″
- End turning up to 24″ dia. (approx.)
- 5 speed "poly V" drive system
- Speed range 425 — 2000 rpm

For Further information ring or write to:-

**Coronet Lathe & Tool Company Limited,
Parkway Works, Sheffield, England.**
Telephone: (0742) 434370. Telex: 547139. Fax: (0742) 434302

86 degrees!

Giving a cool edge to a hot college season — non-student Luke Hughes' stained maple mirror-frame. Through the looking glass: **Top far left**, ash and green laminate wardrobe by Dave Wilson, Suffolk; **above**, sunflower table by John Burr, Brighton; **left**, davenport by Jurgen Kramer, Suffolk. **Below**, the LIFS prize-winning rocking-chair by Oliver Peake, Middlesex; **bottom far left**, the chaiselongue by Julia Tiesteel, RCA, discussed opposite.

Hotter than July or cooler than a cucumber sandwich, College degree shows always herald some good midsummer madness. We review two exhibitions, present a visual feast from some more, and air two contentious views on the value of experiment and tradition in furniture craft. More next month . . .

ROYAL COLLEGE OF ART

Luke Hughes

An observer's expectations are high and scrutiny close at the RCA's annual summer show. It's the only post-graduate College of Art and Design in the country, so it's natural to expect an example; a lead for others to follow in ingenuity, execution, and presentation.

A flamboyant, bold and energetic couch (though 'energy' isn't perhaps the quality one might expect from a resting-place) designed by Julia Tiesteel immediately caught my eye (opposite page). A comforting arm of the couch, formed in opulent curved glass, reminded me of Job resting his head on a stone pillow — solid material, but effective and comfortable. The piece had both a sculptural and a painterly quality which may give some indication of the future direction of this furniture designer.

Much trumpeted in the glossies and already selling well in furniture shops is the folding 'Suzy' stool; a neat, thoroughly professional design that has brought Adrian Reed some acclaim but no riches — a businessman (and Conservative MP) lifted the design and is busy marketing it. Perhaps his conscience will soon be pricked into paying Adrian a suitable royalty . . .

● *The folding 'Suzy' stool in black ash has brought Adrian Reed praise but no cash*

● *Above, sideboard in American black walnut by Michael de Caires, beautifully executed by Andy Whately; left, a curved seat in laminated ash designed by David Williams*

A sideboard in black walnut, designed by Michael de Caires and brilliantly executed by RCA technician Andy Whately, was inspired by discussions with the Property Services Agency about designing dining-room furniture for embassies; there was a pair of circular benches by David Williams for the foyer of a new entrance at the college which owed much to the traditions of Alan Peters, and frosted-glass-topped tables by Catherine Tytherleigh showed a sensitive use of different materials, especially in her patinating of metals.

In mentioning other materials, I have to say that the star of this year's show was not a woodworker but a metalworker. Christopher Robertson, an Australian jeweller and winner of the Ron Lenthal Award (Ron was the chief technician at the RCA for 30 years) is clearly a superlative craftsman and one who really knows how to use his materials. His designs for chairs are the richer for it.

Overall, this was not a classic RCA vintage. Indeed, from a group of students who have now spent six years in full-time design training, it isn't unreasonable to expect greater things. Their show was not aided by being badly displayed, with unflattering lighting, no photographs or promotional literature — after all, promotion is to be paramount for these budding young professionals — and a certain pervasive apathy.

Searching for a lead in ingenuity, execution, and presentation, I ran off for a breath of fresh air — to the Industrial Design Department.

● *Fretwork table in American walnut by Michael de Caires; RCA*

SUFFOLK COLLEGE
Peter Howlett

At Suffolk College of Higher and Further Education the one- or two-year Furniture Studies Course incorporates traditional and contemporary design, but local industry demands a heavier slant on traditional furniture.

First-year students take City and Guilds parts I and II Furniture Crafts. The Advanced Crafts Certificate taken by second-year students carries a college diploma and a special final paper. Although it's principally concerned with reproduction furniture, the core of the course contains elements of original, contemporary design, business management/ organisation and production studies.

Ian Scott, the course tutor, feels the emphasis on traditional design, hand and machine skills, provides a good all-round basis, so sensible and imaginative designs can be realised. He encourages students to design and make furniture with the small scale manufacturer in mind. It must also be functional, well made, production-based and marketable.

Of the first-year students' work, Peter Cooper's elegant concertina card table, 'with fretwork straight out of the back of Chippendale's Director' (his own words) was masterfully made and finished. The Chinese detail on the legs was machined on the over-arm router using a jig he made up himself. Gary Silbert's William and Mary side table in walnut, with its exquisitely cut asymmetrical marquetry inlay, showed all the patience of a mature student.

The second-year work contained the best elements of reproduction and contemporary work: Dave Wilson's Queen Anne chair in walnut would have looked odd in

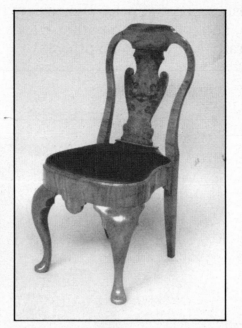

Above left, a walnut chair by David Wilson; above, a sycamore chair by Jurgen Kramer. Left, a cherry table by Jurgen Kramer and below, Stephen Paternoster's beech and grey bookcase

the same room as his detachable semicircular topped wardrobe in white ash with lime green Decamel. Jurgen Kramer's fiddleback sycamore and santos rosewood chair, — overtones of a happy marriage between Mackintosh and De Stijl — couldn't have successfully partnered his heavy Teutonic circular table in stained American cherry. Again, in contrast to these, his oil-finished blanket chest in pale oak, with book-matched fielded panels in brown oak, belonged to the Arts and Crafts movement. Steve Paternoster's fine bookcase had a glazed door in natural beech enclosing the sprayed grey carcase. His companion reproduction piece made, like the pieces by the other students as part of the College's special paper, was a mahogany pedestal desk, fit for any bank manager's office.

All of these Diploma pieces showed a sensitivity born of a wide design vocabulary; it was reassuring that the heavy emphasis on traditional furniture didn't inhibit creative, contemporary design. The ability to move from one idiom to another

● *A walnut kneehole desk by Nigel Betts of Suffolk College*

● **Middlesex Poly: left,** *a chair by Martin Moser, whose entry in the Show catalogue reads: 'Do not imagine, do not meditate, do not reflect; keep the mind in its natural state'; **above,** living-room centrepiece by Oliver Peake*

was evidence of the department's philosophy of allowing 'a bit of freedom' in the second year — the modern stuff works because it's backed up by hand skills. At Suffolk College there is no such thing as a technician's piece; it is all made to high standard by the students, jigs and all.

It seemed to me that the disciplines taught and the discipline learnt, have produced economically and functionally sound pieces, both contemporary and traditional, fit to grace any showroom or home.

MANCHESTER CENTRAL COLLEGE
Jack Hill

Acquiring traditional skills is a vital first step for students — that's the thinking at the college's School of Furniture.

All 40 full-time students — mostly school-leavers — spend a year learning timber preparation, hand cabinetmaking, traditional upholstery, and traditional and modern finishing techniques. In the second year students specialise in one of these areas, and are expected to design and make individual pieces. The one-year full-time course for mature students follows a similar (contracted) pattern, while part-time Furniture Restoration courses are also popular.

The school has strong links with the furniture industry, and block- and day-release courses are available for YTS and apprentice training schemes. Daytime courses all lead to London City & Guilds qualifications in furniture studies at both Craft and Advanced level.

The exhibition, though somewhat confusing and overcrowded, supports the belief that hand skills are still relevant even in today's machine age. I saw some modern designs, but the main emphasis, as I expected, was on the traditional.

● **Manchester: above,** *a small cabinet in olive and ash by Kate Walker; and* **right,** *a second-year drop-leaf table, veneered and inlaid*

● **Manchester Central College** *School of Furniture* **above:** *a tripod table, a buttonback armchair and a small writing table are first-year set pieces*

PARNHAM

● **Above**, 'Siena' chest of drawers in walnut, yew and cherry by David Burke; **above right**, the 'Shogun' table in cherry, rock maple and coloured leather by Timothy Freeman; **right**, 'Swings & Roundabouts' dining table in oak, inlaid in fumed oak, Paul Flowerday; **below**, a teak dining chair, Knut Klimmek; **below right**, the 'Axis' chair and country table by Thomas Overton

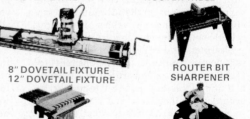

Past defence

Peter Howlett looks at College work and the High Street, and bemoans the lack of intelligent reference to past mastery in furniture design

Clever stuff, some of those latest college designs. But how eminently forgettable. It's my belief that the insular nature of degree courses, with their narrow vision of the way forward, encourages these superficial results.

Of course, there is a place for experiment and innovation, and further education should be fun, a time away from home when students become 'themselves'. But colleges have a duty to direct the studies so they point students towards a vision of a better way of life. I firmly believe that this direction must pay some attention to the past, getting tradition into perspective as well as pushing the contemporary scene forward with vigour and enthusiasm. What happened yesterday is equally important as what will happen tomorrow.

'There must be a better way of doing this,' a craftsman once said to me, referring to some repetitive hand operation. And he meant it! As an apprentice sweeping the floor, then keeping the glue-pots going and working his way up to be a journeyman cabinetmaker of consummate skill, he saw the sense in seeking to improve, of building upon tradition, not forsaking it entirely or sacrificing it for speed and immediacy.

What has happened to this spirit of craft? Our vision appears to be radically impaired by a violent reaction to the materials which we now have at our fingertips. No thanks to the top designers and entrepreneurs, we now see more MDF and — in reaction to it — solid wood abused by college students, and veneered surfaces bastardised by High Street furniture chains.

We are set to drown in a sea of pseudo-Georgian elegance and Jacobean stained oak at one end of the market and bored to tears with joke effects at the other. It seems to me we're missing out on the adventure and are either indulging ourselves in gaudy eclecticism, or bowing low to bad taste.

Designers and college tutors who structure degree courses have a responsibility to make good design and art less of a novelty and more accessible to the buying public. In accord with their role and status, tutors ought to show us clearly what the true potential of their protegés is.

Joe Public deserves more than the trivial offerings that owe more to a straight-line edger and speed-sander than to human need. Unfortunately, the public are largely unaware of designer/craftspeople and what they have to offer, because they're provided with bland and insubstantial offerings

● *Boxing clever – **above**, detachable intersecting boxes; **below**, burr maple integrated squares. Peter's own work shows strong design concepts!*

whose only virtue is quality of finish. It's equally unfortunate that our top designer/craftsmen seem to delight in the bizarre and extreme.

In a spoof radio programme, the script writers sent up Terence Conran in a sketch entitled 'Conran the Barbarian'. I felt the satirists had captured the fundamental elements of 'Conranology' — making money, marketing, empire building and profit margins — and they confirmed the disgust I had felt when I heard that he wanted to rip out the beautiful curved windows of Heal's store. They may not be particularly efficient from a display point of view but they are a surviving testimony to all that Ambrose Heal and his company stood for — quality and style.

My heart sank at the shoddiness of the furniture inside the store; some items were reproductions of Heal's classic 'cottage' furniture, originally made in chestnut. Oak was now being used; doors were badly hung, latches didn't work, some lower drawers were sloppy and melamine lacquer was sprayed inside and out. Such work is a travesty, not a tribute, to one of the great pioneers of the machine age who found a way of mass-producing quality designs to a high standard of craftsmanship and finish.

And yet the influence of Conran is so great that much of what comes out of the

colleges could well be from, or destined for, a Habitat catalogue. Certainly some students ought to have a place in such a team designing contemporary furniture. Visually, most of it is quite pleasing, if not innocuous, but does it have to be made so badly, finished in such severe and awful colours, marketed in a crass and pseudo-precious way and made ultimately to pack into a flat box? Who has decided that this is what the public will have? It is as awful as the current range of Ercol furniture which seems to have abandoned the purity of line developed in the 60s for a pseudo-repro-duction style that has no affinity with any specific historical period.

At the other end of the spectrum stands the giant influential figure of John Makepeace. Unfortunately, much of Makepeace's work which reaches the public eye — through his own promotion work — is the result of a fertile yet wandering imagination. It's hard to know which direction the man will take next! What we tend not to see is his formal work, the traditional, almost conservative, pieces which owe much to a tradition kept alive by Barnsley and Davies, and show the other side of Makepeace's 'whole log' approach. It's also hard to reconcile, in an age of shrinking resources, the use of so much solid timber, and even harder for us lowly mortals to see where the justification for such a high price-tag lies.

Sadly, the colleges seem to be bowing down to these mighty men, encouraging students to cream off all that is superficial in such work. If this is what's happening, and the evidence of another round of degree shows would seem to suggest it is, they can't be acting in a responsible way.

I wonder how many students have had to discover for themselves the work of Mackintosh and the Shakers, or under their own steam badger the curator of furniture at the V&A to open the 20th-century gallery during the week so they can see in the flesh that superb chair by Ponti (incidentally an interpretation of a traditional Italian design) or the subtle laminated work of Alvar Aalto? How many know the work of Jacques Ruhlmann or the superb lacquer-work of the architect and designer Eileen Grey? These past masters still have something to teach us today.

It really is time we saw something better coming out of our colleges, something which owes its form to a wider sphere of influence than the tarty clichés prevalent in the current design scene. It's time we recognised there is a great ocean of influence, past and present, to swim in.

I am as much moved by the superb quality of the late 40s joinery in the refurbished Hunterian Museum as the beautiful veneer work of Martin Grierson. And I'm equally influenced by both. I marvel at the work of Gaudi, with its sinuous and plastic forms and frequently refer to the burial furniture catalogued by Carter when he raided the tomb of Tutankhamun. I continually thirst for knowledge about how such pieces were made, what materials were used and what these discoveries can offer me and my work.

Surely we have reached a point beyond painting MDF in bright colours or bolting together rough hewn billets of elm? There has to be a greater sensitivity to and learning from the past, a definite break with the art-dominated ethos of furniture studies and its severely restricted counterpart — industrial design. It's hard to recognise any of the great historical wealth of work in the degree shows. There are faint glimmers of acknowledgement but in their preciousness, they often miss the point.

I used to think, rather arrogantly, that my pieces had some intrinsic value and would become 'antiques of the future'. Now I've climbed off that ego-trip I'm aiming for a soundness of design which simply says 'that piece is right'. I still have my frivolous moments, and there is a place for such work alongside the rational and pleasing.

But just because we live in a throw-away society we shouldn't allow this to debase our sense of the past — not worship of it — with its timeless pieces and glimpses of genius. Colour, modern materials and an efficient technology are all means to an end and not an end in themselves. We're worshipping false gods if we try to immortalise the past, just as we are if we only look back a few years; there is so much in the 6,000 years of surviving furniture to learn from.

It's also effete to say 'I looked at the log and saw what it wanted to be.' Such an approach is either pure mysticism or an absurd pretension. The true craftsman is searching for honesty, and he/she does it with integrity. The work reflects the true value of the price-tag. There's no need for a philosophical explanation because we can see the person in the work; it has, in James Krenov's words, the 'personal thumbprint'. Ultimately it has style and is superbly made.

I recognise that these qualities, which are born of years of working the material and exploring its possibilities, can't be taught in our colleges overnight. But if we are exposed to it at an early enough stage it will have an effect on us. It might divert us from using materials simply because they exist towards using them because they provide a better solution to old problems. More than ever we have the resources to see first-hand what has been done and what is being done. It would be a shame if lack of direction led to a squandering of these experiences. ∎

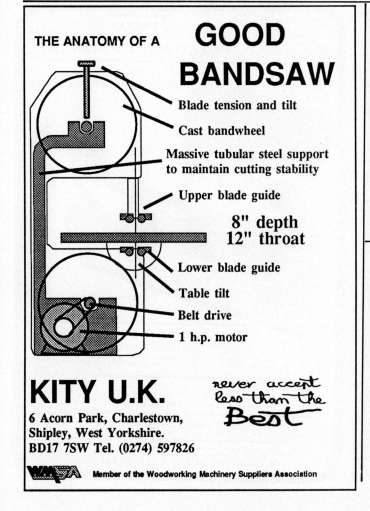

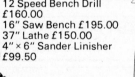
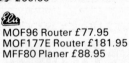

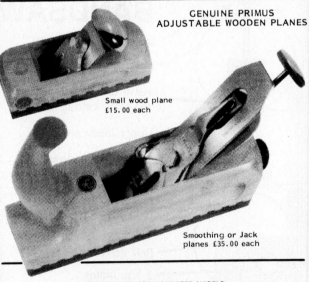

Which way to turn

What's the best machine, you ask. Hugh O'Neill devised a system for deciding what suits you, and applies it to choosing a lathe

Many an experienced woodturner gets asked — 'What lathe should I buy?' It's nice, of course, to know what an expert uses, but someone else's choice is really only of academic interest. The answer to the 'what should I buy?' question should be — what suits you.

Everybody's needs and circumstances are different, and indeed, our needs change over time. You've only to look at the work of, say, Ray Key and Phil Reardon to recognise that they require fundamentally different things from their lathes, and their equipment and tools are bound to be markedly different.

So, though the experts' opinions are interesting, we need to start our *own* decision-making from first principles — our own first principles. Even these change, so each new purchase is likely to require decision-making from scratch. I'm just about to replace my existing lathe, not because it was a poor buy, but because my skills have grown and my needs have changed. My equipment is just no longer suitable and I feel justified in changing it.

Had I foreseen where I was likely to go with woodturning when I bought my second lathe — the first was a 'give-it-a-try' powerdrill attachment — I might have avoided the present change. This must be the first lesson. It isn't easy, but if possible, think ahead. Assess your future requirements and buy up to those; not down to your immediate needs.

The initial step when choosing a lathe — or anything else for that matter — is to be quite clear about your underlying motive. At bottom, what's the basic goal that you're trying to achieve?

My impending decision is choosing a replacement for my existing lathe. I have to ask myself: 'Why? What am I really trying to achieve?'

The 'why' is simply answered. I want to remove the physical/mechanical constraints now limiting my woodturning potential. I have vibration, off-true centres, a flimsy rest, limited (but expensive) fittings, slow adjustments and no long spindle steady. I admit there are also skill constraints, but that is a different matter.

But underlying this reason is my fundamental goal — to produce quality woodturnings (and woodware) of an artistic and commercial nature. Undoubtedly I will end up with a very different lathe from the person whose goal is spare time recreation and a love of working in wood or even from the one who wants to turn components for cabinetmaking.

Obviously I need a lathe capable of high quality work — a machine that is massive and stable — and that also facilitates quantity work — easy to set up and adjust, probably with a copy facility. I am more interested in turning big flat items like bowls than long thin ones; but I expect to make some 36in legs. I do have a limited budget, but cost is less important to me because I expect a return and I can discount the cost over a period.

So my lathe will be different from yours, unless you have similar goals and circumstances.

But the method I use to make my choice will be applicable to everyone, so let's see how it works.

Yardstick

What I need is a yardstick against which to measure the various options. I acknowledge that my 'ideal' lathe doesn't exist, and my decision has to be a compromise.

The yardstick I've developed is a two-part list. First there are the limits beyond which I cannot go and minimum facilities that I must have. On these items I won't compromise. The second section itemises all the things that I want or would like to achieve.

Essentials

I've already made some decisions about absolute constraints. I won't consider a combination machine — I don't like the hassle of changing fittings and I already have some separate items. I will only consider lathes with morse tapers at each end — they're much more convenient and I can use non-proprietary fittings (often less expensive). I need a 36in minimum lathe bed, but not much more — I want to make a four-poster bed but I'll build it up in sections. My power supply is 240v single-phase, so I don't want the bother of installing 440v three-phase, despite possible long-term cost savings.

These constraints automatically eliminate several options.

Preferences

The list of things I want took much longer to complete, but the whole decision relies on how thoroughly you compile the wants list. I used an open-ended approach; so my interest in big bowl turning led me to conclude that I wanted the 'largest overbed turning capacity'.

My final list reads:
- Biggest swing over bed
- Widest range of reasonably priced accessories
- Most solid, vibration-free construction
- Easiest to set up and adjust
- Widest range of speeds
- Most powerful drive
- Best off-bed turning facility
- Proximity of back-up service
- Most transportable
- Lowest price
- Best package of initial inclusions

- Good second-hand value.

These are my requirements — yours will be different. And I also have my own specific interpretations of those requirements. Here's a few examples:
- **Biggest swing over bed** is for large bowls without having to constantly re-set-up over the side or the ends.
- **Widest range of accessories** because I'm fed up with having to get special bits made for a lathe with limited extras and/or pay the earth for spares. So I want morse tapers and various sizes of face-plate to be available; screw-and-cup chucks or a good multi-chuck; a good steady for long spindles (very important); long hole-borer; drill chuck; various lengths and shapes of tool-rest; tool-holder with racking; and robust stand.
- The **most solid construction** will give stability and contribute towards quality turning; it's one of the principle deficiencies of my present equipment. I'm looking for a strong, double-girder (or similar) bed; massive head and tail stocks; substantial drive-spindle and robust bearings; large threads on drive-spindle and on tailstock quill; heavy stand; and heavy overall weight (this conflicts with easy transportability).
- The **easiest to set up and adjust** will speed up quantity output. I'm looking for free access to the tapers; big, clear levers on all adjustments (no knobs or recessed sockets); really easy speed changing; and very handy power switches.
- The **widest range of speeds** would best be met by an infinitely variable range from zero to 5000 revs!
- Assessing the **most powerful drive** is not easy. Some manufacturers rate their motors on short-term peaks, others on continuous running. That's why the 1¼hp motor on one lathe is more compact than somebody else's ¾hp. I want big power to deal with the peaks of a dig-in on rough old burr elm, and also enough there so that the machine doesn't fry after hours of continuous running.
- With **off-bed turning** I am looking at three things. First the facility to do even bigger work; secondly to turn in the standard anti-clockwise direction (all my tools are set for this); and thirdly I want to be able to set it up quickly and easily and not have permanent protrusions awkwardly positioned for big people. Equally I want off-bed to be at the side — I don't have room for end turning.
- **Proximity of back-up service**; ideally I would like there to be a number of agents and suppliers (in case one runs out) grouped all around my home. I'm also looking at the mark-up on spares and the availability of everything from a main casting to a single nut or bolt. Given that other things are at least al-most equal, I believe I should buy British; or at least EEC.
- **Price and value for money** are important and I'll spend as little as I have to to get the quality I require.
- The **best inclusive package** is partly

Which way to turn

concerned value for money, but also with general convenience.

● My final requirement is for a **good second-hand value.** It's nice to know that you are sitting on a marketable asset, and second-hand values are also a measure of how other people regard the machine, and the producer's permanence and reliability.

Weighting

Of course not all these requirements are of equal importance. I'd be prepared to trade off some in order to get more of others. So I've given each factor a weighting or relative value. Using a scale from 10 to one, I've given the most important 10 marks and judged the relative importance of each of the others against that. Here each of us is likely to have extreme variations in our requirements and personal weightings.

Fit for purpose

At last I am ready to get down to looking at individual lathes! I can judge how well a machine meets each of my requirements and how they compare. To work this out I've judged the relative fit of each machine against each of the listed requirements, using a similar 10 to one scale.

Finally I can multiply the 'fit' by the 'weight' to give me a score for each factor, and tot up these scores. This gives me a general idea of how well each machine meets my particular set of requirements.

Checking the result

The process is not completely risk-free, and once the chart is done, study the results carefully. Looking at the lathe that emerges as my initial choice there are some potential problems. The Multistar is a new machine and as yet relatively unproved. The company is small, there are few agents as yet and I would have to go to Colchester for spares. Some of these points could pose problems, but I decided none was overwhelming enough to stop me deciding that my initial choice was to be my final choice.

Going through the process taught me a few things. 'Hard' data isn't always readily available; sales literature is often all 'sizzle and smell' but no factual 'bacon'. I thought I knew most of the facts but found enormous holes in my detailed knowledge, and it was just these details that shaped my final judgement. Had the literature been better, or had I seen the machines at the show, my selection list might have included many more of the 57 lathes I know on the market. The exercise brought home to me just which facts really mattered in the context of what I ultimately wanted to achieve. I learnt the importance of establishing weightings for the requirements and I found myself confronted with fundamental choices such as: which is more important, price or performance, and what is the price of buying British?

Step-by-step guide to deciding which lathe

REQUIREMENTS	Wt	Kity 664	Ft	Sc	Graduate (s/h)	Ft
Biggest swing/length over bed	9	195mm dia. 1000mm long	5	45	12in 30in	3
Most solid construction/ rigidity	10	Fabricated steel alloy bed, lightish	3	30	Massive solid cast iron, big spindle, very rigid	10
Widest range of reasonably priced extras	7	Plates, screw, steady, copy, 3-jaw, rests, mod. prices	10	70	Many but higher prices; not everything	5
Easiest to set up/adjust, start and stop	8	Mix levers and knobs, rotary switch	4	32	Well angled rest, large levers, buttons, easy speed change, big TS wheel	9
Widest speed range	8	3-spd 750/3000, var. 650-3200	5	40	4-spd 425/2250, quick change	6
Most powerful drive	5	1hp mod. size	8	40	¾hp large	8
Best off-bed turning	9	None	0	0	End, clockwise, good rest, 18in	4
Back-up service	4	Some UK dealers	7	28	Few dealers	5
Maker or supplier	3	French	4	12	Heckmondwike	7
Portable	1	Lift as 1 unit 75kg	9	9	560lb lump	1
Lowest comp price (incl. stand/basics)	4	£542 package inc. VAT	10	40	£862 recond. inc. VAT	3
Best package of inclusions	6	Live, stand, 4 point, tool tray	8	48	2 plates, tray, stand, 2 rests, 2 centres	10
Good s/h value	2	Dubious	4	8	Highly sought	10
TOTAL OF SCORES (Wt x F for all categories)				402		

Not the 'best buy'

Finally, I must reiterate what I said at the start. The lathe that I have chosen is *my* choice, for my present circumstances. But as it was made rationally and on a considered basis, I am now committed.

There is no way that I would say that my choice is 'the best buy', only that it is right for me. If your interest is in spindles and small items, if you are more constrained by a limited 'hobby' budget, or if you want the lathe for a school, you may end up with a different machine. But my method still will work, and if you follow it you should find the machine that suits you. ■

We asked for the makers' comments:

Kity

It is most interesting to see how a potential customer views the market quite differently from those of us in the trade. Mr O'Neill appears to have the product comparison correct, but I must make a couple of points.

Kity offers a two year guarantee, and should a problem arise we normally exchange the complete machine for new, without charge.

We have about 180 dealers and agents in the UK, nearly 100 of whom stock more Kity machinery than any other make.

John Farrar

ford ML8	Ft	Sc	Konig	Ft	Sc	Multistar	Ft	Sc	Arundel K600	Ft	Sc	Tyme Avon	Ft	Sc
2in	4	36	16in / 39in	9	81	18in / 54in	10	90	9in / 36/48in	5	45	11in / 36/48in	7	63
d castings, steel bed, spindle,	6	60	Heavy castings, double sq. tube bed, big spindle, very rigid	9	90	Heavy fabricated (½in plate) spindle to choice, rigid	9	90	Mod. castings, 2 small dia. solid rods bed, very smooth	6	60	Mod. castings, 2 sq. sect. steel rods bed, smooth running	7	70
dy, 4-jaw, live, cup, bi, rests, prices	6	42	Rests, steady, copy, expensive	5	35	Steady, copy, many rests, vice, sander, plates, higher price	9	63	Rests, screw, chucks, plate, live, mod. prices	6	42	Rests, steady cup, 4-jaw, Jacobs, bowl, plates, live, least expensive	8	56
ll levers in en holes, ons to side, TS wheel	5	40	Big cam levers, close buttons, mod. wheel	10	80	Mod. levers, drive clutch, small TS wheel, close buttons	9	72	Small rods and clamp, front buttons (big) no swinging, mod. wheel	4	32	Mod. levers, handy buttons, easy change, mod. wheel	6	48
d 700/2850	5	40	5-spd 320/3000, var. also	9	72	5-spd 200/2850	10	80	7-spd 375/2200	8	64	4-spd 470/2200	5	40
mod.	7	35	¾hp mod.	7	35	1hp heavy rated	10	50	¾hp mod.	7	35	¾hp mod.	7	35
, 12in	3	27	Front, good rest, 24in	9	81	Front, floor rest, unlimited	10	90	Far end, strip, 22in	5	45	Front, 23in, fiddly rest	7	63
e, 1 local	8	32	1 UK agent only	3	12	UK mfr. No agents yet	3	12	Many across country	9	36	Very many dlrs, 1 very local	10	40
tingham	8	24	German	4	12	Colchester	10	30	Nottingham	8	24	Bristol	9	27
e 78, stand b + motor	8	8	3cwt lump	5	5	Car-boot units, ½hr to strip	6	6	Lift as 1 unit	10	10	Can lift as 2 units	10	10
package VAT	6	24	£971 package inc. VAT	2	8	£845 package inc. VAT	4	16	£598 package inc. VAT	8	32	£540 package inc. VAT	10	40
, plate, rests, motor)	4	24	Live, 4 prong, plate, divide	6	36	4 prong, live, rests, plate, indexing, tray	7	42	Everything is extra	0	0	Dead, rest, plate, 2 prong	3	18
lar	8	16	Probably good	6	12	Prob. reasonable	5	10	Reasonable	5	10	Popular	6	12
		408			559			651			435			522

Tyme

Mr O'Neill's write-up would be much more useful for the second- or third-time buyer with a clear idea of his/her requirements; a beginner would need different guidance, and is anyway unlikely to consider a £600-£1000 lathe.

This company is privileged that Mr O'Neill has considered our machine, selling at about £540 inc. VAT, alongside others costing close to £1000+VAT, but of course our machine isn't produced to compete with their performance.

I must point out that our company produces a range of lathes, not just one. On the Avon a 1hp motor is available. The motor unit is easily separated, so it lifts as two units.

R. T. Sealey

Arundel

The Arundel K600 uses a full box-construction iron casting, which I think it's unfair to describe as 'moderate' in comparison with light alloy.

Both the K600 and the smaller K450 have a wide range of alternative headstock spindle threads, so people can use existing accessories from their previous machines as well as those made by other manufacturers. This gives enormous choice, in contrast to the policy of making a unique spindle thread which compels the user to buy only that brand of accessory.

Assessment of drive simply on motor size, without considering questions of starting and running torque is far too simplistic. The actual drive-belt arrangement is also of great importance, the modern 'Poly-vee' drives on both the Arundel K600 and Tyme Avon lathes giving more efficient power transmission than the older V-belts or linked belt-drives.

Various accessory packages have been available, all of which have included a four-prong drive centre, a tail centre and a standard tool-rest.

I find it hard to understand how lathes like the Multistar and Konig, which have been on the market for barely 12 months, can be given 'probably good' second-hand values. I can't see how they can be given higher ratings than the Arundel or Myford lathes from companies going back 40 years and whose early models still command high second-hand prices.

Dr E. H. Thomas

745

746

Guild notes

Guild of **WOODWORKERS**

The Guild was set up by *Woodworker* to create a meeting ground for all those involved in working wood, whether professional, amateur, or enthusiastic beginner. Guild members get:

- Access to Guild courses and events
- Free publicity in *Woodworker*
- Specially arranged tool insurance at low rates
- 15% off Woodworker Show entry
- A free display area and meeting point at the Show
- 15% discount off *Woodworker* plans
- Inclusion in our register of members' skills and services

For details, please send an sae to the Guild of Woodworkers, 1 Golden Sq, London W1R 3AB.

GUILD COURSES

● Only Guild members are eligible to go on these courses. You must book in advance, and we must have a cheque for the full cost of the course at the time of booking. If you cancel less than four weeks before the advertised date you will forfeit 50% of the cost, unless there are exceptional circumstances.

Decorative techniques — Ian Hosker

6-7 September, 10-5, Chester, £45.
You read the articles, now do the course. Ian's feature, 'Coats of many colours' in the March and April issues covered wonderful decorative techniques such as dragging, lining, sponging, rag-rolling, marbling, spattering, and (his and our favourite) tortoise-shelling. The cost includes materials, but students should bring a few paint-brushes and jam-jars.

Hand veneering — Bob Grant

Bob's course has run into venue problems, so we have regretfully had to postpone it indefinitely. Please phone the office (01-437 0626) after 1 September for up-to-date information.

Selling space

Here's another possible outlet for your work. A new craft shop in Hitchin, Herts, is seeking local talent whose work can go on display and (you hope) sell.

Allcrafts (Hitchin) Ltd, run by Tim and Barbie Morris, sell craft items and materials. Their aim is to sell unique hand-crafted gifts and provide the means for people to develop a recreational interest in crafts and pastimes.

The couple are also building what they describe as 'a strong international collection of specialist craft books.'

If you live in the area, let us know whether this collection includes books of interest to woodworkers.

Time for a chat

If you are holidaying in Cornwall, Guild member **Duncan Askew** would be pleased to see you. Duncan is a woodturner, living at 31 Station Road, Newlyn East, Newquay, Cornwall. He invited fellow woodturners to call last year, and several turned up. Now he is re-issuing the invitation, so if you've got woodturning problems you need help with, or just fancy a chat with a fellow craftsman, drop in and see him.

Maybe next year other Guild members living in holiday areas would like to follow Duncan's example; drop us a line and we'll include a list in Guild notes.

Local meet?

George Netley, who lives in Purley, Surrey, wants to meet with other local users of the Kity K5 universal, with a view to getting the best out of these machines. So if you use a Kity K5, and live in South London, Croydon, Sutton or Bromley, drop a line to George at 19 Manor Way, Purley, Surrey.

French polishing — Charles Cliffe

2-3 October, 9.30-5, Bexleyheath, £40.
Charles Cliffe, one of our 'Question box' experts and author of *The Woodworker Manual of Finishing and Polishing*, explains preparation, staining, and application of this tricky (and beautiful) finish. He'll also be dealing with using a cabinet scraper, so bring your own, plus any small piece of furniture that you want advice on. Charles can order supplies for you to take away if you tell him in advance.

Wood-machining — Ken Taylor

11 October, 9.30-5.30, Bletchley, Bucks, £25+VAT.
Ken's course on the ins and outs of machining wood is one of our most popular. Find out about (and try for yourself) table- and band-saws, radial-arm saws, planers and thicknessers, spindle moulders, mortisers and universals. Lunch is included in the price.

Say 'cheese'

We love seeing photographs of your work, and we include as many as possible in *Woodworker*. But far too often they are not good enough to print. Here are a few remedies for common problems:

● **Wrong exposure** — photograph comes out too dark or too light. Frequently this happens because your light meter picks up a brighter background, so the subject is under-exposed. Remedy: hold the meter (or camera if it has a built-in meter) close to the part you want best exposed, and go by that reading.

● **Disturbing background** — other furniture, shadows, pools of sunlight, dramatic wallpaper ... Remedy: place your item against a plain background, and check by viewing through a rectangle (a cardboard cut-out or even your hands) to ensure that everything in the frame is what you want there.

● **Depth of field.** If you focus on the middle of a table, say, the front and back will not be in focus. Remedy: the smaller the aperture the greater the depth of field, so take shots at slower shutter-speeds with a small aperture. Lens markings should tell you what depth you have.

London gallery

Don't forget you have a chance to display your work at the **London Woodworker Show**, Alexandra Pavilion, 23-26 October. From August it operates on a first-come-first-served basis, so **send us photos of your work now!**

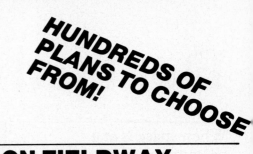

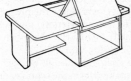
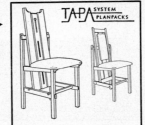
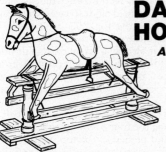

Doubled up

When space is at a premium dual-purpose units are the answer. Leslie Stuttle's ingenious desk converts into a dressing table

Living in a small bungalow, I am always looking for space-saving ideas. My wife wanted some library shelves on which to keep her books and I was looking for somewhere to do some paperwork without having to clear it all away after each session.

The obvious solution was to use our spare room — but how to do this when it was so small and would be needed on occasions for a short-stay visitor?

My idea was a desk unit which would easily convert into a dressing table. The basic idea consists of an 'open' stand with its own drawers, into which fits a reversible top surface which carries its own double-ended drawer sections. One way up, the top presents dressing-table drawers and a backboard; the other way, you get a higher flat surface with drawers below it.

For all large panels I used ¾in blockboard veneered both sides, with matching solid timber for the remainder and for edging strips.

Making the stand

Start by making the stand, followed by the top section and then the drawers. Cut and prepare to size all the pieces for the stand except the drawer-runners and guides and the shaped corner blocks.

Then cut the 1x⅞in shoulders on the top side rails before setting out all the mortises and tenons, being careful to mark the correct mortises on front and back legs.

The stub tenons on the short rails forming the bottom of the drawer openings shouldn't be more than ⅝in long, so their mortises don't run into those of the side rails; this avoids glue getting into them

● *As a dressing table, the piece already has a certain charm. The mirror stores in the space created when the top flips over*

when fitting the side rails and also stops side rail wedges wandering. Don't cut the middle back rail mortises too deep either, as the same applies.

When gauging mortises and tenons, note they are not all the same. Further, the bottom side rails and back rails are set in the middle of 1⅜in square legs, whereas the rails are only ¾in thick, so you must reset the gauge.

Gauge the middle back rail tenons from

its inside edge and the matching mortises from the inside of the legs as the rail is ³⁄₁₆in narrower than the legs to fit the plywood panel.

When you've completed setting out and doubled checked, cut the tenons and chop out the mortises. Check all joints fit and then try a dry run assembly.

To do this, fit the two centre rails into the front and back top rails, then the top and bottom side rails into the legs, followed by the middle and bottom back rails. You should now be able to stand the unit up so that the front and back top rails can be fitted on to the stub tenons on the legs.

Fit the two short rails which form the bottom of the drawer openings, then slip into place the two wide pieces which form the sides of the drawer carcases. These side pieces are ⁷⁄₁₆in shorter than the overall width of the frame to allow a ¼in strip to be glued to the front end to cover the endgrain and leave ³⁄₁₆in at the back for the ply panel. Test everything for squareness, and when you're satisfied dismantle. Number all joints to make gluing up easy.

Before you glue, cut enough wedges for all joints and make cuts in the tenon ends to accept the wedges. As you glue, check that each section is square.

Leave the short drawer-opening rails until the other joints have set and meanwhile cut the four corner-blocks from 1⅛in thick timber.

Now fit the short rails, drawer carcasing sides and the ¼in strips to cover the endgrain, followed by the corner-blocks. These blocks are glued and screwed but those fitted under the top rails can't easily be screwed to the side of the drawer carcasing as there is already a screw passing through the bottom rail into the side piece. A strong glue like Cascamite should do, or screw the blocks on by placing the two screws off centre.

Now clean up the whole job so far, before preparing the four ½x⅜in pieces which are glued and pinned to the top surface of the top rails with mitred corners and ⅛in overhang. Finish by fitting the drawer-runners and guides plus ½x½in softwood

● *In desk form, the top has flipped over and the drawers at the back become the drawers at the front!*

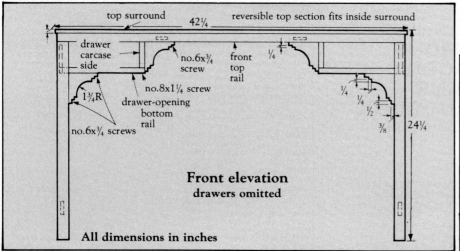

Front elevation
drawers omitted

All dimensions in inches

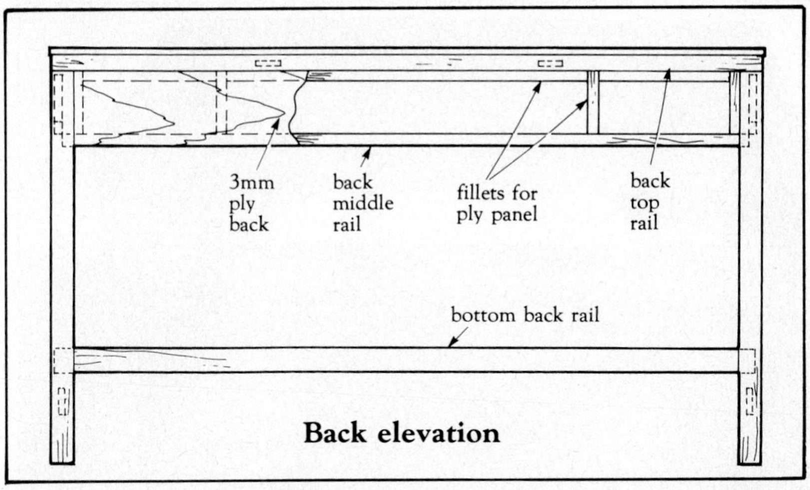

3mm
ply
back
back
middle
rail
fillets for
ply panel
back
top
rail
bottom back rail

Back elevation

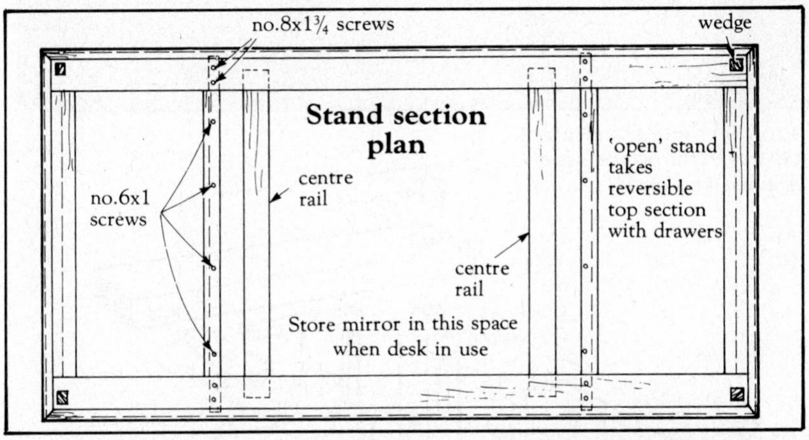

no.8x1¾ screws
wedge
no.6x1
screws
centre
rail
'open' stand
takes
reversible
top section
with drawers
centre
rail
Store mirror in this space
when desk in use

Stand section plan

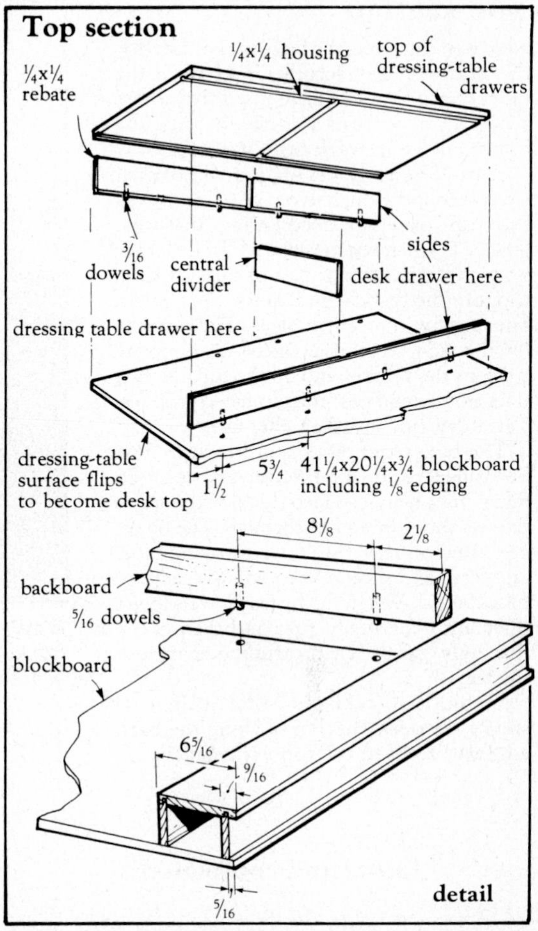

Top section
¼x¼ housing
top of
dressing-table
drawers
¼x¼
rebate
$\frac{3}{16}$
dowels
central
divider
sides
desk drawer here
dressing table drawer here
dressing-table
surface flips
to become desk top
1½
5¾
41¼x20¼x¾ blockboard
including ⅛ edging
8⅛
2⅛
backboard
$\frac{5}{16}$ dowels
blockboard
$6\frac{5}{16}$
$\frac{9}{16}$
$\frac{5}{16}$
detail

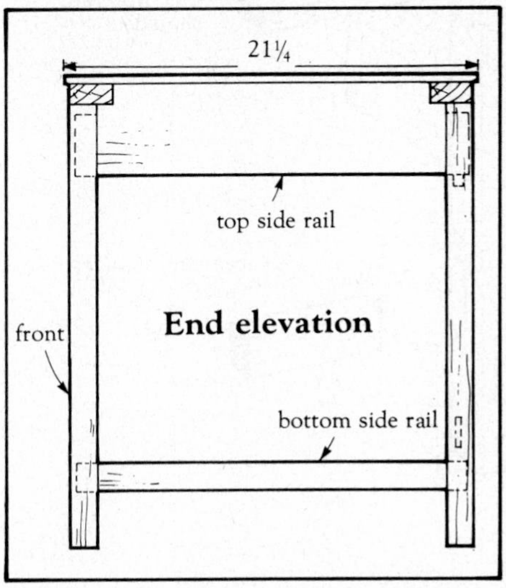

21¼
top side rail
front
bottom side rail

End elevation

Cutting list

Stand			
4 legs	23¾in x	1⅜in x	1⅜in
2 front and back top rails	42	2¼	1
2 top side rails	20½	4⅝	1
1 back middle rail	40½	$1\frac{3}{16}$	¾
1 back bottom rail	41¼	1½	¾
2 bottom side rails	20¼	1½	¾
2 drawer carcase sides	$20\frac{9}{16}$	3⅝	⅜
2 facing strips for above	3	⅝	¼
2 drawer-opening bottom rails	9⅝	1⅜	⅝
2 centre rails	18½	1½	½
4 corner-blocks	3½	3½	1⅛
4 drawer sides	20	3	½
2 drawer-fronts	8⅜	3	¾
2 drawer backs	8⅜	2⅜	⅜
4 drawer runners	18⅝	⅝	⅝
2 drawer side guides	18¼	1¾	⅜
2 drawer top guides	16¾	1	⅝
2 drawer top guides	16¾	1¼	⅝
2 top surrounds	42¼	½	⅜
2 top surrounds	21¼	½	⅜
Top section			
2 edging strips	41¼	¾	⅛
2 edging strips	20¼	¾	⅛
2 drawer carcase tops	20¼	$6\frac{5}{16}$	½
4 drawer carcase sides	20¼	2¼	½
2 drawer carcase central dividers	5½	2¼	¼
1 back board	28⅝	2½	1
4 drawer fronts	5	2	⅝
8 drawer sides	10	2	⅜
4 drawer backs	5	1⅝	¼
1 top	¾in blockboard to fit		

strips to the back legs and the underside of the back top rail. Cut and fit the 3mm ply panel.

Now carefully measure the opening formed by the ½x⅜in strips fitted to the top rails and cut a piece of blockboard to finish $\frac{5}{16}$in smaller. Glue and pin ⅛in edging strip all round it. Lay the board on the frame and check that it fits; there should be roughly $\frac{1}{32}$in clearance on all sides. If it looks good turn the board over, front to back, and provided everything is square it should still fit.

Doubled up

Top section

Now you can make the box-like sections for the drawers. Get accurate sizes from the blockboard top you have just fitted; these boxes must be dead accurate, because the drawers have to work both ways up!

Form ¼x¼in rebates on one edge of each side piece and plough two ¼x¼in grooves in the top panels, remembering that one groove is ¼in from the edge whilst the other is set in ⁹⁄₁₆in. Lay one pair of sides and one top on the bench and mark the ¼x¼in housing for the centre piece. The housing on the side pieces is worked on opposite sides to the rebates and on the top pieces it does not extend past the ploughed grooves. Try a dry run and then glue up.

The boxes and blockboard top can now be drilled ready for the dowels; don't go more than ⅝in deep into the blockboard as dowels shouldn't show through. The boxes are fitted so that the ⁵⁄₁₆in overhang faces outwards and should be in line with edge of blockboard. When fitting the dowels insert them into the boxes first and then check that only ⅝in is left protruding to fit into the top.

To finish off cut a piece of 2½x1in to fit snugly between the boxes along the back edge and fix it to the top with dowels.

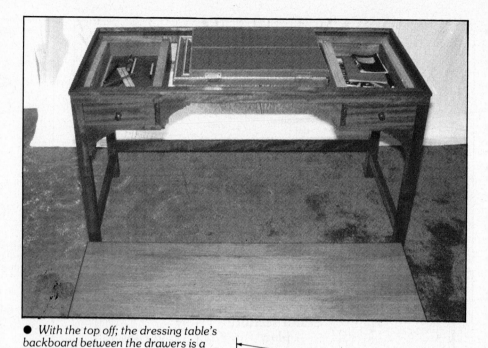

● *With the top off; the dressing table's backboard between the drawers is a 'frontboard' when it's a desk*

Stand — Joints and components

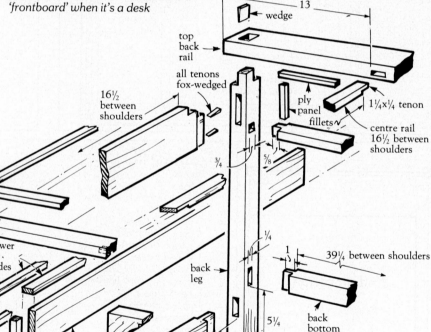

inches

Drawers

The last stage is to make and fit the six drawers. The two large drawers will require stops, whereas the small drawers can stop against the central divider, if their overall length is made to match the length of their respective carcases. You need four drawers 10x5x2in, and two of 20½x8⅜x3in.

After fitting drawer pulls of your choice

— I turned some small knobs with spigot ends, drilled the drawer fronts and glued the knobs in — the whole unit can be rubbed down and finished to your taste.

If you buy a free-standing winged mirror the job is complete. Remember when turning the top over to convert the function to remove the small drawers and put them back in the other way up! ■

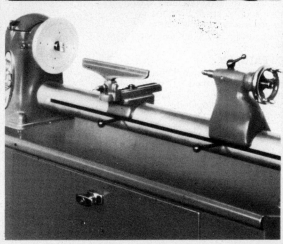

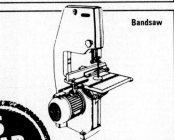
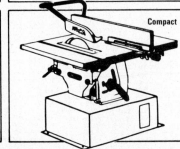

Tapering jigs

It's not as difficult as it sounds. Bob explains how to taper without tears

The taper job which commonly springs to mind is a stool or table leg. Basically it's a matter of removing rather a lot of wood with a plane or saw.

Planing by hand is slow, tedious and hard work. A surface planer is much quicker but has shortcomings, and the finish planing has to be done by hand anyway. Sawing may also be done by hand but again it's hard work and requires a sharp ripsaw.

The circular saw and a good bandsaw make light of this work. It's obviously better to remove the waste material as a piece of wood, rather than end up with a bucket of shavings. The finish is good and needs only light hand planing to clean up an already true surface.

You'll need a jig for machine-saw tapering. There's no standard size but it should be long enough to take a dining-table leg.

Except in certain reproduction work, legs are tapered on the inside only from below the joint, otherwise they end up somewhat pigeon-toed.

Saw the waste from the foot and mark the finished size on the end. Invert the jig and hold the leg in place (wood blocks may be needed for levelling). Measure the jig plus leg at the joint (A). Then adjust the stop so that the finish mark is level with jig plus leg thickness (B). Check this carefully before you start work.

Adjust the fence of the sawbench. Saw as close as possible to the finish line, leaving just enough to hand plane to a finish. Don't remove any guards. Use two push-sticks when approaching the end of the cut. Plan carefully which surface to cut first, so the true face or true edge is always on the table, otherwise the leg will rock on the first cut when making the second.

A convenient method of holding the leg for hand planing is in a sash-cramp fastened to the bench with two packing pieces. ∎

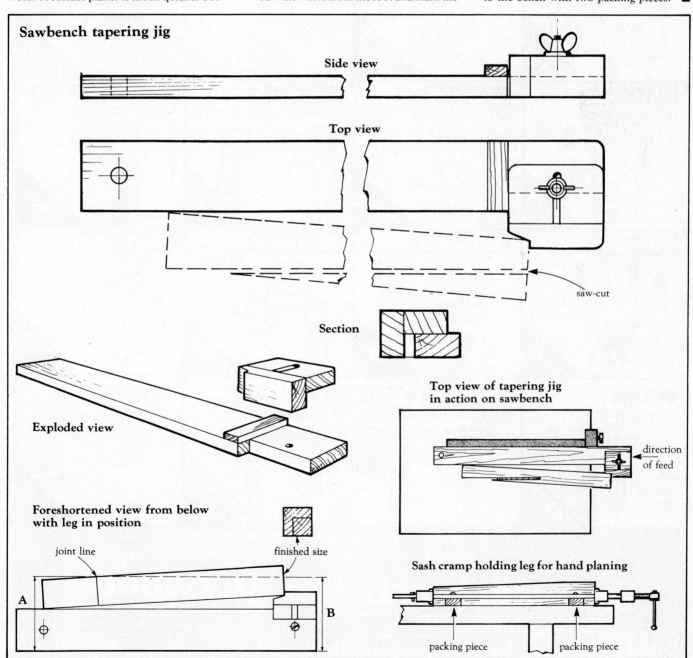

Sawbench tapering jig

Side view

Top view

saw-cut

Section

Exploded view

Top view of tapering jig in action on sawbench

direction of feed

Foreshortened view from below with leg in position

joint line

finished size

A

B

Sash cramp holding leg for hand planing

packing piece   packing piece

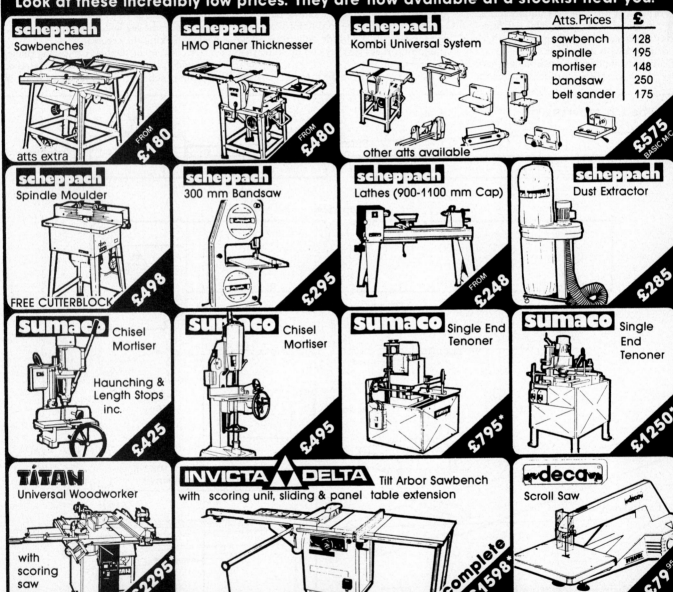
756

Tales out of steel

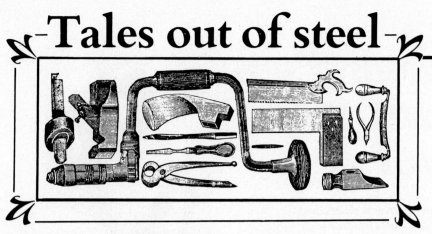

Hot metal and hard graft: Ashley Iles recalls the steel industry's heavyweights

The word 'blacksmith' has a mystique no-one can resist. It simply oozes job satisfaction, tapping primordial urges deep in our souls. Working metals was perhaps the earliest craft and still the war between the smith and the raw material continues. Steel resists being reformed and manipulated and only when it's hot can anything be done at all — as Napoleon said: 'Bring all the forces at your command to the point of attack'.

When I show people round the factory, I like to ask if anyone wants to have a go at forging. The resulting capers are unbelievable; one which really floored us was Ed Gallenstein, the editor of *Chip Chats*, holding the tongs with a red hot blade in the end with both hands at arms' length — 'What do I do now?' The idea of letting go with his right hand to pick up the hammer never occurred to him.

In the 50s, Sheffield forging was very involved and varied from tiny blades for pen-knives to huge crankshafts forged by a team of men on steam hammers. I met some highly skilled men.

Next door to me in Solly Street was the Empire Stamping Company run by Willis Weldon. Inside his long narrow shop was a row of drop stamps in different sizes. The drop stamp is usually associated with mass-production where even a boy can put down 3000 firmer chisels in a shift, but on certain classes of work it's very skilled.

A weight known as a 'tup' is lifted to the ceiling by an electric motor where it trips and falls giving a tremendous blow to the stamp. The size of stamp is determined by the weight of the tup; a 5cwt stamp has a 5cwt tup and every cwt of tup needs a ton of bed. The stamper puts a white hot piece of steel in the bottom die (the top is fixed under the tup) and pulls on a rope which connects the motor to the tup. Up goes the tup, trips and falls by gravity, producing a finished forging in one blow. Then the flash on the joint is cut off on a blanking press.

Not so in Willis' case. He confined himself to difficult work like holloware where he literally made the top die as he went along. If he was making 10in bowls in silver pewter or nickel silver, he'd fix the bottom die on the bed which was correct for the outside of the bowl and make the top die by fixing a large lump of lead under the tup, stamping it into the dovetails, and then start on, say, a hundred bowls from flat circular discs.

The lead lump was stamped into the bottom die a quarter of the depth, then the hundred were done and returned to the muffle furnace to normalise (relieve stresses) one by one. Next time round he would go a little deeper and after about four rounds the lead top die would be touching the bottom of the bottom die and the bowls were finished on the last round. Just going a little too deep, or applying too great a blow, would crack them and prove very costly.

The die-sinkers are worthy of acclaim. A die-sinker I know worked for a firm of hammer-makers. When they made him foreman he told his boss that he could make a pair of stamp dies to do *two* claw hammers at once. He did it — and it was a masterpiece — but something like having £5000 on an outsider to win.

Power hammers were very much in evidence but around the back of Snow Lane was what I christened 'Hell Fire Avenue', where Ridgways produced the blanks for Jennings pattern twist bits. Dozens and dozens of small power hammers rat-a-tatted all down the street.

When I moved from Sheffield to Lincolnshire I had a lot of trouble with a factory inspector over the noise of my hammers and sought the help of a Sheffield man very well informed on such matters and of considerable religious conviction.

He listened carefully to what I had to say then uttered the immortal words 'Tell him to **** off'. Men of stature are men of few words. And it worked!

Making steel go the way you want it to go is sometimes difficult. Take a brick bolster for instance. If the steel was just spread in the ordinary way, only half the width of the bolster blade would be obtained, and much would be lost in the length. The spreading is therefore done on a pair of dies with round faces which force the steel sideways only. Finishing follows on flat faces on the same pair of dies in the same heat. On chisels it is the reverse, drawing out the length without width but the same principle applies.

How were chisels and gouges made before we had mechanical forging machines? Everything was straightforward except for the bolster, that lump on the blade which stops it going into the handle. Before I got a power hammer to do bolstering (mooding), I employed Albert Shaw, an old-timer of 67 retired from Aaron Hildick. He was eight stone of manganese steel and between us we did mooding by hand. First a 'boss' or lump is made in the steel using a simple pair of prints (dies) on the anvil (fig. 1). Next comes the tricky bit where the boss is spread. This is done on a Nellie and is such hard work that the striker and smith have to interchange. As a young man of 28 it was all I could do to keep up with Albert.

The Nellie is fixed in the gate of the anvil and the forging (fig. 2), held by tongs, is rotated vertically in the smith's left hand. While it's revolving the smith holds a sett on a wire handle against the boss with his right hand. The striker working on the slant hits the sett repeatedly, spreading and flattening the boss to a bolster or finished mood (fig. 3). The striker gets a rest while the smith draws the tang to a point.

We are now using these methods to re-produce 17th century tools for the Williamsburg Foundation, Virginia. In fact all the techniques are now of historical interest — most forging today is a matter of progamming a computer! ∎

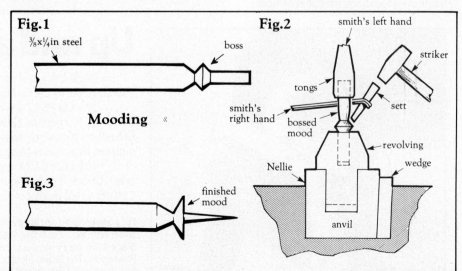

Fig.1 ³⁄₈x¹⁄₄in steel boss

Mooding

Fig.3 finished mood

Fig.2 smith's left hand · striker · tongs · smith's right hand · bossed mood · sett · revolving · Nellie · wedge · anvil

Precision sawing's a push–over with our new pull–over

The **Elu** PS174 Crosscut/Mitre Saw introduces an entirely new and unique approach to precision sawing. It is designed for bench or floor-level operation and will appeal to a wide spectrum of professional users — builders, shopfitters, flooring contractors, signmakers etc., in fact any operation where timber or plastics need to be cut with accuracy using an easily transportable machine.

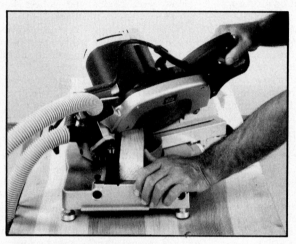

Down

The **Elu** PS174 will crosscut, mitre, bevel and cut combination mitres. On narrow workpieces, the machine is operated like a conventional mitre saw with the sawhead lowered straight down into the work and then allowed to spring-return to its upright position. The safety guard retracts only as far as is necessary to cut the material.

Across

Where the PS174 really comes into its own is on wider material, the telescoping arm giving the machine much wider cutting capacity than an ordinary mitre saw even having a much larger blade.

The whole design of the PS174 exudes quality. The extreme rigidity of its die-cast aluminium construction ensures accurate cutting of widths up to 250mm (174mm in 45° mitre setting) to a depth of 52mm (40mm in 45° bevel setting), which is ample capacity for most applications. Bevel and mitre angle adjustment is simple and quick with clear scales and the most common mitre angles have machined locations for convenience.

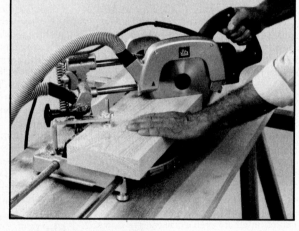

Up and away

Once the job is done, the PS174 weighs only 12.5kg and is therefore easily carried to the next job, even if it's up a ladder.

The **Elu** PS174 is available in both 115V and 220V AC, featuring a powerful 1200 watt low-noise universal motor. Dust extraction tubes are available as optional accessories, as are side support extensions to facilitate cutting of longer material.

The **Elu** PS174 is not like any other mitre saw you have ever seen. Check it out at your **Elu** dealer and see how it can make your cutting a real push-over.

The grand furniture saga: 8

The word 'Baroque' is sometimes used as a term of disparagement, applied to anything with extravagantly florid decoration. But in furniture history, it describes the arts of the 17th century in Europe generally and Italy in particular; the Baroque style had become accepted and established there by 1620.

The principal exponents were artists, sculptors, and architects such as Gianlorenzo Bernini (1598-1680), Francesco Borromini (1599-1667), and Pietro da Cortona (1596-1669); their ideas affected the work of masters like Andrea Brustolon (1662-1732), and Filippo Juvarra (1678-1736).

The Bourbon King Henri IV (1589-1610) was really the father of fine French furniture, as he sent many cabinetmakers to Italy and Flanders, and set up workshops in the Louvre where they could impart their skills to native French craftsmen on their return. In 1598 he granted the Edict of Nantes to give freedom of worship to the Huguenots (Protestants), many of whom were highly skilled craftsmen. This dispensation gave them security to work. During his short reign (he was assassinated in 1610) most French furniture was made in traditional Renaissance styles.

When his son Louis XIII (1610-1643) took over, sculptured decoration of the Italian Baroque style began to permeate French architecture and other arts. Much of this influence was down to his mother,

● An astonishing ebony and pietre dure cabinet, one of a pair made by Domenico Cucci for Louis XIV about 1683. They are now in Alnwick Castle

Photo George Skipper

● An armoire-à-deux-corps in walnut, late 16th century

Maria de' Medici, who dominated the French court until he came of age. She was born in Florence but greatly favoured Flemish art and decoration and encouraged Flemish craftsmen to settle in France.

To curry favour and gain political support she gave away titles and money freely, creating a *nouveau riche* who indulged themselves by building châteaux and houses in the grand manner, with furniture to match. Some pieces were imported from the Netherlands and Italy, but much was made in France and gave a welcome fillip to native craftsmen. To her credit she recalled a French craftsman, Jean Mace, from the Netherlands: he brought with him the art of veneering, practising his skills in the Louvre workshops and becoming the Court cabinetmaker until his death in 1672.

Two other important influences on French furniture styles during the early 17th century were Anne of Austria, who had a liking for Italian culture, and became Louis XIII's queen, and Cardinal Richelieu, an enthusiastic patron of native French arts and the leading minister to Louis.

When Richelieu died in 1642 he was succeeded by Italian-born Jules Mazarin (1602-1661). Louis died in 1643, and though Anne was the nominal ruler, Mazarin really wielded the power. He attacked feudalism, destroying the power of the nobles and demolishing their castles. At the same time he amassed a large collection of works of art and magnificent furniture, including tables with *pietre dure* tops from Italy, and cabinets-on-stands from the Netherlands. He also persuaded Domenico Cucci (1635-1704), the talented Italian cabinetmaker, to work in France.

Mazarin's name was later given to a type of writing table with two pedestals, each with three drawers and on four legs; the pedestals are linked with a central kneehole section and a flat top overall. This style has been known as the *bureau Mazarin* since the 19th century but the first examples appeared only after his death.

Initially the French only used veneering on prestige pieces like their favourite cabinets-on-stands, which had elaborately

759

The grand furniture saga: 8

● *A* walnut *bureau Mazarin, produced after the death of the Cardinal-statesman*

fitted interiors and turned or twisted legs; these became popular throughout Europe and Britain. The idea is supposed to be based on the original twisted columns designed by Bernini to support the *baldachino* (the canopy over the altar) in St Peter's in Rome.

Strangely for a nation which insists on elegance in dining and wining, the French had a tradition of eating at plain, simple tables covered with a tablecloth. This changed during the first half of the 17th century when small rectangular tables appeared which could be used for meals, as writing tables, or to display ornaments. They usually had turned or twisted legs and an underframe, and the frieze rails (top frame rails) were shaped and carved — some examples had the overlapping corners of a tablecloth carved in low relief on the frieze rails!

Frequently these tables had matching backstools (*chaises lorraines*) which were basically stools with the back legs extended upwards and joined with horizontal rails — the back legs were straight, not raked.

At this time furniture began to be made *en suite*, particularly seating. Armchairs had low, square backs upholstered to match the generously-padded seats, the arms assumed voluptuous curves, while the legs were turned or twisted. Thus, the emphasis shifted from chairs as status symbols for important people to chairs that would provide luxury and comfort.

The *armoire-à-deux-corps*, or two-part cabinet which was a French favourite, was also changing. Originally an upper cabinet stood on a lower larger one, both with doors; sometimes the lower section had a row of drawers above the cupboards. Now it developed into a full-length *armoire* or cupboard, like a modern wardrobe; but traditional motifs were used and the early pieces retained the appearance of four small doors, by dividing each door into two panels with a rail. The decoration of wide, heavy mouldings was arranged in diamond, lozenge, or octagonal shapes enclosing a central panel. A new feature was split turning used as ornament, applied lavishly to the vertical stiles or corner posts.

During the same period the *commode* or chest of drawers became popular, superseding the old-style *coffre* or lidded chest.

They were usually partly or wholly veneered and again split turnings were a feature. This convenient piece of furniture was made in large numbers and many survive today in French homes.

In the Netherlands, long and bitter struggles against the Spanish occupying forces resulted in a split between the cultures of north and south. In the north the Protestant doctrines led to restrained and almost austere styles, while in the Catholic south, designs became Italianate, extravagant, and self-indulgent.

One of the most imposing northern designs was the *beeldenkast* (literally figure-cupboard), named from the ornamental carved figures. This superseded the lidded chest which had been the favoured form of storage. The *beeldenkast* was usually made in two sections; an upper, shorter one on a lower, longer one. Dignified by good proportion, well thought-out cornices and geometrically arranged mouldings, the design had figures from contemporary engravings on the panels or the main structural members. Inlays sometimes replaced the mouldings, showing architectural scenes in perspective, and parquetry was skilfully used to represent tiled floors or pavements. These cabinets were popular in Holland and particularly around Middelburg on the island of Walcheren, a well-known centre for furniture manufacture at that time.

The south produced a kind of press-cupboard which was treated in a more sculptural fashion. The upper section was recessed, and its top frieze rail was supported by demi-caryatids or full female figures at the front corners; there were either scrolled brackets (consoles) or more figures at the ends of the cupboards or between the doors. The door panels themselves were frequently embellished with pictorial inlays.

Another cabinet widely used in the south was in one stage only, making it a convenient height as a sideboard. The corner

posts and the dividing stile between the doors often had free-standing massive turned columns with heavy rings standing in front of them. These columns had heavy bases which stood on plinths, and the whole design reflected classical architecture.; incongruous were the heavy 'bun' feet — a feature which the Netherlands craftsmen had borrowed from Spain and Portugal and which was also adopted by the English.

Antwerp was the southern centre for furniture design and construction and was well known for its luxurious cabinets-on-stands. They usually comprised matching sets of drawers, one above the other, flanking a central compartment enclosed by two doors; the stand could have various types of legs — columnar, turned spindle, or twisted. Their chief glory was the drawer-fronts and cabinet doors; these were often lavishly veneered with ebony or tortoiseshell backed with metal foil, or painted with exquisitely detailed allegorical or religious scenes. These beautiful pieces were exported all over Europe and to England (the Dutch East India Company had started in 1602, and Dutch craftsmen were dazzled by exotic veneers, silver, tortoiseshell and ivory imported from the East).

As in France, chairs became increasingly more comfortable, and one armchair in particular became the prototype of a style widely popular in England during Charles II's reign (below). The ordinary side chair had many local variations, the one in the other illustration having a double box-underframe.

Perhaps the most significant innovation was the introduction of split cane and cane work from China, and this was seized on eagerly for caning the seats and backs of chairs and settees.

In the next article we will see what was going on in England at this time, and why the Baroque style passed us by; and examine the impact of exotic materials from India and China on the embellishment of late 17th century furniture. ■

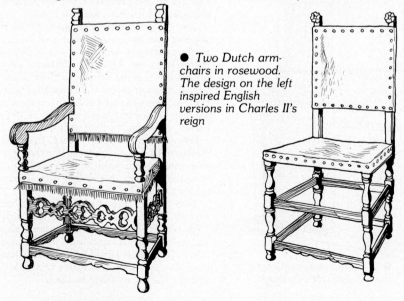

● *Two Dutch armchairs in rosewood. The design on the left inspired English versions in Charles II's reign*

Sit and spin

Old-time spinning chairs inspired Arthur Wood to make a nursing and children's back-stool in the same style. You don't even need a wheel!

Textile museums often display the furniture associated with weaving and spinning, and one often can see spinning stools or chairs which needed to fulfil the same basic requirements as a modern 'nursing chair' — that is, they have to be low, preferably with a good back-rest, and no arms to restrict the elbow movement that goes as much with spinning as it does with changing a nappy!

I was inspired to make a chair/stool along the same lines, which could as well serve its original purpose as be merely ornamental — or be very useful as a nursing chair, the application I had in mind.

Instead of splayed legs — usually four, but some had only three — I decided to use two solid sides which would accommodate a small drawer under the seat. The plan was that it would hold creams, safety-pins and other baby paraphernalia, all in one place and in easy reach. For a spinner, of course, bobbins, yarn and untwisted wool would go very well in the drawer.

Materials

In England, I suppose the traditional timber would be elm or oak. I had neither available, but I did have a piece of imbuia which suited admirably, because of the oil content and the dark attractive grain. The whole chair took no more than a 7ft length of 12x1in plus another 42in of 2x1¼in for the two bottom rails and the cleat under the seat to support the back. Another small item was a 10in square of ³⁄₁₆in plywood for the drawer bottom.

Construction

The back

The spinning stool is little more than a stool with a backrest, and the fitting of this 'splat' needed a bit of thought. If it was to be mortised through near the back of seat, support would have to be added to strengthen the short endgrain. The chair, remember, was designed for regular use as well as ornamental value, although it was to follow the traditional pattern. The grain of the seat would run from front to back, which was why I had the problem of short grain behind the backrest.

I cut the long mortise (see the seat plan, fig. 2), then glued and screwed a shaped cleat on top of the seat which would give additional support to the other angled cleat fixed underneath (side elevation, fig. 1). 80° seemed about right, so I bevelled the mortise to this angle. The overall length of

the backrest is 24in, cut as shown in the side and front elevations, fig. 1. The dimensions for the hand-grip and the other decorative cut-out (I jigsawed them) are of course entirely a matter of preference. I tried to follow a sort of general 'Tudor/ Gothic' style.

The seat

To give a bit of extra width, one of the off-cuts from the backrest was jointed to one edge of a 12in board, and I inserted a loose tongue for better glue-hold and more strength.

The sides

As you can see from fig. 1, these were shaped to take some of the weight away and give a more pleasing appearance. I had to bear in mind I might be dismantling the whole thing and transporting it to England, so the sides weren't mortised but screwed from the inside into cleats fixed under the seat. This proved perfectly adequate, but to give added stability and stop any danger of spreading at the bottom, I fit two rails front and back, two 16in lengths of 1x1¾in finished. My original plan of tusk tenons and wedges was abandoned because they would have projected too far at the sides. I cut a ¼in shoulder all round instead, giving a 1¼x½in tenon. With the rails wedged and glued, the weight and 'weft' are where they need to be — a low centre of gravity rules out any possibility of the chair toppling. The shoulders were bevelled both vertically and horizontally.

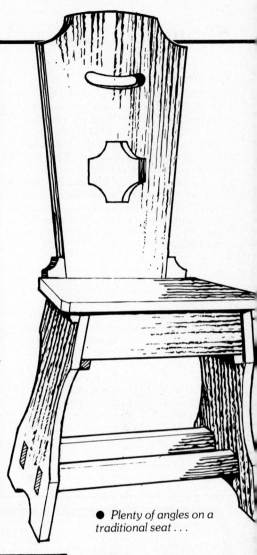

● *Plenty of angles on a traditional seat . . .*

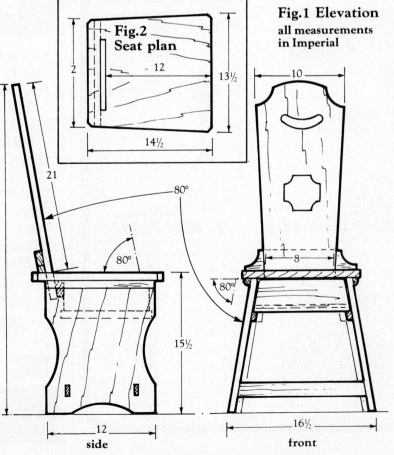

Fig.2 Seat plan

2   12   13½   14½

Fig.1 Elevation
all measurements in Imperial

21   80°   80°   10   80°   8   15½   12   side   16½   front

Sit and spin

The drawer

This involved quite a lot of work because it's bevelled in two ways. It's splayed to the same angle as the sides, and it's also narrower at the back than at the front. If you don't fancy having to hold the drawer up each time you open it, you can simply run the sides parallel back to front (dotted lines, fig. 3). Either way would be suitable, but you'd have to make wedge-shaped long inserts to bring the insides of the seat cavity parallel. Another time I would simplify the drawer, but at the time it offered something of a challenge.

Finish

Two or three applications of beeswax softened in mineral turpentine was all that was needed to give a simple matt finish which suits the original period feel. Imbuia already has a soft oily texture, and it's extremely pleasing to use; the natural grain is all that needs to be brought out.

The chair sat next to the front door in the hall for some years before we moved, and came in for a lot of regular use. It looks and is robust, and where children are concerned, furniture has to do more than just look robust! We'll be using it for many years to come. ∎

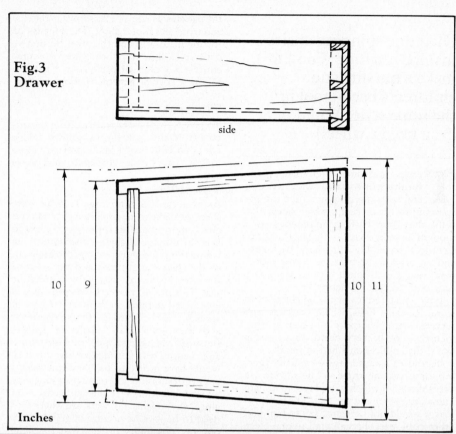

Fig.3
Drawer

side

Inches

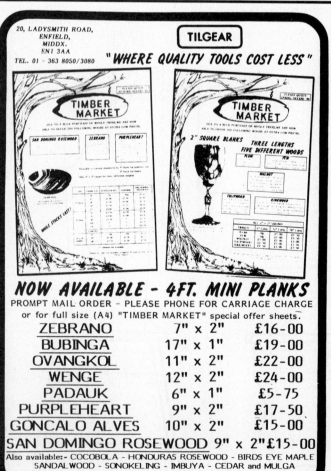

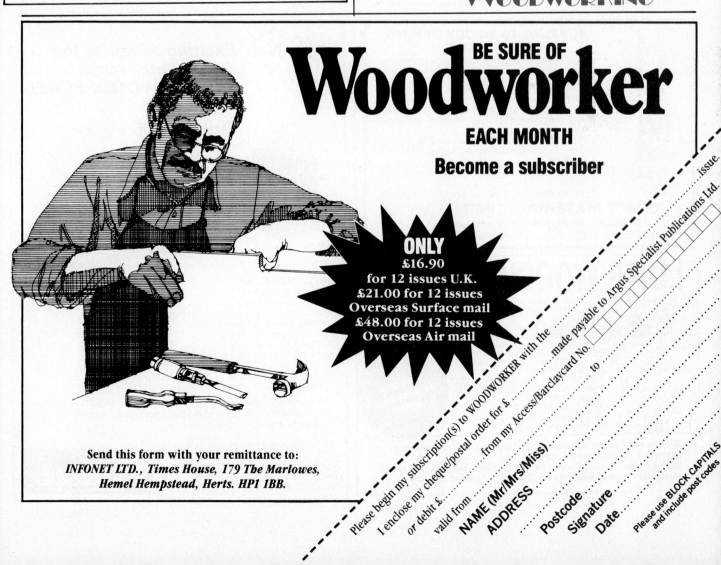

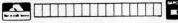

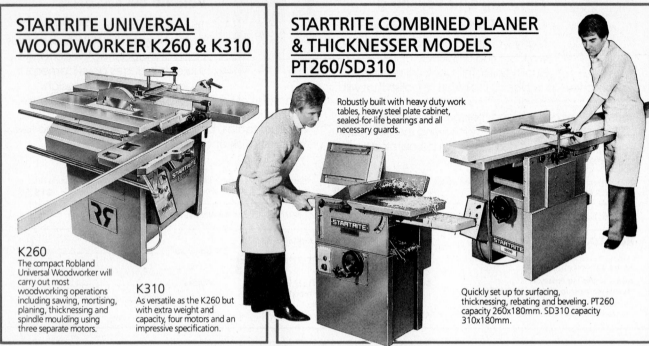

Question box

Our panel of experts solve your woodworking problems

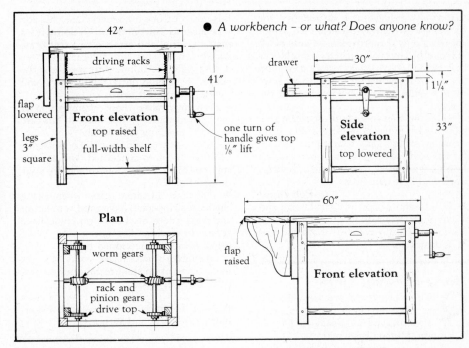

● A workbench – or what? Does anyone know?

driving racks — 42″

41″

flap lowered

legs 3″ square

Front elevation top raised full-width shelf

one turn of handle gives top ⅛″ lift

drawer — 30″ — 1¼″

Side elevation top lowered

33″

Plan

worm gears

rack and pinion gears drive top

60″

flap raised

Front elevation

Curiosity piece

Q *I have an unusual workbench and would like to know its original purpose. It was shown in a recent Byegones programme on Anglia TV but no-one could give me an answer.*

Friends have suggested it might be a veterinary operating table or a coffin-maker's bench but I would like a definitive answer.

P. Crome, Kirby-le-Soken

A I'm afraid I don't know what your bench is, and a search through a number of books and manufacturers' catalogues — German, French, Scandinavian and American, as well as British — has failed to reveal anything resembling it.

However I'm inclined to query the description of it as a workbench. I feel it's unlikely to have been intended for any regular woodworking trade. I'd prefer to call it simply an extending table with top adjustable for height.

Benches for most woodworking trades need something to hold the work — a vice, a hole through the top for a holdfast or carver's screw, or at least a stop of some kind to plane against. Also, for a professional job, as this undoubtedly appears to be, the top is too thin at only 1¼in.

Close inspection might yield some further clues. Does the top surface show any scoring, cuts, indentations, or other wear? Does any dust, smell or stain suggest what was kept in the partitioned drawer?

I will hazard a guess, mainly influenced by the finely geared, four-track elevating mechanism. This suggests to me some instrument which needed to be accurately adjusted for height whilst being kept horizontal — like a laboratory, perhaps, or the old type of slide-projector?

Philip Walker

● Philip Walker is former secretary of the Tool and Trades History Society.

● If anyone has any ideas about this, please write to us at the address above, or the Tool and Trades History Society, 275 Sandridge Lane, Bromham, Wilts SN15 2JW.

Bowling woods

Q *Can you tell me how to grain fill and polish bowling woods?*

J. Hitchen, Wigan

A I've never made bowling woods but would suggest a two-part clear epoxy such as Humbrol which remains just flexible enough to allow wood movement, and can be coloured to suit with 10% by volume dust, sanded from an offcut.

Grain filling wouldn't be necessary and polishing for all outdoor sporting woodware is by successive coats of boiled linseed oil. Three liberal coats should be applied; store in warm, dry conditions for a week between each application, then give it occasional rubs with an oily rag (linseed).

Tobias Kaye

● Tobias Kaye is a professional wood-turner.

Seasoning yew

Q *I have a freshly cut yew tree trunk (10in diameter) which I hope to use for foot-stool components. How should I season it?*

G. N. Mackie, Solihull

A Yew is one of those timbers which season very easily and I've often been able to use pieces successfully which would still be considered unseasoned in other species.

Small pieces of yew can be used in the round, but a piece 10in diameter will need breaking down if it is ever to dry. I suggest you make a breaking cut through the centre using a chainsaw, and cutting horizontally through the log, rather than vertically.

You can then either store the resulting two halves in a cool airy place for a couple of years, or convert them further using your

sawbench. With unseasoned timber any storage must be out of extremes of temperature, and particularly out of the sun.

Alan Holtham

● Alan Holtham is the proprietor of The Old Stores Turnery and an experienced woodturner.

Swivels and plinths

Q *I'm making a revolving bookcase as a project which requires a swivel between the base and the carcase, described as 'a 12.5mm-deep Lazy Susan'. Can you enlighten me on this type of swivel and its manufacturer?*

Also I have a problem of gluing mitred points on a walnut plinth. These blocks break very easily on the horizontal gluing line when pulled together with G-clamps. What do you suggest?

S. Collier, Rugby

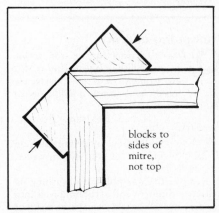

blocks to sides of mitre, not top

A variety of swivel turntable units suitable for your purpose can be obtained from Woodfit of Whittle Low Mill, Chorley, Lancs. PR6 7HB. I recommend that you obtain their catalogue.

Now to your second problem. Unfortunately you don't give the size of the materials that you're using, but I suspect that the blocks are giving way because there is not enough gluing area provided between block and plinth. Thus you might try using blocks that have a much larger surface area. You could also try gluing the blocks to the sides of the members to be joined as shown in the sketch.

Failing all this you could use alternative techniques: mitre cramps; flexible band cramps; string and tourniquet cramp. Details of these are given in Bob Wearing's book *Woodwork Aids and Devices*, published by Evans Bros.

Bob Grant

● Bob Grant is head of Craft Design and Technology at an Oxford comprehensive school and teaches courses for the Guild of Woodworkers.

Horse-chestnut burrs

Q *I have a quantity of large horse-chestnut burrs. Does this timber have any use apart from firewood and would it be possible to wet-turn it before seasoning?*

George Clarke, Swansea

A The horse chestnut is a fine ornamental tree but the qualities of its timber are not sufficiently good for it ever to have taken a major place in the timber market.

It was previously used for brushes and kitchen and dairy utensils — now superseded by plastic. This pale wood can easily become discoloured by sap-staining fungi before it has dried. Since it machines and turns easily you could turn roughly shaped blanks while it is still green, allowing a generous margin for distortion, and turn the final shape when thoroughly seasoned. In this way you could reduce the risks of both staining and cracking during the drying process.

Michael White

● Michael White is a consultant on timber and a former Scientific Officer at the Forest Products Research Laboratory

Removing acrylic

Q *I covered a relief carving with acrylic paint and polished it with Briwax. It's now too dark. How can I remove the wax and acrylic and achieve a light-coloured finish?*

S. Readman, Cleveland

A You couldn't have made the situation more difficult for yourself. However, try the following:

1 Remove the wax polish by brushing on cellulose thinners and scrubbing well into the carving with an old clean paint brush or toothbrush until all traces of wax have gone. Wipe down with absorbent paper or cloth. Cellulose thinners are more effective than white spirit for removing wax.
2 Use a chemical paint stripper to remove the acrylic finish — in this case, one which contains ammonia such as Polystripper. If

this doesn't work try a methylene chloride type such as Nitromors or Cyclone. It's a matter of trial and error. Use a soft brass wire brush to work into the carving.
3 Use cellulose thinners to wash out the gunge, scrubbing into the corners and cavities with a soft brush.
4 Now neutralise these chemicals with methylated spirits — not water in this case as severe cracking may occur.
5 Again, it's trial and error as far as a light-coloured finish is concerned. Use as little stain/pigment as possible to achieve your desired finish.
● Do take adequate care when using chemical strippers to have good ventilation and wear a face mask, or you could have severe headaches. Do not smoke while using the above-mentioned fluids.

To avoid a situation like yours, it's best to try out your finishing technique first on a spare piece of wood.

Noel Leach

● Noel Leach is a professional wood-finisher, lecturer and author.

Ash and beech seasoning

Q *Can you advise on how to season beech and ash logs? I haven't cut the trees yet and have noticed some boring-powder seeping from them. Will this affect the timber?*

P. Jones, Swansea

A When a log dries out it shrinks round its circumference twice as much as it shrinks radially, which causes distortion and cracking. This means that something has to give — either the cells in the middle compress, or the cells around the periphery stretch or, more frequently, the wood splits radially when the tension becomes too great. So never try to dry branch-wood in the round unless absolutely necessary, and then be prepared for high losses. Better to halve the logs longitudinally.

Remove the bark and this will get rid of the insect attack, which is almost certainly some form of bark beetle. Stack the billets well off the ground and separate each layer with softwood stickers. Protect from sun and rain by making a roof of corrugated sheets with a generous overhang.

Michael White

Stain removal

Q *I stained some oak gates with potassium permanganate and finished with linseed oil. After wet weather they've become badly streaked and stained. I tried a high-pressure hose which worked to some extent. How can I remove the stain and what action should I take for future projects?*

R. Kelley, Carlisle

A Although permanganate of potash is sometimes advised for staining oak, and occasionally mahogany, it is not a stain I would ever recommend. It does not give a particularly attractive colour and it fades

markedly. Apart from cheapness there is nothing in its favour.

Linseed oil brings out the beauty of the grain of oak furniture and repeated applications will produce a durable and attractive sheen but a linseed oil finish is not suitable for work which is to be exposed to the weather.

The first thing is to get rid of the black stains. The fact that a high-pressure hose has removed some of the marks suggests that they are not deep seated and can probably be removed by using no. 1 wire wool dipped in white spirit. When the gates have been cleaned they can be glasspapered smooth and stained. A good water-stain for oak can be made by dissolving 2oz bichromate of potash in a pint of water. This is a chemical stain which acts on the tannic acid in the oak and needs daylight and a free circulation of air for the chemical action to take place. It's available from polish suppliers or possibly your local chemist. Bichromate of potash is a poison so use it carefully and wear rubber gloves.

After the stain has dried on the gates you can use an oil varnish but even better for oak gates and window sills exposed to severe weather conditions is Sadolin. Most builders' merchants stock it.

Charles Cliffe

● Charles Cliffe is a professional polisher, author and teacher.

Finishing notice-boards

Q *I've made a church notice-board of 1in Jap oak which has a removable panel with routed-out relief lettering.*

I intended to finish it with 2-pack poly-urethane but I'm unsure about using this on the routed-out areas. What do you advise?

The fastenings, incidentally, are brass and bronze.

R. J. Phillips, Luton

A For maximum durability the board should have at least three coats of yacht varnish (this applies to house-name boards too). Even if the board is being fixed to another board, its back should be given at least one coat of varnish so that the wood is completely sealed. The absorption of moisture makes it contract and swell as the moisture content changes; it then cracks and lets in more moisture, causing the varnish to flake or peel from the surface.

Danish Oil will leave the wood, particularly oak, with a natural low lustre. As oil does not leave a thick surface film, it should be re-oiled at least twice a year. This would still be easier than varnishing.

Exterior matt black would be satisfactory for blacking in the letters. The bronze and brass fastenings could be treated with Rustin's transparent lacquer, based on a polymethacrylic ester, rather than cellulose lacquer. This will prevent tarnishing and won't discolour or craze on ageing.

Ronald Rustin

● Ronald Rustin is the director of Rustin's.

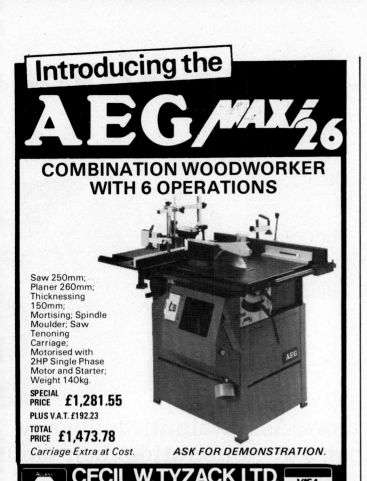

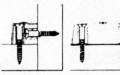

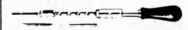

Where Craft Comes Alive...

Beautiful wood... Oak, Sycamore, Ash, Walnut, Mahogany
Versatile wood... see the experts demonstrating their skills
Wonderful wood... admire the competition entries –
from marquetry to cabinet making
LOOK... at the latest woodworking machinery,
tools, supplies and accessories
LISTEN... to the advice of the demonstrators
BUY... from the many exhibition stands

The LONDON Woodworker Show '86

October 23rd – 26th at the
Alexandra Pavilion,
Wood Green, London

For further details contact
Argus Specialist Exhibitions,
Wolsey House, Wolsey Road,
Hemel Hempstead, Herts HP2 4SS
Tel: 0442 41221

Opening Times:
Oct. 23, 24, 25 ..... 10am-6pm
Oct. 26 .... 10am-5pm

French lesson: 1

What's woodworking all about in la belle France? Our cross-channel neighbours have long traditions of proud craftsmanship and fine furniture — but how do they go about their daily work? We visit a clogmaker and a barrelmaker, still practising their rural crafts, look at a one-man furniture business, and view the role of the designer/craftsman — plus a bit of history!

Demand in France for clogs and barrels isn't what it was, but it's still very much alive. Marie-Laure de Montesquieu went visiting

The clogmaker

A honey-gold light bathes the clog workshop; the perfume of freshly worked wood and tannin hangs heavy in the air, and wood shavings form a soft carpet under the feet.

This is the workplace of M. Riboulet, sole surviving clogmaker in the little village of St Clement, set in the mountainous Bourbonnais region of central France.

Bourbonnais, to the north of the Massif Central, has an air of untamed wilderness to this day. Pride of the region is the Tronçais forest, 10,000 hectares of mature oak trees and shady clearings, their beauty reflected in small lakes. Timber from the forest was used in the 17th century to build sailing ships for the French navy, and today it is first choice for many crafts.

The wealth of oak and other deciduous timbers growing in the area has made it a natural home for crafts down the centuries.

One of these is clogmaking. Wooden shoes are very practical footwear, particularly when snow lays or you have to walk through sticky clay — both common features of this area. Wood, of course, is one of the best insulators.

Wooden footwear goes back to Roman times, but over the centuries came to be 'peasant-ware', except for a brief spell after World War II; leather was scarce then and clogs experienced a short-lived revival of popularity.

During the 18th century clogmakers worked in the woods, in temporary cabins made from tree branches and leaves. But about 100 years ago they drifted nearer villages in order to market their crafts more easily. At about that time a clogmakers' guild was formed, a forerunner of today's trades unions.

Local trees are still used, cut down in the autumn when leaves begin to turn (a traditional season for felling), and their bark stripped off. The trunks are cut into one-metre lengths, and each block is then sawn into four pieces.

The wood is worked while it is still fairly

● Sabotier *(clogmaker) M. Riboulet at his automatic equipment – the reluctant machinist*

moist, with final drying-out before or after rough-shaping according to the condition of the wood.

M. Riboulet chooses his wood carefully, frequently using elm, willow or silver birch, all of which are light and not fibrous. He used to love working with elm, but Dutch elm disease has decimated stocks and pushed prices up. So now he uses beech for preference.

A skilled clogmaker can produce four pairs a day, without any mechanical aid. Since the 1920s machines of various kinds have allowed faster production, but M. Riboulet still prefers the traditional handwork that he has practised for 60 years, as his father and grandfather did before.

M. Riboulet also sticks to the traditional measuring device — the thumb. A continental size 45 clog for a tall strong-built man is equivalent to 10 thumb lengths.

Trimming the wood

M. Riboulet rests the block of beech on a larger log and swiftly shapes it roughly with a small trimming axe, locally called *épaule de mouton* or *hache à bucher*. This has a hooked blade and short sleeve with a rounded end; it weighs about two kilograms so it is not easy to manipulate.

Handling the axe deftly, M. Riboulet trims the wood with 16 to 18 chops, giving it the rough shape of the clog. He makes a notch for the heel and then marks the clog's outline on the wood before closer shaping.

● Parage – *odd numbers of paring strokes only!*

Shaping (*parage*)

The paring tool is a long sabre-like knife, with a hook which is attached to a point on the working surface, usually a bench. With a few strokes the outside of the clog is refined.

One of the many rituals of clogmaking demands that in paring an uneven number of strokes must be used — 13 for large clogs, 11 for smaller ones. Never 12, for that would destroy the lovely shape!

Precision is all important here. M. Riboulet sizes, pares and files, with never a sloppy stroke. Occasionally he puts down the parer to cast a keen eye at the clog to ensure the shape is perfect in every detail.

A special kind of parer, the 'heeler' is used for finishing the heel's exterior.

Hollowing

Gouges, augers and special *cuillers* are used to hollow out the clog. These last are spoon-like tools, round metal gouges with wooden T-bar handles so they can twist easily. They come in all shapes and sizes.

Spindle augers start the hollowing, with the spoon gouges removing the bulk of the wood. Curved gouges called *ruines* or

● *Hollowing by hand with a* cuiller

roannes are used for finishing, removing any rough points and leaving a polished finish.

During the hollowing process the clogs are held tightly in a notch in the middle of the workbench, with a clamp to hold them in place.

Decoration

Grooves, notches and ornaments are cut into the surface, using gouges and serrated or embossed cutting wheels. Then the wood may be stained with a dark natural juice — such as bilberry — or painted. The clogs may also be waxed, smoked or varnished, and sometimes a leather strap is attached to secure the clog to the foot.

Sizes of clog were traditionally measured by the quarter-thumb, and the clogs were sold wholesale by the dozen. However, the number of pairs in a dozen varied enormously from 12 up to 18 or more! Grown men's clogs came at 12 to the dozen, but a young girl's size would allow 18 to the dozen.

Very reluctantly, M. Riboulet has had to make concessions to machinery in order to make a living from his trade, but he expresses his feelings clearly.

'The machine has killed friendships within the community, and civilisation has forced us into a solitary existence. We have become machines ourselves, and when that happens love and pride in our work disappears.'

In the old days members of the clogmaking guilds were highly specialised craftsmen. They made different types of

● **Top,** *a set of clogs loaded on the* façonneuse, *or automatic shaper.*
Above, *the machine does the hollowing*

clog — flat or pointed — or concentrated on decoration, and there were even people who made just left-footed or right-footed clogs.

However, with mechanisation the basic processes follow the same path.

He begins by rough-shaping, but using a bandsaw, which can trim several clogs at once. Then an automatic parer, adjusted to millimetre accuracy, finely shapes three clogs at a time.

The hollowing machine also takes three clogs at once, held by their toes and heels. The shanks have spoon-shaped cutters which steadily scoop out the cavity.

Final rubbing down is done on a disc sander, with the abrasive surface vertical. As it rotates, the clogmaker holds the clog against the revolving surface.

In a nearby village is the last remaining shop-window in the area to proclaim 'Clog-maker', its air of antiquity at odds with modern façades around.

Few people now make their living from this ancient trade. But even when the last clogmaker disappears, the French won't forget their colloquial expression: 'Don't put both feet in the same clog'!

The cooper

In the tiny hamlet of Cerilly, bordering the Tronçais forest, one of the last local barrelmakers, Claude Gozard, still plies a trade that has been in his family for over 100 years.

Each barrel was entirely hand-crafted until 1926, when mechanisation was introduced, including a planing machine, a bandsaw, whittler, *gironneuse* (to trace and refine the general convex form of the wood) and the 'spinning top'.

During the last 30 years, glass and plastics have increasingly taken over from wood for many containers, and Claude now gets few orders for butter churns, wooden buckets, cassis (blackcurrant juice) casks and wood containers. He now concentrates on barrels, with the occasional flower tray and vinegar cruet.

Even wine barrels have been affected by the march of civilisation. Horse chestnut, being cheaper, is preferred in many wine-growing areas, and Claude now specialises in cognac barrels, where only the finest oak is suitable.

Chestnut is no good for storing spirits, since it gives off too much tannin, affecting quality and flavour. Tronçais oak, on the other hand, has superb colouring and ageing qualities which help produce the finest cognac.

Wood merchants no longer keep large enough stocks of the oak, so Claude has to calculate ahead, buy his wood green and wait for it to dry in the open air for four years. Each autumn he buys felled oak butts (*merrains*) at auctions round the forest.

● **Above,** *bending by fire and water!*
Below, *braziers go inside barrels*

French lesson: 1

Preparing the staves

Claude first cuts to length the *douelles* or *douvres* (the French name for the staves that form the body of the barrel.) He trims them to thickness using a wooden plane and then shapes them with a taper from the centre towards each end with a *doloire* — a flat-bladed instrument sharpened on one side.

Next grooves (*jables*) are cut in the top and bottom ends of the staves, important later for holding them in position. Another knife called a *jabloir* is used for this.

Once the staves are shaped, Claude stands them upright side by side inside an iron ring ready for the crucial bending.

Bending into shape

Claude places a burning brazier in the circle of staves, and during the four minutes the heat is applied, he splashes the outside with water to prevent the wood burning or splitting; the weather mustn't be too cold for this, because the temperature differential will make the inside burn while the outside stays cold and inflexible.

Now the staves are pressed together and bent into shape using *batissoirs*, strong iron hoops. One at a time they are tapped down around the outside of the ring of staves. As the hoops are hammered into place, the wooden staves close up together into the barrel shape. Claude makes the hoops himself from sheet metal.

Once the shape is obtained, the barrel is put on one side to allow the wood to settle; then the strong moulding hoops are removed for re-use, and a permanent set of hoops tapped into place with a mallet.

Finishing the barrel

Once the wood has stabilised, the circular wooden heads are eased into the top and bottom grooves, the hoops removed temporarily so the staves spring apart enough to allow them to fit.

● **Above**, *the* batissoirs, *the first set of hoops for holding the shape, are fitted;* **below**, *the permanent hoops go on*

The resulting barrels range in size from three litres to 220 litres. A 30-litre barrel, which is sold for 220 francs, takes at least five to eight hours' work, never mind the investment in the wood's storage over four years and the area needed to store the wood.

Claude's workshop now produces about 50 fine barrels a month. He is one of the last barrelmakers, for the craft is facing certain death, killed by the development of glass and plastics containers. Claude's son isn't interested in following the family tradition.

Who knows, perhaps these hand-crafted barrels will soon only be found in antique shops? ■

● *English translation by Katherine J. Britton.*

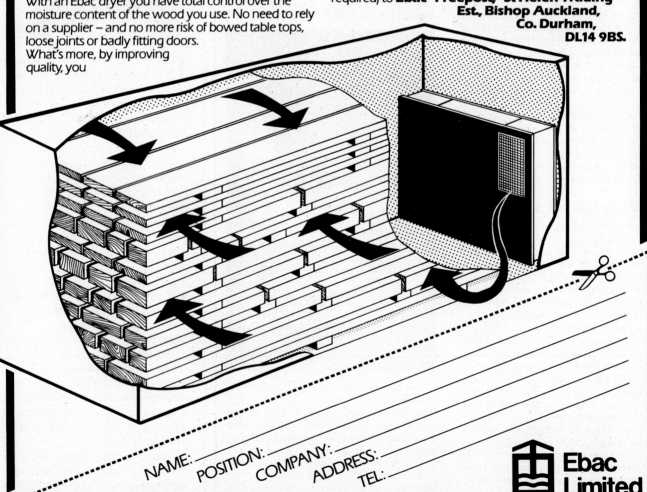

Jigsaw sander

This is a device I put together when I had to clean up the inside edges of a chair splat, writes **Glyn Condick**. The usual practice is to thread some abrasive paper through the holes and pull it to and fro, which is a bit of a bore. So I used a Black & Decker DN31E jigsaw (electronic control is essential) with my adaptor — less elbow-grease and equally effective.

1 Cut a cheap spring-steel 12in ruler in half. You'll probably need a grinding wheel to nick in from both sides — it's tough stuff!

2 Use a tungsten-tipped drill to make holes in one end to match the screw holes in the slide of the jigsaw (fig. 1). Grind three points at the other end — these will prevent the abrasive paper/cloth from slipping off.

3 Make a clip out of ⅟₁₆in (16g) sheet steel (fig. 2). This will hold the abrasive cloth on the rule.

4 Double a strip of abrasive cloth over the metal rule and fasten it with the clip (fig. 3). This is then screwed to the jigsaw slide.

If you want to sand curved shapes, drill screw-holes in the rule and fix complementary shaped pieces of wood covered in abrasive paper (fig. 4).

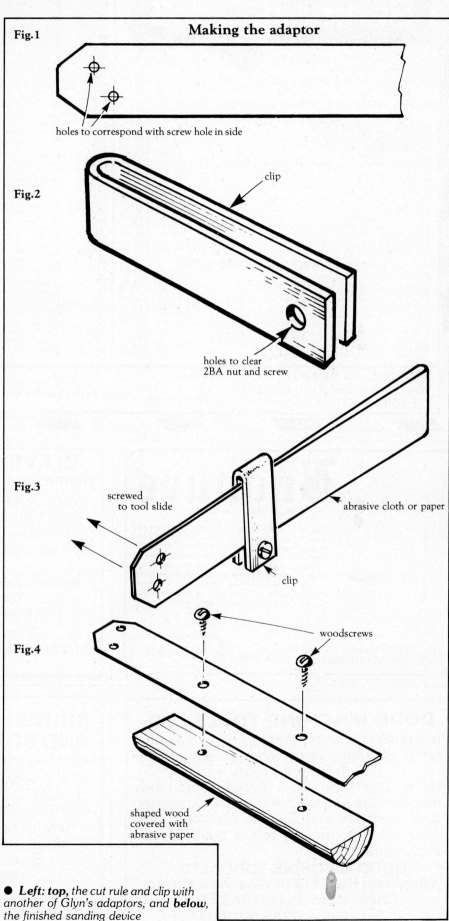

Making the adaptor

Fig. 1

holes to correspond with screw hole in side

Fig. 2

clip

holes to clear
2BA nut and screw

Fig. 3

screwed
to tool slide

abrasive cloth or paper

clip

Fig. 4

woodscrews

shaped wood
covered with
abrasive paper

● **Left: top,** *the cut rule and clip with another of Glyn's adaptors, and* **below,** *the finished sanding device*

778

French lesson: 2

Paul Davis is an *ébéniste* with a difference — he's an Englishman. He describes his launch into the life of a French woodworker, explains some spectacular quirks of technique, and fills in some background

Five and a half years ago, I announced my intention to pack in a well-paid job and set up my own woodworking business. Those who felt entitled to express an honest opinion told me I was mad; my wife, her reticence born of anxious resignation, didn't say much at all.

We grappled beside the precipice:

'Didn't those people who were here for dinner admire the kids' toys and the kitchen shelves? They said I'd make a fortune.'

'Could they have said anything else? Besides, those toys took a week each to make.'

'Wouldn't it be great to have me round all the time, working at home?'

'Ah yes, the swearing . . . the tantrums . . . .'

'Who needs money, anyway?'

'We do.'

The score stood at around deuce when I went out and bought a small, brand-new but 'professional' combination woodworking machine and bandsaw, put them out in the damp and draughty barn, and

● *Some of Paul's own work; a reproduction 18th century parquetry-topped table **above**, and a bookcase **right** 'of vaguely Louis XIII inspiration'*

● *Left, an oak reproduction dining-table in 18th century Auvergne regional style. The moulding is all hand work*

announced that hereafter it was the 'Workshop.' That I had never in my life used such machines, or that I had rarely managed better than a B-minus in woodwork at school were immaterial. The plan was to start making simple wooden toys and bits for the kitchen, progress through plain items of country furniture, and gradually attain experience and the status of 'Designer/Craftsman', a virtually unknown species here in France.

My resignation went in, the formalities for self-employment were completed and a page in history was about to turn. 36 hours

before I was to become my own boss, I was sitting in casualty with a cleft in my thumb big enough to carry a set of VAT forms and a final notice for the electricity bill. I had just learnt something about crosscutting short lengths of timber against the rip-fence on a circular saw. It was not to be my last visit to casualty.

In rural France, Craft fairs and other outlets for wooden toys and spiceboxes are pretty thin on the ground. I quickly concluded that things were fun to think up, stimulating to develop into production, boring to make and difficult to sell. DIY

furniture made for non-DIYers, and other large items like pigsty doors (to be fitted without letting the pigs escape) were scarcely more profitable.

French Income Tax rates are relatively low, but an artisan's compulsory health insurance and pension contributions are astronomically high. VAT at 18.6% doesn't help either, especially because biennial Days of Reckoning mean you can easily find yourself a couple of *millions* (F20,000, about £2000) short of what you expect to pay. So the black economy, although vigorously tracked down, is far from being hunted to extinction. Even the most staid and legitimate operators are suspected of doing a little *au noir*.

All my clients-to-be were, of course, friends, neighbours and contacts, many of whom intimated they were prepared to pay cash and would appreciate it if that were allowed for in my (oral) estimate. Wishing to disappoint nobody I played along with them, but insisted on declaring my complete turnover with an assiduity my rather pragmatic Tax Inspector found positively unnerving.

I wasn't doing myself any good with such self-defeating two-timing, and even after a year, my experience was so lacking that my estimates were still well-nigh 100% out in the client's favour. Apart from converting a Moroccan hall-stand into a hi-fi cabinet and a project to manufacture Aeolian Harp kits, things hadn't been much fun. A return to the salaried ranks loomed ahead; with penury closing in, my wife managed the first smile in a long time when after 16 months I admitted the error of my ways. And then the cavalry rang up.

The 'cavalry' in this case was the *Association de Formation Pour Adultes*, who organise the equivalent of the British TOPS courses as an alternative to traditional two- or three-year apprenticeships. One of my first moves in the Grand Design had been to apply for a place on one of their Furniture-making courses. The application had been accepted, but there were plenty like me, and I should expect to wait seven or eight years before my turn. Wait that long I could not, which partially accounted for the mess we were in now. The AFPA, however, had been monitoring my progress (or lack thereof) and keeping my place in the queue, and it was with exquisite timing that they phoned to say a course had started, one participant had failed to turn up and a place was going begging. They could give me 24 hours to decide; it took just a moment's consultation with my wife. Within three days I had wound up my affairs and was announcing my arrival at the AFPA centre some 100 miles away.

The course instructor made it quite clear he wasn't pleased to see me. A few months' experience with a Lurem didn't count for much in his eyes, and having missed the first two weeks of the course — the basic foundation on the use of hand-tools — I didn't stand much of a chance of becoming a real *ébéniste*. It was not a promising start.

● *The workshop of wheelwright who turned to joinery; M. Planchard's shop uses overhead belts and a planer/thicknesser with a slot mortiser*

● *A clockcase in typical rural style*

Though I managed to emerge at the end with a professional qualification in woodwork, my feelings were still mixed. In one sense, at least, the course was a success — I was now more aware of what I didn't know than what I did. Different timbers and their qualities had only been mentioned in passing and there had been nothing on 'Design' as such; just a slide-show on some period classics, rules of thumb for the choice and dimensions of certain joints, and a free hand in our marquetry work and other ornamentation.

Ébéniste these days means 'Furniture maker', usually of reproduction stuff. Originally it denoted the person who applied the decoration in ebony and other exotic woods to high quality *bourgeois* furniture, the basic carcase of which, along with plain, solid wood country furniture were made by the *menuisier* or joiner. The course was designed with this tradition in mind (although we did our own *menuiserie*), plus

it taught us how to use modern woodworking machinery and techniques and manufactured panel materials. The greatest single thing for me was learning the easy way (well, almost — I visited casualty there as well) about the dangers of such machines, and how to avoid them. I was also greatly impressed with what could be done with just hand-tools, and how quickly some people who had never even tinkered with wood could become competent with them.

We were equipped with a pretty full range of tools, if not exactly rosewood and gunmetal. We had three kinds of plane in beech, the iron and cap wedged in; at least the steel took and kept a good edge, and so did the chisels which we were taught to grind to an angle of more or less 20°, touching the edge up lightly on an oilstone without an additional honing angle.

● **Above**, *M. Planchard's home-made lathe, and **below** some planes*

Perhaps the most striking difference between the *ébéniste's* tool-kit and the cross-Channel counterpart is when it comes to sawing. A single ordinary handsaw hung at the end of the tool-rack for odd jobs and lopping off overlength bits, and we also had a strange kind of gent's saw with a reversible skew handle called a 'Sterling'. It was

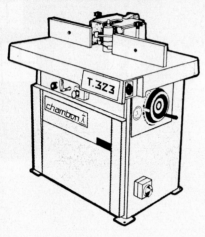

French lesson: 2

● *Choice of bow-saws; Paul's favourite, the* scie à araser, *is on the right*

intended for close work such as dovetails, but I didn't have much success with mine. Then there was the veneer saw, of course, but just about all other sawing jobs were performed with a series of bow-saws, complete with tourniquet for tensioning the blade. I felt like a galley-slave ripping two inches of oak with the biggest of these, holding it vertical with the blade turned through 90°; trying to follow a scrolled line in the same attitude with its smaller brother was equally hard work. The one used for tenon-cutting was very coarse, more of a maid-of-all-work because it doubled as a crosscut. There was one I developed a sneaking affection for; the *scie à araser* has a very fine-toothed blade and is intended essentially for cutting square, clean tenon-shoulders, but once you got the hang of it, it was remarkable how accurately and delicately you could work with what amounted to a picture-frame with a cutting edge.

If there was good emphasis on getting the most out of hand-tools, it was almost equalled by the emphasis on machine safety. For a long time I had believed a push-stick was the answer to everything — until the spindle moulder pushed the push-stick back, and the Head of Casualty spent half an hour with an outside consultant looking for the best way to sew up the hole in my hand!

It would be nice to think someone had invented a perfectly safe woodworking machine, but while the basic principles remain the same, the dangers can only be attenuated by the quality of tooling and guards. I have never seen a British-type chisel-mortiser over here; the French version has three cutters working horizontally. A special centre-chisel shaped like a capital Roman 'I' sweeps from side to side in a slight figure-of-eight, while at each end a square-tipped knife cuts off the shaving in a synchronised stabbing motion. Properly set up (it takes time), this machine can chop out a delightfully clean mortise in seconds, but if you can't afford one, you have to make do with a more conventional slot-mortiser.

Our course instructor was a man of many qualities. We felt secure under his guidance and admired him for his patience, but if there was one thing he got really cranky about, it was what he considered the correct use of the slot-mortiser. No question of drilling a line of holes then linking them with a lateral movement of the table — the cutter is like a router cutter, and the mortise had to be cut accordingly, in a series of

passes as a regularly-deepening groove. Such was his charisma, mild-mannered though he was, no one dared point out that fashioning banana-shaped tenons to fit the mortise thus produced was rather time-consuming. I, for one, have since reverted to the old practice.

The one machine considered indispensable in the French woodworking trade is the spindle-moulder, which is known by the affectionate nick-name of '*bouffe-doigts*', or 'finger-muncher'. It is not only used for shaping and tenon-cutting, but also for certain kinds of dimensioning. Routers are still considered rather limited in comparison for rebating, grooving and scribing. In some workshops the '*bouffe-doigts*' is literally the centre-piece; all employees have equal access to it, and presumably an equal chance of being hit by a flying workpiece or cutter-head. Claiming to own one, albeit as part of a combination machine, has more than once put me on a level with those who doubted my bona fides as a professional woodworker.

Much of an *ébéniste*'s bread-and-sausage-work stems from reproductions and restoration, and 18th-century French country furniture is characterised in part by deeply incised mouldings on the face of the frame. Authentic period mouldings can really only be produced on the spindle moulder, with specially made French-head cutters which the operator usually makes with a special set of files and a leaf-shaped burnisher known as a 'bunny rabbit'. This kind of cutter batters and scrapes rather than cuts through the wood, and making a pass with

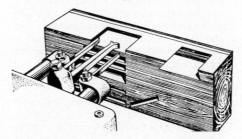

● *The 'Alternax' chisel mortiser*

the workpiece edge down on the table and the face pressed up against the fence is hard and hairy work. In view of the fact that those same edges were hardly ever straight, the need for a *champignon* (mushroom) arose; not for eating, this one. It's a kind of finger pointing over the table to the cutter-head on an extended shaft, up to a foot in the air. The experienced *toupilleur* feeds and guides the wiggly workpiece over the *champignon* with the aid of an extra-high fence, monitoring progress in a mirror mounted behind the shaft! Small wonder this brand of operative was frequently the prima donna of a large workshop, a steely-nerved gymnast who after a long and particularly dicey batch would trim his fingernails on the cutter for an encore!

Risks have been reduced recently with

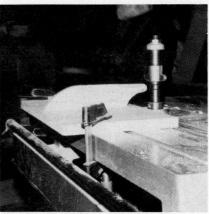

● *The* champignon *is hairy indeed! Curved workpiece runs against the shaft, held vertically . . .*

increasingly sophisticated protectors, fences and power-feeds, while horizontal-axis shapers are diminishing the need to use a *champignon*. One of these, officially referred to as a portable spindle-moulder, is more popularly known as 'the moped' as it looks and feels like a pair of disembodied handlebars — it sounds like a hotted-up 50cc engine too.

Still, most of us have to make do with more traditional approaches, and if one doesn't fancy the risk of home-made accessories on the spindle moulder, there are gouges, scratchstocks and subcontractors. Personally, I'm able to draw from ideas developed using the plunge router in Britain, but experience has taught me a simpler solution yet. A commission that looks too technically demanding can always be gently turned down — and it doesn't

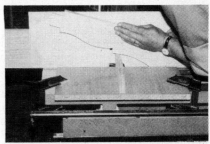

● *Moulding a curved edge on a tenoned rail with the* champignon; *high fence this time!*

necessarily cost you your livelihood.

Another personal solution has been to develop a style that requires neither the high-tech nor labour-intensive production techniques of reproducing French antique furniture. I may not be France's first designer/craftsman yet, but being able to draw inspiration from styles in Britain, Scandinavia and America does make for a certain originality here. Country furniture from Quebec offers a hand reproduction compromise between French and Anglo-Saxon influences.

Little by little, I feel I'm getting somewhere, and more to the point, my wife

● *An old* champignon *for tipping-table spindle moulders; the shaft goes through the hole in the baseboard*

● *The 'moped' is much safer – a hand-held portable spindle moulder! Cutters go on the shaft; note adjustable 'fence'*

thinks so too. I'm not so coy about referring to my work as 'quality' now; at least nothing has been returned. I recently took my eldest daughter, as accident-prone as her father, down to casualty where one of the staff greeted me like a long lost friend and told me that they had been wondering if I had given up woodwork. And finally, I'm even beginning to make a little money.

Designer/craftspeople in France

An eminent *menuisier-ébéniste*, leafing through some back numbers of *Woodworker*, was dismissive. 'You can't really do professional work with the machinery advertised here,' he interrupted, and examined some pictures of pieces by a leading designer-maker. 'Yes, decidedly amateur,' he added. Then he saw something he liked. 'Now that's a professional-looking job.' If he'd been able to read the caption he would have seen it was a Victorian armchair College restoration project.

His comments seemed to confirm the gulf between furniture-making techniques and traditions in the two countries. But one of the reasons I had come to see him was because his son is one of the very few furniture/designer craftsmen in France, and I hoped to find out why there were so few like him.

There are a few contemporary designers, freelance or in design studios, but they mostly work on paper and have to get an *Editeur* (a word synonymous with 'publisher') who will produce and market the product. There are various lamentaions and explanations of why circumstances don't favour a viable alternative to this quasi-industrial process.

The one I was given here was typical of a French self-employed craftsman and small employer. 'Creativity is stifled,' he said, 'by *les charges*.' These are the compulsory contributions to medical insurance and pension funds the self-employed have to pay, social security contributions for their employees, and a multitude of small taxes on specific activities, not to mention overheads and 18.6% VAT. It is reckoned that in a labour-intensive activity such as woodwork, a single self-employed artisan clears less than 30% of his or her turnover. To break even, an employer must ensure an employee's productivity amounts to two and a half times his or her gross wages. Mechanisation helps maintain productivity, the investment can be offset against some of the *charges*, but the administration is time-consuming. The successful craftsman in France is as much as anything a good manager with little time to research new ideas.

To ease the pressures of trying to produce quality furniture at a price the consumer can afford, it's not unusual for some *ébénistes* to have a showroom where they sell factory-made furniture alongside their own products.

All *artisans* (small employers with less than ten employees, plus manual tradespeople) must register with the *Chambre des Métiers*, who run technical apprenticeship classes. But an alternative is not to register with the *Chambre*, and opt for the status of '*Artiste libre*'. The contributions are slightly lower, and since you're considered to be producing works of art rather than goods you're exempted from VAT. However, there are limitations on the batch work you can do, and *artistes* are frequently excluded from government-sponsored financial aid and promotional activities. It's usually a status reserved for the more specialised *métiers d'art* such as carving, gilding and marquetry, and anyway you work more for love than money.

Of those who have tried designing, making and marketing their own furniture, some complain that the interior decorators who account for up to 50% of the market are far too cost-conscious and conservative to give them much encouragement, let alone commissions. And to attract attention in the professional press normally requires heavy, expensive advertising.

Many recognise that training is sadly lacking, too. There are no furniture schools offering courses in design *and* making and even the prestigious École Boulle in Paris is essentially concerned with '*la technologie*'. In fact, with the exception of cabinetmaking and upholstery, none of the *métiers d'art* offer qualifications beyond the basic CAP, the *Certificat d'Aptitude Professionelle*.

This situation is almost certainly rooted in French furniture traditions. 19th-century mechanisation enabled industry to churn out a neo-Renaissance style parallel with the Victorian stuff we now prefer to forget about, but there was no Bauhaus or Arts and Crafts movement in France that today's designer/makers are trying to live up to or live down. The post-Industrial Revolution backlash resulted in the elegant, short-lived *Art Nouveau*, but its followers soon reverted to the traditions of furniture making that originated in the 17th century and developed to the Revolution. Furniture styles are known by the historical periods with which they (more or less) coincided, althought the names of the great French cabinetmakers contemporary with Adam, Chippendale and Hepplewhite are well-known: Boulle (or Buhl, who was Swiss in origin), Oeben, van Reisen Burgh, Cressent, Leleu, Reisener. Before the guilds were abolished and the clearly-defined demarcations between *ébénistes* and *menuisiers* broken down, producing a *meuble d'art* in the 18th century needed a range of craftsmen for marquetry, lacquerwork, gilding, carving and incising. The *maître ébéniste* had a role like a film director's, conceiving overall production and supervising and co-ordinating the production team before finishing the work himself and presenting it to the public. Such an approach persists today in the Faubourg St. Antoine in Paris and in Revel, near Toulouse, where flawless copies of period pieces are made to the same exacting standards as the originals.

While much of such work goes abroad where there is a demand for the very best in French furniture and the money to pay for it, the home market is no less tradition-minded. 80% of the furniture made in France today is reproduction, and in general tastes are for dark-stained 'noble' woods such as oak and fruitwood. Quality workmanship takes a high profile in the form of relief carving, moulded scrollwork and marquetry (or parquetry) along with an antique patina finish.

So the typical established artisan *ébéniste* has a clientèle drawn from the professional and executive classes and is making 'country' furniture for them in a given period or regional style, often adapted for a specific purpose or place. It's not unusual to encounter an 18th-century Basque-style television stand, or Louis XIII cocktail cabinets. I myself have to own up to the occasional 'period' video cabinet!

Woodworking trades in France

Up until the 14th century, woodworkers in France depended directly upon *Le Charpentier du Roi* (The King's Carpenter) and went by the name of *Huchiers-Charpentiers* (bin-makers/carpenters). By 1350 they had split into three branches, *Charpentiers* for heavy constructional woodwork, *Charpentiers de petite cognée*, whose work with *les menus travaux* (light joinery) gave rise to the term *menuisier*, and the *Huchiers-menuisiers*, fore-runners to furniture makers. By the 16th century the term *menuisier* was in current use and the trade had divided into *Menuisier en bâtiment* for building work other than carpentry, and *Menuisier en meubles* for furniture making. By the end of the century a further distinction had been made for those specialising in applying ebony and other rare species to a basic carcase — *Menuisier en ébène*. At this time Henri IV established *Les faiseurs de cabinet du Roi* (The King's cabinetmakers) and gave special privileges to the group of artisans in and around the Faubourg St. Antoine in Paris. In the 17th century the different trades organised themselves into tight-knit *Corporations*, undertaking the training of apprentices who had to execute a *Chef d'Oeuvre* (major or masterpiece!) before being admitted to the rank of *Compagnon* as a first step to becoming a master craftsman. The term *ébéniste* didn't come until the beginning of the 18th century.

Although the French revolution did away with the *Corporations* in 1791 and the jealously-guarded demarcations between the different professions were broken down, the traditional distinctions still exist. The *charpentiers* carry out basic constructional woodwork, the best of which involves impressive feats of large-scale plane and solid geometry. *Menuisiers* work essentially in *agencement* or solid-wood fixed fittings, while *Menuisiers-ébénistes* build furniture in solid wood or do fine panelling and parquet work. Finally, the *Ébénistes* work essentially in veneered furniture.

To the three main branches of woodwork one should add the rural crafts of *charron* (cart- and wheelwright), *tonneleur* (cooper), and *sabotier* (clog maker). The last two are still a common sight in markets other than in the biggest cities, but many *charrons* are now having to turn their hand to *menuiserie* or furniture making.

One professional brotherhood survived the dissolution of 1791 — *Les Compagnons du devoir*. Living in communities with traditions peculiar to them, they are suspiciously regarded by some as a sinister secret society, and indeed there is much distinctive in their manner, language and even their dress. They are strongly associated with the *charpentiers* who wear

● *An old rustic salt-chest/seat*

● *Louis XIII chest, still reproduced today*

● *Régence buffet, c1715*

characteristic baggy corduroy trousers, and (before it became the fashion), older men sometimes wore a single earring. Members are usually recruited following the successful completion of their apprenticeship, and are then sent on *Le Tour de France* — not bikes, but six years travelling and working in a series of towns where they live communally in a *Maison des Compagnons* under the frequently baleful eye of House Mothers, the only women in the society. By day they work with an outside employer and spend their evenings perfecting their technical knowledge and practical skills. After three years they prepare their *Maîtrise*, for which they have to produce a *Chef d'Oeuvre*, an unusually intricate exercise in miniature which they often keep for the rest of their lives. (One *compagnon-menuisier* had a horseshoe double staircase, complete with turned balustrade, which he carried round in pieces in a draw-string bag. With a little encouragement he would bring it out and push-fit it together in about ten minutes.) After the *Maîtrise*, the *Compagnons* stay on for another three years helping junior members prepare for theirs, and then they are free to leave and seek work elsewhere or set up on their own.

Fairly recently the *Compagnons* started offering apprenticeships in addition to their traditional activities, but most apprenticeships leading to the CAP (*Certificat d'Aptitude Professionelle*) are still administered by the Ministry of Education. Apprentices start at 15 or 16 and attend an LEP (*Lycée d'enseignement professionelle*), a kind of technical secondary school, learning their trade as part of the school curriculum. Employers tend, however, to prefer the alternative system where apprentices learn their practical skills working for a nominal wage with an established craftsman, who releases them one week in four to attend technical classes at a CFA (*Centre de formation d'apprentis*), run by the *Chambre*

des Métiers with whom all *artisans* must register.

It's unusual for a young woodworker to set up in business directly after obtaining his or her CAP. Firstly, the financial commitments are enormous — quite apart from the cost of finding and equipping premises, the standing social security charges for the self-employed during the first two years, before they can be assessed on profits, are around £1700 a year. Secondly, it's widely acknowledged that it takes about 10 years to become a '*bonne main*', as an *ébéniste* for example, and so the general trend is to try and find work with an employer or the *Compagnons*. This is not easy in the present economic climate (it never has been) and so the 'wastage' rate among newly-qualified apprentices is high.

Those who persevere and are lucky enough to find stable employment may wish to further themselves and prepare for the *Brevet de Maîtrise*. Organised by the *Chambres des Métiers*, it is open to employees and the self-employed alike. The examination comprises tests in theoretical knowledge and technical drawing as well as producing an exam piece similar to a *Chef d'Oeuvre*.

● *Louis XVI sécretaire, c1760*

The consummate achievement, however, is to earn the title of *L'un des Meilleurs Ouvriers de France* and to place 'MOF' after one's name. Every three years the Ministry of Labour organises a national *Exposition du Travail* of some 4000 entries from no less than 220 crafts. Established in the 1920s, the competition's three-year cycle enables the participants to prepare their entries, which can require 500-2000 hours' work and up to £1000-worth of materials. The entrants receive a detailed brief which allows little or no freedom of interpretation; the entries are judged almost exclusively on the grounds of technical competence. While employees who go in for it are often actively encouraged by their employers, most of the work is done in spare time; but in the 1982 contest, a *charpentier* from near Lyon closed his business for eight months while he and his young employee prepared their respective entries in the workshop. They both won. ■

shop guide

AVON

BATH   Tel. Bath 64513
JOHN HALL TOOLS   ★
RAILWAY STREET

Open: Monday-Saturday
9.00 a.m.-5.30 p.m.
H.P.W.WM.D.A.BC.

BRISTOL   Tel. (0272) 741510
JOHN HALL TOOLS LIMITED   ★
CLIFTON DOWN SHOPPING CENTRE
WHITELADIES ROAD
Open: Monday-Saturday
9.00 a.m.-5.30 p.m.
H.P.W.WM.D.A.BC.

BRISTOL   Tel. (0272) 629092
TRYMWOOD SERVICES
2a DOWNS PARK EAST, (off North View)
WESTBURY PARK
Open: 8.30 a.m.-5.30 p.m. Mon. to Fri.
Closed for lunch 1.00-2.00 p.m.
P.W.WM.D.T.A.BC.

BRISTOL   Tel. (0272) 667013
FASTSET LTD
190-192 WEST STREET
BEDMINSTER
Open: Mon.-Fri. 8.30 a.m.-5.00 p.m.
Saturday 9.00 a.m.-1.00 p.m.
H.P.W.WM.D.CS.A.BC.

BRISTOL   Tel. (0272) 667013
WILLIS
157 WEST STREET
BEDMINSTER
Open Mon.-Fri. 8.30 a.m.-5.00 p.m.
Sat. 9 a.m.-4 p.m.
P.W.WM.D.CS.A.BC.

BEDFORDSHIRE

BEDFORD   Tel. (0234) 59808
BEDFORD SAW SERVICE   K
39 AMPTHILL ROAD

Open: Mon.-Fri. 8.30-5.30
Sat. 9.00-4.00
H.P.A.BC.W.CS.WM.D.

BERKSHIRE

READING   Tel. Littlewick Green
DAVID HUNT (TOOL   2743
MERCHANTS) LTD   ★
KNOWL HILL, NR. READING
Open: Monday-Saturday
9.00 a.m.-5.30 p.m.
H.P.W.D.A.BC.

READING   Tel. Reading 661511
WOKINGHAM TOOL CO. LTD.
99 WOKINGHAM ROAD

Open: Mon-Sat 9.00 a.m.-5.30 p.m.
Closed 1.00-2.00 p.m. for lunch
H.P.W.WM.D.CS.A.BC.

BUCKINGHAMSHIRE

MILTON KEYNES   Tel. (0908)
POLLARD WOODWORKING   641366
CENTRE   ★
51 AYLESBURY ST., BLETCHLEY
Open: Mon-Fri 8.30-5.30
Saturday 9.00-5.00
H.P.W.WM.D.CS.A.BC.

HIGH WYCOMBE   Tel. (0494)
SCOTT SAWS LTD.   24201/33788
14 BRIDGE STREET   ★

Mon.-Sat. 8.30 a.m.-6.00 p.m.

H.P.W.WM.D.T.CS.MF.A.BC.

HIGH WYCOMBE   Tel. (0494)
ISAAC LORD LTD   22221
185 DESBOROUGH ROAD   KE

Open: Mon-Fri 8.00 a.m.-5.00 p.m.
Saturday 9.00 a.m.-5.00 p.m.
H.P.W.D.A.

CAMBRIDGESHIRE

CAMBRIDGE   Tel: (0223) 63132
D. MACKAY LTD.   ★
BRITANNIA WORKS, EAST ROAD

Open: Mon.-Fri. 8.30 a.m.-1 p.m./2.00-
5.00 p.m. Sat. 8.30 a.m.-1.00 p.m.
H.P.W.D.T.CS.MF.A.BC.

CAMBRIDGE   Tel. (0223) 247386
H. B. WOODWORKING   K
105 CHERRY HINTON ROAD
Open: 8.30 a.m.-5.30 p.m.
Monday-Friday
8.30 a.m.-1.00 p.m. Sat.
H.P.W.WM.D.CS.A.

ESSEX

PETERBOROUGH   Tel. (0733)
WILLIAMS DISTRIBUTORS   64252
(TOOLS) LIMITED   K
108-110 BURGHLEY ROAD
Open: Monday to Friday
8.30 a.m.-5.30 p.m.
H.P.A.W.D.WH.BC.

CHESHIRE

NANTWICH   Tel. Crewe 67010
ALAN HOLTHAM   K★
THE OLD STORES TURNERY
WISTASON ROAD, WILLASTON
Open: Tues.-Sat. 9.00 a.m.-5.30 p.m.
Closed Monday
P.W.WM.D.T.CS.A.BC.

CLEVELAND

MIDDLESBROUGH   Tel. (0642)
CLEVELAND WOODCRAFT   813103
(M'BRO), 38-42 CRESCENT ROAD   K

Open: Mon-Sat 9.15 a.m.-5.30 p.m.

H.P.T.A.BC.W.WM.CS.D.

CORNWALL

SOUTH WEST
Power Tools

CORNWALL   Tel: Helston (03265) 4961
HELSTON AND LAUNCESTON   Launceston
                          (0566) 4781
H.P.W.WM.D.CS.A.   K

CUMBRIA

CARLISLE   Tel. (0228) 36391
W. M. PLANT
ALLENBROOK ROAD
ROSEHILL, CA1 2UT
Open: Mon.-Fri. 8.00 a.m.-5.15 p.m.
Sat. 8.00 a.m.-12.30 noon
P.W.WM.D.CS.A.

DEVON

BRIXHAM   Tel. (08045) 4900
WOODCRAFT SUPPLIES   E★
4 HORSE POOL STREET

Open: Mon.-Sat. 9.00 a.m.-6.00 p.m.

H.P.W.A.D.MF.CS.BC.

PLYMOUTH   Tel. (0752) 330303
WESTWARD BUILDING SERVICES   ★
LTD., LISTER CLOSE, NEWNHAM
INDUSTRIAL ESTATE, PLYMPTON
Open: Mon-Fri 8.00 a.m.-5.30 p.m.
Sat. 8.30 a.m.-12.30 p.m.
H.P.W.WM.D.A.BC.

PLYMOUTH   Tel. (0752) 665363
F.T.B. LAWSON LTD.
71 NEW GEORGE STREET
PLYMOUTH PL1 1RB
Open: Mon.-Sat. 8.30 am-5.30 pm.
H.P.W.CS.MF.A.

ESSEX

LEIGH ON SEA   Tel. (0702)
MARSHAL & PARSONS LTD.   710404
1111 LONDON ROAD   EK

Open: 8.30 a.m.-5.30 p.m. Mon-Fri
9.00 a.m.-5.00 p.m. Sat.
H.P.W.WM.D.CS.A.

GLOUCESTER

TEWKESBURY   Tel. (0684)
TEWKESBURY SAW CO. LTD.   293092
TRADING ESTATE, NEWTOWN   K

Open: Mon-Fri 8.00 a.m.-5.00 p.m.
Saturday 9.30 a.m.-12.00 p.m.
P.W.WM.D.CS.

HAMPSHIRE

ALDERSHOT   Tel. (0252) 334422
POWER TOOL CENTRE   K
374 HIGH STREET

Open Mon.-Fri. 8.30 a.m.-5.30 p.m.
Sat. 8.30 a.m.-12.30 p.m.
H.P.W.WM.D.A.BC.

SOUTHAMPTON   Tel: (0703)
POWER TOOL CENTRE   332288
7 BELVIDERE ROAD   K★
Open Mon.-Fri. 8.30-5.30

H.P.W.WM.D.A.BC.CS.MF.

HERTFORDSHIRE

WARE   K★
HEATH SAWS
16 MALTINGS
STANSTEAD ABBOTTS (near Ware) HERTS.
Open: Mon-Fri. 8.30am-5.30pm
Sat. 8.30am-1pm. Sunday by appointment.
P.W.WM.D.CS.A.

HUMBERSIDE

GRIMSBY   Tel. Grimsby (0472)
                58741 Hull (0482) 26999
J. E. SIDDLE LTD. (Tool Specialists)   ★
83 VICTORIA STREET
Open: Mon-Fri 8.30 a.m.-5.30 p.m.
Sat. 8.30 a.m.-12.45 p.m. & 2 p.m.-5 p.m.
H.P.A.BC.W.WMD.

HULL
HUMBERSIDE FACTORING/H.F.C.
SAW SERVICING LTD.
MAIN STREET
Open: Mon.-Fri. 8am-5pm.
Saturday 8am-12.00pm.
H.P.W.WM.D.CS.A.BC.K.

KENT

WYE   Tel. (0233) 813144
KENT POWER TOOLS LTD.
UNIT 1, BRIAR CLOSE
WYE, Nr. ASFORD

H.P.W.WM.D.A.CS.

MAIDSTONE   Tel. (0622) 50177
SOUTH EASTERN SAWS (Ind.) LTD.   ★
COLDRED ROAD
PARKWOOD INDUSTRIAL ESTATE
Open: Mon.-Fri. 8.00 a.m.-6.00 p.m.
Sat. 9.00 a.m.-12.00 a.m.
B.C.W.CS.WM.PH.

LANCASHIRE

PRESTON   Tel. (0772) 52951
SPEEDWELL TOOL COMPANY   E★
62-68 MEADOW STREET PR1 1SU
Open: Mon.-Fri. 8.30 a.m.-5.30 p.m.
Sat. 8.30 a.m.-12.30 p.m.

H.P.W.WM.CS.A.MF.BC.

MANCHESTER   Tel. (061 789)
TIMMS TOOLS   0909
102-104 LIVERPOOL ROAD   ★
PATRICROFT M30 0WZ
Weekdays 9.00 a.m.-5.30 p.m.
Sat. 9.00 a.m.-1.00 p.m.
H.P.A.W.

ROCHDALE   Tel. (0706) 342123/
C.S.M. TOOLS   342322
4-6 HEYWOOD ROAD   E★
CASTLETON
Open: Mon-Sat 9.00 a.m.-6.00 p.m.
Sundays by appointment
W.D.CS.A.BC.

786

WOOD SUPPLIERS

789

Classified Advertisements

FOR SALE

WORKSHOP EQUIPMENT

HARRISON GRADUATE
and JUBILEE Wood Turning Lathes For Sale,
Contact the specialists
L.R.E. MACHINERY & EQUIPMENT Co.
15 Upwood Road, Lowton,
Warrington WA3 2RL.
Tel: (0942) 728208 day or night

THE WHISTON CATALOGUE
Nuts, bolts, screws, washers, bar materials. In brass, alloy, steel, stainless steel, P.T.F.E., nylon, Tufnol, sheet material, electrical and mechanical items. We could go on and on! Better to send for free catalogue No. 114 and see for yourself.
K. R. Whiston Ltd., Dept. WW, New Mills, Stockport, Cheshire. Phone: 0663 42028.

BANKRUPT STOCK
Sandvik circular saw blades tungsten tipped.
5", 5½", 6" .... **£4.00** each
6½", 8¼" .... **£6.00** each
½" to 1⅜" bore any size.
P&P £1 extra per order.
Tel: 01 672 7776
Hannett, 1A Links Road,
Tooting, London SW17 9ED.

£50 MINIMUM Norris/Spiers planer, unusual Stanley models, quality braces. Free comprehensive list (0492) 49019.

LACE BOBBIN turning blanks. Extensive range of exotics, Ivory, lathes, miniature tools, sundries, lace supplies. SAE J. Ford, 5 Squirrels Hollow, Walsall WS7 8YS.

USERS AND COLLECTORS tools for sale at the Old Craft Tool Shop, 15 High Street, Whitton, Middx. Telephone 01-755 0441.

FULGORA WASTEBURNING 'dustbin' stove 10 flue sections angles cowl complete, unused. £80. Tel: 09848 223 (Somerset).

KITY K5 £450, Tyne Cub Lathe plus tools £250. Startrite Bandsaw 301 £200. Warco drill £75. All approx. two years old. Also hand tools sale, due to failed business venture. Tel: Cheltenham (0242) 38704.

BARGAIN PRICE. Home grown, kiln dried timber for sale, most species available also turning blanks. Tel: 0222 861584, S. Wales.

SCHEPPACH HF33 3 speed spindle moulder sliding table. Unused from new. Offers. Campbell, Monmouth 0600 5173.

WADKIN SPINDLE, even wood morticer, Cooksley heavy duty sawbench, Kity planer. Many extras. Tooling etc. Sale/exchange for combination machine and bandsaw. Tel: Torquay 606541.

HARDWOOD HAND SCREWS. Dual metal thread, for strength and versatility, will also clamp long parallel faces. Opening, 3" £13.95, 4½" £16.50, 6" £20.25, 10" £26.00. Woodform, Lezant, Launceston, Cornwall PL15 9PP.

WINDSOR CHAIRS
Full size bends. 50 × 1⅜ × 1⅛" in Ash £6.95.
Childs Windsor Chair bends in Ash 36 × 1⅛ × ⅞" £4.95.
All prices include p&p.
Please send cheque/P.O. with order to:
P. Stuffin, Spurn View, North End Road, Tetney, Grimsnby DN36 5NA.
Tel: (0472) 812576
(Afternoons)

SAMUEL COULTON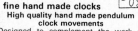
fine hand made clocks
High quality hand made pendulum clock movements
Designed to complement the work of those fellow craftsmen for whom only the best will do. Individually made to order. Send £2.00 for detailed colour brochure.
Samuel Coulton Clocks, Lower Damgate Farm, Stanshope, Nr. Ashbourne, Derbyshire.
Tel: (033527) 367.

FOR SALE
Kity 736 Planer/Thicknesser
Good condition.
Available West Sussex.
Offers over £450.00
Tel: 07983 — 3621

TIMBER BEAMS yellow and pitch pine, very large selection. Can deliver. Tel: 0484 535063.

WOODEN PLOUGH PLANE, Coopers plane. Record Milliplane & cutters. Compass plane, etc. Tel: 01-267-1290.

CLOCKMAKERS
Extensive range of very competitively priced German quartz clock movements, (including standard quartz, pendulum, mini-pendulum, chining, striking and insertion movements). Large selection of quality dials, chapter rings, hands, bezels, clock plans and weather instruments.
Please send 25p stamps for 20 page catalogue.
Bath Clock Company (Dept. W), 13 Welton Road, Radstock, Bath.

BLADES
The specialist mail order supplier of tooling for woodworking machinery and power tools. Spindle tooling, saw blades, dado sets, planer knives, router cutters and accessories, machinery of particular merit, Forstener bits, mortise chisels, etc.
Write NOW for your free copy of our brochure AND competitive price list.
BLADES, Freepost, Petersfield, Hampshire GU32 2BR. (No stamps required)

WOULDHAM SANDSTONE GRINDER, 18 by 3 inch wheel, treadle operated, only three years old. Excellent condition. New price £265 — will sell for £175 o.n.o. Tel: 01-600 7148.

OVERHEAD TRAVEL MONO — saw, will cut sheet material up to 8' × 4', 9" blade, 2hp, single phase, tubular rails, 3 TCT blades, £900. Ring Ware 31176 (7472 evening), for demonstration.

NAEROK BDS46 belt and disc sander, almost new, £50. Chambers, 50 East Street, Alresford, Hants. Tel: Alresford 4769.

CORONET MAJOR LATHE, bench mounted with tenoner, saw, planer, grinder, belt and disc sanders, box combing jig, gearbox etc. Excellent condition £800 o.n.o. Tel: 01-993 7665 daytime.

DANCKAERT semi automatic dove-tailed 3 phase. Danckaert horizontal chisel 3 phase slot mortiser. Each £180. Tel: 445 1611.

CORONET MAJOR with many accessories and tools, chucks £700. Tel: 01-446 2804.

RING ANDREA SMITH ON 01-437 0626 FOR ADVERTISING DETAILS.

FOR ALL SUPPLIES
FOR THE
Craft of Enamelling
ON METAL
Including
LEAD-FREE ENAMELS
PLEASE SEND 2 × 10p STAMPS FOR FREE CATALOGUE, PRICE LIST AND WORKING INSTRUCTIONS

W. G. BALL LTD.
ENAMEL MANUFACTURERS
Dept. W. LONGTON
STOKE-ON-TRENT
ST3 1JW

The best costs less with
BIG DISCOUNTS

off all leading brands of T.C.T. saws, router cutters, planer knives and narrow bandsaws D.I.Y. and Industrial Quality. It pays to check our prices. Same day low cost resharpening service. Visitors Welcome. Free price list on request.

L.M. Saws, Slack Lane, Heanor, Derbyshire DE7 7GX
Telephone: 0773 715616

AN ENTIRE WORKSHOP IN ONE CATALOGUE . . .

WITH THE BIGGEST TOOL MAIL ORDER SPECIALISTS IN THE U.K.
Send 70p for 92 page Tools and Machinery Catalogue No. 12 complete with up to date price list. 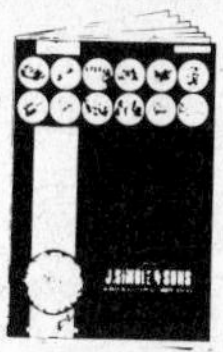
J. SIMBLE & SONS
Dept. WW, The Broadway, 76 Queen's Road, Watford, Herts.   Tel: Watford 26052

GREENJACKETS
TOOL CENTRE

SUPPLIERS OF HAND AND POWER TOOLS AND EQUIPMENT TO GOVT. DEPARTMENTS, LOCAL AUTHORITIES, SCHOOLS, TRADE & INDUSTRY, ETC. ETC.
OFFICIAL MAIN STOCKISTS OF BOSCH — HITACHI — ELU — MAKITA — AEG — DeWALT — BLACK & DECKER (PROFESSIONAL) ALSO STOCKISTS OF CRAFTSMAN — PEUGOT — SKIL — WOLF — RYOBI DISTRIBUTORS OF SUZUKI GENERATORS AND PUMPS — WAVNER SPRAY GUNS, POWER HAMMERS & ACCESSORIES. LOWEST PRICES ON STANLEY — MARPLES — SANDVIK — DISSTON — RECORD — ECLIPSE — ESTWING — DREMELL — ETC.
PHONE FOR LOWEST PRICE.

GREENJACKETS
32-34 St. Mary's Road, Ealing W5 5EU.
Telephone 01-579 1188/9
Prompt Mail Order Service.
Visa & Access accepted - account customers welcomed.

GENERAL

MARKING STAMPS — name stamps branding irons supplied to your requirements SAE for details. Davey, 37 Marina Drive, Brixham, Devon TQ5 8BB.   T/C

793

BUCKINGHAMSHIRE COLLEGE

School of Art and Design, Furniture and Timber

Head of School: Ian M. Barker, BA, Cert. Ed.

Full Time Course for September 1986

B.Sc. Furniture Production — 4 year sandwich course with 1 year in industry.

Diploma in Furniture Craft — 3 year course for the small workshop craftsman.

B.Sc. Timber Technology — 3 year course for the timber and materials technologist.

Details and application forms from:
School of Art and Design, Furniture and Timber, Buckinghamshire College of Higher Education, Queen Alexandra Road, High Wycombe, Bucks. HP11 2JZ   Tel: (0494) 22141

795

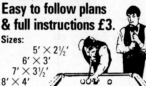
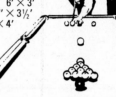

DEMONSTRATIONS

DEMONSTRATIONS
WOODWORKING MACHINERY & POWER TOOLS

Inca, Tyme, Kity, DeWalt, Elu, Naerok, Wolf, Ryobi, Spindle tooling, router cutters.
Friday, 19th September.
Saturday, 20th September.
9 a.m.-6 p.m.
BURCH & HILLS POWER TOOL CENTRE
374 High Street, Aldershot.
Tel: 0252 334422
SPECIAL PRICES FOR VISITORS!

DEMONSTRATIONS OF WOODWORKING MACHINES

Instore demonstrations of hand, carving and power tools.
Tuesday, 21st October, 10am-8pm
Wednesday, 22nd October, 10am-5pm.
Makita power tools — Triton saw benches
Trend router bits — Sandvik hand tools
Ashley Iles edge tools
Record Ridgeway hand tools.

WALKER AND ANDERSON,
Windsor Road, Kings Lynn, Norfolk.
Telephone (0553) 772443

Woodworker Classified Coupon

FROM ....

TEL. No. (DAY) ....

I enclose remittance to the value of ....

Rates — 52p per word (min. £7.20)
Display boxes £8.60 (min. 2.5cm + VAT)

Send to Classified Department, ASP Ltd, No. 1 Golden Square, London W1.

'Fine Craft and Fine Design'

* Seminars and courses
* Comprehensive tool insurance
* Central skills register
* Information and advice
* Show entry discounts

Professional and amateur

Write for application forms to: Guild of Woodworkers, 1 Golden Sq. London W1R 3AB.

798

Letters

De-clogging abrasives

MAY I COMMENT on the article about sanding machines and abrasives ('Machining Wood' Part 8, WW/June). Wire brushing limits the life of the abrasive, as the metal has slight but obvious effects on the cutting potential of the aluminium oxide.

I find a far better solution is to use soft rubber. This can be bought quite cheaply as 'belt saver' from Fiddes of Cardiff and other suppliers, or one can use crêpe rubber, and old shoe-sole or offcuts from a shoe-maker. At a pinch half a washing-up liquid bottle is quite effective.

Whatever material you choose, apply it to the abrasive in motion. Caution must be used, of course, and I use the rubber screwed into a sandwich of wood to avoid rubbing the end of my fingers. Larger discs should not be tackled in this way except by professionals.

Tobias Kaye, Buckfastleigh
● Fiddes & Son, Brindley Road, Cardiff CF1 7TX.

'Fair play!'

I WAS QUITE TAKEN ABACK to read Mr Kenning's letter (WW/July) about advice on hand veneering given by Mr Savage. I wasn't so concerned about the technical details as the tone of the letter.

I feel we are all, professional or amateur, in a learning situation. Some have more knowledge than others, and some have more skill, but there is no better way to block the acquisition of both than become prey to intolerance and pride.

A. Millett, Bracknell

I READ WITH MUCH SADNESS the gritty and abrasive exchange between Mark Kenning and David Savage. Ours is much too nice an occupation — whether absorbing hobby or profession — to be spoilt by dogmatism relating to method.

I wondered if I detected the NIMBY syndrome, or something very close to it — Not In My Back Yard. We are all very familiar with the crying need for motorways, mental hospitals and so on, but strongly oppose their construction close to our own patch.

Perhaps professionals are not very charitable about another professional's work because they might feel threatened in a field of activity where it is notoriously difficult to become competent.

Recently I applied for membership of the Gloucester Guild of Craftsmen, submitting a clock which had been awarded the Gold Medal and Silver Challenge Trophy at the 1985 Woodworker Show. My application was refused on the grounds that my work was 'inappropriate'.

Now winning a cup or medal does not make me the world's finest clock-case maker but nonetheless, the thought-process of that Guild is puzzling. I thought the NIMBY syndrome was a convenient if not necessarily accurate explanation.

What really matters is that our work should be as good as we can possibly make it. None of us is as proficient as we would like to be, nor yet as bad as our critics would perhaps suggest.

I would recommend the gentle whimsical style of James Krenov, who somehow manages to convey his love of craft in a gently suggestive way, offering the reader his own experiences but allowing that there may be — indeed, has to be — room for a contrary viewpoint.

Bill Watts, Lydney, Glos.

Quiet – but hot!

I WAS INTERESTED to read (WW/July) the Tottenham College of Technology's advice on workshop noise and insulation.

I have insulated my 16x8x8ft shed against excessive noise and it was a great success until the recent hot spell. With outside shade temperatures in the 80s, the thermometer rose to over 110° inside my shed, and I haven't been able to work in it.

A solution would have been an electric fan. I opened the double doors and two windows to no avail, and they would have cancelled out any effect of a fan.

This heat has also affected the drying times of paint and glue.

I am now waiting patiently for cooler weather. So my noise insulation stopped one problem but created another. To anyone who works in a small shed, I cry 'Beware!'

D. S. Boulter, Basildon

Tall tales

I'VE BEEN READING Ashley Iles' articles, *Tales out of steel*.

I enjoy them very much, but can't let Ashley get away with all of his tales. I've been a Sheffield tool dealer for 30 years, and as any good Yorkshireman knows, Denby Dale, where they make the world's largest pie, is near Huddersfield. Maybe Ashley is getting confused with Darley Dale in Derbyshire!

The hand forger Tom Merrill could tell a good tale; he'd been taught the trade of pen and pocket blade forging in the 20s. He went out of the trade, but returned about 1939 to do surgical instrument forging — though, like most of his breed, he could produce almost any kind of blade if he set his mind to it. He helped the Sheffield Trades Historical Society to re-create a typical pen and pocket forger's workshop in the Castle Museum, York, and Tom's name board is over the door.

I've heard that story about the discovery of stainless steel many times, and rarely is it told correctly. Harry Brearley, who was a steelworks chemist, recounts the true story in his autobiography *Knotted String* (published in 1941 by Longmans Green & Co), and it has nothing to do with a decimal point error!

High-chrome steel was designed to stop corrosion and fouling in gun tubes, and when etching the polished surface of steel samples for microscopic analysis, it was noticed that the acid etch did not react in the conventional way. Later Brearley suggested the steel could be used for cutlery; this was eventually accomplished by getting cutlers to forge, harden and grind the novel material — no easy matter.

Lastly, Ashley appears to have forgotten Benjamin Huntsman, who 'invented' cast steel — high-carbon steel melted in a crucible and cast into ingots for fine quality tool and other steels. Some readers may have an old chisel- or plane-iron that holds its edge much longer than most modern tools. That will probably be cast steel, made by the crucible process, which dates back 100 years before Bessemer's converter.

It's been said that few other inventions have had as much impact on our world as that of Bessemer's converter. It made possible the machining of metals on a scale previously undreamed of; steam engines and locomotives could be made by mass production; dies for coinage; printing plates for stamps and bank notes. Bessemer gave the world cheap bulk steel!

K. W. Hawley, Sheffield

Ashley Iles replies: I was glad to hear from Mr Hawley, a prominent figure on the history of Sheffield and one of my best customers to boot.

I was also pleased to read that he found my articles readable and enjoyable, and I welcome any extensions or corrections of my remarks. My heart is gladdened to learn as a fellow Yorkshireman that Denby Dale is in Yorkshire, not Derbyshire!

Goering's disgust

I WAS INTERESTED in the article about re-creating the Mosquito aircraft (WW/May), but I must air one or two points.

My interest was riveted at the paragraph on the difficulty in getting suitable plywood, and I took a deep breath when I read it cost £300 for an 8x4ft sheet of 2mm ply. I thought: why not make it? It would have to be to original specifications and by the original method, for authenticity and high quality.

Now the original method was a tapeless jointer invented by a German, Adolf Fritz — which must have been irksome to Hermann Goering when he discovered how Mosquitoes were made. The jointer stuck the veneers with animal glue in layers, and enabled 100% of the super-footage of inner layers to be glued. You can't get this with taped joints, or even tapes with punch-out holes. Fritz's device stood all alone.

I acquired a Fritz tapeless jointer in the 60s when I had to made up some 85thou teak ply, which is how I discovered these machines were used for the Mosquito ply.

I had to get rid of the tapeless in the 70s, and relaced it with a stitcher, which rolls on a hot thread of glue in a zig-zag fashion to

Letters

pull the dry veneer joint together. It's highly efficient and compact, but it doesn't give 100% coverage like the tapeless.

Alan Cranston, London SE17

Touring toolshops

I'M AFRAID M. Marshall ('Question Box' WW/June) won't be able to use his multimeter to measure the moisture content of wood electrically, as it's most unlikely it can measure high enough resistances. Most multimeters lose accuracy above two Megohms; unfortunately wood at 14% moisture content has a resistance (measured over the usual probe spacing of about 20mm) of about 40 Megohms, rising to around 10,000 Megohms for wood at 6% moisture content. A specialist instrument is required.

As summer draws on I'd like to make a holiday request. Could readers recommend interesting toolshops they come across in Europe? It would be helpful to others going abroad to know shops where they can buy tools not generally available in Britain. For a start, I'd like to recommend the basement of BHV, a large department store near the Hotel de Ville metro station in Paris.

Keith Walton, S.W. London

● See 'French lesson: 2', p.780, for some of the unusual tool choices abroad!

Unusual drawknife

I AM THE PROUD OWNER of an 8in drawknife, bought secondhand from a joiner in 1922, my first year as an indentured apprentice. Although many joiners work with drawknives, I haven't come across one like this. It's as good today as when I bought it, and I still use it.

I wonder if any other readers have a similar drawknife?

K. S. Jones, Battle

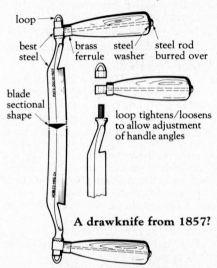

loop

best steel

brass ferrule   steel washer   steel rod burred over

blade sectional shape

loop tightens/loosens to allow adjustment of handle angles

A drawknife from 1857?

Advertisers Index

Apollo Products	764	A. Mills	748
Argus Specialist Exhibitions		Matthew Bros.	782
	729, 770	Multistar	741
Ashford Tool Centre	742	Myford	753
A-Z Tool Sales	739	John Myland	728
Benmail	778	Old Stores Turnery	709
Black & Decker	758		
John Boddy Timber	748	P&J Dust Extraction	765
Builders Direct Mail	753	Plans Service	749
		W.M. Plant	782
Calder Woodworking	800	A. Pollard	764
Canaan Carbides	720		
H. Case Hardware	771	Record Ridgway	716
Charltons Timber Centre	710	E.T. Roberts & Lee	720
Peter Child	765	Rocking Horse Shop	782
Christchurch Power Tools	779		
Cleveland Woodcraft	778	Sanlin	742
Coronet Lathe & Tool	773	Sarjents Tools	769
Craft Materials	764	Scott & Sargeant	746
Craft Supplies	716	Solent Tools	708
Cutwell Tools	782	Southwest Power Tools	771
Cutwell Woodworking	763	Startrite	766
		Steer Dawn	764
Data Power Tools	742	Stobart & Son	764
Dodd Machine Tools	778	Sumaco	713, 757
		Swann Morton	748
Ebac	776		
Elektra Beckum	IFC	Tabwell Tools	774
Excel Machine Tools	728	Henry Taylor	763
		Taylor Bros	774
Heath Saws	779	W. Thatcher	707
J.W. Hoyle	762	Thomas & Willis	765
David Hunt Tools	774	Tilgear 710, 742, 762, 778, 782	
		Tool Centre	771
Ashley Iles	710	Toolmail	771
		Trend	710
Kent Power Tools	774	Cecil W. Tyzack	728, 769
Kity	741		
		Warren Machine Tools	779
Ledbury Craft Supplies	765	Wessex Timber	778
Isaac Lord	769	Whitehall	716
E.W. Lucas	800	Woodfit	741
Luna Tools	707, OBC	Woodworking Mach. Switz.	754
Magh Spa	IBC	X.R. Machines	753

Woodworker CONTENTS

October 1986
Vol. 90
No. 10

design . . . craft . . . and the love of wood

● *Adrian Thompson of the LCF made this desk in American black walnut and silver-blue bird's eye maple; student work galore on pp828ff*

PROJECTS
All with detailed working drawings

813 Hey Presto!
The companion to a dressing table/desk is, of course, the folding wardrobe . . . *Leslie Stuttle*

838 Boulle's rules
Another job for your cover-mounted veneers; mirror-image marquetry, as plain or fancy as you like. *Alan and Gill Bridgewater*

870 La belle table
Make this magnificent parquetry-topped table in period French style — but you'll need some extra veneer! *Paul Davis*

On the cover: a magnificent free gift: you can make the coaster next to the big box with it!

808 Penny plane . . .
It takes more than a few coppers to buy wooden planes now, but someone thinks they're worth their weight in gold. *Rik Middleton*

820 The slice is right
The absorbing craft of parquetry — make a start with your free veneers! *Les Reed*

828 86 degrees . . . plus!
More extreme and exquisite work from the colleges, plus other first-class shows. *Emma Thornton, Peter Anstey, Ian Hosker, Paul Greer*

835 Juror furor
On the subject of student furniture, why did a prestigious bursary just not get awarded for '86?

841 Magic wand
Wave it, make it, or grow it, start your walking stick now and it'll be ready for the Show in '88! *Theo Fossel*

846 JAPAN 7
The 'pull' plane
The last in our in-depth series on tools from the East tells the tale of preparing and using *Hira-kanna*. *Tony Wood*

852 The grand furniture saga: 9
A native style develops in 17th century furniture, and chairs shift down the social spectrum. *Vic Taylor*

856 The eternal turner
How a gargantuan candlestick came to grace a Hertfordshire church. *Ted Reffell*

876 Third World tools
Tools for Self Reliance collect unwanted equipment and ship it to good homes in the developing world. *John Hemsley*

881 Tales out of steel
Millwrights and engineers; meet the elite of the Sheffield tool trade. *Ashley Iles*

REGULARS

802 This month last month, next month

805 Timberline what's on the timber boats

825 Bob Wearing's Workshop Auxiliary faceplates

855 Books *World Woods in Colour*

861 Woodworking wheeze of the month
The jigsaw sander — Mark 2! *Glyn Condick*

863 Question box Fissures in oak, rusting tools, a stail engine . . .

867 Guild notes Ideas, courses, chances

895 Letters Say your piece

896 Advertisers' index

Editor Aidan Walker
Deputy editor John Hemsley
Editorial assistant Kerry Fowler
Senior advertisement manager Paul Holmes
Advertisement manager Trevor Pryer
Graphics Jeff Hamblin
Technical illustrator Peter Holland
Guild of Woodworkers John Hemsley, Kerry Fowler
Editorial, advertisements and Guild of Woodworkers
1 Golden Square, London W1R 3AB, telephone 01-437 0626

Unfortunately we cannot accept responsibility for loss of or damage to unsolicited material. We reserve the right to refuse or suspend advertisements, and regret we cannot guarantee the bone fides of advertisers.
Published every third Friday

ABC
UK circulation
Jan-Dec 85
28,051

Back issues and subscriptions Infonet Ltd, 10-13 Times House, 179 Marlowes, Hemel Hempstead, Herts HP1 1BB; telephone Hemel Hempstead (0442) 48434

Subscriptions per year UK £16.90; overseas outside USA (accelerated surface post) £21.00, USA (accelerated surface post) $28, airmail £48

UK trade SM Distribution Ltd, 16-18 Trinity Gardens, London SW9 8DX; telephone 01-274 8611

North American trade Bill Dean Books Ltd, 151-49 7th Avenue, PO Box 69, Whitestone, New York 11357; tel. 1-718-767-6632

Printed in Great Britain by Ambassador Press Ltd, St. Albans, Herts
Mono origination Multiform Photosetting Ltd, Cardiff
Colour origination Derek Croxson Ltd, Chesham, Bucks
© Argus Specialist Publications Ltd 1986
ISSN 0043 776X

Argus Specialist Publications Ltd
1 Golden Square, London
W1R 3AB; 01-437 0626

This month

Whittle down the wind

Down in the woods something stirred, writes **Jack Hill**; and curious visitors to Black Park country park, Bucks, were fascinated to see what it was — a group of whittlers at work.

July's **whittle-in-the-woods** was organised by **Theo Fossel**, maker of walking sticks and shepherds' crooks, and founder/chairman of the British Stickmakers Guild. His idea was to set up a day-long workshop in a woodland setting for enthusiastic whittlers, people who cut or shape a piece of wood or a stick by paring or shaving with a knife.

Several members of the Stickmakers Guild took their tool rolls along and demonstrated carving sawn handle blanks in yew, elm and walnut. The sun shone in this popular beauty spot, and the group attracted a stream of spectators. Several people got so interested that they had a go themselves; some came to watch and stayed all day to whittle and smooth their chunks of wood.

This was not a competitive event; there was only a booby prize for the person who cut himself/herself most often! The Whittler's Thumb Award was a carved lifesize thumb, complete with sticking plaster.

Theo plans another Whittle-In soon. Why not organise one yourself locally . . .

Thin sliced

Are we good to you or what? Has a gift of nine leaves of exotic veneer on the cover got the class you expect from *Woodworker*, or has it not? Most people would be content with the veneers alone, of course, but we reckon you should have something to make with them as well — so you have two projects this month to cut your parquetry and marquetry teeth on, and one to really stretch you when your skills have developed. 'The slice is right', 'Boulle's rules', and 'La belle table' should keep you busy!

The veneers are zebrano, koto, walnut, Douglas fir, sapele, lime, padauk, purpleheart, and sweet chestnut; and we thank Les Reed of The Art Veneers Co, Ind. Est., Mildenhall, Suffolk IP28 7AY for supplying them. Nicely sliced?

'Oh Africa', one of six chair sculptures by Trinidadian Francisco Cabral, from the recent 'Caribbean Art Now' exhibition at the Commonwealth Institute, London W8

Designers' market

The **Design for Profit** conference on 17 July unearthed some disturbing facts, writes **Hugh O'Neill**.

The revelation that only three of 100 design students present had received any marketing tuition was greeted with stunned silence. Keith Grant of the Design Council, who raised the issue, was clearly appalled — so was his panel of successful designers.

Accountants Arthur Young and the National Westminster Bank sponsored the conference at the Royal Institute of British Architects, in association with the *House & Garden* Young Designer of the Year Award scheme, 'Decorex 86'. The event brought together potential customers, people working in design, students, and tutors.

The highlight was the open forum, chaired by Keith Grant. It was solid, common-sense guidance from a panel of established designers; many had started solo, and all now run significant businesses. Most denied that their personal objectives had changed over the years; Peter Milne explained: 'The emphasis has changed, but not my objective. I started by wanting to produce designer furniture and although I am no longer at the workbench, that is just what my business is doing.'

George Hamlyn of the Patents Office tackled the minefield of patent and design registration, and Priscilla Carluccio (director of styling for Habitat/Heals/Conran) received applause for her illustrated talk on the production of the 'Lifestyle' range. Andy Lord of NatWest made clear 'What the Bank Manager wants to know' when small businesses want finance, but the 'Effective marketing' session by Jan Tellick was too theoretical and general, and did little to fire students' interest in a field vital for survival.

The best of Britain's graduating design talent was featured in the Decorex 86 display; furniture featured prominently, with Parnham House, The Royal College of Art, Kingston, and Rycotewood well represented. Possibly the finest piece in the exhibition was an olive ash chair (below) — part of a dining suite — which won **Nicholas Mortimer** the £500 award from the Worshipful Company of Furniture Makers.

Nicholas, recently graduated from Rycotewood, said he had already become acutely aware of the need to know more about marketing and pricing. So who else?

Diary

Guild courses are shown by an asterisk(*); for further details see the Guild pages.

October

1-15 **Wood Sculpture Symposium**, Connemara West Centre, Letterfrack, Co. Galway, 095 41047

4-5 **Irish Woodturners Guild** annual seminar, Letterfrack; details Tom Dunlop, Shanbough Upper, Kilkenny, Ireland

2-3 **French polishing** Charles Cliffe*

5-9 **Building 86** Earls Court, London

11 **Wood-machining** Ken Taylor*

13-18 **International Creative Marquetry Show** The Corn Exchange, Ipswich. Contact 63 Church Lane, Sproughton, Ipswich IP8 3AY

16-22 **Chelsea Crafts Fair** Old Town Hall, London SW3

25-Nov 22 **Painted Wood**: Cleveland Crafts Centre, 57 Gilkes St, Middlesbrough TS1 5EC, (0642) 226351

19-22 **Style for 87** Furniture Show, Earls Court, London SW5

23-26 **London Woodworker Show** Alexandra Pavilion, London N22

25 **Rough Wood 2**: Forestry and architecture seminar, Parnham House, Beaminster, Dorset DT8 3NA

November

9-13 **Woodmex 86** Woodworking equipment exhibition, NEC Birmingham, contact 01-486 1951

9-13 **NEC International Furniture Show**, NEC, Birmingham

Shoptalk

Build your own Chippendale, Sheraton or Hepplewhite furniture . . . in **miniature**. A new range of 1/12th scale furniture kits is now being imported from Germany. The £2 colour catalogue is being offered free to *Woodworker* readers; send 50p stamps for p&p.
● Dept WWR, Technocentre Ltd, Freepost, Middlesbrough, Cleveland TS5 4BR

A new range of **microporous** stains and finishes — yes, another — is finding its way on to the market from Denmark. Bondex 'stain' and 'sheen', which is slightly more varnish-like, come in a good range of colours — and cost £4.47 for a litre of stain, £5.32 for the sheen, both plus VAT.
● Bondex, SBD Ltd, Denham Way, Maple Cross, Rickmansworth, Herts WD3 2RJ, (0923) 777777

The new Sorby 'Diamond' **sharpening system** consists of a 50gm aerosol of diamond slurry, writes **David Savage**, and a plastic tile on an iroko backing block. Three grades of diamond grit slurry are available, distinguished by a stick-on coloured spot on the can, which could rather easily discolour or peel off. There was no identification system available for the different tiles, which mustn't be muddled up, and which are about the size of a normal bench stone. One was glued askew to the iroko base and a second base had cupped leaving a tile that made sharpening difficult.

The idea is that the diamond embeds itself into the plastic surface; once a build-up occurs, it becomes less important to spray the surface before use, and the diamond-impregnated tile shouldn't then wear. The makers advise against washing off the honing residue as this will remove the diamond.

The system is hardly 'the simple and highly efficient answer to all your sharpening requirements', but it is a useful addition to a workshop.

The red 470/45 or medium grade can could best be compared in cut to a fine India Stone — abrasive lines were clearly visible on the steel. It cut with remarkable speed.

The blue 470/14 or fine grade gave a similar result to a soft white Arkansas stone, again cutting with some speed.

The white 470/6 or extra fine was rather a disappointment, leaving scratches in the steel coarser than a hard white Arkansas. It was marginally finer than a 1200 Japanese waterstone, but not within shouting distance of the 6000 grit Japanese 'gold' polishing stone.

The aerosol is a bit wasteful, as the spray is wide and the tile narrow. In use a dark grey honing residue seems to get everywhere, a far cry from the cleanliness of water-stones. It's not possible to wash it away with honing fluid as one would on an oil system so you have to live with it.

I thought the red medium grit very useful for touching up TCT tooling, but remember the proper sharpening of router bits is best left to the experts. If you have little faith in your local saw doctor, it may serve you very well, but for general sharpening of hand-tools it's expensive, fast and messy, not really cheaper, faster or cleaner than my Japanese stones.

Kit no. 450, the aerosol and tile, costs £20.42; the 460 tile is £7.95, and the 470 Diamond aerosols are £12.51 each, all plus VAT.
● Robert Sorby Ltd, Athol Rd, Woodseats Rd, Sheffield S8 0PA, (0742) 554231

Router bits claimed to last as long as HSS bits costing twice as much are new from Bosch. The 15 'half-price' bits in the Mastersharp range are made from heat-treated alloy steel, and cost from £2.09 to £4.75 inc. VAT.
● Robert Bosch Ltd, P.O. Box 98, Broadwater Pk, North Orbital Rd, Denham, Uxbridge, Middx UB9 5HJ, (0895) 833633

Four new ones for the *Fine Woodworking on . . .* series, collected articles on specific subjects from the US magazine. *Wood and how to dry it; Things to make; Carving;* and *Hand Tools* all cost £7.95.
● The Lion Tool Co. Ltd, 64 Fleet St, Swindon SN1 1RD, (0793) 31361

The Shopsmith Academy is a two day **course** on the respected US universal machine. They take up to eight people on four machines; £65 includes lunches, materials to make a small table, and a manual.
● Sumaco Ltd, Huddersfield Rd, Elland, W. Yorks HX5 9AA, (0422) 79811

A new **woodturning school** in Boroughbridge, Yorkshire is being opened by Allan Batty, who will be running two-day courses; he set up the turning courses at John Boddy's. The new venture is CoSIRA-assisted.
● Allan Batty, St James's Sq, Boroughbridge, Yorks, (09012) 4064

Elu announce a range of heavy duty **drills**; 10mm variable speed up to 13mm two-speed percussion, £75-£110.
● Elu, Westpoint, The Grove, Slough, Berks SL1 1QQ, (0753) 74277

More Show goodies — win a deluxe **power-tool table**, the Triton Workcentre MK3, at the Woodworker Show, 23-26 Oct. Just answer five easy questions based on their on-stand video, wait for the draw, and walk off with £270 of gear!
● M&M, PO Box 128, Bexhill on Sea TN40 2QT, (0424) 216897

Now's your chance to win a Sandvik centenary universal handsaw: send your most original time- and labour-saving workshop or site tip for hand-tool users to 'Shoptalking points', *Woodworker*, 1 Golden Sq, London W1R 3AB

Bench-mounted **mortiser** fills a gap in the maker's range; £475+VAT.
● Multico, (0293) 78244

Re-enter the old **glue-pot**, thanks to popular demand. £23 inc. VAT+ £2.50 p&p.
● Liberon Waxes (0679) 20107

Improved 12x9in version of the Startrite SD310 **planer/thicknesser**, £1342 +VAT single phase.
● Startrite, (0634) 55122

Reduce **wood-waste** volume with the Fercell Refiner; £1550+VAT the complete system.
● Fercell, (0322) 53131

Timberline

Arthur Jones looks at movements in the timber market, and pinpoints a possible threat to softwood price stability

Oak is still Britain's top selling native hardwood, according to a survey by the Forestry Commission. Beech and elm are also popular, but we buy twice as much oak as elm (doubtless now suffering from the results of Dutch elm disease on log production). In the past couple of years sycamore has become more of a favourite, which won't surprise woodworkers, and it's now on a par with ash for popularity among home-grown hardwoods.

An expansion of forestry in the UK is urged in a report from the UK Centre for Economic Environmental Development. The expansion would be part of an integrated land use policy for farms, but with financial support conditional upon good silvicultural planning and practice, and an obligation to respect landscape, amenities and conservation. That could help the hardwood areas.

The political upset in the Philippines is continuing to cause problems with unsettled trading, many areas still being under a logging ban while mills are being investigated for malpractices, and it is known that many logging and sawmill licences have been suspended.

Lauan is far from plentiful and the prices of most *shoreas* have been on the upgrade. Against this there has been a rise in shipments of mahogany from Brazil.

Many tropical hardwoods also find their way to the plywood mills, and here the prices paid have been rising rapidly.

Quotas for export have been introduced in some countries and there are strict controls over minimum selling prices. In Indonesia prices have jumped an amazing 25%, which must soon be reflected in selling prices in the UK. Importers are forced to pay the higher rates to get future supplies, so there are dark clouds over future hardwood and ply prices. Supply will be OK, but at higher prices; in fact selling prices here have been lagging behind the trends overseas, which are distinctly strong and

upwards. So far we've been shielded from steep increases through keen competition among UK stockists for orders on a market which is generally dull, though any increase in sales could quickly produce notable effects upon selling prices.

Higher minimum selling prices for fibreboard can also be expected to be imposed by the EEC to protect European board producers.

The trade is getting jumpy about what happens if the Americans put a hefty tariff on Canadian softwood. This threatened protectionist measure is being demanded by the US lumber industry who want a duty imposed of anything up to 35% because they claim the Canadians pay artificially low log rates. Anything which limits sales of sawn softwood to the US from Canada would immediately send the Canadians scuttling over here to sell us more of their wood, and they could do it only by slashing their prices. That could create quite an upset in the home softwood market; but in the meantime you'll find there are good stocks and steady prices.

Efforts are being made to promote the sale of Canadian hemlock, by grading all stocks and guaranteeing that there will be a maximum moisture content of 18% in any piece.

Efforts are also being made to boost sales of native-grown softwoods and, provided the material has been strength-graded to eliminate problems with trees grown too fast, there is no reason why native softwoods shouldn't be satisfactory.

While importers have not been investing heavily in forward softwood stocks, there are no problems with finding adequate offers of most specifications at prices which show only marginal increases over those quoted six months ago. The forward market, governing wood which will be sold to the woodworker in the first half of 1987, has seen increases from various markets, but none are greater than 7%.

Russian softwood has sold steadily at the prices quoted last month, followed by an offer from the Poles with increases of only £1 per cu. metre on redwood fifths and £2 on whitewood. ∎

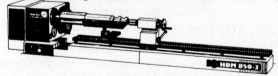

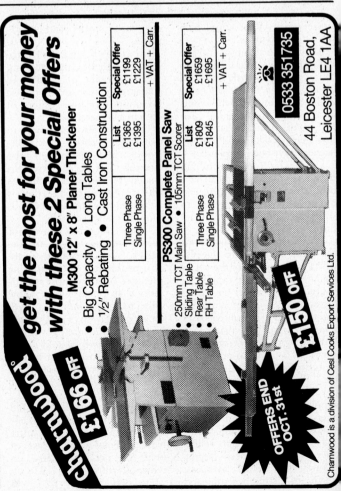
806

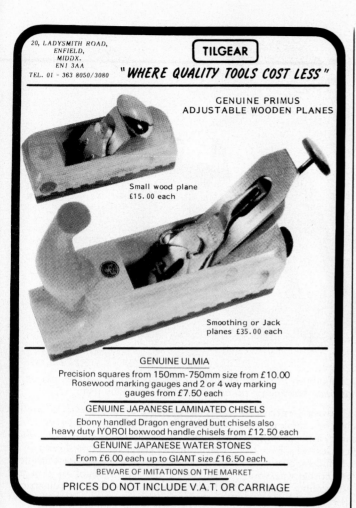

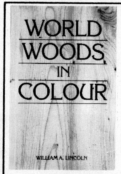

Penny plane...

Wooden planes cost more than pennies nowadays, but they're still plentiful and cheap if you know where to look. Rik Middleton sings their praises, revitalises and uses them

J ust-married and a new home-owner in 1969, I came up against a brick wall whenever I tried to do one of those innumerable vital jobs — no tools to do it with. It seemed to happen every time I tried to lay a carpet or hang a door, which wasn't surprising in view of the fact that on Day One of my new life I possessed no tools at all. So a hurried, piecemeal tool acquisition programme got under way — and cheap too, there were plenty of other things to buy.

I usually bought beech planes — a 1950 ex-WD Marples smoother, for instance, for 15/- as compared with a Stanley metal one for £3 (gasp). After a good few years, my collection has burgeoned embarrassingly — I now have walls full, drawers full, of tools — but I can barely remember my first-bought cheap saws and cheap chisels. My wooden planes, however, have increased in variety and number; they have a firm place in my affections and are used every day. I have at least a dozen, most from market stalls, and most of which have had to have renovation, major surgery, or even an organ transplant. I have refitted many a handle and re-blocked many a bottom to close many a mouth . . .

I've since discovered many woodworkers fight shy of these planes because of the difficulty of adjusting them. I had gained the knack before I heard of this, so it had no psychological effect on me. I had seen my father adjusting a wooden plane as a boy, and although I had no direct instruction in it, and paid it no attention at the time, I seemed to have subliminally grasped the principles. Either that, or it really *is* simple and logical. I gradually realised I was in a minority as a wooden plane user. Most other woodworkers seem to assume I'm masochistically esoteric!

I have often found myself using other peoples' tools, so I have used cast metal planes on many occasions, and I've never had the slightest desire to switch to them. I don't find them at all comfortable to handle. My hands may be gripping the wooden handles (where they are still wooden!) but they rub the metal parts as well, and I get blisters if I have to do a lot of work. In my unheated garage/workshop they would be almost unholdable for a couple of months of the year. Give me a nice well-worn, warm, rounded piece of beech any day. No contest . . . .

Not only are wooden planes kinder to my hands, I'm sure they're kinder to my work as well. Imagine the damage to a job if it's

● *Thousands of you have been throwing away your 'old fashioned' wooden planes, and Rik Middleton has been building up an assortment for everyday use . . .*

accidentally grazed by a worn corner of a beech smoothing plane, then think of the same accident with a sharp cast-iron corner. Perhaps it's only the careless who have to choose tools to cover blunders, but if you claim never to have hit a corner with your plane when you're smoothing down a square jointed framework, you're either a better woodworker than I am, a liar, or an amnesiac. It's not just a case of avoiding accidents; I feel sure that wood-to-wood contact just gives better results, especially at the smoothing-plane stage.

A cast metal plane's adjustability also worries me. It might well be easier and quicker to adjust, but I'm not happy about the principle of using a plane with a blade set up to move up and down. I think it's preferable in a plane to have the blade solidly and immovably fixed, the whole structure locked up as a unit. I can rely on my planes staying at the same setting until I alter it; I find the amount of slop and backlash in the adjustment of ordinary cast planes appalling. They can and do drift out of adjustment. My experience may have been with old, worn and possibly misused cast metal planes, but then the comparison with the planes I normally use is surely all the more valid. I should point out that I haven't used the modern generation of more expensive cast planes, and I know their designers have given these matters serious consideration.

● *Disassemble the smoothing plane by hitting it at the top of the back*

● *Long planes need a blow on top in front of the gullet to loosen them up*

Tuning an English-style beech plane

1 Disassembly

Simply strike the plane body with a mallet. Where you hit it depends entirely on the proportions of the plane. I normally strike smoothing planes on the top of the rear end where your right palm pushes; longer planes respond better to a blow on top, in front of the gullet. Hold the plane free in your left hand, and never hit it when it's resting on anything firmer than your hand. Don't forget to hold it so the wedge and blade/back-iron assembly can't fly out or drop. Give it two blows, then you can lift the wedge and metalwork out. The back-iron unscrews from the blade as in a metal plane, although the fit is different.

2 The blade

Much of what I have to say about the blade applies to cast planes as well. Grinding and honing is essentially identical to any other flat-backed blade and is beyond the scope of this article: Fraser Budd's article 'Plane speaking', WW/Feb, is a good place to start.

Obviously, to avoid one-sided cutting the edge has to be pretty close to 90° to the axis of the blade, but the actual shape of the cutting edge may usefully be varied during honing, especially if, like myself and Alan Thomas (WW/Apr 85) you have more than one plane of each size. Different settings and edge shapes can be used in each one (fig. 1).

I always felt that jointing/trying planes should be 90° and dead flat as at fig. 1a. If you're jointing boards, I'm sure this shape

is best but if you're trying to flatten a large plane surface (mine was a shove-ha'penny board), the precise edge leaves marks which you can't remove without making more. I have honed the blade of one of my longest planes to the shape in fig. 1b so the outside 2mm or so of the blade never makes contact at a fine setting.

I generally hone smoothing-plane blades to the shape in fig. 1c, where only the middle of the blade cuts but the shaving feathers off to nothing both sides. David Savage ('Tools of the trade,' WW/June) also quotes this shape.

As for the jack planes, I keep one blade slightly more coarsely set with profile fig. 1b, and one very fine with profile fig. 1c (a long smoothing plane, in effect).

Fig.1 Honing profiles

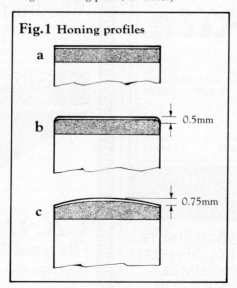

I hone the back-iron from its back. Apart from remedial treatment, I try not to hone the side that comes into contact with the blade. The slightest trace of a hollow middle on the honing stone, or any rocking in the hands, tend to cut back the sides so they aren't firmly in contact with the blade, which causes poor cutting and clogging. Most back-irons seem to be like this when I get them. Once I've got them properly flat and making good contact with the blade-back, I like to leave them that way, so I hone them from the other side. I don't attempt to strop away the edge, but leave it there to bed against the back of the blade (fig. 2).

Don't be frightened to get firm with the screw which joins blade and back-iron. The screw-thread is substantial; only Superman could strip it, and if it isn't tight enough it'll be changed during adjustment of the blade setting.

If I'm setting up a plane with a very close back-iron for difficult timber, I run a well-pointed nail along the junction between back-iron and blade, carefully but firmly. This forces the feather-edge down to completely block any remaining gaps where wood fibres could be forced in.

Since the mouth of most wooden planes isn't adjustable, I keep one specially close-mouthed for difficult timbers.

Fig.2 Back-iron

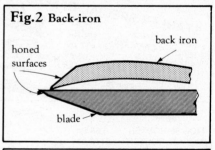

3 Mouth adjustment

There are two ways of adjusting the mouth to make it smaller, a process which may be necessary either to close-mouth a tool for difficult timber, or to renovate one worn down on the sole.

The first method is to stick a thin piece of wood in behind the blade (fig. 3). You might think adhesives would cause problems in well-oiled beech, but with coarse enough scoring of both surfaces I have had good results with Araldite.

Slots must of course be cut to match the existing screw-clearance slots, and the

809

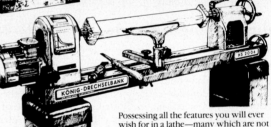

Penny plane...

wedge will then need a good planing-down on the flat side. Check there's enough meat in the wedge to start with, and if not try the second method.

The other way of closing up the mouth is to block it out from below. The front edge of the mouth has to be removed as part of a wide shallow mortise, and a whole new piece dropped in (fig. 4). This can be glued, but a more reliable fixing is four brass screws in recessed holes, a method I prefer. The new piece then has to be taken down flat with the rest of the sole, first with another plane and finally by the following personalised technique.

I take a gouge and undercut the holes slightly (fig. 5), fill them with PVA glue, and leave the plane sole-up to dry. The PVA shrinks into the hole as it dries, leaving a smooth and moderately hard, slightly depressed plug which doesn't pick up wood particles. If you want to get to the screws again, the PVA plug can be lifted out with the same gouge. I notice on some planes that plastic wood has been used for this job, but it doesn't seem to allow access in the same way, and is never as smooth as the rest of the sole.

Fig.4 Blocking mouth from below

screws
new wood

worn away

wedge-shaped insert leaves sides intact

Alternative method

4 Flattening a sole

If you hold a straight-edge to the sole of your plane and it shows fine hairlines of light, don't get neurotic — get on with your woodwork! If the sole is badly out, you might like to look back to Alan Thomas' article in *Woodworker*, April 85, for methods of sorting it out; here is another. If you have no machined surface to use as a reliable flat, you can buy a 4in wide offcut of ¼in plate glass for a nominal sum. It

Fig.5 Covering screw-holes the PVA way

PVA   hardened plug

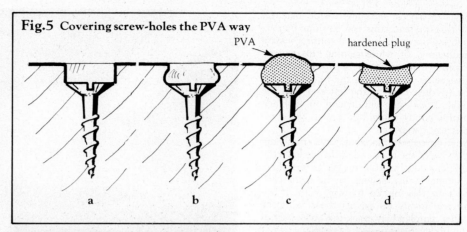

a   b   c   d

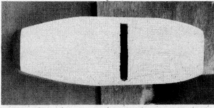

● *Flattening the sole by rubbing it on wet-and-dry paper after emulsioning*

needs to be longer than the plane you intend to work on, and it's also rather springy and needs support, so lay it without any pressure on to numerous blobs of 'Hard' Plastic Padding on a substantial piece of chipboard. Then contact-glue medium wet-and-dry paper to the glass. Wipe the sole of the plane with turps and emulsion-paint it, and when the body is dry, clean the paint off down to the wood across the whole face with a planing action on the wet-and-dry-paper.

5 Reassembly and adjustment

The blade and back-iron assembly is put in position with the body held in the hand. The blade shouldn't extend through the mouth, and the sides must be clear of the wood with an equal gap both sides, or blade adjustments may cause damage to the body. Put the wedge in on top, making sure the rear of the blade extends at least ¼in beyond the wedge. If you have a smaller amount than that because it's an old worn blade, you'll have to cut a piece off the thick end of the wedge.

Hit the wedge home with a hammer; I use a 4oz engineer's tool. If you're worried about hitting beech with a hammer, that weight should stop you hitting it too hard! If you hit the wedge squarely with a hammer no bigger than this, it will suffer no damage. Hit the wedge too hard with a larger hammer or heavy mallet, and you may

● *A plane can easily be damaged if you're not careful with side adjustment*

damage the sides of the gullet (sometimes called the abutment) which hold the wedge in place. This type of damage can be extremely difficult to repair, and if it does occur, it makes the problem of bruises on top of the wedge totally academic! If one firm blow from this small hammer doesn't lock the wedge in place, then it probably doesn't fit correctly and must be reshaped until it does. I know no magic formula for this. You need to find the high-spots, perhaps by rubbing soft pencil graphite on the wedge and seeing where it's rubbed off when you fit the wedge. Then remove them with the lightest touch of a very sharp paring chisel.

To get the plane on 'cut', tap the extended end of the blade squarely with the same 4oz hammer. I do this with my finger-tips over the mouth, to feel the blade coming down. With a bit of experience, this gets you very near the right setting. Sighting along the sole also helps. There is no substitute for the 'scrap timber test', however, ideally the same species you're working on; if you're bold and really confident, risk a test on the actual job!

To get a deeper cut, tap the top of the blade again lightly, and to reduce depth of cut take a mallet and lightly repeat the blow you use to disassemble the plane. Lightly tap the wedge further home again after the 'reduce cut' blow.

With the cut about right for depth, you

Penny plane . . .

have to check the side-to-side balance. With experience this can be done by eye, sighting down the sole. To confirm what's happening, or while gaining this experienced eye, a narrow piece of timber in the vice helps. Cut it with the middle of the blade, then over to the left and then the right. The results will depend on the blade profile you're using, but it must be a symmetrical pattern.

To correct the blade sideways, simply tap the side of the back end of the blade on the side that cuts thickest (fig. 6). This is where you may cause damage if the metalwork isn't in the middle to start with. If it's already firmly up against the side of the gullet, tapping may crack this weak part of the body.

Sideways adjustment may change the effective depth of cut slightly, so re-check that and adjust it if necessary. In practice, adjusting both ways is a see-saw process while you look for the best setting. One does tend to overshoot and overcorrect, but with experience the time taken soon becomes seconds rather than minutes.

And there it is, that wooden plane, spreading ribbon shavings all over the floor. There are absolutely no loose parts to rattle back and forth, it's one solid unit and it won't move till you decide to change it. You've gained another skill — and doesn't a wooden plane *feel* nice? It's wood in your hands, after all . . . . ■

● **Next month:** Rik compares some modern wooden adjustable planes with his collection of oldies but goodies.

● *Above right, putting the plane on 'cut'; **right**, when making side adjustments, check there is room for the blade to move or you can cause serious damage*

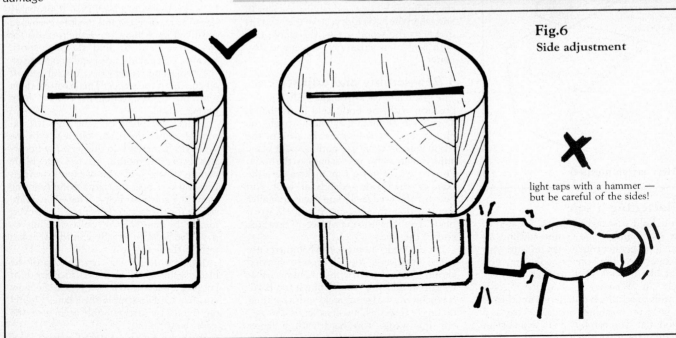

Fig.6
Side adjustment

light taps with a hammer — but be careful of the sides!

Hey Presto!

From the man who brought you last month's dual desk/dressing table, we give you the incredible shrinking wardrobe. Leslie Stuttle does it again

My latest space-saving idea for the spare room of our bungalow is a wardrobe that folds back to less than 4in from the wall when not in use. It complements last month's desk/dressing table unit, and with a convertible settee/bed, means we have a most useful spare storage/office room that can easily be turned into a bedroom for visitors.

For all large panels I used ¾in blockboard veneered both sides, and matching solid timber for the rest plus the edging strips.

I suggest you start by cutting out a 3ft section of the skirting board, which is the easiest way of dealing with potential scribing problems. If you scribe round the skirting, you'll have to add a piece to it inside the cupboard on which to store the top and floor of the cupboard when it's closed up — but that comes later.

Make up all the metal plates and the hanger fittings (see the list at end) so they are ready when they're needed.

● *Now you see it, now you don't . . . well it's certainly slimmed down! This ingenious design would be a bonus in any small home*

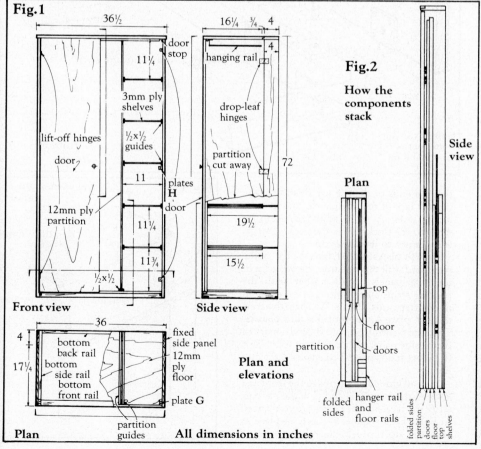

Fig.1

Front view — 36½, 11¼, 3mm ply shelves, lift-off hinges, door, ½x½ guides, 11, 12mm ply partition, ½x½

Side view — 16¼, ¾, 4, 4, door stop, hanging rail, drop-leaf hinges, partition cut away, plates **H**, door, 11¼, 11¾, 19½, 15½, 72

Fig.2

How the components stack

Side view

Plan

top, floor, partition, doors

Plan and elevations

folded sides, hanger rail and floor rails

folded sides, partition, doors, floor, top, shelves

Plan — 36, 4, 17¼, bottom back rail, bottom side rail, bottom front rail, fixed side panel, 12mm ply floor, plate G, partition guides

All dimensions in inches

Carcase panels

Cut two pieces of blockboard for the fixed side panels, to finish 71¼x3¾in, then glue and pin ¼in edging strip to one long edge of each. Set in and screw three plates **H** to the opposite long edges; plates **E** go at the bottom of each panel, ½in from the front edge. Fix the panels to the wall through plates **H**, making sure that they are upright, hard down on the floor and that the overall width is 36in.

Cut another piece of blockboard 36x4¾in for the fixed top panel (fig. 3), and form a rebate ¾x⅞in along one long edge; then attach the plates **C** as shown in fig. 3, and two wall-fixing plates **H**. Place the fixed top panel on top of the side panels and, making sure the ends are flush with the outside of the side panels, fix it to the wall. Then drill and dowel the top to the sides. Glue and pin edging strip to each end.

Now you can start on the folding sides. Measure the distance from the underside of the top panel to the top of the carpet pile; when these panels are fitted they should appear to reach the floor yet be capable of moving without rubbing too hard on the carpet. If you have hard flooring, arrange clearance by using a thin piece of cardboard.

Deduct ⅝in from this height measurement to obtain the moveable side-panel length. This allows for edging strip top and bottom, plus ⅛in clearance at the top when

Hey Presto!

the panels are folded in. The panels are 16½in wide. After cutting them, test for length and adjust if necessary; then glue and pin ¼in edging strip all round and attach plates **E** 2½in from the front edges.

Next fit three drop-leaf hinges to each panel, but let in only the knuckles; don't recess the whole hinge as it wouldn't leave enough wood to screw to. If you can't get hold of drop-leaf hinges, backflaps will do if you fit them wrong way round using round-headed screws; if you use backflaps you'll have to be careful when stacking the components inside to avoid catching them on the screw heads.

Now you can attach the folding panels to the fixed sides with the hinges. Keep the panels tight up together and again let in only the knuckles, and don't forget the ⅛in clearance at the top.

Base

Prepare three bottom rails 1½x¾in and one back rail 1¾x1½in. Make sure that the length of the side rails exactly matches the combined width of the wide and narrow side panels, and that the back and front rails fit neatly between the side panels. Make halving joints at the ends of the rails (fig. 4).

Now fit plates **D**, **F** and **G**. Place the side rails against the panels and mark the positions of plates **E**. Square the marks across the rails and cut recesses ³⁄₁₆in deep. Test fit the rails to ensure a snug fit over plates **E**. Lay plate **F** in the recess, mark the slot and cut it out. Place the rail in position, insert a Whitworth screw through plate **F** and engage the thread in the plate **E**. Now you can line up plate **F** and fix it with no.4 screws. Then you can fix plates **G** to the tops of the side rails.

Fit the side and front rails together and drill ³⁄₁₆in holes through both rails at the corners. Insert the Whitworth screw through the hole and engage the thread in plate **D** so you can mark this plate's position before cutting out a ³⁄₁₆in recess for it. Trial fit in case some slight adjustment is necessary to get a really close-fitting joint.

When you're happy with it, place the back rail in position, screw the front and side rails together, and drop them into place. Press one side rail hard down on to the floor and fix it to the side panel with a Whitworth screw; repeat on the other side.

Removable top

Cut a 36x16¾in piece of blockboard and form a ¾x⅜ rebate on one long edge to match the rebate in the fixed top panel (fig. 5).

As the folding side panels are set down ⅛in from the top, you should make ¾x⅛in packing strips to go each end under the removable top panel to compensate; these strips extend the width of the panel, including the rebate and the front edging strip that is fitted later. Don't attach the strips, just lay them on the top edges of the side panels before putting the top panel in position; check that the rebate fits properly,

that the ends of the top are flush with the outside face of the side panels, and that the top is level. A slight adjustment can be made to the thickness of the packing strips if necessary to level the top.

Now fit plates **A** flush into the top of the panel and drill through into the top edge of the side panels; don't bother with the packing strips since holes can be made in these afterwards. Pass a Whitworth screw through plate **A** and thread it into plate **B**. Then the position of plate **B** can be marked on the side panel and a recess cut for it. Test fit before fixing plate **B** to ensure the plates line up.

Pin and glue edging strips to the front and ends of the top panel and glue the packing strips in place. For the next stage you'll need to hold the top panel securely in place as you drill up through the rebate; a heavy

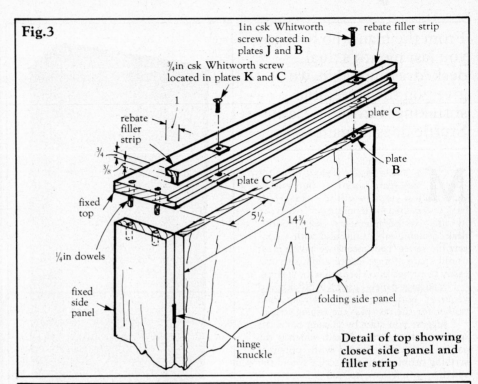

Fig.3

1in csk Whitworth screw located in plates **J** and **B**

¾in csk Whitworth screw located in plates **K** and **C**

rebate filler strip

plate **C**

plate **B**

rebate filler strip

¾

⅜

1

fixed top

¼in dowels

fixed side panel

plate **C**

5½   14¾

hinge knuckle

folding side panel

Detail of top showing closed side panel and filler strip

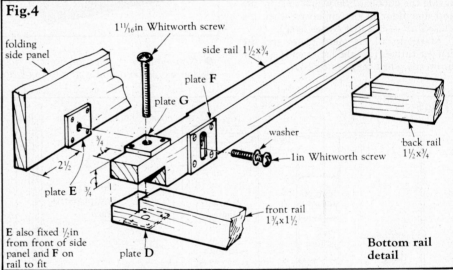

Fig.4

folding side panel

1¹¹⁄₁₆in Whitworth screw

side rail 1½x¾

plate **F**

plate **G**

washer

1in Whitworth screw

back rail 1½x¾

¾

2½

plate **E**   ¾

front rail 1¾x1½

E also fixed ½in from front of side panel and F on rail to fit

plate **D**

Bottom rail detail

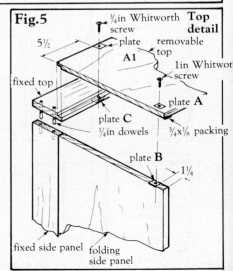

Fig.5   **Top detail**

¾in Whitworth screw

plate removable top

A1

1in Whitworth screw

5½

fixed top

plate **C**

¼in dowels

¾x⅛ packing

plate **A**

plate **B**

1¼

fixed side panel   folding side panel

weight may do the job. Use the largest drill you have which will pass through the hole in plate **C** without damaging the thread. After drilling through into the top panel, put plate **C** on one side and enlarge the hole with a ³⁄₁₆in drill. Pass a Whitworth screw down through plate **A1** and engage the thread in plate **C**. Mark the position of plate **A1**, cut recess and fix. Recess for and fix plate **C** as well. Now with all the sections fitted and secured together, the job should be fairly rigid.

● *Ample hanging and shelf space for that weekend guest*

Internal fittings

Cut and fit the plywood floor; the front edge which acts as a stop for the doors should be in line with the front edges of plates **G** and you'll have to cut the corners out to fit round them. Attach the vertical partition guides by screwing up from the underside of the floor and fix them at the top to the removable section only. The top guides should be kept back from the front at least 1¼in to allow for the thickness of the doors and fitting the door stop.

Now, working from the top, screw the pairs of shelf guides to the right-hand folding side panel only. The guides should be kept back about 1in from the front edge and stop ½in short of the joint with the fixed side panel. Use a piece of plywood intended for the shelves to get the spacing right between each pair of guides. The shelves are removable so don't make them too tight a fit. I found that a piece of paper pasted to a scrap of ply gave just the right amount of clearance. The guides must be level, and an easy way to get even spacing between them is to use a piece of hardboard or ply cut to match the distance between each set of guides.

Next cut the vertical plywood partition and fit the shelf guides by screwing through the ply into the guides. The partition

shouldn't protrude beyond the front end of the top guides. To complete, cut the shelves to size and slide them into position.

Hanging rail

The hanger is made from ¼in round steel rod, cut to 19in long and threaded at each end, and two ¾x⅛in steel right-angle brackets. Take two 3in lengths of steel and drill a ¼in hole ½in from one end and a ³⁄₁₆in hole centred, ⅜in from the other; then bend the strip at right angles ¾in from the end with the larger hole. Use ¼in Whitworth nuts to secure the rod between the brackets.

These brackets are held in position by 1¼x1¼x³⁄₁₆in plates, tapped with a ³⁄₁₆in hole in the centre, and four holes for countersunk no.6x¾ screws.

Secure one of these plates to the top fixed panel centrally between the left hand side of the partition and 1in from the wall. Attach the bracket with a Whitworth screw, insert the rod and place a nut on the end. Attach the other plate to the remaining bracket, slide the bracket on to the rod and thread on a nut. Hold this end against the removable top when it's in position and mark the position of the plate. Now separate bracket and plate and screw the plate to the top panel.

Doors

Finally you can tackle the doors. Cut two pieces of blockboard ½in undersize, glue and pin edging strip all round, and hang them with lift-off hinges; these must be staggered or they will clash when the doors are folded up. Fit flush bolts to the edges of the left-hand door top and bottom and ball catches to the right-hand door to lock into the left-hand one. Fit a ½x½in batten to the underside of the top to act as a stop for the doors and fix detachable handles or knobs to the doors.

One extra item is needed. When the wardrobe is not in use and the sides are folded in, the fixed top panel will show a

rebated edge. To hide this, and to lock the sides in the closed position, prepare a piece 36½x1x¾in, and rebate it ¾x⅜in (fig. 3).

With the top removed, place this filler strip in position, drill up through plate **C** and fit plate **K**. Insert Whitworth screws, and then, with the sides folded in, mark the position of plate **B** on the front edge of the filler strip. Using a square, draw lines across the edge and on to the top of the strip. Set in plates **J** with their edges flush with the back edge and drill a ³⁄₁₆in hole through the filler strip and the rebate in the fixed top panel. Use a Whitworth screw to hold the sides closed. Don't overtighten these screws or you will pull the sides up and strain the hinges.

Now you can rub the whole job down and finish it to match the dressing table unit.

Putting it together

A special sequence is used to assemble the wardrobe.

Remove the screws from the front edge of the top and take off the filler strip. Open out the sides and take out all the components. Place the bottom back rail in place, then assemble the side and front rails and set them in place. Press down on one side rail and secure it with Whitworth screws; repeat on the other side. Store the filler strip inside, then lay the floor. Stand the partition in place, fit the top and screw down. Insert the shelves, fit the hanger rail, hang the doors and fit the door knobs.

When dismantling the pieces must be stacked in the correct order. The floor and top are placed with the guides between them, and the partition is stacked with shelf guides to the front so the side panel guides fit between them (fig. 2).

I hope you will enjoy making and using this wardrobe; I'm sure there are detail improvements that can be made, but the general idea works very well. And it makes good use of very limited space! ∎

Metal plates

Use brass or stainless steel for preference, but mild steel is also fine. I used ³⁄₁₆in Whitworth screws because I had a tap that size, but you can use any suitable thread.

Notice that plates **A**, **A1**, **C**, **J** and **K** are not drilled for fixing screws because the wood isn't thick enough to screw into; I used Superglue for these.

2 Plates **A**	1in x	¾in x	¹⁄₁₆ in	centrally drilled ³⁄₁₆in & csk
2 Plates **A1**	1	¾	¹⁄₁₆	centrally drilled ³⁄₁₆in & csk
2 Plates **B**	1	¾	⅛	centrally drilled & tapped; drilled & csk for 2 no.4 screws
2 Plates **C**	1	¾	⅛	centrally drilled & tapped
2 Plates **D**	1½	1	³⁄₁₆	centrally drilled & tapped; drilled & csk for 4 no.4 screws
4 Plates **E**	1½	1	³⁄₁₆	centrally drilled & tapped; drilled & csk for 4 no.6 screws
4 Plates **F**	1½	1	⅛	centre slotted 1x³⁄₁₆in; drilled for 4 no.3 rd/hd screws
2 Plates **G**	1	¾	³⁄₁₆	centrally drilled ³⁄₁₆in; drilled for 2 no.4 rd/hd screws
8 Plates **H**	1½	1	⅛	drilled & csk for 2 no.6 screws and 1 no.8 screw
2 Plates **J**	1	¾	¹⁄₁₆	centrally drilled & csk ³⁄₁₆in
2 Plates **K**	1	¾	¹⁄₁₆	centrally drilled & csk ³⁄₁₆in

You only need two hands with a MAXi 26

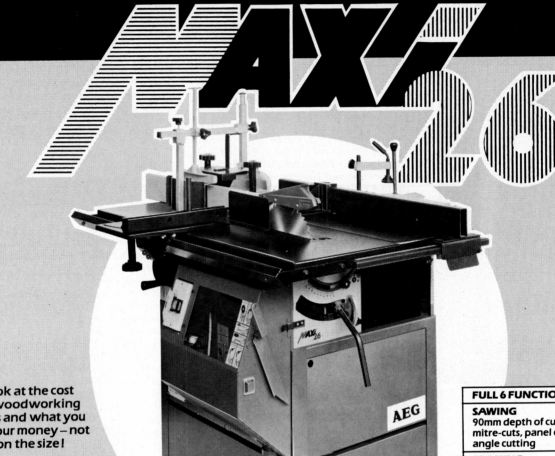

Just look at the cost of some woodworking machines and what you get for your money – not to mention the size!

CAPACITY, COMPACTNESS, COST and CONFIDENCE come together in the universal Maxi 26 – the ideal woodworking machine for the light professional and the keen hobbyist.

Look at the CAPACITY. Six functions – sawing, thicknessing, tenoning, planing, moulding and mortising – all effortless, with flexibility, precision and safety, and driven by a powerful and reliable 2 HP motor.

Look at its COMPACT design. The Maxi 26 is easily moved, even in the smallest of workshops.

Look at the COST. Buy a Maxi 26 and you still get change from £1350 (plus VAT, of course).

Look at the COMPETITION – and you **must** come back to the Maxi 26.

You can have every CONFIDENCE in the Maxi 26 – in its performance, and because it comes fully guaranteed for 2 years.

Designed and built to the highest standards, the Maxi 26 is the best value woodworking machine available today.

FULL 6 FUNCTIONS	
SAWING 90mm depth of cut, edging, mitre-cuts, panel cuts, 45° angle cutting	✓
PLANING On edge or flat, 260mm width of cut. Easy machining of any woods.	✓
THICKNESSING Up to 150mm capacity, depth of cut adjustable 0-4mm, automatic feed.	✓
MORTISING Deep, with both movements controlled by a single lever. Lateral and depth.	✓
MOULDING Moulding, rebates, grooving and all shaping tasks to a professional standard, 30mm diameter spindle shaft.	✓
TENONING Bearing mounted carriage 0-45° adjustable fence for precision square or angular cuts.	✓

AEG (UK) Limited
217 Bath Road, Slough, Berkshire SL1 4AW
Telephone: Slough (0753) 872101

AEG

Where Craft Comes Alive...

Beautiful wood... Oak, Sycamore, Ash, Walnut, Mahogany
Versatile wood... see the experts demonstrating their skills
Wonderful wood... admire the competition entries –
from marquetry to cabinet making
LOOK... at the latest woodworking machinery,
tools, supplies and accessories
LISTEN... to the advice of the demonstrators
BUY... from the many exhibition stands

October 23rd – 26th at the
Alexandra Pavilion,
Wood Green, London

For further details contact
Argus Specialist Exhibitions,
Wolsey House, Wolsey Road,
Hemel Hempstead, Herts HP2 4SS
Tel: 0442 41221

Opening Times:
Oct. 23, 24, 25 ..... 10am-6pm
Oct. 26 .... 10am-5pm

817

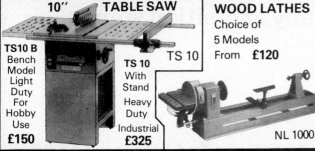

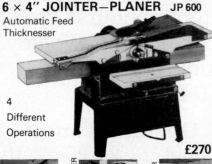

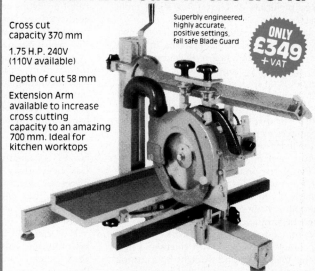

The slice is right

If you're already fired up to use your veneer cover gift, try a start in the challenging craft of parquetry. Les Reed of the Art Veneers Co. explains

As an introduction to working with decorative veneers, parquetry has everything to recommend it. You may not be inclined towards pictorial marquetry, but with some veneers — like the ones on the cover — a ruler, and a sharp knife you can create myriads of patterns for large furniture or (just for a start) table mats.

Parquetry is the art of designing and constructing geometric patterns in wood veneer, using the same tools and materials as marquetry, but making different demands on skills, especially in the cutting.

Marquetry calls for a well developed artistic sense to produce top quality original work. It involves freehand cutting, and beginners usually start with kits to develop knowledge of veneers and technical skills before moving on to their own designs.

Parquetry, on the other hand, will appeal to everyone who enjoys veneers, particularly if you also enjoy maths! You will be designing your own patterns almost from the beginning; there are no kits or recommended designs to work through. Accuracy is achieved with rulers and jigs, using measuring and straight-line cutting techniques familiar to all woodworkers.

You'll fine here a series of logical exercises showing how to produce the basic patterns. Using a little imagination, you can then develop your own designs and assemblies, playing mathematical games.

Learning is by doing — and enjoying the process. As you experiment, you'll find yourself wondering how to produce specific effects you want. You might start looking into the elements of mathematics which are the essential background to the craft, but many people prefer to work out practical solutions of their own.

You can use the nine veneers on this month's cover for some of the exercises, or why not treat them as a 'starter pack' to make a table mat about 6½in wide like the one in the photograph.

Parquetry tools

Since the shapes to be cut — straight lines or regular curves — are straightforward, use a more robust knife than you would for marquetry, like a Swann-Morton craft knife with nos. 1 & 2 blades (or other makers' equivalents). Use an engineer's rule for cutting accurate straight lines. It is graduated and has two good straight edges, parallel to each other, which are essential. You won't normally require a specific size. When you do need a specific width, as in tile assembly, you may have to make a metal parallel cutting guide using a guillotine, or one in 6mm ply using a panel or circular saw for accuracy. Finish the plywood edge by hand, using file and sandpaper.

For measuring and setting the angles required, use clear plastic 90/45° and 60/30° set squares, large ones for accuracy. Use clear sticky tape for holding veneer pieces in position and/or joining strips together, but choose a cheap tape with limited stick, generally found on market stalls.

You can use any wood glue for final assembly, and balsa cement is suitable when you're sticking piece by piece direct to the baseboard using the 'tile method'. For generally sticking taped assemblies use PVA, Cascamite, Contact glue or Gulfilm.

Choosing veneers

Limit yourself to a few timber species, looking for marked contrast in colour and pieces with either little grain marking or striped parallel grain. I recommend:

● *Start with the suggested design using your free veneers, then try a cube-illusion tray; soon you'll be making box-lids like the one **above left**. Above, the veneers on the cover will make this pattern*

ash	ayan	boxwood
cedar of		
Lebanon	cherry	oak
opepe	padouk	purpleheart
sapele	sycamore	teak
walnut	zebrano	

Two parquetry methods are covered here:
1 Strip method: all cutting and assembly is done using strips of veneer. This method is relatively easy, calls only for the accurate cutting of parallel strips of veneer, and avoids any build-up of cumulative errors.
2 Tile assembly method: shapes are cut either in strips or individually, but assembled piece by piece. This requires greater accuracy since only small individual mistakes in cutting will accumulate to produce significant errors.

In each case you need to make simple jigs for repetitive cutting of parallel strips to a specific size and with accurate angles.

Strip method

Make a simple jig for strip cutting from a plywood or chipboard base (6-12mm thick) with a metal or ply guide strip about 1in wide. Cut the ply strip with a panel or crosscut saw to produce a straight edge, and then true it with sandpaper and a file, before pinning and glueing it to one edge of the board as a stop.

You'll understand how the jig is used if you follow the stages in making the chessboard pattern (fig. 1).

Place a piece of veneer on the board against the guide stop, with the grain at 90° to the edge. Place your ruler on top of the veneer, tight up to the guide and cut a strip across the grain the width of the ruler. This first strip is waste unless the original edge was straight and true. Now repeat the procedure, cutting a number of parallel

Fig.1

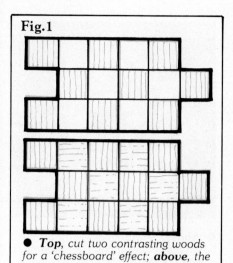

● **Top**, cut two contrasting woods for a 'chessboard' effect; **above**, the same veneer is cut with and across the grain for subtle contrast

strips of the first veneer. Then you can cut strips of a contrasting veneer. As you cut the edges take care the veneer doesn't break out; ease the pressure on the knife or use a number of gentle cuts. Try sticking small pieces of tape on the veneer surface as reinforcement.

For the second stage, tape strips of the two veneers in an alternating pattern, with sticky tape along the joins on the face side. Feed this composite veneer into the jig up to the guide stop, using a set-square to check that the strips are exactly at right angles to the guide. Using the ruler as before, cut a series of strips parallel to the guide edge, rejecting the first one as waste. The strips of squares can now be taped together, displacing them alternatively to the left and right for the pattern you want (fig. 1).

Fig.2

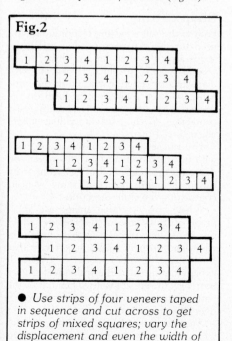

● Use strips of four veneers taped in sequence and cut across to get strips of mixed squares; vary the displacement and even the width of the strips, and thus the squares, for numerous effects

Fig.3

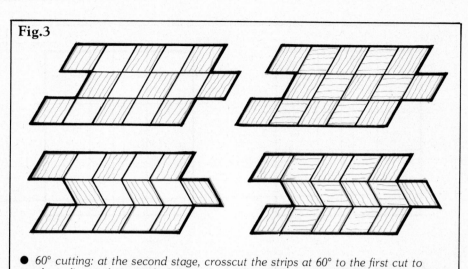

● 60° cutting: at the second stage, crosscut the strips at 60° to the first cut to produce diamonds instead of squares – and a whole new range of patterns. 'Chevron' effects come from turning alternative diamond-cut strips end for end

Fig.4

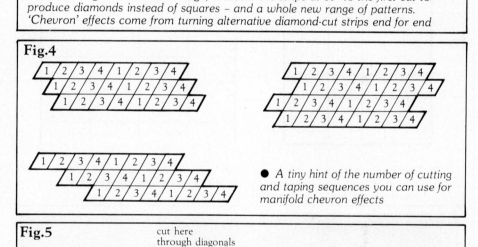

● A tiny hint of the number of cutting and taping sequences you can use for manifold chevron effects

Fig.5

cut here through diagonals

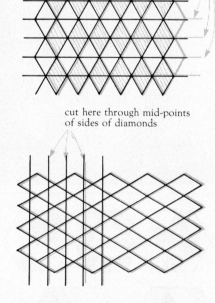

cut here through mid-points of sides of diamonds

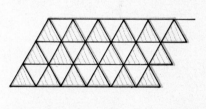

● **Top**, cut the diamonds from fig. 3 diagonally for triangles; **top right**, reverse alternate strips for another triangular effect. **Above**, cut strips of diamonds through the mid-points of their sides for yet another variation

This is the basic strip method technique. By varying the angle of the second cut (60° and 45° on set squares) and other modifications, you can produce the patterns in figs. 1-9.

When you've done these initial exercises you'll have worked out that there are three main variables:

a the number of different veneers used
b the angle of the second cut
c the width of strip used.

By shuffling the combinations you'll get a vast range of different effects.

Once you've practised this method and recognise its potential you might want to construct patterns which can't be built up from simple strips.

Tile method

You can actually cut some patterns (fig. 7) by the strip method, but others (figs 8, 9) involve geometric shapes which must be cut individually. Since both groups are

Fig.6

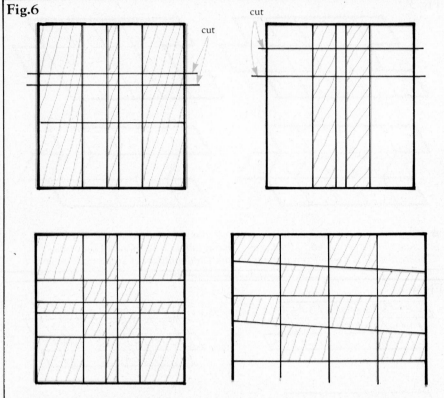

cut

cut

● **Top**: make two mirror-image assemblies and cut three widths of strip and you can get a pattern like the one **above left: above right**, the result of using equal-width strips but tapering second-stage cuts

● **Above**, a mere handful of the diamond-based patterns you can cut. **Middle left**, samples of the different cutting methods

individually assembled you have to cut really accurately. The width of squares and diamonds and hence the length of the sides must be precise and, where angles join at a point, they must add up to exactly 360°.

To improve the accuracy of angle cutting, I add a second guide to the strip-cutting jig. It is pinned and glued at the required angle to the first guide (generally 90°, 60°, or 45°) depending on the shape you want. Get the angle absolutely accurate with a large plastic set-square, and allow a gap between the ends of the guides to suit the width of your ruler. This second guide enables you to make sure the angle of the second-stage cut is right every time, because you check the fit against both guide edges before cutting each parallel strip.

If you mount guides at different angles on each side of a baseboard, each base can provide two different jigs.

Strip cutting

Follow the same cutting technique as you used for the strip method, but rejoin the strips after the first cut and then cut the second stage to produce a basic stock of diamonds or other shapes, all in the same veneer. I keep them in strip form on the sticky tape for ease of handling and protection, peeling off individual shapes when I need them.

You can see various combinations made with 60° diamonds in fig. 7. I suggest you make up the single-colour hexagons from three diamonds of the same veneer, contrasting the grain directions.

When you assemble them, use small pieces of sticky tape on the face side to hold the individual pieces together, lining up edges and corners to get a perfectly true final shape. I often assemble freehand, experimenting with the individual shapes until I get the effect I want. Then I draw the pattern on a sheet of paper and reassemble over this plan to get it right.

Another assembly technique, useful when patterns become more complex, is to cover the design with clear sticky-back plastic, sticky side up, held in place with a few pieces of tape. It's easier to experiment

Fig.7

● Work on these 60° variations, or make your own. Use the same coloured veneer but alter grain direction for a 'secondary' pattern appearance

with and rearrange shapes on this material than use sticky tape on single pieces or combinations.

Individual cutting

Now look at the patterns using 45° diamonds mixed with squares (fig. 8), and you'll notice a new problem.

In previous designs, once you'd chosen the width of ruler the resulting shapes all had a common edge length. When you start mixing diamonds and squares, this no longer holds true. A practical solution to this problem is to draw the pattern out on a sheet of paper, using the actual diamonds as a guide to size. Draw the best square through the tips of the diamonds; small differences in the cutting and assembly of the diamonds will lead to a degree of 'averaging' here.

Now you can cut the squares individually and hand fit them to the pattern; that's how I did these examples. This is accurate enough to construct quite complicated assemblies (fig. 9) but it does take time.

There is an alternative mathematical method; make a parallel cutting guide 1.414 times the width of the ruler used to cut the diamonds. Thus if the ruler were $\frac{3}{4}$in wide, you'd need a cutting guide $\frac{3}{4} \times 1.414 = 1.061$in. Cut a 6mm ply strip to size and trim it carefully, using a vernier gauge to check the width.

Fig.8

● *Mixing diamonds and squares; use the diamonds you have already cut as a guide for size on paper*

Fig.9

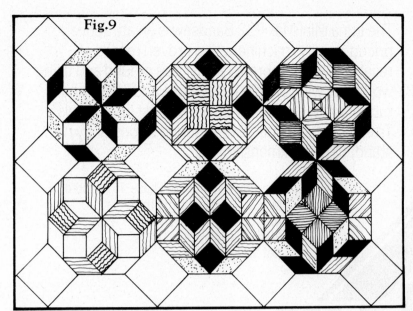

● *Drawing the best square you can get through the tips of your laid-out diamonds, plus a 'degree of averaging' for six octagons can get you to this patience-testing conglomerate!*

Assembly and finishing

Normally you should assemble the whole veneer surface complete with surrounds and borders as a veneer lay-on, held together with tape ready for glueing down in a single operation. This is straightforward with contact glue, and no clamping is required. Water-based contact glues tend to curl the veneer and cause some laying problems, so take care if you're using these.

You can also use water-based glues such as Cascamite and PVA, but the veneer will naturally curl when it absorbs water from the glue. So it must be held flat and in contact with the base surface with good cramping while the glue dries.

For large surfaces you'll have to use a press or temporary cramping arrangement with boards and G-cramps, since the forces involved are quite large. With areas up to about one square foot, you can get enough pressure with weights or even by standing on the board. I often lay marquetry pictures of this size by inverting the glued assembly face-down on to a flat surface and standing on it for 15-20 minutes!

Check the work after 20-30 minutes of clamping and if there are any bubbles, blisters or wrinkles in the veneer surface, cover it with brown paper (*not newspaper!*) for protection and iron over the surface lightly to press out air, flatten the veneer and speed the setting of the glue. On medium heat, iron it from the centre outwards, taking care not to overheat the veneer, or it'll shrink and crack. After ironing, press for at least another 10-15 minutes.

When the glue has dried, sand the surface; obviously you can't sand wholly with the grain, but this is no problem if you finish progressively, ending with a 320-grit paper.

You can use any normal clear woodworking polishes, from matt to gloss, but many people prefer a satin finish to highlight the beauty of the contrasting grains, which catch the light at different angles.

Traditionally, parquetry and marquetry were used to decorate items from long-case clocks and bureaux down to boxes, table mats, trays and coasters. On some items — even long-case clocks — parquetry was used to cover the whole surface, while elsewhere it was used as a decorative feature to relieve an otherwise plain veneer face.

Beware of over-decoration. Compare the examples shown here, from the face of the box covered in parquetry to the circular tray where it's used as a central decorative feature.

You might consider using parquetry as a decorative feature for other applications, including kitchen units, internal doors, bedroom furniture, coffee tables, desk-top accessories, boxes and even personal jewellery. Although normally laid as an integral part of the surface, small tasteful decorative features can be used as overlays on an already existing surface. ■

● The Marquetry Society Chairman, 67 Pickhurst Park, Bromley, Kent BR2 0TN.
● *The Marquetarian*, editor Ernie Ives, 63 Church Lane, Sproughton, Ipswich, Suffolk IP8 3AY.

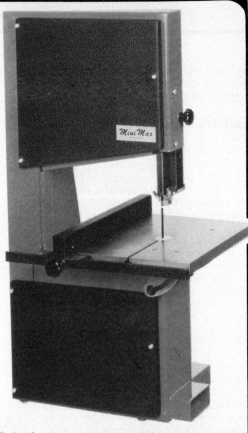

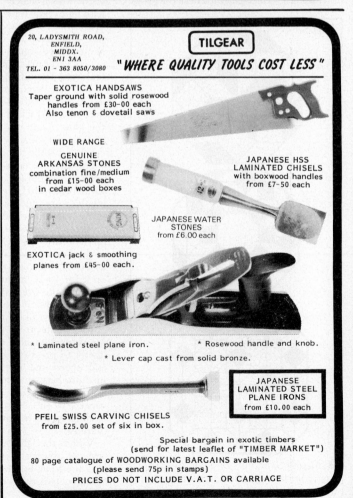

Base methods

Turn a flat-based bowl over, and chances are you'll find green baize. Unnecessary, and here's why . . .

I don't like bowls with flat bases covered with green baize. Baize is there for one reason only — to cover up the screw-holes where the bowl was attached to the faceplate, fixed to be turned both inside and outside at one fitting.

Any self-respecting bowl should have a foot or base ring, which means turning the outside, reversing, then turning the inside. The simplest way of reversing is on to a thick wood faceplate, with a slight upstand or a shallow depression to suit the already-turned base ring. The bowl is scotch-glued on with a paper washer between it and the faceplate, but the process does mean a frustrating overnight wait and the risk of across-the-grain shrinkage. Mechanical chucks overcome these problems, but they don't come cheap, and you have to decide for most lathes on inboard or outboard models. Is there a cheaper alternative, avoiding the overnight break? Yes: the intermediate faceplate.

This is a simple engineering job. You need an aluminium disc, cast or from thick sheet. A standard faceplate is generally true enough to hold by its rim in the chuck while you turn a shallow recess just larger than the threaded bore on which it mounts; then hold the aluminium disc in a chuck or temporarily on a faceplate, and turn up a face with a small upstand for a good fit in the recess you have just turned on the standard faceplate. Now drill through the faceplate screw-holes, and tap them to secure the aluminium auxiliary to the main faceplate with small hexagon-headed bolts. Face up the second side of the auxiliary, making sure the screws don't come through, and shortening them if necessary.

Next turn either one or two upstand rings about 2mm tall, and drill for four screws outside each to fix the bowl, countersinking deeply. File an index mark on both faceplates for exact re-assembly.

While you're set up, it's worth making several of these auxiliary faceplates using different spacings. Leave a 20mm space between the locating rim for a 16mm base ring, enough for most purposes. The screw-hole centres are 8mm from the rim, to position the screws near the centre of most base rings.

If you're making enough auxiliary faceplates for a communal workshop, part-finished bowls can be removed and stored on their auxiliary faceplates in a tightly tied-up plastic bag with shavings from the bowl itself. The slightly moist shavings reduce the amount of shrinkage.

Now for the use. Fix the bowl blank to the normal faceplate and roughly turn the outside, then turn a base recess to fit outside the chosen rim of the auxiliary faceplate. You have two possible bowl-base sizes for each auxiliary faceplate. Having obtained a good fit, complete the turning and polishing of the outside of the bowl; within the base ring, the curve should be convex, following the inside shape of the bowl. If it's concave, either the internal capacity of the bowl is reduced, or the bottom of the bowl becomes very thin.

Unscrew the bowl, locate it on the auxiliary faceplate and fix it with the four screws. Assemble the faceplates, return the whole thing to the lathe, and finish both the inside and outside of the bowl.

Finally, remove the bowl and drill out the screw-holes, into which you can put small rosewood or ebony plugs. These can be quite decorative, particularly if one or two incised rings can be put on the base during the first phase of turning.

No overnight wait, no shrinkage problems — and a process which is completely safe at all stages. ∎

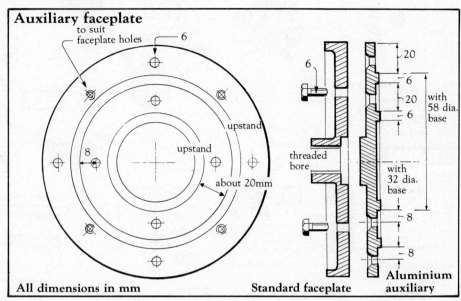

Auxiliary faceplate
to suit faceplate holes
6
upstand
upstand
8
about 20mm
6
threaded bore
with 58 dia. base
20
6
20
6
with 32 dia. base
8
8

All dimensions in mm   Standard faceplate   Aluminium auxiliary

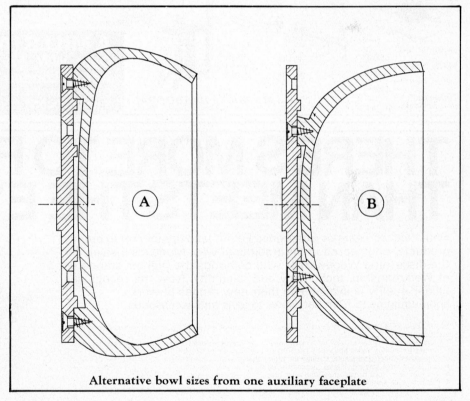

A   B

Alternative bowl sizes from one auxiliary faceplate

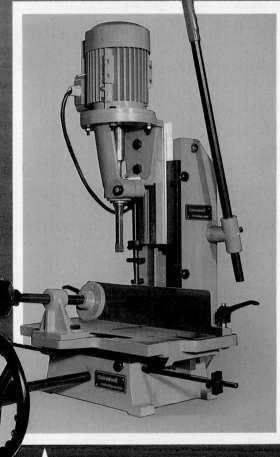

86 degrees...plus

A nd the rest ... more work, startling and straightforward, from College degree shows; plus a tasty *hors d'oeuvre* from two other topical exhibitions

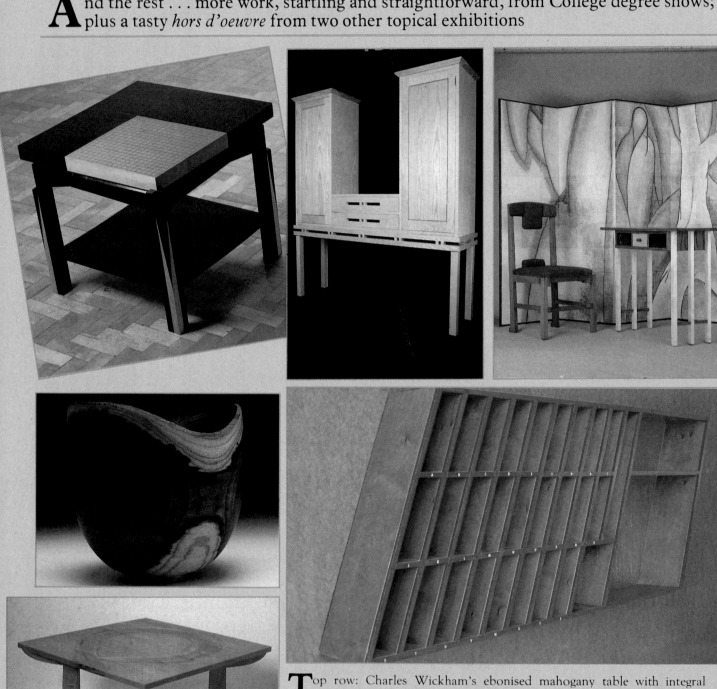

T op row: Charles Wickham's ebonised mahogany table with integral Go-board; Lucinda Leech's magnificent ash cabinet; their work with a screen by Michael Dunwell, all at the recent **Furniture and Screens** exhibition in Bampton, Oxon. 'British crafts are in a revolution,' claim the organisers of **Chelsea Crafts Fair,** 11-20 Oct, Old Town Hall, London SW3; 'craft has finally shed its raffiawork and knotted plant-holder image.' Featured will be work by (among a host of others) Bert Marsh (**above left**), Guy Martin (**left**), and Martin Fraser, who made the eccentric storage unit **above**

Photo Lynn Werner

London College of Furniture, top: John Werner's 'Butterfly chest' in lacquered MDF and Jim Travers' 'Buccaneer chair'. **Leicester Poly, middle left:** map cabinet in sycamore and rosewood by Richard Thorpe. **Bucks College, middle right:** Andrew Ball's supremely elegant sycamore cabinet on a stand. **Shrewsbury, above:** P. Saunders' 'business project' flat-pack coffee table in grey stained ash with red suede details; **right,** Chris Ayres' outstanding satinwood secretaire. The Craftsmanship of the Year Award?

86 degrees...plus!

Photos Tony Blackburn, George Crane

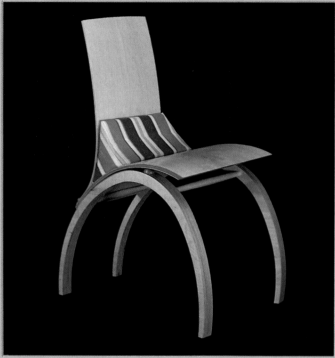

Kingston Poly (thanks to **Francesca Graham**): **above left**, Beverley Payne's Pugin-esque bureau; **above**, Adam Weir's laminated ply and upholstered chair. **Far left**, chair by Dominic Seddon in sycamore, with ebony and pink inlays; **left**, another sycamore chair by Huren Marsh. **Rycotewood: below left**, Richard Ash's ash coffee table, and **below**, Christine Wood's unusual ladies' book cheveret

86 degrees . . . plus!

LONDON COLLEGE OF FURNITURE
Emma Thornton

Career aims of LCF students vary widely, and were reflected in the types of work on show in the college in the heart of London's East End furniture district. Most students intend to work independently in small workshops, so one-off craft pieces were abundant. A small but increasing number, however, are aiming for batch or large-scale production, often through sub-contracting their designs. Their prototypes reflect this aim, but it's probably more of an ideal than a probability, given the unwillingness of British manufacturers to take on new ideas and the lack of guidance for students on how to contact them. Some students aim to become production managers or technicians in large firms, so their displays demonstrated the relevant skills — complex jigs, computer router programmes, and so on.

Design-wise, the show included much beautifully made, traditional-style furniture. This year the favourite period for inspiration seems to be Empire/Regency. Post-modernism has also got a grip on the LCF; there were lots of brightly coloured, space-agey pieces, and no line that could be bent was left straight. Some of the most interesting work is in metal or a combination of materials. There were very few examples of the deliberately slapdash neo-primitive- and baroque-influenced work becoming fashionable elsewhere. The pieces tended to be safer and less way-out in appearance than those in other student shows, but it isn't difficult to appreciate that the college's close relationship with industry gives a more realistic understanding of the production and marketing operations of the furniture business; LCF designs are perhaps more influenced by this realism than those in other colleges.

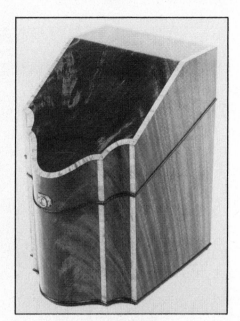

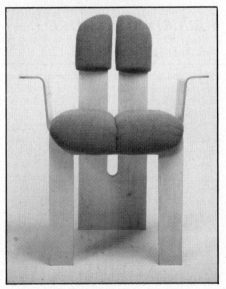

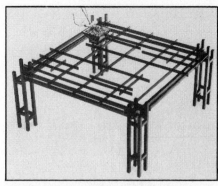

● **Clockwise from left:** Scott Bowran's curl mahogany knife box, Andrew Wilson's padouk table, Rod Tizzano's lacquered cabinet, Bruce High's laminated chair

BUCKINGHAMSHIRE COLLEGE
Peter Anstey

Furniture college shows often provide insights into how both teachers and taught are responding to external pressures and contributing to future trends at the same time. The first graduations from Bucks College's three-year diploma course in Furniture Craft and Management were a milestone for the college, and a case in point. Philip Hussey, lecturer in charge of the course, points to the growing demand in this country for well-designed and -made furniture, the products of craftspeople who try to steer between cheap mass production on the one hand and 'bespoke', exotic and expensive commissions on the other. 'One of our aims,' he says, 'is to play our part at the training stage in the regeneration of small-scale craft industry. Wycombe College has facilities for training only in wood technology but in other related craft areas such as plastics and metal. We aim to equip students first and foremost to be good craftspeople, so whether they are subsequently concerned with restoration, making and selling their own products, or simply fitting kitchens, they can realistically expect to make a living under today's conditions.' A particular opportunity, he believes, lies in persuading retailers to look at well-made craft furniture with a workable balance between quality and quantity.

The exhibits showed encouraging progress in achieving these objectives. There was no artificial 'Wycombe' style imposed by the college, and many of the pieces bore eloquent witness to craft skills in depth. Of 15 graduates from the course, 12 already had firm job prospects at the time of the show.

● The Bucks tradition: Adrian Jacobs' re-working of a Victorian idea in upholstered chairs

831

● **BUCKINGHAMSHIRE's** *trad or modern styles always show elegance;* **left,** *flautist Petra Fiehland's ash music stand, and* **above,** *Matthew Morris' writing table and chair in English walnut*

SHREWSBURY COLLEGE

Ian Hosker

The quality of Shrewsbury's training was demonstrated in the classic designs, the best of which was Chris Ayres' lady's satinwood secretaire, a copy of a 1790 piece. It is quite extraordinary, faithfull to the period, superbly made, and the best item I saw. The multiplicity of secret drawers and other contrivances are a credit to Chris' craftsmanship. He even made the lock on the tambour front; the whole job took him 300 hours!

A rather neat 'flat pack' coffee or occasional table by first-year student P. Saunders has four trestle-like legs which slot through the top and are secured with wedges. Dark grey stain contrasts with the red suede hinging and wedges. Obvious commercial possibilities here. There were also two splendid cabinetmaker's tool chests by Edwin Jones and I. Whitehead. Edwin's was the less functional in appearance — in a bedroom it would easily pass for a blanket chest. The contrasting applied work to the front and sides (ash is the carcase timber) gives it an oriental air. An excellent example of good design in that this decoration doubles as drawer-pulls, disguising the lid and drawers.

The second year 'design for business' project was a folding chair that could be mass produced. Bruce Robertson's result — woven cane seat and flat-pack potential — was ideal for corners, though I doubt its comfort. Edwin Jones' chair is along modern classic lines, comfortable and saleable, while Ron James designed his for back sufferers. Both chairs were laminated,

and looked rather similar — an example of a specific function resulting in a convergence of design? Ron's chair can be adjusted to a variety of positions like a deck chair.

The free hand the students got after the business project yielded little that was bizarre, thankfully, but there was more than a smattering of Deco influence. I. Whitehead, for example, produced a rather splendid desk in sycamore. The use of box sections, secret dovetail mitres and flush drawer-fronts with continuity of figure gave the work a wonderful overall coherence.

Terence Alexandre produced a novel extending table; from a round shape it extends to form a figure-of-eight in about the same length of time it takes to read this sentence aloud. The waist inevitably creates

an area unusable as seating space, but it is a well-thought-out, and relatively simple mechanism and Terence has buyers.

The exhibition reflects course leader John Price's great emphasis on good design, and every exhibit was based on sound constructional techniques. I expected to see a greater use of strong colours (dyes) but they were little used and then with restraint.

Nothing is completely original; all designs draw on the past, and many exhibits had a familiar look about them. This is no criticism; it's good that students can identify a trend or take the best of Deco or whatever and incorporate it into their own work. I believe the art of good design lies in choosing what works or is acceptable, adopting and adapting.

● **Below left,** *Bruce Robertson's cane-seat folding chair, and* **right,** *Ron James' adjustable laminated version for back sufferers*

LEEDS POLYTECHNIC
Paul Greer

Chairs were among the most attractive and interesting designs from the Leeds graduating class, particularly Paul Stott's hardboard design, distinguished by its angular planes and arresting shade of blue. It looks fragile, but a duplicate has withstood robust use in the students' common room!

Andrew Kennedy's boardroom chair was one of the most sculpturally pleasing exhibits; laminated in beech and ash, and upholstered in 100% wool fabric, the chair's muted colour tones allow the high-backed shape to be enjoyed.

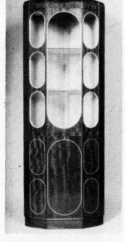

● *Shrewsbury's traditions: a superb mahogany and inlay corner cabinet right, and a reproduction carver below*

Graham Chaffer produced the most attractive and versatile items of furniture for children. His 'Toy Robox' in bright primary colours shows an inventive use of space, but more impressive was his 'Play Surface', a storage-cum-working top for playthings. It allows a child to keep toys handy and change the surface (it can take shallow or deep receptacles) to suit different activities. It looks ideal for home or school, particularly good for messy activities like painting. Several can easily be joined so children can play together.

RYCOTEWOOD
Kerry Fowler

Business acumen is on its way but tradition and craft are still the mainstays of the Rycotewood approach.

Solid, useable pieces like Brian Todd's steam-bent and laminated yew chair and Stuart Harris' child's integral desk-bench in beech were handsomely practical. This sort of established design in a modern context formed the main strand of the exhibits, while trendier pieces like Katherine Scott's one-armed chair and traditional beauties like Christine Wood's hand-painted ladies' book cheveret fall either side.

'Japanesey', heavy masculine tables had caught some imaginations; the chunky ash coffee-table from Richard Ash and Giles Elliot's 'Mackintosh table' were both more for display than function.

'Playing it safe'? It was a critical phase I overheard, but the students have jobs to go to, and caution has also knocked the boring and pretentious firmly on the head.

● *Mackintosh and MDF . . . Katherine Scott's chair just might be sat upon!*

Also eye-catching were Elizabeth Yates' 'Thai Tables', the name a pun on the feature of vertical and horizontal surfaces secured with cords. Christopher Lupton's corner shelving in grey and primrose could house ornaments, but is really too attractive to do anything but stand and be admired. Jane Wilson's mirror, with its near pocket-sized glass supported by a sideboard-sized frame, provided a note of humour.

All the students I talked to appeared to have enjoyed the course, feeling it had been right to encourage and promote creativity at the occasional expense of technical know-how which could be acquired later. Several students saw a future working for themselves, or as part of a group of like-minded designers, but most of them felt that at least a year or two in industry would provide a useful preparation for such a venture.

● *Far left, Elizabeth Yates' 'Thai tables', middle, Andrew Kennedy's boardroom chair, below, Graham Chaffer's imaginative Play Surface for children*

86 degrees...plus!

● More from **Rycotewood**: Stuart Harris' charming child's desk and integral seat in beech, **above left**, Brian Todd's yew chair suggests traditional style and shows curvaceous subtlety

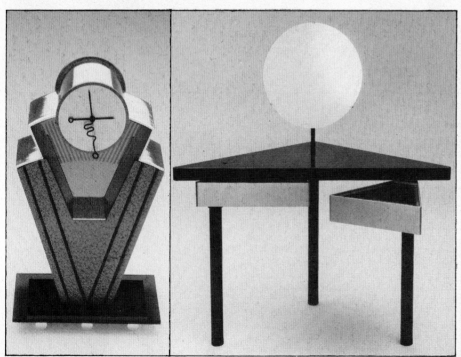

● **Above left**, Beverley Payne's clock from impressive **Kingston Poly** uses metal finishes and a version of classical form; **above, Leicester Poly's** Kate George won the London International Furniture Show's Student Award with this triangular dressing table MDF top and cast aluminium cantilevered drawers. It's part of a project devised by
● **Geoffrey Harcourt**, chairman of the RSA jury who refused to give a student bursary this year . . . see 'Juror furor'. **Right**, Michael Shutte's maple collector's cabinet was made to a brief set by **Martin Grierson** at Leicester

Juror furor

A sting in the tail of this year's college story . . .

Scathing criticism is directed at college tutors and furniture design education by the jury of the Royal Society of Arts Furniture Design Bursaries Competition. The jury, whose members are drawn from the design and furniture industries, decided the standard of entries was so low that none of them deserved an award!

'On the evidence we saw this year, we seriously question the colleges' success in the training of potential designers and their ability to educate designers who could benefit from such awards,' declare the jury in a special three-page report explaining their decision.

The report drew attention to what the jury saw as 'an overall deterioration of design education standards in this area' and expressed concern at the 'consequent likely future effect on the UK furniture industry.'

Furniture design students have consequently lost out on the £3850 awards and two attachments which the RSA had on offer, a possible helping hand into a design career. But the jury's remarks are pointed at college departments, who, they say, are not providing basic training or teaching broad principles of design.

Many colleges were thrown by the jury's decision. 'We were slightly upset initially,' says Derek Carpenter, Director of Studies in furniture design at Leeds Polytechnic,

which submitted the work of 13 students. 'I felt the quality of the ideas and the presentation was as good as any in the past. I'm not so sure now, however.' He accepts the jury's decision and respects it, but has reservations about the quality of the briefs.

Colleges who didn't submit designs have been more robust in their comments. It's perhaps significant that while 17 colleges sent in entries, several well-known furniture design establishments who didn't get involved include Brighton Poly, Kingston Poly, Leeds' Jacob Kramer College, Manchester, Middlesex Poly, Parnham, the RCA, Rycotewood, Shrewsbury, and Suffolk College.

The poor standard of the design brief was the reason no students from Kingston put in entries. *Cabinet Maker and Retail Furnisher*, 13 June, quotes Mick Warren, head of the School of 3D Design: 'The brief was awful. We would like a piece of work that allows a little more involvement from students on an intellectual level.'

A tutor from another of these colleges commented: 'The projects are very limited in the scope for creative and imaginative input. In some cases they tend to relate too closely to mass production. We found the limitations of the projects don't encourage students to enter.'

The final versions of the 1986/87 briefs have taken note of these criticisms, concedes jury-member John Barden of the Design Council.

'I thought the standard of entries this year was very poor,' he said. 'There was very little sensitivity to the briefs, especially

in upholstery.'

He said the jury was looking for good craftsmanship as well as innovation. 'We asked for a well-designed chair with upholstery, and we expected to see some good stitching,' he said.

The report was useful, he pointed out, because it sparked off a good debate. Has it really created 'a national forum on furniture design'; or has it merely pointed up the gap between an unadventurous UK furniture establishment and the thrusting and admittedly sometimes unrealistic design consciousness of our colleges?

● **RSA Jury's report in full overleaf**

TRENT POLY

● **Right**, Philip Fenton's laminated ash chairs; the black one is knock-down. **Far right**, David Hingley's ash veneered vanity unit; **below**, Ulf Pedersen's chaise longue, painted MDF and upholstered

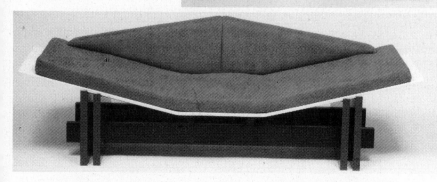

Why we gave no bursary awards
— Geoffrey Harcourt, chairman

The problems set in 1985/86 were:

a to design a chair for a boardroom setting, for a 'design conscious' company where support for the chair was not to be a standard pedestal type

b to design a piece of furniture to house the various components of a domestic computer system.

A large majority favoured the chair problem, but in both cases the jury had difficulty in finding more than two or three entries where candidates were worthy of being called for interview. Almost without exception there seemed to be a total lack of understanding of the design problems involved in seating, or in the storage and use of computer equipment (problems which, though not stated in the brief, are critical to all questions of seating or cabinet design). Solutions submitted lacked ideas beyond the trivial and there seemed to be an alarming ignorance among students of the nature of good design, its historical base, its capacity to delight by wit, simplicity and attention to detail, and to represent all these characteristics by clear, straightforward presentations.

In the case of the chair, the phrase a 'design conscious' company seemed to have been misunderstood by students and led to outlandish, bizarre suggestions for seating, irrespective of its functional or visual suitability for boardroom use. The jury had in mind a client devoted to the idea of design as a vehicle to demonstrate the company's aesthetic awareness and commitment to modern products through good proportion, elegance, attention to detail and quality of materials — qualities valued by both designers and manufacturers alike.

There should have been no misunderstanding, however, about the intention of the home computer brief and while these solutions were, in the main, more sensible in concept, they fell down badly on poor detailing and a reliance on MDF to solve all constructional problems.

Some designs in both categories were clearly either impractical, contrived or devoid of any real creative merit or, worse still, a combination of all three.

It is, of course not easy for students to set the right criteria for themselves when starting a project — nor is it easy to avoid setting their sights too high. However, the jury were surprised to find that so little guidance had apparently been given to students during the early stages of developing their solutions which would have prevented unsuitable attempts at originality for its own sake.

We would hope to encourage originality as an aspect of the Design Bursaries Competition and appreciate that very often the competition is seen as a 'brain storming' exercise where students can experiment with ideas (which need not be totally solved in practical terms) but where creativity within the subject brief is recognised and rewarded. We would, however, question the 'springboard' from which many students embarked on their projects — many solutions seemed to be based purely on visual imagery or currently fashionable ideas, rather than on a firm knowledge of materials and their use in industry. Basic ergonomic or structural considerations seemed also to be absent. For instance, there seemed to be little awareness of ergonomic criteria in chair design — backs were often totally vertical, either in ignorance of the requirements of comfort or in pursuit of some Mackintosh-inspired visual statement.

In short, we could see little evidence that reason and common sense had played any significant part in the conceptual process.

There was no lack of skill of presentation in *some* submissions, where much effort had clearly been made on this aspect of the entry. In others, however, the work would have been more appropriate to an unskilled amateur, both in presentation and content, showing the telltale signs of the ill-informed and ill-tutored, slavishly imitating current idioms irrespective of their meaning or origin. This was perhaps the most worrying aspect of the submissions.

While we cannot and do not expect students at this stage of their studies to produce highly professional solutions, finished to a high degree of presentation, we should, however, expect from students (the majority of whom were BA Hons undergraduates) a knowledgeable approach that reflected both elements of basic training in their own subject, and tutelage on the broad subject of design. Absence of these qualities gave us cause for concern both for the health of this area of design training and for the wellbeing of the furniture industry in the future. It appeared to the jury that although the ideas and presentations should rightly emanate entirely from the students, the level of maturity needed to interpret and realise these ideas should be influenced in large measure by direction and criticism by the tutors — this rarely seemed to have been the case.

Throughout the competition the society asks tutors only to submit work of a good standard for a national competition and the jury felt that a large proportion of the furniture entries should never have been submitted. Some colleges adhere to this practice and hence only submit work whose standard reflects well on their establishment. A minority of jury members even felt that some colleges should be put 'on notice' should their submissions not improve — while this was not a majority view, it is true that in the jury's opinion the obsessional preoccupation with real or imagined novelty, the ignorance of the manner of manufacture and its consequent reflection in trivial, impractical forms, and the ignorance of historical antecedents, can all be attributed to a lack of guidance from college staff.

We accept that industrial design in general, and furniture design in particular, is concerned with originality and the exploration of innovative forms. These factors are important in the final appraisal of design, but we would, however, question whether the students are being well served by the encouragement of these factors to the exclusion of all else. Very few designers innovate intuitively with any degree of success and the majority must rely on other, no less important, aspects of the design process, such as a good basic knowledge and common sense, to lead to new images and forms.

A critical understanding of the factors which go to make up the tenets of design worth, including the old adage 'fitness for purpose', plus simplicity, economy, delight, wit, scale, weight, structure, detailing and aesthetic pleasure, should be as much a part of a designer's education and training as an ability to use a pencil, hand-tool or computer if he or she is to become a good designer. The responsibility for instilling these critical faculties into students lies with the colleges.

The Design Bursaries Competition exists to provide students with the maturing influence of both travel and work experience in industry, thus enabling them to absorb other influences in preparation for their future careers. On the evidence we saw this year, we seriously question the colleges' success in the training of potential designers and their ability to educate designers who could benefit from such awards.

837

Boulle's rules

Alan and Gill Bridgewater
introduce the mirror-image
mystique of Boulle
marquetry, and
demonstrate the techniques
in a step-by-step project

The exotic names and splendid
colours of rare decorative veneers
like some of those on the *Woodworker* cover this month must inspire you to
try them in a suitable starter project. Why
not have a go at a little Boulle marquetry?
The nine leaves you've got on the cover will
do for a small piece — plus you need
another bit of 'waster' veneer. Boulle, boule
or buhl describes a type of repeated and
reversed marquetry very popular in 17th
and 18th century France. Similar
techniques of counterchanging coloured
veneers had been used before, but the
technique as we now understand it was
named after Charles André Boulle, a French
cabinetmaker (1642-1732) who produced
his most characteristic work while
decorating walls, panels and floors for
Louis XIV at Versailles.

The main feature that sets Boulle work
apart from the more ordinary marquetry
techniques is the very clever, time-saving
and economical process of sandwiching
together thin sheets of wood, brass, silver,
copper, tortoiseshell and so on, and then
cutting a design through all the layers. The
pieces can then be swapped around
(counterchanged). This method calls for
considerable prior design work.

If you study the illustrations, you'll see
the central motifs are nearly always made
up of four (or eight) identical counterchanged cuttings. It follows that for every
design produced, there is an opposite
possibility. For example, if four dark and
four light sheets of veneer are used to create
a design of brown tendrils on a light ground,
then the 'waste' from that design will
produce an alternative motif with light
tendrils on a dark ground. This repeat and
mirror-image potential sets Boulle work
apart from most other marquetry
techniques.

Tools and equipment

For this project you need a fretsaw with a
pack of 4/0 or 6/0 jeweller's piercing
blades, a fine-point craft knife, a metal
straight edge, a ruler, a workboard, a cutting
board, a fine-point pen, a lightweight hammer, a pair of wire snips or pliers, a fretsaw
cutting table or vice, a small hand-drill, a
fine needle-bit, two clamping boards,
battens, G-clamps, a cork sanding-block
and a selection of pencils.

● *Right*: This dramatic pair of matched
silhouettes makes a good project for
beginners

● *This 17th century French cabinet shows Boulle at its best*

● *Working drawing for the project, with four identical cuttings; scale up to suit*

Materials

You need some contrasting veneers, a compensating veneer, black waterproof ink, white cartridge paper, a sheet of good wet-strength tissue paper (such as long-fibred mulberry paper), tracing paper, a water-based starch/flour paste (wallpaper paste is fine), a few drops of vegetable oil, veneer pins, white PVA glue, brown paper, lick-and-stick parcel tape, masking tape, newspapers, glass/garnet papers, wax polish and methylated spirits.

Design technique

Look carefully at the working drawings and see how the motif has been quartered, mirror-imaged and counterchanged. The seemingly complex motif has in fact been built up from four simple repeats. Now take a pencil and layout pad, and analyse the design and working implications. Then look at the working drawings and the various 'hand-on-tool' details and note the order of working.

At this stage, it would help if you visited a suitable museum and searched out examples of Boulle-inspired works and any you can find by the master himself. The Victoria and Albert Museum, London, has several pieces by Boulle. Also search through magazines and handouts to make a collection of inspirational clips — pictures of antique furniture and so on.

When you feel you have a good understanding of the Boulle technique, work out your own modified design. With waterproof black ink, a fine-point pen and white cartridge paper, draw up a full-size design grid of the project, and think about how you will arrange the contrasting veneers. Then make three careful ink tracings of the master design on mulberry paper. Mark details of sizes, colours, texture and placing of the pieces on the master design and put similar labels on the tracings.

● *What the project could look like, with the negative/positive pieces all matched, placed and interchanged; you'll need eight veneer slips for this quartered design*

Preparing the veneer

With this motif of four repeats, you'll need eight veneer thicknesses. Take the eight veneer slips, four of each colour, and arrange them in a stack or sandwich. Add the 'waster' veneers to each side of the stack, then strap the whole block up with masking tape so that all the sheets are well contained and stable. Generously brushing one of the tracings with water-based paste, wait a few minutes for the paper to stretch and settle, and then arrange it on the topmost veneer of the sandwich, smoothing it down. When the paste is completely dry, rub the now crisp tissue with a few drops of vegetable oil until the paper becomes transparent and the ink lines can be clearly seen. Then take the lightweight hammer and veneer pins, and with the greatest of care, nail through the outside waste margins of the slab. Finally take a pair of snips and nip off the pins so they're flush with the veneer.

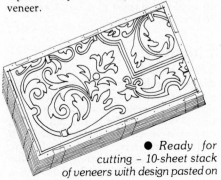

● *Ready for cutting – 10-sheet stack of veneers with design pasted on*

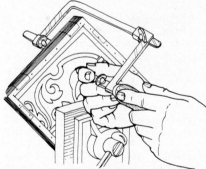

● *Cutting: fix the blade through the pilot hole, and hold at 90°; slow even strokes*

Multiple sawing

Clear the work surface of all clutter, then pin up the inspirational drawings and the master designs so they can be seen from the working area, and set out all the tools and materials so they're to hand.

Place the slab of veneers in vice jaws or on a fretsaw cutting table. Before you start cutting, get acquainted with the fretsaw, noting how the blade is fixed and tensioned. See how best the blade can be swiftly removed and replaced, and set the blade so the teeth point towards the handle and so cut on the 'pull'. When you have done this, drill small pilot holes on the lines to be cut, pass the blade through a hole and tension it in the frame. Work the saw with a steady action, cutting along the drawn guide lines, and keeping the saw-blade at 90° to the working face of the wood.

Boulle's rules

Continue cutting, keeping the saw moving and only stopping to change a blade, or to manoeuvre the stack in the vice so the saw is presented with the line of next cut. When you come to a tight acute angle, keep the blade moving on the spot while you change the direction of cut. Work with care and caution, and above all, don't try to force the pace — if you rush, you will only twist and break the blade.

As each little motif or part-motif is cut out, place it in a labelled container, then move on to the next area to be worked. Finally, when you've cut all the 'windows', carefully cut the waste margins away from the ground; keep the margin offcuts for repair work.

Setting the veneers

Trim up all the rags and burrs on the cut-outs, and then group them, with reference to your master design, so they are matched according to type, shape, colour and placing. With the working drawings you'll see how two designs are made, one positive and the other negative.

Fix two tracings of the master design to the workbench with masking tape and start the whole jigsaw puzzle by setting out the main blocks of base or ground veneer. As each piece is found and identified, locate it on one or other of the tracings, then butt-joint it to its neighbouring piece of veneer with a tab or two of brown lick-and-stick parcel tape.

When all eight ground pieces have been tape fixed, select a 'window' in one of the grounds and search around for its piece of counterchange veneer. Work in this manner through all the windows, reversing, changing, fitting and taping, until the whole puzzle is complete. Each small 'window' piece has at least four possible placings; try each in turn, and then settle for the best fit. When you've completed both designs, trim them to size, remove and re-work any unnecessary tape, then place them under weighted boards and put them to one side to dry out and settle.

Glueing up

Arrange the two designs on the workbench. Set out PVA glue, the baseboard, the clamping boards, the battens, the G-clamps, some clean newspaper and a pencil and measure. We use PVA glue, but if you want to use hot glue, hot irons and all the rest, and don't mind glue in your hair, on the wall and seemingly everywhere — then the best of luck! Start by measuring up and placing the designs so they are square with your baseboard, then have a trial dry-run fitting; set out in order the clamping board and battens, a few sheets of newspaper, the sheet of compensating veneer, the baseboard, the Boulle design, more newspaper, and finally the top clamping boards. Check you have enough clamps.

Spread an even layer of lump-free PVA on the compensating veneer and the

● *Starting the jigsaw puzzle,* **above**; *arrange the veneer ground, position the motif pieces in the 'windows' and tape in place.* **Below**, *getting the sandwich ready for pressing – clamping board, newspaper, compensating veneer, PVA glue, baseboard, PVA glue, Boulle marquetry, newspaper, clamping board*

baseboard, then bring them together and place them, veneer down, on the newspaper-covered clamping board. Now generously glue the baseboard and carefully lower the Boulle design into position. When you're sure the placing is correct, cover the Boulle with more newspaper, lower the other clamping board and then clamp up. Don't overtighten and risk twisting the marquetry off-true, just screw up until the surplus glue oozes out from between the various layers.

Finishing

When the glue is dry (about 24 hours), dampen the brown paper tape, and clean the face of the work. Give the marquetry a light coat of grain/wood sealer once it is dry. When the sealer is dry, use a sharp cabinet scraper to remove the slight variations and steps. Work with a firm but delicate touch, all the while making sure that the corners of the scraper don't drag,

and removing only the finest wisps of wood.

Rub down the work with a sanding block and graded papers, using a smooth backwards-and-forwards action. Continue until the wood is completely smooth and looks slightly burnished. Stop and inspect the work from time to time, just to make sure the thinner veneers haven't been worn through.

After rubbing it down, wipe the marquetry over with methylated spirits to bring out the colours and texture, and check the work for faults and blemishes. Leave the marquetry for a day or two to make sure the veneers haven't lifted or buckled. Finally, when all is correct, give the wood a good waxing, burnish with a smooth cotton cloth and the job is done.

As with all craft processes, there are many different ways of tackling the job. You might use different saws, you might use a different method of taping up or clamping and so on — no matter, enjoy the doing! ■

Magic wand

Grow and shape your own
unique walking stick with
the help and advice of
stickmaker *extraordinaire*
Theo Fossel

I f you're keen on walking sticks,
you're likely to have seen some
reports of giant walking-stick cab-
bages, and perhaps been tempted to try
growing your own ('Shoptalk', WW/Aug
85). They can grow to 5 or 6ft, taking two
years to fully mature; in the same length of
time, why not grow your own totally
individual one from 'real wood'?

All you need is a small corner of garden
or another private spot — even a hedgerow
or neglected corner of a field will do. If you
can find suitable already-established plants,
you're at least two years ahead of seeds, but
you may need to sow your own or bring in
your own transplants. At least this gives
you the opportunity to prepare the ground
properly with a good balance of fertiliser
and humus, but remember that you need
permission to dig up plants, even on the
roadside.

Seeds come from a variety of sources,
and if all else fails you always have the
specialist supplier. Gather your own, or
why not buy hazelnuts or sweet chestnuts in
the shops during autumn? Walnuts are
rather a waste of time because although they
grow well enough at first, their wood is very
pithy and insubstantial.

Breaking dormancy

Many seeds lie dormant until the weather
turns favourable for the seedling, which
usually means they must go through a
period of winter-like cold before they will
germinate. The trouble is, if you sow seeds
in the autumn mice and birds will have a
field day; there'll be few left to germinate in
spring.

So we have to persuade the seeds they've
been through a winter. With some, like
hazel, this actually means putting them in
the fridge for a few months; with others it's
enough to hang them out of doors. To avoid
mould growth and keep the seeds viable,
they should be mixed with about two parts
sand and kept in a sealed plastic bag; add a
fungicide, because mould will grow quite
well even in a fridge. The sand should be
just damp enough to keep its shape when
you squeeze it in your hand. Then either put
the bag in the fridge or hang it outside in a
cool but not windy place. Even those hung
outdoors may need the fridge treatment for
a given time before they're sown, to really
break dormancy. Just by the way, storage in
damp sand is also the best way to keep hard-
shell nuts fresh and sweet till Christmas.
This method of breaking dormancy is
known as 'stratification'.

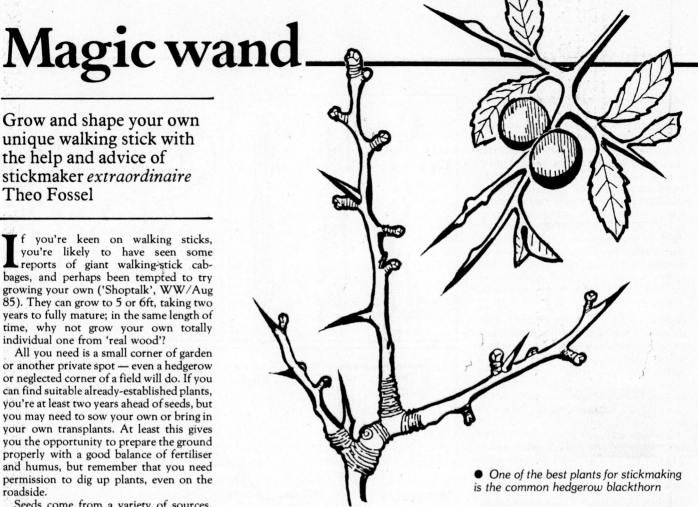

● *One of the best plants for stickmaking
is the common hedgerow blackthorn*

Woods to use

Here are some of the woods worth trying:
Ash (*Fraxinus excelsior*). Pick the seeds
during dry weather and stratify them for
16-18 months before sowing them in
March or April. Neutral soil is best for good
growth.

Cherry (*Prunus avium & spp*). Sow the
seeds immediately after collection if you
can protect them against rodents. Otherwise store them in sand and put them in the
fridge in about January for sowing late
March/early April. Cherry is tolerant of
most soils, but it's best over chalk.

Hazel (*Corylus avellana*). Store the seeds in
damp sand inside a sealed plastic bag
hanging in a cool place, until you put the
bag in the fridge in January. Sow them in
early April. Towards the end of stratification, check them frequently for moisture
and break of germination. Hazel will grow
in most friable soils.

Blackthorn (*Prunus spinosa*). These seeds
are the same family as cherry, so treat them
similarly. This is one of the most desirable
walking-stick woods; it suckers freely from
roots, and all you need to do is transplant
the suckers — but beware, this species isn't
easy to eradicate later!

Chestnut (*Castanea sativa*). This is the
sweet chestnut; horse chestnut isn't much
good for sticks. Store the chestnuts in a dry
cool place, but in the New Year check to see
if the seeds are shriveling. When this
happens, sprinkle them with water to keep
them plump until you sow them in late
March. You can also sow them in the

autumn, if the soil isn't likely to become
waterlogged and you can protect them
against rodents; if you do this, cover the
chestnuts with an extra 100mm of soil,
which should be removed in early spring.
Chestnut needs fairly neutral well-drained
soil, but grows faster than any of the other
trees listed here.

Growing techniques

If all this seems rather laborious (it isn't
really!), then go for wild seedlings in the
garden or scrubby corners. Always remember that everything in the countryside
belongs to *someone*, and anyway it doesn't
make sense to start digging up seedlings in
the woods. As long as the soil has been well
prepared in advance, you should be able to
get a decent size for a walking stick in three
or four years — assuming you sow seeds
about 500mm apart and don't transplant
them. Once the sapling is approaching a
usable size, you can consider the
refinements.

The best time of the year for any of these
specialised growing techniques is April-
June, when the wood is most flexible from
the maximum flow of sap. It also allows
time for the growth that comes in response
to your 'stimulation'.

Corkscrew twists Some young growth
lends itself to training round a pole, or even
a stiff plastic pipe (fig. 1). Slowly wind the
young shoot round the former, being
careful to avoid straining and breaking the
internal fibres. Do this in stages if
necessary, over some days or even weeks.
Take great care to avoid strangling the wood

Magic wand

and causing 'die-back' by tying it too tightly.

Spiral grooves are also naturally caused in woods, usually by honeysuckle (fig. 2). You could use wire or string, but it mustn't have any stretch. Wind it up the shank in a spiral; it must be firm, and eventually force the wood to bulge round it. The start and finish shouldn't be tied in a tight ring round the stem, as this would strangle the upper growth. Well-placed side branches provide the best anchorage. You could achieve a similar effect by cutting a spiral groove up the stem, but in that case it's probably best to apply a fungicide such as Benlate to exposed wood to protect it against fungal attack.

Plaited sticks If you find two or three shoots of roughly equal thickness growing close together, they can be twisted or plaited together and left to grow into a fusion (fig. 3). These shoots needn't necessarily come from the same root stock, or even the same species. The fusion can be helped along by wounding the bark with coarse folded sandpaper at the line of contact. A graft can only form between related species, and with different species you just get a callus. Take precautions to stop the wind rocking loose any graft that may form.

Pearling Scar tissue can be induced by wounding the bark and cambium of a stem with wide-jawed pincers; sharpen the noses into three or four shallow points (fig. 4). Remove all the side branches, and pinch the stem on opposite sides at about 50mm intervals, all the way from top to bottom. Repeat the procedure at right angles to produce four rows of wounds vertically up the stem (fig. 5). Do this in late spring during dry weather, because rain or damp may cause fungal infection. In a really dry summer, water the plants liberally. The faster the scar tissue forms, the better the effect. Sweet chestnut is one of the best for this, since it grows so quickly. The stick should be ready for cutting the following winter, but you could leave it another year. Peel the stick after seasoning it to show the pearling at its best.

It's vital that none of these methods should damage or constrict growth completely round the stem, since this would stop all sap flow and kill the growth above the constriction. The only 'living' part of a tree is the cambium layer just below the bark, and if this is blocked or parted all the way round, die-back will surely be the result. Nor should you remove any actual bark if possible, which would let fungi in and cause rot. Bruising or scoring the bark is usually enough to achieve the scarring you want.

Cross handles Ash is still grown from seed specifically to use for sticks; 'cross-head' walking sticks are produced by digging up the two-year-old seedling, trimming it back to a bud and planting it horizontally (fig. 6). The bud then grows into an upright shank

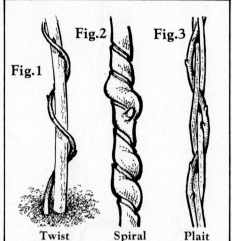

Fig.1   Fig.2   Fig.3

Twist   **Spiral**   **Plait**

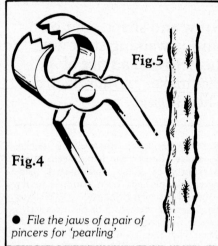

Fig.4   Fig.5

● *File the jaws of a pair of pincers for 'pearling'*

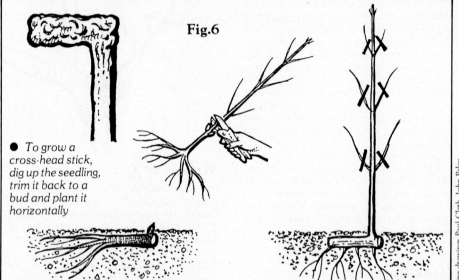

Fig.6

● *To grow a cross-head stick, dig up the seedling, trim it back to a bud and plant it horizontally*

Line drawings Paul Clark, John Paley

with the rootstock eventually forming a very strong, naturally-shaped handle rather like an upside down 'L'. Unlike steam-bent handles, these will never straighten out, even if you leave them in the damp for long periods.

Another way of producing cross-head sticks is to peg low branches down, after pruning them back to an upward-facing bud or side shoot. You can use a garden bamboo to train the shaft to grow straight, and trim away any side branches before they grow too big.

You might like to explore other ways of growing 'specials', such as grafting, which offers plenty of scope for experiment. It's the same in stickmaking (or should we say 'stick-growing'?) as in any form of woodwork — or any form of enjoyable craft at all, come to that — the only limits are those imposed by your own imagination. All you have to do is make sure you follow the two basic stick premises: use the right timber species for the job, and be sure the finished stick fits comfortably in your hand. ■

● See Jack Hill's review of Theo Fossel's new book *Walking and Working Sticks*, 'Books', p855.

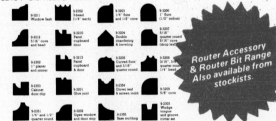
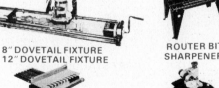

844

JAPAN 7
The 'pull' plane

How to set up and use *Hira-kanna*, the 'back-to-front' wooden plane. Tony Wood concludes our introduction to the tools of Japan

Once you've bought your Japanese wooden plane, you'll have to do some preparation on both blade and body before the tool can be used.

The first step is to sharpen the blade, which is done in much the same way as for Japanese chisels (WW/May). Flatten the back of the blade first on the flattening plate to remove any high spots left by forging, starting with a coarse grit. Continue with progressively finer grades of grit and then water-stones until you get a mirror finish. Once the back has been flattened, you can sharpen the single bevel on the front of the blade on a water-stone. Take great care when sharpening the bevel to avoid rocking the blade, which will alter the original bevel angle or round off the face.

The most critical preparation is probably on the body or *dai* of the plane, which because it's made of solid wood, can change in shape between manufacture and use as it seasons. This is why the *dai* is sold 'unfinished', and it's up to the owner to 'tune' it. It's really not that much of a hardship, and repays the trouble with outstanding results.

Usually, when you first get a Japanese wooden plane, you'll find the blade will not fit right down into the mouth, and the cutting edge of the blade won't protrude through the sole. Don't be tempted to drive

● *Japanese craftsmanship begins with preparing tools to precise individual specification.* **Above**, *mouthing a plane:* **above right** *cutting the mouth;* **below right**, *chopping the edge grooves*

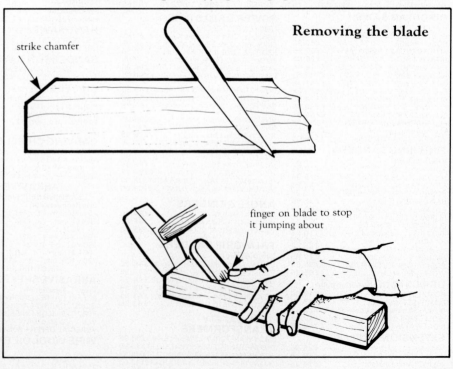

Removing the blade

strike chamfer

finger on blade to stop it jumping about

the blade tight into the body to see if it can be made to fit just that bit more deeply. The *dai* is made of fairly tough wood, but it isn't tough enough to cope with the forces of a blade being hammered in too tightly, and split *dais* aren't easy to repair!

So the first operation is to open up the blade grooves in the side of the throat. Like most of the preparation tasks, this isn't one to rush at; if too much wood is removed, the blade will move when the plane is used, giving uneven results. The correct fitting is when the blade is gripped snugly, but permits fine adjustment when the end is tapped lightly with a hammer.

To find out how well the blade marries up with the *dai*, first remove the blade and chip-breaker by sharply tapping the front of the body at an angle parallel to the blade. Don't strike the endgrain of the *dai*, or you may split it; the place to hit is on the chamfered top front edge of the *dai*, which is itself parallel to the blade.

When you take the blade out, grip the edges of the body, applying slight pressure with the index finger to the front of the

Checking seating

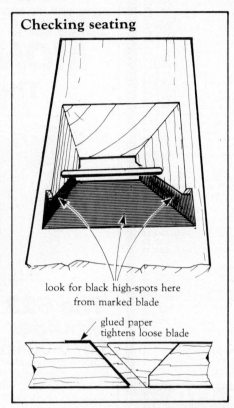

look for black high-spots here
from marked blade

glued paper
tightens loose blade

blade. This keeps your fingers away from the nice razor-sharp edge you created earlier, and it stops the blade flying out of the body when it comes free.

Once the blade and chip-breaker are out of the body, remove the retaining pin by drifting it out slightly from the side, and pull it right out with a pair of pliers. Be careful not to bend the pin when you take it out, or you'll have problems re-seating the chip-breaker later. Now 'paint' the sides and bottom face of the blade with drawing ink or a soft pencil. Place the blade back in the body and tap it on top lightly, to seat it as far as it will go without jamming. Remove it again in the way I've described, and check the bed and blade-grooves in the body. The high-spots should show up coated in your ink or pencil; pare them down carefully with a chisel, making only the very smallest of cuts. Be particularly careful not to alter the blade-angle line of the grooves, or you'll get bad seating, the wrong cutting angle, and poor results. Repeat the marking and paring process until all the high-spots are gone. Don't rush this job by forcing the blade further into the *dai* than it wants to go — patience is the name of the game! If you do inadvertently pare too much away, you can remedy it by gluing a thin piece of paper to the area you want to pack out. This will also work, of course, if the blade loosens up as the *dai* ages and shrinks.

You can judge just when a blade is nicely seated by listening to its resonance as you tap it into the body. If it's loose, the sound is quite hollow, but as it tightens up the note increases in pitch. When the blade 'rings' and the note remains constant, the seating is correct and snug.

Preparing the sole

Because of the natural changes in the body, the sole must be checked periodically, and flattened if necessary. A wooden 'sole ruler' is the traditional tool, but any good straight-edge will do.

When you're checking the sole for flatness and straightness, position the blade just shy of the sole, so the pressure it exerts on the body is the same as when you're using the tool. Hold the straight-edge across the sole in front of a bright light, and tilt both body and straight-edge, looking for chinks of light created by a gap from a high-spot. Mark it with a pencil; move the straight-edge to check the sole front to back, side to side, and corner to corner.

The traditional tool for truing up the sole is a *daianoshi*, a small scraper-plane-like tool with the blade perpendicular to the sole, which removes paper-thin shavings. You can also use a 1in chisel, held like a scraper; the aim is to get the sole perfectly flat without any steps. Try it out on a piece of scrap hardwood before you go to the *dai* itself. Make frequent checks with the straight-edge so you don't overdo it and just make new high areas! Don't be tempted to remove fine high areas with glass- or garnet paper, because you'll very likely embed abrasive particles in the sole, which will mark the surfaces you will be planing.

Other features of the sole include the

Checking the sole

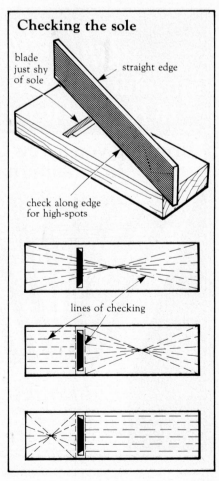

blade
just shy
of sole

straight edge

check along edge
for high-spots

lines of checking

The 'pull' plane

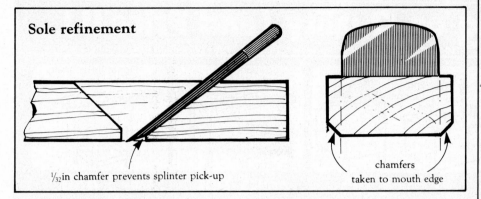

Sole refinement

¹⁄₃₂in chamfer prevents splinter pick-up

chamfers taken to mouth edge

bevels which run along each side. They are there to reduce the contact area between sole and workpiece, reducing friction and making the job easier, and can safely be extended right up to the edge of the mouth to make the contact area smaller and the friction still less. Put a slight chamfer on the sharp edge where the blade-bed meets the sole to prevent the sole 'picking up' splinters and tearing the work, but *never* chamfer the bottom front or back edges of the sole — dust and waste would collect there and be pushed along and into the surface of the work as you planed it.

Using *Hira-kanna*

With blade, chip-breaker and pin all safely back in the prepared *dai*, and the blade well seated, you have merely to adjust the cut and then get used to the action. The squareness of blade to sole and the depth of cut you take are a matter of light taps with a small hammer, much the same as on the wooden planes that have long been in use in this country (see 'Penny plane . . . ' in this issue). The blade will in fact work without the chip-breaker at all; it doesn't hold the blade in the body like the wooden wedge on traditional English-type wooden planes. It acts more like the back-iron of a cast plane, and so should be adjusted accordingly, again with a small hammer. Put the blade in, then set the chip-breaker so the bottom edge comes to within about ¹⁄₃₂in of the cutting edge — a 'fine cut' adjustment familiar to any discerning plane user. Again as with English-type wooden planes, you must be sure there is room to move the blade side to side if you need to, without putting undue pressure on the body. Tap the top front-edge chamfer to take the blade back a bit if you're cutting too much, and tap the top of the blade itself to give extra depth of cut. The beauty of these tools is their fineness of cut; they aren't for taking off a lot of stock in a short time. The friction-polished hardwood sole give a superb finish, which leaves the work looking as if it has already been waxed!

Hold the plane with your right hand over the top of the body in front of the blade and your left hand cupped over it behind the blade. Start with the tool at arm's length, and pull it towards you in a long sweeping motion; you're bound to find yourself on the wrong foot at first, but it's perhaps best to ignore the abstruse, even philosophical, treatises on body (yours) positioning and moving, and just work out how it works best for you. The same foot is forward as when you use a 'push' plane; you're just pulling your body and arms back instead of pushing them forward. It wouldn't really be right to claim that it's easier to do, or less hard work, than using a 'push' plane; it's just different. For some people, throwing the weight back instead of forward might work out a more natural and smooth movement; it's certainly easier to start the stroke, because your weight is pulling from the point where (more or less) the stroke ends, rather than pushing away from where it starts. This suggests that you might be less likely to fall into the 'downward curve' trap, a natural result that any plane user has to counteract when pushing a plane; but other bad habits can just as easily develop. Enjoy the sound and feel of a sharp blade in a light tool cutting the wood cells, just as you do with an 'ordinary' plane; and enjoy the work!

Endpiece

Which brings us to the end of our introductory series to Japanese tools, how they're made, how they're used, and how to get the (sometimes astonishing) best out of them. Our series seems to have raised a lot of passions, many of which have been voiced on our letters pages; the hoary old arguments about which steels are best and which tools are best have been fuelled, but we doubt they'll ever be settled. It's a matter of personal experience and personal taste, after all. What we have tried to do is supply you with information, where before there has been merely a lot of wild claims and a lot of pooh-poohing. *Woodworker* isn't going to get into Japan *vs* Britain recommendations; our job is to tell you what's good, why it's good, and how you can do good work with it. We don't believe something is superb just because it's Japanese any more than we believe something's superb just because it's English; the answer is, try it yourself — if you want to!

● Many thanks to Roger Buse of Roger's of Hitchin who has been a great help in the preparation of this series.

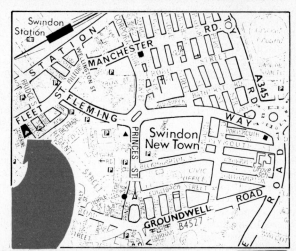

The grand furniture saga: 9

Religion, royals and
revolution; Vic Taylor
looks at the impact of the
transitional Stuart years on
home furniture

One of the results of Henry VIII's
break with the Pope in 1531
was a decline in the influence of
Italian and French styles on English furniture. The struggle between the Protestant
and Roman Catholic religious was long and
bitter, and cultural links between England
and the Holy Roman Empire were actively
discouraged. Consequently, Baroque had
little impact on our native furniture styles
and any influence it did have was anglicised.
Englishmen still travelled abroad, but
mainly to the Low Countries and the Protestant, north German states.

The closing years of Elizabeth I's reign,
which ended in 1603, were a period of
comparative affluence which spread down
from the aristocracy to the yeoman and
artisan classes. William Harrison, a contemporary writer, noted the change in
trend: 'The furniture of our houses also
exceedeth, and is grown in manner even to
passing delicacy . . . The inferior artificers
and many farmers have learned also to
garnish their cupboards with plate, their
joined beds with tapestry and silk hangings,
and their tables with carpets and fine
napery.' It's interesting to note how carpets
were used as table coverings, a tradition
followed until recently in New England.

Around the turn of the 16th century
many fine houses were built, such as those
used by Elizabeth I and her successor, James
I, on their travels round the country.
Longleat (1580) was the first of a long list:
Audley End, Burghley House, Haddon
Hall, Hardwick Hall, Hatfield House,
Montacute House, and Wollaton Hall.
They were primarily status symbols, and in
contrast to their predecessors, designed to
be seen for miles around; the aim before
had always been to build large houses
hidden from view, so they could be more
easily defended.

Wilton House, near Salisbury in
Wiltshire, was designed under the supervision of Inigo Jones, although it was
probably built by another architect, Isaac
de Caus, in the 1630s. It contains the
famous 'Double Cube' and 'Single Cube'
rooms; Jones seems to have been almost
obsessed with cubic proportions.

In the pre-Civil War years, native
craftsmanship flourished, and royalty gave
the lead. James I (1603-1625) founded the
magnificent Mortlake tapestry works, and
his son, Charles I, was the patron of Rubens
and Van Dyck and an enthusiastic,
discriminating collector of works of art of

● *A chest of drawers from the late 17th
century; continental-style mouldings give a
'tremidos' ripple effect*

Victoria and Albert Museum

all kinds, including superb furniture, much
of it from the Continent.

The style of furniture most favoured by
the people, however, was a blend of
Elizabethan and Jacobean (dubbed
'Jacobethan' by the well-known furniture
historian, Margaret MacDonald-Taylor).
The emphasis was on comfort, and the
period saw the development of furniture
upholstered with silks, satins, brocades,
gold and silver fringes, and similar exotic
fabrics. In particular, beds (always prime
status symbols) became more and more
luxurious; bedsteads were often richly
carved and inlaid, or painted and gilded;
and the hangings were equally rich in velvet,
satin, and silk.

A favourite design of chair was the
'wainscot' which carried a heavily
carved and ornamented crest rail and was
invariably made in oak (fig. 2). Another
design still proving popular was the X-
frame chair, which was now fitted with a

back and arms, only the supports being X-
shaped; it was sumptuously upholstered in
rich fabrics and often bore gold or silver
fringes fixed on with gilt nails.

The period also saw a revolution in the
customs of seating. Formerly, to sit on a
chair was the prerogative of the highest
social class only. There's a story that when
Princess Margaret, daughter of Henry VII,
dined with James IV of Scotland on the
night before their wedding, the King sat on
the only chair while the Princess sat on a
stool. The King noticed she was uncomfortable, and insisted they change places.

The general form of seating was the stool.
It was joined, with pegged tenons and a
heavy framework of oak rails and turned
legs (often splayed outwards for stability)
on which a thick piece of plank made the
seat — when not used they were pushed
under the table. Between 1600 and 1630
the back legs were extended upwards to
form a back frame, and 'back-stools' came
into existence as our first side, or single,

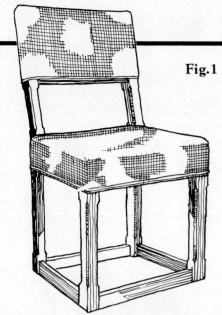

Fig.1

● *A farthingale chair in oak, 1645, designed to cope with the skirts of the same name*

chairs (as distinct from the armchairs used formerly). They were not thought of as chairs, however, and the name survived until the second half of the 18th century — Ince and Mayhew describe single chairs with upholstered backs as back-stools, and in America, 'backstools' were being advertised as late as 1786.

The design was so utilitarian that variations soon appeared: the 'farthingale' chair (fig. 1), the 'Cromwellian-style' chair (fig. 4), and the 'Yorkshire' chair, (fig. 3), with its close relations, the 'Shropshire' and 'Derbyshire' chairs. The farthingale chair was specially designed without arms and with a broad seat to accommodate the voluminous farthingale skirts of the time. They are also known as 'imbrauderers' or 'upholsterers' chairs. All back-stools have one characteristic which betrays their origin; the lower part of the back foot is not raked, but stands vertically on the floor.

Fig.2

● *An oak wainscot chair, with ornately carved and inlaid decoration*

Fig.3

● *Yorkshire back-stool, late 17th century*

The long oak tables which first appeared in Elizabethan times continued to be popular; those with four legs usually had extending leaves, but six- and eight-legged tables were common. Although the legs retained their bulbous shape, they tended to become baluster-shaped instead of the 'cup-and-cover' style of the earlier designs. They were still ornately carved with acanthus and gadrooning; the rails were intricately inlaid with contrasting woods and decorated with lunette or fluted motifs. Folding flap tables were also in existence, although they didn't really come into their own until after the Restoration in 1660.

The other essential piece of dining furniture was the dreser, used to 'dress' (carve) the meat. The dresser was of table height and up to 7ft long by about 2ft deep; there was a row of drawers beneath the table-top and the whole thing was supported on several baluster-turned legs along the front, with plain square legs at each back corner. Early examples often had fielded panels in the drawer-fronts, or plain fronts edged with a narrow moulding.

The traditional chest was still widely employed, mainly for storing clothes and domestic linen, although books and other treasured articles were often put in them for safekeeping, as most chests could be locked. It was during this period that press cupboards developed into what we today erroneously call a 'court cupboard' (see Saga 5, WW/June). About 1610 the canted cupboard which was incorporated into the upper section gave way to a flat straight cupboard; this was sub-divided into three sections by pilasters, often made to slide or lift off to reveal secret compartments. The heavy 'cup-and-cover' pillars used to support the canopy were replaced by slimmer ones which were either baluster or double-baluster turned but they were eventually eliminated altogether and the

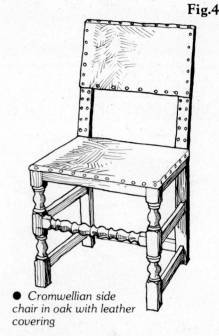

Fig.4

● *Cromwellian side chair in oak with leather covering*

canopy retained simple bosses or terminals at the front corners.

As you can imagine, chests were never very convenient for storing clothes; by 1650 a more suitable, hybrid design had emerged. The 'mule chest' was a marriage of drawers and a chest; in its earliest stage, it consisted of a chest with drawers fitted inside it which could be lifted out to reach the storage space beneath. It then developed into a chest which was mounted on a long drawer, or two drawers set side by side, the whole thing supported on a low frame of turned 'bun' feet or simple bracket feet. By the end of the 17th century, it had become a full-blown chest of drawers, and the chest section had disappeared entirely.

A different kind of storage was the 'press' cupboard with solid doors, fitted either with shelves for folded linen and clothes, or with pegs for hanging cloaks and coats (Saga 5, WW/June). About 1600 they became more elaborate and were, in effect, tall cupboards up to 7ft high and about 4ft wide, with sliding drawers or shelves in the upper part enclosed by doors, and a row of long drawers in the bottom section.

From 1649 until 1660, the country was ruled by Council of State and Parliament, 'The Commonwealth'. Oliver Cromwell was Lord Protector and it has been fashionable to portray him as a puritanical Philistine; but although he couldn't exactly be called a devoted patron of the arts, he actively encouraged the tapestry factory at Mortlake, was a lover of organ music and a patron of portrait painters.

Admittedly furniture produced during the Commonwealth was simple, unpretentious, and more or less devoid of ornament, but this doesn't necessarily condemn such designs. We must remember that the American Puritan styles stem from them, and the functional beauty of Shaker furniture reflects a similar religious feeling in its makers. ■

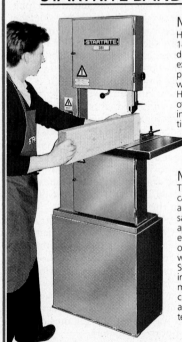

Books

William A. Lincoln
World Woods in Colour
Stobart & Son Ltd, £19.50
Reviewed by John Hemsley

The publishers must be congratulated on tackling the daunting task of rendering the colours of wood on to the printed page. Printed colour is fundamentally a poor relation to colour photographs, but this Mount Everest of a challenge has been squarely faced by the publishers, and they have firmly planted their flag at the peak. Just as well, for anyone paying £19.50 for a book calling itself *World Woods in Colour* would expect high quality colour.

The publishers have also used full-size reproductions which is invaluable if you are trying to identify an unknown specimen of wood by leafing through the illustrations. These photographs show the structure as well as the colour; rather they show the appearance of a polished specimen of wood — more useful if you want to know what a certain wood will look like when it's finished rather than identify timber in its raw state.

Wood expert Bill Lincoln — he's been in veneers more than 30 years — points out in his introduction that 70,000 different woods exist. Fewer than 400 of these are commercially available, and some of them never leave their native shores. This book contains information related to 275 different commercial timbers, each illustrated in full colour.

The format is straightforward and clear. The woods are arranged alphabetically, with each page usually devoted to one wood. The top half of the page has a generous 5x4in illustration, with the rest of the page crammed with useful information.

Listed are alternative commercial names and the botanical name, where the wood is grown and a general description of the timber — three or four sentences which describe colour of heart and sapwood, grain and figuring, and the weight. For each wood there is also a section on its reaction to seasoning, its mechanical properties, working properties, and durability. Finally there is an entry about the wood's common usages, perhaps the most fascinating for the woodworker.

A fact-filled eight-page introduction gives background to each of these factors, and is highly illuminating.

Another useful general section at the back of the book includes a table of usages, and which woods are suitable for what; sources of further information; and a five-page bibliography listing scores of books.

Finally there's a three-part index, listing timbers alphabetically under standard names, botanical names and vernacular or trade names.

The book, necessarily, has some limitations. A photograph can't show you the texture of the surface, which is a handicap in identification.

Even more significant is that generally only one picture is given of each type of wood. Now, as the introduction points out, logs can be flat sawn or quarter sawn; decorative veneer can be sliced in four different ways; and five rotary methods are used to peel logs for veneer! With some timbers in particular, these different methods result in very dissimilar appearances.

Some kind of key-tracing chart would have made identifying unknown timbers easier than having to look through the entire book — but perhaps that was not practicable.

But these are slight deficiencies — and probably unavoidable — in a 320-page book that I wholeheartedly recommend to every wood-lover. You'll find yourself picking it up time and time again, and for my money it's in the running for the woodwork book of the year.

● John Hemsley is *Woodworker*'s deputy editor, an ex-newspaper journalist and professional woodworker.

Theo Fossel
Walking and Working Sticks
4-Shot Ltd, £8.70 hardback,
£4.95 softback
Reviewed by Jack Hill

The ancient craft — or is it the art? — of making walking sticks and shepherd's crooks seems to be as popular today as ever. The British Stickmaker's Guild, formed only two years ago with less than 50 founder members, now has over 600 devotees.

The Guild was conceived and co-founded by Theo Fossel, who has written a book about stickmaking, covering the whole subject of making walking sticks and shepherd's crooks in all their different forms.

Beginning with a useful section on the merits and demerits of different species of wood, Theo goes on to discuss cutting, seasoning and straightening. Sticks with bark and without, sticks stained and fumed come next. He explores different materials for handles; wood and horn, and how to bend, carve and dress them. Jointing handles to shafts — a problem area frequently passed over too quickly in other books on stickmaking — is well covered, as are finishing and ferrule-fitting. A glossary of stickmaking terms, a bibliography, a list of useful addresses and an index complement this highly informative book, which has 128 pages and over 200 illustrations.

Phil Drabble has contributed a foreword, saying the book will 'whet the appetite of every country lover to have a sturdy stick to accompany you wherever you go.' And I agree — this book tells you how to choose and make that indispensable 'third leg'. There are other books on stickmaking, but none quite so comprehensive as this one.

● The book is available from 4-Shot Ltd, Freepost, Station Rd, Beaconsfield, Bucks HP9 1BR.

● Jack Hill is a well-known chair and stickmaker.

In brief

Turning wood with Richard Raffan
(Richard Raffan; Bell & Hyman, £12.95 softback)
The first English edition of this book, highly praised by Tobias Kaye in April's *Woodworker*, is £2 cheaper than the American edition Tobias reviewed, *Woodworker* will be publishing an exclusive extract — keep your eyes open!

Picture framing made easy (Penelope Stokes; Blandford Press, £5.95)
Useful primer covering mounts as well as mouldings, with non-technical text and clear but badly drawn diagrams. The author presumes little basic knowledge, and acknowledges that mistakes are a valuable part of learning by suggesting remedies and actually writing in the foreword, 'This book is for the inveterate bungler'! If the hat fits, buy the book.

The Complete Home Improvement Manual (Richard Wiles ed; Dragon's World, £14.95 hardback)
Disappointing, but maybe that's because it follows hard on the heels of the superlative Collin's Manual (WW/July).

Making Authentic Craftsman Furniture (Gustav Stickley; Constable, £4.45 softback)
Instructions and plans for making 62 pieces of furniture which first appeared in Stickley's seminal American woodworking magazine *The Craftsman* from 1901-1907. 'The simple, straightforward Craftsman approach to furniture . . . became a classic American style in its own right' says the blurb; most of the projects are very simple, but there are a few American classics.

The Book of Toymaking (Pamela Peake; Ebury Press, £8.95 hardback)
Over 35 projects including 14 wooden toys, very clearly presented; a good beginner's book.

Woodcarving – An introduction (Maurice Woods; A & C Black, £5.95 softback)
Softback reprint of the 1981 standard — a useful basic introduction to tools, techniques and ideas. Outlining, planning, relief, letter, in-the-round, heads, small bowls and dishes, carving for casting . . .

The eternal turner

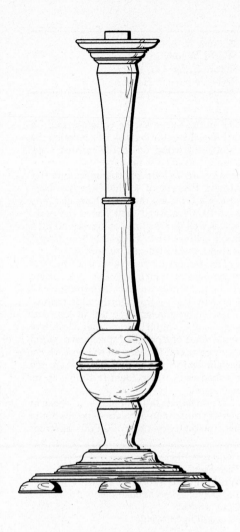

● **Above left**: Ted Reffell and Father Melvyn Barnsley ceremonially place the 3ft-long candle on top of Ted's giant candlestick. Profile **above**

Ted Reffell was inspired to put his new-found enthusiasm for turning at the service of his local church — and found himself making this Goliath of a candlestick!

Ted Reffell's boyhood hobby of woodwork has been a lifelong interest, and when he was 60 he took up woodturning. He made a wooden lathe with a wooden bed and headstock, took a basic course at Roger's of Hitchin, and since then has not looked back.

Ted is an engineering craftsman working on space projects, so naturally he aimed his work at celestial orbits. He asked the minister of the Church of St. Andrew and St. George in Stevenage to set him a project for the church, and the result was this paschal-candlestick. A single paschal-

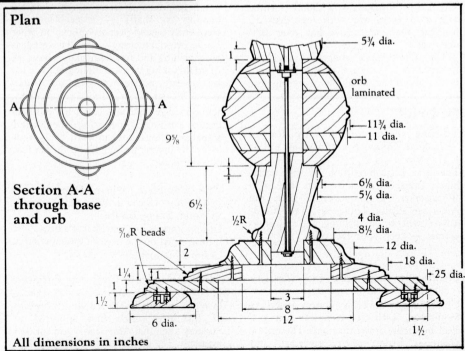

Plan

Section A-A through base and orb

$\frac{5}{16}$R beads

$\frac{1}{2}$R

$5\frac{3}{4}$ dia.

orb laminated

$11\frac{3}{4}$ dia.
11 dia.

$6\frac{1}{8}$ dia.
$5\frac{1}{4}$ dia.

4 dia.
$8\frac{1}{2}$ dia.

12 dia.

18 dia.

25 dia.

$9\frac{5}{8}$

$6\frac{1}{2}$

1

1

2

$1\frac{1}{4}$ 1

1

$1\frac{1}{2}$

6 dia.

3

8

12

$1\frac{1}{2}$

All dimensions in inches

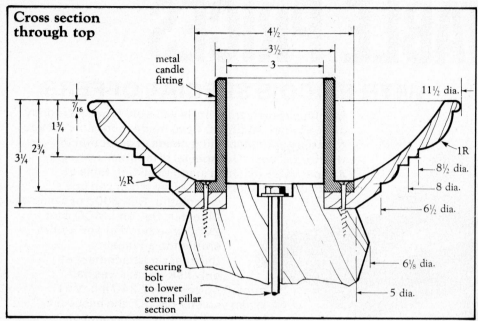

Cross section through top

metal candle fitting

$4\frac{1}{2}$
$3\frac{1}{2}$
3
$11\frac{1}{2}$ dia.
$\frac{7}{16}$
$1\frac{3}{4}$
$2\frac{3}{4}$
$3\frac{1}{4}$
1R
$\frac{1}{2}$R
$8\frac{1}{2}$ dia.
8 dia.
$6\frac{1}{2}$ dia.
$6\frac{1}{8}$ dia.
5 dia.

securing bolt to lower central pillar section

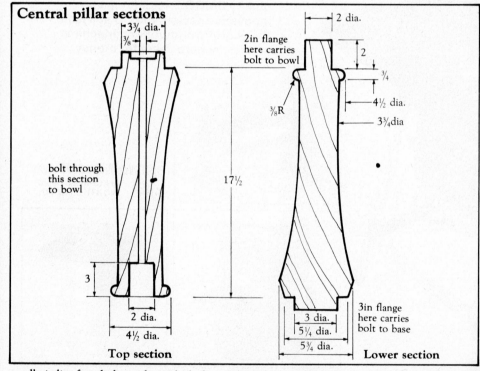

Central pillar sections

$3\frac{3}{4}$ dia.
$\frac{3}{8}$
2 dia.
2in flange here carries bolt to bowl
2
$\frac{3}{4}$
$\frac{3}{8}$R
$4\frac{1}{2}$ dia.
$3\frac{3}{4}$ dia

bolt through this section to bowl

$17\frac{1}{2}$

3
2 dia.
$4\frac{1}{2}$ dia.

Top section

3 dia.
$5\frac{1}{4}$ dia.
$5\frac{3}{4}$ dia.
3in flange here carries bolt to base

Lower section

Level adjustment

$1\frac{1}{2}$ dia.
threaded studs in base
4 holes $\frac{7}{32}$
2 holes $\frac{7}{32}$
$\frac{3}{8}$BSW
threaded inserts in feet

Threaded assembly flanges

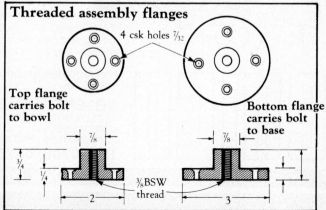

4 csk holes $\frac{7}{32}$

Top flange carries bolt to bowl

Bottom flange carries bolt to base

$\frac{7}{8}$
$\frac{3}{4}$
$\frac{1}{4}$
2
$\frac{3}{8}$BSW thread
$\frac{7}{8}$
3

---

display at the Stevenage Leisure Centre before being taken to the church for the morning service on 16 March.

Ted didn't get a penny for the project, but he reckons the gains exceeded mere financial reward. It greatly extended his skill and gave him confidence for other projects.

Construction

The candlestick is mounted on four feet, each with threaded metal inserts; screwed studs are attached to the base to allow adjustments for level by turning the feet.

The base is made up of circles 25in and 18in across, which have 12in and 8in central bores to reduce weight. The candlestick weighs 63lbs.

The three base layers and the short $6\frac{1}{2}$in length of the central pillar are fixed with screws, which will allow for subsequent movement more effectively than glue.

The orb is laminated; Ted turned each layer to the appropriate radius and bored a 3in hole through it. Then he glued the pieces together, using the bores for location before blending them into a sphere with abrasive paper.

The central column consists of two sections, each $17\frac{1}{2}$in long, joined by a turned 2in pin and bore; the join is hidden by a double bead.

The bowl has an aluminium fitting counterbored into it for the candle, which Ted machined on an engineering lathe. He bronze lacquered it, and used four wood-screws to secure the fitting and the bowl to the upper part of the central pillar.

Then he moulded a removable fibreglass insert to fit the space between the candle holder and the bowl; the mould was turned in pine, a tricky dimensioning job to get the exact internal profile.

The lower part of the central pillar has threaded metal flanges attached to each end for the long bolts that go through the top and base to complete the assembly. The candlestick can be disassembled for transport or storage.

Ted finished all the individual turnings with coats of Danish oil, and wax polished them before assembly. Presentation details are on a small engraved brass plate attached to the base. ∎

---

candle is lit after dark on the night before Easter Sunday and is left burning until after Easter. For the rest of the year, the candlestick is kept near the font and used at christenings.

Ted's design is 5ft tall and takes a 3ft-long 3in-diameter candle. As he designed it, Ted was conscious that our cultural heritage has been handed down through libraries, museums and the church; arts and crafts have played their part in this process, and Ted determined to make his personal contribution.

The task, fitted in among other work, was spread over three months. The candlestick was finally presented to the minister on 20 January 1986, and then put on public

The jigsander

Swirls and scratches could be yesterday's nuisance with this home-made linear finishing sander

My Black & Decker palm sander is a most useful tool for finishing timber, writes **Glyn Condick,** but unfortunately it tends to leave swirl marks which only show up after I've applied stain. It's really hard work to get rid of them, and is time-consuming if I'm finishing a lot of timber.

Then I spotted the potential of my DN 533E jigsaw, and produced this device to turn it into a linear sander.

Materials:

1 Sheet steel L-shape, $^{13}/_{14}$ gauge (fig. 1)
2 Sheet steel angles from $^{13}/_{14}$ gauge (fig. 2)

● *Prototype of Glyn Condick's de luxe linear finishing sander, showing additional features*

1 Piece plywood, 6x2x½in
1 Nut and bolt, 4BA
2 Round-head screws, ½in
Screw the metal angles to the plywood base with the round-head screws, and bolt the L-shaped piece between them (fig. 3).

Glue glasspaper on to the bottom. The bolt joining the pieces shouldn't be too tight; a little play allows the plywood base to tilt when you use the tool. Run the saw on speed one.

By altering the angle of the tool slightly, the cut can be increased; it gets into corners, and gives a most acceptable finish.

Since this first prototype, I have also built a de luxe version. I stuck foam rubber on the base of the plywood, and shaped the wood back at the ends (fig. 4).

I also adapted two bulldog clips so I can change glasspaper easily. I filed the teeth down and bent the grippers (fig. 5), then screwed the bulldog clips to the plywood (fig. 6). Inexpensive and effective! ■

● *The linear sander ready for action. The deluxe version has a padded base, cut-back ends and a quick-release device for the glasspaper*

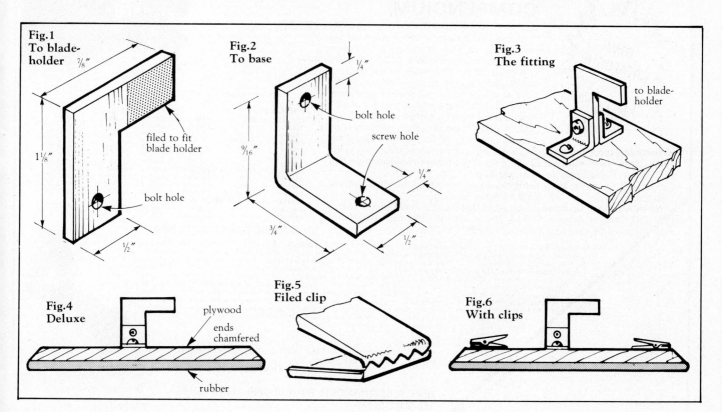

Fig.1
To blade-holder $^{7}/_{8}$″
$1^{1}/_{8}$″
filed to fit blade holder
bolt hole
½″

Fig.2
To base ¼″
bolt hole
screw hole
$^{9}/_{16}$″
¼″
$^{3}/_{4}$″
½″

Fig.3
The fitting
to blade-holder

Fig.4
Deluxe
plywood
ends chamfered
rubber

Fig.5
Filed clip

Fig.6
With clips

862

Question box

We will try to answer any questions you can throw at us, but the ones we publish are the ones of most general interest to readers.

Please type your question double-spaced with generous margins, and include a stamped self-addressed envelope. Send it to: Question Box, Woodworker, 1 Golden Sq., London W1R 3AB.

Weathered oak

Q *I have cut oak slats for two garden chairs from 60 year-old weathered fence palings, previously creosoted. Planing has produced a surprisingly smooth finish, and the wood is strong enough. I would like to prevent the spread of fissures, if this is possible, and keep the good looks and feel. What do you recommend?*

D. Ambrose, Surbiton

A The fissures still present after planing have been caused by alternate expansion and contraction of the surface over many years. There's no reliable way to prevent them spreading further, or new ones developing. When wood is used outside in this condition, water tends to collect, creating areas of dampness which may extend the fissures, lead to staining and destroy a finish. To keep the good looks and 'feel' to some extent, I suggest you:

1 Ensure the wood is dry and creosote-free, then apply two or three coats of quality yacht varnish.

2 If possible, fix the slats with the original heartwood uppermost.

3 Store the chairs under cover when they're not being used.

4 Periodically examine the surface for finish failure, particularly around fissures. Sand and recoat when it's necessary. Examine like this every few months; if you leave it longer, replaning, sanding and re-finishing may be necessary.

Oak is particularly susceptible to surface fissuring when it's exposed to the weather. The most you can expect is to keep the surface relatively smooth.

Ron Hooks

● Ron Hooks is a professional timber consultant.

Cellulose finish

Q *I'm making fishing tackle boxes out of birch plywood. I want a low sheen black paint finish similar to the effect of* spraying auto-cellulose on to metal.

I've tried cellulose paint, sanding sealer and filler/primer – in various combinations – but the grain still comes through even after five coats of paint.

A. W. Taylor, Kidderminster

A Whatever finish is applied to wood it's essential to prepare the surface so it's absolutely smooth and free from blemishes. Any prominent grain must be glasspapered level or defects will be noticeable when the finishing coats are applied. This is probably why the grain of the plywood has shown through the lacquer.

Glasspaper the plywood using progressively finer grades of abrasive paper wrapped round a cork block. Test the smoothed surface by lightly rubbing the tips of your fingers over it when any ripples or inequalities in the surface will be apparent.

The surface should now be lightly sponged with warm water to raise the grain and, when completely dry, glasspapered smooth in readiness for staining with a water stain. Let the stain dry overnight before spraying on a coat of cellulose grain sealer which will be ready for glasspapering after about an hour. If necessary the work can be touched in with some stain to achieve a uniform colour. It can now be finally sprayed with black cellulose.

There is a helpful chapter on spraying techniques in *Staining and Polishing* by Charles Hayward.

Charles Cliffe

Colouring mahogany

Q *How can I achieve a good rich brown colour on Brazilian mahogany? I've been using bichromate of potash, finishing with french polish, but the result is too red. I'm worried about the edges wearing thin and going light; would it be enough to use garnet polish on its own here and let the mahogany darken by itself?*

Also can you tell me how to obtain an antique look to furniture made from this wood, and how should I finish off the insides of cabinets where I've used various woods – pine for backs, oak for drawer-sides?

T. Butterworth, Cumbernauld

A Generally a solution of 2oz of bichromate of potash dissolved in a pint of water gives mahogany a pleasing brown shade. But some varieties of mahogany turn red, so always experiment with the stain on some waste pieces from the job. If the result is too red, try a walnut stain instead. Make this by dissolving vandyke crystals in ammonia and adding water to give the required shade.

An alternative is a brown mahogany oil stain. But you will probably achieve deeper penetration with water-stain, especially with ammonia.

Garnet polish adds a little warmth to the finished colour, and as long as you apply both stain and polish evenly, there shouldn't be any danger of wearing away the colour from the edges.

For an antique appearance you should let the french-polished surface harden for a week or two before dulling it slightly with rottenstone. Wipe away all traces of the rottenstone with a chamois leather and then wax with a light-coloured antique wax polish. This reduces the brilliance of the french polish and gives the furniture mellower appearance.

Leave the oak sides of drawers unstained and unpolished apart from the ends of drawer-fronts, which may show if the drawers are left slightly open. Stain the pine with a colour to hide the grain completely; for mahogany mix red ochre with water and add glue size as a binder, about 2oz to ½ pt of water.

Charles Cliffe

● Charles Cliffe is a professional polisher, author and teacher.

Colouring MDF

Q *Can you tell me how to colour furniture made from MDF with lacquer, and the advantages of this over stain or paint?*

Ms P.A. Harris, Sunderland

A This finish is ideal for MDF because of the particle board's fine texture; it has no grain texture or figure. Stains are generally transparent to highlight the natural markings of wood, and stained particle board looks ghastly! I suggest you think about using paint however. I recommend you read *Paint Magic* by Jocasta Innes which covers all forms of decorative painting, not just furniture. Also look up my recent decorative finish articles (WW/March, Apr).

Modern lacquers are highly volatile and fast drying — a considerable fire risk — and there are basically two types. Cellulose lacquers harden by evaporation of the solvent; catalyst lacquers harden by chemical reaction, and are very resistant to heat, water and alcohol. They are all designed to be sprayed but there are brushing varieties. For home use I suggest cellulose unless you really need the catalytic qualities described above. You can get coloured lacquer from industrial paint suppliers who will be listed in the Yellow Pages. The standard range includes the 100 British Standard colours, but a good supplier can match any colour you take as a sample.

Proceed as follows:

1 Seal the surface with two coats of cellulose sanding sealer, allowing two hours between coats and sanding both smooth with fine garnet paper.

2 Thin your coloured lacquer with enough 'brushing thinners' in in a metal container to make it workable without running (experiment on scrap).

3 Use a soft-bristled brush and charge it generously with lacquer. Don't discharge the surplus or allow it to drip. Flow, not brush, the lacquer on to the surface with long straight strokes. Cover the surface quickly to keep a wet edge; if you miss a spot, ignore it and catch it with the next coat. Take care on vertical surfaces to prevent runs. Allow to dry for two hours.

4 Cut back with 600-grit wet-or-dry, using soapy water as a lubricant, to remove brush-marks and dust specks. Allow the surface to dry and recoat it. Two or three coats should be enough, allow the last coat to harden for 24 hours.

5 Burnish the finish to a high gloss with T-Cut or burnishing cream, using long straight strokes. Alternatively you can get a satin or matt finish by rubbing gently with a damp felt pad sprinkled with fine pumice powder. You may need to use 800-grit wet-or-dry to remove stubborn brush marks before burnishing.

Clean all brushes and equipment with thinners between coats. Don't attempt this process in your home. You need an enormous amount of ventilation, and you must take stringent precautions against fire, such as a dry powder extinguisher. You'll really need a well ventilated garage or workshop. I do recommend paint rather than lacquer!

Ian Hosker

● Ian Hosker is a professional finisher and a Guild course tutor.

Stail engine

Q *After a fruitless search trying to find a stail engine for making hay-rake shafts, I've decided to make my own. Can you advise?*

Andrew Robinson, Ayrshire

A There are many variations of the stail engine and its close cousin, the rounder. The drawings show a fairly large one from my collection, suitable for shaping rake handles from coppice-type stakes.

You can use any plane blade, slightly curved and with the bevelled cutting edge face down on the bed. The angle of the blade in this case is about 280°. You'll notice the tool is in two halves, held together and adjusted with two bolts with wing-nuts; this allows for different-diameter handles to be shaped, and allows you to set a coarse or fine cut. The mouth is slightly tapered to help the work on its way.

Further information:

Woodland Crafts in Great Britain, Herbert L. Edlin; David & Charles
Dictionary of Tools, R.A. Salaman; George Allen and Unwin.

Stuart King

● Stuart King is a miniaturist and an expert on country craft history.

Scratch-stock blades

Q *I have a box of cast-steel Victorian/Edwardian scratch-stock blades. As each piece has been scored with a grinder and broken from a larger piece, I assume the cutting edges have been ground with the steel fully hardened – the edges are ground to about 40%.*

When used in an ordinary scratch stock, these cutters judder across the length of the wood but when drawn towards the operator they cut rather than scrape. Were they actually intended for a scratch stock?

B. Ratcliffe, Leicester

A The point you make about the cutters having been shaped after the steel had been hardened clearly suggests that they were one-off, home-made, jobs. It's likely that the original stock, or stocks, to hold them were also one-offs and we are unlikely to find them in a catalogue.

You don't mention how long the cutters are, or whether they're tailed like moulding plane irons but, assuming they have parallel sides and aren't more than 3in long, two possibilities exist. One is that they were plane irons, used in the type of short-soled plane — confusingly known as a 'router' — designed for curved work (*Salaman's Dictionary of Woodworking Tools*). In this case they would cut at a pitch of about 45°.

The other possibility is that they were scrapers, held between finger and thumb, for the final surface finishing of mouldings cut with ordinary moulding planes. If so, they would have been pushed or dragged with the flat face downwards.

In either case the angle of pitch should prevent the juddering experienced when the cutters are held almost vertically in the scratch-stock.

Philip Walker

● Philip Walker is a founder member of the Tool and Trades History Society

---

Guitar fingerboard

Q *I want to remove the metal frets on the fingerboard of my bass guitar, which is rosewood laid on maple, and fill the slots with plastic, to get a 'fretless'. I'm concerned about the effects of the metal strings on the fingerboard; can I treat the rosewood to improve its durability and yet retain the natural wood feel? I've heard of one instrument repairer who uses yacht varnish for this.*

B.S. Farley, Bishop's Stortford

A The vertical and horizontal movement of stopped down strings will wear any surface finish in time. Rosewood wears quicker than ebony, being softer; you might think about replacing the fretted rosewood with an unfretted ebony fingerboard. Sand the ebony and burnish it with a soft cloth to get a polished surface.

Varnishing won't greatly extend the usable life of the fingerboard. When the finish breaks through, which it will do fairly rapidly, you'll get problems of string buzz because of the uneven surface, as well as a poor appearance.

Phil Chambers

● Phil Chambers teaches musical instrument technology at Merton College.

Bending timber

Q *I need information on bending and laminating timber around a former. I am thinking of building up to thickness with sheets of plywood and finishing with veneer. What type of glue do you recommend?*

J. Burgess, Houghton-le-Spring

A Various techniques are suitable for the small workshop, such as saw-kerfing, brick build-ups, stave and

---

Stail engine

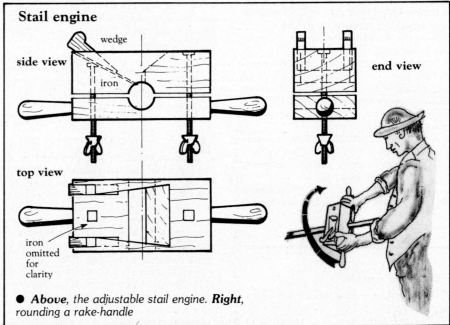

● *Above*, the adjustable stail engine. *Right*, rounding a rake-handle

veneer laminating, multi-ply drums and coopering. These processes are too complex to describe here and I suggest you refer to *Practical Veneering* by Charles Hayward, published by Evans (chapter 11) and *The Practical Carpenter and Joiner* by N.W. Kay, published by Odhams Press (chapter 13). Both books deal exhaustively with the various methods and advise on the use of suitable for most processes because of the flexibility it allows in laying up the veneers. See also David Savage's 'Craft of cabinetmaking' article on laminating in *Woodworker*, July 85.

Bob Grant

Rusting tools

Q *Have you any advice for keeping rust at bay, both in hand-tools and machines? This is a particular problem with an outside workshop.*

Parry Davis, Northwich

A The most effective answer is to ensure you have a thermally well-insulated workshop which will protect the contents in a stable envelope and exclude vapour. In addition some form of background heating would help; I find the small industrial type of black element heater (like Dimplex) useful and cheap to run.

If this is impossible, or you lay up the workshop for the winter, then you'll have to resort to various expedients to prevent moisture condensing on the metal. Coat all surfaces with grease, Vaseline, or engine oil. Bags of silica gel will help, but remember that you will have to continually dry these as they become saturated with moisture. On machine beds I have found that the silicone-based sprays, such as WD-40 (obtainable from motorists' shops), particularly good at dispelling moisture. You might also consider wrapping tools in a special vapour inhibiting paper which is treated for anti-corrosion (from Whistons, New Mills, Stockport, Cheshire).

Bob Grant

● Bob Grant is head of Craft Design and Technology at an Oxford comprehensive school and is a Guild course tutor.

Wooden threads

Q *I having great difficulty turning a thread on wood. Even if I manage to cut a decent form, it just tends to crumble.*

I have made cutters of different forms using various rake angles, and I also made a hollow cutter like the ones in screw-boxes. I still find that all these cutters tend to tear the wood rather than cut it.

I want to cut a thread 2in OD and 12tpi, only about .032in deep, on an oak bar. Although this is mainly cosmetic, I still need a strong thread form.

Andrew King, Beckenham

A I feel this is almost impossible, particularly using wood as coarse-grained as oak. It seems you're attempting this in an engineer's screwcutting lathe, but wooden threads are normally cut using a screwbox, the equivalent of the engineer's die.

12tpi is the pitch for ½in Whitworth threads, unusually fine for wood. A depth of .032in? — well, .0312 is only 1/32in. A 2in Whitworth thread is 4tpi, a great deal coarser than the 12tpi you require. Wooden threads are in any case coarser than Whitworth, the coarsest common metal thread. You could try with a screwbox, but I doubt whether such a fine wood thread could be produced with one.

Bob Wearing

● Making a tap and screw-box is described in *Fine Woodworking Techniques vol. 1*, Taunton Press, £14.95 softback, from Stobart & Son, 67-73 Worship St, London EC2A 2EL, 01-247 0501.
● Bob Wearing is a woodwork lecturer at Shrewsbury College and a regular *Woodworker* contributor.

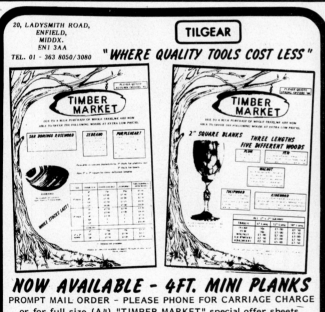
865

WHATEVER YOUR HOBBY...

Guild notes

WOODWORKERS

T he Guild was set up by *Woodworker* to create a meeting ground for all those involved in working wood, whether professional, amateur, or enthusiastic beginner. Guild members get:

- Access to Guild courses and events
- Free publicity in *Woodworker*
- Specially arranged tool insurance at low rates
- 15% off Woodworker Show entry
- A free display area and meeting point at the Show
- 15% discount off *Woodworker* plans
- Inclusion in our register of members' skills and services

For details, please send an sae to the Guild of Woodworkers, 1 Golden Sq, London W1R 3AB.

GUILD COURSES

● Only Guild members are eligible to go on these courses. You must book in advance, and we must have a cheque for the full cost of the course at the time of booking. If you cancel less than four weeks before the advertised date you will forfeit 50% of the cost, unless there are exceptional circumstances.

French polishing — Charles Cliffe

2-3 October, 9.30-5, Bexleyheath, £40. Charles Cliffe, one of our 'Question box' experts and author of *The Woodworker Manual of Finishing and Polishing*, explains preparation, staining, and application of this tricky (and beautiful) finish. He'll also be dealing with using a cabinet scraper, so bring your own, plus any small piece of furniture that you want advice on. Charles can order supplies for you to take away if you tell him in advance.

Wood-machining — Ken Taylor

11 October, 9.30-5.30, Bletchley, Bucks, £25+VAT.
Ken's course on the ins and outs of machining wood is one of our most popular. Find out about (and try for yourself) table- and band-saws, radial-arm saws, planers and thicknessers, spindle moulders, mortisers and universals. Lunch is included in the price.

Hardy crew

Some Guild members braved the elements to visit Parnham House and the new School for Woodland Industry back in April — and here's a picture to prove it! Beastly cold, reports **John Odom** of Kenley, Surrey, who took the photograph **right** of the prototype house at Hooke Park (WW/Mar, Apr). 'But I enjoyed it very much and am grateful to you for arranging the visit,' writes John.

All aboard

Fancy helping to restore a vintage luxury railway carriage? The Dart Valley Railway Association is appealing for volunteers with woodwork skills to assist with a major restoration of the 1931-built Great Western Railway Ocean Liner Saloon no.9111, 'King George', said to be the finest vehicle ever built by the G.W.R.

It's timber-framed with steel panelling outside, luxuriously appointed inside with magnificent walnut veneers. To bring it back to its original condition, the association needs people with general woodwork skills, and especially with experience in veneering and french polishing. There's also plenty of semi-and unskilled work to do.

No cash in it, of course. But the satisfaction of challenging work, and the reward of knowing you have helped restore a superb example of yesteryear's railway vehicles. The coach is based at Buckfastleigh, Devon, and volunteers work mainly at weekends. One perk is free travel on the Dart Valley Railway.

If you live in the south west, contact Tim Searle at 52 College Avenue, Mannamead, Plymouth PL4 7AN.

Power routing — Roy Sutton

22 November 1986, Herne Bay, £25+VAT.
Another popular course from this well-known expert on the subject. Roy starts from first principles and covers housing, grooving, rebating, straight and circular moulding, tenoning, mortising, and rule-joint and template work; he also deals with designing and setting up your own jigs.

Jewel of a box

The unusual jewellery box at **left** is the work of Guild member **Richard Hague**, from Blofield, Norfolk. Unusual, because it's got ample space compared with most of the titchy boxes you see; the built-in mirror is a very useful component.

It's also unusual because Richard used 12mm MDF for the carcase, trying his hand at veneering for the first time with rosewood. Drawer fronts are solid sycamore, inlaid with rosewood and with rosewood handles; the sides and bottoms are Cedar of Lebanon.

The mirror is hinged at the top, folding back to allow the lid to close; in use it can be positioned at any of eight angles, the dowels at the bottom locating in cut-outs at the base.

As well as cutting his teeth on hand veneering, Richard also dived into traditional french polishing for the first time. Looks fine to us.

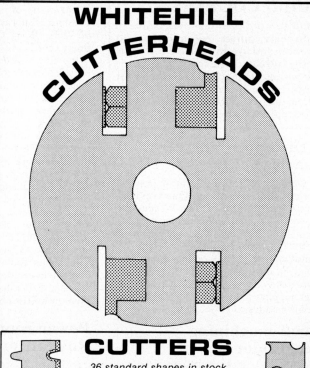

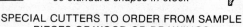

La belle table

Paul Davis' *table chiffonier* in late 18th century French style will really test your parquetry skills — and there's some tricky shaping too

In France around 1770 furniture styles were in transition between Louis XV and Louis XVI. The relatively simple geometric lines of this *table chiffonier*, or worktable, are typical of Louis XVI, while the curved legs are a vestige of a Louis XV style.

I have simplified the design slightly, which would annoy the French, who stipulate that a reproduction is an exact copy of an existing piece of period furniture. You could modify the design even further if you wished, using four instead of three legs, for example.

Medium to dark, fairly close-grained hardwoods were used at that period, and mahogany or walnut are ideal; oak and ash would be unsuitable. You could always stain a lighter-coloured wood such as maple or cherry; I chose walnut veneer and plain, unpretentious beech.

Setting out

Start by drawing a full-scale plan of the apron and leg assembly (fig. 1). This will help you see where the joints should be and make you realise the massive dimensions of wood required for the delicately curved segments. You could glue up layers with an expensive wood on the *parement*, or outside, and a baser wood of similar density on the inside; the outer layer must be thick enough so the baser wood doesn't show through after shaping.

● *Louis XV or Louis XVI, the walnut parquetry and curved components are a challenge in any language*

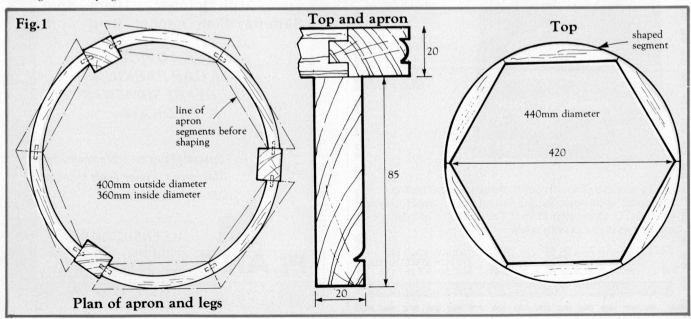

Fig.1

line of apron segments before shaping

400mm outside diameter
360mm inside diameter

Plan of apron and legs

Top and apron

20

85

20

Top

shaped segment

440mm diameter

420

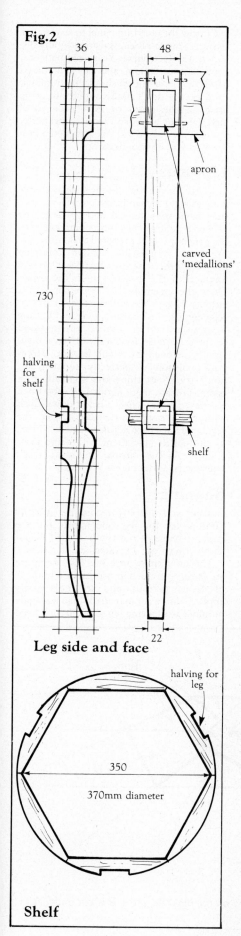

Fig.2

36 48

apron

carved 'medallions'

730

halving for shelf

shelf

Leg side and face

22

halving for leg

350

370mm diameter

Shelf

Dowel joints are adequate throughout, as the apron isn't expected to do much load bearing. You could use mortise and tenon joints, but cutting them on a 60° angle while trying to maintain symmetry is quite a headache and short grain in the tenons can cause them to snap off. Whichever you choose, the joints need to be quite strong to withstand the subsequent shaping and finishing processes, and besides, tight joints look neat.

The 60° mitres on each segment have to be cut perfectly accurately; drilling holes for the dowels freehand, or even with a jig, risks being a bit hit-or-miss, but a slot-mortiser with a 60° template in chipboard or thick ply clamped to the table can give perfect results. Fit a drill bit into the mortiser, block the sideways movement of the table and set it to the appropriate height. Fix the template on the table with one segment in place so that the first series of holes will be positioned correctly, drill them and reposition a segment on its other edge so the second hole will be vertically aligned with the first. Turn the template over, clamp it down and drill the second series of holes. When drilling the legs, make sure the holes are the same distance apart as on the segments.

Now you can glue up the segments in pairs. To clamp you need firm but gentle pressure inwards at the ends of the pieces and downwards on the joint. You can use a pair of sash-cramps, or even a Workmate and a large G-cramp. The two pressures

need to be balanced so that no gaps appear in the joint (fig. 3).

A French cabinetmaker or *ébéniste* would test-fit the carcase construction before the lengthy shaping process to check the joinery is adequate. Test it for symmetry by placing the assembly upside down on the plan and also check that the feet are equidisant. You might correct minor faults by bending and twisting, but this could force joints apart if the misalignment is more than 4-5mm.

Shaping

Cutting curves in 85mm hardwood is tough going, so a finely tuned bandsaw with a thin blade is virtually indispensable in this project. Use a template for shaping the legs — quicker and more accurate than struggling with tracing or carbon paper. Another effort-saver is to make the leg slightly overlength at the bottom and saw down towards the foot, stopping before the blade comes through the end of the wood. Then cut the other taper and the whole profile shape. The waste 'wedges' of the taper will fall away when you cut the leg to length. This method avoids having to tape the waste back on for the second cut.

To mark out the inside and outside diameters of the apron, lay the paired segments on the plan; then fix a block of wood on the drawing the same height as the apron with its centre directly above the centre of the plan and mark out the two circles with conventional compasses or a trammel bar.

Shaping involves cutting, rasping, filing, scraping and sanding. Aim for maximum accuracy from the start; the bandsaw blade should just 'kiss' the pencil lines.

Veneering

This kind of parquetry, or *marqueterie de fond*, depends largely on good matching and the joints intersecting at a perfect point. An 18-piece *soleil*, or sunburst (fig. 4) is a real challenge. Curly or wild-grained veneers are more difficult to use effectively than straight-grained wood and, like all things beautiful, they tend to have a will of their own! A simple hexagon made of six equi-lateral triangles can be more difficult to produce satisfactorily with a fine burr or crotch veneer than the more complex designs with humbler quarter-cut stuff.

Whatever design you opt for, don't try to cut the segments from a single large leaf, however straight the grain; use a packet of smaller leaves that have been cut in sequence from the leg and number the sequence in pencil. Set out the design full-size on a spare piece of board with the lines extending beyond the intersections to help align the straight-edge you cut against. This should be perfectly straight and quite thick (a strip of 6 or 8mm bakelite is ideal), and a veneer saw is better than a cutter or craft knife. As you can push as well as pull the saw, there is less risk of delicate grain

Fig.3
Assembly

clamps in two directions hold angled joints

Test-fitting the apron and legs before assembly

Fig.4
Choices for parquetry designs

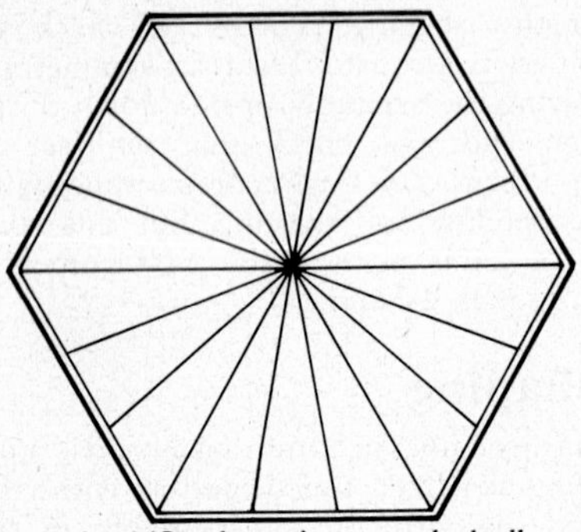

● *18-leaf 'Sunburst' – a real challenge*

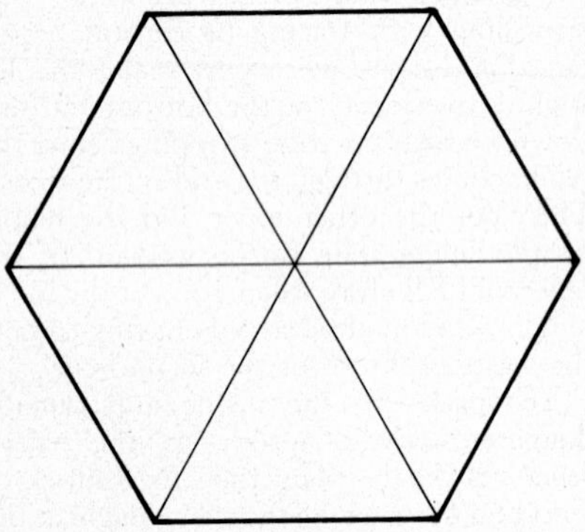

● *The simple hexagon*

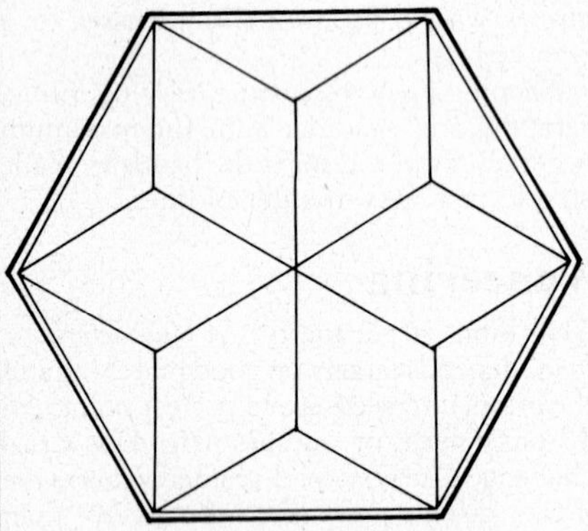

● *Diamond patterns go well with regular grain*

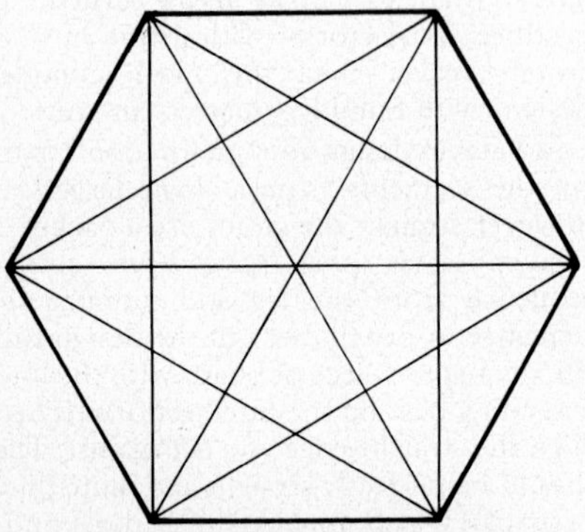

● *Triangles and rhomboids: just join up all the corners!*

breaking out at the edges when crosscutting or cutting on the bias.

Matching the last segment with both its neighbours is the biggest problem with a polygon. With a six-segment design, say, it helps to cut the leaves in the order 1-6-5-4-3-2 and so avoid having to fit the top or bottom leaf of the packet last.

Cut the first segment and fix it to the drawing with fine headless veneer pins (fig. 5); the pin holes won't show after laying, but position them carefully as they are fiddly to handle and you won't want to keep moving them if you find they get in the way. Slide the second leaf under the first segment until the grain matches, cut it to shape, fix it and so on. Taping up as you go along will minimise the need for pins; remember that dampened veneer tape shrinks as it dries out, and pulls the join together, which may result in a difficult overlap if segments have been forced together too hard to ensure a 'good' join. You could add a thin veneer stringing in a contrasting colour to heighten the effect of the parquetry work; it also gives rise to some additional fun when staining!

You'll find it's virtually impossible to align a geometric veneer assembly on a ground that has been pre-cut to the final shape. It's best to leave the ground oversize and cut it to shape after laying. The ground needs to be 19mm thick, so the finished piece (with a balancing veneer on the reverse side) will be about 20mm. You can lay the work, taped side up, between home-made cauls with large cramps. Urea formaldehyde glues (Cascamite) are irreversible and virtually indestructible, but they allow for no rectification later on and show up as black glue lines. PVA is probably easier to handle but the risks of 'lifting' are greater, especially if you need to re-dampen the work to remove tape and paper used to prevent the work sticking to the cauls. Allow the glue to cure fully before cleaning up and cutting to shape.

Cutting the glued-up panel to shape after laying is a nerve-racking business — any slip and you're in trouble. You need patience, good co-ordination and a well tuned bandsaw. Cleaning up should be minimal; hand planes don't really appreciate being used on the edges of man-made panel materials but a coarse file, used properly, will do the job. Keep the parquetry face towards you as you clean up.

Lippings

Lippings for the top and the shelf are made from straight segments and are shaped once they have been mitred and glued to the veneered panels. They can be butt-joined to the panels if you're prepared to take the risk of them 'wandering' under clamping pressure; otherwise use tongue-and-groove joints with the groove cut in the panel. Once the assembly has been cut into a circular shape, the intersections between segments are only 10mm wide and butting is your only course. Jointing with plywood feathers or false tongues will have them coming through the circumference. Unless your polygon is perfectly symmetrical, don't try to machine the segments in a batch. Prepare them about 1mm too thick so they can be gently planed down flush with the veneered surfaces. After the segments have been adjusted and test-fitted to the panel, glue them with three sash-cramps. As they are to be cut to shape afterwards, softening isn't necessary.

Shaping

Cutting and shaping techniques are the same as for the legs and apron, but the circumference of the top and shelf would allow you to use a spokeshave this time.

The mouldings on Louis XVI furniture are fairly restrained in comparison to those of earlier periods, and are more easily applied with a scratch stock than a spindle moulder with a ring fence and french-head

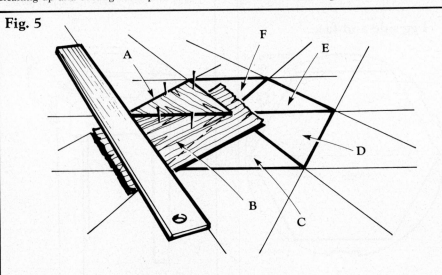

Fig. 5

● *Segment **A** has been cut and positioned on the plan. Segment **B** is put under **A** to match the grain, and then cut; and so on*

cutter. If you go round both faces, the simple 'hook' pattern can be used to produce a profile on the top and shelf as well as on the apron. Alternatively, you could use a router to run a light cove moulding round the upper edges of the top and shelf and the lower edge of the apron, avoiding cutting off the polygon points.

Simple halving joints are used for shelf and leg assembly, but check with the plan to ensure the notches are positioned correctly, and cut to the right depth so the legs are parallel, neither tapering in from the top nor splaying out.

In *ébénisterie* (nearest equivalent to cabinet-making) all the finishing except staining and varnishing is done before final assembly. So in the latter stages your handiwork is in a very delicate state and it's a good idea to have plenty of bits of carpeting around to line the vice and lay on the bench-top to protect against knocks and grime.

All surfaces should be scraped down with a properly sharpened cabinet scraper and the *parements*, or visible surfaces, should be sanded with 100, 150 and 240-grit abrasives. Between sandings, raise the grain by wiping down with a sponge wetted (not soaked) in water as hot as you can bear it.

Final assembly

Bear in mind that the top goes on last. Gluing up is a tricky business, as the sanded components are very vulnerable to bruising and stain does not take well on glue smears, even if they have been carefully wiped. The dowel joints on the apron may not bear up under the strain of three-way pressure under clamps, but if you make sure the fit is not too tight you can push the joints home and hold them in place with a tourniquet. Protect all protruding parts with pieces of thin plywood or cardboard softening, remembering string or webbing bruise wood just as metal does. The lower shelf would withstand clamping but you can just as easily use a second tourniquet.

You shouldn't get much movement in a table-top constructed like this so, having ensured the tops of the legs and apron are plane and flush, glue down the top using some locating dowels. The radial joints on the lipping should be in vertical alignment with the joints in the apron.

Finishing

If you're using a stain — I recommend water-based — check the colour on a piece of scrap and then, working quickly, apply the stain liberally with a sponge from the bottom up. Before it has time to dry right out, wipe off excess stain with the squeezed-out sponge and make sure no stain subsequently leaches out of tight corners and makes a tear-drop.

If you intend to colour-match a light wood in the carcase with a dark veneer and/or have a contrasting stringing, the areas not to be stained must be masked before applying the stain. The surest method is to apply a coat of sealer to the isolated areas before staining. Go round the outline with a steady hand and a signwriter's brush, for sealer, like stain, creeps under masking tape. Make sure the protective coat has dried properly before staining and allow at least twelve hours' drying time for water-stains before varnishing.

French polishing — known as *vernis au tampon* — is regarded in France as being beyond the scope of amateurs or young professionals. A very good finish can be obtained with a *fond dur*, or sanding sealer, rubbed down and given three thorough waxings. When the final coat has been buffed up, step back and say — inevitably — 'Voila!' ∎

875

Third World tools

John Hemsley tracked down an unusual charity

If you ever feel frustrated because you can't afford the tools you want, spare a thought for Ali Muhumbi. Ali, who lives in Singida, Tanzania, made his first saw from scratch by filing teeth into a flat piece of steel he found. He set to with it to cut 20 logs into planks, and sold them to buy his pride and joy — a smoothing plane. Now, with a tiny tool-kit, he practises carpentry and joinery, producing simple but well-put-together pieces for his village's needs.

Tanzania has no iron deposits of its own, and imported tools cost a small fortune. Ali's plane cost around £200 and a simple spanner is about £10 in the nearest market town, once you've got there.

Ali was one of the craftsmen Glyn Roberts met when he visited Tanzania last summer. Glyn — a sociologist by profession, a practical bloke who has built part of his own house — was one of the founders of Tools for Self Reliance, a unique no-frills organisation that now collects and refurbishes 20,000 unwanted hand-tools a year and ships them out to craftsmen in Third World countries.

The organisation, brainchild of a group at Portsmouth Polytechnic, only started in 1980, but is rapidly arousing interest all over Britain, and is being copied in other European countries. In the UK there are 65-70 local groups collecting tools and passing them on to the headquarters in Netley Marsh, near Southampton.

The idea is simple. In many parts of the world local craftsmen struggle with worn-out or inadequate hand-tools — using nails in hand-drills because they can't afford bits, or sharing one handsaw among five people. Here in Britain, virtually every household has an unused tool somewhere rusting — not counting superseded and idle pieces in workshops and factories.

'We reckon there must be 65 million tools lying unused in Britain,' says Glyn.

The challenge came in collecting these unwanted tools and getting them out to where they were desperately needed. Tools for Self Reliance took up this challenge, and now sends small tool-kits of 25-30 tools to many parts of the world. So far it has sent about 70,000 tools abroad, and about 30,000 kilos of scrap tool steel, enough for local blacksmiths to produce 125,000 hoes (the universal digging tool in developing countries).

• *The mural outside the Tools for Self Reliance HQ shows some of the 1000 jobs village craftsmen can do with a basic kit of 25-50 hand-tools;* **right**, *these two well-used handsaws are all one village group of six carpenters has got!*

The organisation's appeal to public goodwill in Britain has two sensible and attractive themes; you can give practical aid with no risk of your donation ending up in somebody's personal Swiss bank account, and they help you find a use for tools and metal that are simply going to waste here.

Glyn's own interest in providing simple tools developed as he became increasingly critical of UNESCO aid programmes he observed at first hand abroad. Expensive, highly sophisticated machinery needs imported spare parts and imported oil; he realised that this kind of contribution makes people more dependent, not independent. All too often he found machinery was lying idle through lack of spare parts or ignorance of how to use it. Even when it was working, the equipment was often being used at only 25% of capacity.

A small kit of hand-tools, on the other hand, is extremely versatile, and contributes towards genuine independence at grass-roots level. With simple hand-tools village craftsmen can build carts, housing, furniture . . . and other tools.

'Villages are often surrounded by abundant raw materials — timber, skins, plant fibres, stone, scrap metal — but all are virtually useless until you can process them,' says Glyn. 'Tools are the keys that unlock the value in the materials.

'Handing out finished goods to people in need can actually be destructive, creating apathy and dependency,' claims Glyn. 'Of course, there are crises when food and blankets are the immediate priority.

'But for development of dependence you

have to hand the initiative back to communities. I see tools as akin to seedcorn. You know they aren't going to end up lining the pocket of the rich. In a real sense, tools have no value till you start to use them.'

As well as providing kits of hand-tools — primarily to groups of craftsmen working co-operatively, rather than individuals — the organisation wants to spread knowledge about repairing damaged tools and even making them from scratch.

Many villages have their own primitive forges, with simple goatskin push-pull bellows capable of heating iron to a high temperature for working. Blacksmiths with initiative make bill-hooks, scissors, knives, axe-heads, hammer-heads, adzes, tin-snips, spokeshaves and plane blades; Tools for Self Reliance encourage them by sending instructions.

The blacksmiths use scrap steel from broken-down vehicles, and some have their own methods of case-hardening — heating up a poor quality steel, and rubbing cow horn on it so some natural carbon seeps into the hot metal.

The desperate need for simple tools was brought home to Glyn when he visited a school in Tanzania where 30 students were being taught masonry without a single trowel between them. Each morning they walked five miles to a Catholic school, borrowed five trowels for the day's practice, and then took them back in the evening!

The tools collected by local groups are sorted, cleaned up, sharpened, assembled into kits, greased and wrapped in newspaper before being crated. The organisation buys some specific tools to make up kits — in particularly short supply are planes, chisels, drill-bits, saw-files, oil-stones, rules (metric preferred), braces and claw-hammers.

Obviously not all the tools collected are suitable for sending abroad. About one in five is, in Glyn's word, 'rubbish' because it is completely worn out or not worth the time it would take to renovate; such judgments vary according to the tool, for a vice is worth spending time on. Another one in five of the tools collected is in 'spanking good condition', ready to be sent abroad as it comes in.

That leaves three out of five needing de-rusting, securing handles, sharpening and oiling, before greasing and packing. This is done by a small army of volunteers. About 30 of the local groups refurbish the tools they collect, but the main centre is in a group of buildings on what used to be a greyhound racetrack at the end of the M27 near Southampton, a stone's throw from the New Forest. Some local volunteers help two days a week, while others from further

● **Above**, *packing refurbished tools for the journey from the Netley Marsh workshops;* **below left**, *saws and an old pedal fretsaw await the treatment before despatch*

afield stay a week or two, sleeping on the floor and sharing simple meals. A recent International Voluntary Service workcamp of 12 people refurbished about 1500 tools in their two-week visit.

Many of the volunteers are good-willed rather than highly-skilled, concedes Glyn, but he points out that it needs little skill to scrape paint off old screwdrivers that have been used as stirrers for 20 years, or paint addresses on crates. They now have saw-sharpening machinery, donated by the local Rotary Club, with a guillotine that punches out a new set of teeth in 45 seconds.

If you've got unused tools, why not find them a good home with a fellow craftsman through Tools for Self Reliance? Bring them along when you visit the **London Woodworker Show** (Alexandra Pavilion, London N22, 23-26 October), where we'll have a reception point and a display of refurbishing by Tools for Self Reliance volunteers. If you can manage it, please clean them up first!

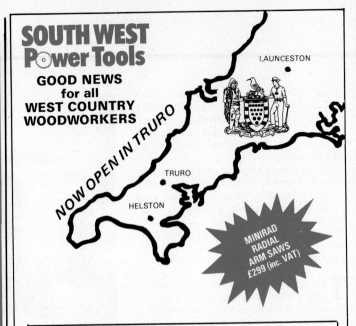

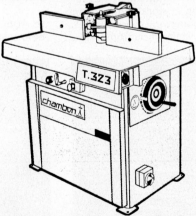

878

Third World tools

Really skilled people are needed for some sharpening jobs, and any woodworker who can spare an hour or two occasionally can get a list of local groups from Tools for Self Reliance headquarters.

In the substantial warehouse behind the refurbishing workshops at Netley Marsh are racks and bins of tools — around 2000 handsaws, an equal number of hammers, and perhaps a total of 30,000 individual tools stacked there at any one time.

If you live in the area you're welcome to visit the workshops, which are intended to play an educational function as well as being practical — helping people understand the value of tools. In a 'museum' gallery there is a display of tools and household items made and used in East Africa, and a fascinating selection of antique and curious tools which are unsuitable for sending abroad; no one knows what some of them even are, so the organisation would be grateful if visitors can throw light on them!

The organisation does get given antique tools, embarassing if the donators don't know they are of collector's interest. Tools for Self Reliance is definitely not in the business of selling tools (hovering dealers are no longer a problem since this stance was made clear), but it is hoping to hold an auction occasionally.

'All the tools we collect are sent abroad

unless they are unusable or unsuitable,' stresses Glyn.

What sort of person gives their tools to Tools for Self Reliance? One donator was retired joiner and fitter Robert Besselt of Lee-on-Solent. He wouldn't give away his best set of tools, because he still uses them for making fine furniture. Nor would he let them have his 'seconds', as he might need those from time to time.

Somewhat apologetically he offered his 'thirds', a box of 30 tools in perfect condition, steel honed razor-sharp, wood handles glowing from years of careful use, and among them a plane he had made as an apprentice in 1920! ∎

● For more information, write with SAE to Tools for Self Reliance, Netley Marsh Workshops, Netley Marsh, Southampton SO4 2GY, (0703) 869697.

TFSR's standard kit of carpentry tools for a village craft workshop of 4-6 workers

4 crosscut saws	4 clamps
4 tenon saws	7 rasps and files (wood and metal)
2 ripsaws	2 oilstones
1 keyhole saw (or similar)	1 slipstone
1 hacksaw + 4 blades	2 carpenter's braces
1 bow-saw (optional)	1 hand-drill
3 saw-files	10 bits for brace (1in to ¼in)
2 jack planes	2 long auger bits (optional)
2 smoothing planes	1 set of drill-bits
1 block plane	3 pincers
1 drawknife or spokeshave	2 pliers
2 knives	2 awls/gimlets
2 claw-hammers	5 screwdrivers
4 hammers, various	1 pair dividers
1 mallet (optional)	1 pair calipers
1 rebate plane (optional)	1 rule (folding or metal tape)
12 chisels and gouges	2 axes
(1in to ¼in, inc. mortising)	1 square
1 woodworker's vice	

Extra tools as available such as sliding bevel

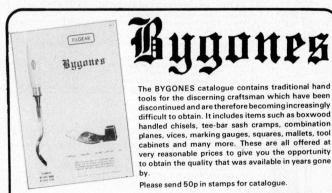

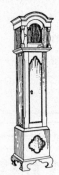

Tales out of steel

Immortal millwrights and engineers . . . Ashley Iles opens doors down Sheffield's memory lane

This month I pay tribute to the engineers; those shadowy overalled figures lurking in the background twiddling micrometers, very few of whom ever enjoyed 'The hour of crowded glory worth an age without a name'.

During my apprenticeship at a large South Yorkshire steel works, I was in daily contact with the mechanical and electrical engineers who built and maintained the mills and furnaces. The maintenance shops started at the main gate and extended in a straight line through the electricians' shop, the machine and fitting shop, iron foundry, brass foundry, fettlers, patternshop, blacksmiths and boilershop. The drawing-office and that rare breed, the millwrights, were at the far end of the works a 10-minute walk away (class distinction).

The variety of work going through the maintenance shops was tremendous. The smaller rolling mills were driven by large electric motors, but the larger billet mills were driven by huge steam engines with 24in cylinders producing 1500hp, reversing as the steel went back and forwards through the rolls. I began to realise that Watt and Stevenson had really started something; one of the engines was controlled by the Stevenson Link Motion, in fact.

After a fire we had in the patternshop, new machinery arrived from Wadkins along with a motley crew — the immortal millwrights. There was a bow-legged little man with a sledge-hammer over one shoulder and crowbar over the other; a little fat chap with a bag full of rollers and wedges; and a tall thin labourer wheeling a barrow containing a chain hoist and a coil of rope. I never saw such a decrepit bunch of men in my life, but what an education to see them at work!

The shop was on the first floor and a girder jutted out of a door for lifting. The millwrights worked by placing steel rollers under the machines, then inching them forwards with a crowbar; by placing the rollers at angles the machine could be made to go in any direction. As a roller came out at the back it was returned to the front. The chain-hoist was attached to the girder and the machines went up one by one. This job was a piece of cake for the millwrights — they were the troubleshooters of the firm, like the Marines, and were held in suitably high esteem. When an impossible job came up, it was: 'Send for the Millwrights'.

The engineers of North Yorkshire were greatly underestimated. In the six woollen towns there were some remarkable engineering works serving the mills and collieries and most of the men I worked with had served their time in places like Halifax, Huddersfield, Bradford, Leeds and Wakefield.

The accent was on simplicity in the engineering of the Sheffield Tool Trade. Take the set-up for a typical Sheffield grinder, nothing more than an arrangement of rough-machined castings — only the axle and the steel plates either side of the grinding-wheel were machined. The axle-end seated itself in the 'V' of the bolster and ran trouble-free for years.

It was possible to walk into Farrers on Devonshire St and buy all the parts to build a wheel, along with all the advice you needed. A pair of bolsters cost 25/-. Sad to say they were even cheaper if you knew the right face in the right pub.

You didn't have to look far for an axle and plates. I once bought a set from a grinder outworking for Tyzack Sons and Turner, the saw people. He rented a shop at their works and did so much for them and so much for his other customers. £5 was too much for him — more than he could live with or work with, and he suggested we go and 'ave one. He took me to a Stones house and got on to 'Draggons Blood', a very strong beer brewed in Sheffield. I had two and a half; he had five. I spent the rest of the day in an alcoholic daze and later walked into a chemist's thinking it was a café.

One of the best machine shops was Pattinsons, the power hammer and forging machine people. You could get an old hammer casting and buy all the parts needed from Pattinson; Mr Sharpe, the proprietor, showed me round and I was very impressed with the size and quality of machines being made. I was even more taken with Mr Sharpe who had a command of the works seldom found in management today.

Walter and Dobson were a similar firm for machines for the cutlery trade. They made some ingenious machines for grinding and buffing; one, a 'double header', worked like the clutch plates on a car. Knife blades were fixed radially from the centre on one plate and when the two plates came together dozens of blades were buffed at once.

Little did anyone realised then how quickly the engineers — nurtured by the war experience — would produce machines to eliminate skilled men. I was in a firm some years ago and saw a large custom-built hydraulic press for straightening chisels hundreds at a time before they went for machine grinding. It cost £50,000 — just to eliminate a man on an anvil. ∎

shopguide

AVON

BATH   Tel. Bath 64513
JOHN HALL TOOLS   ★
RAILWAY STREET

Open: Monday-Saturday
9.00 a.m.-5.30 p.m.
H.P.W.WM.D.A.BC.

CUMBRIA

CARLISLE   Tel. (0228) 36391
W. M. PLANT
ALLENBROOK ROAD
ROSEHILL, CA1 2UT
Open: Mon.-Fri. 8.00 a.m.-5.15 p.m.
Sat. 8.00 a.m.-12.30 noon
P.W.WM.D.CS.A.

HERTFORDSHIRE

WARE   K★
HEATH SAWS
16 MALTINGS
STANSTEAD ABBOTTS (near Ware) HERTS.
Open: Mon.-Fri. 8.30am-5.30pm
Sat. 8.30am-1pm. Sunday by appointment.
P.W.WM.D.CS.A.

BRISTOL   Tel. (0272) 741510
JOHN HALL TOOLS LIMITED   ★
CLIFTON DOWN SHOPPING CENTRE
WHITELADIES ROAD
Open: Monday-Saturday
9.00 a.m.-5.30 p.m.
H.P.W.WM.D.A.BC.

HIGH WYCOMBE   Tel. (0494)
SCOTT SAWS LTD.   24201/33788
14 BRIDGE STREET   ★

Mon.-Sat. 8.30 a.m.-6.00 p.m.

H.P.W.WM.D.T.CS.MF.A.BC.

DEVON

BRIXHAM   Tel. (08045) 4900
WOODCRAFT SUPPLIES   E★
4 HORSE POOL STREET

Open: Mon.-Sat. 9.00 a.m.-6.00 p.m.

H.P.W.A.D.MF.CS.BC.

HUMBERSIDE

GRIMSBY   Tel. Grimsby (0472)
58741 Hull (0482) 26999
J. E. SIDDLE LTD. (Tool Specialists)   ★
83 VICTORIA STREET
Open: Mon-Fri 8.30 a.m.-5.30 p.m.
Sat. 8.30 a.m.-12.45 p.m. & 2 p.m.-5 p.m.
H.P.A.BC.W.WMD.

BRISTOL   Tel. (0272) 629092
TRYMWOOD SERVICES
2a DOWNS PARK EAST, (off North View)
WESTBURY PARK
Open: 8.30 a.m.-5.30 p.m. Mon. to Fri.
Closed for lunch 1.00-2.00 p.m.
P.W.WM.D.T.A.BC.

HIGH WYCOMBE   Tel. (0494)
ISAAC LORD LTD.   22221
185 DESBOROUGH ROAD   KE

Open: Mon-Fri 8.00 a.m.-5.00 p.m.
Saturday 9.00 a.m.-5.00 p.m.
H.P.W.D.A.

CAMBRIDGESHIRE

CAMBRIDGE   Tel. (0223) 63132
D. MACKAY LTD.   ★
BRITANNIA WORKS, EAST ROAD

Open: Mon.-Fri. 8.30 a.m.-1 p.m./2.00-
5.00 p.m. Sat. 8.30 a.m.-1.00 p.m.
H.P.W.D.T.CS.MF.A.BC.

PLYMOUTH   Tel. (0752) 330303
WESTWARD BUILDING SERVICES   ★
LTD., LISTER CLOSE, NEWNHAM
INDUSTRIAL ESTATE, PLYMPTON
Open: Mon-Fri 8.00 a.m.-5.30 p.m.
Sat. 8.30 a.m.-12.30 p.m.
H.P.W.WM.D.A.BC.

HULL
HUMBERSIDE FACTORING/H.F.C.
SAW SERVICING LTD.
MAIN STREET
Open: Mon.-Fri. 8am-5pm.
Saturday 8am-12.00pm.
H.P.W.WM.D.CS.A.BC.K.

BRISTOL   Tel. (0272) 667013
FASTSET LTD
190-192 WEST STREET
BEDMINSTER
Open: Mon.-Fri. 8.30 a.m.-5.00 p.m.
Saturday 9.00 a.m.-1.00 p.m.
H.P.W.WM.D.CS.A.BC.

CAMBRIDGE   Tel. (0223) 247386
H. B. WOODWORKING   K
105 CHERRY HINTON ROAD
Open: 8.30 a.m.-5.30 p.m.
Monday-Friday
8.30 a.m.-1.00 p.m. Sat.
H.P.W.WM.D.CS.A.

PLYMOUTH   Tel. (0752) 665363
F.T.B. LAWSON LTD.
71 NEW GEORGE STREET
PLYMOUTH PL1 1RB
Open: Mon.-Sat. 8.30 a.m.-5.30 pm.
H.P.W.CS.MF.A.

KENT

WYE   Tel. (0233) 813144
KENT POWER TOOLS LTD.
UNIT 1, BRIAR CLOSE
WYE, Nr. ASFORD

H.P.W.WM.D.A.CS.

BRISTOL   Tel. (0272) 667013
WILLIS
157 WEST STREET
BEDMINSTER
Open: Mon.-Fri. 8.30 a.m.-5.00 p.m.
Sat. 9 a.m.-4 p.m.
P.W.WM.D.CS.A.BC.

BEDFORDSHIRE

BEDFORD   Tel. (0234) 59808
BEDFORD SAW SERVICE   K
39 AMPTHILL ROAD

Open: Mon.-Fri. 8.30-5.30
Sat. 9.00-4.00
H.P.A.BC.W.CS.WM.D.

PETERBOROUGH   Tel. (0733)
WILLIAMS DISTRIBUTORS   64252
(TOOLS) LIMITED   K
108-110 BURGHLEY ROAD
Open: Monday to Friday
8.30 a.m.-5.30 p.m.
H.P.A.W.D.WH.BC.

ESSEX

LEIGH ON SEA   Tel. (0702)
MARSHAL & PARSONS LTD.   710404
1111 LONDON ROAD   EK

Open: 8.30 a.m.-5.30 p.m. Mon-Fri
9.00 a.m.-5.00 p.m. Sat.
H.P.W.WM.D.CS.A.

MAIDSTONE   Tel. (0622) 50177
SOUTH EASTERN SAWS (Ind.) LTD.   ★
COLDRED ROAD
PARKWOOD INDUSTRIAL ESTATE
Open: Mon.-Fri. 8.00 a.m.-6.00 p.m.
Sat. 9.00 a.m.-12.00 a.m.
B.C.W.CS.WM.PH.

BERKSHIRE

READING   Tel. Littlewick Green
DAVID HUNT (TOOL   2743
MERCHANTS) LTD   ★
KNOWL HILL, NR. READING
Open: Monday-Saturday
9.00 a.m.-5.30 p.m.
H.P.W.D.A.BC.

CHESHIRE

NANTWICH   Tel. Crewe 67010
ALAN HOLTHAM   K★
THE OLD STORES TURNERY
WISTASON ROAD, WILLASTON
Open: Tues.-Sat. 9.00 a.m.-5.30 p.m.
Closed Monday
P.W.WM.D.T.C.CS.A.BC.

GLOUCESTER

TEWKESBURY   Tel. (0684)
TEWKESBURY SAW CO. LTD.   293092
TRADING ESTATE, NEWTOWN   K

Open: Mon-Fri 8.00 a.m.-5.00 p.m.
Saturday 9.30 a.m.-12.00 p.m.
P.W.WM.D.CS.

LANCASHIRE

PRESTON   Tel. (0772) 52951
SPEEDWELL TOOL COMPANY   E★
62-68 MEADOW STREET PR1 1SU
Open: Mon.-Fri. 8.30 a.m.-5.30 p.m.
Sat. 8.30 a.m.-12.30 p.m.

H.P.W.WM.CS.A.MF.BC.

READING   Tel. Reading 661511
WOKINGHAM TOOL CO. LTD.
99 WOKINGHAM ROAD

Open: Mon-Sat 9.00 a.m.-5.30 p.m.
Closed 1.00-2.00 p.m. for lunch
H.P.W.WM.D.CS.A.BC.

CLEVELAND

MIDDLESBROUGH   Tel. (0642)
CLEVELAND WOODCRAFT   813103
(M'BRO), 38-42 CRESCENT ROAD   K

Open: Mon-Sat 9.15 a.m.-5.30 p.m.

H.P.T.A.BC.W.WM.CS.D.

HAMPSHIRE

ALDERSHOT   Tel. (0252) 334422
POWER TOOL CENTRE   K
374 HIGH STREET

Open Mon.-Fri. 8.30 a.m.-5.30 p.m.
Sat. 8.30 a.m.-12.30 p.m.
H.P.W.WM.D.A.BC.

MANCHESTER   Tel. (061 789)
TIMMS TOOLS   0909
102-104 LIVERPOOL ROAD   ★
PATRICROFT M30 0WZ
Weekdays 9.00 a.m.-5.30 p.m.
Sat. 9.00 a.m.-1.00 p.m.
H.P.A.W.

BUCKINGHAMSHIRE

MILTON KEYNES   Tel. (0908)
POLLARD WOODWORKING   641366
CENTRE
51 AYLESBURY ST., BLETCHLEY   ★
Open: Mon-Fri 8.30-5.30
Saturday 9.00-5.00
H.P.W.WM.D.CS.A.BC.

CORNWALL

**SOUTH WEST
Power Tools**
CORNWALL   Tel: Helston (03265) 4961
HELSTON AND LAUNCESTON   Launceston
(0566) 4781
H.P.W.WM.D.CS.A.   K

SOUTHAMPTON   Tel: (0703)
POWER TOOL CENTRE   332288
7 BELVIDERE ROAD   K★
Open Mon.-Fri. 8.30-5.30

H.P.W.WM.D.A.BC.CS.MF.

ROCHDALE   Tel. (0706) 342123/
C.S.M. TOOLS   342322
4-6 HEYWOOD ROAD   E★
CASTLETON
Open: Mon-Sat 9.00 a.m.-6.00 p.m.
Sundays by appointment
W.D.CS.A.BC.

shop guide

LANCASHIRE

LANCASTER Tel: (0524) 32886
LILE TOOL SHOP — K
43/45 NORTH ROAD
Open: Monday to Saturday
9.00 a.m.-5.30 p.m.
Wed. 9.00 a.m.-12.30 p.m.
H.P.W.D.A.

LANCASHIRE Tel: (070 681) 4931
'TODMORDEN' ★
TOWNLEY TIMES, HAREHILL STREET
OFF BURNLEY ROAD
Open: Mon.-Fri. 8.30 am-5.30 pm
Sat. 9.00 am-1.00 pm.
H.P.W.D.A.BC.

BLACKPOOL Tel: (0253) 24299
FLYDE WOODTURNING SUPPLIES ★
222 HORNBY ROAD (BASEMENT)
BLACKPOOL FY1 4HY
9.30-5.30 Monday to Saturday
H.P.W.WM.A.MF.C.B.C.D.

ALL THOSE SHOPS WITH ASTERIX HAVE MAIL ORDER SERVICE ★

LINCOLNSHIRE

LINCOLN Tel: (0522) 689369
SKELLINGTHORPE SAW SERVICES LTD.
OLD WOOD, SKELLINGTHORPE
Open: Mon to Fri 8 a.m.-5 p.m.
Sat 8 a.m.-12 p.m.
H.P.W.WM.D.CS.A.*.BC.
Access/Barclaycard

LONDON

ACTON Tel: (01-992) 4835
A. MILLS (ACTON) LTD ★
32/36 CHURCHFIELD ROAD W3 6ED
Open: Mon-Fri 9.00 a.m.-5.00 p.m.
Saturdays 9.00 am-1.00 p.m.
H.P.W.WM.

LONDON Tel. 01-723 2295-6-7
LANGHAM TOOLS LIMITED
13 NORFOLK PLACE
LONDON W2 1QJ

LONDON Tel. (01-636) 7475
BUCK & RYAN LTD
101 TOTTENHAM COURT ROAD W1P 0DY
Open: Mon.-Fri. 8.30 a.m.-5.30 p.m.
Saturday 8.30 a.m.-4.00 p.m.
H.P.W.WM.D.A..

WEMBLEY Tel. 904-1144
ROBERT SAMUEL LTD. (904-1147
7, 15 & 16 COURT PARADE after 4.00)
EAST LANE, N. WEMBLEY ★
Open Mon.-Fri. 8.45-5.15; Sat. 9-1.00
Access, Barclaycard, AM Express, & Diners
H.P.W.CS.E.A.D.

LONDON

HOUNSLOW Tel. (01-570)
Q.R. TOOLS LTD 2103/5135
251-253 HANWORTH ROAD
Open: Mon-Fri 8.30 a.m.-5.30 p.m.
Sat. 9.00 a.m.-1.00 p.m.
P.W.WM.D.CS.A.

FULHAM Tel. (01-385) 5109
I. GRIZZARD LTD. E
84a-b LILLIE ROAD, SW6 1TL
Open: Mon-Sat 9.00-5.30 p.m.
Half day Thursday
H.P.A.BC.W.CS.WM.D.

MERSEYSIDE

LIVERPOOL Tel. (051-207) 2967
TAYLOR BROS (LIVERPOOL) LTD K
195-199 LONDON ROAD
LIVERPOOL L3 8JG
Open: Monday to Friday
8.30 a.m.-5.30 p.m.
H.P.W.WM.D.A.BC.

MIDDLESEX

RUISLIP Tel. (08956) 74126
ALLMODELS ENGINEERING LTD. E★
91 MANOR WAY
Open: Mon-Sat 9.00 a.m.-5.30 p.m.
H.P.W.A.D.CS.MF.BC.

ENFIELD Tel: 01-363 2935
GILL & HOXBY LTD.
131-137 ST. MARKS ROAD ADJ.
BUSH HILL PARK STATION, EN1 1BA
Mon.-Sat. 8-5.30
Early closing Wed. 1 p.m.
H.P.A.M.MC.T.S.W.

NORFOLK

NORWICH Tel. (0603) 898695
NORFOLK SAW SERVICES
DOG LANE, HORSFORD
Open: Monday to Friday
8.00 a.m.-5.00 p.m.
Saturday 8.00 a.m.-12.00 p.m.
H.P.W.WM.D.CS.A.

KINGS LYNN Tel. (0553) 2443
WALKER & ANDERSON (Kings Lynn) LTD.
WINDSOR ROAD, KINGS LYNN K
Open: Monday to Saturday
7.45 a.m.-5.30 p.m.
Wednesday 1.00 p.m. Saturday 5.00 p.m.
H.P.W.WM.D.CS.A.

NORWICH Tel. (0603) 400933
WESTGATES WOODWORKING Tx
61 HURRICANE WAY, 975412
NORWICH AIRPORT INDUSTRIAL ESTATE
Open: Mon.-Fri. 9.00 a.m.-5.00 p.m. weekdays
9.00 a.m.-12.30 Sat.
P.W.WM.D.BC. K

KING'S LYNN ★
TONY WADDILOVE WOODCRAFT
HILL FARM WORKSHOPS
GT. DUNHAM
(NR. SWAFFHAM)
Tues.-Sat. 9.00am-5.30pm.
H.P.W.D.T.MF.A.BC.

NOTTINGHAMSHIRE

NOTTINGHAM Tel: (0602) 225979
POOLEWOOD and 227064/5
EQUIPMENT LTD. (06077) 2421 after hrs
5a HOLLY LANE, CHILLWELL
Open: Mon-Fri 9.00 a.m.-5.30 p.m.
Sat. 9.00 a.m. to 12.30 p.m.
P.W.WM.D.CS.A.BC.

OXON

WITNEY Tel. (0993) 3885
TARGET TOOLS (SALES, & 72095 OXON
TARGET TOOLS HIRE & REPAIRS) ★
SWAIN COURT
STATION INDUSTRIAL ESTATE
Open: Mon.-Sat. 8.00 a.m.-5.00 p.m.
24 hour Answerphone
BC.W.M.A.

SHROPSHIRE

TELFORD Tel. Telford (0952)
ASLES LTD 48054
VINEYARD ROAD, WELLINGTON EK★
Open: Mon. Fri. 8.30 a.m.-5.30 p.m.
Saturday 8.30 a.m.-4.00 p.m.
H.P.W.WM.D.CS.BC.A.

SOMERSET

TAUNTON Tel. (0823) 85431
JOHN HALL TOOLS ★
6 HIGH STREET
Open Monday-Saturday
9.00 a.m.-5.30 p.m.
H.P.W.WM.D.CS.A.

TAUNTON Tel. 0823 443766
CUTWELL TOOLS LTD. ★
CREECH HEATHFIELD
SOMERSET TA3 5EQ
Mon-Fri 9 a.m.-5 p.m. and also by appointment.
P.W.WM.A.D.CS.

STAFFORDSHIRE

TO FILL THIS SPACE. PHONE 01-437 0626

TAMWORTH Tel: (0827) 56188
MATTHEWS BROTHERS LTD. K
KETTLEBROOK ROAD
Open: Mon-Sat 8.30 a.m.-6.00 p.m.
Demonstrations Sunday mornings by
appointment only
H.P.WM.D.T.CS.A.BC.

SUFFOLK

SUFFOLK
LOCKWOOD WOODWORKING MACHINERY
WHITE GATES BUNGALOW
THE COMMON MELLIS
NEAR EYE/DISS IP23 8DY Tel: (037983) 8126
Open: Mon., Wed., Thurs., Fri. 8am-8pm
Tues. & Sat. 8am-5pm.
*Lathe demos every Saturday morning.
We cover both Norfolk and Suffolk*
H.P.W.D.A.

IPSWICH Tel. (0473) 40456
FOX WOODWORKING KE★
142-144 BRAMFORD LANE
Open: Tues., Fri., 9.00 a.m.-5.30 p.m.
Sat. 9.00 a.m.-5.00 p.m.
H.P.W.WM.D.A.B.C.

SUSSEX

BOGNOR REGIS Tel. (0243) 863100
A. OLBY & SON (BOGNOR REGIS) LTD.
"TOOLSHOP," BUILDERS MERCHANT
HAWTHORN ROAD K
Open: Mon-Thurs 8 a.m.-5.15 p.m. Fri.
8 a.m.-8 p.m. Sat 8 a.m.-12.45 p.m.
H.P.W.WM.D.T.C.A.BC.

WORTHING Tel. (0903) 38739
W. HOSKING LTD (TOOLS & KE★
MACHINERY)
28 PORTLAND RD, BN11 1QN
Open:-Mon.-Sat. 8.30 a.m.-5.30 p.m.
Closed Wednesday
H.P.W.WM.D.CS.A.BC.

TYNE & WEAR

NEWCASTLE Tel. (0632) 320311
HENRY OSBOURNE LTD. E★
50-54 UNION STREET
Open: Mon-Fri 8.30 a.m.-5.00 p.m.
H.P.W.D.CS.MF.A.BC.

W. MIDLANDS

WOLVERHAMPTON Tel. (0902)
MANSAW SERVICES 58759
SEDGLEY STREET K ★
Open: Mon.-Fri. 9.00 a.m.-5.00 p.m.
H.P.W.WM.A.D.CS.

YORKSHIRE

BOROUGHBRIDGE Tel. (09012)
JOHN BODDY TIMBER LTD 2370
FINE WOOD & TOOL STORE ★
RIVERSIDE SAWMILLS
Open: Mon.-Thurs. 8.00 a.m.-6.00 p.m.
Fri. 8.00am-5.00pm Sat. 8.00am-4.00pm
H.P.W.WM.D.T.CS.MF.A.BC.

SHEFFIELD Tel. (0742) 441012
GREGORY & TAYLOR LTD KE
WORKSOP ROAD
Open: 8.30 a.m.-5.30 p.m.
Monday-Friday
8.30 a.m.-12.30 p.m. Sat.
H.P.W.WM.D.

HARROGATE Tel. (0423) 66245/
MULTI-TOOLS 55328
158 KINGS ROAD K★
Open: Monday to Saturday
8.30 a.m.-6.00 p.m.
H.P.W.WM.D.A.BC.

THIRSK Tel. (0845) 22770
THE WOOD SHOP
TRESKE SAWMILLS LTD.
STATION WORKS
Open: Seven days a week 9.00-5.00
T.H.MF.BC.

LEEDS Tel. (0532) 574736
D. B. KEIGHLEY MACHINERY LTD.
VICKERS PLACE, STANNINGLEY
PUDSEY LS2 86LZ
Mon.-Fri. 9.00 a.m.-5.00 p.m.
Sat. 9.00 a.m.-1.00 p.m.
P.A.W.WM.CS.BC.

shop guide

WOOD SUPPLIERS

WOOD SUPPLIERS

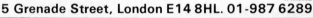

Classified Advertisements

FOR SALE

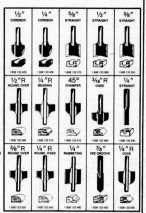

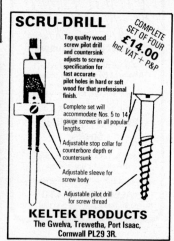

889

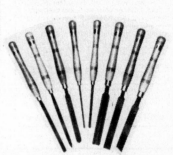

891

892

Letters

Weather strip

FURTHER TO THE JUNE 'Question box' on weatherproofing windows, I recently fitted a proprietary weather/draught strip (Magnet Southerns) in a window I made. I didn't have thick enough timber to make the frame with closing rebates, so I laminated the members, which made it easy to cut a small rebate in the 'upstand' pieces of the L-shaped frame members before I glued them to the larger, full-width pieces. The sash also needed a rebate in its outside corner to allow drainage separation between sash and frame.

The window performed excellently in last winter's cold winds.

John Crossthwaite, Plymouth

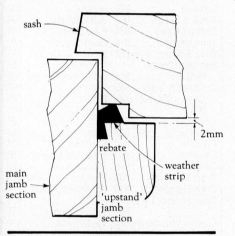

Spectacular safety

I'M SURE I'M NOT ALONE in finding plastic safety glasses distort vision and scratch easily, so may I recommend to other readers one manufacturer for exceptional efficiency and a first-class product despatched by return of post? Occupational Kite Safety Ltd, Unit 1, Hilton Main Ind. Est., Cannock Road, Featherstone, nr Wolverhampton, Staffs WV10 7HP. Plain toughened glass spectacles cost £7.13 inc. p&p, a bargain since I had been quoted £30 by an optician; the firm will also supply prescription lenses.

R.J. Leigh, S.E. London

Veneering faults?

HAVING RECENTLY BENEFITED enormously from a David Savage weekend veneering course, I've got a few comments to make on Mark Kenning's points in 'Letters', *Woodworker* July.

Of course David uses his veneer hammer back to front. Anyone who has examined the cover picture on Charles Hayward's *Practical Veneering* would spot that at once. But to say so forthrightly that he's wrong reminds me of the character in pre-war adverts by Desoutter, the power toolmakers. Opposing change in any form, the little man in the ad was wont to exclaim, 'Pah Tools! Make work easy?! Work wasn't meant to be easy! Work was meant to be 'orrible otherwise we shouldn't never want to leave orf.'

David's method has at least one vital factor going for it — it works! And it gives the beginner an almost instant precision control over the hammer which otherwise could take hours to acquire.

I went on the course to learn something of laying veneer, not to practise traditional methods of using particular tools. I brought away with me a board veneered on both sides with wild-grained mahogany, joined invisibly (well, almost!) by the method David advocates, and with one side strung and cross-banded.

I also acquired knowledge of related woodworking problems, learnt how to cope with the difficulties that arise in laying decorative veneers, and gained the confidence to start tackling my next job — veneering a grandfather clock case I've built from scratch.

Pretty good value from a two-day course, I would say. Thank you David and keep up the good work.

F.G.T. Brown, Andover

Workshop to share

IS ANYONE OUT THERE interested in sharing my riverside workshop in the Lake District? I moved into this building — my fourth workshop since I started 12 years ago — a few months ago and am currently fitting out and equipping it.

My area of woodwork is furniture and fittings, with interior design as well, and now I've got a decent-sized workshop I hope to develop ideas and seek out new markets to extend myself.

Working long days alone, however, isn't the cheeriest of prospects, and having some like-minded workmates would be very welcome. I can offer to shoulder all the workshop costs until my new workmates have found their feet.

The younger generation of woodworkers may not regard the Lake District as Milan, but it is an area with unequalled surroundings in this country. I believe there is much to be said for the line that if the product is right, the world will beat a path to your door.

If I can help anyone make a start, and in the process gain for myself some like-minded, interesting, enthusiastic workmates and friends, I shall be highly delighted.

Peter Goldthorp, Fenton Holme, Fenton, Keswick, Cumbria CA12 4AZ

Tricky drilling

HERE'S A TIP for people facing a particular drilling problem. A coffee table I am making has an undershelf of ½in dowelling fixed into rails only ½in thick. I found an ordinary drill-bit went through the rail before it had cut the hole.

My son suggested I used my chisel-mortiser, with the drill lowered about an inch below the chisel. I tried it out, using it as a vertical drill, and it worked perfectly. I lightly pre-drilled with an ordinary ½in drill to give a mark. The flat-bottomed mortising bit enabled me to cut good ¼in deep holes without break-out.

G. F. Elliott, W. London

Bleaching oak

I MUST COMMENT ON 'Question box' advice (WW/Aug). It's not possible to neutralise oxalic acid or any other acid with vinegar, which contains acetic acid. Perhaps the strong oxalic acid is washed away with the vinegar, but neutralised — never!

Geoffrey Smart, Kingswinford

● To neutralise oxalic acid, use one part ammonia in 10 parts water. Add ammonia to water, not the other way round!

Chisels and steels

'TOOLS OF THE TRADE 4' comparing chisels, and the manufacturers' responses (WW/Aug) was fascinating, and ties in with comments in Ashley Iles' articles.

Mr Davidson of Sorby says steel used today is better than in the past, and Mr Iles remarks that tool steel is as good as ever and sometimes better. But the point complainants are making is surely that it is not the steel that goes in, but the steel that comes *out* in the end product is not as good as it was. Mr Davidson doesn't explain why the old Ward chisel outperformed his own. Mr Iles seems to suggest that the modern stamping process, instead of forging, may affect the steel; I've heard that stamping plays old Harry with the molecular structure.

Mr Jewitt of Footprint appears to imply that their products must be made to a price, and Mr Davidson mentions 'an affordable price' which may mean the same thing. Mr Buse touches on the same point, saying that manufacturers today look for a mass market and accordingly make their tools to stand up to a lot of abuse.

As I understand it, small Sheffield toolmakers were put out of business in the 50s by the introduction of mass production, with lower prices than hand methods allow. If that is so, then the tools produced by the new machinery would be of consistent quality, but of lower quality than those produced by the old tool men. The market for these lower quality cheaper tools came from the growing DIY field, and tradesmen working on site, where good tools get stolen.

So manufacturers are supplying one or at most two qualities for a market which seems to need three or four — for tip-top craftsmen, keen amateurs, handymen and site-workers. Colleges might use the second grade and schools the third. This fits in with Mr Buse's comments (p. 661).

895

Letters

Perhaps the makers should look again at their market research. Maybe there should be British Standards for different grades. Certainly, for a nation that must make its living by exports, there's little point in carrying on with the status quo. Making fine points about this and that will not improve the products to the point where they are eagerly sought all over the world, as was once the case.

J. Holiday, Cardiff

I'D LIKE TO ANSWER some of the points Roger Buse makes about Japanese tools, in August's *Woodworker*. My original letter on Japanese chisels was prompted because I have some Marples registered-pattern firmer chisels, hoops on the handles and rugged construction — similar in these particular ways to Japanese chisels. Apart from honing, they haven't required any of the elaborate preparation a Japanese chisel needs; they're beautifully made; they haven't bent, snapped or even chipped. My response would have been the same if the article had been about Swedish chisels, rather than Japanese.

Mr Buse raises the subject of steel quality. This is dependent on steel composition and heat treatment. The steel-making process may now more closely control the proportion of constituents in a steel than was possible say, 30 years ago. Heat treatment may also be more accurately controlled. Consequently steels of a required hardness and ductility may be consistently produced. Steels of today are not inferior to those of years ago.

I have been very interested in this series of articles. Perhaps through such discussion Mr Buse's 60% figure for stock from foreign sources may be reduced!

Dr R.W. Page, Guildford

● An important point in this connection made by Nick Davidson of Sorby (Tools of the Trade 4; WW/Aug) is that the old tools that have survived were the highest quality originally. The many poor quality tools that were produced in the less-consistent manufacturing process have long ago been dumped.

The reviewer reviewed

I WOULD APPRECIATE the opportunity to respond to Michael O'Donnell's review of my book *The Practice of Woodturning* (WW/Aug).

'He uses the skew almost continuously': I have a wide range of all types of turning tools and use each when it's appropriate. Sadly neither I nor any other turner is able to produce a finish straight from the skew which doesn't require sanding.

'Many of the sections don't fulfill a function or come to any definite conclusion': The function of each section is to impart knowledge. Later sections assume that the reader has absorbed earlier sections and built on that. It's not possible to impart a large body of knowledge instantaneously — a major text book is not a collection of short stories.

'Terminology is also a problem, more because of the tems he doesn't use than those he does': The book uses the standard woodturning jargon wherever possible, and there is a section on terminology at the front.

There is a movement, led from America, to raise the status of turning; to break out from the corral of furniture, architectural components and utilitarian domestic ware into the lusher pastures of the fine arts. Your reviewer and I both support this movement, but the famous names in contemporary turning are not the norm. allow me to quote from my 'design guidelines': 'I and others have found these guidelines valuable in the production of designs and in analysing designs which do not look quite right. However, the guidelines are not rigid rules which must be followed blindly, and indeed many successful pieces do not conform'.

The criticisms of the turning theory sections further illustrate Mr. O'Donnell's attitudes to information which is unfamiliar to him. Had he bothered to consult the comprehensive index he would have learned that discussion of bevel support occurs on at least eleven pages.

In the 100 pages on bowl turning I fully describe how gouges work, how to use the bevel, and the problems associated with excessive bevel pressure. Those who are receptive will find their reading rewarding.

Mike Darlow, Sydney, Australia

● *The Practice of Woodturning* from Ruskin Book Services Ltd, 15 Comberton Hill, Kidderminster, Worcs DY10 1QG, (0562) 515151, £15.95 hardback.

Advertisers' Index

AEG	816	Limehouse	869
Apollo	874	Isaac Lord	810
Art Veneer Co	824	E. W. Lucas	848
ASE	817	Luna Tools	824, 879
Ashford Tools	859	Matthews	878
Axminster Power Tools	844, 845	A. Mills	826
A-Z Tool Sales	843	MRM Distributors	874
Benmail	880	Multistar	881
Black & Decker	IFC	John Myland	894
Bedford Saws	881	Myford	860
John Boddy	818	P & J Dust	804
Buck & Ryan	819, 868	Plans Service	880
Builders Direct Mail	818	W. M. Plant	869, 875
Canaan Carbides	865	A. Pollard	862
H. Case	804, 805, 806, 807	Old Stores Turnery	860
		Rogers	862
Charltons	879	Sanlin	826
Charnwood	806, 827	Sarjents	851
P. Child	807	Scott & Sargeant	837
Cleveland	806	Solent	858
Christchurch	878	Startrite	854
Craft Materials	862	Steerdawn	850
Craft Supplies	810	Stobart & Son	807
Craft Tools & Tackle	862	Sumaco	850, 873
		Southwest Power Tools	878
Cutwell Woodworking	859	Tabwell Tools	875
Data Power Tools	859	Taylor Bros	868
Dodd Machines	850	Henry Taylor	859
Elektra Beckum	IBC	Third World Tools	879
Excel	818	Thomas & Willis	804
Henry Flack	OBC	Tilgear	807, 824, 865, 879, 896
Gill & Hoxby	878	Tool Centre	819
Heath Saws	869	Tool Mail	869
Home & Video Workshop	807, 874	Treebridge	850
		Trend	896
David Hunt	875	C. Tyzack	804
Ashley Iles	848	Warren Machine Tools	819
Kent Power Tools	875	Wessex Timber	806
Kity	848	Whitehill Spindle	868
Ledbury Craft	869	Woodfit	804
		XR Machines	806

Woodworker

CONTENTS

November 1986
Vol. 90
No. 11

design . . . craft . . . and the love of wood

904 Show of shows
What's to see, who's to watch, and what's to win at woodworking's biggest event of the year. *Mary White*

912 Raffan's rules
One of the marks of a master is making the art seem simple. Try this extract from an important new woodturning book. *Richard Raffan*

916 Bent on steam
Country craft furniture with modern style and engineering overtones — in the depths of Wales! *John Hemsley*

923 EXCLUSIVE OFFER
Raring to go with the dowels you got free on this month's cover? This dowelling jig is a hard-to-beat bargain

PROJECTS

All with detailed working drawings

908 Out of sight . . .
An unusual TV/video cabinet that gives you a chance to use your free dowels — and then some. *Alan Fell*

926 Taking the biscuit
A 'cottage-style' corner cabinet which makes extensive use of a very uncottagey power tool. *Eric Colwell*

962 Take a chair
Loads of choice and a lot of flair in a selection of chair designs. *Tim Ashby*

966 Country colossus
An elegant sideboard/cabinet, made to show just what you can do with a small universal machine. *Guy Rendel*

On the cover: David Colwell eyes one of his creations: see his classical country style **left** and more on p916. **Plus:** free dowels for your delectation!

Editor Aidan Walker
Deputy editor John Hemsley
Editorial assistant Kerry Fowler
Senior advertisement manager Paul Holmes
Advertisement manager Trevor Pryer
Graphics Ian Bottle
Technical illustrator Peter Holland
Guild of Woodworkers John Hemsley, Kerry Fowler
Editorial, advertisements and Guild of Woodworkers
1 Golden Square, London W1R 3AB, telephone 01-437 0626

Unfortunately we cannot accept responsibility for loss of or damage to unsolicited material. We reserve the right to refuse or suspend advertisements, and regret we cannot guarantee the bone fides of advertisers.
Published every third Friday

ABC
UK circulation
Jan-Dec 85
28,051

Back issues and subscriptions Infonet Ltd, 10-13 Times House, 179 Marlowes, Hemel Hempstead, Herts HP1 1BB; telephone Hemel Hempstead (0442) 48434

Subscriptions per year UK £16.90; overseas outside USA (accelerated surface post) £21.00, USA (accelerated surface post) $28, airmail £48

UK trade SM Distribution Ltd, 16-18 Trinity Gardens, London SW9 8DX; telephone 01-274 8611

North American trade Bill Dean Books Ltd, 151-49 7th Avenue, PO Box 69, Whitestone, New York 11357; tel. 1-718-767-6632

Printed in Great Britain by Ambassador Press Ltd, St. Albans, Herts
Mono origination Multiform Photosetting Ltd, Cardiff
Colour origination Derek Croxson Ltd, Chesham, Bucks
© Argus Specialist Publications Ltd 1986
ISSN 0043 776X

Argus Specialist Publications Ltd
1 Golden Square, London
W1R 3AB; 01-437 0626

942 Propcraft
The craft of the white shaper, or airscrew maker, explained by an expert in aviation woodwork. *Jim Kingshott*

949 Scarfing it
The scarf — not just a joint to lengthen timber; there's tricks in this too. *Malcolm Wintle*

956 The grand furniture saga: 10
The age of the Sun King in France brought outrageous ornament, and the work of Louis Boulle. *Vic Taylor*

972 Soled on wood
Wooden planes, old and new; we look at what's available now and how it compares with traditional designs. *Rik Middleton*

REGULARS

898 This month Takes a view

899 Shoptalk How to spend your money

901 Timberline Trade news

921 Books Carving, cramping, the Shakers

935 Question box Keruing, rebate/rabbet, colour matching

945 Bob Wearing's Workshop Router gauges

953 Woodworking wheeze of the month Rout-a-slide

976 Guild notes Not just for members!

991 Letters Talkback

992 Advertisers' index

This month

Fair shares?

Are woodworkers getting a fair share of **setting up grants** from the Crafts Council? The Council's annual report for 1985/86 shows that three people in this field received them in the period: Tom Kealy (furniture), Ralph Ball (furniture/lights), and Alan Ward (musical instruments). That's three out of a total of 41 such grants given by the Crafts Council during those 12 months. By far the largest number of grants went to people in ceramics (17), followed by textiles (eight), and glass (four).

Does this mean the Crafts Council has a bias away from woodworkers, or simply that craftspeople in this field aren't applying for grants? Latest news is that Guy Martin (*WW/Oct*) and Robin Williams, both furniture makers, have got setting up grants in July 86.

Minster Oak Donors of the oak used in the York Minster restoration (*WW/June*) were invited to inspect the work by suppliers Henry Venables

Fiord fashion

So what do you know about **Norwegian design**? Peter Vickers of Trent Polytechnic, who has been studying design in several European countries on a travel scholarship from the Worshipful Company of Furniture Makers, says three principal aspects are very apparent in Norway.

'These are the relationship between architecture, interior design and furniture; the development of national craft skills into production pieces; and the rapport between users and designers, their lifestyles and complementary products.'

These key elements of Norwegian design will be highlighted by two speakers at a 'Style for Living' seminar being held on 21 October at Style 87, the furniture show in London.

Fancy a 'Tree chair' that 'bridges the gap between adventure playground and bar stool'? See it at Style 87.

Do the dowel

Your wonderful freebie this month is 10 fluted beech **dowels**, a useful addition to your stock when you get into your next project that needs them. Why not try them out with 'Out of sight . . . ', the video cabinet with a difference on p908. Then if you want a first-class **jig** at an unbeatable price, go for the offer on p923 . . . . Many thanks **Wolfcraft** for your generosity.

Chaos . . .

. . . Is a new London showroom and sales/display centre, 'bringing together the best of well-known designers in furniture, lighting, ceramics, jewellery' . . . yes, but why 'Chaos'?
● 170 Royal College St, London NW10SP, 01-267 1747.

Diary

Guild courses are shown by an asterisk(*); for further details see the Guild pages.

October
25-Nov 22 **Painted Wood:** carved/painted birds, bowls and furniture, Cleveland Crafts Centre, 57 Gilkes St, Middlesbrough TS15EC, (0642) 226351
19-22 **Style 87** Furniture Show, Earl's Court, London SW5
23-26 **London Woodworker Show** Alexandra Pavilion, London N22
25 **Rough Wood 2:** Forestry and architecture seminar, Parnham House, Beaminster, Dorset DT8 3NA

November
9-13 **Woodmex 86** Woodworking equipment exhibition, NEC Birmingham, contact 01-486 1951
9-13 **NEC International Furniture Show**, NEC Birmingham
12-13 Dec **Timber In Architecture Exhibition**, Strathclyde University, Dept. of Architecture and Building Science, contact (091) 235424

December
6-23 **Surrey Guild of Craftsmen Annual Exhibition** Guildford House, 153 High St, Guildford, (0483) 57128
12-14 **Basic picture framing and mounting**, West Dean College, Chichester, Sussex, (02463) 301
13-14 **Christmas Craft Fair**, Alexandra Palace, London N22, contact (0727) 23176

Power danger

Users of portable power tools have been urged to invest in automatic cut-out systems to save themselves from electrocution. The warning came from a Norwich coroner after hearing how a man died as he was about to use an electric paint stripper outside his home; he was tampering with the extension lead socket when he was electrocuted.

The inquest was told that automatic cut-outs, which cost around £30, switch off power faster than a heart beat when any interference is detected. Recording a verdict of misadventure, the coroner said their use was a 'necessity.'

Iron road Keir Smith's sculpture from 20 railway sleepers in the Forest of Dean project, sponsored by the Arnolfini Gallery and the Forestry Commission with support from the Henry Moore Foundation

Winner table Paul Flowerday, Parnham House graduate, won this year's Smallpiece prize for the piece best suited to production with his 'Zee' table

Workbench winner

Congratulations to **John Green**, of Camborne, Cornwall, on winning our Workbench of the Future Competition. John's futuristic idea is more like a 'work environment' than a bench. See next month's issue, and a prototype or part prototype at the Woodworker Show. Many thanks, **Sjöbergs!**

At last . . .

The International Tropical Timber Organisation comes to life. The much-disputed place for the HQ (*WW/Jan*) of ITTO — the first international commodity arrangement to openly recognise the value of conservation — will be Yokohama. Now for trade co-operation and responsible forest management. See 'Timberline'.

Shoptalk

Ryobi's new AP10 **thicknesser**, a dinky little item for £375+VAT. Small enough to carry on site, yet 10x5in capacity.
● Luna, (0908) 70771.

The 'Peerless' **plane** from Roger's of Hitchin, launched last year to great acclaim by — among others — Fraser Budd in February's *Woodworker* — is back on the market after a lamented disappearance. The no.4 is £75.95 inc. VAT, and Roger will be doing a no.5 too.
● Roger's, 47 Walsworth Rd, Hitchin, Herts SG4 9SU, (0462) 34177.

Even small shops use a lot of board materials that need **edgebanding**, reason Jaydee Machine Sales; so they've brought in Brandt's KTV11 from Germany for under £500. The bigger KTV12 will do odd shapes as well.
● Jaydee, Old Exchange, New Pond Rd, Holmer Green, Bucks HP15 6SU, (0494) 714448.

Real news, this one: Kity's 'Combi-star' is a portable **combination** saw and planer/thicknesser. On site with ease for £500+VAT — see it at the Woodworker Show.
● Kity UK, 6 Acorn Pk, Charlestown, W. Yorks BD17 7SW, (0274) 597826.

Improvements to Nobex' popular **mitre saw** include what was conspicuously missing; a clamp to hold the work. It's now called the 202 pro, and costs £79+VAT.
● Luna, 20 Denbigh Hall, Bletchley, Bucks MK3 7QT, (0908) 70771.

Winter's round the corner and the workshop's getting colder; consider the Fercell GX15 woodwaste burning **space heater**, complete with circulating fan for £699+VAT. They also do a **briquetter** which won't break the bank if your operation can bear an investment of £4500 +VAT; remember you can sell the briquettes for a couple of quid a bag.
● Fercell, Unit 60, Swaislands Drive, Crayford Ind. Est., Crayford, Kent DA1 4HU, (0322) 53131.

Cub's the name of P&J's new **mini-dust extractor**, which can be mounted virtually anywhere in the workshop — even on the bench — and at £150 should attract the smallest of 'small users'. It can take two types of filter for fine or coarse waste, and it's claimed it will 'work with' a 14in ripsaw!
● P&J, Unit 1, Revenge Rd, Lordswood Ind. Est., Chatham, Kent ME5 8PF, (0634) 684526.

Free **tooling set** from Startrite when you buy a K260 or K310 universal machine: it's worth £59.50+VAT.
● Startrite, Waterside Works, Gads Hill, Kent ME7 2SF, (0634) 55122.

Cutting speeds of 1000-5000 cuts per minute; 'vibration-free' drive; maximum cutting height 50mm, throat 390mm. That's the Deca Dynamic **scroll saw** for £79.95+VAT.
● Sumaco, Suma House, Huddersfield Rd, Elland, W. Yorks HX5 9AA, (0422) 79811

A free leaflet on **timber pests** you may find around the home has been published by the Timber Research and Development Association (TRADA). With colour photographs you can identify 15 of the more common insects to be seen, and find out how to get rid of them. TRADA point out that many insects discovered lurking indoors are no danger all to wood. A useful leaflet.
● Publications Dept, TRADA, Stocking Lane, Hughenden Valley, High Wycombe, Bucks HP14 4ND.

Shoptalking points: first winner of the Sandvik Centenary handsaw is Mr J. I. White of Sheffield. Put a large belt through a hole in the bench, loop another smaller one to the floor, and you have a foot-tensioned holdfast for any shape. Is that clever or what?

Lightweight **belt sander** from Bosch: the PBS 60 weighs 2.1kg and has a 60mm-wide belt. £60+VAT.
● Robert Bosch, PO Box 98, North Orbital Rd, Denham, Middx UB9 5HJ, (0895) 833 633.

Timberline

Arthur Jones gives the low-down on the world timber market

Woodworkers may find they are not immune from the effects of foreign exhange rate fluctuations if recent events are a guide. The Swedish and Finnish currencies have both been weak against sterling and there have even been rumours of devaluation in Finland. If the Swedish krona falls below a stated level against sterling then the price of Russian softwood already under contract (but not delivered) automatically rises. And that means the consumer will pay more for the same wood.

Timber is always at the mercy of exchange rate fluctuations which can make a nonsense of prices negotiated earlier between buyers and sellers.

You'll know that few retail outlets offer more than a limited range of dimensions and grades in anything but a few species of timber. Most woodworkers are interested in only a small number of species anyway and only shortages of well-known woods would be sufficient reason to buy unfamiliar timber. However, there's now mounting concern within the hardwood trade that much more will have to be done to encourage use of secondary hardwoods in the UK.

This is a theme of the Friends of the Earth and it is accepted that proper management of tropical forests must mean fuller use of all the species, rather than taking just a few trees of select quality and species from every acre.

The long-term interests of the timber trade and the FoE are identical in this respect; both want to see the survival of the tropical rainforests and welcome the fully-operational International Tropical Timber Organisation back into the arena. The international bickering over the appointment of an executive director and home for the organisation is at last over: a forestry expert from Malaysia has been appointed to the post and the headquarters will be set up in Yokohama.

First on the agenda for the ITTO is to secure international agreement on expansion of trop-ical forest usage within a framework of sustained yield — which will be aided by modern forest management techniques. This way the organisation will ensure the future growth of the tropical rainforests for the benefit of the developing countries and those who use the hardwoods from the forests, which would be good news all round.

But at present, we're all aware that hardwood prices have been creeping up despite official chatter about the rate of inflation being under 3%. Stockists claim that even these higher prices do not cover replacement costs; they know what is being paid today for fresh supplies from the southern hemisphere — wood which won't be in their stocks, ready for sale, for at least another four months.

Brazilian mahogany and lauan are showing signs of supply-shortage which will affect forward selling prices. Most of the favoured hardwoods will stay firm in price at least until the end of the year. There can be the odd exception, like keruing or the serayas (sometimes used as a slightly cheaper form of mahogany and even called a mahogany in some quarters).

American ash and oak are fairly readily available, but Japanese oak seems to have faded almost entirely from the market-place, solely on the score of rising prices. The loss of this export trade to the UK does not appear to worry the Japanese as they're not making any effort to regain their share of the oak market here.

Price agreements made by the producers in the Far East for plywood exports seem to be holding well — previous attempts at quotas and price controls have usually failed.

Canadian plywood prices have been firmed by strike problems, so US yellow pine plywood is now a better buy, price-wise. Imports from Canada now attract duty until the end of the year, so there's no expectation of lower selling prices here, especially as stocks are no longer too large.

A new British Standard (BS6566) has been issued covering all types of imported commercial plywoods which should form the basis of better consumer protection and ensure quality — interesting reading for those who use ply. ■

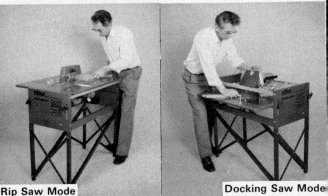

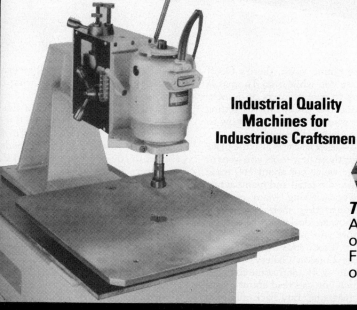

Show of shows

Don't miss it — the 1986 Woodworker Show, previewed by Show organiser Mary White

Here's the show you've all been waiting for. Alexandra Pavilion will be bustling with woodworkers for four days from Thursday 23 October, at Britain's premier show for seeing all that's best in the woodworking field.

The shows have gone from success to success since they started seven years ago, proving that in this age of high technology more and more people want the deep satisfaction that comes from using their hands to design and make in wood.

The show's centrepiece is the competition; the entries are from some of Britain's

● Among this year's exhibits: Paul Anderson's unusual clock (see it in next month's issue too!), 'King of Clubs' carving by Julian Cox, and a cabinetmaker's tool chest by Keith Stephenson; **below** and **right**, all eyes on the demos

best craftspeople in turning, carving, cabinetmaking and marquetry. You'll find yourself drawn back again and again to admire individual pieces, to take pleasure in the innovative designs, to be awed by the technical intricacies, and perhaps to be inspired to emulate their achievements.

Demonstrations are always a crowd-drawer at Woodworker Shows, and this year we've got an excellent line-up of craftsmen. Maurice Lund, whose carvings have frequently won him prizes, will be showing how he works. Not to be missed are the demonstrations of traditional country crafts by Stuart King, Mike Abbott and Jack Hill; they'll be covering Windsor chair making, chair bodging, pole lathe turning of green wood, skills that are in danger of disappearing.

If you've got problems in woodworking, we've got the people with the answers. Who better to ask about restoring than Charles

Cliffe? For re-caning work, there's Geoff Berry to advise you while Stan Thomas is always willing to give pointers on joinery and sharpening old tools. Not forgetting Zach Taylor, who will be showing how to make and play musical instruments.

The Woodworker Show is also the place to look out for those new tools you want to buy. This year we've got about 160 trade exhibitors from the retail and manufacturing side of woodworking. Many of them will be demonstrating their equipment, making the Show an ideal place to see tools in action before you purchase.

On our own *Woodworker* magazine stand there'll be the London Gallery, showing Guild members' work, and some items of furniture which you can read about in this issue of the magazine. Buy back numbers and binders, get a deal on subscriptions, and win **super prizes** in the draw — see p990.

Colleges and societies will be exhibiting their work and telling you what courses they have on offer.

There's a new ingredient in this year's Show. Tools for Self Reliance is a charity which collects unwanted tools in Britain, refurbishes them and then sends them abroad to equip village craft workshops — they were featured last month. They will have a stand at the Show to receive any tools you are willing to contribute; please bring them along, cleaned up and sharpened if possible, and hand them in at the stand. Your unwanted tools could have a second lease of life helping somebody else practise their skills.

Above all, the Show is a place to meet other people who are as enthusiastic about woodwork as you are. *Woodworker* staff look forward to meeting you at the Alexandra Pavilion, Wood Green, 23-26 October.

How to get there:

By public transport. You can take either the British Rail service to Alexandra Palace station, or the underground to Wood Green.

Main line: service from King's Cross every half hour, alighting at Alexandra Palace. Journey time is about 10 minutes, and you'll find a free bus service from Alexandra Palace station to the Alexandra Pavilion, and back.

Underground: take the Piccadilly line from Piccadilly Circus or King's Cross to Wood Green, journey time about 30 minutes. Free bus service available from Wood Green to Alexandra Pavilion and back.

By road. With the M25 nearly complete around London, this is the quickest route for most drivers, turning off at Junction 25. Alexandra Pavilion is just off the North Circular, and AA signs are being posted from the bottom of the M1. Ample car parking is available, with a park-and-ride shuttle service to the Show, or an easy stroll if you prefer.

Woodworker Show, Alexandra Pavilion, London N22, Thursday 23 October to Sunday 26 October; open 10-6 daily (till 5 on Sunday). Admission £3.25, children/OAPs £2.95 (reductions for party bookings and Guild of Woodworker members). Argus Specialist Exhibitions, P.O. Box 35, Wolsey House, Wolsey Rd, Hemel Hempstead, Herts HP2 4SS, (0442) 41221

● *Miniature horsedrawn caravans, exquisite turned bowls – there's something for everyone at the show of shows. And you can still get that £100 saving on the* **Sjöberg 1900** *bench,* **below left**; *you've read about it in* **Woodworker**, *now see it on the* **Sarjents'** *stand*

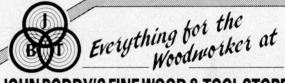
907

Out of sight...

Want a unit to house your video? Alan Fell's prize-winning design could be the answer — and you can use your free dowels making it!

● *Close the door firmly on the one-eyed monster with this simple-to-build unit. It houses TV, video, and your favourite tapes. You could have a lot of fun working out your own decorative ideas; Alan's solution is green ink motifs under a clear polyurethane, but MDF is notably good for lacquering to a high gloss or a flat colour*

Side elevation

49

castors

20   145   245   90

This project, which won fourth prize in the 1985 *Woodworker* MDF competition, uses 16mm MDF joined with 6mm dowels, except for the load-bearing shelves which are slotted into housing joints cut in the board.

I wanted a functional cabinet to house my particular television and the heavy video, but the design could be adapted to suit any models.

I decided to have the video above the television to avoid having to crouch down

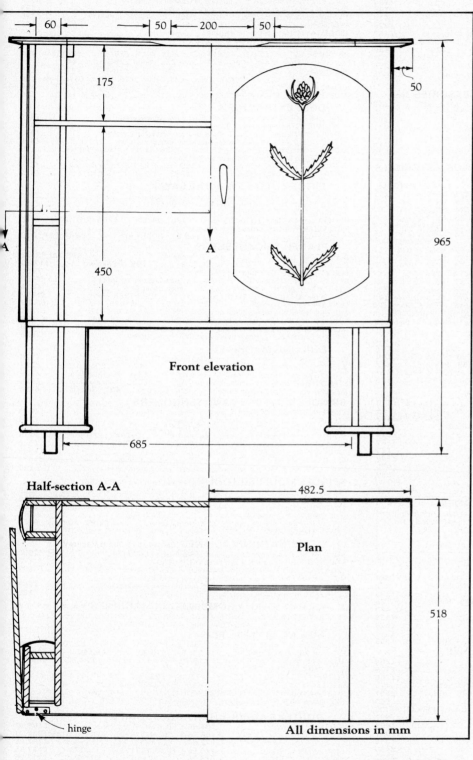

60 | 50 | 200 | 50

175

450

A

A

Front elevation

965

50

685

Half-section A-A

482.5

Plan

518

hinge

All dimensions in mm

legs continue under the television shelf, they do provide extra strength.

The curve of the arch in each end panel matches, in ratio of height to width of curve (1:5), the curves on the ends of the feet, the rounded edges of the boards and the curves on the ends of the door hinges; this makes a common feature running throughout the design. To avoid the square, box-like appearance of many units made from board materials, I rounded all the full width edges of the boards on the front and sides of the unit to soften their appearance. Where the television and video shelves continue through the sides (with a bridle joint) to provide tape shelves, the rounded edges again soften the right angles of these joints. I found the MDF ideal for forming these rounded edges which were all planed to shape before final sanding.

I gave the overhang of the top a more delicate edge to produce a lighter appearance. A finger-pull groove in the hinged lid was worked by hand with gouges and then sanded. I angled the door edges so they overlap by 5mm and routed a V-groove on

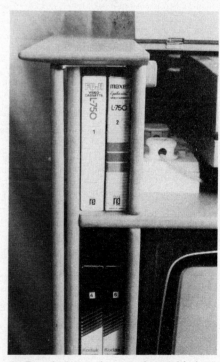

● *Detail of unit showing door folded right back and lid hinged up for access to video recorder*

when loading tapes and because the video is a top-loading model. To have it mounted below the television would mean either having a large gap above the video (unsightly) or putting it on a sliding shelf (risky because of weight). A hinged lid in the top provides access to the video. The television and video shelves are fitted into 5mm deep housings to provide maximum strength.

I don't have a large collection of video tapes so I limited the storage space to 16

tapes (including the space below the doors). By doing this I was able to avoid having a drawer for tape storage (although one could easily be accommodated between the legs of the unit) and instead keep them on shelves fitted in the box section legs, which I think make a more interesting feature. The back legs don't provide tape storage but match the front legs in appearance and are turned through 90° to leave a wider panel between the front and back legs. This was for purely aesthetic reasons although where the back

the front, highlighting with green ink to provide a frame for the teasel motif. The curves of the groove again matching the other curves of the unit.

I worked the door handles by hand from MDF because, although it's not ideal for the purpose, I wanted a perfect colour match with the rest of the unit. The joints were dowelled or screwed and glued as appropriate and the whole unit mounted on castors for easy movement. I finished the unit in clear varnish. ∎

Raffan's rules

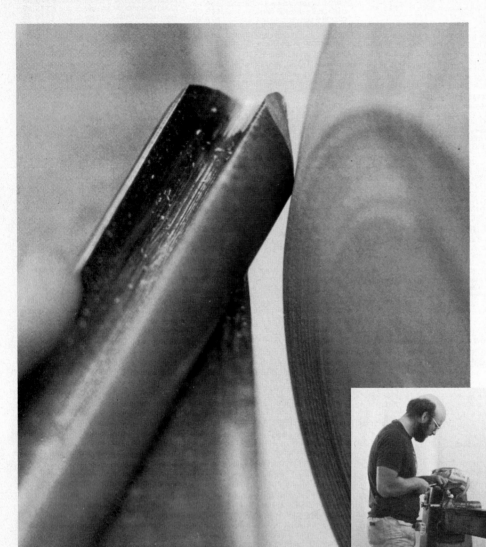

Richard Raffan, one of the world's best-known woodturners, talks stance and cutting practice in this extract from his new book *Turning Wood*

support it while still approaching the lathe safely. If you don't apply the general principles of tool handling, you'll find it difficult to control the cutting edge, and the wood will dictate the path of the tool.

Consider yourself apprenticed to the lathe. You can't just stand before it and produce excellence. As a musician practices scale, so the turner should practice routine exercises until mastered. When I first started I turned lots of small repetitious shapes: scoops, bowls, honey dippers, meat bashers.

Try to resist the temptation to make something; it's more important at first to develop good form and work habits than it is to produce a functional object. Practise cutting wood away and enjoy the shavings that result as you develop basic tool handling skills.

Stance

To move the cutting edge precisely where you want, you must get your weight behind the tool and guide it through space on a predetermined trajectory, regardless of the wood it meets on the way. On metal lathes, control is achieved by cutters that move in a

● *Top left: bevel shoulder to work before the edge cuts.* **Above,** *right and wrong stances*

It's fairly easy to achieve a bowl that functions as a bowl, a box with a passably fitting lid, or a spindle covered with beads, grooves and coves. What is not so easy is to produce a really beautiful, well-balanced bowl that is a joy to hold as well as to look at, or a box with just the right degree of suction in the fit of the lid, or a slender, elegant spindle with a few beads in just the right places.

To produce this kind of result takes time. It was at least five years before I developed real speed in my turning and another year or so before I had the fluent technique to

convert my ideas readily into woodturnings.

Practising the fundamentals — tool handling, stance, cutting — provides a solid basis for all turning work.

Tool handling

There is more to woodturning than simply maintaining the correct angle of the cutting edge to the wood. The angle is important, but you must also be aware of what is happening behind the edge, how the tool is held and how to position your body to

rack-and-pinion system. In woodturning, you hold the tools yourself, and support comes from the tool rest and your body.

In manipulating the tools, your movement should not come so much from your hands, wrists and arms, as from your shoulders, hips and legs. Aim for a compact stance with your elbows tucked into your sides. Stand in a balanced position, with your feet placed comfortably apart, and the tool handle aligned along your forearm for maximum control (above left). Never stand in front of the lathe with your elbows waving about in space (above right).

 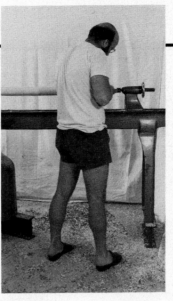 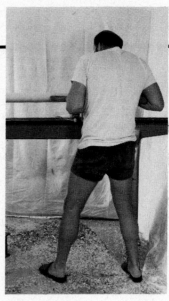

● *Right, a good stance, tool handle along forearm, feet comfortably apart. Following sequence **right** and **below** the weight shifts from foot to foot turning a long cylinder*

NOTE: the strapless sandals worn in these photos are not recommended!

It's good practice to keep your upper hand on the rest, but try to maintain contact between other parts of your anatomy and the machine as well. Lean your hip against the bed or press a leg against the stand. This stance will not only give you extra support and stability, but also establish physical points of reference between you and the lathe.

Develop and enjoy the control gained from this approach by moving the cutting edge with a little squeeze or push, in conjunction with broader support movements from the rest of your body. As in steering a bicycle, control in woodturning is essentially a matter of shifting weight and coordination.

If you want to move the tip of a tool slightly to the left, the movement should come from a nudge from your hip pushing the handle to the right. To move the tip to

● *Bowl exteriors: plant your feet and swing your body with the tool*

913

Raffan's rules

the right, draw your right elbow in close to your side, nudging the tool handle to the left. Keep your lower hand close to your side, and you remain compact.

If you want the tool edge to drop, extend your side by stretching upward, standing on tiptoe if necessary, to bring the handle up (and the tip down) with the weight of your entire torso and shoulders behind the tool. If the handle must leave your side, align it along your forearm for support.

Most beginners are very inhibited about moving their bodies along with the tool handle; it pays to overcome this self-consciousness. Practise the movements a few times at the lathe to get the feel of it, even before you pick up a tool or turn the machine on.

Cutting

There is absolutely no right or wrong way to turn. The correct way for you is one which feels comfortable and produces a clean surfaces.

But there are several important rules you ought to be aware of, and refer back to again once you've begun turning:
● Wood is essentially a bundle of long fibres lying generally in the same direction. Your cleanest cut will be across the bundle (the grain) where any one fibre is supported by others (fig. 1). Unsupported fibres will splinter away, as anyone who has cross-

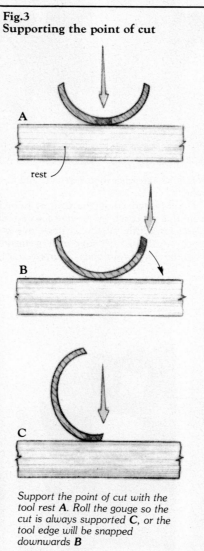

Fig.1 Clean shearing cuts

Centrework

Cleanest cuts across the grain where fibres are supported; shown by arrows

Facework

sawn a board will know. Plan your cuts so there is support for the area being cut by following the directional arrows in the drawing.
● The tool must contact the rest first, before moving forward to bring the bevel shoulder into contact with the wood (fig. 2). If the edge contacts the revolving wood first, the downward force will slap the tool on to the rest and you'll almost certainly have a catch. This will either leave a mess on

the wood, or with a light lathe might even cause a broken tool rest (I did this twice early on in my turning career). Don't allow one side of a scraper or parting tool to rise

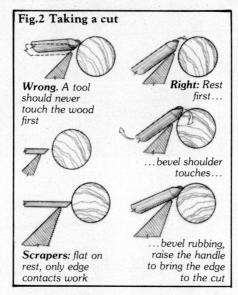

Fig.2 Taking a cut

Wrong. A tool should never touch the wood first

Right: Rest first ...

... bevel shoulder touches ...

Scrapers: flat on rest, only edge contacts work

... bevel rubbing, raise the handle to bring the edge to the cut

Fig.3 Supporting the point of cut

A

rest

B

C

*Support the point of cut with the tool rest **A**. Roll the gouge so the cut is always supported **C**, or the tool edge will be snapped downwards **B***

off the rest.
● When the bevel shoulder is in contact with the wood, tilt the handle up about 10° to bring the edge down through an arc and into the cut. Don't simply move the tool horizontally across the rest into the wood. This procedure applies when using skew chisels and parting tools as well as gouges. (Set the scraper flat on the rest and push it into the cut; the bevel is on the underside of the tool and cannot rub. Because only the cutting edge contacts the wood, you should ease the scraper forward with great care to make light cuts.) Rubbing the bevel is often impossible when you enter the wood, as there is no cut surface on which to rub, but do this whenever possible. The bevel shoulder can be used as a secondary fulcrum against which the tool pivots to bring the cutting edge into play.
● Roll gouges in the direction of the cut (fig. 3). Many nasty catches result from the pressure of the wood on the unsupported edge of a gouge. You shouldn't find any problem when cutting with the centre (lower edge) of the gouge, because the point of cut is directly supported by the tool rest (fig. 3A). It's more difficult when the point of cut moves up to the unsupported corner of the tool (fig. 3B). Adjust for this by rolling the tool so it contacts the rest below the point of cut (fig. 3C).
● Cut with the tool moving parallel or at a tangent to the axis on which the wood

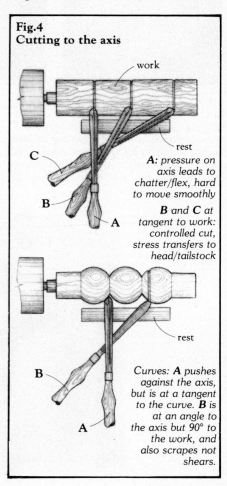

Fig.4 Cutting to the axis

work

rest

C

B

A

A: pressure on axis leads to chatter/flex, hard to move smoothly

B and C at tangent to work: controlled cut, stress transfers to head/tailstock

rest

B

A

Curves: A pushes against the axis, but is at a tangent to the curve. B is at an angle to the axis but 90° to the work, and also scrapes not shears.

rotates, rather than against it (fig. 4). This allows the force that is applied as the tool moves forward to be transferred to the headstock or tailstock. The idea is to put as little pressure against the axis as possible; too much pressure can cause chattering, flexing or breaking of slender work, or it may even weaken a fixing. In practice cuts are rarely made parallel to the axis because you have to compromise and consider grain direction.

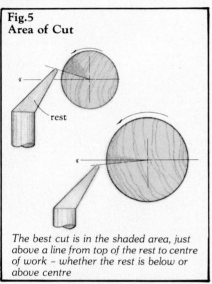

Fig.5
Area of Cut

rest

The best cut is in the shaded area, just above a line from top of the rest to centre of work – whether the rest is below or above centre

● Always cut above a line from the top of the tool rest to the centre (fig. 5). If you cut below this line, the wood tends to grab at the tool. I raise the tool edge a maximum of 10° during a cut before bringing the edge down to finish at the centre. As you cut into the centre of the work, slow up and float the edge in gently, rolling the tool to maintain the most effective cut. Stop at the centre; don't push and overshoot the centre or the tool will meet wood travelling upwards on the other side and you'll risk tearing or pulling out fibres.
● Initial cuts should be exploratory until you determine where the wood and the orbit of its extremities are. If the tool is pushed in too fast, too much wood will contact the edge at once, making the tool clear more wood than is advisable. That sudden force will lead to a catch. As you cut, you want to control the leverage and path of the edge rather than forcing the tool forward against the work. The tool should move forward only when the wood in its path has been removed. In the hands of an expert this is a rapid flowing action; it's like a moving picture or animated cartoon where slightly different static images in each frame run in quick succession to produce a single, fluid movement.

A sharp tool held in the optimum position will produce a large shaving with virtually no forward pressure. If a sharp tool begins to cut less efficiently or even stops cutting altogether, don't push it hard to find an edge. Instead adjust the tool angle or roll it to a different position where it will

cut. If you push hard at the wrong angle, the tool will often skate up and over the surface with little or no effect. The tool should never shoot forward and ride on the bevel if you lose an edge; this indicates lack of control and too much pressure against the wood. The aim is to move the tool precisely and evenly along a definite path, removing all that it encounters. Don't try to cut too much at one go.

Practice stopping in mid-cut by easing pressure so that the edge is barely in contact with the wood. In this position the bevel still rubs while the edge produces light, fluffy shavings. Then proceed and stop again. Soon you should be able to withdraw the tool and return it to exactly the same position.

As you do this, practise bringing the bevel shoulder in contact with the wood first and letting it rub. Then gradually rotate and adjust the angle of the edge downwards to pick up the cut. Move the tool into the wood slowly with precise control. Whenever you succeed in producing a good shaving and leaving a smooth surface, try to

repeat the action. Do it over and over until you are confident you can make that cut at will, then build on it.

Here's five questions to ask yourself when you find yourself in difficulties:
1 Does the tool need sharpening?
2 Is it the wood (difficult grain) or a foreign particle (silica, wire or a nail)?
3 Could I use the tool differently with better results?
4 Would a different tool be better?
5 Is it just me?
If you decide you are the culprit, keep practising. Or go for a walk and try again later. Everyone has off days.

As your skill develops, beware of complacency. Aim to get things right the first time. Don't poke or jab at the wood; any shape poked at and messed about with looks it. When you achieve flowing movements and sounds, flowing forms will follow.

Never be afraid to risk ruining a job with a final cut. It's all too easy to find turnery where a shape just misses because the woodworker has settled for a surface that is more or less okay, but where one or two more cuts could have made all the difference. Too many people say 'that'll do' and either don't care about achieving

● *Above, scoops in radiata pine; left, natural-edge bowl in holly*

quality or don't want to put at risk an hour's work in looking for it.

But it is worth pushing yourself to develop your skill so that if you want to try something technically outrageous you can tackle it with some prospect of success. I can recall a 4x10in burr elm bowl I had turned with a ¼in thick wall that, upon inspection, I found to be less than ⅛in thick near the base (easy to check for it had holes in the side). I held my breath and turned the whole wall down to the much thinner section. It was cut in one minute and not bludgeoned into submission with 20-grit abrasive in 10. That venture was successful. Other, smaller, bowls have shattered with the final cut, but it is always worth the risk.

Decide what you want to make and go for it. Don't be satisfied with less. You will always know when you could have done better, even if others don't. Learn to be hypercritical and enjoy the long-term results. I find I am rarely satisfied with yesterday's masterpiece because it becomes today's run-of-the-mill. The better you get, the smaller your steps forward will be, but progress is always possible. And rest assured, you will never reach perfection — but you might have glimpses of it!

Turning Wood by Richard Raffan is published by Bell & Hyman at £12.95 paperback; we are grateful for permission to use this extract.

Bent on steam

● *A folding upright chair in natural ash*

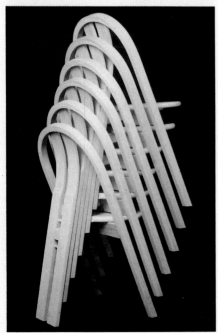

● *Stacking dining chairs, also in a natural finish*

How an idea for a cast aluminium chair led designer David Colwell on a trail that involved green ash and a change of lifestyle; John Hemsley reports from the depths of Wales

Nobody would call David Colwell a traditional craftsman. But his personally developed technique of bending unseasoned ash does derive from the traditional methods of Windsor chair-making.

His choice of wood — young ash in particular — is the result of a logical appraisal of suitable materials for chairs, rather than an obsessive infatuation with timber *per se*. 'I was looking for a material that would combine durability, high strength-to-weight ratio and low capital cost of manufacture,' he told me, removing hot pieces of ash from a steamer in his converted school workshop in mid-Wales.

From this 1000sq ft workshop, with a modicum of simple equipment, David and his two assistants will this year produce about 300 chairs in three different designs, and a tightly limited range of other furniture.

His designs show the influences of Michael Thonet, the 19th century pioneer of mass-produced steam-bent furniture, and Alvar Aalto, the Swedish architect whose three-legged stools remain 'modern' classics. The designs are deceptively simple,

● *Classical reclining chair and footstool, ash and rattan*

choose it as his target. Indeed, all his designs stem from chairmaking techniques (turning, mortise-and-tenon joints), including his three-legged tables.

David talked me through the process of production from green timber to comfortable chairs — which takes three to four months — and revealed the techniques of steam bending which are the culmination of persistent trial-and-error work.

The setting of Trannon Furniture Makers, David's trade name, is idyllic, halfway up a mountain at the edge of the Upper Severn valley, in a hamlet between Shrewsbury and Aberystwyth. He converted the workshop from a redundant school nine years ago, and lives with his family in the school house next door. The only sounds are the rushing of the nearby stream ... and the throbbing of the bandsaw.

Chairmaking starts with selecting the timber, all local material from the Border Counties and Welshpool. Only fast-grown ash butts are suitable for the high quality wood he needs (it's actually stronger than slow-grown), and he chooses them standing or recently felled, before immediately having them sawn into $1\frac{1}{2}$, $1\frac{1}{4}$ or 1in planks. 'Just like the Windsor chair tradition,' he points out, 'it's the steaming that seasons the timber.' The butts are 12-15in across.

David declined to reveal how much the timber costs him (you'd be envious), but because it is local and virtually an agricultural product, it is cheap. He buys from three local timber mills regularly, having it cut to his requirements.

Apart from a tiny amount of air-dried elm (its resistance to splitting makes it suitable for the threaded knobs on the reclining chairs), other wood that will not be steamed is bought kiln-dried. This

based on a few bent members and mortise-and-tenon joints, but they rely on high quality materials, extended perfecting of the design, and skilled development of the bending techniques.

He generally produces batches of 30-50 at a time, achieving economies of scale and using alternative finishes (natural/black-stained, rattan/upholstered) to add variety to the deliberately limited range; his business head tells him this is the most effective approach.

David is basically a designer-entrepreneur, who stumbled across wood nine

years ago as the most suitable medium for a reclining chair; his previous experience had largely been in steel and plastic. Timber also fits in with his strong concern for conservation of resources; it's a low-energy material to work, and the young ash grows quickly, so the 500cu. ft he uses in a year is rapidly replaced. 'I make sure not to use very much material in the chairs I design,' he asserts.

Most of us probably agree that the chair is the single most challenging piece of furniture, so it's not really surprising that a person who is primarily a designer should

Bent on steam

includes oak and sycamore for table tops and chair seats. 'Generally I specialise in domestic timbers, locally grown; it's convenient, it's appropriate and it's also economic.'

The batch method of production means suitable wood is selected from the wood store, crosscut outside the shop by chainsaw or electric hand-saw and ripped by bandsaw into blanks before being left to dry out naturally for another two months. This releases some of the tension in the timber, and shows up any natural bending which can be capitalised on.

His machine shop has small equipment, all single-phase: a Startrite 352 bandsaw, a radial-arm saw, planer/thicknesser, two lathes (a metalworking lathe used to produce some wooden components and an ancient wooden-bed lathe which can turn 78in between centres), an overhead router, a chisel-mortiser and a spindle moulder.

Mortise and tenon joints are at the heart of David's chairs. The chisel-mortiser cuts rectangular mortises, while the tenons are cut on the spindle moulder. The shoulders are bevelled only on the long edges, an outside chamfer to give a neat finish; the narrow edges aren't bevelled but fit very tightly. The position of the tenon on cylindrical components is marked when turning on the lathe, the slight incision stopping the joint from breaking out and leaving a neat decorative detail.

This kind of attention to detail runs right through David's work. 'I try to achieve character of appearance from convenience of making,' he points out.

Next to the miniscule machine shop is the open assembly area, where the steamer was already warming up when I arrived. A sawdust burning stove heats water in what looks rather like a double dustbin lid, with the steam fed through into a 4ft-long plywood box, lined with three inches of insulation and stainless steel. It takes about an hour to soften a batch of timber, and condensation dripping from an overflow is tinged brown by sap.

Before the timber is stacked in the steamer it has been sorted into pairs of potential legs with matched grain, the faces to be bent already planed; the edges are left sawn, for they will distort in the process and can be trimmed afterwards. Each pair of components are put in face up; this face will be on the outside after bending.

While the timber was softening, David cleared the assembly table and got out the jigs. For legs he uses stainless steel straps which keep the outside of the bend under compression and prevent the wood from cracking. The components only stay in the straps for 20 minutes and are then put into racks which keep them in shape and allow them to dry out on all sides.

The bend itself is achieved in one of several ways, his equipment including a pneumatic ram with pairs of wooden moulds and a giant wooden lever-cam device. With thin sections of wood, straps

are unneccessary, since compression and tension are more balanced.

David was bending a batch of chairbacks. Into the steamer went dozens of leaf-shaped pieces of flat wood, about ½in thick (these were wide in the middle, trimming down to about 2in at the ends). When they were hot, he brought them out a pair at a time, and secured the ends in the wooden jigs with wing-nuts. In the space between the two backs was a V-shaped piece of timber, with metal dowels protruding from the top. Once the backs were secure, David inserted a long wooden beam into the metal dowels, and with one steady heave turned

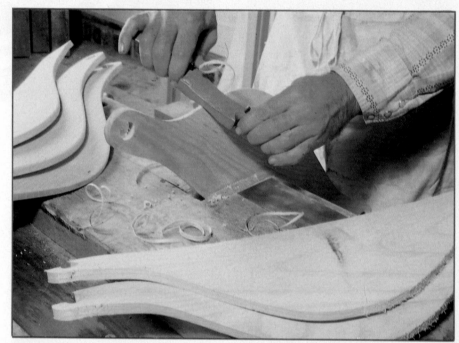

● *Spokeshaving bent chair backs*

the V-shape so it was at right angles to the backs. Before my eyes those flat backs developed a curve in two directions at once, like leaf-sections cut from a giant hollow ball. The jigs were removed from the holding device, but kept the backs in shape.

In just 20 minutes David had produced 14 chairbacks, with only one of them splitting in indignation at this severe treatment! Sure beats laminating, as David points out.

The shape is made permanent by subsequent curing. The pieces are piled up, covered with a polythene and blanket tent, and a fan heater is left running in the middle overnight to keep the temperature at 100°F. 'The steaming gets the inside moisture moving,' explained David. 'The curing then coaxes out the outer layer of moisture.'

After curing the pieces are taken out of the setting jigs and left for about a month before use. Using these bent components in designs which are based on triangular shapes (much stronger than rectangles) allows some natural 'give' to what is essentially a very rigid structure. This means that the chairs are ergonomically sound (sought

out by people with bad backs) as well as being durable (sought out by people with children who test furniture to destruction).

Alas, like all handmade furniture, David's work is in the top price bracket. The dining chair with turned wooden seat in natural finish costs £96; the folding upright with hide seat £144; the reclining chair with rattan seat and back £168; all prices are exclusive of VAT, plus a delivery charge of £15 per piece. 'For the quality and the durability this is cheap,' claims David.

The majority of his business is through direct order, in response to editorial mentions and, more recently, advertising in

● *David twists the V-shaped jig to turn flat blanks into curved backs*

magazines; he does sell some through shops, and also through contract work and specifiers.

David, now 42, grew up in south-west London and studied furniture design at Kingston College of Art before going to the Royal College of Art in London, under David Pye ('a major influence on me and many other people').

After graduating in 1969 he set up his own practice in London, designing commercial interiors and doing work in plastic for firms like ICI.

'I've always been more interested in manufacture than in craftsmanship,' he says. 'Processes fascinate me. In plastics the process is moulding, a form-change process. In metal it can be melting or fabrication. In woodwork you're involved in cutting and removing wood to get the shape you want, which is comparatively wasteful.'

His interest in wood, which led to a complete change of lifestyle, developed when he was designing a reclining chair. Originally he envisaged it in cast aluminium — and someone else producing it — but engineering criteria nudged him towards the benefits of timber.

'Steam-bent ash turned out to suit the criteria best, and when I started making

While he was working on the chair prototype he rented a house in mid-Wales, fell in love with the locality and saw the advantages of moving. Property was cheaper and there was a ready abundance of the raw material he needed. The rest, as they say, is history. That first reclining chair remains one of his best-sellers. He now has two assistants; Simon Moorhouse, an ex-furniture student at Shrewsbury College of Art and Technology, and Sally Clayton, a YTS trainee who's going to Shrewsbury next year. Simon is virtually in charge of day-to-day production, leaving David freer to develop his ideas and concentrate on marketing.

Marketing is absolutely vital now that he's in the business of manufacturing, albeit on a small scale. He feels that craftsmen producing one-offs for individuals are really more of a service industry.

David has traditional views on design as a creative and innovative activity whose solutions to problems embody a visual language. From this position he views with dismay what he sees as a general decline in design today. 'Design is increasingly allied to the persuasion market,' he claims. In mass markets the 'creative act' is identifying the symbols in the popular imagination and then devising a product which embodies

or convenience of making. Hand-made furniture usually relies on elaborate detailing, which means it is a virtuoso individual achievement by the craftsman. That may be fine, but it doesn't make much sense in terms of the furniture design tradition. Most furniture isn't even comfortable,' he adds, 'but strangely this doesn't seem to bother furniture makers or customers. The point I'm making is that at the coarsest level most designs don't deal with fundamental problems — comfort, makeability, good use of resources.'

David's designs are very much to do with comfort, durability, and appropriateness of material and production. Ash is strong, impact-resistant, comparatively cheap and ideal for steam-bending. He makes use of triangulation, which takes stress off joints. And he has no unnecessary superficial detailing.

As an aside he pointed out that virtually nobody designing cabinets exploits the strength of drawer bottoms, potentially the strongest part of the drawer, if plywood is used. Instead people still use solid wood grooved into the sides, which doesn't help to keep the drawer carcase together at all.

'Furniture designers have hardly started in the real sense,' he claims. 'They are piddling about with colours or details.'

David builds on his experience in industry, rather than turning his back on it, in design as well as in processes.

He is fond of citing the bicycle as an example of good design. 'A bicycle is very, very close to what you want from furniture,' he says. 'Minute variations on a standard object in the hand-built end of the market, which is the sharp end of design development, produce a very high performance object. I like to think that my own furniture is similar.'

He now feels a slightly larger output would be more appropriate to his small-batch production methods. Batching makes sense with the chair-based techniques he uses, but the economies of the method are pushing him towards a larger team — perhaps double the size — in order to get the maximum cost effectiveness out of his investment.

He is interested in making the scale harmonious with the manufacturing process, and suggests furniture manufacture could go in the direction of more, smaller, units if consumers want increasing variety, and there are signs that they do. Large manufacturing units, he points out, find themselves more and more trapped at the bottom of the market. 'But if they compete on price, they will have to compete with furniture from other parts of the world where wages are lower . . . '

David Colwell has a refreshing breadth of vision rare among furniture makers. I left his workshop feeling he has only just begun to tap a great reservoir of innovation, and that he will be an increasingly important figure in the furniture scene. ■

● *Even David's tables involve chairmaking techniques*

prototypes I discovered it was better to use it green rather than seasoned.

'This was a whole voyage of discovery for me, and I found it fitted in with my personal preference for the country furniture tradition rather than cabinetmaking — the pragmatic approach rather than the stylistic. After a while I was getting such a buzz from the material that I got hooked, and ended up deciding to manufacture myself. From the engineering point of view, the low capital cost and ecological arguments, the process had so much going for it.'

these aspects. For example, in his view Japanese learner motorcycles sell largely on their styling, borrowed inappropriately, from racing machines; the colour of the paintwork and the diagonal stripes are the triggers that get people to buy. In the fashion world these superficial aspects are described as 'hanging appeal', and motorcycles in this sense have become fashion items.

'Most furniture today falls into the category concerned with style, which I regard as superficial,' says David. 'Very rarely has it to do with convenience of use

FASTEST SERVICE +++ BEST ADVICE +++ FASTEST SERVICE +++ BEST ADVICE +++ FASTEST SERVICE +++ BEST ADVICE +++ FASTEST SERVICE

NATIONWIDE TOOLS & MACHINERY

ROUTERS

BLACK & DECKER		Ex. VAT £	Inc. VAT £
SR100	¼" Plunge Action C/W Fence & Cutter fits MOF96 Accessory Kit	60.83	69.95
ELU			
MOF96	¼" Router 600W	75.22	86.50
MOF96E	¼" Router 750W	93.48	106.95
MOF96	Accessory Kit	58.69	67.50
MOF96	Dovetail Kit	58.69	67.50
MOF31	¼" Router 1200W — ½" capability	118.70	136.50
MOF177	½" Router Single Speed 1600W inc. ¼" collet	150.88	173.50
MOF177E	½" Router Variable Speed 1850W inc. ¼" collet	176.62	198.50
MOF112	½" Heavy Duty Router 2000W	152.62	175.50
ELU551	Combination Bench used as Spindle Moulder	86.05	98.95

SAW BENCHES

SCHEPPACH TKU 12" 3HP c/w TCT blade	178.27	205.00
ROYAL Mk3B 10" TCT blade, cast iron, made in G.B.	573.07	659.00
ROYAL Mk3DS as above with sliding table	955.69	1099.00
ELU TGS 172 Sawbench & Mitre Saw c/w TCT blade	352.19	405.00
ELU TGS 171 Sawbench & Mitre Saw c/w TCT blade	287.81	331.00
STARTRITE TA/SP145 9" 1HP 1PH	625.00	718.00
STARTRITE TA/SP275DS 3HP 3PH c/w sliding table	1202.00	1382.00
STARTRITE TA300PS Tilt Arbour Scoring Saw 1PH	1198.00	1377.00
WADKIN AGS250/300 Tilt Arbour 3HP 3PH 1024.00 1PH	1100.00	1265.00
WADKIN AGSP Tilt Arbour Scoring Saw 1PH	1261.00	1450.00
WADKIN SP12 Tilt Arbour Scoring Saw 4' return on table	2224.00	2557.00

RADIAL ARM SAWS

DW320 10 Foldaway Saw with TCT Blade	199.14	229.00
DW1251 10" Saw 1.5 HP 15" Crosscut	345.22	399.00
DW1501 10" Saw 1.5 HP 18" Crosscut	406.00	467.00
DW1751 10" Saw 1.5HP 24" Crosscut	467.00	538.00
DW8101 12" Saw 2HP 15" Crosscut	503.48	579.00
DW8101 12" Saw 2HP 24" Crosscut	575.65	662.00
WADKIN BRA Mod. I with Long Arm 28" X-Cut 14", 4HP	1545.00	1776.75
ELU PS174 Crosscut Mitre Saw 8" TCT Blade	233.92	269.00

BANDSAWS

DeWALT DW100 with Disc Sander + 2 Blades	129.57	149.00
DeWALT DW3401 2 Speed 6" Under Guides	225.63	259.00
DeWALT DW3501 Variable Speed 6" U Guides	229.57	264.00
STARTRITE 301 6×12 c/w Stand & 3 Guides	346.97	399.00
STARTRITE 351 8×13 c/w Stand & 3 Guides	430.45	495.00
STARTRITE 352 11×13 Cast Table, 3 Guides, Brake + 2 Speed	607.00	699.00
WADKIN C5 3HP 3PH 16" under guides, 19" Throat	1246.00	1433.00

We also stock Monniger Longlife blades in most popular sizes & lengths.

SPINDLE MOULDERS & TENNONERS

SCHEPPACH HF33 2HP, 3 Speed, 30mm Spindle	433.93	498.00
STARTRITE T30 2HP c/w Sliding Table for Tennoning	825.25	949.00
STARTRITE TZ30 Combined Spindle & Saw, 2 Motors + free block	1042.00	1199.00
SEDGWICK GW Spindle Moulder 1PH 2HP	940.00	1081.00
WADKIN BEL 5.5. HP, 30mm Spindle, Automatic Brake	1738.33	1999.00
MULTICO TM/1 Tennoner 2HP 1PH	1347.00	1549.00
SEDGWICK TE TENNONER	1560.00	1794.00

OMAS TOOLING

392 100×50 Tiger Head Blocks c/w box, stones & keys £62.10; Block only £46.00; 390 boxed set, inc. 9 pairs profiles & 4 blanks £99.00; Rebate Blocks with TCT cutters & scribes 125×50 £109.00; OM275 Panel Fielding blocks 200m £157.00; 10" TCT Wobblesaw 4-24mm £94.00.

UNIVERSALS

LUNA Z40 6" with TCT blade	633.93	729.00
STARTRITE K260 3 motors, PLUS FREE TIGER HEAD	1734.00	1990.00
STARTRITE K3104 motors NEW 12" machine 1PH + free kit	2695.00	3099.00

PLANER/THICKNESSERS

DeWALT DW1150 10×6 2HP	412.19	474.00
DeWALT DW600 Slot Mortice Attachment		69.00
SCHEPPACH HM2 Combi Planer Thicknesser	517.41	599.00
STARTRITE PT260 10×7 Plus FREE Pressure Guard	708.72	815.00
STARTRITE SD310 12×7 Plus FREE Pressure Guard 1PH	1213.00	1395.00
SEDGWICK PT 10X7 Cast Iron Planer Thicknesser 1PH	955.00	1098.25
MULTICO NS300 Surface Planer 2.4m Table 1PH	1390.00	1599.00
MULTICO CPT310/230 new Combined Machine 2 Motors 3PH	1564.50	1799.00

TCT Planer Knives: 10" — £110.00; 12" — £120.00 other sizes available — Phone.

LATHES

CORONET No. 1 Woodturning Lathe ½HP, 24" between centres	191.27	219.95
CORONET MAJOR ¾HP Lathe 33" between centres, 5 speed	521.72	599.95
TYME CUB 30" Bed ½ HP with Tuning Headstock	243.45	279.95
TYME Cub 36" Bed ½ HP with Turning Headstock	254.75	292.95
Tyme Avon 36" ¾ HP with Tuning Headstock	346.97	399.95
TYME Avon 48" ¾ HP with Turning Headstock	356.10	409.95
ELU DB180 1 Metre Bed	258.27	297.00

SORBY precision combination chucks stocked in many threads £56.90. Salt & Pepper mill mechs.; Sorby HSS turning tools. Liberon waxes; finishes; Drive centres; Tail centres; PLUS hundreds of other bits and pieces. Speedeneez friction polish £5.99.

MORTISERS

MULTICO HM bench mortiser 91/16 cap	320.00	369.00
MULTICO HMT New Bench Mortiser with Compound Table	430.45	495.00
MULTICO M/I 1" cap. New version 1.5HP 1PH	543.50	625.00
SEDGWICK 571 1" cap Mortiser 1PH	538.28	619.00
WADKIN EDA-2 1" cap including single wheel compound table	520.00	599.00
WADKIN DM/V Mortiser with Vibro Head	2342.00	2693.00
Ridgeway mortise stand	169.00	146.96

DUST EXTRACTION

DeWALT Twin Bag C/W Hose & Adaptors	229.57	264.00
MULTICO DEA New Mod, 2 Bag Extractor 15 cu. M/min. 1PH	299.00	343.85
LUNA W178 16cu. M/min 1PH	236.53	272.00
LUNA NF243 25cm M/min 1PH	346.97	399.00
STARTRITE Cyclair 75 single phase	433.93	499.00
P&J Mite wall-mounted extractor	180.00	207.00
P&J Mini Mobile twin-bag	280.00	322.00

MISCELLANEOUS MACHINES

ORTEGUIL ORC-55 mitre trimmer	199.00	229.00
ORTEGUIL ORC-100 Mitre Trimmer with Compound Table	339.14	390.00
MULTICO ORC-100 Mitre Trimmer with Compound Free Standing	480.00	552.00
LUNA YKV1200 Face & Edge Sander 1PH	647.85	745.00

INDUSTRIAL PREMIUM QUALITY TCT BLADES

SAME DAY SAW SHARPENING SERVICE AVAILABLE.

Diameter	5"		6"				7"				8"				9"			
No. of teeth	20	36	16	24	36	48	12	30	42	56	20	36	48	64	24	40	54	72
Price £	19	28	16	19	22	27	14	22	24	29	20	27	29	33	22	27	33	37

Diameter	10"				12"				14"				16"				18"	
No. of teeth	24	42	60	80	32	48	72	96	36	60	84	108	40	72	96	120	42	72
Price £	23	24	36	39	28	36	42	48	34	42	46	52	44	55	64	79	46	58

Diameter	18"		20"				22"		24"			26"	28"	30"
No. of teeth	108	140	48	80	120	160	50	84	56	72	100	56		60
Price £	76	90	52	69	86	105	66	81	70	80	95	105		139

Up to £1000 of Instant credit for personal callers — ask for written details.
Open 6 days a week 8.30-5.30. Second hand machines bought and sold.
PLEASE TELEPHONE FOR PRICE LIST AND BROCHURES.

TO AVOID DISAPPOINTMENT PLEASE PHONE FIRST TO CHECK AVAILABILITY.

THOUSANDS OF OTHER ITEMS ALWAYS IN STOCK

DEMO DAY SATURDAY 6th DECEMBER

HAND TOOLS

(£1.50 p&p per order)

PLANES

Stanley 04 Smooth Plane	£18.50
Stanley 04½ Smooth Plane	£20.00
Stanley 05 Jack Plane	£27.50
Stanley 05½ Jack Plane	£29.50
Stanley 06 Fore Plane	£36.00
Stanley 07 Fore Plane	£40.00
Stanley 10 Rebate Plane	£38.00
Stanley 60½ Block Plane	£18.00
Stanley 78 Duplex Rebate Plane	£22.00
Stanley 13050 Combination Plane	£60.00
Stanley 92 Cabinet Rebate Plane	£26.00
Stanley 92 Shoulder Plane	£23.60
Record 020C Circular Plane	£76.00
Clifton 3 in 1 Rebate Plane	£67.00
Clifton Rebate Plane 42D	£57.00
Stanley 90 Two-hand scraper	£8.90
Stanley 151M Flat spoke-shave	£8.00
Stanley 151RM Rounded spoke-shave	£8.00

Plane Irons — Jap laminated 2" £18.95 2⅜" £19.95

JAPANESE "SAMURAI" CHISELS "Superlative quality"

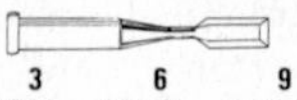

Size (mm)	3	6	9	12	15	18	24
"Silver Seal" (Ebony handled)	£17.95	£17.95	£17.95	£18.50	£18.95	£19.50	£20.95
"Bronze Seal" (Oak handled)	£7.40	£7.40	£7.40	£7.55	£7.75	£8.15	£9.05

WATER STONES

King Deluxe 800	£9.95
King Deluxe 1200	£9.95
King S3	£10.95
Henry Taylor slipstone set	£4.95
Soft Arkansas (medium) GP	£19.95
Hard Arkansas (fine)	£28.50
King Deluxe Slipstone	£4.95
Sun Tiger Slipstone	£9.95

SAWS

Atkinson Walker Gold flight 22 x 8pt	£6.95
Sorby 22 x 10pt	£14.95
Diston 22 x 10pt	£33.69
Diston 24 x 7pt	£30.33
Diston 26 x 6pt	£37.73
Diston D8 Tenon 12 x 12pt	£17.99
Tyzack	£12.63
Sanders 12 x 14pt 12 x 14pt	£13.28
A. Walker Gold flight	£4.50
Samurai 9½"	£15.99
Nobex Mitre saw 202	£44.00
Nobex Mitre Saw 303	£69.95

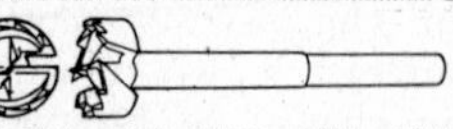

BITS, AUGERS, PLUG CUTTERS

Size ins.	⅜"	½"	⅝"	¾"	⅞"	1"	1⅛"	1¼"	1⅜2"	1½"	1⅝"	1¾"
Clico sawtooth bit	7.70	7.90	8.70	9.50	10.20	10.90	12.80	15.60	16.20	17.10	19.70	22.40
Plug cutter (tube type)	23.00	26.00	29.00	32.00	—	38.00	—	43.00	—	55.00	—	60.00

Ridgeway expansive bits: ½" - 1¾" med. duty £16.49; ⅞" - 2" H.D. £24.13; 1⅜" - 3⅛" H.D. £37.66
T.C.T. Plugmakers (specify head size 6 8 or 12) £18.35 Drill & Counter bore (specify head size 6, 8 or 12) £22.00

	6mm	8	10	12	13	14	16	18	19	20	22	25	28	32	36
W.S. Slot mortise cutters:	2.75	2.75	2.95	3.55	4.30	4.50	5.10	5.75	6.50	6.95	—	—	—	—	—
Augers, med. length. fit ½" ch'ks:	3.80	3.85	3.85	4.55	—	4.55	4.85	—	—	6.05	6.30	7.10	9.85	13.15	17.95

SORBY H.S.S. TURNING TOOLS — Handled

	⅛"	¼"	⅜"	½"	¾"	1"	1¼"
Roughing out gouges	—	—	—	—	19.46	—	23.38
Bowl gouges	—	11.57	14.58	18.42	—	—	—
Spindle gouges	5.97	7.43	8.41	9.98	14.80	—	—
Skew chisels	—	—	—	9.37	9.95	12.06	14.70
Square ended chisels	—	—	—	9.37	9.95	12.06	14.70
Scrapers square ended	—	—	—	8.90	10.37	12.11	14.70
Scrapers round nosed	—	—	—	8.90	10.37	12.11	14.70

Parting Tools: Standard ⅛" £7.20; Diamond sec 3/16" £15.27; Fluted 3/16" £15.92.

TURNING CENTRES

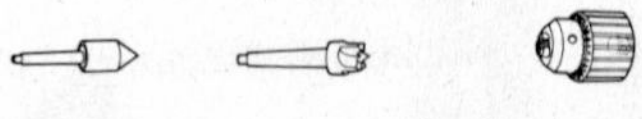

	1M	2M
4 Prong drive ctr. 1" dia.	7.94	8.17
4 Prong drive ctr. ⅜" dia.	7.48	7.71
2 Prong drive ctr. ¾" dia.	£7.19	£7.42
2 Prong drive ctr. ⅜" dia.	6.44	6.67
Jacobs Drill chuck ½" dia.	15.35	15.64
Jacobs Drill Chuck ¾" dia.	£32.78	£33.35
Revolving ctr.	19.26	19.49
Lace Bobbin Drive	7.76	7.99
Deluxe Rev. ctr.	28.41	29.56
Cup centre	4.03	5.06

Sorby Precision Combination Chuck £52.00.

CARVING TOOLS, ADZES, MALLETS

EMIR 210 3½" Beech mallet	£7.50
EMIR 211 3" Lignum Vitae mallet	£9.89
EMIR 211 3½" Lignum Vitae mallet	£12.94
Ridgeway 680 Carvers Adze curved	£19.29
Ridgeway 681 Carvers Adze straight	£16.79
Henry Taylor set of 8 Riffles	£44.00
Henry Taylor set of 6 Chisels	£34.00
Henry Taylor set of 12 Chisels	£62.00

VICES & SASH CRAMPS

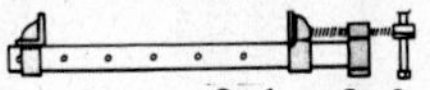

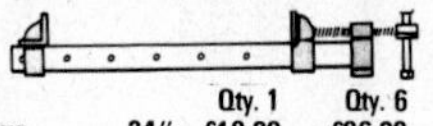

Record 52E 7" Wood Vice	£56.00
Record 52½E 9" Wood Vice quick Ret.	£65.00
Record 53E 10½" Wood Vice	£71.00
Record 141 Corner Cramp	£20.00
Record Cramp Heads	£10.30

Record Sash Cramp	Qty. 1	Qty. 6
24"	£19.00	£96.00
36"	£20.00	£102.00
42"	£21.00	£108.00
48"	£22.00	£114.00

TREND GRIPPER CLAMPS

Length:	8"	12"	15"	19"	23"	31"	39"	59"	79"
+D Gripper clamps	5.95	9.75	10.95	12.75	—	14.95	17.25	22.95	28.95

Deep Throat Gripper — Clamps

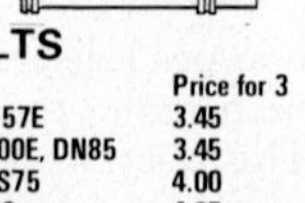

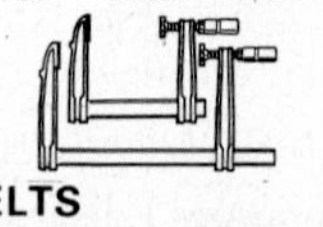

Throat depth	8"	12"	15"	19"
23" capacity length:	23.10	39.60	47.00	48.00
39" capacity length:	28.50	47.00	48.00	49.00

BANDSAW BLADES

	¼"	⅜"	½"	⅝"	¾"
Burgess 57"	3.20	3.30	—	—	—
Bed 59.5"	3.20	3.30	3.40	—	—
Coronet 67.5"	3.40	3.50	3.70	—	—
Inca 73"	3.70	3.80	3.90	4.50	4.70
DW3401 82.5"	3.95	4.10	4.20	5.10	—
Kity 612 83.5"	3.95	4.10	4.20	5.10	5.30
Minimax P32 85.5"	3.95	4.10	4.20	5.10	5.30
Startrite 301 88"	3.95	4.10	4.20	5.10	—
Startrite 351 102"	4.50	4.60	4.80	5.90	—
Startrite 352 112"	4.80	4.90	5.10	6.30	7.00

SANDING BELTS

Size	To Fit	Price for 3
75 × 480	Elu MHB157E	3.45
75 × 520	B&D SR100E, DN85	3.45
75 × 533	Bosch PBS75	4.00
100 × 560	Elu MHB90	4.95
100 × 610	Wolf, Makita, Ryobi	4.75

WIRE WOOL (Liberon, oil free)

	0000	000	00	0	1	2
250g	1.58	1.58	1.45	1.45	1.42	1.42
1kg	4.73	4.73	4.35	4.35	4.25	4.25

Coronet

SCOTT & SARGEANT

26 EAST STREET, HORSHAM, SUSSEX RH12 1HL

Tel: (0403) 53761, 65386, 50280. AFTER HOURS (0293) 84362

FASTEST SERVICE +++ BEST ADVICE +++ FASTEST SERVICE +++ BEST ADVICE +++ FASTEST SERVICE +++ BEST ADVICE +++ FASTEST SERVICE

Books

Patrick Spielman
Gluing and cramping
Sterling, £9.95
Reviewed by Bob Wearing

Patrick Spielman, who's written more than 14 books and is well-known in the American market, should be congratulated for putting this difficult subject into print. Not only does he avoid confusing jargon but provides a good glossary for the less technical-minded.

It is an American publication, so the adhesive brands are unknown to us with the exception of Aerolite. However the types of glues, characteristics and uses are covered in great detail along with the selection of wood for gluing.

There are a number of projects and illustrations of finished work but the basic designs are poor; it's mostly reproduction furniture which is probably popular in America. But the technical material is excellent. Even the experienced should learn from the detailed section on gluing, which deals with most kinds of jointing. Plastic laminates are fully explained including the useful method of 'bubble' removal.

Modern methods and equipment are prescribed for veneering and laminating and there is a handy section on repairs and equipment-making at the end of the book. It's clear from the large chapter on clamps (cramps) and gluing equipment that there's a far greater range in America than here — not only of cramps but kits and components to make yourself. I'm sure the American pipe clamp, a form of cramp-heads running on electrical conduit, and handscrew kits, would go down well here. There are some ingenious cramping methods for awkward jobs but the rubber bag press (vacuum press), an amazingly versatile tool that an amateur could make, isn't mentioned at all.

The layout is well designed and clear, with over 500 superb illustrations, both photographic and line-drawing, in 250 pages. It's both a good technical read and permanent reference.
● Bob Wearing is a regular contributor to *Woodworker* of vast experience.

E. J. Tangerman
Woodcarvers Pattern and Design Book
Sterling, £8.95 softback
Reviewed by Alan Bridgewater

E. J. Tangerman rides again! What a book! What an exciting, stimulating and inspirational read. Good old E.J., his books are always jam-packed full of patterns, motifs, little step-by-step tips, excellent illustrations and bags of black and white photographs. The problem with this book is not what to carve, but which of the 500 or so ideas to go for.

The book opens with a couple of sections on tools, materials and techniques, then launches into hundreds of inspirational patterns and ideas. Ball-in-cage folk whittling, cowboy reliefs, gargoyles, ogres, elves, horses, silhouettes, marquetry, mobiles, walking sticks, masks, netsuke toggles, Balinese figures — this book really is, as the cover blurb suggests, a treasury of ideas. And as with all E.J's books there are acres of details, plans, close-ups and notes.

This particular little Tangerman package seems to encapsulate the full flavour and spirit of traditional folk, tribal and ethnic woodcarving. On Balinese carving the drawings are worked with enthusiasm, the photographs good, if a little grainy, and the text is full of little gems. E.J. has been to Bali, and knows about prices, styles, tools and materials. He seems to appreciate the plight of the Balinese carvers who are highly skilled and underpaid. E.J. knows what to say about woodcarving techniques or types of carvings, and how to say it.

So whether you're a beginner or an experienced woodcarver, this book is a must.
● Alan Bridgewater is a multi-skilled craftsman and author who works with his wife Gill.

Well, we always have a problem when it comes to 'What's next month'. Not one of finding things to put in the country's best-selling woodwork journal; but one of saying 'You can't afford to miss it.' Face it, you can't afford to miss **any** *Woodworker*; but December's is a real cracker (not just the Xmas kind), even by our standards.

We visited **Martin Grierson**, maker of the quietly classical, subtly beautiful chair **above**; and we have a profile of **Sid Hatton**, a very unusual carver.

We have some **Christmas specials**, offers galore; plus your very own free **Woodworker wall planner** for 1987, to show you the year and remind you of the best days. We have some charming things you can easily **make for the children** for Christmas; we have details of Show entrant Paul Anderson's **clock.**

We have, in fact, just about anything you, as a woodworker who loves the style, the craft and just plain the wood itself, could ask for — it's only natural. December's *Woodworker* — don't miss it!

ON SALE 21 NOVEMBER

In brief

Shaker Design (*June Sprigg: W. W. Norton & Co., £32 hardback*)
This is an absolutely magnificent book. Page after luscious page of superb colour photographs of many and varied Shaker artefacts — not just furniture, but household equipment, tools (a mortiser included), boxes, graphic art and textiles. It is a catalogue of an exhibition at the Whitney Museum of Modern Art; June Sprigg, who has lived and worked with the surviving Shakers (12 left) of New England since 1972, has the authority of both personal experience and meticulous scholarship. A powerful and colourful insight into the lives and works of these mild-mannered and deeply religious people; their commitment to excellence and rejection of adornment has made their design and craft an abiding inspiration for all who love cleanliness of line and simplicity of form. We can't recommend it too highly — worth every penny and more. See a future *Woodworker* for an even better taste!

Federal Furniture (*Michael Dunbar: Taunton Press, £15.95 softback*)
Appearing in the office at the same time as *Shaker Design*, this book gives a fine opportunity to see what the Americans in the 'Outside world' were doing in the late 18th and early 19th centuries, when their new-found independence — so it's claimed — was inspiring craftsmen to embrace a 'dramatically different' furniture style; light, graceful, yet sturdy. Challenging but rewarding repro designs, particularly if you want to limit yourself to hand tools only; well written, well drawn, well photographed, but no colour. A good burst of history as an introduction; 20 projects for 'parlor', dining room, kitchen and bedroom. Good value.

You only need two hands with a MAXi 26

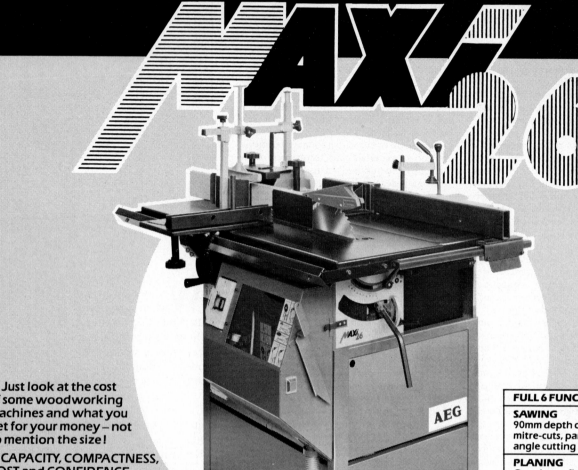

Just look at the cost of some woodworking machines and what you get for your money – not to mention the size!

CAPACITY, COMPACTNESS, COST and CONFIDENCE come together in the universal Maxi 26 – the ideal woodworking machine for the light professional and the keen hobbyist.

Look at the CAPACITY. Six functions – sawing, thicknessing, tenoning, planing, moulding and mortising – all effortless, with flexibility, precision and safety, and driven by a powerful and reliable 2 HP motor.

Look at its COMPACT design. The Maxi 26 is easily moved, even in the smallest of workshops.

Look at the COST. Buy a Maxi 26 and you still get change from £1350 (plus VAT, of course).

Look at the COMPETITION – and you **must** come back to the Maxi 26.

You can have every CONFIDENCE in the Maxi 26 – in its performance, and because it comes fully guaranteed for 2 years.

Designed and built to the highest standards, the Maxi 26 is the best value woodworking machine available today.

FULL 6 FUNCTIONS	
SAWING 90mm depth of cut, edging, mitre-cuts, panel cuts, 45° angle cutting	✓
PLANING On edge or flat, 260mm width of cut. Easy machining of any woods.	✓
THICKNESSING Up to 150mm capacity, depth of cut adjustable 0-4mm, automatic feed.	✓
MORTISING Deep, with both movements controlled by a single lever. Lateral and depth.	✓
MOULDING Moulding, rebates, grooving and all shaping tasks to a professional standard, 30mm diameter spindle shaft.	✓
TENONING Bearing mounted carriage 0-45° adjustable fence for precision square or angular cuts.	✓

AEG (UK) Limited
217 Bath Road, Slough, Berkshire SL1 4AW
Telephone: Slough (0753) 872101

AEG

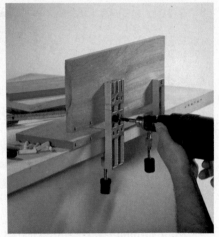

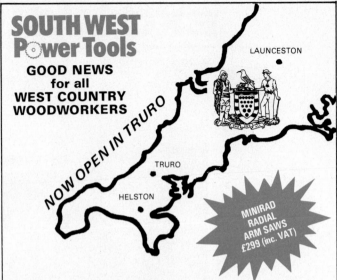

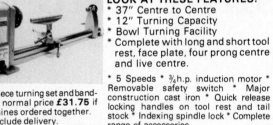

924

925

Taking the biscuit

Eric Coldwell is a fan of the biscuit jointer. He built this attractive pine corner cabinet with one, just to show what it can do

The style of this pine corner cabinet is derived from around the 18th century. The two sections, upper and lower, can be put together as a complete dresser, or you could use them individually as a corner display cabinet fastened to the wall, and a standing corner cabinet.

Unlike most corner cabinets, this design uses no screws or nails for joining; the method I used is more accurate, easier to assemble and there are no holes to stop up. My favourite secret fastening is biscuit jointing, a technique widely used in kitchen fitting, panel joining, and small-scale production.

The Elu DS140 biscuit jointer, as does the 'Lamello' tool, cuts neat half-moon grooves in matching positions in the faces to be joined. The 'biscuit' is an oval-shaped beech dowel, compressed in one direction only. Under the action of a water-based adhesive such as PVA, it expands laterally to fill the grooves, quickly forming a strongly bonded joint while the faces are clamped together.

I hadn't heard of this tool being used much for solid wood, so it was fascinating to try it out; it may give you ideas for other pieces of furniture where it could be useful. Another unusual aspect of this variation on 'cottage' corner cabinets is that the two sections can stand in their own right — as a corner wall display cabinet and a floor-standing cupboard.

Colour photos Guy Woollatt

● **Above**, this fine piece in traditional style will be at the Show for you to examine. **Above left**, the lower unit looks well on its own; **left**, a corner detail where
● it all meets. **Above right**, the first step; marking out the shelves from the dimensioned template

Our thanks to Elu Power Tools, Westpoint, The Grove, Slough, Berks SL1 1QQ, (0753) 74277 for their generosity in the preparation of this feature.

926

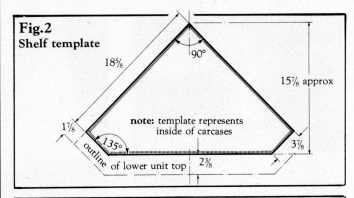

Fig.1 All dimensions in inches

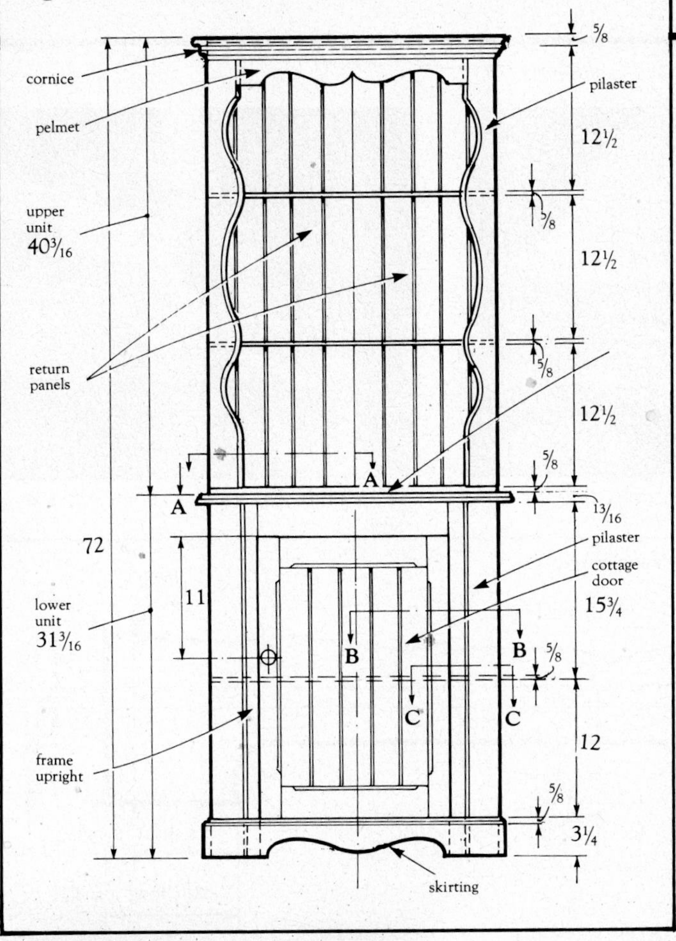

cornice

pelmet

pilaster

12½

upper
unit
40³⁄₁₆

7⁄8

12½

return
panels

5⁄8

12½

5⁄8

13⁄16

A — A

A

A

pilaster

cottage
door

15¾

72

11

lower
unit
31³⁄₁₆

B

B

5⁄8

C

C

12

frame
upright

5⁄8

3¼

skirting

Fig.2
Shelf template

18⁵⁄8

90°

15⁷⁄8 approx

1⁷⁄8

135°

note: template represents
inside of carcases

outline of lower unit top

2³⁄8

3⁷⁄8

Fig.3

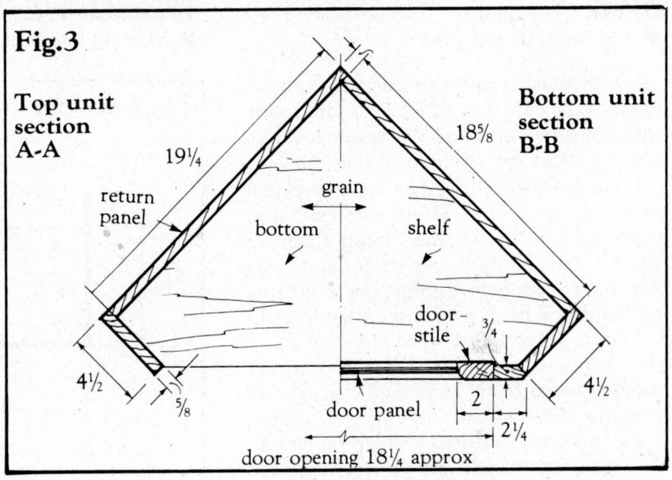

**Top unit
section
A-A**

**Bottom unit
section
B-B**

19¼

18⁵⁄8

return
panel

grain

bottom

shelf

door-
stile

¾

4½

5⁄8

door panel

2

2¼

4½

door opening 18¼ approx

Timber

Pine is the obvious choice for this 'cottage' piece, but it must be fully seasoned (preferably air-dried and old unused stock) and really flat — no perceptible wave in, say, a 14ft length of 8x⅞in sawn. Oak, ash and chestnut would also be suitable if they are as stable. If you are doubtful about your wood's stability, keep the boards in a warm room for 3-6 months before using it; central heating isn't friendly to newly made solid furniture.

Consider what finish you want before you start, for it's best to finish inner surfaces before gluing to avoid difficulties. You don't have to stain, but people usually do; try out stains on scrap pieces, sealing and waxing to discover the results.

Construction

The main dimensions and features are shown in fig. 1. To allow for wood movement the shelves aren't glued to the return panels, though the biscuit dowels are; the result is good rigidity and strength. The overall heights of the units, 31in and 40in, are quite arbitrary, and so is the shelf spacing. I used ⅝in timber for the shelves and return panels, with slight variations elsewhere, but it depends what you have.

Before you start, make the shelf template (fig. 2) which is vital at many stages; if you stick on a label with the dimensions it saves time. The widths of the return panels and pilaster are arbitrary, but the right angle must be 90°, and the template should be perfectly accurate, cut from hardboard or ⅜in ply. The grain of the solid timber shelves and bottoms must run as shown in fig. 3. To avoid warping, you should assemble the units soon after cutting.

Cut the lengths for the four return panels first, since only fairly short pieces are needed for the shelves. Cut the lengths about 1in oversize, prepare and thickness them so you have enough to make up the upper panels, 20x40in and the lower 20x31in. You can use equal or various widths of wood. After planing, square off one end and cut all the pieces to exact length — it's easier than trying to cut square ends on the 20in glued-up width. Clamp a planed batten across the bench, and butt the pieces up to it in sets, reversing alternate grain direction. Make reference marks across the joins, then stack all the pieces in four sash-

cramps dry to resist warping and set them aside.

Shelves

Choose the better faced pieces of wood for the upper unit shelves, for they will be on show. Referring to fig. 2, and particularly the template, cut to the different lengths you need, and finish them to ⅝in thick. As you'll notice in fig. 2, the top of the lower unit is larger and thicker than the shelves.

Mark the face sides, and then fit the pieces together to make up the triangular shelf shapes; put reference marks, using letters or numbers, at the joins so you know how they will fit together. Now lightly mark the outline of the template, and decide where the biscuit dowel slots should go. To mark these, draw vertical lines at the centre of where the slot will be cut. Use no. 20 biscuits and a 'pitch' of about 4½in.

I set the fence close up to the vertical face of the groover, which makes it cut more or less centrally in ⅝in wood. It doesn't matter if the slot is slightly off-centre, provided each cut is made with the fence against the face side; all similar slot cutting should be done with the fence on the face. For these biscuits the groover depth should be set to 12 on the scale.

I use a vice for holding the pieces while cutting, because it's quicker than clamping the wood to the bench, but you need a little practice. Keep the machine steady and in line, plunging slowly. With longer pieces cut half the slots at a time, and then move the wood along in the vice so it is held rigidly. When the cutter is fully engaged,

Taking the biscuit

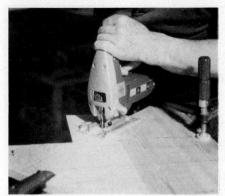

● *Cutting out the shelf*

● *Planing shelf edges, apex first*

● *Biscuiting a shelf edge – it takes a knack*

move it forwards and then backwards about 2mm; this cuts a slightly elongated slot which allows for small discrepancies, but doesn't affect the strength of the joint.

Glue the pieces together, using a pencil brush to apply the PVA; glue one slot, insert and tap down the biscuit firmly. I glued biscuits into alternate slots on matching edges before gluing the projecting halves of the biscuits and the edge areas in between. After pressing the pieces of wood together, you can cramp them up, using the other pieces from the shelf triangle as packing. Clean off surplus glue with a damp rag immediately. When you have glued up one complete panel, leave it in cramps for about two hours before assembling the next.

Once all these are assembled, lay the template on each blank in turn and mark its outline. Using a jigsaw or bandsaw, cut out each one about 1mm oversize, before trimming on the planer, using light cuts and checking with the template regularly. If you use a planer for this, you must be careful not to drag the apex of the blank over the cutters, or you could have substantial breakout — so feed in from each direction, apex first, to about a halfway point.

Use a bench saw and fence to trim the shorter pilaster edges at 90° to the panel edges. The groover fence needs a smooth surface to slide along, so sand both sides of each shelf. The best figured panels should be chosen for the upper unit shelves and bottom, and marked as such.

Now for grooving them all. Take up the biscuit jointer again, without altering the fence setting or depth, and groove along the return panel edges from the apex to just short of the front edge. Change the depth setting for no. 0 biscuits and groove along the pilaster edges. In the *top* of the upper unit and the *bottom* of the lower unit, cut a suitable number of slots for no. 8 or 10 biscuits so you can secure the pelmet and lower stretcher rail respectively. Radius the front edges where required, but not the lower unit shelf. Now you can set the six shelves aside, stacked flat under weights to prevent warping.

Return panels

Make up the return panels one at a time,

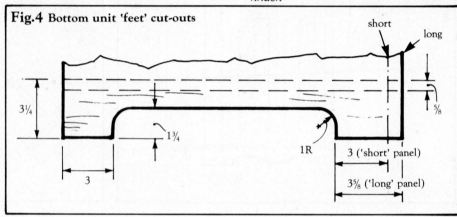

Fig.4 Bottom unit 'feet' cut-outs

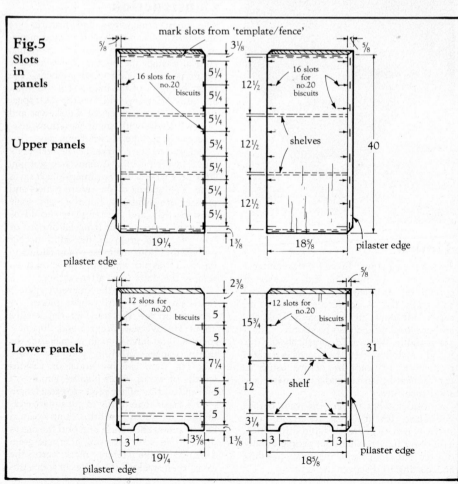

Fig.5 Slots in panels

Upper panels

Lower panels

● Cutting V-grooves in the panels: enlarged router base avoids 'wander'

● Cutting slots for biscuits in the panels against the 'template/fence' – note the registration lines

**Fig.6
Lower unit
front corner
detail**

shelf cut
back to
take door
frame

⅝

1

pilaster

¾

2¼

remove
waste
after
joining

door stile

upright

no.10 biscuit

using four sash-cramps. First clamp a stout edge-faced batten across and near the end of the table at 90° to the front edge, and place the top ends of the machined stock squarely to it, alternating the grain, and with face side up; put reference marks at the joins. Mark positions of the shelves on the edge of the front piece, and draw dotted lines across, giving the line of the slot for no. 20 biscuits (fig. 5). Mark the position of the slots — about a 5in pitch — but make sure you don't clash with the shelf dowel slots. Draw vertical lines across the mating edges, and then use a planer or shooting board to obtain good edges. After cutting the slots — remember the fence should always be on the face side — set up the four sash-cramps with two sturdy protective laths for the outside.

Put the panel pieces on the cramps, and glue up as before, taking two pieces at a time and using the remainder as packing. You have to make sure the ends match exactly, for they are already cut to length. Even if you only have four cramps, you can complete four panels in a day using this system, at say two hours per cramped panel. Finally take the completed panels out of the cramps and lay each piece flat, stacked up on top of each other, and leave overnight.

Now you should do some preliminary sanding on both sides of the panels, using nothing coarser than 100-grit paper; you could use an orbital sander for this. Choose the front edges and cut them to width, remembering that one of each pair should be ⅝in wider to allow for the back overlap. Skim the sawn edges square, and mark the four top edges (with a felt tip pen) for quick positive identification.

The next job is to join these panels, and you should deal with one unit at a time. With back edges against one another, re-mark the parallel lines across the inside faces indicating the shelf positions. Mark out the slot positions for the no. 20 biscuits which will join the panels; also mark biscuit positions matching the grooves already cut in the shelves and for the pilasters on the front edges (fig. 5).

For locating the shelf and bottom positions, prepare the template/fence you can

see in the photo above. It is hefty, straight, and the biscuit centres are marked all round.

Working on the upper unit, cut the top and bottom slots first, using the previously set fence position — but check that the depth is suitable — and then those for the panel and pilaster joints. Repeat the process for the lower unit.

Now remove the groover fence. Clamp the template/fence into position on the wood, and use the etched centre lines on the groover's face to cut the slots across the widths.

The three bracket feet in the lower unit are produced by making the simple cut-outs shown in figs 4 and 5; I think they suit the 'cottage' style and minimise damage if you move the piece.

The V-grooves, about 2mm deep, in the inside faces of the return panels (fig. 1) are produced with a router — they aren't strictly necessary with the lower unit, since they won't show with the door closed. These V-grooves are a bit tricky. I enlarged my router base to prevent wandering, and use a long piece of 1in thick ply as a fence. My slow light cuts were about 3½in apart, and certainly improve the appearance of the cabinet.

Sand the inner panel surfaces, using 150-grit paper, and apply soft wax stopping where necessary, before trying a dry assembly. Put biscuits in all the slots, and lay the carcases on the sash cramps. Check the shelves are parallel, that everything is correctly at right angles, that biscuits fit, and that the short pilaster edges of the shelves aren't proud of the return panel front edges.

If all is well, dismantle and prepare for staining. With pine I use a brush coat of 50/50 linseed oil and white spirit around knots and other wild grain to encourage more even staining. I applied Jackson's Weathered Pine oil stain with a rag and left it for 24 hours, thinning to give a lighter shade for the interior faces. Then I finished with two or three coats of transparent

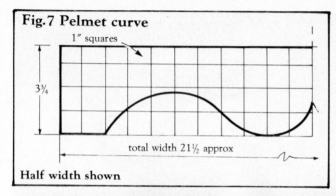

Fig.7 Pelmet curve

1" squares

3¾

total width 21½ approx

Half width shown

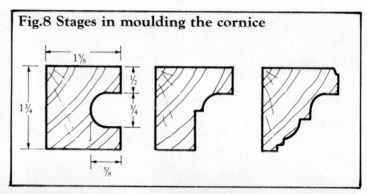

Fig.8 Stages in moulding the cornice

1⅝

½

1¾

¾

⅝

● *Cutting out the curved pelmet*

● *Jigsaw shoe at 45° for the bevelled uprights*

● *Cutting the cornices at an accurate 26½°*

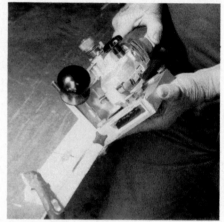

● *A bit tricky – slotting in a bevelled edge*

polish, sanding lightly between coats and afterwards. When it's thoroughly dry, stack under weights as before.

Pilasters

Prepare the four pieces to the same thickness and lengths as the panels, and mark the positions of the biscuit slots by transference from the panel edges. I added two no. 0 slots at the top of the upper ones to fix the mitred edges of the pelmet, though you don't have to have a pelmet. I also transfer-marked the slots to be used to join on the frame uprights in the lower units (see figs 1 and 6). Cut all the slots, then clamp the upper pilasters together and use a full-size grid to establish and mark out the curved profile, ensuring the lobes fit in with the shelf positions. Cut out both together, sand, stain and seal the inside surfaces.

Assemble the units dry again, adding the pilasters and securing with sash cramps. Now you can measure, make and fit the pelmet (fig. 7); this should be from ½in timber. If you use biscuits in the mitres, slot in the same way as the lower unit uprights (described below), but you may need to make shallow grooves in the pelmet and deeper ones in the pilasters.

Each unit should be glued up in three stages, starting with the upper unit. Glue the biscuits into the panel faces and leave them to set; no glue is used on the shelf biscuits. Fix the corner joint; after gluing it, insert the shelves, the top and the bottom and the pilasters (unglued), cramp and leave to set. Then uncramp and glue on one

pilaster, no. 1 biscuits glued in the shelves but not the pilasters. Glue the other pilaster.

Cornice

You can use either a cutter block or a router for shaping this. Fig. 8 shows the profile I used, but you can choose whatever shape you want, depending on what cutters you have; I used a combination of bench saw, small router table and two main cutters. Having worked out your design, plan how you're going to achieve it. Allow extra length and make some additional pieces in case you need them.

The mitre joints are at 67½°, not 45°; cut them, and the appropriate no. 0 slots. Sand

the unit top and the pilasters, dry assemble to test fit, and finally glue the three parts to the unit (³⁄₁₆in proud if you wish) to complete the upper unit.

Now for the lower unit. Prepare pieces for the top, for the pilasters and for frame uprights (figs 1/6). The top should be ⅞in thick, but use fig. 2 to determine the make-up lengths and check with the template. Make up similarly to the shelves, and set aside.

The lower unit is assembled the same way as the upper, but bevel the edges of the two uprights which will join to the pilasters. The door frame is 1in thick, so recess the shelf front to both accommodate it and to serve as a stop. Mark the shelf front with the uprights laid in place, and cut out the recesses with a router end-mill cutter before finally radiusing the edge. Glue up as you did before, leaving the shelf and bottom loose. Mark the slot positions for no. 10 biscuits in the frame uprights, transfer-markings from the pilasters; cut these by hooking the side fence over the bevel edge. Dry-fit the assembly of the uprights to the pilasters with biscuits in place; the over-hanging lip of the bevel is removed later. Glue the pilasters to the return panels, with non-glued biscuits in the shelf and bottom.

The top horizontal stays are 2¾x¾in in section, the bottom ones 3¼x¾in, and cut overlength. Replace the uprights and cut the stays to fit flush. Mark out and cut slots for no. 12 biscuits in the stay ends, four in all, and the frame uprights. Do a final dry assembly check, then cut three slots for

Fig.9 Skirting curve

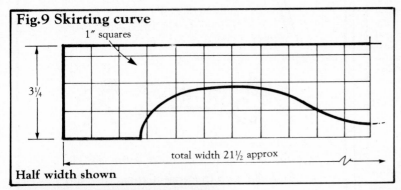

1″ squares

3¼

total width 21½ approx

Half width shown

Fig.10 Skirting slots

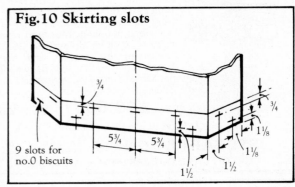

9 slots for
no.0 biscuits

¾

¾

5¾ 5¾

1⅛

1⅛

1½ 1½

1½

Fig.11 Door rail end

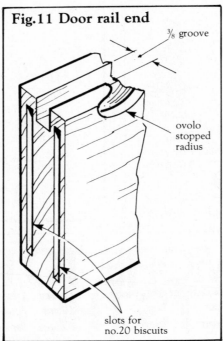

⅜ groove

ovolo
stopped
radius

slots for
no.20 biscuits

● *The 'double biscuit tenon', one biscuit in*

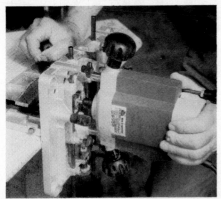

● *Moulding edges is easy with a
right-angled router base*

no. 0 biscuits in the edge of the bottom shelf and the corresponding face of the stay before gluing the pieces to the carcase. You'll find angular cramping pads made up from scrap help here, and the overhanging lips will accept two sash-cramps if you're careful. When set, remove waste from uprights and sand flush.

Skirting

Prepare a piece to 3¼x⅝in and about 34in long, and mould the top edge with a simple ogee cutter. Sand the outside face and cut the three 67½° mitred pieces. Mark these out for no. 0 biscuits (fig. 10). After checking dry, glue all pieces to the carcase. Mark and cut the profile (fig. 9) in both rail and skirting simultaneously, noting that the

centre portion of the skirting clears the floor line.

Door

Make the stile lengths to suit the door opening; the square-ended top and bottom rails should fit exactly between them to give the correct overall width. The panel should be the right thickness to fit loosely inside the ⅜in rail grooves. The rail thickness allows slots for no. 20 biscuits, two at each end (fig. 11) and lying between the slot and the groove and the outside rail edges. This gives a double biscuit which is really strong. It's a joint I developed by experiment when I first got a groover years ago; I joined two pieces of wood at 90° using two biscuits, then tested the joint to destruction over several days. The assembly finally broke down, but the bulk of the actual joint remained intact. So I've used it frequently since.

Cut the 16 slots with the fence close to the groover face, operating from each face. Plunge the blade into the end grain slowly and carefully, holding the machine very steady; I find holding the work in the vice is best for this. Dry assemble with the biscuits

in place using sash cramps. If you've done the job correctly, you'll hear satisfying friction noises as the biscuits settle in the groove. Mark the joints and set aside.

Prepare the panel, allowing ⅜in extra all round. I used four lengths slightly less than ⅜in thick, joining them with no. 0 biscuits and cutting the slots with the aid of a packing strip to get them central.

For the grooves in the door I used the biscuiter, which is ideal; in the stiles the wood between the slots must not be removed, so I did some chiselling out at the corners.

Use the router to produce the stopped radii on the front-facing inner rail edges. Then change to a V-cutter to make four shallow equidistant grooves on the sanded outside panel face. Finish both sides of the panel to the touch-dry stage, then glue the door together with the panel inserted freely in the grooves and allow to set.

Fit the door to the opening, using 2/2½in brass butt hinges — old ones if you have them. Fit a suitable door catch; I used a 'cupboard turn' after antiquing the brass knob, and consequently had to pad out the inside of the upright with ¼in wood to catch the lever.

Lower unit top

Hold your breath and fit the upper unit on top of the lower; I hope the fit is acceptable! Now mark out the top using the template, again referring to fig. 2; cut and fit it to the carcase and sand both sides. Mould the overhanging edges and then completely finish the underside. Secure it to the carcase with shrinkage plates; I made my own from ½x½in 16 gauge brass angle.

The upper unit needs to lightly hold on the lower, but obviously screw holes won't do. I made two brass plates. secured at the centre of the return panels. They are unobtrusive, and the screw holes can be filled if the units are used separately.

Put a mild radius on the back corner edges and sand and stain the outside of the return panels. Complete by waxing; I used Jakpol, which the surfaces readily accepted, applying three coats inside and out.

It's a satisfying piece to make, and the biscuiter speeds up jointing no end. ■
● Polish and waxes; J. Jackson and Co. Ltd, 76-9 Alscot Rd, London SE1 3AW, 01-237 2862.

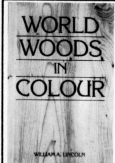

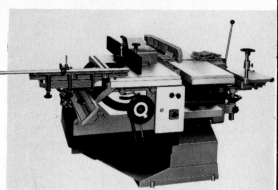

932

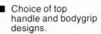

933

Question box

Unusual wood

Q *I made a goblet from a local timber, ilex, and am fascinated by its interesting grain. It's referred to in Glossary of Woods as 'holly' and in Chambers Dictionary as 'holm oak'. Can you put the record straight?*

A The timber which you've used is probably holm oak, also known as evergreen oak. This timber is indigenous to the Mediterranean area but has been extensively planted in the UK. Holm oak has the same uses as European oak, although it is denser and harder.

The confusion between your two references, is due to the botanical nomenclature of holm oak and holly. Holm oak is botanically *Quercus ilex* of the family *Fagaceae*. Holly is *Ilex aquifolium* of the family *Aquifoliaceae*. The word 'Ilex' is used as the genus in holly and the species in holm oak, but in no way relates to timbers.

Both woods are referred to in *The Handbook of Hardwoods*, published by the Department of the Environment.

Ron Hooks

● Ron Hooks is a professional timber consultant.

Japanning

Q *Could you tell me how to make and apply Japan lacquer?*

P. Rafferty, Australia

A Japanning is a process originating from China, around 2000BC, but developed by the Japanese who became the masters of the technique. The method was simply to cover a substrate with 15-20 layers of lacquer; each coating film was flatted and burnished before further coats of lacquer were applied. The original lacquer was shellac varnish over black pigment. When dry and burnished the substrate was decorated with gold or gilt. English lacquer was later developed, made up of copal resins and drying oils such as linseed or tung. The first British DIY book on the technique, by John Stalker and George Parker in 1688, was called 'A Treatise of Japanning'.

Back to the questions — it's rather wasteful in time and expense to make your own lacquer. I suggest a good quality copal varnish or lacquer: Japan varnish or John Mylands No. 8 Lacquer are fast drying varnishes and will do the job.

Workshop procedure:
● Prepare substrate to a fine smooth surface. Damp down to raise the grain, fill, and stop all imperfections; sand down and dust.
● Apply one coating of spirit black pigment and allow to dry out.
● Apply one coat of your choice of lacquer and allow to dry out.
● Flat down this film with either 320-grit silicon carbide papers (Lubrisil) used dry, or 400-grit silicon carbide wet or

dry used with soft water (rain or distilled) or white spirit.
● Clean off with a dry cloth and apply further coatings of the lacquer, flatting down between each film of lacquer until the satisfactory surface is obtained, at least five coats.
● The final coating can be flatted down using 600-grit wet-and-dry papers, dusting off and burnishing using medium and fine burnishing pastes until you have a full mirror-gloss finish; use a well-washed mutton cloth.

Don't stint on materials and tools — use the best. Buy varnish brushes or mops and use the right abrasive papers, not glasspapers. Good japanning needs all the patience and skill you can muster.

Noel Leach

Polish on polyurethane

Q *I have a mahogany table brush-finished in polyurethane which I want to french polish. Will I have to strip it or can I just rub it down?*

D. Tinch, Orkney

A You can't french polish over polyurethane, because the materials are incompatible. You can either remove all the polyurethane and french polish from scratch, or keep the polyurethane as a base and produce an effect similar in appearance to french polish.

1 Keeping the polyurethane finish:
● Flat down the whole surface using 400 or 600-grit wet-and-dry silicon carbide abrasive papers with distilled water or soft rainwater and a little dissolved household soap to remove all brush marks. Do this carefully so you don't rub through the polyurethane.
● Using a standard light brown furniture wax polish (silicon-free) burnish the whole surface using fine steel wool, grade OOO. Dip the steel wool in the wax and apply it in the direction of the grain until you get a smooth finish.
● Remove all traces of the wax polish using a clean piece of mutton cloth.

This will give you a smooth satin patina with the original surface coating undisturbed.

2 French polishing from scratch:
● Strip off all traces of polyurethane varnish with paint or varnish stripper.
● Neutralise the substrate with either water, white spirit or methylated spirits, depending which type of stripper used (follow the manufacturer's instructions).
● Sand down the surface using 240-grit garnet paper.
● Re-stain if required: fill the grain, sand down, re-colour and allow to dry.
● French polish to a full gloss. Finish off using either the 'spiriting off' method or the 'acid finish' — the choice is yours.

Noel Leach

● Noel Leach is a professional woodfinisher and lecturer.

Rabbet, rabbet

Q *David Savage's article on planes (Tools of the Trade, WW/Jul) provoked several questions. Firstly, why is the mouth of a rabbet plane at a different angle from most other planes?*

In my collection of planes – rabbet, larger shoulder, smaller shoulder, bull nose – I found that the vertical angle of the irons differs in all four. Why is this?

Finally, the word 'rebate' instead of 'rabbet' was used throughout the article – have both words always been used or is one older?

P. Tonks, Bromsgrove, Worcs

A Your letter illustrates the great diversity of styles, sizes, patterns and tastes in planes throughout the ages. Really one can do no better than consult the marvellous book *Dictionary of Tools used in the Woodworking and Allied Trades*, by R. A. Salaman.

● The skew mouth of the rabbet/rebate plane is not a consistent feature of all such planes but does seem to be more common in wooden planes than in metal ones; one benefit of the skew mouth with its correspondingly 'skewed' chip clearance aperture is that the shavings are deflected to the side and are less likely to choke. There are both left-skewed and right-skewed models.

Another possible explanation lies with manufacturing advantage rather than with benefit in use; a skewed cut engages the wood to be planed with less of the cutter on a series of initial cuts. Thus the shock to the plane of entering the wood with a portion of the width of the plane is reduced when compared with the shock across the whole width of the plane with a square mouth/cutter. This would reduce the danger of damage to the wooden point of the plane immediately behind the cutter, which would otherwise receive a constant battering in the direction of the grain (of the plane) across a width of say, $7/8$in. Imagine a head-on confrontation between a possibly suspect beech plane and mahogany!

● The iron is set at a low angle of about 20° but since the sharpening bevel is uppermost, the effective angle remains at about 50°. The object of this is to support the iron right up to the cutting edge and so avoid 'chattering' when working endgrain.

The variations between 16° and 27° can, I think, be ascribed to maker's and possibly users' preference, as craftsmen frequently adjust tools to their own style of working.

● The words 'rabbet' and 'rebate' are interchangeable and both come from the Latin via the French 'rabat' which is in between the two. Incidentally, the Scottish name for such a plane is 'geelum', clearly a corruption of the French *guillaume* — the name in France for a rabbet/rebate plane.

Alan Reid

● Alan Reid is managing director of Clico Tools, Sheffield.

Question box

Our panel of experts solve
your woodworking problems

We will try to answer any questions
you can throw at us, but the ones we
publish are the ones of most general
interest to readers.
Please type your question double-
spaced with generous margins, and
include a stamped self-addressed
envelope. Send it to: Question Box,
Woodworker, 1 Golden Sq., London
W1R 3AB.

Protecting keruing

Q *I have a five-barred gate in Malayan
keruing, with oak supports, and have
used teak oil as weather-proofing.
What other precautions can I take?*
J. Humble, Winchcombe

A Whatever preservative is applied to
your gate and posts, it should be put
on when the wood is dry after a spell of
good weather. If the wood is wet when
treated the moisture will be trapped inside
and the life of the gate considerably
shortened.

The posts are most liable to rot just above
ground level where the wood suffers greatly
from alternating between being wet and
dry. It will help if the concrete in which the
posts are bedded slopes downwards away
from the posts to assist drainage.

A reliable wood preservative such as
Cuprinol or Solignum should be brushed
liberally all over the gates and posts; make
sure that all endgrain is well soaked. Brush
plenty in around the mortise-and-tenon
joints and where the braces cross the bars. If
treatment is carried out annually the gates
and posts will last for many years.

Most wood preservatives are obtainable
in a choice of colours, or colourless, so you
can keep the natural colour of the wood if
you want.

You will find keruing an extremely
durable timber.

Charles Cliffe

Colour matching

Q *I have made a Welsh dresser in parana
pine and red deal and found that a clear
polyurethane varnish darkens the pine
but has no effect on the deal. (Luckily I used
scrap wood first).*
How do I achieve a colour match?
J. Bramham, Clwyd

A Making furniture from mixed timbers frequently gives rise to difficulties at the finishing stage. The colour may be
even but the different grain patterns are
noticeable, particularly to the trained eye.
So even if your parana pine is the same

colour as the red deal, the more
pronounced grain in the deal will show
through.

Most woods can be made lighter by
bleaching. You'll need to experiment on
some scrap pieces of parana pine to see how
light it must be so that it's the required
colour after it's been varnished. Polish
suppliers sell a two-part bleach for lighten-
ing wood. Follow the manufacturer's instructions carefully regarding wearing
rubber gloves, avoiding splashes, methods
of application and neutralising when the
work is done.

If you can't get a two-part bleach, you
could bleach with oxalic acid which your
chemist should stock. Dissolve 2oz oxalic
acid crystals in hot water and apply evenly
to the wood. You may need to go over the
work a second time. Neutralise with diluted
ammonia and wash clean with cold water.

Oxalic acid is poisonous so wear rubber
gloves and protective overalls and never use
it with wire wool.

Having bleached the wood and glasspapered it smooth you can varnish a test
piece to compare its colour with the red
deal. If it's too light you can stain it with a
weak solution of walnut stain to deepen its
colour.

Charles Cliffe

Rosewood chair

Q *I plan to make a rosewood chair to match
three I bought dating from around 1830.
Can you tell me where to buy the wood
and how to obtain the mellow patina of the old
rosewood surfaces?*
A. K. Jones, Tunbridge Wells

A The chairs are probably of Brazilian
rosewood and to make an exact match
you really need a supply of old rosewood of
the same species. As this is highly unlikely, I
suggest you approach rosewood suppliers
who advertise in *Woodworker* to see what's
available.

When you've completed your chair, you
will need to experiment with various stains
on pieces of scrap wood to see which stain
gives the best colour match. A very old
method for rosewood was to boil 8oz of oak
bark and a similar amount of walnut shells
in half a gallon of water to give a pleasing
brown stain.

A chemical stain to give a similar shade
can be made by dissolving 1oz permanganate of potash in a pint of warm water,
but it is likely to fade in time. Many polish
houses supply water-soluble aniline
powder stains in rosewood and various
brown shades and with a blend of these
colours you should get a close match.

Let the stain dry for at least 24 hours
before french polishing and do not use any
raw linseed oil on the face of the polishing
rubber when bodying up; otherwise you
will have trouble later on with oil 'sweating'
through the polish. The turned and reeded
legs together with the fretted back rail will
have to be brush polished. Allow the polish

to harden for about two weeks before
gently matting with OOOO wire wool; dust
thoroughly ready for waxing. Use a light
coloured antique wax and after five or six
applications, well rubbed in, you will have a
deep, mellow polish.

Charles Cliffe
● Charles Cliffe is a professional polisher,
author and teacher.

Timber conversion

Q *I have a small workshop, with little
power equipment, and need to convert
timber for sculpting. How do I convert a
plain bench, with apron vice, to handle 4ft logs
of 12in dia.? Can a small chainsaw tackle logs
this size which have been air-dried?*
J. D. Ralphs, Herefordshire

A In view of your limited facilities it
might be best to get a local sawmill to
convert your timber. However, there are a
number of techniques you could try
although it is easier to convert timber from
the round when it's first felled, i.e. not dried
out. The simplest way to reduce the logs to
manageable halves and billets is to split the
timber with a beetle and and wedge. This
and other age-old techniques — using the
adze, side axe, draw knife — are described
in *Woodland Crafts of Britain* by Herbert
Edlin, available as a David & Charles
reprint. It also illustrates the horse and the
shaving break; two devices for cradling the
timber being worked on, which should be
of use to you.

You could modify your bench top to
carry a number of 'dogs' so you could grip
your smaller timber for secondary sawing.
Cut a row of 1in square mortises in the top
close to the front edge and spaced 6in apart,
and drive temporary dogs or wedges into
them. The timber then overhangs the front
of the bench; secure it lengthwise by
trapping it between the nearest dogs. Then
you can rip off lengths parallel to the bench
edge.

You've probably heard of sculptor Willie
Soukop who works directly into the log
with a chainsaw, producing interesting
textural effects. These saws need very
careful handling for converting timber and
the electrically driven DIY models are not
up to ripping baulks of hardwood on a
continuous basis. The cradle-mounted
petrol-driven chainsaws which make up a
portable timber mill are much better at the
job, but, of course, represent a larger
financial investment.

Confronted with a similar problem to
yours I have hand-sawn small baulks to size
using a 26in ripsaw of four teeth per inch. If
you do buy one, specify the above to your
tool merchant and ask for a well-known
brand name.

Bob Grant
● Bob Grant is head of Craft Design and
Technology at an Oxford comprehensive
school and teaches courses for the Guild of
Woodworkers.

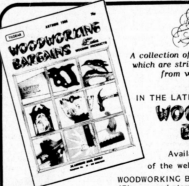

939

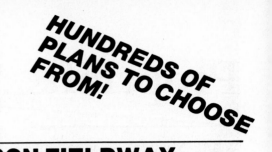

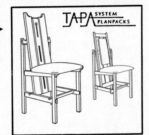

Propcraft

White Shapers — wooden propeller makers — had a brief but vital role in aviation history, as Jim Kingshott reveals

You may think the wooden aircraft propeller is just a simple engineering creation, possessing a classic simplicity reminiscent of a fine sculpture. You couldn't be more wrong. The propeller has always been one of the most difficult parts of an aircraft to design, and is anything but simple to construct. The craft of the white shaper probably reached its zenith during the 1914-18 war, when production was still mainly by hand, and many regard it as the greatest achievement of technical woodwork. It took more than 800 man-hours to make a propeller or airscrew, depending on how many blades were involved.

There are several ways in which engine power can be turned into propulsive thrust

● *Checking the profile on a massive wind tunnel blade, and,* **inset,** *an aircraft blade*

for an aircraft. Early designers of balloons proposed the use of oars. In 1836 one inventor was convinced the right answer was paddle wheels. In 1852 the first screw-propelled airship made headway against a moderate wind.

Until this century the propeller was a series of straight beams rotating about a centrepoint with curved plates fixed to their outermost tips. By 1900 simple wind tunnels were being used and the science of aerodynamics had begun; propellers could be designed based on actual measurements, not just on vague hunches. The internal combustion engine made it possible to drive the propeller much faster.

The result was a much neater and smaller propeller carved from wood instead of the huge end-plate screw used by the early pioneers. These early carved propellers were made from one solid lump of ash,

spruce or mahogany, but the makers soon found that they could be made much stronger and more stable if they were cut from a laminated block.

Stresses

There are two steady stresses on an airscrew blade and hub, due to the centrifugal pull of the blades — the force which tends to pull the rotating blades from the hub, and the bending force produced by the thrust which tries to bend the blades forward. Yes, forward; the propeller's thrust, or pull, comes from pushing back the air, and this air has a resulting equal thrust on the *back* of the blades. The centrifugal force on the blades is useful because the more the blades deflect forwards because of increased thrust, the more the outward centrifugal force tries to return them to their original plane of rotation. That's why wooden

blades frequently have forward rake or tilt; as soon as the blades rotate, the centrifugal force relieves the bending. Centrifugal force is also responsible for very severe loads on the roots of the blades.

Apart from these steady stresses, there are two vital considerations in the strength of an airscrew — flutter and vibration. Certain aerodynamic influences attempt to make the blade flutter, and if it is not stiff enough, a major structural failure may result. The fluctuating torque of an internal combustion engine, caused by the interval between successive power strokes, leads to severe vibrating stresses in the driving airscrew. Obviously a propeller must be in perfect balance, otherwise it vibrates when rotating; for this reason all the components of an airscrew are built to very close tolerances, and are balanced at various stages of manufacture.

● *Glued-up laminations for a 24ft wind-tunnel blade*

● *A close shave! The blade's shape is finished to superfine tolerances to ensure balance*

Timber

The timber used to make propellers is very carefully selected. Several British Standard Specifications were specially drawn up; for instance, BSS 3V5 of December 1928, modified by a war emergency amendment in 1943, laid down the following specification for selecting walnut:

Quality. The timber shall be of the best description of American black walnut.

Freedom from defects. The timber shall contain no deleterious knots, shakes, curls, burrs, rammy figure, or caney grain, and shall show no signs of rot or decay. Sapwood may be permitted in any part if it is sound, bright, tough and strong.

Dryness. The timber should not be converted to its final size until the moisture content has been reduced to 13% or less, when calculated on the dry weight of the timber.

Straightness of grain. The maximum inclination of the grain to the length shall not exceed 1:12.

Density. The weight per cubic foot shall be not less than 35lb at 15% MC.

There are also levels laid down for Young's Modulus of Elasticity, Modulus of Rupture and Brittleness. Similar specs were drawn up by the Ministry of Supply. Bulk inspection of boards was carried out before delivery to the manufacturer, but individual planks were inspected immediately before use and often condemned. Whilst walnut and mahogany were the main timbers used, birch, oak, Queensland silk, Grand bassam, Lagos and Benin mahogany, African iroko, English ash, Japanese walnut, silver spruce, and Benin walnut were also used.

Laminating

The wooden fixed-pitch airscrew is constructed from a number of planks, or laminations, glued together, fanwise, parallel to the plane of rotation. The ¾in planks were roughed out with the grain running lengthwise and parallel to the surface to be glued, then stored for at least three weeks under the same humidity and temperature as in the workshop. Each lamination was balanced on a knife edge at its centre point to determine the heaviest end; this was marked, so heavy ends could be alternated with light in assembly, helping to balance the prop.

Laminations, shot up on the flat faces to fit the next, were individually inspected and stamped by the Aeronautical Inspection Department (A.I.D.). The shot joints were inspected by shining a bicycle torch behind

943

the joint and trying to insert a 2-thou feeler gauge into the joint. The boards were then bandsawn to the profile — about ¼in oversize for a two-bladed propeller and ½in for a four-bladed. Boards for a four-bladed prop would have a halving joint cut at the centre.

Assembly

Gluing-up was done in a workroom free from draughts and dust, kept night and day at 70°F. Pearl glue was supplied in special sealed bags, marked 'A.I.D. approved'. A weighed quantity of glue was added to a measured amount of water and heated; boiling of the glue was prohibited, and mixed glue discarded at the end of each day's work. The work of gluing-up was carried out on a specially prepared jig; this was a bed plate with special cramping bolts attached along its edges. The boards were heated in an enclosure for about ten minutes at 100°F to help prevent chilling of the glue. After rapid gluing and assembly on the jig, the men waited three minutes before clamping up so the glue penetrated the timber. Then all the cramp screws were tightened down, starting from the centre and working out. The block of laminations was left in the cramps for 24 hours. On very large airscrews the laminations were first glued up in pairs and then the pairs together, but as each pair had to stay 24 hours in the cramps this was a long-winded job. On removal from the cramps the block was allowed to rest for at least two days.

Then the hole in the hub was bored with a boring bar; typically plus or minus 20-thou was allowed on this hole diameter. Wasting away down to a rough shape, using a small side axe, a hand adze and a draw knife, was followed by a further rest of about a week for the block to settle down.

Shaping

Shaping was then started in earnest, using a number of templates and shaping the propeller at specified points to fit them, and fairing in the intervals. Special spokeshaves made by the white shaper himself were used for the accurate shaping; these were like small planes with handles on the sides, something like a cooper's Jarvis but with a flat sole.

A surface table, fitted with a spigot which was a push fit in the centre bore, was now used to mount the airscrew on and final shaping and checking took place, with tolerances of about ¹⁄₆₄in.

After checking the tracking of the airscrew around the spigot in the centre bore, the centre ring bolt-holes were bored; these had to be centred correctly within ¹⁄₆₄in but could be drawn by this amount towards the direction of rotation — the permitted limit for gun synchronisation. For balancing, the propeller was mounted on a centre mandrel supported on knife edges, this balancing jig set over a hole in the floor so the centre of the airscrew was at a comfortable working level. A very small weight — about 1oz — was put in one of the centre boss bolt-holes to check that it would turn the propeller; this was carried out with each blade horizontal in turn. Small amounts of wood were removed from the pitch face of heavy blades to achieve final balance; abrasives were not allowed, all work having to be smooth and fair straight from the cutting edges.

Finishing

Wood by itself is not a very suitable material for resisting abrasion, by rain, dust, stones or spray thrown up during take-off; and it tends to warp when subjected to changes in humidity and temperature. So wooden propellers were covered with cellulose and fabric, and usually with a metal sheath over the tip and leading edge of the blades. Linen was hot glued, first on to the pitch face, beginning at the leading edge, taken round over the trailing edge and back to the leading edge, overlapping the beginning by an inch; the linen was smoothed down with a hot iron and a wooden roller. It was a highly skilled job to get rid of the wrinkles particularly as no snipping was permitted. The edges of the linen had threads removed so that the edge was frayed and this edge was worked into the general surface where the joint occurred. One of several proprietary finishes were then applied, the most common being three coats of primer/filler, each being cut back before the next coat was applied. When these coats had hardened they were flattened and a coat of copal varnish applied.

The final production stage, known as 'tipping and beading', followed — covering the leading edge and the tip with 24swg annealed brass sheet, fixed with ⅝in x no.4/5 brass screws in staggered rows through spun dipple holes, the screw-heads soft soldered to the brass covering. Drain holes were drilled in the very tip of the brass covering so that any trapped rain water would be thrown out.

The final job was a coat of varnish or enamel, burnished to a high gloss until 1918, but left semi-matt thereafter, either because of the time taken, or for aerodynamic reasons.

A propeller shaping machine which worked on a pantograph principle was introduced in 1918, but much of the final shaping and balancing was still done by hand right up until the late 40s.

A number of World War I props were used as headstones to mark airmen's graves, and it is a tribute to the craftsmen who made them that after more than half a century some are still standing the ravages of time.

Today these wooden airscrews are only made for restoration jobs, but the craft lives on in some fields. The large fans used in wind tunnels are a direct descendant of the airscrew, and pose even bigger problems in construction though modern glues have helped enormously.

And you never know about the future. Could the search for alternative power sources lead to resurrecting in quantity this most elegant and technical woodwork — the craft of the white shaper? ∎

● *Nearly there; templates in foreground*

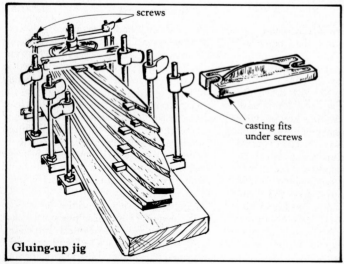

Gluing-up jig

screws

casting fits under screws

In the groove

Routing gauges help locate those difficult housings

Sometimes we want to cut a groove or housing at a distance from the edge greater than the fence adjustment of the machine. The remedy is to cramp or pin a wooden straight-edge to the work and run the router, with its fence removed, along the straight-edge as a fence. But how do you work out the precise place the fence should go? You can do it by trial and error, or by calculation, but neither is very satisfactory.

Here is a simple-to-make permanent gauge that avoids any chance of error.

You need to make a temporary construction table from scrap materials (fig. 1); don't worry about sizes, except that the fence should be about ½-⅝in high, and a block nailed below enables you to fit the table in a vice.

The gauge itself is made from ³⁄₁₆ or ¼in plywood, with one edge accurately planed; don't use solid wood, for it may shrink and become inaccurate. Pin this rectangle of ply down with its true edge firmly in contact with the fence (fig. 2).

Choose an appropriate cutter and then run the router along the fence in the following way to get a clean cut. Place a thin steel rule between the router and the fence, cutting halfway through the ply at the first pass. Increase the depth and cut right through, so the bit bites into the base very slightly. Remove the loose section of ply (fig. 3), take away the steel rule, and make a third pass with the router to get a very fine finish.

Prise off the completed plywood gauge, which is the exact width between the edge of the router base and the particular cutter. Cut a hole to hang it on a nail, and mark it with the size of the cutter you used; you will need different width gauges for different sized cutters. It's worthwhile making a gauge for each size of straight router bits you have while you've got your temporary table set up.

To use the gauge, first mark the position of the groove or housing on the work, preferably with a knife-line. Lay a straight-edge on the work, parallel to your marked line, and interpose the gauge in between the straight-edge and the line. It's easier to use the gauge at one end and then the other (fig. 4), moving the straight-edge and gauge so the edge of the gauge is exactly on the marked line. For real accuracy, hold a marking knife on the line as you push the straight-edge and gauge up to it. When both

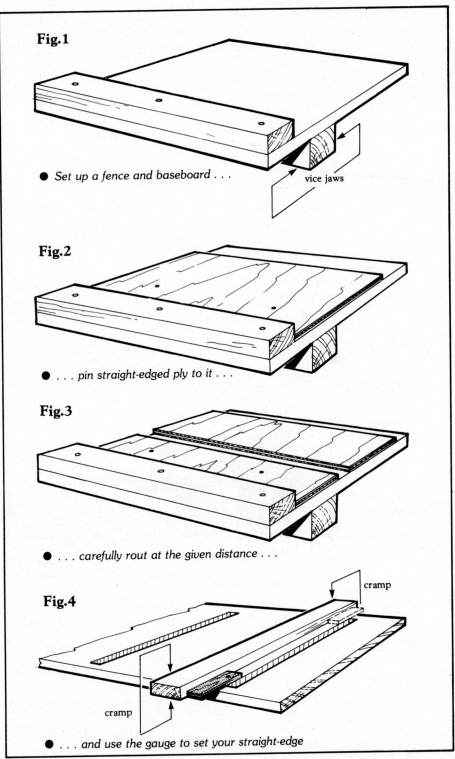

Fig.1
● *Set up a fence and baseboard . . .* vice jaws

Fig.2
● *. . . pin straight-edged ply to it . . .*

Fig.3
● *. . . carefully rout at the given distance . . .*

Fig.4
cramp

cramp

● *. . . and use the gauge to set your straight-edge*

ends are in the correct position, cramp up the straight-edge. Using that as a fence, you can now rout the groove precisely where you have marked it.

Occasionally you may want to cut a groove for which you don't have an appropriate cutter, or you'll want to cut wider grooves from a router taking only ¼in shank cutters. You can do this by interposing a thin strip of steel of appropriate thickness between the router base and the fence.

To make a ⅝in groove when you only have a ½in cutter, for instance, make a cut first as outlined to make a ½in groove. Then interpose an ⅛in metal strip between the router base and the fence and make a second cut to widen to groove to ⅝in.

It's helpful to collect offcuts of bright drawn mild steel, say ⅜in or ½in wide and in thicknesses of ¹⁄₁₆in, ⅛in, ³⁄₁₆in and ¼in.

When cutting grooves in this way, you need to concentrate well to prevent the router wandering from the fence. ■

If you work with wood you need

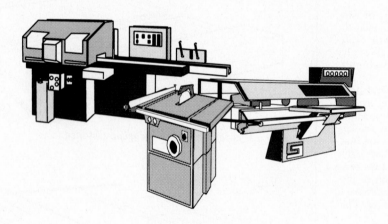

A

GUIDE TO

WOODWORKING

MACHINERY

for the smaller

BUSINESS

Write or phone for your free copy

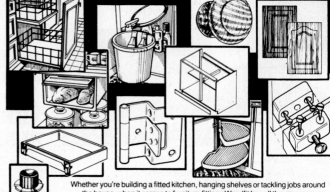

Scarfing it

Just a cheap way of making a long bit of wood, you say? Scarfing is a great deal more than that, says Malcolm Wintle — with a host of drawings to back him up

The scarf rarely receives a mention in carpentry manuals, which is a pity because it's a useful joint. With a knowledge of the method and a little care, the average woodworker can make good use of it.

The form shown in fig. 1 is in effect a butt joint with the butt ends cut not at right angles to the grain, but at an acute angle. The faces are glued and the pieces clamped together. It sounds very easy and it is; but there are pitfalls.

Why make such a joint? The scarf has long been common in clinker-built (i.e. planked) boat-building, where longer planks than the ones available may be needed. It's also used when repairing such boats, when a section of planking is scarfed in. If a boat has a plywood skin, scarfing can extend standard sheets, giving a stronger and fairer outer surface than a butt-and-lap joint would. Domestic skirting-boards are usually joined on a long run by a crude scarf joint, generally rough-sawn and not glued. Broken masts, oars, paddles and even broom- and tool-handles can be repaired by scarfing. Bad patches in timber too — knots, shakes, bends, or areas where the grain runs off badly — can all be cut out and the wood re-joined. Then you might come across an unexpected job for which pieces to hand are too short, so you can just join up the available wood rather than make a special journey to a timber yard.

I sometimes need pieces longer than I can easily carry home, so I buy two lengths and scarf them together when I get them on the bench. This actually makes it easier to get the timber straight on a long run. For instance, if a long piece develops a bad bend on the flat, it may be impossible to pull it straight. Planing the edges wastes a lot of wood, as fig. 2a shows (it's exaggerated for clarity). But if you cut the wood in half and scarf together again, the bend can be greatly reduced which in turn increases the useful thickness of wood left after planing (fig. 2b).

The strength of the finished joint is determined by the angle of taper. The finer the taper, the stronger the final result. If the joint is purely decorative, as in a skirting-board or unstressed panelling, then a 1:2 taper may be adequate (fig. 3a), but in a shelf, mast or broom-handle for example, where bending forces have to be withstood, a taper between 1:6 and 1:10 would be more suitable (fig. 3b).

The total length of timber will have to be at least the finished length plus the length of

the scarf. To make a strong joint in 25mm timber would require an extra length of wood of 200mm for a 1:8 joint, plus safety margins.

The method

There are two problems in forming the tapers: making the two tapers true and identical, and getting a good feather edge. The stock should be cut slightly wider and thicker than finished to allow it to be trued up square before the joint is started and also for some wood to be left for planing off in final cleaning up. The two ends to be joined are marked with the intended taper (fig. 4a). Save effort by sawing the scrap off on the waste side (fig. 4b). A rigid flat working

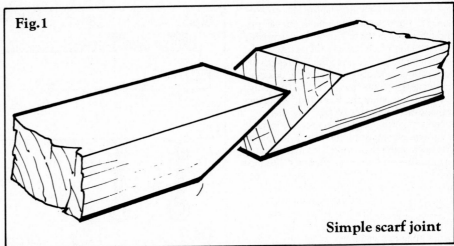

Fig.1

Simple scarf joint

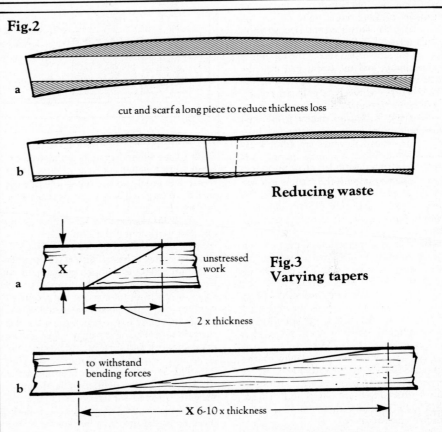

Fig.2

a

cut and scarf a long piece to reduce thickness loss

b

Reducing waste

a

X

unstressed work

2 x thickness

Fig.3 Varying tapers

b

to withstand bending forces

X 6-10 x thickness

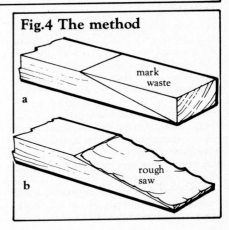

Fig.4 The method

a

mark waste

b

rough saw

Scarfing it

surface is essential for planing the tapers; clamp the two parts to be joined one on top of the other as in fig. 5. The bottom, straight flat packing-piece raises the work high enough to be planed over the full length of both tapers, and also supports the delicate feather edge. This piece should be only slightly wider than the work, and its front end should be square to the long sides.

Next, position the two pieces to be joined as shown, one face up, the other face down. The lines of the two tapers are lined up with one another and with the corner (**C**) of the packing-piece. Align the long edges of the two workpieces with one another, parallel with the long edge of the packing-piece.

Then clamp a flat pad to spread clamp-action in two places, to bring the work-pieces together right up to the tip of the upper one, and the lower one in contact with the packing-piece right up to the corner (fig. 5). This is essential to get good feather edges. The final planing line must be clear of the upper pad and of the top of the nearer clamp, and the lower pad must be thick enough to stop the plane hitting the bench before you reach the end of the taper.

Using a sharp plane, cut the tapers back to the mark. It doesn't matter if the final taper isn't exactly what you intended, pro-viding the rough sawcuts are completely planed away. Nor, if a small margin has been left on the overall length of the work-pieces, does it matter if the planing is taken a little too far; apart from shortening the work slightly, the only other result is a slight nick off the corner of the packing-piece.

There are two important points to watch during planing. Firstly, the planed face of each taper must be *quite flat* so they will eventually lie in good contact over the whole area. Second, both ends of each taper must finish at right angles to the long sides of the work. An angled cut (seen from above in fig. 6) results in an error of double the angle when the two pieces are glued together, so you need more planing on the right side **R** to bring the ends of the tapers perpendicular to the long edges of the work. The feather edges are sharp and delicate when you unclamp them, and must be handled carefully.

Gluing

Lay the two pieces flat and offer them up for a trial fitting in the final position. When the pieces are slid together and aligned, the two bevels should come together over the whole area. If they don't, then the planing was out of true, the work wasn't initially planed square, or the pieces weren't clamped up accurately for planing the tapers — or any combination of these. So clamp up again and repeat the planing. You can make slight corrections by planing one of the tapers only, the feather edge supported this time with a single workpiece.

When the pieces meet accurately, mark them across the join (fig. 7b) to aid length-wise positioning when gluing. It can be dif-

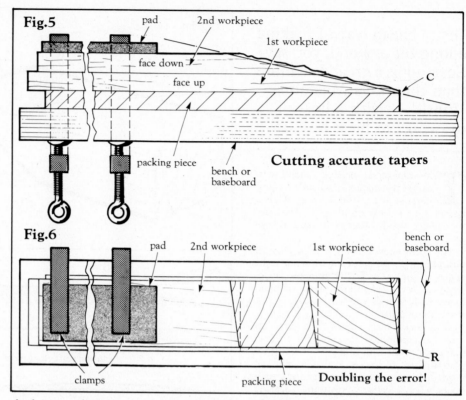

Fig.5 — pad — 2nd workpiece — 1st workpiece — face down — face up — C — packing piece — bench or baseboard — **Cutting accurate tapers**

Fig.6 — bench or baseboard — pad — 2nd workpiece — 1st workpiece — R — clamps — packing piece — **Doubling the error!**

ficult to see when the tapers are mated cor-rectly with a generous layer of glue. Then score thoroughly across the whole of each surface to be glued with a saw or sandpaper to provide a key.

Cascamite is suitable for 'undercover' outdoor work, but if the joint will get wet, a fully waterproof glue such as Aerolite 300 or a resorcinol is best. The clamping secret is that each piece is clamped individually to a common base before being clamped to the other — it's important to get the sequence right or the joint is just squeezed apart. Clamp one piece to the bench (or other flat surface with a good straight edge) so the edges of work and surface coincide and the glued face of the work is uppermost (fig. 7a). Slide a piece of plastic film under the feather edge before tightening the clamp so the glue squeezed out later doesn't stick the work to the bench. Offer the second work-piece up to the first, in a line guided by the edge of the bench, the two previously made

marks coinciding (fig. 7b); then clamp this piece to the bench as well. Put a second piece of plastic film over the upper feather edge, and clamp the joint together with one or two clamps on a flat pad (fig. 7c).

If the joint has been well prepared and comes together correctly, glue will squeeze out all along both sides, but don't clamp too tightly or you'll starve the job of glue and weaken it. Don't clean the excess glue off until it's rubbery, which shows curing is well advanced. With a glue like Cascamite which sets finally like glass, it's easier on the plane to do most of the cleaning-off before the glue is fully hard.

The alternative way to prevent the parts slipping under clamps — temporarily pin-ning them together — apart from leaving holes, puts pins in the way and is best avoided by the fig. 7 method. But it's some-times useful; two well-spaced pins are driven through the upper piece when both are dry and clamped in position (fig. 8). The

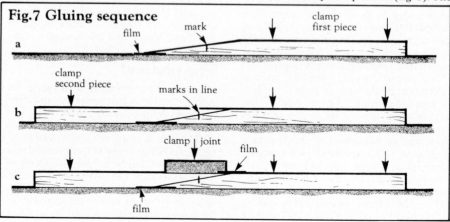

Fig.7 Gluing sequence — film — mark — clamp first piece — a — clamp second piece — marks in line — b — clamp joint — film — c — film

pins should just enter the lower half; mark the joint across as before. Then separate the parts and glue them, and relocate the points of the pins in the same holes in the lower workpiece, using the pencil marks as a guide. The pins can be driven in further if necessary and the joint clamped. Remove the pins when the glue has set.

With a good taper (1:8 at least) and careful gluing with good glue, the joint should be as strong as the original wood. It's always worth making one or two practice joints and testing them to destruction, in which you'll see that with a fine taper, it should be the wood and not the joint that fails. If the scarf is so you can remove a bad section at a knot or where the grain runs off, the finished job will certainly be stronger than the original.

If the stock is round (a mast for example), it's difficult to plane the two parts together as in fig. 5, so they must be planed separately after roughing out the joint. It's essential to support each feather edge on a packing-piece as it is planed, and the two parts have to be fitted together by trial and error until each is planed to the same angle and you get an accurate fit all over the faces.

The sequence of clamping is as before, but it is necessary to make shaped packing-pieces like those in fig. 9 to provide a firm bearing surface for the clamps.

Double scarf joint

Sometimes, it's worth considering a double scarf as shown in fig. 10. It uses a smaller additional length of material, and for a given length of joint is likely to be stronger than a single scarf because of the second pair of mating surfaces. A disadvantage is that the faces of the slot have to be finished by hand after roughing out, but this isn't too difficult. I've used this joint successfully to extend a wooden mast.

The slotted part is marked out as in fig. 11. There's a flat at the bottom of the slot, easier than working an acute-angled recess right down to a sharp point. Make the width of the flat equal to the diameter of whatever drill you have around 5-6mm. Drill through the work halfway from each side at **X**, then rough out the tapers by making two saw-cuts to end at the hole. Finish the slot off to the line with hand chisels. The other part is marked out as in fig. 12 with the same width of flat and angle of taper, roughed out by sawing, and finished to the line. This part is comparatively easy as the tip can be left rough-sawn, the tapers can be planed till you get a good fit with the slot, and there's no feather edge to protect. If the faces are planed too far, you'll have to plane a little off the tip. Score and join as before.

Some cosmetic uses

An easier job is the repair of a damaged corner, of a door or door-lining for example. If the damage is more than filler can cope with, you can scarf a new piece in.

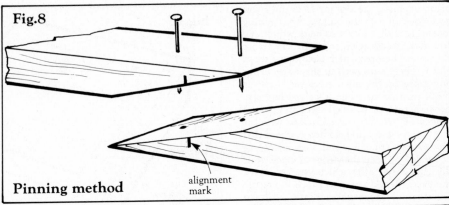

Fig.8

Pinning method

alignment mark

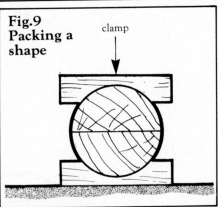

Fig.9
Packing a shape

clamp

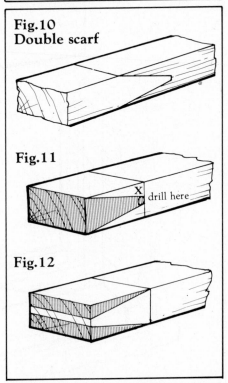

Fig.10
Double scarf

Fig.11

X drill here

Fig.12

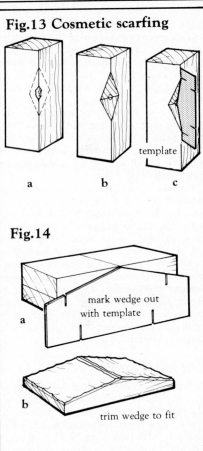

Fig.13 Cosmetic scarfing

template

a   b   c

Fig.14

mark wedge out with template

a

b

trim wedge to fit

Cut a gash (fig. 13a) out along the dotted lines. Depending on its position, the enlarged hole can sometimes be roughed out with a saw and cleaned up with a chisel, but it's just as easy to do the whole thing by chiselling from each end alternately, enlarging the hole from the centre outwards till the damage is cut out or at least surrounded by good wood. It helps if the

angles of the two tapers are about equal, and the line where the tapers meet is at right angles to the edges of the frame or door (fig. 13b). As this is a cosmetic job, a taper of 1:2 or 3 is adequate. It's easy to check each taper is flat by laying the back of the chisel on it, which immediately shows up any bumps or hollows for further paring.

Next make a template of the angle by cutting a piece of cardboard and adjusting it until it's a good snug fit in the angle. Mark the extent of the hole on it (fig. 13c), and mark the width of the hole on the opposite edge of the card.

Mark out a broad wedge with the template (fig. 14a) on a well-seasoned oddment of wood with lengthwise grain, slightly wider than the base of the hole. Cut off the waste on the tapers (fig. 14b) and either

Scarfing it

plane or chisel the sloping faces until you get a good fit with the hollow. After getting a good fit, don't forget to mark which way round the wedge goes, and also mark across the join as before to help positioning when glued. There's no need to shape the wedge any more on the other faces yet — this is more easily done when it's glued in place. Score across all inclined faces and glue as before. When the wedge is mated with the work and lightly pressed home, check that glue squeezes out all round. Very little force is needed to keep the wedge in place while the glue cures, after which you can plane the excess wood and glue off. If the repair and surrounding area are well rubbed down and painted, the new wood is undetectable.

My most frequent use of the scarf is to repair a piece of wood on the flat. Examples are: cutting out knots in work I'm preparing, cutting out unsightly or resinous knots in existing fixtures, and filling holes in floors under carpets where knots have shrunk and fallen through.

Mark two lines on the work along the grain on each side, clear of the defect (fig. 15a). Starting from the centre, chisel out a shallow vee progressively until there is sufficient depth all over the fault to make a good repair (fig. 15b).

As before, cut a piece of card to make a template for the angle of the base of the hole, and mark the width of the hole on it as in fig. 13c. Mark out the replacement wood as in fig. 14a, but this time the width (fig. 14b) is the same as the hole. After you've cut the tapers, adjust the plug by trial-and-trim to fit the hole easily but snugly; make a locating mark across the join as before. Score across all sloping faces, glue all mating faces and press the plug lightly home until glue comes out all round, especially under the overhang at each end.

Larger repairs

Rotted areas of window and door linings or frames, usually at the bottom, require replacement of rather larger volumes of wood. Awaiting my attention now is a bad patch in an oak porch (fig.16) where the rain has got up into the endgrain and caused shakes if not actual rot. I shall cut out a vee as indicated and scarf in a new piece of oak, using Aerolite. If the part to be mended includes a rebate, the scarfed insert can be shaped before gluing in place, but it may be easier to leave the section slightly oversize and finish it to match after fixing.

I recently repaired a window lining, rotten round a bottom corner, by cutting out the whole corner with about 1:4 tapers, then jointing up a complete new corner on the bench with the rebate roughed out to size and the two scarfs accurately fitting the fixed tapers. It was glued and clamped in place, and finished in situ flush with the old wood. It was undetectable when completed and painted. It was much cheaper than replacing the whole frame; and although it took a long time, it was still quicker than waiting for the builders!

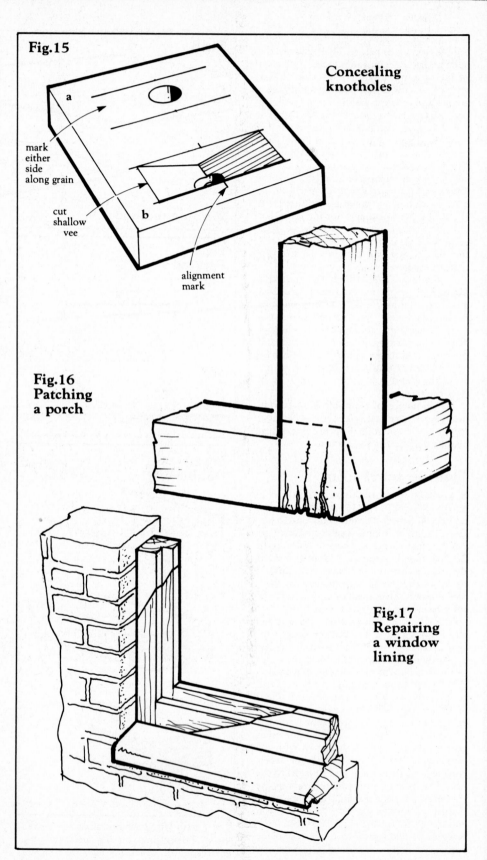

Fig.15

a
mark either side along grain

cut shallow vee

b

alignment mark

Concealing knotholes

Fig.16 Patching a porch

Fig.17 Repairing a window lining

Motivation!

I've tried to give an idea of the range of uses of this versatile joint — please don't be put off because it sounds just too much trouble. It really is a case of easier done than said, and once you've tried it, you'll find you can knock off a good joint remarkably quickly. I find it very satisfying, when stripping a job for repainting, to find a scarf joint or repair I've made many years before, forgotten and hidden under the old paint. ∎

Rout-a-slide

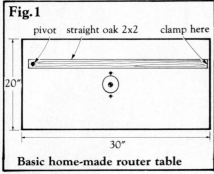

Fig. 1

pivot straight oak 2x2 clamp here

20"

30"

Basic home-made router table

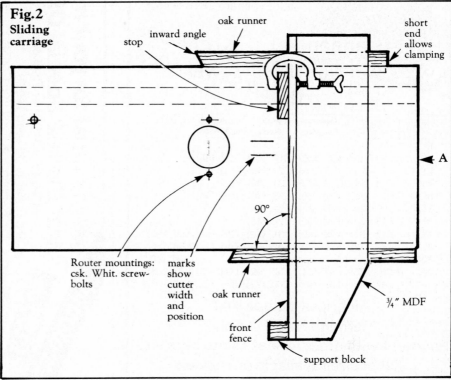

Fig. 2
Sliding carriage

oak runner

inward angle

stop

short end allows clamping

A

90°

Router mountings: csk. Whit. screw-bolts

marks show cutter width and position

oak runner

¾" MDF

front fence

support block

A recently accepted quote for a kitchen with a cock-bead detail on the inside edges of the door frames, writes **Grant Pearce**, faced me with cutting 158 45° mitres where the beads met, without fouling the mortises or tenons. I came up with a sliding carriage (figs 2, 3) for my 'ordinary' home-made router table (fig. 1). The recess for the router base is cut in underneath ⅜in, and the machine is held with oak turn-buttons.

The carriage was fun to make, and produced excellent mitres on my cocked beads time after time. The router-crazy could extend its uses to tenoning, half-lap joints, even dovetailing without a jig.

I lipped the ply/Formica table very carefully with oak and flushed it off exactly top and bottom, then routed a rebate in the lipping a bit more than half the thickness. I planed the runners for the carriage slightly

thinner than the table thickness so the one which runs on the bench side wouldn't foul the bench, to which the table is clamped; then rebated them to marry with the rebate in the table lipping. I cut a hefty piece of ¾in MDF for the top 'plate' of the sliding carriage, fixed the front fence (also good quarter-cut straight oak) to that, waxed the rebates in the table lippings and the matching ones in the runners, set the carriage up perfectly square on the table, and glued and clamped the runners to the carriage. The location for a precise sliding fit is given by the rebates themselves. The wax helps sliding, of course, and also ensured I wouldn't glue the runners to the table as well as the sliding carriage. The runners' front ends are offset one from the other, and cut at an angle to help when you mount the carriage on the table. The 'bench side' runner is slightly shorter than the

outside one to allow for a G-cramp at the back of the table, holding it to the bench; my main fixing is a 2x2in oak batten on the underside of the table, held in the vice.

There is also a block glued under the outside end of the carriage, flush with the top surface of the table, to hold longer lengths up in perfectly alignment with the table surface.

The marks on the table (fig. 2) are a reference for the point where the edges of the 45° cutter meet the table — the width of cut, in other words. This is for pieces of non-standard length, so you can just line them up. It's worth making a moveable stop (fig. 2) for a run of pieces all the same length; and also worth remembering to work out the position of the beads and do all the 45° cutting *before* you rout or spindle-mould the beads. Otherwise you risk nasty breakout in the mouldings. ∎

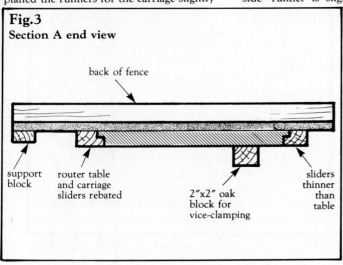

Fig. 3
Section A end view

back of fence

support block

router table and carriage sliders rebated

2"x2" oak block for vice-clamping

sliders thinner than table

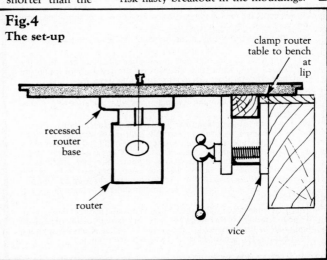

Fig. 4
The set-up

clamp router table to bench at lip

recessed router base

router

vice

Canaan Carbides Ltd.

Peewit Road, Hampton, Evesham
Worcs. WR11 6NH
Tel: Evesham 2818 & 45302

QUALITY TUNGSTEN CARBIDE TIPPED SAWBLADES

Dia.	Rip	General Purpose	Multi Grain	Plastics & Laminates	Alumin -ium
5″	£7 (12)				
6″	£13 (20)	£17 (30)	£17 (40)	£28 (48)	
6¼″	£13 (20)	£17 (30)	£21 (40)		
7¼″	£13 (24)	£17 (30)	£21 (40)		
8″	£15 (20)	£20 (30)	£23 (40)	£35 (64)	
8¼″	£15 (20)	£20 (30)	£23 (40)		
9¼″	£16 (24)	£22 (30)	£24 (40)		
10″	£17 (30)	£30 (40)	£35 (48)	£38 (60)	£50 (80)
12″	£32 (32)	£38 (48)	£42 (60)	£44 (72)	£56 (96)
330mm					£60 (96)
14″	£36 (36)	£43 (54)	£52 (72)	£59 (108)	£67 (108)
16″	£42 (40)	£54 (60)	£63 (72)	£70 (96)	£88 (128)

All prices include VAT
Carriage Free (UK only)
Payment with order   Please state bore size!
Other sizes available on request
Trade enquiries welcome

get the most for your money with these 2 Special Offers

Charnwood

£166 OFF

M300 12″ x 8″ Planer Thickener
- Big Capacity • Long Tables
- ½″ Rebating • Cast Iron Construction

	List	Special Offer	
Three Phase	£1365	£1199	+ VAT + Carr.
Single Phase	£1395	£1229	

PS300 Complete Panel Saw
- 250mm TCT Main Saw • 105mm TCT Scorer
- Sliding Table
- Rear Table
- RH Table

	List	Special Offer	
Three Phase	£1809	£1659	+ VAT + Carr.
Single Phase	£1845	£1695	

£153 OFF

OFFERS END OCT. 31st

0533 351735
44 Boston Road, Leicester LE4 1AA

Charnwood is a division of Cecil Cooks Export Services Ltd.

MAIL ORDER ADVERTISING

British Code of Advertising Practice

Advertisements in this publication are required to conform to the British Code of Advertising Practice. In respect of mail order advertisements where money is paid in advance, the code requires advertisers to fulfil orders within 28 days, unless a longer delivery period is stated. Where goods are returned undamaged within seven days, the purchaser's money must be refunded. Please retain proof of postage/despatch, as this may be needed.

Mail Order Protection Scheme

If you order goods from Mail Order advertisements in this magazine and pay by post in advance of delivery, Argus Specialist Publications Ltd will consider you for compensation if the Advertiser should become insolvent or bankrupt, provided:

(1) You have not received the goods or had your money returned; and

(2) You write to the Publisher of this publication, summarising the situation not earlier than 28 days from the day you sent your order and not later than two months from that day.

Please do not wait until the last moment to inform us. When you write, we will tell you how to make your claim and what evidence of payment is required.

We guarantee to meet claims from readers made in accordance with the above procedure as soon as possible after the Advertiser has been declared bankrupt or insolvent (up to a limit of £2,000 per annum for any one Advertiser so affected and up to £6,000 per annum in respect of all insolvent Advertisers. Claims may be paid for higher amounts, or when the above procedure has not been complied with, at the discretion of this publication but we do not guarantee to do so in view of the need to set some limit to this commitment and to learn quickly of readers' difficulties.

This guarantee covers only advance payment sent in direct response to an advertisement in this magazine (not, for example, payment made in response to catalogues etc., received as a result of answering such advertisements). Classified advertisements are excluded.

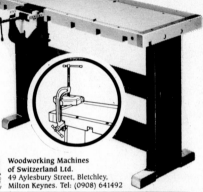

955

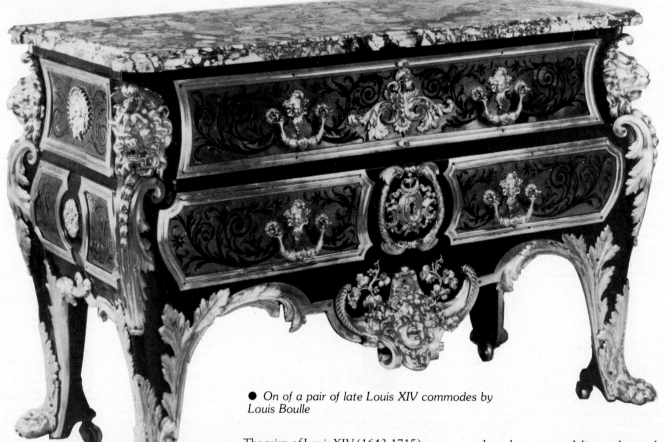

● On of a pair of late Louis XIV commodes by Louis Boulle

Grandeur and flamboyance were Louis XIV's trade-marks. Vic Taylor looks at some shining examples from the Sun King's reign of conspicuous patronage

One of the outstanding figures in late 17th century French furniture was André-Charles Boulle (1642-1732), who developed the intricate style of decoration bearing his name (see WW/Oct). It consisted of sheet brass laid into a tortoiseshell background, or vice-versa; the metal was beautifully engraved and the shell was backed with coloured paper or mica, or even painted on the reverse, to enhance the colours. He didn't invent the process — Italian furniture of the early 17th century was similarly embellished — but he did refine and improve it.

The reign of Louis XIV (1643-1715) saw the creation of his palace at Versailles, which was to symbolise the grandeur of the French monarchy. His minister, Jean-Baptiste Colbert, who helped in the project, appointed Charles Le Brun as the first director of the royal factory 'Manufacture Royale des Meubles de la Couronne' — which approved all furnishings for the Court. Le Brun trained as an artist in Rome and had absorbed the High Baroque influence to which he applied pure classical principles. The result was what is today called 'Louis XIV style'.

Jean Le Pautre was the King's chief furniture designer who left a large collection of engraved designs notable for their florid, ornate Baroque decoration — startling designs used for beds with elaborate canopies, and console tables of carved/gilded wood adorned with grotesques and nymphs. Another influential designer, Jean Berain, took over the directorship from Le Brun and was instrumental in introducing Chinoiserie. This use of Chinese figures and landscapes as decoration was later adopted by Thomas Chippendale and others in the 18th century. Le Brun's penchant had been singeries — flat-panel scenes incorporating monkeys, imitating human beings.

Italian-born craftsman Domenico Cucci worked in France, and took marquetry probably to its highest level with the lavish use of exotic woods, precious metals and semi-precious stones, tortoiseshell, and ormolu mounts. These gilded mounts were cast in bronze from carved wooden moulds,

and used to protect delicate edges and add strength to the construction.

In 1685 the King ordered all furniture in the royal palaces to be recorded in the Journal du Garde-Meubles; this practice carried on for the next century. Along with the revised rules of the French cabinetmakers' guild in 1741 — which required cabinetmakers to mark their work — a method was introduced to trace the provenance of French furniture relatively accurately. Life for English furniture historians would be much easier if the same had happened here!

The same year saw the revocation of the Edict of Nantes, which withdrew freedom of worship from the Huguenots. Thousands of them fled from the savage persecution that ensued, some going to the Netherlands and many coming to England. They brought with them a reputation for skill, hard work, and sobriety, and they contributed greatly to the superb workmanship of the 18th century English cabinetmakers.

Late 17th century French case-furniture tended to be predominantly square in outline, though Boulle was partially involved in the development of the bombé front. The chest of drawers, then known as a commode, was the commonest means of storing linen; tall wardrobes, bureaux, and armoires (double cupboards) were also popular. Chairs and settees were still restricted to the rich and were massive in form, with gilded wood and gesso carving, sumptuous damasks and silks for the upholstery. Tables appeared in a variety of sizes and shapes, all of them heavily ornamented, often with marble tops and sinuous S-shaped legs, particularly on console tables.

At the end of the 17th century many novel designs were being produced in Holland using exotic oriental decoration and materials, no doubt as a result of their trading activities in the Far East. Thus, the first cane was imported from the Malay Peninsula about 1660 and its use quickly spread throughout Europe. They also brought in complete pieces of ebony furniture which were made in the Dutch East Indies and Ceylon. After the Portuguese were expelled from Japan, the Dutch established trading connections there and, amongst other things, imported lacquered cabinets from Japan and China. Spa, a town near Liège, was the most famous centre for japanning and the work of some of the craftsmen was almost indistinguishable from genuine oriental pieces.

The highly-skilled craftsman, Daniel Marot (1633-1752),probably worked for Boulle in Paris, and fled to Holland as a Huguenot refugee. He became principal designer to William, Prince of Orange, and worked on furnishings for the Royal Palace at Het Loo. When William came to England to rule jointly with his wife, Mary, Marot came with him — later returning to Holland. Inspired by Louis XIV style, he was particularly keen on luxurious fabrics for upholstery and drapery; one of his best-known designs is a bed with a tester upholstered in voluminous flounces, the entire thing being cantilevered from the wall so no bed posts were needed at the foot. His chairs had tall, narrow backs which were

● *Typical Louis XIV arm chair, c1670; carving, gilt and brocade*

either upholstered or in fretted wood carved with scroll motifs; the seats were either stuffed or caned to support loose squab cushions. He favoured turned legs which had a swelling at the top, rather like an inverted cup; or designs which incorporated a hook-like scroll. Although some of his pieces were gilded, many were left in the natural walnut wood which was extremely popular then.

The Dutch, great flower-lovers, had a passion in the 17th century for floral marquetry, brought to a fine art by Jan van Mekeren (working 1690-1735). Such marquetry was used to adorn the doors of large cabinets and the tops of tables which were intended to stand in the centre of a room and to be regarded as works of art too precious for ordinary purposes.

The other Dutch passion was Chinese porcelain which they imported in large quantities. This led to the invention of the display cabinet, which had a glazed upper portion and a cupboard below, with panelled doors. These cabinets often had the distinctive characteristic of angled-ends so the contents of the glazed section could be viewed to their best advantage. The tops were usually arched, with the doors, cornice, and ceiling of the glazed section all following the shape. And, as you would expect, the door panels were decorated with marquetry. ■

● *A bureau Mazarin, c1680, in tortoiseshell veneer, coloured mica and brass Boulle marquetry*

● *Dutch walnut armchair, c1670, with typical pierced carving and twist-turning*

958

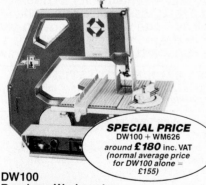

959

960

Take a chair...

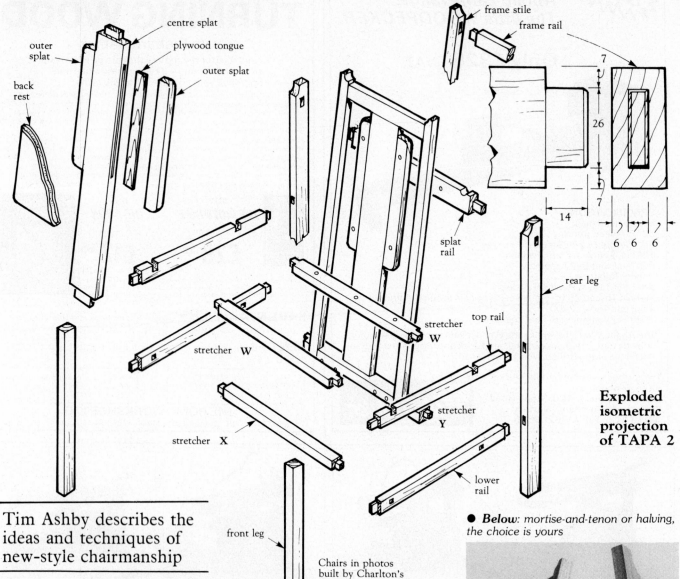

outer splat
centre splat
plywood tongue
outer splat
back rest
frame stile
frame rail

7
26
7
14
6 6 6

splat rail

rear leg

stretcher W

top rail

stretcher W

stretcher X

stretcher Y

Exploded isometric projection of TAPA 2

lower rail

front leg

Chairs in photos built by Charlton's Timber Centre, Radstock — see them at the **Woodworker Show!**

Tim Ashby describes the ideas and techniques of new-style chairmanship

Chairs are the most challenging construction projects for the woodworker — and arguably, the most commonly used piece of furniture. It's vitally important when you design and make a chair that it is comfortable; that it fits the human frame (given certain variations!), as well as be strong, well-proportioned, and aesthetically pleasing. It's no easy job, designing a chair; more difficult, perhaps than the actual making. But if you work from a basic plan that allows you numerous choices, as well as giving accurate guidance on cutting lengths and widths, component positions and other data, much of the difficult work is taken out of the job. The idea of TAPA packs is that you choose a basic construction style — halved joints or mortises and tenons — then go for the various other options open. These are:

1 Shaped wooden splats and upholstered seat
2 Upholstered back rest and seat
3 Caned seat and back
4 Fanned back splats and sculpted wooden seat.

But the options go further than this; you can adapt the basic designs yourself, limited only by your imagination. For instance, you could use leather or canvas strapping horizontally across the back framework, or make laminated back rests, designed to fit the profile of the typical human back.

If you are going to introduce more personal elements, however, you must consider the effects these might have on construction, comfort, appearance and material requirements.

The impact of the designs will also be affected by your workmanship and personal decisions on finishing. You could keep arrises sharp, bevel them or round them. Your joints may be tight or sloppy (affecting the stability). You could leave the wood natural or stain it; apply teak oil or polyurethane or fill the grain and use french polish.

● **Below**: *mortise-and-tenon or halving, the choice is yours*

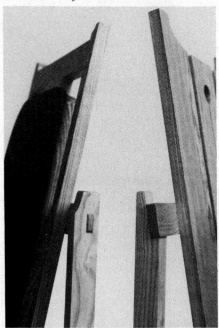

Construction

The TAPA dining chair planpack comprises fully measured drawings for all four chair styles, full size profiles, a cutting

962

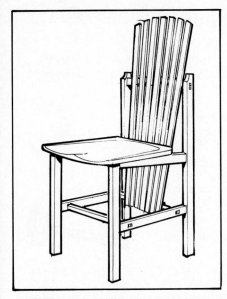

● TAPA 4: fanned back splats and a sculpted wooden seat

● TAPA 1: shaped wooden splats and an upholstered seat

● TAPA 2 with an upholstered back and seat

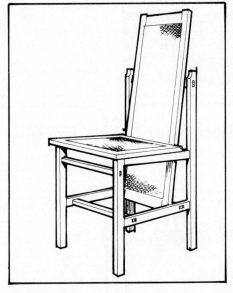

● TAPA 3: a caned seat and back make up the team

Cutting list

2 rear legs	721mm	x	32mm	x	22mm
2 front legs	434		32		22
2 top rails	482		30		18
2 lower rails	456		30		18
1 splat rail	414		40		18
3 stretchers: W, X	406		15		18
1 stretcher: Y	406		22		15
1 plywood seat	407		380		18
2 back rails	330		40		18
1 centre splat	747		88		18
2 outer splats	370		45		18

These are finished sizes, all in metric.

list and a suggested schedule of operations. The ash timberpacks also have cutting instructions; these packs are not kits, but three or four oversized boards from which you can cut the various components.

You obviously have to make your mind up which design you want before you start work and also choose whether to use mortise-and-tenon jointing or the simpler halving joint/screw and glue method.

Preparing the timber

Familiarise yourself with the working drawings and check you have all the necessary seasoned timber. Convert the boards to planed stock, either by hand or with a planer/thicknesser. All surfaces should be flat, straight and square, and free from major blemishes.

Framework

The exploded diagram of chair no. 2 shows the construction using mortise-and-tenon joints. The two side frames (front leg, rear leg, top rail and lower rail) are connected with horizontal components; stretchers and splat rail. You should start with the side frames, marking and cutting the joints, and assembling dry to test fit, and to check that the frames are flat, square and in alignment with each other. Don't overwork the joints at this stage. Number or letter the components before dismantling.

Now you can mark and cut the joints for the stretchers and splat rail, pre-planing stretcher Y to the correct angle. Assemble the whole framework dry to check alignment.

For this chair I would advise sanding and finishing the components before gluing up, taking care to mask off all surfaces to be glued. Finally glue and cramp together.

Splats and seat

In all four design suggestions, the splats or back rest frames are screwed to the splat rail and stretcher Y in pre-drilled holes; fill these plug holes afterwards. The back frames are not glued to the chair frame, to allow for wood movement.

The seats are screwed to the framework from underneath the stretchers W and top rails. Any upholstery, caning, rushwork or strapwork for the seats or back rests should be carried out before screwing the components to the framework.

These chairs have been designed to give pleasure in making and using and are quite straightforward if you stick to one of the suggested designs. If you want to get those brain cells working, devise your own adaptation and have a completely individual design. ∎

● TAPA planpack costs £5.75 plus 40p p&p from Woodworker Plans Service, Wolsey House, Wolsey Rd, Hemel Hempstead, Herts HP2 4SS, Ashby Design Workshop, 34a Catherine Hill, Frome, Somerset BA11 1BY, or ABW stockists. For details of ash timberpacks send SAE to above address.

Country colossus

Guy Rendel put 2cwt of timber through his universal to produce this beautifully proportioned dresser

T his project was designed to demonstrate the ability range of a universal woodworking machine. I chose white ash as it is attractive, strong and matches my other furniture. The dresser dismantles into two halves for easy transport, and is a suitable width and height for an exhibition stand — you'll see it at the 1986 Woodworker Show.

● We wish to thank Kity (UK), 6 Acorn Park, Charlestown, Shipley, West Yorks BD17 7SW, for the company's generous help in preparing this article.

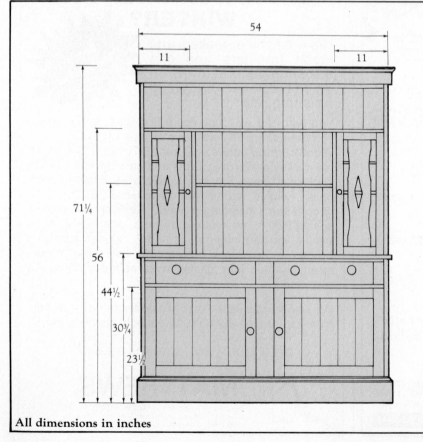

All dimensions in inches

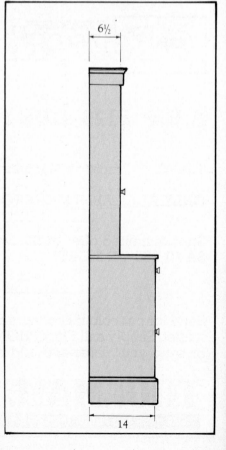

A believer in good proportions, I started by consulting a dictionary of 19th and early 20th century furniture. I liked the proportions of a dresser made by Norman and Stacey in 1910, but it was much too fussy in general, so I refined it to what you see here. I left the colour natural, with a Melamine catalytic lacquer finish.

With my design drawn up in detail I prepared a cutting list. The general rule with buying sawn hardwood is that the effective yield is around one-third of the original rough sawn volume. This dresser uses a fair amount of timber, which in total weighed about 2cwt when it arrived. One restriction of my universal, the Kity K5, is the 6in planer width, which meant planking would be required sometimes; I find this no great disadvantage with a small workshop.

A universal machine provides no short cuts from the conventional cabinetmaking work. But it enables you to start from rough-sawn timber and end up with flat boards to specific thickness and squareness. To achieve this you need accurate marking out in the first place, appropriate selection of timber grain direction, and careful and

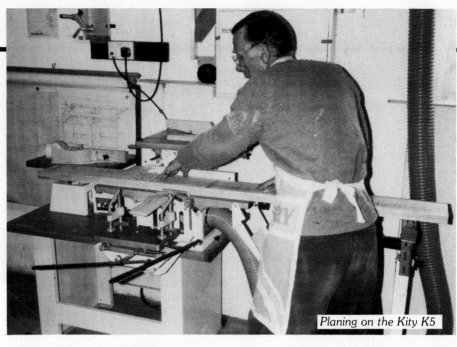

Planing on the Kity K5

accurate use of the machine during each process.

The finish you get from the planer/thicknesser — however sharp the blades and fine the cut — is not a final finish. To get fair faces you must hand-plane, scrape and hand-sand.

Hand-trimming is also necessary with mortise and tenon joints. The square mortise requires accurate hand finishing, and with tenons it's not safe to try to cut to a marked line; saw the crosscuts first to the mark and machine, leaving, say, 2mm to be finally hand-trimmed; this takes little time.

Machining tenons

1 Bottom carcase

After preparing boards for the two carcase sides, I made them up into panels with loose ply tongues by cutting 5mm grooves in the edges on the spindle moulder with a tungsten carbide grooving cutter, slotting from the fair face of each board to produce an almost perfect joint. I had previously trimmed the edges with a shooting plane, for the planer table was too short to give a straight enough edge for a clean joint.

With the other bottom carcase components prepared, I cut 12mm tenons on the spindle moulder, using the tenoning plate and the two tungsten carbide cutters ganged up with 12mm spacers. I used the slot mortiser for the matching holes,

squaring them out after by hand. I had to cut the mortises on the sides of the carcase with a router. Then I rebated the back edges of the sides, and hand-cut lap dovetails in the horizontal top pieces and the sides.

Before gluing up I finished all the wood, using a David Savage tip to identify components. The problem I had had in the past was that despite using a BB pencil, marks remained after finishing. The tip is to use

tiny coloured self-adhesive circles which you can buy from any stationer; these are easily removed after assembly, requiring only a slight scrape to remove any residual adhesive.

Having marked all components in this way, I glued up the whole carcase and cramped it in one; it's a bit arduous if there's only one pair of hands, and it takes a lot of cramps!

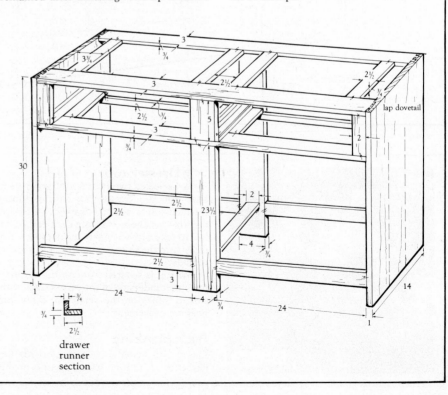

drawer
runner
section

Country colossus

Slot mortising

2 Top carcase

After preparing the wood for all components, I made up the sides and base in a similar fashion to the bottom side panels, rebating both at the back. I used the spindle moulder again for the tenons, and routed the mortise slots on the sides and base. I find cutting tenons by machine gives me consistent dimensions, so I only have to make a short test-piece tenon as a model for the mortises, and achieve a good tight fit every time. I used no screws except where the verticals are mortised into the base, and these don't show. Then I glued and cramped the top carcase together.

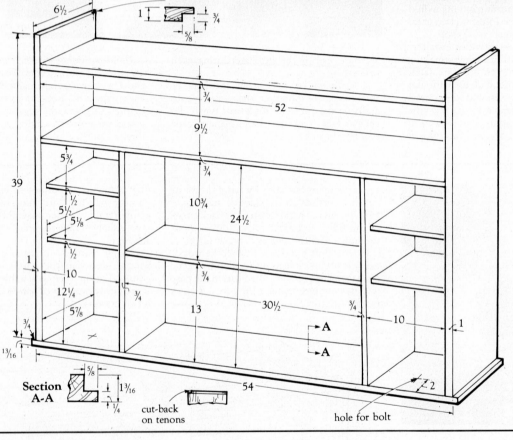

Section A-A

cut-back on tenons

hole for bolt

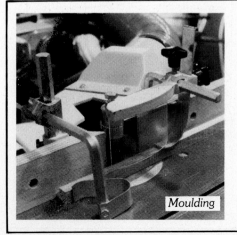
Moulding

3 Dresser top

I selected two boards with good grain for the dresser top, using loose-tongued joints again; however, I stopped the slots for these 2in from each end, and I had to take care when feeding in the leading edges into the slotting cutter on the spindle moulder.

The top is secured by screwing through from the underside of the carcase top, with slotted holes at the front to allow for possible movement.

Back planking

I used ½in material, selecting boards for best effect. I cut tongues and grooves on the spindle moulder with paired 5mm cutters, setting the far edge of the guide 1mm proud of the leading one to allow for the cut taken on the face of the board.

As ash has a tendency to move, I allowed a 2mm gap in each join when screwing the boards centrally to the carcase horizontals.

Drawers

I constructed the drawers in the conventional way, with lapped front and through back dovetails, cutting them all by hand. I rebated the bottom fronts and sides on the spindle moulder for the 5mm ply bottoms.

4 Cupboard doors

I shaped the centre panels of the top cupboard doors with a bandsaw, finishing by hand. After making the slot mortises on the spindle moulder, I finished squaring them up with a chisel.

With the bottom cupboard doors I machined rebates for the panels, using an 8mm carbide grooving cutter. The panels are of ½in material, tongued and grooved as for the top back planks. After gluing up the frame, I screwed on the planks, again using 2mm gaps for expansion. I finished the doors by fitting hinges, catches and locks.

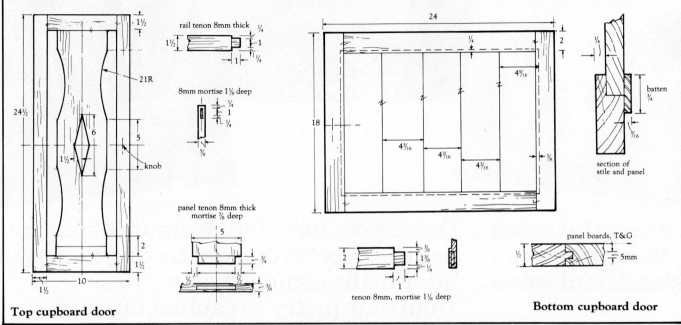

Top cupboard door

Bottom cupboard door

5 Top frieze and skirt

I find that deep mitre joints in particular are difficult to get looking presentable, so I cut and planed them by hand. I glued and cramped them in situ, using band cramps which are invaluable for this kind of job.

Mouldings

Before making these on the spindle moulder, I checked the direction of the grain to ensure the best finish I could get. Then I mitred the corners by hand, leaving them overlength for fitting.

Assembly

I fitted the drawers into the carcase, and then screwed on the top frieze and bottom skirting from behind, before fitting and gluing the top and bottom mouldings. The bottom cupboard back and floor were hand-sawn from 5mm ply, trimmed to fit and screwed to the carcase. I fitted the cupboard doors, and drilled and recessed holes for bolting the top carcase to the bottom. I turned cupboard and drawer knobs.

Now for the finishing touches. I scraped all wood surfaces and hand-sanded, finishing with 320-grit garnet paper, and ironing out the inevitable dents you seem to get with a lengthy project. After damping down to raise the grain, I sanded again with worn 320 garnet.

Then I lacquered all over, inside and out, using pre-catalysed acrylic lacquer diluted 50/50 with thinner, and applying with a squirrel mop. When this first coat was dry I took off the nibs with 0000 steel wool, and vacuumed off all dust before rubbing over with worn 320 garnet and applying a second coat of base lacquer. I de-nibbed this as before when thoroughly dry, and then left it a day to harden off.

The final coat was in satin finish, again diluted 50/50. And when this was dry I de-nibbed very lightly again.

Incidentally I did the whole finishing operation in the open under cover in warm dry weather, as the lacquer gives off considerable fumes. If you do it indoors, make sure you have plenty of ventilation.

Finally I applied a coat of Myland's Centenary wax which gave an excellent result. ■

Cutting list Planed sizes: lengths include working allowances

Top carcase sides	2 x	40in x	6½in x	1in
Bottom carcase sides	2	32	14	1
Base skirting	1	58	5	¾
	2	16	5	¾
Top frieze	1	58	4½	¾
	2	16	4½	¾
Top back planking	11	38	5¼	½
Top cupboard frames	4	24½	1½	¾
	4	10	1½	¾
Top cupboard panels	2	24	5	½
Shelves and top verticals	2	54	6½	¾
	1	32	6½	¾
	2	28	6½	¾
Bottom door panels	10	16	5	½
Drawer fronts	2	22	5	¾
Drawer sides	4	12	5	½
Drawer backs	2	22	5	½
Mouldings	2	58	1	¾
	4	16	1	¾
Bottom cupboard frames	4	19	2	¾
	4	22	2	¾
Dresser table top	1	58	6½	15/16
	1	58	7½	15/16
Drawer fascias and runners	1	54	2½	¾
	4	16	2½	¾
Front filling fascias	1	24	4	¾
	1	6	4	¾
	2	6	2	¾
Top cupboard shelves	4	11	5⅛	½

Where Craft Comes Alive..

Beautiful wood...   Oak, Sycamore, Ash, Walnut, Mahogany
Versatile wood...   see the experts demonstrating their skill
Wonderful wood...   admire the competition entries –
from marquetry to cabinet making
LOOK...   at the latest woodworking machinery,
tools, supplies and accessories
LISTEN...   to the advice of the demonstrators
BUY...   from the many exhibition stands

October 23rd – 26th at the
Alexandra Pavilion,
Wood Green, London

For further details contact
Argus Specialist Exhibitions,
Wolsey House, Wolsey Road,
Hemel Hempstead, Herts HP2 4SS
Tel: 0442 41221

Opening Times:
Oct. 23, 24, 25 ..... 10am-6pm
Oct. 26 .... 10am-5pm

The London Woodworker Show is organised by Argus Specialist Exhibitions
and sponsored by Woodworker Magazine

EUMENIA

The most versatile and safe Radial Arm Saw in the world

Cross cut capacity 370 mm

1.75 H.P. 240V (110V available)

Depth of cut 58 mm

Extension Arm available to increase cross cutting capacity to an amazing 700 mm. Ideal for kitchen worktops

Superbly engineered, highly accurate, positive settings, fail safe Blade Guard

ONLY £349 + VAT

With this amazing machine you can add accessories to rout – plane – mortice – mould – groove – tenon

Available from your local stockist. Send for comprehensive colour brochure. Full demonstration facilities at our Guildford and Warrington showrooms.

U.K. DISTRIBUTOR
WARREN MACHINE TOOLS
Middle Street, Shere, Nr Guildford, Surrey GU5 9HF.
Phone: 048 641 3434 (24 hours). Telex: 859455.
Adlington Court, Risley Industrial Estate, Birchwood, Warrington, Cheshire WA3 6PL.
Phone: 0925 821616. Telex: 629397

SEE TRY BEFORE YOU BUY

"BRIDGE HOUSE"
69 STATION ROAD,
CUFFLEY,
HERTS. EN6 4TG
CUFFLEY (0707) 873545

TILGEAR

"WHERE QUALITY TOOLS COST LESS"

EBONY HANDLED "EXOTICA" CHISELS

MULTI FLUTED – FORGED LAMINATED – BUTT CHISELS

The Butt chisel is the most common Japanese chisel being used in all general workshops. The blade is bevel edged and both the blade and handle are shorter than on heavy duty models for easier handling. Made of laminated steel, hand forged to a very high temper. The backs are hollow ground and require only light honing to maintain the perfect cutting edge even on the hardest woods. They have been tested by independent sources and have proved that they will last up to six times as long as conventional chisels.

NOW AVAILABLE INDIVIDUALLY!

OUR PRICES

3mm	£9.00
6mm	£9.50
9mm	£10.00
12mm	£11.00
15mm	£12.00
18mm	£13.00
24mm	£14.00
30mm	£15.00
36mm	£16.00
42mm	£17.00
48mm	£18.00

Exotica

These chisels have been included into our "EXOTICA" range of tools as they meet the exacting standards required. They will soon display our distinctive GOLD on purple Exotica labels.

Rear view showing multi-flutes

LAMINATED STEEL

This is made by hammering soft steel to hard steel by a hot forging process. The edge of the blade is thin, extremely hard and brittle but is supported by the thick soft steel which absorbs the shock. The backs of the chisels are hollowed out by a hammering process which retains the hard outside layer.

PRICES DO NOT INCLUDE V.A.T. OR CARRIAGE

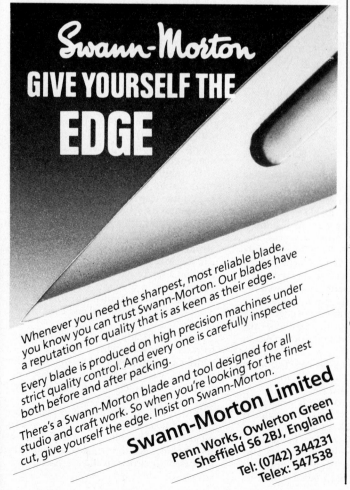

Swann-Morton
GIVE YOURSELF THE EDGE

Whenever you need the sharpest, most reliable blade, you know you can trust Swann-Morton. Our blades have a reputation for quality that is as keen as their edge.

Every blade is produced on high precision machines under strict quality control. And every one is carefully inspected both before and after packing.

There's a Swann-Morton blade and tool designed for all studio and craft work. So when you're looking for the finest cut, give yourself the edge. Insist on Swann-Morton.

Swann-Morton Limited
Penn Works, Owlerton Green
Sheffield S6 2BJ, England
Tel: (0742) 344231
Telex: 547538

carry away a bargain in our month of LUNA deals.

This lucky chap has just snapped up one of our **LUNA** package deals — FREE tooling, FREE extractor & special prices are up for grabs — so snap up a bargain, but our offers must end November 30th.

WRITE OR PHONE FOR OUR OFFER PRICE LISTS.

HEATH SAWS, LEESIDE WORKS, STANSTEAD ABBOTTS, Nr. WARE, HERTS.(0920) 870230/ 870636.

Soled on wood

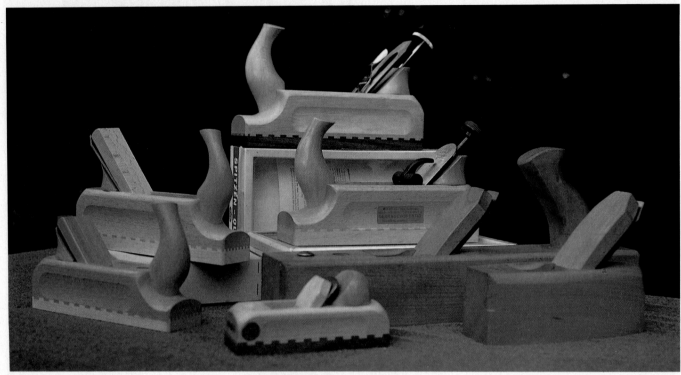

Rik Middleton's examination of wooden planes continues with a close and critical look at modern models

While I've built up my collection of wooden planes largely from market stalls, you don't have to go through the work of resurrecting worn-out old planes. There's a wide range of good quality, robust, bench planes available new, but you might not find them in your local tool shop.

Wooden planes today seem to come from either West Germany or Japan. I've looked at a range from a single West German manufacturer, E. C. Emmerich, who produces a wide variety of styles (above). These include copies of the English pattern smoothing and jack plane, while the rest are markedly mid-European in style, with a rounded hand-guard behind the blade and a beautifully tactile and functional 'horn' front handle.

I haven't tried to compare similar tools, but give you an idea of the range available, with the strengths and weaknesses of each type.

Although most of the German planes were labelled 'Gebrauchsfertig' (ready for use), they all needed a bit of attention to get them working well.

Wooden wedges, where these were fitted, all fitted poorly and needed re-shaping with a paring chisel. Some of the blades needed considerable rubbing down to make them flat.

Don't let that put you off; with a bit of tuning they all worked well.

English-style smoother

After modifying the wedge and rubbing down the coarsely ground blade, it should have been in good order. But it was very disappointing; it seemed unable to take any sort of fine cut, taking a very small amount off at the front and back of a pass, but nothing in the middle. I checked the sole with a piece of 1/4in plate glass, lightly oiling it with linseed oil, and laying it on the upturned sole of the plane. This showed the problem; the oil spread out in a line a few millimetres wide all around the edge of the sole with no contact in the middle — the sole was concave and the mouth was not in contact with the workpiece. I rubbed the sole down on my plate-glass-based abrasive board, as explained last month, and it was flat within a few minutes.

After curing this problem it performed comparably in every way with my own old smoothing planes with which it is almost identical. In fact with a blade of harder steel it held an edge noticeably better; it was also more sensitive to light hammer blows for fine setting than my old ones. It could be very finely set and easily removed a very fine shaving.

The mouth was rather wide at over 4mm for its specialist smoothing function and the blade and wedge come out to almost exactly the same point; I would like to remove about 1/2in from the thick end of the wedge.

At about £18 it is cheaper than the cast metal type and if this kind of plane is what you want I thoroughly recommend it.

English-style jack plane

This was slightly smaller in cross-section than my old ones (70x70mm compared with 78x78mm) but it was exactly the same length (430mm). It showed no sole distortion and the blade back was flat.

The fault with this one was strange and inexplicable. The top of the handle intersects a line upward through the blade axis; the result is that you can't hit the back of the iron squarely with a hammer. I found this inconvenient and annoying; I had to put it 'on cut' by alternate taps either side of the handle. My solution was to take a coping saw and a spokeshave to the handle top and remove 1/2in in a curve. There's plenty of room to do this and still have room for your hand as it is a substantial and comfortable handle.

Once I had adjusted it, the plane performed very well, with a suitable mouth width of 2.8mm. Again I recommend this to the wooden plane enthusiast not frightened to take a saw to the structural modification; it costs about £28.

Both of these English-style planes are made of what looks like excellent quality oiled beech. The following mid-European-styled planes are all varnished and all those imported into Britain have a harder sole jointed on.

Scrub plane

This is a very narrow plane fitted with a 33mm wide single iron, ground to a 33mm radius curve cutting edge, and simply wooden-wedged in place. The instructions say the plane removes a lot of stock quickly from the surface, may be used with or across the grain, and should be set between ¹⁄₁₆in and ⅛in, or enough to leave hollow grooves in the work. A new one on me.

Unfortunately, as supplied, it won't work! The effective mouth size of the model I had was about 1mm measured on the centre-line with the blade on zero cut depth. Since the plane is designed to cut grooves of more than 1mm thickness there is no way that the thick shavings produced could pass through into the gullet — so the plane jams solid if you attempt to use it as described. The only way I could make it work was to take a gouge to the front of the mouth and cut away a curve to match the blade, making the effective mouth opening about 4-5mm at the centre (see below). I checked a shelf-full and found they all had the same mouth setting. Michael Sarjent says he has not had any returned with complaints — either everybody is quite happy to take a gouge to their new plane or there are a lot of highly polished planes decorating mantelpieces or holding doors open.

'Gents' plane

This is a reduced-size German plane and the cheapest of the range available in this country. It has a simple wooden wedge and a single 39mm blade, both of which needed work. Once it was sharpened I couldn't get a fine cut; thick shavings or none at all. I found the side of the blade on which the bevel is ground was covered with a black scaley deposit, presumably from the heat treatment; this made the blade quite unresponsive to small adjustment taps.

After rubbing down it adjusted well and cut really very nicely within the limitations imposed by a single iron. Such a plane cannot deal well with wild or crossed grains such as knotty pine or mahogany, but on straight-grained wood it cuts very fine shavings. The mouth width of 2.5mm is not close enough to help it overcome its lack of back iron.

If slightly reduced-size tools appeal to you (I love them) then this is a very charming and useable novelty tool as well as being the cheapest available in this country at just under £16. For serious smoothing functions on a variety of timbers the English smoother is only £2 more and has a back iron and a wider blade.

Block plane

Much of what I have said about the 'gents' plane also applies to this one. Its wedge needed some reshaping, its blade took a bit of flattening and had the same scale on the back of it. It also has a 39mm blade, in this case a rather short one which needed considerable care to hit with the hammer without catching the wedge or rounded back handle. Of course, it's even smaller than the 'gents'; but once fettled it's a delight to use on straight-grained timber. I had the wooden-wedged version at just under £17; there's also a steel-wedged wheel adjustable version at around £24.

Oh for a back iron on the 'gents' or block planes and I could fall in love all over again!

'Primus' planes

These have double irons and a spring-tensioned fine-adjustment mechanism. They range through smoothing and

● *The jack-plane handle after modification,* **below**; *a profusion of blades,* **right**

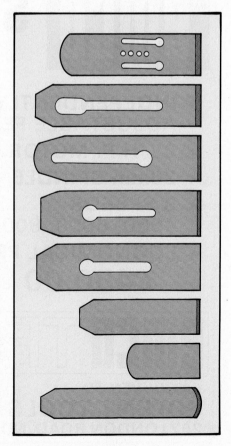

Soled on wood

German-style jack planes to a try plane, and include rebate planes.

I tested the Primus 703p, one of three very similar planes in this range; two are almost identical, including price. The 703p is a 240mm-long jack plane; also in the range is a smoother (704p), an 'improved' smoothing plane (711p) and a 600mm-long try plane.

I found the mechanism for fixing and adjusting the blade a little confusing at first. Instructions for tightening up the spring tension screw are not very specific, so I did it fairly tight. Lateral adjustment is done by eye with the blade showing, but I found the adjustment lever too crude, so I removed it, rubbed it down on a flat stone and remounted it with a smear of vaseline. Even so the leverage is not great, and soon I found I was adjusting by hand, levering the back end of the blade against the rear hand guard. On the model I tried, I lost lateral adjustment when I changed the vertical adjustment by more than a small amount, and it kept cutting to the right.

I was also disappointed with the vertical adjustment wheel. Taking it apart, I removed two metal studs with pincers, and pared some wood from the slot in the back of the gullet — you need the courage of your convictions to do this to a new £50 tool. But it worked, and vertical adjustment was immediately better.

Having looked at other models I've discovered mine was a bad one. Once I had this plane set to my satisfaction it cut really beautifully. It has a certain smooth weight to it (it weighs 2lb 14oz). With its back iron close set and its mouth width of about 1mm it made a better job of difficult grain than anything I have ever had before. Tiny turns of the adjusting wheel produced shavings whose differences could only be found using a micrometer. At £50 I feel it should be worth anyone's serious consideration.

Expert jack

The Expert jack plane is a screw-adjustable plane at a cheaper price than the 'Primus' range. The single iron has two slots to fit over screws in the gullet and a row of holes to fit over the spigot of the adjustment mechanism. All this is held in place by a cap iron. This is not a back iron as it stops about 10mm short of the cutting edge and doesn't present a close-fitting profile.

The vertical adjustment is precise and positive, better than any cast plane I have used. Lateral adjustment is by hand. The sole was flat and it planed well within the limitations of a single iron.

The blade fixing mechanism is just not firm enough for my liking. You can easily move the back end of the iron from side to side; not surprisingly it can move itself while planing. I found a noticeable tendency to 'chatter marks' on difficult patches of grain and on the start of a cut, because of the blade fixing method. This one at around £30 should not be chosen as an 'all purpose' plane.

Conclusions

On German styles of plane generally, I find the front handle a very functional device; it allows much more contact and 'feel' from the left hand. It also greatly facilitates pulling when you need to.

The sole pieces are cunningly and prettily jointed on at the bottom. Most models come as either beech with a hornbeam sole or hornbeam with a lignum vitae sole. I recommend the lignum vitae soled models; this wood refuses to accept any dirt or discolouration no matter how tatty the timber being planed and simply burnishes to an ever greater and more friction-free gloss; hornbeam just gets scruffy.

As well as these flat work planes there are others for specialist functions. A very classy-looking rebate plane with the Primus mechanism and a double iron is ahead of my old English ones. It has a readily adjustable mouth and lignum vitae sole; quite mouth-watering in fact — but £55.

There's also the big, meaty-looking 'old woman's tooth' router with three blades and a real handful of beechwood body, and a pair of tongue-and-groove cutting moulding planes. More esoteric is a dovetail plane for insetting shelf ends. Who doesn't do this with an electric router?

Missing, to my regret, is a German designed body for those wanting the cutting quality of a double iron and the security of a wooden wedge. I'm sure not all woodworkers are frightened of hammer adjustable planes.

● **N.B.:** Rik tells us that the Primus plane with the lignum vitae sole has turned **convex in length** by about 1mm in 12 weeks. Recommendation reconsidered . . .

● Thanks to Michael Sarjent of Sarjent's Tools of Reading, Roger Buse of Roger's of Hitchin, and Dick Warren of Lanchester Polytechnic Metallurgy department for help in preparing this feature.

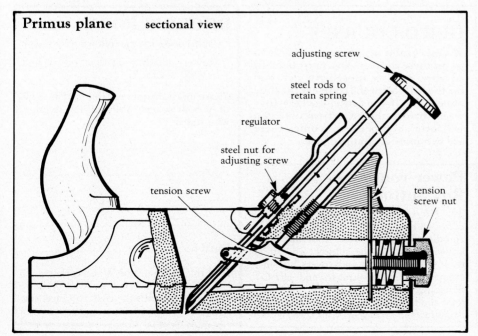

Primus plane   sectional view

adjusting screw

steel rods to retain spring

regulator

steel nut for adjusting screw

tension screw

tension screw nut

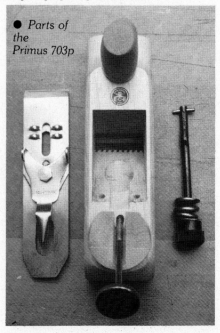

● *Parts of the Primus 703p*

Guild notes

Guild of WOODWORKERS

The Guild was set up by *Woodworker* to create a meeting ground for all those involved in working wood, whether professional, amateur, or enthusiastic beginner. Guild members get:
- Access to Guild courses and events
- Free publicity in *Woodworker*
- Specially arranged tool insurance at low rates
- 15% off Woodworker Show entry
- A free display area and meeting point at the Show
- 15% discount off *Woodworker* plans
- Inclusion in our register of members' skills and services

For details, please send an sae to the Guild of Woodworkers, 1 Golden Sq, London W1R 3AB.

Christmas is coming . . .

And we'd like some festive help from you. If you know of a special event or place worthy of a woodworker visit, let us know and we'll try and arrange a yuletide get-together for Guild members.

Come up with a good idea — anything from a country-house to a working museum, preferably with a hostelry in sight — and send us the details of location, entrance fees and why it will be of interest to Guild bods.

And the incentive: if we use your suggestion, there'll be a genuine **plum-pudding** in the post to you!

Selling yourself

If you're in business for yourself or trying to sell your work you'll need to find the right outlets. The Independent Craft Galleries Association has supplied us with details of galleries interested in woodcrafts.
- Holly House Gallery, 14 Front St, Tynemouth, North Shields, Tyne & Wear NE3 04DX, (0632) 592753, contact Timandra Gustafson
- Chestnut Gallery, High St, Bourton-on-the-Water, Cheltenham, Glos, (0451) 20017, contact Peter and Mary O'Connor
- Fenny Lodge Gallery, Simpson Rd, Bletchley, Milton Keynes MK1 1BD, (0908) 642207, contact Sophie Rathsach.

A passage to India

I've just spent six months in Madras, writes Guild member John Chambers, training apprentices in a carpentry shop for orphans The trainees, 16-23 years old, spend three years in the school, with conventional teaching as well as craft training. They make items for the community, as well as toolkits for when they leave to work in the local furniture industry or as contract carpenters. The kits include smoothing, jack, rebate and plough planes, mallets from mango trees, chisel handles and marking gauges. Saws, chisel and plane blades are supplied by the charity, Intermission.

I got a shock when I saw an apprentice sharpening his chisel on a piece of wood. They use a 1m long piece of hardwood laid flat on the bench, with yellow sand rubbed into the grain. They grasp the chisel in both hands and move it from left to right across the surface until they get a keen edge.

Almost all carpentry and furniture in India is in hardwoods — there don't seem to be any native softwoods. Teak is very common, and is used for all good furniture, doors and windows. At the cheaper end is 'country wood' — a mixture of many varieties (no choice) including venteak, teak, karumuruthu, red padauk, yellow wood, mango, silver oak, white suclam and vengay. This costs about 100 rupees per cu. ft (about £6.50). I found vast quantities of rosewood in timber yards, costing 400-550 rupees a cu. ft (£23-32).

Our workshop had a circular saw, a thicknesser, bandsaw and lathe; first thing I did was get guards made for them all!

I took some plans from *Woodworker* and designs I had collected over the years, and helped the trainees make toys, kitchen items and laminated bowls. To give and receive as a craftsman was a delight; it's a great privilege to do such work in India.

House style

Cardiff Guild member Sid Lye sent us this rags-to-riches story proving that the pioneering spirit and the friendly postman are still alive and kicking.

'About time you had a house-name that doesn't need a magnifying glass to find it,' said the helpful Post Office driver. So having done a night-class in woodcarving and been given some odd bits of timber, I set to with my carving gouges, mallet and Workmate, transforming a 8x1½in plastic 'Heathcliff' into a 26x7x1in name-plate out of a piece of very white sycamore. A coat of Rustin's mahogany stain/varnish and a matching family name on the bell-push — and the offers came flooding in (poetic licence).

So what made the postman/doctor/gas-man happy again, has mushroomed into quite a little sideline. From my customers' remarks there seems to be a dearth of house-name makers in this patch of South Wales and it also seems that these days most people like one-upmanship in most things — like: 'the neighbour's slice of pine-log with pyrographed lettering won't do for ower house, mun!'

Experience wanted

Could you use an extra pair of hands in your workshop?

We've had a request from a young Guild member hoping to go to Rycotewood and eager to enhance his skills in the meantime.

He's asked if we can find a professional Guild member, within reasonable distance of Reading, who will take him on as an unpaid apprentice. Replies, in the first instance, to The Administrator, Guild of Woodworkers, 1 Golden Sq, London W1R 3AB.

shop guide

AVON

BATH Tel. Bath 64513
JOHN HALL TOOLS ★
RAILWAY STREET

Open: Monday-Saturday
9.00 a.m.-5.30 p.m.
H.P.W.WM.D.A.BC.

BRISTOL Tel. (0272) 741510
JOHN HALL TOOLS LIMITED ★
CLIFTON DOWN SHOPPING CENTRE
WHITELADIES ROAD
Open: Monday-Saturday
9.00 a.m.-5.30 p.m.
H.P.W.WM.D.A.BC.

BRISTOL Tel. (0272) 629092
TRYMWOOD SERVICES
2a DOWNS PARK EAST, (off North View)
WESTBURY PARK
Open: 8.30 a.m.-5.30 p.m. Mon. to Fri.
Closed for lunch 1.00-2.00 p.m.
P.W.WM.D.T.A.BC.

BRISTOL Tel. (0272) 667013
FASTSET LTD
190-192 WEST STREET
BEDMINSTER
Open: Mon.-Fri. 8.30 a.m.-5.00 p.m.
Saturday 9.00 a.m.-1.00 p.m.
H.P.W.WM.D.CS.A.BC.

BRISTOL Tel. (0272) 667013
WILLIS
157 WEST STREET
BEDMINSTER
Open Mon.-Fri. 8.30 a.m.-5.00 p.m.
Sat. 9 a.m.-4 p.m.
P.W.WM.D.CS.A.BC.

ALL THOSE SHOPS WITH AN ASTERIX HAVE A MAIL ORDER SERVICE.

BERKSHIRE

READING Tel. Littlewick Green
DAVID HUNT (TOOL 2743
MERCHANTS) LTD ★
KNOWL HILL, NR. READING
Open: Monday-Saturday
9.00 a.m.-5.30 p.m.
H.P.W.D.A.BC.

READING Tel. Reading 661511
WOKINGHAM TOOL CO. LTD
99 WOKINGHAM ROAD

Open: Mon-Sat 9.00 a.m.-5.30 p.m.
Closed 1.00-2.00 p.m. for lunch
H.P.W.WM.D.CS.A.BC.

BUCKINGHAMSHIRE

MILTON KEYNES Tel. (0908)
POLLARD WOODWORKING 641366
CENTRE
51 AYLESBURY ST., BLETCHLEY
Open: Mon-Fri 8.30-5.30
Saturday 9.00-5.00
H.P.W.WM.D.CS.A.BC.

HIGH WYCOMBE Tel. (0494)
SCOTT SAWS LTD. 24201/33788
14 BRIDGE STREET ★

Mon.-Sat. 8.30 a.m.-6.00 p.m.

H.P.W.WM.D.T.CS.MF.A.BC.

HIGH WYCOMBE Tel. (0494)
ISAAC LORD LTD 22221
185 DESBOROUGH ROAD KE

Open: Mon-Fri 8.00 a.m.-5.00 p.m.
Saturday 9.00 a.m.-5.00 p.m.
H.P.W.D.A.

CAMBRIDGESHIRE

CAMBRIDGE Tel: (0223) 63132
D. MACKAY LTD. ★
BRITANNIA WORKS, EAST ROAD

Open: Mon.-Fri. 8.30 a.m.-1 p.m./2.00-
5.00 p.m. Sat. 8.30 a.m.-1.00 p.m.
H.P.W.D.T.CS.MF.A.BC.

CAMBRIDGE Tel. (0223) 247386
H. B. WOODWORKING K
105 CHERRY HINTON ROAD
Open: 8.30 a.m.-5.30 p.m.
Monday-Friday
8.30 a.m.-1.00 p.m. Sat.
H.P.W.WM.D.CS.A.

PETERBOROUGH Tel. (0733)
WILLIAMS DISTRIBUTORS 64252
(TOOLS) LIMITED K
108-110 BURGHLEY ROAD
Open: Monday to Friday
8.30 a.m.-5.30 p.m.
H.P.A.W.D.WH.BC.

CHESHIRE

NANTWICH Tel. Crewe 67010
ALAN HOLTHAM K★
THE OLD STORES TURNERY
WISTASON ROAD, WILLASTON
Open: Tues.-Sat. 9.00 a.m.-5.30 p.m.
Closed Monday
P.W.WM.D.T.C.CS.A.BC.

CLEVELAND

MIDDLESBROUGH Tel. (0642)
CLEVELAND WOODCRAFT 813103
(M'BRO), 38-42 CRESCENT ROAD K

Open: Mon-Sat 9.15 a.m.-5.30 p.m.

H.P.T.A.BC.W.WM.CS.D.

CORNWALL

SOUTH WEST Power Tools

CORNWALL Tel: Helston (03265) 4961
HELSTON AND LAUNCESTON Launceston
(0566) 4781
H.P.W.WM.D.CS.A. K

CUMBRIA

CARLISLE Tel: (0228) 36391
W. M. PLANT
ALLENBROOK ROAD
ROSEHILL, CA1 2UT
Open: Mon.-Fri. 8.00 a.m.-5.15 p.m.
Sat. 8.00 a.m.-12.30 noon
P.W.WM.D.CS.A.

DEVON

BRIXHAM Tel. (08045) 4900
WOODCRAFT SUPPLIES E★
4 HORSE POOL STREET

Open: Mon.-Sat. 9.00 a.m.-6.00 p.m.

H.P.W.A.D.MF.CS.BC.

PLYMOUTH Tel. (0752) 330303
WESTWARD BUILDING SERVICES ★
LTD., LISTER CLOSE, NEWNHAM
INDUSTRIAL ESTATE, PLYMPTON
Open: Mon-Fri 8.00 a.m.-5.30 p.m.
Sat. 8.30 a.m.-12.30 p.m.
H.P.W.WM.D.A.BC.

PLYMOUTH Tel: (0752) 665363
F.T.B. LAWSON LTD.
71 NEW GEORGE STREET
PLYMOUTH PL1 1RB
Open: Mon.-Sat. 8.30 a.m.-5.30 p.m.
H.P.W.CS.MF.A.

ESSEX

LEIGH ON SEA Tel. (0702)
MARSHAL & PARSONS LTD. 710404
1111 LONDON ROAD EK

Open: 8.30 a.m.-5.30 p.m. Mon-Fri
9.00 a.m.-5.00 p.m. Sat.
H.P.W.WM.D.CS.A.

GLOUCESTER

TEWKESBURY Tel. (0684)
TEWKESBURY SAW CO. LTD. 293092
TRADING ESTATE, NEWTOWN K

Open: Mon-Fri 8.00 a.m.-5.00 p.m.
Saturday 9.30 a.m.-12.00 p.m.
P.W.WM.D.CS.

HAMPSHIRE

ALDERSHOT Tel. (0252) 334422
POWER TOOL CENTRE K
374 HIGH STREET

Open Mon.-Fri. 8.30 a.m.-5.30 p.m.
Sat. 8.30 a.m.-12.30 p.m.
H.P.W.WM.D.A.BC.

SOUTHAMPTON Tel. (0703)
POWER TOOL CENTRE 332288
7 BELVIDERE ROAD K★
Open Mon.-Fri. 8.30-5.30

H.P.W.WM.D.A.BC.CS.MF.

HERTFORDSHIRE

WARE K★
HEATH SAWS
16 MALTINGS
STANSTEAD ABBOTTS (near Ware) HERTS.
Open: Mon.-Fri. 8.30am-5.30pm
Sat. 8.30am-1pm. Sunday by appointment.
P.W.WM.D.CS.A.

ENFIELD Tel: 01-363 2935
GILL & HOXBY LTD.
131-137 ST. MARKS ROAD ADJ.
BUSH HILL PARK STATION, EN1 1BA
Mon.-Sat. 8-5.30
Early closing Wed. 1 p.m.
H.P.A.M.C.T.S.W.

HUMBERSIDE

GRIMSBY Tel. Grimsby (0472)
58741 Hull (0482) 26999
J. E. SIDDLE LTD. (Tool Specialists) ★
83 VICTORIA STREET
Open: Mon-Fri 8.30 a.m.-5.30 p.m.
Sat. 8.30 a.m.-12.45 p.m. & 2 p.m.-5 p.m.
H.P.A.BC.W.WMD.

HULL
HUMBERSIDE FACTORING/H.F.C.
SAW SERVICING LTD.
MAIN STREET
Open: Mon.-Fri. 8am-5pm
Saturday 8am-12.00pm.
H.P.W.WM.D.CS.A.BC.K.

KENT

WYE Tel. (0233) 813144
KENT POWER TOOLS LTD.
UNIT 1, BRIAR CLOSE
WYE, Nr. ASFORD

H.P.W.WM.D.A.CS.

MAIDSTONE Tel. (0622) 50177
SOUTH EASTERN SAWS (Ind.) LTD. ★
COLDRED ROAD
PARKWOOD INDUSTRIAL ESTATE

Open: Mon.-Fri. 8.00 a.m.-6.00 p.m.
Sat. 9.00 a.m.-12.00 a.m.
B.C.W.CS.WM.PH.

LANCASHIRE

PRESTON Tel. (0772) 52951
SPEEDWELL TOOL COMPANY E★
62-68 MEADOW STREET PR1 1SU
Open: Mon.-Fri. 8.30 a.m.-5.30 p.m.
Sat. 8.30 a.m.-12.30 p.m.

H.P.W.WM.CS.A.MF.BC.

ALL THOSE SHOPS WITH ASTERIX HAVE MAIL ORDER SERVICE ★

977

shopguide

LANCASHIRE

LANCASTER Tel: (0524) 32886
LILE TOOL SHOP K
43/45 NORTH ROAD
Open: Monday to Saturday
9.00 a.m.-5.30 p.m.
Wed. 9.00 a.m.-12.30 p.m.
H.P.W.D.A.

LANCASHIRE Tel: (070 681) 4931
'TODMORDEN' ★
TOWNLEY TIMES, HAREHILL STREET
OFF BURNLEY ROAD
Open: Mon.-Fri. 8.30 am-5.30 pm
Sat. 9.00 am-1.00 pm
H.P.W.D.A.BC.

BLACKPOOL Tel: (0253) 24299
FLYDE WOODTURNING SUPPLIES ★
222 HORNBY ROAD (BASEMENT)
BLACKPOOL FY1 4HY
9.30-5.30 Monday to Saturday
H.P.W.WM.A.MF.C.B.C.D.

ROCHDALE Tel. (0706) 342123/
C.S.M. TOOLS 342322
4-6 HEYWOOD ROAD E★
CASTLETON
Open: Mon-Sat 9.00 a.m.-6.00 p.m.
Sundays by appointment
W.D.CS.A.BC.

LINCOLNSHIRE

LINCOLN Tel: (0522) 689369
SKELLINGTHORPE SAW SERVICES LTD.
OLD WOOD, SKELLINGTHORPE
Open: Mon to Fri 8 a.m -5 p.m.
Sat 8 a.m-12 p.m.
H.P.W.WM.D.CS.A.*.BC.
Access/Barclaycard

LONDON

ACTON Tel: (01-992) 4835
A. MILLS (ACTON) LTD ★
32/36 CHURCHFIELD ROAD W3 6ED
Open: Mon-Fri 9.00 a.m.-5.00 p.m.
Saturdays 9.00 am-1.00 p.m.
H.P.W.WM.

LONDON Tel. 01-723 2295-6-7
LANGHAM TOOLS LIMITED
13 NORFOLK PLACE
LONDON W2 1QJ

LONDON Tel. (01-636) 7475
BUCK & RYAN LTD ★
101 TOTTENHAM COURT ROAD W1P 0DY
Open: Mon.-Fri. 8.30 a.m.-5.30 p.m.
Saturday 8.30 a.m.-4.00 p.m.
H.P.W.WM.D.A..

WEMBLEY Tel. 904-1144
ROBERT SAMUEL LTD. (904-1147
7, 15 & 16 COURT PARADE after 4.00)
EAST LANE, N. WEMBLEY ★
Open Mon.-Fri. 8.45-5.15; Sat. 9-1.00
Access, Barclaycard, AM Express, & Diners
H.P.W.CS.E.A.D.

LONDON

HOUNSLOW Tel. (01-570)
Q.R. TOOLS LTD 2103/5135
251-253 HANWORTH ROAD
Open: Mon-Fri 8.30 a.m.-5.30 p.m.
Sat. 9.00 a.m.-1.00 p.m.
P.W.WM.D.CS.A.

FULHAM Tel. (01-385) 5109
I. GRIZZARD LTD. E
84a-b LILLIE ROAD, SW6 1TL
Open: Mon-Sat 9.00-5.30 p.m.
Half day Thursday
H.P.A.BC.W.CS.WM.D.

MANCHESTER

MANCHESTER Tel. (061 789)
TIMMS TOOLS 0909
102-104 LIVERPOOL ROAD ★
PATRICROFT M30 0WZ
Weekdays 9.00 a.m.-5.30 p.m.
Sat. 9.00 a.m.-1.00 p.m.
H.P.A.W.

MERSEYSIDE

LIVERPOOL Tel. (051-207) 2967
TAYLOR BROS (LIVERPOOL) LTD K
195-199 LONDON ROAD
LIVERPOOL L3 8JG
Open: Monday to Friday
8.30 a.m.-5.30 p.m.
H.P.W.WM.D.A.BC.

MIDDLESEX

RUISLIP Tel. (08956) 74126
ALLMODELS ENGINEERING LTD. E★
91 MANOR WAY
Open: Mon-Sat 9.00 a.m.-5.30 p.m.
H.P.W.A.D.CS.MF.BC.

NORFOLK

NORWICH Tel. (06D3) 898695
NORFOLK SAW SERVICES
DOG LANE, HORSFORD
Open: Monday to Friday
8.00 a.m.-5.00 p.m.
Saturday 8.00 a.m.-12.00 p.m.
H.P.W.WM.D.CS.A.

KINGS LYNN Tel. (0553) 2443
WALKER & ANDERSON (Kings Lynn) LTD.
WINDSOR ROAD, KINGS LYNN K
Open: Monday to Saturday
7.45 a.m.-5.30 p.m.
Wednesday 1.00 p.m. Saturday 5.00 p.m.
H.P.W.WM.D.CS.A.

NORWICH Tel. (0603) 400933
WESTGATES WOODWORKING Tx
61 HURRICANE WAY, 975412
NORWICH AIRPORT INDUSTRIAL ESTATE
Open: 9.00 a.m.-5.00 p.m. weekdays
9.00 a.m.-12.30 Sat.
P.W.WM.D.BC. K

KING'S LYNN Tel. (07605) 674
TONY WADILOVE WOODCRAFT
HILL FARM WORKSHOPS
GT. DUNHAM
(NR. SWAFFHAM)
Tues.-Sat. 9.00am-5.30pm
H.P.W.D.T.MF.A.BC.

NOTTINGHAMSHIRE

NOTTINGHAM Tel. (0602) 225979
POOLEWOOD and 227064/5
EQUIPMENT LTD. (06077) 2421 after hrs
5a HOLLY LANE, CHILLWELL
Open: Mon-Fri 9.00 a.m.-5.30 p.m.
Sat. 9.00 a.m. to 12.30 p.m.
P.W.WM.D.CS.A.BC.

OXON

WITNEY Tel. (0993) 3885
TARGET TOOLS (SALES, & 72095 OXON
TARGET TOOLS HIRE & REPAIRS) ★
SWAIN COURT
STATION INDUSTRIAL ESTATE
Open: Mon.-Sat. 8.00 a.m.-5.00 p.m.
24 hour Answerphone
BC.W.M.A.

SHROPSHIRE

TELFORD Tel. Telford (0952)
ASLES LTD 48054
VINEYARD ROAD, WELLINGTON EK★
Open: Mon. Fri. 8.30 a.m.-5.30 p.m.
Saturday 8.30 a.m.-4.00 p.m.
H.P.W.WM.D.CS.BC.A.

SOMERSET

TAUNTON Tel. (0823) 85431
JOHN HALL TOOLS ★
6 HIGH STREET
Open Monday-Saturday
9.00 a.m.-5.30 p.m.
H.P.W.WM.D.CS.A.

SUFFOLK

SUFFOLK
LOCKWOOD WOODWORKING MACHINERY
WHITE GATES BUNGALOW
THE COMMON MELLIS
NEAR EYE/DISS IP23 8DY Tel: (037983) 8126
Open: Mon., Wed., Thurs., Fri. 8am-8pm
Tues. & Sat. 8am-5pm.
Lathe demos every Saturday morning.
We cover both Norfolk and Suffolk.
H.P.W.D.A.

IPSWICH Tel. (0473) 40456
FOX WOODWORKING KE★
142-144 BRAMFORD LANE
Open: Tues., Fri., 9.00 a.m.-5.30 p.m.
Sat. 9.00 a.m.-5.00 p.m.
H.P.W.WM.D.A.BC.

TO FILL THIS
SPACE. PHONE
01-437 0626

SUSSEX

BOGNOR REGIS Tel. (0243) 863100
A. OLBY & SON (BOGNOR REGIS) LTD.
"TOOLSHOP," BUILDERS MERCHANT
HAWTHORN ROAD K
Open: Mon-Thurs 8 a.m.-5.15 p.m. Fri.
8 a.m-8 p.m. Sat 8 a.m.-12.45 p.m.
H.P.W.WM.D.T.C.A.BC.

WORTHING Tel. (0903) 38739
W. HOSKING LTD (TOOLS & KE★
MACHINERY)
28 PORTLAND RD, BN11 1QN
Open: Mon.-Sat. 8.30 a.m.-5.30 p.m.
Closed Wednesday
H.P.W.WM.D.CS.A.BC.

TYNE & WEAR

NEWCASTLE Tel. (0632) 320311
HENRY OSBOURNE LTD. E★
50-54 UNION STREET
Open: Mon-Fri 8.30 a.m.-5.00 p.m.
H.P.W.D.CS.MF.A.BC.

W. MIDLANDS

WOLVERHAMPTON Tel. (0902)
MANSAW SERVICES 58759
SEDGLEY STREET K★
Open: Mon.-Fri. 9.00 a.m.-5.00 p.m.
H.P.W.WM.A.D.CS.

YORKSHIRE

BOROUGHBRIDGE Tel. (09012)
JOHN BODDY TIMBER LTD 2370
FINE WOOD & TOOL STORE ★
RIVERSIDE SAWMILLS
Open: Mon.-Thurs. 8.00 a.m.-6.00 p.m.
Fri. 8.00am-5.00pm Sat. 8.00am-4.00pm
H.P.W.WM.D.T.CS.MF.A.BC.

SHEFFIELD Tel. (0742) 441012
GREGORY & TAYLOR LTD KE
WORKSOP ROAD
Open: 8.30 a.m.-5.30 p.m.
Monday-Friday
8.30 a.m.-12.30 p.m. Sat.
H.P.W.WM.D.

HARROGATE Tel. (0423) 66245/
MULTI-TOOLS 55328
158 KINGS ROAD K★
Open: Monday to Saturday
8.30 a.m.-6.00 p.m.
H.P.W.WM.D.A.BC.

THIRSK Tel. (0845) 22770
THE WOOD SHOP ★
TRESKE SAWMILLS LTD.
STATION WORKS
Open: Seven days a week 9.00-5.00
T.H.MF.BC.

LEEDS Tel. (0532) 574736
D. B. KEIGHLEY MACHINERY LTD. ★
VICKERS PLACE, STANNINGLEY
PUDSEY LS2 86LZ
Mon.-Fri. 9.00 a.m.-5.00 p.m.
Sat. 9.00 a.m.-1.00 p.m.
P.A.W.WM.CS.BC.

LEEDS Tel. (0532) 790507
GEORGE SPENCE & SONS LTD.
WELLINGTON ROAD
Open: Monday to Friday
8.30 a.m.-5.30 p.m.
Saturday 9.00 a.m.-5.00 p.m.
H.P.W.WM.D.T.A.

HUDDERSFIELD Tel. (0484)
NEVILLE M. OLDHAM 641219/(0484)
UNIT 1 DALE ST. MILLS 42777
DALE STREET, LONGWOOD ★
Open: Mon-Fri 8.00 a.m.-5.30 p.m.
Saturday 9.30 a.m.-12.00 p.m.
P.W.WM.D.A.BC.

shopguide

WOOD SUPPLIERS

Classified Advertisements

FOR SALE

THE FINEST SELECTION ON DISPLAY IN SCOTLAND!

WOODWORKING & METALWORKING MACHINERY POWER TOOLS HAND TOOLS

THE SAW CENTRE

LARGE STOCKS COMPETITIVE PRICES. PHONE AND TRY US NOW!

Eglinton Toll, Glasgow
G5 9RP
Tel: 041-429-4444

38 Haymarket
Edinburgh
EH12 5J2
Tel: 031-337-5555

OPEN Mon - Fri 8am - 5pm Sat 9am - 1pm

CLOCKMAKERS

Extensive range of very competitively priced German quartz clock movements, (including standard quartz, pendulum, mini-pendulum, chining, striking and insertion movements). Large selection of quality dials, chapter rings, hands, bezels, clock plans and weather instruments.
Please send 25p stamps for 20 page catalogue.
Bath Clock Company (Dept. W), 13 Welton Road, Radstock, Bath.

USERS AND COLLECTORS tools for sale at the Old Craft Tool Shop, 15 High Street, Whitton, Middx. Telephone 01-755 0441.

TEAK SHORTS square edged. ¾" × 1½" × 3". 1" × 2¼"/2½"/3"/4". 3" × 5" at £15.00 cu.ft. V. J. Penson Ltd., Ware, Herts. Tel: 0920 4163.

WOODCARVING tools

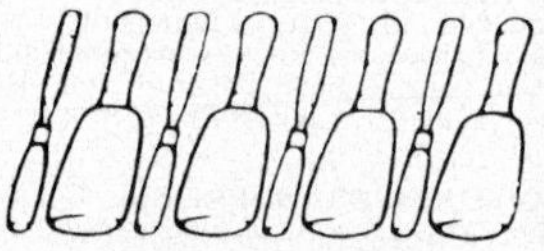

LARGEST STOCK IN EUROPE

Ashley Iles & Henry Taylor
Arkansas Bench & Slip Stones
Strops & Strop Paste
Bench Screws, Carvers' Vices

WOODTURNING tools

Complete range of
Henry Taylor & Ashley Iles
handled or unhandled

send 40p in stamps for illustrated catalogue

ALEC TIRANTI LTD
70 High St, Theale, Reading, Berks RG7 5AR
21 Goodge Place, London W1.

BLADES

The specialist mail order supplier of tooling for woodworking machinery and power tools. Spindle tooling, saw blades, dado sets, planer knives, router cutters and accessories, machinery of particular merit, Forstener bits, mortise chisels, etc.
Write NOW for your free copy of our brochure AND competitive price list.
BLADES, Freepost, Petersfield, Hampshire GU32 2BR. (No stamps required)

BANKRUPT STOCK

Sandvik circular saw blades tungsten tipped.
5", 5½", 6" .... **£4.00** each
6½", 8¼" .... **£6.00** each
½" to 1⅜" bore any size.
P&P £1 extra per order.
Tel: 01 672 7776
Hannett, 1A Links Road, Tooting, London SW17 9ED.

SAMUEL COULTON

fine hand made clocks
High quality hand made pendulum clock movements
Designed to complement the work of those fellow craftsmen for whom only the best will do. Individually made to order.
Send £2.00 for detailed colour brochure.
Samuel Coulton Clocks, Lower Damgate Farm, Stanshope, Nr. Ashbourne, Derbyshire.
Tel: (033527) 367.

BUSINESS FOR SALE

NORTH YORKSHIRE. Well established timber machine shop. 2,500sq.ft. low rent. Good lease. For sale due to business expansion. Ideal for fir furniture making or special joinery. It is anticipated that the volume of sub contract machine work will be made available to purchaser. Outstanding opportunity for ambitious woodworker. £7,000. Box WW120, Classified Dept., ASP Ltd., No. 1 Golden Square, London W1R 3AB.

WINDSOR CHAIRS

Full size bends. 50 × 1⅜ × 1⅛" in Ash £6.95.
Childs Windsor Chair bends in Ash 36 × 1⅛ × ⅞" £4.95.
All prices include p&p.
Please send cheque/P.O. with order to:
P. Stuffin, Spurn View, North End Road, Tetney, Grimby DN36 5NA.
Tel: (0472) 812576 (Afternoons)

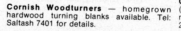

GREENJACKETS TOOL CENTRE

SUPPLIERS OF HAND AND POWER TOOLS AND EQUIPMENT TO GOVT. DEPARTMENTS, LOCAL AUTHORITIES, SCHOOLS, TRADE & INDUSTRY, ETC. ETC.
OFFICIAL MAIN STOCKISTS OF BOSCH — HITACHI — ELU — MAKITA — AEG — DeWALT — BLACK & DECKER (PROFESSIONAL) ALSO STOCKISTS OF CRAFTSMAN — PEUGOT — SKIL — WOLF — RYOBI DISTRIBUTORS OF SUZUKI GENERATORS AND PUMPS — WAVNER SPRAY GUNS, POWER HAMMERS & ACCESSORIES. LOWEST PRICES ON STANLEY — MARPLES — SANDVIK — DISSTON — RECORD — ECLIPSE — ESTWING — DREMELL — ETC.
PHONE FOR LOWEST PRICE.

GREENJACKETS
32-34 St. Mary's Road, Ealing W5 5EU.
Telephone 01-579 1188/9
Prompt Mail Order Service.
Visa & Access accepted - account customers welcomed.

Cornish Woodturners — homegrown hardwood turning blanks available. Tel: Saltash 7401 for details.

CORONET Mk2 LATHE (long) with saw, moulder, planer/thicknesser, bench, tools, accessories, £500. Gainsborough 890189.

CORONET MAJOR on cabinet stand with circular saw/slot morticer/planer/sander/face plates/tools etc. £800 as new. J.H. Tuck, Fakenham (0328) 3626.

MYFORD ML8 for sale, fair condition with turning tools and accessories. £230 o.n.o. Tel: (041) 956 5192.

HANDSAW SHARPENING EQUIPMENT: 1 recutting machine; 1 automatic setting machine, 1 automatic filer, only 21 months use, £1,900 the lot. 36" planer blade, grinder £500, chain saw grinder, riveter and breaker and some chain £250. Phone 0703 — 766207 evenings.

PLANER ATTACHMENT 4½ for Coronet Minor, thicknessing attachment, rebating guard, combination table £200 o.n.o. Saw table with blades £50. Portsmouth 734963.

THE WHISTON CATALOGUE

Nuts, bolts, screws, washers, bar materials. In brass, alloy, steel, stainless steel, P.T.F.E., nylon, Tufnol, sheet material, electrical and mechanical items. We could go on and on! Better to send for free catalogue No. 114 and see for yourself.
K. R. Whiston Ltd., Dept. WW, New Mills, Stockport, Cheshire. Phone: 0663 42028.

LARGE ELM bowl blanks roughed out, air dried. Some natural edged. S.A.E. For details of these and other blanks. Michael Harbron, Longlands, Ennerdale, Cumbria. Tel: 0946 861662.

DeWALT DW320 Powershop, very little use £150 o.n.o. B&D Skill Saw without blade, needs attention £15. Upright panel saw (single phase) with Wadkin dust extractor £750 o.n.o. Buyer collects. Nailsea 852240 evenings/weekends.

INCA 7½" saw including morticer, 8⅝" planer, both on motorised stand, £450. Tel: 074-488-4729.

GRANDFATHER clock movement c.1790 by Wenham, Dereham, Norfolk. Complete, excellent condition, £220. Phone 0959 62110. (Kent).

DOMINION UNIVERSAL WOODWORKER. Is operations £950.00 o.n.o. Also Fairburn morticer £200.00 o.n.o. Tel: Longsridge, Nr. Preston, Lancs. 2377.

FOR SALE. Antique chopper morticer. Good working order. Brockwood, Harrogate (0423) 780901.

LUNAR BANDSAW LBS 720. 700mm throat. 6 months old. Little use. 3 phase. £950 ono. Also AEG C2600 Universal single phase woodworking machine. Various extras. 6 months old. Very little use. £1,200 ono. Everyman Theatre Workshop, Cheltenham (0242) 512515.

BRIAR AND MEERSCHAUM pipes by post — free brochure: "Pipeline," 10 Milton Crescent, Heswall, Merseyside.

CORONET MAJOR with many accessories (circular saw, belt sander, planer/thicknesser), tools and chucks. £650. Tel: 01-446 2804 evenings.

MARQUETRY

MARQUETRY stars, shells and fans, made to order inlays for restoration and reproductions. Send design and colour scheme for quote to: S. Rockwood, 13-15 Seel Street, The Courtyard, Liverpool L1 4AU or Telephone 051-708 5200. Send large S.A.E. for details.

PACKAGING

TERRY ANDREWS Packaging and printing. bags. boxes and stationary. Any quantity supplied! Send 95p for comprehensive samples or SAE for prices only. 53A Parsons Street, Banbury, Oxon. OX16 8NB.

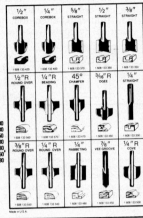
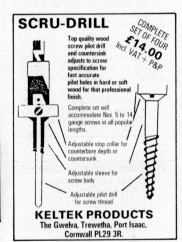

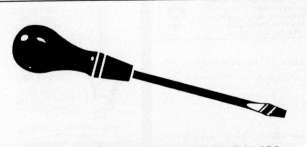

983

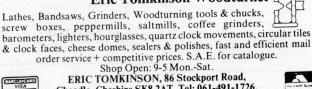

AUCTIONS

SITUATIONS VACANT

DECOY DUCKS

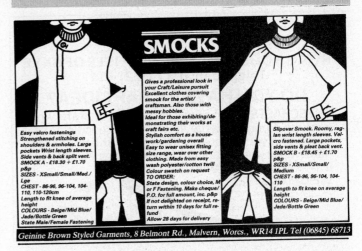

989

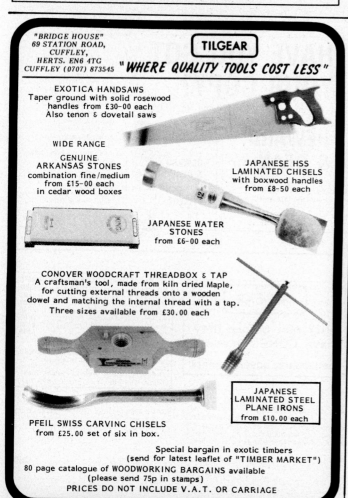

ON TWO WINNERS!
PRIZE DRAW AT THE SHOW

The tradition of having mouth-watering prizes in a draw on the **Woodworker Stand** at the **Woodworker Show** isn't a long one, but it's certainly popular. Who wouldn't leap at the chance to win these goodies:

A Sears Craftsman Radial Arm Saw: 10in blade, 2½hp induction motor, blade brake; this highly respected machine has just come back on to the UK market, and it's worth £549 + VAT!

3 Dunlop Powerbases. New entrant in the highly competitive field of workstations for hand-held power tools, the Powerbase offers the unusual facility of using a standard jig or pattern for repeat work. This attractive little number is worth £130 retail — and there's three to be won!

Winners, no? Just come to the **Woodworker stand** and fill in your name and address . . . it's as easy as that.

● Thanks to **A-Z Tool Sales** and **Dunlop**

Above, the Sears Craftsman radial arm right: the Dunlop Powerbase

Letters

Steel – old versus new

IN THE DEBATE over the quality of edge tools and old versus new steels, some consideration should be given to the effects of modern metal-making practices. While the alchemy of alloying has provided solutions to metallurgical problems, an insidious and unintentional alloy production has been occurring in steels, probably since World War I.

At this time scrap began to be used increasingly in steel production, with a consequent permanent rise in the proportions of copper and tin in UK steel. Neither of these elements can be removed from steel by conventional processing and both are associated with problems; copper reduces weld strength and tin reduces durability and toughness.

Today first generation steel scrap may contain up to 0.6% copper. This level, and those of metals such as tin, lead and aluminium, can be expected to rise still further with the appeal of recycling now firmly in place.

I have no data on the effects these metals may have on the durability of a cutting edge, but it is established that this doping is detrimental to the structure of steel. I feel that a gross characteristic like hardness may only tell part of the story; the rest may lie in something of the crystal structure of a sharp edge. So it may not be illogical to seek out 'pre-atomic' steel in the form of defunct bridges and anchor chain (Roger Buse, *Letters, WW/Aug*). However, I suspect the term 'pre-atomic' has less to do with the Bomb than defining an era in our technical history.

We are at a critical position in our relationship with the remaining stands of hardwoods. Should we not also see to it that there is a continuing adequate supply of edge tool steels for fine simple tools?

Rodney Hayward, Bundanoon,
New South Wales

File it

I HAVE BEEN greatly interested in the 'Tools of the Trade' series, particularly the August one on chisels. I don't propose to enter the argument on Japan v Europe, but I have made my finest chisels from old flat files — as many others before me have done. For longer and wider sizes of chisel I grind smooth a suitable file, grind the edge to a suitable angle, anneal and temper to suit. The best chisel I have is my skew, made from a 1¾in file.

I sharpen all my chisels on flat sheets of wet-and-dry glued to a ply disc in place of my grindstone, finishing off on a leather sheet glued to the other side — I could shave with the resulting edge!

Jack Wear, Prestatyn

Miscellany 1

A FEW POINTS ON the splendid Tools of the Trade series: not necessarily in order!

Duck guru replies

AS BRITAIN'S ONLY full-time teacher of decoy carving I think I am in the target area for the disparaging reference by Alan Bridgewater to the '"my way is best" duck gurus' (*Art ducko 2, WW/Aug*).

Mr Bridgewater says he refuses to get involved in 'the confusing debate about how decoy ducks should be described.' There is no debate and no confusion among people who know. The hundreds of decoy carvers who came to the 1986 British Decoy Festival and Competition at Stowe School in April this year seemed to experience no confusion in knowing where to enter their carvings, nor do they in shows and competitions across America. Perhaps the Bridgewaters should do some homework.

I have searched their article for any sign of guidance which might actually help a beginner with a first duck, and can find only vague laid-back assurances 'that anything goes'. Statements such as 'when you have carved and worked (!?) a good head — a head that says all you want it to say . . . ' are bland in the extreme.

I have helped well over 1000 absolute beginners in this country to carve and paint their first decoy. I know the problems they will encounter and can give them positive guidance. When they finish their course with a completed duck to take home, they have the confidence and knowledge to go on carving and to find their own artistic identity and style.

I only hope the Bridgewater project didn't put off too many would-be duck carvers. A mortise-and-tenon head-joint for someone without a workbench, vice or chisels could be a real turn-off.

Bob Ridges, Farrington Gurney

July, p.568: Mr Reid of Clico Tools is out of order in asserting a thicker blade will narrow the mouth of a shoulder plane. This only applies to planes where the cutting iron is 'bevel down' (as the diagram on p. 565 of that issue makes clear).

May, p. 434: I wonder why Mr Savage did not include the sliding head square, or combination engineer's square in his survey. Really useful and accurate tools, some of these. And though no square should be dropped, the sliding head squares are most unlikely to go out of true if it does happen. August, p. 659: Mr Savage refers to the 'curious hollow ground' on the backs of Japanese chisels. What happens when you reach that — surely one can't lightly dispose of them at these prices?

(● *You rub the back of the blade on a stone to increase the flat area.*)

My own view is that the advantages of Japanese tools have been unmercifully hyped. The fact that the pre-war Ward chisels compared so well shows two things: pre-war tools, though more variable, were better than those made today; and, secondly, only the better specimens have survived consistent use.

I think tools were vest in the 1920s.

F. Seward, London W7

Stripping

AN ANSWER IN 'Question box', *Woodworker* July, was the second recent recommendation to use a water-washable chemical stripper for removal of a non-paint finish.

With a french polish finish, might I suggest a varnish remover, which is washable with methylated spirits rather than water. I am apprehensive about using water on oak, particularly as any tiny rusty piece of embedded iron could lead to a permanent, disfiguring dark stain. I would also avoid using water on quality veneer.

Ron Kimber, Ruislip

Bandsaw motor

I OWN A WHITEHEAD BJ Bandsaw similar to the one described by Mr R. A. Law in May's *Woodworker*, and I can add to the helpful information given by Mr Hugh O'Neill in August.

Parry's catalogue of 1970/71 shows two sizes of the machine described as 'Type 12in BJ' and 'Type 15in BJF'. The former cost £135.37 and the latter £174.25 in their 1971 price list.

Main details given were:

	Type BJ	Type BJF
Table size	16in x 15in	19in x 18in
Throat capacity	11½in	14½in
HP of motor	½hp	1hp
Max. width of blade	¾in	¾in

Some of Mr O'Neill's figures seem to relate to the large 15in model.

I bought my machine, fitted with a ½hp motor, secondhand in the early 1950s, and it came with the metal cutting attachment. The result is that I have two pulleys for the motor, the ODs of which are 2⅞in and 3⅜in respectively. I can't remember which was on the motor when I bought it! I generally use the larger of the two. The drive shaft pulley is 6⅜in OD.

With V-belts the speed ratio depends on the pitch diameter, not the OD. I imagine that the original idea, for purposes of calculation, was that the pitch diameter was ⅜in less than the above figures (2½in, 3in and 6in). A lot of useful information, including pitch diameters for V-belts, is in *Model Engineers Handbook* by Tubal Cain, Argus Books.

The original blade guides were made of perspex for wood cutting and of brass for metal. The side of the guides bearing on the blade were about 1in long. My blades are about 88in long, but 86in could well be the correct length.

I still have the original instructions for adjusting the machine, and will endeavour to send him a legible copy if Mr Law would contact me through the *Woodworker* office.

R. B. Monteath, Haslemere

Letters

Miscellany 2

I WAS INTERESTED in the letter from Mr K. S. Jones on the drawknife with detachable handles (Letters, Aug). I used to have a drawknife which had the handles fixed on with cup square screws and wing nuts. This was made by American Pexto, and was evidently intended for issue to the US Army. The handles could be either attached in the normal position for using the drawknife, or they could be turned across the blade for safe carrying. The blade was about 8in across.

I was also interested in the saws article. I don't come across mention these days of the 'thumb hole' which was provided on rip saw handles, particularly the Disston D8 range. This was a small hole just above the hand hole, to facilitate overhand ripping. The thumb was placed through this small hole, with the fingers round the back of the handle to improve what could be an uncomfortable job.

On a completely different subject, I'd like to warn readers of the dangers of induction motors which are not totally enclosed. A neighbour had an open frame type which caught fire; it had been used on a small saw bench, and wood dust which had got in through the ventilation slots had been ignited by the flashover at the centrifugal switch. So I advise anyone thinking of buying induction motor-driven machinery to insist that the motors are totally enclosed.

Roland Hill, Stockport

Back to basics

I HAVEN'T ANY ideas for the 'Workbench of the Future' competition, but it seems to me that simplicity is what is most needed for a universal workbench; any specialisations would probably limit its usefulness.

Apart from Workmates or machine specialist peripheries, I'd say the best accessory to a simple workbench is a good stable carpenter's stool or trestle. It's a bench in miniature and a remote-portable. Because it's got a good base it's useful for other jobs like tiling, paper-hanging, ceiling fixtures, wiring and so on. A trestle like this makes for an extra 20% output just by being around.

The answer for a better workbench and a better world is primarily down to how we improve ourselves and the personal standards and morals of living harmoniously and without any fuss.

Terry Board, Welling, Kent

Advertisers Index

AEG	922	Lervad UK	902
Apollo	961	Isaac Lord	962
Argus Exhibitions	955	E. W. Lucas	959
Ashford Tools	955	Luna	964, OBC
Asles	924	Matthews	965
Axminster	910, 911	A. Mills	940
A-Z Tool Sales	933	M&M Distribution	902
Benmail	933	Multistar	907
Black & Decker	933, 937,	John Myland	938
	939, 959, 961	Old Stores Turnery	900
John Boddy	907	P&J Dust Extraction	939
Brimarc	960	A. Pollard	955
Buck & Ryan	925	Plans Service	941
Canaan Carbides	954	W. M. Plant	964
H. Case	900, 902, 903	E. T. Roberts	932
Charltons	903	Rogers	947
Charnwood	954	Sanlin	932
P. Child	937	Sarjents	958
Christchurch Tools	965	Scott & Sargeant	920
Clam Brummer	907	Solent	974
Cleveland	907	Southwest P. Tools	924
Craft Materials	925	Startrite	IBC
Craft Supplies	937	Steerdawn	965
Craft Tools & Tackle	955	Stobart & Sons	932
Cutwell W/wking	939	Sumaco	906
CZ Scientific	948	Swann Morton	971
Data Power Tools	955	Tabwell Tools	924
Dunlop	IFC	Taylor Bros	925
Edgemaster	933	Henry Taylor	939
Excel	901	Thatcher	964
Henry Flack	924	Thomas & Willis	925
Gill & Hoxby	974	Tilgear	907, 937, 955,
Heath Saws	971		971, 990
Home Video Workshop		Toolmail	965
	938, 961	Treebridge	959
W. Hoskins	259	Trend	903
J. W. Hoyle	906	Cecil W. Tyzack	902
D. Hunt	964	Warren	971
Ashley Iles	925	Wessex Timber	932
Jarrett & Son	939	Whitehill	900
Kent Power Tools	974	Woodfit	948
Kity	946	XR Machines	948

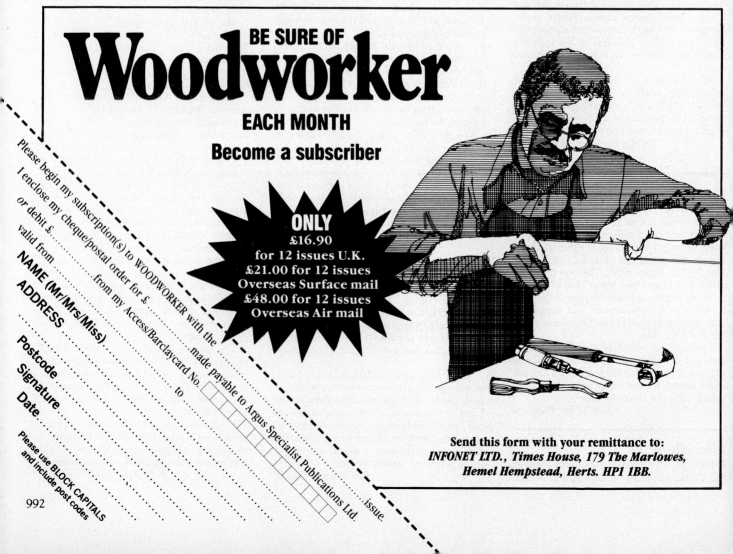

CONTENTS

Woodworker

December 1986
Vol. 90
No. 12

design . . . craft . . . and the love of wood

● *Framed and panelled chest in yew and Indian laurel by Martin Grierson . . . see p1012*

1000 Making it plane
Making your own wooden planes.
Rik Middleton

1005 Adjust in a moment
Wooden planes with adjusting mechanisms . . . *Bob Wearing*

1011 XMAS OFFERS!
Tools and **videos**

1012 Class out of time
Martin Grierson is making classical modern furniture of outstanding beauty. *Aidan Walker*

1019 Shaker Design
Truth and simplicity were and are life principles for the Shakers, and for their furniture. *June Sprigg*

1026 Workbench of the future
The winning design in our ideas-for-a-bench competition is full of innovations; plus three more

1036 The grand furniture saga: 11
Furniture time-travel in Europe and America. *Vic Taylor*

1043 Smoke your own
Add flavour to your Christmas cheese with fruitwood shavings and humour! *John Turner*

1049 Tales out of steel
Sheffield stories. *Ashley Iles*

1053 Magical mystery school
London's Victorian School of Woodcarving — where is it now? *John Hemsley*

1066 Rough-hewn history
Trapper, traveller and adopted Red Indian; carver Sid Hatton's story *David Saunders*

1070 Butting up
Take a chainsaw, a tree-trunk, and control of your own bowls. *Michael O'Donnell*

PROJECTS
All with detailed working drawings

1008 Count the days
Fascinate the children and test yourself with this pre-Christmas project — a wooden Advent Calendar. *Martin Bulger*

1031 Chunky charming chair
Gift for a turner's offspring; a well-proportioned, sturdy child's chair that you can make as a rocker. *Dennis Rowlinson*

1039 Style in time
This clock caused a lot of interest at October's Woodworker Show; here's the chance to make it yourself. *Paul Anderson*

1058 Smoke screen
Lots of fun and easy to make, the puffer-train screen will be Xmas favourite with yet more children! *Paul Austin*

1062 Design for display
Postscript to our 'Japan' series; design story and plans for the impressive Woodworker Show Japanese tools display cabinet. *Peter Dines*

On the cover: A Shaker 'table swift', used for winding yarn. See p1020.
Photo Paul Rocheleau

REGULARS

994 This month Out and about

995 Shoptalk Packed with new products

997 Timberline An eye on the trade

1045 Bob Wearing's Workshop Stones and stops

1051 Guild notes Join and learn

1055 Books Boxes, the radial-arm, decoration

1065 Woodworking wheeze of the month Easy planing

1073 Question box Wooden threads, a chess table, parabolas . . .

1088 Letters Readers write lively

1088 Advertiser's index

Editor Aidan Walker
Deputy editor John Hemsley
Editorial assistant Kerry Fowler
Advertisement manager Trevor Pryer
Graphics Jeff Hamblin
Technical illustrator Peter Holland
Guild of Woodworkers John Hemsley, Kerry Fowler

Editorial, advertisements and Guild of Woodworkers
1 Golden Square, London W1R 3AB, telephone 01-437 0626

Unfortunately we cannot accept responsibility for loss of or damage to unsolicited material. We reserve the right to refuse or suspend advertisements, and regret we cannot guarantee the bone fides of advertisers.
Published every third Friday

ABC

UK circulation
Jan-Dec 85
28,051

Back issues and subscriptions Infonet Ltd, 10-13 Times House, 179 Marlowes, Hemel Hempstead, Herts HP1 1BB; telephone Hemel Hempstead (0442) 48434

Subscriptions per year UK £16.90; overseas outside USA (accelerated surface post) £21.00, USA (accelerated surface post) $28, airmail £48

UK trade SM Distribution Ltd, 16-18 Trinity Gardens, London SW9 8DX; telephone 01-274 8611

North American trade Bill Dean Books Ltd, 151-49 7th Avenue, PO Box 69, Whitestone, New York 11357; tel. 1-718-767-6632

Printed in Great Britain by Ambassador Press Ltd, St. Albans, Herts
Mono origination Multiform Photosetting Ltd, Cardiff
Colour origination Derek Croxson Ltd, Chesham, Bucks
© Argus Specialist Publications Ltd 1986
ISSN 0043 776X

Argus Specialist Publications Ltd

1 Golden Square, London
W1R 3AB; 01-437 0626

This month

Woodworker Award

Your favourite magazine is co-sponsoring an award for the most comfortable chair at the **Direct Design Show**, Kensington Town Hall, London. The show is a shop window for about 100 designer/makers who make and sell all sorts of crafts direct to the public. In a strict selection procedure, 60% of applicants for places were turned down, which means that what's there will be really good.

The Woodworker Award will go to the most comfortable non-upholstered chair in the show, and will be judged by (among others) editor Aidan Walker, and a distinguished orthopaedic surgeon, Bernard Watkin.

The whole show will be well worth visiting if you're around; it's open 9am-8pm, 28-30 November in the Great Hall of Kensington Town Hall, Hornton St, W8, and costs just £1.50.

And if you're interested in taking part in next year's shows — June and November — contact show organiser Joe Tibbetts, Jardines, The Canteen, 1 Lawn Lane, London SW8 1UD.

Link up

Between furniture and textiles ... the people at the Contemporary Textile Gallery in central London had the bright idea of putting tapestries and textile hangings with the work of leading furniture designer/ makers. **Jeremy Broun**, who made the clock above, recently exhibited with **Grace Erickson**, an artist from the west country; 'Designer Showcase', a monthly series, currently has dining chairs by **Martin Grierson** (see 'Class out of time'), upholstered in fabrics by **Jennie Moncur**. More of this, we say.
● Contemporary Textile Gallery, 10 Golden Sq, London W1R 3AF, 01-439 6971.

Up the ladder

The joinery industry is introducing a pattern of training for management. The scheme is jointly sponsored by the British Woodworking Federation, the Joinery Managers' Association and the Construction Industry Training Board. It is not a training package in itself, but outlines a pattern of experience and training under various modules.
● Further information from Scheme Administrator, c/o British Woodworking Federation, 82 New Cavendish St, London W1M 8AD, 01-580 5588.

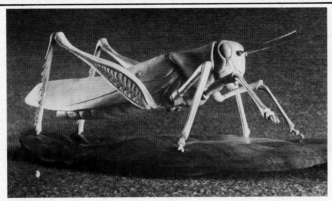

Hocus locust by carver **Ian Norbury's** student D. Johnson; see more at Ian's open weekend at the White Knight Gallery, Painswick Rd, Cheltenham, 5-7 December

Hazards

Did you realise it's safer to work down a coal mine than in the furniture and timber industries? The sobering fact is that anyone working in wood stands a 1:550 chance of being injured this year.

Accidental deaths have dropped substantially, reveals the annual report of the Chief Inspector of Factories (from 14 in 1984 to five last year), but major injuries are still around the same level at 363. Furniture and timber industries are the third most dangerous in Britain, behind construction and metal manufacturing.

The Chief Inspector, David Eves, blames management for giving a low priority to their employees' safety: 'managers must arm themselves with better information about what can go wrong.

He warned companies that the inspectorate is prepared to take action to improve matters. 'We are having to take a tough attitude where we find inattention to basic legal requirements and decent standards of safety,' he said. There were 1,534 convictions under health and safety legislation last year, still a 7% drop on 1984.

Royal Designer

Eileen Gray, whose furniture was first produced in France in the 1930s, and Gordon Russell are among Royal Designers for Industry whose work will be exhibited at the Victoria & Albert Museum, London, in the next few months. An exhibition, **Eye for Industry**, marks the 50th anniversary of the founding of Royal Designers for Industry by the Royal Society of Arts in 1936.

● Eye for Industry, V&A, 26 Nov. to 1 Feb., daily except Fridays.

LCF success

Four students at the **London College of Furniture** scooped all the top prizes in the Design and Industries Association competition for socially-aware design. The four are students on the college's diploma course in design for disability, which is supported by the charity 'Demand'.

Diary

Guild courses are shown by an asterisk (*); for further details see the Guild pages.

November
12-15 Dec **Designer Showcase** furniture and textile designs from Martin Grierson and Jenny Moncur, Contemporary Textile Gallery, 10 Golden Sq, London W1R 3AF, 01-439 9071
12-3 Dec **Timber in Architecture Exhibition**, Strathclyde University, Dept of Architecture and Building Science, (091) 2358424
22 **Power Routing** Roy Sutton*
26-1 Feb **Eye for Industry**, Royal Designers for Industry 1936-86, Victoria & Albert Museum, London
28-30 **Direct Design Show**, Kensington Town Hall, London W8

December
5-7 **Open Weekend**, White Knight Gallery, 28 Painswick Rd, Cheltenham, Glos, (0242) 38582
6-23 **Surrey Guild of Craftsmen Annual Exhibition** Guildford Hse, 153 High St, Guildford, (0483) 57128
12-14 **Basic picture framing and mounting**, West Dean College, Chichester, Sussex, (02463) 301
13-14 **Christmas Craft Fair**, Alexandra Palace, London N22, contact (0727) 23176

January
7-1 Feb **Timber in Architecture Exhibition**, Smith Art Gallery and Museum, Stirling, (091) 2358424
13-18 **International Furniture Fair**, Cologne, W. Germany

February
1-3 **British Toymakers Guild 8th Toy Fair**, Kensington Town Hall, Hornton St, London W8, 01-549 1483
8-13 **Shipwright's Workshop**, traditional boat repair, West Dean College, Chichester, Sussex, (02463) 301

March
12-13 **French polishing** Charles Cliffe*

Young blade 18-year old **Trevor Baker** has already been running his own Sussex cabinet-making business for 10 months — set up with CoSIRA's help — and is doing so well he's thinking of taking on an apprentice . . .

Shoptalk

Good news for the woodwork teacher and chairmaker alike! The arcane and elusive **rotary plane** is on the market after being out of production for five years — if you couldn't buy one, you had to make your own.

The rotary plane works like a giant pencil sharpener, turning wood from square — you don't need a lathe, and they're also cheaper and safer than lathes, both selling points for classroom use.

The planes are £190 + VAT for a set of five plus a trapping plane, and a 'Twizzler' is also available.
● PIK (Castings), Necarne Ind. Est., Irvinestown, Co. Fermanagh, N. Ireland, (03656) 28055

Very scholarly, comprehensive to a degree, impressive indeed ... if you want to **make a spinet** or early musical instrument, John Barnes' plan/booklet/photo pack could hardly be bettered. The spinet information is culled from a detailed inspection of John's own spinet, made by Stephen Keene and Charles Brackley in 1715; the photos are of details of that instrument. It amounts to, claims John, more information about the construction of this particular spinet than is currently available on any other early keyboard instrument. We don't doubt it.

The drawing on plastic is £22, on paper £16; the booklet £4.50, the set of 10 photos £7. He has a range of other instrument plans.
● John Barnes, 3 East Castle Rd, Edinburgh EH10 5AP, 031-229 8018

Happy birthday, Craft Supplies — rapidly expanding, computer all installed and working correctly . . . this woodturner's haven has been operating for 10 years now, and to celebrate they've brought out a full colour catalogue. Nicely produced for £2.
● Craft Supplies, The Mill, Millers Dale, Buxton, Derbys. SK17 8SN, (0298) 871636

If any of you who were at the Show last year liked the MAGOmagh **workshop-in-a-cupboard** and couldn't find out where to buy it, your troubles are over.
● Crownall Systems Ltd, 21 Ostler Gate, Maidenhead, Berks SL6 6SG, (0992) 468868

Ground, hardened and crossed high-technology teeth for new veneer and backsaws (left) as well as ordinary handsaws, from Danish company Jack; 13in veneer saw 13ppi, £8.48, tenon saws from £7.61, also 13ppi; both plus VAT. Saxon Tools, Brierly Hill, W. Midlands, (0384) 262424

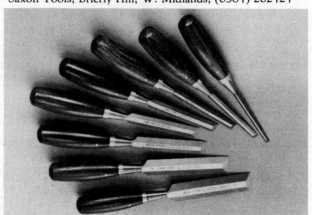

New Clay chisels with rosewood handles — Paramo's upmarket offering; £30.50 for four in a wallet, £45.00 for six in a box, both plus VAT. Paramo, Rockingham St, Sheffield S1 3NW, (0742) 25262

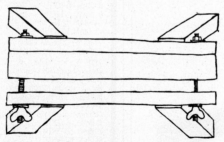

Shoptalking points Winner of the **Sandvik** Centenary Handsaw this month is Stephen Bostock, a sub-contract joiner in Manchester, who rarely needs a vice on site — but when he does he uses his 'Trice', a trestle with a 5x2 top on edge, ripped down the middle and held together with coach-bolts and wingnuts. Numerous holes let him set the two halves in different relative positions for different jobs; an extra bit of 3x2 in the middle gives him a wider surface. Nice one, Stephen.
Send those clever-clogs ideas for hand-tool users to **Shoptalking Points**, Woodworker, 1 Golden Sq, London W1R 3AB, and win a Sandvik Centenary 22in 8ppi saw!

Stop Press! Show Prizewinners! Lucky ones out of the hat on the *Woodworker* stand at the Show: Mr. G. N. Sillman got the Sears Craftsman **radial-arm saw**, and Messrs Peter Hunt, R. Marlow and R. Dixon took the **Dunlop Powerbases**. Thanks, A-Z Tool Sales and Dunlop. J. Grayson won a **Triton.**

We've put the first cordless glue gun on the market, say Camping Gaz — the P500 takes the new CV360 compact gas cartridge, which should last for four hours. £35.50 inc. VAT the gun, £1.70 the cartridges.
● Camping Gaz, 126-130 St Leonards Rd, Windsor, Berks, (075 35) 55011

PRODUCT DIGEST

Woodworker binders £5.20 inc. p&p from A.S.P., Wolsey Ho., Wolsey Rd, Hemel Hempstead HP2 4SS — make cheques to A.S.P. Ltd.

Dunlop Powerbase New and versatile workstation for portable power tools — jigs, patterns, clamps, fences — around £125. Dunlop, 140 Fielden St, Glasgow G40 3TX, 041-554 3811

Instant boats Simple boat plans for proper craft from £12.50. Dick Moore, PO Box 38, York YO12 1EG, (0904) 3898

Mitre saw New Sandvik 309 has 20in blade, 10ppi; £14.75 + VAT. Sandvik, Manor Way, Halesowen, B62 8QZ, 021-550 4700

Router guide system Stop router-wander with Trend's range of stops, rods and blocks, ranging from £3.95 to £7.80 + VAT per piece. Trend, Unit N, Penfold Works, Imperial Way, Watford WD2 4YY, (0923) 49911

Screwdriver/drill Elu's new ESD705K has 320w, 10mm chuck, variable speed/torque; £90 + VAT. Elu, Westpoint, The Grove, Slough SL1 1QQ (0735) 74277

Woodturning video British made by ex-lighting cameraman Kevin Baxendale, it promises to be a goodie; £29.95 inc. VAT, plus p&p. Knowhow Productions, PO Box 43, Greenford UB6 8TX, 01-578 8716

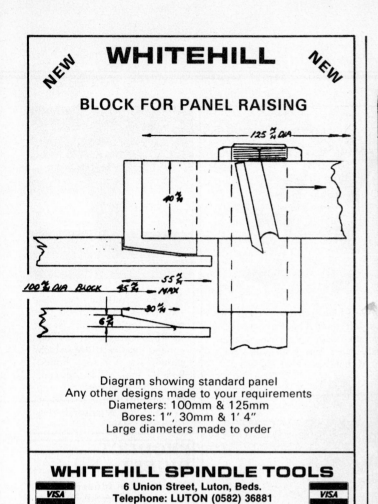

996

Timberline

Arthur Jones examines the world timber market

It used to be that softwood shippers in Scandinavia cleared their stocks in the autumn ready for the new season's production, and offered the wood at discount prices. No such sales took place this year, which marks the solidarity of the current softwood market. The shippers have been having a tough time in the Middle East, where their sales have slumped, but they cut back production at the mills to allow for this rather than try to flood the European market with extra supplies.

Timber merchants are currently keeping a fairly tight hold on softwood prices, with whitewood generally a little firmer than of late. There should be only marginal price movements over the coming months and supplies this winter will be plentiful — but not enough to force prices down.

On the other hand, a little shopping around for hardwoods could pay dividends. There are bargain prices being asked on the UK market for tropical hardwoods and they're unlikely to be repeated next year. Stocks of some species are too high for present demand, so merchants are forced to reduce their prices to keep up the level of sales. However, the prices being paid for forward shipments of many Far Eastern and tropical hardwoods indicate that the selling prices here must rise quite sharply.

Brazil has freed log exports at the same time as pegging prices on the home market, so the forest owners are selling mahogany logs for export and supplies to the home mills are dwindling. This will affect the stocks of sawn mahogany being offered to our importers, and so we could see prices rise.

Incidentally, some of the lauan shipments currently reaching our yards are at the old prices under contracts closed before the new ·government came into power in the Philippines. But don't expect these to last.

Conditions in the Philippine mills and plywood factories are still not back to normal, with outputs well down. By late summer there was still a hefty chunk of duty-free Philippines plywood available for sale under the quota systems, whereas a year earlier the quota had been sold out by the summer.

The new official prices for exports set by Indonesia have held, and other Far Eastern markets have been quick to follow their example, seeing that UK importers were prepared to pay the higher prices. Which means that you will pay more in the near future for plywoods from the Far East.

There has been a lot of concern in official quarters about the levels of formaldehyde emission from chipboard, and the manufacturers have been desperately seeking a solution before sales are affected. Now there comes news from a Finnish particleboard manufacturer that a chemical solution has been found so that chipboards can be produced with no more of a formaldehyde problem than solid wood. Presumably we shall soon find that the solution can be applied to all panel products.

Last year an anti-dumping duty was imposed by the EEC on certain Eastern block chipboard manufacturers following complaints from European producers, and this led to a fall in imports from these countries. Trade is now reviving, apparently because of barter agreements with firms selling machinery from the West, so more cheap chipboard might find its way here. On the other hand, currency fluctuations might negate price advantages.

Stock and price conditions should remain favourable over the next few months but some species, especially hardwoods, will become more costly. ∎

14

998

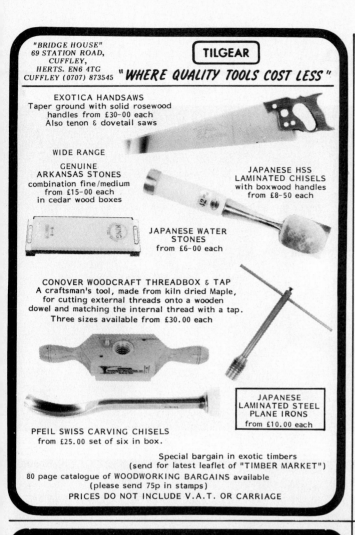
999

Making it plane

Rik Middleton, exponent *extraordinaire* of the pleasures of wooden planes, explains how to make your own

The first time I went out to buy myself a mallet I came home a bit shaken by the price and hit the chisel with a chair leg instead. Some people might say I was tight. (I eventually got round to making a mallet when I came by an offcut suitable for the head.)

Much the same happened with bench-hooks, saw-handles and other wooden tools. I reasoned that I wouldn't go out and buy a coffee table, so why buy any other timber fabrication?

The frustrations of buying planes on secondhand stalls in markets caused this approach to be extended from plane repair to manufacture. Some, quite desirable, planes were irreparably damaged, avariciously priced or couldn't be found at all. I was inspired to my first attempts when I wanted a toothing plane. I couldn't find a secondhand one but had some tatty old spare blades, so I set about making one. It was a good example to start on because I don't believe much accuracy or sophistication of finish is needed to make it work. That first plane isn't very precisely cut, and if it were a smoothing plane I wouldn't rate its chances. But progress has been made and lessons learned — I do it better now.

I have seen very small smoothing planes which appeal to me, but they've always been overpriced or not for sale, so I decided to make one. So if you want a wooden plane to some specific design, you are too tight to buy, or can't afford those reviewed last month, or if you just fancy it as a woodwork project, here's the way I go about it.

Materials

Most of my planes are beech, but I know other timbers such as hornbeam and pear are used. I would like to try sweet chestnut but I haven't any big enough. So I decided to use cherry for my mini-smoothing plane. I have based it around a Stanley 1¾in blade made for a cast plane; I don't have any other double irons this narrow and this type of blade is readily available — mine was just under £7 in a local tool shop. The highly arched back-iron is less easy to deal with than the older flatter style but it's not a big problem.

Preparing the wood

You could use 3x3in beech, perhaps from old school table legs, but I used a cherry half log. I took this tree down for a neighbour about six years ago — long enough, I hope, for it to be stable. I split the log up with an axe and side-axed it into rough shape. I

● **Top**: the oiled cherry grain has given Rik's little smoother 'a bit of novelty and a whole lot of looks'. **Above**, complex marking out round the centre line; the mouth is quite near the middle of the length

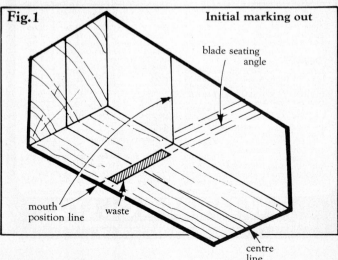

Fig. 1   **Initial marking out**

blade seating angle

mouth position line

waste

centre line

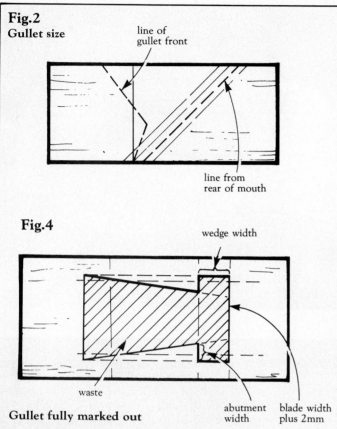

Fig.2
Gullet size

line of gullet front

line from rear of mouth

Fig.3

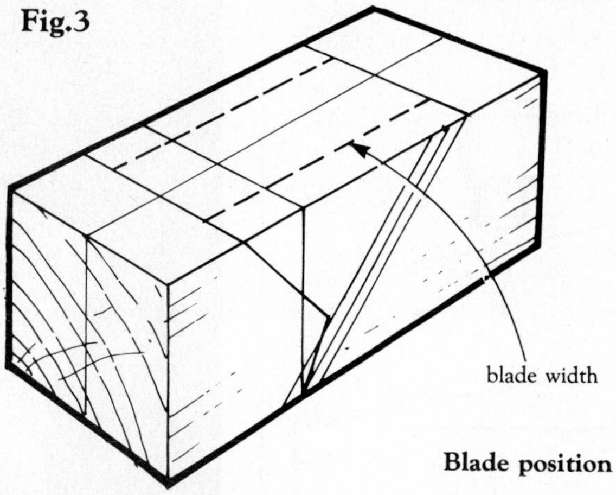

blade width

Blade position

Fig.4

wedge width

waste

Gullet fully marked out

abutment width

blade width plus 2mm

would have liked it square parallel and true before going further but the piece took on coffin-shaped proportions naturally as the grain split so I went along with it. I planed the wood all round. Ideally you do need it square in cross section to facilitate marking out. The sides don't have to be good, as it all gets skimmed down later, but fairly square does help.

Draw a line down the axis of the sole, marked up the front and back and along the top. All subsequent markings are done symmetrically off this centre-line (fig. 1). Planning where to put the mouth, I initially marked 45° lines down the body sides. Now I like the mouth nearer the middle of the sole than is conventional. For this reason and to keep the whole thing small I changed my mind and decided to make the blade angle 50°.

Then I marked out the mouth at blade-width plus 2mm either side. I made it 6mm deep after comparison with my old ones but the very thin steel of the new type blade and the steeper angle left me, when the plane was finished, with more mouth in front of the blade than I had wanted — goofed again!

Tracing the blade angle up the sides of the body, you can mark the rear of the gullet (fig. 2). Plan the front of the gullet up the sides of the body from the front of the mouth. Having marked these across the top (fig. 3), mark the blade-width plus 2mm along the top (all measurements done as half measures off the centre line).

Decide on a wedge width and mark this in (fig. 4). I know of no formula for the thick-

● *Right,* *wedging the body up underneath the drill stand gives the right angle for the mouth*

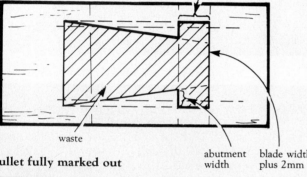

ness. Mine is 19mm as marked along the top, and the wedge at this point is 12mm thick; but remember this is a very small plane. Having marked this across, decide on an abutment thickness, erring on the generous side. Mine is 7mm — quite substantial for a little one. The rest of the gullet can then be lined in as shown (fig. 4).

Cutting the mouth

I knifed and chisel-cut the mouth outline to prevent breakout. Then, using a wedge to get the angle, I drilled out the mouth to about 10mm from the edge (fig. 5a overleaf). I used a 5mm drill but it should have

been smaller.

Turning the body over, and with it flat on the drill-stand base, I drilled through from the top (fig. 5b) to meet the first line of holes; I ensured continuity by blowing through.

Then I was ready to remove most of the waste. This is a fairly hefty job, needing really good clamping down and careful work with the mortise chisel. Pare the middle of the blade bed down to a very good flat smooth surface from top to sole. Err on the side of caution and work gradually — overcutting this bit wrecks it.

I laced up a bowsaw through the job to

Making it plane

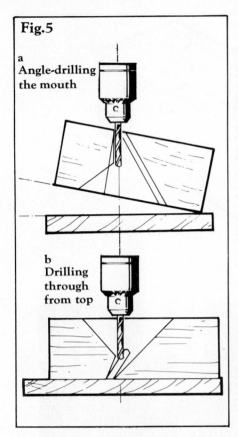

Fig.5

a Angle-drilling the mouth

b Drilling through from top

extend the blade and wedge slot behind the abutment, cutting at right angles to the central axis to extend the blade bed through to the sole at the rear of the mouth. Cut to the full 'blade plus 2mm' line top and bottom. Similarly cut the abutment line through to the front of the mouth. You could use a coping or keyhole saw but each needs a lot more care in use to keep a straight line.

You must then remove all remaining waste with a narrow chisel. For final smoothing and flattening of the blade bed you can use the plane-blade as a wide chisel blade.

The highly arched back-iron on this particular blade means that a bit of the abutment needs removing just inside the mouth so that the arch doesn't foul the woodwork. It also limits the length of the wedge.

Now you must make a slot in the top centre of the blade bed for the back-iron screw. If this is made a very snug fit from side to side it will act as a pivot point; lateral adjustment can then be done with no risk of hammering the blade assembly against the thinnest side of the gullet (*see 'Penny plane'*, *WW/ Oct*).

Contouring the coffin-shaped sides is easy with a disc sander; I also used it to chamfer the top edges until it felt right.

Fitting the wedge

The wedge is less amenable to rules of marking out and rather more a matter of eye. I planed a piece of the timber to a wedge

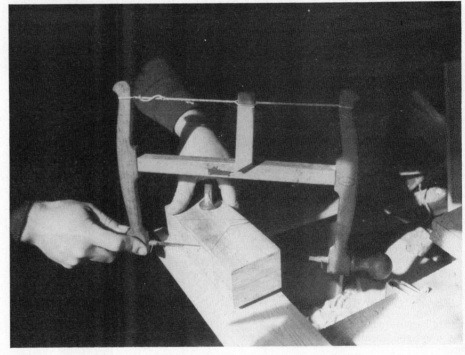

● **Top**: *remove most of the waste with a hefty mortise chisel – but be careful!* **Middle**: *a bowsaw is best for the flat surfaces when cutting out the blade and wedge slot behind the abutment.* **Right**: *the body after final smoothing, the plane iron used as a wide chisel*

sheet of the same abrasive on a cork block.

Then comes the very satisfying stage of covering it in lots of linseed oil and watching all that lovely grain leap into life!

So there it is: 165mm long, 70mm high and 62mm wide at the widest point. The grain in the cherry has given it a bit of novelty and a whole lot of looks. I've taken the blade down to a gentle arc of about 0.5mm on a medium oilstone and honed it on a 6000-grit waterstone.

What's more, it actually works. Shavings drift down to the workshop floor like gossamer. It adjusts very sensitively and is very resistant to any suggestion of chatter; it must all fit!

One thing is for sure. The only place you will come by a quality wooden plane ergonomically custom-built to your own design is in your own workshop. ∎

● **Left**: *cut the slot for the cap-iron screw tight to avoid 'adjustment damage';*
below, *and it works well with no chatter*

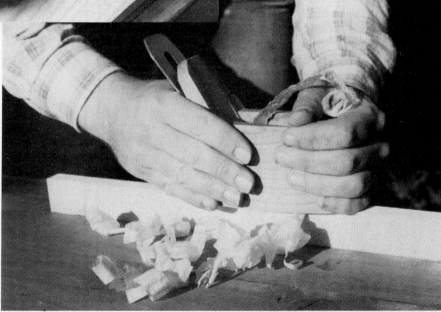

shape which approximately matched the hole for the taper angle.

Before you can trial-fit the wedge, a groove has to be cut for the back-iron screw. Plane the wedge till it will drop in to within an inch of the back-iron arch. Then cut away the middle to leave two legs which fit under the abutments either side.

Making sure the blade and back-iron are firmly screwed together, push the wedge in and look closely. Pare off wood where it makes good contact with the abutment, making sure to remove none where the surfaces are not in contact. Progressing slowly in this way, you should be able to get good contact down the whole length of both legs. To check, push the wedge firmly in by hand then push it from side to side to remove it; if it moves easily one side and pivots about a point on the other this indicates where to remove more material. Chisels need to be super sharp and parings gossamer thin when you're nearly there. If the wedge fits, a light pin-hammer tap should make it difficult to remove by hand; a modest rap with a small hammer should make it impossible.

The wedge must stop short of the back-iron arch, otherwise tightening the wedge will pre-empt blade adjustment. Wedge the blade firmly at least 2mm 'off cut' to check this.

Finishing

I flattened the sole with silicon carbide paper, glued down on a flat surface — a supported sheet of plate glass (*WW/Oct*). I gave the top and sides a final sanding with a

The Rhino

Here is the big brother to the little cherry plane; I call it 'the Rhino', and you may think that it looks as if its gone through the design stages popularly attributed to a camel! Clearly it owes something to my recent aquaintance with German planes. It couldn't be called pretty in the way the cherry smoothing plane is, but it is anatomically fitted to my hands, it has an accurate right-angled flat right side for shooting, and with an old Ward laminated 2in blade it cuts every bit as well as the smaller one.

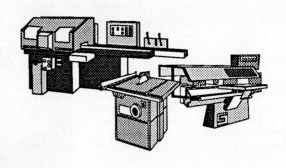

Adjust in a moment

For the ambitious and really inspired wooden plane maker, Bob Wearing has some (relatively!) simple suggestions for adjustable models

It's always a great pleasure to make something which actually performs — even more so if it performs well. This is why planes are such satisfying projects. The sweetness in action and the very feel are the attractions of wooden planes, but when it comes to easy and convenient adjustment, the metal plane is generally the winner.

Before WWII there was an attempt to bridge the gap by fitting Norris mechanisms to otherwise standard wooden planes, but the idea didn't survive the war. Continental makers are producing adjustable wooden planes (*WW/Nov*), but their mechanisms don't lend themselves to one-off making with a woodworker's set of metalworking tools; the mechanisms described here, plus the laminated construction of the planes themselves, put these fully adjustable tools well within average capability, if you work carefully.

Materials

The basic requirement, before any woodwork starts, is an old, thick plane-blade. In theory it should be parallel in thickness, but in practice the tapered blade seems to work, since the amount of taper in the length of movement required is negligible. The smoothing plane shown here takes a 2in cutter and the jackplane a 2¼in, not the 2⅜in of the iron planes. Many different hardwoods are suitable, so before you tell me that any fool knows planes are made of beech, let me remind you that very successful planes are made in lands where no beech tree ever grew. Fruitwoods are particularly successful — but don't discard a nice block of imported timber, either.

Ideally the body should come from a quarter-sawn board, but in the past many wooden plane makers ignored this. If the material is old and dry it will hardly distort anyway. A quarter-sawn block, of course, will not distort, but as these planes aren't intended to be used on their sides, a slight distortion shouldn't affect the performance.

The body

The entire plane can be cut from one block, or if you don't have timber of such a size, saw the sides from 1in material. You need the sides, a single piece which is cut into two for front and rear blocks, and enough for the handle. Make sure you arrange the grain of the blocks so that when you plane the sole to finish it you are working from front to rear.

● *Fancy a custom-made wooden smoothing plane . . .*

● *Or perhaps you prefer to make your own ebony-soled jack?*

Face and edge the main block, then carefully thickness it to ⅛in more than the cutter is wide. Saw it into two on an angle, and plane the 'bed' face to 45°. You can give the smoother a cabinetmaker's 'York pitch', 50°. The front block is angled to 60°, then reduced in height (fig. 1).

Now shape the handle from 1in material; hands differ as widely as preferences, so the handle is such an individual matter that I can only give approximate guidance. Don't skimp on the time you work on it, for a really comfortable handle goes a long way towards making a plane a firm favourite.

The rear block nears completion when you cut it away to take the low-set handle. Clean up the curve, then mortise it and glue

in the handle. Skim over the 45° bed again, finishing the handle in line.

The mechanism

It's wise now to put aside the woodwork and make the mechanism, about which there is nothing particularly difficult. All the work can be done with hand-tools, though a lathe is a help. I have shown two versions in fig. 3; the double screw gives the finer adjustment, but there is more slack in the mechanism. Be sure that the central block (fig. 3C) is a match in size for the bit which will drill the hole in the angled face of the handle/bed.

I recommend you draw a full-size view of the blade, cap-iron and mechanism, which

Adjust in a moment

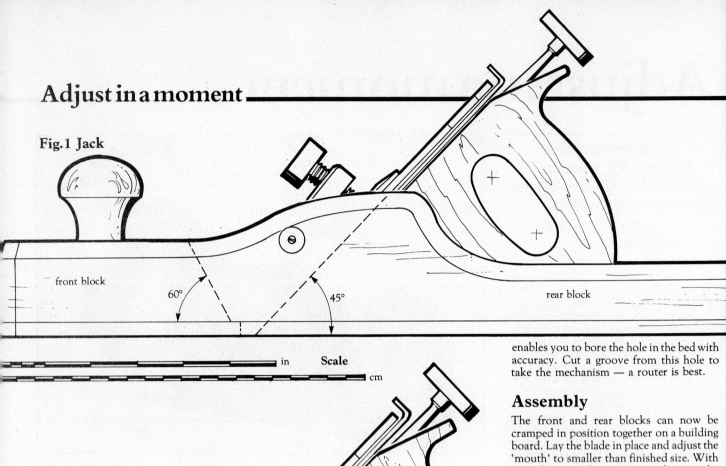

Fig.1 Jack

front block

60°   45°

rear block

in   **Scale**

cm

Fig.2 Smoother

in

cm

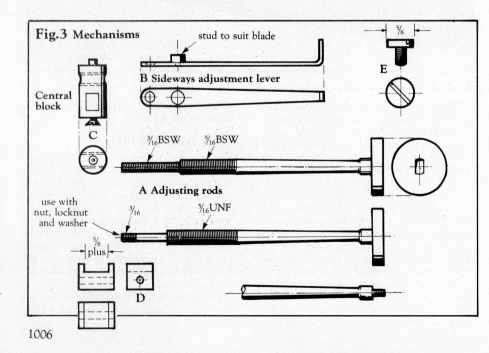

Fig.3 Mechanisms

stud to suit blade

⁵/₈

E

Central
block

B Sideways adjustment lever

C

³/₁₆BSW   ⁵/₁₆BSW

A Adjusting rods

use with
nut, locknut
and washer

³/₁₆   ⁵/₁₆UNF

⁵/₈
plus

D

1006

enables you to bore the hole in the bed with accuracy. Cut a groove from this hole to take the mechanism — a router is best.

Assembly

The front and rear blocks can now be cramped in position together on a building board. Lay the blade in place and adjust the 'mouth' to smaller than finished size. With everything in this position, glue on the roughly shaped sides; Aerolite is my preference, with Cascamite second. Use plenty of cramps and possibly the vice as well. A router with an edge-trimming cutter brings down the rough sides to the base of the blocks, or they can be whittled down to shape. The front knob is routine turning; aim rather at a mushroom shape to take good downwards pressure comfortably.

The cap-iron (fig. 4B) is simply made from bright drawn mild steel, the end hammered over a round bar to produce the curve. If an old cap-iron is used, you'll need to remove its large brass nut. A Record/ Stanley cap-iron can be modified to suit. The wedge (fig. 4A) can be cut and filed from the solid, bought as an aluminium casting, and cleaned up. The two screw-knobs for wedge tension and blade-adjustment (fig. 4D) can be engineered from brass, or made up as described in my 'Workshop' article, 'Making professional knobs', *Woodworker* February 1986. The end of the wedge screw (fig. 4D) must be finished to a smooth dome; if it's left square-ended, it will grip the cap-iron and slightly alter the setting of the cutter when rotated.

The two round bushes to pivot the wedge (fig.5B) are made from round brass or aluminium bar, and are glued into their holes with Araldite. One way of finding out their position is to glue on only one side of the plane, assemble all the metal components, and mark the centre through the wedge with a sharp piece of ³/₁₆in rod. The other side is then glued on and trimmed. Alternatively, work from a full-size drawing. Fit the wedge pivot-rod (fig. 5A) alone directly in the wood first, to check its position and movement. If it proves necessary to move the pivot, the ½in hole you will have to drill for the bush will displace the unwanted hole. The wedge should fit as close as possible to the cap-iron, but still allow easy removal of the cutting unit. I can't give exact details, as wedge, cap-iron and blade are all variables.

When all the metal components are made, they can be fitted into place. The screw beneath the central block (fig. 6C) is adjusted to bring the mechanism slightly below the wood surface.

Finishing

It's now time to plane up the sole and to pare out or file the mouth to the smallest aperture which doesn't clog. The jack plane, for rather rougher work, can possibly be given a slightly wider mouth. Now you can try the plane out. When you're satisfied with the feel and action of the plane, you can fit the ebony or rosewood sole. (Those who have had enough can of course get off here and leave well alone!) Remove ⁵⁄₁₆in from the sole, preferably by machine planing, and glue the new sole on, slightly overlapping. This is the best method to follow for a first plane, but experienced plane makers will avoid this by doing the main body glue-up with a larger gap, which will permit an escapement as in fig. 7. Drill a series of small holes and file out the final mouth with a large warding file. A number of timber suppliers advertise rosewood and ebony; pieces sold as guitar fingerboards will make two smoothers, but they are just too narrow for a jack plane.

When you've thoroughly tested and all is well, the plane can be finished, either with raw linseed oil and lots of rubbing or with polyurethane — but not on the sole!

Observations

If you definitely decide to fit an ebony sole, you can laminate the rear block by adding two shaped blocks to the completely shaped handle, thus avoiding mortising. Similarly, if thick enough material isn't available, both the body blocks can be made from two thinner pieces laminated together. The endgrain pattern should be arranged symmetrically.

The cylindrical centre block (fig. 3C) can be left as a tight fit in case you need to remove it later, or a ³⁄₁₆in pin can be put through it; the very confident may decide to glue it in with Araldite, for which two flats must be filed on it.

For final truing up of the sole, fit the blade in with the screw at normal working tension but with the blade *well withdrawn*. Check and double check this before you pass the tool over the planer on fine cut. Often these soles don't respond well to hand-planing, but they will finish well on a machine. Or you can sand the sole true with a length of belt-sanding material on a machine surface, or on a piece of plate glass.

To set the plane, the wedge-screw is slightly slackened, the cut adjusted (always finishing with a clockwise movement to take up any slack), then the wedge-screw re-tightened. This isn't as messy as it sounds — with experience you'll become quite slick.

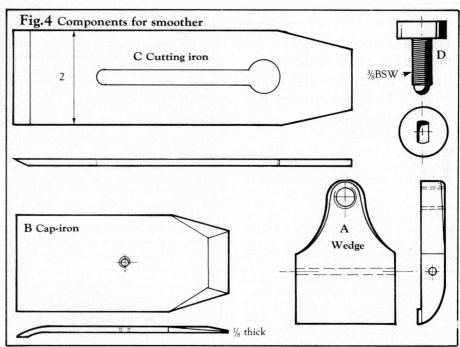

Fig.4 Components for smoother

C Cutting iron

2

D

³⁄₈BSW

B Cap-iron

A Wedge

⅛ thick

Fig.5 Positioning pivot pin — draw full size

thickness of screw-head plus ease

B

bushes: one threaded one clear

½

³⁄₁₆ BSW

⁵⁄₁₆

³⁄₁₆

A

height above sole

cutting unit thickness

pivot rod to fit plane

distance behind mouth

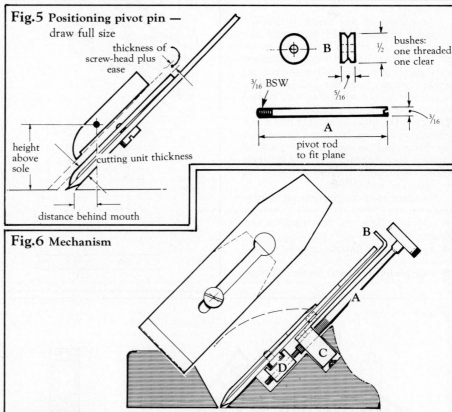

Fig.6 Mechanism

B

A

C

D

Enormous tension will distort the sole; the screw should be just tight enough to prevent easy sideways movement of the blade with the fingers. ∎

● Wedge castings can be obtained from The Bloxwich Aluminium Casting Co, Straight Rd, Short Heath, Willenhall, W. Midlands. The cost including postage is:

Size	Pattern no.	Aluminium	Gunmetal
2in	RW37	£3.40	£5.46
2¼in	RW38	£4.20	£7.10

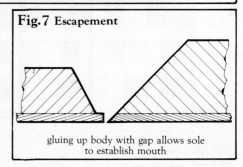

Fig.7 Escapement

gluing up body with gap allows sole to establish mouth

Count the days

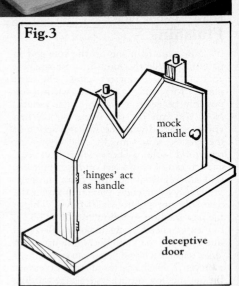

Here's a novel project to delight your children in the run-up to Christmas. Martin Bulger explains his ingenious design

Have you looked at the Advent calendar cards in the shops? Not very impressive, either in quality or value. That's my opinion, and if you agree you could make this wooden design. But get cracking, because it should be ready by 1 December. You'll recall that an Advent calendar has 24 'windows', one to be opened on each day of December leading up to Christmas Day.

I decided to plan the project as a Tudor-style house, with 20 windows, two doors and two chimneys (fig. 1) which open to reveal little surprises. Each window, door and chimney is numbered, for which you can use 'Letraset' numeral transfers or a fine-tipped pen.

The delight of this design is that the openings remain locked tight until the appropriate day. It's really rewarding to see the excitement on children's faces when they go to open the window — and bewilderment as to how the door or window which was locked when they went to bed can be opened in the morning. And when they open the little doors, they find a tiny gift such as a rubber, birthday cake candle, a 5p piece and so on, together with a miniature greeting card from the Christmas gnomes and fairies. It's definitely great fun to make and and fill!

The three main design problems to solve were:
● a simple hinge for the windows and doors
● a secret access into the calendar so only you can unlock the windows
● a simple locking device for the 24 places.

Hinges

For the hinges I used a pivot of very thin dowel; you could use weaving cane or even headless panel pins. The front is made in sections (fig. 2) so you can fit the stubs in as you put it together.

Secret access

The back of the house (fig. 3) with its single odd-shaped door, two butt hinges at one side and a small lathe-turned knob at the other, is a deception — the hinges are in fact false and act as handles. There are hidden pivots on the knob side of the door; they should fool the most inquisitive child, or adult for that matter. Pull the knob and nothing happens; only you will know to pull the 'hinges' in order to open the access door.

Fig.2

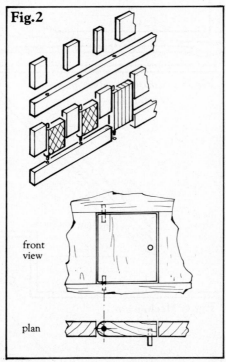

front view

plan

Locking device

The device I have used on the windows and doors to prevent them being opened before the right day is shown in fig. 4. Stuck to the rear of the windows and doors are L-shaped pieces of wood into which individual locking bars fit. So it's easy to open the back access door and lift the appropriate bar to make that window accessible.

The chimneys use a different mechanism — in fact, two different mechanisms to make it harder for children to find the secrets. Both operate from the outside. Chimney A is unlocked by sliding the top backwards, while chimney B requires a 90° rotation of the chimney pot to release it.

Fig.3

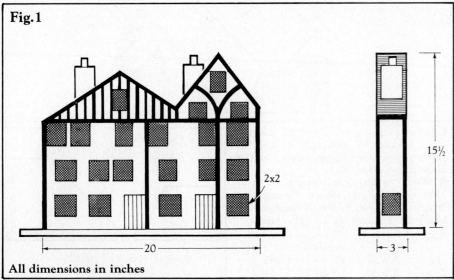

mock handle

'hinges' act as handle

deceptive door

Fig.4

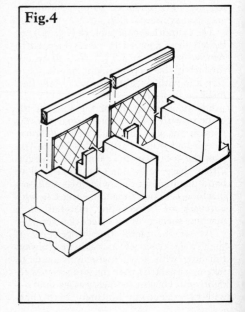

Fig.1

All dimensions in inches

20

15½

3

2x2

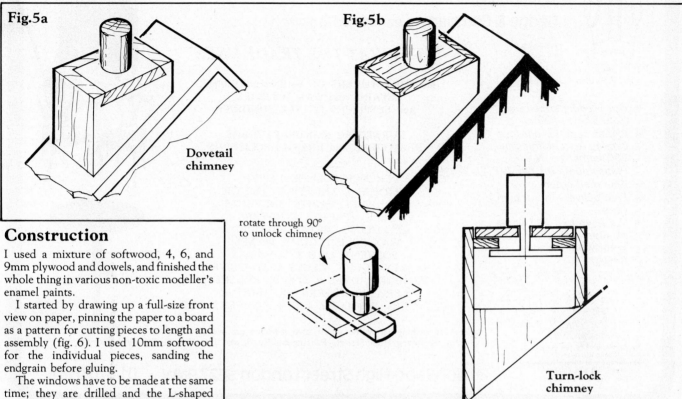

Fig.5a

Dovetail chimney

Fig.5b

rotate through 90° to unlock chimney

Turn-lock chimney

Construction

I used a mixture of softwood, 4, 6, and 9mm plywood and dowels, and finished the whole thing in various non-toxic modeller's enamel paints.

I started by drawing up a full-size front view on paper, pinning the paper to a board as a pattern for cutting pieces to length and assembly (fig. 6). I used 10mm softwood for the individual pieces, sanding the endgrain before gluing.

The windows have to be made at the same time; they are drilled and the L-shaped pieces glued on before the front is assembled.

There's no need for cramping; I simply laid the various pieces on the paper diagram, then applied a thin smear of PVA adhesive and rub-jointed the edges. Once the pieces were joined, I lightly planed the front and back and sanded them ready for finishing.

With the front complete, I made wooden blocks up to the height of the first row of windows (fig. 7) with gaps for the doors. Screw the base to these blocks.

Now you can make the side walls and fix them in position. You'll also need floors and room dividers for all upstairs windows (fig. 4); I glued pieces of 9mm ply in for these.

Using the part-assembled house as a guide, measure and cut the one-piece back door in 9 or 12mm ply. Fit mock hinges, a small door knob and a magnetic catch. Since the back door is pivoted in the same way as the windows, make up the roof sections and fit them and the door at the same time. Finally make and fit the chimneys.

To complete the locking device for the windows and doors, cut 24 bars from 8x4mm material (fig. 4). These will probably vary in length to match the irregular layout of the windows and doors, so number them to match door and window numerals.

Once the construction is complete you can have fun painting it, and putting the numerals on. Scour the shops looking for suitable tiny gifts. Then sit back and wait for the delighted smiles of the children as they open the places day by day! ∎

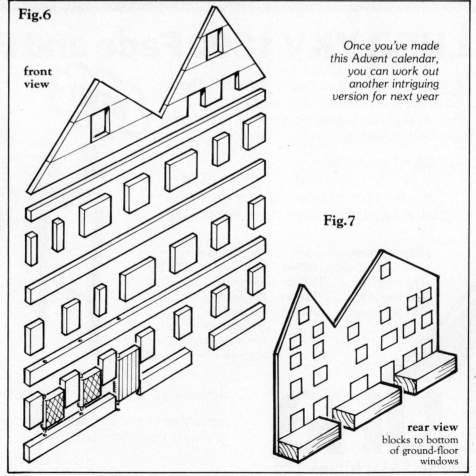

Fig.6

front view

Once you've made this Advent calendar, you can work out another intriguing version for next year

Fig.7

rear view
blocks to bottom of ground-floor windows

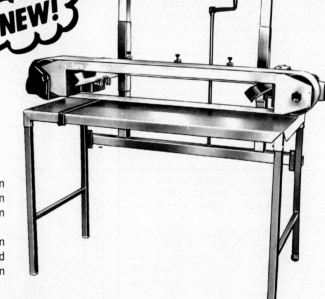

EXCLUSIVE XMAS OFFERS!

Woodworker has put together this enticing range of Xmas gifts for home and workshop — from you to yourself, or drop a hint to your nearest and dearest!

Dowelling set

Last month's offer continued — the Wolfcraft universal set includes jig, clamp, dowels, and drill depth-stops

Retail price £21.50

Woodworker price inc. p&p £17.95
ORDER CODE ROWW 2

Heavy-duty drill stand

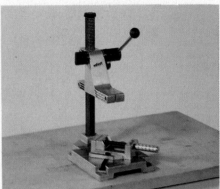

The popular Wolfcraft stand is strong as an ox — and we include a machine vice and bolts

Retail price £49.95

Woodworker price inc. p&p £39.95
ORDER CODE ROWW 3

Variotec work table

Unique flip-over table: guard and fence included: and we're throwing in the extra safety switch

Retail price £107.70

Woodworker price inc. p&p £87.95
ORDER CODE ROWW 4

MASTER CLASS VIDEOS

All videos VHS only

Learn bowl turning with an acknowledged professional, teacher and artist. 120 minutes

Retail price.......£31.95 inc. p&p

Woodworker offer price................£28
Order Code WV1

Carving with experts — lettering, scallop shell, tools, tips, techniques. 90 minutes

Retail price.......£31.95 inc. p&p

Woodworker offer price................£28
Order Code WV2

Wood finishing — stain, oil, varnish, lacquer, french polish, refinishing. 100 minutes

Retail price.......£31.95 inc. p&p

Woodworker offer price................£28
Order Code WV3

Router techniques galore — joints, jigs, a project, drawings included. 60 minutes

Retail price.......£26.95 inc. p&p

Woodworker offer price................£24
Order Code WV4

Turning wood with Richard Raffan — demonstrations from the book featured last month; tools, cutting, six projects. 117 minutes

Retail price £31.95
Woodworker offer price £28
Order Code WV5

Small shop tips and techniques — new ideas and angles, ingenious solutions to common problems in the small workshop. 60 minutes

Retail price.......£26.95 inc. p&p

Woodworker offer price................£24
Order Code WV6

To A.S.P. Reader Services, Wolsey House, Wolsey Rd, Hemel Hempstead, Herts HP2 4SS (0442) 211882
Please rush me the following goods in time for Christmas!

Order code(s) ....

Name ....

Address ....

....Post Code............................

I enclose a cheque/PO for ....

● Make cheques payable to Argus Specialist Publications Ltd   ● We accept Access/Barclaycard

Class out of time

Martin Grierson is
unquestionably one of
Britain's finest makers of
classical modern furniture.
Aidan Walker met him

'**I**'m a designer first and a maker second really . . .'. Martin Grierson was watching his colleagues and employees, Robin Furlong and Jonathan Baulkwill, work on the last stages of shaping and dry-fitting the current job in his workshop; a 2100x1100mm elliptical dining table in American black walnut and Honduras mahogany, with ten dining chairs. No ordinary table. To narrow down to 'buffet' width, the top has hanging side-flaps, the pieces for the rule joints routed and let into the edges of the table-top substrate. Two lift-out sections, also with their hinged flaps, set into the top to expand it to 3000mm long, locating on rounded tongues and grooves. The sliding-bar mechanism underneath for the top to extend is a masterpiece of dovetail grooving and brass inserts.

An expanding ellipse? 'It's two ellipses, really. Each quarter has three arcs.' To illustrate, Robin — 'a better maker than I am', says Grierson — searches out the templates he has shaped to Grierson's original curves. They have inlaid crossbanding and stringing round the edge of the top, setting themselves the problem of making sure not only that the curves flow free and perfect in any one of the table's three lengths, but also that all the inlays meet and match exactly. The mahogany veneers on the top itself also match with the table closed, half or fully extended; of course, of course.

Martin's gaze turns to the chairs. 'The client said she wanted a shield back — well, what can you do with a shield back that isn't Hepplewhite?' The backs have six splats each, cross-halved where they meet, curving in two planes — up and over, and in towards the sitter's back. Grierson points to the human back-shaped former over which they have laminated the 3mm thicknesses; hand-carving and shaping, then two laminating processes for the back of each chair, all the right-hand pieces and all the left. Then the jointing and fitting . . .

All of which says most that needs to be said about the quality of Martin Grierson's work, and his approach to it. He is as uncompromising as he is unassuming; without a hint of the ego or self-advertisement you would half-expect from a designer with a piece in the Victoria & Albert Museum's 20th century collection, he explains carefully that his commitment to quality is overriding. He will never make down to a price, which is one reason why he isn't rich. Detailing and quality of making are crucial; the piece must be beautiful and it must be beautifully made. 'I like my clients,' says his leaflet, 'to know that the high quality of craftsmanship and design applies as much to the back as to the front, and opening a door or a drawer reveals a hidden richness of detail'.

His comments on this subject are illuminating, particularly when it comes to his respect for the craft of his colleagues. 'I design the craftsman into the piece. I get as much pleasure in seeing a piece come together when Robin's making it as if I was doing it.' But the craftsman *into* the piece? There is a quality of design which doesn't demand a great deal in the making, and no one can say it isn't good design. But Grierson thinks the quality of making itself into the design; his philosophy includes the pleasure of the well-made as part of the beautiful. 'A hidden richness of detail' that industry couldn't handle, the personal hand-made feel that comes from overcoming technical challenges the production accountants would drop like hot cakes. Tiny moulding worked round corners, a panelled drawer bottom; faced with

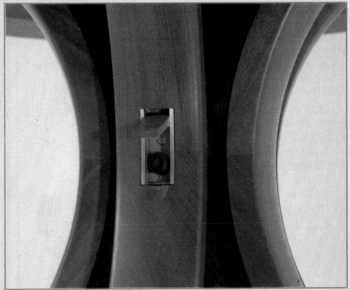

● **Opposite page**: A medal collector's cabinet in macassar ebony – 'a bit of Barnsley in mind': the mahogany and walnut 'buffet table' and dining chairs: the 'Golden Section' table in macassar ebony is in the V&A.

This page: top, a round table in Cuban mahogany with rosewood crossbanding extends with one 5ft leaf; the detail is of the bolt-lock (behind a brass flap) that locates the legs or removable stretcher. **Right**, a 'Thai influenced' chest in rosewood; **below**, a 10ft long sideboard in Cuban mahogany veneer and rosewood crossbanding

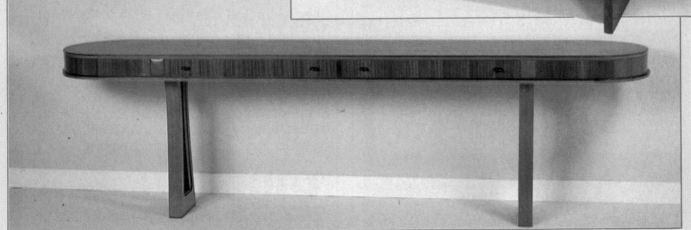

Class out of time

matching the grain of veneers over all the flat surfaces of a light oak desk with dark oak framework, he rejected using manufactured board for the drawer-fronts because hand-cut dovetails would look horrible, and edge-lipping them with endgrain pieces (to look right) spelt movement horrors; so it was cross-veneering then length-veneering all the solid oak drawer-fronts. 'Furniturey furniture.'

Grierson trained as a designer in the early 50s, and worked in architectural and design practices on interiors, furniture and architectural models. In 1960 he set up his own practice doing much the same, and designing domestic and office furniture for industry (he still does this). But by the early 70s he was beginning to baulk at being cast in one mould, and felt a growing dissatisfaction with industry's production and cost limitations. Seeking more variety, more control over the realisation as well as the conception of his designs, in 1975 he set up in a workshop in Covent Garden to make his own furniture — at the age of 43. At the time he was sharing with Rupert Williamson (*WW/Apr 85*) and David Field (*WW/Oct 85*). A decision that has led to the production of some of Britain's finest one-off furniture, but not to riches for Martin Grierson.

One-offs are difficult to price. Grierson has a rough costing/estimating formula — basically, the piece will cost three times the price of the labour — but he can't charge design time to private clients, and his unswerving search for 100% perfection in the making will always lead him towards the more difficult and time-consuming techniques. He is also concerned to save his favourite woods, more from a fear of not being able to work with them than from an overall worry about wiher conservation issues. He will form (say) vertical members in a cheaper solid hardwood, then cover with some precious Macassar ebony or Rio rosewood, veneers when possible, let in as edges or corner mouldings where not. Generally, veneer for Grierson is not a way of 'cheating', making a wood look like something else. His celebrated veneered tables, one of which is in the V&A, are outstanding examples of veneer-as-ornament, decorative woods used decoratively, in some cases almost luridly.

He blames the furniture industry for pushing market prices so low that people think £4000 is 'expensive' for a table. Always producing to a price, manufacturers have corrupted the idea of 'affordability' in the buyer's mind. 'People don't think twice about paying £7000 or even £15,000 for a car that depreciates by 20% as soon as it's on the road, and will any way be replaced after two years.' Grierson's furniture isn't built-in obsolescent; it won't depreciate. And it costs a great deal to make, which is why the market for work from makers like him can be slack at times. Speculative pieces, made with a price tag and the hope of a sale, cost far too much; working to

● **Above**, the walnut and macassar ebony 'Carlton House style' desk and 'Chinese' chair: **left**, these library steps owe something to Thai temple architecture

commission is a better solution, but private clients are comparatively few, and so Grierson is investigating the idea of corporate customers for prestige furniture — a route some of his contemporaries also follow.

His influences? 'I started life as a committed modernist, no respect for the past. All I wanted to do was experiment with new materials and ideas' — the zany 60s. 'When I started to make I became more interested in traditional, formal furniture that is functional, and more relevant to today — but I won't be bound by a particular style.' Hepplewhite, Sheraton, Chippendale, of course: classical proportions: Mackintosh: the eye on the East. 'Yes, the library steps . . . I wanted a light-looking structure without heavy diagonals, and ultimately got the answer from Thai temple architecture; their panels are narrow and high, with half-drop staggered horizontals. I like their tapering vertical spaces, too . . .' So the steps are properly placed and housed, but the lightness of the piece is preserved. The subtle details at the base are all Grierson. His favourite piece, the walnut and Macassar ebony desk, a 'development of a version of a Carlton House piece', is probably his favourite because it has lightness, elegance, that 'richness of detail' . . . and it is a working piece of furniture. The chair that goes with it is what Grierson calls 'Chinese'; he takes care to receive an idea without letting the original plant itself too firmly in his mind, so he can develop it freely. 'I turned up this picture of a 16th century Chinese chair and then put it away quickly

Class out of time

and worked something out from that.'

'If I do have a style, I certainly don't want it to be self-conscious. If you take style to mean a particular kind of detail, then people tend to inflict design exercises on their customers — I'll take ideas from anywhere that's relevant. People say "that's an interesting design" — but what is "interesting"? To make beautiful things with an enduring quality is my wish — things that won't go out of fashion.'

Which might just be the key to understanding what Martin Grierson the furniture maker is all about. He's a modern classicist, a designer/maker with no desire to follow trends or even create them — but one eye is on the past, and the other is very definitely on the future. He signs all his work, as do his colleague/employees on the pieces on which they have worked; it's easy to see he is making with a sense of future history. He has no qualms about making expensive furniture for rich people, partly because of the cockeyed idea of 'expensive', partly because to live he has to sell his stuff to people who can afford the idea as well as the artefact. I'm convinced he is one of Britain's greats, in a distinctly English — an eclectic — tradition; however they're paid for, pieces from the Grierson workshop make the world a better place. If Christie's or Sotheby's are still operating in 300 years' time, Martin Grierson's work will be the cream of the crop, clamoured over by collectors. They'll be fighting tooth and nail for the timeless quality that can only be found in perfectly honest design and utterly uncompromising craftsmanship — truly classical furniture. ■

● Martin Grierson, Barley Mow Workspace, 10 Barley Mow Passage, London W4 4PH.

● **Above**, *Grierson veneered the solid drawer-fronts of this Partners' desk in light and dark oak to get a match all round;* **below**, *the top of a round table on a coopered-style base in Indian laurel with yew inlays*

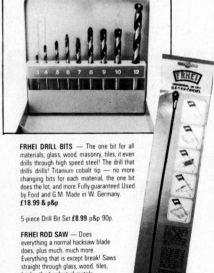

1018

Shaker design

Self-isolated communities of deeply religious people in 19th century America designed and made furniture and much else according to their own inspiration — to the enduring inspiration of succeeding generations. June Sprigg, who has lived and worked with the surviving Shakers of New England, studying their life and art, presents an insight into their work

Shaker Design is a superbly produced scholarly catalogue of an exhibition at the Whitney Museum of American Art, New York, and the Corcoran Gallery of Art, Washington DC, copyright © 1986 Whitney Museum of American Art. It is published in the UK by W. W. Norton & Company, £32 hardback. We are grateful for the permission to use this extract.

● *Left, a rocking chair, unusually in natural bird's eye maple; the Shakers generally painted their pieces, thinking grain pattern somewhat frivolous. Above, a 10in-deep case of drawers, c1840, red-orange stained pine. Right, a blue and orange painted tailor's counter with swallowtail-joined oval boxes in maple*

Photos Paul Rocheleau

I t was not design for which the Shakers were known in their own day. Rather, they were remarkable as the largest and most successful Utopian venture in existence, with an estimated 4-6000 members in 18 principal communities from Maine to Kentucky by 1840. The United Society of Believers — or Shakers, as they were better known — peacefully pursued the vision of their English founder, Ann Lee. They turned away from the rest of society, which they simply called the World. They lived in large Families that were both celibate and communal, devoted their lives to work, and celebrated their love of God in the rousing dance worship that gave them their name. Simplicity was their hallmark. They cared little for possessions. 'Set not your hearts upon worldly objects,' they said, 'but let this be your labour, to keep a spiritual sense.'

But as they created a new, more perfect society, the Shakers also produced a visual environment of such quiet power that it continues to impress the observer even as they themselves are passing from the American scene. Today, fewer than a dozen

Shaker design

● *'The joiners Orren and Joseph are making a morticeing machine, to mortice the Doors and window sash for the new shop . . .' **Right**, a cupboard and case of drawers in ochre-yellow stained pine. Note the asymmetrical drawer arrangement, for a practical but unknown purpose*

Shakers remain in two communities — Canterbury, New Hampshire, and Sabbathday Lake, Maine — yet Shaker work endures. It is unadorned, functional, and well made. But these qualities by themselves do not account for the excellence of design. What really distinguishes Shaker design is something that transcends utility, simplicity, and perfection — a subtle beauty that relies almost wholly on proportion. There is harmony in the parts of a Shaker object.

How did the Shakers create the design that remains distinctively their own, born of American traditions, infinitely refined and simplified? The Shakers were not an aesthetic movement, but a religious sect. To understand Shaker design, we must look at the inner life that created it.

Shaker history began in America in 1774, when a thirty-nine-year-old working-class woman brought eight followers to New York from Manchester, England. Ann Lee sought to establish a new order of beings, more like angels than men. Free from the evils of the corrupt Old World, they would live without violence, war, greed, poverty, lust, and intemperance. As in her vision of Eden before the Fall, men and women would live together in chaste love, at one with each other and God.

Celibate Brothers and Sisters would own all property in common, giving what they could and taking what they needed.

The principal community at New Lebanon, New York, was influential in shaping the visible world of the Shakers — clothing, buildings, village planning, and household articles of all sorts. For the sake of union, Shaker communities sought to look alike, as well as to think, act, and worship alike. Their standards of simplicity and excellence were based on the teachings of 'Mother' Ann Lee. She was concerned with the eternal life of the soul, not with ephemeral things of the earth, such as chairs. Nevertheless, she believed that the outward appearance of things revealed the inner spirit. She cautioned her followers to shun the ultimately hollow pursuit of material goods. She taught them to recognise their true wants — to love and be loved, to live in harmony with oneself and others — and to eliminate other wants accordingly. She told them to avoid excess and needless luxuries (ever more readily available since the advent of the Industrial Revolution) because they drained energy from the real pursuit of life. 'Never put on silver spoons, nor table cloths for me,' she exhorted, 'but let your tables be clean enough to eat from without cloths, and if you do not know what to do with them, give them to the poor.'

Ann taught her followers how to work. Because they were building for the Millennium, it was essential to do their best. The purpose of work was as much to benefit the spirit as it was to produce goods. Believers learned that the mastery of a craft was a partnership with tools, materials, and processes; they also gained experience in patience, all of which served as well in the business of communal living. 'Do all your work as though you had 1000 years to live, and as you would if you knew you must die tomorrow,' Ann said; and, simply: 'Put your hands to work, and your hearts to God.'

It is easy to see the harmony of proportion in Shaker design that transforms common objects into works of uncommon grace. The reasons for this quiet beauty are less apparent, particularly because the Shakers themselves were not self-conscious about it. Their journals, rich in detail on many topics, are almost mute on aesthetics and design. The unassuming diary entries of even the finest craftspeople — 'Made a table,' or 'Finished a silk handkerchief' — yield few clues to the source of their inspiration. No more revealing is the simple praise — 'nice,' 'neat,' or 'well done' — that Shakers gave each other.

The men and women who became Shakers were ordinary people, but the circumstances in which they chose to live produced an extraordinary opportunity for creativity. To a degree that we can scarcely imagine, the Shakers were free of distractions. They stayed at home, worked quietly, and gave part of each day to meditation.

They eliminated the tyranny of petty decisions. Communal life provided uniform clothing, meals, a daily routine, and job assignments. It also freed them from financial worries. No one relied solely on his or her work for survival, and none made cheap second-rate goods to get by. With ample work space, the best of materials, and business-minded colleagues to market what they made, Shaker artisans could concentrate wholly on their work. Celibacy released Shakers from the demands of conventional marriage and parenthood.

Above all, Shaker life freed Believers from the whimsical, merciless prison called style. They did not care what the World considered fashionable. The first Believers, of course, knew about worldly style when they entered Shaker life, but with the passage of time, those worldly design traditions faded for these artisans. The children raised in Shaker villages were even further removed from the influence of fashion. It is no accident that the best, purest examples of Shaker design date from the second quarter of the 19th century, when the first generation of Shaker children reached their prime active years. Shakers did not so much create a new design as endlessly refine an inherited one. As worldly taste grew increasingly ornate in the mid-19th century, the difference between Shaker and worldly homes became more pronounced, Shaker furniture-makers continuing to produce simplified versions of the plain, Federal-style country furniture prevalent around 1800.

Not surprisingly, the Shakers' contemporaries found their buildings, furnishings, and clothing old-fashioned and utterly lacking in style. In 1842 Charles Dickens

---

A rare glimpse of Shaker cabinet-makers sharing information; from a letter dated 23 December 1846, Thomas Damon (1819-1880) to George Willcox (1819-1910):

Not having anything of importance to write about, I will proceed to comply with your request respecting the desk, although I fear you will hardly obtain 5 cts. worth of information. Length 23 in. Width 21 ½ in. as wide as the bench would admit. Depth, back side 4½ in. front side 2¾ including lid & bottom. The desk is made precisely as any common desk, and slides in & out exactly like one of the drawers. When it is shoved in, it slides sufficiently far to admit of a false drawer face (about ½ in. in thickness) which is hung with brass butts so as to turn down to admit the desk's slide out & in freely: this and all the rest that I have said relative to it, would no doubt have occurred to your mind, but as you requested the particulars I have been thus explicit. You will please suit yourself as to size and information, 'For where there is no law there is no transgression.'

---

scorned their 'stiff high-backed chairs,' and likened their dwellings to English factories or barns. A few years later, Nathaniel Hawthorne admitted grudging admiration for the quality of built-in drawers and cupboards, but dismissed the whole as 'so neat that it was a pain and constraint to look at it.' A modish Englishwoman said that Shaker dress would 'disfigure the very Goddess of Beauty,' and humorist Artemus Ward called one Sister a 'last year's bean-pole stuck into a long meal bag.'

Such carping did not matter. It might even have pleased the Shakers, as proof of their own freedom from passing fancies. 'The beautiful, as you call it, is absurd and abnormal,' as one Shaker informed a visitor. 'It has no business with us.' The Shakers did not spurn beauty; they simply reinvented it. It is wrong to suppose that Shaker design was bound by endless restrictions. The Shakers had just one: do not make what is not useful. They saw every reason to make necessary things beautiful, according to their own understanding of beauty. Of the elements universally available to designers, the Shakers rejected only applied ornament as unnecessary. The rest — colour, pattern, line, form, proportion — they freely and joyously used. Perhaps the elimination of superficial decoration gave Believers a keener eye for the shape of a thing and the relationship of its parts.

One cannot say with certainty why the Shakers made beautiful things; perhaps that is unknowable. The source of inspiration has had many names in human history, from the muse to the unconscious. The Shakers themselves had a simple answer. They called the creative spirit a gift. 'If you improve in one talent, God will give you more,' they said. The Shakers were not conscious of themselves as 'designers' or 'artists,' as those terms are understood in modern times. But they clearly worked to create a visible world in harmony with their inner life: simple, excellent, stripped of vanity and excess. Work and worship were not separate in the Shaker world. The line between heaven and earth flickered and danced. 'A Man can Show his religion as much in measureing onions as he can in singing glory hal[le]lu[j]ah,' observed one Believer. Thomas Merton attributed the 'peculiar grace' of a Shaker chair to the maker's belief that 'an angel might come and sit on it.'

The most appealing thing about Shaker design is its optimism. Those who would lavish care on a chair, a basket, a clothes hanger, or a wheelbarrow clearly believe that life is worthwhile. And the use of every material — iron, wood, silk, tin, wool, stone — reveals the same grace, as if the artisans were linked in their collective endeavour in ways that transcend understanding. It is no exaggeration to call Shaker design other worldly. In freeing themselves from worldly taste, the Shakers created a purity of design that endures. ■

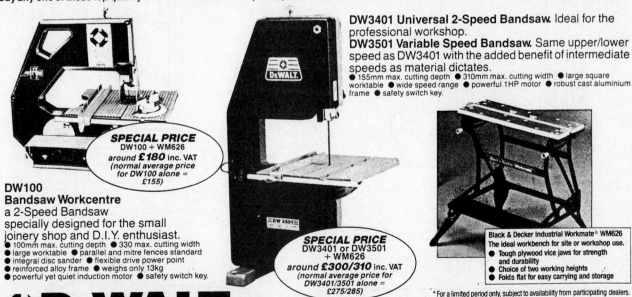

Workbench of the future!

Our *Woodworker*/Sjöberg Workbench of the Future Competition obviously struck a chord with readers. We had dozens of entries; here's the winner and runners-up. Congratulations all!

Outright winner of the competition was John Green, of Camborne, Cornwall, whose design incorporated a wide variety of innovations to make life easier for woodworkers.

John wins a long weekend for two in Sweden, plus a Sjöberg 2000 workbench. The trip to Sweden includes two nights at the Hook Herrgard Resort Hotel and a visit to the Sjöberg factory.

John took first prize because in the opinion of the judges — *Woodworker* and Sjöberg — his idea makes the greatest overall contribution in terms of design advancement.

Many thanks to Sjöberg, and to all the other *Woodworker* readers who submitted designs. Here we present the winning design and the three runners-up.

Innovations galore in the winning design from John Green

John's design incorporates many ingenious ideas:

- Pull-out extension for supporting 8x4ft sheets while marking out and cutting, with rules and pins for measuring and squaring
- Dust extraction system: no more wood shavings on the floor; simply sweep them back into the full-length slot and they will be sucked into a dustbag hanging under the bench
- Built-in lights so the work is never in your own shadow
- Noise reduction; bases of legs are generously insulated to prevent noise from handwork reverberating to the floor below or through the house
- Worktop protection: a roll of plastic film (like extra-wide cling film) unwinds across the bench to protect the wood while gluing and finishing. When the job is over you tear off the length used
- Anti-pollution device; odours from gluing and finishing are sucked through a carbon filter (like a cooker hood unit) using a silent motor so it can be run at night
- Concealing mechanism: when you're not using the bench, you can pull down the blinds
- Controlled environment: infra-red heaters and a thermostat keep temperature constant when the blinds are pulled down; the control panel also gives a humidity reading
- Electric power on hand: the bench has its own electric sockets, all fed from one 13amp plug to the mains, with reinforced cable for this trailing flex. All electric wires run inside the steel framework to avoid damage, with sockets placed high so power-tool leads hang down. The electrics have an on/off key and earth-leak circuit-breakers for safety, backed up by an emergency-push 'off' switch on the bench leg
- Safety equipment to hand: a built-in pack holds goggles, ear-muffs, dust-mask and first aid kit.

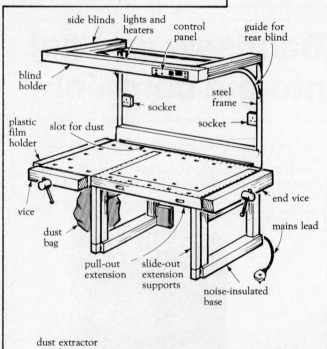

side blinds, lights and heaters, control panel, guide for rear blind, blind holder, socket, steel frame, socket, plastic film holder, slot for dust, vice, dust bag, pull-out extension, slide-out extension supports, end vice, mains lead, noise-insulated base

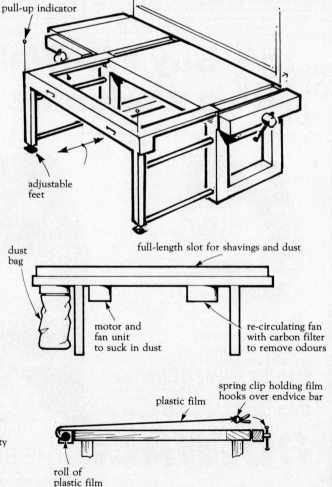

pull-up indicator, adjustable feet, dust bag, full-length slot for shavings and dust, motor and fan unit to suck in dust, re-circulating fan with carbon filter to remove odours, plastic film, spring clip holding film hooks over endvice bar, roll of plastic film

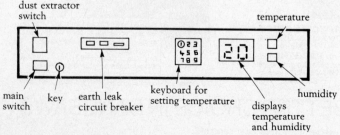

dust extractor switch, temperature, main switch, key, earth leak circuit breaker, keyboard for setting temperature, displays temperature and humidity, humidity

ohn describes his Workbench of the Future

Many people have to use the same bench for making things from start to finish — cutting the wood up, working it, then sanding and finishing. The Sjöberg benches are really so good for the classic woodworking operations that I have kept to their design and construction. The extra features of my bench enable sheet material to be cut safely and squared up accurately, with just one pair of hands.

When woodworking operations are over, the bench converts to a controlled environment for sanding, finishing and painting, with the working surface protected against glue and paint.

The controlled environment of the workbench suits many of the modern glues and resins, which require known conditions of temperature and humidity. It also prevents dust and odours pervading the rest of the house, a boon when you don't have a separate workshop. The bench is almost a piece of furniture, so it needn't be banished to the garage!

Incorporating these ideas into a workbench of the future will enable us to use high-tech materials, but retain the traditional feel and pleasure of a wooden bench that has proved itself over the years.

Reversible modules

Kim Gyr of Hedgehog Design, Wadhurst, East Sussex, devised this module system so machines can be permanently fixed without taking up floor space. This dual height system uses a pivoting mechanism, with the pivoting points close to the machine's centre of gravity for easy change-over.

With the worktop locked in the lower position, machines such as a bandsaw, radial-arm saw or a small planer/thicknesser would be at a suitable height for working. Flip the worktop over and it locks into a conventional workbench; he has incorporated a neat foldaway handle for the end vice. Construction is in laminated beech. Kim suggests the modules should be at standard heights so you can make one unit and add others as budget, available space and workloads increase. The flipover system, he suggests, makes optimum use of space in a small workshop.

Design copyright © Kim Gyr

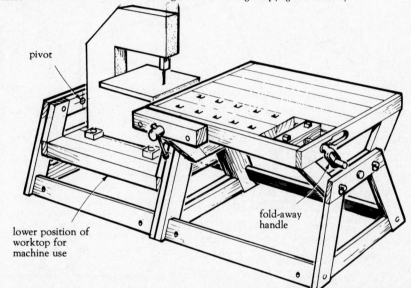

pivot

lower position of worktop for machine use

fold-away handle

Frame-up

The design of Mr L. Hannah of Newcastle, Co. Down, Northern Ireland is both a general purpose woodwork bench and an assembly device for framing up. It incorporates removable sash-cramps and bench-length cramping.

The top is made of two 9x3in boards, in soft or hard wood, slotted to take three heavy-duty T-bar sash-cramps, and grooved at their top outside edges for the 'Ultra' sliding clamp system.

The planks are screwed to a 12mm plywood sheet, nearly 7ft long, to produce a full-length tool well open at each end. The unconventional panel framework is of blockboard and ply, with a plywood panel down the centre to give cupboard space each side. The bench has a pull-out rod to give tail-end support to timber held in the front vice. It also has a slide-out frame for sawing timber.

sash cramps

bench top boards

Ultra clamp

ply

end panel

shelf

sawhorse

slide-out frame

Design copyright © L. Hannah

Workbench of the future!

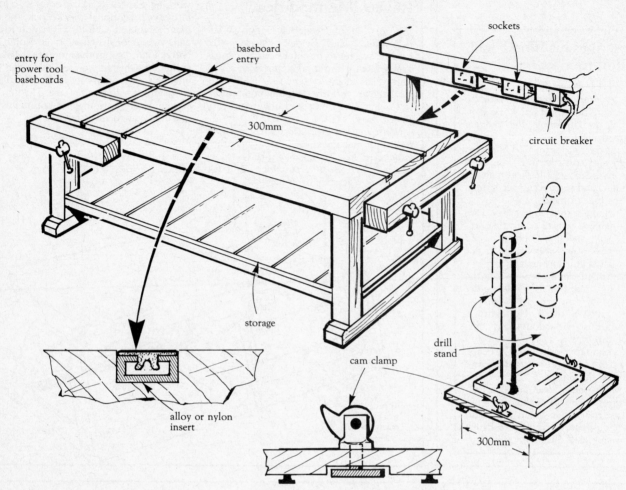

entry for power tool baseboards

baseboard entry

300mm

sockets

circuit breaker

storage

alloy or nylon insert

cam clamp

drill stand

300mm

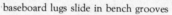

baseboard lugs slide in bench grooves

Double entry

John Atkinson of Allerton, Yorkshire, put in entries for two different benches ... and we liked them both.

The first has alloy or nylon groove inserts in the top of the bench, into which slide power tools mounted on individual baseboards. Simple cam devices front and rear hold the machine firmly in place. At the back of the bench a generous overhang protects electric outlets from damage by falling tools, and the electrics have a built-in circuit breaker.

The second entry, a development of the first, is a bench for use by disabled people, including those restricted to wheelchairs. Half the bench is conventional, except for a long vice with wheel adjustment instead of the usual tommy bar. The other half has full wheelchair access, and the work surface adjusts in height by scissor-jack risers. This side of the bench incorporates a small central vice, again with wheel adjustment. Although this workbench is designed with disabled people in mind, John points out that most woodworkers would enjoy the benefits of a variable height work surface.

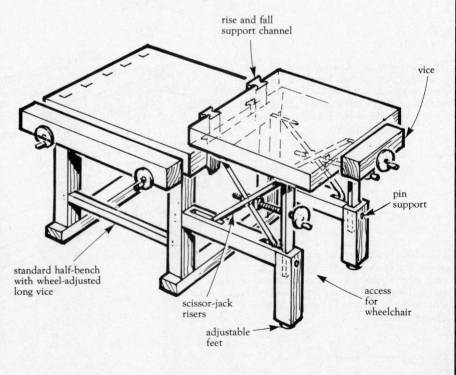

rise and fall support channel

vice

pin support

standard half-bench with wheel-adjusted long vice

scissor-jack risers

adjustable feet

access for wheelchair

1029

1030

Chunky charming chair

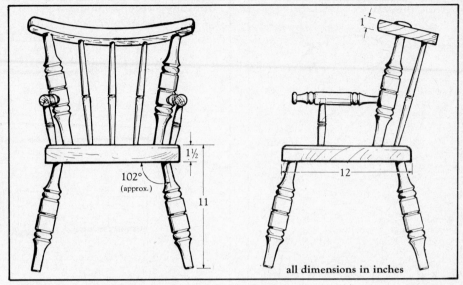

all dimensions in inches

An ideal Christmas gift for turners' young families — Dennis Rowlinson exploited his lathe to the full to produce this child's delight

If you like turning, you'll enjoy making this child's armchair, for every component bar one uses the lathe; only the back rest needs to be worked by hand. You could add rockers, but be warned; left by themselves, children can overdo things. Someone might rock it over backwards and get hurt.

Although this was designed for a child, you could scale it up to produce a full-size armchair or rocker. If you do, try to keep its distinctive chunky appearance. Economising on timber would be a mistake with this project.

Choose whichever timber you want. I used natural ash, but almost any hardwood is suitable. I do recommend you use a reasonably attractive wood, so it can be finished in its natural colour; staining can cause problems, as I'll explain later.

I must point out that I don't claim to be an expert in this kind of work. I just like to explore the many varied aspects of woodturning, and this chair is yet another project in this way. You might devise better methods of doing the job yourself.

Seat

Begin by turning the 12in diameter seat. I prefer to glue two pieces of 6½in wide wood together, reducing the possibility of twist, but 12½in wide can be used, providing it is well seasoned. True up one face and screw it to the faceplate; clean up the edge first with a ½in deep-fluted gouge at about 800rpm. When it's running true, increase the speed to 1000rpm. The same tool can be used to clean up the face and also to cut the ½in

deep depression, but I prefer to use a heavy 1½in scraper, slightly rounded, for the final finish before sanding; sharpen the tool frequently and take a very light cut with the handle raised. Avoid a bump in the middle, which would stick out like a sore thumb when you put the finish on. Finish the coved edge of the depression with a 1in round-nosed scraper. (Some may prefer to use a deep-fluted gouge throughout, but the speed difference between centre and edge makes this extremely difficult, unless you've had vast experience. With large-diameter work even scrapers have a tendency to dig in.)

Sand the seat with fine aluminium oxide paper and finish it off with steel wool. You won't need the faceplate again, so leave it in position; then if the wood gets damaged you can easily re-mount it on the lathe and sand it again.

Legs and backs

Next rough out the legs and back supports from 2in square wood, finished at 1¾in. These are all the same length and pattern. Cut them to length (11in) before turning and use a prong centre smaller than the 1in finished diameter of the ends.

Set external calipers off a 1in Forstner bit and part down to this diameter at each end. Then you can cut the half coves with the ½in spindle gouge. Make sure that the final inch at each end is parallel. Drill a hole with the Forstner bit in a waste piece and use this as a gauge. Allow some play, for in this type of work there is bound to be some inaccuracy in drilling. (These inaccuracies

work against one another, making the whole thing very rigid when assembled, even if the joints individually are slack. It's all too easy to knock it together dry and find you cannot get it apart again without damage.)

Now mark and cut the ⅝in beads. I make a ¼in-deep vee-cut at each side with the point of a skew chisel and shape it with a ¼in beading and parting tool. Finish off the first one and use that as a pattern for the remainder; they must all look similar but a few thousandths of an inch one way or the other won't make much difference! If you take too much off one end and it's a bit slack you can always use the other. For this reason bevel each end slightly with the point of the skew chisel.

Fitting the seat

Now you can drill the holes in the seat base, but first make a jig by drilling a hole in a length of 2x1, using a sliding bevel set at the correct angle as a guide. Drop a leg in and make sure that it doesn't lean either way out of alignment.

Mark the position of the holes 1in in from the edge to the centre, and position the jig as shown. Clamp seat and jig in the vice, and drill to about ¾in deep at the shallowest point. Take away the jig and continue drilling to 1in deep.

Place the four legs in position in the holes, invert the chair, stand it on a level surface and check it for rock. Remove a little from one or other of the holes until it stands firmly.

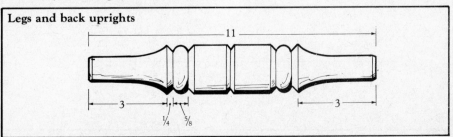

Legs and back uprights

Chunky charming chair

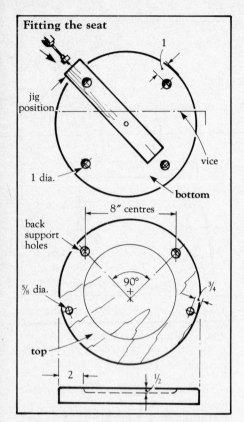

Fitting the seat

jig
position

1 dia.

vice

bottom

8" centres

back
support
holes

90°

⅝ dia.

¾

top

2

½

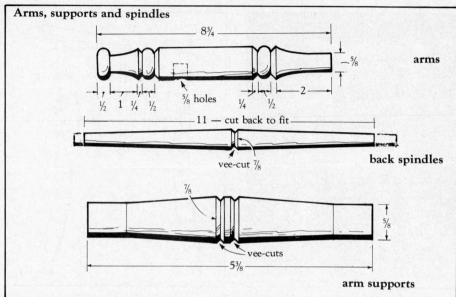

Arms, supports and spindles

8¾

~⅝

arms

½   1   ¼   ½

⅝ holes

¼   ½

2

11 — cut back to fit

vee-cut ⅞

back spindles

⅞

⅝

vee-cuts

5⅜

arm supports

Using the same jig, you can now drill the holes for the back supports. These may run slightly into the leg holes but this doesn't matter. However, accurate marking out at 8in centres is important, so when the assembled chair is viewed from the rear the back supports match up with the two rear legs. The back supports shouldn't be too tight a fit in the holes; some movement is essential to allow for inaccuracies.

Back rest

You'll find the back rest can just be squeezed out of 6x1in timber. The radius for the inside curve (7in) is 1in larger than that of the seat; make a template out of hard-board. Drill the holes for the back support before cutting to shape, again using the

bevel as a guide, the holes should be about ¾in deep at 12in centres.

Cutting out the back rest is no problem if you have a bandsaw; I haven't, so I used a well-sharpened padsaw, finishing off with internal and external spokeshaves to round off the inside curve slightly.

Now you can temporarily assemble the back rest, uprights and seat. The uprights may have to be 'sprung in', which is when you'll realise why I recommend some play on the joints. Before dismantling, mark the position for the holes in the uprights to take the arms, 4½in in from seat to centre. Place the uprights in the vice at the correct angle, determined by placing the stock of the bevel against the vertical blade of a set square, and drill with a brace and ⅝in Jennings-type bit to about ¾in deep; keep the bit vertical during drilling.

Arms

For the arms you need two pieces of 1½x1½in timber, about 9½in long. Turn these to a finished size of 1¼in. Keep the rear end, which needs to be ⅝in, to the tail-

stock, so you can remove it from the lathe to check the fit and re-mount it if necessary.

It's important that these joints are strong; make them a nice sliding fit with no taper. Part down to ⅝in, checking with calipers set from the drill. Cut the half cove, check for fit, and if it's satisfactory mark off 8¾in from the end and part down to ½in diameter. Measure ½in inwards and part down again to about ⅝in. Cut the beads as previously described. Finish the half cove which adjoins the button with a ⅜in spindle gouge used on its edge, so you can cut right up to the corner.

When one arm is completed and sanded, part down to ⅛in and repeat the operations for the second one; they must be a good match. Now you can cut off the waste and finish the ends of the buttons with a flat file and sandpaper. You should also drill the ⅝in hole for the arm support to about ⅝in deep; this is just a straight hole, with the centre 1in inwards from the bottom of the vee-cut. Clamp the arm parallel in the vice and keep the bit vertical.

Assemble the arms into the uprights and square the centre of the holes down to the seat. Drill similar holes in the seat, using the bevel as a guide; the holes are ¾in deep and ¾in in from the edge to the centre.

Next turn the arm supports, which need to be 5⅜in overall, finished to ⅞in diameter. Part down to ⅝in at each end and then taper from the centre down to this, making sure that enough of the length at each end is parallel. Make small vee-cuts with the point of the skew chisel.

For the sticks, measure the distance between the back rest and the seat, and add 1in. Turn them from 1x1in timber to a finished size of ⅞in. Part down at each end to ½in, and again taper from the centre. If the piece is springy and bends away from the chisel, you can overcome this by running the lathe at 2000rpm, using a square-ended deep-fluted gouge and

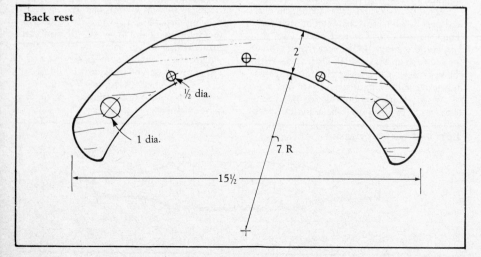

Back rest

2

½ dia.

1 dia.

7 R

15½

supporting it behind the piece with your fingers. Move the tool smoothly; a drop of oil smeared along the toolrest helps a lot. You could use a skew chisel, but it's a bit tricky to do this while also supporting the piece with your fingers. Make vee-cuts and sand off. Now you can use the first one as a pattern for the other two, checking that the vee-cuts line up accurately.

Mark the position of the holes in the underside of the back rest ½in from edge to centre, drilling to about ½in deep. Do the same with the seat holes, but ⅝in deep and 1½in to centre from edge of seat. You'll find it's easy enough to guess the angles for these holes.

Assembly

Now you can assemble and check the whole thing. Sight across the arms to make sure they are parallel with one another; you should be able to move the arms so they both point outward at the same angle. When everything is reasonable, mark the various components so they can be reassembled the same way; I use pieces of masking tape which can be easily removed after gluing up. As well as gluing, I screwed the back rest down into the top of support with 1½in screws; drill the holes for these and countersink them before assembly.

To cover the screwheads and enhance the chair's appearance I turned two 1½x¼in domed buttons and glued them in place. To make the buttons, first turn a short length of waste (about 3in) down to 1½in diameter. Screw another piece of waste about 4x4x1¼in on to the faceplate, and cut a 1½in diameter hole 1in deep. Transfer the exact diameter measurement with calipers, then tap the 1½in piece (if it's a bit slack masking tape will tighten it up). The buttons can then be domed and parted off.

Remember to saw-kerf the legs to take the fox wedges; these need only to be ⅛in at their thickest point, any thicker may cause a split.

Gluing up

Now you can glue up the whole thing. I use Cascamite, mixed to a thick batter consistency; it is very strong and also fills gaps.

Fit the legs first. Place wedges in the saw-cuts, glue both the leg and the inside of the hole and whack in with a wood block and hammer. Check that the chair stands level and the legs all look at the same angle; if not, ease them out or in to suit. Remove surplus glue with a damp cloth and leave the assembly for 12 hours for the glue to set.

Before gluing up the remainder, you may need to clean out the bottom of the back support holes with the Forstner bit. Glue the arms into the uprights and the arm supports into the arms, tapping them into position. Next, fit the sticks, and finally, the back rest and screws.

Check carefully from a distance that everything looks correct; you may need to rack slightly to get it right. Glue the buttons

into position and all is complete. Remove surplus glue with a damp cloth, and allow it to set.

Finishing

Before finishing clean off any gluey finger marks with steel wool and then apply a couple of coats of Ronseal Satin Coat polyurethane or similar, rubbing down lightly with steel wool between coats; brush it well out to avoid runs. This will give a first-class, professional-looking finish and enhance the beauty of the wood. A coat of Briwax or something similar gives a nice feel.

Bad finishing, and particularly bad staining, can ruin a project, no matter how good the construction is or how much patience and skill has gone into it. With turned work in particular any scratches will be across the grain and hit you in the eye when the stain accumulates in them. If you must stain the chair, then do so before assembly, covering the parts to be glued with masking tape; if any scratches show up, you can re-sand the pieces in the lathe. If you want a dark colour, it will look best on oak, preferably air-dried. Instead of stain, brushing oak with household ammonia will give a lovely, even antique finish and scratches will not show up. This treatment does raise the grain, but as the coloration is deep, there's no problem in sanding down. Again, it is best to do this before assembly so that most of the sanding can be done in the lathe. Kiln-dried oak can be used but the colour produced does have a brownish tinge which may not be to everyone's taste.

This treatment with ammonia works only with oak, but you can obtain a good stain to use on other woods by soaking oak

sawdust in ammonia for a day or two and then straining it through a stocking.

Assemble the 'stained' components as previously described and finish with one coat of varnish to seal. Rub down and apply several coats of wax. The result can be very attractive — I was told of this method by an organ builder many years ago.

Rockers

Although I have reservations about converting the chair to a rocker, I have included the dimensions of the pieces in case you want to make them.

Drilling the holes in the rockers for the legs is a bit tricky, for you need to make compound-angled holes in an already angled surface. To add to the problem, the centre of the holes must be ¼in inward from the centre of the rocker to avoid the danger of the butt coming through the side. I just clamp the rocker in the vice, use two sliding bevels to align the bit, offer up a suitable prayer and press on; it seems to work. If you do make a mistake, a very useful feature of the Forstner bit is that it is possible to re-direct a hole with it.

You'll also have to turn the 1in-diameter spacers for the front and rear of the rockers. Make these long enough to tension the assembly, for it's preferable not to use fox wedges when fitting rockers.

Having completed this project, you'll realise these woodturning techniques have considerable potential and could be used for many items of furniture — coffee tables, stools and, for anyone really ambitious, even a dining room suite. You'll often need ingenuity, but for those who like a challenge, it all adds to the interest. ∎

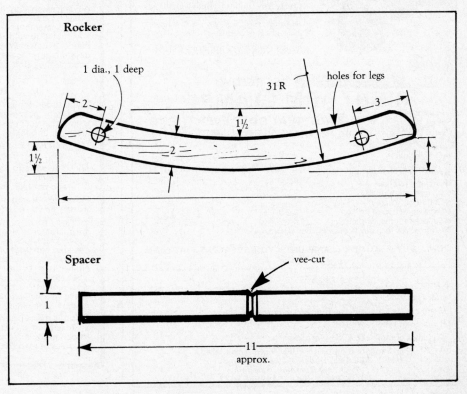

While High Baroque dominated the German states, simplicity reigned supreme in the New World. Vic Taylor looks at furniture from both sides of the Atlantic, and ponders on the origins of the Windsor chair

The Thirty Years' War from 1618-1648 created turmoil among the German States, and by the end the country was virtually divided into two cultures. In the north, the large towns were dominant and their culture was reflected in their middle-class attitudes, while the south and east were still governed by the aristocratic ruling class; there were also areas near the border with the Netherlands which imitated Dutch and Flemish furniture styles. Despite all these tendencies, the Baroque influence persisted from about 1630-1750 as a major factor — much later than in France or England.

The most representative piece of furniture of the time was the *schrank*, or large cupboard, which had several regional manifestations. There was the *Barockschrank* (Baroque cupboard) in southern Germany which was richly ornamented with mouldings, carving, and intricate turning — like all *schranken* it was ponderous, massive, and obviously derived from architectural forms.

There was also the *wellenschrank*, its front distinctly decorated with a series of mouldings arranged geometrically like picture frames. The mouldings were carved to show facets so that when the light played on them they seemed to ripple like waves (from *wellen*, waves or shafts). There were two more designs, the *geschirrschrank* and the *stollenschrank*, a china cabinet and a cabinet on a stand respectively. The first was a low cupboard with carved doors and a shelf rack for china above it; the second was a cabinet, the front covered with *wellen* mouldings, supported on a stand with twist

● *Above*, the Barockschrank; *top*, *a superb* wellenschrank *with calendric motifs centred around the fallen Adam and Eve*

legs and X-stretchers.

One of the most important designers of the period was Gerhard Dagly, who worked between 1687 and 1714. He became Director of Ornaments to Friedrich Wilhelm, the Elector of Brandenburg, and is particularly remembered for his lacquered furniture. Although he sometimes used the dark-coloured backgrounds, typical of others' work, he also painted *chinoiserie* decoration on to white or cream lacquer to a delicate porcelain effect.

Martin Schnell, at one time Dagly's assistant, was an eminent craftsman who worked between 1703 and 1740. When Dagly was dismissed from his post in 1713, Schnell returned to Dresden (his birthplace) and worked for Augustus the Strong, King of Poland and Elector of Saxony. He continued Dagly's method of painting lacquered furniture and specialised in decorating *schreibkommoden* (bureaux).

During the latter half of the 17th century, Bavaria's strong royal-marriage links with Savoy and Piedmont in Italy led to the manufacture in Munich of furniture of the most extravagant High Baroque style. The particular emphasis was on tables consisting of marble mosaic tops supported on caryatids and other sculptured human figures. But by the early 18th century such Italian influences were being supplanted by those of Paris, and Boulle work was imported and imitated by the Munich craftsmen.

Another result of the Italian influence in the south of Germany was the introduction of the *tabernakel-schreibkommode*. This had a base which could be either a chest or a commode (usually with a serpentine front), with a sloping fall-front bureau section above it. On top of this was a *tabernakel*, a central cupboard with banks of four or five drawers at each side. The design was not finally developed until about 1750, but even at this late date the Baroque inspiration survived in the use of walnut veneer, wide cross-bandings, and marquetry.

Across the ocean in the New World, the American settlers were developing their own styles and types of furniture. Obviously, the first settlers found it difficult enough just to survive and could spare little time for the aesthetics of furniture design. The furniture they made was basic in the extreme and it was not until the second half of the 17th century that any distinguishable designs appeared.

Despite the pitifully meagre inventories of contemporary households' goods and chattels, the one material the settlers were not short of was wood. Their earliest tables consisted of oak or elm planks laid on trestles; they could be dismantled, the top planks scrubbed, and the whole thing stacked against the wall to make more space in the one-room living quarters. Table utensils were maple, (including trenchers to eat from), pine went for buckets and tubs, birch for brooms and window coverings,

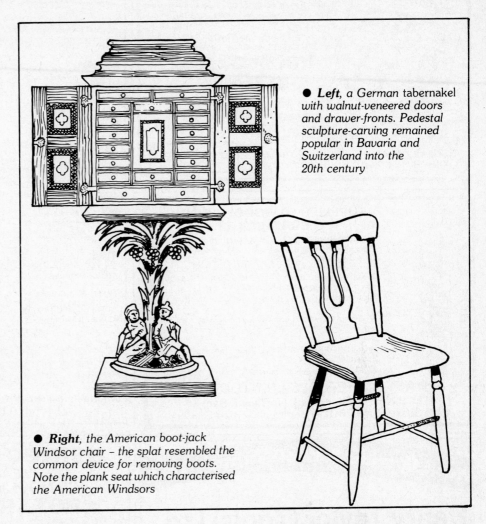

● *Left*, a German tabernakel with walnut-veneered doors and drawer-fronts. Pedestal sculpture-carving remained popular in Bavaria and Switzerland into the 20th century

● *Right*, the American boot-jack Windsor chair – the splat resembled the common device for removing boots. Note the plank seat which characterised the American Windsors

and cedar for washtubs.

There was usually only one chair per household, reserved for the man of the house. It was reminiscent of the European 'joyned' chair with its box-like form, solid arms, plank seat, and splat back; the rest of the family made do with three-legged 'cracket' stools or benches. Later in the century the stools were fitted with sloping backs to become a species of backstool.

The original Pilgrims had landed in 1620 and were followed by other settlers — mostly British, though there were some Dutch, German, and Swedish settlements. Each community had to make most of the artefacts it needed; ships were small and bulky goods like furniture could not be imported. Furniture designs were based on mother country's and were generally 10 to 20 years behind the times. From about 1650 onwards many European styles were being reproduced, more or less faithfully. American furniture always tended to be smaller and slimmer than European counterparts, with less emphasis on frills.

There is one design common to America and England (and, to a lesser degree, France) which has intriguing origins — the Windsor chair. Although American and English Windsors had common ancestors in the 'thrown' and 'stick' chairs which had

been made by English village wheelwrights and woodturners for centuries, it is not certain which country originated the actual Windsor chair. Probably the earliest type of Windsor chair in England was the 'comb back', which dates back to about 1700; the earliest record of American Windsors is about 1725, in Philadelphia. They wouldn't have been known as 'Windsors' then; the first recorded use of the name is 1724 when, as Ivan Sparkes tells us in *English Windsor Chairs*, '. . . Lord Percival's wife was carried around the grounds of Hall Barn, Buckinghamshire, "in a Windsor chair like those at Versailles".' There were still strong associations between the Americans and the French and it's conceivable that the style was introduced to America from France rather than England.

There are many variations of the American Windsor chair, probably more than of the English, but it had one distinguishing characteristic; the back never contained any form of splat, until 1851 when Jacob Royer introduced the 'boot-jack' chair. Although the English-style saddle seat was used at first, later models in the 19th century used 'plank' seats which were also peculiar to American chairs. ■
● Ivan Sparkes, *English Windsor Chairs*, Shire Publications Ltd.

1038

Style in time

Take an offcut of a good hardwood, a glass tumbler and a simple quartz movement, put them together and you get this unusual clock by Paul Anderson — it took silver at the Woodworker Show

I've had a life-long interest in clocks and a passion for the unusual. These two strands have come together in this design. The idea of using vertical motion shafts and rotating chapter cylinders may not be original, but I hope and believe my interpretation of it is.

The overall dimensions are governed by the choice of glass cover or lens — a novel use for a household tumbler. If you can't find a tumbler the same size as I used you'll have to scale the other dimensions to fit what you can get.

● *Novelty time*

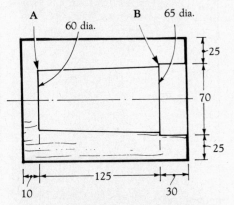

1 Plane and cut the timber for the case of the clock, ensuring that one face of each block is perfectly flat so you get a good joint between the two. Mark out these faces as shown.

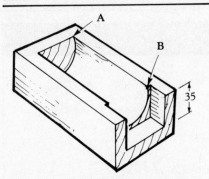

2 Cut two semi-circular cardboard templates corresponding to the top and bottom diameters of the glass lens. Hollow out the two blocks, using the templates to achieve the correct shape at points A and B.

Then use a straightedge to check the shape is achieved between these points. When the hollowing is done, temporarily clamp the two halves together and check the fit of the glass lens. A small clearance allows for possible shrinkage.

3 Cut the rectangular recesses at the base of each side for the quartz movement. When this is complete, carefully clean up the interior faces, which will be difficult to reach later. Glue and clamp the two halves together.

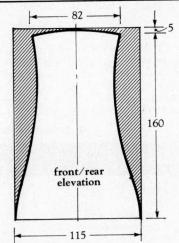

4 Once the glue has completely set, you can start the final shaping of the case. First carve both sides to the profile shown. I mark profiles on the front and back faces and then make multiple saw cuts down to these lines, which helps keep the correct shape and reduces the danger of splitting out during carving. Shape and smooth both faces to a fair finish.

all measurements in mm

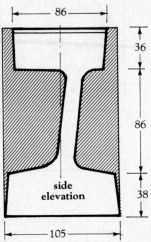

5 Repeat this procedure for the initial shaping of the front and back faces. Use a fine-toothed tenon saw — but carefully, because the cuts penetrate the inner face of the case.

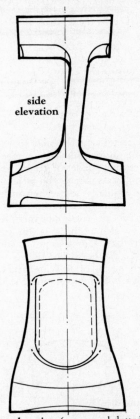

front elevation (rear reveal dotted)

6 The areas to be relieved for the final shaping should now be marked out on all sides.

You'll need patience and a selection of small, sharp carving chisels and gouges; make small cuts, and do frequent checks on shape and symmetry. Take care not to cut too much wood away at the top of the reveals, because you might expose the base of the glass lens.

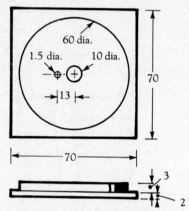

7 Use glasspaper to finish, being careful not to round off the crisp edges too much; they are elemental to the design. After you've worked down through the grades to a flour paper, the case can be polished. Then cut the movement mounting board from 5mm stock as shown, and polish it to match the case.

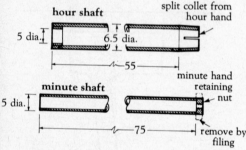

hour shaft | split collet from hour hand
5 dia. | 6.5 dia. | 55
minute shaft | minute hand retaining nut
5 dia. | 75 | remove by filing

8 Carefully cut the brass split collet from the hour hand that comes with the movement. Solder it to the end of the 6.5mm brass tube so you get accurate alignment. Similarly, solder the knurled minute-hand retaining nut to the end of the 5mm brass tube. File down the nut flush with the outside of the tube so it will fit inside the larger tube. Cut a 2mm length of 5mm internal dia. brass tube and solder it to the remaining end of the 6.5mm tube. This will act as a bush for the minute shaft.

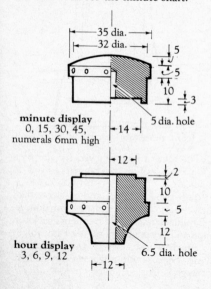

minute display
0, 15, 30, 45,
numerals 6mm high
5 dia. hole

hour display
3, 6, 9, 12
6.5 dia. hole

9 Now turn the top and bottom parts of the chapter cylinder on the faceplate to the dimensions shown. Use a screw chuck to hold one end while you turn the other. You can also drill the shaft holes at this stage. Then reverse the pieces and hold them in a cup chuck machined from scrap timber while you do the final shaping.

10 Now mark out both parts of the chapter cylinder with the hour/five min. divisions, which is easy enough on a lathe with a dividing head. If you aren't a lucky owner of such equipment, you'll have to do some careful marking in 30° divisions with a protractor. Drill a 1.5mm hole at each division, 5mm deep. Cut the 1.5mm brass rod into 4mm lengths; true up the end of the rod and polish it before you cut each length, because the pieces are a little small to hold for this operation once they're cut. Fix them into the prepared holes with a drop of adhesive, ensuring that the top surface is flush with the wood.

11 Now cut the numerals from sheet brass. Draw them on paper first, then stick the paper down on to the sheet using a water-soluble adhesive. For cutting you can use a fretsaw (preferably electric) fitted with a fine metal-cutting blade. Drill out the centres of the numerals 0, 6 and 9 before you cut them. Do the final shaping and finishing with a selection of needle files. Soak off the paper templates before final polishing.

Mark the outline of each numeral in turn on to the relevant position on the two halves of the chapter cylinder. You can inlay them, using either a fine craft knife to 'cut in', or a small dentist's type burr on a modelling drill. Hold the numerals in place with a drop of adhesive. Now polish both parts of the chapter cylinder.

12 Assemble the movement to the mounting board, followed by the hour and minute shafts. The hour shaft is a push fit, and the minute shaft is firmly screwed on. The indicator pointer is formed from 1.5mm brass rod, glued into

● *Sideways glance*

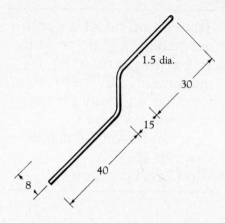

the hole in the mounting board. Now you can fix the two parts of the chapter cylinder with adhesive to the shafts in the 12 o'clock position, as indicated by the pointer. Finally make two small retainer blocks and screw them to the inside of the case, hard against the underside of the movement mounting board. ■

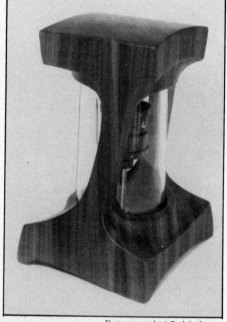

Design copyright © Paul Anderson

Materials list

Timber

Sides	2	170mm	x	125mm	x	55m
Mounting board	1	75		75		5
Chapter cylinders	1	c150		40		40

Other parts
1 Junghans 938 quartz movement
1 pair of hands
1 straight-sided glass (65mm rim, 60mm base, 125mm high)
1 sheet thin gauge brass (0.5mm)
brass tube, 55x6.5mm outside dia.
brass tube, 75x5mm outside dia.
brass tube, 2x5mm inside dia.
brass tube, 200x1.5mm outside dia.

You only need two hands with a MAXI 26

Just look at the cost of some woodworking machines and what you get for your money – not to mention the size!

CAPACITY, COMPACTNESS, COST and CONFIDENCE come together in the universal Maxi 26 – the ideal woodworking machine for the light professional and the keen hobbyist.

Look at the CAPACITY. Six functions – sawing, thicknessing, tenoning, planing, moulding and mortising – all effortless, with flexibility, precision and safety, and driven by a powerful and reliable 2 HP motor.

Look at its COMPACT design. The Maxi 26 is easily moved, even in the smallest of workshops.

Look at the COST. Buy a Maxi 26 and you still get change from £1350 (plus VAT, of course).

Look at the COMPETITION – and you **must** come back to the Maxi 26.

You can have every CONFIDENCE in the Maxi 26 – in its performance, and because it comes fully guaranteed for 2 years.

Designed and built to the highest standards, the Maxi 26 is the best value woodworking machine available today.

FULL 6 FUNCTIONS	
SAWING 90mm depth of cut, edging, mitre-cuts, panel cuts, 45° angle cutting	✓
PLANING On edge or flat, 260mm width of cut. Easy machining of any woods.	✓
THICKNESSING Up to 150mm capacity, depth of cut adjustable 0-4mm, automatic feed.	✓
MORTISING Deep, with both movements controlled by a single lever. Lateral and depth.	✓
MOULDING Moulding, rebates, grooving and all shaping tasks to a professional standard, 30mm diameter spindle shaft.	✓
TENONING Bearing mounted carriage 0-45° adjustable fence for precision square or angular cuts.	✓

AEG (UK) Limited
217 Bath Road, Slough, Berkshire SL1 4AW
Telephone: Slough (0753) 872101

AEG

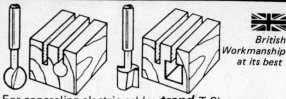

Smoke your own

An interesting special for the Christmas cuisine — benefit from guest cookery editor John Turner's sagacity and add an individual shavings flavour to your cheese

I'd long thought about having a go at smoking my own food, cheese in particular, but it was having a floor full of apple shavings that launched me into action. I filled an 8in-high flowerpot with them, set them alight, and put the pot in a clean oil drum. I had cut some ash laths ½in longer than the drum diameter, and I braced these into the ridges, and balanced some more small-section pieces across these as a makeshift grid.

This is when I learnt lesson one. Do all the leaning into the barrel and fiddling about that you have to do *before* you light the shavings.

Eyes smarting, I ran to fetch the pound of tasty cheese we had in the fridge, and balanced it on the sticks. The wind blew the smoke out as fast as it was generated so I shook out an old sack and covered the drum with it; 10 minutes later the shavings went out.

Lesson two: carbon dioxide is heavy and extinguishes fires. Solution — drill some holes round the bottom of the barrel.

Two hours later I tasted the cheese, refilled the flowerpot and put it back to get a bit more flavour. Three hours after that I was jubilant. The cheese was delicious — if a little strong.

Next day I bought 3lb of mild and tried again. I also put two bacon rashers in to try that. Smokey those rashers certainly became, nice when chopped into a sauce — cauliflower with smoked cheese and smoked bacon sauce, delicious — but bacon really needs smoking as a joint before slicing. The cheese was such a success with friends and it seemed so easy I immediately did another 3lb.

This time I took slices of it to a couple of local delicatessens, to get an opinion and investigate the idea of supplying them. I carefully memorised the wholesaler's phone number on the cheese block in one shop, and wrote it down once I got out of the shop. When I rang him to ask if he could supply cheese for my new smoking business, he suggested he might buy it back once it was smoked. This seemed a brilliant idea, since distribution costs were already threatening to destroy my potential profits.

The wholesaler came to see me, liked the cheese and heard the reports I had received from my 'deli' tasters. He suggested it would be easier to pay me to smoke it, rather than selling it and buying it back; so I found myself holding 40lb of cheese, waving good-bye to trusting salesman.

It was raining, so I moved my smoker indoors. It was also obvious that 40lb of cheese was going to take up more space than 3lb, so I wedged in another rack, only to discover that the cheese took up so much space I couldn't get the flowerpot in. So out it all had to come; the dog knocked the flowerpot over and broke it.

I had a failed applewood bowl lying round, so I drilled some holes in that, filled it with shavings and lit it; bending into the smoke, I braced in the racks, put the cheese in and covered it over. The shavings in the bowl burnt a bit fast, and though the cheese didn't actually melt, it did take on some of the shape of the sticks and coloured somewhat patchily. Visions of paying out fat cheques and finding myself with six months' supply of cheese began to flash uncomfortably in my mind.

A remedy was needed — and quick. A smoke spreader? Cutting a circle from an old roofing sheet with scissors (hard work but needs must), I punched it full of holes and put that in the barrel.

Now what to put the shavings in? Metal causes condensation and extinguishes the smoulder, no more flower pots . . . what? Ring round the libraries: a book on smoking? No, not giving it up; *food* smoking. Yes? I'll be right over.

I set to and re-equipped myself, going by the book.

Proper 1in welded mesh racks, iron bars, more holes in the barrel, a door cut in the bottom, self-tapping screws, a hinge, a heavier lid to cover — but for the shavings container, no easy answer.

Try the wooden bowl again, this time controlling airflow into the barrel; I also put a yoghurt-making thermometer in the top. Chuck that sack, dust on the cheese doesn't look good.

This time it burnt too cool, and the cheese smelled a bit sharp as a result, so I discarded the lid and decided on a clean candlewick cloth to cover.

Still doesn't look right, 40 quid's worth of cheese . . . what to do?

Ring round the market traders: Look, I may have some good smoked cheese coming up, a pound a pound, doesn't look perfect that's why it's not going out the usual way, but it tastes good, the price is right, you interested? Good. Yes, I'll let you know.

Smoked cheese seems best about four days after it comes out, so I bagged up the results to season. On Wednesday I'll open the bags, cut one block in half and taste it. I'll look the other blocks over, and any that meet a high standard will go to the wholesaler. Some I shall swop with a friend for an old fridge — the wholesaler only comes past once a week — some will go to the market unless there's been a flavour disaster, then . . . well, suck it and see, as they say. ∎

● Cheese is less complicated to smoke than meat. The book from the library is called *Home Smoking and Curing* by Keith Erlandson, Barrie & Jenkins 1977.
● Don't put the smoker in your workshop unless you want a sore throat!

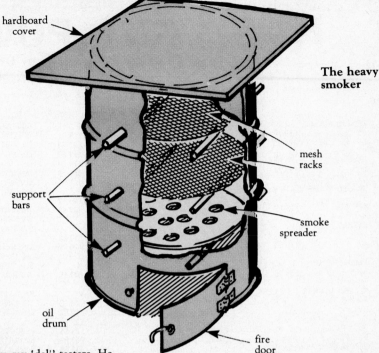

The heavy smoker

- hardboard cover
- mesh racks
- support bars
- smoke spreader
- oil drum
- fire door

Stones and stops

Bob Wearing's Workshop

For the aficionado of Japanese waterstones and hand-planing techniques, some useful ideas to make life easier

Managing waterstones

In spite of many years of practice, I'm still a very dirty sharpener. I can get oil up to the elbows, and transfer it to the workpiece with the greatest of ease, particularly if it happens to be sycamore. So I was delighted by the arrival of the Japanese waterstones and quickly bought a pair, the red medium and the whiter fine finishing stone.

These stones require to be kept in water for daily use.

A particularly successful container is the plastic bacon box for fridges and freezer, about 1½x3½x2in deep, with its snap-on lid. With a benchful of rustable tools the last thing one wants is a bench top swimming with water, so this seems to be quite a successful method of working; take the wet stone from its box and put it on the inverted lid, which is pushed against a planing stop — not the usual small square block, but the type illustrated. A squeezy detergent bottle provides the water supply. These stones are extremely soft, and so unsuitable for communal workshops; even with the best care they quickly wear hollow from the sharpening of narrow chisels. Minimise this by scratching identifying marks on the stones and using one side solely for plane cutters and the other side for chisels and other tools. The surface of the stone should be wiped clean after sharpenings and the water in the boxes changed frequently.

Hollow stones are quite easily corrected, so easily in fact that they shouldn't be allowed to deteriorate much before you level them out. Get a piece of plate glass, rub off the sharp corners with an oilstone, and fix it to a scrap of plywood or blockboard by small pins round the edges, their heads below the glass surface. Grind the stones on a sheet of wet-and-dry paper using plenty of water, which also serves to grip the paper to the glass. Coarse paper can be used at the start; work up the grades and finish with something comparable with the grade of the stone. Slightly chamfer the edges of the reconditioned stone. 6000 or 8000 finishing stones can be kept in good form by rubbing down on 320 to 600 grits; a slight hollow can be corrected with 150-180 grit paper. A stone in a really poor condition can be brought back to level with 80 or 100 grit paper, finishing off with the finer grades.

Planing stops

If you don't have an end vice, you'll find this a help when planing boards — quite an improvement on the traditional adjustable endgrain planing block. It can also be conveniently used for holding Japanese water stones when sharpening. I suggest you make several sizes, which will cover, say, drawer-bottom stuff to quite substantial components.

Cut strong blocks about 1½in thick to about the same length as the vice jaws. The top edges are angled very slightly, shown exaggerated in fig. 1. The stop boards are plywood in a variety of thicknesses. Glue and cramp these square to the length on the angled face (fig. 2). The act of tightening the vice rotates the block slightly, forcing the ply strip firmly against the bench top. Fig. 3 shows the device in use. ■

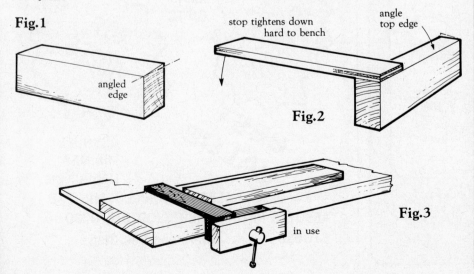

Fig.1 — angled edge

Fig.2 — stop tightens down hard to bench / angle top edge

Fig.3 — in use

COMING NEXT MONTH!

It's a New Year, and January's *Woodworker* will give us a flying start for sure. Keith Krause's magnificent **cabinet** (above) in black-finished beech, with its bevelled glass panels, created a stir when it appeared in last year's student shows; we've got full details on the construction. Deputy editor John Hemsley will be taking a personal view of all that was seen and heard at the October **Woodworker Show**; we have a **green wood special**, featuring the work of **chair bodger** Mike Abbott and an introduction to the **Green Wood Centre** in Shropshire.
For the turners, Lech Zielinski was at the recent **Letterfrack Symposium**, and brings us his report; plus we were at **Style 87**, the furniture preview show, and we'll show you what caught our eye.
In short, January's *Woodworker* is all you need when it comes to your monthly reading diet — all this and more, more than enough for even the most voracious appetite!

ON SALE 19 DECEMBER

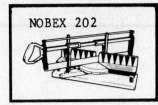

Woodworker PLANS SERVICE

JOHN THOMPSON FIELDWAY COLLECTION — OVER 40 DESIGNS

ALL ILLUSTRATED IN THE WOODWORKER PLANS HANDBOOK

YORKSHIRE WAGON
This example is of the Vale of Pickering type, very robustly built, a handsome vehicle. Model is 16ins. long.
Plan JT/40   4 Sheets   Price £3.30

HEREFORD WAGON
A small size plank sided wagon, it is now in the reserve collection at the Museum of Rural Life at Reading. Model is 15in. long.
Plan JT/14   1/8 scale, 2 large sheets   Price £2.95

HOP TUG
The high ladders fore and aft are a feature of this unusual wagon. Model is 19in. long.
Plan JT/15   1/8 scale, 2 large sheets   Price £2.95

OXFORDSHIRE WAGON
To many people this is the epitome of the English farm wagon. Used on Blackwood farm, the original is now in the Oxford County Museum this 1/8 scale model is 18ins. long.
Plan No. JT/18   1/8 scale 4 sheets plus photo sheet £3.60

GLAMORGAN WAGON
A most elegant wagon. This wagon was built around 1870, now renovated and on display at St. Fagans.
Plan JT/38   1/8 scale   Price £3.30

HAMPSHIRE WAGGON
Constructed about 1900, this is an unusual wagon with double shafts. A superb subject for someone who wants a wealth of detail. Model is 17in. long.
Plan JT/10   1/8 scale, 2 large sheets   Price £2.95

1850 EAST ANGLIAN WAGON
This massive and stately vehicle dates from 1850, now in the reserve collection at the Reading museum of Rural Life. Model is 19ins. long.
Plan JT/20   1/8 scale, 5 sheets plus sheet of photos
Price £4.50

HOW TO MAKE WHEELS
The chart MODEL WHEEL CONSTRUCTION gives step-by-step instructions to enable the average handyman to produce excellent scale wheels Available only with one other plan order.
Plan No. JT/001   Price 80p

ASHBY DESIGN WORKSHOP — TRADITIONAL FURNITURE FOR HOUSE & GARDEN

FULL LIST SENT WITH EVERY ORDER OR ON RECEIPT OF AN SAE.

NEW!

TAPA SYSTEM PLANPACKS

NURSERY PLAY TABLE
This versatile table has a number of features that make it ideal for the nursery. The working height of the table which varies with the height of the blackboard, will suit children between three and ten years old. There is a storage space for large and small toys and an optional posting box may be built into the system. A simple screw and glue construction is used needing less than two sheets of plywood & 4.5 metres of softwood batten.
Plan ADW110   Price £4.00

TAPA SYSTEM PLAN PACKS
Each Pack comprises:
A1 size Plan   2 Frameworks
3 A3 Plans   4 Chair designs
Full-size profiles   Cutting List
Joint details   Schedules
Featuring a series of modern furniture designs for the home, the TAPA system of plan-packs is a new concept in woodworking projects. Each plan-pack focusses on a specific object and explores many alternatives to the original model. The Dining Chair is the first in the series, featuring ideas based on the simple halving joint prototype.
Plan ADW134   Price £5.75

DAVID BRYANT CRAFT DESIGN PLANS HOME & LEISURE, TOYS, SPINNING WEAVING

ALL ILLUSTRATED IN THE WOODWORKER PLANS HANDBOOK

DRUM CARDER
Sooner or later spinners graduate to a drum carder. This design takes the toil out of hand carding. It uses a positive gear/sprocket drive which also reduces the drag which the belt drive alternative imposes. A little metalwork as well as woodwork involved. One sheet plan.
Plan No. DB54   Price £3.70

TABBY LOOM
A simple tabby loom having rollers, warp and cloth beams and fitted with a rigid heddle, and canvas aprons. Basic weaving width 380mm but plan can be adapted for other widths if desired. Ideal for beginners and it is surprising what can be achieved with warp and weft variations tufting etc.
Plan No. DB 2   Price £3.20

SLOPING STYLE SPINNING WHEEL
This design is a replica of an authentic spinning wheel doem olden days, having a 486mm (19in.) diameter wheel with bent

wood rim. Plan is complete with mother-of-all, distaff, treadle operation etc. A feature of this wheel is its attractive turnings which make it a most decorative piece besides being functional. A design for the enthusiast woodturner. Two sheet plan.
Plan No. DB12   Price £5.40

UPRIGHT SPINNING WHEEL
In this vertical style spinning wheel the mother-of-all arrangement is situated above the main wheel. The latter is 460mm diameter and the rim is of segmented design. Simpler lines than the sloping wheel but nevertheless graceful in appearance and of course functional.
Plan No. DB13   Price £5.40

SPINNING STOOL
A spinning stool specially suited for use with the sloping bed wheel. Four legged arrangement, with richly carved seat and back. A good example of chip carving.
Plan No. DB20   Price £2.20

WARPING MILL
This warping mill design consists of a vertical revolving drum supported within a floor standing frame. The drum is fitted with pegs for securing the warp to, and the frame is complete with heck block for spreading warps up to 15-20 metres.
Plan No. DB9   Price £3.20

Tales out of steel

Ashley Iles takes time out from his own memory banks and samples history in the raw at Sheffield's working museums

Museums are changing, thank goodness. The stuffy rooms, glass cases and specimen drawers are giving ground to the working museums where the machines and methods of producing artefacts are demonstrated by craftsmen with traditional expertise. Here the Sheffield museums have led the field in being true working museums.

Not far from Sheffield city centre the Don swirls round Kelham Island which houses the Kelham Island Museum. The building itself is old and gaunt with bricks blackened by age and pollution. The roads are cobbled and the atmosphere as thick as black pudding. Inside the entrance hall the walls and showcases are festooned with the products of leading Sheffield manufacturers. From then on the rich tapestry of Sheffield unfolds itself and you feel that in some dark corner lurks the ghost of Vulcan himself.

The first working exhibit is an enormous gleaming steam engine. The flywheel, which must be 20ft across, runs in a deep pit and is used to drive a steel mill. On the left down a passage is a full-size working model of a 'buffing lass' in full regalia swaying backwards and forwards to the running buffing wheel.

Further on are the 'little mesters' in their tiny workshops with doors and latticed windows on to the 'street' where the public watch through the windows. The grinders sit on horsings, grinding and glazing pocket knives in an authentic grinding shop. Next door is a pen and pocket knife forger blowing away with hand bellows and then banging on an old anvil, and at the same time answering questions through the open window. It's all so very real and rather a strange experience.

On the south side of the city in much more pleasant residential surroundings the Abbeydale Industrial Hamlet is complete and working right down to the typical boss' furnished cottage. In its day, 1714-1933, it was one of the largest water-powered works on the river Sheaf producing scythes, hay knives and general agricultural tools. It was founded by the Goddard family; the dam was enlarged in 1777 and the tilt hammer followed in 1785. The grinding shop or 'hull' arrived in 1817 and by 1830 the site included a crucible steel furnace of the type designed by Benjamin Huntsman — hence 'cast steel' found marked on old tools. The site also included numerous hand-forges, warehouses and offices.

During the 19th century the works had more than its share of industrial problems. The grinding shop was blown up with gunpowder because non-union labour was suspected of being used; one managing director was shot at five times — but the shots all missed!

Steel was melted in crucibles which were made in the pot room from locally mined fireclay together with china clay and coke dust mixed together by bare-foot treading. The pots were stored and fired just before use and each pot was used only twice before discarding. In later years the crucible was only used for non-ferrous metals.

An interesting character was the 'pot lad' who controlled the air draught in a cellar below the furnaces. He also did all the fetching and carrying including the barrel of beer drunk to assuage the thirst of the furnace men.

Next came the charge room (nothing to do with military police) where the pots were loaded. The metal would be either blister steel, a low quality steel, or wrought iron imported from Sweden. This was broken into small pieces on the anvil. A normal charge would be 60lb.

The crucible furnaces were sunk into the floor and were fired first by coal then coke to get the intense heat. Being in a crucible the steel was not in direct contact with the fuel as in a blast furnace. After melting, the steel was poured into bars or ingots, which were then forged on the tilt hammer or rolled to smaller sizes. A scythe was made by welding a piece of steel between two pieces of iron. The roughly forged scythes were then finished, straightened and hardened in small forges with smiths using hand bellows.

These days you can walk into a mill furnisher and buy an electric blower complete, but at Abbeydale the draught was achieved by a pair of water-powered pistons. The tilt hammers, grindstones and most of the other machinery were all driven by water-wheels. At Abbeydale the grinding wheels, running in water, revolved towards the grinder. Just think about it! Personally I would rather face a 15in gun.

Why not go and see it for yourself with hammers banging away, machinery going, water wheels driving the lot through cycloidal gears and skilled old-timers working away? It's a fantastic experience.

Write for Leaflet 1977 with sae (to Abbeydale Industrial Hamlet, Sheffield — not me!). ∎

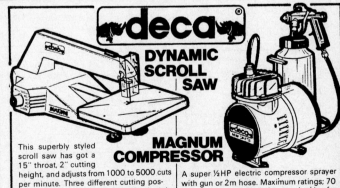

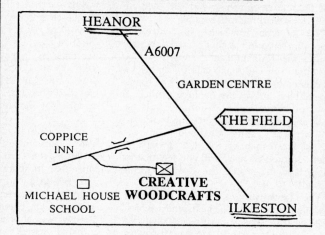

Guild notes

WOODWORKERS

Guild of

The Guild was set up by *Woodworker* to create a meeting ground for all those involved in working wood, whether professional, amateur, or enthusiastic beginner. Guild members get:

- Access to Guild courses and events
- Free publicity in *Woodworker*
- Specially arranged tool insurance at low rates
- 15% off Woodworker Show entry
- A free display area and meeting point at the Show
- 15% discount off *Woodworker* plans
- Inclusion in our register of members' skills and services

For details, please send an sae to the Guild of Woodworkers, 1 Golden Sq, London W1R 3AB.

GUILD COURSES

● **Only Guild members are eligible to go on these courses. You must book in advance, and we must have a cheque for the full cost of the course at the time of booking. If you cancel less than four weeks before the advertised date you will forfeit 50% of the cost, unless there are exceptional circumstances.**

Power routing — Roy Sutton

14 February, 9.30-5.30, Herne Bay, Kent; £25+VAT.
Roy is an expert on this subject. Starting from first principles, he covers housing, grooving, rebating, straight and circular moulding, tenoning, mortising, and rule-joint and template work; he also deals with designing and setting up your own jigs.

French polishing — Charles Cliffe

12-13 March, 10-4, Bexleyheath, £40.
This is a popular course by one of our 'Question box' experts and author of *The Woodworker Manual of Finishing and Polishing*. Charles explains preparation, staining and the techniques of French polishing itself; he'll also show you how to sharpen a cabinet scraper, so bring yours along. Charles will offer advice on any small piece of furniture you want to refinish, and can also order supplies for you to take away if you tell him in advance.

Wizard of Oz

We hear there's a lot of interest and enthusiasm for woodwork and woodturning 'down under'. Rob Ripley, who works for the Hawthorn Institute of Education in Hawthorn, Victoria, Australia, and is very much involved in woodturning, tells us that turners he meets are very keen to get in touch with fellow enthusiasts. He has started nine woodturning clubs since December, and the first question members ask is 'Is there anyone else about?'

If you know of turners in Australia — or if you are one! — Rob Ripley can be contacted at the Hawthorn Institute of Education, 442 Auburn Road, Hawthorn 3122, Victoria, Australia.

Turn of the month

Woodturners in West London/South Bucks are invited to a 'Talking Turning' evening by craft woodturner, Mike Cripps, on 4 December. If you're interested in sharing ideas, triumphs, and disasters (you can bring along up to four pieces of work) then send an SAE to: Mike Cripps, 41 The Greenaway, Ickenham, Middx UB10 8LS. He is planning a demonstration evening for February — so now is a good time to get involved.

Your local?

Several members have volunteered to act as local representatives who will encourage get-togethers of members in their areas. If one of these lives near you, please contact him.

South-east London: Mr M. J. Belcher, 30 Rusholme Grove, London SE19 1HY
West Sussex: Mr Clive Green, The Lychgate, 20 Broadmark Lane, Rustington, West Sussex BN16 2HJ
Nottingham: Mr B. Harmer, Westbridgford, Nottingham, 0602 815046
Suffolk: Mr S. Lloyd Jones, Varne, New Street, Stradbroke, Eye, Suffolk

Thriving

Good to hear that one local group is holding regular meetings. 'Small but enthusiastic' — that's how Paul Smith describes the Herefordshire group. There are six people involved, spread all round the county. After an initial meeting for 'natter and coffee' at his house early this year, the group decided it wanted an informal style, and now meets about every two months in turn at each address. That way members see each other's work and workshops, and they can exchange ideas. One or two family friendships have ensued, so Paul feels the initial efforts to get started have been really worthwhile. Numbers aren't everything, he comments. Any other Guild members living in Herefordshire can contact Paul Smith at Dinmaur, Hope-under-Dinmore, Leominster.

Congratulations to Paul and to this group who are showing how useful and enjoyable local meets can be.

London Gallery

Congratulations to all Guild members whose work was in the London Gallery at the Woodworker Show. Sadly we didn't have room for all the entries we received; better luck next time.

Visitors to the stand enjoyed the variety of work, including Clive Green's magnificent rocking horse and Charles Beresford's Shaker-style table. Pity we missed G. Ray's model of a Churchill tank in mahogany and brass; it has 3,500 parts and took over 1500 hours to make! On the turning front, William Jamieson showed some lovely hour-glasses, and there was some first-class cabinet work from last year's Robbins Rose bowl winner, Waring Robinson (*WW/Mar*). We were intrigued by the miniature furniture from K. G. Paskell, including this $1/12$ scale Shaker log box in pine.

Magical mystery school

From gentleman's playground to exemplar of progressive craft education — the School of Woodcarving was of a rare breed. John Hemsley wonders why it disappeared

In calf-length smocks, heads bent over their wood, dozens of carving students crowded the tiny workshop of the unique School of Woodcarving, in South Kensington, London. Started in 1878, when technical education was in its infancy, and the influence of Morris was yet to be felt, the school evolved from a haven for dilettantes pursuing a gentleman's hobby into a training body for the trade, an alternative to the time-consuming and often narrow apprenticeship training.

More than 2500 students passed through these workshops between 1878 and 1937. Some of these students may still today be practising their craft, and it would be interesting to hear from them. We learnt about the school from Mr. C. F. Yeates, of Norwich, who was given a brochure by the granddaughter of a student of 1906, and we thought readers might like this glimpse of the past.

The school started in 1878 to 'encourage the art of woodcarving as a branch of the fine arts' funded by the Society of Arts, with help from the Worshipful Company of Drapers and Gillow & Co — 'a well-known furnishing and decorating firm.' Sir Edwin Lutyens was chairman from 1921-37.

The first full-time tutor, 'that eminent Florentine artist, Signor Bulletti', resigned within five years, and the school took the unusual step of using English staff after that. 'It was customary at the time to look abroad for anything that was good in art or artists', recounts the unnamed author of the brochure about the school. 'Little impression had so far been made by the Morris pioneers. Can anything good come out of England was a question invariably answered by a double negative.

'The work of the Italian Renaissance in the realm of applied art was alone considered worthy of study. Taste in decorative art to be good had to be taste for Italian work, and examples of this work were analysed with rule and compass and the grammar of the ornament worked out on a meticulously mathematical basis.'

Even the English successors to Signor Bulletti were unable to avoid this heavy influence for many years.

'No considered system of instruction had been thought out or adopted by the school.

Instruction began and ended in the mere manipulation of wood; notions of design, line and form might be picked up in copying graded models, and too often these examples of so-called Italian Renaissance, when they were not genuine fragments torn from their settings, were debased products of the early 19th century and conspicuous only as *tours de force* of technical skill.

'Nevertheless, in the late 80s the carving of wood became a popular as well as a society hobby.'

Sometimes as many as 70 students were taking either daytime or evening classes there, but with only two staff nobody could have got much individual attention, and the work was almost exclusively technical.

This started to change about the turn of the century, when the school moved into premises rented from the Royal School of Art Needlework, and obtained grants from the London County Council and the Board of Education. As a condition, the school agreed to provide free scholarships for Board nominees and to open its doors to 'all Masters and Mistresses employed by London County Council' — presumably teachers. Saturday classes rapidly became popular.

The method of teaching had changed appreciably by this time. Originally students did slavish copy work for architects and other specifiers, and were often paid for it. Now design and drawing were studied as well, and carving, if no less technical, had become more expressive and individual.

By the time the school moved to its new and permanent premises at 39 Thurloe Place, South Kensington, in 1908, the Italian Renaissance was no longer such an obsessive preoccupation in Britain. People were beginning to appreciate what England had achieved in the age of Gothic art, and in the 17th and 18th centuries in architecture, interior decoration and furniture; other countries apart from Italy were acknow-

ledged as useful to study. The preponderant dilettante element was giving way to an increasing number of serious students. LCC inspectors helped sort out a more comprehensive curriculum. It was now firmly understood that as well as helping students who wanted to study woodcarving as a cultural interest, the school was primarily concerned to train students so they could enter workshops as professional craftsmen, and to help those already in the 'trade.' The school's three-year course was beginning to take the place of traditional apprenticeships, and woodcarving firms eagerly sought out ex-students.

This movement gathered pace after the Great War, when new ideals and methods, a re-examination of traditions and an experimental approach became the order of the day. Coloured carving was introduced, and the conception of design changed so much that in 1925 students' work won one of the few gold medals of the Exposition Internationale des Arts Décoratifs et Industriels Modernes, Paris.

The author of the brochure comments:

'Students are trained to do the work of the workshop, but a higher ideal is maintained than is, unfortunately, too often required there, and a better understanding of the significance of carving is inculcated.'

After a deputation from the Wood-Carvers' Trade Union visited the workshop, the school principal reported: ' . . . they looked to us to play an important part in improving the calibre and standard of the carver as a craftsman and a man, so that in the not far distant future their self respect, backed by their organisation, would lead to a stoppage of all forms of bad workmanship.'

The records of this school seem to have stopped after 1937. What happened to it, and what influence did the school have for the thousands of students who learned the craft there? ∎

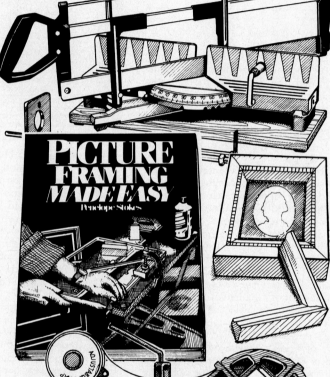

1054

Books

James A. Jacobson
Making Small Wooden Boxes
Sterling, £7.95
Reviewed by Peter Howlett

James Jacobson's book on box-making is another one of those well-meaning and enthusiastic American publications that should never have reached the press, let alone been exported to England. The text is sprawling and in some cases quite unintelligible, with no clear direction on either design or manufacture. Techniques are dealt with vaguely, and the only technical photograph of cutting mitres on a radial-arm saw is poorly lit and confusingly illustrated with bald, inadequate line drawings.

The bulk of the book is taken up with 42 depressingly naff projects, mostly indifferent music-box after indifferent music-box. Inlay of the grossest sort is dealt with in torturing detail, and as for hints on turning boxes, goodness knows how he managed to produce what appears in the photographs. The only redeeming feature of the book is the interesting section on spalted timbers native to Illinois — great if you live there.

It is quite impossible to take this book seriously, as it fails to inspire or give direction to the person seriously thinking of making boxes, either for pleasure or for a living.
● Peter Howlett is a professional box maker and a contributor to *Woodworker*.

Alan and Gill Bridgewater
The Complete Guide to Decorative Woodworking
Phaidon, £17.50 hardback
Reviewed by Aidan Walker

Anyone who reads *Woodworker* for more than a few months will know the work of Alan and Gill Bridgewater. They are set fair to become a craft tradition themselves, and this book will do a lot for that development. Their multi-talents abound, and the woodworking ones are here beautifully presented in a superb book, imaginatively and luxuriously designed and attractively illustrated with colour photography and the Bridgewaters' own drawings. A showcase worthy of them, in other words.

Variations on the themes of decorative construction — dovetail joints, Shaker boxes (*see 'Shaker Design' in this issue*), windsor chairs; veneering, inlay, marquetry; relief woodcarving, carving in the round; french polishing, stencilling, water gilding.

That isn't all that's in the book, but they give step-by-step instructions as practical projects for everything they describe as well. The word 'Complete' in any title remotely connected with woodworking always arouses suspicious; one can think of various techniques they haven't covered — but who cares, it's a lovely book and will be relished by experienced woodworker and newcomer alike.
● Aidan Walker is *Woodworker's* editor.

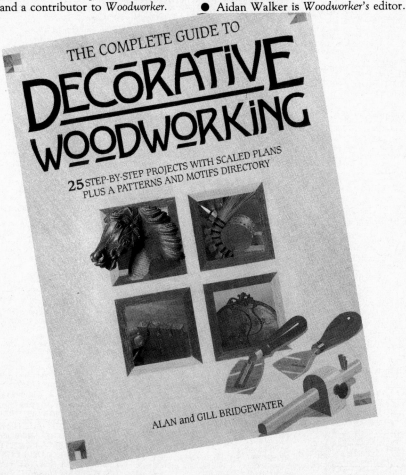

THE COMPLETE GUIDE TO
DECŌRATIVE WOODWORKING
25 STEP-BY-STEP PROJECTS WITH SCALED PLANS
PLUS A PATTERNS AND MOTIFS DIRECTORY

ALAN and GILL BRIDGEWATER

Michael A. Stone
Contemporary American Woodworkers
Gibbs M. Smith, £25.50 hardback from Stobarts, London EC2
Reviewed by Kerry Fowler

The ten woodworkers detailed in Michael Stone's compilation of American talent divide into established giants and innovators. Giants such as Wendell Castle, Tage Frid and James Krenov should be familiar, but newcomers to the grand parade like Garry Knox Bennett won't ring too many bells here.

Styles and attitudes of the top ten are varied to say the least: George Nakashima delights in free-form (slabs of burr for table-tops); Krenov prefers an 'orchestration of details and subtleties' and Knox Bennett, one of the 'innovators', thinks wood 'a convenient medium for making large objects . . . '

It's a well-presented and unpretentious book with good photography (a bit short on colour shots) and needs no translation from the American; a good work of reference.
● Kerry Fowler is *Woodworker's* editorial assistant.

Roger W. Cliffe
Radial Arm Saw Techniques
Sterling, £11.95 softback
Reviewed by Luke Hughes

Encyclopaedic coverage, 1100 photos and drawings, and voluminous text make this the definitive book on the radial-arm saw. There are excellent chapters on saw-blades, accessories, ingenious jigs to make, and even some woodworking projects at the end of the book. But I am confused about what market the book was intended for. Professionals will have more equipment; amateurs frequently do too. Who wants a whole book on one tool? Normally a chapter is enough. (I recommend the chapter in Alf Martenson's *The Woodworker's Bible*.)

Meticulous and thorough as the author is, it seems he would have a world of radial-arm sawyers diligently changing accessories and making jigs just to prove any woodwork operation can be done on the RAS. Much energy and ingenuity is spent devising means to mould, spline, drill, rout, sand, and taper. Radial sawing is to be a way of life.

This is nonsense. With the high cost of accessories, the time needed to change them, and the remarkable value of small modern power tools, most aspirant woodworkers will prefer to have the best tool for the job. The jobs for which the RAS is best will always be crosscutting, mitring, bevel and compound cuts. It is also an excellent tool to have for site-work, carpentry and joinery. But don't be deceived, either by the claims of manufacturers or by this book, that you will want for nothing more.
● Luke Hughes is a professional designer and maker of furniture in London.

AXMINSTER POWER TOOL CENTRE

WOODTURNING LATHES — *OUR PRICE INC. VAT*

TYME STUDENT 10" swing 30" centres (With accessory voucher £20) **£219**
CARLZEISS HMD Wood Lathe 5" swing 24" centres asstd. accs. **£199**
CORONET HOBBY 10" swing 39" centres 1MT ½HP 3 speed **£199**
CORONET No. 1 Cast const. 12" swing 24" centres 1MT 3 speed **£218**
ELU DB180 39" centres 15" swing 1½HP motor 3 speed **£299**
TYME CUB 30" centres (With accessory voucher £30) **£296**
TYME AVON 36" centres (With accessory voucher £45) **£419**
MYFORD ML8 36" centres (no rear turning) 5" swing **£376**
MYFORD ML8B 36" centres 9" Rear turning .... **£432** ML8C 42" centres **£467**
MOTOR for Myford lathes ¾HP .... **£80** Starter .... **£26** Cabinet Stand **£289**
MINIMAX Centre lathes T90 ...... **£421** T100 ...... **£497** T120 ...... **£538** Legs **£67**
MINIMAX COPIERS for above lathes CT90 .... **£484** CT100 .... **£514** CT120 .... **£560**
LUNA SPKA 900 COPIER medium duty copier for all lathes **£256**
CORONET CMB600 33" Centres 23" bowl cap .... **£599** Bowl rest **£49.95**
HARRISON GRADUATE 30" Centres .... **£1175** 42" Centres .... **£1232** Shortbed **£1037**

WOODTURNING FITMENTS CHISELS & ACCESSORIES (State m/c)

Coronet collet chuck sets **£69**
Coronet collet bodies .... only **£29**
Collets 5/8", ¾", 1" .... each **£12**
Expanding Jaws 3", 2", 1" .... each **£27**
Spigots 5/8", ¾", 1" .... each **£14**
Speedaneez polish std/wht **£5**
Coronet planer blades 4½" .. **£20** 7" .. **£23**
Revolving centres 1MT or 2MT **£18**
0-½" Drill chuck 1MT or 2MT **£15**
Craft supplies chuck **£52**
Long hole boring kit 5/16" **£32**
2½" Woodscrew chuck **£22**
Sorby sizing tool **£6**
Carnuba wax turning stick **£1.80**

WOODTURNERS "AT LAST PERFECTION"

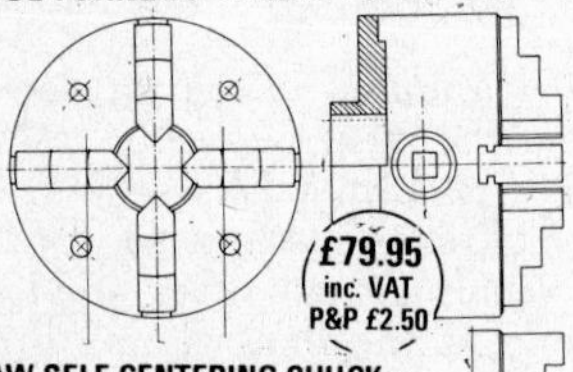

4 JAW SELF CENTERING CHUCK
AVAILABLE IN THREAD SIZES FOR MOST LATHES.
SPECIFICATION: GRIPPING CAPACITY 1/8"-4" DIAMETER 4" WEIGHT 2KG. SUPPLIED READY THREADED (LH OR RH) WITH TWO SETS OF PRECISION JAWS (INTERNAL & EXTERNAL).
5" 4 Jaw S/C **£99.95**
4" 3 Jaw S/C **£69.95**

HENRY TAYLOR HSS CHISELS

(P&P £1.20 per order)

GOUGES	PARTING TOOLS
HS1 Superflute **£24**	HS2 Fluted **£15**
HS3 ¾" D/Fte . **£14**	HS11 ¼" Std. **£5**
HS4 1½" D/Fte **£24**	HS12 3/8" Std. **£7**
HS5 ¼" Spindle . **£5**	HS13 ¾" × ½" .. **£10**
HS6 3/8" Spindle . **£7**	HS33 Diamond **£13**
HS7 ½" Spindle . **£9**	HS32 ½" × 1/8" **£6**
CHISELS	**SCRAPERS**
HS8 ½" Skew **£7**	HS26 ½" Rnd **£7**
HS21 ¾" Skew .. **£8**	HS38 ¾" Rnd **£8**
HS22 1" Skew ... **£9**	HS27 1" Rnd **£10**
HS9 1¼" Skew **£14**	HS28 ½" Sq **£7**
HS23 ½" Square **£7**	HS29 ¾" Sq. **£8**
HS24 ¾" Sqre ... **£8**	HS30 1" Sq. **£10**
HS25 1" Sqre .. **£10**	HS15 HD Round **£20**
HS10 1¼" Sqre **£15**	HS16 HD Domed **£20**

ALL PRICES INCLUDE HANDLES
LUNA Ring Gouge 16mm **£17** 25mm **£19**

WOODTURNING CHISEL SETS (P&P £1.80)

HENRY TAYLOR Carbon Steel Sets, 3 Piece .... **£17** 5 Piece .... **£29** 8 Piece **£46**
SORBY Carbon Steel Sets 5 Piece (51c) ...... **£24** 6 Piece (61c) ...... **£33** 8 Piece (82c) **£46**
SORBY High Speed Sets 5 Piece (51h) ...... **£34** 6 Piece (61h) ...... **£59** 8 Piece (82h) **£77**
LUNA Swedish Steel Sets GOOD VALUE 3 Piece ...... **£14** 4 Piece ...... **£27** 5 Piece **£37**
MINIATURE SETS SORBY HSS set of 5 .... **£25** HENRY TAYLOR SUPER FIVE **£18**

BANDSAWS

BURGESS BK111+ 45° 3" cut jigsaw fretsaw .... (inc. P&P) **£115**
7" Sanding attachment for Burgess .... **£20** Mitre fence .... **£6** Rip fence **£5**
DeWALT DW100 45° tilt 4" cut c/w sanding table .... (P&P £2.50) **£149**
DeWALT 6" cut 14" throat 45° DW3401 .... **£256** DW3501 .... **£264**
LUNA BS320 45° tilt 6" cut 14" throat cast iron table **£324**
MINIMAX P32 45° tilt 6" cut 14" throat cast iron table **£367**
Mitre fences for above .... **£12** Stands for above **£29**
KITY 613 8" cut Large table 1½HP Very Sturdy .... **Special Price**
MINIMAX S45 45° tilt 10" cut 17" throat **£615**

★ ★ **SPECIAL OFFERS ON STARTRITE 301 — 351 — 352** ★ ★ ★
5 FREE BLADES WITH EACH MACHINE

STARTRITE 301 45° tilt 6" cut c/w rip & mitre fence floor standing **£399**
STARTRITE 351 45° tilt 8" cut c/w rip & mitre fence floor standing **£495**
STARTRITE 352 45° tilt 10" cut c/w rip & mitre fence floor standing **£699**

★ ★ **Carriage To Be Advised Mainland Each Startrite Bandsaw** ★ ★

★ ★ ★ ★ ★ SWEDISH STEEL BANDSAW BLADES ★ ★ ★ ★ ★

THE FINEST RANGE OF SWEDISH STEEL BANDSAW BLADES WELDED AND PRECISION GROUND FOR PERFECT RUNNING ENSURING ONLY THE BEST PERFORMANCE FROM YOUR BANDSAW. WHY SETTLE FOR LESS?
SEND NOW FOR CURRENT PRICE LIST
OVER 4000 BLADES IN STOCK FROM 57" — 144" IN ALL WIDTHS

METAL BLADE GUIDES for DeWalt DW100, 1310, 3401, 3501, Luna & Minimax **£5.20**

RADIAL SAWS

EUMENIA 9" blade 1¾HP 15" C/cut .... **£320** 24" C/cut **£384**
EUMENIA Stand .... **£93** Router Bracket .... **£65** Wobble Washers **£12**
DeWALT 1201 Portable 10" TCT Folding Radial Saw 1½ HP **£295**
DeWALT DW1251 10" TCT blade 1½ HP 16" C/cut .... **£399** Stand **£25**
DeWALT DW1501 10" TCT blade 1½ HP 18" C/cut **£469**
DeWALT DW1751 10" TCT blade 1½ HP 24" C/cut **£538**
DeWALT DW8001 12" TCT blade 2HP 18" C/cut floor standing **£579**
DeWALT DW8101 12" TCT blade 2HP 24" C/cut floor standing **£661**
DeWALT DW1600S 14" TCT blade 24" C/cut 1PH .... **£993** 3PH **£956**

PORTABLE AND WORKSHOP SAWBENCHES

MAKITA 2708 8" Portable tilt arbor bench saw **£204**
ELEKTRA 12" Sawbench floor standing TCT blade 3HP **£179**
SCHEPPACH TKU 12" Sawbench floor standing TCT blade 3HP **£205**
Elektra & Scheppach Sliding Table .... **£80** Panel Cutting Extension **£75**
ELU TGS Sawbench/Mitre Saws c/w TCT blade TGS 172 .... **£405** TGS 171 .... **£331**
Sliding table for TGS .... **£98** Aluminium cutting kit **£60**
KITY 618 10" tilt arbor sawbench floor standing .... **SPECIAL PRICE**
MULTICO NTA300 3HP 12" .... **£1123** Sliding table 48" cap. **£316**
WADKIN AGS250/300 3HP 1PH .... **£1199** Sliding table 35" cap. **£450**
STARTRITE Scoring Saw 1PH .... **£1377** Sliding table 48" cap. **£327**
LUNA L18 12" 3HP 1PH .... **£840** Sliding table 24" cap. **£140**

ROLLER SUPPORT STANDS (P&P £3.00)

LUNA 10" support roller adjustable height sturdy construction **£28**
LUNA 16" combined roller support adjustable height **£39**

INDUSTRIAL QUALITY T.C.T SAWBLADES

ALL PRICES INCLUDE V.A.T. AND P&P
GENERAL DUTY (MADE IN SHEFFIELD) PREMIUM QUALITY FOR CONTINUOUS USE (MADE IN W. GERMANY)

BLADE DIAMETER	6"				7"-7 1/4"				8"				9"-9 1/4"			
NO OF TEETH	16	24	36	48	18	30	42	56	20	36	48	64	24	40	54	72
GENERAL DUTY	£16	£17	£20	£26	£16	£17	£21	£26	£20	£25	£27	£32	£24	£26	£29	£36
PREMIUM QUALITY	-	£26	-	£34	-	-	-	-	-	£31	£36	£42	-	£39	£44	-
BLADE DIAMETER	10"				12"				14"				16"			
NO OF TEETH	24	40	60	80	32	48	72	96	36	60	84	108	28	36	60	96
GENERAL DUTY	£23	£26	£35	£38	£28	£36	£42	£48	£34	£42	£50	£57	-	-	-	-
PREMIUM QUALITY	£32	£36	£41	£50	£36	£42	£51	£60	£41	£48	£59	£68	£47	£50	£60	£70

PLEASE STATE BORE SIZE WHEN ORDERING

MORTICING MACHINES — *OUR PRICE INC. VAT*

SMITHS BCM 75 bench morticer c/w lateral table ¾" cap. **£399**
SMITHS CM75 floor standing morticer dual table movement ¾" cap. **£499**
MULTICO HM bench morticer 5/8" capacity precision morticer **£356**
MULTICO HMT bench morticer dual table movement **£499**
MULTICO M floor standing 1" capacity dual table movement 1PH **£626**
WADKIN EDA-2 floor standing 1" capacity dual table **£599**
RYOBI portable chain morticer .... **£365** Portable chisel morticer **£395**
WOLF Drill mortice stand C/W ½" chisel & sharpener **£135**
RIDGEWAY mortice/drill stand (requires ½" power drill) **£169**

MORTICE CHISELS & BITS

JAPANESE ¼" ...... **£16** 3/8" ...... **£17** ½" ...... **£20** 5/8" ...... **£25** ¾" ...... **£37** 1" **£45**
8mm **£21** 10mm **£24** 12mm **£25** 16mm **£29** 20mm **£44**
RIDGEWAY ¼" ...... **£19**; 3/8" ...... **£23**; ½" ...... **£24**; 5/8" ...... **£35**; ¾" ...... **£37**; 1" **£45**
6mm ... **£21**; 8mm ... **£22**; 10mm ... **£25**; 12mm ... **£26**; 16mm ... **£31**; 20mm ... **£46**
CHISEL BITS ONLY ¼" ..... **£6**; 3/8" ..... **£7**; ½" ..... **£8**; 5/8" ..... **£10**; ¾" ..... **£14**; 1" **£18**
MORTICE CHISEL SHARPENING SETS set 1 (¼"-½") .... **£21** Set 2 (3/8"-¾") **£26**

DUST EXTRACTORS

LUNA SPSS400 460m/hr portable suitable for low volume waste **£215**
LUNA W178 975m/hr excellent general purpose extractor c/w hose **£324**
LUNA NF243 1500m/hr mobile 5" hose ideal for high volume waste **£429**
LUNA NF259 2000m/hr heavy duty suitable for up to 3 machines **£599**
LUNA 4" × 3m hose ...... **£18** 5" × 4m hose ...... **£36** LUNA dust bags (per 10) **£3**
MULTICO DEA 960m/hr mobile extractor 4" hose **£335**
DeWALT DW60 500m/hr 5" hose .... **£265** ELEKTRA 1000m/hr 4" hose **£256**
STARTRITE CYCLAIR 55 960m/hr 4" .... **£399** CYCLAIR 75 1800m/hr 6" **£499**

MITRE CUTTERS & MITRE SAWS

ELU PS174 8" Portable mitre crosscut saw 10" crosscut **£268**
DeWALT DW250 Portable mitre saw 1¼HP 10" Blade **£194**
HITACHI CF10A 10" Portable precision mitre saw **£259**
ORTEGUILLE MITRE CUTTERS ORC55 .... **£230** ORC80 .... **£286** ORC100 .... **£430**
LION MITRE TRIMMER Excellent for clean cuts and mitres **£249**
NOBEX 202 Hand Mitre saw .... **£68.95** NOBEX 303 .... **£44** (P&P £2.50)

PLANER THICKNESSERS

DeWALT DW1150 10" × 6" 2HP 2 speed power feed .... **SPECIAL PRICE**
Stand for DW1150 .... **£25** Slot Morticer .... **£65** HSS knives **£17.50**
ELECKTRA 10" × 6" floor standing power feed **£495**
SCHEPPACH HMO SOLO 10" × 6" 2HP floor standing Adjustable fence **£490**
STARTRITE PT260 10" × 7" floor standing 5/8" rebate capacity **£834**
STARTRITE SD310 12" × 7" 3 cutter block 1PH .... **£1370** 3PH **£1317**
LUNA 3HP Planers 10" × 9" .... **£1399** 12" × 9" .... **£1499** 16" × 9" **£2299**
MULTICO NS300 surfacer 3 cutter block 2HP 1PH .... **£1388** 3PH **£1271**
MULTICO THA300 12" × 10" thicknesser only 1PH .... **£1399** 3PH **£1299**
MULTICO CPT 12" × 8" Combined planer/thicknesser ¾" rebate 1PH .. **£1749** 3PH .. **£1649**
WADKIN BAOS 12" × 7" Heavy duty planer 3PH (1 only to clear) **£2699**

DRILLING MACHINES

WARCO HOBBY ½" 5 speed rack and pinion table bench mounting **£125**
WARCO 5/8" cap 2MT 12 speed 2B12 bench mounting .... **£179** 2F12 floor standing **£222**
FOBCO STAR ½" precision drill bench mounting .... **£340** floor standing **£385**
STARTRITE SP250 ½" 5 speed bench mounting .... **£356** floor standing **£398**
Morticing attachments Warco 2B/2F .... **£24** Fobco .... **£61** Startrite **£110**

SPINDLE MOULDERS AND TENNONERS

SCHEPPACH HF33 3HP 30mm 3 speed with adjustable fences **£549**
ELEKTRA TF100 3HP 30mm 3 speed 4" Rise and fall **£584**
KITY 623 2HP 3 speed 4" Rise and fall C/W sliding table **£776**
STARTRITE T30 30mm C/W sliding table 1PH 2HP .... **£943** 3PH 3HP **£915**
LUNA L28 30mm 3 speed 3HP Heavy duty 1PH 3HP .... **£999** 3PH 3HP **£988**
WADKIN BURSGREEN BEL 5HP (3PH only) 4 speed 30mm **£1999**
MULTICO TENNONER TM1 240v twin motors (excluding tooling) **£1579**
MULTICO TENNONER Spindle moulder conversion kit (new m/cs only) **£220**

SPINDLE MOULDER TOOLING (State bore size P&P £1.50)

OMAS "TIGER" BLOCKS 392 .... **£46** BLOCK in wooden case with stone etc. **£56**
OMAS cutter profiles .... **£11.50** CUTTER BLANKS .... **£6** SAW SEGMENTS **£16**
KITY PROFILE Door set .... **£96** OMAS ART 176D1 DOORSET complete **£139**
WHITEHILL Cutter blocks 4 7/8" × 15/16" .... **£47** 5 3/8" × 15/16 .... **£66**
LEITZ 488 Cutter block 100mm .... **£56** 40mm blanks ...... each **£2.80** 60mm ...... ea **£5**
TUNGSTEN REBATE BLOCKS 125mm × 50mm ...... **£98** 6" Wobble saw 3-21mm .. **£89**

COMBINATION MACHINES (Carriage £10.00 UK Mainland)

STARTRITE K260 saw spindle planer etc. FREE TIGER HEAD SET **£1990**
STARTRITE TZ30 saw spindle only FREE TIGER HEAD only **£1170**
LUNA MASTER COMBINATIONS 240v W59 ..... **£2650** W64 ..... **£3100** W69 ..... **£3899**
NB. Luna combinations are exclusive of sliding table & slot morticer.
SCHEPPACH HM2 COMBI saw spindle planer (other accs. available) **£969**
LUNA Z40 light duty combination saw planer spindle morticer **£685**

★ ★ ★ ★ ★ ★ ★ ★ KITY COMBINATION MACHINES ★ ★ ★ ★ ★ ★ ★ ★

K5 COMBINATION K5 BASIC K704 TABLE COMBINATION K704 DIRECT DRIVE AND ACCESSORIES ALL AT SPECIAL PRICES SEND FOR LATEST PRICE LIST.

BORING BITS (inc. P&P)

CLICO SAW TOOTH & FORSTNER BITS (State type) 6" long ½" shank 3/8" .... **£7.70**; ½" **£7.90**
5/8" .... **£8.70**; ¾" .... **£9.50**; 7/8" .... **£10.20**; 1" .... **£10.90**; 1 1/8" .... **£12.80**; 1¼" **£15.60**;
1 3/8" ... **£16.20**; 1½" ... **£17.10**; 1 5/8" ... **£19.70**; 1¾" ... **£22.40**; 1 7/8" ... **£24.80**; 2" ... **£26.20**;
2¼" .... **£32.90**; 2½" .... **£43.70**.
CLICO PLUG CUTTERS 3/8" .. **£20** ½" .. **£23** 5/8" .. **£26** ¾" .. **£28** 1" .. **£34** 1⅓ .. **£37.80**
CLICO SAW TOOTH set ½", ¾", 1" .... **£25** ECONOMY 5 piece set ½"-1½" × ¼" **£53**
RIDGEWAY ADJUSTABLE FORSTNERS WR10/2 ½"-1¾" ...... **£14** WR10/3 7/8"-3" **£16**
RIDGEWAY ADJUSTABLE FORSTNERS (h/duty) WR20/2 7/8"-2" **£28** WR20/3 1 3/8"-3" **£32**

ROUTERS AND ROUTER ACCESSORIES

ELU MOF96 ¼" 600W **£86.50**
ELU MOF31 ¼, 3/8, ½" 1200W **£135.95**
ELU MOF177 ¼, ½" 1600W **£172.95**
HITACHI TR8 ¼" 730W **£79.95**
RYOBI R150 ¼" 730W **£75.95**
HITACHI FM ¼" 550W **£46.95**
MAKITA 3600B ¼, ½" 1500W **£154.95**
ELU MOF96E ¼" Var. speed **£106.95**
ELU MOF11/2 ½" 2000W c/w base **£337.33**
ELU MOF177E ½" Var. speed **£197.95**
HITACHI TR12 ¼, ½" 1300W **£137.95**
RYOBI R500 ¼, ½" 1500W **£113.95**
BOSCH POF 52 ¼" 520W **£50.24**
BOSCH 1604 Fixed base 1300W .. **£163.95**

ROUTER ACCESSORIES

ELU DOVETAIL KIT TCT cutter **£66.00**
ELU MOF96 Accessory kit **£66.00**
STAIR JIG (General duty) **£69.00**
ELU ROUTER BRKT. for DeWalt **£37.00**
ELU 96 Dust extraction kit **£29.00**
ELU MOF96 Height adjuster **£3.95**
RYOBI Dovetail jig fits above **£99.95**
ELU ROUTER COMBI BENCH **£97.00**
STAIR JIG (heavy duty) **£160.00**
ELU 12 piece Guide bush set **£29.95**
ELU MOF 98, 31, 177 Height adjuster **£15.95**
ELU 96 177 side fence adjuster **£6.30**

★ ★ ★ ★ ★ ★ ★ ★ ELU ACCESSORIES ★ ★ ★ ★ ★ ★ ★ ★

10% OFF ALL ELU ACCESSORIES 90% STOCK AVAILABILITY POST PAID ON MOST ITEMS. EXCELLENT RANGE OF ROUTER ACCESSORIES SEND NOW FOR FREE LIST.

HSS ROUTER BIT SETS (inc. P&P)

SAVE 30% ON HSS ROUTER BIT SETS AND GET A FREE ROUTER BIT CASE.
13 PIECE SET **£59.95**
8 PIECE SET **£37.95**
5 PIECE SET **£21.95**
ROUTER BIT CUTTER BOX .... ONLY **£4**

ROUTER CUTTERS

20-25% OFF LEADING BRANDS EXCELLENT STOCKS OF HSS & TCT ROUTER CUTTERS OVER 500 PROFILES IN STOCK. SEND NOW FOR FREE CUTTER CHART:- TECHNIQUES OF ROUTING £6.95 (inc. P&P)

IMMEDIATE DESPATCH ON CREDIT CARD PHONED ORDERS — CREDIT TERMS AVAILABLE OVER £120

0297 33656 CHARD STREET AXMINSTER DEVON EX13 5DZ 6.30-9pm 34836
BARCLAYCARD VISA

Smoke screen

Time and more to make this one for the Christmas children to hide behind — Paul Austin's amusing puff-a-screen

You'll find this screen simple and fun to make — and fun for the kids to use, too. You'll get the four sections from a single 8x4ft sheet of ½in best quality plywood; use birch-faced WBP multiply. It's cut first into four equal 4x2ft sections, which are joined by nine 2x½in hinges, fixed alternately for the screen to fold up.

The basic tools you need are a drill, jigsaw or keyhole saw, a pencil, a drawing pin and string. Use the drill to make the starting holes for the saw-blade. Pencil, string and drawing pin is the tried and tested method for drawing the large circles and curves. You can leave the screen with a plain wood finish, or carefully stain or paint, in which case you must use non-toxic paints.

Before you start, study the plans carefully so you get the hang of the method. Extreme accuracy with measurements is not important, and once you start on the project everything will soon become clear. The instructions show how to mark out and cut each of the four sections; triangular stabilisers are fixed to the base of each.

Section 1

Measure from the top and mark lines A, B, C, D and E in pencil. To mark out the funnel or chimney-stack, measure across the top from the left, making small marks at 1¼in and 16in. Then measure in along line A, putting marks at 4¼in and 13¼in. Join up the marks to give the funnel shape as shown. To get the curve at the top of the funnel, measure in 8¼in along line C; stick a drawing pin in and extend the string and pencil out 31¾in to draw the arc.

For the curved front of the engine, insert the drawing pin in line B, ¼in from the right-hand side. Extend the string and pencil out 21½in and draw the arc.

To position the wheel circles, measure 12in in on line D to the centre. Put the pin in at this point, and draw circles 2¾in, 5½in and 8¼in.

The wheel spokes are drawn by this simple method: make a mark along line C 2in to the right of the centre-line. Measure up 2in from line D and mark. Draw a line from each of these marks through the centre of the hub. To produce the remaining spokes, you can cut out the shaded area and use it as a template, or mark out the whole wheel as you did the first spoke.

Once all your lines are marked in pencil, you can cut out section 1. The wheel on section 1 is a useful template for wheels on sections 2 and 3.

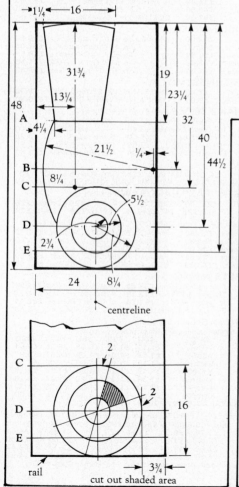

centreline

cut out shaded area

rail

Section 2

Measure and draw lines F, G, H, I and J as you did with section 1. To produce the dome shape, measure and mark 9½in along line G, stick your drawing pin in and scribe an 11in arc. If you've already cut out section 1, you can use it as a template for the wheel. Now you can cut out section 2.

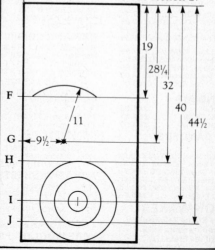

Section 3

Draw lines K, L, M, N and O as shown on the plan. Measure and draw the window cutouts as shown, and mark out the wheel. You can now cut out section 3.

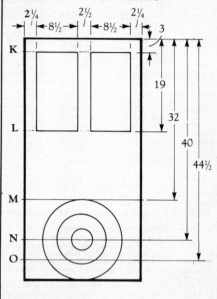

Section 4

Mark out the windows as you did for section 3; you could use that section as a template if you wish.

For the small wheels, draw lines P and Q 7½in and 3½in from the bottom respectively. Put marks on line 7in and 18¼in in from the left. Put the drawing pin in on the 7in mark and draw circles with 1¾in and 5in radii; repeat on the 18¼in mark. Cut out the centre circle, or hub, which is shaded in the diagram.

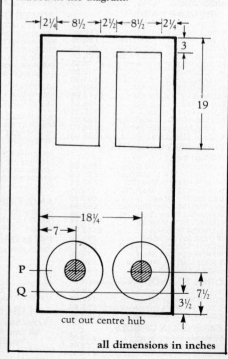

cut out centre hub

all dimensions in inches

Rail supports

You can use the scraps from the window and wheel cut-outs to produce 4x3½in triangles. Draw and cut out one to start with, then use it as a template for 16 in all. These are glued together in pairs to produce eight triangles. These rail supports can be straight or with a curved top edge; draw it freehand on the first triangle, then cut out and use this as a template for the rest.

Fix two rail supports on each section, one on each side, 4in from the ends. Screw them into place from the other side of the sections, using 1½in x no.8 screws. Using screws without glue means you can detach the supports for storage.

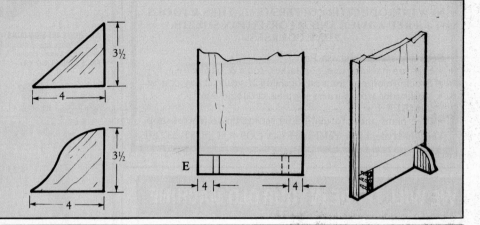

Hinging

If your screen is going to be folded a lot, you should lip the edges that will be carrying the hinges with ¾x½in softwood; it will probably be thicker than the ply, so pin and glue it then plane it flush. Now you can fix the hinges; stand the four sections up in line, angle the way you want them to fold, and mark alternate faces to show which side the knuckle will be, fix three hinges at appropriate places on one edge, then mark off the positions on the neighbouring one and bradawl or pilot-drill the screw-holes. Screw them all up, and you have your folding puffer. Prime and paint, or clear varnish as you like; perhaps the young passengers and crew would like to choose the colour scheme! ■

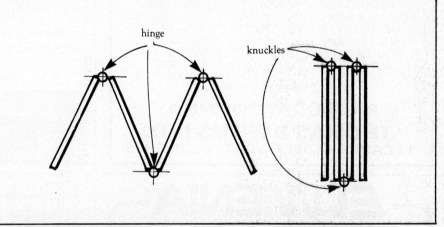

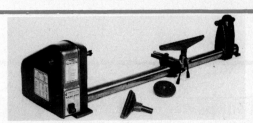

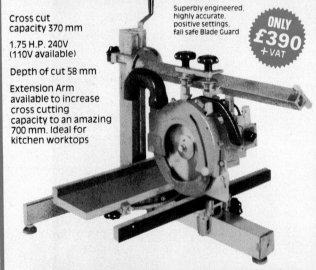

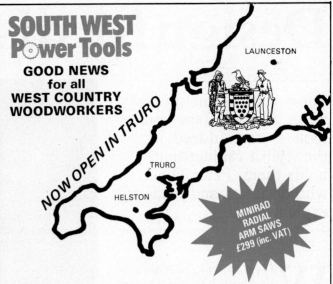

Design for display

Show visitors' mouths may water at classy Japanese tools — and, indeed, at the stylish cabinet that holds them. Peter Dines, who designed and made it, explains how

When Roger Buse of Roger's of Hitchin needed a display cabinet for his range of Japanese hand tools, his brief was clear. The cabinet was required:

- to occupy 2sq ft of floor, no more than 78in high
- to give maximum display area for tools, showing them clearly from each side, from above and below
- to be easily dismantled for safe, convenient transport and quick assembly for exhibitions
- to be secure, with access via a lockable rear door
- to be finished in black, in contrast with the red silk display material
- to reflect in style the Japanese hand tools displayed
- to be made to a limited budget.

I felt the finished cabinet should in no way distract attention from the contents; Roger wants to sell tools, not cabinets. The brief was full of conflicting ideas — how to make a cabinet strong and secure, yet light and easily dismantled; how to enhance the contents without distracting from them; how to create a feeling of space without bulk.

● Peter Dines captured a Japanese flavour in this temple of tools. Wedges, commonly used in Japanese joinery, hold the panels together, **left**

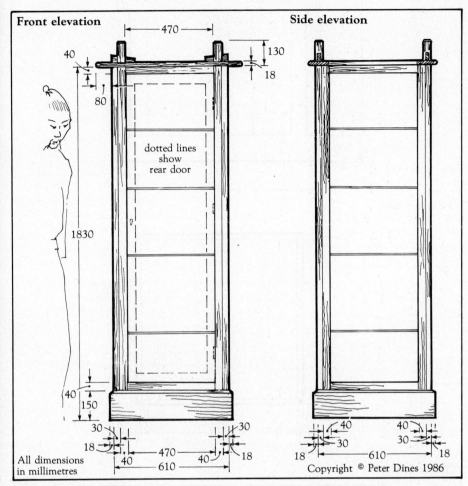

Front elevation

470

40

130

18

80

dotted lines
show
rear door

1830

40

150

30

30

18

18

40

470

40

610

All dimensions
in millimetres

Side elevation

40

40

30

30

18

610

18

Copyright © Peter Dines 1986

The design process

I ruled out traditional forms of display furniture construction because the cabinet had to be easily transportable. My first step was to look at Japanese joinery, but I had to reject Japanese joints because time is very important with a limited budget. I felt that as long as the flavour of a Japanese piece was achieved it would work.

My initial idea was a folding screen, using the four panels as four sides, but this had to be ruled out because it would have been too heavy to carry as one unit. However, the appearance of the panelled screens was promising. If the panels could be separated and then quickly assembled on a base and held in place at the top this could be the basis for its construction. Wedges seemed a good way to fix pieces quickly, and they are commonly used in Japanese joinery so I thought I would try to incorporate them.

I decided the main elements would be: four separate glazed panels with traditional mortise-and-tenoned frames, one including a door; a base plinth to raise the panels off the ground for protection, to locate them, and to provide some weight for stability (it would be a tall cabinet); a top piece to secure the panels using wedges; and four shelves.

I chose beech for the frames because it is strong, dense, cheap and good for ebonising; MDF for the top panel and

plinth because it is easy to machine, heavy and dense and stains well; laminated glass rather than Perspex because it's much cheaper and very strong. The shelf edges would be ground for safety of handling.

The most difficult part of the job was specifying the exact dimensions and construction details. The timber frames had to be strong enough to hold large sheets of heavy glass, but must be as slim as possible to show the contents.

I decided to make the main frames 40x40mm and to set the sides slightly inside the front so that the frame did not look too bulky, but without greatly reducing the internal space. After considering many arrangements with blocks and spacer timbers I decided the best way to locate the panels in the plinth was to extend the stiles through mortises in the plinth right to floor level. The plinth would have solid top and bottom panels for weight so this could be done easily. I realised this would only be necessary for two out of the four panels if they could be held steady while the last two panels were fixed securely to the first two. This could be done by extending the stiles upwards as well as downwards, through a top panel, and then driving wedges through mortises in the stiles to hold this panel tight against the top rails. I decided to put the back panel containing the door and the front panel in first, so that the wedges seen

from the front would make an interesting visual feature.

I needed a method to fix the other two panels in place. It would kill two birds with one stone if this fixing could be spaced in such a way as to serve also as shelf supports and cut down on interference with the simple look of the cabinet. I decided to use small metal angle brackets, carefully aligned and fixed on all stiles, so that when each side panel was held in place, located by rebates against the front and back panels, a machine screw could be simply inserted (not threaded) through both brackets, firmly locking the panels in place as well as providing strong and inconspicuous supports for the glass shelves. As commercially available brackets were not accurate enough I made them out of mild steel angle and blued them by heating to red heat and quenching in oil (chemical gun blue didn't work). With black machine screws, the fixings hardly showed.

With my ideas worked out, I reached for the drawing board. Everything seemed to be perfectly feasible on the construction side. I just needed to decide its final visual appearance. I had thought of tapering the plinth but using MDF it would have meant a lot of extra work; I could achieve a similar visual effect by simply chamfering the top edge, which also meant the plinth only exceeded the size of the cabinet by its own thickness and would not need any extra floorspace. I also decided to chamfer the outside edges of the stiles as these were most likely to get knocked. The top panel (also a standard mortised-and-tenoned frame) could have fitted flush but had a more Japanese appearance if it was extended and had a gently moulded edge. I had originally planned a more elaborate curved shape to the wedges and stile tops but decided at this stage that simple straight lines and chamfers on the wedges and stile tops would be both more practical and more in keeping visually with the rest of the cabinet. I would use brass butts and escutcheon on the door which would only be seen from the rear and would look good, polished and tidied up, against the black. I would use 'blued' steel pins to fix the glazing beads (this didn't work very well because hammering in the pins removed the blue colour). I would use 18mm MDF for the plinth; the top panel would be 18mm MDF in a 1in-thick timber frame, with the mortises for the frame stiles cut in the timber. I would use black spirit stain, sanding sealer and wax for the finish. This would not chip and would be easy to renew if it was damaged, but would still give an ebonised look if worn along the edges.

Construction

My newly bought universal machine would not plane flat or square so I took out my hand plane, blessing the hours of enforced practice at college. First I sawed all materials to size and hand-planed them to finished sizes. I gauged rebate sizes, marked the mor-

Design for display

tises and tenons, cut the mortises and ripped the tenons. (Incidentally, I've never got on with the traditional method of ripping tenons, by angling the timber in the vice, cutting part down one side, reversing the timber and cutting the other side. I find it far better to fix the piece vertically in the vice and cut the cheek in one operation to the shoulder line. It saves time opening and closing the vice and repositioning the timber, and avoids saw cuts that fail to meet. Also after some practice you can cut both cheeks from the same side, sawing on opposite sides of the waste).

Next I cut the rebates using the circular saw. I know it's now common practice to form rebates with a router or spindle moulder, but all that waste disappearing up the chute really hurts. Besides, the waste pieces can be used as glazing beads. The rebates can then be cleaned up with the router, but a shoulder plane is quite fast and much more sympathetic to the ears. I cut the tenon shoulders, not forgetting the offset to fill the rebates. (I filled in the rebates on the stile extensions afterwards; these small infill pieces are invisible on the finished cabinet.)

On the top panel I set the MDF panel into grooves instead of rebates. I ran these straight through on the tenoned rails and from mortise to mortise on the other rails. I cut the through mortises for the stiles into the main frame, chamfering the outer edges to ease assembly and prevent damage during continual assembly and dis-assembly.

I made the rear door to the same sequence as the main frames, and then fitted them to the frame, fitting the lock and escutcheon. A tip about fitting locks: if you gauge the distance from lock face to pin position and mark this on the door stile, then drill a small hole through the stile, this hole can be used to locate the lock pin. All other measurements are taken from the lock held in this position and this makes for fine lock fitting.

I clean and polish all brassware before fitting, and I also practice an idea from Edward Barnsley's workshop; I use a small triangular file to produce a small chamfer on every rubbing surface on the knuckle part and a small round to the outside showing ends, and gauge to halfway through the knuckle so as to see the minimum of hinge. How often I have seen beautiful pieces of furniture spoilt because these small attentions to detail are forgotten; brass butts straight from the shelf, fitted showing the whole knuckle, joinery style, have a surprisingly crude appearance on fine furniture.

The plinth is basically a mitred box with thin plywood tongues, and with top and bottom permanently fixed. The top and bottom have offset tongues that fit grooves in the side pieces. I cut the through mortises for the front and back panel stiles before assembly, and formed chamfers to the side pieces.

Top panel: Plan

Plinth: Plan

MDF 5mm in groove

front

Plinth: Elevation

location for long stiles

I made a full size drawing showing the actual tapered mortise dimensions to make a template for the wedges.

I dry assembled all pieces, in order to make any adjustments, although I aim to make every joint fit first time. At this stage, I also cleaned up, stained and polished all the pieces difficult to get at after assembly. Then I glued up and cleaned up.

I partly assembled the cabinet to mark out the shelf distances (for best display of the tools) on the front and back panel stiles, and gauged the position of the bracket screws. I marked and fitted the first brackets, making due allowance in both cases for the thickness of the metal. The side panels were held in place while I marked the positions of the remaining brackets (my web-cramps came in very useful here) and then fitted them.

Finishing

I sanded all surfaces, inside and out, with 120-grit and then 240-grit paper. I raised the grain by dampening it, and then cut back with 320-grit paper. For colouring I used black spirit stain which is powerful, fast and cheap, though some find it difficult to use. Indian ink is a very good black stain and being water soluble is very easy to apply. When staining MDF I first size the edges with weak glue size to stop it absorbing stain like a sponge. Next came two coats of sanding sealer, lightly cut back when dried with 320 paper. Finally everything had a coat of my own wax polish.

All that remained was to position the glass and pin the glazing beads on, and replace all the fittings which had been removed for finishing. I marked the underside of the bottom rails with coloured dots to match their location on the plinth, for quick and easy assembly. When the moment came for final assembly it worked perfectly.

Roger was very pleased with the cabinet, a unique piece of furniture; it fulfils all his requirements, and attracts attention to his Japanese tools both in his shop and at exhibitions. It was fun to make, too. ■

Section at shelf level

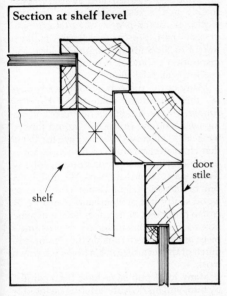

shelf

door stile

Cutting list

Finished sizes

Posts, front & back	4	1960mm x	40mm x	40mm
Posts, side	4	1680	40	40
Rails	8	550	40	40
Door stiles	2	1590	45	22
Door rails	2	470	45	22
Top frame, front & back	2	770	100	22
Top frame, sides	2	530	60	22
Glazing beads, posts	6	1610	25	10
Glazing beads, rails	6	490	25	10
Door stile beads	2	1520	10	8
Door rail beads	2	400	10	8
Wedges	4	120	40	20
Top panel	1	570	490	18
Plinth panel	2	620	620	18
Plinth side	4	646	150	18
Glass, laminated				
Panel	3	1614	485	6.4
Door panel	1	1525	395	6.4
Shelves	4	520	520	6.4

Plane and simple

WOODWORKING WHEEZE *of the* **month**

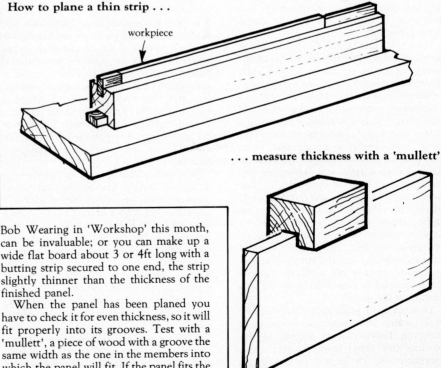

How to plane a thin strip . . .

workpiece

. . . measure thickness with a 'mullett'

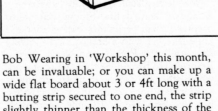

Planing thin strips of wood, writes **Charles Cliffe**, particularly the edges, is by no means easy. Unless you work out some way of supporting the strips, the number of breakages will be disappointingly high. The simple device shown holds the strips firmly and enables straight and square edges to be planed. Plough the length of the supporting strip, and glue a wooden stop into one end of the groove.

To hold wide, thin, flat work such as a solid drawer-bottom securely in position, a 'planing board' like the one suggested by

Bob Wearing in 'Workshop' this month, can be invaluable; or you can make up a wide flat board about 3 or 4ft long with a butting strip secured to one end, the strip slightly thinner than the thickness of the finished panel.

When the panel has been planed you have to check it for even thickness, so it will fit properly into its grooves. Test with a 'mullett', a piece of wood with a groove the same width as the one in the members into which the panel will fit. If the panel fits the mullett it is bound to fit its grooves. ■

Rough-hewn history

Six decades of adventurous travel have left Sid Hatton with a head full of rich images to carve. David Saunders talked to him

'When I was trapping for the fur trade in Canada in the 30s, we were told to shoot as many wolves as possible. I refused. I could see the good they did keeping their prey strong and their numbers down. I knew about conservation even 50 years ago.' That remark is typical of artist and woodcarver Sid Hatton; it demonstrates his defiance of accepted values and his confidence as a *raconteur*.

It's difficult to imagine any man having packed a more diverse life into 74 years. Merchant seaman, taxidermist's assistant, fur-trapper, soldier, circus rider, knife-thrower, mortuary attendant, cabinet-maker, signwriter and additionally a woodcarver of international renown. He was the winner of the Ashley Iles original wood carving competition, the 'Robin on a post' held at the Woodworker Show in 1977, and in the late 1970s went on to win major carving prizes in Frankfurt, Cologne and Paris.

A lean, wiry man with enough energy and verve to make him the envy of a man several decades younger, Sid speaks of his life and times and passes quickly over the spectrum of emotion — anger at some past or present injustice, the humour of a remembered anecdote. Bearded, bespectacled, with a large gold maritime-fashion hoop in each ear, and sporting buckskin trousers and moccasins, he is by no means the archtypal septuagenarian.

Sid was born in Dover, Kent, educated at Barton Road school and admits to a certain failure to excel on the academic side. However, a talent for art was acknowledged by his tutors since they advised his parents to send him to the Royal College of Art. It didn't happen. Not considering drawing a proper career, Sid's father apprenticed him to a local electrical engineering firm, 'humping accumulators about'. But he soon shipped anchor from this repetitive job and joined a ship, the *Pathfinder*, a pilot cutter out of Dover harbour ferrying pilots around from ship to ship. One foggy day an Italian steam freighter collided with a Russian training vessel causing the loss of all hands, bar one. This tragedy made a lasting impression on the young boy, and six decades later he still recalls the sight of those 'bloated bodies swollen by the sea, floating in the water'.

A short spell as an apprentice cabinet-maker came next, but again boredom of humping heavy objects around al day (coffins this time) made another move inevitable. At 15 he was in London in search of another ship, with the prospect of a more glamorous destination than the foggy straits of Dover. A chance meeting in a waterside cafe with the skipper of a short-crewed cargo carrier bound for Canada answered the boy's dreams.

He jumped ship on reaching Quebec and took a job as a taxidermist's assistant, getting to know animal anatomy first hand. Six months later he moved on to a lumber camp in Northern Ontario. Here daily contact with the local Indians gave him a chance to fulfill a boyhood dream, shaking off the fetters of the western world to live a completely different life. In that virgin vastness he escaped from the authoritarian ways he had so loathed in his formative years in England. Some boys dream of running away with gypsies, others with the circus (more of that later); young Sid found his escape with the Indians. Romantic the notion may have been, but in reality life with the Swampey Cree was tough and unrelenting. He stayed for 12 years, working as a fur trapper operating under licence from the Hudson Bay Company. Living among the Indians, Sid studied them carving all manner of woodland creatures — beaver, bear, lynx and wolves delicately formed in their native bass-wood, a type of lime. He tried his hand and 'took to it like a duck to water', developing a strong personal style very much in evidence today. The tough existence with the Indians in the great outdoors was as hard as could be found anywhere; while he was never fully accepted into the tribal family, they still described him as 'more Indian than the goddam Indians'. Adopting their habits, clothing and values, Sid's transition was so complete that visitors from England didn't believe him one of their own — until he opened his mouth!

In 1938 he returned to his birthplace, got married and had two sons and a daughter. At the outbreak of war he joined the army where his talent for outdoor survival and taste for adventure led to a posting with a demolition squad handling high explosives. However, for once, Lady Luck deserted him, and in 1943 he was invalided out for a wound received during a raid. The rest of the war years he spent in the building trade as a joiner repairing bomb damaged buildings.

Wanderlust struck again in 1955 after a decade of settled life. Sid moved on to become Indian performer, horse rider and knife-thrower with a French circus, giving shows all over Europe and North Africa. Returning to Britain, he took a line of work which other artists have tried; six months as a mortuary attendant in a Maidstone hospital provided invaluable anatomical experience, this time human!

In 1958 he married for the second time, to an aristocratic Prussian lady; she died last year.

As one would expect from a man of such energy, Sid works quickly and accurately with a vigour undiluted by repetition of the subject matter; he roughs out many quite large carvings in a day or so. His fine creations are actually born of quite primitive conditions; no heated studio for this master carver, merely an 8x6ft garden shed or, weather permitting, an outside bench. The shed itself is strewn with semi-shaped carvings, chisels, rifflers, drawings and cardboard templates. A pungent smell of woodstain, polish and sawdust hangs thickly in the restricted space. This tiny world, a hotch-potch of artefacts and projects past, present and future, is like a mirror of Sid's mind, a jumble of ideas and inspirations, some as if on ice awaiting his spark to rekindle their life.

Many of the subjects echo his early days in the Canadian wilderness. Howling timber wolves, hissing rattle-snakes, piercing-eyed birds of prey, liquid-limbed weasels — all carved with an eye for detail that characterises much of his work. Many of the carvings adorn his home in one of Kent's most beautiful towns, West Malling. But his artistic talent is not restricted to wood sculptures of woodland creatures, he is also proficient in netsuke, both ivory and boxwood. His classic curled rat is as fine a piece as can be seen outside the Orient, and much of the furniture in his home is his own work.

Many local pub signs have been painted by him, and his delicate lettering on interior walls will guide you to the right bar or toilet. He also makes Indian artefacts and clothing in authentic style, the moccasins painstakingly decorated with beadwork, the powder horns decorated scrimshaw style.

Examples of Sid's carvings are to be found in places too numerous to mention. By the altar of a local Catholic church, a 7ft high oak statue of Sir Thomas More stands guard. Hunting lodges of rich American ranchers display his horses and eagles; there's hardly a church in Maidstone which doesn't possess some of his carving or script-work. Sid has even restored some of Grinling Gibbons' work.

What is it about his work that sets him apart? It's not just technical skill; there's something that's hard to define in what Sid Hatton does which conveys an ideal. His human faces are not merely moon-shaped objects with features carved on as afterthoughts.They reveal an understanding of what lies beneath the surface, the unseen forces that shape and govern any portrayal of a living creature, animal or human. His carving of two American bison locked in combat clearly shows the stress and muscle-tension of battle as the powerful hindquarters strain with bursting effort. The wild eyes are wide open in fear of defeat; you can almost hear the snorting and see the rising dust as hoof and horn clash and scrape.

A true artist not only captures a moment in time, a frozen action in whatever medium he chooses, but also conveys to the spectator what has gone before, and hints at what is to follow. Sid Hatton is such an artist. ∎

... howling timber wolves, hissing rattle-snakes, liquid-limbed weasels ...

... life with the Swampy Cree Indians was tough ...

● *Sid Hatton's life has been a walk on the wild side; now surrounded by mementos in his shed, he recreates vivid moments from his wilderness adventures*

Photos Applied Photographics

1068

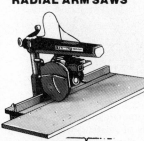

Butting up

● *A selection of Michael O'Donnell's bowls:* **top left**, *small elm bowl in foreground, turned from an air-dried slab, cooking-oil finish,* **top right**, *sycamore bowl from kiln-dried blank, Danish oil finish;* **left**, *elm bowl, at back, turned in one operation from the log, cooking-oil finish;* **right**, *sycamore bowl turned from the log, sprayed with melamine*

It's back to the roots — or in this case, the trunk — if you want to save on turning blanks. Leading woodturner Michael O'Donnell has some suggestions

Just what I needed on a Friday morning. A phone call from a customer, asking if her fruit bowl would be ready the following Tuesday. The 14 dia.x4in elm bowl, ordered months before, was to have been part-turned green, allowed to dry, then finish-turned. I don't know why it had been overlooked, but it was too late to start

now — as the drying would take six to eight weeks.

I thought hard for an alternative strategy — buy a piece of kiln-dried wood. My usual supplier was out of town and the local sawmills didn't have what I wanted, so I looked through a woodturning supplier's catalogue. There they were, bowl-turning discs of the size I was looking for: problem solved! So I thought, until I looked at the price — almost £25+VAT+delivery. And I had quoted a price of £28 *total* for the finished item!

Fortunately my customer was quite happy to wait another week while I completely finished a bowl 'green', dried and oiled it. That's all it took; maybe it wasn't round, but the distortion was even and balanced, because I planned the cutting for that.

This slight panic situation made me think about the plight of amateurs who pay these prices for bowl blanks. There are plenty of different ways to start on a bowl; you can make your turning easier, much more exciting and healthier, without the need to go to this expense. Generally different methods produce different products, but there are enough methods to try which can all produce similar and even better bowls than when you start from a kiln-dried blank.

If I had bought the blank, all the decisions on the bowl would already have been made, except which side was to be the top — that's if there are no faults or knots in the way. All I would have had to do is mount the blank on the lathe and turn it.

Suppose I went back a stage further and bought a kiln-dried plank. There would have been a few splits and knots and a waney edge, but the price for a bowl would have been much less and I could have got a little more involved in the planning; examining the plank, picking out any interesting grain patterns or features and incorporating them in the bowl when the circle was drawn. If you do this, you can begin to understand the wood, and spend a little more time selecting suitable planks for the next bowl down at the woodyard.

Part-seasoned

You can also buy planks part-seasoned or air-dried, usually with a moisture content of 20-25%; there's probably a slightly larger choice, particularly in thicknesses up to 4in, with a further reduction in costs.

There are three different ways of dealing with part-seasoned wood in the making of a bowl:

1 Complete the turning and sanding in one operation, then allow the bowl to dry gradually over, say, 7-14 days; in this time a very low moisture content can be achieved. Splitting during drying is said to be a problem, but I haven't found it so using home-grown woods such as ash, elm, sycamore, beech and so on. Holly does present a splitting problem, so more time and care is needed in drying it. Of course, the final result isn't a perfectly round bowl; there's usually some distortion, but it can be kept to a minimum if the cut in relation to the grain is planned correctly, and you can make it a feature rather than a fault.

2 Part-turn, roughing out to 1-1¼in thickness all over, drying the rough-turned piece slowly to a low moisture content, then remounting and completing the turning on what is now a dry piece of wood. Again splitting problems are minimal, and drying takes a little longer, four to six weeks. The result this time would be a round bowl.

3 Seasoning with PEG. Again the bowl is part-turned, possibly a little thinner, as there should be no distortion during seasoning, then soaked in a warm solution of PEG for around 20 days at 70°F; shorter times for higher temperatures and vice versa. The wetter the wood the better the penetration. A special tank and heating element are needed, plus the PEG solution. On removing, the part-turned bowl will take a further 20 days to dry before remounting for finish turning. As PEG is a waxy solution it changes with temperature and humidity and is liable to ooze out with changes in the weather unless it's held with a hard finish. A polyurethane is usually recommended, but I think this is an unwelcome restriction on the method of finishing.

Photos Joanne O'Donnell

● *With sawn planks you can mark out bowl sizes to optimise use of timber and avoid faults*

Fresh-sawn timber

Fresh-sawn timber is, as it says, sawn fresh from the log and with a very high moisture content. Again the choice of sizes will be much the same as for part-seasoned stock, with an appropriate reduction in price, but you may have to purchase a complete slab or even the whole log. The treatment of the timber would also be similar, but you can expect a little more distortion on part-turning and a better penetration when using PEG. A wonderful bonus is that the turning is so much easier, cleaner, healthier — and consequently, more fun.

If a whole log is purchased then the sawmill will cut it to your exact requirements and the price will probably be the same as fresh-sawn. This is where turning really becomes exciting — examining the log, planning the cutting to give nice grain patterns when it's turned into bowls, wondering just what you will find inside and experiencing the tense moments waiting for the planks to fall apart as they leave the saw-blade. Bowls of any size are now possible, the only restrictions being the size of the tree and the capacity of the lathe.

From the tree

If all this now sounds far too production-orientated and beyond the scope and storage capacity of the hobbyist, then let's go back a stage further. Go out to find the timber at its source, where it grows. It's a sad fact that there are hundreds of trees cut down every day — they're too near houses, have grown too tall for the garden, or are being cleared for buildings. Most of this timber has no commercial value and is either left to rot where it is cut down or cut up for firewood. To obtain this almost endless supply of timber you may have to pay the price of rough firewood, or as I often find happens, offer an exchange for a finished piece from the tree. It's really a matter of keeping your eyes and ears open and being as quick as possible on the spot.

● *A small chainsaw could be the key to future supplies of timber*

Butting up

leave severe restrictions on methods of finishing. Why do we buy it?

When I started working with green wood I was losing around 60% of the bowls from the various problems I encountered throughout the process, a period of about three months. But I was determined they could all be overcome, so I carried on, and now my losses are minimal. From much contact with turners who do it for a hobby, it seems they usually start with one piece of wood, expecting to make one bowl; naturally it becomes a 100% disaster when things go wrong.

There's a little more to woodturning than operating a lathe: it's a whole new way of looking at and using timber, a way of thinking about problems and solving them. All the answers are in your head and hands, not the catalogues. Be a conservationist, save some of the wood from trees otherwise destined for the rubbish heap or firewood — and keep most of your hard-earned money in your pocket! ∎

● *If you saw the timber yourself you can even make decisions on site about the potential of a particular log*

Dealing with logs does raise problems. If they can be carried and are up to 8-9in diameter, then most bandsaws will cope; above this size a small chainsaw, which can be bought for not much more than the price of a few kiln-dried bowl blanks, will be the key to future tree supplies.

A piece of chalk, a pair of dividers, a rule and a sense of adventure are all you need to plan bowls from the log — flat-topped or natural-edged, turned in one operation or part-turned for seasoning and completion later. Understanding the growth patterns of the tree and knowing the kind of problems to look for — like stones in the roots at the base of the tree, or hidden nails which once supported a washing line or child's swing — are all a matter of experience. The planning and decisions are made on site, the rest is a process to be performed at leisure.

PEG

This is an odd man out among suggested methods of timber seasoning. I did buy some in about 1978, before I started working with green wood, as a magic solution to problems I hadn't yet encountered. As it turned out, the potential problems were much more satisfactorily solved in the planning stages of the work by understanding the wood and how it was likely to move — knowledge which has come from experience. My PEG equipment is still gathering dust, and will so remain until I have a problem that only PEG will solve — like making bowls the Ed Moulthrop way (*WW/June*) or preserving archaeological wrecks like the *Mary Rose*. Otherwise it will increase the cost of a bowl, usually more than the cost of the wood, and

Question box

Our panel of experts solve
your woodworking problems

We will try to answer any questions you can throw at us, but the ones we publish are the ones of most general interest to readers.

Please type your question double-spaced with generous margins, and include a stamped self-addressed envelope. Send it to: Question Box, Woodworker, 1 Golden Sq., London W1R 3AB.

Crazy veneers

Q I had the pleasure last year of attending Bob Grant's veneering course, on which I made a veneered panel, and Charles Cliffe's polishing course, on which I french polished it. I kept it out of the sun, but notice that the surface is crazed in all directions. Why – and how to stop it happening again?

A. Nichols, Billericay

A I have to admit that the practice panels we veneered on that course were made from ½in birch ply, which for economy reasons were cut with the top ply veneer running in the same direction as the applied face veneer. I pointed out at the time that under normal circumstances this was the wrong procedure; the grains should be laid at right angles, not only to preserve the balance of the structure but to avoid the inherent tendency of the top applied veneer to shrink and pull at the ground. In your case the classic fault has emerged with time — minute stress cracks appearing.

The problem is compounded when a finish is applied to the veneer. As the surface on which the finish is bonded moves, the polish film begins to exhibit the crazed pattern. This is particularly noticeable with some glazes based on copal varnish and certain nitro-cellulose lacquers, but I hasten to add that my colleague Charles Cliffe is entirely blameless in this specific incident!

Bob Grant

● Bob Grant is head of Craft, Design and Technology at an Oxford comprehensive school, and teaches Guild of Woodworkers' courses.

Teak and teak

Q I am making a teak-veneered cupboard unit, and want it to match some other teak furniture which has a golden look – what would be the best way to do this? I was going to use teak oil, but would like to polish the external surfaces, and doubt whether teak oil would take a polish.

Also, I'd like a quick way of finishing my craftwork, which I do in batches – I'm presently filling the grain, applying two coats of white polish and rubbing down with OO wire wool and wax, but it's time-consuming waiting for the coats to dry.

R. Edmunds, Rowlands Castle, Hants

A You will have a number of waste pieces on which you should experiment with different finishes. Number each piece and make notes of the finish you have used, so when you achieve a good match you'll know how you got it.

Teak oil darkens with each application, which could mean your unit would end up darker than the other furniture. With plenty of rubbing you can bring up quite a good polish using oil.

A wax finish looks well on teak, and good and quick results can be obtained by the following method:

Glasspaper the work smooth with progressively finer grades of abrasive paper. Dust off thoroughly, and brush on three coats of brushing french polish, rubbing down lightly between coats with OOO wire wool. Allow about half an hour for drying between each coat. This should give you the golden tone you require. Now apply a thin, even coat of wax polish and let it stand for about a quarter of an hour before rubbing briskly with a soft duster to bring up the shine. Three or four waxings will give a deep mellow finish. It is unnecessary to use a grain filler. The grain is partially filled by the brush polish and the remaining open pores are soon filled with wax.

Charles Cliffe

Outside wax?

Q We have a new pair of part-glazed oak doors at our local church, which were treated with beeswax in turpentine. No sealer was applied to the south-facing doors. The treatment has virtually disappeared after only a short while on those parts exposed most often to bright or hot sun, giving a patchy effect.

Can you suggest any means of bringing the woodwork back to a common colour and absorbency and a subsequent treatment that is likely to be more durable in these circumstances?

K. R. Darby, Norwich

A Although wax is a highly suitable finish for oak furniture, it cannot be used outside. Wax isn't weatherproof, which is why the parts of the doors exposed to direct sunlight have suffered most.

Remaining traces of wax polish must be washed off with a rag moistened with white spirit, then the doors can be smoothed and cleaned by rubbing first with no.1 steel wool, and finishing with grade 000. The doors will now be back to their original colour and after thoroughly dusting off will be ready for finishing.

I have found that oak doors and entrance gates treated with Sadolin not only have a good appearance, but stand up well to severe weather conditions. It is stocked by most builders' merchants. I also recommend Sikkens Cetol THB, which has a satin finish and comes in several different colours including light and dark oak.

Charles Cliffe

● Charles Cliffe is a professional finisher, author and teacher.

Born-again oak

Q I have been asked to clean and 'revive' some Victorian oak panelling in the sanctuary of my parish church. It doesn't show any indication of the finishes which may have been used, though it may have been waxed at the time of installation. It now appears dull, lifeless and neglected.

I propose cleaning the panelling with turpentine substitute, a soft cloth, and if necessary fine grade steel wool. I would then finish it by polishing lightly with Briwax. A carved frieze at dado height would be cleaned with a soft brush.

Do you think this is a satisfactory method of work for such panelling?

Kenneth May, Chester

A I would recommend the following method:

● The oak panelling must first be cleaned with a standard textbook five-part 'reviver'; equal parts by volume of raw linseed oil, paraffin oil or turpentine, methylated spirits, water, mild acetic acid or white vinegar, and a little fine pumice powder to give a little abrasive power. Mix it all up by shaking the contents in a glass bottle.

● Apply the reviver liberally with waste cotton wool to really clean off all the dirt and grime from the oak. Use a 2in paint brush to scrub into the mouldings and carvings, clean it off with clean cotton wool or white paper towels, and allow to dry for at least 24 hours.

● Apply raw (not boiled) linseed oil very liberally with a paint brush to soak the oak, and allow it to soak in for two to three hours, making sure the corners and mouldings are soaked. Wipe off all surplus oil from the oak with clean washed mutton cloths and polish it dry.

Use a soft brush (like a shoe-brush) for the moulding and carving. I don't recommend steel wool on this type of work, as bits can get trapped in the corners. Turpentine is really not strong enough for cleaning down. An oil finish is far superior to wax polish for this type of work.

After a few days the oak will take on a lovely mellow patina which will be a joy to behold.

Noel Leach

● Noel Leach is a professional wood finisher and lecturer.

Wooden threads

Q I am making a nutcracker in the style of an 'old village well'; I have tried teak, oak, apple, yew, beech and mahogany for the screw, but the threads break when I cut them; 8tpi is the coarsest thread I can cut. What wood should I buy?

J. Gavin, Stevenage

A You don't state the diameter of the thread you are attempting to cut, but I'm afraid you are on to a loser anyway. The wooden threads in the older handscrews

Question box

were generally of hornbeam, but I don't feel you would have fared any better with this wood.

Instead of cutting, the action in hand turning, you are scraping — and across the grain at that — so you are merely knocking the fibres out. You get away with it on the internal thread because the cut is always against well-supported wood.

The woodworker's screwbox, the equivalent of the engineer's die, succeeds because it is really cutting and not scraping. Screwboxes and taps are expensive, though; they are available from good tool merchants. I would suggest making the screw component in brass. Several of the woodturning suppliers offer a very elegant brass fitting.

Bob Wearing

Parabolic problem

Q *I have to set out a parabola 10ft diameter by 1.0416ft high. Could you tell me, in layman's language, how to find the lengths of the ordinates and the distances between them, also the length of the focal arm or point?*

John Sheenan, Co. Tipperary

A Working inside a 10x1ft rectangle will certainly present great difficulties in drawing, while a dimension in tenths of thousandths of a foot is unachievable in wood, an unstable material anyway, and graphically.

Anyway, here is a standard method which should help: Lay out a rectangle to the dimensions of the parabola and divide it in two longitudinally. Divide the two long halves vertically into the same number of equal divisions; the more you make the more accurate will be your plotting. Now draw horizontal lines parallel to the central axis; now join the end point 0 to each end of the vertical divisions. Where those diagonal lines cross the horizontal lines are points on your parabola — 01, 02, 03 and so on.

Bob Wearing

● Bob Wearing is a regular contributor to *Woodworker* of great experience.

Against the elements

Q *I want to use a sycamore tree trunk, which I found washed up on the beach, for small carvings. I had to saw and split it and many of the pieces are now starting to crack from the heart.*

How should I protect them from the weather and stack for seasoning? Also is there any way of removing the sea-salt from the timber?

D. T. Knapman, Penzance

A Don't worry about the salt — it's unlikely to have penetrated far into the wood and if it has, there's no way of removing it. In any event, for your purposes it won't do much harm.

Your main concern is to dry the wood without it splitting. Normally this is a slow process, but while the wood remains wet it

Setting out parabolas

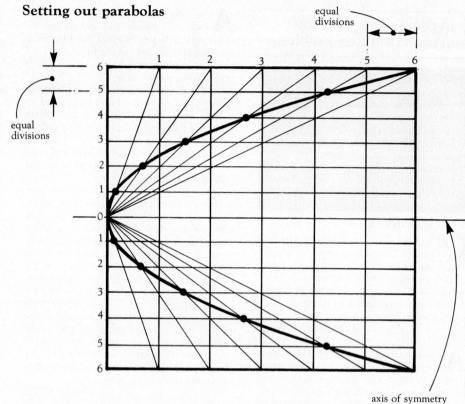

axis of symmetry

will be liable to attack by sap-staining fungi which may spoil the colour of the wood.

I suggest you make a stack with the billets laid horizontally side by side, each layer being separated by softwood 'stickers'. Keep the bottom layer clear of the ground and place the stack in a well-ventilated spot. The ends of the billets shouldn't be exposed to the sun (if you're lucky enough to have that problem!). Lay sheets of corrugated iron on top of the stack leaving a generous overhang as a rain shield. Be prepared for a long wait, and resign yourself to losing a fair proportion through cracking.

Michael White

Yew or non-U

Q *I have been offered five 4ft logs of yew, about 12in diameter. I would imagine there would be 8in of usable wood in each.*

How should it be sawn? How long should it be seasoned for (the log has been down about six months)? Is there anything particular/peculiar that I should know about it?

Alison Gravatt, Westerham

A The logs should be sawn in half longitudinally, which will pre-empt any tendency to split as they dry out. If the wood at the centre is sound, you can obtain maximum-width boards by sawing the halves through and through at the thickness you want, remembering to allow a little for shrinkage. If the centre is unsound the halves should be halved again to produce

quarters, and the boards can then be sawn alternately from each face to produce high quality quarter-sawn timber.

The boards should be air-dried first, in an unheated environment. They must be stacked with softwood stickers between them so that air can circulate, and weighted down to reduce any tendency to distort. If this air-drying is out of doors, the stack must be clear of soil moisture and protected from rain and direct sunlight by covering it with corrugated iron, leaving generous overhangs. Boards less than 1in thick should be air-dry by the end of next summer. The final stage of drying (or seasoning) is to prepare the wood for the conditions in which it will be used, i.e. indoors. Commercially this is done fairly quickly in a kiln. If you lack such facilities, the alternative is to restack the boards somewhere inside a heated building until they cease losing moisture. You can tell this by weighing a test board at intervals until there is no further loss of weight. Yew is a beautiful timber with no hidden vices, but it has high density and fine grain, so requires sharp tools. Watch out for wild and curly grain when planing — you will often find the only way to get a decent final finish is with a cabinet scraper. If you have a thicknesser or surface planer, put sharp knives in and take only very fine cuts.

Michael White

● Michael White is a consultant on timber and a former Scientific Officer at the Forest Products Research Laboratory.

shopguide

AVON

BATH   Tel. Bath 64513
JOHN HALL TOOLS   ★
RAILWAY STREET

Open: Monday-Saturday
9.00 a.m.-5.30 p.m.
H.P.W.WM.D.A.BC.

BRISTOL   Tel. (0272) 741510
JOHN HALL TOOLS LIMITED   ★
CLIFTON DOWN SHOPPING CENTRE
WHITELADIES ROAD
Open: Monday-Saturday
9.00 a.m.-5.30 p.m.
H.P.W.WM.D.A.BC.

BRISTOL   Tel. (0272) 629092
TRYMWOOD SERVICES
2a DOWNS PARK EAST, (off North View)
WESTBURY PARK
Open: 8.30 a.m.-5.30 p.m. Mon. to Fri.
Closed for lunch 1.00-2.00 p.m.
P.W.WM.D.T.A.BC.

BRISTOL   Tel. (0272) 667013
FASTSET LTD
190-192 WEST STREET
BEDMINSTER
Open: Mon.-Fri. 8.30 a.m.-5.00 p.m.
Saturday 9.00 a.m.-1.00 p.m..
H.P.W.WM.D.CS.A.BC.

BRISTOL   Tel. (0272) 667013
WILLIS
157 WEST STREET
BEDMINSTER
Open Mon.-Fri. 8.30 a.m.-5.00 p.m.
Sat. 9 a.m-4 p.m.
P.W.WM.D.CS.A.BC.

BERKSHIRE

READING   Tel. Littlewick Green
DAVID HUNT (TOOL   2743
MERCHANTS) LTD   ★
KNOWL HILL, NR. READING
Open: Monday-Saturday
9.00 a.m.-5.30 p.m.
H.P.W.D.A.BC.

READING   Tel. Reading 661511
WOKINGHAM TOOL CO. LTD.
99 WOKINGHAM ROAD

Open: Mon-Sat 9.00 a.m.-5.30 p.m.
Closed 1.00-2.00 p.m. for lunch
H.P.W.WM.D.CS.A.BC.

BUCKINGHAMSHIRE

MILTON KEYNES   Tel. (0908)
POLLARD WOODWORKING   641366
CENTRE   ★
51 AYLESBURY ST., BLETCHLEY
Open: Mon-Fri 8.30-5.30
Saturday 9.00-5.00
H.P.W.WM.D.CS.A.BC.

HIGH WYCOMBE   Tel. (0494)
SCOTT SAWS LTD.   24201/33788
14 BRIDGE STREET   ★

Mon.-Sat. 8.30 a.m.-6.00 p.m.

H.P.W.WM.D.T.CS.MF.A.BC.

BUCKINGHAMSHIRE

HIGH WYCOMBE   Tel. (0494)
ISAAC LORD LTD   22221
185 DESBOROUGH ROAD   KE

Open: Mon-Fri 8.00 a.m.-5.00 p.m.
Saturday 9.00 a.m.-5.00 p.m.
H.P.W.D.A.

CAMBRIDGESHIRE

CAMBRIDGE   Tel. (0223) 63132
D. MACKAY LTD.   ★
BRITANNIA WORKS, EAST ROAD

Open: Mon-Fri. 8.30 a.m.-1 p.m./2.00-
5.00 p.m. Sat. 8.30 a.m.-1.00 p.m.
H.P.W.WM.D.T.CS.MF.A.BC.

CAMBRIDGE   Tel. (0223) 247386
H. B. WOODWORKING   K
105 CHERRY HINTON ROAD
Open: 8.30 a.m.-5.30 p.m.
Monday-Friday
8.30 a.m.-1.00 p.m. Sat.
H.P.W.WM.D.CS.A.

PETERBOROUGH   Tel. (0733)
WILLIAMS DISTRIBUTORS   64252
(TOOLS) LIMITED   K
108-110 BURGHLEY ROAD
Open: Monday to Friday
8.30 a.m.-5.30 p.m.
H.P.A.W.D.WH.BC.

CHESHIRE

NANTWICH   Tel. Crewe 67010
ALAN HOLTHAM   K★
THE OLD STORES TURNERY
WISTASON ROAD, WILLASTON
Open: Tues.-Sat. 9.00 a.m.-5.30 p.m.
Closed Monday
P.W.WM.D.T.C.CS.A.BC.

CLEVELAND

MIDDLESBROUGH   Tel. (0642)
CLEVELAND WOODCRAFT   813103
(M'BRO), 38-42 CRESCENT ROAD   K

Open: Mon-Sat 9.15 a.m.-5.30 p.m.

H.P.T.A.BC.W.WM.CS.D.

CORNWALL

**SOUTH WEST
Power Tools**
CORNWALL   Tel: Helston (03265) 4961
HELSTON AND LAUNCESTON   Launceston
  (0566) 4781
  K
H.P.W.WM.D.CS.A.

CUMBRIA

CARLISLE   Tel: (0228) 36391
W. M. PLANT
ALLENBROOK ROAD
ROSEHILL, CA1 2UT
Open: Mon.-Fri. 8.00 a.m.-5.15 p.m.
Sat. 8.00 a.m.-12.30 noon
P.W.WM.D.CS.A.

DEVON

BRIXHAM   Tel. (08045) 4900
WOODCRAFT SUPPLIES   E★
4 HORSE POOL STREET

Open: Mon.-Sat. 9.00 a.m.-6.00 p.m.

H.P.W.A.D.MF.CS.BC.

PLYMOUTH   Tel. (0752) 330303
WESTWARD BUILDING SERVICES   ★
LTD., LISTER CLOSE, NEWNHAM
INDUSTRIAL ESTATE, PLYMPTON
Open: Mon-Fri 8.00 a.m.-5.00 p.m.
Sat. 8.30 a.m.-12.30 p.m.
H.P.W.WM.D.A.BC.

PLYMOUTH   Tel. (0752) 665363
F.T.B. LAWSON LTD.
71 NEW GEORGE STREET
PLYMOUTH PL1 1RB
Open: Mon.-Sat. 8.30 am-5.30 p.m.
H.P.W.CS.MF.A.

ESSEX

LEIGH ON SEA   Tel. (0702)
MARSHAL & PARSONS LTD.   710404
1111 LONDON ROAD   EK

Open: 8.30 a.m.-5.30 p.m. Mon-Fri
9.00 a.m.-5.00 p.m. Sat.
H.P.W.WM.D.CS.A.

GLOUCESTER

TEWKESBURY   Tel. (0684)
TEWKESBURY SAW CO. LTD.   293092
TRADING ESTATE, NEWTOWN   K

Open: Mon-Fri 8.00 a.m.-5.00 p.m.
Saturday 9.30 a.m.-12.00 a.m.
P.W.WM.D.CS.

HAMPSHIRE

ALDERSHOT   Tel. (0252) 334422
POWER TOOL CENTRE   K
374 HIGH STREET

Open Mon.-Fri. 8.30 a.m.-5.30 p.m.
Sat. 8.30 a.m.-12.30 p.m.
H.P.W.WM.D.A.BC.

SOUTHAMPTON   Tel: (0703)
POWER TOOL CENTRE   332288
7 BELVIDERE ROAD   K★
Open Mon.-Fri. 8.30-5.30

H.P.W.WM.D.A.BC.CS.MF.

HERTFORDSHIRE

WARE   K★
HEATH SAWS
16 MALTINGS
STANSTEAD ABBOTTS (near Ware) HERTS.
Open: Mon.-Fri. 8.30am-5.30pm
Sat. 8.30am-1pm. Sunday by appointment.
P.W.WM.D.CS.A.

HERTFORDSHIRE

ENFIELD   Tel: 01-363 2935
GILL & HOXBY LTD.
131-137 ST. MARKS ROAD ADJ.
BUSH HILL PARK STATION, EN1 1BA
Mon.-Sat. 8-5.30
Early closing Wed. 1 p.m.
H.P.A.M.MC.T.S.W.

HUMBERSIDE

GRIMSBY   Tel. Grimsby (0472)
  58741 Hull (0482) 26999
J. E. SIDDLE LTD. (Tool Specialists)   ★
83 VICTORIA STREET
Open: Mon-Fri 8.30 a.m.-5.30 p.m.
Sat. 8.30 a.m.-12.45 p.m. & 2 p.m.-5 p.m.
H.P.A.BC.W.WMD.

HULL
HUMBERSIDE FACTORING/H.F.C.
SAW SERVICING LTD.
MAIN STREET
Open: Mon.-Fri. 8am-5pm.
Saturday 8am-12.00pm.
H.P.W.WM.D.CS.A.BC.K.

KENT

WYE   Tel. (0233) 813144
KENT POWER TOOLS LTD.
UNIT 1, BRIAR CLOSE
WYE, Nr. ASFORD

H.P.W.WM.D.A.CS.

MAIDSTONE   Tel. (0622) 50177
SOUTH EASTERN SAWS (Ind.) LTD.   ★
COLDRED ROAD
PARKWOOD INDUSTRIAL ESTATE

Open: Mon.-Fri. 8.00 a.m.-6.00 p.m.
Sat. 9.00 a.m.-12.00 a.m.
B.C.W.CS.WM.PH.

MAIDSTONE
HENSON AND PLATT
TOKE PLACE
LINTON

Open Mon.-Fri. 8.00 a.m.-5.00 p.m.
Saturday 8.00 a.m.-1.0p.m.
H.P.W.T.CS.A.

LANCASHIRE

PRESTON   Tel. (0772) 52951
SPEEDWELL TOOL COMPANY   E★
62-68 MEADOW STREET PR1 1SU
Open: Mon.-Fri. 8.30 a.m.-5.30 p.m.
Sat. 8.30 a.m.-12.30 p.m.

H.P.W.WM.CS.A.MF.BC.

ROCHDALE   Tel. (0706) 342123/
C.S.M. TOOLS   342322
4-6 HEYWOOD ROAD   E★
CASTLETON
Open: Mon-Sat 9.00 a.m.-6.00 p.m.
Sundays by appointment
W.D.CS.A.BC.

shopguide

LANCASHIRE

LANCASTER Tel: (0524) 32886
LILE TOOL SHOP **K**
43/45 NORTH ROAD
Open: Monday to Saturday
9.00 a.m.-5.30 p.m.
Wed. 9.00 a.m.-12.30 p.m.
H.P.W.D.A.

LANCASHIRE Tel: (070 681) 4931
'TODMORDEN' ★
TOWNLEY TIMES, HAREHILL STREET
OFF BURNLEY ROAD
Open: Mon.-Fri. 8.30 am-5.30 pm
Sat. 9.00 am-1.00 pm.
H.P.W.D.A.BC.

BLACKPOOL
FLYDE WOODTURNING SUPPLIES ★
255 CHURCH STREET
BLACKPOOL FY1 4HY
9.30-5.30 Monday to Saturday
H.P.W.WM.A.MF.C.B.C.D.

LINCOLNSHIRE

LINCOLN Tel: (0522) 689369
SKELLINGTHORPE SAW SERVICES LTD.
OLD WOOD, SKELLINGTHORPE
Open: Mon to Fri 8 a.m.-5 p.m.
Sat 8 a.m.-12 p.m.
H.P.W.WM.D.CS.A.*.BC.
Access/Barclaycard

LONDON

ACTON Tel: (01-992) 4835
A. MILLS (ACTON) LTD ★
32/36 CHURCHFIELD ROAD W3 6ED
Open: Mon-Fri 9.00 a.m.-5.00 p.m.
Saturdays 9.00 am-1.00 p.m.
H.P.W.WM.

LONDON Tel. 01-723 2295-6-7
LANGHAM TOOLS LIMITED
13 NORFOLK PLACE
LONDON W2 1QJ

LONDON Tel. (01-636) 7475
BUCK & RYAN LTD ★
101 TOTTENHAM COURT ROAD W1P 0DY
Open: Mon.-Fri. 8.30 a.m.-5.30 p.m.
Saturday 8.30 a.m.-4.00 p.m.
H.P.W.WM.D.A..

WEMBLEY Tel. 904-1144
ROBERT SAMUEL LTD. (904-1147
7, 15 & 16 COURT PARADE after 4.00)
EAST LANE, N. WEMBLEY ★
Open Mon.-Fri. 8.45-5.15; Sat. 9-1.00
Access, Barclaycard, AM Express, & Diners
H.P.W.CS.E.A.D.

HOUNSLOW Tel. (01-570)
Q.R. TOOLS LTD 2103/5135
251-253 HANWORTH ROAD
Open: Mon-Fri 8.30 a.m.-5.30 p.m.
Sat. 9.00 a.m.-1.00 p.m.
P.W.WM.D.CS.A.

LONDON

FULHAM Tel. (01-385) 5109
I. GRIZZARD LTD. **E**
84a-b LILLIE ROAD, SW6 1TL
Open: Mon-Sat 9.00-5.30 p.m.
Half day Thursday
H.P.A.BC.W.CS.WM.D.

MANCHESTER

MANCHESTER Tel. (061 789)
TIMMS TOOLS 0909
102-104 LIVERPOOL ROAD ★
PATRICROFT M30 0WZ
Weekdays 9.00 a.m.-5.30 p.m.
Sat. 9.00 a.m.-1.00 p.m.
H.P.A.W.

MERSEYSIDE

LIVERPOOL Tel. (051-207) 2967
TAYLOR BROS (LIVERPOOL) LTD **K**
195-199 LONDON ROAD
LIVERPOOL L3 8JG
Open: Monday to Friday
8.30 a.m.-5.30 p.m.
H.P.W.WM.D.A.BC.

MIDDLESEX

RUISLIP Tel. (08956) 74126
ALLMODELS ENGINEERING LTD. **E★**
91 MANOR WAY
Open: Mon-Sat 9.00 a.m.-5.30 p.m.
H.P.W.A.D.CS.MF.BC.

NORFOLK

NORWICH Tel. (0603) 898695
NORFOLK SAW SERVICES
DOG LANE, HORSFORD
Open: Monday to Friday
8.00 a.m.-5.00 p.m.
Saturday 8.00 a.m.-12.00 p.m.
H.P.W.WM.D.CS.A.

KINGS LYNN Tel. (0553) 2443
WALKER & ANDERSON (Kings Lynn) LTD. **K**
WINDSOR ROAD, KINGS LYNN
Open: Monday to Saturday
7.45 a.m.-5.30 p.m.
Wednesday 1.00 p.m. Saturday 5.00 p.m.
H.P.W.WM.D.CS.A.

NORWICH Tel. (0603) 400933
WESTGATES WOODWORKING Tx
61 HURRICANE WAY, 975412
NORWICH AIRPORT INDUSTRIAL ESTATE
Open: 9.00 a.m.-5.00 p.m. weekdays
9.00 a.m.-12.30 Sat.
P.W.WM.D.BC. **K**

KING'S LYNN Tel. (07605) 674
TONY WADILOVE WOODCRAFT ★
HILL FARM WORKSHOPS
GT. DUNHAM
(NR. SWAFFHAM)
Tues.-Sat. 9.00am-5.30pm
H.P.W.D.T.MF.A.BC.

NOTTINGHAMSHIRE

NOTTINGHAM Tel: (0602) 225979
POOLEWOOD and 227064/5
EQUIPMENT LTD. (06077) 2421 after hrs
5a HOLLY LANE, CHILLWELL
Open: Mon-Fri 9.00 a.m.-5.30 p.m.
Sat. 9.00 a.m. to 12.30 p.m.
P.W.WM.D.CS.A.BC.

OXON

WITNEY Tel. (0993) 3885
TARGET TOOLS (SALES, & 72095 OXON
TARGET HIRE & REPAIRS) ★
TOOLS SWAIN COURT
STATION INDUSTRIAL ESTATE
Open: Mon.-Sat. 8.00 a.m.-5.00 p.m.
24 hour Answerphone
BC.W.M.A.

SHROPSHIRE

TELFORD Tel. Telford (0952)
ASLES LTD 48054
VINEYARD ROAD, WELLINGTON **EK★**
Open: Mon. Fri. 8.30 a.m.-5.30 p.m.
Saturday 8.30 a.m.-4.00 p.m.
H.P.W.WM.D.CS.BC.A.

SOMERSET

TAUNTON Tel. (0823) 85431
JOHN HALL TOOLS ★
6 HIGH STREET
Open Monday-Saturday
9.00 a.m.-5.30 p.m.
H.P.W.WM.D.CS.A.

STAFFORDSHIRE

TAMWORTH Tel. (0827) 56188
MATTHEWS BROTHERS LTD. **K**
KETTLEBROOK ROAD
Open: Mon.-Sat. 8.30-6.00 p.m.
Demonstrations Sunday mornings by
appointment only
H.P.WM.D T.CS.A.BC.

SUFFOLK

SUFFOLK
LOCKWOOD WOODWORKING MACHINERY
WHITE GATES BUNGALOW
THE COMMON MELLIS
NEAR EYE/DISS IP23 8DY Tel: (037983) 8126
Open: Mon., Wed., Thurs., Fri. 8am-8pm
Tues. & Sat. 8am-5pm.
*Lathe demos every Saturday morning.
We cover both Norfolk and Suffolk.*
H.P.W.D.A.

IPSWICH Tel. (0473) 40456
FOX WOODWORKING **KE★**
142-144 BRAMFORD LANE
Open: Tues., Fri., 9.00 a.m.-5.30 p.m.
Sat. 9.00 a.m.-5.00 p.m.
H.P.W.WM.D.A.B.C.

SUSSEX

BOGNOR REGIS Tel. (0243) 863100
A. OLBY & SON (BOGNOR REGIS) LTD.
"TOOLSHOP," BUILDERS MERCHANT
HAWTHORN ROAD **K**
Open: Mon-Thurs 8 a.m.-5.15 p.m. Fri.
8 a.m.-8 p.m. Sat 8 a.m.-12.45 p.m.
H.P.W.WM.D.T.C.A.BC.

WORTHING Tel. (0903) 38739
W. HOSKING LTD (TOOLS & **KE★**
MACHINERY)
28 PORTLAND RD, BN11 1QN
Open: Mon.-Sat. 8.30 a.m.-5.30 p.m.
Closed Wednesday
H.P.W.WM.D.CS.A.BC.

TYNE & WEAR

NEWCASTLE Tel. (0632) 320311
HENRY OSBOURNE LTD. **E★**
50-54 UNION STREET
Open: Mon-Fri 8.30 a.m.-5.00 p.m.
H.P.W.D.CS.MF.A.BC.

TYNE & WEAR

NEWCASTLE-UPON-TYNE ★
J. W. HOYLE LTD
CLARENCE STREET
NEWCASTLE-UPON-TYNE
TYNE & WEAR
NE2 17J
H.P.W.WM.D.CS.A.BC.K.

W. MIDLANDS

WOLVERHAMPTON Tel. (0902)
MANSAW SERVICES 58759
SEDGLEY STREET **K★**
Open: Mon.-Fri. 9.00 a.m.-5.00 p.m.
H.P.W.WM.A.D.CS.

YORKSHIRE

BOROUGHBRIDGE Tel. (09012)
JOHN BODDY TIMBER LTD 2370
FINE WOOD & TOOL STORE ★
RIVERSIDE SAWMILLS
Open: Mon.-Thurs. 8.00 a.m.-6.00 p.m.
Fri. 8.00am-5.00pm Sat. 8.00am-4.00pm
H.P.W.WM.D.T.CS.MF.A.BC.

SHEFFIELD Tel. (0742) 441012
GREGORY & TAYLOR LTD **KE**
WORKSOP ROAD
Open: 8.30 a.m.-5.30 p.m.
Monday-Friday
8.30 a.m.-12.30 p.m. Sat.
H.P.W.WM.D.

HARROGATE Tel. (0423) 66245/
MULTI-TOOLS 55328
158 KINGS ROAD **K★**
Open: Monday to Saturday
8.30 a.m.-6.00 p.m.
H.P.W.WM.D.A.BC.

THIRSK Tel. (0845) 22770
THE WOOD SHOP ★
TRESKE SAWMILLS LTD.
STATION WORKS
Open: Seven days a week 9.00-5.00
T.H.MF.BC.

LEEDS Tel. (0532) 574736
D. B. KEIGHLEY MACHINERY LTD. ★
VICKERS PLACE, STANNINGLEY
PUDSEY LS2 86LZ
Mon.-Fri. 9.00 a.m.-5.00 p.m.
Sat. 9.00 a.m.-1.00 p.m.
P.A.W.WM.CS.BC.

LEEDS Tel. (0532) 790507
GEORGE SPENCE & SONS LTD. ★
WELLINGTON ROAD
Open: Monday to Friday
8.30 a.m.-5.30 p.m.
Saturday 9.00 a.m.-5.00 p.m.
H.P.W.WM.D.T.A.

HUDDERSFIELD Tel. (0484)
NEVILLE M. OLDHAM 641219/(0484)
UNIT 1 DALE ST. MILLS 42777
DALE STREET, LONGWOOD
Open: Mon-Fri 8.00 a.m.-5.30 p.m.
Saturday 9.30 a.m.-12.00 p.m.
P.W.WM.D.A.BC.

shop guide

WOOD SUPPLIERS

1077

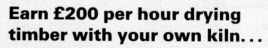
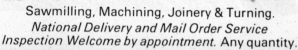

WOOD SUPPLIERS

THE WOODSTORE

Suppliers of Native Hardwoods

MOST HOMEGROWN SPECIES IN STOCK
LARGE AND SMALL QUANTITIES
SUPPLIED FRESH SAWN, AIR DRIED
AND KILN DRIED

MACHINING FACILITIES AVAILABLE

Send sae for Price List to

TREEWORK SERVICES LTD

CHESTON COOMBE, CHURCH TOWN,
BACKWELL, Nr. BRISTOL
OR PHONE FLAX BOURTON
(027583) 3917 OR 3078

We also offer a tree milling service

H.B. LACEY & SON

Whitemoor Farm, Doddiscombsleigh,
Exeter, Devon. Tel: (0647) 52268

Air dried Oak £14 cu.ft. Ash £18 cu.ft.
Olive Ash £12 cu.ft. Most stock has been
air dried for 2 years.
Cheap delivery and "cut-to-size"
service available.

LOTHIAN TREE SERVICES Ltd.

Scottish Suppliers of Native Hardwoods

A personal service at competitive prices.

Fresh sawn, air dried & kiln
dried stock available.

Send SAE for
further information to:
Whitehil Sawmill, Thornton, Rosewell,
Midlothian EH24 9EF.
Or Tel: 031 440 4175 (24 hours)

Small quantities of Oak, Walnut,
Apple, Ash, Cedar, Tuliptree and
Elm for sale.

Job lot, or individually. Also onsight
sawmilling using portable bandmill.
Very efficient and ideal for users of
de-humidifyer kilns.
80 cu.ft. approx. of 1" Oak, fresh
sawn at **£8** per cube.
Tel: Dorking 886933 (Evenings)

Berkshire Hardwoods

Seasoned British hardwoods for the woodworker
and turner. Prime oak,
ash, beech, chestnut,
cherry, yew. Waney edge
boards, bowl blanks or
fully finished stock. Cutting lists quoted for:
Prices from £10 cu.ft. kiln dried.
Allan Morris, Crowthorne 772157
Steve Dooley, Crowthorne 773586

English Hardwoods — kiln dried
English Oak and Elm. Air dried
Ash 1¼", 3" and 4". Walnut 1".
Yew 1" and 2". Elm and Oak Burrs.
M. Griffin, 'Wesleyan House',
Alstonefield, Ashbourne,
Derbyshire.
Tel: Alstonefield (033527) 249

WELSH OAK and ASH

Kiln dried, small — medium
quantities. Deliveries arranged.

Valley Timber Company,
Cwm Cych near Newcastle Emlyn,
Dyfed. Tel: (023977) 200

Classified Advertisements

SPECIALIST SERVICES

SkyeCrafts

ROAG HOUSE · DUNVEGAN · ISLE OF SKYE
Telephone: (047 022) 411

DO YOU HAVE A CRAFT IDEA?

SKYECRAFTS offer a unique service to craft/wood
workers. Phone or write in with your specific project
needs and we can supply top quality British or Exotic
hardwoods made up to your exact specifications.
IF IT'S MADE OF WOOD
WE CAN SUPPLY.

DEMONSTRATIONS

Hegner (UK) Ltd.

*For accurate cutting, intricate shaping, smooth finishing on
2" wood. Also thick plastic, metal, etc, a HEGNER saw
does it all and more with*
MAXIMUM SAFETY
*Send a stamp for
our brochure, you will see at once..
...this is no ordinary fretsaw.*

< DIRECT SALES ONLY >
111 Sutton Road, Southend-on-Sea, Essex SS2 5PB tel (0702) 617298

*Demonstrations at Model Engineer Exhibition, Wembley Conference Centre
1st-8th January and Practical Woodworking Exhibition, Wembley Conference
Centre 15th-18th January.*

Classified Advertisements

FOR SALE

WINDSOR CHAIRS

Full size bends. 50 × $1\frac{3}{8}$ × $1\frac{1}{8}$" in Ash £6.95.
Childs Windsor Chair bends in Ash 36 × $1\frac{1}{8}$ × $\frac{7}{8}$" £4.95.
All prices include p&p.

Please send cheque/P.O. with order to:
**P. Stuffin, Spurn View, North End Road, Tetney, Grimby DN36 5NA.
Tel: (0472) 812576
(Afternoons)**

THE WHISTON CATALOGUE

Nuts, bolts, screws, washers, bar materials. In brass, alloy, steel, stainless steel, P.T.F.E., nylon, Tufnol, sheet material, electrical and mechanical items. We could go on and on! Better to send for free catalogue No. 114 and see for yourself.
K. R. Whiston Ltd., Dept. WW, New Mills, Stockport, Cheshire. Phone: 0663 42028.

UNIQUE CRAFT BUSINESS

For sale due to owner's retirement. Offers complete with goodwill; order book, machinery, tools and tuition as going concern, for siting at purchaser's premises. Unlimited potential £27,000 plus stock at valuation.
Alternatively, complete existing set-up including three-bedroomed detached Tudor cottage and workshops, in idyllic surroundings. Available at **£115,000** + stock.
Tel: 0449 740 211.

Quality Movements for Quality Cases

Eight Day Long case clock movements hand made of traditional design and very high quality, suitable for fitting in reproduction clock cases. These should appeal to the craftsman who requires the quality of the original Long Case movements. Dials and hands available made to your requirements. Brassware for clock cases including capitals, escutcheons, etc. available.

RICHARDS OF BURTON

Woodhouse Clockworks
Swadlincote Road, Woodville
Burton-on-Trent   Tel: (0283) 219155

CLOCKMAKERS

Extensive range of very competitively priced German quartz clock movements, (including standard quartz, pendulum, mini-pendulum, chining, striking and insertion movements). Large selection of quality dials, chapter rings, hands, bezels, clock plans and weather instruments.
Please send 25p stamps for 20 page catalogue.
**Bath Clock Company (Dept. W),
13 Welton Road, Radstock, Bath.**

WOODCARVING tools

LARGEST STOCK IN EUROPE

Ashley Iles & Henry Taylor
Arkansas Bench & Slip Stones
Strops & Strop Paste
Bench Screws, Carvers' Vices

WOODTURNING tools

Complete range of
Henry Taylor & Ashley Iles
handled or unhandled

send 40p in stamps for illustrated catalogue
ALEC TIRANTI LTD
70 High St, Theale, Reading, Berks RG7 5AR
21. Goodge Place, London W1.

SAMUEL COULTON

fine hand made clocks
High quality hand made pendulum clock movements
Designed to complement the work of those fellow craftsmen for whom only the best will do. Individually made to order. Send £2.00 for detailed colour brochure.
Samuel Coulton Clocks, Lower Damgate Farm, Stanshope, Nr. Ashbourne, Derbyshire.
Tel: (033527) 367.

BANKRUPT STOCK

Sandvik circular saw blades tungsten tipped.
5", $5\frac{1}{2}$", 6" .... **£4.00** each
$6\frac{1}{2}$", $8\frac{1}{4}$" .... **£6.00** each
$\frac{1}{2}$" to $1\frac{3}{8}$" bore any size.
P&P £1 extra per order.
**Tel: 01 672 7776
Hannett, 1A Links Road, Tooting, London SW17 9ED.**

BLADES

The specialist mail order supplier of tooling for woodworking machinery and power tools. Spindle tooling, saw blades, dado sets, planer knives, router cutters and accessories, machinery of particular merit, Forstener bits, mortise chisels, etc.
Write NOW for your free copy of our brochure AND competitive price list.
BLADES, Freepost, Petersfield, Hampshire GU32 2BR. (No stamps required)

SALE: Solid Cuban mahogany table tops, leaves, legs. Long veneers, fiddle-back sycamore, mahogany, rosewood. £200 ono. Planes: Norris panel, moulding. 13 circular. 45 Multi complete. 30 Addis carving chisels. Ernest Gimson, 'His Life and Work' No. 2.7.6. £250. Details Phone D/N 0742/553782.

THE FINEST SELECTION ON DISPLAY IN SCOTLAND!

WOODWORKING & METALWORKING MACHINERY POWER TOOLS HAND TOOLS

THE SAW CENTRE

LARGE STOCKS COMPETITIVE PRICES. PHONE AND TRY US NOW!

Eglinton Toll, Glasgow
G5 9RP
Tel: 041-429-4444

38 Haymarket
Edinburgh
EH12 5J2
Tel: 031-337-5555

OPEN
Mon - Fri
8am - 5pm
Sat 9am - 1pm

SURPLUS machine for sale. Reconditioned Wadkin high speed Router LS £1500, ono. Evenings 021-552 2334.

SHARPENSET whetstone grinder. 10" grinding jig. Spare stone. £200. Tel: 01-567 9571.

SCHEPPACH Prima HMI 10" planer/thicknesser with circular saw, disc sander, and spindle moulder attachments. Tel: 0823 490841. £650 complete.

RECORD three in one shoulder plane No. 311 Brand New. £45. Chester 679304 (Evenings).

SWEDISH woodworkers bench. Excellent condition. Reasonable offers accepted. Tel: Reading (0734) 697152. Evenings.

MYFORD ML8B woodturning lathe. $\frac{3}{4}$hp 1 phase, cabinet stand, starter, chuck, etc. All new and unused. £620. Marlow 72094.

CORONET Major with many accessories. Saw, planer, mortiser, etc. £500. Tel: Romford 61673.

EBAC wood dryer model LD82 complete with universal controller. Excellent condition. £500 including VAT. Tel: 070-681 7716 (West Yorks).

SEVENTY moulding planes, etc. Will sell separately. Details: SAE 30 Mount View, Oakworth, Keighley. Tel: 0535 42710.

SCHEPPACH HMZ Icombi combined planing machine with spindle moulder attachment as new. £420 ono. Tel: Southport 36485.

RECORD 405 40 cutters plus 5 special bases. Unpacked. £220 ono. Also Wolfcraft milling table unused. £20. Tel: 0400 50176. (Grantham area.)

USERS AND COLLECTORS tools for sale at the Old Craft Tool Shop, 15 High Street, Whitton, Middx. Telephone 01-755 0441.

INCA 10in Circular saw sliding table. Two TCT blades. Morticing table chuck. £475. 01-340 4837.

LUNAR 190 woodturning lathe — New 36in centres, revolving 13in swing, face plate, Multi-Star chuck, screw chuck with stand and tool tray, etc. £550, ono. Mr. Foakes, 24 River View Park, Catford, London SE6. 01-690 2444.

MARQUETRY

MARQUETRY stars, shells and fans, made to order inlays for restoration and reproductions. Send design and colour scheme for quote to: S. Rockwood, 13-15 Seel Street, The Courtyard, Liverpool L1 4AU or Telephone 051-708 5200. Send large S.A.E. for details.

KITS & HOBBIES

Everything for the home craftsman

Clock movements, hands, faces, dials, ceramic tiles kits. Woodturning accessories. Miniature power tools, etc. Send £1.95 for 128 page catalogue and £5 voucher against first order.
**Toolmail (WWD) Ltd.
Dept. WS, 170 High Street, Lewes, East Sussex.
Telephone: (0273) 477009.**

SHARPENING SERVICES

WHY throw away those expensive router cutters when they can be re-ground correctly at a fraction of new price? Ring Woodcutter Services for details. 061 4324294 (after 6pm).

PLANS

MODEL ROCKING HORSES

The book, kits, plans, quality accessories to make or restore fine, traditional wooden rocking horses.

Full details from:

**The Rocking Horse Shop,
Holme Upon Spalding Moor, York.
YO4 4AB. Tel: (0696) 60563**

1081

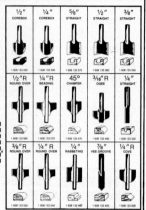

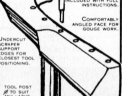

1082

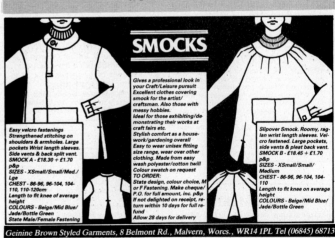

1086

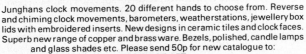

Letters

Turned off

I MUST PROTEST about yet another article on lathes, 'Which way to turn' (*WW/Sept*). What is it about lathes and turning that fascinates woodworking magazines and their readers so much?

The article doesn't touch upon turning (the main purpose of a lathe) and I'm quite capable of assessing the models on offer without reference to an individual's personal feelings. I also find it difficult to justify the prices quoted. A lathe is the most basic woodworking machine (the old chairmakers' lathes had few metal components and were operated by muscle-power) so why so expensive?

My own lathe was made by an engineer, in his spare time, using standard section steel channel for the bed. The head- and tailstock are in steel plate with four speeds in both; it has outboard turning facility and truly massive bearings. The tailstock and tool-rest are adjusted by a ring-spanner — but it's in no way crude and would measure up against any advertised model — at a fraction of the price.

If people turned as much as they wrote, argued, and raved about it, we'd be knee-high in turned ware! (The only book I've ever bought on turning was Dale Nish's *Creative Woodturning* which says or rather shows it all.)

May we have more hard-hitting articles to the standard of Peter Howlett's piece on design (*WW/Sept*) and leave the manufacturers to market their own products?

T. K. Findley, Wincanton

Dusty designs

WHILST I ADMIT to being a traditionalist, I do nevertheless try to keep an open mind on the unusual and sometimes radical designs which emerge from the various training establishments, and try to view them objectively.

However, I find some of the student pieces (*WW/Sept*) way over the top, particularly the skeleton and fretted designs which must surely be absolute dust-traps.

It seems to me that the fundamental principles involved are being ignored by some students and their mentors as they strive to be 'different'. It is so easy to change a basic design — the skill is demonstrated by improving it.

H. Hillier, Beaminster

Sitting comfortably?

I WOULD LIKE TO ENDORSE everything Peter Howlett says in 'Past Defence' (*WW/Sept*) relating to modern 'way-out' design.

I was a student from 1923-1926, at the old Shoreditch Technical Institute, under the direction of Percy A. Wells, and was instilled with a love and respect of our craft — which was difficult to practise in the ensuing years (the General Strike, the Depression and the war in 1939). I ended up eventually in joinery and shop-fitting.

My design idol throughout has been Sir Gordon Russell and I must mention the inscription at the Victoria & Albert Museum which goes something like 'The excellence of every art must consist in the complete accomplishment of its purpose'. Which surely means no matter how you design a chair, it must be comfortable to sit on.

Mr Howlett mentions the beautiful curved windows of Heals' store and questions their efficiency for display purposes. I worked for the shop-fitters who installed these 'non-reflecting windows' and believe me, they were wonderful; you could see the display through the window without realising there was any glass there — but they were expensive and needed a lot of dusting!

B. Chapman, Bromley

Where are they now?

I WONDER IF any of your readers can help me locate a firm who used to advertise in *Woodworker*. Their name is Ferropine and their old trading address was 8 Temple Park Crescent, Edinburgh EH11 1HT. They produce something called the Ferropine Burnisher, a cabinet-scraper sharpener, and I need a replacement for one which was stolen.

Alan Biggs, Lesmurene,
Dark Lane, Swindon Village,
nr. Cheltenham, Glos. G51 9RW

Thanks for the memories

I MUST CONGRATULATE Ashley Iles for his excellently related series, 'Tales out of steel'.

It took me back some 60 years and refreshed my memory of similar outstanding characters, specialists and oddities from all the different trades in our district. I feel that in the present micro-chip world we somehow lack the individuality that once flourished.

H. Aquatias, Knutsford

Advertisers Index

AEG	1042	Machine Sales	
Apollo	996	Southampton	1082
Argus Books	1024	Martek	1017
Ashford Tools	1046	Matthews	1068
Asles	998	A. Mills	1069
Axminster	1056, 1057	M&M Distrib.	998
A-Z Tools	IBC	Model Wheel	1049
BDM	1030	Multistar	1030
Bedford Saws	1030	John Myland	1110
Benmail	1024	Ocean West	1034
John Boddy	1061	Old Stores Turnery	1004
Clam Brummer	1061	Nortec	1038
Burch & Hills	1060	P&J Dust	1018
Canaan Carbides	1029	Plans Service	1048
H. Case	996, 997, 998, 999	W. M. Plant	1019
Charltons	1047	A. Pollard	1050
P. Child	1060	Rogers	1035
Christchurch Tools	1019	Sanlin	1087
Cleveland	1014	Sarjents	1054
Craft Materials	1038	Scott & Sargeant	1052
Craft Supplies	1018	Smiths	1018
Craft Tools & Tackle	1030	S/West Power Tools	1061
Cutwell W/Wking	1046	Steerdawn	999
Data Power	1038	Sumaco	1034, 1049
DeWalt	1025, 1029	Tabwell Tools	1044
DIY Supplies	1054	Taylor Bros	1014
Dunlop	IFC	Henry Taylor	1038
Elektra Beckum	OBC	Thomas & Willis	1060
Elu	1017, 1019, 1025	Tilgear	999, 1018, 1038,
Excel	998		1042, 1068
Fox	1061	Timber P'chasing	1050
Gill & Hoxby	1068	Toolmail	1014, 1029
Heath Saws	1046	Treebridge	1025
Home Video W/Shop		Trend	1050
	1042, 1047	Trimbridge	1034
J. W. Hoyle	1017	L. H. Turtle	1047
D. Hunt	1060	Cecil W. Tyzack	996
Ashley Iles	1046	Waymek	1025
Kent Power Tools	1019	Warren	1060
Kity	1004	Whitehill	996
Lervad UK	1087	Woodfit	997
Isaac Lord	1014	XR Machines	1050
E. W. Lucas	999		
Luna	1110, 1068		

A wider radial arm

AS A SMALL-TIME cabinetmaker/joiner (I work alone) I miss the value of others' experience, and much appreciate *Woodworker* as a medium for ideas and techniques from seasoned craftspeople and novices alike. It's often the simplest of ideas that turn out to be good solutions to the problems — and working them out provides the real thrill of what for me is a profession, craft and hobby.

So I hope this radial-arm saw idea will be of use to readers with a machine whose limited ripping width is frustrating when it comes to wide boards. I often have to cut sheet material more or less in half down the middle — a cut of 24in or thereabouts — and the limited arm length on my DeWalt DW110 occasionally upsets me. Resorting to a hand-held power saw is tiresome, time consuming and not all that accurate.

The standard fence is about 6½in in front of the rise-and-fall pillar; I have just fitted a fence right up against the pillar, about ¾in higher than the standard fence, and added two removable supports the same height as the standard fence which sit either side of the blade under the piece being cut. End blocks stop them moving as you pass the board over. It gives a potential ripping width of 25¾in — just what we need.

Grant Pearce, N. London

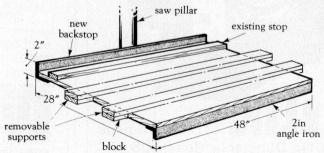